The BEAULIEU ENCYCLOPEDIA of the AUTOMOBILE

The BEAULIEU ENCYCLOPEDIA of the AUTOMOBILE

Volume 1
A-F

Editor in Chief
NICK GEORGANO

Foreword by
LORD MONTAGU *of* **BEAULIEU**

FITZROY DEARBORN PUBLISHERS
CHICAGO · LONDON

© The Stationery Office 2000

Published in the United Kingdom by
The Stationery Office Limited, St Crispins, Duke Street, Norwich NR3 1PD.

Published in the United States of America by
Fitzroy Dearborn Publishers, 919 North Michigan Avenue, Chicago, Illinois 60611.

The information contained in this publication is believed to be correct at the time of manufacture. Whilst care has been taken to ensure that the information is accurate, the publisher can accept no responsibility for any errors or omissions or for changes to the details given.

A Cataloging-in-Publication record for this book is available from the Library of Congress.

ISBN 1-57958-293-1 Fitzroy Dearborn

First published 2000.

Reprinted with amendments 2001.

Produced and designed by The Stationery Office.

Design by Guy Myles Warren.

Reproductive services by Colourscript, Mildenhall, Suffolk.

Printed and bound by Butler & Tanner, Frome, Somerset.

Dedication

To the memory of George Ralph Doyle, John Pollitt, and Michael Sedgwick.

G.R.Doyle (1890–1961) was the first man to compile a worldwide address list of car manufacturers. *The World's Automobiles*, first published privately in 1932, stimulated the interest of countless enthusiasts. Without Doyle's pioneering work, the compilation of this encyclopedia would have been a near impossibility.

John Pollitt (1892–1958) was one of the most painstaking of researchers into motoring history. After his retirement from the Rover company in 1945, he devoted his entire time to investigations and correspondence on the subject, the fruits of which he wrote up in twenty eight files, running to several million words. These files, generously lent by the late Dennis C. Field) were among the most important cornerstones of the encyclopedia.

Michael Sedgwick (1926–1983) was the most tireless researcher into motoring history from the early 1960s to the day of his death in October 1983. He was Curator of the Montagu Motor Museum (today the National Motor Museum) from 1958 to 1966, and subsequently the Museum's Director of Research, Assistant Editor of *The Veteran & Vintage Magazine*, and a regular contributor to practically every old car magazine in the world. His enthusiasm and knowledge extended to any period and variety of road vehicle. He would have loved this book.

Contents

Alphabetical List of Biographies included in Volume 1

Alphabetical List of Biographies included in Volume 2

Alphabetical List of Biographies included in Volume 3

Alphabetical List of Colour Illustrations included in Volume 2

1995	Daimler Double Six saloon	National Motor Museum
1978	Datsun 260Z coupé.	National Motor Museum
1901	De Dion-Bouton vis-à-vis	National Motor Museum
1975	De Tomaso Pantera GTS coupé	National Motor Museum
1937	Delage D8 coupé	National Motor Museum
1947	Delahaye 135 MS 2-door cabriolet	National Motor Museum
1929	Duesenberg Model J convertible roadster	Nicky Wright/National Motor Museum
1988	Excalibur Series VI sedan	Nicky Wright/National Motor Museum
1960	Facel Vega HK500 2-door coupé	National Motor Museum
1950	Ferrari 166 Barchetta sports car	Nicky Wright/National Motor Museum
1960	Ferrari 250GT cabriolet	National Motor Museum
1964	Ferrari 330GT coupé	National Motor Museum
1974	Ferrari Dino 246GT spyder	Nicky Wright/National Motor Museum
1982	Ferrari BB512 coupé	Nicky Wright/National Motor Museum
1985	Ferrari Testa Rossa coupé	National Motor Museum
1996	Ferrari F50 coupé	National Motor Museum
1937	Fiat Topolino 500 saloon	Nicky Wright/National Motor Museum
1977	Fiat 127 hatchback	National Motor Museum
1983	Fiat Uno 55S hatchback	National Motor Museum
1981	Fiat X1/9 targa sports car	National Motor Museum
2000	Fiat Multipla MPV	Fiat SpA
1914	Ford Model T 2-seater	National Motor Museum
1930	Ford Model A phaeton	National Motor Museum
1933	Ford V8 cabriolet	National Motor Museum
1956	Ford Thunderbird 2-door convertible	National Motor Museum
1957	Ford Zodiac Hyline saloon	National Motor Museum
1964	Ford Mustang 2-door convertible	Nicky Wright/National Motor Museum
1978	Ford Capri Ghia 3-litre coupé	Nicky Wright/National Motor Museum
1996	Ford Mondeo GLX saloon	National Motor Museum
1964	Ginetta G4 sports car	National Motor Museum
1965	Gordon Keeble 2-door coupé	National Motor Museum
1950	Healey Silverstone sports car	Nicky Wright/National Motor Museum
1963	Hillman Imp 2-door saloon	National Motor Museum
1912	Hispano-Suiza Alfonso sports car	Nicky Wright/National Motor Museum
1924	Hispano-Suiza Tulip Wood H6C dual phaeton	National Motor Museum
1967	Honda S800 convertible	Nicky Wright/National Motor Museum
1992	Honda NSX coupé	National Motor Museum
1950	Hotchkiss 2-door cabriolet	National Motor Museum
1957	Hudson Hornet 4-door sedan	Nicky Wright/National Motor Museum
1903	Humberette 5hp 2-seater	Nicky Wright/National Motor Museum
1934	Invicta 4-litre S Type Salmons drop-head coupé	National Motor Museum
1937	Jaguar SS100 2-seater sports car	National Motor Museum
1950	Jaguar XK120 2-seater sports car	Nicky Wright/National Motor Museum
1954	Jaguar MkVII saloon	Nick Georgano/National Motor Museum
1962	Jaguar Mk2 3.4 saloon	Nick Georgano/National Motor Museum
1963	Jaguar E Type roadster	National Motor Museum
1985	Jaguar XJ6 saloon	Nick Georgano/National Motor Museum
1997	Jaguar XK8 convertible	National Motor Museum

1974	Jensen Interceptor coupé	Nicky Wright/National Motor Museum
1953	Jowett Javelin saloon	Nick Georgano/National Motor Museum
1938	Lagonda V12 4-door saloon	Nicky Wright/National Motor Museum
1968	Lamborghini Miura P400 coupé	National Motor Museum
1993	Lamborghini Diablo coupé	National Motor Museum
1908	Lanchester 20hp landaulet	National Motor Museum
1928	Lancia Lambda 8th series tourer	National Motor Museum
1937	Lancia Aprilia 4-door saloon	National Motor Museum
1973	Lancia Stratos coupé	National Motor Museum
1941	Lincoln Continental club coupé	National Motor Museum
1962	Lotus Elite 2-seater hard-top	National Motor Museum
1972	Lotus Elan Sprint 2-seater sports car	National Motor Museum
1996	Lotus Elise 2-seater sports car	National Motor Museum
1949	Maserati A6-1500 coupé.	Nicky Wright/National Motor Museum
1973	Maserati Bora coupé.	Nick Georgano/National Motor Museum
1982	Mazda RX7 Elford Turbo coupé.	National Motor Museum
1995	Mazda MX5 2-seater sports car.	National Motor Museum
1907	Mercedes 40/45 Simplex tourer.	National Motor Museum
1929	Mercedes-Benz SS 38/250 tourer.	National Motor Museum
1935	Mercedes -Benz 500K convertible coupé.	National Motor Museum
1957	Mercedes-Benz 300SL Gullwing coupé.	National Motor Museum
1965	Mercedes-Benz 600 limousine.	National Motor Museum
1993	Mercedes-Benz S280 saloon.	National Motor Museum
1955	Messerschmitt KR200 bubblecar.	National Motor Museum
1930	MG M Midget sports car.	National Motor Museum
1933	MG J2 Midget sports car.	Nick Georgano/National Motor Museum
1947	MG TC Midget sports car.	National Motor Museum
1955	MGA 1600 MkI sports car.	National Motor Museum
1971	MGB roadster.	Nicky Wright/National Motor Museum
1995	MGF 1.8i sports car.	Rover Group
1948	Morgan 4/4 sports car.	Nicky Wright/National Motor Museum
1990	Morgan Plus 8 sports car.	National Motor Museum
2000	Morgan Aero 8 sports car.	Morgan Cars
1926	Morris Bullnose saloon.	National Motor Museum
1949	Morris Minor saloon.	Nicky Wright/National Motor Museum
1960	Morris Minor Traveller estate car.	National Motor Museum
1964	Morris Mini Cooper 'S' saloon.	National Motor Museum
1974	NSU Ro80 4-door saloon.	National Motor Museum
1912	Opel 5/14 2-seater.	National Motor Museum
1971	Opel GT coupé.	National Motor Museum
1920	Packard Twin 6 3-35 landaulet.	Nicky Wright/National Motor Museum
1939	Packard 120 Series 1700 convertible.	Nicky Wright/National Motor Museum
1947	Packard Clipper Custom Super 8 sedan.	Nicky Wright/National Motor Museum
1899	Panhard 6hp wagonette.	Nick Georgano/National Motor Museum
1955	Pegaso Z102B coupé.	Nicky Wright/National Motor Museum
1937	Peugeot 402B 4-door saloon.	Nick Georgano/National Motor Museum
1989	Peugeot 205 Gti 1.9 hatchback.	National Motor Museum
1996	Peugeot 306 Gti-6 hatchback.	Peugeot
1913	Pierce Arrow Gentleman's Roadster.	National Motor Museum

Alphabetical List of Original Manufacturers' Promotional Images included in Volume 1

Alphabetical List of Original Manufacturers' Promotional Images included in Volume 2

Alphabetical List of Original Manufacturers' Promotional Images included in Volume 3

Foreword
by Lord Montagu of Beaulieu

It has long been a dream of mine that the National Motor Museum at Beaulieu should be closely associated with a major international motoring work of reference. The opportunity came after a meeting at Beaulieu with Rupert Pennant-Rea shortly after he took over as Managing Director of Her Majesty's Stationery Office (HMSO), soon to be privatised and relaunched as The Stationery Office.

The *Beaulieu Encyclopedia of the Automobile* can trace its roots back to a slim volume, published privately in 1932 by George Ralph Doyle entitled *The World's Automobiles*. Keen-eyed readers will notice that this encyclopedia is dedicated to Ralph Doyle. 'Doyle', as this work of reference became known, was just a listing of manufacturers, dates, and addresses – the first ever to be published. Whilst studying at Oxford, Nick Georgano found a copy of Doyle and realised that with fuller facts that he had accumulated from his own researches, he could enlarge on that slim volume. The two enthusiasts met and became firm friends. When he died in 1961, Ralph Doyle left all his research notes to Nick Georgano, and the fourth and last edition of Doyle was put together by Nick for publication. Throughout this time, he had been developing ideas for a much more comprehensive book which would have biographical details of all manufacturers as well as photographs. A chance meeting in 1965 with British motoring historian Tim Nicholson resulted in Nick being introduced to the publishers George Rainbird Ltd, who had been thinking along similar lines. Thus was born the great *Complete Encyclopædia of Motor Cars*, published by Ebury Press in 1968, and this now famous work of reference has soldover 90,000 copies and been translated into five languages. There have been three editions, the last being in 1982, and to quote the words of Michael Lamm, Editor of *Special-Interest Autos* (and a contributor to this encyclopædia), in 1971:

'If an auto historian were sentenced to life in prison and allowed only one book in his cell, that book would have to be Georgano's *The Complete Encyclopædia of Motor Cars, 1885-1968*. I consider it the single most important work ever published in the field of automotive history – the one book about 20th century cars that 25th century historians will still keep handy. The dog-eared copy I bought in 1968 stands in the most accessible spot on my desk.

Even aside from the encyclopedia's reference value, I find myself picking it up constantly and reading it for pure pleasure – or just looking again and again at the 2000-odd photos. Anyone who has even glanced through this book has marvelled at the monumental job it must have been to compile.'

That splendid bible of motoring knowledge has long been out of print and second-hand copies change hands at inflated prices. We all knew that Nick Georgano was capable of great things and I persuaded him to put his name forward again as the editor for a brand new reference work which we were to propose to The Stationery Office. The result is a book of tremendous detail, produced from many years of research by many different people and three years of concentrated effort by Nick Georgano. So many people have helped over the years that it would be invidious of me to single out any one person but I would like to pay tribute to the late Michael Sedgwick, for so long my historical mentor at Beaulieu and the Museum's Director of Research. Sadly, Michael died in October 1983 but his memory lives on in many ways, including much of the background work in these volumes.

I am delighted that the National Motor Museum at Beaulieu was chosen by The Stationery Office to be its partner in this important work. Beaulieu has been connected with motoring from the earliest days. My father, who had a lifelong interest in all forms of transport, purchased his first car in 1898, followed a year later by the first 4-cylinder Daimler to be built in England, which is now owned by the Science Museum but is a prize exhibit on display at the National Motor Museum. Motoring is in the blood here at Beaulieu, in terms of both driving motor cars and recording their history. My father wrote a number of books about driving in the early days and in 1902 became founder editor of the weekly magazine *Car Illustrated*, which he continued to edit until the beginning of World War I. Many years later, in August 1956, I started *Veteran & Vintage* magazine, which ran through until August 1979 and is now incorporated with *Thoroughbred and Classic Cars*.

Palace House opened to the public in April 1952 with just a few old cars on show, and from this grew the Montagu Motor Museum and latterly the National Motor Museum. In 1960

I opened a Library of Motoring at Beaulieu based on my father's collection of books and in 1962 this was supplemented by a Photographic Library and later, in 1979, a Film and Video Archive. These Libraries are now renowned as important research establishments throughout the motoring world and much of the background research for that first encyclopædia was done by Nick Georgano at Beaulieu, whom I first met when he was trawling through the Montagu Motor Museum Library in Palace House for photographs to use in that first edition. I am pleased that the majority of the photographs in this book have come from our own files here at Beaulieu, supplemented from the private collection of Nick Baldwin, who is Chairman of the National Motor Museum's Advisory Council.

There are motoring historians in practically every country in the world, many of whom are members of the Society of Automotive Historians, and I know that much research in the future will start with a look into this encyclopedia. The study of motoring history is not adequately covered by Universities, one reason being because it is a new subject, but even so its impact on design, engineering and social history has been tremendous. The development of motoring has profoundly influenced the landscape around us and the way we live; the motor vehicle has carried goods to help keep the wheels of industry turning and has completely revolutionised personal mobility. We remember with affection not only our first car and those which have given us good service but also all the bad vehicles that stick in our minds.

Whilst there are nearly 1000 motor museums in the world, relatively few can claim to also be academic institutions, as we strive to do at Beaulieu. As competition increases for people's leisure time, motor museums find themselves struggling to stay afloat and have relatively few resources available for future research or publication. I hope we can reverse this trend in the next few years and I am confident that this great work of reference will be a catalyst for future research.

Montagu of Beaulieu

Acknowledgements

My thanks are due, first and foremost, to the contributors who not only delivered their material on time, but also answered the many queries that inevitably arose during preparation of the entries for the publishers.

I would like to thank Lord Montagu of Beaulieu and Michael Ware, former director of the National Motor Museum, for their tireless efforts to revive the encyclopedia over a number of years, culminating in the successful link with The Stationery Office.

Annice Collett, Marie Tieche, and Mike Budd of the National Motor Museum's Reference Library were always painstaking and prompt in replying to my abstruse queries, as was Jonathan Day of the Photographic Library in providing last-minute photos. Caroline Johnson, Library Secretary, was very helpful in rapid delivery of photocopies and information. The bulk of the illustrations have come from the collections of the National Motor Museum or Nick Baldwin, but others who have provided many excellent and rare photos include Mike Worthington-Williams, Bryan K. Goodman, John A. Conde, Keith Marvin, Halwart Schrader and Ernest Schmid, who lent a number of photos used in his excellent book on Swiss cars. Mike has also been very helpful with additional information and picture identification, as have Malcolm Jeal and Peter Heilbron. Gary Axon and Richard Heseltine gave valuable help with small postwar makes. Philip and Sue Hill toiled for many hours preparing a list of *Automobile Quarterly* entries for the further reading sections. Countless other people have provided help in many ways; to name some would be invidious but to name all would be impossible.

On the publishing side I am deeply grateful to Mick Spencer, Editorial Manager at The Stationery Office; always patient with last-minute changes and additions, he has enabled the encyclopedia to be up-to-date to within three months of publication. The layout has been the responsibility of Designer Guy Myles Warren, who has worked wonders fitting some 3500 photos of assorted shapes and sizes and a text of almost 1.5 million words into something under 2000 pages. The complete text was checked by Editor Sallie Moss, and the galley proofs were read by freelance proof reader Lynne Davies.

Finally, I should thank my wife Jenny without whom this book could never have been produced. She has been responsible for dealing with all correspondence, filing, packing and posting proofs, often at very short notice, as well as providing a steady flow of tea, coffee, and, sometimes, stronger beverages.

NICK GEORGANO
Guernsey, May 2000

Introduction

According to the Oxford English Dictionary, an encyclopedia is 'an elaborate and exhaustive reportory of information on all branches of some particular art or department of knowledge, especially one arranged in alphabetical order.'

This seems as good a definition as any for what we have set out to do in this encyclopedia, although some limitations have to be placed on the concept of exhaustiveness. For a name to qualify as a 'make of car', there must be some evidence of an intention to manufacture, even if it was not a success, and resulted in no more than a single prototype. This is clearly not a water-tight definition, for to establish 'intention to manufacture' one would have to read the minds of men long dead. In the early days many people built a car to prove to themsleves that they could do so, and to make some improvements on what had gone before. Their friends might say "That's nice, will you make one for me?" and some sort of production would follow. Louis Renault might never have become a manufacturer had friends not admired his first effort and asked for replicas. Many of his contemporaries took a stand at the Paris Salon on which to show their hastily-assembled prototype, and if no customers came forward they went no further, and never formed a company. These must, nevertheless, be considered as makes.

On the other hand there were countless backyard tinkerers who built a car or two purely for their own amusement, but through lack of capital or interest in business never planned to make cars for sale. They flourished chiefly in the years up to 1914, though some appeared up to World War II, such as Willard L. Morrison of Buchanan, Michigan, who built a Ford V8-powered streamlined sedan in 1935.

Also in this category are the 19th century steam car makers, with the honourable exception of Thomas Rickett, who not only buiilt two 3-wheelers to the order of British aristocrats, but placed an advertisement in *The Engineer* offering replicas for sale. This earns him a place in the encyclopædia, unlike his contemporaries Yarrow & Hilditch or on the Continent, Etienne Lenoir, Gustav Hammel, or Siegfried Markus, whose vehicles were purely experimental.

Other categories not included are the following;

1   Motorcycles are obviously ruled out, though some 2-wheelers with car-like bodywork, such as the Atlantic, Monotrace and Whitwood Monocar, are included. A more difficult problem is posed by the distinction between a tricycle and a 3-wheeled car. Early tricycles, such as the De Dion-Bouton, were no more than motorcycles with a third wheel, but from about 1903 a type of vehicle appeared which used the frame, saddle, engine and final drive of a motorcycle with two wheels in front, and a body, often of wickerwork, for a passenger. Known as tri-cars, they were still of motorcycle descent, but gradually the driver's saddle became a seat and the handlebars were replaced by a steering wheel, giving them the appearance of a tandem car on three wheels. With makes such as Riley it is almost impossible to decide at what point they became cars. The more car-like vehicles, such as the Bat or Rexette are included, while the many makes which never progressed beyond saddle, handlebars and wickerwork, are not.

2   Cars built purely for racing, and not usable on public roads, such as Formula One and Indy cars.

3   A number of makes listed in earlier encyclopedias are absent as research has placed them in the one-off experimental category. Sometimes evidence is lacking that they ever built even one car, despite advertising that they did. An exception is made for the Owen of Comeragh Road, which persisted on paper for 36 years, and is one of the great conundrums of motoring history.

No attempt has been made to describe every model made by any firm, large or small. In 1927 Daimler listed 27 models, and to mention them all would be tedious and wasteful of space. However, we have endeavoured to indicate the range of models, highlighting any unconventional or unexpected designs, and technical features which were unusual for the period. Up to about 1900, when there was great diversity, and engines might be at the front, centre or rear of the frame, vertical or horizontal and cooled by water or air, these features are generally mentioned. With the coming of a relatively standard layout of front-mounted vertical water-cooled engine, driving by a 3- or 4-speed sliding pinion gearbox and propeller shaft to a bevel rear axle, it is only the exceptions which are noted. Front wheel brakes were noteworthy in the early 1920s, but later were noteworthy only by their absence, as on the 1950 Bond Minicar or its contemporary, the Mochet.

The dating of cars, especially in the illustration captions, may cause confusion because of the discrepancy between the model and calendar year. Normally the date represents the year in which the car was made, a practice followed by the Dating Committee of the Veteran Car Club of Great Britain. An exception has to be made for American cars, which were generally announced in September or October of their model year. The Mercury was introduced in November 1938, (hence a starting date of 1938 in our entry) but even the first cars were always thought of as 1939 models. Similarly, Ford Thunderbird enthusiasts will not recognise that there was a 1954 Thunderbird, though quite a number were made in that calendar year.

The nationality of a make is indicated by the letter(s) used on touring plates, and refers to the country where the parent firm was located. An exceptions is EU which is not yet a nation state, but is used for Fords built in various European factories and which are quite international in design. The Fiesta is no more British than it is German, Belgian, or Spanish. Dual nationality may occur in two ways:

- Cars like the Pennington which had factories in two countries at the same time, are indicated by (US/GB).
- Cars whose nationality changed for political reasons, such as Bugatti and Mathis, which were German up to 1918 when the province of Alsace became French, are indicated by (D;F).

The makes are listed in alphabetical order, but the following points should be noted:

- Makes which consist of Christian and surnames are listed under the Christian name e.g., Georges Irat, not Irat, Georges.
- Makes beginning with Mc are listed between MCC and M.C.M., not at the beginning of the letter 'M'.

- Makes beginning with De are listed under the letter 'D'. Thus De Lavaud is found in 'D', not 'L'.
- Makes using initial letters joined by 'and', such as S & M Simplex are treated as if they were spelt S M.
- Chinese names are romanised using the Pinyin system.

We hope that this encyclopedia will be not only readable, but accurate. Some familiar stories have been corrected. For example, it was long held that Ned Jordan started his upward progress by marrying the daughter of his boss, Thomas Jeffery. Not so; recent research has revealed that his bride was Lotta Hanna whose father ran a furniture store in Kenosha, Wisconsin. History is being rewritten all the time, and it would be unrealistic to suppose that production figures and other statistics may not be revised in the future. More generally, one cannot do better than quote the words of the great historian and journalist Laurence Pomeroy Jr. 'It is manifestly desirable that any reference book should be wholly free from error, but this is an ideal which it seems impossible to realise. The author can only plead that he, like others, has found that "sudden fits of inadvertancy will surprise vigilance, slight avocations will seduce attention. and casual eclipses of the mind will darken learning"'.

NICK GEORGANO
Guernsey, May 2000

Further Reading

Readers seeking more detailed information are referred to marque histories or serious historical articles in magazines. For obvious reasons of space, we are not including contemporary magazine announcements or road tests. These can be found in the Reference Library at the National Motor Museum, which offers a photocopying service and is happy to answer queries by post, telephone, fax or e-mail.

The Reference Library, National Motor Museum, Beaulieu, Hampshire SO42 7ZN, tel. 01590 614652; fax. 01590 612655; e-mail motoring.library@beaulieu.co.uk

Photographic enquiries should be made to the Photographic Library at the same address, tel. 01590 614656; fax as above; e-mail motoring.pictures@beaulieu.co.uk

Again, for space reasons we have not referred under each entry to the many excellent books devoted to the makes of one country or era. Among the more valuable of these are:

Great Britain

A to Z of Cars of the 1920s, Nick Baldwin, Bay View Books, 1994.

A to Z of Cars of the 1930s, Michael Sedgwick and Mark Gillies, Bay View Books, 1989.

A to Z of Cars, 1945-1970, Michael Sedgwick and Mark Gillies, (revised by Jon Pressnell), Bay View Books, 1993.

A to Z of Cars of the 1970s, Graham Robson, Bay View Books, 1990.

A to Z of Cars of the 1980s, Martin Lewis, Bay View Books, 1998.

The Complete Catalogue of British Cars, David Culshaw and Peter Horrobin, Veloce Publishing, 1997.

Germany

Autos in Deutschland 1885-1920, Hans-Heinrich von Fersen, Motorbuch-Verlag, Stuttgart, 1965.

Autos in Deutschland 1920-1945, Werner Oswald, Motorbuch-Verlag, Stuttgart, 1981.

Autos in Deutschland 1945-1975, Werner Oswald, Motorbuch-Verlag, Stuttgart, 1980.

France

In First Gear. The French Automobile Industry to 1914, James M. Laux, Liverpool University Press, 1976.

French Cars 1920–1925, Pierre Dumont, Frederick Warne, 1978.

Toutes les Voitures Francaise 1935, René Bellu, Herme-Vilo,1984.

Toutes les Voitures Francaise 1939, René Bellu, Edita Vilo, 1982.

Les Voitures Francaise des Annees 50 (actually covers 1945-1959), René Bellu, Editions Delville, 1983.

Switzerland

Automobiles Suisses des Origines à nos Jours, Ernest Schmid, Editions du Chateau de Grandson, 1967.

Schweizer Autos, (expanded version of above, in German) Ernest Schmid, Editions du Chateau de Grandson, 1978.

Netherlands

Autodesign in Nederland, Jan Lammerse, Waanders Uitgevers, Zwolle, 1993.

Belgium

Histoire de l'Automobile Belge, Yvette and Jacques Kupélian and Jacques Sirtaine, Editions Paul Legrain, c.1972.

Austria

Gesichte von Oesterreiche Kraftfahrt, Hans Seper, Oesterreiche Wirtschaft Verlag, 1968.

Spain

El Automovil en Espana, Pablo Gimenez Vallador, RACE, Madrid, 1998.

Historia de l'Automobilisme a Catalunya, Javier del Arco, Planita, 1990.

Italy

Marche Italiane Scomparse, Museo dell' Automobile Carlo Biscaretti di Ruffia, Turin, 1972.

Hungary

A Magyer Auto, Zsuppan Istvan, Zrini Kiado, 1994.

Canada

Cars of Canada, Hugh Durnford and Glenn Baechler, McLelland & Stewart, 1973.

United States

There are many titles, but none can rival the incomparable:

The Standard Catalog of American Cars 1805-1942, Beverly Rae Kimes and
Henry Austin Clark Jr, Krause Publications, 1996.

For more recent cars, and in the same series:

The Standard Catalog of American Cars 1946-1975, edited by John A. Gunnell,
Krause Publications, 1982.

Japan

Autos made in Japan, Jan P. Norbye, Heicher Verlag, 1991.

Terms and Abbreviations Used

Throughout the encyclopedia technical and other terms are generally described according to current English usage. For the convenience of American readers a short list of the more frequently-used terms whose meaning differs in American usage is given below.

English	American	English	American
bonnet	hood	paraffin	kerosene
boot	trunk	petrol	gasoline
capacity (of engine)	displacement	saloon	sedan
coupé de ville	town car	sedanca de ville	town car
dickey (seat)	rumble seat	shooting-brake	station wagon
engine	motor	silencer	muffler
epicyclic (gears)	planetary (gears)	track	tread
estate car	station wagon	two-stroke	two-cycle
gearbox	transmission	windscreen	windshield
hood	top	wing	fender
mudguard	fender		

The following have generally been used in the text for frequently-repeated terms.

bhp	brake horse power
cc	cubic centimetres
cr	compression ratio
CV	cheveaux-vapeur (French horsepower rating)
fwd	front-wheel drive
GP	Grand Prix
GT	GranTurismo
hp	horse power
ifs	independent front suspension
in	inch(es)
ioe	inlet over exhaust
km	kilometre(s)
km/h	kilometres per hour
kg	kilogram(s)
lb	pound(s)
LPG	liquid petroleum gas
lwb	long wheelbase
mm	millimetre(s)
mpg	miles per gallon
mph	miles per hour
ohc	overhead camshaft(s)
ohv	overhead valve(s)
PS	Pferdestärke (German horsepower rating)
psi	pounds per square inch
rpm	revolutions per minute
rwd	rear-wheel drive
sv	side valve(s)
swb	short wheelbase
TT	Tourist Trophy

A.A.A. (i) **(D)** 1919–1922

Aktiengesellschaft für Akkumulatoren- und Automobilbau, Berlin.
This battery manufacturer turned to making electric cars and also vans, for which it was better known. Large numbers were used by the German Post Office. Petrol cars were later produced under the name ALFI.
HON

A.A.A. (ii) **(F)** 1920

Ateliers d'Automobile et d'Aviation, Paris.
This company made a few large 4-door electric saloons, though they were better known for truck manufacture.
NG

AAC COBRA (US) 1993–1995

All American Classics, East Berlin, Pennsylvania.
AAC built a 427 Cobra replica with a round-tube frame designed around Ford or Chevy engines. They were sold in kit or assembled form.
HP

A.A.G. (D) 1900–1901

Allgemeiner Automobil-Gesellschaft Berlin GmbH, Berlin.
Professor Klingenberg from the Berlin Technical University introduced the *Kapselmotor*, in which engine, gearbox and differential were fixed to the rear axle. The engine was a single-cylinder 5PS unit. After limited production under the AAG name, the design was taken over by the AEG electrical concern, who put it into production as the first NAG. AAG also made 2-seater electric cars and petrol-engined tricycles.
HON

AB1 *see* A. F. (ii)

A.B.A.M. *see* KRIÉGER

ABADAL (E) 1912–1923; 1930

F.S. Abadal Cia., Barcelona.
Francisco Serramelera Abadal became the Madrid agent for the newly-announced HISPANO-SUIZA cars in 1904, extending his dealership to Barcelona in 1908. Four years later he announced a car under his own name. Cylinder dimensions were similar to those of the Hispano-Suiza Alfonso, at 80 × 180mm, as was the T-head valve layout, but they were not made by Hispano. Instead Abadal bought them from the Belgian IMPERIA company, who also made the chassis. Abadals wore handsome vee radiators and were mostly seen with sporting bodywork, particularly skiff tourers by Labourdette and Alin et Liautard. About 90 Abadals were made until the outbreak of World War I abruptly ended supplies from Belgium. Abadal also offered a 4.5-litre 6-cylinder car; its origins are unknown as such a model was listed neither by Imperia nor Hispano-Suiza. During the war Abadal built a number of bodies on Hispano-Suiza, Mercedes and Peugeot chassis, but soon concentrated on the 6-cylinder Buick, for which he became Spanish agent from 1916. These bodies often concealed the American origins of the chassis, with exotic town car or racing styles, being sold as Abadal-Buicks. The longstroke fours were made in Belgium by Imperia, and sold under the Imperia-Abadal name. There was also a 5.6-litre straight-8 Imperia-Abadal, of which only three or four were made. Imperia dropped the Spanish designs in 1923 after about 170 had been made and the Abadal-Buicks faded away at about the same time. The last car to bear the Abadal name appeared in 1930. It was a 4-door saloon of very American lines, powered by a 3.5-litre Continental six engine, though a European feature was a 4-speed gearbox. It never went into production.
NG

ABARTH (I) 1949–1971

Abarth & Co., Turin.
Karl Abarth was born in 1908 in Austria and his family moved to Italy just after World War I. In the 1930s Abarth was five times a European motorcycle champion. He built his first car in 1928, when only 20 and, significantly, he also designed his first exhaust system – with a high efficiency silencer – about the same time. Exhaust systems were to become Abarth's speciality.

1900 A.A.G. Klingenberg 5PS vis-à-vis.
HANS-OTTO NEUBAUER

1914 Abadal 15.9hp Skiff sports tourer, with coachwork by Labourdette.
NICK BALDWIN

Abarth's competition successes were embraced by the Italian government and, since Karl loved Italy, he gradually became Carlo.

In October 1939, Abarth was injured in a race in Yugoslavia and, when he was released from hospital, World War II had begun and he decided to stay where he was. During the war Abarth worked on engines and, afterwards, his old friend, Ferry Porsche, employed him in his design studio. Abarth was part of the Cisitalia Formula One project – and was especially useful since he was fluent in both German and Italian. When Cisitalia's patron, Piero Dusio, left Italy in 1949, Guido Scarliarini (a Cisitalia customer) persuaded his father to set up Abarth in business.

At first, Abarth continued the Cisitalia customer car programme, and then he made dual-purpose sports/racing cars under his own name. The first of these, the Abarth 204, owed much to the Cisitalia 202. The first 204 Spyder appeared at the Madrid (sports car) Grand Prix in 1949, but it was so slow that orders were cancelled and Abarth nearly folded. The problem was traced to the special, alcohol-based, fuel which deteriorated in transit.

By the end of the year, however, Abarth could claim 16 race wins and had lived down its early problem. It proved to Karl, however, how fickle competition success could be and, thereafter, he ensured that competition cars were only a part of a broader portfolio.

The Abarth 204 faded as a competition car after 1951, but road-going versions were made until 1956.

From the start, Scuderia Abarth made tuning accessories, and Abarth exhaust systems and silencers became available for many cars. To drum up publicity, Abarth turned to record breaking, but it was not until 1955 that the company again built a new competition car, the Tipo 207 Spyder. The T207 used modified Fiat 1100 running gear in a chassis based on the 204-series.

The Spyder was competitive in America until Coventry Climax-powered cars from Cooper and Lotus arrived – but they made no impact in international racing. Road versions were offered.

When Fiat introduced the 600 in 1956, Abarth made a 750cc version which was followed by the 850 TC (Turismo Competizione). Fiat supplied part finished

1957 Abarth 500 coupé.
NATIONAL MOTOR MUSEUM

1962 Abarth 1000 coupé.
NATIONAL MOTOR MUSEUM

1960 Abarth 2.2-litre coupé.
NATIONAL MOTOR MUSEUM

1917 Abbott tourer.
JOHN A. CONDE

cars and, in return, received a great deal of publicity – in 1972, Fiat claimed that Abarth-modified Fiats had taken 7200 outright and class wins.

It is impossible to say how many models Abarth made because so many cars were in a constant state of development and change – most authorities simply put the figure at 'between 150 and 250'. The most famous, however, were small coupés, based on the Fiat 600, with bodies by Zagato which had distinctive 'twin bubble' roofs.

Production estimates of these cars range from 600 to 1800 units. Then Abarth and Zagato quarrelled – neither man was flexible – and while that ended one line, Vignale, Viotti, Pininfarina, Bertone and Allemano also built bodies on a Fiat-Abarth base.

The engine was gradually enlarged to 1-litre and the range included one with a double-ohc cylinder head and another with a cross-over pushrod system similar to the BMW 328 unit.

In 1960 came another link with Ferry Porsche in the Porsche-Abarth Carrera GTL. This was a Porsche 356B with a body by Abarth which was lighter (by 150 kg) than the standard shell and probably more aerodynamically efficient. Most of the 18 made were used for racing.

Abarth was unusual among the small Italian makers in that it did not make a car for Formula Junior, and it was one of the few Italian specialist makers to survive the onslaught of Lotus-Ford and Cooper-BMC in 1960.

A nominal partnership with SIATA, 1959–61, produced no cars, but in 1961 Abarth joined with Simca to make modified versions of the Simca 1100 and special bodies on Simca chassis. As with the Fiat cars, there was a long menu of engine options up to a double-ohc 2-litre version. When Chrysler bought Simca in 1965, the relationship ended.

These affairs with other makers did not weaken the marriage with Fiat, and there were rebodied Abarth versions of many of the larger Fiats from the 1100 to the 2300. The engine of the Fiat 850 of 1964 is believed to have been derived from Abarth's own work on the Fiat 600, and is a classic 'chicken and egg' scenario.

By the mid–1960s, Abarth was making double-ohc 4-cylinder 1300cc and 1600cc engines some of which found their way into Fiat 850 chassis.

Against its natural inclination, the company became directly involved with motor racing and undertook a number of ambitious projects which included a 3-litre Formula One engine and a 6-litre V12 sports car unit. Karl Abarth had succumbed to the pride which afflicts many makers of performance cars – he had to measure himself against the best, but the exercise drained his company.

In 1970 Abarth produced its last distinct model, the Scorpione, a mid-engined wedge-shaped coupé which used an enlarged Fiat 124 engine and, by 1971, the company was in such a perilous state that Fiat took it over, retaining Karl as technical consultant.

Karl Abarth, for so long his own master, was unhappy working for a large corporation, and he returned to Austria, where he died in 1979. Abarth, the company, developed the successful Fiat rally cars of the late 1970s and the equally successful Lancias of the 1980s.

In 1984, Fiat used the Abarth name on the double-ohc Strada 130 TC which used the 2 litre double-ohc engine from the Mirafiori Sport. The result was the quickest hatchback of its time, although it was the least refined. The Abarth badge went into abeyance when the Strada ceased production in 1988.

In the late 1990s Fiat revived the name, but only for cosmetic accessories, and then only on its smaller cars.

MJL

Further Reading
'Automobile Piccola, Gran Brio! The small wonders of Carlo Abarth',
Alfred S. Consentino, *Automobile Quarterly*, Vol.13, No.1.

ABBEY (GB) 1922

Abbey Auto Engineering Co., Westminster, London.

Assembled close to Westminster Abbey, from whence presumably it was named, the Abbey Ten was a conventional light car powered by a 1498cc 4-cylinder Coventry-Simplex engine, with friction disc transmission and chain final drive. Only one body style was offered, a two seater with dickey; a hood could be erected to cover front seats and dickey. *The Light Car & Cyclecar* had doubts about its appearance, saying 'To those who may have been brought up on aestheticism to a fine art it may even appear to be ugly, but the fact remains that it fulfils its purpose'. Priced at £315, the Abbey was announced in February 1922 and does not seem to have survived the year.

NG

ABBOTT-DETROIT; ABBOTT (US) 1909–1918
1909–1915 Abbott Motor Car Co., Detroit, Michigan.
1915–1916 Consolidated Car Co., Detroit, Michigan.
1916–1918 The Abbott Corp., Cleveland, Ohio.
The Abbott-Detroit was a conventional car, initially powered by a 30hp 4-cylinder
Continental engine, and with one body style, a 5-seater tourer priced at $1500.
Founder Charles Abbott left his company in 1910, but by 1912 the range had
expanded to five styles on two wheelbases, 110 and 120in (2972 and 3046mm),
priced from $1275 for a 4-door roadster to $3000 for a 7-passenger limousine.
That year the company built 1817 cars, its best output ever as it turned out, and
the slogan was 'Built for Permanence'. Abbott-Detroits were of very conventional
appearance, apart from the 1913 Battleship Roadster which had a striking vee
radiator. A 6-cylinder engine, also by Continental, joined the range in 1914 when
the company was reorganised. New owner Edward F. Gerber left in 1915 and
was replaced by R.A. Palmer who had formerly managed CARTERCAR. He
changed the name to Consolidated Car Co., and expanded the range to include
the Model 8-80, powered by a Herschell-Spillman V8. The four was dropped
after 1915. In order to increase production Palmer relocated the company to
Cleveland in April 1917, a few days before America entered World War I, changing
the name of both company and car to Abbott. He acquired a large factory taken
on a ten-year lease, but sales never justified the move and were lower than they
had been in Detroit. Very few of the 8-80 were made and none at Cleveland,
where a small number of sixes were built before Abbott went bankrupt in January
1918. Just 312 cars were made that year. Total production of Abbotts and
Abbott-Detroits over a twelve year period was 12,244. The Cleveland plant was
acquired by the National Electric Lamp Works, and it is believed that a few
cars were assembled by this company from parts left behind by The Abbott
Corporation.
NG

A.B.C. (i) (US) 1905–1910
1905–1908 Autobuggy Manufacturing Co., St Louis, Missouri.
1908–1910 A.B.C. Motor Vehicle Manufacturing Co., St Louis, Missouri .
This car took its name from the initials of its maker Amédée B. Cole. Early
cars were called Autobuggy, not to be confused with the AUTO-BUGGY, also
a high-wheeler and also made in St Louis at the same time. The A.B.C. was a
typical high wheel buggy with 10/12hp 2-cylinder engine and friction transmission
by cone and two bevel wheels, one for forward motion and one for reverse. This
enabled the car to be driven at 30mph (48km/h) in reverse, if anyone wanted to
do such a thing. Final drive was by single chain. For 1908 power went up to
16/18hp and the wheelbase was extended considerably, from 72in (1827mm) to
90in (2284mm). The 1909 range was very complex, with ten 2-cylinder models,
offered with air- or water-cooling and pneumatic as well as solid tyres, and a
30/35hp 4-cylinder car on a 112in (2843mm) wheelbase. These were continued
into 1910 when Cole's company went bankrupt.
NG

A.B.C. (ii) (GB) 1920–1927
A.B.C. Motors (1920)Ltd, Hersham, Surrey.
The origins of the A.B.C. company lay in a small factory at Redbridge, near
Southampton, where motorboat and aero engines were made before World War I.
In 1911 they moved to Brooklands to be nearer to the few firms that were
making aircraft then, and soon afterwards added to their range flat-twin engines
for motorcycles and cyclecars. Complete motorcycles were then made by A.B.C.
Road Motors Ltd of Walton-on-Thames, and this company also made aero
engines during World War I, including the famous Dragonfly, Gnat and Wasp.
    In 1919 A.B.C. began to make the Scootamota, one of the first motor
scooters, and in 1920 a new company, A.B.C. Motors (1920) Ltd was formed
to make aero engines, motorcycles and a new light car. All were to be powered
by flat-twin engines designed by Granville Bradshaw, who had been involved
with A.B.C. since 1910. The car had a 1203cc air-cooled ohv engine, 4-speed
gearbox and shaft drive to a spiral bevel rear axle. 2- and 4-seater tourers and a
Super Sports with 1320cc engine and pointed tail were made. They performed
well but the engines were rough and noisy and none too reliable at first, being
very prone to breaking pushrods. Planned sales of 5000 per year never materialised,
and not more than 1500 were made altogether. Although the A.B.C. was listed until

c.1911 Abbott-Detroit tourer.
NATIONAL MOTOR MUSEUM

1907 A.B.C.(i) motor buggy.
JOHN A.CONDE

c.1922 A.B.C.(ii) 12hp 2-seater.
NICK BALDWIN

1927, production may not have lasted beyond 1925. In 1929 the company
made a single example of an aeroplane, the Robin, and continued to maker aero
engines and, from 1932, a flat-twin auxiliary engine designed by Lord Ridley,
who had joined the company in 1929. This was widely used during World War
II for driving dynamos and compressors. A.B.C. became part of Vickers in 1951
and was closed down in 1971.
NG
Further Reading
'Sixty Years of A.B.C. Motors', David Hales,
The Veteran & Vintage Magazine, September and October, 1970.

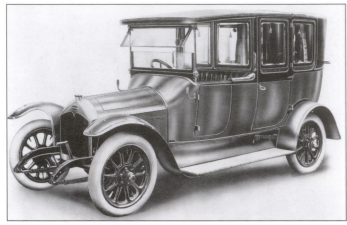

1913 Aberdonia 15hp landaulet.
NATIONAL MOTOR MUSEUM

1923 A.B.F., 2-seater.
BRIAN DEMAUS

A.B.C. (iii) (GB) 1969–1973
1969–1971 Auto Body Craft, Kingswinford, West Midlands.
1971–1973 Auto Body Craft, Brierley Hill, Staffordshire.
The ABC Tricar probably qualifies as the first-ever road-going Mini-based trike. The whole front end of the Mini was retained, but the rear half was chopped away and fitted with half a rear Mini subframe. A glassfibre open 2-seater body was bonded on top. Later Tricars had all-glassfibre bodywork, and the whole front end swung forwards for access to the engine. Around 25 were made in total.
CR

ABEILLE see A.M.

ABERDONIA (GB) 1911–1915
Aberdonia Cars Ltd, Shepherd's Bush, London; Park Royal, London.
The Aberdonia was made by the coachbuilders Brown, Hughes and Strachan, the bodies coming from their Park Royal coachbuilding department, while chassis were made at Shepherd's Bush. Only one engine size was offered, a 3160cc 16/20hp 4-cylinder with side-valves and monobloc casting. Tourers and landaulets were made, and in 1911 Brown, Hughes & Strachan showed on their own stand at Olympia an extraordinary 'Park Royal town landau' in which the driver was located ahead of the engine which was concealed between him and the passenger compartment. This was of barouche layout, with the passengers facing each other. It was almost certainly a one-off.
NG

A.B.F. (GB) 1923
Albert O. Ford, Kenilworth, Warwickshire.
Canadian-born Albert Ford called his car the A.B.F. (All-British Ford) to make sure no one confused it with the better-known products of Henry Ford. A quick

look under the bonnet would have dispelled any confusion, for the A.B.F. had a V4 2-stroke engine, each cylinder delivering a charge to its neighbour while on the firing stroke, as in the Trojan. Capacity was 1216cc, and the 3-speed gearbox was in unit with the engine. Drive was by shaft to a worm rear axle, but this was to have been replaced by a spiral bevel. The body was from a racing 10/30 Alvis, but production cars would have had a 3-door 4-seater tourer body. Ford also built a more conventional light car with 4-stroke flat-twin engine. Only one of each was made, but the 2-stroke survives today.
NG

ABINGDON (i) (GB) 1902–1903
John Child Meredith Ltd, Birmingham.
This company were well-known makers of ignition equipment and accessories, but they briefly offered two models of car. The Abingdon was a voiturette with 3½hp single-cylinder engine, 2-speed gearbox and single chain drive, gaining its name from the fact that it was sold by Coxeter & Sons of Abingdon, Berkshire. Also made was a larger car called the Meredith, a 4-seater tonneau with 9hp 2-cylinder engine.
NG

ABINGDON (ii) (GB) 1922–1923
Abingdon Works Ltd, Tyseley, Birmingham.
Made by a firm better known for the Abingdon King Dick spanner, and also for A.K.D. motorcycles, this was a light car powered by a 1490cc Dorman S4 4-cylinder engine with 3-speed gearbox and spiral bevel rear axle by Wrigley, who also supplied the steering gear. It seems that this reliance on Wrigley proved unwise, for when that company was taken over for manufacture of the Morris Commercial, Abingdon lost their supplier and did not bother to look for another. Probably they found car manufacture unprofitable anyway, and only 12 Abingdons were built.
NG

ABLE (F) 1920–1925
Paul Toulouse, Orgon, Bouche-du-Rhône; Avignon, Vaucluse.
The Able was one of many regional makes which flourished briefly in the 1920s, but faded in the face of competition from the mass producers. It was a tourer powered by various proprietary 4-cylinder engines, including the 1095cc ohv Chapuis-Dornier and 1494cc single-ohc C.I.M.E.
NG

ABLE EIGHT see VERNON

A.B.S. (GB) 1988–1991
Auto Build-Up Services, Wimborne, Dorset.
The A.B.S Scorpion was a revival of the BROADBEST Primo Countach replica with American V8 power. A.B.S. also made an open-topped Countach, which they called the Monaco. Both models were subsequently re-engineered by PRESTIGE.
CR

A.C. (GB) 1908 to date
1908–1911 Autocars & Accessories Ltd, West Norwood, London.
1911–1922 Autocarriers (1911) Ltd, Thames Ditton, Surrey.
1922–1984 A.C. Cars Ltd, Thames Ditton, Surrey.
1984–1985 A.C. (Scotland) Ltd, Glasgow.
1986–1990 C.P. Autokraft Ltd, Weybridge, Surrey.
1996 to date A.C. Car Group Ltd, Weybridge, Surrey.
Autocars & Accessories was formed in 1904 to make a 3-wheeled trade carrier in which the driver sat behind the load. A passenger version was introduced in 1908, in which the passenger took the place of the box van, and in 1910 this was replaced by the Sociable in which driver and passenger sat side by side at the front of the vehicle. There was also a 3-seater version in which the driver sat behind, with two passengers ahead of him. Mechanically, the Sociable followed the same pattern as the earlier vehicles, with a 648cc single-cylinder air-cooled engine driving by chain to a 2-speed epicyclic gearbox mounted on one side of the rear wheel. The brake drum was mounted on the other side of the wheel. The wooden frame was of ash, and the body of birch.

The A.C. Sociable was the first of the cyclecars, and sold well, at a price of only £90. A 1913 advertisement said that 1800 had been delivered, but it was not clear whether this figure referred to the year's production, or to the total made since 1908. However the builders, John Weller and John Portwine, had higher ambitions, and in 1913 there appeared Weller's 4-wheeled car. This was a quality light car with nothing of the cyclecar about it. The engine was a 1096cc French-built Fivet, and transmission was by a transaxle, or combined gearbox and rear axle which characterised all A.C. cars up to 1930. The standard body was 2-seater with dickey seat, but there was also a sports model, strictly a 2-seater with pointed tail and no weather protection. A team of these took part in trials and hill climbs, but few were sold to the public, and indeed total production of the prewar A.C. probably did not exceed 100. As well as the 1096cc engine, a 1327cc was offered. Artillery or wire wheels were available.

After the war Weller and Portwine considered putting a flat-twin engine in the 10hp chassis, but decided to continue with the four. A few cars were completed using the prewar Fivet engine, after which A.C. turned to British Anzani. They placed an order for 2000 of Anzani's 1496cc engines, and in recognition of such important business, both men were given places on the board of British Anzani. More significant than the four, though, was Weller's brand-new 1477cc 6-cylinder engine. Made by A.C. themselves, this had a chain-driven overhead camshaft, inclined overhead valves, light alloy cylinders and wet liners. It was announced in 1919, but needed a lot of development before it was quiet and smooth enough to be acceptable for use in a quality touring car. However, when it did get into production in 1922, enlarged to 1991cc, it remained in A.C.'s range until 1963, without major design change. During the period, output rose from 40bhp at 2800rpm to 103bhp at 4500rpm.

While the six was being developed, the Anzani-engined four kept A.C. going very satisfactorily. It was aimed above the Morris Cowley market, and with attractive 2- or 4-seater bodywork, the A.C. was one of the best-looking light cars of its period. Particularly eye-catching was the sports 2-seater with pointed tail and polished aluminium body. As delivered from British Anzani, the 1496cc engine gave about 25bhp, but tuning by A.C. enabled it to deliver 40bhp, and the sports model was known as the 12/40.

A.C.'s attraction for the sportsman was enhanced by a number of competition successes, particularly in the field of record breaking. With a special racing chassis and very slim single-seater body, Harry Hawker covered the flying half mile at 105mph (169km/h) in 1921, and in November 1922 J.A. Joyce became the first man to cover 100 miles (160 kilometres) in an hour in a light car. This was achieved with a streamlined Hawker body in an underslung chassis powered by a 16-valve engine. Joyce's actual speed in the hour was 101.375mph (163.112 km/h). Replicas of this car with a standard Anzani engine were offered for sale up to 1926 at £1000. It is not known if any were sold. The 16-valve engine was used in the works entries for the Brooklands 200 Mile Race in 1923 and 1924, Joyce finishing 3rd in 1923 and 4th in 1924.

There were considerable changes in A.C.'s management in the early 1920s. In February 1921 the dynamic and often controversial S.F. Edge, who had promoted Napiers so successfully before the war, joined the board of directors. He clearly did not get on with the original partners, Weller and Portwine, and in September 1922 they both resigned, leaving Edge in command of the company. He began to make 4-cylinder engines of Anzani type in the CUBITT factory, and never took the full 2000 engines from Anzani that A.C. had agreed to buy in 1919. By the mid–1920s A.C. was in difficulties; the cars had sold well in the first few years, but there was little modernisation, and front wheel brakes were not standardised until 1927. Sales dropped, especially of the 4-cylinder car, and Edge had to put £135,000 of his own money into A.C. It was reformed as A.C. (Acedes) Ltd in 1927, but three years later it went into liquidation, and car manufacture ceased. Edge left, having lost all his investment.

The 6-cylinder car did not get into serious production until the end of 1923, but once on the market it quickly took over from the ageing 4-cylinder model. Several body styles were offered, including A.C.'s first saloon (from 1926)and the popular Aceca drophead coupé. One of these was owned by the Hon. Victor Bruce who made a number of well-publicised long-distance journeys, and in 1926 gave Britain its first victory in the Monte Carlo Rally. Mrs Bruce followed this with 6th place in 1927 and 5th in 1928.

Saved by the Hurlocks
It would not have been surprising if A.C. had vanished for ever after the liquidation of 1930. Many other car makers, some older than A.C., were killed off by the

c.1914 A.C. Sociable.
NATIONAL MOTOR MUSEUM

1926 A.C. 2-litre 2-seater; the Monte Carlo Rally winner.
NATIONAL MOTOR MUSEUM

1938 A.C. 16/80 sports car.
NATIONAL MOTOR MUSEUM

Depression. The name was saved by the brothers William and Charles Hurlock who ran a successful haulage business combined with sales and service of cars and trucks, and bought the A.C. factory in order to obtain more depot space. They allowed the service department to carry on, and towards the end of 1930 the service manager completed a car for William Hurlock. He was sufficiently pleased with it to decide on limited production, though on a much more modest level than in Edge's day. The 6-cylinder engine was continued, but the transaxle gave way to a conventionally-placed 3-speed gearbox. For a chassis they approached John Black of Standard, who let them have a number of the frames he was supposed to be supplying exclusively to SS. From the end of 1930 to the middle of 1932 a handful of cars, fewer than 50, were built, using left-over components to start with, so that some cars of the Hurlock regime still had transaxles. An important improvement, from 1932, was the adoption of a 4-speed

A.C.

1958 A.C. Ace-Bristol sports car.
NATIONAL MOTOR MUSEUM

1967 A.C. 428 convertible.
NATIONAL MOTOR MUSEUM

1976 A.C. ME3000 coupé.
NATIONAL MOTOR MUSEUM

gearbox which they bought from E.N.V. In June 1932 the first dropped-frame sports tourer was made, using a chassis identical to that of the SS1. Fitted with a light 4-seater body with polished aluminium bonnet and wings, it was built for Charles Hurlock, who used it widely in rallies and trials over the next few years. It was the ancestor of a line of attractive, low-slung A.C.s which were made up to the outbreak of World War II. Nearly all had factory-designed bodywork, some built at Thames Ditton, others contracted out to various firms when demand was too great for A.C.'s own coachwork department to cope. However, very few A.C. chassis carried entirely custom-made bodies. By 1935 seven body styles were listed, including 2- and 4-door saloons. Mechanical improvements were mostly in the gearbox department, with an optional pre-selector from 1934, and synchromesh from 1935.

A.C.s of the later 1930s were among the best-looking British cars, particularly the 2- and 4-seater drophead coupés. The 4-door Greyhound saloon bore some similarity to the SS Jaguar. However, it was considerably more expensive, at

£495, compared with £295 for the 1½-litre Jaguar, and £375 for the 2½-litre. AC owners were a select group, and only 678 cars were made between the Hurlocks' arrival and the outbreak of World War II. The rarest model was the short-chassis sports 2-seater, called the 16/80, or 16/90 when fitted with an Arnott supercharger. Only four supercharged cars were made, out of a total of 44 sports models. Small production meant that customers' wishes could be accommodated, so that very few A.C.s were exactly the same. At least one had a Scintilla Vertex magneto instead of the standard coil ignition, and a fixed-head coupé was fitted with a 16/80 engine. In 1939 a new A.C. appeared using the familiar engine in a Flying Standard chassis. The engine and radiator were moved further forward, and most of the elegance of the earlier models was lost. It was probably a good thing that the war ended production before more than a handful were made.

As with so many firms, World War II proved very profitable for A.C. who bought a new factory at Taggs Island in the Thames in 1940. Their work included making parts for Fairey Aviation, which continued into the 1950s, and also fire pump trailers, bodies and cabs for Ford and Bedford fire engines, 6-pounder guns, glider undercarriages and flame throwers.

The completion of wartime contracts prevented work on cars starting immediately, and it was not until October 1947 that the postwar A.C. appeared. It had the same familiar 1991cc engine with a new cooling system, the traditional 1930s chassis instead of the unfortunate Flying Standard one, and a new streamlined 2-door saloon body. As before the war, the wooden framed body with light alloy panels was made in A.C.'s factory. The A.C. 2-litre looked modern enough, but the semi-elliptic suspension gave a very firm ride in comparison with the independent systems which were becoming widespread. Nevertheless, it sold well in a car-hungry world, and was exported in larger numbers than any prewar A.C. had been. A 4-door saloon and a drophead coupé were made, but in much smaller numbers than the 2-door (about 35 dropheads). For 1950 there was also the Buckland 4-seater tourer. Buckland Body Works Ltd was a small coachbuilder at Buntingford, Hertfordshire, a place that was later to be of great significance to A.C. The 2-litre A.C. was made up to 1958, though few were built in its last years as demand for the new Ace took up most of the factory space. There were few changes in its lifetime, apart from hydraulic brakes taking over from hydro-mechanicals from November 1951. Total production was about 1300.

In 1947 A.C. began to make invalid cars for the Ministry of Pensions, single-seaters powered by a rear-mounted single-cylinder B.S.A engine. Built at Taggs Island until 1965, they proved a very important source of revenue for A.C., and production continued, with improved bodies, up to 1976. Later models had Steyr-Puch engines. A.C. made a 2-seater 3-wheeled coupé called the Petite, powered by a 346cc 2-cylinder engine, of which about 2000 were made between 1953 and 1958. They also made several prototypes of 3- and 4-wheeled minicars in the 1970s, none of which saw production.

Ace and Aceca

By 1952 sales of the 2-litre saloon were slowing down, and the Hurlocks realised that a new car was essential if the company was to survive. The market for quality sporting saloons was increasingly dominated by Jaguar, so they needed a new direction. One day, when they were visiting the Buckland works at Buntingford, they noticed a workshop run by a young racing car builder called John Tojeiro. Among his cars was a tubular chassis sports car with all-round independent suspension, clothed in a Ferrari-like aluminium body and powered by a 2-litre Bristol engine. It had already made a name for itself in sports car racing, and A.C. management saw it as the basis of a production sports car. Tojeiro agreed to cooperate in developing the car, and a private owner, Vincent Davison, lent his Connaught-powered Tojeiro. At the 1953 Earls Court Motor Show the new car was launched as the A.C. Ace. The chassis on the stand was A.C. built, but the complete car was, in fact, Davison's Tojeiro fitted with an A.C. engine.

The production Ace appeared early in 1954; its lines were somewhat modified from those of the Tojeiro, and it was fitted with Michelin radial tyres. It was an important addition to the ranks of British sports cars, though it needed more power than the old A.C. engine could provide. This was now giving just over 100bhp, pretty good for a unit which had begun life with 40bhp in 1922. Remembering that the original Tojeiro sports had used a Bristol engine, A.C. offered the 135bhp Bristol 2-litre in the Ace from March 1956. The Ace-Bristol was £240 more expensive, but it had performance to match its looks and handling. Any customer with competitions in mind bought the Bristol-engined car, though

1999 A.C. Aceca 4.6-litre coupé.
A.C. CAR GROUP

the A.C. was available until 1961. In 1959 Bristol discontinued their engine, and A.C. turned to the Ford Zephyr. This was available in five stages of tune, by Ken Rudd, the most powerful giving 170bhp and a top speed of 125mph (201km/h). Untuned, the Ace-Ford was £500 cheaper than the Ace-Bristol, and even the highest degree of tune cost only £225 extra, so the last Aces were good value. Only 37 were made as they were supplanted by the Ford V8-powered Cobra. There were two closed variants of the Ace, the Aceca 2-seater coupé (1955–1963) and the Greyhound 4-seater saloon (1959–1963). The Aceca could be had with A.C. or Bristol engine, but the Greyhound was almost always Bristol-powered, though a handful had the old A.C. unit, and two or three were Ford-powered. Production figures were 223 Aces and 463 Ace Bristols, 151 Acecas and 169 Aceca-Bristols, and 83 Greyhounds.

The Ace gave A.C. a more competitive car than ever before, and they took full advantage of it. They competed successfully in races, sprints and hill climbs all over Britain and ran in the Reims 12 Hour Race and Mille Miglia, and one was 2nd in the 2-litre class at Le Mans in 1957. Ken Rudd won the 1956 *Autosport* Production Sports Car Championship in a very early Ace-Bristol. In America the Ace-Bristol had an even better career, winning the SCCA Class E production category in 1957, 1958, and 1959, so for 1960 they were put into Class D, and promptly won that too. In 1961 they were in Class C, competing against cars like the Mercedes-Benz 300SL and Porsche Carrera, but nevertheless Pierre Mion's Ace-Bristol took the Championship.

The success of the Ace in SCCA racing attracted the attention of racing driver Carroll Shelby who reckoned that with a powerful V8 engine it could compete successfully even in Class A. In February 1962 an engineless Ace was flown to California, where Shelby fitted a 4260cc Ford V8. He christened the result the Cobra; officially the cars were called Shelby-A.C. Cobra, but Cobra usually sufficed.

Shelby has always maintained that the cars were American, as he had to re-work the A.C. chassis completely to make it acceptable for the greater power of the V8. Nevertheless the cars were marketed in Britain and Europe as the A.C. Cobra, capitalising on the good reputation earned by the A.C. Ace. For further history of the Shelby-developed car, see SHELBY.

Later V8s and other models

In 1966 A.C. returned to the high-speed tourer with the 428 coupé and convertible. These used a lengthened Cobra chassis, a 7014cc Ford V8 engine and handsome bodies by the Italian coachbuilder, Frua. With a top speed of 142mph (228km/h), the 428 was an interesting alternative to cars like the Aston Martin DB6 or Jensen Interceptor, but several factors worked against it. Labour problems at Frua made the supply of bodies very spasmodic, A.C. found it increasingly difficult to obtain Ford engines, and finally the oil crisis of 1973/4 made large-engined cars unfashionable. Only 51 convertibles and 29 coupés were made before production ended in March 1973.

The 428's replacement was, like the Ace, based on a prototype conceived outside the company. In 1972 Peter Bohanna and Robin Stables built a mid-engined coupé with transverse-mounted BL Maxi engine and gearbox, called the Diablo. A.C. took over the design, replaced the Maxi engine and gearbox with a more powerful 2994cc Ford V6 engine and their own 5-speed gearbox, and announced the result at the 1973 Earls Court Show as the ME3000 (ME = Mid-Engined). Development problems and difficulties in obtaining Type Approval delayed the start of production until 1979. Only eight prototypes were built between 1973 and 1979, and 68 production cars between 1979 and 1984. In April 1984 a Scottish businessman, David McDonald, bought the car interests of A.C., forming a new company, A.C. (Scotland), with a factory at Hillington, near Glasgow. A further 30 ME3000s were made between September 1984 and

A.C.

1906 Academy TT tourer.
JOHN SPICER

June 1985, when a re-styled coupé named the Ecosse was announced, powered by a 2½-litre V6 Alfa Romeo engine. However, the necessary finance was not forthcoming, and the Ecosse never saw production. The design was later taken up by a new company, ECOSSE Cars of Knebworth, Hertfordshire.

Meanwhile, CP Autokraft were making Cobras in a factory within the old Brooklands Track. Headed by Brian Angliss, this company was the only one licensed to use the Cobra name which was owned by Ford; indeed Ford and Angliss were joint owners of A.C. Cars from 1987 to 1990. The Cobra Mk IV was built on the original jigs and used a 225bhp 4942cc Ford V8 engine. Some were adapted by agents in the USA to take the full-blown 7-litre engine, which gave them the performance equal to that of the old Cobra 427.

In 1986 Angliss announced a new Ace, a traditional front-engined sports car using a 2.9-litre Ford V6 engine. This was later adapted for a 2-litre Ford Cosworth turbo and 4-wheel drive from the Ford Sierra, but Ford cancelled the project in 1990 after only a few prototypes had been made. The Ace languished until A.C. was bought by a car leasing company, Pride Automotive in 1996. Under its new chairman, South African Alan Lubinsky, the Ace was re-launched with a 32-valve 4601cc Ford V8 engine developing 326bhp. An alternative engine was the older 16-valve 4942cc V8 which, with belt-driven Eaton supercharger, also gave 326bhp. At the 1998 Birmingham Motor Show the Aceca name was revived for a coupé version of the Ace. It was a full 4-seater coupé on a wheelbase 10in (254mm) longer than the Ace's. These were no longer made at Weybridge; the chassis came from South Africa, and the cars were assembled in Coventry by Cam Special Vehicles.

At the same time, Lubinsky launched the Superblower, a Cobra in all but name (which still belonged to Ford), powered by a 4942cc Ford V8. This cost £69,795, but still more expensive were the 25 replicas of the Cobra Mk II with polished aluminium bodies, selling for £150,000. However, in the summer of 1999 A.C. launched the CRS (Carbon Road Series) using fibreglass in place of aluminium for the same body shape as the Superblower, but selling for under £40,000. Unlike the Ace and Aceca, the Superblower and the Mk II replicas were built at Weybridge, with the fibreglass mouldings for the CRS being made by Protech Motorsport in Hampshire. For 2000, A.C. offered an additional engine option, a 350bhp, 3506cc four-ohc V8 by Lotus.

NG

Further Reading
A.C. and Cobra, John McLennan, Dalton Watson, 1982.
'A.C.'s Winning Hand', David Burgess-Wise,
Automobile Quarterly, Vol. 29, No. 4.
'A.C. 428', John Heilig, *Automobile Quarterly*, Vol. 29, No. 4.
A.C. Heritage: from three-wheeler to superblower, Simon Taylor and Peter Burn, Osprey, Oxford, 1999.

A.C. (P) c.1983–c.1988
Cacao Automoveis Lda, Figueira da Foz.
The A.C. Sportcar was a close copy of the gullwing G.P. Talon. It too was based on a VW Beetle chassis with all VW mechanicals.
CR

A.C. (GB) 1992
A.C. Auto Replicas, Porthleven, Helston, Cornwall.
The A.C. Challenger had nothing to with the more famous eponymous manufacturer, but was one of a multitude of Lamborghini Countach replicas. Only one V8 prototype was ever seen.
CR

ACADEMY (GB) 1906–1908
E.J. West & Co. Ltd, Foleshill, Coventry.
The Motor Academy of Notting Hill, London, must have been one of the first driving schools, almost certainly the first to offer dual-control cars. These were built for the Academy's proprietor, Mr Turbeville-Smith, by WEST of Coventry, and had 14/20hp 4-cylinder White & Poppe engines and tourer bodies. Turbeville-Smith also sold cars with single controls under the Academy name to the general public, and entered one in the 1906 Tourist Trophy Race, but it retired after three laps. In February 1907 the Academy of Motoring became a limited company, but went into liquidation in May 1908.
NG

ACADIA (US) 1903–1904
Ernest R. Kelly, Wilmington, Delaware.
This was a simple 2-seater runabout with 5hp single-cylinder engine under the seat and single-chain drive. It had wheel steering and a Renault-style bonnet. Kelly quoted a price of $600 (wings, lights and horn extra), but he never even formed a company. Possibly no more than one Acadia was made.
NG

ACADIAN (CDN) 1962–1971
General Motors Corp. of Canada, Oshawa, Ontario.
Acadian was the brand name of General Motors cars sold in Canada. Although initially based on the Chevy 11, it was sold by Pontiac-Buick dealers, and had a certain element of Pontiac styling, including a split grille. 1962 Acadians were made in two series, the base-line Invader and the up-market Beaumont. For 1963 there were two more distinct lines, the Acadian, now available with 4637cc V8 engine, and the larger Beaumont which was based on the Chevrolet Chevelle, and came in five body styles and four engine options. These cars were being sold by Pontiac-Buick dealers at the same time as regular Chevy 11s and Chevelles were being sold by Chevrolet dealers, but the Acadians had the bulk of the market, 70 per cent or more.

From 1965 to 1969 the Beaumont was sold as a separate line, making the dealerships Acadian-Beaumont-Pontiac-Buick franchises. About 70,000 Beaumonts were sold in six years, but the line was then dropped. The 1967 Acadians were the last to be built in Canada; after that they were assembled at Willow Run, Michigan, alongside the Chevy 11 and Nova. The line was discontinued early in 1971, being replaced by the Pontiac Ventura which took over on the Willow Run assembly line on March 11th. Four years later the name was revived for a badge-engineered Chevette, sold in Canada as the Pontiac Acadian. This was a model rather than a marque in its own right, as the earlier Acadian had been. It lasted until 1987.
NG

A.C.A.M. (I) 1984–1988
A.C.A.M. SpA, Catania.
The Nica conformed to the mores of the Italian microcar market, being an enclosed 2-seater of compact dimensions. While the 3-wheeler version was a monobox design, the 4-wheeler, although looking very similar, had a 2-box style. Piaggio 125cc or 218cc air-cooled engines were fitted. A 50cc microcar called the Galassia or Zeta arrived in 1987.
CR

A.C.A.P *see* PODVIN

A.C.B (F) 1982–1985
Ateliers de Carrosserie Broual, Courbevoie.
Taking the name of a postwar coachbuilder (Ateliers de Carrosserie de Bécon, Courbevoie), museum director M. Broual produced replicas of great French coachwork. Unlike most replicas, many of the components used were authentic,

in this case Delage and Delahaye items. Replicas included the Delage D6, Delahaye 135 and prewar Talbot. More modest versions were built with Renault 18 or 20 units or, in the case of the Talbot replica, Peugeot 505.

CR

ACCELERA *see* FOSTER (ii)

ACCLES-TURRELL (GB) 1899–1902

1899–1901 Accles-Turrell Autocars Ltd, Perry Bar, Birmingham.
1901–1902 Pollock Engineering Co. Ltd, Ashton-under-Lyne, Lancashire.
Accles Ltd was a well-known engineering concern when Charles McRobie Turrell joined it. He had been one of the organisers of the 1896 London– Brighton Emancipation Run, and was responsible for a light 2-seater, bodied by Mulliners of Northampton, powered by a 3½hp single-cylinder engine mounted horizontally under the seat, with the cylinder facing forwards. This drove by a belt to a 3-speed constant-mesh gearbox, with final drive by chain. Top speed was 20mph (33 km/h). They also offered the 3½hp engine to other car makers, and a 1¼hp engine for tricycles and quadricycles. By 1901 Turrell was living in Ashton-under-Lyne, where he built a larger car. This had a 10/15hp engine also under the seat, and also driving through a constant-mesh gearbox, but the body was a 4-seater tonneau. The design was taken up by the Pollock Engineering Co. who sold it under the name Turrell. In 1910 Thomas Pollock joined Accles to form the well-known tube-making company, Accles & Pollock, and the Turrell design was taken up by the Autocar Construction Co. who sold it as the HERMES (i).

NG

ACCUMULATOR INDUSTRIES (GB) 1902–c.1903

Accumulator Industries Ltd, Woking, Surrey.
This company made a few light electric cars similar in appearance to the American Columbia or Riker cars, but with solid tyres. They were powered by two 2½hp Lundell motors. They also made a heavy electric coach with a range of 80 miles.

NG

ACE (i) (GB) 1912–1916

Salmon Motor Co. Ltd, Burton-on-Trent, Staffordshire.
This company was formed by P. Salmon, who was chief designer for BAGULEY Cars, and the Ace was in fact built in the Baguley factory. It had a very small monobloc 4-cylinder engine of 748cc, a 2-speed gearbox and chain drive. The 2-seater was priced at £100, which seems very reasonable, but it did not sell well, though it was apparently made up to the third year of World War I. The company also made larger cars under the names Salmon and Baguley.

NG

ACE (ii) (US) 1920–1923

Apex Motor Corp., Ypsilanti, Michigan.
The Ace was initially supplied in early 1920 to a dealer in Seattle, Washington, who had ordered a consignment during mid–1919, the cars not being available to other buyers until later in 1920. The cars featured engines by Herschell-Spillman, or one with rotary disc valves, which had been designed by Fred Guy and O.W. Heintz. In 1921 two sixes were available on wheelbases of 117in (2970mm) and 123in (3122mm), with a coupé added to the touring cars. For 1923, Ace's last year, they introduced a 4-cylinder series with a Gray engine and a wheelbase of 114in (2893mm), plus a 6-cylinder addition to its 6-cylinder Herschell-Spillman line with a wheelbase at 120in (3046mm), 3in (76mm) longer than the existing series. The Ace Four was priced at $1295 for both its Pup touring car and Pup roadster, its other two models priced at $2260 to $3150. The coupé was discontinued for 1923. Ace production ended in 1923 after the completion of an estimated 250 cars.

KM

ACE (iii) *see* FRONTENAC

ACE (iv) (US) c.1996

American Car Craft Enterprises, Marietta, Georgia.
As if a Corvette was not big enough already, ACE stretched them out to full 4-seater size. A full-length frame kept the Corvette 2+2 rigid. The body was based on the 1970–82 Corvette, with custom features like dual rectangular headlights. ACE also sold a Ferrari Dino replica kit for VW Type 3 chassis.

HP

1903 Achilles 8hp 2-seater.
DOUGLAS FITZPATRICK

ACE (v) (F) 1998 to date

Automobiles Contemporaines d'Exception, Seclin.
The Ace was a replica of the A.C. 289 using a British-manufactured glassfibre body (by HAWK) on a French chassis. Ford V8 engines were used in three versions, the 289 MkII, 289 FIA, and fixed-head 289 Le Mans limited edition, while a fourth version called the Ace Bristol used a BMW 6-cylinder engine.

CR

ACE 427 ROADSTER (US) 1991–1994

Ace Auto Services (USA) Ltd, Reseda, California.
Ace assembled and sold a Cobra replica built by Graham Berry in New Zealand. They were available only in assembled form and built to a very high standard, with leather interiors and Jaguar rear suspension.

HP

ACE COBRA (US) c.1996

Ace Cobra, Canoga Park, California.
Yet another Cobra replica kit, this one was sold as a rolling chassis or completely assembled. Offered a choice of Ford live axle or Jaguar IRS.

HP

ACEDO (E) 1941

Auto Acedo, Madrid.
This light car was designed by Manuel Ortega and combined a single-cylinder engine of 2.2hp with pedal drive delivering almost 95mpg. It was the attempt to build a car using national components in a country surrounded by World War II. The Acedo was subject to a lot of tests controlled by the Real Automobile Club, but only a few prototypes were built.

VCM

A.C. EXOTIC CARS (US) c.1994

A.C. Exotic Cars Inc., Cleveland, Ohio.
Although no relation to A.C. in England, this company sold replicas of the Cobra 427, Cobra Daytona Coupé, and the 1936 Ford pick-up truck, either in kit form or as fully-assembled vehicles.

HP

ACHENBACH *see* HEXE

ACHE *see* LASSOUGADE

ACHILLES (GB) 1903–1908

B. Thompson & Co. Ltd, Frome, Somerset.
This firm advertised a range of vehicles from 6hp upwards. Most cars sold utilised single-cylinder De Dion-Bouton engines, though a White & Poppe-

1904 Acme (i) Type VI tonneau.
JOHN A.CONDE

1979 Acoma Super Comtesse.
NATIONAL MOTOR MUSEUM

engined 2-cylinder 12hp was also offered. Other major components originated from the leading contemporary suppliers such as Lacoste et Battman and Malicet et Blin, and only bodies and smaller fitments were manufactured in Frome. Agencies for other marques were also held, and other engineering work was undertaken, including iron and bronze castings for various purposes. Some cars were marketed under the name 'G.P.'. A sound reputation was achieved locally, which is upheld by the existence of a survivor from what must have been a comparatively small total production.

DF

A.C.M. *see* BONITO

ACME (i) **(US)** 1903–1911
Acme Motor Car Co., Reading, Pennsylvania.
Acme cars were made by James C. Reber who had founded the Acme Bicycle Manufacturing Co. in 1892. For one year, 1902, he made a car under his own name, then used the bicycle name for all his subsequent cars. A 16hp twin (the Reber re-named) was made in 1904 and 1905, but later Acmes were larger cars with 4-cylinder engines of 30, 30/35, and 45/50hp, and from 1909, 6-cylinder engines of 48 and 60hp. These were expensive cars, costing up to $6000 for a 60hp tourer in 1909. Frederick Moscovics joined Acme as sales manager late in 1904, although he was to achieve much greater fame more than 20 years later when he saved STUTZ from probable extinction. Acme survived a receivership in 1906, but succumbed in 1911. Their factory was bought by the makers of the S.G.V. car.

NG

ACME (ii) *see* M.B. (i)

ACME (iii) **(CDN)** 1910–1911
Acme Motor Carriage & Machinery Co. Ltd, Hamilton, Ontario.
This company was founded to make cars and commercial vehicles with engines and running gear imported from the United States and bodies built in Canada. All that came of these ambitious plans was a single 30hp tourer.

NG

ACME (iv) **(AUS)** 1917
Holding & Overall, Drummoyne, New South Wales.
Erroneously known earlier as the 1904 Ace, the Acme was a 2-seater with a 4-cylinder 10/12hp engine; only the magneto and carburettor being imported. The Acme Motor Works began in 1906 at Lavender Bay as marine engineers, being sold to V.A. Holding in 1916. No more was heard of the car, but the business was solely owned by F.R. Overall in Sydney by 1920.

MG

ACOMA (F) 1975–1984
Acoma sarl, Angers.
As one of the pioneers of the new wave of French microcars, Acoma's tiny Mini-Comtesse was popular, but this had little to do with the merits of its design, as it was proven to be unstable in independent tests. A single-seater, it used a 50cc Motobécane engine in the front and a single front wheel. The polyester body incorporated a folding gullwing door for entry. The 4-wheeled Mini-Comtesse of 1978 looked even more bizarre, being very upright, and the Break version was uncompromisingly boxy. More conventional designs followed, including the Comtesse Super Coupé, Comtesse Super Sport, Star, and Starlette, all being powered by a 50cc engine, except for the Star which had 125cc power. In its heyday, Acoma was one of the largest microcar makers, selling 3500 cars in 1979.

CR

A.C. PROPULSION (USA) 1997 to date
A.C. Propulsion Inc., San Dimas, California.
Produced by an electric vehicle systems manufacturer, founded in 1992 by ex-GM electrics specialist Alan Cocconi, the Zero was introduced at the 1997 Los Angeles Auto Show. It was a zero-emissions sports car with an electric engine and lead–acid batteries producing the equivalent of 220bhp. A 0–60mph (0-96 km/h) time of 4.9 seconds and a range of 80–100 miles (130-160 km) was quoted. The bodywork incorporated a removable roof and small upward-hinging doors with removable screens. Also offered was the Long Ranger, a hybrid trailer that provided the capability for unlimited autonomy in electric vehicles.

CR

A.C.S. (F) 1991 to date
Automobiles Classiques Sportives, Objat.
This was a local French version of the G.T.D. 40 (Ford GT40 replica). For the French market it was homologated with a 3.0-litre Peugeot V6 engine or Ford/Rover V8 power.

CR

A.D. (GB) 1982–1986
1982-84 Automotive Design & Development, Colchester, Essex.
1984-85 Ferrante Cars, Peterborough, Cambridgeshire.
1985-86 Trident Autovet, Peterborough, Cambridgeshire .
Before it entered kit car manufacture this firm was called Perry Automotive Developments, importing the US-made KARMA, a vague Ferrari Dino replica, to Britain. As A.D., the company stretched a Karma shell, made its own chassis and turned it into a convertible, calling the new model the A.D. 400. Mechanically it was based on Ford parts, and V8 and even V12 power options were mooted. It was later marketed by Ferrante and Trident Autovet as the Chimera. A.D. also made a Cobra 427 replica on Ford Capri or Jaguar parts.

CR

ADAMS (i) **(US)** 1899–1900
Myron D. Adams, Lansingburgh, New York.
Myron Adams was a bicycle repairer and gramophone salesman who built his first car in 1899. No details are known, but he had to get special police permission to operate the car on the streets of Troy, New York. This was granted in September

1899, and was possibly the first registration of a motor car in the State of New York. In 1900 he built another car with a 2-cylinder engine, and offered replicas for sale in the local press. It seems there were no takers, but he continued to operate this car for ten years or so.

KM

ADAMS (ii) (GB) 1903–1906

Adams & Co., Tunbridge Wells, Kent.

H. Adams began by making an *avant-train* conversion set for motorising horse-drawn vehicles. It consisted of a petrol engine mounted on a swivelling fore-carriage, with steering by wheel and vertical column. In 1905 he showed a 9hp 2-seater light car at the Agricultural Hall Show, under the name 'One of the Best'. This was on the same stand as the Adams Patent Quick Lift Motor Jack.

NG

ADAMS (iii) (GB) 1905–1914

Adams Manufacturing Co. Ltd, Bedford.

A.H. Adams founded the Igranic Works at Bedford in 1899 to make electrical equipment, and when he met American Edward Ringwood Hewitt, they decided on a joint production of cars, with the engines and epicyclic transmissions being made by Adams, with axles and other components being made in New York and shipped to Bedford. The first Adams-Hewitt car was launched in 1905, having a 1724cc 9/10hp single-cylinder horizontal engine mounted under the front seat, and the 2-speed epicyclic transmission which gave rise to the slogan 'Pedals to Push, That's All'. Most of the cars had short bonnets, despite the engine position, but some were forward-control landaulets for town use.

In 1906 a range of 2- and 4-cylinder cars with vertical front-mounted engines was introduced, and sliding mesh gearboxes came in 1907, when a car was supplied to the Emperor of Abyssinia. There was also a short-lived 32hp V8 of 7270cc, based on a French Antoinette aero engine which was also used in the ANTOINETTE car. The main difference between the English and French versions was that the Adams version had automatically-operated inlet valves, while on the French engine they were automatic. The V8 was also offered in the New York-built HEWITT, but probably no more than 11 V8s were made altogether. Two were mounted on a common crankcase to make a V16 engine for a racing boat ordered by a New Zealand customer in 1908.

The single-cylinder car was dropped in 1909 and replaced by a 10hp twin called the Varsity. The Adams became more conventional, with Coventry-Simplex and Aster engines used in a range of 4- and 6-cylinder models from 14/16 to 30hp. A new light car appeared in 1913 which reverted to the old horizontal underfloor position for its 10/12hp 2-cylinder engine, It even revived the epicyclic transmission and single-chain drive of the Adams-Hewitt made nearly ten years earlier, but found few buyers. A.H. Adams had perished on the *Titanic* (like another car maker, Washington Roebling of Mercer). The Adams car did not survive World War I, but the Igranic Works continued to make electrical equipment, later becoming Brookhirst-Igranic and continuing to the present day.

NG

ADAMS (iv) (US) 1910–1911

Adams Bros Co., Findlay, Ohio.

Only one model of the Adams car was made, a 30hp 4-cylinder tourer with Renault-style dashboard radiator. It was built for barely one season before the Adams brothers decided to concentrate on commercial vehicles, which were made up to 1916.

NG

ADAMS (v) (GB) 1986 to date

Adams Roadsters, Frome, Somerset.

Dennis Adams, the celebrated designer of virtually all Marcos cars, created his own Roadster as a neo-classic, drawing on British and American themes. It used Jaguar XJ6 components in a ladder frame chassis with a glassfibre body. It was sold either in kit form, or as a Jaguar XJ conversion.

CR

1908 Adams (iii) 10hp tourer.
NATIONAL MOTOR MUSEUM

1906 Adams-Farwell 40/45hp tourer.
NICK BALDWIN

ADAMS-FARWELL (US) 1905–1911

The Adams Co., Dubuque, Iowa.

The brothers Herbert and Eugene Adams founded a company in 1883 to make grave markers and park benches, later turning to milling and general foundry equipment. The idea of car manufacture came from their partner Fay Oliver Farwell, who was dedicated to the rotary radial engine. Between 1898 and 1904 he built four experimental vehicles, one of which was sold to a Dubuque resident, and his Model 5 was the prototype of the car offered for sale in February 1905. It had a 20/25hp 3-cylinder engine mounted at the rear. The cylinders and crankcase revolved horizontally around a fixed shaft, with power transmitted by bevel gears to the 4-speed gearbox, and then by single chain to the rear axle. For 1906 the 3-cylinder engine was joined by a 40/45hp 5-cylinder unit. In the Gentleman's Speed Roadster it gave a top speed of 75mph (121km/h). An unusual feature of the brougham was that the controls could be detached from the exposed front seat and slotted into the floor of the rear compartment, which was fully protected from the weather. The steering wheel could slide sideways to give left- or right-hand drive at will. From 1907 onwards only the 5-cylinder model was made. Later Adams-Farwells had frontal bonnets, though the engine remained at the rear. Not more than 200 were made in all, before the brothers decided that their foundry and gear cutting work was more profitable. Farwell stayed with them until 1921, when he left to promote a merry-go-round he had invented. (Still faithful to the rotary principle!) He died in 1942.

NG

Further Reading
'Adams-Farwell', Beverley Rae Kimes, *Automobile Quarterly*, Vol. 8, No. 2.

1914 Adamson 8hp cyclecar.
M.J.WORTHINGTON-WILLIAMS

1902 Ader 15hp double phaeton.
NATIONAL MOTOR MUSEUM

ADAMSON (GB) 1912–1924
R. Barton Adamson & Co. Ltd, Enfield Highway, Middlesex.
This was a cyclecar built by a well-known firm of transport contractors. It had a 2-cylinder Alpha engine, a 3-speed gearbox and belt drive. Its underslung frame gave it a very low appearance. The postwar Adamson was much less conventional, the body being virtually two sidecars side by side, with the driver seated in the offside one. They were powered by a 1075cc 2-cylinder British Anzani engine with chain drive, though a light car with 1330cc 4-cylinder Alpha engine was also made up to 1922.
NG

ADAMS PROBE see PROBE

ADAYER (AUS) 1981–1985
Dominion & International Automobiles Pty Ltd, Braeside, Victoria.
Originally intended to be called Phantom and have a classical-styled grille, those plans were upset by a court order obtained by Rolls-Royce. Mechanically it was totally Holden, being built on the chassis of the 1-tonne commercial; only five were made. The Sportif, a modified Holden Commodore with a 2-door coupé body, appeared in 1985, of which 11 were produced.
MG

A.D.D. see NOVA

ADELPHI (AUS) 1945
Automobile Manufacturing Industries Pty Ltd, Fitzroy, Victoria.
An initiative prompted by Government moves to encourage Australian motor manufacture, it utilised the resources of two engineering firms owned by Greek-born Constantine Couttoupes. Cascall Industries and Toll Engineering built two examples of a 4-cylinder vehicle which, it was believed, could be produced economically. The prototypes were run, with utility (pick-up) bodies, by the businesses for durability testing, but the plans obviously did not gain the required support.
MG

ADELPHIA (US) 1920
Winfield Barnes Co., Philadelphia, Pennsylvania.
The Adelphia was a light car intended for the export market. It had a 4-cylinder Herschell-Spillman engine and was only offered as a right-hand drive five-seater tourer. The advertised price was $1695, but very few cars were made. The Adelphia was announced in the summer of 1920, and by October the company admitted that it had insufficient capital to continue.
NG

ADEM (I) 1912
This was an Italian-built car marketed in Britain by Adolf de Martini after he had left the MARTINI company. It had a 2.9-litre 4-cylinder monobloc engine and a 4-speed gearbox. Cooling was by fan blades on the flywheel. Few, if any, were actually sold in England.
NG

ADER (F) 1900–1907
1900–1904 Sté Industrielle des Téléphones-Voitures Système Ader, Levallois- Perret, Seine.
1904–1907 Sté Ader, Levallois-Perret, Seine.
Clement Ader (1841–1925) achieved more fame from telephones and aeroplanes than he did from cars, though these were not lacking in interest. He started making bicycles as early as 1869, and his Société Générale des Téléphones Ader installed many of the most important lines in France and elsewhere in Europe. The money he made from this enabled him to experiment with aviation, though he also received some help from the French War Office. Between 1890 and 1897 he made two steam-powered aeroplanes called *Eole* and *Avion*. They were not successful, though they were the first attempts at heavier-than-air flight in France.
In 1900 Ader formed a separate company to make cars, starting with a 904cc 6hp V-twin light car, with chain drive, tubular frame and tonneau body. In 1901 he brought out a new 7hp of 795cc; this had a channel steel frame and shaft drive. In 1902 Ader built his first 4-cylinder engine, which was, in effect, two of the 904cc V-twins coupled together, and he repeated the process for his Paris–Madrid racing cars of 1903, coupling two V4s to make a 3616cc V8. This engine was never used in a production car, but it was significant in being the first V8 engine used in a car. Also in 1903 Ader made a 1570cc 12hp V-twin, and a shaft-driven motorcycle sold under the name Moto-Cardan.
In 1904 he separated car production from telephones, forming a new company called simply Société Ader. He also started using vertical engines, a 10hp twin and a 14/20hp four, though he hedged his bets by making a 14/20hp V4 as well. He continued this regime until 1907, when he went over to vertical engines entirely, a 2923cc 16/20 and a 5398cc 28/32hp. This was the last year for Ader cars, though he continued to make V4 engines for use in motorboats, and supplied some engines to other car makers, notably Royal Enfield in England. Ader cars were sold in England under the name Pegasus.
NG

Further Reading
'Automobiles Ader', J.-R. Dulier, *L'Album du Fanatique,* September, 1972.

AD-HOC (F) 1984
Sté Ad-Hoc, Annecy-le-Vieux.
Created by M. Arié (of SUNCAR fame), the Ad-Hoc rode the wave of the microcar boom of the 1980s. It was a basic open fun car with a rear-mounted Sachs 125cc petrol or diesel engine, 4-wheel disc brakes, variable transmission, and MacPherson strut front suspension.
CR

A.D.I. (D) 1950
Fahrzeugbau Arthur Diebler, Berlin-Neukolln.
This company began by making light 3-wheeled goods vehicles just after the war, and in 1950 announced a passenger version. It had a 120cc single-cylinder engine mounted over the front wheel, a bench seat for two between the rear wheels, and handlebar steering. There were no doors or roof.
NG

A.D.J. (GB) 1989
This company offered A.C. Cobra 427 and Ford GT40 replicas, as well as an original Jaguar-based roadster called the Merlin.

CR

A.D.K. (B) 1922–1931
SA des Automobiles de Kuyper, Brussels.
Robert de Kuyper set up in business as a car maker in 1922, and made a variety of machines, all with bought-in engines. His first, the 10CV Type Y-22, had a 1692cc 4-cylinder single-ohc S.C.A.P. engine, and this was followed by the WB-16 with pushrod ohv S.C.A.P. engine of 1615cc. Though of lower performance, it was up to date in having 4-wheel brakes. Other 4-cylinder models included one with a 1846cc Sergant engine, and in 1927 de Kuyper went over to six cylinders, using a 1682cc C.I.M.E. engine. At the end of 1928 he went further up-market with a small straight-8, a 2340cc S.C.A.P. This was the cheapest 8-cylinder car sold in Belgium at the time. Like the smaller A.D.K.s, it carried attractive bodywork, especially the coupés, but the chassis lacked rigidity, and the use of inferior steel for some components, such as the rear axle housing damaged the make's reputation. The Depression was the final blow, and A.D.K. closed during 1931.

NG

1929 A.D.K. 2.3-litre straight-eight coupé.
NATIONAL MOTOR MUSEUM

ADLER (D) 1900–1939
1900–1906 Adler Fahrradwerke vorm. Heinrich Kleyer AG, Frankfurt-am-Main.
1906–1939 Adlerwerke vorm. Heinrich Kleyer AG, Frankfurt-am-Main.
Heinrich Kleyer (1853–1932) founded a bicycle business in Frankfurt in 1880, initially importing American machines which he sold under the name Herold. By 1885 he had acquired a six-storey building, at the time the tallest business premises in Frankfurt. Five floors were used for manufacture, with the top floor reserved for riding lessons for new owners. Though he did not start car manufacture until 1900, he was involved in the very beginning of the German motor industry, for he supplied wire wheels to both Carl Benz and Gottlieb Daimler for their pioneer vehicles. In 1895 he adopted the name Adler (Eagle) for his cycles, and also started to make typewriters, which were to outlast cars by many years.

In 1898 he acquired a licence to make De Dion Bouton engines, but did not do much with it, apart from using a De Dion engine in his first car. This was designed by Franz Starkloph, and had a front-mounted 400cc single-cylinder engine, with tiller steering and full-elliptic springing all round. Like the contemporary Renault, it was advanced in having shaft drive. Adler never used chain drive, even on his biggest 9-litre cars. 1901 cars had wheel steering and slightly larger engines of 510cc, and from 1902 they made their own engines, an 850cc single and a 1730cc twin. Again following Renault, they had lateral radiators. In 1903 Starkloph moved to Polyphon who made the Curved Dash Oldsmobile, and was replaced by Edmund Rumpler (1872–1940), later to be famous for his rear-engined teardrop cars. His contribution to Adler was not so spectacular, but he kept them in the forefront of design with 4-cylinder engines in unit with gearboxes, light-alloy crankcases and, from 1905, pressure lubrication. There was a single-cylinder light car up to 1905, and a twin was still listed in 1909, but the standard Adler had an L-head 4-cylinder engine. In 1905 these were of 2796, 4016, and 7440cc, the latter being the model used in the 1906 Herkomer Trial and attracting an order from the Kaiser in 1907.

In 1904 Adler expanded their premises but still could not keep up with demand, so they imported Clement-Bayard cars from France to keep their customers happy. In Britain they were represented by Morgan & Co., the coachbuilders of Leighton Buzzard, who mounted their own bodies and sold the cars under the name Morgan-Adler. A wide variety of cars was made up to 1914 including the popular 1555cc 7/15PS, sold in England as the 12hp, some larger sporting fours such as the 2070cc 8/22PS and 3886cc 15/40PS, the latter the basis for Adler's unsuccessful 1914 Tourist Trophy racing cars, and at the top of the range a 9081cc 35/80PS, which had a vee-radiator in 1914. Knight-engined cars were tried in 1911, but did not pass the prototype stage. 1913 saw a new light car, the 1292cc 5/13PS Model K with monobloc 4-cylinder engine and a choice of tandem or side-by-side seating. It was sold in England as the Morgan-Adler Carette. In 1914 Adler was also making the bicycles on which their prosperity had been founded, motorcycles and 3-ton trucks.

1907 Adler Herkomer Trophy tourer.
NATIONAL MOTOR MUSEUM

1914 Adler Model K 5/13PS light car.
NATIONAL MOTOR MUSEUM

During World War I Adler built trucks, transmissions for tanks, and aero engines under Benz licence. Heinrich Kleyer made an interest-free loan of 4 million Marks to the government, but it was never fully repaid, so that in 1920 Adler came under the control of the Deutsche Bank. The postwar car range, which did not get into production until 1921, was smaller than before, consisting of the Modell K, enlarged to 1550cc and no longer offered with tandem seating, and larger fours of 2298cc (9/24PS), 3115cc (12/34PS) and 4700cc (18/60PS). Like all contemporary German cars they had vee-radiators, changing to a flat shape in 1925. That year saw Adler's first sixes, the 2580cc monobloc 10/50PS and 4704cc bi-bloc 18/80PS. They had alloy pistons, detachable cylinder heads and front wheel brakes. Assembly-line production arrived with the 1943cc 4-cylinder Favorit, of which more than 14,000 were made up to 1934. It had hydraulic brakes from 1929, also seen on the 2540/2916cc Standard 6 and 3887cc Standard 8. The latter was Adler's top model of the inter-war years, and was often seen with custom coachwork by Glaser, Neuss, and others. Some

1931 Adler Standard 6A 12/50PS saloon.
NICK BALDWIN

1938 Adler Trumpf Junior cabrio-limousine.
NICK GEORGANO/NATIONAL MOTOR MUSEUM

1939 Adler 2.5-litre saloon.
NATIONAL MOTOR MUSEUM

chassis carried unusual, functional coachwork designed by Walter Gropius of the Bauhaus movement, and built by Neuss and Karmann. Only 1720 8s were made between 1928 and 1934, compared with nearly 21,000 Standard 6s.

By 1928 Adler had a workforce of 6000, and was making 60 cars a day, as well as commercial vehicles and bicycles. They were Germany's third largest car maker, after Opel and BMW, and in order to keep this position the directors decided to move towards a more popular market. After considering and rejecting (probably wisely) a rear-engined minicar designed by Josef Ganz, they commissioned Hans-Gustav Rohr to design a front-drive car powered by a 1504cc 4-cylinder engine, with all-round independent suspension and all-steel

body by Ambi-Budd. Introduced at the 1932 Geneva Show as the Trumpf, it became the best-known Adler. Capacity went up to 1645cc in 1934, and 25,603 were made up to 1938. Body styles included 2- and 4-door saloons, a cabriolet, and an attractive sports model with power boosted from 38 to 47bhp. The Trumpf was made under licence in France by ROSENGART and in Belgium by IMPERIA. The Trumpf's little sister, the 995cc Trumpf Junior, was an even better seller, with 102,840 being sold between 1934 and 1941. Styling and range of bodies followed closely those of the Trumpf.

Larger rear-drive Adlers were made in the 1930s, including the Primus which used the Trumpf's 1645cc engine, the 2916cc 6-cylinder Diplomat (1934–1940) and the 2494cc 6-cylinder 2.5-litre which was made with striking streamlined bodies from 1937 to 1940. 5295 of these advanced cars with swing axles were made. Like most Adlers they were bodied by Ambi-Budd.

Passenger production virtually ended with the war, though a few Trumpf Juniors were made up to 1941, and the factory made staff cars and ambulances based on the Diplomat, as well as half-tracked vehicles of Demag design. Some 2.5-litre engines were used in TRIPPEL amphibious cars. After the war two prototypes of Trumpf Junior with restyled bodies by Karmann and Wendler were built, but production never started. When the factory had been rebuilt, it was used for manufacture of typewriters and, from 1949 to 1957, a range of motorcycles from 98 to 250cc. Adler's considerable dealer network was taken up by Volkswagen.

NG

Further Reading
Adler Automobile 1900–1945, Werner Oswald,
Motorbuch Verlag, Stuttgart, 1981.
'Adler – The Eagle from Frankfurt', Stan Grayson,
Automobile Quarterly, Vol. 15, No. 4.

ADLER 300 SLR (US) c.1994

Adler Industries, Sandy, Utah.
One of the few American kit car companies that did not build Cobra replicas. Instead they sold a pseudo-replica of the Mercedes 300 SLR that looked more like a 300 SL roadster with a 300 SLR nose. It used a tubular space frame with Chevrolet 5700cc or 7400cc engines. Sold as rolling chassis or in assembled form.

HP

ADRIA (US) 1921–1922

Adria Motor Car Corp., Batavia, New York.
The Adria was a good-looking car for the price, and it had a gimmick, including a 3-section chassis and cross springs, not unlike the Parenti which had surfaced about the same time. The Adria was powered by a 2932cc Supreme L-head engine which developed 396bhp at 2200rpm. Built on a wheelbase of 120in (3046mm) and equipped with wooden artillery spoke wheels or, as an option, wire, the 5-passenger touring car was listed at $1495. Adria had planned to include a roadster and a sedan in its plans, but failed before they were built. Adria was sued by Parenti for patent infringement, and the factory was temporarily closed. The lawsuit added to insufficient financial support, and the sharp Depression of 1921 finished off the Adria. As production had never really got underway, the only cars completed, numbering an estimated 20 to 40, constituted Adria's total output.

KM

A.D.T. (GB) 1990–1995

Automotive Design Technology, Saffron Walden, Essex.
First seen in 1990 as the Macintosh, this mid-engined Mini-based sports car had a steel tube space frame chassis. After the death of the designer, the project was acquired in 1991 and re-emerged with a steel monocoque chassis and part-stressed body under the name A.D.T. Sprint. It appears that it never entered proper production.

CR

ADVANCE *see* KAUFMAN

ADVANCED AUTOMATIVE TECHNOLOGIES *see* AMORE

ADVANCED CHASSIS (US) 1991–1992

Advanced Chassis, Alameda, California.

This kit car manufacturer built a sophisticated round-tube chassis for their Cobra replica. They also made a mid-engined kit called the Anthem, which was an attractive convertible resembling modified Ferrari Testarossa with a Camaro nose grafted on. Sold in kit or assembled form.

HP

ADVANCED GENERATION MOTORS (US) c.1992–1994

Advanced Generation Motors, Miami, Florida.

The AGM Rhino, an off-road vehicle, was their most popular model. They also made a beach buggy conversion for a Geo Metro or Suzuki Swift.

HP

A.E.C. ANGER (US) 1913–1915

Anger Engineering Co., Milwaukee, Wisconsin.

Three models were made by the Anger Engineering Co., a 4-cylinder 4-40 and two sixes, the 6-50 and 6-60. The former had a 6-litre 38hp L-head engine, the latter a 6.9-litre 43hp T-head; it was unusual to have the two layouts offered at the same time, especially as the T-head was distinctly old fashioned by 1913. The maker was Walter A. Anger, and the cars were known as A.E.C. or Anger. Perhaps he felt that his surname was not the best appellation for a motorcar. They seem to have been built mostly to customers' specifications.

NG

A.E.D. see BONITO

A.E.M. (i) (F) 1926–1927

Applications Electro-Mécanique, Neuilly, Seine.

This company produced the ELECTROCYCLETTE cyclecar in 1923, and three years later launched a light car and delivery van with front-wheel drive from a motor which lived under a short, Renault-like bonnet. The batteries were under the seat and gave a range of 50–60 miles. It had independent front suspension by transverse leaves.

NG

A.E.M. (ii) see SCOUT (iii)

A.E.R. see B.N.C.

AERIC see LA LICORNE

AERO (i) (F) 1925

Ans. Ets. Aero, Paris.

This is a mysterious 'make' which may never have existed. The company claimed in advertising that several of their cars were exhibited at the 1925 Paris Salon, of which they would describe their torpedo as a typical example. It was said to have a new principle of engine with opposed, mechanically-operated valves (*soupapes opposées commandées*) and a new type of magneto and carburettor. Prices were given for different versions of the torpedo, with 2- and 4/5-seater bodies, and with or without electric lighting and starting. These prices were very low, even the most expensive model being below the 5CV Citroën. Apart from the sketchiness of the details, there is the awkward fact that the Salon was not held in 1925!

KB

AERO (ii) (CS) 1929–1947

Aero, tovarna letadel Dr Kabes, Praha-Vysocany.

The Aero aircraft firm was mainly in the business of airplane production and repairs, but in periods of weak demand for airplanes, other products were made: airscrews, motorcycle sidecars of both American and their own design, and car bodies built under licence from 1925. The Aero's trade director Josef Sorel invited Bretislav Novotny, constructor of the Enka, to produce his small car in the Aero works. Some cars were assembled from parts made by the ENKA factory, but the first true Aero was produced in May 1929.

Dr Kabes's firm entered the motor industry with a simple unitary-construction cyclecar, the Aero 10 HP powered by a 490cc single-cylinder water-cooled two-stroke

Strikingly Beautiful
Price $1495

1921 Adria tourer.
KEITH MARVIN

1932 Aero (ii) Type 30 2-seater.
HANS-OTTO NEUBAUER

1939 Aero (ii) Type 50 sports car.
NATIONAL MOTOR MUSEUM

engine. This transmitted its 10bhp to a back axle without differential, through the medium of a cone clutch and a 3-speed gearbox. There were no front-wheel brakes, and a starter was extra – the standard equipment was a rope device with dashboard control. Three main body styles were available: an open roadster, faux-cabriolet and a hard-top coupé, all 2+1 seaters, and with one door only. About 1500 Aero 10 HPs were built.

This lightweight had grown up by 1932 into a more sophisticated 18bhp 662cc twin with 4-wheel brakes. Aero's production that year was 1317 units. The most popular was a 2-door 2+1 roadster, but 4-seater sedans with a steel tin-plated body on a wooden frame were also built. At the end of this range was the Aero 1000 (1932–1934) with 999cc 26bhp twin-cylinder engine and 2-seater roadster body. 4210 cars of the 500/662/1000 range were made. Many sporting successes were achieved by these cars, and Bohumil Turek was the best-known

1950 Aero Minor 615cc saloon.
NATIONAL MOTOR MUSEUM

1907 Aerocar (i). The front car was the first arrival in the New York–Boston Endurance Run, 12 March 1907.
NATIONAL MOTOR MUSEUM

Aero driver. For the route from Prague to Venice and back he took only 43 hours, Prague–Paris 16.5 hours, and at the 1934 Monte Carlo Rally he finished as 3rd in his category. Another driver, F.A. Elstner, visited Africa and Afghanistan travelling 35,000km (21,735 miles) without any trouble.

It was, however, the 1934 Aero A30 that was to make the most impression. The work of Ing. Basek, these front-wheel drive cars used all-independently sprung platform frames, with mechanical brakes and friction dampers. As before, the engines were two-strokes and water-cooled (by pump and fan), but unlike contemporary DKWs, the Aero had light alloy deflector-type pistons. Another vital difference between the German and Czechoslovak designs was that Aero's engines were always longitudinally mounted. The 999cc twin-cylinder A30 developed 28bhp at 3500rpm, and was capable of 105km/h (65 mph). The production in 1934, 1935 and 1937 was 920, 820 and 1277 cars respectively. B. Turek drove more than 10,000km in 6 weeks in the USSR in 1935 with the A30. After World War II the A30 was briefly revived, and about 500 cars with redesigned grilles and a synchromesh gearbox were produced in 1946 and 1947. 200 of them were exported to France and 100 to Belgium.

The Aero A50 had a 4-cylinder engine of double the capacity (1997cc) giving 48bhp. Such features as alloy cylinder heads, 6v coil ignition, and gravity feed were common to both types. The ratios of the Aero's 3-speed gearbox were selected by the usual clumsy lever on the dash. An A50 sedan weighed 1050 kg (a roadster 950-980 kg) and was capable of 125km/h (78mph), though it proved less smooth than the twin, and suffered from severe oversteer on full power. Aero's annual sales in the later 1930s were around a thousand cars, and some were sold to the Baltic States, Hungary and Romania.

After the War a new generation was intended to replace the faithful twin A30 and the 2-litre A50. These were smaller cars than their predecessors, with capacities of 745cc (21bhp, developed already in 1939) for the twin-cylinder Ponny, and 1491cc (39bhp, developed in 1942) for the companion 4-cylinder Rekord. Engines were, of course, two-stroke, with deflector-type pistons, but the gearboxes were given synchromesh and an extra forward ratio, and the brakes were hydraulic. Both types were designed by Vladimir Kabes, but they did not go into production when the automobile industry in Czechoslovakia was nationalized.

MSH

AEROCAR (i) (US) 1906–1908

1906–1907 The Aerocar Co., Detroit, Michigan.
1907–1908 Aerocar Motor Co., Detroit, Michigan.
The Aerocar was designed by Milton O. Reeves, later famous for his 6- and 8-wheeled cars, and financed by Alexander Malcolmson, who had been an early backer of Henry Ford. Aerocars were made with both air- and water-cooled engines, the latter designed by Leo Melanowski. Three models were offered, of 20, 20/24 and 40hp. After production ended the factory was bought by Hudson.
NG

AEROCAR (ii) (GB) 1919–1920

Aero Car Engineering Co., Upper Clapton, London.
This was a cyclecar powered by a 5/7hp air-cooled flat-twin Blackburne engine, with Sturmey-Archer motorcycle gearbox. It was of sporty appearance, with a bullnose radiator, pointed tail and disc wheels.
NG

AEROCAR (iii) see REESE

AEROCAR (iv) (US) 1948 to date

Aerocar Corp., Longview, Washington.
This flying car was the long-term dream of Molt Taylor who built his prototype in 1948, though it was not certified for flight until 1956. It was a two-seater coupé powered by flat-four aero engines by Franklin or Lycoming. Detachable wings, which could be towed behind the car on a trailer, gave a top speed of 125mph (200km/h) in the air, but only 56mph (90km/h) on the ground. Five were built, and as recently as 1993 Taylor was hoping to get a new version into production, based on a modern car such as the Geo Metro or Honda CRX.
NG

AÉROCARÈNE (F) 1947

Designed by the engineers Desbenoit and Bodu, the Aérocarène 700 was a curious-looking 3-wheeled coupé powered by a 684cc 2-cylinder (in-line) 2-stroke engine giving 23bhp. Transmission was via a Cotal electromagnetic gearbox to the single rear wheel, and top speed was 77mph (125km/h). There were no doors, as the front part of the body slid forward to give access to the seats. The body was made of light alloy and the cockpit of plexiglass. The headlights were mounted above the spatted front wheels.
NG

AEROFORD (GB) 1920–1925

Aeroford Cars, Bayswater, London.
This was one of many attempts to disguise the homely appearance of the Model T Ford, and to market the result at a much higher price. The Aeroford had a distinctive body and radiator, and was made as a 2-seater, 4-seater and coupé, at prices 'from £288' in 1920, but dropping to £168–214 by 1925. Others on the same theme included the ALBERFORD, CREWFORD and MAIFLOWER.
NG

AEROLITHE see COADOU-FLEURY

AERO-MINOR (CS) 1946–1951

Letecke zavody, n.p., Praha-Letnany.
After the war, Czechoslovakia's automobile industry was nationalized, but even before this step was taken, production had been concentrated on the 1100cc Skodas, the rear-engined Tatras, and the Aero-Minor.

The Aero-Minors were not, however, Aeros, though the Aero works delivered the engines. The mechanical elements were entrusted to the former Walter company, and bodies were built either in Skoda Kvasiny or in the main plant. They were in fact direct descendants of the 2-cylinder 615cc JAWA Minor, of which a few were run off after World War II, the designer being Jawa's Rudolf Vykoukal. Prototypes were actually built during the war. Cylinder capacity was unchanged, though output was up to 19.5 bhp. An unusual feature for a water-cooled engine was cooling ribs on the block. Gravity feed was still standard practice in this class, and the frame was a typical Czechoslovak forked backbone, independently suspended at both ends by transverse springs. In the interests of compactness the radiator was positioned behind the engine. The brakes were hydraulic, and the 4-speed gearbox incorporated an overdrive top, but no synchromesh or free-wheel.

Bodied variously as sedans, estate cars, small delivery vans and even roadsters, 14,187 Aero-Minors were built, about half of them being exported to western European countries. For example, Sweden and the Netherlands took about 2000 cars each, Belgium 1300, Switzerland 600, and Austria about 500. After the production ceased in Czechoslovakia, they were assembled in Egypt, and BSA toyed briefly with the idea of making Aero-Minors in England.

A special version, bored out to 744cc and with a racing body, was successful at Le Mans and Spa in 1949. The famous Aero-driver F.A. Elstner used the production Aero-Minor for his travels through the Sahara desert to the Guinea Gulf, making an average 426 km (265 miles) a day in a landscape without roads. Another car reached the Arctic circle.

MSH

AERO-TYPE *see* VICTOR PAGE

AERO VISIONS (US) c.1981–c.1986
Aero Visions Inc., Irvine, California.
Having been involved with daredevil Evel Knievel's motorbike stunts, partners Doug Malewicki, Richard Long and Gary Cerveny set up a company to make a highly economical single-seater 3-wheeler. The California Commuter was based around a Honda 85cc power train, and returned a claimed average of 155mpg, while being capable of reaching 82mph (132 km/h). The car's Buck Rogers-style appearance was claimed to be aerodynamically efficient. After the open-roof prototype, it was planned to sell a fully-enclosed version with a flip-up canopy, but this never got beyond the planning stage.

CR

A.F. (i) *see* AUSTRO-FIAT

A.F. (ii) **(GB)** 1971–1980
1971 Antique Automobiles Ltd, Baston, Peterborough.
1971-72 A.T. Fraser Ltd, Sleaford, Lincolnshire.
1972-80 A.F., Marlborough, Wiltshire.
Alexander T. Fraser's Mini-based trike arrived in 1971 with the name AB1. Its marine ply monocoque body/chassis was mated to a standard Mini front subframe, with a single Mini trailing arm supporting the pointed tail. The definitive version was the 1971 A.F. Spider, which differed only in detail from the AB1, and was sold in kit form. The company was wound up in 1972 with very few cars sold. A further four examples of a redesigned model, called the A.F. Grand Prix, were subsequently made, distinguished by cycle-type front wings and rounded rear bodywork.

CR

A.F. (iii) **(GB)** 1987–1990;1994–1996
1987–1990 Auto Forge Automobiles, Coventry.
1994–1996 A.F. Sports, Coventry.
The ancestry of the A.F. Sports lay in the BURLINGTON Berretta, but its design was completely overhauled. The chassis was a space frame, designed to accept Ford running gear and other parts, although engine options encompassed a wide variety of units, including Fiat and Toyota twin cams. The bodywork was mostly aluminium, with glassfibre wings and came in 2-seater or 2+2 guises. Production ceased after around 40 had been made, but the A.F. was later revived using Ford Sierra mechanicals.

CR

A.F.A. (E) 1942–1944
Juan Aymerich Casanovas, Barcelona.
The AFA was an ambitious project to build a completely Spanish car in the difficult circumstance of World War II. The only type was a 2-seater with a 5/13hp 4-cylinder monobloc engine and simple leaf springs. The company planned to build 100 cars annually, but only some prototypes were finished.

VCM

AFFORDABLE COMPANY (US) 1997 to date
The Affordable Company, division of New England Exotic Rebodies, East Hampstead, New Hampshire.
Low-cost kits were the forté of this company. They sold a replica of a Mercedes 500SL for Chrysler Le Baron or Ford Mustang running gear, a basic T-bucket hot rod kit, and a Ferrari 308 GTSi replica to fit Pontiac Firebird or Chevrolet Camaro mechanicals. All are available in kit or fully assembled form.

HP

A.F.M. (D) 1951
Alex von Falkenhausen, Munich.
Former BMW engineer von Falkenhausen made BMW-based sports cars and single-seater racing cars which did well in Formula 2 events in the years 1948–50. In 1951 he built a prototype 4/5-seater luxury coupé powered by a 2½-litre 6-cylinder Opel Kapitan engine, and using the tubular frame and all-independent suspension from his competition cars.

NG

AFRICAR (GB) 1982–c.1988
1982–1987 Africar, Coalville, Leicestershire.
1987–c.1988 Africar, Lancaster.
The world is littered with attempts to create a 'Third World' car, and Anthony Howarth's Africar came closer to production than virtually any of them. Ultimately it did not succeed, although things got off to a good start with a highly-publicised expedition from the Arctic to the Equator in three prototypes in 1984. The method of construction allowed for numerous body styles – saloon, estate, pick-up and coupé – and construction was of layered plywood and epoxy resin reinforced with steel subframes and a roll cage. The intention was for the car to be constructed with little skilled labour and no need for expensive chassis jigs. All wheels were driven and 4×4, 6×6, and even 8×8 versions were planned. Suspension was by front leading arms and rear trailing arms with Citroën-type nitrogen gas spheres. The engines in the prototypes were Citroën, but later Volkswagen 1.7-litre fuel-injection and Subaru engines were used. There were even plans for self-made powerplants, initially centring on a flat-four design with rotary valves, then an air-cooled supercharged 2- or 3-cylinder engine of 1.3-or 2.0-litres fuelled by petrol or diesel.

CR

Further Reading
Africar, the Development of a Car for Africa, Anthony Howarth, The Ordinary Road, Ltd, 1987.

A.F.S. (US) c.1994
American Flywheel Systems, Seattle, Washington.
The A.F.S.20 was an experimental electric luxury car based on the Chrysler LHS sedan. It had an aerodynamic aluminium or fibreglass body with a system of carbon-fibre flywheels that were spun up by electricity and stored energy for powering the car. Total weight was 2538lb and it had a projected 0–60mph time of 6.5 seconds. The flywheel batteries were being jointly developed by A.F.S and Honeywell Satellite Systems.

HP

A.G. (i) **(I)** 1925–1927
Istituto Feltrinelli, Milan.
This was a small sports car designed by Giuseppe Alfieri, powered by a 1093cc Chapuis-Dornier engine. It was very low-built, and the design featured independent suspension all round. In 1927 Alfieri built a competition model with Cozette-supercharged 1084cc S.C.A.P. engine. Only one of these was made, later converted for road use. Production of all A.G.s was very limited.

NG

A.G. (ii) **(P)** 1988–c.1995
Auto Reparadora da Graça, Lisbon.
This company (which specialised in cabriolet conversions) also made licence-built buggies and a VW Beetle-based Bugatti Type 35 replica from 1988. It then moved into an unusual area of replication, producing a Citroën Traction Avant look-alike on a 2CV chassis. The bodywork was realised in steel and the 2CV engine could be supplemented by a supercharger to take its power up to 40bhp.

CR

1921 AGA 6/16PS tourer.
NATIONAL MOTOR MUSEUM

1913 Ahrens-Fox Battalion roadster.
KEITH MARVIN

A.G. (iii) (GB) 1992

A.G. Fabrications, London.

This was a traditional-style roadster designed for Triumph Spitfire or Herald chassis. It was launched at the 1992 Stoneleigh kit car show and the company intended offering a range of components for kit car builders, but in fact the car was never productionised.

CR

AGA (D) 1919–1928

1919–1926 AG für Automobilbau, Berlin-Lichtenberg.
1926–1928 AGA Fahrzeugwerke, Berlin-Lichtenberg.

This company entered car manufacture with the 1418cc 6/16PS Typ A which was based on a prewar F.N. design. It was not successful and was replaced for 1921 by the Typ C which had the same capacity engine, but with power upped from 18 to 20PS. It was made in open and closed models, and like all German cars had a vee-radiator to start with, going over to a more rounded shape in about 1925. It was reasonably priced and sold quite well. In order to obtain more factory space, the DINOS firm was taken over in November 1925, both companies belonging to the Hugo Stinnes group. However this coincided with a downturn in the car market, and the reformed AGA company made relatively few cars. Power was increased to 24bhp in 1927, and there were plans to make a 10/45PS 6-cylinder car, but nothing came of this idea. A 6/30PS sports car was built for the 1924 Targa Florio, in which they finished 2nd and 3rd in their class. From 1920 to 1924 the Swedish THULIN company made about 300 AGAs under licence.

HON

AGERON (F) 1908–1910

Constructions d'Automobiles Ageron et Cie, Lyons.

This was a conventional car powered by a 10/12hp 4-cylinder engine, with chain drive. It had a compressed air starting system design by M. Ageron, and it is possible that he built only a few chassis to demonstrate his system.

NG

A.G.R. (GB) 1911–1912

Ariel & General Repairs Ltd, Camberwell.

This company was the agent for HURTU and the car they sold under the A.G.R. name was in most respects identical to the 12hp Hurtu, though it was slightly longer and had larger tyres. The only body style offered was an open 4-seater.

NG

AGUZZOLI (I) 1964–1965

Aguzzoli, Parma.

Sergio Aguzzoli and Luigi Bertocco collaborated to create a new GT coupé called the Aguzzoli Condor. In a tubular chassis, a tuned (128bhp) Alfa Romeo Giulietta 1300 engine was mounted centrally and coupled with a ZF 5-speed gearbox. First presented at the 1964 Geneva Salon, it was soon uprated to a 160bhp 1.6-litre Giulia engine and Hewland 5-speed transmission. The Condor failed to enter series production.

CR

AHRENS-FOX (US) 1913

The Ahrens-Fox Fire Engine Co., Cincinnati, Ohio.

Ahrens-Fox was a well-known fire engine maker whose horse-drawn pumpers dated back to 1868. In 1913 they followed the example of their rivals American La France in announcing a roadster, intended for the personal use of fire chiefs. The Model E-C Battalion Roadster had a 44hp 6-cylinder engine and carried some fire equipment. Unfortunately the orders from fire chiefs nationwide did not materialise, and only six Battalion Roadsters were made, all delivered to the Cincinnati Fire Department. Ahrens-Fox remained in business making fire engines until 1956.

NG

AI FIBERGLASS (US) c.1985

AI Fiberglass, Elkridge, Maryland; Anderson Industries, Elkridge, Maryland.

This company was stuck in the 1920s, building replicas of 1923–25 Ford pick-ups, 1926–27 Ford roadsters, and a 1923 Ford Track T hot rod. All were intended to use V8 engines.

HP

AILEF (F) 1997 to date

Ailef, St-Martin le Vinoux.

This company was a racing car operation for several years before it launched the 696, a road-going sports car inspired by the Ferrari 206S racer. Of very high quality, it was powered by a centrally-mounted 250bhp Peugeot/Renault 2.85-litre V6 engine and was claimed to reach a top speed of 174mph (280km/h).

CR

AILLOUD; AILLOUD ET DUMOND (F) 1897–1904

1897–1900 Automobiles Ailloud, Lyons.
1900–1904 Automobiles Ailloud et Dumond, Lyons.

Claude Ailloud was a bicycle maker who began to build a small car in 1897. It had a 618cc vertical-twin engine, originally mounted at the rear, but later moved to the front to obtain better cooling. It had a tubular frame, 3-speed gearbox and single-chain drive. Ailloud won a diploma and silver medal for the car at the Lyons Cycle and Automobile Show in December 1899, but probably did not build a second example.

In 1900 he joined forces with Francisque Dumond, and together they made five cars with 2-cylinder engines, four of 1004cc with hot-tube ignition, and one of 1105cc with low-tension magneto ignition. They then made a number of tricycles with single-cylinder De Dion Bouton engines, and in 1904 one final car. This had a 2798cc 4-cylinder engine with 4-speed gearbox and double-chain drive. It was sold to a customer in Paris where it was in use at least until 1914. The partners later sold other makes of car, particularly De Dietrich, Gregoire, Mors and Turcat-Méry.

NG

AILSA see KENNEDY (ii)

AILSA CRAIG see CRAIG-DORWALD

A.I.M.S. *see* FERGUS

AIR DYNAMICS (US) 1993 to date
Air Dynamics, Conasauga, Tennessee.
Riding on the success of the movie *The Wraith*, Air Dynamics built a prototype of the car featured in the movie. The Wraith II was originally intended to have a custom chassis with Corvette and Fiero suspension components and a Ford SHO V6 for power. Revised prototypes were shown during 1995, but only 2 cars were built. Air dynamics also built replicas of Ferraris.
HP

AIREDALE (GB) 1919–1924
1919–1922 Nanson, Barker & Co., Esholt, Yorkshire.
1922–1924 Airedale Cars Ltd, Esholt, Yorkshire.
This company was founded in 1911 by Guy Nanson and Norman Barker to make the TINY cyclecar. Barker's father was a fellmonger or dealer in skins and hides, and it was in part of his premises nicknamed 'The Skinyard' that the cars were made. The Airedale was named after the nearby River Aire and also the terrier which took its name from the same district. The first four cars had American-built Sterling 4-cylinder engines which had been bought during the war. Later Airedales had 1794cc Dorman KNO ohv engines, and the last 33 cars, made in 1923–24, had 2120cc Meadows engines. All frames were supplied by Rubury Owen, but Nanson Barker did have a small forge where 4-speed gearboxes and rear axles were made. Bodies came mostly from local suppliers in Bingley and Bradford, though at least two cars were bodied by John C. Beadle of Dartford, Kent. Exact production figures are not known, but probably fewer than 100 Airedales were made.
NG

Further Reading
'The Tiny and the Tyke from Esholt', M. Worthington–Williams, *The Automobile*, October 1995.

AIREX *see* REX

AIRFLOW MOTORSPORTS (US) c.1988
Airflow Motorsports, Charlotte, North Carolina.
Although they began by assembling other manufacturers' kits for customers, Airflow built a prototype of an aluminium-bodied Lamborghini Countach replica that was intended to wrap around a Buick V6. They also announced plans to add a V12-powered version, but actual production, if any, is unknown.
HP

AIROMOBILE *see* LEWIS AIROMOBILE

AIRPHIBIAN (US) 1950–1956
Continental Inc., Danbury, Connecticut.
Like the Aerocar (iv) the Airphibian was a flying car powered by a 165bhp engine, with an air speed of 121mph (195km/h) and road speed of 88mph (141km/h). It had four independently sprung small wheels on struts. It was fully licenced by the Federal Aviation Agency and offered for sale, but few, if any, were bought. It was also known as the Fulton Airphibian.
NG

AIRSCOOT (US) 1947
Aircraft Products, Wichita, Kansas.
The aptly-named Airscoot was designed to fold up and be carried on an aeroplane to provide road transportation away from the airport. It weighed 72lb and had an overall length of 37in. Seating was for two and it had a rack that held two suitcases. It never caught on with the flying public.
HP

AIRWAY (US) 1948–1950
T.P. Hall Engineering Corp., San Diego, California.
T.P. Hall had been associated with the Convair flying car, but his Airway was strictly earthbound. Powered by an air-cooled aluminium block 2-cylinder engine, it was available in two forms, fastback 2-seater coupé and notchback 3-seater sedan, both priced at $750. Only one example was made of each.
NG

1921 Airedale 11.9hp all-weather tourer by Dixons of West Bromwich.
NICK BALDWIN

c.1983 Aixam 325D Microcar.
JOHN FILSELL

A.I.S.A. (E) 1955
Actividades Industriales SA, Barcelona.
The rather grandly named Pullman-Biscuter resembled the German Fuldamobil in form, being a very compact 3-wheeler with a single rear wheel. The 2-seater had a Hispano-Villiers 197cc single-cylinder 2-stroke engine mounted in the rear, together with a 3-speed gearbox. Weighing only 220kg, a top speed of 50mph (80km/h) was claimed.
CR

AIXAM (F) 1983 to date
Aixam Automobiles, Aix-les-Bains.
This enterprise grew out of the ashes of the failed AROLA company, and occupied the old Arola factory. It relaunched production with the diesel-powered 325D, joined a year later by the faster 400D. By 1987 it had displaced Microcar as France's largest microcar maker, with 35 per cent of the market. In 1988 the new 325i passed the 30mph (48km/h) EC crash barrier test, and the following year a 3-cylinder 600i and a 2-cylinder 500i were launched. The 400i Twin of 1991 was France's first ever water-cooled twin-cylinder microcar. A new range for 1992 (the A540 and A550) boasted expanded bodywork with seating for four people. In 1992 Aixam created a new marque, MEGA, building a diametrically-opposed supercar. A completely new microcar range appeared in 1997 under the names A300, A400 and A500, with bodywork resembling the Renault Twingo. The A500 was a 4-seater. Aixam remains Europe's largest producer of microcars, boasting 49 per cent of the French market.
CR

AJAM (F) 1921
Designed by Nemorin Causan and Rene LeGrain-Eifel, the Ajam was a cyclecar powered by a V-twin or 6/8hp 4-cylinder engine, with ifs by semi-elliptic springs which took the place of the front axle. It was shown as the 1921 Paris Salon, but did not go into production. The suspension was later used on the M.A.S.E. light car.
NG

1908 Ajax (ii) Type A 8/16CV landaulet.
ERNEST SCHMID

1925 Ajax (vi) Six sedan.
NATIONAL MOTOR MUSEUM

1931 A.J.S. Nine saloon.
NATIONAL MOTOR MUSEUM

AJAX (i) (US) 1901–1903

The Ajax Motor Vehicle Co., New York, New York.
Built on West 36th Street in the centre of Manhattan, the Ajax was a light electric runabout with bicycle-type wheels and full-elliptic suspension, a transverse spring at the front and two conventionally placed at the rear. The price was $1100, reduced to $800 for 1903.
NG

AJAX (ii) (CH) 1906–1910

1906–1907 Automobilfabrik Dr G. Aigner, Zürich.
1907–1910 Ajax AG, Zürich.
The first Ajax passenger car of 20/27PS was ready in 1906. Its 4-cylinder monobloc engine with L-head had a capacity of about 4-litres. The big flywheel served as a fan to complement the thermosyphon water-cooling. Power was

transmitted via wet multiple-disc clutch and a long shaft to the 4-speed gearbox located in the rear of the chassis, and final drive was by chains. After one year a financial group took over the faltering small enterprise and founded Ajax AG in Zürich. Two 4-cylinder and a 6-cylinder model were developed by D. Siebenmann, the engineer responsible for their design. The 16PS had shaft-drive, whereas the 24PS with square cylinder dimensions of 100 x 104mm, 3266cc, and the 24PS six, with two groups of three cylinders, of 3403cc, could be delivered optionally with shaft or chain drive. All Ajax cars had a sophisticated mechanical starting device which was actuated by stepping on the running board. The engines were said to run so smoothly that they could be compared only with electric cars. Two 6-cylinder Ajax delivering about 50bhp were prepared for the Targa Florio of 1907, one with shaft, the other with chain drive. The gallant effort was not successful. One car suffered mechanical problems and the other crashed. Four cars only were sold in 1908, but then Ajax participated financially with the newly-founded Taxi company of Zürich and supplied ten landaulets at SFr.15,000 each. Two new models were launched in 1909–10. The 4-cylinder engine of 3084cc offered 24bhp at 1600rpm. No details are known of the 6-cylinder. The costly development, expensive manufacturing and high investments into the development of an airplane created liquidity problems. When the Taxi companies of Vienna, Munich and Zürich, where the fleet consisted of 32 Ajax landaulets, ran into financial troubles, the days of the marque were numbered. In February 1910 the company went broke. A pity Siebenmann could no longer pursue his plans for a gearless automobile, where he intended to place a rotary engine in the back of the chassis to directly drive the rear wheels. One single Ajax has survived. An 8/16PS landaulet is in the Transport Museum of Lucerne, Switzerland.
FH

AJAX (iii) (F) 1913–1914

Briscoe Frères, Neuilly, Seine.
After resigning from the US Motor Corporation, Benjamin and Frank Briscoe went to France where they planned to make the Ajax cyclecar on a large scale. 'The workmanship will be French but the business management American' they said. The car had a 980cc 4-cylinder engine with friction drive, and sold for the equivalent of £78. The war interrupted their plans and they returned to America where they made the ARGO (ii). This was similar to the Ajax, apart from having a conventional gearbox in place of the friction drive.
NG

AJAX (iv) (US) 1914–1915

1914–1915 Parker Motor Car Co., Seattle, Washington.
1915 Ajax Motors Co., Seattle, Washington.
A variety of options characterised this limited production car; a choice of poppet- or sleeve-valve 6-cylinder engines, left or right hand drive and three wheelbases. Body options were roadster, tourer or limousine. Steel for its construction was said to have come from Krupp in Germany, and the company claimed to have extensive foundries for iron, bronze and aluminium components. However they lasted barely two years.
NG

AJAX (v) (US) 1920–1921

Ajax Motors Corp., Boston, Massachusetts.
This Ajax was made only as a 5-seater tourer powered by a 55bhp 6-cylinder Continental engine. Few were made; some sources suggest that the factory was in Hyde Park, Massachusetts.
NG

AJAX (vi) (US) 1925–1926

Ajax Motors Co., Racine, Wisconsin.
This Ajax was a NASH product, though a separate company was formed for its manufacture, which took place in the former Mitchell factory in Racine. Offered in two styles only, tourer and sedan, it had a 2786cc side-valve 6-cylinder engine, unusual among cars in its price bracket in having a 7-bearing crankshaft. First year sales were an encouraging 22,122 cars, but there didn't seem to be much point in selling a car which was just a small Nash under a different and less familiar name, and with the costly complexity of a separate company. So for 1926 the Ajax was renamed the Nash Light Six. Nash dealers were provided with new nameplates and hubcaps to re-name the Ajaxes they had in stock.
NG

A.J.P. *see* C.P.C.

A.J.S. (GB) 1930–1932

1930–1931 A.J. Stevens Ltd, Wolverhampton, Staffordshire.
1932–1933 Willys-Overland-Crossley Ltd, Stockport, Cheshire.
A.J. Stevens Ltd was founded in 1909 and by the mid–1920s had become one of Britain's leading makers of motorcycles. In 1924 they added radio sets to their products, and in 1929 brought out a range of buses powered by 6-cylinder Coventry-Climax engines. When they decided to enter the car market in 1930 they also went to Coventry-Climax for their engine, in this case a 1018cc 4-cylinder side-valve unit, with 3-speed gearbox and offered in three body styles: open 2-seater, fabric saloon, and coachbuilt saloon. It was a quality light car with several luxury features such as interior roof light, ash tray and map net, but at prices from £210 to £240, it did not seem good value compared with a Morris Cowley saloon at £160. Price reductions in February 1931 did not help all that much, though A.J.S. had sold about 3000 cars when they went into liquidation in October 1931. Production of the Nine was taken over by Willys-Overland-Crossley in Stockport, and the line was pruned to just the coachbuilt saloon with a fabric top and 4-speed gearbox. About 300 were made. W-O-C itself went into liquidation in 1933, and probably no A.J.S. cars were made after the summer of 1932. A prototype 1½-litre 12hp saloon was shown at Olympia in October 1932, but never went into production.

NG

Further Reading
'The A.J.S. Car', M. Worthington-Williams, *The Automobile,* August, 1994.

A.K. (GB) 1992 to date

A.K. Sportscars, Peterborough, Cambridgeshire.
This company made the KF 427, a Cobra replica, using a steel ladder frame chassis, glassfibre body, a choice of V8 power plants and Jaguar running gear. It was marketed as a low-cost kit.

CR

AKA (US) c.1981–1991

AKA, Anaheim, California.
Kelly Motors, Riverside, California.
This sports car project was started by entrepreneur Al Kelly with a leftover body shell from the Ford Bordinat Cobra show car. Stylist McKinley Thompson, who had worked on the project at Ford, reworked the shape to fit a shortened Mustang unibody that had been modified into a chassis. The fibreglass body was to have been built by PACIFIC COBRA, with final assembly by AKA and with sales to be handled through a network of Ford dealers. They were intended to sell in the $35,000 to $40,000 range. Although 3 prototypes were completed by 1985, the AKA 100, also known as the Kelly Python, does not appear to have made it into full production. Kelly was still developing the Python in 1991.

HP

AKRON (i) (US) 1899–1901

1899–1900 Akron Machine Co., Akron, Ohio.
1900–1901 Akron Motor Carriage Co., Akron, Ohio.
The Akron Machine Co. made mower knives, sickles and similar goods, offering a 'motor carriage' in the form of a light 2-seater stanhope powered by a single-cylinder engine. Several examples were tested, and a company formed for manufacture, but production never started. The brothers Albert and George Woodruff, who designed the car, later went into business with their own WOODRUFF car.

NG

AKRON (ii) (US) 1905

Akron Two-Cycle Automobile Co., Akron, Ohio.
This small company was formed by Albert Woodruff after the death of his brother George and the failure of their Woodruff Automobile Co. They made mostly engines, but four touring cars were also built.

NG

ALAMAGNY (F) 1948

M. Alamagny was an ex-Renault engineer who presented an extraordinary design in 1948. Its four wheels were arranged in a diamond pattern and the enclosed

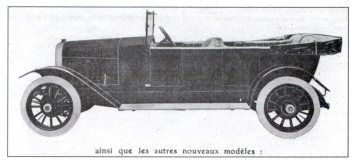

c.1924 Alba (ii) 8CV tourer.
NICK BALDWIN

bodywork was absolutely symmetrical front-to-rear; the entire front and rear bodywork sections opened up for access to the back-to-back 4-seater interior. A Simca 5 engine was centrally-placed, driving the centre pair of wheels, while the front and rear wheels steered. The two headlamps were stacked vertically in the centre of the bonnet.

CR

ALAN (D) 1923–1925

J. Mayer, Bamberg.
This was one of many German makes which tried to crack the market in the 1920s, and did not succeed for long. The only model was the 6/30PS, powered by a 4-cylinder Siemens & Halske engine.

NG

ALAND (US) 1916–1917

Aland Motor Car Co., Detroit, Michigan.
The Aland Four, made as a 5-seater tourer or 2-seater roadster, was a conventional-looking car, but had a very advanced engine, featuring a single ohc and four valves per cylinder. This gave a high output of 65bhp from 2540cc. Another advanced feature for 1916 was that of diagonally-connected 4-wheel brakes. The two models of Aland were not overpriced at $1500, but few were sold.

NG

ALATAC (B) 1913–1914

Automobiles Catala, Braine-le-Comté.
Etienne Catala sold Model T Fords before setting up as a car maker in his own right, choosing an anagram of his surname for the cars. They were assembled machines, using Chapuis-Dornier engines in two sizes, a 1526cc 9/12hp, and a 2296cc 12/16hp, both 4-cylinder monobloc side-valve units in conjunction with 4-speed gearboxes. The chassis came from Malicet et Blin, and bodies – 2-seaters, tourers and saloons – were built locally, with an attractive vee-radiator.

NG

ALBA (i) (A) 1906–1908

Automobile-werk Alba AG, Trieste.
Made in the former Austrian port of Trieste, Italian since the end of World War I, the Alba was a conventional car made with two sizes of 4-cylinder engine, 25 and 45hp.

NG

ALBA (ii) (F) 1913–1928

Constructions Métallurgiques, Usines Alba, Suresnes, Seine.
The Alba was a conventional light car made with a variety of 4-cylinder engines. These included a 1170cc side-valve S.C.A.P., 1994cc side-valve Altos, 1476cc pushrod ohv S.C.A.P. and 1994cc pushrod ohv Altos. The usual range of bodies – 2- seaters, tourers and saloons – was made, including a 4-seater torpedo sport with pointed tail. In 1921 they introduced a smaller car called the Bobby Alba, with a 1243cc side-valve Altos engine, 3-speed gearbox, and shaft drive. Front-wheel brakes were an unusual feature. The following year it was offered in two models, the 1243cc and a 1725cc unit, both on a 104in (2650mm) wheelbase. The larger was close to an Alba in engine size, but had a 3-speed gearbox, whereas Albas had four, and the Alba's wheelbase was 118in (3000mm).

NG

23

1972 Albany (iii) replica roadster.
NATIONAL MOTOR MUSEUM

1903 Lamplough-Albany 12hp steam tonneau.
NATIONAL MOTOR MUSEUM

ALBA REGIA (H) 1955
Székesfehérvári Motorjavitó Vállalat, Székesfehérvár.

During the 1950s only a few privileged persons were allowed to possess passenger cars in Hungary. Other cars were confiscated and scrapped or found new homes among communist party leaders. But the desire to have an individual and closed means of transport remained, and lots of skilled craftsmen (blacksmiths, engineers, etc) tried to fabricate something out of left-over parts and motorcycles. COMECON prohibited car production in Hungary, so the myriad of one-off vehicles built between 1948–1953 were either registered as motorcycles or as vehicles for the disabled. In 1953 the Ministry of Metallurgy and Engineering decided it was time to have an official Hungarian microcar. Three engineers: Ernö Rubik (the father of the inventor of the Rubik cube and himself a very talented engineer with lots of aircraft experience), Pál Kerekes, and Géza Bengyel were sent to a former aeroplane repair company in Székesfehérvár to realise this project. At Székesfehérvár they found that work had already started on a microcar, as a local engineer, József Horváth brought his own drawings to the factory. Horváth's creation became the Alba Regia and a second model was also built after an idea by one of his friends, József Zappel. The latter was called the BALATON.

Both cars had aluminium bodies, airplane tail wheels, Csepel 250cc motorbike engines and Isetta gearboxes, with Messerschmitt reverse. The Alba Regia had torsion suspension sourced from Csepel motorcycles and suicide doors. It was a neatly-styled 2+2 seater.

When the Ministry decided to use the Székesfehérvár plant as the headquarters of the Hungarian microcar project, a third Hungarian microcar, the ÚTTÖR (Pioneer) was shipped there, along with an Isetta, a Goggomobil, and a Messerschmitt Kabinroller. Lots of tests followed, and the Goggomobil was chosen as the most capable. But to let the general public have its say (it was a People's Republic, after all) a microcar design competition was announced during the autumn of 1956. However, the Revolution intervened and put an end to all work. All cars were sent to the scrapyard and the Székesfehérvár company was renamed and became an arm of the Ikarus bus company. Rumours circulate that both the Alba Regia and Balaton might have survived.

In 1957 passenger car ownership was again allowed and with cars like the Trabant and the Wartburg, Hungary entered into a new era.

PN

Further Reading
'Hungarian microcars, part II', *Classic Car Mart*, December 1996.

ALBANI (AUS) 1921–1922
Albani Motor Construction Pty Ltd, Melbourne, Victoria.

An assembled car, which used such US components as a 6-cylinder 25hp Continental engine of 3671cc. Initially called Albany, as known in the Alpine Trial, it also took part in an Alternative Fuels Demonstration and sought publicity with a 5000 mile run with its bonnet sealed by the Automobile Club of Victoria. Dealers were sought for the more exotically named car in 1922, but nothing more was heard.

MG

ALBANY (i) (GB) 1903–1905
Albany Mfg Co. Ltd, Willesden, London.

This company's first car was a steamer called the Lamplough-Albany after its designer Frederick Lamplough. It was shown at the Crystal Palace Show in February 1903, having a semi-flash boiler using petrol or paraffin fuel, a 24hp 4-cylinder engine and a choice of wheel or tiller steering. With a frontal bonnet and 4-seater tonneau body, it looked very like a petrol car. Probably few were made, as it was not listed after 1903, when Albany were offering petrol cars, a 10hp single-cylinder model being promoted as the Silent Albany. This had a silencer in which the exhaust gases drove a fan to cool the engine before passing into a conventional silencer. It was offered up to 1905, after which Albany concentrated on making radiators and selling Talbots.

CR

ALBANY (ii) (US) 1907–1908
Albany Automobile Co., Albany, Indiana.

This was a typical high-wheeler, originally with 6/7hp single-cylinder engine, tiller steering and steel-shod wheels. After very few had been made in this form there came improvements such as wheel steering and solid rubber tyres. There was also a dummy bonnet, though the engine was located under the seat. For 1908 the engine was increased to two cylinders (18/20hp), and was mounted under the bonnet. Total Albany production was about 850.

NG

ALBANY (iii) (GB) 1971–1981
Albany Motor Carriage Company, Christchurch, Dorset.

Launched by an engineering company with spare capacity, the Albany followed an American trend to produce replicas of veteran cars. In this case it was inspired by the 1908 Buick 2-seater. Into a special tubular steel chassis were placed the components of a Morris Minor, including its 948cc engine with a special governor in place to limit the top speed to 40mph (64km/h). The replication was convincing, if expensive. A governed Triumph Spitfire 1500 engine arrived in 1974, and a long wheelbase 5-seater followed in 1976. Faced with competition from cheaper replicas, the company folded in 1981.

CR

ALBAR (CH) 1978–1993
Alois Barmettler, Buochs.

Alois Barmettler (b. 1931), driving instructor and owner of a workshop, began converting Volkswagen Beetles into Buggies and cross-country vehicles in the 1970s. Still on the VW-chassis, but with a fibreglass body made in Austria, he produced a small number of rather pleasing sports coupés. They had VW or Porsche engines and were offered in Switzerland as Albar Jet and in Austria as Strato. In 1982 Albar launched their Sonic model, which still had the VW rear engine but, instead of the platform-chassis, it received a space-frame on which the fibreglass targa body of very modern lines was fitted. Later a fixed head coupé with upward swinging doors – as on the Lamborghini Countach – was available. Improved versions of the Sonic followed. The VW flat-4 was replaced by VW-Audi 4-cylinder in-line engines and then by the Renault 25 engine of 2165cc and 110bhp, always mounted in the rear. Production of these specialist cars was limited.

FH

ALBATROS (i) (F) 1912
Henri Billouin, Paris.
This company was chiefly known for its bicycles and motor cycles, but they offered a light 4-cylinder car in 1912. In an advertisement in *La Vie au Grand Air* in June 1912 they spoke of 91 victories in 92 races, but this achievement presumably referred to their 2-wheelers.

NG

ALBATROS (ii) (GB) 1923–1924
Albatros Motors Ltd, Coventry.
This was a conventional light car powered by Coventry-Climax engines of 1247 or 1368cc, with 3-speed unit gearbox and shaft drive to a spiral bevel rear axle. 2- and 4-seater bodies were listed, and the utility 2-seater with the smaller engine had no differential. Probably no more than 12 were made, of which there are two known survivors. The name is thought to have come from a Mr Albert Ross rather than from the large bird, the killing of which brought so much woe to the Ancient Mariner.

NG

ALBATROSS (US) 1939
Albatross Motor Car Co., New York, New York.
Conceived by *New Yorker* cartoonist Peter Arno, the Albatross had a rakish, 4-seater convertible body, built by J.S. Inskip, New York City Rolls-Royce distributor, and was mounted on a Mercury chassis, described in the company's advertising as re-engineered and greatly accelerated. Arno had planned to market the Albatross commercially, and releases to the automotive press listed plans for a town car and a 2-passenger speedster in addition to the 4/5-seater convertible which Arno used as his personal car. Plans to market the 137in (3477mm) wheelbase Albatross on New York City's Automobile Row failed to appear.

KM

ALBERFORD (GB) c.1924
Albert Bridge Garage, Chelsea, London.
This was one of a number of 'improved' Model T Fords, in this case having an English clover-leaf body and racing wings, with an ohv engine and 'special gear ratio' which it was claimed gave a top speed of 75mph (121km/h). The frame was said to be underslung, but from a photograph it appears to be no lower than a standard Model T. A new car was said to cost £500, very high when compared with the contemporary Aeroford at £148–194, and must have been hard to sell as the garage was offering a brand-new example at £250 in February 1924.

NG

ALBERT (GB) 1920–1924
1920 Adam, Grimaldi & Co. Ltd, Vauxhall, London.
1920–1924 Gwynne's Engineering Co Ltd, Chiswick, London.
The Albert was a high quality light car powered by a 1495cc 4-cylinder ohv engine with 4-speed gearbox, designed by A.O. Lord who later was involved with the LOYD-LORD car. Bodies made extensive use of aluminium, and were mostly all-weather 4-seater tourers. The builders of the first Alberts, Adam, Grimaldi & Co., made aircraft parts during the war, and bought their engines from GWYNNE. They ordered 3000 engines, but only 250 cars had been made by March 1920, when Adam, Grimaldi were bought up by Gwynne, who transferred production of the Albert to their works at Chiswick. They made about 1450 cars up to 1923, but were more interested in their little 850cc Gwynne Eight, of which they made 2250. In 1923 they replaced the Albert with an enlarged version which they called the Gwynne-Albert. This had a 1944cc engine and, from 1925, front wheel brakes. About 200 were made, production lasting spasmodically up to 1929.

NG

ALBION (GB) 1900–1913
Albion Motor Car Co. Ltd, Scotstoun, Glasgow.
Albion was founded in December 1899 by Norman Osborne Fulton and Thomas Blackwood Murray. Both had worked at ARROL-JOHNSTON, and their first car was a dogcart in the same idiom as the Arrol-Johnston, with horizontally-opposed 2-cylinder engine under the seat, single-chain final drive, and solid tyres. It incorporated Murray's patent automatic engine governor, and

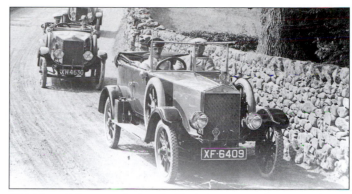

1921 Albert 11.9hp tourer in the Lake District.
NATIONAL MOTOR MUSEUM

1923 Albatros (ii) 10hp 2-seater.
MIKE ERROLL

1908 Albion 24/30hp tourer in Scottish Reliability Trials.
NATIONAL MOTOR MUSEUM

a patent lubricator, whereby all working parts could be lubricated from the driver's seat while the car was in motion.

The Albion works in Finnieston Street, Glasgow, were on the first floor and had only seven employees, yet by July 1903 they had turned out nearly 160 cars with 8 or 10hp engines. In that month they moved to larger premises on the outskirts of Glasgow, where they were to remain until 1972, when commercial vehicle production ended. The mid-engined dogcarts were made up to 1904, and were replaced for the following season by a more conventional-looking car with a 3115cc 16hp vertical-twin engine mounted at the front. Solid tyres were still general, though pneumatics soon became optional, and were standardised on the next Albion. This was a large touring car with 4175cc 24hp 4-cylinder engine and double-chain drive. This and the 16hp twin made up most of Albion's passenger car production up to 1913, though for 1912 a smaller 15hp four of 2490cc with monobloc engine and shaft drive was announced. Albion made 553 vehicles in 1912, but only about 150 were passenger cars. The last of these, a 15hp coupé, left the factory in November 1913.

In 1920 Albion announced that their estate vehicles were again available, but these were more in the nature of small buses than private cars. Commercial vehicle production flourished, and Albion enjoyed an excellent export market.

1913 Alco 60hp limousine.
JOHN A. CONDE

1907 Alcyon single-cylinder 2-seater.
NATIONAL MOTOR MUSEUM

They were taken over by Leyland in 1951, who closed down truck and bus production in 1972, though they kept the Scotstoun factory for manufacture of axles.

NG

ALBO (GB) 1998 to date
Albo Engineering, Batley, West Yorkshire.
Distinguishing itself from the plethora of other kit-form Lotus 7 lookalikes, the Albo had all-aluminium bodywork. It was also unusual in that it could be tailored around the individual customer. Most of the mechanicals were derived from Ford, including a live rear axle and a wide variety of engine choices.

CR

ALBRUNA (GB) 1908–1912
Brown Brothers, London.
This was one of the range of cars marketed by Brown Brothers, and was a light car powered by a 1592cc 4-cylinder monobloc engine, in conjunction with a 3-speed gearbox and shaft drive. From 1910 a slightly larger engine of 2120cc was used. They were not listed after 1912, by which time all Brown cars had been discontinued, the company concentrating on their business as motor factors.

NG

ALCO (US) 1909–1913
American Locomotive Co., Providence, Rhode Island.
The American Locomotive Company was one of the leading producers of steam locomotives in the United States. In June 1905 company president Albert S. Pitkin announced that the French Berliet car would be manufactured in one of Alco's rolling stock factories, at Providence, Rhode Island (see AMERICAN BERLIET). In 1909 the name of the car was changed to Alco and the three Berliet designs continued under this name. They were a 22 and 40hp four and a massive 60hp six. This had a capacity of 9488cc, rode on a 134in (3401mm) wheelbase and cost $6000 for a tourer. For 1910 the 22hp was dropped, and the larger cars were listed with a wider variety of coachwork, including a landaulette and limousine which cost $6750 on the 60 chassis. This rose to $7250 by 1912. Alcos were meticulously made, the company claiming that it took six months to build the rear axle alone, and that a complete car could not be made in less than 19 months. Bodies were also made by Alco, being distinguished by a white stripe around the body at the top of the doors. In 1913 Alco asked the Crane Motor Car Co. to design a smaller and cheaper car, with a 6178cc 6-cylinder engine to sell at around $3400. Only three prototypes were made, as Alco were about to leave the car business. Though the cars had a wonderful reputation Alco's accountants found that they were losing $460 on each car sold. They ordered an immediate end to the car division, though the company's locomotives continued to grace America's railroads for many years.

NG

Further Reading
'The Mighty Alco: a history', Beverley Rae Kimes,
Automobile Quarterly, Vol. 11, No. 2.

ALCRE (RA) 1960–1961
Alcre Automotores SAIC, Parana, Entre Rios.
Only a few examples of the Alcre automobiles were made. The Argentine Alcre company planned to make the cars in association with the German Heinkel and Bellino companies. There were two models. The Alcre Susana 500, was a small 2-door 4-seat saloon powered by a rear-mounted Heinkel 452cc 2-stroke engine. The Alcre Sport Luis 700 was a sportier 2-seater coupé, powered by a rear-mounted 3-cylinder 2-stroke 677cc engine.

ACT

ALCYON (F) 1906–1929
1906–1912 Edmond Gentil, Neuilly, Seine.
1912–1914 Edmond Gentil, Courbevoie, Seine.
1914–1929 Automobiles Alcyon, Courbevoie, Seine.
Edmond Gentil began manufacture of bicycles in about 1890 and motorcycles in 1902. For the latter, and for his cars, he chose the name Alcyon (kingfisher). At the 1906 Paris Salon he showed two models of 4-wheeler, a 2-seater voiturette with 950cc 7/8hp single-cylinder engine and a light car with 1.4-litre 10/12hp 4-cylinder engine suitable for 4-seater bodies. They had 3-speed gearboxes and shaft drive. The engines were built by Gentil, and the chassis came from Surleau. These were of advanced design, with the sides of the frame extending upwards to form the seat squab, in the manner of the later Lancia Lambda. A factory was set up at Neuilly, separate from the manufacture of cycles and motorcycles which continued at Courbevoie. In 1907 the range was extended, with two singles of 725cc and 1-litre, and a 2.7-litre four. This had monobloc casting, but in 1909 Alcyon turned to Zurcher for their engines, a 1205cc twin and a 1943cc four. The single-cylinder engines were still made by Alcyon, and lasted at least until 1911. Some larger singles of 942 and 1038cc were built for the 1907 and 1908 Coupe des Voiturettes races, and the latter was used in the 1909/10 production cars. From 1912 to 1914 only 4-cylinder cars were made, notably the L-head 2120cc Type E. This carried some quite heavy coachwork, saloons and landaulets, including a modern-looking completely enclosed saloon with centre door as on the 1915 Dodge. Engines continued to be made by Zurcher, and chassis by Surleau, though the advanced semi-monocoque construction was not continued on these larger cars. For 1914 two smaller fours were added, a 1356cc 8hp and 1846cc 12hp.

The first postwar Alcyon did not appear until the end of 1921. It was a conventional 1994cc 4-cylinder car, which made little impact on the market and might have been forgotten had not the Lyons agent, M. Giroux, prepared some examples with enlarged and tuned engines, which he sold under the name Alcyon-GL (Giroux Lyons). They were bodied in Lyons, in open and closed versions, and some did well in sprints and hill climbs. One covered the flying kilometre at 66.97mph (107.784km/h), which was well beyond the ability of an ordinary Alcyon.

Towards the end of 1923 the 4-cylinder Alcyon was dropped in favour of a 2-cylinder cyclecar which was a SIMA-VIOLET design made under licence. The engine was a flat-twin of 496cc, though other sizes may have been offered as well. It remained available until 1929, but Alcyon realised that the cyclecar's day was over, and concentrated production on motorcycles. They were sold under a variety of names, from the companies they had acquired. The Labor marque, which was used for the Sima-Violet type cars, lasted until 1960, and a few mopeds were sold under the Alcyon name up to the mid–1960s.

NG

Further Reading
'Les Voitures Legères Alcyon', Jacques Rousseau,
L'Album du Fanatique, January–March, 1982.

ALDA (F) 1912–1922
1912–1920 Fernand Charron, Courbevoie, Seine.
1920–1922 Automobiles Farman, Billancourt, Seine
Fernand Charron was one of the three founding partners in the C.G.V. company, which he left in 1907. After a spell as manager of the CLEMENT-BAYARD works, he took on dealerships for a number of makes, including HURTU, REYROL, S.C.A.R. and TH. SCHNEIDER. In 1912 he acquired the E.N.V. factory and decided to go back into car manufacture. His initial plan to call the cars F. Charron was dropped because of possible confusion with the cars being made by C.G.V.'s successor, CHARRON, so he chose the name Alda (Ah, la Délicieuse Automobile). He had acquired the rights to the Henriod rotary-valve engine, and he offered his customers the choice of this or a conventional side-valve unit in the 3176cc 15hp 4-cylinder car that he launched in 1912. Originally there was to have been a 25hp as well, but this was not put into production. The Henriod engine was soon dropped as being too troublesome, but the L-head 15hp was made up to the outbreak of war. It was a handsome car, with a long wheelbase, wire wheels and a Renault-type dashboard radiator. A variety of bodies was offered from 2-seater to landaulet and town car. Charron entered a team of two cars in the 1913 Coupe de l'Auto. They had the same 85mm bore as the production cars, but a stroke reduced to 132mm gave a capacity of 2995cc. Their best position was 6th. For the 1914 French Grand Prix he entered three cars with 4440cc single-ohc 16-valve engines, but all three retired.

Charron imported Federal trucks from America during the war, and in 1920 launched his postwar car. The radiator was moved to the front and was of vee shape, and the engine was larger than before the war, at 3550cc. A small number were made in the FARMAN factory, but production ended in 1922.

NG

ALDEN SAMPSON (US) 1904
Alden Sampson Mfg Co., Pittsfield, Massachusetts.
Alden Sampson built the prototype of the MOYEA car whose factory was not ready, and was so impressed that he bought the design and put it into production under his own name. It was a high-quality 16hp 4-cylinder chain drive car, with a variety of open and closed bodies available. Few were made as Sampson turned to truck manufacture after one year.

NG

ALDEN THOMAS GTO (US) c.1986–1991
Alden Thomas GTO, Santa Ana, California.
This kit car consisted of a Ferrari 288 GTO-lookalike body to fit the Pontiac Fiero chassis. It was redesigned in 1987 to make it look less realistic due to pressure from Ferrari.

HP

ALDINO (US) 1993 to date
Aldino Car Company, Brookfield, Wisconsin;
Contender Car Company, Racine, Wisconsin.
An original-design body with styling cues from several Ferrari models graced this kit car body for the Pontiac Fiero. Offered in kit or assembled form with Fiero or Chevrolet V8 engines.

HP

ALDO (US) 1910
Albaugh Dover Co., Chicago, Illinois.
The Aldo was a typical high-wheel motor buggy, powered by a 12hp air-cooled flat-twin engine. Transmission was by planetary gears and final drive by chain. One of the partners, Gilbert R. Albaugh, had designed the Cleveland-built STAR (iii) and the Detroit-built WOLVERINE (i)

NG

ALEAT (GB) 1992
Classic Car Panels, Frome, Somerset.
This slab-sided sheet steel Jaguar-based roadster was based on a KOUGAR chassis. Priced at £12,000 for the kit, its lifespan was very short. This company also produced the TRIPACER.

CR

ALENA (US) 1922
Alena Steam Products Co., Indianapolis, Indiana.
This company planned to build steam cars, trucks and tractors, but the only cars completed were two prototypes of a 2-cylinder tourer, for which a price of $2750 was announced.

NG

ALES see OTOMO

ALESBURY (GB) 1907–1908
Alesbury Bros, Edenderry, King's County, Ireland.
Exhibited at the 1907 Dublin Motor Show, the Alesbury was a light car powered by an 8/10hp 2-cylinder Stevens engine. It had solid tyres and a 4-seater body said to be constructed entirely of Irish wood.

NG

ALEU (E) 1954–1956
Manufacturas Mécanicas Aleu SA, Esparraguera, Barcelona.
The Aleu Bambi was a very small roofless, doorless 3-wheeler weighing only 145kg (320lb). The rear-mounted 200cc single-cylinder 2-stroke engine drove the single rear wheel. After a showing at the Feria de Muestras in Barcelona, the Aleu operation went very quiet, and it is believed no production run occurred.

CR

ALEX (GB) 1908
Alexander & Co., Edinburgh.
This company proposed to make a tourer powered by a 14/18hp 4-cylinder Gnome engine with Rubury Owen chassis. They found that production costs would be too great, and only one prototype was made.

NG

ALEXANDRA see PHOENIX (iv)

ALEXIS (GB) c.1905–1906
T. & R. Taig, Alexandria, Dumbartonshire.
The Alexis was a wheel-steered tricar made with two sizes of engine, the 3½ hp single-cylinder Tricar and the 6½ hp 2-cylinder Motor Carette. The Tricar had a 2-speed gearbox and the Motor Carette 3 speeds, with final drive by chain to the rear wheel. Both had frames of combined tubular and angle steel, and seated two, though the Carette could be made to seat three, at a cost of an additional 5 guineas (£5.25) over the price of 85 guineas (£89.25). The makers also advertised the Alexis 4hp motor launch.

NG

A.L.F.A. ALFA ROMEO (I) 1910 to date
1910–1918 A.L.F.A. (Anonima Lombardo Fabbrica Automobili), Milan.
1918–1930 SA Italiana Ing. Nicola Romeo & Cia, Milan.
1930–1942 SA Alfa Romeo, Milan.
1942 to date Alfa Romeo SpA, Milan.
Alfa Romeo is one of the greatest names in the history of motoring and motor sport, having engaged almost continuously in competitions from 1911 to the 1990s. Although hand-built in small numbers for the first 40 years of their history,

1910 Alfa 24hp tourer.
NATIONAL MOTOR MUSEUM

1926 Alfa Romeo RLSS 22/90 4-seater sports car by Vanden Plas.
NATIONAL MOTOR MUSEUM

completed in 1920, as well as a few examples of the first 6-cylinder Alfa Romeo. This Tipo G1 had the largest engine Alfa Romeo ever made, with a capacity of 6597cc. At 100 x 140mm, its cylinder dimensions were the same as those of the Hispano-Suiza H6, but it delivered less than half the power of its French rival. It was followed in 1921 by the slightly smaller G2, of which about 50 were made. The first specifically sporting Alfa Romeo was the 20/30 ES of 1920, which had a larger bore than the prewar model, giving a capacity of 4250cc, and power increased from 49 to 67bhp. With a top speed of 87mph (140km/h), it was the fastest road-going Alfa until the supercharged twin-cam 1500 of 1928.

In 1920 Alfa Romeo had their first racing victory when Giuseppe Campari won the Circuit of Mugello in a pre-war 40/60, a feat he repeated in 1921. Enzo Ferrari was 2nd in the 1920 Targa Florio in a 20/30 and Campari 3rd in a 40/60. Thus Alfa Romeo were well-launched on their sporting career, though they had not yet achieved any international fame.

Merosi's pushrod cars

In 1921 the Grand Prix formula was for engines up to 3-litres capacity, and Merosi, who had been bitterly disappointed that his 1914 Grand Prix car had not raced, determined to get the Alfa Romeo name onto the circuits of Europe. However, before a new car was ready, the formula was reduced to 2-litres for 1922, so his 3-litre pushrod engine was used for touring and sports cars. This was the RL, which was the first Alfa to achieve international renown. It was made in two sizes, the 75×110mm 2916cc RLN (RL Normale), and the 76×110mm 2996cc RLS (RL Sport). The RLN had a flat radiator and the RLS a pointed one with two badges, one on each side of the point. Both had 4-speed gearboxes in unit with the engine, with central or right-hand change. The single carburettor RLN gave 56bhp and 68mph (109km/h), and the twin carburettor RLS 71bhp and 75mph (120km/h). Early cars were braked on the rear wheels only, but front wheel brakes were fitted to the 3rd series models from September 1923 onwards. In 1926 the 6th Series were given greater power and new names; the RLN became the RLT and the RLS the RLSS. This gave 83bhp, or about the same as a contemporary 3-litre Bentley.

A wide variety of bodies was seen on the RL, from limousines and coupés de ville on the 135in (3426mm) RLN/RLT chassis to 2-seater sports cars on the 123in (3122mm) RLS/RLSS chassis. Among prominent owners of the RLSS was Benito Mussolini who declared that his car had a magnificent engine. There were also companion 4-cylinder cars of similar layout, the 1944cc RM and 1996cc RMS, with flat radiators on the touring RM and pointed ones on the sporting RMS. A total of 2538 RLs and 424 RMs was made, the last RLSS being delivered in 1928.

Numerous sporting successes were gained by the RLS and RLSS, but the cars which really brought honours to Alfa Romeo were the special racing machines derived from the RLS, known as the Targa Florio models. These had much lighter chassis with a wheelbase 12in (305mm) shorter than the RLS, and more powerful engines. Five TF cars were made, three with 88bhp 2994cc engines, and two with 95bhp engines of 3154cc. The team drivers were Campari, Alberto Ascari and Ugo Sivocci, known as 'the three musketeers', with Enzo Ferrari being the team manager and sharing the driving. It was at the wheel of a TF Alfa that Ferrari won the 1923 Circuit of Savio, which so impressed the parents of fighter pilot Francesco Baracca that they gave Ferrari their son's prancing horse badge. This was carried on all the team cars which Ferrari managed for Alfa Romeo, and later on Ferrari's own cars.

The Jano era

In 1926 Merosi gave up his post as chief designer at Alfa Romeo to take up a similar position with Mathis at Strasbourg. His place was taken by Vittorio Jano (1891–1965) who had joined Alfa from Fiat in 1923. Jano was undoubtedly one of the greatest designers of competition cars ever, giving Alfa Romeo all its Grand Prix cars from 1924 to 1937, as well as the single and twin-cam sports cars, and Lancia's Aurelia, D23/4 sports cars and D50 Grand Prix cars. His first task on joining Alfa was to produce a competitive GP car for the 1924 season. Known as the P2, this 1987cc twin-cam supercharged straight-8 car won the first Grand Prix in which it was entered, at Lyons in August 1924, following this with many successes in the rest of the season and in 1925, when Alfa won the Manufacturers' World Championship, awarded for the first time that year. In honour of this a laurel wreath was added as a surround to the radiator badge, which has been worn by all Alfa Romeo cars since 1926. Jano designed several other successful racing cars for Alfa Romeo, particularly the Tipo B Monoposto of 1932–35, unofficially called the P3, and the 8C-35 and 12C-36, with straight-8,

they aroused the admiration of that apostle of mass production, Henry Ford. 'Every time I see an Alfa Romeo pass by', he said, 'I raise my hat'.

The original company, whose name translates as Lombardy Car Manufacturing Co., was set up in 1910 to make an all-Italian car in a factory which had made French DARRACQS for some four years. Only the small models of Darracq were assembled at the Portello factory, and they proved under-powered for local conditions, so the founders of A.L.F.A. were determined to build a worthy competitor for Fiat, Isotta Fraschini and Itala. Two models were made initially, the 2413cc 15/20 and the 4084cc 20/30, both with monobloc 4-cylinder side-valve engines designed by Giuseppe Merosi (1872–1957). In 1913 they were joined by a 6082cc 40/60 sporting model with overhead valves operated by twin camshafts in the crankcase. Like most Italian car manufacturers, A.L.F.A. could not keep away from competitions, and two cars ran in the 1911 Targa Florio, although neither finished. However, in 1914 they finished 3rd and 4th in the Targa. A 4½-litre twin-ohc car with 16 valves and eight plugs, designed by Merosi for the 1914 French Grand Prix, was not ready in time, and did not race until after the war.

Within a few years of its opening, the Portello factory had 300 employees and was making about 350 cars per year. However, finances were not very strong, and the company received a much-needed boost when it was taken over in December 1915 by Nicola Romeo (1876–1938), an industrialist who was already manufacturing mining equipment and portable compressed-air plants. These and other military goods were made in the Portello factory until the end of World War I. In February 1918 the company name was changed to SA Italiana Ing. Nicola Romeo e Cia, and when cars began to be made again they carried the name Alfa Romeo.

At first the prewar models were made, ten 15/20s and 95 20/30s being and V12 engines respectively. Brilliantly successful in 1932 and 1933, Jano's cars struggled valiantly against the growing might and efficiency of the German teams up to 1938, but with decreasing success. In 1938 the Alfa Romeo directors thought that, at 46, their famous designer was too old. Jano moved to Lancia where he had a further 20 years of successful work.

At the same time as the Grand Prix cars, Jano designed a succession of touring and sports cars which earned just as much glory for the Milan company. These began with a 1487cc single-ohc 6-cylinder car known as the 6C-1500. The 44bhp engine was largely of aluminium alloy and had a 5-bearing crankshaft. Two wheelbases were available, 122in (3096mm) for touring bodywork and 114in (2893mm) for sports. Announced in 1925, the 6C did not go into production until 1927, and it was joined in 1928 by the Gran Turismo which had twin ocs and was available only with the shorter wheelbase. Next came the Gran Sport with a still shorter wheelbase of 108in (2741mm)and a Roots supercharger turning at 1¹/₂ times engine speed. An unsupercharged car gave the 6C its first success when Ferrari won the 1927 Modena Circuit, but it was the blown Gran Sport which really established Alfa Romeo as a successful sports car. They won four major events in 1928, but in 1929 were overshadowed by the even more

successful 1750. This had a capacity of 1752cc, giving 45bhp in single-cam touring form, 55 in twin-cam sports and 85bhp in the supercharged Super Sports. As with most Alfas, the 1750 could be had with fairly staid saloon bodies, but it is as a 2-seater, especially when bodied by Zagato, that the 1750 is best known. These beautifully functional cars were also very successful in competitions, winning the Mille Miglia, Belgian 24 Hours and Irish GP in 1929, and the Mille Miglia, Belgian 24 Hours and Tourist Trophy in 1930.

The 1750 was made up to 1934, the final development being the 1920cc Gran Turismo. A total of 2776 were made, of which 369 were the classic 2-seater sports models. In 1931 came the 8C-2300 which had the 2336cc engine from the Monza racing car. An unusual feature was that the drive for the twin overhead camshafts was taken by a train of gear between cylinders 4 and 5. Output was around 140bhp in standard form, but competition engines bored out to 2632cc gave up to 165bhp. A Roots supercharger ran at 1¹/₂ times engine speed. The 8C-2300 was probably the best-performing sports car in the world in the early 1930s, but in price it was the equivalent of today's Lamborghini Diablo. Only 188 were made in four years, and it is said that Alfa Romeo made no profit from them.

NICK BALDWIN

JANO, VITTORIO (1891–1965)

Vittorio Jano was one of the greatest Italian engineers, especially in the field of competition cars, producing milestone designs for Alfa Romeo and Lancia. Though his family had been settled in the Turin area since about 1760, they came originally from Hungary, where the name is believed to have been the not uncommon one of Janos. His father was a soldier in charge of one of Turin's arsenals, and young Vittorio inherited a technical aptitude, which led him to a career as a draughtsman with Rapid, and also an early interest in motorcycling. From Rapid he moved to Fiat in 1911 where he worked in the design department under Carlo Cavalli. He was a very good organiser as well as a technician, and played some part in the running of Fiat's racing teams, both in 1914 and after the war. He also helped Cavalli with touring cars such as the Tipos 501, 510 and 520.

In 1923, when Jano was in charge of the Fiat racing team, he was invited to join Alfa Romeo, with particular responsibility for designing a Grand Prix car. For the time being, the road cars were left in the hands of Giuseppe Merosi. It was a wrench for him to leave Turin, and the pleas of Enzo Ferrari were not sufficient to persuade him to make the move. He insisted that Nicola Romeo come to see him, but after a visit from Romeo's assistant, Giorgio Rimini, he consented, and in September 1923 Jano and his family moved to Milan. He quickly gathered a staff of ten men, including some ex-Fiat people and a young man already at Alfa Romeo, Luigi Fusi, who later wrote an excellent

history of Alfa Romeo. Their first design was a 2-litre twin-ohc straight-8 engine which powered the P2 racing car, the car that put the name of Alfa Romeo on the map. This won for Alfa the World Manufacturers' Championship in 1925. Jano's confidence in his cars was shown in an episode during the Belgian GP. The Delage cars had all retired and the crowd were jeering at the Italians; Jano called his team in, made the drivers sit down and eat a meal while the cars were cleaned and polished, then sent them off to complete the race and win.

In 1925 Jano was appointed chief designer, succeeding Merosi who moved to the less prestigious firm of Mathis in France. He replaced Merosi's pushrod ohv engines with the single-ohc 1500 design, following this with the beautiful twin-ohc 1500 and 1750 which had much in common with the P2, except that they had six cylinders in place of eight, and plain instead of roller bearing crankshafts. In the spring of 1931 he began work on the twin-ohc straight-8 engine which powered the 8C 2300 sports car and Monza and P3 Tipo B Monoposto (single seater) racing cars. The 8C 2300 was almost unbeatable in sports car events and the racing cars also dominated the field until the arrival of the state-sponsored Mercedes-Benz and Auto Union teams in 1934. From 1930 to 1937 the Alfa Romeo team cars were run by the Scuderia Ferrari, which piqued Jano who wanted to have sole control. His last design for Alfa was the 12C 4¹/₂-litre V12 of 1937. It was raced without being properly tested, and retired in the Italian GP. His friends predicted 'This will be the end of Jano' and so it turned out. The management at Alfa Romeo decided that, at 46, he was too old to be designing racing cars, and he was replaced by the Spaniard Wilfredo Ricart.

Jano soon found another job at Lancia, which involved a return to Turin. This should have pleased him but he was never as happy at Lancia as he had been at Alfa Romeo. The Torinese resented him for having moved to Milan in the first place. However he produced some excellent designs, in particular the Aurelia with its classic B20 coupé version, the Appia and the D50 Grand Prix car of 1954. In Fusi's opinion this was Jano's best design, but its first season was a disaster, and Lancia went into liquidation before it could be sorted out. The D50 was taken over by Ferrari, for whom Jano worked as a consultant for several years

His end was tragic; he had watched his brother die painfully from cancer, and a persistent cough convinced him that he also suffered from the disease. On 13th March 1965 he shot himself. The post mortem revealed nothing more serious than bronchitis.

Jano married Rosina Ramella in 1920; they had one son, Francesco, who died in his early twenties.

NG

Further Reading
Great Designers and their Work, Edited by Ronald Barker and Anthony Harding, David & Charles, 1970.

1933 Alfa Romeo 1900 Gran Turismo saloon.
NATIONAL MOTOR MUSEUM

1933 Alfa Romeo 6C-2300 sports car by Zagato.
NATIONAL MOTOR MUSEUM

1947 Alfa Romeo 2500 Freccia d'Oro saloon.
NATIONAL MOTOR MUSEUM

The 8C's competition record was outstanding, with wins at Le Mans every year from 1931 to 1934 (1-2-3 in 1933), and in the Mille Miglia from 1932 to 1934. Alfa Romeo's success in this event was remarkable. They won every year from 1932 to 1939, taking the first three places in every race but one, when Laurie Schell's Delahaye came 2nd in 1937.

The successor to the 8C-2300 was the 8C-2900 which used a 2905cc Tipo B engine in an all-independent chassis, with coil springs at the front and transverse leaves with swing axles at the rear. The original 2900A was a very stark 2-seater, in effect a road-equipped racing car. Only six were made and they were raced by the Scuderia Ferrari. Their most notable success was a 1-2-3 victory in the 1936 Mille Miglia, but Pintacuda was also successful in the 1936 Sao Paulo GP. In 1937 came the 2900B which had more streamlined bodies and came in two wheelbases, the Corto of 108in (2741mm) and the Lungo of 118in (2995mm). A total of 30 of these were made, 20 Cortos and 10 Lungos. These figures disprove the once-current theory that the 2900 was conceived to use up surplus Tipo B engines, for Alfa Romeo would hardly have made as many as 36 engines

surplus to requirements. It is more likely that the chief motive behind the 2900 was to maintain the marque's success in the Mille Miglia, which they did, and to tackle other events such as Le Mans, which brought fewer rewards. A 2900B coupé ran at Le Mans in 1938, but retired before the end of the race. However Pintacuda and Severi won the 1938 Belgian 24 Hours, and Biondetti and Romano drove a Lungo coupé to victory in the 1947 Mille Miglia. With the highest axle ratio and a light body, a 2900 could exceed 125mph (200km/h), a very high figure for a prewar production car.

In 1939 four examples were built of the Tipo 412 sports car, which used a 4492cc V12 12C-37 racing engine in a 2900A chassis, with bodies by Touring similar to those of the 2900B Corto. Farina won the Antwerp GP, with Sommer in 2nd place, and Biondetti was 2nd in the Luxembourg GP. After the war the Swiss driver Willy Daetwyler drove a 412 successfully in hill climbs.

The dramatic straight-8 sports cars were backed up by a range of twin-ohc 6-cylinder cars, the 2300 (1934–39) and 2500 (1939–53). They were the first Alfa Romeos to have synchromesh gearboxes, and came in two wheelbases. Coachwork varied from the Pescara 2-door saloon which was a replica of the team cars which took the first three places in the 1934 Targa Abruzzo, to heavy limousines and cabriolets in the style of the Lancia Astura. The later factory-bodied saloons were rather pedestrian in appearance, with pressed steel wheels, but some beautiful custom bodies were made as well by the leading Italian coachbuilders. The 2300B of 1936–39 had hydraulic brakes and all-independent suspension like the 2900B. The short-wheelbase 6-cylinder cars had quite a respectable racing career; coupés were 1st and 2nd in the 1937 Mille Miglia, while a 2500 Super Sport driven by Mussolini's chauffeur Ercole Boratto won the 1939 Mille Miglia held in Libya. 1606 of the 2300 were made, and 652 of the 2500 before the war and a further 300 between 1946 and 1953.

In 1933 Alfa Romeo was bought by the IRI (Istituto Ricostruzione Industriale), a government organisation which allowed the directors almost complete autonomy, while the company still remained the financial property of the government. This situation remained essentially unchanged until ownership passed to Fiat in November 1986.

Postwar change to mass production
Passenger car production continued in Italy further into World War II than in any other country, the United States included. It is surprising to learn that in 1943 Alfa Romeo built 47 6C-2500 touring cars, and even in 1944 18 were turned out. Only three cars left the factory in 1945, but in 1946 they were back in production with new bodies on the 2500 chassis. Mechanically, the main difference was an all-synchromesh 4-speed gearbox (prewar 2500s had synchro on top and 3rd only) operated by a steering column gearchange. As in 1939, two wheelbases were available, and bodies ranged from sports coupés to limousines. There was the Competizione coupé, smaller, lighter and more powerful than any production model, with 145bhp and a top speed of over 120mph (195km/h). Three of these were made, and Fangio drove one into 3rd place in the 1950 Mille Miglia.

Up to 1950 the Alfa Romeo had been a limited production car, largely hand-built and with output seldom exceeding 800 per year, but the arrival of the 1900 saw a complete change at Portello. This car and its successors were designed by Orazio Satta (1910–1973) who had joined the company in 1938. Put into mass production on a new assembly line, the 1900 had a twin-ohc 4-cylinder engine of 1884cc, a unitary-construction 4-door saloon body, and was the first Alfa to have left-hand drive. For a family saloon the 1900 performed well, with top speeds of 90mph (145km/h) with the 80bhp single-carburettor engine and 105mph (170km/h) in 93bhp twin-carb form. In 1951 came the 1900TI (Turismo Internazionale) with 100bhp and this engine went into the short-wheelbase 1900C Sprint. This was made as a coupé by Touring or a cabriolet by Pinin Farina, as well as with numerous custom bodies. These specialists welded their bodies onto platform frames supplied by Alfa Romeo. The 1900 saloon was made up to 1955, with 17,243 being built, and the 1900C Sprint up to 1958, their numbers being only 1796. There were also about 2000 4x4 Jeep-type models called the 1900M.

In 1954 Satta produced his second design for Alfa, which was to prove even more important than the 1900. This was the Giulietta, powered by a twin-ohc engine of only 1290cc, the smallest twin-camshaft engine to be made in quantity. The body was an integral construction 2-door coupé. This nippy and attractive little car had a top speed of 102mph (165km/h) in its original form, and 110mph (177km/h) with the Sprint Veloce engine introduced in 1956. There

1936 Alfa Romeo 6C-2300 coupé by Pinin Farina.
NATIONAL MOTOR MUSEUM

was also an open Spider Veloce. A 4-door saloon Giulietta Berlina was made from 1955 to 1962, the majority being the higher performance TI model. The Berlina was the first Alfa to reach a six figure production total, as 192,917 were made. More limited models were the Giulietta SS and SZ, the former a long-tailed coupé by Bertone (1366 made) and the latter a short-tailed coupé by Zagato (210 made).

The last few SS and SZ coupés had disc brake at the front, and these were standard on the Giulia which came out in 1962, replacing all the Giuliettas except the TI Berlina. The Giulia had a slightly larger engine of 1570cc, and 5-speed gearbox with floor change replacing the 4-speed column change of the Giulietta. Most of the Giulietta styles were continued in the larger range, including the saloons, open roadsters and special coupés. The Zagato coupé differed from the standard car more than previously, with tubular spaceframe body and irs. It was raced by the Autodelta team and some had fibreglass bodies. The Giulia was made in even larger numbers than its predecessor, thanks to a new factory at Arese, near Milan, which opened in 1963. A total of 836,323 saloons were made between 1962 and 1972, as well as 144,213 1300TI saloons, which used the Giulietta's 1290cc engine in a Giulia body shell. One of the most attractive models was the Pinin Farina-styled Duetto 2-seater sports which was introduced in 1966, received a 1750cc engine in 1967 and a 2000cc engine in 1970. The latter model was made with little change up to 1994. Like the saloons, the Duetto and coupé were available with the 1290cc engine, though only up to 1972. An unusual variation on the Giulia was the 4R Zagato, a replica of the classic 1750 with modern components, of which 92 were made between 1966 and 1968.

Larger Alfas were also made, the 1975cc 4-cylinder 2000 in saloon and sports models from 1958 to 1961, and the 2584cc 6-cylinder 2600 in saloon, coupé and sports models, from 1962 to 1968. The 2000 saloon was unusual in having a 5-speed all-synchromesh gearbox with column change. This was continued on the 2600 saloons, but the coupés and sports models, having no bench seat, had floor change, as did the right-hand drive saloons sold in the UK.

A more unusual large Alfa was the Montreal coupé, named after the 1967 Montreal World Exhibition at which the prototype 'dream car' was shown. It went into production in 1970, powered by a 2593cc four-ohc V8 engine derived from that of the Tipo 33 sports/racing cars. Output was 200bhp, and top speed around 140mph (225km/h). The Montreal was quite separate from other contemporary

1962 Alfa Romeo Giulia T1 saloon.
NATIONAL MOTOR MUSEUM

1975 Alfa Romeo Alfasud T1 saloon.
NATIONAL MOTOR MUSEUM

1983 Alfa Romeo 33 saloon.
ALFA ROMEO SPA

1977 Alfa Romeo Spider Junior Sports car.
NATIONAL MOTOR MUSEUM

Alfas, though its suspension was standard, and much more expensive. The UK price in 1973 was £5549, more than double that of a 2000 Veloce coupé. The Montreal was made from 1970 to 1976, output reaching 3925 cars.

Return to Sport

In a sense Alfa Romeo never totally abandoned the competition field. Their cars were raced and rallied somewhere in the world, at least by private owners, from the 1950s to the present day. After the abrupt withdrawal of the Tipo 159 Grand Prix cars in 1951, they attempted a return to sports car racing with the Disco Volanté (Flying Saucer), so named after its unusual curved streamlined body. They first used a 1900 4-cylinder engine, but later versions had specially-built 6-cylinder engines of which the largest was a 3576cc unit developing 260bhp. They were not very successful, their only important win being that of Fangio in the 1953 Supercortemaggiore GP. Four road-going coupé versions were made.

In 1965 Alfa Romeo chose Autodelta, which had been set up to assemble the Zagato-bodied Giulia TZ competition coupés, to be their self-contained racing department, and a year later it was absorbed into Alfa, with Carlo Chiti as its Director General. In 1967 they announced a car for the Sports Prototype category which would be a challenger for the World Manufacturers' Championship. Known as the Tipo 33, it was a mid-engined car with an unusual chassis consisting of large diameter tubes, the side members and main cross members being fuel tanks. The engine was a 1995cc 4-camshaft V8 developing 270bhp and driving through a 6-speed gearbox. The 2-seater body could be open or closed, and there were short- and long-tailed versions. The latter was capable of nearly 186mph (300km/h).

After a disappointing 1967 season, revamped 33s won at Mugello and Imola in 1968, and had enough good placings in other events to give them 3rd place in the Manufacturers' Championship, behind Ford and Porsche.

A road-going version of the 33 called the Stradale was made between 1967 and 1969. The closed bodywork was designed and built by Scaglione, and 18 were made. The 33 chassis was also the basis for several concept cars exhibited at motor shows, of which the best-known was the Bertone Carabo. The 1970 33/3 had a

2992cc V8 engine derived from a Formula 1 project, and a conventional riveted duralumin platform chassis. They had only one win, but nevertheless were again 3rd in the Championship. The 1971 33/3TT reverted to tubular construction, though with smaller diameter tubes which did not act as fuel tanks; this was Satta's last design before his death in 1973. Several 3rd places were achieved in 1972, and Alfa Romeo were 2nd in the Championship, behind Ferrari but ahead of Porsche. In 1973 a new 2993cc flat-12 engine was used, the cars being known as the 33 TT12. They had no successes in 1973, and only one win in 1974, but in 1975 six victories in Championship events gave Autodelta the World Manufacturers' Championship they had been seeking for so long. The 33's last season was 1977, when two versions were campaigned, the 2993cc flat-12 which was giving 520bhp at 12,000rpm, and a 2134cc turbocharged unit which gave 640bhp at 11,000rpm. Eight wins were achieved in various races, Championship and non-Championship, and the Manufacturers' Cup came to Alfa Romeo again. A total of 64 Tipo 33s were made, 30 33/2 coupés, 20 33/3 spiders, six 33 TT12 spiders, six 33 SC12 spiders and two 33 SC12 turbo spiders.

In 1976 Autodelta began to supply their 3-litre flat-12 engine to Brabham for their BT45-46 Formula 1 cars, and in 1979 a new V12 engine went into the first Formula 1 Alfa Romeo since 1951. Although raced over the next seven years, it had little success.

The Alfasud and its contemporaries

In 1972 Alfa Romeo took a step quite as drastic as they had done with the 1900. They launched a completely new car in a new factory which was far from the traditional area of Northern Italy. To reduce unemployment in the South, the Italian government provided substantial subsidies to companies which would open factories in the area. As Alfa Romeo already had a factory making aero-engine parts at Pomigliano d'Arco, near Naples, they built their new car factory on an abandoned airfield nearby. To supervise the factory building, and to design the new car, they engaged the Viennese-born engineer Rudolf Hruska, who had spent eight years with the company in the 1950s.

The new car, called the Alfasud (Alfa South), had a 1186cc flat-4 engine driving the front wheels. Each pair of cylinders had its own overhead camshaft, driven by cogged tooth belts, and output was 63bhp at 6000rpm. The engine was mounted ahead of the 4-speed gearbox/differential casing, and there were disc brakes all round. The 4-door saloon body was designed by Giugiaro of Ital Design. The Alfasud was an advanced small car, just the sort of machine one would expect from Alfa Romeo when they entered the popular car market, but it was not without problems. Early models rusted badly when they were exported to damper climates than their native Naples, and the factory suffered endless labour troubles, with absenteeism up to 20 per cent while in 1977 alone there were 78 major strikes and 882 minor ones. When they were being made, Alfasuds sold well, particularly after they had received 5-speed gearboxes and larger engines; 1286cc from 1977 to 1980, and 1490cc from 1978 to 1983. There was also a 2-door saloon in which all the engine options were available. In 1983 the Alfasud was replaced by the larger 33, after 825,301 had been made. A curious hybrid was the Arna (Alfa Romeo Nissan Automobiles), which used an Alfasud engine in the bodyshell of the Nissan Cherry. It was not a success, as the Cherry was a more pedestrian car than the Alfasud, and customers for the latter were not attracted by its staid looks. Also the Italian-built Cherry bodies lacked the quality of the Japanese versions. Neither Alfa nor Nissan dealers liked selling it, and it was dropped in 1985, after about 50,000 had been made.

The development of the Giulia continued into the 1970s, with the 1750 engine up to 1971 or 1972, and the 2000 up to 1977. There were numerous permutations on this theme, such as the 1600GT Junior which had the Giulia Super's 1600 engine in the bodyshell of the larger 1750. In 1972 a new medium-sized saloon appeared, named the Alfetta after the Tipo 158 racing cars of 1939–1950. This used the 1600, 1750 and 2000 engines in new bodies, with rear-mounted gearboxes and all-round independent suspension. The Alfetta was made as a 4-door saloon or Giugiaro-styled 2-door coupé. The saloon was replaced in 1984 by the 90 which had the same platform and new styling, but the coupé was continued up to 1986 under the name GTV. From 1985 it was available with a 2496cc V6 engine as an alternative to the 1962cc four.

The Alfasud's replacement, the 33, had a similar conception of 4-door saloon, but a roomier body. Engines were 1351 and 1490cc, joined in 1986 by a 1717cc unit and also a vertical 3-cylinder diesel of 1779cc. Three bodies were offered, saloon, estate car and Sprint coupé, the latter being carried over from the old

Alfasud range. The saloon and estate were available with 4-wheel drive. It was restyled for 1990, with lines closer to those of the 164, and made until 1995.

In 1976 the Giulietta name was revived for a medium-sized saloon using the Alfetta 1600 and 1750 engines, transmission and suspension with a new, high tail body shell. For the Italian market only there was a 1357cc engine, and a full 2-litre unit joined the Giulietta range in 1980. They were replaced in 1985 by the 75, named to celebrate the 75th anniversary of the company. This was a similar car to the Giulietta, made in turbocharged form with the 1750 engine which was renamed the 1800 Injection Turbo. A competition version with KKK turbocharger and twin intercoolers developed 300bhp.

At the top of the Alfa range was the 6, a saloon with 2496cc V6 engine with, unusually, six carburettors, one for each cylinder. Automatic transmission and power-assisted steering indicated that it was aimed at the luxury market, not catered to by Alfa Romeo for a long time. It was not altogether a new car, for the floorpan, doors, roof and windows came from the Alfetta, extra length being provided by extensions at the front and rear. The complex carburation was replaced by Bosch L-Jetronic fuel injection in 1984, and the 6 was dropped in 1987. Sales had never approached the anticipated 9000 per year, being only 6528 in seven years, of which just 128 were sold in Britain.

In November 1986 Alfa Romeo was sold by the government-backed IRI to Fiat, who announced that they would aim Alfa products at the BMW market. The first fruit of the merger was the 164, Alfa's version of the front-wheel drive Type 4 car which was also made in a Fiat version as the Croma, by Lancia as the Thema, and by Saab as the 9000. Careful attention to styling, particularly at the front, gave each car a measure of individuality, and the 164 had its own engine, a 185bhp 2959cc V6. The engine range was later broadened to include a 1962cc four, 1996cc V6 and a 2500cc 4-cylinder turbo diesel. The 164 was made until 1998 when it gave way to the 166. This was of similar size, and came with 4-cylinder and V6 petrol engines, the largest being a 2959cc V6, and a 2387cc 5-cylinder turbo diesel.

A curious limited production car was the SZ coupé, conceived on the 75 chassis with a 210bhp version of the 164's V6 engine and chunky styling by Zagato. It was introduced in 1989, and was still listed in 1992, though sales were slow due to its controversial appearance and high price. It was replaced in 1993 by the RZ convertible on similar lines though at a lower price.

In January 1992 came the 155, a medium-sized saloon sharing mechanical elements with the Lancia Delta Integrale, with 1775 and 1996cc fours, and a 2482cc V6 also used in the Lancia Thema. It was made until 1997 when it gave way to the 156, a similar-sized 3-box saloon with a choice of three 4-cylinder engines from 1598 to 1970cc and a 2492cc V6. It was voted Car of the Year in 1998, the first time that an Alfa Romeo had won this title. In 1999 buyers of the 156 had the option of the 5-speed Selespeed clutchless push-button gearchange, and a high-performance Cloverleaf version of the 156 was planned for 2000.

The 33 was gradually phased out in favour of the similar sized 145 from 1994, though the two were made alongside for a while. The 145 was a 3-door hatchback, joined in 1996 by the 5-door 146 on a longer wheelbase, both having flat-4 engines of 1351, 1596 and 1712cc, as well as a vertical 1929cc turbo diesel. For 1997 the flat-4s gave way to vertical engines of approximately the same size, and the body styling remained unchanged. They were still made in 1999, and featured the Twin Spark system in which a second, smaller, sparking plug fired at the end of the exhaust phase to ensure that any unburnt fuel was eradicated before leaving the engine. For 2000 a new range was planned, the 147, which had 3- and 5-door models on a common wheelbase.

In 1994 the evergreen Spyder 2-seater sports car, whose styling dated back to 1966, finally gave way to a new sports, the Pininfarina-styled GTV which was made in open and coupé forms, with two 4-cylinder engines, 1747 and 1949cc, and two V6s, 1997 and 1959cc and in November 1996, 2959cc.
NG

Further Reading
Alfa Romeo, Peter Hull and Roy Slater, Transport Bookman Publications, 1982.
Le Vetture Alfa Romeo dal 1910, Luigi Fusi, Editrice Adiemme, 1965.
'Alfa Romeo: the Merosi and Jano years', Pat Braden,
Automobile Quarterly, Vol. 3, No. 4.

ALFA (I) 1907
Anonima Lombarda Fabbricazione Automobile, Novara.

1998 Alfa Romeo 146 Twin Spark 16-valve saloon.
ALFA ROMEO SPA

1999 Alfa Romeo Spider 2.0TS 16-valve sports car.
ALFA ROMEO SPA

Though this company's name was very close to that of the Alfa Romeo's predecessor, there was no link between the two. The Alfa from Novara was a rare example of an Italian steam car, with a vertical double-acting 4-cylinder engine mounted at the front under a bonnet, and final drive by shaft. A prototype was built by Olivari & Duse of Milan, but it is not known if any were sold.
NG

ALFA-LEGIA (B) 1914–1921
Klinkhammers, Liège.
M. Klinkhammers was a sportsman who assembled a few cars just before the war. They had 4-cylinder engines of 1327 or 1888cc. After the war he assembled a few cars, using Austro-Daimler components for which he also used the name Alfa-Legia, and also made modified Buicks with vee-radiators, which he sold under the name Buick-Sport. In 1930 he was making petrol-engined locomotives under the name A.L.F.A.
NG

ALFI (i) (D) 1922–1924
Automobil- und Akkumulatorenbau GmbH, Berlin; Driesen-Vordamm.
This company's first cars were electrics sold under the name A.A.A. When they decided to turn to petrol cars they adopted the name Alfi, from that of Alex Fischer, the owner of the firm. They made 5/20 and 7/35PS models, using proprietary engines of various makes. Production was limited, but the cars took part in number of sporting events including the early AVUS races.
HON

ALFI (ii) (D) 1927–1928
Alfi Automobile GmbH, Berlin.
This was also a product of Alex Fischer, but the company was quite separate from his earlier venture. The new cars were 3-wheelers with single-cylinder DKW engines driving the single front wheel. The steering could be turned through 180 degrees to give reverse drive. More were made as light delivery vehicles than as passenger cars. A single example of a 4-wheeled 'Alfi-Sport' was made.
HON

1949 Allard (ii) L-type tourer.
NATIONAL MOTOR MUSEUM

ALFIBRE (ZA) 1990s

Alfibre, Cape Town.

This was a kit-built Austin-Healey 100 replica using wishbone front suspension and a live rear axle on a steel chassis with glassfibre bodywork. The engine was a Nissan in-line 6-cylinder unit.

CR

ALKEN (US) 1958–1959

Alken Corporation, Venice, California.

One of the first kit car bodies for the VW Beetle platform, the Alken was a high-quality fibreglass convertible with a removable hardtop. Penned by industrial designer Bill Pierson, it was attractive and sold well after a positive road test by *Road & Track* magazine in 1958. It could be assembled in 19 hours – much better than the average kit in 1958.

HP

ALLARD (i) (GB) 1899–1902

Allard & Co. Ltd, Coventry.

The Allard Cycle Co. was formed in 1891 and eight years later they began to experiment with powered vehicles, a De Dion-Bouton powered tricycle and a 4-wheeled car based on the Benz, which they called the Express. They later made voiturettes with 500cc single-cylinder engines based on De Dion designs, with belt drive and tubular frames. One was a narrow tandem 2-seater, with the passengers facing each other in the *vis-à-vis* position. In late 1900 Allard agreed to make the belt-driven Charette for INTERNATIONAL (i). A new 9hp Allard with single-cylinder engine, shaft drive and flitch-plate frame appeared in 1902, and in June Allard joined forces with the Birmingham Motor Manufacturing & Supply Co., who made the REX (i). The Birmingham factory was sold and subsequent Rex cars were made in the Allard factory in Coventry.

NG

ALLARD (ii) (GB) 1937–1960

1937–1945 Adlards Motors Ltd, Putney, London.

1946–1960 Allard Motor Co. Ltd, Clapham, London.

Sydney Allard (1910–1966) was a London garage owner and a brave and robust racing driver. In the late 1930s he was very successful with trials cars powered by Ford V8 or Lincoln V12 engines, which featured split axle front suspension designed by Leslie Ballamy. A dozen were made for sale.

During World War II Allard's garage business (confusingly called Adlards Ltd) rebuilt Ford military vehicles and, when hostilities ended, Allard had a well-equipped machine shop and masses of engines and spare parts.

In 1946 Allard announced the 2-seat K1 (151 made) which had a box section chassis, transverse leaf and split axle ifs, a transverse rear leaf spring and live axle, and a 2-seater steel body. With either an 85bhp 3662cc L-head Ford V8, or a 95 bhp side-valve 3917cc Mercury unit, both made by Ford in Britain, it had an excellent power/weight ratio and acceleration.

The L1(191 made), also introduced in 1946, was a K1 with a longer wheelbase and four seats. As would become Allard practice, some cars went abroad without an engine or gearbox, which were fitted by the customer. The factory usually fitted a Ford or Mercury V8, sometimes with an Ardun ohv conversion created by Zora Arkus Duntov. Duntov was Allard's technical adviser, and a works driver, from 1950 until 1953 when he joined GM to save the Chevrolet Corvette.

In 1947 came the J1, a shorter and slimmer version of the K1, designed for trials and sprints, made in a limited edition of 12.

The Allard M1 of 1947 was a 4-seater coupé and 500 were made in 1947–50. Allard production peaked in 1948 when 432 cars were made. From 1949, the M1 had coil spring ifs and hydraulic brakes.

The Allard J2 of 1950 was based on the J1 chassis, but with a De Dion rear axle suspended on coil springs and located by radius arms. A peculiarity of the J2 was that the front track was 4in (102mm) wider than the rear. Most of the 90 made went to America as rolling chassis and Oldsmobile and Cadillac engines were the popular choices. A works J2 finished third at Le Mans in 1950, despite losing all gears bar top.

The K2 of 1950 (119 made) was a more refined version of the K1, with coil spring front suspension. The Allard P1 was an amalgam of the J1 and M1 models and, with 569 made, it was the company's most popular model. It was in an Allard P1 that Sydney Allard won the 1952 Monte Carlo Rally – the only man to win a major rally in a car of his own make.

A long wheelbase convertible version, the MX2, was made in 1951–2, but found only 25 buyers.

Allard introduced a new chassis in 1952 when it launched the J2X. The frame was made from small diameter tubes with the sides stiffened by plates, it retained the De Dion rear axle of the J2 and some had enveloping bodies. Most of the 83 J2X went to America for competition use, but they were soon outclassed by new cars from Jaguar and Ferrari.

After 1952, Allard sales, in common with other British specialist makers, went into a sharp decline as mainstream car production got up to speed, and just 132 cars were sold in 1952. During 1952–5, the P2 Monte Carlo saloon sold only 11 examples while the Safari station wagon sold ten.

Better sales were enjoyed by the K3, which was a sporting tourer with a pretty body built on the 'X' chassis frame, but only 62 were made. They were criticised in America, the target market, for their poor detail design. The market shifted from sellers to buyers and Allard did not have the resources to compete.

Allard tried to revive its fortunes with the Palm Beach of 1952 which was built on a shortened 'X' frame, but with a live rear axle. The 21C (eight made) had a Ford Consul engine while the 21Z had a Zephyr engine. The 60 cars in the 21Z production run included at least one streamlined coupé and several were fitted with fibreglass bodies made by the American firm, Anchorage Plastics.

Before the Palm Beach reached the market, however, the Triumph TR2 and Austin-Healey 100 had arrived and the Palm Beach could compete neither on performance nor on price. One was fitted with a 4.4-litre Dodge V8 to tempt the Chrysler Corporation, but Chrysler declined the bait.

The J2R of 1953 was the fastest of all Allards, and was the first competition car designed for automatic transmission. It had the shortened 'X' frame of the Palm Beach, but with a De Dion rear axle located by an A-frame, and an enveloping body. It was too little, too late, to save Allard's reputation, and just seven were made.

Allard entered the economy car market in 1955 with the three-wheeled 346cc Clipper, and perhaps 50 were made. A revised Palm Beach with a curvaceous body and torsion bar suspension was offered in 1956, and the choice of engines included Jaguar. Production of the Palm Beach officially ended in 1959 after seven had been made, but most were show or demonstration cars.

Sydney Allard then became an enthusiastic proponent of drag racing in Britain, while also marketing Allardettes, which were modified Ford Anglias. Allard himself died in 1966 and, soon afterwards, a fire destroyed most of his factory.

In 1981 a Canadian company which styled itself 'Allard' made copies of the Allard J2X which it called the J2X2.

Rights to the Allard name were acquired by a new company in 1991. It intended to market a range of sports and GT cars, but the project got no further than an unsuccessful Group C/IMSA sports racing car.

MJL

Further Reading
The Inside Story of Allard, Tom Lush, Motor Racing Publications, 1977.

ALLARD (iii) (CDN) 1981

Allard Motor Co., Mississauga, Ontario.
This was a replica of the Allard J2X powered by a 5.2-litre Chrysler V8 engine, using a fibreglass body and coil suspension all round. A turbocharger was an option.
NG

ALLARD (iv) (GB) 1994–1997

Allard Replicas, Harpenden, Hertfordshire.
This Allard J2X replica had connections with the HARDY Allard, but featured a chassis and body engineered by Dennis Adams (designer of the Marcos) and accepted Jaguar XJ12 mechanicals, including the V12 engine. Cars were sold in kit form or fully-built. The Allard name was used by agreement with the then-holders of the title.
CR

ALLARD-LATOUR (F) 1899–1902

E. Allard-Latour, Lyons.
Edouard Allard-Latour had a small factory making machine tools, in which he built a few cars of his own design. A belt-driven model was shown at the Salon de l'Auto et du Cycle at Lyons in December 1899, and later cars had double-chain drive. The engines were under the seat, they had tiller steering and one example had a *vis-à-vis* body.
NG

1951 Allard (ii) J2 sports car.
NATIONAL MOTOR MUSEUM

1952 Allard (ii) 21Z Palm Beach sports car.
NATIONAL MOTOR MUSEUM

ALL BRITISH (GB) 1906–1908

All-British Car Co., Bridgeton, Glasgow.
This company was founded by George Johnston, formerly a partner in ARROL-JOHNSTON. He built a complex 8-cylinder engine on the same opposed-piston lines as the early Arrol-Johnston unit, and installed it in a car exhibited at the 1907 Agricultural Hall Show. He announced plans to make 75 cars per year, but the Show car may have been the only All-British, though Johnston also built a bus with a 4-cylinder engine on similar lines, which ran in London for a short time.
NG

ALL CARS (I) 1978–1985

All Cars srl, Pianoro, Bologna.
The Charly was first offered by AUTOZODIACO in 1974 and was taken over by All Cars in 1978, a company that was itself affiliated to AUTOMIRAGE. The Charly was renamed the Snuggy and fitted with a 50cc Morini engine. A convertible version called the Snuggy Tobrouk was also offered. Later versions had Motobécane 50cc and 250cc engines.
CR

ALLDAYS (GB) 1898–1918

Alldays & Onions Pneumatic Engineering Co. Ltd, Birmingham.
This company had an older ancestry than any other British car maker, being descended from two Birmingham engineering firms, Onions founded in 1650, and Alldays founded in 1720. By the 1880s their premises covered more than eight acres, and was a major supplier to blacksmiths, foundries and railway companies. Their first motor vehicle was the Alldays Traveller of 1898, a quadricycle powered by a 4hp De Dion Bouton engine. It seated two in tandem and was unusual for that type of vehicle in having wheel steering. A proper car followed in 1903, a single-cylinder 2-seater with shaft drive, but the car which made Alldays' name came in 1905. This was the 10/12hp, a side-valve vertical-twin which lasted up to 1913, and was made with 2- and 4-seater bodies, and in commercial traveller form. A 16hp 4-cylinder car was introduced in 1906, and

1901 Alldays Traveller voiturette.
NATIONAL MOTOR MUSEUM

1912 Alldays 16hp landaulet.
NATIONAL MOTOR MUSEUM

1913 Alldays Midget light car.
NATIONAL MOTOR MUSEUM

two years later Alldays acquired the Enfield Autocar Co., another Birmingham concern which made the ENFIELD car. The acquisition cost them £10,000, for which they got the factory and machinery and also three finished cars and ten partly-completed chassis.

The purchase of Enfield led to a rationalisation of the two ranges, with the Enfield name being generally used for more upmarket models. The 990cc V-twin 1914 Alldays Midget was a badge-engineered Enfield Nimble Nine, though priced the same at £138, while the 3018cc Alldays 16/20 was equivalent to the 18.4hp Enfield, but was £25 cheaper. The largest Alldays was the 4786cc 30/35hp 6-cylinder, sold from 1911 to 1914; this had no Enfield equivalent, though, confusingly, there was a 6104cc 4-cylinder Enfield called the 30/35, made in 1909–10. Other models in the 1914 Alldays range included an 8/10hp twin, which was an enlarged version of the Midget, and pair-cast side-valve fours of 10, 12/14, 16/20 and 25/30hp. These had their Enfield equivalents called the Ten, 14.3, 18.4 and 24.9hp. In November 1918 the motor activities of the two companies were fully merged as Enfield Alldays Motors Ltd. Alldays & Onions continued with general engineering, and also made motorcycles under the name Allon from 1915 to 1924. The chairman was Hyam Marks who was also a director of Austin. The company was reformed in 1925 as New Alldays & Onions, but closed down in 1927.

NG

ALLEN (i) (US) c.1895–1900
G. Edgar Allen, New York, New York.
Allen was a carriage builder who made a few cars in his workshops on West 53rd Street. There are indications that he was in business as early as 1895, but details are only known of a surviving car made in 1900. This was a light runabout powered by a 7.5hp Aster single-cylinder engine, with tiller steering and chain drive.
NG

ALLEN (ii) (US) 1913–1922
Allen Motor Co., Fostoria, Bucyrus, Columbus, Ohio.
The Allen was a well-known 4-cylinder car of its time, powered by an own-design 4-cylinder 3.1-litre side-valve engine. A complete line of open and closed bodies were available, and Allen production peaked in 1920 with more than 2000 units completed. Production during Allen's ten-year existence is estimated at between 15,000 and 20,000 cars.
KM

ALLEN (iii) (US) 1914
Allen Iron & Steel Co., Philadelphia, Pennsylvania.
Although sometimes described as a cyclecar, this Allen was more of a light car, with 4-cylinder water-cooled engine. Transmission was more like that of a cyclecar, with friction discs for the gear change and final drive by double belts. The price was $450. A shaft-drive model was announced for 1915, but only a prototype was made.
NG

ALLEN (iv) (US) c.1982–1987
Mike Allen Specialties, Boise, Idaho.
Allen built a 427 Cobra replica with a few differences, like a nose that tilted up like a Jaguar XKE. The tube frame could accept Ford Mustang II front suspension, with Corvette suspension at the rear, or 1984 Corvette suspension all around. Sold in kit or assembled form.
HP

ALLEN-KINGSTON (US) 1908–1910
Allen-Kingston Motor Car Co., Kingston, New York.
Walter C. Allen was an importer of foreign cars who built three cars in 1907 which were branded as New Yorks. The following year he changed the name of his New York Car & Truck Co. to Allen-Kingston Motor Car Co., and the cars were henceforth known as Allen-Kingstons or A.K.s. They had large 48hp 4-cylinder T-head engines, and were available in tourer, limousine or Gunboat roadster forms, with prices between $3900 and $5000. Allen admitted that they were built on Mercedes lines, though the engines were modelled on the Isotta-Fraschini and the front axles on those of Fiat. He built 100 of the big cars in 1908, and they were joined by a smaller 17hp town car in 1909, and in 1910 a 36hp Junior which was built by George J. Grossman and was virtually the same as the smaller G.J.G. In 1910 Allen-Kingston moved to Bristol, Connecticut, but it is not certain how many cars were made there. One Allen-Kingston employee was Fred Moscovics, later to achieve fame with the Stutz Vertical Eight.
NG

ALLIANCE (i) **(D)** 1904–1905
Automobil- und Motorenwerke Alliance Fischer & Abele, Berlin.
This short-lived company used 2- and 4-cylinder engines bought from outside suppliers, but also provided components such as chassis to other firms.
HON

ALLIANCE (ii) **(F)** 1905–1908
Alliance Automobiles B. Baud, Paris.
This company made cars with Tony Huber engines, a 10/12hp 2-cylinder and 12/14 and 18hp 4-cylinder units, with shaft drive. They were also listed under the name Aiglon in 1905, and were sold in England by the Alliance Manufacturing Co. of Holborn, London.
NG

ALLIED FIBERGLASS (US) c.1965–1970
Allied Fiberglass Co., Sacramento, California.
Allied took over production of the KELLISON coupés and roadsters in the mid–1960s. They marketed them under the Astra name, and made several versions. The J-5 coupé was the longest and was sized to fit full-size American chassis. The J-4 coupé was for medium-length frames like the Corvette, while the J-3 roadster fitted short European chassis like VW and MGA. The J-2 coupé had a double bubble top and fitted on the Triumph TR3 chassis, among others. The last Astra variation was purely their own design and was not shared with Kellison. This was the X-300GT, a J-5 coupé with a raised roof for more headroom. All were available with special steel tube chassis that took Corvette or Plymouth suspension, and there were many variations in headlight configuration and headrests. Some were raced in the 1950s. The coupés were very popular and many were sold. Allied also built a dune buggy and a VW-based sports car kit called the VW-GT 2+2, which was similar to the Fiberfab Aztec.
HP

ALLIED INDUSTRIES (US) c.1967–1985
Allied Industries International, Fremont, Nebraska and Michigan City, Indiana; Sportsland Unlimited, Lincoln, Nebraska.
Allied was one of the most prolific kit manufacturers, with at least a dozen models. They built the first 289 and 427 Cobra replicas in 1967, when authentic Cobras were still sitting in the showrooms. They followed that with a replica of the Bill Thomas CHEETAH. Later additions included Bugatti, GT-40, MG-TD and Porsche Speedster replicas, as well as a number of original designs. These included a 3-wheeler and a hybrid gas/electric power van to fit a VW floorpan. Under the guise of Sportsland Unlimited, they sold a replica of the AMT PIRANHA called the CRV. In 1983 they moved to Michigan City, Indiana.
HP

ALLISON REPLICARS (US) 1973–c.1980
Allison Replicars Inc., Port Orange, Florida.
An MG-TD replica on a Volkswagen floorplan was built by this company.
HP

ALLORA *see* CORSE

ALLRIGHT (ALLREIT) (D) 1908–1911
Köln-Lindenthaler Metallwerke AG, Cologne-Lindenthal.
This was a well-known manufacturer of bicycles and motorcyles who took up production of light cars in their extensive factory. They had 1-litre 2-cylinder engines, and were sold outside Germany under the name Vindec. This name was also used for motorcycles sold in England. In 1924 the Cologne company bought up another motorcycle maker, Cito, who had also previously made cars.
HON

ALLSTATE (US) 1952–1953
Kaiser-Frazer Corp., Willow Run, Michigan.
The Allstate was a Kaiser Henry J built by Kaiser-Frazer exclusively for sale by Sears Roebuck, either by mail order or from Sears retail stores. The idea came from Sears vice-president Theodore V. Houser who also had a seat on the board of Kaiser-Frazer. Carrying a 90-day guarantee, the Allstates were mechanically similar to the Henry J, though they had different grilles and badging, and superior

1920 Allen (ii) Model 43 tourer.
NATIONAL MOTOR MUSEUM

upholstery. The basic Allstate Four undercut the equivalent Henry J by just $12, while the De Luxe Six was $29 more than the Henry J Corsair De Luxe. The project was not a success, possibly because of the limited marketing approach, and only 2363 cars were sold in two seasons.
NG

ALL-STEEL *see* MACON

ALLWIN (GB) c.1920
Allwin Cyclecars, Bournemouth, Hampshire.
The seaside resort of Bournemouth was an unusual location for car manufacture, though the PERFEX (ii) and URECAR also hailed from there. The Allwin cyclecar had an air-cooled engine and final drive by chains or belts to a differential less rear axle. The body was very narrow.
NG

ALMA (i) **(F)** 1926–1927
Sté Alma, Courbevoie, Seine.
The initials of the company stand for Automobiles Legères et Moteurs d'Aviation, and its co-founder Vaslin had been involved with aircraft engines for several years. His double flat-twin unit had been tried in the BELL (v) cyclecar before being used in a Dewoitine aeroplane and he also designed a 6-cylinder engine for Avions Albert and a replacement for two Bugatti Brescia engines that were used in the De Monge aeroplane. This company closed its doors before the engine was built, and Vaslin turned his attention to cars, forming ALMA with his friend Maurice Coquet.
The first ALMA was a low-built coupé powered by a 1640cc pushrod ohv engine, each cylinder having two inlet valves and one exhaust. The inlet valves had separate ports, each with their own induction system and carburettor. At slow speeds, only one inlet valve was working, but at maximum revs both valves and their carburettors were in operation. The engine was so flexible that only two forward speeds were provided. This may not have been satisfactory, as within a few months, before the end of 1926, the car was given a larger engine of 1850cc and a 3-speed gearbox. About a dozen cars were made during 1926, and engines were supplied to a few other firms such as Harris Leon Laisne, Rally, and even Citroën. However, the small company closed its doors at the end of 1927. One further car was made in 1928, not strictly an ALMA, as the company no longer existed. Still the work of Coquet and Vaslin, it had a 2460cc straight-8 engine in a similar chassis to the smaller cars, with a 4-door saloon body. Capable of 86mph (138km/h), it survived at least until 1951. Vaslin did more aero engine work, designed a motor scooter in 1941, and from 1945 worked for Matra.
NG

ALMA (ii) **(H)** 1995–1996
Pápa & Pápa Kft, Biharkeresztes.
In 1990 a Hungarian sculptor clothed a Trabant in a plastic body and named his creation Papillon (Butterfly). Four years later, entrepreneur Imre Pápa bought

1927 Alma (i) 1600 chassis.
NATIONAL MOTOR MUSEUM

"ALPENA FLYER."

1911 Alpena Flyer 33.6hp tourer.
NICK BALDWIN

the manufacturing rights. He possessed a can-making factory at a rural city, Biharkeresztes, and the workers attempted to learn how to make plastic bodies and other components. The transition was not successful, the quality of the car was awful and it was too old and expensive to succeed. It was a strange idea: a car on a Trabant floorpan, gearbox brakes mated to a Fiat 127 engine, with a price tag matching a Suzuki Swift, built by workers trained to fabricate cans–the project soon collapsed with only a few Almas (Apple) built.

PN

ALMAC (NZ) 1985 to date
Almac Cars, Wellington, North Island.
Beginning in 1985 with the 427 SC Cobra replica, which used Holden Torana front and Jaguar rear suspensions and 7-litre Chevrolet or Ford V8 engines, Alex McDonald moved on, in 1986, by adding a model inspired by the MG T-series, which also had a 1-piece fibreglass body, built on a Triumph Herald base. The Sabre, a roadster with contemporary styling and V8 power built on a Ford Cortina mechanical base, appeared in 1995 and was offered as a complete car, rather than as a kit, like the earlier types.

MG

ALMQUIST (US) 1952–c.1964
Almquist Engineering, Milford, Pennsylvania.
Almquist made the bulk of their money from their large mail-order hot rod parts catalogue. They got into the kit car business when they purchased a lot of fibreglass bodies from defunct Clearfield Plastics, who had designed them to fit modified Fiat Topolino chassis. This design became the Saber I, and was their biggest seller. A shorter version with a higher rear deck, the Saber II fitted VW and Renault chassis. There were also three longer versions of the same basic shell, the Speedster I, II and III. To fit full-size Detroit running gear, Almquist produced the glitzy El Morocco, which had tall rear fins in the Detroit idiom. They also sold a 1932 Ford roadster kit and a Sports Rod with cycle mudguards. The last Almquist body was the Thunderbolt, which resembled the newly-introduced 1963 Corvette Stingray.

HP

A.L.P. (B) 1919–1921
SA des Automobiles Leroux-Pisart, Brussels.
This was a light car made by French-born André Leroux and Belgian André Pisart, who had met during the war. Designed by Leroux, it had an 1846cc 4-cylinder side-valve engine made by Ballot or Decolange, a chassis from Dyle et Bacalan, and a Rolls-Royce shaped radiator. The partners fixed a price of BFr9800, the same as the Fiat 501 which they saw as their main rival, but it proved too low, and although some cars were sold, no profit was made. In 1920 a financial group called SOMEA took over the design and made it for a while as the Leroux-Pisart. In 1921 Leroux left to join Citroën, and SOMEA engaged Paul Bastien to design a new car which went on the market as the SOMEA.

NG

ALPENA (US) 1911–1914
Alpena Motor Car Co., Alpena, Michigan.
This was a conventional 30hp 4-cylinder car made in four open models (Alpena never offered a closed body), and known in its first year as the Alpena Flyer. The 4-cylinder engines were made in house, but for the 1913–14 season a 50hp six by Rutenber was offered. However, the firm petitioned for bankruptcy in February 1914. Touring and roadster models were sold in Canada under the names Canada Tourist and Canada Roadster by Canadian Motors of Galt, Ontario. Although some sources claim that they were made in Galt, it is more likely that they were imported from Michigan.

NG

ALPHA 1 (US) 1983–c.1985
Alpha Design & Engineering, Huntington Beach, California.
Produced by Ferrari expert Joe Alphabet, the Alpha 1 was a convincing replica of the Ferrari 250GTO Series I based on a Datsun 240Z chassis. The kit had been developed by EAGLE MANUFACTURING, and Alpha bought the project in 1983. They were sold with Datsun or Chevrolet engines in kit or assembled form.

HP

ALPHI (F) 1928–1931
Sté Alphi, Paris.
This small company gained its name from the men who made it: Automobiles Luart, Poniatowski, Hougardy, Ingénieurs. They aimed to build cars to order, and only completed four. The first was a sports car with 1485cc C.I.M.E. engine which ran at Le Mans in 1929, retiring after 45 laps, the second a racing car with supercharged version of the C.I.M.E. engine, the third a 4-seater coupé powered originally by the same C.I.M.E. engine, but when this proved insufficiently powerful it was replaced by a 2.6-litre 6-cylinder Continental. The fourth also used a Continental unit, a 4.8-litre straight-8 and carried a 2-seater body with bolster tank and behind it two spare wheels. It is not known who ordered this, but in 1936 it came into the hands of the world champion weightlifter Charles Rigoulot, who altered the body and renamed the car the Rigoulot Speciale.

Out of the four Alphis made, two survive, the supercharged racing car and the 2.6-litre coupé.

NG

ALPINE (F) 1955–1995
Automobiles Alpine sri, Dieppe.
In the 1950s, Renault was open to a relationship with a small sports car outfit along the lines of the relationship that Simca once had with Gordini. There were several suitors, but Alpine was chosen.

Société Automobiles Alpine was founded in 1955 by Jean Redélé, an engineer who had competed in events such as the Alpine Rally and the Mille Miglia in a modified Renault 4CV saloon.

The first Alpine was a 2-seater fibreglass coupé body, styled by Michelotti, on a Renault 4CV floorpan, but with the option of a 5-speed gearbox. Redélé drove one in the 1955 Mille Miglia and it was launched as the A106 'Mille Miles'.

A version with a steel body, the A107, did not go into production but, by 1957, Alpine A106s were made at a rate of two a week. 1957 saw the short-lived A108 cabriolet, 1959 saw the arrival of a tubular backbone chassis, and 1961 saw a 2+2 coupé and the Berlinette Tour de France.

As on the Renault 4CV, the backbone chassis had the engine mounted behind the rear axle line and the running gear was always Renault, although it would be

1961 Alpine Mille Miglia coupé.
NATIONAL MOTOR MUSEUM

1990 Alpine - Renault GTA V6 coupé.
RENAULT UK

years before there were formal links between the two companies. Detail specifications of Alpines changed as Renault cars changed and, from 1957, these included Gordini versions of the engines.

A breakthrough came with the A110 of 1963, a car which established the classic Alpine shape. It was available as a cabriolet, but most buyers preferred the coupé. The A110 began with an 1108cc 87bhp Renault R8 engine but, by the time production ceased in 1977, engines of up to 180bhp were used, and these cars were particularly successful in rallying.

Other Alpines were successful in long-distance sports car events. Alpine also made Brabham single-seaters under licence, and developed the design as a distinct line. From 1965 Alpine road cars were sold through Renault agencies with full warranties and, by 1969, production had reached ten cars a week.

In 1971 Alpine was nominated as Renault's competition arm and it became part of Renault in 1974 when it suffered a fall in sales following the OPEC oil crisis. The car which won Le Mans in 1978 was designated the Renault Alpine A442, but it was more Renault than Alpine.

Alpine introduced the A310 coupé in 1971 and it became the company's main production car for the next 14 years. It also set the agenda for its successor, the Renault GTA. Unlike the fast but flimsy 2-seaters Alpine had previously made, the A310 was a well-appointed 2+2 coupé which followed usual Alpine practice with a backbone chassis and a rear engine.

Power came from a 127bhp version of the 1605cc Renault R16 engine which drove through a modified Renault 5-speed transaxle – top speed was 129mph (208km/h) and 0–62mph (0–100km/h) could be achieved in 8.1 seconds. Suspension was by coil springs and double wishbones all round, and brakes were discs at the front, drums at the rear.

In late 1976, the 1.6-litre engine was replaced by the 150bhp 'PRV' (Peugeot/Renault/Volvo) V6 of 2664cc and this boosted top speed to 137mph (220km/h), 0–62 mph (0–100km/h) in 7.5 seconds. Disc brakes were fitted at the rear and production was increased. Alpines were also assembled by Renault associates in Bulgaria, Brazil, Mexico, and Spain.

Renault replaced the A310 with the GTA in 1984, which retained the overall layout: a 2+2 fibreglass coupé on a backbone chassis with a rear-mounted V6 engine. The styling was related to the A310, but the car had been conceived by a major manufacturer and not a specialist maker. The fibreglass body was bonded to the chassis, thus creating a semi-monocoque addition to the pressed steel backbone.

It was the first Alpine to be made with rhd – it was called the Alpine V6 GT in France but, in Britain, it had to be marketed as the Renault GTA because the name Alpine was owned by Peugeot, which owned the remnants of the Rootes Group which had made the Sunbeam Alpine.

America was the target market for the GTA, but that came to nothing when Chrysler bought Renault's stake in American Motors. Chrysler decided that the GTA was too close to a Maserati-based car which was then on the drawing board, but which did not materialise. That quirk of fate, outside of Alpine's control, changed the history of the marque.

The standard engine of the GTA was a 160bhp 2849cc version of the PRV V6, but a 200 bhp turbocharged 2458cc unit was the option preferred by many and, in this form, the GTA would touch 149mph (240km/h) and sprint to 62mph (100km/h) in 6.3 seconds.

In 1990 Renault introduced a limited edition, the 'Le Mans', with body bulges to accommodate wider wheels. It was fitted with a catalytic convertor so the performance figures were slightly down: 146mph (235km/h), 0–62mph (0–100km/h) in 6.8 seconds.

In 1992 GTA was replaced by the A610 which was essentially a thoroughly revised version built on similar lines. A slightly longer stroke increased engine size to 2983cc and, in turbocharged form, it would reach 165mph (265km/h) and cover 0–62mph (0–100km/h) in 5.7 seconds. The A610, the fastest road car ever made by Renault, remained in production until 1995.

As a marque, Alpine then passed into abeyance.

MJL

ALSACE (US) 1920–1921
Automotive Products Co., New York, New York.
The Alsace was in fact a Piedmont built for the export market, changes from the parent car including magneto rather than coil ignition and a Rolls-Royce type radiator. Right hand drive would indicate that the exports were intended for Great Britain or its colonies. The regular body style was a 5-seater tourer, though at least one sedan was made, and shown at Olympia in 1920.

NG

ALTA (i) (GB) 1931–1947
Alta Car & Engineering Co. Ltd, Surbiton, Surrey.
The Alta was a sports car made in very limited numbers by the perfectionist Geoffrey Taylor, who made his own engines, with an aluminium block, hemispherical combustion chambers and shaft-driven twin overhead cam-shafts. He used an A.B.C. frame on his first car, but for production models he bought frames from Rubery Owen. His first model used a 1074cc 4-cylinder engine which gave 49bhp unblown or 76bhp with supercharger. A choice of 4-speed non synchromesh or pre-selector gearboxes was available on the 13 cars made between 1931 and 1935.

The next Altas were even more select, with only six made from 1935 to 1939. They had 1496 or 1961cc engines with chain drive to the overhead-camshafts, and, from 1937, coil independent front suspension. With supercharger, 180bhp was produced, giving a top speed of 120mph (193km/h). This made the Alta one of the fastest prewar sports cars, probably the fastest in the 2-litre class. Of the 19 cars made, nine survive. In 1947 an aerodynamic 2-seater and even saloon were offered, but it is unlikely that any were actually built. Taylor concentrated on racing cars in the post-war years, in particular a Formula 2 contender made in 1951–2.

NG

ALTA (ii) (GR) 1968–1977
Alta Inc., Athens.
After the ATTICA project ended in financial difficulty, Alta picked up the pieces and modified the design. Notably there was more angular rear bodywork for more generous 2+2 seating and a 198cc Sachs engine with 10bhp. In this form, the Alta became one of the stalwarts of the Greek motor industry but,

even in that protectionist market, its attractions steadily faded. Even so, the last Altas were made as late as 1977. Alta also made an open 3-wheeler and a larger BMW 700-engined enclosed 3-wheeler.

CR

ALTENA (NL) 1904–1907

1904–1906 NV Haarlemsche Automobiel en Motorrijwielfabriek, voorheen A. van Altena, Haarlem.

1906–1907 A. van Altena, Haarlem.

At the turn of the century A. van Altena started the production of motorcycles after being service-engineer at the MORS and BENZ importer Aertnijs. In April 1901 he published an advertisement in which he confirmed that he built and repaired motorcars. During the RAI exhibition at Amsterdam he had a three-and-a-half person 2-seater Duc Voiturette on display, probably with a De Dion engine. Soon after he started the production of his own engine. Around 1902 the board of directors gained two new members, Mr C.L. de Veer and his son C.deVeer Jr; the name of the firm changed to NV Haarlemsche Automobiel en Motorrijwielfabriek, voorheen A. van Altena. At first the manufacturing of cars was a minor activity; mainly they built motorcycles. In 1903 visitors to the Amsterdam RAI exhibition could see, next to Altena motorcycles, French HENRIOD cars, of which they were importer. Two years later Altena built its first real cars, including an 8hp 2-cylinder and three 4-cylinder types of 12, 24 and 40hp. The largest one with a 4-speed unit gearbox could reach a top speed of 60mph (96km/h). Motorcycle manufacture was discontinued, but resumed soon afterward in 1906, when the largest Altena car was a 12/14 2-cylinder. Bankruptcy led to a factory auction later in the year, but van Altena himself was the purchaser, and 8hp and 12hp models were offered briefly in 1907. Some 40 or 50 cars of all types were made.

FBV

ALTER (US) 1914–1917

1914–1916 Alter Motor Car Co., Plymouth, Michigan.

1916–1917 Alter Motor Car Co., Grand Haven, Michigan.

Alter began production in August 1914 of conventional cars powered by 23hp 4-cylinder or 28hp 6-cylinder engines. Body styles were limited to a 5-seater tourer or 2-seater roadster. A V8 was planned for 1916, but production was delayed while the company moved to a new purpose-built factory at Grand Haven. Bankruptcy ensued in January 1917. About 1000 cars were made. One of the partners, Guy Hamilton, made a similar car which he called the HAMILTON, but this failed to survive the year.

NG

ALTERNATIVE AUTOMOTIVE (US) c.1980

Alternative Automotive, Tempe, Arizona.

The Tracker was a Jeep-like body kit for Volkswagen bus running gear. The body was a fibreglass replica of the CJ-5 model, and it had a custom steel tube frame. It was one of the few kits designed for bus, rather than beetle, components.

HP

ALTMANN (D) 1905–1907

Kraftfahrzeug-Werke GmbH, Brandeburg/Havel.

This was one of the few German-made steam cars. It was an advanced design using the Gardner-Serpollet valve-timing system, though the engine was entirely original. It was a 15/25hp 3-cylinder unit with a condenser which gave low water consumption, about 125 miles per tankful. Adolf Altmann was killed when a steam engine exploded, and his work was not carried on.

HON

ALTO (i) (GB) 1983–1984

Peerhouse Cars, Surrey.

This 2-seater glassfibre coupé, based on a VW Beetle chassis, looked almost identical to the AVANTE. There was an optional chassis for mid-engined Alfa Romeo Alfasud power. A plan to revive the car in 1988 by Cardo Engineering was unsuccessful.

CR

1921 Alsace 19.6hp tourer.
NICK BALDWIN

1933 Alta (i) 1074cc sports car.
NATIONAL MOTOR MUSEUM

1938 Alta (i) 2-litre sports car.
NICK GEORGANO

ALTO (ii) (GB) 1985–1988; 1994–1996

1985-87 & 1994 Alto Component Cars, Preston, Lancashire.

1987–1988 Automotive Concepts, Portsmouth, Hampshire.

1995–1996 Rhino Engineering, Newburgh, Lancashire.

David Gornall designed the unusual Alto Duo kit car. This was a tiny 2-seater city car based on Mini subframes, mounted on a space frame chassis and clothed with a GRP body, which incorporated a glass hatch. Gornall sold the project to journalist Alexander Graham Pipe of Automotive Concepts, who also built an electric version. In 1994 Gornall presented the Alto Boxer, a radically body-kitted Mini, while the Duo was taken up by Rhino Engineering.

CR

1922 Alva A-76 sports car.
NICK GEORGANO

ALTONA (B) 1938–1946
Altona Motors, Antwerp-Bergerhout.

This company was mainly concerned with making trailers and a 3-wheeled van with single front wheel on the lines of the German Goliath, but they also made a few private cars with single rear wheel. In 1946 they showed a new 3-wheeler with open 2-seater body and single rear wheel called the Condor, but it remained a prototype.

NG

ALVA (F) 1913–1923
Automobiles Alva, Courbevoie, Seine.

The Alva was a conventional car made with a variety of proprietary engines, mostly by S.C.A.P. These included a 1690cc with single-ohc and a 2292cc side-valve unit. Front wheel brakes were available as early as 1921. A variety of bodies was available, particularly on the larger chassis, including a 6-light saloon, a town car and a pointed-tail sports car.

NG

ALVECHURCH (GB) 1911
Alvechurch Light Car Co., Alvechurch, Birmingham.

This was a cyclecar built by DUNKLEYS, the pram makers who dabbled in cars from time to time, from their 1896 coal-gas-powered vehicle onwards. They formed a separate company to make the Alvechurch, which had an air-cooled V-twin Matchless engine, pram wheels, and belt drive. This slipped badly and as a result only two cars were made. This debacle was said to have bankrupted the company, which must have referred to the Alvechurch Light Car Co., as Dunkleys themselves carried on with their prams, making powered versions in the early 1920s.

NG

ALVIS (GB) 1920–1967
1920–1921 T.G. John Ltd, Coventry.
1921–1937 Alvis Car & Engineering Co. Ltd, Coventry.
1937–1967 Alvis Limited, Coventry.

The company's first products were engines, not automobiles. T.G. John (1880–1946) had purchased the sole manufacturing and marketing rights to a line of single- and 2-cylinder Electra engines from the Hillman Motor Car Co., and he registered the company in April 1919 with a paid-up capital of £4240. A machine shop on Holyhead Road was acquired, followed by a foundry on Lincoln Street and a factory on Hertford Street where the Holley Bros Co. Ltd formerly made carburettors. Former works manager of SIDDELEY-DEASY, John held the title of managing director, with E.F. Peirson as chairman. By the end of the year, the company had a 200-strong work force.

Geoffrey P.H. de Freville, the son of a clergyman, was born at the Chartham Vicarage in Kent, and received a classical education. In 1902 he went to work for Long Acre Motor Car Co., and four years later he took over the DFP agency in London. In 1914 he established his own company, Aluminium Alloy Pistons Ltd at Wandsworth, with the word Alvis as his trademark, written in a red triangle.

He designed a 1498cc side-valve 4-cylinder engine which he showed to T.G. John, and they decided to build a car for it; the first Alvis was ready for the road

in March 1920. For the production model which followed, the displacement was reduced to 1460cc in order to meet the 10hp bore limit. It put out 30hp at 3500rpm and was sold as the Alvis 10/30. The engine was notable for its integral head and block, roller cam-followers, and 6-point engine mounting on a sub-frame. Bodies were built up on a wire-braced steel-tubing structure and clothed with aluminium panels. They were produced by Morgan of Long Acre, London. By the end of 1920 the company was turning out two cars a week.

T.G. John realised he was in the car business to stay, sold the foundry on Lincoln Road in June 1921, and discontinued Electra engine production in July 1921. This overlapped with production of some motor scooter engines for the Stafford, and assembly of the BUCKINGHAM Cyclecar under contract with J.F. Buckingham. The Hertford Street factory was sold before the end of 1921, when some 150 Alvis cars had been built and the company had made a £3317 net profit. G.P.H. de Freville had left in order to become manager of the Rolls-Royce showrooms in Hanover Street, London, but later went to America and held a position with Lafayette Motors Inc. in 1923–24, after which he settled in Paris and worked in advertising.

On 14 December 1921, the company was reorganised as Alvis Car & Engineering Co. Ltd, with T.G. John as chairman and managing director, and a board composed of H.B. Tarford, L.W. Adams, and H.W. Harding.

In 1922 the Alvis engine was bored out to 1598cc for an additional model sold as the 11/40, with a choice of tourer, coupé, and dickey-seat roadster bodies.

On 8 July 1922, T.G. John hired G.T. Smith-Clarke as chief engineer and works manager, and W.M. Dunn joined Alvis shortly afterwards as chief draftsman.

At the end of the war, Smith-Clarke went to Daimler as assistant chief engineer (under A.E. Berriman). When he met T.G. John in 1921, he had no praise for the Alvis car, which led to his engagement to draw up a better one.

He revamped the 10/30 as a 12/40 and designed a new 1645cc engine with pushrod-operated ohvs, which powered a new model, the 12/50. Production stabilised at approximately 12 cars a week. Most of the bodies were produced by Cross & Ellis.

At the time, the Alvis plant had no proper organisation. There were 300 workers, but no control over materials flow. Production costs were excessive and the company was in a financial squeeze. By 16 July 1924, Alvis owed its creditors £219,000 and a bankruptcy petition from Cross & Ellis for £5000 put the firm into court-ordered receivership.

The debts were restructured, and in February 1925, the big creditors accepted payment mainly in the form of debentures, while small claims were paid in cash. Sir Arthur Lowes-Dickinson, who had good banking connections, was made chairman of Alvis, T.G. John continuing as managing director.

A shorter-stroke 1496cc sports version of the 12/50 had been in production since 1923 and was selling well. Alvis shipped 922 chassis in 1924, 640 in 1925 and 914 in 1926.

Smith-Clarke wanted to explore the possibilities of front-wheel drive, and designed a racing version of the 12/50 with a 1482cc supercharged engine mounted back-to-front in a duralumin chassis frame. A street version was prepared for 1926, with a steel frame, and lower-pressure supercharging. The complete 12/80 front-wheel drive 2-seater was offered at a flat £1000, but none were sold.

The racing version was successful, and it was decided to build a front-wheel drive Grand Prix racing car. It had a 1496cc straight-8 engine with integral head and block, double-ohc with horizontal valves on opposite sides, Roots-type supercharger and a circular-web crankshaft running in five main bearings. It was claimed to put out 125hp at 6500rpm. The engine was redesigned for 1927 with hemispherical combustion chambers and the valves splayed at 90 degrees. The racing career of the 8-cylinder model can be summed up as a failure.

With an output of 1002 cars and a net profit of £25,000 in 1927, business was good, but Alvis did not really have an adequate budget for major racing projects. Yet the experience was fruitful, for it led to both 4- and 8-cylinder production models with front-wheel drive.

In 1927 Alvis also began production of a 6-cylinder model, the 14/75. The 1868cc overhead-valve engine had a chain-driven camshaft and put out 60hp at 4000rpm. It was mated with a separately-mounted 4-speed gearbox and spiral-bevel final drive in the rear axle. With saloon bodywork, it could top 63mph (100km/h) and cruise indefinitely at 47–50mph (75–80km/h).

Since John aimed to sell front-wheel drive cars on the strength of faster cornering, it became important to have enough power. A new engine was laid out, with the usual 12/50 cylinder dimensions and 1482cc, but very different in construction. The cylinder head was detachable, with a single-ohc driven by a train of gears at the front end of the crankshaft. The forged-steel crankshaft had four counterweights and ran in three main bearings. The basic version put out 50hp, and the supercharged one 75hp. The FD roadster, on a 102in (2589mm) wheelbase, went into production in May 1928, followed by the FE 4-passenger tourer, on a 120in (3046mm) wheelbase, in September. These cars also featured all-independent suspension, with four transverse quarter-elliptics on each side for the front wheels, trailing arms, and reversed quarter-elliptics at the rear. They commanded a premium price, £597 for the basic FD and £625 for the supercharged FD, compared with £535 for the 12/50 sports. Production continued until 1930, with a total count of 142 cars.

The engine for the 8-cylinder sports car made in 1929–30 was directly derived from the Grand Prix racing unit, supercharged, with twin-ohc. Modifications included the use of roller bearings on the crankshaft and the adoption of steel con-rods. It came with a list price of £975 (roadster or 4-seater), but only ten cars were produced. Before the Autumn of 1930, Smith-Clarke's exploration of front-wheel drive was over. He fell ill and took a leave of absence which lasted until July 1931.

The 14/75 continued for 1929, the main modification being a change from fuel tank on the scuttle to a rear-mounted tank with Autovac feed. In March 1929, however, Alvis introduced the Silver Eagle 16/95, with a 2148cc version of the 6-cylinder engine (bored out). It delivered 65hp at 4000rpm on a 5.85:1 compression ratio. The Silver Eagle was built in five body styles: 4-light saloon, 6-light saloon, coupé, 4/5 passenger tourer, and roadster.

But Alvis was not making enough money to sustain its ambitions. Profits slid from £32,000 in 1928, to £22,000 in 1929, and for most of 1930 the company was operating at a loss, clearing only £1,600. By October 1930, Alvis owed the banks £60,000 and its creditors £85,000.

Charles Follett came to the rescue. He was a prominent motor trader, with showrooms in London's West-End, and a keen competitor at Brooklands. John levelled with him as to the troubles with Alvis, and Follett agreed to finance its recovery. He did a lot more, for he was able to advise the Alvis management on the types of car that were in demand and suggest a realignment of the Alvis product range. He signed a contract to sell one out of every three cars Alvis could produce, and made styling sketches which became the basis for new bodies built by Vanden Plas on Alvis chassis. Alvis models were soon noted for their fresh appearance, and the Alvis image began to change.

The 12/60 was added in 1931, essentially a twin-carburettor 1645cc 12/50 with more fashionable styling, and the Silver Eagle Sports had a 3-carburettor 2148cc six, and a 2511cc version (bored out) was offered in the 1931 Silver Eagle 19/82, delivering 72hp at 4000rpm.

A new project called the Ace was intended as a replacement for the 12/60. Arthur F. Varney designed the chassis and Andrew Kemp drew up a new 4-cylinder ohc engine (with a timing chain) of 1500cc and 55hp. But when Smith-Clarke returned, he turned down the Ace. Instead he ordered his staff to prepare a front-wheel drive car with the 2148cc six turned back-to-front. It never became a production model. The prototype was given to John's daughter.

Developed by A.F. Varney, the Speed Twenty went into production in November 1931, with triple SU carburettors on the 2511cc, high (6.33:1) compression engine, and an output of 80hp at 4000rpm. It was initially called Silver Dart, but Charles Follett persuaded John that the Speed Twenty name would sell better. It had a low, double-drop frame on a 123in (3122mm) wheelbase and 5.25×20 tyres. Capable of speeds up to 92mph (145 km/h), it was priced at £750 with saloon body.

The 14/75 model was taken out of production at the end of 1929, but its engine, bored out to 1991cc, became an economy-option in the Silver Eagle during 1931.

Two important technical innovations arrived in 1933: revised ifs and the synchromesh gearbox. The ifs appeared first on the Crested Eagle, which made its debut in June 1933, replacing the Silver Eagle. It had an upper transverse leaf spring and lower A-arms. W.M. Dunn had been working for years to make gearshifts easier, and invented a type of constant-mesh gearbox where changes were made by floating bushings. Alvis held a patent on it, which brought in several licence fees in the years up to 1939. It was first mounted on the 1934 model Sixteen, with double-helical gears (except for spur gears on first), introduced in November 1933.

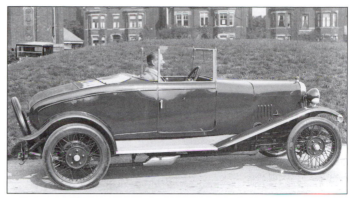

1924 Alvis 12/40 2-seater.
NATIONAL MOTOR MUSEUM

1926 Alvis 12/50 tourer.
NICK BALDWIN

1938 Alvis Crested Eagle limousine.
NICK GEORGANO/NATIONAL MOTOR MUSEUM

The synchromesh gearbox was not ready in time for the Crested Eagle, and this was equipped with an ENV pre-selector gearbox. The Sixteen inherited the 2148cc six in triple-carburettor form, mounted in a new frame with X-bracing ahead of the gearbox and under the bulkhead. Engine size was increased for 1935 (longer stroke) to 2362cc, raising output to 66hp at 4200rpm. At the same time, the model name was changed from Sixteen to Silver Eagle.

The Firefly 12 replaced the 12/50 in September 1932, its 1496cc engine now putting out 48hp at 4000rpm. The 1645cc engine from the 12/60 was also offered, and buyers had a choice of a 4-speed pre-selector or a conventional gearbox.

For 1934 the Speed Twenty was given ifs and an all-synchromesh gearbox. Coachwork by Charlesworth, Holbrook, Offord, Tickford and Mulliner became more common on Alvis chassis. In 1934 the company invoiced 1110 chassis and declared a record profit of £41,107.

1928 Alvis FD 12/50 sports car.
NATIONAL MOTOR MUSEUM

In 1935 the company was recapitalised at £370,000 and purchased a licence to produce Gnome-Rhone radial aircraft engines. That year T.G. John also made a £35,000 bid for control of Lagonda, after he had recovered his chairman's title at Alvis. He also entered a joint venture, Alvis-Straussler Ltd, in 1936, to produce military vehicles designed by Nicholas Straussler, formerly of Manfred Weiss at Csepel, Hungary, and an expert on all-terrain vehicles, but it lasted only until 1938.

For 1935 the Crested Eagle and the Speed Twenty had engine displacement increased to 2762cc. The single-carburettor engine put out 77hp at 3920rpm and the triple-carburettor version 87hp at 4380rpm. The Speed Twenty was offered in three body styles: 4-light saloon, 4-passenger tourer, and drophead coupé.

The Firebird replaced the Firefly in September 1934, with the engine bored-out to 1842cc and fitted with bigger main bearings and water-pump circulation. An all-synchromesh gearbox was standard. The Firebird could reach 75mph (120km/h) and was priced at £510. The factory turned out 322 Firefly cars in 1934 and 134 Firebirds in 1935. In September 1937 the Firebird was renamed 12/70 after a complete redesign by George Lanchester. Mulliners of Birmingham made the bodies.

George Lanchester also had a hand in the Speed 25 and 4.3-Litre, both launched in 1937, with 7-bearing 6-cylinder engines of 3571 and 4387cc. Both had the same 110mm stroke as the smaller engines and differed mainly in bore size: 83mm and 92mm. The TA-series Speed 25 engine ran with a 6.35:1 compression ratio and triple SU carburettors, putting out a maximum of 106hp at 3800rpm. It was the first Alvis on which the accelerator pedal was moved from the left to the right-hand side of the brake pedal. The bigger engine peaked at 3600rpm, delivering 123hp on a 6.25:1 compression ratio. Both were built on a 127in (3223mm) wheelbase, with X-braced frames and separately mounted gearboxes. The 4-wheel brakes were cable-operated. On the 4.3-Litre the pedal was assisted by a Dewandre vacuum servo system.

A new 17, with the 2362cc six, was also added in 1937, with a new all-box-section frame looped above the rear axle, which had under-slung springs. The gearbox was moved up and bolted to the clutch housing. For 1938 the 17 was renamed Silver Crest and the 2511cc engine became an option.

On account of the company's commitment to the military defence industries, John renamed it Alvis Limited in 1937. He was able to report shipments of 750 cars in the fiscal year ending 31 July 1937, 656 cars the following fiscal year, and 561 from July 1938 to August 1939. The net profit for 1939 was only £21,000.

Car production for the civilian market came to a halt in July 1940 and the Holyhead Road works were damaged by air raids in November 1940 and April 1941.

John retired in 1944 to his Kenilworth estate, but died on 9 August 1946 in his home, Dunster House, on Putney Hill. A.E. Nicholson served as chairman from 1944 to 1946, when John Joseph Parkes joined the company and was named chairman. Preliminary planning of the postwar cars had in fact begun before John's departure, and Vanden Plas made scale models for Alvis in 1944. In 1945 Arthur F. Varney was detached from his wartime duties to tackle the new car project, under the supervision of Lt-Col John Chaytor, a director of Alvis Limited and also chief constable of North Riding, Yorkshire. Production of the Leonides radial aircraft engine for civilian aircraft also began in 1945. W.M. Dunn also rejoined the Alvis car engineering staff.

The 1946 Alvis Fourteen was closely based on the prewar 12/70. The 1892cc engine was the same as the 1842cc unit, except for a 1mm bigger bore and higher compression (6.9:1). It put out 66hp at 4000rpm. The standard body (by Mulliners) was a 4-door saloon, but the coachbuilders showed great interest in alternative styles on the Alvis chassis. Duncan built a Hamblin-designed coupé reminiscent of the B.G. Bowden-styled Healey coupé; Langenthal built a Riley (RM) style cabriolet, Graber a classic drophead coupé.

F.J. Bidee designed a streamlined special sports tourer and contracted with AP Metalcraft for the production of 100 units; and Airflow Streamlines Ltd proposed their Alvis Woodland saloon. From 1946 to 1950, Alvis produced 3311 cars.

William Michael Dunn (1894–1969) took charge of the TA-21 car project, which was marketed as the 3-Litre, beginning in 1950. Smith-Clarke retired in 1950, soon after production got under way.

Dunn had begun at an early date to prepare a completely new short-stroke (90mm) 6-cylinder ohv engine, and a chassis for it was ready in 1948. The 2992cc unit put out 93hp at 4000rpm with a 7.1:1 compression ratio and twin SU carburettors. Mulliners built the 4-light 4-door saloon and Tickford the drophead coupé.

The first Graber coupé on the 3-Litre was shown in Geneva in March 1953, revealing a great deal of Bentley Continental styling influence. Graber's next one came in 1955, with a Studebaker-type roofline, and the Berne-based coachbuilder also offered a TA21 drophead coupé in 1954.

Alec Issigonis joined Alvis upon leaving Morris when the merger with Austin had been decided, and began design work on a new saloon suitable for both a 2000cc 4-cylinder and a 3500cc V8 engine. The chassis featured all-independent suspension with rubber springs and a gearbox-cum-differential unit mounted between the rear wheels and consisting of a 2-speed gearbox with Laycock-de-Normanville overdrive on both ratios, so providing four speeds. The body shells were to have been supplied by Pressed Steel, who were ready to make 5000 units a year, but the whole project was shelved as Alvis could not foot the development and tooling costs.

Issigonis had a hand in developing a high-performance version of the 3-litre saloon, which became the TC 21/100, marketed as the Grey Lady. With higher (8.0:1) compression, it was rated at 100hp, which enabled it to use a 3.77:1 final drive rather than the standard ratio of 4.09:1. The Grey Lady was distinguished by its Dunlop wire wheels and special paintwork.

Alvis also revived its military-vehicle activity by launching the Saracen 6-wheeler with all-wheel drive in 1952. It was powered by Rolls-Royce, with a Daimler fluid flywheel and 5-speed Wilson planetary transmission. Other versions, some with heavy armour, or with extra fordability, were known as the Saladin, Salamander, and Stalwart.

Production of the TA-21 and the TC-21/100 came to an end in 1955, when Mulliners came under contract to work exclusively for Standard-Triumph, after a run of just 1310 3-Litre saloons and 475 Grey Ladies. Parkes arranged with Willowbrook to produce the Swiss-designed coupé under licence from Graber in 1956, but they were priced at £3500 and only 16 were built.

An agreement to switch production to Park Ward was reached in March 1958, and body deliveries began late that year for the new model, called the TD-21, and powered by a triple-SU version of the 3-litre engine, rated at 120hp.

In August 1962, it became the TD-21 Series II, and was equipped with 4-wheel disc brakes, and a choice of a Borg-Warner automatic transmission or a 5-speed ZF gearbox. But it was not available with power steering. When TD-21 production ended in October 1963, 1060 units had been built.

It was replaced by the TE-21 (or Series III), with a new front end design featuring stacked headlamps. The engine had a modified crankshaft and bigger valves, and delivered 130hp. The steering effort was eased somewhat by the adoption of recirculating-ball steering gear.

Concurrently, Graber was making his cabriolet on Alvis chassis in small numbers, and in 1963 showed a new coupé with a Maserati-like grille and a headlamp arrangement copied from the Mercedes-Benz 230 SL. Dunn had retired in 1959, but Parkes talked him into going back to work in 1961, and he spent another two years trying to modernise the engineering on Alvis cars.

Parkes realised that Alvis, even with its aircraft-engine and military vehicle departments, was no longer viable without a partner. Negotiations with Rover chairman George Farmer led to Alvis being taken over by Rover in July 1965. Rover paid for the total share capital of Alvis Limited by a new stock issue. Parkes was given a seat on the Rover board, and Rover's general manager A.B. Smith became a director of Alvis.

During 1965 ZF power steering became optional on the Series III. It was replaced in March 1966 by the TF-21 (Series IV) which had a 150hp triple-SU-equipped engine. But the demand for Alvis cars was drying up under the pressure of competition. Rover and Alvis engineers worked together in 1967 on a new sports coupé with a Rover V8 engine mounted inboard at the rear, but the project was abandoned at the prototype stage.

Chassis production for the TF-21 was halted in May 1967, and the final Alvis car was completed on 29 September 1967. Only 105 cars of TF-21 specification were built, and the total from 1953 to 1967 of Graber-built bodies mounted on Alvis chassis did not exceed 150.

Along with Rover, Alvis Limited passed under British Leyland control in 1973. Alvis was still making the 6-wheel Saladin and the tracked Scorpion, now using Jaguar engines, but in 1981 Alvis Limited was sold for £27 million to United Scientific Holdings, a small enterprise best known for making military sighting systems. Alvis Vehicles Ltd was formed as a separate subsidiary and moved into a new factory in 1990. By 1995 the workforce had been reduced from around 500 to 160. But the parent company was not without resources, for Unipower Ltd was taken over in 1994 and combined with Alvis. In 1997 Alvis took over Hägglund AB of Sweden, builders of special-purpose all-terrain (and snow-going) vehicles, and sales volume for the year reached £233 million. In 1998 Alvis Vehicles Ltd also acquired the tank division of GKN.

1947 Alvis TA14 saloon.
NATIONAL MOTOR MUSEUM

1952 Alvis TA21 3-Litre saloon.
NATIONAL MOTOR MUSEUM

1963 Alvis TE21 3-Litre saloon.
NATIONAL MOTOR MUSEUM

The last attempt to develop a 4-wheeled vehicle was made in 1995 with the Alvis 8, proposed in military and civilian forms, with Mercedes-Benz 6-cylinder diesel engines and Unimog transmission systems. But it was priced at £125,000 and production never began.

JPN

Further Reading
Alvis, K.R. Day, Lewis Cole and Company, London, 1966.
The Alvis Car, K.R. Day, published privately.
The Vintage Alvis, Peter Hull and Norma Johnson, Alvis Register, 1995.
'The Hare and the Eagle: A History of Alvis', David Owen, *Automobile Quarterly*, Vol. 16. No. 4.

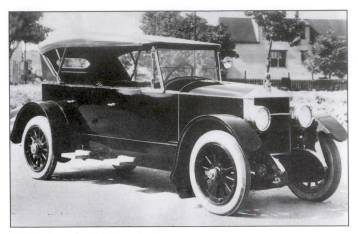

1921 Ambassador tourer.
KEITH MARVIN

A. & M. (GB) 1996 to date
A. & M. (Specialist Cars) Ltd, Redditch, Worcestershire.
The EX2 sports coupé was a smoothly-styled kit-built mid-engined car. Its chassis was a semi-space frame backbone utilising specially-fabricated double wishbones with cast aluminium uprights, rose joints and disc brakes all round. The 4-cylinder engine came from Vauxhall (1.3–2.0 litres), as did the 5-speed transaxle, and the bodywork was in self-coloured glassfibre.
CR

A.M. (i) (F) 1906–1915
Ateliers Veuve A. de Mesmay, St Quentin, Aisne.
This company was mainly known for their Abeille engines which were supplied to a number of car makers, including BRUSH (i), LAMBERT (ii), PASSY-THELLIER, VELOX (i), and others. They were listed in directories as car makers during the years 1906 to 1915, 1906 models including a 12hp 2-cylinder car sold under the Abeille name, and 12 and 24hp 4-cylinder cars. There was little evidence of these cars in contemporary journals.
NG

A.M. (ii) (F) c.1922–1936
Alfred Maridet, St Martin d'Estreaux.
Maridet was a wealthy amateur driver and engineer who made a small number of cars, probably not more than seven, over a long period. The first had a 5-litre 4-cylinder T-head Janvier engine, a light 2-seater body and gas headlamps. He entered another car with a smaller 4-litre engine, also by Janvier, in the 1922 Touring Car Grand Prix, but it was burnt out early in the race. Some of his cars bore the badge of a bat and went by the name of Chauve Souris. His last known car was a 2-door coupé with cycle-type wings, made in 1936.
NG

A.M.A. (B) 1913–1914
These initials stood for American Motorcar Agency, and the cars had American-made engines and chassis which were imported from an unknown source, and Belgian bodies by Minet with a Métallurgique-inspired vee-radiator. The engine was a 4500cc, 4-cylinder rated at 18/24hp. It is not known how many were made, but an open tourer finished 2nd in a race at the Ostend Meeting in 1913.
NG

AMALFI (GB) 1994 to date
Amalfi Sportscars, Ammanford, Wales.
This was a highly unusual Countach lookalike, with a spaceframe chassis to accept a Fiat X1/9 engine and running gear (alternatively a Lancia Beta engine). The dimensions were much smaller than the original Lamborghini and there were some tweaks in its appearance, such as having six headlamps.
CR

AMALGAMATED STEAM CAR (US) 1919
The Amalgamated Machinery Corp., Chicago, Illinois.

The Amalgamated Steam Car was one of several attempts in the US to revive an interest in steam cars, immediately following World War I. Unfortunately, the project failed shortly after the completion and during the testing of a prototype.
KM

AMANTE GT (US) c.1969–1975
1969–1970 Hebina Plastics, Santa Clara, California.
1970–1971 Voegele Industries, Santa Clara, California.
1971–1973 Performance Designers, Daytona Beach, Florida.
1973–1975 Amante Cars, Chamblee, Georgia.
This popular kit sports car had a long life with a number of manufacturers. It was an attractive original design usually installed on the VW Type III floorpan. This gave it disc brakes and a fuel-injected engine, which the more common Beetle lacked. The body was smooth and clean, without excess ornamentation. First named the Gazelle, it was quickly changed to Amante. In 1970 Hebina changed their name to Voegele Industries and added a tube frame for mounting Corvair or V8 engines in the middle. The V8 Ford-powered GT/XM used a ZF transaxle and sold for more than a new Corvette. In 1971 the Amante project was sold to Performance Designers, who built them until 1973 when they sold out to Amante Cars.
HP

AMARETTA COACH (US) c.1981
Amaretta Coach, Van Nuys, California.
The T-Era was a replica of the 1957 Thunderbird that came with a custom tube frame. It used running gear from Ford Pintos and Mustangs, including 4-, 6- or 8-cylinder engines. The T-Era was sold in kit and assembled form.
HP

AMAZON (i) (GB) 1921–1922
Amazon Cars Ltd, London.
The Amazon was a cyclecar powered by a 6/9hp flat-twin Coventry-Victor engine, with Juckes 3-speed gearbox and chain drive. The engine was mounted at the rear, but to give the car a conventional appearance it had a dummy radiator at the front.
NG

AMAZON (ii) (MALTA) 1979–c.1986
Vintage Cars Ltd, Lija.
Produced by a company engaged in pleasure boat construction, the Amazon was a disfigured 'replica' of the Mercedes SSK based on a VW Beetle chassis and licensed from an American producer.
CR

AMBASSADOR (US) 1921–1925
Yellow Cab Manufacturing Co., Chicago, Illinois.
The large Ambassador cars of 1921, 1922, and 1923 were simply leftover SHAW cars with a new emblem and Continental 6-T L-head engine, Yellow Cab having taken over Shaw early in 1921. This was in line with Yellow Cab's desire to use up existing parts of the Shaw and, although the supply was small, sales were slow. In an effort to expedite the disposal of the remaining stock, Ambassador completed the cars from the remaining parts and strong-armed their disposal to those who held Yellow Cab franchises in the larger cities of the US at cost. In late 1923 designs were completed for a smaller Ambassador model for general sale. This plan was abandoned and further efforts were channelled toward a smaller taxicab which could also be used for rental purposes. The Ambassador D-1 was debuted in late 1924, and within months the plan for taxis was abandoned and John Hertz, erstwhile head of the Walden W. Shaw Livery Corporation, who was in charge of operations, decided to market the car exclusively for rental, where the car would be available on a dollar-and-cents basis for one day, a week or any other period, as needed. Shortly after the idea was put into service, Hertz renamed the car after himself and made it available for both lease and sale for private ownership. The Hertz subsequently became a GM product when General Motors took over Yellow Cab, and it remained in production into late 1927. Approximately 4000 Hertz cars were manufactured, primarily in sedan form, but also available as an open touring car.
KM

1885 Amédée Bollée steam mail coach built for the Marquis de Broc.
NATIONAL MOTOR MUSEUM

AMBERSON (US) c.1991

Amberson Classics, Gadsden, Alabama.

The Amberson SSK was a Mercedes SSK replica that was more accurate than most, due to being modelled from an original SSK and having an all-Mercedes drive train. A single Mercedes sedan was used for all parts, including the 6-cylinder engine, and the body panels were stainless steel. Another nice touch was the use of 20in wheels and tyres, which gave the right stance. They also bought the LASER 917 kit car project, which was a replica of the Porsche 917, based on VW components or a custom chassis with a General Motors V6 engine.

HP

AMBRO see DIO

A.M.C. see ANDERSEN

AMCO (US) 1917–1922

American Motors Inc., New York, New York.

Like the Alsace, the Amco was an American car built for export only. Various 4-cylinder engines were used, G.B. & S, Herschell-Spillman, or Rutenber, and a 5-seater tourer was the only body offered. Drive was left or right hand. The factory was at Norwalk, Connecticut, later being relocated to Stamford.

NG

AMECTRAN (US) 1979

American Ecological Transportation, Dallas, Texas.

After several years of experiment, Amectran felt confident enough to release details of a forthcoming electrically powered 4-seater sports coupé called the Exar-1. It obtained the prototype of the Frua-designed BMW 3000 coupé show car and took moulds from it with the intention of producing bodies in Kevlar. With a 19hp GE motor, regenerative braking and a 4-speed semi-automatic

1906 Amédée Bollée Type E 30hp tourer.
BRYAN K. GOODMAN

transmission, the Exar-1 was quoted as having a top speed of 85mph (137 km/h) and a maximum range of 100 miles (160 km). It appears that production did not commence.

CR

AMÉDÉE BOLLÉE (F) 1885–1921

Amédée Bollée fils, Le Mans.

The Bollée family were bell founders whose business dated back to the 1820s. Three members of the family were connected with the motor business, Amédée père (1844–1917), Amédée fils (1867–1926), and his brother Léon (1870–1913) (see LÉON BOLLÉE). Amédée père was a pioneer builder of steam carriages, making such famous vehicles as L'Obéissante (1873) with ifs, and Marie-Anne (1879), a 4-wheeler with shaft-drive to a two-wheeled tender. His son's first vehicle was built with his father's aid in 1885 when he was 18 years old. It was a

1920 América (ii) Type C sports car.
NATIONAL MOTOR MUSEUM

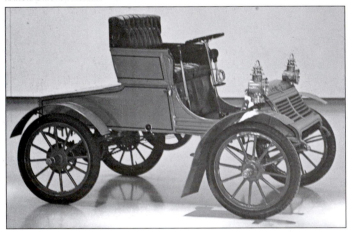

1902 American (ii) runabout.
NATIONAL MOTOR MUSEUM

massive steam mail coach built to the order of the Marquis de Broc, and in the same year he built a much smaller steam carriage of his own design. He made a petrol engine intended for use in airships in 1889, but did not offer petrol cars for sale until 1896, when he announced a 6hp horizontal twin- engined car with belt drive. The engine and transmission were mounted below the frame which was carried on long springs, giving a low centre of gravity. The first car made took part in the 1896 Paris–Marseilles–Paris Race, but was eliminated by an accident. Production models followed later in the year; closed bodywork as well as open 2- and 4-seaters were made. In 1897 Baron de Turckheim took out a licence to make these cars in his German DE DIETRICH factory at Niederbronn, Alsace, and LEESDORFER also acquired a licence for Austria. Some of these Bollées were raced, including one with a pioneering streamlined body which competed in the 1898 Paris-Amsterdam Race. Though another racing car of 1899 had a 6.3-litre 20hp 4-cylinder engine, touring models had 10hp twins or 12hp 4-cylinder engines, all horizontal, and from 1899 were characterised by large curved gilled-tube radiators. Most of the bodies were made by the local firms of Gaston Dauplay or Pouriau, with the later 4-cylinder Bollées being bodied by Gaudichet et Turquet who also worked on Léon Bollée chassis. Bollée turned to the vertical 4-cylinder engine in 1904 and the cars took on a more conventional appearance, with round radiators not unlike those of Delaunay-Belleville. The 6333cc Type E, made from 1907 to 1914, had a number of advanced features including steering column gearchange which could be operated with one finger, the makers claimed. Hydraulic tappets, later used by Rolls-Royce on the Phantom III, were adopted in 1910. Bollée had many aristocratic customers

including two princes, a duke and several marquises including de Broc who bought seven Bollée cars as well as his steam coach. The cars were very expensive and exclusive, a Type E chassis costing just a little less than a Rolls-Royce Silver Ghost. Production was lower than that of his brother Léon. Amédée said that in good years he made no more than 25 to 30 cars. A little over 200 Type Es were made, being joined in 1912 by the smaller 4-litre Type F. Production was suspended during the war, when Amédée Bollée made shells for the Belgian and British armies. He also transformed a number of cars into ambulances. A small number of Type Fs was completed from existing parts between 1919 and 1921, but Bollée realised that demand for his high-quality cars would be very limited in the postwar world. He turned to the manufacture of piston rings, in which he was very successful, being joined by his son Pierre Amédée (1894–1980).

The company still flourishes, being known since 1977 as the Société Mécanique de Précision du Maine, but still in the hands of the Bollée family.
NG

Further Reading
L'Invention de l'Automobile, Jean-Pierre Delaperelle,
Éditions Cenomande, 1986

AMERICA (i) (US) 1911

Motor Car Co. of America, New York, New York.
The America 40 was a low-slung car powered by a 40hp 4-cylinder engine, and made in torpedo, touring, roadster or landaulette forms. An auxiliary 1.5 gallon fuel tank was provided for emergencies. Almost as soon as production began, or possibly before, the design was taken over by the W.H. McIntyre company of Auburn, Indiana. They were makers of high-wheelers who wanted to add a standard car to their range, so the America 40 became the McIntyre Special.
NG

AMÉRICA (ii) (E) 1917–1922

América Autos SA, Barcelona.
Designed by the talented Manuel Pazos, who held a great number of patents for different automotive components, the first América Type A was a prestige car, but very complex, with a patented valveless 4-cylinder engine, synchronised 3-speed gearbox of own design, and internally sprung wheels. This very complex car only sold in a small number, but it demonstrated the excellent knowledge of Manuel Pazos. From 1919 América built the Type B, a light car with a small 4-cylinder 760cc engine of 6/8hp. Fitted frequently with sporting bodywork, the B sold well and was often entered in several races and hill climbs, where it won the Gold Medal of the Royal Automobile Club of Catalonia in the Test of Regularity in 1921. The Type B was offered in several lengths from 4.3 to 5 metres. In 1921 the new Type C was entered in the famous Penya Rhin Grand Prix, but it had to retire. Based on the Type B, the C was specially designed for competition with lighter bodywork and more power. Only one prototype was built.
VCM

AMÉRICAINE see COHENDET

AMERICAN (i) (US) 1899–1901

American Automobile Co., New York, New York.
A 4-seater car powered by a 3-cylinder engine, this was the first independent design by J. Frank Duryea after he parted company with his brother Charles. The New York address was an office, the factory location being unknown. Duryea apparently developed the car near his home in New England, and possibly this was the 'factory', such as it was. In 1900 he left American to make the HAMPDEN and, later, STEVENS-DURYEA. The American Automobile Co. became the United Power Vehicle Co. which offered a wide range of vehicles under the name UNITED POWER.
NG

AMERICAN (ii) (US) 1902–1904

American Motor Carriage Co., Cleveland, Ohio.
Also known as the American Gas, this was a light runabout powered by a 7hp single-cylinder engine mounted under the seat, with planetary transmission and single-chain final drive. At $1000 it was seriously over-priced for such a car, and though the price was cut to $750 for 1904, the company went bankrupt that year. Factory capacity of 200 cars per year was never reached
NG

AMERICAN (iii) **(US)** 1904

American Manufacturing Co., Alexandria, Virginia.

Headed by Frank L. Carter, this company bought up patents on a variety of products, of which cars were only one. Other machinery sold by them included French fry potato cutters and fire extinguishers. Their car was a conventional-looking machine with 4-cylinder front-mounted engine and offered in touring, runabout or commercial form. Frank Carter's brother, Howard, built the later CARTER TWIN ENGINE, while another brother, A. Gary Carter, made the WASHINGTON (i)

NG

AMERICAN (iv) **(US)** 1906–1914

American Motors Co., Indianapolis, Indiana.

The products of this company are often referred to as American Underslung, because the best-known models had underslung frames. However, the first cars had conventional frames, and these were made alongside the underslung versions certainly up to 1911. The first American had a 35/40hp 4-cylinder T-head engine; the car was designed by Harry C. Stutz and the engine was made by a small company owned by the Teetor brothers. This contract set them on the road to becoming major engine manufacturers under the name Teetor-Hartley. Most subsequent Americans used their engines, in varying sizes. These early Americans used Garford axles and frames from A.O. Smith. Stutz left in 1907 and was succeeded by Fred Tone. He is said to have gained the idea of the underslung frame by seeing a conventional frame being carried into the factory upside down. The first Underslung was made in 1907; it was a 2-seater roadster powered by a 40/50hp engine which, with the gearbox, was mounted on a sub-frame. It was priced at $3250, the same as the conventional tourer. About 100 cars were made in 1907, later output averaging 150–200 per year, with a peak of 1000 cars in 1912. Larger engines of 50 and 70hp were offered in 1908, when the first underslung 4-seaters were made. Closed models were made on the conventional chassis, and by 1911 there was a closed coupé on the underslung frame as well. This cost $5250, and the American was being priced out of the market. For 1912 a smaller car, the American Scout, was listed. This had a 20hp L-head engine made by American, and sold for $1250, but it was too late to save the firm. Fred Tone left in 1913, and American Motors Company was declared bankrupt in the spring of 1914 when two sizes of 6-cylinder engine were listed. About 50 unsold cars were marketed by the Auto Parts Company of Chicago for as little as $600–900.

NG

AMERICAN (v) **(US)** 1914

American Cyclecar Co., Detroit, Michigan.

This was a light car rather than a cyclecar despite the company name. Designed by Harry J. Stoops, it had a 14/18hp 4-cylinder engine and shaft drive. Few were made in Detroit, as the design and the company were bought by the Trumbull brothers and made at Bridgeport, Connecticut under the name TRUMBULL.

NG

AMERICAN (vi) **(US)** 1916–1924

1916–1924 American Motors Corp., Plainfield, New Jersey.

1920–1921 American-Southern Motors Corp., Greensboro, North Carolina.

1922–1924 Bessemer-American Motor Corp., Plainfield, New Jersey.

The American, with its Miles of Smiles slogan, was a standard 6-cylinder assembled car, marketed at various times as the American, American Six or American Balanced Six, its earlier output equipped with a Rutenber engine. Louis Chevrolet served as chief engineer during this period, and the advertising emphasized that all Americans sold had to pass muster by Chevrolet first and carry a badge inscribed OK, Chevrolet. In 1920 the Rutenber engine was replaced by a more powerful and updated one by Herschell-Spillman, production of 1500 cars peaking that year. The same year, American-Southern Motors was formed, ostensibly to produce the American for a southern clientele plus manufacturing a sporting luxury car called the VAUGHN, the latter of which died a-borning after the completion and exhibition of a single car in 1921. In 1923 American merged with the Bessemer Truck Co., also of Plainfield, to form the Bessemer-American Motor Corp., of which American proceeded as its passenger car division. The car was phased out of production early in 1924.

KM

1913 American (iv) Type 54A tourer.
NATIONAL MOTOR MUSEUM

1919 American (vi) tourer.
KEITH MARVIN

AMERICAN AIR PRODUCTS (US) 1959–1960

1959–1960 American Air Products, Fort Lauderdale, Florida.

1960 Gaslight Motors, Detroit, Michigan.

The only model built by this company was a replica of the 1902 Rambler. It used a single-cylinder air-cooled engine. In 1960 the project was taken over by Gaslight Motors in Detroit, Michigan, who built them through 1961.

HP

AMERICAN AUSTIN; AMERICAN BANTAM (US) 1930–1940

1930–1934 American Austin Car Co. Inc., Butler, Pennsylvania.

1937–1940 American Bantam Car Co. Inc., Butler, Pennsylvania.

Built in the former Standard Steel Car factory this make began as a licence-built English Austin Seven chassis clothed in striking roadster and coupé bodies styled by Alex de Sakhnoffsky and built by Hayes Body Co. of Detroit. The roadster sold for $445, ten dollars more than a Model A Ford, so from the start the American Austin was a novelty rather than serious transport for budget-minded buyers. They were popular in Hollywood, and the sedan delivery offered eye-catching mobile publicity for florists and the like, but this was not nearly enough to earn hoped for sales of 180,000. In fact the company's best year, 1930, saw only 8558 cars delivered, and not more than 10,000 were sold before the factory closed early in 1932. It was rescued by Georgia car dealer Roy S. Evans who remaindered off unsold cars at only $295. This earned enough money to restart production, but only 4726 were made in 1933, and 1057 up to June 1934. Bodies were now made at Butler. No cars were made in 1935 or 1936, but in September 1937 the car was re-launched under the name American Bantam, or simply Bantam. It was restyled, again by Sakhnoffsky, with pointed radiator grille and spatted rear wheels on the roadster, so that its Austin origins were completely disguised. The engine was worked on by racing car expert Harry A. Miller; a redesigned manifold enabled Evans to avoid paying a $10 per

49

1933 American Austin sedan.
KENNETH STAUFFER

1939 American Bantam roadster.
ELLIOTT KAHN

car royalty to Austin. Pressure lubrication and mechanical pump feed were featured, and prices were $469 for the coupé and $479 for the roadster. A station wagon was added to the range for 1939, and 1940 models had 3-bearing crankshafts and 800cc engines compared with 747cc for the Austin unit. Only about 2000 were made of the new generation American Bantam in 1938, 1225 in 1939 and 800 in 1940, when production ended, though a 1941 catalogue was issued. The company's most important contribution to history was their development of the first Jeep. Designed by Karl Probst and powered by a Continental engine, 2675 of these were made before much larger production was undertaken by Ford and Willys. Bantam subsequently made two-wheeled trailers up to 1956, when they were taken over by American Rolling Mills. Roy Evans sold out in 1946.

NG

Further Reading
'Good Things Did Come in Small Packages', George Edward Domer, *Automobile Quarterly*, Vol. 14, No. 4.

AMERICAN BERLIET (US) 1906–1908

American Locomotive Automobile Co., Providence, Rhode Island.
In 1905 one of America's leading locomotive makers signed an agreement with the French car manufacturer BERLIET to build automobiles in their Providence factory. Production began in 1906, initially of two fours, a 24/30hp and a 40/50hp. Prices were very high, at $5500 to $8500. Even more expensive was the 60hp six added to the range for 1908, and costing $10,000 for a tourer, landaulette or limousine. This was shaft-driven, as were the smaller models for 1908, though previously they had chain drive. For 1909 the Berliet licence was discontinued and the cars were re-named ALCO.

NG

AMERICAN BUCKBOARD (US) 1955

American Buckboard Corp., Los Angeles, California.
This small fibreglass-bodied car was unique in having five wheels. The fifth one was at the rear and drove the car via a chain drive from a 2-cylinder air-cooled

motorcycle engine. The body style was a 2-seater roadster. In 1956 the Buckboard was renamed the BEARCAT.

HP

AMERICAN CLASSICS (US) c.1991

American Classics Corp., Fargo, North Dakota.
Not to be too subtle, American Classics named their 1957 Thunderbird replica Big Thunder. It used a ladder frame set up for Ford or Chevrolet V6 and V8 engines. Running gear was based on Ford Mustang parts, and the trim was so original it was also purchased by restorers.

HP

AMERICAN COACH CRAFT (US) c.1980–c.1985

American Coach Craft Inc., Lemont, Illinois.
The Marcotte Vision was a very attractive fibreglass kit car body designed to fit the Volkswagen Beetle or Ghia chassis. A sweeping fastback top gave it a dramatic rear profile. They could be ordered in several stages of assembly.

HP

AMERICAN CUSTOM & COMPONENT CARS (US) c.1982

American Custom & Component Cars, Boise, Idaho.
ACC sold a kit car replica of the Jaguar XK-120 and also carried the Pantera replica built by LONG AND NEWMAN.

HP

AMERICAN CUSTOM CARS (US) c.1981

American Custom Cars Inc., Houston, Texas.
This company built MG-TD and Porsche Speedster replicas on Volkswagen chassis. They were sold in kit or assembled form, and the factory-built cars came with a 12,000-mile warranty.

HP

AMERICAN CUSTOM INDUSTRIES (US) c.1967 to date

American Custom Industries, Sylvania, Ohio
ACI specialised in Chevrolet Corvette custom body and performance items, and built several series of special Corvettes. They teamed up with famed Corvette racer John Greenwood in the late 1970s to build a turbocharged Corvette with wildly stylised body panels called the Greenwood Turbo. These could be purchased complete or in kit form. Later these were renamed the American Turbo. ACI also built the Duntov Turbo in 1980, a turbocharged Corvette convertible with large mudguard flares, a custom bonnet and upgraded chassis and suspension. It was a different body than the Greeenwood Turbo. The turbocharged engine was not much more powerful than stock, but the Duntov handled much better than the standard Corvette. It was endorsed by Zora Arkus-Duntov, the legendary 'father' of the Corvette. Another ACI product was the American Turbo Sportwagon, a turbocharged Corvette with a raised rear deck for increased carrying capacity. ACI continued building custom fibreglass body panels for the Corvette.

HP

AMERICAN EAGLE *see* EAGLE (vi)

AMERICAN ELECTRIC (US) 1896–1902

1896–1900 American Electric Vehicle Co., Chicago, Illinois.
1900–1902 American Electric Vehicle Co., Hoboken, New Jersey.
This company issued a catalogue in May 1896, and ten months later they said that the department store Montgomery Ward had been using one of their carriages for over a year. This is sometimes listed as a Montgomery Ward. Cars were offered as 2-seaters at $900 or 4-seaters at $1250, with a top speed of 12mph (19km/h). Some cars were built for the company by the Elgin Sewing Machine & Bicycle Company. Early models had wooden spoked wheels, but by 1900 a runabout was offered with wire wheels. Manufacture was removed to Hoboken, New Jersey, with sales office in New York City, 'to find more wealthy buyers' the company said. They offered no fewer than 21 body styles, from the runabout at $1500 to an 8-seater omnibus at $3500, but were out of business by 1902.

NG

AMERICAN ENTERPRISES (US) c.1952

American Enterprises, Baltimore, Maryland.

This company made an early fibreglass body kit to fit MG-TC and TD chassis. The envelope-style body featured a tilt-forward nose and a large, rectangular grill.

HP

AMERICAN FIAT (US) 1910–1918

Fiat Automobile Co., Poughkeepsie, New York.

The American Fiat was unusual in that, unlike other US-built versions of European cars such as Berliet and Mercedes, one model was made which had no European equivalents. The company was American-financed, and practically all components were made at Poughkeepsie. However, the Italian company received royalties on every American Fiat built. The first cars were delivered in the summer of 1910, and up to the end of the 1911 season there was just one model, the 5.7-litre 4-cylinder Tipo 54. For 1912 it was joined by the 8.6-litre 6-cylinder Tipo 56, the largest American Fiat and the only one to have no equivalent made at Turin. It was an impressive and expensive car, on a 135in (3426mm) wheelbase and selling at prices from $5000 for a tourer to $6100 for a landaulette. It was made up to 1916. Other American Fiats included the 4.4-litre Tipo 53 and the 9-litre Tipo 55, a 4-cylinder car with a shorter wheelbase than the slightly smaller engined Tipo 56. For the final 1917/18 season this was the only model listed. From 1914 onwards, many American Fiats had the pear-shaped radiator adopted at Turin, though the Mercedes shape was still available. In theory American Fiats could not be exported outside the United States, to protect the Italian company's markets elsewhere. However, a batch of 50 Tipo 55s with armoured car bodies destined for Czarist Russia was detained in England in 1917 because of the Russian revolution, rebodied and sold in 1920 as 'new 40/50s'. American Fiat production ended in March 1918 when the factory was sold to Rochester-Duesenberg who moved the machinery to their plant at Elizabeth, New Jersey, for the manufacture of aero engines.

NG

AMERICAN FIBER CRAFT (US) 1981–c.1984

American Fiber Craft, Cupertino, California.

The Aquila was one of the better-looking kit car bodies designed for the VW chassis, as it had been inspired by the BMW Turbo show car of 1972. The Aquila was a low, sleek coupé with gull-wing doors and a lowered floorpan, providing more room for tall drivers. In 1982, an electric power package was introduced which used a 20hp motor, powered by a 96v battery pack. Range was 45–50 miles.

HP

AMERICAN FIBERBODIES (US) 1994 to date

1994–1998 American Fiberbodies International, Xenia, Ohio.

1998 to date American Fiberglass International, Xenia, Ohio.

This kit car manufacturer made a wide variety of kits. The AFI 5000S was a Lamborghini Countach replica based on Pontiac Fiero running gear. In addition to the Fiero chassis, a special tubular frame was offered that used a longitudinally-mounted V8 with a Porsche or ZF transaxle. AFI also advertised a variation that would accept the BMW V12. Their second car was a Ferrari F40 replica called the AFI 40 Euro Coupé which was based on the same chassis. In 1998 they changed their name to American Fiberglass International and introduced Cobra, Lamborghini Diablo, Ferrari Testarossa and Ferrari F-50 replicas to their line-up. All were available in kit or assembled form.

HP

AMERICAN FIBERGLASS (US) c.1990

American Fiberglass, Fort Lauderdale, Florida.

Not to let a good project go to waste, this company bought the MERA moulds and re-introduced it as the 308AF/GT. This was a Ferrari 308 GTB replica for the Pontiac Fiero chassis. AFI added a convertible version as well. Unlike the Mera, which was always sold completed, the 308AF/GT was only available as a kit.

HP

AMERICAN JUNIOR (US) 1916–1920

American Motor Vehicle Co., Lafayette, Indiana.

This was a very small 2-seater powered by a single-cylinder Davis Motor Wheel at the rear, in the manner of the later SMITH FLYER and BRIGGS & STRATTON

1914 American Fiat Type 55 tourer.
ELLIOTT KAHN

buckboards. Unlike these, though, it had a bonnet at the front. Priced at only $160 it was claimed to be suitable for adults as well as children, though it seemed to be aimed mainly at the latter. The makers also offered a genuine buckboard powered by the Smith Motor Wheel, but soon sold the whole design to the A.O. Smith Co. who sold it as the Smith Flyer. In 1918 American Motor Vehicle offered a roadster with a 10/12hp 4-cylinder engine marketed under the name Greyhound.

NG

AMERICAN JUVENILE (US) 1906–1907

American Metal Wheel & Auto Co., Toledo, Ohio.

As the name implies this was a child's car, an electrically-powered 2-seater with a box body and wheelbase of only 41in (1041mm). Top speed was 10mph (16km/h) and the price was a hefty $800, too high for any but the most indulgent parents.

NG

AMERICAN LAFRANCE (US) 1907–1914

American LaFrance Fire Engine Co., Elmira, New York.

America's best-known fire engine maker made a few passenger cars which were called 'chief's cars'. Their production, such as it was, was just a continuation of the estimated half-dozen cars which were built by the company's earlier title, the International Fire Engine Company, and which carried the LAFRANCE badge. Unlike the earlier cars, of which both chain-and shaft-drive cars were completed, the American LaFrance cars were exclusively shaft-driven. Of them, at least two and possibly more, were built as roadsters and used by fire chiefs, the others presumably being made to special order for officers of the American LaFrance company. The cars were well-designed, carefully built, very fast and very expensive. One chief's car survives, but the numerous so-called roadsters around today have been converted from fire engines.

KM

AMERICAN MATHIS *see* MATHIS

AMERICAN MERCEDES *see* MERCEDES

AMERICAN MICROCAR (US) 1979–c.1981

American Microcar Inc., Farmingdale, New York.

Also known as the Tri-Ped, the American Microcar was an extremely basic 2-seater runabout with a single front wheel. It was little more than a 3-wheeled moped with a roll cage and windscreen; snap-on doors/side panels and roof were optional. Both 49cc petrol and electric models were offered, the latter boasting a range of 30 miles (48km) at up to 20mph (32km/h).

CR

1969 American Motors AMX coupé.
NATIONAL MOTOR MUSEUM

1979 American Microcar 49cc 3-wheeler.
NATIONAL MOTOR MUSEUM

AMERICAN MORS see MORS

AMERICAN MOTORS (US) 1968–1987

American Motors Corp., Kenosha, Wisconsin.

American Motors was founded in May 1954, as a merger between HUDSON and NASH, and cars continued to be marketed under both names until the 1958 season, when they were renamed RAMBLER. Ten years later came the first car which was not sold as a Rambler. This was the Javelin, a 4-seater sports coupé aimed at the pony car market dominated by Ford's Mustang and Chevrolet's Camaro. The AMC Javelin was offered with a 3802cc six or V8s of 4752 or 5620cc, the latter with 4-barrel carburettor and dual exhausts. The Javelin sold 55,124 units in its first year, but the figures dropped after that, down to 26,184 in 1972. AMC dropped the Javelin in 1974 because it could not meet Federal bumper standards without a costly redesign. A shorter derivative of the Javelin was offered from mid–1968 to the end of the 1970 season under the name AMX. It was 12in shorter in wheelbase and, unlike other pony cars, seated only two passengers. To fit its more sporty image it was not offered with the 6-cylinder engine, only two V8s, 5620 and 6390cc, giving 280 and 315bhp. The AMX gave Corvettes a hard time on the race track, and with development could have been a great car. Unfortunately it did not sell well, only 19,134, compared with 236,379 Javelins, and AMC president William Luneburg complained that it was cluttering up the line.

Meanwhile AMC was pursuing its philosophy of making different cars from the Big Three. Company president Robert Evans said 'We can't be just another pretty face on the road - we've got to be different'. April 1970 saw the arrival of the Gremlin, a stubby little coupé on a 96in (2436mm) wheelbase with a sharply sloping hatchback rear mated to the front of the compact Hornet. *Car & Driver* said of its styling 'It's brisk and efficient and it borrows from no one'. Powered by a 3802cc six, it was the first of the sub-compact cars, followed by Ford's Pinto and Chevrolet's Vega five months later. The Gremlin was made up to 1978, when it was available with a 1983cc 4-cylinder Audi engine, as well as the 3802 and 4228cc sixes. Total Gremlin production was 700,000. Even more different than the Gremlin was the Pacer, conceived as a roomy small car, 'the first wide small car'. The bonnet was very short, as it was designed for a Wankel rotary engine, and the 2-door body was bulbous with an enormous glass area. Richard Teague's styling earned few plaudits; comments included 'a football on wheels' and 'a great big frog'. The GM-built rotary never materialised, and the Pacer went into production in 1975 with AMC's old 88bhp 3802cc six, which made for a heavier car with inferior performance and handling. A 130bhp 4982cc V8 was an option from 1978, and a station wagon joined the coupé in 1977, but the Pacer never sold well and was dropped in 1980, after just over 280,000 had been made. In addition to the smaller cars, AMC made the full-size Ambassador sedans, inherited from the Rambler range, up to 1974, and also the compact Hornet and medium-sized Rebel, which became the Matador in 1971, with three body styles and six engine options, from the 3802cc six to a 5900cc V8. The V8s were dropped after 1979, and in 1980 AMC launched a range of 4-wheel drive cars called Eagles, with 2474cc 4- or 4228cc 6-cylinder engines and made in sedan and station wagon forms, joined by a 3-door hatchback for 1981. They were America's first regular cars, as opposed to Jeep-type vehicles, to have 4-wheel drive. In 1978 Renault began to buy into AMC, acquiring a 46.9 per cent interest in 1982. AMC dealers sold the Renault 5 under the name Le Car, and also the Fuego coupé, and in 1982 the Renault 9 sedan and 11 hatchback went into production at Kenosha, under the names Alliance and Encore. They sold well to start with, more than 208,000 in 1984, and outsold the Eagles by ten to one. They were joined in 1985 by a convertible Alliance, which was unique to the US, and at $10,295 was the cheapest American-built convertible. However, quality problems caused sales of the Renault models to drop, and in 1987 both AMC and Renault were in serious trouble. A saviour appeared in the form of Chrysler's Lee Iacocca who bought AMC for $600m, largely to obtain the lucrative Jeep side of the business. The only survivor from the old AMC range was the 4x4 Eagle which disappeared after the take-over along with the Renaults, apart from the Canadian-built 25-based Premier which Chrysler marketed under the name Eagle. They also sold the French-built Renault 21 as the Eagle Medaillon (*see* EAGLE (x)).

NG

Further Reading
American Motors – The Last Independent, Patrick R. Foster,
Krause Publications, 1993.
'Change of an Image: behind the scenes at AMX and Javelin', Robert C. Ackerson,
Automobile Quarterly, Vol. 19, No. 1.

AMERICAN NAPIER *see* NAPIER

AMERICAN POPULAIRE (US) 1904–1905
American Automobile & Power Co., Lawrence, Massachusetts;
Sanford, Maine.
This was a 4-seater touring car in which the front seats folded back to give access to those at the rear. The engine was a piston-valve four designed by Edward O. Mosher. The prototype and first production cars were made at Lawrence, and later ones in a new factory at Sanford, but by April 1905 this had been sold to the Maine Alpaca Company and used for weaving.
NG

AMERICAN POWER (US) 1899–1900
American Power Carriage Co., Boston, Massachusetts.
This company made a single-cylinder runabout with a top speed of 25mph (40km/h). Not more than 15 were completed.
NG

AMERICAN ROADSTERS 427SC (US) c.1994
American Roadsters, Tempe, Arizona.
A Cobra replica built on a ladder frame with Mustang II running gear was the sole product of this kit manufacturer. Sold in kit or assembled form.
HP

AMERICAN SIMPLEX (US) 1906–1910; AMPLEX (US) 1910–1913
1906–1910 Simplex Motor Car Co., Mishawaka, Indiana.
1910–1912 Amplex Motor Car Co., Mishawaka, Indiana.
1913 Amplex Manufacturing Co., Mishawaka, Indiana.
This car used 2-stroke engines for most of its life, starting with a 40hp twin in 1906, and progressing to a 6.8-litre 30/50hp four in 1908. They were expensive cars, priced up to $5400 for a landaulette. In 1910 the name of car and company was changed to Amplex to avoid confusion with the better-known Simplex made in New York City. A 40hp 4-stroke poppet-valve six was offered for 1913, and a sleeve-valve version was announced but never made. Two well-known names showed short-lived interest in Amplex in its last days; William Wrigley of chewing gum fame bought the company in 1914 and sold it two years later to razor blade magnate William Gillette, who considered making the sleeve-valve-engined car. Possibly one prototype was built, but he then made the engine alone for sale to other companies under the name Wilmo; this venture lasted only to 1917.
NG

AMERICAN STEAM CAR (US) 1926–1942
American Steam Automobile Co., West Newton, Massachusetts.
The American Steam Car was built by Thomas S. Derr, a graduate and former faculty member of the Massachusetts Institute of Technology. Derr's initial contribution to steam car enthusiasts was in the rebuilding of Stanley Steam Cars, many of which were still in operation in the Greater Boston area. In addition, he offered complete service and repairs to these cars. Derr subsequently perfected a V4 poppet-valve engine and boiler which he introduced as the American Steam Car, and which consisted of Hudson chassis, but with the condenser badge and hubcaps identifying the cars accordingly. Derr completed a number of these cars for the dwindling market of steam car aficionados. At least one of the American Steam Cars was exported to England, where it was featured in the automotive press.
KM

AMERICAN STEAMER (US) 1922–1924
American Steam Truck Co., Chicago, Illinois.
The American Steam Car debuted in the late spring of 1922 as a companion product to the American Steam Truck. The car itself was a continuation of an experimental unit which had been completed six years earlier. Actually, there

1971 American Motors Gremlin coupé.
NATIONAL MOTOR MUSEUM

1979 American Motors Pacer hatchback.
NATIONAL MOTOR MUSEUM

1912 (American Simplex) Amplex tourer.
JOHN A. CONDE

was a marked difference between the prototype which had been widely publicised in the automotive press, and the finished product, the latter sporting a condenser similar in appearance to the radiator on the contemporary Lincoln. Listed price for the touring car, probably the only body style available, was $1650. The company initially had planned a complete array of both open- and closed-body options, but the quoted price of the touring model implies that only the lone touring type was technically available. Production is believed to have consisted of 16 units before the venture folded.
KM

AMERICAN THUNDER TRYKE (US) 1992 to date
American Thunder Tryke Inc., Sante Fe, New Mexico.
This kit car was a strange 3-wheeler that looked like a prop from a science-fiction movie. It combined a motorcycle front end with an automobile engine and rear axle. The first model used a 7400cc Chevrolet engine and a General Motors automatic transmission. Later models slimmed down with a 5700cc Chevy and either automatic or manual transmissions. Available ready to ride or in kit form.
HP

AMERICAN TRI-CAR (US) 1912
Tri-Car Company of America, Denver, Colorado.
As its name implied, this was a 3-wheeler with chain drive to the single rear wheel, with epicyclic transmission and powered by a 10/12hp 2-cylinder engine mounted under a Renault-type bonnet. Like Henry Ford, they called their first car the Model A, but the makers did not last out the year, and there were no succeeding models. In fact, a Denver resident said that only one car was made.
NG

AMERICAN UNDERSLUNG see AMERICAN (iv)

AMERICAN VOITURETTE see CARNATION

AMERICAN WALTHAM (US) 1898–1899
American Waltham Manufacturing Co., Waltham, Massachusetts.
This was a light steam car with 2-cylinder engine under the seat, tiller steering, and single-chain drive to the rear axle. The makers were better known for their Comet bicycles, made for a number of years before and after the cars. They should not be confused with the Waltham Steamer made by John Piper and George Tinker from 1898 to 1902 and sometimes known as the Piper-Tinker.
NG

AMES (US) 1910–1915
1910–1911 Carriage Woodstock Co., Owensboro, Kentucky.
1912–1915 Ames Motor Car Co., Owensboro, Kentucky.
Frederick Ames was a carriage builder who added cars to his range in 1910 with a conventional 30hp 4-cylinder tourer, adding a roadster and a 40hp tourer on a longer wheelbase the following year. A 50hp 6-cylinder was listed for 1913 only, and the 1914 40hp roadster was called the Kentucky Thoroughbred. After car production ended, Ames made bodies for Model T Fords, and from 1922 concentrated on upholstered furniture, in which business the Ames Corporation continued until 1970.
NG

AMES-DEAN (US) 1909–1910
Ames-Dean Carriage Co., Jackson, Michigan.
A builder of horse-drawn carriages, Ames-Dean announced that they would make 200 high-wheeler motor buggies. It is not known if they completed this many.
NG

A.M.G. (S) 1903–c.1905
AB Motorfabriken, Gothenburg.
This company, founded in 1897, began their involvement in cars by importing the GEORGES RICHARD from France. They took out a licence to manufacture these, but also built a prototype of their own powered by an air-cooled 2-cylinder Fafnir engine. About ten production cars followed, with locally-made wooden bodies. One survived in regular use until 1928.
NG

AMG (US) 1992 to date
AM General, South Bend, Indiana.
The AMG Hummer was the civilian version of the Humvee military multipurpose vehicle. Due to the publicity that the Humvee received during the televised Gulf War in 1990, AMG decided to launch a modified version for street use. Although bucket seats, seat belts, roll-up windows, keyed ignition, optional air conditioning, steel doors, revised lighting, improved hardtop and other civilian niceties were added, the interior was still stark and military-like. There were four versions, a 2-seater hard top, four door utility, 4-seater hard top and a 4-seater open version with a canvas top. Price was $40,000 to $45,000 when introduced. The 1992 Hummer used a 6200cc diesel engine with a 3-speed automatic transmission and all-wheel drive. This engine was upgraded in 1994 and an improved overdrive transmission was added. A 5700cc Chevrolet petrol engine was optional in 1995, and the steering boxes were strengthened. A more powerful turbo diesel was introduced the following year, and in 1997 it replaced the petrol-powered engine. However, at 6200lb (2818kg) curb weight and with only 195hp, the Hummer was one of the slowest vehicles on the road. In1999 production of the Hummer was running at about 3500 a year, of which 1000 were for civilian use, and the rest for the military. The design was taken over by GM at the beginning of 2000, and a new, smaller Hummer was planned for a 2002 introduction.
HP

AMHERST (CDN) 1911–1912
Canadian Two in One Capital Auto Co., Amherstburg, Ontario.
The Amherst 40 was a conventional 40hp 4-cylinder tourer, but with the unusual feature of a demountable body behind the front seats so that it could be converted into a light truck. It was financed by Detroit capital, but the backers lost enthusiasm before production in a brand new factory could start, and only three cars were completed. The factory later became the home of Brock Motors Ltd who made a single example of the BROCK Six in 1921.
NG

AMILCAR (F) 1921–1939
1921–1927 Sté Nouvelle pour l'Automobile Amilcar, St Denis, Seine.
1927–1935 Sté Anonyme Française de l'Automobile, St Denis, Seine.
1935–1939 Sté Financière pour l'Automobile, Boulogne-sur-Seine.
Together with Salmson, the Amilcar was the quintessential small French sports car of the 1920s, and like its compatriot the company moved on to heavier touring cars in the next decade. The name was an amalgam of the two backers' names, Joseph Lamy and Emile Akar, though the first car was designed by Edmond Moyet who worked for Citroën. The driving spirit was a Le Zèbre employee and former Berliet test driver, André Morel, and the first two prototypes of Moyet's design were called Borie, after Borie & Co., makers of the Le Zèbre. Further finance came from Le Zèbre dealers, who seemed keener to back the new design than the staider cars they were already selling. Moyet's design was a small tourer with an 18bhp 903cc 4-cylinder side-valve engine, a basic lightweight car with quarter-elliptic springs and no differential. This was the Type CC. Inevitably it was taken to hill climbs, and Morel's successes persuaded the cautious Lamy that it would not be irresponsible to add a sporting model to the range. This was the CS with a slightly larger engine of 985cc and 23bhp, 5bhp more than the CC. A longer chassis, the CO, had a 1004cc engine and was suitable for touring bodies. These could carry a 3-seater body, which, with the sporting 2-seaters, were made by Charles Duval of Paris. The best-known body was probably the Petit Sport, with staggered seating for two, but from 1923 there was also a touring car, the 1485cc Type E. This was also made under licence by Le Zèbre from 1923 to 1925. Unlike the smaller French sporting makes, such as Rally and Sénéchal, Amilcar made their own engines. By the end of 1924 they had made over 15,000 cars. In 1925 they built 3700 cars, moving into larger premises and investing heavily in new machinery.
1924 saw a new model, which became one of their best known. This was the CGS, with 1074cc 30bhp engine, pressure lubrication and front wheel brakes. These cars, which became very popular in England and gained many competition successes, had a top speed of 75mph (121km/h). In 1927 came the CGSs, or Surbaisse, with a lowered chassis and radiator, and usually sold with cycle-type wings. It looked a much more modern car, though made alongside the CGS. Amilcar also offered several touring chassis, including the Type E enlarged to 1578cc in 1925 and to 1875cc in 1926, the 1188cc Type L (1928) and the 1266cc Type M (1929–1933). The peak production year was 1926 when some 1200 employees built around 4800 cars. Amilcars were assembled in Italy by the Compagnia Generale Automobili of Rome from 1925 to 1927, and by S.I.L.V.A. of Verona from 1927 to 1928, as the Amilcar Italiana, and made in Germany as the Pluto (1924–1927) and in Austria as the Grofri (1922–1927). They were sold in the USA by Maybach Motors of New York, alongside the massive German cars.
Amilcar moved towards more cylinders with the 6-cylinder 1089cc twin-ohc supercharged CO racing car. The engine was used in a production car called the C6, of which 50 were sold to private customers in 1926. However 1927 saw a downturn in the company's fortunes, caused by falling demand and over expenditure in the competition department. The latter was radically cut back, Morel left, Lamy and Akar both withdrew their support, and the company was reorganised under the bland name Société Anonyme Française de l'Automobile. Although the CGS and CGSs were continued into 1929, Amilcars became predominantly touring cars from the late 1920s. A straight-8, the C8 was introduced in 1929, initially of 1875cc on the prototype, enlarged to 1994cc in 1930 and to

2330cc in 1931 (C8bis). It had a 5-bearing crankshaft, single ohc, 4-speed gearbox and carried some very attractive coachwork, but most of the bodies were too heavy for the 58bhp engine, and performance was unexciting. The straight-8 was dropped in 1933, after 350 had been made. The year of the C8's demise saw a return to small cars, with the tiny Type C 5CV, with an 850cc 4-cylinder side-valve engine and 2-seater bodywork. Capacity was enlarged to 877cc on the 1934 models and to 977cc for 1935, when a 4-seater saloon and cabriolet were available, as well as a 2-seater roadster. Total production of all the Type Cs was 2455. The range also included the 1244cc 7CV Type M3, descended from the Type Ms of the 1920s. It had a 4-cylinder side-valve engine and similar lines to the Type C, though a longer wheelbase permitted 4-door coachwork. Both the Types C and M3 were discontinued in 1936, being joined the previous year by a new more up-market model, the Pégase. This was a competitor for the Salmson S4 or the smaller Delages and Delahayes, and originally had a 2-litre ohv engine designed by Grillot who had been responsible for the straight-8s, and built by Janvier. Announced in 1934, this proved too expensive to make, and was replaced by the 2150cc engine used in the Type 134 Delahaye, the first time a production Amilcar had an engine from an outside supplier. A Cotal gearbox was an option. The prototype Pégase at the 1934 Paris Salon had headlights mounted in the top of the radiator and a streamlined body with no running boards, but production models had conventionally-mounted lights and running boards. Bodies were quite handsome 2- and 4-door saloons and a cabriolet, but they did not stand out in an overcrowded market, and only about 200 were made, up to the end of 1937. There was also a competition model with a 2470cc Grillot-designed engine which had some success in sports car racing. The company was reorganised again in 1935 and moved to much smaller premises at Boulogne-sur-Seine. For 1938 a completely new Amilcar was announced, helped by finance from Hotchkiss who had bought the firm. Named the Compound, and sold in Britain as the Hotchkiss Ten, it was designed by Jean Grégoire and had unitary construction in Alpax alloy, a 4-speed synchromesh gearbox ahead of the engine driving the front wheels, all independent suspension with torsion bars at the rear, and rack-and-pinion steering. The engine was a side-valve 1185cc four whose identical dimensions to those of the Hillman Minx has led some historians to say that it was based on the British unit. There is no reason to suppose this, and it was almost certainly an in-house design in the tradition of earlier Amilcar fours. In the summer of 1939 it gained overhead valves, but few of these were made. The 2-door saloon and cabriolet bodies looked not unlike those of the Type GS Hotchkiss, both being styled by Vinciguerra. There was also a 2-seater roadster, and total production was 681. Hotchkiss planned a more roomy 5-seater successor to the Compound after the war, but the French government decided that there were enough cars in this field already, and decreed that Hotchkiss must make large 6-cylinder cars only. However, the Compound's ohv engine was used by Imperia in Belgium for a few years.

NG

Further Reading
Le Grande Livre Amilcar, Gilles Foumier, Retroviseur, 1994.
'Amilcar – Red Ones and Blue Ones and Tooled Aluminium Jobs',
Stan Grayson, *Automobile Quarterly,* Vol. 3, No. 1.

AMIOT-PENEAU (F) 1898–1902

L'Avant Train Amiot et Peneau, Asnieres, Seine.

The *avant train* system of motorising a horse-drawn vehicle was popular in France at the turn of the century. Among the first was the Amiot, which appeared in 1897 as a crude 4-wheeled vehicle which could be attached to a horse carriage. The Amiot-Peneau which succeeded it was a slightly more sophisticated 2-wheeled *avant train* which could be fitted to a variety of brakes and broughams, as well as to commercial vehicles. Petrol versions used Augé engines, and electric models used motors by Patin.

NG

AMOR (D) 1924–1925

Amor Automobilbau GmbH, Cologne.

This was one of many German light cars of the early 1920s. It was powered by a 4/16PS 4-cylinder engine, and sales were restricted largely to the local district.

HON

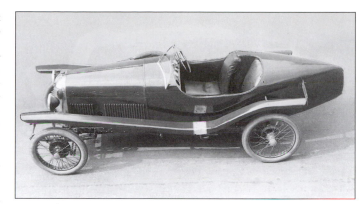
1924 Amilcar GS sports car.
NATIONAL MOTOR MUSEUM

1927 Amilcar CGS sports car.
NATIONAL MOTOR MUSEUM

1936 Amilcar Pégase 14CV drophead coupé.
NICK GEORGANO/NATIONAL MOTOR MUSEUM

1939 Amilcar Compound 7CV convertible saloon.
NICK GEORGANO/NATIONAL MOTOR MUSEUM

1965 Amphicar cabriolet.
NATIONAL MOTOR MUSEUM

1967 Anadol 1.2-litre saloon.
NATIONAL MOTOR MUSEUM

AMORE CIMBRIA (US) 1978–1990
Amore Cars, Milwaukee, Wisconsin.
The Cimbria was one of the most stunning kit cars ever built. The design was clean and striking, without the over-ornamentation common to many kits. Originally designed to fit the Volkswagen floorpan, it later acquired a tube frame for mounting V6 and V8 transverse engines, along with 4-wheel disc brakes. The Cimbria was a sales success, and in 1984 it was joined by the Viper 2000, a deluxe version of the Cimbria sold only in fully assembled form. Equipped with a Porsche 930 Turbo engine, the Viper 2000 cost $62,000 in 1985. Other engines were available at lower prices. In 1990 the Cimbria project was bought by NEREIA Yachts, where it was still in production in 1999.
HP

AMPÈRE (F) 1906–1909
Sté des Éts. Ampère, Billancourt, Seine.
The Ampère was powered by a 10/16hp 4-cylinder engine which had an electrically-operated clutch transmitting power to the gearbox. Its appearance was very similar to that of a Renault, with dashboard radiator and an identical bonnet. It is possible that it was a Renault fitted with the Ampère electric clutch.
NG

AMPHICAR (D) 1961–1968
1961–1962 Deutsche Industrie-Werke, Lubeck-Schlutup.
1962–1968 Deutsche Waggon- und Maschinenfabriken GmbH, Berlin.
This amphibious car was designed by Hans Trippel who had built amphibious cars under his own name before and during the war. He obtained the support of the Deutsche Industrie-Werke for his project, which was originally called the Eurocar. It had a chassisless steel 2-door cabriolet body with electrically-welded joints and was powered by a 1147cc Triumph Herald engine mounted at the rear and driving the rear wheels. Two propellers were activated for driving when the car was in the water. Top speed was about 6½ knots (7mph or 11km/h) in the water,

and 68mph (109km/h) on land. Steering in the water was by using the front wheels as rudimentary rudders. Of about 800 cars made, 600 were exported to the USA, and the rest sold around Europe. Two Amphicars crossed the Channel in 1962, though they ended up one towing the other.
HON
Further Reading
'Where the highway doesn't go', John A. Heilig, *Automobile Quarterly*, Vol. 35, No. 1.

AMPLAS *see* SN1, LEMAZONE, and PULSAR

AMPLEX *see* AMERICAN SIMPLEX

AMS-STERLING *see* STERLING-NEW YORK

AMT PIRANHA (US) 1966–1968
AMT Corporation, Phoenix, Arizona.
The Piranha was the big brother to the millions of plastic model cars sold by AMT and, like a model car, it had a plastic body. Conceived by the Marbon Chemical Division of Borg Warner, it used fibreglass and Cycolac ABS thermoplastic for both body and chassis. AMT obtained the production rights from Marbon and built six production models plus two race cars. A modified Piranha was used in the popular TV show *The Man From U.N.C.L.E.* The body was very futuristic, with gull-wing doors. Running gear was Corvair in the street and road-race cars, but a Chrysler 7000cc Hemi V8 was used in a one-off dragster version. AMT also sold a model of the Piranha. AMT dropped the project after they were unable to build them for appreciably less than the sale price of $7000. Ironically, they were only sold in fully-assembled form. In 1971 the Piranha body popped up in ads for Sportsland Unlimited, a division of ALLIED INDUSTRIES. The plastic chassis was gone and it had been adapted to Volkswagen running gear.
HP

AMX *see* AMERICAN MOTORS

A.N. (F) c.1921–1923
Automobiles Allain et Niguet, Kremlin-Bicetre, Seine.
This was a cyclecar powered by a 994cc water-cooled V-twin engine, with 2-speed gearbox and shaft drive. Lighting was by acetylene, very antiquated for the 1920s.
NG

ANADOL (TR) 1966–1986
Otosan Otomobil Sanayii, Istanbul.
Reliant specialised in planning and setting up car factories in countries without an indigenous motor industry. Having established Autocars of Haifa in Israel, makers of the SABRA, they did the same thing in Turkey with the Anadol. Originally known as the Reliant FW5, the Ogle-styled 5-seater fibreglass saloon was powered by a 1198cc Ford Anglia Super engine, and had front disc brakes. The prototype was driven to Istanbul in December 1965, and was named Anadol after a national competition. The first Otosan-built car was completed on 7 December 1966, and by November 1970 10,000 had been made, with annual production reaching 5000, close to the factory capacity of 6000. A Ford 1300cc engine was standardised in 1969, and a 1600cc engine was added to the range in 1974, as was a 2-door coupé and, later, a station wagon. However, production declined as more cars were imported; in 1982 only 407 cars were made, and in 1986 the Anadol was replaced on the production lines by the Otosan Ford Taunus 1.6, which used the body of the 1982 Cortina with a 1.6-litre Ford engine.
NG

ANAHUAC (US) 1922
Frontenac Motor Corp., Indianapolis, Indiana.
The Anahuac was an export car built on consignment for Compania Automobiles Anahuac of Mexico City, which planned to continue production in Mexico. It never happened. The four Anahuacs completed were 4-cylinder cars with a wheelbase of 115in (2919mm), all identical touring cars, weighing 2450lb (1114kg). The car was designed in the style of a contemporary Polish automobile.
KM

ANASAGASTI (RA) 1911–1915

Horacio Anasagasti & Cia., Buenos Aires.

Even though in 1909 Ing. Horacio Anasagasti had not made a single car, he had already proclaimed himself as a tractor and automobile manufacturer. During a later trip to Paris he contacted the Ballot brothers, who agreed to ship several of their 12hp and 15hp engines and also a set of wooden patterns of castings which they hoped Anasagasti could reproduce in Buenos Aires. Other French firms supplied additional components, and soon cars started to be built at the 1670 Alvear Avenue workshop. A prototype with 12hp engine was driven by Le Patron himself in the Rosario-Cordoba–Rosario Rally of 17 September 1911. The car was abandoned in Cordoba with mechanical trouble.

Production Anasagastis made their appearence in 1912. After a while the Ballot engines were dropped in favour of Picker-Janvier units. Anasagasti was determined to transform his scissors-and-paste operations into a truly Argentinian car, but this proved very difficult with the limited mechanical know-how available at the time in South America.

Anasagasti cars competed in Europe, as their creator believed that no matter how much it might cost, racing would improve the breed – and also sales. His advertisements, published in the Argentine press in 1913 and 1914, stressed the racing background of the cars. But sales were unspectacular and the writing was on the wall: when World War I broke out in Europe and the flow of parts from France came to a halt, production stopped. Somewhere around the middle of 1915 Anasagasti became a lost cause of motoring. Some 30-odd cars were made. Of these, apparently only two survive, one in private hands, the other belonging to the Argentine Air Force, which received it new, as a gift, from Horacio Anasagasti himself.

ACT

ANCHOR (US) 1910–1911

Anchor Motor Car Co., Cincinnati, Ohio.

The product of a carriage builder, the Anchor was a short-lived and very conventional touring car powered by a 35hp 4-cylinder T-head engine and selling for $1850.

NG

ANDERHEGGEN (NL) 1901–1902

Ferdinand Anderheggen, Amsterdam.

At the turn of the century Ferdinand Anderheggen built a prototype of a motorcar. That light car pleased him so much that he decided to build a second one in the construction workshop of the Willink brothers. This car was a *vis-á-vis* model: 4 seats placed opposite each other so that passengers could easily have a conversation. It was a simple construction, with gear-shifting by the help of belts that worked like two gears. The 4hp engine was a French-made water-cooled single-cylinder, built by Abeille. Anderheggen registered his gearbox system with chain-driven gears and tried to make arrangements with a French manufacturer to build it under licence, but without any results. In 1901 the Konings machine factory at Swalmen in the province of Limburg started building the Anderheggen construction under licence. Anderheggen himself became an employee in the factory to help assembly and to improve his design, including the special epicyclic gearbox. In 1902 the first registrations became a reality, but after a short time the company decided that car manufacturing did not bring any positive financial results, and they stopped production.

FBV

ANDERSEN (GB) 1985 to date

Andersen Motor Company, Liverpool.

The Cub was a fairly close Mini Moke replica with a steel chassis and galvanised welded steel body panels. The Mini donated its mechanicals, although any A-series engine/gearbox could be used, including Metro and Allegro. Long-wheelbase and even 6-wheeled versions were on offer, and the car was sold in kit form and also complete (mostly for export). CLASSIC REPLICAS also marketed a version, later called the Mule.

CR

ANDERSON (i) (US) 1906

Anderson Machine Co., Bedford, Indiana.

This was a runabout on solid tyres powered by an air-cooled 2-cylinder engine. Announced in October 1906, a month later the company was taken over by Fred Postal who made another high-wheeler under his own name.

NG

c.1912 Anasagasti tourer.
ALVARO CASAL TATLOCK

1909 Anderson (iii) Model B high-wheeler.
NATIONAL MOTOR MUSEUM

ANDERSON (ii) (AUS) 1906

W. Anderson & Sons Pty Ltd, Richmond, Victoria.

This foundry and engineering works was established in 1870 and made machinery for industry and mines, as well as the huge winding pulleys for Melbourne's cable tram system. It made a 16hp car in 1906 for its own use, but the publicity was intended to attract further orders. Apparently none were forthcoming, but the firm was still operating in the 1980s.

MG

ANDERSON (iii) (US) 1907–1910

Anderson Carriage Mfg Co., Anderson, Indiana.

This was a typical high-wheeler buggy powered by a 12 or 14hp air-cooled 2-cylinder engine with friction transmission and solid tyres. Standard wheel size was 36 inches, but the makers offered one model with smaller wheels and pneumatic tyres. Prices were $500 and $650 respectively.

NG

ANDERSON (iv) (US) 1916–1925

The Anderson Motor Co., Rock Hill, South Carolina.

The best-known of the four Anderson marques, and the most successful of all cars made in the Southern United States, the Anderson was made by a former carriage company founded in 1889. John Gary Anderson's first car venture was the ROCK HILL of 1910, but this was simply a NORWALK renamed, and lasted barely a year. The car that bore his own name was designed by Joseph Anglada (also responsible for the LIBERTY(i)) and was a medium-sized machine with a 3.7-litre Continental 6/40 engine and offered with tourer,

1920 Anderson (iv) tourer.
NATIONAL MOTOR MUSEUM

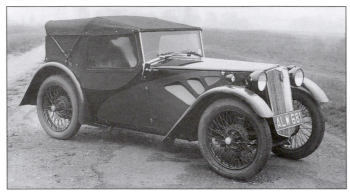

1933 André V6 sports car.
M.J.WORTHINGTON-WILLIAMS

roadster or racer bodies. These were built by Anderson from oak and ash grown in the company's own woods. Unusual colour combinations gave the conventional-looking cars some distinction, and they also traded on local patriotism with their slogan 'A Little Bit Higher in Price but Made in Dixie'. Wartime production included trailers for carrying aircraft, but they still made 811 cars in 1918. Closed bodies were listed from 1919, when there were two sedans, a 'convertible sedan' and an 'ultra-convertible sedan', the latter costing $100 less. The convertible 3-seater dickey seat was patented not only in the United States, but also in Great Britain, France, Italy, Canada, Japan, Argentina and New Zealand. Anderson sales were quite encouraging to start with, rising from 317 in 1916 to 1875 in 1923, their peak year. Most were sold locally, but they found buyers in northern states as well, and were sold in Great Britain for a few years. For 1923 a smaller Continental engine was adopted, the 3.2-litre Model 6Y. These suffered seriously from cylinder-block warpage, and damaged Anderson's reputation. Like many other small firms, they were suffering from competition from big manufacturers like Buick, and the lure of 'made in Dixie' could not save the Anderson. Only 136 cars were made in 1925, and in September the factory closed down. The assets were sold in 1926 and the factory was empty for two years, after which it was used for textile manufacture. Total production was about 10,000 cars.

NG

Further Reading
'Nothin' finer in Carolina: the Anderson Motor Company', Ron Chepesink, *Automobile Quarterly*, Vol. 34, No. 3.

ANDERSON INDUSTRIES (US) c.1985

Anderson Industries Inc., Elkridge, Maryland.
In the 1950s and 1960s, many American dragsters used small fibreglass bodies to save weight and reduce aerodynamic drag. Among the most popular bodies were the 1932 Austin Bantam, the 1948 Fiat Topolino, and the 1948 Anglia. Anderson made kits based on these bodies, as well as the 1923 Ford Model T C-cab, 1926 Ford roadster, and the 1933–34 Ford roadster. All were intended to be built into hot rods with V8 power.

HP

ANDRÉ (GB) 1933–1934

T.B. André Ltd, London W11.
Despite its name, the André V6 had only two cylinders, using a 728cc V-twin J.A.P. engine which developed 28bhp, and a 4-speed gearbox. The front wheels were independently sprung by a single transverse leaf, and there were cantilever springs at the rear. It had a 2-seater sports body and a punt-type frame in which the floor of the body acted as a chassis. Only six were made. T.B. André was better known for sponsorship of the MARLBOROUGH (i), and for the manufacture of shock absorbers. The André car was built in a little factory near Notting Hill Gate underground station, which is now a London Electricity Board property.

NG

ANDRÉ PY (F) 1899

Cie des Automobiles du Sud Ouest.
This was a 3-wheeled voiturette with a superficial resemblance to a LÉON BOLLÉE, with tandem seating and a 3½hp horizontal single-cylinder engine. However, it differed in having front-wheel drive and rear-wheel steering.

NG

ANDREAS (D) 1900–1902

Sachsische Accumulatoren-Werke AG, Dresden.
A small number of electric cars designed by Dr Ernst Andreas were built for a short time.

HON

ANGELI (F) 1922–c.1927

Automobiles Angeli, Neuilly-Plaisance, Seine.
The Angeli, or Angely as it was sometimes spelt, was a small car powered by a 7hp 4-cylinder engine driving the front wheels, with the 4-speed gearbox between the engine and the radiator. It had independent suspension all round by double superimposed transverse leaf springs, which took the place of axles. When it was described in *The Motor* in April 1924, the prototype was said to have been around for two years and to have covered about 60,000 miles. It is not certain if any production models were made.

NG

ANGER see A.E.C.

ANGLADA (E) 1901–1904

Anglada, Puerto de Sta Maria, Cadiz.
Francisco Anglada Gallardo produced bicycles from 1896 and started with car production in 1901. He offered single-, 2- and 4-cylinder engines of 6, 10, 14, 18, 24 and 36hp, but only the smaller ones were definitely built. The first was a 2-seater with 6hp single-cylinder and tiller steering, with a round radiator looking like the Renault. The 2-cylinder 10hp was sold to Argentina and Uruguay, and King Alfonso XIII bought the big 4-cylinder 24 hp, with tonneau bodywork, shaft drive to the rear wheels, and brakes only on the rear wheels. Anglada closed his factory in 1904 due to financial problems and started a car repair shop in Madrid. He died in 1917 leaving 14 children.

VCM

ANGLO-DANE (DK) 1902–1917

H.C. Fredericksen, Copenhagen.
Fredericksen started in business by assembling bicycles from English parts, hence the name Anglo-Dane. When he began car manufacture he used a single-cylinder Belgian-built Kelecom engine in a light car with friction transmission based on that of the German MAURER UNION. He used a 4.5hp engine of his own design, also a single-cylinder, in later cars, with a double friction disc transmission giving 12 forward speeds. Later cars used 2-cylinder engines, but passenger car production was sporadic as Fredericksen concentrated increasingly on commercial vehicles. About 70 Anglo-Danes were made up to 1917, mostly commercials, after which the company combined with two others, JAN, and THRIGE, to form Triangel, which was well-known in the truck and bus field up to 1945.

NG

ANGLO-FRENCH see ROGER

ANGLO-SPHINX *see* SPHINX (i)

ANGUS *see* FULLER (i)

ANGUS-SANDERSON (GB) 1919–1927

1919–1921 Sir William Angus, Sanderson & Co., Birtley, Co. Durham.
1921–1927 Angus-Sanderson (1921) Ltd, Hendon, Middlesex.
The Angus family had been coachbuilders in Newcastle upon Tyne since the second half of the 18th century, and Sanderson was an apprentice with the firm, eventually becoming a partner and adding his name to the business. A branch based in Carlisle, Henry Angus, Sanderson Ltd, made a few Aster-powered cars in 1905–07, sold as SANDERSON-ASTER, and the Newcastle firm built a number of bodies for Armstrong-Whitworth, and 46 on Rolls-Royce Silver Ghost chassis between 1910 and 1914.

They planned to build complete cars before the end of World War I, and prototypes were running in December 1918. They had 2265cc 4-cylinder engines supplied by the London firm of Tylor, who also made lavatory cisterns as well as engines for London buses. Gearboxes, axles, steering gear and radiators (styled by Cecil Kimber, later founder of MG) came from Wrigley in Birmingham, and frames from Mechins of Glasgow. The bodies were, naturally, made by Angus-Sanderson themselves. Wood for these bodies came from the company's own forests. There were three body styles, tourer, open 2-seater and closed 4-seater coupé. In May 1919 engine capacity was increased to 2306cc and remained the same for the rest of the car's life.

Production began at Thomas Street, Newcastle, but in the summer of 1919 was moved out to a large site at Birtley, about 6 miles from the city centre, which had been built for munitions work during the war. It had a capacity of 20 cars per day, but never turned out more than 48 in a week, and often fewer than 30. Partly-completed bodies and chassis sat in the factory for up to a year, waiting for vital components to be delivered. Angus-Sanderson was under-capitalised, and in 1921 a new company was formed under the control of S.F. Edge. Fresh capital was raised, they bought their engine suppliers, Tylor, and moved to new premises at Hendon which had formerly housed the Grahame-White company, coachbuilders and cyclecar makers. In fact, about 300–500 cars were completed at Birtley under the new regime before the move to London. Bodywork was mostly made by J.E.B. Hall & Co. of Hammersmith, though a few were made by Mann Egerton of Norwich.

A 990cc 8hp light car of 1922–3 never progressed beyond the prototype stage, and production of the larger cars dwindled during the 1920s. By 1925 another reorganisation saw Angus-Sanderson come under the control of Tylor, a reversal of the previous position. The make's last year was 1927, when 4-wheel brakes were offered, pretty late compared with rival makes. Probably the cars had been assembled from existing parts for several years; they certainly could not have bought components from Wrigley after 1924, when William Morris acquired the firm for his own cars. Total production of Angus-Sandersons was about 3000 cars, of which six are known to survive.
NG

Further Reading
'Mass Production and the Angus-Sanderson Car', M. Worthington-Williams, *The Automobile*, October 1991.

ANHUT (US) 1909–1910

Anhut Motor Car Co., Detroit, Michigan.
Backed by Michigan State Senator John Anhut, this company made a 2-seater roadster and toy tonneau powered by a 3.7-litre 6-cylinder Brownell engine. Early sales were encouraging, but Anhut found politics more rewarding and turned over the business to his factory superintendent H.C. Barnes. He reorganised the company under the name Barnes Motor Car Co. in September 1910. He was bankrupt two months later, and it is not known if any cars were built under the Barnes name. A link with the Barnes Manufacturing Company of Sandusky, Ohio, is possible.
NG

ANIBAL (E) 1990–1992

Anibal Auto SL Motril, Granada.
Having presented from 1986 several prototypes under the name of Raider, the Spanish designer Francisco Podadera finally set up a production plant for his

c.1921 Angus-Sanderson tourer.
NATIONAL MOTOR MUSEUM

2-seater coupé based on the Seat Ibiza hatchback. Podadera changed the front with retractable 'eyelid' covers, and the rear with a deep spoiler on the boot lid, cutting out two seats to form a coupé. From 1990, on the car was called the Anibal F-100. Production was planned to be about 500 a year, but only 50 were finished in two years, when production finished. The F-100 used the 1.5-litre Ibiza engine and, given 90bhp or 100bhp with injection, was good for 120mph (193km/h). Podadera continues with the design of special cars and was preparing the launch of a new company in 1999.
VCM

ANKER (D) 1918–1920

Anker Automobilfabrik Paul Griebert, Berlin.
This was one of the earliest German firms to start production after World War I, making their own chassis and using various proprietary engines. Being early in the field did not help in the Anker's case, and the limited production ended in 1920.
HON

ANN ARBOR (US) 1911–1912

Huron River Manufacturing Co., Ann Arbor, Michigan.
Like the Canadian Amherst, the Ann Arbor was a dual-purpose car, with the rear seats removable to give a useful load space for the small merchant or farmer. It was powered by a 2-cylinder engine under a conventional bonnet in the 1911 models, and a very short bonnet for 1912. In passenger form it had three rows of seats, accommodating up to eight passengers. Top speed was 25mph (40km/h).
NG

ANNA (US) 1912

Anna Motor Car Co., Anna, Illinois.
The Anna was a very short-lived car featuring a 2.8-litre 2-cylinder engine and what was described as a 2-seater 'Democrat' body.
NG

ANNESLEY (US) 1899; 1914

Charles G. Annesley, Detroit, Michigan.
Charles Annesley showed an early interest in cars when he became the first purchaser of a Ford, buying Henry's original prototype for $200 in 1896. Three years later he made four electric and three petrol cars, but could not get the finance to go into production. He moved to Buffalo, but was back in Detroit by 1914 when he tried to launch a light 2-seater to sell for $500.
NG

ANSALDO (I) 1919–1936

1919–1932 SA Ansaldo Automobili, Turin.
1932–1934 Costruzione e Vendita Automobili Ansaldo, Turin.
1934–1936 Ansaldo-Ceva SA, Turin.
Ansaldo was one of Italy's largest engineering groups, dating back to 1852, with interests in ordnance, railway locomotives, shipbuilding and aero engines. The latter were made in Turin, and it was in order to keep them busy after World War I

1925 Ansaldo Model 6 BC 16/50 tourer.
NATIONAL MOTOR MUSEUM

that Ansaldo decided to enter the car business. Chief engineer Guido Soria designed an up-to-date small car with 1847cc single-ohc 4-cylinder engine, and 3-speed gearbox with American-type central gear lever. The bodies on the early models were angular and unattractive, but the Tipo 4 sold quite well, 287 in 1920 and 443 in 1921. The 1980cc Tipo 4CS arrived in 1922, and 1923 saw 4-wheel brakes and a 6-cylinder model, the 1990cc 6AN. The fours were continued up to 1930, as was the six, enlarged to 2179cc as the 6BN in 1927. This model had a 4-speed gearbox and coil ignition, features which were adopted on the fours by 1928. From 1926 to 1929 there was a lower-priced four, the 1496cc Tipo 10.

Annual production in the mid–1920s varied between 1000 and 2000. There was a reorganisation in 1927, when the car division of Ansaldo came under the control of aircraft makers Macchi. This was because Ansaldo's aircraft division passed into Fiat hands on the orders of Mussolini, who wanted to break up the enormous conglomerate, said to be Europe's largest. Soria left in 1927 and Ansaldo design stagnated thereafter, with very little progress, though two more luxurious models appeared in 1929, the 2782cc 6-cylinder Tipo 18 and 3540cc straight-8 Tipo 22. The latter was a handsome luxury car on a 134in (3401mm) wheelbase, distinguished by disc wheels with quick-detachable rims. Designed by Soria before he left, they had the single-ohc that he had used from the first cars. Four hundred of the Tipos 18 and 22 were laid down, but they were not all sold until 1936, by which time they needed more modern bodies than they had been designed to carry. In 1932 the company was reorganised under the name CEVA (Costruzione e Vendita Automobili Ansaldo – construction and sales (of) Ansaldo cars), though there was not much construction taking place. A small number of trucks was made from 1930 to 1932, and Ansaldo sold a licence for their ohc engine to the WIKOV company in Czechoslovakia. CEVA was sold to bus builders Viberti in 1937, and a few Viberti-bodied trolleybuses carried the Ansaldo name up to about 1950. There were also some Fiat-powered Ansaldo 6-wheeled armoured cars in the 1930s, but these were made by a separate division in Genoa.
NG

ANSBACH (D) 1910
Fahrzeugfabrik Ansbach, Ansbach.
This company built trucks under the Ansbach name from 1906, and in 1910 launched a short-lived small car with 4/14PS 4-cylinder engine, called the Kauz. It was dropped after a year to concentrate on commercial vehicles. In 1919 the company name was changed to Fahrzeugfabriken Ansbach und Nurnberg AG (FAUN) which made mostly commercials, though some cars were also built in the 1920s (see FAUN).
HON

ANSERMIER (CH) 1906
1906 Louis Ansermier, Geneva.
As owner of the Sporting Garage in Geneva, Louis Ansermier represented Renault and Darracq. In 1906 he presented his own light car at the 2nd Geneva Salon. It was a well-finished 2-seater with the trusted De Dion single-cylinder engine of 8bhp, a 3-speed gearbox and shaft drive. Only a handful of cars was produced, and none seems to have survived.
FH

ANSTED (US) 1921–1927
Lexington Motor Car Co., Connersville, Indiana.

The Ansted was named after F.B. Ansted, President of the Ansted Engineering Co. and the Lexington Motor Car Co., both of Connersville, Indiana, and enjoyed two series of cars, six years apart. The initial series was restricted to a sports roadster which was, in effect, a LEXINGTON T offering with sporting lines, a special radiator, its own nomenclature and a hefty price of $4000 f.o.b. Connersville. The second series comprised a handful of the last Lexingtons in 1927, probably 1926 cars remaining in stock which were given Ansted badges and marketed in the Chicago area. Elsewhere, the final Lexington cars carried the Lexington badge and were regarded as such.
KM

ANTIQUE & CLASSIC (US) 1972–1990
Antique & Classic Cars Inc., Buffalo, New York;
British Motor Cars, Buffalo, New York.
Replica would perhaps be too strong a word for these kit cars. Perhaps caricatures. A&C built simple, inexpensive kits based on the Bugatti T-35, Chain Gang Frazer Nash, Alfa Romeo Monza, SS-100, and Blower Bentley. All were based on Volkswagen running gear. They later cut back to just the SS-100, their most accurate replica, for which they added a tube frame to take Ford Pinto or Mustang II running gear. A Jaguar XK-120 replica followed. They closed in 1990, and their assets were purchased by ANTIQUE & COLLECTIBLE AUTOS.
HP

ANTIQUE & COLLECTIBLE AUTOS (US) 1991 to date
Antique & Collectible Autos, Buffalo, New York.
Owner Joe Trombley had been building fibreglass bodies for ANTIQUE AND CLASSIC CARS, and when they closed he bought the assets and began expanding the line-up. Saving the SS-100 and XK-120 models, he added replicas of the Cobra 427, 1934 Ford Coupé, and the 1941 Willys. All were based on steel tube frames with Ford suspension and Ford or Chevrolet engines.
HP

ANTOINE (B) 1900–1902
Sté Victor Antoine et Fils, Liège.
This company was best known for the manufacture of Kelecom engines (named after their designer), which were sold to a variety of car makers. They also showed a tricycle and quadricycle at the 1900 Brussels Salon, both with 2½hp water-cooled engines, and also a voiturette with front-mounted 4hp engine, 2-speed gearbox and a tubular chassis. They made motorcycles up to 1905, but the voiturette did not last beyond 1901 or 1902.
NG

ANTOINETTE (F) 1906–1907
Sté Antoinette, Puteaux, Seine.
This company was better known for its aero engines than for cars. They exhibited a 7270cc 32hp V8 at the 1906 Paris Salon. This had a hydraulic clutch with variable slip in place of a gearbox, and was shown again in 1907, alongside a 16hp 4-cylinder car. The engine, which was designed by Levavasseur and named after the daughter of Jules Gastambide, one of the partners in the firm, was also used in the British ADAMS (iii) and American HEWITT cars, though probably no more than 11 examples of the V8 were made in all. By December 1909 Antoinette were making complete monoplanes at the rate of six to seven per month, as well as engines.
NG

ANTONY (F) 1921–1932
Automobiles Antony, Douai, Nord.
Louis-Auguste Antony (1885–1958) came from a prosperous cycle-dealing family, and his cars were largely financed by his mother. After building single examples of a motorcycle and tricycle, he launched into car production in 1921, using a 1095cc 4-cylinder Ruby engine which he badged as his own make, followed by a 1494cc single-ohc C.I.M.E., which he treated in the same way. His catalogue of 1924 listed an 8-cylinder model; this was to have used a straight-8 S.C.A.P. engine, but no examples of this car were ever built. He also made some isolated examples of smaller cars with 350 or 500cc Hannisard engines, as well as a number of racing specials, one of which ran in the Bol d'Or as late as 1947. His standard production car had a 4-seater touring body, but he also made a pointed sports 4-seater, and offered 'all types of body on demand'. Antony's total

output was about 60 cars. He was an early enthusiast of older cars, restoring and racing two Edwardian Grand Prix cars, a 1907 Fiat and 1908 Porthos.

NG

Further Reading
'Antony et ses Voitures', Fabien Sabates, *L'Album du Fanatique,* March–April 1982.

ANZAC (AUS) 1916

Keep Bros & Wood, Melbourne, Victoria.
The Anzac (from Australian & New Zealand Army Corps) was presumably an American export car featuring a 4-cylinder engine, cantilever rear springs, a fully-floating rear axle and a monobloc fixed-head engine. The Australian Government, however, prohibited the use of Anzac as a trade name and the name 'Victory' was substituted. *See* VICTORY (i).

KM

ANZANI *see* MAUVE

AOSHEN (CHI) 1992–1993

Luoyang Bus Works, Luoyang City, Henan Province.
A small bus factory, which produced 4x4 station wagons and 18-seat and 45-seat buses, also produced, in small quantities, two different 4-door 4-seat minicars, one with some kind of miniaturised VW Santana styling, called the Aoshen LYK 6420. The other was called the Aoshen LYK 5010XH.

FVIS

APACHE (US) 1966

Interco Development Corp., New York, New York.
This 2-passenger convertible was to have been a competitor to European sports cars. Unfortunately, it never made it into production.

HP

A.P.A.L. (B) 1964 to date

A.P.A.L. S.a.r.l., Blegny-Trembleur, Liège.
In 1964 Apal offered a two-seater coupé based on a VW Beetle chassis with a tuned (50bhp) 1.3-litre engine. Subsequently, a 95bhp 1.6-litre Renault engine was used.
Apal also made beach buggies and Jeep-style vehicles which were exported to 20 countries.
In 1978 Apal made the 'Jet Corsa' which was a gull-wing coupé based on VW running gear. For many years it has also made, in kit and turn key forms, a copy of the Porsche 356 Speedster, which was also built under licence by other companies. The Apal Speedster had a fibreglass body, reinforced by a tubular frame, on a shortened VW Beetle floor pan with either an air-cooled VW flat-4 engine or a VW Golf water-cooled unit. Other VW-based cars included the Replicar, styled after a Bugatti T35, and the Aruki, a 4-seater retro-styled convertible.
By 1990 Apal was also listing the Francorchamps, a 2-seater roadster on a tubular steel structure, a fibreglass body and Mercedes-Benz 190 running gear. It was available on special order only. With the standard 122bhp engine, a top speed of 127mph (205km/h) was claimed, but options included a 16-valve 160 bhp engine or a 185bhp turbocharged version.
There were few takers for the Francorchamps, and Apal has since focused on its VW-based cars.

MJL

APOLLO (i) (US) 1906–1907

Chicago Recording Scale Co., Waukegan, Illinois.
This was a conventional car with 35hp 4-cylinder engine, 3-speed gearbox and shaft drive. The only body offered was a 5-seater Roi-des-Belges tourer.

NG

APOLLO (ii) (D) 1910–1927

1910–1912 A. Ruppe & Sohn AG, Apolda.
1912–1927 Apollo-Werke AG, Apolda.
When the makers of the PICCOLO moved up to a larger car they chose a new name, Apollo. Designed by Karl Slevogt, the new car, called the Typ B, had a 960cc ohv 4/14PS 4-cylinder engine, and was followed by the 2040cc 8/28PS Typ F. They had a number of competition successes, often with Slevogt at the wheel.

1924 Antony 11CV tourer.
NICK GEORGANO

1911 Apollo (ii) Type B sports car.
HANS-OTTO NEUBAUER

There were also larger Apollos with side-valve engines, the 2612cc Typ K and 3440cc Typ L, both made from 1912 to 1914.
The smaller car was revived after the war, and made up to 1925, together with a 2597cc 10/40PS. The 4/14PS was claimed to have the first German-made example of a swing axle at the front. Some Apollos were fitted with Jaray streamlined bodies. A 12/50PS V8 engine was built in 1921, but remained a prototype. The last Apollos were the 1221cc 5/25Ps which was developed from the 4/14, and the 1551cc 6/24PS. This was the first to use a proprietary engine, a side-valve Steudel.

HON

APOLLO (iii) (US) 1962–1965

1962–1964 International Motorcars Inc., Oakland, California.
1964–1965 Apollo International Corp., Pasadena, California..
The Apollo was a Californian sports car of 1962, designed by Milt Brown and styled by Ron Plescia. It resembled a longer, cleaner MGB GT, but the MGB had not been launched when the Apollo was styled.
Buick V8 engines of 3.5-or 5-litres were used in a tubular ladder frame with suspension and other components from the Buick Special. With the larger engine fitted, top speed was claimed to be 150mph (240km/h), 0–62mph (0–100km/h) in 7.5 seconds, but the company was not sufficiently strong to advertise nationally, or to establish a dealer network.
Production ceased in 1964 and the body was then supplied by its Italian maker, Intermeccanica, to a firm in Texas which used them to make a car called the VETTA VENTURA.

c.1909 Apperson Jack Rabbit roadster.
NATIONAL MOTOR MUSEUM

1919 Apperson V8 Model 8–19 tourer.
NATIONAL MOTOR MUSEUM

1923 Apperson V8 Model 8-23S sedan.
NATIONAL MOTOR MUSEUM

Production of the Apollo was resumed later in 1964, but the Ventura was soon dead – 88 cars (77 coupés, 11 convertibles) were made.

An Apollo GT was driven by the bad hats in the Disney film, *The Love Bug*.
MJL

APOLLO (iv) (GB) 1971–1972
Allen Pearce, Hornchurch, Essex.
This Chevron Can-Am inspired gull-wing coupé used a space frame chassis over a VW Beetle floorpan and glassfibre bodywork. There was seating for 2+2, but the car never reached intended production in kit form.
CR

APOLLO (v) (AUS) 1973
Apollo Fibreglass Industries, Blacktown, New South Wales.
A late entrant to the VW-based street buggy field, the Apollo had a sports-orientated appeal but, apart from having a T-roof, it differed little from other buggies. It seems to have been succeeded by the 1974 Kalita, an equally short-lived attempt to promote the buggy as a sports car.
MG

APOLLO (vi) (US) 1979–1993
Apollo Motor Cars, Berkeley, California.
This company was started by Milt Brown and Ron Plescia, who had engineered the International Motors Apollo sports car project in the 1960s. This time they designed a handsome roadster along the lines of the British Morgan, but with a Jaguar XK-150 grille, called the Verona. It used a steel tube frame which took General Motors suspension. Engine choices included Chevrolet or Ford V8, Buick V6 or BMW in-line 6. Veronas were initially sold only in fully-assembled form, but in 1984 kits were added to the line. In 1986 they added the Verona Cabriolet, which was only sold in kit form. It was similar to the roadster, but had more room for V8 or Jaguar V12 engines. It had more interior room, roll-up windows and a longer wheelbase for greater comfort.

In the late 1980s the Verona was built in Germany under the name Warmouth. Warmouth made its own multi-tubular chassis frame and, because it used BMW 5-series running gear, some of the dimensions were changed.

In 1990, Warmouth was one of only a tiny handful of companies to whom BMW was prepared to supply components. The company later changed its name to Verona Automobile GmbH.
HP/MJL

A.P.P see TEILHOL

APPENNINE (GB) 1995 to date
Appennine Car Co. Ltd, Eckington, Pershore, Worcestershire.
Few replicas have ever been as painstaking or evocative as the Appennine Three Nine. It duplicated the style and specification of the 1938 Alfa Romeo 2.9B sports car. Most interesting was its straight-8 engine, created by Weslake by joining two Alfa Romeo Alfetta 4-cylinder units together (forming a 3.9-litre engine with an output of 251bhp). Suspension was by torsion bars, with a De Dion rear axle. The bodywork was carefully re-created in aluminium, using Touring Superleggera principles, and the chassis was made by SPYDER. Only one car had been produced by the end of 1998.
CR

APPERSON (US) 1902–1926
1902–1924 Apperson Brothers Automobile Co., Kokomo, Indiana.
1924–1926 Apperson Automobile Co., Kokomo, Indiana.
After leaving the HAYNES-APPERSON Company, and Elwood HAYNES, Elmer (1861–1920) and Edgar (1869–1959) Apperson established their own Apperson Brothers Automobile Company in November 1901. Thereafter the Appersons and Haynes would studiously ignore the contributions of the other when referring to the Haynes-Apperson experiments and production cars of 1897 to 1901. The Appersons' own cars, the first of which appeared in July 1902, used a Sintz engine, the same brand adopted for the early Haynes trials. Twin-cylinder cars were built until 1903, at which time a four appeared. By 1904, only fours were offered. Prices in this period ranged from $2500 to $5000, considerably higher than the levy asked by Haynes for what were still called Haynes-Appersons until mid-year.

A 6-cylinder Apperson was built in 1908, though this did not become a production model until much later. The most noteworthy Apperson of the period was the Jack Rabbit speedster, introduced in 1907. Smaller and cheaper than the STUTZ Bearcat (which would not appear until 1912), and also less powerful, the Jack Rabbit was produced through 1913. Although not winning any major racing events, Jack Rabbits regularly contested in such events as the Vanderbilt Cup series, the last chain drive car to do so. By 1909 a touring-bodied Jack Rabbit had appeared, and in the epochal year of 1913 all Appersons, six models on four wheelbases, carried the name.

The 6-cylinder engine reached production in 1914, in models called 6-45 and 6-55, both on 128in (3249mm) wheelbases.

In 1916, a V8 engine, Apperson's own, was introduced, and the fours were retired. For 1917, the name Roadplane was adopted for all models, which continued to include touring cars and roadsters. Closed cars, however, had been absent from the line since 1907. From 1919, all Appersons were V8s; closed cars reappeared in 1920. New York dealer Conover T. Silver put together a long, low 'Silver Special'

1913 Aquila Italiana 12hp 2-seater.
NATIONAL MOTOR MUSEUM

roadster for the 1918 New York Auto Show – a similar car, which has accrued far greater renown, was done on the chassis of Silver's other car line, KISSEL and became the famed Kissel Gold Bug.

A new six, its engine built by Falls, entered the line-up for 1923. This Model 6-23 was, at $1535, the least expensive Apperson ever. The Falls engine was a 3206cc unit, also used by COURIER, DORT, ELGIN, and FARNER. Production peaked in 1916, at about 2000 units.

The Apperson brothers always worked as a team, so the death of Elmer in March 1920 upset the company's situation. Production took a downturn, and the company turned to outside capital. In 1924 it was reorganised as Apperson Automobile Company, but not for long. A Lycoming straight-8 appeared in 1925, powered by a 4528cc engine making 65bhp. The V8 stayed in production that year, and actually had more body styles available that did either the six or the new straight-8. Models for 1926 had 4-wheel brakes, a first for the marque. The V8 was now gone, and the six and Straightaway Eight stumbled along until mid-year. A receivers' sale was conducted on July 20th in Kokomo.
KF

APPLE (US) 1915–1917
W.A. Apple Motor Car Co., Dayton, Ohio.
The Apple was a conventional-looking 5-seater tourer distinguished by a Paige-like vee-radiator. The power unit was a 44bhp V8, make unspecified but unlikely to have been Apple's own as they were a very small company. Possibly only prototypes of the $1150 Apple 8 were made.
NG

APTA see ELIZALDE and RICART-ESPAÑA

AQUILA ITALIANA (I) 1906–1917
Fabbrica Italiana d'Automobili Aquila, Turin.
The Aquila Italiana (Italian Eagle) was not widely known, being made in small quantities, but its design was very advanced. The founder was the Marques Palavicini di Priola. The chief engineer was Giulio Cesare Cappa who later worked for Fiat and Itala, and among the features of his early cars were monobloc casting of cylinders, the first use of aluminium pistons (in 1908), overhead inlet and side exhaust valves (as used by Henry Royce), ball bearing crankshaft, and engine and gearbox carried on a common tray. Though the first cars were announced in 1906 – two fours of 12/16 and 28/40hp and two sixes of 18/24 and 60/75hp – production was delayed by two years because of the death of the chief backer and a move to a larger factory. Models listed for 1908 were similar to those of 1906. Initially STORERO agreed to buy the whole of Aquila's production, but they ended this agreement in 1909. The 1912 30/45hp six had an output of 60bhp from 4.2-litres. There was also a smaller 12/15hp four. One of these, with a streamlined aluminium body, had numerous hill climb and sprint successes driven by Eugenio Beria d'Argentina. They also competed in the Targa Florio, and three cars with 4-litre single-ohc 6-cylinder engines were entered in the 1914 French Grand Prix, though only one started. Aquila Italiana also made aero engines, under licence from Salmson and SPA, and car production ended in 1917 when SPA took over the company.
NG

AR (E) 1980–1985
Autoreplica SA, Madrid.
The first Spanish company dedicated to replicas, AR took the MG TD as pattern, built up from Seat components. The prototype was made in 1980, but production did not start until 1984 due to homologation problems. The classic car specialist, Francisco Pueche, developed the AR using Seat 1430cc engines with 77bhp, and 1600cc with 98bhp. After having sold 11 cars the company closed.
VCM

ARAB (GB) 1926–1928
Arab Motors, Letchworth, Hertfordshire.
This was a very advanced sports car designed by Reid Railton, who had worked with J.G. Parry Thomas on the LEYLAND Eight, and was later to give his name to a sports car in the 1930s. It had a 1960cc 4-cylinder engine with a single-ohc operating inclined valves. The valve springs were of transverse leaf type, as in the MARLBOROUGH-THOMAS, and in the Thomas Special racing cars. It is not certain that Parry Thomas was directly involved in the Arab engine design, but clearly Railton would have been influenced by the ideas of 'the Master'. The rest of the design was conventional, with a Moss 4-speed gearbox and ENV spiral-bevel rear axle. Two Arabs were made in low-chassis form, out of the 10 or so which were made.

1928 Arab 2-litre sports car.
NATIONAL MOTOR MUSEUM

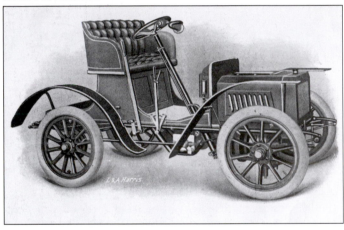

1904 Arbee 6hp 2-seater.
NATIONAL MOTOR MUSEUM

The first Arab was made in the Letchworth steel foundry of Kryn & Lahy, and subsequently about six in the works of the PHOENIX company. The final few were assembled from existing parts by Thomson & Taylor at Brooklands.

NG

ARABIAN (US) 1915–1917

William Galloway Co., Waterloo, Iowa.

William Galloway made high-wheelers (see GALLOWAY (i)), and when he chose to make more conventional cars he bought them from ARGO (ii), renaming them Arabian. They had 4-cylinder engines, of 12hp in 1915 and then of 22hp. Most were 2-seater roadsters but a 5-seater tourer on a longer wheelbase was added in 1917.

NG

ARAWAK (BS) 1976–1980

Arawak Motors Ltd, St Johns, Antigua.

The local Chrysler importer for the tiny Caribbean island of Antigua commissioned the Hustler, an open-topped leisure vehicle, for production. Mechanically it was entirely based on the Hillman Imp, including its rear-mounted 875cc engine. The Terry Tyrrell-designed bodywork was in glassfibre and a hardtop was available. Just as it was launched, Chrysler stopped production of the Imp and Arawak was forced to redevelop it into the Hustler II for a front-mounted Vauxhall Viva 1256cc engine but it is believed that this model never surfaced in production.

CR

ARBEE (GB) 1904

Rodgers Bros., New Kent Road, London.

Rodgers Brothers were makers of the Dreadnought cycle and motorcycle, and platers to the trade. Their short-lived light car had a 6hp engine, tubular frame and 2-speed gearbox.

NG

ARBEL see SYMETRIC

ARBENZ (US) 1911–1918

1911–1912 Scioto Car Co., Chillicothe, Ohio.
1912–1918 ArBenz Car Co., Chillicothe, Ohio.

This car was named after its maker Fred C. Arbenz, but was usually spelt ArBenz, presumably to hint at a connection with the famous German company. The original company name, Scioto, came from the river that runs through Chillicothe. The cars were conventional tourers and roadsters powered by a 30/40hp 4-cylinder engine. From 1916 they were replaced by a smaller and cheaper car powered by a 17hp Lycoming four. At $625 the tourer was one third the price of the larger ArBenz. It was the only model listed up to the close of production in 1918. Despite being a car maker, Fred Arbenz generally travelled in a horse-drawn buggy.

NG

ARCHER (i) (GB) 1920

This car bore a famous name as its designer M. Archer was responsible for the invention of the trench mortar. His car had an 8/10hp 2-cylinder engine and tandem 2-seater body.

NG

ARCHER (ii) (US) c.1984–1989

Archer Coachworks, Valparaiso, Indiana.

This was a neoclassic kit car based on a Lincoln chassis, Chevrolet engine and Fiat 124 Spyder body. The Fiat body, boot, doors and interior were used, but the body was cut off at the firewall and a long fibreglass nose was grafted on. Running boards and a vertical grill were added to give an appearance similar to a CLENET or EXCALIBUR. Could be purchased in basic kit, rolling chassis or full-assembled form.

HP

A.R. DA GRAÇA see A.G.

ARDEN (GB) 1912–1916

Arden Motor Co. Ltd, Balsall Heath, Coventry.

This was a light car powered by a 2-cylinder engine, either an 8hp air-cooled V-twin J.A.P. or a 10hp water-cooled vertical-twin Alpha. In 1914 a 10hp 4-cylinder Alpha was offered, the extra power of which justified adding a 3-seater cloverleaf body to the 2-seater already on the market. The twins were dropped after 1914, and a new model for 1916 was an 11.9hp four of 1704cc. All Ardens had 3-speed gearboxes and shaft drive.

NG

ARDENT see CARON

ARDEX (i) (F) 1934–c.1937

Automobiles Ardex, Nanterre, Seine.

This was a small 3-wheeler of slightly Morgan-like appearance, though with less performance as it used 2- or 4-stroke motorcycle engines of under 500cc. In 1937 they announced a 4-wheeler with streamlined body which, at 5500 francs, was the cheapest car on the French market. Production of all Ardex cars was very limited, from a small workshop in Nanterre. Demonstrations were limited to Mondays and Saturdays.

NG

ARDEX (ii) (F) 1952–1955

Ardex, Nanterre, Seine.

This was a microcar with very simple, slab-sided bodywork, no doors and seating for four passengers. The rear-mounted engine was either a Saab 100cc or 125cc single-cylinder 2-stroke, driving through a 3-speed transmission. An even smaller Sachs 50cc engined 2-seater was also listed.

CR

ARDITA (I) 1918

Costruzioni Automobili Ing. A. Gallanzi, Milan.

Garage proprietor Alfredo Gallanzi bought up the stock of parts left over by Antonio Chiribiri when he gave up car manufacture for the first time. He assembled a few light cars powered by 1100 and 1300cc 4-cylinder side-valve engines. But although they were credited with 'all the latest improvements' he did not sell many. The name Ardita was later taken up by Fiat for one of their medium-sized models.

NG

ARDIURME (E) 1905

La Maquinaria Bilbaina, Deusto.

This was a comfortable Landaulet with two small extra seats and separate place for the driver, looking like a carriage. Built by Artiñano D'az y Hurtado de Mendoza, the Ardiurme was the first car built in Vizcaya equipped with an electric engine. The car was very robust, and though the complete technical data are not known, it seems this car had sufficient power to climb a 1 in 7 hill with four people on board.

VCM

ARDSLEY (US) 1905–1906

Ardsley Motor Car Co., Yonkers, New York.

Advertised as 'Made in New York by New Yorkers for New Yorkers', the Ardsley was a large and expensive car, made only in tourer form and powered by a 35/40hp 4-cylinder engine, and selling for $4000. In January 1905 25 cars were said to be under construction, with another 50 to follow.

NG

ARGEO (D) 1925

Argeo Fahrzeugwerk Georg Kulitsky, Berlin.

The Argeo was a 3-wheeled cyclecar with single front wheel. Although it was light, it was underpowered with the 123cc 2-stroke engine, and few were sold.

HON

ARGO (i) (US) 1912–1914

Argo Electric Vehicle Co., Saginaw, Michigan.

The Argo was quite advanced for an electric car, with wheel steering on all models and a long wheelbase of 110in (2792mm). Westinghouse motors were used. The initial model of 1912 was a typical closed brougham, but a roadster and delivery truck were added for 1913. An advertisement that year claimed that 300 Argo Electrics had been sold, but it was a hotly-contested market, with the better-known DETROIT taking much of the field. In 1914 Argo merged with BROC and BORLAND-GRANNIS to form the American Electric Car Co. Production of all three makes was concentrated in the Argo plant, but did not last beyond November 1916. The factory was later used for manufacture of the YALE (ii), and then the Nelson Motor Truck Company's Jumbo truck.

NG

ARGO (ii) (US) 1914–1918

Argo Motor Co., Jackson, Michigan.

The Argo was originally a cyclecar based on the AJAX (iii) which Benjamin Briscoe built in France. His American-built version had an identical 12hp 4-cylinder engine, and the main difference between the two cars was that the Ajax had friction transmission, and the Argo a conventional sliding gearbox. Briscoe planned to build the Argo in New York City, but chose the Jackson plant of the recently-defunct STANDARD (vii) electric car. For 1916, with the cyclecar boom over, Briscoe offered a larger car with 22hp engine, in roadster and touring forms, sold under the name WEGO. He soon sold the company to Mansell Hackett, who began to build his own HACKETT car, though he assembled the Briscoe-designed cars up to 1918, renaming them Argos. Meanwhile Benjamin Briscoe continued with the manufacture of cars under his own name, which lasted until 1921.

NG

1913 Arden 8.96hp 2-seater.
NATIONAL MOTOR MUSEUM

1916 Argo (ii) tourer.
KEITH MARVIN

ARGON (GB) 1908

Grannaway Engineering Co., Earls Court, London.

The Argon was a fairly large tourer powered by a 25hp 6-cylinder Coventry-Simplex engine. Priced at £750, few were sold. In 1905 the same company was planning to build a car called the Grannaway, and this may well have become the Argon.

NG

ARGONAUT (US) 1959–1963

Argonaut Motor Machine Corp., Cleveland, Ohio.

One of the most ambitious attempts to market the 'super car', the first planned models of the make were to have been called the Argonaut State Limousine. The first prototype was built on a Chrysler chassis, and one Argonaut is known to have reached private hands. Price listings were quoted from $26,800 to $36,000, and

1920 Argonne roadster.
KEITH MARVIN

1906 Argus tourer in the Herkomer Trial.
NATIONAL MOTOR MUSEUM

these behemoths were to have been built of stainless and special steels, magnesium titanium alloys and duralumin, and to feature a 12-cylinder ohc aluminium air-cooled engine developing 1020hp. Argonauts were to carry a four-year guarantee. In the concern's elaborate illustrated catalogue both closed and open models were shown, the Smoke and Raceway open styles having a claimed maximum speed of 240mph (386km/h).

KM

ARGONNE (US) 1919–1920
Argonne Motor Car Co., Jersey City, New Jersey.
The Argonne was an assembled car powered initially by a 3710cc 4-cylinder Buda engine, and made for the Argonne company by the Jersey City Machine Co. It was of striking appearance, with disc wheels and a pointed radiator closely resembling that of the prewar Austro-Daimler. Both tourer and roadster models were offered, but the roadster was the most familiar. In 1920 a more powerful 4950cc Rochester-Duesenberg engine was used, and only the roadster was offered. Not more than 24 cars were made before Argonne went into receivership in July 1920, but parts were bought by a garment manufacturer who assembled about ten more Argonnes in a garage in the Bronx. In contrast to the previous cars, these all had closed bodies.

NG

ARGSON (GB) 1922–c.1952
1922–1926 Argson Engineering Co. Ltd, London.
1926–c.1952 Stanley Engineering Co. Ltd, Egham, Surrey.
This company was founded in 1919 by A.R. Garnett and S.O. Needham to make hand-propelled invalid tricycles. In 1922 they built their first powered car,

the Beaufort, using a 172cc engine of their own design and manufacture, and followed this in 1923 with an electric model with 24v battery and three forward speeds. During the 1920s and 1930s they were probably the largest manufacturers of invalid tricycles in Britain, with the standard pattern of single front wheel. The most popular engine in the 1930s was the 147cc Villiers 2-stroke, used in the Standard, De Luxe and Runnymede models. They received a large order from the Ministry of Health in 1949, but in the early 1950s they were taken over by HARPER Engineering who transferred production to Exeter Airport and made new models under their own name.

NG

ARGUS (D) 1902–1906
1902–1904 Internationale Automobil-Zentrale KG Jeannin & Co., Berlin-Reinickendorf.
1904–1906 Argus Motoren-Gesellschaft Jeannin & Co. KG, Berlin-Reinickendorf.
Paul Jeannin was the man behind the Argus, and he began by importing Panhards from France in 1901. His first cars of 1902 used Panhard engines and other components, but from 1903 he began using his own engines, a 2380cc 12PS 2-cylinder, 4960cc 20PS 4-cylinder and 9260cc 40PS 4-cylinder. Argus also made marine engines. Production was on a small scale, but the cars were of good quality. Some Argus models were sold in England under the name BEAUFORT.

In 1906 Jeannin left Argus and with his brother Emil set up the Sun Motorengesellschaft Jeannin & Co. KG which made SUN (i) cars for two years. Argus concentrated on marine and aero engines, but returned to the car field in 1929 when they manufactured straight-8 engines for HORCH.

HON

ARGYLL (i) (GB) 1899–1928
1899–1905 Hozier Engineering Co. Ltd, Bridgeton, Glasgow.
1905–1906 Argyll Motors Ltd, Bridgeton, Glasgow.
1906–1914 Argyll Motors Ltd, Alexandria-by-Glasgow.
1915–1928 Argyll Motors Ltd, Bridgeton, Glasgow.
Together with Arrol-Johnston, Argyll was the most important of the 50-plus Scottish car makers. The first Argyll, a Renault-inspired light car with 258cc 2¾ hp single-cylinder MMC-De Dion engine, and tubular steel frame, was designed by Alexander Govan (1869–1907) in 1899, a year before the Hozier Engineering Co. was formed to make it. This was financed by W.A. Smith of the National Telephone Co. A 5hp MMC engine was used in the 1901 Argyll, which had wheel steering in place of handlebars, and a new radiator with two horizontal radiators linked by vertical tubes. For 1902, 8hp engines by MMC or Simms were offered, and before that year was out larger cars were available, with 10 and 12hp 2-cylinder and 16hp 4-cylinder engines listed. Their chief drawback was a difficult gearbox with separate lever for reverse; a Govan design, it was not replaced until 1910. Production rose quickly, with 15 cars a week being made in January 1904, and in the second quarter of the year Argyll made 156 cars, which Govan considered a record for the British industry. A variety of engines was used: Argyll's own 12hp 3-cylinder, an 8hp single by De Dion Bouton, and 10hp twin and 16hp four by Aster. 1905 saw a larger car with a 20/24hp 4-cylinder Argyll-built engine of 3684cc. With longer stroke giving 3825cc, it was made until 1908. Larger still were the 4846cc 26/30hp of 1906–07 and 6330cc 40hp of 1908–09. These were the largest-engined Argylls ever made.

The optimism generated by an output of 1200 cars in 1905 led to a classic case of over-expansion. Argyll bought a 25-acre site at Alexandria in the Vale of Leven, where they erected a vast factory with marble staircase in the main hall leading to the directors' offices, Georgian style for the managing director and Elizabethan for the board. The southern wing contained a dining hall and a lecture theatre large enough to hold orchestral concerts. The workers' washrooms and lavatories were of unheard-of size and quality. 'The space devoted to lavatory and cloakroom accommodation for the workpeople occupies as much ground, and must have cost as much money, as many a factory complete' marvelled *The Autocar* at the opening in June 1906. It is debatable if the extravagance of the marble halls, as the Alexandria factory became known, was responsible for Argyll's subsequent problems, but the cost of around £220,000 cannot have helped the balance sheet. By contrast, Napier's new works at Acton cost only £32,000.

A more immediate blow was Govan's early death in May 1907, which robbed the firm of much of its drive. The extravagance of the marble halls could only

66

1902 Argyll (i) 8hp tonneau.
NATIONAL MOTOR MUSEUM

1907 Argyll (i) 26/30hp tourer in 1907 Criterium de France.
NATIONAL MOTOR MUSEUM

1927 Argyll (i) 12/40hp tourer.
NATIONAL MOTOR MUSEUM

have been justified by mass production, and Argylls were still very much built by hand. In August 1908 the company was in liquidation, though the factory remained open and cars continued to be made.

There was a largely new range for 1910, starting with a 10hp monobloc twin, a 12/14 four which was used as a taxicab, not only in London and other British cities, but in New York, the old 14/16hp four and a new Twenty four and Thirty six. Production rose from 240 cars in 1909 to 452 in 1910, but they were still far short of the heady days of 1905. A new 12hp monobloc four of 1911 had four-wheel brakes, the pedals operating on the front wheels and the lever on the rear. The system was designed by Argyll employee J.M. Rubury, who was later co-designer of the R.L.C. light car. Argyll's next experiment was with sleeve valves, not Charles Knight's double-sleeve variety, but a single-sleeve design patented by Peter Burt and J.H.K. McCollum. Argyll made two sizes of sleeve-valve engine, a 2612cc 15/30 and a 4082cc 25/50. These were made up to 1914, together with a single

poppet-valve engine, the 1953cc 12/18. Argyll hoped to sell licences for their engine to other car makers (rumours spoke of licencees in France, Switzerland and Canada), but only PICCARD-PICTET actually made any engines. Although there were considerable differences in design between the Knight and Burt-McCollum systems, Knight sued Argyll for patent infringement. Argyll won the case, but suffered heavy legal expenses. Coupled with the drain on their resources from the Alexandria works, this led to another liquidation, in June 1914. Argyll shares dropped from 10 shillings (50p) in February to only 7d (2.8p) in June. The marble halls were sold to the Admiralty, becoming the Royal Naval Torpedo Factory, and continuing as such until they were sold to Plessey Ltd in the 1970s.

This seemed like the end of the road for Argyll, but in November 1915 the former works at Bridgeton were bought by John Brimlow, manager of the repair works, and after the war he restarted production on a modest scale. The first model was a slightly modified 15/30 with electric starting, but only 11 were made. It was joined in 1922 by the Twelve, a smaller car with 1495cc sleeve-valve engine made by Greenwood & Batley of Leeds, though some were also supplied by Wallace of Glasgow. A sports model with front-wheel brakes, the 12/40, was offered for 1926 and these were standardised on the Argylls shown at Olympia in 1927. That was their last show appearance, and production probably ended in 1928, though the name was carried on a number of lists up to 1932. Not more than 300 cars were made after the war.

NG

Further Reading
Lost Causes of Motoring, Lord Montagu of Beaulieu, Cassell, 1960.

ARGYLL (ii) **(GB)** 1976–c. 1990
Minnow Fish Carburettors, Lochgilphead, Argyll.
The British turbocharger pioneer, Bob Henderson, created this mid-engined 2+2 coupé in 1976.

The Argyll had a box section chassis, Triumph 2500 all-independent suspension, and a 4-cylinder Saab or a Rover V8 engine (both turbocharged and transversely mounted) driving through a 5-speed ZF gearbox. A top speed of 160mph (257km/h) was claimed for the Rover version, 130mph (209km/h) for the Saab-engined variant. A PRV (Peugeot/Renault/Volvo) V6 engine was a later option.

Not many people were seduced by the Argyll's looks, its specification, or the grandiose claims made by the company, but it was theoretically available until the mid–1990s.

CR

ARH **(E)** 1970–1972
Huertas, Almagro, Bienvenida y Albisa, Madrid.
Ricardo Huertas designed a sportscar called Condor using the mechanical base of a Simca 1200, a car financed by Chrysler. It participated in several races driven by Miguel Righetto. After having built three or five cars, Chrysler withdrew financial support, and the company closed.

VCM

ARIA **(US)** c.1992
Aria Motor Co., Getty Design, Riverside, California
The strangely named Aria Phantom CACHET V12 was a mid-engined sports car that looked like a mildly restyled Jaguar XJ-13 prototype. They were built to customer specifications with aluminium or composite bodywork. The first one built had a Porsche 6-cylinder engine.

HP

ARIANE **(F)** 1907
Automobiles Ariane, Suresnes, Seine.
This light car used a 6hp single-cylinder engine and friction transmission, differing from most in having the friction discs by the rear axle instead of closer to the engine.

NG

ARIÉ **(F)** 1983–1985
Arié, Annecy-le-Vieux.
The Arié Hopi microcar was designed by the creator of the SUNCAR. It was a very boxy cabriolet design, with a rear-mounted 125cc Sachs engine. Other features included MacPherson strut front suspension and 4-wheel disc brakes.

CR

ARIEL (i) **(GB)** 1898–1915; 1922–1925
1898–1906 Ariel Motor Co. Ltd, Birmingham.
1906–1911 Ariel Motors Ltd, Birmingham.
1911–1915; 1922–1925 Coventry Ordnance Works Ltd, Coventry.

The Ariel name dates back to 1847 when the London firm of Whitehurst & Co. marketed the Ariel wheel fitted with Thompson's pneumatic tyre for horse-drawn vehicles. It was not successful, but the name was taken up by James Starley and William Hillman in 1871 for their bicycles and sewing machines. They named their Coventry factory the Ariel works, but the name lapsed from the late 1870s, to be revived in 1897 by Harvey duCros' Dunlop Group of companies as the Ariel Cycle Co. Ltd. When powered tricycles were added in 1898 this became the Ariel Motor Co. Ltd. They showed a tricycle at the Crystal Palace Show in November 1898; this was a licence-built De Dion Bouton, but Ariel soon started making vehicles of their own design, though still showing De Dion influence. At the 1901 National Show they exhibited a 3hp quadricycle and also their first car. Designed by Charles Sangster, one of the founders of the Ariel Cycle Co., it had a 9/10hp vertical twin engine and 4-seater tonneau body. A 16hp 4-cylinder followed in 1902, but sales were not encouraging, and the company concentrated on motorcycle manufacture by the Ariel Cycle Co. Two-wheelers were to outlast all the cars, continuing until merger with B.S.A. in the 1960s.

In 1906 the Ariel Motor Co. was reorganised as Ariel Motors, and began to make a range of large, Mercedes-like cars called Ariel-Simplex. These ran from the 6330cc 28/38hp four to the 12,875cc 40/50hp six. Financial problems continued, and in 1907 Ariel sold its factory to LORRAINE-DIETRICH who were looking for a way into the British market. Ariel were said to be making three Lorraine-Dietrich cars a week in 1908, but the arrangement was short-lived, and by 1910 the British Lorraine-Dietrich was no more.

Ariel Motors were in receivership in 1911, and arrangements were made for their cars to be built by the Coventry Ordnance Co., a branch of shipbuilders Cammell Laird. Smaller models were made up to 1915, from the 1328cc 10hp of 1915 to the 4082cc 25hp of 1912–13. During the war Ariel made motorcycles in their Birmingham factory while the Coventry Ordnance Works were given over to bombs and other armaments. Car production did not restart immediately after the Armistice. Charles Sangster's son Jack designed a flat-twin light car which was put into production by ROVER as the Rover Eight. In 1922 he rejoined Ariel as assistant managing director to his father, and designed a light car with 996cc flat-twin similar to the Rover, though with water-cooling instead of air-cooling. It had a 3-speed gearbox in unit with a spiral bevel rear axle, and was made mostly with 4-seater 'chummy' body. About 700 were made from 1922 to 1925, and it was joined in 1924 by a 1097cc 4-cylinder Ten of similar appearance, and with the same combined gearbox and rear axle. About 250 of these were made up to 1926, when Ariel abandoned 4-wheelers.
NG

ARIEL (ii) **(US)** 1905–1907
The Ariel Motor Co., Boston, Massachusetts; Nutley, New Jersey;
Bridgeport, Connecticut; Baltimore, Maryland.

Four factory locations in less than three years in business cannot have made for continuity of production, which was a pity because the Ariel was an advanced car featuring an early use of a single-ohc engine built by the Trebert Auto & Marine Motor Company of Rochester, New York. Two models were launched at the 1905 Boston Automobile Show, a 15hp 3-cylinder roadster and a 25hp 4-cylinder tourer. These had rectangular radiators, but the 1906 Ariel, now a 4-cylinder only, had a handsome oval radiator, giving rise to the slogan 'Look for the Oval Front'. It was now called a 30hp, but was probably the same engine as the 1905 25hp. In January 1907 the Ariel was relaunched as the MARYLAND (ii) in Baltimore.
NG

ARIEL ATOM (GB) 1999 to date
Ariel Motor Co. Ltd, North Perrott, Somerset

Designed by Simon Saunders, a lecturer in three-dimensional design at the University of Exeter, this was a very light (1100lb) sports car with a simple mono space steel chassis clad with fibreglass panels. The chassis formed a protective shoulder-high cage around the occupants, and there were no doors. Engines were the 1.6- or 1.8-litre Rover K series, transversely mounted behind the driver, and mated to a MGF 5-speed gearbox driving the rear wheels. It was available complete or in kit form.
NG

1976 Argyll (ii) coupé.
MINNOW FISH CARBURETTORS

c.1904 Ariel (i) 15 or 20hp landaulet.
NATIONAL MOTOR MUSEUM

1908 Ariel (i) 40/50hp tourer.
NATIONAL MOTOR MUSEUM

ARIÈS (F) 1903–1938
SA Ariès, Villeneuve-la Garenne; Courbevoie, Seine.

The Société Anonyme Ariès was a relatively small company which had the distinction of being founded and directed for the whole of its 35-year life by one man, Baron Charles Petiet (1879–1958) who had worked briefly for Panhard et Levassor. The small factory at Villeneuve-la Garenne was quite near the Aster factory at St Denis, and there were strong links between the two concerns. The first Ariès had 8/10hp 2-cylinder and 12/16hp 4-cylinder Aster engines, and these power units were used by Ariès for many years. Some of the early models were sold in England by Sidney Begbie under the Aster name, while others were

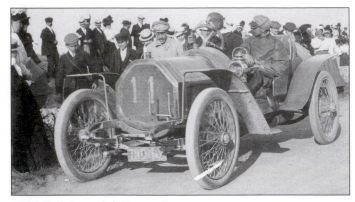

1908 Ariès in Coupe de la Normandie.
NATIONAL MOTOR MUSEUM

1925 Ariès 15hp tourer by Établissements Privat.
BRYAN K. GOODMAN

1935 Ariès Super 10-50 cabriolet.
BRYAN K. GOODMAN

1956 Arista (ii) coupé.
NATIONAL MOTOR MUSEUM

marketed from 1904 to 1906 by a firm in Beccles, Suffolk under the name Anglian. Ariès was not a large concern, having only 95 employees in 1904. The smaller Ariès had De Dion axles, while larger cars used chain drive up to 1912. A 6-cylinder engine was introduced in 1908, and also a narrow-angle V4 of 1130cc. In 1910 Ariès were offering two fours, of 1130 and 2880cc, and a 3444cc V6. All had monobloc cylinders and chain-driven gearboxes. An additional factory was opened at Courbevoie, and used largely for commercial vehicle manufacture, which was more significant than that of passenger cars. 350 vehicles were made in 1913, but fewer than half of these were cars. Five models of 4-cylinder car were offered in 1914, from a 1327cc 10/12hp to a 4487cc 20/30hp, the latter with Knight sleeve-valve engine. A large contract for army trucks during World War I helped Ariès to make good profits, and they also made Hispano-Suiza aero engines. Quite a wide range of cars was made in the 1920s, 12 and 15CV side-valve models, and three with single ohc-engines, from the 960cc (later 1085cc) 5/8CV to the 3178cc 15/20CV. The 3-litre sixes that ran at Le Mans and other long-distance races with some success from 1925 to 1927 had a capacity of 2952cc to bring them within the 3-litre limit, and gave up to 96bhp. These ohc engines were made by Ariès rather than Aster, though the latter were used in trucks up to the early 1930s. The 7CV and 15/20CV were replaced in 1930 by a single model with a new engine designed by Henri Touté, who had been responsible for the ohc Chenard-Walcker engines of the 1920s. His 1496cc CB4 had overhead inlet and side exhaust valves, and grew to 1628cc in 1934, 1767cc in 1935 and 1977cc in 1936. The gearbox was a regular 3-speed synchromesh unit, but from 1935 there was a 2-speed rear axle controlled by a button on the gear-lever knob, giving six forward speeds. Called the Super 10-50, this model was made up to 1938. Ariès never abandoned their vertical radiator, though from 1935 they offered a streamlined fastback coupé whose body was made by Antem. Other body styles were a 4-light saloon, 6-light limousine, cabriolet and roadster. They were considerably more expensive than mass-produced cars of the same size, 36,000 francs compared with 22,900 for a Peugeot 401. Fewer than 100 were sold per year, and even fewer in 1937 and 1938. Baron Petiet was president of the Chambre Syndicale d'Automobiles and the Paris Salon for many years, the latter up to his death in 1958.

NG

ARIMOFA (D) 1921–1922

Ari-Motorfahrzeugbau GmbH, Plauen.

This company offered a single 2-seater powered by a 4/12PS proprietary engine.

HON

ARISTA (i) (F) 1912–1915

Établissements Ruffier, Paris.

This ambitious firm offered seven different models in 1913, one single-cylinder 6hp of 720cc and six fours from 8 to 12hp. They had friction transmission or conventional gearboxes. The *Catalogue des Catalogues* mentioned the make in 1919.

NG

ARISTA (ii) (F) 1952–1967

Automobiles Arista, Paris; Vigny.

Like several other small French marques (D.B., MARATHON, RAFALE, R.E.A.C.) the Arista used Dyna-Panhard mechanical components, with sporting bodies of their own design. It was developed from the CALLISTA, and the former Callista Ranalagh became the Arista Le Mans, made as a steel roadster or fibreglass coupé. The latter were sold in 2-seater (Rallye) or 2+2 (Passy) models. The Dyna engine was used in 42bhp normal or 50bhp Tigre versions for the more sporting Aristas. When the Dyna engine was no longer available, a few Aristas were made with Ford Corsair or 20MTS V4 units. Total production of the Arista was 106 units.

NG

ARISTON (US) 1906

L.D. Sheppard, Chicago, Illinois.

Two models of the Ariston were offered, the 30/35hp Model S and the 40/50hp Model G, but the make did not survive the year (1906).

NG

ARIZONA Z-CAR (US) c.1992

Arizona Z-Car, Mesa, Arizona.

Something different in kit car circles was this company that specialised in kits based on the Datsun/Nissan Z-car chassis. The Proto Z was a clean convertible conversion on an early 240/280Z with a more rounded nose and side vents. The ZX IMSA gave the later ZX a racer look, with wide wheel flares, covered headlights, a wide nose spoiler, and a rear wing. The GTO body kit for the 240/280Z was similar to the Ferrari replica sold by ALPHA. They also offered V8 conversion kits.

HP

ARKLEY (i) (GB) 1970–1995

1970–1987 Arkley Engineering (John Britten Garages), Arkley, Herefordshire.
1987–1995 Arkley Sportscars (Peter May Engineering), Halesowen, West Midlands.

The Arkley was an extremely popular way of transforming the appearance of the MG Midget for not much outlay. The front and rear bodywork was taken off and replaced with new glassfibre panels with a fun car/traditional cross-over flavour. The earliest examples had cut-away doors – later ones used standard Midget doors – and there were two models: an S version with narrower wheel-arches for standard MG wheels and an SS for wider alloy wheels. Almost 1000 were made in all.

CR

ARKLEY (ii) (US) c.1980 to date

North American Arkley, Portland, Oregon.

The popular British Arkley kit car was built under licence by this American company. They were based on MG Midget chassis, but Datsun and Mazda RX-7 engines were optional.

HP

ARKON (GB) 1971

Richard Moon, Purley, Surrey.

Probably inspired by the PROBE, this was an extremely low coupé that used a Hillman Imp rear-mounted engine and rear suspension in a Triumph Spitfire chassis with extra strengthening. A slightly larger version was intended to enter production, but this did not proceed.

CR

ARMAC (US) 1905–1906

Armac Motor Co., Chicago, Illinois.

Archie McCullen was a motorcycle maker who offered side- and fore-car attachments to his cycles, and also a 6hp buckboard-type light car with belt drive. The engine was, not surprisingly, one of his motorcyle units. After a few had been built he returned to 2-wheelers.

NG

ARMADALE (GB) 1906–1907

1906 Armadale Motors Ltd, Northwood, Middlesex.
1907 Northwood Motor & Engineering Works, Northwood, Middlesex.

The first product of this company was a tri-car powered by either a single-cylinder Aster or 2-cylinder Fafnir engine. It also went under the name Toboggan. In 1906 they also made a conventional car with 16hp 4-cylinder engine and chain drive.

NG

ARMOR *see* ALCYON

ARMSTRONG (i) (US) 1896

Armstrong Mfg Co., Bridgeport, Connecticut.

This was a 2-cylinder car with wheel steering (advanced for 1896) and belt drive. It is not known how many were made, but one survives today.

NG

ARMSTRONG (ii) (US) 1901–1902

M. Armstrong & Co., New Haven, Connecticut.

This company made electric cars with two Eddy motors and Willard batteries. Maximum speed was 14mph (22 km/h).

NG

1971 Arkley (i) SS sports car.
NICK GEORGANO/NATIONAL MOTOR MUSEUM

1906 Armadale 14hp 2-seater.
NATIONAL MOTOR MUSEUM

ARMSTRONG (iii) (GB) 1913–1914

Armstrong Motor Co., Birmingham.

The Armstrong cyclecar could be had with air- or water-cooled engines, both 8hp 2-cylinder units by Precision. The air-cooled model had belt drive and cost 95 guineas (£99.75), while the water-cooled model was more car-like with shaft drive, and cost 100 guineas (£105.00).

NG

ARMSTRONG (iv) (US) c.1991

Armstrong Motor Works, Rancho Cucamonga, California.

The Armstrong Titan was a high-quality Lamborghini Countach replica powered by a Chevrolet V8 engine. It used a steel space frame and high quality components throughout, including an optional supercharger.

HP

ARMSTRONG-SIDDELEY (GB) 1919–1960

Armstrong-Siddeley Motors Ltd, Parkside, Coventry.

Armstrong-Siddeley Motors Ltd was founded after World War I in October 1919 as a fully-owned subsidiary of Sir W.G. Armstrong Whitworth Development Co. Ltd. This had been registered in May 1919 as a joint venture between John D. Siddeley of Coventry and Sir W.G. Armstrong, Whitworth & Co. of Newcastle upon Tyne to take over and combine assets and operations of the Siddeley-Deasy Motor Car Co. Ltd and the motor car and aircraft departments of Armstrong-Whitworth. Sir W.G. Armstrong, Whitworth & Co. Ltd paid out £419,750 to the Siddeley-Deasy shareholders, and operations were centralized at Parkside.

John D. Siddeley was named managing director of Armstrong-Siddeley Motors Ltd but did not have a seat on the board of Sir W.G. Armstrong Whitworth Development Co. Ltd.

In February 1920 J.D. Siddeley proposed that aircraft production should be handled by a separate subsidiary, and the Sir W.G. Armstrong Whitworth Aircraft Company was duly registered. Yet aircraft production remained at Parkside until 1923, when it was transferred to new premises at Whitley.

c.1923 Armstrong-Siddeley 30hp limousine by Hooper.
NATIONAL MOTOR MUSEUM

1934 Armstrong-Siddeley 12hp coupé.
NATIONAL MOTOR MUSEUM

1935 Armstrong-Siddeley 17hp Wingham cabriolet by Martin Walker.
NATIONAL MOTOR MUSEUM

1935 Armstrong-Siddeley 20 saloon.
NICK GEORGANO

J.D. Siddeley was equally attached to automobiles and aircraft engines. From a financial viewpoint they were logical partners, tending to stabilize annual turnover across the cyclical fluctuations in the car market and the ups and downs of national defence spending. Civil aviation was insignificant in 1920, and an aircraft-engine maker was entirely dependent on military orders, either from Whitehall or overseas.

There was no thought of resumed production of prewar Siddeley-Deasy models. Having been impressed by American cars in service in Britain during World War I, J.D. Siddeley decided to build cars of American type; that is, orthodox in layout, large and powerful, using top-quality materials.

Prior to the end of 1918, his son Ernest was able to arrange the purchase of a Marmon Series 34 through British agents for Delco electrical equipment, to serve as a basic reference.

F.R. Smith (1882–1930) was named chief engineer for the car project. He had accepted an offer from J.D. Siddeley to become chief engineer of Siddeley-Deasy in 1916. One of his first tasks was to redesign the BHP (Beardmore-Halford-Pullinger) 6-cylinder in-line ohc 18,000cc aircraft engine, which Siddeley-Deasy produced as the Puma for two years, building a total of 3225 units. He also designed the Tiger V12 aircraft engine.

Ernest Hall Siddeley (1895–1985) also had a great deal of influence on the design of the company's first car. He had joined his father at Siddeley-Deasy in 1913, but volunteered for military service in October 1914 as a lieutenant in the Royal West Kent Regiment. Having fought in the Somme offensive and contracted Trench Fever he was invalided out near the end of 1916. He made a study tour of the American motor industry and its suppliers in 1919, visiting 32 factories. On his return to Coventry, he was named assistant to the works manager, A.G. Asbury, who had worked for Swift before joining Vickers at the Crayford plant, where he first met J.D. Siddeley.

In addition to producing engines and assembling the chassis, the Parkside plant manufactured its own gearbox and rear axle, steering gear, and suspension systems, and built its own clutch and brakes from purchased components. Bodies were designed at Parkside, where Mr Inglis had the title of coach manager, and were produced by the Burlington Carriage Co., which J.D. Siddeley had acquired in 1913 and by the British & Colonial Aeroplane Co. (which became the Bristol Aeroplane Company in 1920).

F.R. Smith made no effort to copy the Marmon engine, which had a 1-piece aluminium block and 5-bearing crankshaft. The Armstrong-Siddeley Six, also known as the 30 for its taxable hp-rating, had two cast-iron 3-cylinder blocks and a 3-bearing crankshaft. What it had in common with the Marmon was a long stroke (stroke/bore ratios were 1.366 in the Marmon and 1.5:1 in the 30) and pushrod-operated overhead valves. The Marmon's displacement was 5574cc against 4960cc in the 30. Marmon's all-aluminium engine construction was not trouble-free, however, and, in a 1920 redesign, it was given two cast-iron 3-cylinder blocks and three main bearings!

On the 30 the engine blocks had open sides with aluminium water plates and external pushrods enclosed in light-alloy tubes. Each block had its own cylinder head. Hollow steel con-rods carried cast-iron pistons. A big water pump was mounted near the front of the engine, drawing water from the bottom of the radiator and feeding it to the blocks. A front-mounted flywheel of open-spoked pattern was intended to draw some air through the radiator. Peak output was 60hp at 2000–2250rpm, compared with 74hp in the Marmon.

A Lucas starter motor had chain drive with a free-wheel to the crankshaft, and the Lucas generator was belt-driven from the input side of the clutch. The car from Coventry had a dry multi-plate clutch, which compared favourably with Marmon's old-type cone clutch. Both cars had 3-speed (and reverse) gearboxes with the common H-form shift pattern. But drive lines were quite different. The Marmon had Hotchkiss drive with a double-jointed open propeller shaft. On the 30 a short shaft separated the gearbox from the engine, and the propeller shaft was enclosed in a torque tube that was rigidly fixed to the gearbox, which meant putting the full driving thrust into the gearbox mountings.

The rear axle casing was made of aluminium, with final-drive gearing of 3.69:1. The gearbox gave direct drive in third, with a 1.63:1 second and 3.36:1 first.

There was no similarity in chassis design. In fact the Armstrong-Siddeley frame was unusual in having integral running boards, and the cantilever rear springs laid inside the channel-section side members.

The front end with its V-shaped radiator was designed by F.G. Crosby, the famous motor-racing illustrator who also designed the Bentley's radiator. The

Sphinx on the radiator cap was inherited from Siddeley-Deasy and registered as a trademark in 1920. Siddeley-Deasy had begun using Daimler sleeve-valve engines in 1911, and when a press report stated that the car was as silent and inscrutable as a Sphinx, J. D. Siddeley began showing a Sphinx in his advertising campaign.

2000 cars were scheduled for production in 1920, and the Parkside works easily turned out 1000 chassis, but cars could not be completed due to a constant shortage of bodies. Nevertheless, by the end of the year they were turning out 75 cars a week.

Production of a medium-priced 18hp model with a 2318cc 6-cylinder ohv engine began towards the end of 1921. Its technical specifications read like a downscaled version of the 30, built on a 120in (3046mm) wheelbase, compared to 135in (3426mm). Plans to build 20 18hp cars a week proved over-optimistic, but the situation was solved by the suspension of 30 production in 1922–23.

In 1922 E. Siddeley was named superintendent of car testing and finishing, his elder brother Cyril having joined the firm in 1919 to take up administrative and commercial duties. Cyril Davenport Siddeley (1894–1958) was educated at St Lawrence College and was a trainee with Lloyds Bank from 1911 to 1914. He spent World War I as an officer with the Royal Warwickshire Regiment.

Aiming for a broader section of the market, Armstrong-Siddeley introduced a 14hp model for 1923, with a flat-face honeycomb radiator to emphasize its poor relation status. It was powered by an 1852cc 4-cylinder ohv engine with a one-piece cylinder block, had a simple frame, front and rear quarter-elliptic springs, and stood on a 111in (2817mm) wheelbase.

In 1924, when 500 14hp chassis had been built, J.D. Siddeley scheduled another 1000, plus 500 18hp chassis. The 30 re-entered production, with optional Perrot front-wheel brakes. No models had bumpers as standard equipment, as C. Siddeley felt they were a sign of bad driving. 'Good drivers don't need bumpers', he declared.

Big changes were made for the 1926 models, distinguished by Mk II designation. 4-wheel brakes became standard on all models. The 18hp engine grew in size to 2872cc and both the 18hp and 30hp engines were made with one-piece blocks and one-piece heads. Aluminium pistons were fitted across the board. Bigger valves were put into the 30hp engine. On the 18hp models, the cantilever rear springs were replaced by semi-elliptics, shackled at both ends.

At the business level, 1926 was also an important year. J.D. Siddeley expressed dissatisfaction with the way profits from Armstrong-Siddeley Motors were being used to prop up a mismanaged parent organisation, after millions of pounds had been wasted on a paper-mill project in Newfoundland.

He secured the financial backing of the Midland Bank and offered to purchase the Sir W.G. Armstrong Whitworth Development Co. Ltd. The sale was arranged in November 1926 for the sum of £1,500,000. J.D Siddeley immediately took a seat on the board and was selected chairman in February 1927. In March 1927 he changed the company name to Armstrong-Siddeley Development Co. Ltd. He wanted to keep the Armstrong name for the firm as well as its products, even though the Armstrong connection had been severed (the Armstrong Whitworth Aircraft Company became part of the Vickers group in 1928).

The model range continued to evolve, and Armstrong-Siddeley preceded Austin and Hotchkiss in giving geographical names to their body styles. In the 14hp line-up for 1926 were the Mendip wide-bodied roadster with 3-abreast seating and the Sandown sports tourer with slanted doors and a hint of a boat-tail. The following year one could also buy a Broadway saloon and a Lonsdale 4-door 6-light saloon on the 14hp chassis. A 14hp Cotswold tourer and Manston fabric saloon were added for 1928. The 14hp line was phased out in 1929.

The 1926 Long 18 chassis provided a base for the Ascot all-weather 4-seater, the Chester Landaulette and York limousine. In addition, there were the Maidstone folding-head limousine and the Malvern 7-passenger limousine. Buyers of the 1927 chassis had a choice of the Shrewsbury touring landaulette, Richmond limousine, and Cheltenham Pullman limousine.

Late in 1927 Armstrong-Siddeley brought out a 15hp model with an L-head 6-cylinder engine of 1900cc, sharing the 14hp chassis and choice of body styles. At the same time all models were fitted with central chassis lubrication.

For 1928 the 18hp model was renamed Short 20 and the Long 18 became Long 20. The Short 20 introduced the Sterling saloon and Cranwell fabric saloon. All 1928 models were given instrument panels with a central cluster.

In October 1928 a 12hp 1236cc 6-cylinder L-head model went into production with a new chassis on a 105in (2665mm) wheelbase, featuring a separately

1937 Armstrong-Siddeley 20/25 saloon.
NICK GEORGANO

1938 Armstrong-Siddeley 16 saloon.
NICK GEORGANO

1950 Armstrong-Siddeley Whitley 18hp saloon.
NATIONAL MOTOR MUSEUM

1956 Armstrong-Siddeley Sapphire saloon.
NATIONAL MOTOR MUSEUM

mounted gearbox, cast-iron torque tube, and banjo-type pressed-steel rear axle. Due to inadequate performance, the engine was sent to Ricardo for testing and analysis, but it was simply bored out to 1434cc for 1931.

The Wilson pre-selector gearbox was available on the 20hp and 30hp model before the end of 1928. J.D. Siddeley had become convinced of the merits of the planetary transmission and decided to back it financially, becoming a co-founder and governing director of Improved Gears Ltd in December 1928.

The central gear lever on the floor was replaced by a small stick moving in a quadrant on the steering-wheel, the positions being marked Reverse, Neutral, Low, Medium, Normal and High. What looked like a normal clutch was simply a gear-engagement pedal.

On the 1929 30hp cars, the fuel tank was moved to the tail end of the frame, with an Autovac fuel supply system. The rear suspension on the 20hp chassis was redesigned, with the leaf springs slung below the axle casing.

Works manager A.G. Asbury died in May 1928, and was succeeded by F. Baron, who went to Bristol after a quarrel with J.D. Siddeley but returned after a brief absence. E. and C. Siddeley were appointed board members of Armstrong-Siddeley Motors Ltd in 1928, and Cyril was named sales director. Late in 1929 E. Siddeley was promoted to technical manager for Aero Engines and Special Projects.

When Baron died in 1931, Harold Thomas Chapman (1898–1985), who had joined the company in 1926 as an aircraft-engine designer, was transferred to the production side, while C.S. Oliver was hired from Humber to take over as works manager. At the same time, E. Siddeley engaged F.W. Allard, son of the manufacturer of Rex Motorcycles, as chief engineer for motor cars.

During 1929 an indoor 3-in-one test hill was built at the Parkside works, and chrome-plating facilities were also installed.

In March 1930 the 4-speed Wilson pre-selector gearbox became standard equipment on the 20hp and 30hp models, followed by the 15hp models in May 1930. In 1931 Daimler's 'Fluid Flywheel' became a £50 option for pre-selector-equipped cars, but a year later it was no longer available. In 1933 the Newton centrifugal clutch was installed on all models.

The 30hp model was taken out of production at the end of 1931 after a cumulative 12-year total of 2700 units.

Beginning with the 1930 models, all cars had anti-dazzle headlamps, automatic spark advance, and Triplex safety glass. A 12hp 4-door 4-light fabric saloon was added to the line-up. A Special 20, with cantilever springs, was offered, and in March 1930 the rear axle on the 15hp chassis was reinforced and mounted on underslung springs.

For 1931 the 15hp line was split into Normal 15 and Short 15, the latter on a 109in (2766mm) wheelbase with a 3-speed pre-selector gearbox, and the Normal 15 with 115in (2919mm) wheelbase and a 4-speed pre-selector. The reworked engine had a new cylinder head, revised cam contours, and an air cleaner. The chassis was lower, with a redesigned front axle, pivots and steering gear, while Silentbloc bushings replaced several grease points in the automatic chassis lubrication system. The steering column was adjustable for rake, and the starter was operated by pushbutton and solenoid switch.

The 3-speed pre-selector became optional on the 1931 12hp, which was further improved in April 1931 (rubber engine mountings; generator on the timing case).

On the 1932 12hp models Autovac was adopted with a rear-mounted fuel tank, and the 3-speed pre-selector gearbox was standard, with an optional 4-speed pre-selector. A year later, the Autovac was replaced by a mechanical fuel pump on the engine.

The 20hp engine was enlarged to 3190cc (longer stroke) and fitted with a belt-driven fan for 1932. Late in 1932 the 15hp engine was given a new long-stroke crankshaft, raising displacement to 2169cc.

The Siddeley Special

This was E. Siddeley's dream car, an over-ambitious bid to join the world elite of prestige cars. It was big, with wheelbases of 132in (3350mm) and 144in (3655mm), and a weight approaching 2 tons in the tourer-bodied version.

The 6-cylinder engine had the same 4960cc displacement as the original 30, with the same bore and stroke, but the construction could not have been more different. Most of the castings were Hiduminium, a new aircraft-engine metal developed jointly by Rolls-Royce and High Duty Alloys. They included the crankcase, block, head, con-rods and pistons. Still the engine weighed 303kg (including flywheel and clutch).

The piston ran in wet liners, and the fully counterbalanced crankshaft had a vibration damper at the front end and seven main bearings. Fabroil timing gears were used, and the camshaft also drove the oil- and fuel-pumps. Hydraulic tappets were adopted after about 18 months. The gear-driven generator had an extended shaft to drive the water pump. A hot-spot manifold and twin exhaust system were fitted. Output was 145hp at 2700rpm. The gearbox was separately mounted, linked with the torque tube by a ball-joint.

The chassis had a double-dropped channel-section frame with outrigger semi-elliptics on the rear axle.

The original Siddeley Special was introduced in October 1932, and the Mk II appeared in June 1935. The changes for the Mk II included replacement of the single Claudel-Hobson carburettor with twin SUs, and moving the engine 2in (51mm) forward in the frame. The front springs were mounted on roller slides instead of shackles at both ends, and the axle was braced by hefty radius rods. The rear springs were increased in length. Vacuum-assisted power brakes and Bijur automatic chassis lubrication were standard. Bumpers were optional – but only if made by Wilmot-Breeden.

Siddeley Special production ended in 1937 after a run of 252 cars. Ninety of the chassis carried bodies by Burlington, and ten were bodied by Weymann. Hooper and Vanden Plas each made eight bodies for the Siddeley Special, Martin Walter produced 14 bodies of various styles, and Park Ward built five sedancas. Lancefield produced a slab-sided streamliner, and other one-off bodies were made by Gurney Nutting, Mann Egerton, Barker and Saoutchik.

The Hawker-Siddeley Period

Realizing that he was approaching the end of his career, J.D. Siddeley began preparations for Armstrong-Siddeley to continue without him. He approached Handley-Page with a merger proposition in 1934, which proved fruitless. But in 1935 he reached an agreement with T.O.M. 'Tommy' Sopwith for the outright sale of Armstrong-Siddeley, with all its subsidiaries, to the Hawker Aircraft Company.

Thomas Octave Murdoch Sopwith (1888–1989) was a pioneer aviator who set up the Sopwith Aviation Company at Kingston-on-Thames in 1912 and led its growth, with reorganization as the Hawker Aircraft Co. in 1923. Armstrong-Siddeley Development Co. Ltd then went out of existence, being absorbed into a new group, Hawker-Siddeley Aircraft Ltd.

J.D. Siddeley stayed on as chairman of Armstrong-Siddeley Motors Ltd until his formal resignation on 30 September 1936, and E.H. Siddeley left in June 1937. T.O.M. Sopwith became chairman of the new board, which included Frank S. Spriggs, H. K. Jones as managing director, A.J. Austen, and C.S. Oliver as general manager.

The 1935 model line-up was composed of the 12hp, 15hp, 17hp, Long 20, and Siddeley Special. The 17 had gone into production in August 1934, with an ohv 2394cc engine and 4-speed pre-selector gearbox, torque tube drive, and a new frame with parallel semi-elliptic springs all around. The saloon was built on a 116in (2944mm) wheelbase, and the 17 Sports on a wheelbase of 111in (2817mm), with its own double-drop frame. The 15 was discontinued at the end of 1935, effectively replaced by the 17. The 12 was phased out during 1936, its place taken by 12-Plus powered by a new ohv 1666cc 6-cylinder engine. The chassis was a downscaled version of the 17, with a 105in (2665mm) wheelbase (increased to 108in (2741mm) in December 1935).

The Long 20 was taken out of production at the end of 1936 and replaced by the 20/25 with a new ohv 3670cc short-stroke (114.3mm vs 127mm in the Long 20) 6-cylinder engine. It was not scaled down from the Siddeley Special power unit, but a separate design with four main bearings, cast-iron block, Invar-strur Bohnalite pistons, and steel con-rods. On the 1937 model, the 4-speed pre-selector gearbox was mounted separately, but for 1938 it was combined with the engine. Instead of a torque tube, the 20/25 had an open, universal-jointed propeller shaft and Hotchkiss drive. C. Siddeley designed the Atalanta 4-door sports saloon bodies for the 17 and 20/25 chassis. He remained with the company until 1939, when he rejoined the Royal Warwickshire Regiment.

The 12-Plus was renamed 14 for 1937, without any material change in specifications. But for 1938, the 14 pre-selector gearbox was joined to the engine, a modification that was also applied to the 17 at the same time.

A new short-stroke (105mm, reduced from 114.3mm) 2780cc ohv engine appeared in the 1938 Ensign 20, which was short-lived, and the 1939 New 20 had the same engine in a conventional chassis, derived from that of the 17. The 20/25, renamed 25 on the same occasion, and a new 16 Six with a 1991cc ohv engine was introduced.

Early in 1943 Armstrong-Siddeley began planning their new postwar products. A new engineering team went to work on the car project, with Sidney Thornett as chief engineer, G. Mervyn Cutler in charge of development, and Percy Riman as body designer. The car itself was ready early in 1945, when the factory was still fully occupied with military orders. Production start-up was planned for December 1945, and Armstrong-Siddeley was first by far in announcing new postwar cars, with public presentation of the Hurricane on 11 May 1945.

The Hurricane coupé was quickly followed by the Lancaster saloon. The Typhoon hardtop-style 2-door saloon was added late in 1946. The 1991cc engine came from the 16-Six introduced in 1939, updated with hydraulic tappets. It had a 4-speed gearbox, with synchromesh on top, third, and second. The chassis featured independent front suspension with longitudinal torsion bars, an x-braced channel-section frame underslung at the rear axle, and hypoid-bevel final drive. The bodies were built on a steel floorplan with a steel cage at the rear end, but most of the structure had a timber framework. Body panels were mostly steel, but the doors had aluminium skins and the hindquarters were aluminium-panelled.

For export models, the engine was bored out to 2309cc in 1948 and fitted with wet liners. Six Tempest saloons were made in 1949, from the idea of using the Typhoon styling on a 4-door saloon. They led to the development of the Whitley 6-light saloon, on a longer wheelbase, with a body that was also wider on the inside because the doors were thinner. The Whitley was powered by the 2309cc engine, which became standard for all models in 1950. It also had a 4-speed pre-selector gearbox with a new fingertip H-pattern electric switch on the left of the steering hub. The Whitley replaced the Typhoon, and the Whitley was taken out of production in 1952 because its successor was ready.

The Station coupé and Utility coupé added in 1949 were a compromise between the business coupé and pick-up truck, sharing the saloon sheet-metal from the grille to the B-post, with a cargo bin in place of the back seat. Some Station coupés built in 1949 had the 1991cc engine, but most of them, produced up to 1954, had the 2309cc engine. The Utility coupé had a longer club cab body, and all 708 units made had the 2309cc engine.

The project which led to the Sapphire started in 1950. W.O. Bentley was consulted in the planning stages, and he drew up a twin-ohc engine (much like the Lagonda's), which ran into timing-chain trouble in the early testing period and was eliminated. The production engine had a crossflow head and operated by unequal-length (for inlet and exhaust) pushrods from a single chain-driven camshaft in the side of the block. The 3435cc in-line six had four main bearings and a fully balanced crankshaft, producing 120hp in its initial version, which was first shown to the public at Earl's Court in October 1952. A twin-carburettor engine rated at 150hp followed. The styling, closely supervised by C. Siddeley who retired in 1952, was a compromise between Armstrong-Siddeley traditions and the Austin Sheerline look.

The initial Sapphire 346 had the same electric-switch pre-selector as the Whitley, open propeller shaft, and parallel semi-elliptics underslung at the rear axle. The front suspension changed from torsion bars to coil springs, with similar geometry, and power steering was standard from 1955 onwards. The pre-selector was dropped for the Mk II, which had a 4-speed synchromesh gearbox made by the Rootes Group (shared with the Humber Hawk) as standard, with an optional 4-speed Hydra-matic made by Rolls-Royce.

A long-wheelbase Sapphire Limousine was made from 1955 to 1959. In 1959 the engine was bored out to 3990cc for the Star Sapphire, which was built only with a 3-speed Borg-Warner automatic transmission. A 5000cc V8 was in the planning stage when the decision was made to stop car production.

A total of 7246 Sapphires and 1284 Star Sapphires were produced. The last Star Sapphire saloon was made on 5 July 1960, and the last Star Sapphire limousine on 6 September 1960.

The company introduced two cross-breed lower-priced Sapphires late in 1955, the 234 and the 236, with shorter wheelbases and their own, not entirely happy, styling. The Sapphire 236 was powered by the former Whitley 2309cc 6-cylinder engine, rated at 85hp at 4500rpm. The 4-speed synchromesh gearbox was made at Parkside, and options included Manumatic (clutchless drive) and Laycock-de Normanville overdrive. The 234 had a new 4-cylinder engine of 2290cc, created by chopping two cylinders off the Sapphire 346 unit, producing 120hp at 5000rpm, available only with a conventional clutch and 4-speed gearbox. The Parkside works turned out 803 cars of 234 specification, and 609 cars of 236 specification, until their demise in 1958.

In 1959 Armstrong-Siddeley Motors Ltd merged with Bristol Aero Engines Ltd to become Bristol-Siddeley Engines Ltd, which was taken over by Rolls-Royce in 1967. The Parkside plant was used for turbo-jet engine maintenance and repair work until 1975, when it was closed.

JPN

1912 Armstrong-Whitworth 15/20hp landaulet.
NATIONAL MOTOR MUSEUM

1914 Armstrong-Whitworth 28hp tourer.
NATIONAL MOTOR MUSEUM

Further Reading
Armstrong-Siddeley, The Parkside Story, Ray Cook, Rolls-Royce Heritage Trust, Derby, 1988.
Armstrong-Siddeley, The Postwar Cars, Robert Penn Bradly, Motor Racing Publications, 1989.

ARMSTRONG-WHITWORTH (GB) 1906–1914

Sir W.G. Armstrong, Whitworth & Co. Ltd, Newcastle upon Tyne.

This company was one of Britain's leading makers of armaments as well as having substantial interests in shipbuilding with yards at Barrow-in-Furness. William Armstrong was a solicitor who began making hydraulic machinery in 1847, followed by rifles from 1855. In 1897 his company merged with that of Sir Joseph Whitworth, pioneer of the standard screw thread. The Elswick works at Newcastle made two 'foreign' designs of car, the ROOTS & VENABLES from 1902 to 1904, and the WILSON-PILCHER from 1904 to 1907. The car department was set up by works manager Charles Englebach (1876–1943) who was later works director at AUSTIN.

The first Armstrong-Whitworth car was the 4522cc 28/36hp with 4-cylinder T-head engine of oversquare dimensions (120 x 100mm), 4-speed gearbox and shaft drive. It was only listed in 1906 and 1907, being followed by the 5064cc 30hp and 7698cc 40hp. In 1909 these were joined by a smaller 18/22hp of

1896 Arnold dog cart at the start of the Emancipation Run.
NATIONAL MOTOR MUSEUM

1955 Arnolt-Bristol 2-litre coupé.
NATIONAL MOTOR MUSEUM

3400cc with a 5-bearing crankshaft. 1910 saw a still smaller model, the 2412cc 12/14hp with monobloc engine and pressure lubrication. In 1912 they made their first 6-cylinder car, the 5150cc 30/50, which was enlarged to 5722cc for 1913, though as the bore was unchanged it was still rated as a 30/50. It had a 4-speed gearbox, dual magneto ignition, an engine-operated tyre pump and optional electric lighting. It was made up to the outbreak of war, together with three 4-cylinder cars, a 15/20, 17/25, and 20/30. The motor department was in a separate factory, with 750 employees in 1914. Output was about 10 to 12 chassis per week.

In 1919 Armstrong-Whitworth merged their car division with SIDDELEY-DEASY to form ARMSTRONG-SIDDELEY Motors Ltd. In 1927 the armaments division was merged with Vickers to form Vickers-Armstrong Ltd. Their aircraft division made the Spitfire and, as Vickers Ltd, they owned ROLLS-ROYCE from 1980 to 1998.

NG

ARNAULT (F) 1968–1972
Éts Arnault, Garches.
The Arnault K5T was a fun/utility car very similar in concept to the Renault Rodeo. It had glassfibre bodywork mounted over a Renault 4 platform and was offered in three versions: Tarantelle (basic 2/3-seater), Taïga (solid roof cabin) and Toundra (fixed cabin).

CR

ARNO (GB) 1908
Arno Motor Co., Coventry.
The Arno was a medium-sized tourer powered by a 35hp White & Poppe engine. It probably did not pass the prototype stage.

NG

ARNOLD (GB) 1896–1898
Arnold Motor Carriage Co., East Peckham, Kent.
The agricultural engineering company of William Arnold & Sons dated back to 1844. In 1895 Walter Arnold brought back a Benz from Germany and acquired a licence to build and sell them in England. He entered five cars and a van in the London–Brighton Emancipation Run in November 1896, but only one was British made, the others being imports. In 1897 and 1898 11 Arnold cars were built, all basically Benz in design but with Arnold-made engines, which differed in cylinder dimensions and in having bronze castings instead of iron. The 1896 prototype was bought by electrical engineer H.J. Dowsing, who fitted it with an electric starter, the world's first. It was a dynamotor coupled to the flywheel, which was supposed to assist the car up hills as well as to start it. This car survives today.

NG

ARNOLT (US) 1953–1963
S.H. Arnolt Inc., Chicago, Illinois.
Stanley Howard 'Wacky' Arnolt was a mid-west distributor of British cars whose first offerings were a 2-door coupé and convertible, styled and built by Bertone, on the MG TD chassis. He sold 65 coupés and 35 convertibles in two years, then turned to a more powerful car which became much better known than the Arnolt-MGs. The Arnolt-Bristols' distinctively-styled light steel bodies were again built by Bertone, and the engine was the 1971cc 6-cylinder Bristol in 130bhp form (regular Bristol engines gave 100–125bhp at this time). Three coupés were made, and 254 roadsters, of which half were the De Luxe fully trimmed models, and the others were the Bolide stripped-down version with no hood. These did very well in SCCA racing. At $3995 a Bolide cost half the price of the Bristol 404 on which it was based.

NG

Further Reading
'Wacky: Stanley Harold Arnot and his cars', Rick Taylor, *Automobile Quarterly*, Vol. 15, No. 4; Vol. 16, No. 3; Vol. 16, No. 4.

ARNOTT (GB) 1951–1957
Arnott's Garages (Harlesden) Ltd, London.
Daphne Arnott was heiress to a London garage that specialised in tuning equipment and superchargers. In 1951, together with her works manager, she designed a 500cc Formula Three car which had a simple ladder frame and all-independent suspension. Six were made, and achieved no great success, but they were notable for their fibreglass bodies and for being the first European single-seaters which had seat belts as standard.

In 1955, the Formula Three car was used as the basis for a fibreglass-bodied sports car, although the engine was at the front. It was designed for an Austin A35 engine, but buyers of the seven cars made chose their own units.

Much was made in the press that a mere girl could build a sports car. Daphne became the first female constructor for a World Championship class when an 1100cc Coventry Climax-powered Arnott was entered at Le Mans in 1955. It crashed during practice.

A single sports racing car, with a spaceframe and cross-over suspension, was made in 1956, but was sold on as a road car. The company's swansong came in 1957 with a Climax-powered GT car which was entered at Le Mans (its only contemporary race), but it failed to last the distance.

MJL

ARNTZ (US) 1971–1981
Arntz Engineering Co., San Francisco, California.
Steve Arntz deserves the credit (or blame) for popularising Cobra replicas, which have been the largest segment of the kit car market in the US ever since. Although not the first Cobra clone on the market, the Arntz kits were the best-promoted and were a reasonably good product. Chassis development was done by Huffaker Engineering, who had been building successful racing cars for some time. The Arntz replicas used a rectangular-steel ladder frame with MGB front suspension and a Jaguar XKE IRS at the back. Ironically, most were fitted with Chevrolet V8s. Several were raced with success in amateur club racing. They sold in impressive numbers, and were exported all over the world, but Arntz still went out of business in 1981. The project ended up in the hands of BUTLER RACING, and later was passed on to G & S MOTORSPORTS.

HP

ARO (RO) 1957 to date

Aro SA, Campalung.

This factory originally made aircraft during World War II and built the first Rumanian motorcycle in 1953. From 1957 off-roader production had started. From day one models were based on the Russian GAZ off-roaders. Both were mainly destined for the Army, but slowly civil production increased. In 1963, following the updated GAZ 69, the new Aro (Automobil Romanescu, or Rumanian Car) M-461 was introduced. This was the first car to be exported to China and Columbia. The first self-designed Aro, the 24 series, was launched in 1966. It was a rugged and boxy construction, but was roomier than its predecessor and had serious off-road abilities. The model's career spanned almost two decades. It was one of the most successful East European off-roaders, having been exported to almost everywhere from Canada to Australia. One Aro won the Pharao Rally Raid. It was made under licence in Portugal by Portaro. The second generation of Aro off-roaders was born in 1980. It was the 10 series which became a popular fun car in Italy, France, and other places. It looked like a Suzuki Samurai, but was even more rugged and cheaper and, for some, more stylish. The Aro 10 shared many components, e.g., engines, with the DACIA 1310. The 24 series was reborn in 1989 with Ford, Daewoo, and Toyota engines. It was sold in Western Europe as the Aro Spartana or Dacia Duster.

PN

AROLA (F) 1976–1983

1976–1982 Arola sarl, Lyon-Corbas.

1982–1983 Arola sarl, Aix-les-Bains.

This was one of the most successful French makers of microcars. The first Arola's simple but elegant glassfibre enclosed bodywork marked it as a short step up from a moped, and indeed it used a 47cc Sachs engine in the rear. There was a single front wheel or, soon after, a 4-wheeled version with a Motobécane 50cc engine. As it grew longer and heavier, a BCB 125cc engine was offered. The 1982 Minoto was a model taken over from BEL-MOTORS. Having at one time sold over 4000 units per year, Arola went bankrupt in 1983 but rose from the ashes in the form of AIXAM.

CR

ARROL-JOHNSTON; ARROL-ASTER (GB) 1895–1931

1895–1901 The Mo-Car Syndicate Ltd, Bluevale, Camlachie, Glasgow.

1901–1905 The Mo-Car Syndicate Ltd, Paisley, Renfrewshire.

1905–1913 The New Arrol-Johnston Car Co. Ltd, Paisley, Dumfries.

1913–1927 Arrol-Johnston Ltd, Heathall, Dumfries.

1927–1931 Arrol-Johnston & Aster Engineering Co. Ltd, Heathall, Dumfries.

The Mo-Car Syndicate was formed by locomotive engineer George Johnston, his cousin Norman Fulton and Thomas Blackwood Murray, with finance coming from Sir William Arrol, an eminent consulting engineer who was the architect of the Forth Bridge. Johnston had conceived his car in 1894, and probably built it in 1895, several months before the formation of the company in November. This gave him a lead of several months, perhaps a year, over Frederick Lanchester, who is so often credited with making the first British car, but did not get onto the road until February or March 1896. Johnston's car was an unusual design, with an opposed-piston flat-twin engine. The connecting rod of one piston worked directly on the crankshaft, while the other acted through a rocking lever. The gearbox was driven by chain, with another single, central chain taking power to the rear axle. The dogcart-type body seated six passengers in three rows, with the driver in the second row. The solid tyres and high build were not out of the ordinary in 1895, but Johnston's design was still being made in 1906, by which time it was the most antique-looking car on the market. However, it sold reasonably well, being popular in the Scottish Highlands where it coped well with atrocious road surfaces. One was supplied to the Sudan as a military vehicle, towing a large searchlight on a 2-wheeled trailer.

In 1905 a new model was added to the range, with three cylinders, of which the central one had a larger bore than the other two. It was front-mounted and inclined and had the advanced feature of unit construction of engine and gearbox. Not so advanced was the continuing use of solid tyres, and it did not survive the new regime ushered in by the formation of the New Arrol-Johnston Co. in 1905. This was backed by Sir William Beardmore, later Lord Invernairn, head of the engineering company which made cars and taxis in the 1920s. There were several changes in personnel; Fulton and Blackwood Murray had left in 1899 to make

1956 Arnott sports car.
NICK GEORGANO/NATIONAL MOTOR MUSEUM

c.1995 Aro 10 Spartana utility.
NICK GEORGANO

c.1978 Arola microcar.
NICK GEORGANO

the ALBION, and George Johnston left in 1906 to make the unsuccessful ALL-BRITISH car and bus. A new designer was J.S. Napier, no connection with the London car makers of the same name. His first car had an 18hp front-mounted horizontal-twin engine of 3792cc; fitted with a light tourer body and, driven by its designer, it won the first Tourist Trophy Race in September 1905. Another similar car finished 4th. A smaller 12/15hp went into production, and in 1907 came two large vertical L-head fours, the 4650cc 24/30hp and 9760cc 38/45hp. In 1907 a special car was built for Ernest Shackleton's Antarctic expedition; it had an air-cooled Simms engine, which no production Arrol-Johnston used, and two sets of wheels, with wooden tyres and with Dunlop pneumatics; the latter proved much more successful. A foretaste of the future was its coal-scuttle bonnet which, combined with a dashboard radiator, characterised Arrol-Johnstons from 1909 to 1914.

The first of the new range was the 2412cc 15.9hp designed by T.C. Pullinger, who came to Arrol-Johnston from Sunbeam. The 15.9 was largely conventional apart from its use of Allen-Liversidge 4-wheel brakes. These were not popular as they were not linked, and synchronisation of working the front brakes by pedal

1902 Arrol-Johnston 12hp dog cart.
NATIONAL MOTOR MUSEUM

1912 Arrol-Johnston 24/30hp tourer.
NATIONAL MOTOR MUSEUM

1920 Arrol-Johnston 15.9hp tourer.
NATIONAL MOTOR MUSEUM

1928 Arrol-Aster 17/50hp fabric saloon.
NATIONAL MOTOR MUSEUM

and the rear ones by lever proved beyond many drivers. Other models in Pullinger's range were two fours, a 1794cc 11.9hp and a 3640cc 20.9hp, and a 3618cc 23.8hp six. In 1914 electric lighting and starting were available. Car production ended soon after the outbreak of World War I, and a new 17.9hp car with frontal radiator remained a prototype. An electric coupé based on the DETROIT ELECTRIC, but with coal-scuttle bonnet, was planned in 1913. Arrol-Johnston contracted to make 50, but probably only a single example was made.

Arrol-Johnston were among the first firms to get a postwar car onto the market. The appropriately-named Victory was an advanced design, with 2650cc single-ohc 4-cylinder engine, central gear and handbrake levers, and a streamlined tourer body fronted by an oval radiator. On paper it was an attractive proposition, but it was disastrously unreliable. This was highlighted when a car provided for the Prince of Wales for a West Country tour broke down at Yeovil and had to be withdrawn. The Victory was soon withdrawn from the market altogether, and replaced by a warmed-over prewar 15.9hp, now with frontal radiator. In 1920 this was being made at the rate of 50 cars a week, and it acquired a monobloc engine for 1922. Arrol-Johnston was also making the GALLOWAY in a separate factory to cover the cheaper end of the market, and one model of this shared the 1668cc engine of the Arrol-Johnston Twelve introduced for 1925. This was close to duplication of models, though the Galloway Twelve was cheaper by £80. There was also a larger Arrol-Johnston, the 3290cc Empire model for the Colonial market. Front wheel brakes arrived, not before time, on all models for 1926, and these also had ohv engines.

In April 1927 Arrol-Johnston merged with the ASTER Engineering Co. of Wembley, Middlesex, who were making more expensive cars, some with Burt-McCollum single sleeve-valve engines. Far from rationalising the two ranges, Arrol-Johnston simply added them together, so that for 1928 they offered six different models, from the Galloway at £360 to the 24/70 Aster at £1200. The 12hp Galloway, 15/40hp Arrol-Johnston, and 21/60hp Arrol-Aster had pushrod ohv engines, while the 17/50hp Arrol-Aster and 21/60 and 24/70hp Asters had sleeve-valves. For 1929 all models except the six-cylinder Arrol-Aster and the two sleeve-valve Aster sixes were dropped, but there was a new 23/70hp straight-8 Arrol-Aster of 3273cc. This was made as a saloon, coupé, or sports model, the latter available with cozette supercharger. Few were sold, and in July 1929 the company went into liquidation, though production limped on for about another 18 months. By September 1931 the factory was said to be making industrial machinery.

NG

ARROW (i) (US) 1907
Arrow Motor Buggy Co., St Louis, Missouri.
This was a typical high-wheeler, with horizontal 2-cylinder engine and chain drive. Its price was $250.

NG

ARROW (ii) (US) 1914
M.C. Whitmore Co., Dayton, Ohio.
One of two cyclecars sold under the Arrow name in the same year, this was offered in single- or 2-seater forms (tandem or side by side), as well as a light delivery van. The engine was a 12hp Spacke V-twin, and the Arrow had a 2-speed planetary transmission, shaft final drive, and an ash frame. Triple transverse springs took the place of a front axle. The Arrow was marketed through the National United Service Co. of Detroit, who also made their own cyclecar in 1914. Confusingly this was also named Arrow.

NG

ARROW (iii) (US) 1914
National United Service Co., Detroit, Michigan.
Not content with distributing the Dayton-built ARROW (ii) cyclecar, as well as the BEISEL built in Monroe, Michigan, and carburettors, sparking plugs and batteries, this company made a cyclecar of their own. With an 18hp 4-cylinder engine it was in a larger class than the Dayton product. Although both were listed in 1914, possibly the Detroit car took the place of the Dayton one, as two different cyclecars could hardly be sold simultaneously under the same name.

NG

ARROW (iv) see E.G.

ARROWBILE (US) 1937–1938

Waterman Arrowplane Corp., Santa Monica, California.

Waldo Waterman was a pioneer of aviation in California, and his Arrowbile was a flying car powered by a Studebaker Dictator Six engine that drove a pusher propeller. It had three wheels, with the single wheel at the front. Top speed in the air was 125mph (200km/h) and on land, 75mph (120km/h). It was to have been sold by selected Studebaker dealerships for $3000, but Waterman found that it cost him considerably more than that to manufacture it. A crash landing during a demonstration to Studebaker executives destroyed any hope of their selling it, though Waterman subsequently made five himself. How much he sold them for is not known. In 1958 he built another flying car, this time powered by a flat-6 Franklin engine and called the Aerobile.

NG

ARROW LOCOMOTOR (US) 1896

Adolph Moesch & Co., Buffalo, New York.

This was a 2-seater phaeton powered by a single-cylinder engine of Moesch's own design, located under the seat and driving the rear wheels by chains. Claimed top speed was 15mph (24km/h). Production was planned but probably only the one car was made.

NG

ARSENAL (H) 1980 to date

1980–1994 Frigyes Bank, Soltvadkert.
1994–1998 Frigyes Bank, Szentgotthárd.
1998 to date Imperial, Budapest.

Frigyes Bank, a talented car repairman, created a Lada Shiguli-based 2-seater sportscar in 1980. It used all standard Lada mechanics and a GRP body. He dreamt about the 1920s Mercedes racers, and it shows in style.

The car was a brave attempt, as individual creations were usually dismissed by the authorities. However, he somehow managed to get it through technical examination and built about a dozen examples, despite the envy of neighbours and the political climate. In 1994 he had moved to the northern part of Hungary, close to the General Motors assembly plant, hoping to gain the interest of Opel, but it never materialised. The car was reintroduced at the 1998 Budapest Autoshow.

PN

ARTES (E) 1966–1970

José Artes de Arcos, Barcelona.

Artes was a well-known component company, but an interest in sportscars induced it to finance some car projects. First was the production of Formula 4 racing cars under the name of Guepardo, followed by a rear-engine GT coupé with fibreglass body, in the style of the Ford GT40, called Campeador. The prototype used a 1100cc Gordini engine, but production models were powered by the Spanish-built Seat 1500 engine, tuned to give 140bhp. Another project of Artes was a buggy, developed in 1971, and the Gato Montes, a small 6-wheeler all terrain amphibious car using Citroën mechanical parts.

VCM

ARX INDUSTRIES *see* BREMEN

ARZENS (F) 1951

Paul Arzens, Paris.

Artist, sculptor and designer, Paul Arzens became famous during wartime Paris for driving his self-designed electric car, the extraordinary l'Oeuf. This near-spherical car predated the bubble car idiom by more than ten years, but it remained a one-off. In 1951 Arzens built another small car called the Carrosse. Its ingenious method of construction – an exterior tubular chassis with flat metal panelwork between – was intended for cheap reproduction without heavy industrial equipment. It had a rear-mounted 125cc engine and could exceed 45mph (72 km/h). However, it remained a prototype.

CR

A.S. (i) (F) 1926–1928

1924–1926 Voiturettes Automobiles A.S., Courbevoie, Seine.
1926–1928 Voiturettes Automobiles A.S., La Garenne Colombe, Seine.

1962 A.S.A. GT coupé.
NATIONAL MOTOR MUSEUM

An attractive sporting light car, produced in small numbers. One model used a twin ohc engine of 1100cc, and proprietary Chapuis-Dornier or C.I.M.E. engines were also used.

NG

A.S. (ii) (PL) 1928–1930

Towarzystwo Budówy Samochodów AS, Warsaw.

In 1927 Czesław Zbieranski, the owner of Warsaw's Autoworkshops, joined Jan Laski in the manufacture of cars designed by Mr Zbieranski. The first prototype was ready in January 1928, and production began in March. Most of the components were Polish-made apart from the engines which came from France. The Model S-1 (mainly used for taxi work) had an 18bhp 950cc Chapuis–Dornier engine, while the S-2 used a 1095cc Ruby, replaced in later versions by a 24bhp 1203cc CIME. Both models had the same chassis with 3-speed gearbox, semi-elliptic leaf springs all round, hydraulic shock absorbers and 4-wheel brakes. Top speed of the S-2 was 56mph (90km/h). Bodies were made by Szydlowiecka Fabryka Powozów Braci Wegrzeckich i Spotka.

About 50 cars were made in 1928, but only 20 in 1929. Sales were slow, and more were bodied as taxicabs than as passenger cars. In January 1930 new owners took over, the cabs were refurbished, and three new chassis were delivered. The depression put an end to the company within a few months.

RP

A.S.A. (I) 1962–1967

Autocostruzioni SpA, Milan.

The originator of A.S.A. was Ferrari which, in 1958, made a double-ohc 4-cylinder engine of 850cc. In 1961 the engine was mated to a chassis designed by Giotto Bizzarini – it was virtually a scaled down GTO – and was bodied by Bertone. Ferrari decided not to proceed further and the project was taken over by some enthusiastic industrialists.

In 1965 A.S.A. launched the Mille, which was available as a coupé or a cabriolet. Unusually for the time, there were 4-wheel disc brakes and the engine, which was virtually two thirds of a bank from a Ferrari V12, was increased to 1032cc. It produced 84bhp, which gave the car a top speed of 115mph (185km/h), but the torque curve was peaky and the car was expensive.

After two years, the Mille was replaced by the Rollbar GT Spyder which had a 6-cylinder 1.3-litre version of the engine (there was a 140bhp 1754cc version for export) and costs were cut by having the body made in fibreglass. Like the Mille, it had a 4-speed transmission with double overdrive but, like the smaller car, it found few takers. The project folded in 1967 after not many more than 50 had been made.

MJL

Further Reading
'La Ferrarina', Lowell Paddock, *Automobile Quarterly*, Vol. 21, No. 3.

ASAHI (JAP) 1937–c.1939

Miyata Works Ltd, Tokyo.

This was a short-lived venture into car building by a company better known for bicycles and who had made two experimental motorcycles in 1916. A 730cc 16bhp air-cooled 2-cylinder engine drove the front wheels, and all four wheels were independently sprung.

NG

1999 Ascari Écosse coupé.
ASCARI

ASARDO (US) 1959

American Special Automotive Research & Design Corporation,
North Bergen, New Jersey.

This was an aerodynamic sports coupé with tubular space frame, fibreglass body and gull-wing doors. It was powered by an Alfa Romeo Giulia 1300 engine bored out to 1485cc and giving 135bhp, and also had Alfa Romeo transmission and rear suspension. Only one prototype was built, though this was later fitted with a 3528cc Buick aluminium V8 engine.

NG

ASC MCLAREN (US) 1984 to date

ASC, Los Angeles, California.

ASC McLaren was a division of ASC, which made convertible and sunroof conversions for the major Detroit automakers. In addition to one-off prototypes like the ASC Vision (1985), they also produced short-run speciality cars for major manufacturers. One project was a line of modified Ford Mustangs and Mercury Capris sold from 1984 to 1990. Improvements included special suspension, wheels, aerodynamic body panels, trim and a rear spoiler. Coupé and convertible bodies were offered, and they proved to be quite popular. In 1987 ASC built the Grand National GNX for Buick, which was a more powerful version of the turbocharged Regal Grand National sedan. The GNX also had a stronger transmission and revised suspension geometry. All 547 built were 2-door coupés.

HP

ASCARI (GB) 1995 to date

Ascari Cars Ltd, Blandford Forum, Dorset.

Designed by Lee Noble, the Ascari FGT was a very high performance coupé designed both as a luxury road car and a competition tool. A prototype competed at Le Mans and finished third in its class. The prototype car's centrally-mounted engine was a 600bhp modified Chevrolet Corvette V8. Production cars gained a 4.6-litre BMW V8 developing 350bhp, although a Hartge-tuned 4.7-litre V8 developing 400bhp and a less powerful 300bhp version were also listed. Weighing only 1250kg, the Ascari Écosse was claimed to be able to exceed 200mph (320km/h) and do the 0–60mph (0-96km/h) sprint in 4.1 seconds. The race-derived suspension was independent by double wishbones and co-axial springs all round. The chassis was a steel tube space frame with riveted and bonded alloy panelling and a full roll cage, clothed in a glassfibre coupé body. Ten cars had been completed by 1998.

CR

ASCORT (AUS) 1958–1960

Continental Coachwork Pty Ltd, Sydney, New South Wales.

After difficulty in choosing between Ascot and Escort for its name, the TSV 1300, a fibreglass coupé, appeared on a Volkswagen base and with Okrasa performance fittings. Although double-skinned, insulated, and with a large luggage space, plush upholstery, and even a first-aid kit in an arm-rest, its weight was no greater than the regular Beetle. The idea of Mirek Craney, who was involved with fibreglass production through his Hermex company (the agents for Okrasa), it attracted much attention. Being expensive, it could be personalised to the point of having monogrammed doors. Although a fine concept, and built with the latest fibreglass technology, the loss of commercial terms for the VW components, and with the Karmann-Ghia taken into consideration, it became unprofitable to continue after 19 were made, although orders were in hand.

MG

ASCOT (i) (F) 1914–1915

Sté Buchet, Levallois-Perret, Seine

This car had a 10hp side-valve 4-cylinder engine with unit gearbox which, with the chassis, were built by BUCHET. They were sold to the Hollingdrake Automobile Co. of Stockport, who fitted their own bodies, mostly 2-seaters and coupés, and sold the result under the name Ascot.

NG

ASCOT (ii) (GB) 1928–1930

Ascot Motor & Manufacturing Co., Letchworth, Hertfordshire.

This company was formed to exploit the patents of Eugen FEJES, a Hungarian who had invented a car with chassis and engine made of welded sheet steel, eliminating the need for casting. A factory was acquired from the recently defunct PHOENIX (iii) Motor Co. and Ascot was floated with a nominal capital of £400,000. Plans for an initial production of 1500 cars were made, at which the selling price for a 10hp tourer would be £130. However, the necessary finance was never raised, and only a few prototypes were made at Letchworth though several hundred Fejes cars were said to be in use in Hungary.

The next venture was a much more conventional car called the Ascot Gold Cup Six. This used a 2423cc 6-cylinder side-valve engine, probably by Continental, a Warner 3-speed gearbox, and Dewandre servo brakes. Some of the components were alleged to come from the unsuccessful 18hp Phoenix. It was available as a fabric saloon, coupé or 2-seater sports, but very few were made. Another short-lived project was the advanced Ascot-Pullin motorcycle, which also did not last beyond 1930.

ASCOT (iii) *see* GLASSPAR

A.S.D. (GB) 1984 to date
Automotive Systems Development, Leeds, Kent.
This firm built and prepared racing cars, then produced a string of specialised road cars. The first was the TRIPOS, but its own branded products followed. One promising car was the 1984 Minim, a small Mini-based mid-engined roadster with a steel backbone chassis, bolt-on glassfibre body and half-doors, but only a handful were made. Another Mini-based project was the 1990 Hobo, a glassfibre-bodied utility car in the Mini Moke vein. A.S.D. also produced the CK 427 (a heavily re-engineered version of the GRAVETTI Cobra replica) and undertook licensed production of the American HUNTER. Perhaps its most enticing products were fabulous replicas of racing classics such as the Maserati 250F and Aston Martin DBR2.
CR

ASHEVILLE (US) 1914–1915
Asheville Light Car Co., Asheville, North Carolina.
This was a cyclecar built by bicycle-shop proprietor E.C. Merrill, powered by a 7hp air-cooled Indian V-twin engine located under a remarkably long bonnet, big enough to contain a 6-cylinder engine. Final drive was by a one-inch belt, with suspension by cantilever springs.
NG

ASHLEY (GB) 1954–1962
Ashley Laminates Ltd, Loughton, Essex; Harlow, Essex.
One of the first of the British wave of glassfibre bodyshell builders, Ashley produced a range of basic shells for fitment over Austin Seven and Ford Ten chassis. One such body, sold in open and coupé forms and with a long or short wheelbase, could be fitted over the company's own Regent coil-sprung ladder chassis from 1958. Engine options spanned Ford, BMC A-series, and MGA/MGB. Ashley grew up with the times and began offering a full component form model, the Sportiva, from 1961. Again this was sold in coupé and convertible forms with two or four seats. An Ashley shell formed the basis of the shape of the Reliant Sabre, but the company's glassfibre hardtop business could no longer support a decreasingly popular car range, and the marque disappeared in 1962.
CR

ASHTON-EVANS (GB) 1919–1927
Ashton-Evans Motors Ltd, Birmingham.
This car was made by an engineering company whose products included locomotives, tools, castings and aeroplane components. It was a generally conventional light car, though the 3-speed constant-mesh gearbox operated by dog clutches, and narrow rear track of only 8in were unusual. It was powered by a 1498cc 4-cylinder Coventry-Simplex engine, and 2- or 4-seater bodies were offered. From 1920 a conventional full-width rear axle was offered, the cars being briefly known as Ashton, before reverting to Ashton-Evans the following year. Production was 'discontinued *pro tem*' in 1927, and never resumed. Possibly as many as 250 cars may have been made.
NG

ASIA (ROK) 1994 to date
Asia Motors, South Korea.
This KIA-owned company was formed to make small-medium sized commercial vehicles, and in 1994 launched the Rocsta, a Jeep-like vehicle powered by a 2184cc 4-cylinder diesel engine with either 2- or 4-wheel drive. It was joined in 1997 by

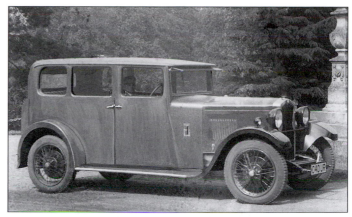

1930 Ascot (ii) 18/50hp saloon.
NATIONAL MOTOR MUSEUM

c.1920 Ashton-Evans 10.5hp 2-seater.
NATIONAL MOTOR MUSEUM

the Retona, a similar design, but on a longer wheelbase and with a more powerful 16-valve twin-ohc petrol engine of 1998cc, with the option of a single-ohc turbo diesel of the same dimensions.
NG

ASP (AUS) 1973–1975
Alpha Sports Productions, Adelaide, South Australia.
Usually a constructor of competition cars, such as the Model 330 Formula 3 and 340 racing clubman, the Model 310 was road-going. In 1963 Ray Lewis and a partner, Mr Ivy, had built a series of Bacchus clubman cars but, this time, designer Rory Thompson was associated. A 1166cc Toyota Corolla engine and transmission line, Triumph Herald front suspension and Morris Minor rack and pinion steering were installed in a tubular space frame, although a Ford Cortina engine was optional. Like the racing cars, it was well regarded, but after some 40 had been made, it was a financial loss.
MG

ASPA (CS) 1924–1929
Pribramska strojirna a slevarna, a.s., Pribram.
This was an attempt to build simple, light cars using engines and electrical equipment from various producers. The small 4-seater ASPA passenger car (for Akciova Spolecnost Pribramske Automobilky - Pribram Automobile Co. Ltd) was introduced in 1924. Its predecessor was the two cylinder STELKA. The 4-cylinder 1327cc 15bhp water-cooled engine powered the rear wheels of 650kg light open tourer with only one door at the left side. About 40 Type B passenger cars were produced, and a few delivery vans and ambulances ended the short history of this marque.
MSH

ASPEN (US) c.1985
Aspen Car Company, Fontana, California.

This company built a sports car utilising styling cues from a number of Porsche racing cars from the 1950s. Called the Aspen 550 RSK Spyder, it was part 550 Spyder, part RS-61 and part Speedster. Initially sold only as a fully-assembled car, most Aspens were built on a VW platform with a variety of air- or water-cooled VW engines. A mid-engine chassis that would use a Porsche 914 engine and transmission was in development in 1985.

HP

ASPER (CH) 1908–1911
1901 Ernst Asper, Dietikon, Zürich.
1908–1911 Ernst Asper, Küsnacht, Zürich.

Ernst Asper resigned from his post as a director of ROCHET-SCHNEIDER in Lyon and founded his own company in 1908. He built a conventional tourer with a round radiator-shell quite similar to the DELAUNAY-BELLEVILLE or HOTCHKISS. It had a 4-cylinder engine and shaft drive. In1910 part of the liquidated AJAX factory was purchased. After having built about 30 cars, Asper ceased production and turned to the manufacturing of railroad equipment and light rail vehicles.

FH

ASQUITH (i) (GB) 1901–1902
William Asquith Ltd, Halifax, Yorkshire.

This company was a well-known maker of machine tools which built a prototype light car powered by a single-cylinder De Dion Bouton engine. In its original form it was belt-driven, but this was later modified to shaft drive. The body was a 4-seater tonneau.

NG

ASQUITH (ii) (GB) 1987 to date
Asquith Brothers, Dewsbury, West Yorks.

Conceived by a Yorkshire-based Riley restoration specialist, the Asquith Vista was an exacting Riley MPH replica designed to use original prewar Riley components. Since this was not practical for most kit car builders, Asquith engineered a Mk2 chassis to accept modern Ford parts.

CR

ASQUITH (iii) (GB) 1991 to date
Asquith Motor Carriage Co. Ltd, Great Yealdham, Essex.

In the antique-style commercial vehicle market, the Asquith name was active and respected from 1982. Its first purely passenger vehicles were a Taxi (designed to conform to London Taxi regulations) and a Limousine, both launched in 1991. Both used a purpose-built steel chassis based on Ford Transit components, including the engine (2-litre and 2.9-litre petrol or 2.5-litre diesel) and manual or automatic transmission. The Limousine could also be purchased with landaulette type coachwork. A prototype of an all-new Taxi with modern bodywork was displayed in 1996.

CR

A.S.S. (F) 1919–1920
SA des Automobiles A.S.S, Lyons.

Like Henry Ford and, in his own country André Citroën, Bernard Verdy planned to mass-produce popular cars. For his power unit he chose the little-known 1240cc vertical-twin 2-stroke Thomas engine, driving through a 2-speed epicyclic gearbox and shaft to a bevel rear axle. It had electric lighting and starting but, as one would expect from a light car of its date, brakes were only on the rear wheels. The standard body was a 4-seater tourer, but a 2-seater, convertible to a coupé, was mentioned in the catalogue. The A.S.S. was launched in March 1919 at a price of FFr4750. This was clearly unrealistically low, and by February 1920 it had risen to FFr10,950, which was unrealistically high, and damaged sales prospects. In March 1920 it was announced that A.S.S. had merged with the Société des Moteurs Thomas, and no more was heard of the car. A few months later the factory was sold to Charles Beck-Maillard, who was to make the equally short-lived BECK car there.

NG

ASTAHL (F) 1906–1908
Lêvéque et Bodenreder, Boulogne-sur-Seine.

This is a shadowy make, said by a British journalist to be the same as the HELBE, hence the Helbe address at the beginning of this entry, though the Astahl was advertised from the Rue des Labourdonnais in Paris. Like the Helbe, it was listed with 6 and 8hp single-cylinder De Dion Bouton engines, as well as a 10/12hp 4-cylinder unit by Amstoutz. Helbe listed a 12hp four in 1907, though they did not specify the maker. The Astahl name seems to have been used particularly for the British market, and one Astahl survives in England today.

NG

Further Reading
'Astahl is Born', M. Worthington-Williams, *The Automobile*, April 1987.

ASTATIC (F) 1922–1923
Automobiles Astatic, St Ouen, Seine.

The Astatic was described by *The Light Car & Cyclecar* as 'perhaps the most interesting cyclecar at the 1922 Paris Salon', though they observed that it showed certain traces of hurried preparation. The 894cc S.C.A.P. engine and 3-speed gearbox were conventional enough, but there were no axles in the ordinary sense. Instead each wheel was separately sprung on a bell crank arm with a large horizontal coil spring enclosed in a cylinder. At the front there were separate steering rods to each wheel, and at the rear the differential casing was bolted to the rear of the chassis, with a drive shaft to each wheel.

NG

ASTER (i) (F) 1900–1910
Ateliers de Construction Mécanique l'Aster, St Denis, Seine.

This company was one of the best-known suppliers of engines in France, and a number of cars were marketed as Asters from time to time, though they never made complete cars. They exhibited a 3½hp quadricycle at the 1900 Paris Salon, and a 12hp car was shown at the 1903 Crystal Palace Show. Though Aster did make chassis, this one had a British-built chassis. Other cars sometimes marketed as Asters were the WEST-ASTER and WHITLOCK-ASTER, while among the better-known British cars which used Aster engines were ARGYLL, DENNIS, SINGER and SWIFT. In France ARIÈS and GLADIATOR were prominent Aster customers, and the 'Asters' sold in the UK by their British agents were almost certainly Ariès.

NG

ASTER (ii) (GB) 1922–1930
1922–1927 Aster Engineering Co. Ltd, Wembley, Middlesex.
1927–1930 Arrol-Johnston Ltd and Aster Engineering Co.Ltd, Heathall, Dumfries.

These cars were originally built by the British branch of ASTER (i). They were high-quality machines with 6-cylinder ohv engines, 4-speed gearboxes and Lanchester-like cantilever rear suspension. The original 18/50 engine had a capacity of 2618cc, and the car was expensive at £850 for a tourer. Balloon tyres and Perrot front wheel brakes arrived in 1924, and in 1926 the engine was enlarged to the 3048cc 21/60. Saloons and coupés were also available, one of the former being supplied to the Duke of York (later King George VI). Among features of these bodies were electric cigar lighters in the doors and continuous winding windows.

For 1927 the 21/60 was joined by the 3466cc 24/70 with Burt-McCollum single sleeve-valve engine. During the year Aster merged with ARROL-JOHNSTON; Lord Invernairn of the Scottish company had had an interest in Aster since before World War I. A complicated range resulted from the merger; the 21/60 became an Arrol-Aster, and there was also a 17/50hp sleeve-valve Arrol-Aster as well as two sleeve-valve models, the 21/60 and 24/70 which were sold as plain Asters.

NG

Further Reading
Lost Causes of Motoring, Lord Montagu of Beaulieu, Cassell, 1960.
'Aster and Arrol-Aster: The Anglo-Scottish Alliance',
M. Worthington-Williams, *The Automobile*, January 1989.

ASTON (US) 1908–c.1910

Aston Motor Car Co., Bridgeport, Connecticut.

This company advertised cars built to order, and little is known of their activities. Two cars, a 25 and a 40hp, were registered in Connecticut in 1915.

NG

ASTON MARTIN (GB) 1921 to date

1921–1926 Bamford & Martin Ltd, Kensington, London.
1926–1947 Aston Martin Motors Ltd, Feltham, Middlesex.
1947–1957 Aston Martin Limited, Feltham, Middlesex.
1957–1974 Aston Martin Lagonda Ltd, Newport Pagnell, Buckinghamshire.
1975–1981 Aston Martin Lagonda (1975) Ltd, Newport Pagnell, Buckinghamshire.
1981 to date Aston Martin Lagonda Ltd, Newport Pagnell, Buckinghamshire.

The decision to name the future cars Aston Martin was taken in 1913 when Lionel Martin's race-tuned Singer Ten won its class in the Aston Clinton hill climb.

With a capital of £1000, he and Robert Bamford founded Bamford & Martin Ltd on 13 June 1913, as Singer agents with premises in Callow Street, off the Fulham Road in London. They also sold and serviced Calthorpe and GWK cars. Before the end of the year they moved to 12–16 Henniker Place in South Kensington.

In 1914 Martin acquired a 1908 Isotta Fraschini chassis into which he installed a 4-cylinder 1390cc side-valve Coventry Simplex engine and planned to go racing. Those plans evaporated when World War I began, and Martin went into service in the Admiralty. Bamford had been a member of a Cyclist Battalion in the reserves since 1911, and joined the Royal Army Service Corps. They closed the shop, gave up the lease, and sold all the equipment to the Sopwith Aviation Company. Reunited after the war, Bamford & Martin Ltd moved into premises at 53 Abington Road in Kensington.

A new car was designed, and the first vehicle to carry the Aston Martin name was ready for the road in May 1921.

The partnership with Bamford ended in May 1920 and Martin's wife Kathy took over the vacant director's chair. The business was refinanced by Count Louis Vorow Zborowski, and Martin planned to build 100 cars over a three-year period. R. Bamford went to live in Torquay, and subsequently retired to Ditchling in Sussex.

Actual production did not begin until 1922, with a light sports car of simple design. A light ladder-type steel frame with channel-section side members carried both axles on parallel semi-elliptic leaf springs. The 4-cylinder L-head 1496cc engine had a 3-bearing crankshaft, Zephyr iron pistons, and steel con-rods drilled for lightness. The clutch was of Hele-Shaw type, and the 4-speed gearbox was made by E.G. Wrigley & Co. The propeller shaft was enclosed in a torque tube, and brakes were fitted on the rear wheels only. The bare chassis weighed approximately 483kg. Perrot 4-wheel brakes were adopted later in 1922.

When Count Zborowski wanted a competitive car, he arranged with Clive Gallop, who knew Marcel Gremillon from his days with Ballot, to have Gremillon draw up a 4-cylinder derivative of the Ballot Grand Prix straight-8 for Aston Martin. It had hemispherical combustion chambers, the 16 valves being actuated by two ohc driven by vertical shaft and bevel gears. At least two of these engines were made by Rover and mounted in special Aston Martin chassis in 1923.

The Aston Martin name became well known in racing circles, but few customers bought their cars for road use. Only 69 cars were built in the initial three years, and by mid–1924, the company was bankrupt.

On 11 July 1924, Bamford & Martin Ltd was sold to Lady Charnwood for £2600. Her son, John Benson, was a great car enthusiast who became her representative on the board of directors. Lionel and Katherine Martin remained directors, with the addition of George E. R. Shield. But the company failed again, fell into receivership in November 1925, and the factory was closed in May 1926.

The Martins then withdrew and Martin decided to put an end to his career, turning down several offers from other companies.

J. Benson developed a new scheme to refinance the business and formed an alliance with the engineering firm of Renwick & Bertelli Ltd of Birmingham. Augusto Cesare Bertelli and William Somerville Renwick, both formerly of Enfield-Allday, founded their company on 8 December 1924, and put their prototype, the R & B Special, on the road in May 1926. It was to be the basis for a new type of Aston Martin.

1923 Aston Martin 1½-litre sports car by Compton & Hermon.
NATIONAL MOTOR MUSEUM

Lady Charnwood's company was reorganised in October 1926, as Aston Martin Motors Ltd, capitalised at £14,000, and established in the former Citroën assembly plant at Hanworth Air Park, Feltham. Renwick & Bertelli Ltd also moved to Feltham at the same time.

The first Bertelli-designed Aston Martin appeared at Olympia in October 1927. The big news was an ohc 1488cc engine plus worm-drive rear axle and a rugged frame, made by Vickers, with two channel-section and five tubular cross-members. It was also a big step for the company to produce its own bodies. A.C. Bertelli's brother Enrico (known on the shop floor as Harry) was head of the body department which became an independent company, E. Bertelli Ltd, in 1931.

Thirty cars were built in 1928, and in October of that year, the Touring model was launched, on a 114in (2893mm) wheelbase, which was stretched to 118in (2995mm) for 1930.

For 1931 the frame was underslung at the rear and both axles were given the benefit of torque-resisting cables tying them to the frame. Sales fell to 30 cars for that whole year, and the threat of bankruptcy became imminent. Renwick resigned and later became a member of Singer's engineering staff. Early in 1932, L. Prideaux Brune, owner and chief executive of the Automobile Service Company, rescued the firm with a healthy injection of working capital. The 1932 models had a Moss gearbox attached to the engine and an ENV spiral-bevel rear axle.

The new 56hp International was launched in May 1932, replacing the Touring. The 12/70 Le Mans on a 102in (2589mm) wheelbase went into production at the same time, replacing the Sports Model.

But sales fell to 25 cars in 1932, and Prideaux Brune could no longer carry the financial burden. He persuaded Sir Arthur Sutherland to take over, and early in 1933 his son was named joint managing director. Robert Gordon Sutherland was born in Newcastle upon Tyne on 10 January 1908, and educated at Malvern College and the Automobile Engineering Training College at Chelsea. He had worked briefly with Alvis in 1931–32.

Production climbed to 105 cars in 1933, including 57 Le Mans cars. Over a two-year stretch, 81 Internationals were produced. For 1934, Aston Martin launched the 12/50 Standard, but could not sell more than 20 of them. The 12/70 Le Mans continued, being upgraded to Mk II status in May 1934, with a lot of technical refinements, including a revised cylinder head, a better balanced crankshaft, vertical rubber-block engine mountings, transversely mounted front-axle dampers, and needle-roller bearings on the propeller shaft. A new full 4-passenger car with the 70hp Le Mans engine on a 120in (3046mm) wheelbase was added.

The 1934 line-up also included the 12/80 Ulster, with a high-compression (9.0:1) twin SU carburettor engine in a 103in (2614mm) wheelbase. The Feltham factory turned out 85 Le Mans and 24 Ulster cars in 1934. Those models were also produced in 1935 and part of 1936.

In 1935 A.C. Bertelli and his closest collaborator Claude Hill began designing a 1949cc version of the 4-cylinder single-ohc engine. Bertelli resigned, however, in November 1937, leaving R.G. Sutherland as sole managing director. Twelve

1933 Aston Martin 1½-litre Le Mans sports car.
NATIONAL MOTOR MUSEUM

1935 Aston Martin MkII coupé.
NICK GEORGANO

Speed Model cars with the new engine were built in 1936, but the base model 15/98 was not shown publicly until October of that year, with bodies by E.D. Abbott Ltd of Farnham.

The Speed Model had hydraulic brakes, Scintilla Vertex magneto ignition and a non-synchromesh gearbox. The plain 15/98 had twin SU carburettors, fuel feed by dual electric (alternative) pumps from a 14-gallon rear-mounted tank, 4-speed gearbox with synchromesh on second, third and top, Girling mechanical brakes with Al-fin drums, centre-lock wire wheels, and permanent Jackall hydraulic jacks. From 1936 to the end of 1939, the Feltham factory turned out 174 15/98s.

Hill was named chief engineer on Bertelli's departure and set about modernising the car. First he created the 1938 Type C as a successor to the Speed Model, with a cowled radiator, V-form split windshield, headlamps faired into the wings, and a long, tapering tail. It was put on the market at £775, compared with £495 for the 15/98 Long Tourer. Only about six Type C cars were built.

Next, Hill created a compact sports saloon which he called the Atom. It had a space frame welded up from rectangular-section steel tubes and independent front suspension, with coil springs and trailing links, patented by Gordon Armstrong. The engine was the same as in the 15/98, matched with a Cotal electromagnetic-shift epicyclic gearbox.

The company spent the World War II years fulfilling contracts from Lord Beaverbrook's Ministry of Aircraft production, and in 1945 the factory was moved to another part of Hanworth Air Park. C. Hill designed a new 1970cc 4-cylinder engine with pushrod-operated overhead valves and a 5-bearing crankshaft. It put out 90hp at 4750rpm, with a 7.5:1 compression ratio. He also reworked the Atom frame to suit open as well as closed bodywork.

Near the end of 1946, before postwar production actually began, R.G. Sutherland sold the company to the Yorkshire industrialist David Brown. In February 1947 it was capitalised and re-titled, and the new car, identified simply as the Two-Litre, took shape, with a stylish modern body designed by Frank Feeley. R.G. Sutherland

remained a director of Aston Martin, and in 1949 also became chairman and managing director of E.D. Abbott Ltd, the coachbuilders who supplied the bodies.

Production of engines, gearboxes and chassis frames was transferred to the factory of David Brown Tractors Ltd at Farsley near Leeds, and 15 Two-Litre cars were assembled at Feltham from 1948 to 1950.

C. Hill was busy with the development of a 6-cylinder 2445cc engine with pushrod-operated overhead valves and a bigger chassis to carry it. The space-frame concept was kept, redesigned by Ted Cutting who had just joined the company, with a multitude of box-section members, and extra reinforcement in the doorsill areas. The chassis became the basis for the DB2, but the engine was discarded in favour of a twin-ohc 2580cc Lagonda 6-cylinder unit. It was chiefly in order to get this engine that David Brown had purchased the Lagonda company in 1947. But Claude felt insulted at the substitution, and left Aston Martin in 1949.

David Brown engaged Robert Eberan von Eberhorst as chief engineer in 1950, fresh from two years with ERA, but he came in too late to have any influence on the initial version of the DB2.

The DB2 was first shown to the public in April 1950. It was a new type of car for Aston Martin, with a slab-sided aluminium 2-passenger coupé body styled by Frank Feeley. With the 105hp Lagonda engine, it had sparkling performance.

The DB2 Mk II arrived in 1951, with a number of minor improvements. In all, 411 DB2s were made, from 1950 to October 1953, when it was replaced by the DB2/4, so-called because of its 2+2 seating arrangement. The roomier DB2/4 bodies, which introduced a form of hatchback design, were produced by Mulliners of Birmingham. For 1954, a bigger engine (140hp 2922cc Lagonda) was mounted in the DB2/4, raising top speed to 112mph (180km/h).

The DB3 was an open sports/racing machine designed by R.E. von Eberhorst, with a 140hp 2580cc engine and a De Dion-type rear suspension system, appearing in June 1952. Its successor, the DB3S, appeared in the spring of 1953 with a 164hp version of the 3922cc engine and all-independent suspension with torsion bars. At that time, R.E. von Eberhorst returned to Germany and Harold Beach, who had joined the company as a draftsman/designer in 1950, was named chief engineer of Aston Martin. By 1956 Ted Cutting had developed the DB3S engine to the point where it put out 210hp at 6000rpm on an 8.68:1 compression ratio. It was adopted for the new DBR1 sports/racing prototypes raced in 1957–59.

On the production side, Aston Martin was forced to change coachbuilders in 1954, because Mulliners came under contract to work exclusively for Standard-Triumph. The contract went to Tickford, along with the tooling, and within months, David Brown bought the company.

A total of 566 DB2/4s (including 75 cabriolets) were made, from October 1953 to October 1955. The DB2/4 Mk II was built from then until August 1957 with a total number of 109 units.

Then came the DB2/4 Mk III, restyled by Frank Feeley with elements from the DB3S, and equipped with Girling disc brakes with a Baldwin hydro-booster on the front wheels. The 178hp engine raised top speed to almost 140mph (225km/h). Aston Martin built 551 Mk III cars, including 84 cabriolets, from March 1957 to July 1959, the final series being assembled at Newport Pagnell, where the Tickford plant was undergoing vast expansion to take over all production processes for Aston Martin and Lagonda cars.

In July 1955, after five years' activity as racing manager and development engineer, John L. Wyer was made technical director of Aston Martin, with the additional duties of general manager a year later.

Beach had been working on project 114 since 1954. It was given tremendous impetus by Wyer's take-charge attitude, and evolved into the DB4. It was new from the ground up, with no carry-over components from earlier models. It was to be a 2+2 coupé, bigger and with more generous passenger accommodation than the Mk III. The new engine would also be considerably bigger, though still a six, powerful enough to rival even a famous Italian V12 in terms of performance.

It was to have not just a new body, but a new type of body construction. At J.L. Wyer's initiative, the styling contract was given to Carrozzeria Touring, along with the purchase of a licence for their Superleggera type of body construction, with a steel cage and aluminium-panelled skin.

In 1956 Touring had built two roadster bodies on the DB2/4 Mark III chassis which had impressed Wyer. They supplied the tooling for making the complete body at Newport Pagnell.

1937 Aston Martin 2-litre long chassis sports tourer.
NICK GEORGANO

NICK BALDWIN

MARTIN, LIONEL (1878–1945)

One of the two originators of Aston Martin, Lionel Walker Birch Martin was born to a well-off family whose fortune derived from the English China Clay mines in Cornwall. He was educated at Eton, and at a small private college at Oxford. Presumably he failed to gain entrance to the University. He took to cycling, a sport which he pursued for the rest of his life, and raced against William Morris who was starting to make bicycles. Cycling brought him into contact with Montague Napier, and he bought several Napier cars. Shortly before World War I he began competing in hill climbs in a 10hp Singer, one of his favourite venues being Aston Clinton in Buckinghamshire. In 1912 he went into partnership with Robert Bamford, and built a special which consisted of a 1389cc Coventry-Simplex engine in the chassis of a 1908 Isotta-Fraschini racing voiturette. To name it he combined that of the hill climb with his surname. It was completed in 1914 and took part in a few trials before the war broke out. Martin used it throughout the war, when he was working for the Admiralty, and in 1918 re-formed Bamford & Martin Ltd, though Robert Bamford left in 1921. They had made very few cars, probably no more than four, but with Bamford's shares bought up by Martin's wife they took new premises in Abingdon Road, Kensington, where several racing cars were built with twin-ohc engines. Martin obtained about £10,000 in support from Count Louis Zborowski who drove the cars, but the bulk of finance came from Martin himself, probably £100,000 to £150,000 (equivalent to at least £2 to 3 million today). In 1924 the company was re-formed, this time with finance from another old Etonian, the Hon. John Benson, who persuaded his mother, Lady Charnwood, to put up £2600. Even this did not help, and after making about 50 cars, on each of which they lost money, Bamford & Martin as it was still called, went into receivership. Martin left the works for the last time on 13 November 1925, and played no part in subsequent Aston Martin history. He concentrated on his mining interests, though he continued to take an interest in racing as an RAC steward. He died in 1945 after being knocked off his tricycle in Kingston-on-Thames.

NG

Further reading
Lionel Martin, a Biography, A.B. Demaus,
Transport Bookman Publications , 1980.

1938 Aston Martin 2-litre sports car.
NICK GEORGANO/NATIONAL MOTOR MUSEUM

Wyer's original intention was to use a type of space-frame, but the Touring specialists explained that their body construction demanded a very stiff platform type of frame, which led to a hurried redesign of the whole chassis. The DB4 frame became a fabricated floor structure with integral bulkhead, welded up from a plurality of individual steel pressings.

Tadek Marek designed the 3670cc twin-ohc engine with aluminium block and head. It weighed 216.3kg and put out 240hp at 5500rpm. It was matched with a David Brown 4-speed synchromesh gearbox and a Salisbury hypoid-bevel rear axle. Brakes were 4-wheel discs, with Dunlop calipers and Lockheed vacuum-servo. The front suspension had upper and lower A-arms with coil springs, and the rear axle was tied down by trailing arms with coil springs and a Watt linkage. Road-testing began in July 1957, and production started in September 1958.

The DB4 GT was released on 30 September 1959, its Vantage engine having bigger valves, revised cam contours, and higher compression, giving 302hp at 6000rpm. A Powr-Lok differential was added. Wheelbase was shortened and the headlamp areas rounded off.

A 314hp version was prepared for the DB GT Zagato, first shown in London in October 1960. It was the result of another Wyer initiative, by which Aston Martin shipped the complete chassis to Milan where Zagato put on an ultra-lightweight aluminium body which saved 170kg when compared with the regular DB4 GT.

In 1962 the basic DB4 engine was uprated to 266hp at 5750rpm. The DB4 was taken out of production in September 1963 after a run of 1119 units, plus 75 DB4 GTs and a mere 19 GT Zagato models.

Wyer left Aston Martin late in 1963 to join Ford Advanced Vehicles, and Dudley Gershon, the former service manager, became director of engineering. Fred Hartley was brought in to take over as general manager. Ted Cutting resigned and later became head of engine design for Ford (GB).

Beach led the development of both the DB5 and the DB6. Powered by a 3995cc 282hp version of the DB4 engine, the DB5 coupé and Volanté convertible replaced the DB4 in October 1963.

The base engine had a peak output of 282hp at 5500rpm, and the Vantage engine delivered 325hp at 5750rpm.

At first the DB5 was offered with the David Brown 4-speed gearbox and Laycock de Normanville overdrive, but the company soon listed the 5-speed ZF as an option and standardised it later. A 3-speed Borg-Warner automatic transmission was also optional on the DB5. The DB5 was produced up to November 1965, with a total of 1021 coupés and 120 Volantés (including 37 short-chassis cabriolets). In addition, 13 DB5 chassis had been built with shooting-brake bodies by Harold Radford.

The DB6 was intended as a true 4-passenger coupé and built on a 101.75in (2582mm) wheelbase. It gained some weight, tipping the scales at 1474kg. The engines were inherited from the DB5.

Production of the DB6 Mk I totalled 1325 coupés, 140 Volanté cabriolets, six shooting brakes by Harold Radford, and three by Panelcraft.

The MK II arrived in September 1969. The changes included wider tyres, better seats, power steering, and optional AE Brico fuel injection. The DB6 Mk II was in production for just 16 months, with a total of 235 coupés and 36 Volanté cabriolets.

It overlapped with the DBS, wider and lower, with updated styling by William Towns, on a 102.75in (2608mm) wheelbase, which was launched in October 1967. The body had light-alloy skin panels, but without the Superleggera cage. The engines were shared with the DB6, the 5-speed ZF gearbox was standard, and Borg-Warner's Type 8 automatic was optional. The Salisbury axle was replaced by a De Dion-type rear suspension with vertical coil springs.

The DBS was actually designed around a future V8 engine, whose 5064cc racing version was developed for Lola in 1967. It was designed by Tadek Marek with two-stage timing chains to the four ohcs, and a fully-counterbalanced 5-bearing hardened steel crankshaft with forged-steel con-rods. Block and heads were light alloy.

NATIONAL MOTOR MUSEUM

BROWN, DAVID (1904–1993)

Aston Martin has had many saviours during its troubled 86 year history, but none lasted so long as David Brown. He was a member of a family business founded by his grandfather, also David, in 1860, making gears. With the arrival of the motor car they contributed gearboxes and rear axles in large numbers, and were also involved with two makes of car, the Dodson and the Valveless. David was educated at Rossall and then joined the family firm as an apprentice. He designed a twin-ohc 1½-litre straight-8 engine, which proceeded no further than the casting of the block, then assembled a car with a Meadows engine, which he christened the Davbro, but there was no question of manufacture. In 1929 he was given a seat on the board of David Brown Gear Co. Ltd, at the age of 25. Three years later, when his uncle died he became managing director.

In 1934 he acquired the site for a new factory at Meltham, five miles south of Huddersfield, where, later, tractors were to be built. As a farm owner, he was most impressed with Harry Ferguson's design of a tractor with three-point hydraulic linkage and automatic depth control. Ferguson demonstrated the system on David Brown's land, with a view to selling the design to a Sheffield steel firm. Instead, Brown took the design over himself. He made about 1350 Ferguson-Brown tractors, the last 20 in the Meltham factory, then, in 1939, turned to making his own, more powerful and heavier tractors, which were known as David Browns. More than 7700 were made up to 1945, including 2400 industrial versions which were widely used as aircraft tugs by the RAF.

By the end of the war David Brown was a very wealthy man, and could afford to look for something a little more inspiring than making gears and tractors, though these undoubtedly provided the company's bread-and-butter. In the autumn of 1946 he saw an advertisement in *The Times* for a car company that was for sale. He was surprised to find that it was Aston Martin; 'After all, that was a very famous name', he said. Famous or not, he haggled with Aston's owner Gordon Sutherland, offering £14,000 initially, and

1955 Aston Martin DB2 saloon.
NATIONAL MOTOR MUSEUM

The production-model V8 was a 5340cc unit with an estimated output of 360hp, which became available in the DBS in 1969, the redesign and development being led by Alan Crouch. With no distinction for engines, Aston Martin produced 787 DBS cars up to September 1972, when it was renamed the Vantage.

Major events had occurred on the corporate front earlier in the year. While retaining the title of group president, David Brown made his son Christopher chief executive officer of the David Brown Group in 1969. The president got worried when the group lost £10 million in 18 months, and put the group under new management, with John Boex as chief executive, in July 1971. One of the new directors, John Montgomery, was also given a seat on the board of Aston Martin Lagonda, and hired John McKillop from Ford to take over as production manager at Newport Pagnell.

Discreetly, Brown also began searching for someone to take Aston Martin Lagonda off his hands. He found him in William Willson, chairman of Company Developments, who agreed in February 1972 to settle the company's debts, estimated at £5 million, in addition to paying a nominal £100 for the shares. Willson also put in £500,000 in fresh capital to finance the development of the V8 engine, the Lagonda car project, and factory improvements. W. Willson took the title of Managing Director.

Beach succeeded Dudley Gershon as technical director in 1974 and Mike Loasby, who had joined the company as a development engineer in 1967, was named chief engineer.

eventually settling for £20,500. The purchase was announced in February 1947, and a few months later Brown bought Lagonda for £52,500, largely, it is said, for the advanced 2½-litre twin-ohc engine which W.O.Bentley had designed. Brown married the Aston Martin chassis with the Lagonda engine to produce the immortal DB2 coupé, ancestor of a line of 6-cylinder Aston Martins made in successive versions up to 1959. In 1954, to ensure a continued supply of bodies, he bought Tickford of Newport Pagnell, and moved car production there in 1957. It has remained the home of Aston Martin ever since.

David Brown was keenly interested in the Aston Martin racing programme, and was rewarded by winning Le Mans and the Sports Car Constructors' Championship in 1959.

He was also keen to keep the Lagonda name alive; four years before the original 2.6-litre went out of production in 1958, he ordered a new car with full-width 4-door saloon body and sophisticated dual-rate rear suspension which he used regularly. He approved the production of the 4-door 4-litre Rapide of 1961–65, though only 55 were made. In 1969 another Lagonda, essentially a 4-door Aston Martin DBS V8, was made for David Brown, now Sir David.

He received his knighthood in 1968 and four years later he sold Aston Martin-Lagonda Ltd to Company Developments Ltd. AML was deeply in debt, to the tune of about £450,000. The company had seldom made a profit, but in the easier days of the 1950s this did not matter so much. Now, as he later said 'Naturally it was a wrench losing Aston Martin, but it was pretty obvious at the time that it would be difficult to produce a motorcar of that kind and make a profit out of it'. Brown merely divested himself of the debts, for all he gained from the sale was £100 for his shares and a nominal £1.00 for the debts. In 1978, after his shipbuilding company, Vosper-Thornycroft, was nationalised, he moved to Monte Carlo, but remained full of enthusiasm for Aston Martin, and was delighted when, in 1993, Walter Hayes, head of the company, which was now owned by Ford, revived the initials DB for the new Jaguar-powered DB7. He died in Monte Carlo in September 1993.

According to a colleague, Bill Ladbrooke, David Brown was 'in many ways a difficult man to work for, and at times hard to please. He worked hard at projects, brought them to success, and then moved on. This applied to tractors, cars, polo, horse racing, hunting, boating, helicopters, even farming'. Though he loved motor racing, his Yorkshire reserve meant that he did not react to victories with the exuberance of, say, Colin Chapman.

He was married three times, in 1926 to Daisy Muriel Firth (marriage dissolved 1955), in 1955 to his secretary Marjorie Deans (marriage dissolved 1980) and in 1980 to model Paula Benton Stone. He had two children by his first marriage, David Jr ('Bill') who followed him into the family firm, and Angela who also went into the firm, working hard in the Tractor Division, and was a successful competition driver. She married George Abecassis, one of his team drivers.

NG

Further Reading
'Life at Full Throttle', Chris Nixon,
Thoroughbred & Classic Car, December 1993.

1965 Aston Martin DB5 saloon.
NICK GEORGANO

1968 Aston Martin DBS saloon.
NICK GEORGANO

1981 Aston Martin V8 Volante convertible.
NATIONAL MOTOR MUSEUM

1989 Aston Martin Virage coupé.
ASTON MARTIN LAGONDA

But the company did not prosper. One symptom of its ills was the slow rate of production – a car could spend seven to nine weeks on the shop floor before being completed. As Christmas 1974 approached, production was halted, the 500-strong workforce laid off, and the company placed in receivership. Over 600 creditors were owed £580,000, the assets did not exceed £2.5 million, and Willson reckoned that it would take £1.5 million to keep the company afloat.

In March 1975 an international group of businessmen bid $1.4 million for the company. They were Peter J.S. Sprague, chairman of the National Semiconductor Corporation, Santa Clara, California, George Minden, Canadian importer and distributor of Aston Martin and Rolls-Royce, owner of the Windsor Arms Hotel in Toronto and a restaurant chain, and Jeremy Turner of London, operator of an executive jet charter service.

When the bid had been raised to $2.5 million, the board approved it. The firm was reorganised as Aston Martin Lagonda (1975) Ltd, with Alan Curtis as managing director and Fred Hartley as general manager. Turner took charge of running the factory.

Production resumed early in 1976, with the V8 coupé in basic and Vantage versions. In February 1977, the base-model engine had its output boosted by 15 per cent and the Vantage by 40 per cent (to about 475hp) with 10 per cent greater torque. Prices began at £15,954 and Hartley claimed an average building rate of six cars a week, with a workforce of just 175.

Beach retired in April 1978, and Mike Loasby left to join the De Lorean Motor Co. Tadek Marek retired in 1979. The 45-year-old former head of Pressed Steel, John Symonds, replaced Curtis as managing director in the summer of 1979. Steve Coughlin was made chief engineer in 1980.

One of Curtis' pet projects was the Bulldog, which was first seen in prototype form in April 1980, powered by a mid-mounted twin-turbo V8 engine. The body was designed by William Towns, Keith Martin was project manager, and Steve Hallam, development engineer.

Production plans were hinged on making a deal with British Leyland, and negotiations between Alan Curtis and Michael Edwardes also included plans for a more moderately-priced Aston Martin to be built in the MG factory. It all came to nothing, for in February 1981 Peter Sprague and his partners sold the company to Victor Gauntlett and Tim Hearley for $3.5 million.

Gauntlett was a former executive of BP and Total who had founded the Pace Petroleum Co. in 1972, and Hearley was chairman of C.H. Industrials Ltd, a minor conglomerate. Pace Petroleum and C.H. Industrials had a combined annual turnover in the region of $125 million. The new owners decided to spin off Tickford as coachbuilders and engineering consultants, free to work for outside clients.

Production continued. All models now came with Chrysler's TorqueFlite automatic transmission, and after difficulties with Bosch (and other) electronic fuel-injection systems, the V8 was equipped with four Weber 42 DCNF carburettors.

In mid-year 1983 Gauntlett sold his 55 per cent holding in Aston Martin Lagonda to Automotive Investments Inc. of Greenwich, Connecticut, formed in 1981 to act as US importers and distributors for Aston Martin (and other makes). It was jointly owned by George Livanos, a Greek shipowner whose personal fortune was estimated at $2 billion, and the brothers Papanicolaou (John and Nicholas), owners of the Titan Shipping & Brokerage Co. Peter Livanos, son of George, became a director of Aston Martin, and Gauntlett agreed to stay on as chief executive. In October 1983 he sold Pace Petroleum.

In 1984 Automotive Investments ceded its 50 per cent stake in Aston Martin Tickford to C.H. Industrials, who still held 45 per cent of Aston Martin Lagonda. When the Titan Shipping & Brokerage suddenly fell into receivership, the Papanicolaou brothers sold their holdings in Aston Martin Lagonda to G. Livanos, who thus owned 75 per cent of the company by October 1984.

In March 1986 a new Vantage Zagato was presented, powered by a 438hp version of the V8 engine. It carried a price tag of £87,000 and Gauntlett daringly scheduled 50 of them for production. They were built and sold within six months. In November 1986 Aston Martin Lagonda took a 50 per cent stake in the Zagato company. Gauntlett also tried to buy Rayton-Fissore, but failed. A Zagato cabriolet was shown in prototype form at Geneva in March 1987, and Gauntlett announced plans to build 25 units to sell at £120,000 each.

That summer when the 400 workers at Newport Pagnell were turning out five cars a week, the Livanos family decided to sell its Aston Martin Lagonda shares. The Ford Motor Company agreed to buy 75 per cent majority control for an amount approaching £20 million, and the deal went through in September 1987. Gauntlett was asked to stay on.

1993 Aston Martin DB7 coupé.
ASTON MARTIN LAGONDA

The final V8 cars were built in the summer of 1988. Dating back to 1969, the V8 engine had powered 405 DBS cars made up to 1972. From 1972 to 1988 a total of 1615 V8 models were turned out, plus 245 Vantages, starting in 1977, 610 Volantés, starting in 1978, and 44 Vantage Volantés.

An entirely new V8 engine with 4 valves-per-cylinder was in preparation. It was designed by Arthur Wilson, and the cylinder heads were developed by Callaway Engineering in Connecticut. The 5341cc engine was rated at 335hp and mounted in the Virage, which was introduced in October 1988.

The Virage chassis was developed with assistance from the department of finite-element analysis at Cranfield Institute of Technology, and the aluminium body was styled by John Heffernan and Ken Greenley.

A.E. Woolner, former product engineering director of Freight-Rover, became director of engineering at Aston Martin Lagonda in 1989. A Virage Volanté was added in September 1990, followed by Virage Volanté 2+2 in March 1991. The 557hp Vantage with 6-speed gearbox was introduced in October 1992, and for 1993 a 4-speed GM Hydra-matic transmission was offered in the regular Virages, the 5-speed Getrag gearbox being standard.

Wilson was named manager of Powertrain Engineering in 1992. At first he thought his V8 had potential for 460hp, but by fitting two Roots-type Eaton superchargers, geared to run at 1.8 times crankshaft speed, and air-to-water intercoolers, he was getting 500hp in 1991, and the production-model Vantage put out 557hp at 6500rpm.

Gauntlett resigned on 20 September 1991, and Bob Dover became chief executive, with Walter Hayes as chairman. Nick Fry, a former Ford plan manager, was named operations director. Gauntlett's best year had been 1989 when approximately 240 cars were sold, but the sales curve began dropping, and only 127 cars were delivered in 1992.

Hayes gave full support to Gauntlett's idea of a smaller Aston Martin, to be assembled away from Newport Pagnell, where there was no room for further expansion. The project, which became the DB7, started under code name NPX late in 1991, and the first prototype stood ready in November 1992. It was first seen in public at the Geneva Salon in March 1993.

The engine was an in-line six, retrieved from a cancelled Jaguar project, and developed in the laboratories of Tom Walkinshaw Racing. Responsibility for production was given to Jaguar. With an Eaton supercharger and 8.3:1 compression ratio, the 3239cc 24-valve engine put out 340hp at 6000rpm.

A 5-speed Getrag was standard and a 4-speed GM Hydra-matic optional. The DB7 had all-independent coil-spring suspension, power steering, 4-wheel ventilated disc brakes and magnesium-alloy wheels.

1997 Aston Martin V8 Volanté convertible.
ASTON MARTIN LAGONDA

The sleek coupé was designed by Ian Callum, formerly of Ford's Ghia Operations in Turin. Complete DB7 body shells, with their steel platform, were supplied by Motor Panels in Coventry and shipped to Crewe for painting by Rolls-Royce.

DB7 assembly was assigned to the Bloxham factory, once a seed mill, where Jaguar had built the XJ-220, with a schedule of 625 cars a year, starting in 1994. They were building 15 cars a week in 1995. The DB7 cabriolet was first shown in January 1994.

Nick Fry was named managing director in 1995, and Dan Parry-Williams was put in charge of Project Vantage, a V12 version of the DB7, with David King as project engineer. Neil Ressler, of Ford's Research and Vehicle Technology Group, played a vital role in the development.

The V12 engine was first seen at the Turin show in April 1994, alongside the Lagonda Vignale prototype. The 48-valve 5995cc 408hp unit was based on the idea of combining two Ford V6 Duratec engines (from the Contour and Mondeo), and developed by Cosworth Engineering, who were also engaged for its production.

Project Vantage was unveiled in January 1998, with a 420hp version of the V12 which was 5kg lighter than the DB7s turbocharged six, and by March 1999, the rating had increased to 450hp. The transmission was a 6-speed paddle-shift Tremec (formerly Borg-Warner) gearbox, with an optional ZF 5hp 30 automatic. In 1999 the V12–engined model accounted for 95% of DB7 output.

1998 Aston Martin Vantage Project V12 coupé.
ASTON MARTIN LAGONDA

The Vantage car did not share the DB7 platform, but was built up on an aluminium honeycomb floor, with aluminium tubes running forward from the bulkhead on both sides of the engine. The body was mainly aluminium panels, with a carbon-fibre roof panel.

The 5341cc V8 was still made in 1999, in coupé, Volanté convertible and Vantage coupé forms, the latter with power up to 600bhp.

JPN

Further Reading
Aston Martin, Dudley Coram, Motor Racing Publications, London, 1957.
Aston Martin and Lagonda V-engined cars, David G. Styles,
Crowood AutoClassics, 1994.

ASTRA (i) (US) 1920
Astra Motors Corp., St Louis, Missouri.
The Astra Corporation was initially formed to take over the DORRIS Motor Car Co., and its product was a companion car to the larger make. It was exhibited at the St Louis Auto Show in February 1920. It featured an attractive pointed radiator, a Le Roi 4-cylinder engine, and wire wheels. Its wheelbase measured 108in (2741mm); an estimated five to ten prototypes were completed. The planned take over failed to materialise and Dorris continued until 1925.
KM

ASTRA (ii) (F) 1922
E. Pasquet, Paris.
This was a cyclecar with 496cc 2-cylinder 2-stroke engine, friction transmission and chain drive. The frame was of armoured wood, and had independent rear suspension by quarter-elliptic springs.
NG

ASTRA (iii) (B) 1929–1931
Sté Astra Motors SA, Liège.
The Société Astra was formed to manufacture the small front-wheel drive JUWEL TA-4 designed by M. Simon which was shown at the Brussels Salon in December 1928, but which never went into production under the Juwel name. Made in the same factory, the Astra had a 1171cc S.C.A.P. engine instead of the 1130cc Juwel, but used the same front-drive which was a very close copy of the French TRACTA. However the transverse leaf spring rear suspension was quite different from the Tracta's. Several body styles were offered, including a 4-door saloon and 2-door coupé and roadster. A small number were built, but the proposed 6- and 8-cylinder Astras were never marketed, though a single prototype six was built.
NG

ASTRA (iv) (US) 1955
Jay Everitt, Los Angeles, California.
The Astra coupé had a hand-formed aluminium body on a tubular frame, and was powered by a modified Oldsmobile V8 engine, with Lincoln 3-speed gearbox

with overdrive. The most striking aspect of its appearance was the extremely low bonnet, so low that the radiator was mounted behind the engine. Only one prototype was made, and, no price was ever quoted.
NG

ASTRA (v) (GB) 1956–1959
Astra Car Co. Ltd, Hampton Hill, Middlesex.
Originally launched as the Jarc Little Horse with a 250cc Excelsior engine, the Astra was made by a subsidiary of the British Anzani Company. It was a miniature utility vehicle with swing axle independent suspension all round, hydraulic brakes and Burman steering. Later examples used an under-floor 322cc Anzani engine. Its alloy bodywork was sold only in 2-seater station wagon form in Great Britain (complete or in kit form) but other types, notably a 4-seater saloon, were apparently built, as well as a 2-seater coupé under the GILL name.
CR

ASTRA (vi) *see* ALLIED FIBERGLASS

ASTRA-GNOME (US) c.1956
Richard Abib, New York, New York.
This odd car looked like a prop from a science-fiction movie. With a glass bubble top and no mudguard openings, it was certainly distinctive. Side trim was anodized aluminium. Based on a Nash Metropolitan chassis, its standard equipment included a celestial time zone clock and a record player. It was built by industrial designer Richard Abib with bodywork by Andrew Mazzara.
HP

ASTRAL (GB) 1923–1924
Hertford Engineering Co. Ltd, Barking, Essex.
This company was unusual for a small firm in that they made most of the car themselves, including the 1720cc single-ohc 4-cylinder engine with unit construction 3-speed gearbox. A ball-bearing crankshaft, Lucas coil ignition, Dynastart and 4-wheel brakes were featured, with 2- or 4-seater open bodies. Very few were made; one customer was Capt. D. Drummond of the banking family, who raced his Astral, nicknamed 'Goshawk', at Brooklands in 1923.
NG

ASTRO DESIGNS (US) 1979–c.1990
Astro Designs Coach Builders, Canoga Park, California.
Started as an assembly shop for Sterlings (the American version of the British NOVA kit car), Astro also assembled the Witton Tiger and Mercedes 540K replicas made by THOROUGHBRED MOTORCARS and ROARING TWENTIES. They began building a car of their own design in 1985, with the introduction of the Garrish Countach, designed by Ray Garrish. It was based on a Sterling body with Lamborghini Countach nose, wheel flares and spoiler grafted on. The chassis was steel tube with Cadillac Eldorado running gear. They were available in kit or assembled form.
HP

ASTRON (GB) 1984–1985
Astron Motors Ltd, Telford, Shropshire.
This was a rather brick-like 4-seater sports car with an open glassfibre body. It was offered for sale in kit form and was based on Ford Cortina mechanicals. Only one car was ever built.
CR

ASUNA (CDN) 1992–1993
General Motors Canada, Oshawa, Ontario.
This was a very short-lived GM brand consisting of the Asuna Sunfire 2+2 coupé, a badge-engineered GEO Storm which was itself based on the ISUZU Impulse, and the Asuna Sunrunner 4x4 (Geo Tracker, *aka* Suzuki Samurai). Dealerships were set up under the name Pontiac-Asuna-Buick-GMC, and a new model appeared for 1993, the SE and GT (Pontiac Le Mans built by Daewoo in Korea). There were no 1994 Asunas, the Sunrunner being rebadged as a Pontiac. Confusion over badging, and consequent loss of trade-in values, was blamed for the demise of the brand.
NG

A.T.A. (B) 1914
Ateliers de Construction d'Automobile Texeira, Trooz.
This short-lived car, whose career was cut short by World War I, was listed in four models; the 1469cc 10CV, 2154cc 12CV, 3014cc 16CV and 4070cc 20CV, all with 4-cylinder engines. The factory was managed by Mathieu van Roggen who was to take over IMPERIA in 1919, and in which the Texeira business was merged.
NG

ATALANTA (i) *see* OWEN (i)

ATALANTA (ii) **(GB)** 1916–1917
Atalanta Light Cars Ltd, Greenwich, London S.E.
This company launched their 9hp 4-cylinder light car in the summer of 1916, when World War I was at its height. They managed to stay in business until February 1917, but few cars were built.
NG

ATALANTA (iii) **(GB)** 1937–1939
Atalanta Motors Ltd, Staines, Middlesex.
The Atalanta was one of the last British marques to appear before World War II, and had a short life. The company was largely backed by Peter Whitehead, and engine designer Albert Gough, whose single-ohc 4-cylinder units powered some Atalantas, as well as being used by FRAZER NASH. Atalanta used two sizes of the 3-valves-per-cylinder Gough engine, 1496cc (78bhp) and 1996cc (98bhp). A Centric supercharger was optional. The X-braced channel chassis with tubular cross members front and rear had coil independent suspension all round, with rear coils mounted horizontally. The gearbox was a 3-speed dual overdrive Warner, or a 4-speed Cotal. These Atalantas came with attractive 2-seater drophead coupé or stark roadster bodies, the latter with cycle-type wings. Later 4-cylinder Atalantas had 2-valves-per-cylinder engines modified by A.C. Bertelli. In 1938 Atalanta offered the 4387cc Lincoln Zephyr V12 engine in the same chassis, lengthened to accommodate the 4-seater sports saloon bodies made, like the smaller bodies, by Abbott. The drophead and sports bodies were also available with the V12 engine, and these more powerful cars cost little more than the fours. Indeed the most expensive 2-litre model was £37 more costly than the V12 saloon. Not more than 20 Atalantas were made. The company became Atalanta Pumps, then Atalanta Engineering Ltd, moving from Staines to Chertsey where they were still active in 1993.
NG

ATHMAC (GB) 1913
Athmac Motor Co., Leyton, Essex.
The Athmac was a fairly typical cyclecar in its friction transmission, though it used a cone-shaped driving disc instead of a flat one, and final drive by long belts. Less usual was a 1109cc 4-cylinder engine with single-ohc. Despite this advanced power unit, the Athmac, which was to be offered in 2-seater form for 120 guineas (£126), did not survive the year of its introduction.
NG

ATHOLL (GB) 1907–1908
Angus Murray & Sons, Glasgow.
The Atholl was a conventional shaft-driven tourer powered by a 25hp 4-cylinder engine. It was distinguished by a radiator shaped like a Scottish bluebell. About a dozen were made at the Craigton Engineering Works.
NG

ATKINSON & PHILIPSON (GB) 1896
Atkinson & Philipson, Northumberland Coach Factory, Newcastle upon Tyne.
This company was one of the oldest-established coachbuilders in the north-east of England, having been founded in 1774. They built mail coaches and, in the early 19th century, railway carriages for George Stephenson. In 1896 they advertised a crude-looking steam brake with iron-shod tyres, but few, if any, were sold.
NG

1939 Atalanta (iii) V12 coupé.
NATIONAL MOTOR MUSEUM

1908 Atholl 25hp chassis.
NATIONAL MOTOR MUSEUM

A.T.L. (I) 1969–1976
A.T.L. Autotecnica del Lario, Mandello.
Ercole Zuccoli established A.T.L. in 1969, initially to produce beach buggies derived from the American EMPI. In 1971 Zuccoli expanded the A.T.L. buggy range and added a couple of VW Beetle-based roadsters, including a 1936 Riley MPH-inspired replica with a glassfibre body and Volkswagen Beetle chassis.
CR

A.T.L.A. (F) 1958–1961
A.T.L.A., Garches.
This was a pretty small coupé with a multi-tubular chassis and bodywork in plastic, featuring gullwing doors. There was a choice of Panhard 850cc or Renault 750cc/850cc engines, permitting good performance because of its low weight of just 500kg.
CR

ATLANTIC (D) 1921–1923
Atlantic AG für Automobilbau, Berlin.
This was a curious 2-wheeled single-track car powered by a 1.8/6PS air-cooled 2-cylinder engine. It seated two in tandem, and had small auxiliary wheels at the sides which could be let down when the vehicle was at rest.
HON

ATLANTIS (GB) 1982–1986
Atlantis Motor Co. Ltd, Attleborough, Norfolk.
This very well conceived 1930s style touring car was created by Michael Booth, initially in complete form at prices from £39,000, but soon after as an up-market kit as well. The Figoni & Falaschi-inspired bodywork was initially sold as a

1908 Atlas (ii) taxicab.
NICK BALDWIN

fixed-head with four seats, but from 1985, a full drophead coupé was available. Mechanicals derived from the Jaguar XJ, but at least one Atlantis was fitted with a V8 engine. Although the Atlantis was theoretically available throughout the 1980s, the last of approximately 15 cars built emerged in 1986.

CR

ATLAS (i) (US) 1906–1907

Atlas Automobile Co., Pittsburgh, Pennsylvania.
This company offered a 25/30hp 4-cylinder car in touring or runabout form, with 3-speed gearbox and shaft drive.

NG

ATLAS (ii); ATLAS-KNIGHT (US) 1907–1913

Atlas Motor Car Co., Springfield, Massachusetts.
This Atlas was made by Harry A. Knox who had left the car company bearing his name to set up the Knox Motor Truck Company. He built a 2-ton truck called the Atlas, but the Atlas car that he introduced in 1907 was designed by the Sunset Automobile Company of San Francisco whose factory had been destroyed in the 1906 earthquake. It went into production at Springfield as the Atlas Model R Runabout with 20hp 2-cylinder 2-stroke engine on a 90in (2284mm) wheelbase, and was joined in 1908 by 34hp 3-cylinder and 46hp 4-cylinder models, with longer wheelbases that could carry 5-seater tourer bodies. The 2-cylinder model was also offered as a taxicab and delivery van. The Atlas grew in size up to 1911, when the largest model was the 40hp 4-cylinder Model O on a 128in (3249mm) wheelbase. By then the 2-stroke engine was out of fashion, and as Harry Knox still did not wish to embrace conventional poppet-valves, he opted for the sleeve-valve Knight engine, calling his cars Atlas-Knights. A 50hp four was made for two seasons, after which Knox moved to Indianapolis to join the Lyons brothers in making the LYONS-KNIGHT.

NG

ATLAS (iii) (F) 1949–1951

Sté Industrielle de Livry, Paris.
Launched at the 1949 Paris Salon, the Atlas was a 2-seater minicar powered by a 125cc AMC engine, replaced on production cars by a 175cc developing 8.5bhp, and giving a top speed of 43mph (69km/h). It was also known as the Coccinelle (Ladybird); confusingly the name was also applied to another French minicar of the same era, the SOFRAVEL. The Société Industrielle de Livry also sold the KOVER and LE PIAF minicars.

NG

ATLAS FIBER-GLASS (US) c.1952

Atlas Fiber-Glass Inc., Los Angeles, California;
Allied Fiber-Glass, Los Angeles, California.
Atlas was a kit car company formed by Roy Kinch and his helper Mickey Thompson, who would later find fame in speed record cars. They pulled a set of moulds from a Pininfarina-bodied Cisitalia 202 Gran Sport and adapted them to fit the MG-TC and TD chassis. These bodies were made in coupé and convertible styles, and were popular on V8 powered specials raced at the Bonneville salt flats. The company changed its name to the Allied Fiber-Glass Company (no apparent relation to Allied Fiberglass in Sacramento, California) soon after it was formed.

HP

ATOMO (I) 1947–1949

S.A.M.C.A., Parma.
Made by the impressive-sounding Società Applicazioni Meccaniche Costruzioni Automobilistiche, the Atomo was a small 3-wheeler powered by a 246cc 2-cylinder 2-stroke engine mounted over, and driving, the rear wheel. It had a 3-speed gearbox and top speed of 47mph (75km/h). Few were made, and by October 1949 S.A.M.C.A. was out of business.

NG

A TO Z CAR EMPORIUM (US) c.1994

A to Z Car Emporium, Davie, Florida.
This diversified kit company manufactured bodies to fit several donor chassis. These included replicas of the Lamborghini Countach (ESC 5000) and Ferrari 308 (350GTB) built on Pontiac Fiero chassis, and Ferrari Testarossa replicas called the Fire-Rossa for 1982–92 Chevrolet Camaro and Pontiac Firebird running gear. Their low-cost Lamborghini replica called La Grande Spyder XT had a simple one-piece body that slipped over a Fiero chassis. Their only original design was the Concept 2000, an attractive coupé body that fitted onto Fiero running gear. Designed by David Tidwell, it was available in kit or assembled form. It was later sold by EXOTIC ENTERPRISES.

HP

A.T.S. (i) (I) 1962–1964

Automobil Turismo Sport SpA, Bologna.
Following ructions at Ferrari in 1961, when a number of key personnel left the company, Count Volpi di Misurata, Giorgio Billi and Jaime Ortez-Patino formed Automobili Serenissima in 1962, but Volpi quickly departed to found his own separate SERENISSIMA concern. The others founded A.T.S. to pursue a Formula 1 project which, despite the input of Carlo Chiti as engineer and Phil Hill and Carlo Baghetti as drivers, failed badly. An ambitious road-going GT car was also developed by Chiti for launch at the 1963 Geneva Salon. The A.T.S. 2500 GT was only the second road-going mid-engined car ever made (after the René Bonnet Djet) and closely followed racing practice, using a tubular chassis and triangulated suspension. The mid-mounted engine was an ohc 2468cc V8, claimed to produce 210bhp, sufficient for a top speed of 150mph (241km/h). The exceptionally handsome coupé bodywork was created by Allemano. A GTS version, with lightweight bodywork and a 245bhp engine, was shown in 1964 and competed in the Targa Fiorio, but the A.T.S. adventure was all but over by then. It is estimated that between six and twelve cars had been completed.

CR

Further Reading
'ATS 2500GT and GTS', Winston Goodfellow,
Automobile Quarterly, Vol. 39, No. 4.

A.T.S. (ii) (F) 1994–c.1996

A.T.S. Evolution, Arcueil.
Presented at the 1994 Geneva Motor Show, the A.T.S. was a painstaking replica of the Shelby Cobra Daytona coupé. The aluminium bodywork was an absolutely faithful reproduction. It used a 308bhp, 4.7-litre Ford V8 engine mated to a 4-speed manual transmission, and the makers claimed a top speed of 191mph (307km/h).

CR

ATTERBURY see AUTOCAR

ATTICA (GR) 1964–1968

Vioplastic, Piraeus.
The German FULDAMOBIL was made under licence in numerous countries, but in Greece it managed to stay in production for an inordinate number of years. A plastics manufacturer, Georgios Dimitriadis, took on licensed production in 1964, and named the car Attica. The 3-wheeler used a 198cc Heinkel single-

cylinder engine (top speed 60mph/96km/h). In 1966 it was joined by the open Cabrioletta version, as well as a beach model that had no doors or windscreen. About 100 saloons and a handful of convertibles were made before the manufacturing firm had to sell the project on to a new firm, ALTA, in 1968. Attica also assembled the Israeli SABRA Carmel, and Dimitriadis went on to build the DIM in 1977.

CR

ATTILA (D) 1900–1901
Attila Fahrradwerke AG vorm. Kretschmer & Co., Dresden–Lobtau.
The Attila bicycle works tried to enter car production with a 2-seater 3-wheeler powered by a 2½hp Aster engine. Only a few prototypes were made.

NG

ATVIDABERG (S) 1910
Atvidabergs Vagnfabrik, Atvidaberg.
This was an old-fashioned-looking car with the appearance of an American high-wheeler, and based on an imported HOLSMAN. Designed by Martin Eriksson, it was powered by a horizontally-opposed 2-cylinder engine which could be moved forwards or backwards to engage forward or reverse gear. Top speed was 28mph (45km/h). An advanced feature was electric lighting, the lights turning with the front wheels. A production run of 35 was planned, but not more than 12 Atvidabergs were made.

NG

ATW (D) 1983 to date
ATW Autotechnik Walther GmbH, Bad Rappenau.
This company – partly owned by Ligier of France – specialised in microcars for a special clientele, eg handicapped people, holders of moped licences, and 16- to 18-year-olds who could not get a full licence.

Other microcars, mostly Italian and French, were converted according to the requirements of the buyers, mostly using small German 2-stroke moped engines of 50cc. However, ATW also developed their own model, the 'Charly', a single-seater with a 4-stroke engine of 160cc. Electric versions were available to special order. ATW claims production of more than 7000 units.

HON

AUBURN (i) (US) 1902–1936
Auburn Automobile Co., Auburn, Indiana.
One of America's best known cars after its acquisition by Errett Lobban Cord in 1924, the Auburn became a style leader for the next dozen years until the end of production at the end of 1936. It was generally considered the flagship of E.L. Cord's automobile empire which also included CORD and DUESENBERG cars.

Formerly the Eckhart Carriage Company, the Eckhart brothers – Frank and Morris – began experimenting with a projected automobile in 1900, and by 1902 they had formed the Auburn Automobile Company and were building single-cylinder tiller-steered runabouts. These were assembled before production officially commenced and were sold in and around Auburn. Actual production began a year later with an updated design comprising a single-cylinder chain-driven runabout with the engine under the body, the fuel tank under the bonnet, and a steering wheel in place of a tiller.

In 1904 a rear-entrance tonneau model was introduced, and a year later a 2-cylinder engine was introduced, which would remain on all Auburns until 1910.

In 1910, this engine was supplanted by a Rutenber 4-cylinder type and a vee-type radiator. A complete line of open and closed body types was also made available that year. The company branched out in 1912 by buying the Zimmerman Manufacturing Company of Auburn, erstwhile builders of high-wheelers, and continued production of them into 1915. In 1912, Auburn added a 6-cylinder series to its fours, and both fours and sixes would be produced until 1917, when the four was dropped. Left- or right-hand steering was optional, and by this time both Continental and Teetor engines were added to Rutenbers in Auburn cars.

In 1921, Auburn introduced its 'Beauty Six' series, which featured bevelled edges on the sides of the open cars and a streamline motif. Especially noted in the Beauty Six line was the sporting-type phaeton with cycle-type mudguards, step plates, disc wheels, and a largish luggage holder – more akin to a small trunk–directly behind the front fender. The three 6-cylinder series, the Model

1964 A.T.S. (i) V8 GT coupé.
NATIONAL MOTOR MUSEUM

1904 Auburn (i) 20hp tonneau.
NICK GEORGANO/NATIONAL MOTOR MUSEUM

6-43 for this year, was fitted with a Continental 6Y L-head engine or a Weidely ohv type – the owner's choice – or a Supreme for the larger sixes. Despite their attractive appearance, Auburn production for 1923 totalled 2443 cars, a formidable drop from the 6062 cars which found buyers in 1919.

By 1924 Auburn was in trouble, with production down to six cars a day and a large number of completed but unsold cars parked next to the factory. The company's future was bleak indeed, but its destiny would abruptly change at this point.

This change occurred when the Auburn Automobile Company was purchased outright by E.L. Cord, an aggressive and highly successful salesman of Moon cars, who had a set vision for the future of the nearly moribund Auburn. Cord immediately had the piled-up unsold Auburns repainted in attractive, brighter colours, exposing the nickelled radiators and other brightwork, and successfully selling them at slightly above cost. Simultaneously, his stylists were busily working on designs for a completely new line of cars. Thus ended 1924, with Auburn production exceeding that of the previous year by about 30 cars.

Designed by J.M. Crawford, the 1925 Auburns exemplified modern design completely throughout, featuring 2-toned colour schemes and a novel belt moulding which extended from the cowl, over the top of the bonnet, with its apex at the radiator cap. The external design was not exclusive in the Auburn's 'Second Coming' for, although a six was continued with a Continental engine, the new cars were largely promoted by a Lycoming straight-8, which would also be used at this time in the ELCAR, GARDNER and the KISSEL 8-75. Although 6-cylinder Auburns would be manufactured until 1930, and from 1934 until 1936, the eight would become more closely associated with the make.

Crawford's design was so far ahead of most automotive design that it remained only minutely changed through 1930.

1930 Auburn (i) 8-95 cabriolet.
NATIONAL MOTOR MUSEUM

1932 Auburn (i) speedster.
NATIONAL MOTOR MUSEUM

The lithe sporting appearance for Auburn's 1931 cars was a design by 26-year old Alan H. Leamy, who had been instrumental in designing Cord's higher priced Cord L-29 and Duesenberg Model J cars. This new Auburn was widely considered to be a great bargain. Low and rangy in concept, it was priced from $945 to $1395, with production rocketing to a total of 34,228 units.

This figure is of major importance historically. As 1931 was the first year of the Great Depression, automobile production plummeted, but in face of this only Auburn and Plymouth would see an increase over their 1930 figures – 34,228 compared with 1930's 12,985 for Auburn.

But despite the introduction of a twelve in 1932, the future would follow a downhill direction with a drop to 11,145 cars leaving the factory in 1932.

Auburn's prices for 1932 reflected the times, listed from $725 to $1005 for the three series of eights and $975 to $1175 to $1275 for the two twelves. Without any perceptible change for 1933, overall prices were listed at $745 to $1495. Production dropped to 5038.

A new design was debuted, and a six added to the Auburn line for 1934, overall prices ranging from $695 to $1545 with an increase in production to 7770.

For 1935 a new and handsome sports design was announced, and a supercharged line of Auburns augmented the existing sixes and eights, with prices set between $745 and $1725, plus $2245 for a sporting 2-passenger boat-tailed speedster which was generally accepted by most pundits as the sportiest production car of all standard-priced American automobiles, but which, continued into 1936, would herald Auburn's swan song. Production for 1935 reached 6316.

The 1935 Auburns were continued into 1936 with prices unchanged and a major drop in production to 1263 units. Plans were underway, however, for a new range of cars for 1937.

E.L. Cord dropped Auburn later in 1936, such 1937 models as were presumably built being prototypes. Cord continued the Cord and Duesenberg cars into the next year, both of them becoming casualties of 1937. Approximately 180,000 Auburn automobiles were manufactured in 34 years of production.

KM

NICK BALDWIN

CORD, ERRETT LOBBAN (1894–1974)

A classic entrepreneur who rescued two car makers from the doldrums (Auburn and Duesenberg) and gave his name to a third, Cord was born on 20 July 1894 in Warrensburg, Missouri. His parents moved to Los Angeles where he graduated from high school, and was immediately involved in a number of business ventures. These included running garages in Los Angeles, making racing cars from junked Fords and driving them on dirt tracks up and down the West Coast, running truck lines through Death Valley and selling new and used cars. It was his ability as a salesman that ignited his career. In the early 1920s he went to Chicago and became a salesman for Moon Cars. By 1924 he was vice-president and general manager of Quinlan Motors, the Chicago distributor for Moon cars. His success there attracted the directors of the failing Auburn Motor Co., which was turning out a dismal six cars a day, and pretty dull ones at that. 'They all thought Auburn was a little bum' said Cord, but he could see possibilities in the car, and obtained a deal whereby his salary was modest, but if he salvaged the company he would gain control. There were 500 unsold Auburns at the factory; Cord had them repainted in dual colour schemes, gave them nickel-plated door handles and sold them in batches of 100 to a dealer in Brooklyn. This brought in much-needed cash and enabled more attractive models to be produced for the 1925 season. Like Harley Earl, Cord realised sooner than most that style sold cars, and also that it was the woman who passed final judgement on the purchase of the family car. Though no engineer, he was aware of the appeal of the 8-cylinder engine over the six, and used some of the money earned from the sale of the refurbished 1924 cars to commission a straight-8 from Lycoming for 1925.

The 1925 Auburns were the first to be completely restyled, with a beltline gracefully curving from the bonnet sides over the top to meet at the radiator. Sales increased nearly tenfold between 1924 and 1930, but like all entrepreneurs, Cord was soon looking for fresh pastures. In 1926 he cast his eye on Duesenberg which was making the high-class Model A in dwindling numbers. He wanted to take a step into the top ranks of American cars, but the Model A was not the car to take that step. Having bought the Duesenberg company for a claimed $1 million, Cord then bought Lycoming, thus ensuring a supply of the engines he wanted, and also an entry into the aircraft engine business, which he was sure Lycoming would do very well at. Along the way he bought the Stinson Aircraft Corp. and body builders Central Manufacturing Co. He ordered from Lycoming the famous 6.9-litre twin-ohc straight-8 engine that powered the Model J Duesenberg, and was never to be used in any other car.

Further Reading
'Auburn–from Runabout to Speedster', Beverly Rae Kimes,
Automobile Quarterly, Vol.5, No.4.
Errett Lobban Cord–his Empire, his Motor Cars: Auburn, Cord, Duesenberg,
Griffith Borgeson, Automobile Quarterly Publications.

AUBURN (ii) (US) 1912–1915

Auburn Motor Chassis Co., Auburn, Indiana.
Made in the same town at the same time as the better-known AUBURN (i), this
was a high-wheeler sold mostly as a truck or Handy Wagon which could be used
for taking produce to market on weekdays and for church going and social
activities on Sundays. It was very precisely priced at $487.50, while one of the
wagons was even more precise at $365.62. They also offered a buggy on a 65in
(1650mm) wheelbase at $293, and a runabout on a 77in (1954mm) wheelbase
at $390.
NG

AUBURN (iii) (US) 1967–1975

Auburn-Cord-Duesenberg Co., Tulsa, Oklahoma.
Former schoolteacher Glenn Pray started this company after a mildly successful
attempt at building Cord replicas (*see* CORD 810). He replicated the 1935 Auburn
boat-tail speedster with a fibreglass body on a Ford chassis with a 7000cc Ford
V8. A 4-door boat-tail phaeton was added in 1975. These were very high quality
cars, and were sold in assembled form.
HP

AUBURN MOTORCAR COMPANY (US) 1996 to date

Auburn Motorcar Company, Port Richey, Florida.
This company built a replica of the Auburn Speedster with a rectangular steel
tube frame using Chevrolet Caprice suspension and a Chevrolet V8 engine.
Sold in turn-key form from 1996 to 1997, then offered in kit form as well.
HP

In September 1929 he launched the first car to bear his own name, the
Model L-29 Cord. He had been impressed by the front-drive racing cars
of Harry Miller, but probably the greatest attraction of the system was
that it allowed for a low, long-bonnetted line that made the cars stand out
from all others. He missed most of the launch parties as he was busy
testing a car across the country, but he was present at the introduction of
the car at the Paris and London Motor Shows in October. Sales were
disappointing, largely because of the aftermath of the Wall Street crash,
but Auburn sales were holding up in 1930, and in 1931 they almost
tripled, an unparalleled success during the Depression. Cord was hailed as
a business genius and as a beacon to others. However things were not so
good by the end of 1932, with sales in Auburn and Duesenberg seriously
down (the Cord L-29 had been discontinued at the end of 1931). E.L.
began to distance himself from cars, and spent a lot of money buying up
aviation and shipbuilding companies. However in August 1933 he
bought the Checker Cab Co., and November 1935 saw the launch of his
dramatic Gordon Buehrig-styled Cord 810. Sales of that were
disappointing too, and in August 1937 he got out of the car business
altogether. He sold his holdings in the Cord Corp. for $2,632,000 to a
group of bankers who promptly discontinued production of the 810. E.L.
had no more involvement with cars, but made a further fortune in real
estate on the West Coast and uranium mining in Utah. He also started an
all-music radio station and in the mid-1950s became a senator for the
state of Nevada. Despite these achievements he remained, as he had
always been, a very private man, preferring to sit with the crowd rather
than at the top tables, and revealing little about his personal life.
NG
Further Reading
*Errett Lobban Cord, his Empire, his Motor Cars: Auburn, Cord,
Duesenberg,* Griffith Borgeson, Automobile Quarterly Publications.
'E.L. Cord and his Empire', Beverly Rae Kimes,
Automobile Quarterly, Vol.18, No.2.

1936 Auburn (i) 654 sedan.
NATIONAL MOTOR MUSEUM

1923 Audi Type K 14/50PS tourer.
NATIONAL MOTOR MUSEUM

AUBURN SPEEDSTERS (US) 1973

Auburn Speedsters Co., Buffalo, New York.
Very similar to the Glenn Pray Auburn, this replica also used a Ford chassis and
running gear. However, it had a smaller 5700cc engine. This project was sold to
GLASSIC, who renamed it the Romulus.
HP

AUDAX (i) (F) 1914

Lenefait et Cie, Rouen.
The Audax was a conventional 4-cylinder light car. The makers were still listed
in 1920, but it is not known if any postwar cars were made.
NG

AUDAX (ii) (F) 1997 to date

Société Audax Ingénierie, Gallargues le Montueux.
Launched at the 1997 Geneva Salon, this open 2-seater roadster featured a
BMW 4.4-litre V8 engine and 6-speed gearbox, after initial plans for a tuned
Peugeot V6 engine proved too expensive. The multi-tubular chassis was clothed
in a low-slung but aesthetically challenged body created by Olivier Moret-Bailly,
although the company envisaged multitudinous coachbuilt bodywork designs.
One novelty was so-called 'mono-interactive' suspension, which used a single
coil spring/damper for each axle, which was double-triangulated.
CR

AUDI (D) 1910–1939; 1965 to date

1910–1939 Audi Automobilwerke GmbH, Zwickau.
1965–1969 Auto Union GmbH, Ingolstadt.
1969 to date Audi AG, Ingolstadt.
The Audi marque came about because of August Horch's disagreement with the
other directors of HORCH Motorwagenwerke. He believed strongly in competitions:

1937 Audi Front 225 Spezial-Cabriolet by Glaser.
NATIONAL MOTOR MUSEUM

1929 Audi Zwickau Pullmann limousine.
NATIONAL MOTOR MUSEUM

1965 Audi L saloon.
NATIONAL MOTOR MUSEUM

they thought them a waste of time and money; so he left to form his own company, August Horch Automobilwerke, in the same town. He was promptly told that he could not use the same name as the existing company, so he chose Audi, which is the Latinised version of Horch, meaning 'hark' or 'listen'.

The first product of his new company was the 2612cc Typ A 10/22PS with overhead inlet and side exhaust valves which Horch had used on his 18/22PS cars. It retained dual ignition and other Horch features, and in 1911 became the Typ B 28PS. Larger models followed quickly, the 3560cc Type C, 4680cc Typ D and 5699cc Typ E. The Typ C was made in sporting form, with a light aluminium body, and these cars were entered in the Alpine Trials from 1911 to 1914. Two cars were unpenalised in 1912, though the team prize went to Opel, but in 1913 they won this, the Typ C earning the name Alpensieger (Alpine Victor).

The Typs B to E were made up to the outbreak of World War I, joined in 1914 by the smaller 2084cc Typ G. From 1913 electric lighting and starting by Bosch were available. Audi also made trucks powered by the Typ C engine, and these kept them busy during the war. The Typs C, E and G were revived in 1919, and were made up to 1924. All postwar models had vee-radiators which seemed mandatory on German cars at that period. In 1921 technical director Hermann Lange brought out his first postwar design, the 3560cc Typ K. This had the same dimensions as the C, but was a more modern concept, with block, pistons and axle casing in light alloy. The engine gave 50bhp, compared with 35bhp from its predecessor. Transatlantic influence was evident in the central gearchange and left-hand drive, Audi being one of the first German manufacturers to adopt this feature. About 200 Typ Ks were made between 1921 and 1925, and in 1923 it was joined by the more ambitious and expensive Typ M. This had a 4655cc single-ohc 6-cylinder engine with three pumps for pressure lubrication, one-shot chassis lubrication, and servo-assisted hydraulic brakes on all four wheels. About 230 of these advanced cars were sold between 1923 and 1928, but it was said that Audi lost money on all of them because of the expense of manufacture.

For their next model Audi added more cylinders; the Typ R Imperator (1928–1932) had a 100bhp straight-8 engine of 4872cc. The design was less sophisticated than that of the Typ M, with side valves, a 3-speed gearbox and mechanical brakes. This enabled the price to be kept down to RM16,575 for a pullman-limousine, compared with RM22,300 for the same style on a Typ M chassis.

Changes of ownership

In 1920 August Horch left Audi to join the Ministry of Economics in Berlin. The company was then led by a consortium of directors under Ernst Baus. In 1928 the majority of the shares were acquired by Danish-born Jurgen Skafte Rasmussen (1878–1964) who had been making DKW motorcycles since 1920 and was about to launch the DKW light car. He needed factory space for car assembly, and this was his main reason for taking control of Audi. However, he continued production of the Imperator at a modest level (only 150 were made altogether), and also launched three new models, the 3838cc 6-cylinder Dresden and two sizes of the 8-cylinder Zwickau, 4371 and 5130cc. These had side-valve engines of Rickenbacker type. Rasmussen had acquired manufacturing rights to these after the RICKENBACKER company ceased car production in 1927. The engines used in the Audis were very similar to the American designs, though Capt. Eddie Rickenbacker always denied that they were his. About 450 Zwickaus and 70 Dresdens were made up to 1932. The last Audi of the Rasmussen era was the 4-cylinder Typ P, which had a Peugeot 201 engine in the chassis and body of the V4 DKW. Very few were made.

Audi sales were very low at this time; only 77 cars were delivered in 1931 and 22 in 1932. Horch were also at a low ebb, so in the summer of 1932 they merged to form a new group, Auto Union, taking on the Chemnitz firm, WANDERER, as well. This gave them an effective market coverage, from the popular-priced DKW through the middle-class Wanderer to the prestige Horch. With Horch making several straight-8s and a V12 there was no point in continuing the American-engined Audis, and the name might well have disappeared. However, the Auto Union directors decided to use it on an interesting new car which combined the components and ideas of several others in the group. The 1950cc 6-cylinder engine came from Wanderer and drove the front wheels as in the little DKW, while styling was on the lines of the smaller Horchs. The chassis was a central backbone frame, and all wheels were independently sprung by transverse leaves. Early models had Deutsche Perrot mechanical brakes, later replaced by ATE hydraulics.

The new car was named the Audi Front, and prototypes were running in 1932, with production starting in February 1933. Up to April 1934 they were made in the Audi factory, and after that in the Horch factory. In 1935 capacity went up to 2257cc, this model being known as the Audi Front 225. More were made than any previous Audi, production totalling 3519 between 1933 and 1938. However, it was not altogether a success, suffering from heavy steering and gearchange, and it was dropped in April 1938. For 1939 there was another Auto Union cocktail – the Audi 920 had a 3281cc 6-cylinder engine which was a straight-8 Horch with two fewer cylinders, in the body of the 6-cylinder Wanderer. This time there was no flirting with front-wheel drive, and the conventional 920 was pleasanter to drive than the Front, as well as being more powerful and faster, with a top speed of 80mph (129km/h). Two bodies were offered, a factory-built 4-door saloon and a 2-door cabriolet by Glaser. Production lasted into World War II, ending in April 1940, when 1282 had been made.

Delayed revival

All the factories of the Auto Union group fell into the Eastern Zone of Germany after the war, and the names of Audi, Horch and Wanderer disappeared. Horch was briefly seen on heavy trucks, and on the short-lived 6-cylinder car made in the Zwickau factory from 1956 to 1959. The DKW was revived at Ingolstadt in West Germany, making a rebodied version of the prewar 2-cylinder Meisterklasse. The makers were once again called Auto Union, and in 1958 Daimler Benz became the majority shareholder. By the early 1960s the DKW 2-stroke engine was becoming outmoded, and just before Volkswagen came to Auto Union's rescue in 1965 they introduced a new 1696cc 4-cylinder engine which went into the body shell of the current DKW, the F102 saloon. The engine was designed by Ludwig Kraus, formerly with Daimler Benz. As the name DKW was irrevocably associated with 2-strokes and cheap cars, and as the new model was aimed at the BMW market, a new name was needed. Audi was chosen as the new car was in roughly the same position in the market as the pre war Audis had been.

The first Audi had no model name, being simply called the limousine. Apart from grille and trim, the 2- and 4-door saloons were similar in appearance to the DKW F102, which was continued into the 1966 season. The 72bhp 4-cylinder engine was inclined at an angle of 40 degrees, to fit under the low bonnet, and the front wheels had disc brakes. In 1966 came a luxury version, the Audi L, and a higher performance model, the 80bhp 80L. An additional body style was an estate car called the Variant. From September 1967 the L, 80L and Variant had dual-circuit braking with optional servo assistance. For 1968 a smaller engine of 1496cc was available in the 60L and there was also the Super 90 with 90bhp 1770cc engine. The last of the first series Audis was made in 1972, but meanwhile a larger model had appeared. Made from 1968 to 1976, the 100 had a longer wheelbase, larger bodies and engines of 1760 and 1871cc. In 1971 came a 2-door fastback coupé available only with the larger engine.

By the early 1970s Audi were not only moving successfully upmarket, they were also becoming volume manufacturers. Production of the first series cars up

1983 Audi Quattro coupé.
NATIONAL MOTOR MUSEUM

1990 Audi 200 Quattro 20-valve 2-litre saloon.
AUDI AG

to 1972 was 41,685 and 827,474 of the 100 were made. The millionth Audi was made in May 1973, in which year the company made 409,743 cars. In 1969 they merged with NSU to form Audi NSU Auto Union AG, which was under the control of Volkswagen. The last NSU was made in 1977. There was some sharing and overlapping of models between VW and Audi. The most obvious was the Audi 50/VW Polo which used the same bodyshell with an 895cc engine in the Polo and 1093 or 1272cc in the Audi. Introduced in 1974, the Audi predated the Polo by a year, but was dropped in 1978 after 190,828 had been made. The Polo then received the larger engine.

The other example of badge engineering was the Audi 80, a new 4-door saloon made from 1972 to 1978, which had its VW equivalent in the Passat. Both shared a new vertically-mounted Audi-designed single-ohc engine and McPherson strut suspension, though they had different body styling. In 1978 the original 80 gave way to a second generation model, which was more upmarket and was no longer linked to the Passat. Before it was dropped, the first generation 80 was the first Audi to exceed the million mark, with 1,103,766 made.

In 1976 came the 'new 100' saloon, larger and completely restyled, with single-ohc 4-cylinder engines of 1588 and 1984cc, and in 1977 this car received Audi's revolutionary in-line 5-cylinder engine of 2144cc, the first to be fitted to a passenger car. With power steering and optional automatic transmission, the 100 represented another move upmarket, and was a worthy rival to the medium-sized cars from BMW and Mercedes-Benz. In 1977 a 5-door hatchback joined the 100 range; known as the 100 Avant, it was available with a 1986cc 5-cylinder diesel engine in addition to the petrol units. By the time the 100 was replaced in 1982, production had reached 948,114, a high figure for a relatively expensive car. The bigger 200 of 1980 had the same 5-cylinder petrol engine, with a 170bhp turbocharged option, and featured all-disc brakes, power steering and electric windows.

Four-wheel drive

Today the ordinary touring car driven on all four wheels is by no means uncommon, but the pioneer in this field was Audi, with a range developed from their remarkable Quattro coupé. The genesis of the Quattro came in 1977 when a group of Audi saloons was being tested in Northern Scandinavia together with

1999 Audi TT coupé.
NICK BALDWIN

1999 Audi A8 saloon.
NICK BALDWIN

a Volkswagen Iltis utility vehicle. This had an Audi 80 engine with less power than any of the saloons, yet it outperformed them with ease, making the maximum use of its power. The reason was that it drove on all four wheels. This led development engineer Jurg Bessinger to consider 4-wheel drive for road cars, but before going into mass production it needed to be tested in a small series model. With the encouragement of senior manager (and former rally driver) Walter Treser, work went ahead, first on an Audi 80 saloon with the Iltis' transmission, then on a new competition coupé. This used the 170bhp turbocharged 100 5-cylinder engine in the floorpan of the 80, with a crisply-styled 2-door coupé body. Drive to the front wheels was through an integral differential, as on the other front-drive Audis, while a 2-piece shaft and Iltis-derived rear axle drove the rear wheels.

The Quattro made its debut at the 1980 Geneva Show, where international journalists were enthusiastic about its performance on snow. An intercooler boosted engine output to 200bhp, and the first rally Quattros gave 285bhp. The car made its rally debut in the Algarve in October 1980, its first full season being 1981 when three major event victories were achieved. Quattros won the Championship for makes in 1982 and 1984, their leading drivers being Hannu Mikkola, Stig Blomqvist and Michele Mouton. A more powerful KKK turbocharger and a larger intercooler increased power to 370bhp. In 1984 came the Quattro Sport with four valves per cylinder and wheelbase shortened by 12.5in (317mm). In works form the engine developed nearly 500bhp, but the cars were difficult to handle and less successful than the standard Quattro. The latter won 21 World Championship rallies in four years, the Sport only two. Once 200 had been made for homologation purposes, production ceased. They were very expensive, costing DM198,000, compared with DM75,915 for the regular Quattro. A 2-wheel drive coupé of similar appearance to the Quattro cost only DM24,340 (1985 prices).

In 1982 a new 100 appeared, with the same 4- and 5-cylinder engines and a more aerodynamic body with flush glass windows. An Avant estate car version joined the saloons in March 1983. They were joined by the similar-styled 200 in June 1983 and 80 in September 1986. By then all Audis could be had with 4-wheel drive, including the coupé which was called the Coupé Quattro. This was not to be confused with the original Quattro Coupé which was still made and was a more powerful and expensive car. Engines ranged from a 1595cc 70bhp four to a 2226cc 220bhp turbocharged five used in the top model 200 and Quattro.

A new model in 1988 was Audi's first V8 with a 250bhp 3562cc engine in a body which bore a strong family resemblance to those of the smaller saloons. The V8 was available in long-chassis limousine form, while Lorenz & Rankl made extra-long limousine conversions of several Audis, including the V8. A Lorenz & Rankl converted Audi was the basis of the 1990 HONG-QI CA-7225. The V8 was made up to February 1994 when it was replaced by the A8. This advanced saloon, with light alloy space frame construction, could be had with a 2771cc V6 or 4172cc V8 engine, with a 3697cc V8 being added in June 1995. In its most powerful S8 version of 1999, the 4.2-litre V8 gave 360bhp from a 40-valve engine (three inlet valves per cylinder).

Since the A50 had been discontinued in 1978 Audi had no contender in the small car class, but this was remedied in 1996 when they introduced the A3 3-door hatchback, available with four engines from a single-cam 1597cc to a twin-cam 20-valve 1781cc, as well as an 1896cc turbo diesel. In 1998 came turbocharged 1781cc engines giving 150 or 180bhp, while still more powerful was the 209bhp S3 introduced in the Spring of 1999. These more powerful A3s could be had with 4-wheel drive, and a 5-door hatchback joined the range in 1999. Also using the turbocharged 1781cc engine was the TT 2-seater coupé with engine options up to 224bhp. Introduced in September 1998, this and the later roadster version were made at Gyŏr in Hungary.

Among larger Audi saloons were the A4 with its Avant estate version, introduced in 1994 and available with several engines from a 101bhp 1595cc four to a 265bhp 2671cc V6, the latter being known as the S4. Filling the gap between the A4 and the A8 was the A6 saloon with five petrol engine options from 1781 to 2671cc as well as two sizes of turbo diesel. A high performance S6 version with 360bhp 3697cc V8 was launched at the 1999 Frankfurt Show. For open air fans Audi offered the Cabriolet which had no model number. Introduced in 1991 it could be had with 1781cc four or V6 engines up to 2771cc. The Cabriolet earned fame as the favourite car of the late Diana, Princess of Wales.

Although Audi had been the leading company offering 4-wheel drive on a variety of road cars, they did not enter the on/off-road 4x4 field until 1999, when they announced the Allroad. This was based on the A6 Avant, but had a higher ground clearance. Engine options were the V6 turbo or V6 turbo diesel, with the possibility of a V8 as well. Production was due to start in February 2000.

For 2000 Audi extended their range at both ends of the spectrum. Smaller and cheaper than the A3, and pitched against the Mercedes-Benz A Class, the A2 was a 5-door hatchback with radical lines, based on the AL2 concept car of 1997 and powered by a 1.2-litre 3-cylinder direct-injection petrol engine, and also a similar sized diesel as used in the Volkswagen Lupo. A 3-door version was planned for 2001. At the other end of the range was an A8 powered by a 408bhp 5.6 litre W12 engine, with more power than rival V12s from BMW or Mercedes Benz. It had four overhead camshafts, 48 valves and was only available in the long wheelbase version of the A8.

NG

Further Reading
Alle Audi Automobile 1910–1980, Werner Oswald, Motorbuch Verlag, 1980.

AUDIBERT-LAVIROTTE (F) 1896–1902

1896–1898 Sté des Voitures Audibert et Lavirotte, Lyons.
1898–1902 SA des Anciens Établissements Audibert et Lavirotte, Lyons.
Maurice Audibert worked for the Scotte company which made wagonettes in Paris before joining Emile Lavirotte in car manufacture. Both young men had been destined for careers in the silk industry but, like so many others, they were lured by the idea of the car. Their early models, which were the first petrol cars to be made in Lyons, were closely based on Benz designs, though they soon began making their own 2- and 4-cylinder engines and carburettors. Production was very small, to customer demand only, until they set up their company in 1896. Two years later they offered seven models, from a 2-seater *petit duc* to a large enclosed 4-seater coupé. From 1899 the engines were front-mounted, with 3-speed gearboxes and chain final drive. Four models were listed in 1900, of 7, 12, 16 and 32hp. The largest was a 4-cylinder racing car capable of 50mph (80km/h). About 50 cars a year were made in 1899–1900 before the partnership split up. More than 150 vehicles were made in all, of which three survive. Maurice Audibert became commercial manager of another Lyon firm, ROCHET-SCHNEIDER, while Emile Lavirotte became a partner of Marius BERLIET in return for providing him with the Audibert–Lavirotte factory.

NG

AUDINEAU (F) 1897

The Parisian coachbuilder Paul Audineau built a voiturette powered by a rear-mounted Pygmée engine.

NG

AUGÉ (F) 1899–c.1901

Daniel Augé et Cie, Levallois-Perret, Seine.
Augé built a range of engines which, according to *The Autocar* report on the 1899 Paris Salon 'attracted a great deal of attention on account of their simple, and at the same time robust, appearance'. They were 2-cylinder horizontal units called Cyclops (or Cyclope) after the one-eyed giant of mythology, because the platinum tubes for the ignition were heated by a single lamp. One was fitted to a chassis, which was bodied later in the year. From 1899 electric ignition was used. Transmission was by belt to a countershaft and thence by chains to the rear wheels. Later models used engines of 4½, 5, 7 or 8hp, both horizontal and vertical. Body styles included a 3-seater known as the Troika. One surviving example has a frontal bonnet and the appearance of a car of about 1904, but this is probably a modernised earlier car.

NG

AULTMAN (US) 1901–1905

The Aultman Co., Canton, Ohio.
Henry J. Aultman built a steam car in Cincinnati in 1898, but moved to Canton for his production cars, which were ready for sale by March 1901. They were typical light steam buggies with single-chain final drive. In September 1901 he was experimenting with a petrol-engined buggy, but decided to stick to steam, and continued small-scale production up to October 1905. He also made at least one large 4-wheel drive steam truck.

NG

AUREA (I) 1920–1933

1920–1922 Società Italiana Ferrotaie, Turin.
1922–1933 Fabbrica Anonima Torinese Automobili, Turin.
Designed by Effren Magrini, the Aurea began life as a conventional small car with 1460cc 15/18hp 4-cylinder side-valve engine which developed 22bhp in

1899 Audibert-Lavirotte.
NATIONAL MOTOR MUSEUM

1899 Augé Troika.
NATIONAL MOTOR MUSEUM

touring form, and 30–35bhp in the sporting model. Essentially it remained the same throughout the company's life, though gaining 4-wheel brakes and a 4-speed gearbox in 1925, when an improved model 4000 with 1497cc ohv engine joined the sv car, now called the 600 and also enlarged to 1497cc. Also in 1925 the company moved into larger premises which had formerly been occupied by NAZZARO. Production dwindled from the late 1920s, and in 1932 F.A.T.A. was bought by Giovanni Ceirano who ended car manufacture in favour of components. One of his biggest contracts was for Alfa Romeo. The factory was very badly damaged during World War II, and Ceirano closed the business in April 1945.

NG

AURIGA (i) (US) 1980–c.1995

Auriga Corp., Gainesville, Florida.
The Auriga GS was a simple, doorless convertible sports car based on the VW floorpan. It was also sold as the Vokaro 4 by VOPARD in California. It was inexpensive and easy to assemble. The Auriga later reappeared as the Dauphin 2+2, sold by REDHEAD ROADSTERS.

HP

AURIGA (ii) (GB) 1990 to date

1990–98 Auriga Designs, Chelmsford, Essex.
1998 to date Espero Ltd, Burton Latimer, Northamptonshire.
This Lotus 23-inspired sports car was originally designed by Lee Noble and offered by him, briefly, as the NOBLE 23. The chassis was a fully triangulated space frame and the suspension was specially designed around Ford Cortina uprights. The bodywork was made in glassfibre and there was a variety of donor parts: mid-mounted Ford or Lotus 4-cylinder or Renault 4-cylinder or V6 engines, plus an Alfasud transaxle and brakes.

CR

1909 Austin (i) Model 45 45/60hp tourer.
NICK BALDWIN

AURORA (i) (US) 1905–1906

Aurora Automobile Co., Aurora, Illinois.

This was a 30hp 4-cylinder tourer with friction transmission and shaft drive, made by the former Aurora Carriage Top Company. The change of direction to automobiles seems to have been unwise, for the automobile company was out of business by the end of 1906.

NG

AURORA (ii) (US) 1907–1909

Aurora Motor Works, Aurora, Illinois.

The demise of the Aurora Automobile Company conveniently left the name free for another manufacturer to use. Their product was more modest than the previous Aurora, having a horizontally-opposed twin engine and a 2-seater body. In 1909 they decided to go for four cylinders after all, and launched the EMANCIPATOR. One of the partners, Dr James Selkirk, was involved with the KIRKSEL car.

NG

AURORA (iii) (US) 1957–1958

Custom Automobile Corp. of America, Branford, Connecticut.

Links between the clergy and motor manufacture have been few, though an early example was the steam car built by the Revd Hiram FRANTZ. In 1957 it was the turn of the Roman Catholic church, when Father Alfred Juliano (1919–1989) built a bizarre-looking safety car. It was a 4-door sedan with sculptured wings flowing from back to front, giving the impression that the car was being driven in reverse. The driver sat behind an enormous bulbous wrap-around windscreen. Advanced features for 1957 included seatbelts, a telescopic steering column and foam-filled bumpers on shock rams. Options included fuel injection and supercharging. The prototype used a 1954 Buick Roadmaster V8 engine, but a choice of Cadillac, Chrysler or Lincoln V8s was offered, the complete car priced at $15,000. Since a regular V8 from these prestigious manufacturers cost around $5000 at this time, one imagines that Father Juliano, like the Revd Frantz, soon returned to full-time pastoral duties. However, financial problems and allegations of mis-appropriation of funds led to his leaving the Order of Holy Ghost Fathers. The car survives in Poole, Dorset, England.

NG

Further Reading
'The Aurora Safety Car', Michael Lamm, *Special-Interest Autos*, May/June 1993.

AURORA (iv) (CDN) 1977–c.1988

Aurora Cars Ltd, Richmond Hill, Ontario.

This Canadian operation produced one of the world's first A.C. Cobra replicas. Unusually, it was not the later 427 style so often copied by specialist manufacturers, but the early narrow-bodied 289 style, realised in glassfibre by a yacht-making specialist. A Ford 5-litre V8 engine and 4- or 5-speed transmission (manual or automatic) were fitted in a space frame chassis with all-independent suspension and 4-wheel disc brakes. Complete cars and kits were sold.

CR

AUSCAR (AUS) 1939

Australian Car Syndicate, Adelaide, South Australia.

When the possibility of Australia becoming a motor manufacturer was being seriously canvassed, Adelaide motor trade figure, George Bateup, promoted his plans for a medium-sized car to be built in South Australia. Early in 1939 he revealed his prototype, wholly built in that state, with a body by J.S. Lawton & Sons, which featured a 15hp 4-cylinder, ohc engine of 2200cc installed in a chassis of 2640mm wheelbase. Local industry was praised for its capabilities by the Premier (Mr Playford) when he ceremoniously started the car at its unveiling. It was confidently predicted that it would be priced keenly enough to be a people's car, but the onset of war ensured that the promise would not be tested.

MG

AUSFOD (GB) 1947–1948

Ausfod Motor Engineering Ltd, Chorlton-on-Medlock, Manchester.

This was the first of a small number of trials specials which were offered for sale, rather than being built up by their owners. It used a Ford Ten engine in an Austin Seven chassis, with LMB trials front axle designed by Leslie Ballamy, and remote control gearbox. An aerodynamic sports car was advertised as well, but it is not known if any of these were made.

NG

AUSONIA (I) 1903–1906

Camone, Giussani Turrinelli e Cie, Milan.

A small number of electric cars were sold under this name, with a range of 90 miles, but at the low speed of only 15mph (24km/h).

NG

AUSTIN (i) (US) 1902–1920

Austin Automobile Co., Grand Rapids, Michigan.

James E. Austin was a lumberman who bought the Michigan Iron Works at Grand Rapids in 1900 for his mechanically-minded son Walter. After experimenting with a shingle cutting machine and a chainless bicycle, they decided that cars were the coming thing, changed the company name to Austin Automobile Co., and had a prototype ready by December 1902. Priced at $2000 it had a 16hp 2-cylinder engine under the seat, epicyclic transmission and chain drive. They sold 11 during 1903, then proceeded to a larger car with 25hp 2-cylinder engine and shaft drive. Their first fours came in 1904, 35 and 50hp models, of which the larger sold for $4500. This was almost in the Locomobile and Peerless segment of the market, though the Austin never became as widely known. Production was very low, about 25 per year up to 1906, rising to a 30 per year average up to the end of 1918. There were never more than 35 workers. The 60hp 4-cylinder Model LX came in 1906 and the 90hp 6-cylinder Model XC in 1907. This was priced at up to $7000 for the detachable top limousine, though one owner managed to get his for $5000 in cash, paid on the stand at the 1909 Chicago Auto Show. The XC had an enormous Weidely engine of nearly 13-litres, and was capable of 7 to 90mph (11 to 145km/h) in top gear. Wheelbase was a massive 147in (3731mm). Electric lighting was adopted in 1911, and a two-speed rear axle in 1913, just ahead of Cadillac, who were unable to claim infringement of patent, though it took until 1916 to settle the matter.

The 4-cylinder cars were dropped after 1908, and by World War I Austin was offering two large sixes, the 66 and 77hp, on a 141in wheelbase. The name Highway King was adopted in 1916, when they listed a smaller engine rated at 36.04hp, though the wheelbase remained the same. Their final model, also called Highway King, had a 6.4-litre Weidely V12 engine and was offered in seven body styles. The Austins struggled in the postwar years, and sold only ten cars in 1920. Walter offered his two-speed axle as an accessory for Ford and Chevrolet, and they also prospered in real estate. Both lived to a ripe old age; James was 95 when he died in 1936, and Walter was within a few months of his 100th birthday when he died in 1965.

NG

AUSTIN (ii) (GB) 1906–1989

1906–1970 Austin Motor Co. Ltd, Longbridge, Birmingham.
1970–1975 Austin-Morris Division, British Leyland Motor Corp. Ltd, Longbridge, Birmingham.
1975–1978 British Leyland UK Ltd, Longbridge, Birmingham.
1978–1982 BL Cars Ltd, Longbridge, Birmingham.
1982–1989 Austin-Rover Group, Longbridge, Birmingham.

Herbert Austin was no stranger to the motor industry when he formed his company in 1906 (*see* Biography). Ironically he left WOLSELEY because he refused to design a vertical engine for them, yet when he built his own cars they had vertical engines from the start. His first model had a 5182cc 24/30hp 4-cylinder T-head engine with separately-cast cylinders and chain drive. There was nothing particularly unusual about the design, but doubtless Austin's reputation helped sales. In the first full year 31 cars were made, and annual production up to 1910 ran at about 200 cars. The chain-drive 25/30 was replaced by the smaller shaft-driven 18/24 of 4396cc in 1907, and this was made for the next three years. There was also a 5838cc 40hp four and a 60hp six of 8757cc. The latter engine, enlarged to 9657cc, was used in the cars built for the 1908 Grand Prix. At a time when the only British firm seriously contesting the Grand Prix was Napier, it was surprising for a newcomer like Austin to enter the fray, but they ran three 100hp cars, two with chain drive and one with shaft. They finished in 18th and 19th places, not very distinguished, but they were the only British cars to complete the course.

At the other end of the scale was the 7hp single-cylinder Austin, of which 182 were made from 1910 to 1911. This was really a SWIFT design with an Austin radiator, which came about because the du Cros family had links with both Austin and Swift. Austin also made French-designed GLADIATORS for the British market in this period. Between 1910 and 1912 the Austin company expanded greatly; production rose from about 200 cars in 1910 to 1100 in 1912, from a workforce of 1800. 1914 models were a 1616cc Ten, a 3168cc Twenty and a 5883cc Thirty, all with 4-cylinder side-valve engines and shaft drive. The Thirty had electric lighting and starting.

During World War I Austin expanded greatly, the workforce rising from 2638 to more than 22,000. Vast quantities of shells, heavy guns, trucks, aero engines and complete aircraft were made, so that by the end of hostilities Herbert Austin found himself a very wealthy man with a large factory at his disposal. Greatly impressed by American cars and their mass production, he decided on a one-model policy, in which a single design of engine would power a car, a commercial vehicle and a tractor. He chose a modified version of his prewar Twenty, with capacity increased to 3620cc, detachable cylinder head, unit construction of engine and gearbox, and central gearchange. The footbrake now worked on the rear wheels, though a transmission handbrake was retained. A wheelbase of 150in (3807mm) allowed plenty of room for 7-seater bodies, both open and closed, and even the standard tourer had a fully disappearing hood. The Twenty was a strong and reliable car, but was too expensive to sell in the numbers that Herbert Austin planned. He had made 12,500 by the early summer of 1920, and two years later production was running at 4000 per annum, but this was more than the market would bear. In 1921 the firm went into receivership, but was restructured and handed back to Austin and Harvey du Cros.

In order to widen his market, Austin introduced a smaller version of the Twenty for the 1922 season. This was the 1661cc Twelve, destined to become the most famous Austin of the inter-war years, apart from the Seven. It had the larger car's virtues of reliability and ruggedness, but cost its owner appreciably less in purchase, tax and running costs. A 1923 tourer cost £450, compared with £695 for a Twenty. The Twelve lived on until 1935, by which time it had acquired 4-wheel brakes, a synchromesh gearbox and an engine enlarged to 1861cc. In its best year, 1927, the Twelve sold around 14,000 units, and even in 1934, when it was distinctly old-fashioned, more than 3000 found customers. After 1935 the engine lived on in the London taxicab, of which nearly 7000 were made between 1929 and 1940. The Twelve had little performance, with a maximum speed of around 55mph (88km/h), but its reliability endeared it to many customers, and thousands were still giving good service into the 1950s. Of all Austin models, it best epitomised the slogan 'You buy a car, but you invest in an Austin'.

The Baby Austin

No sooner was the Twelve launched on its way than Austin began to think about a still smaller car, one which would offer the maximum accommodation for a family in the smallest possible wheelbase. At first he envisaged a 2-cylinder engine similar to that of the Rover Eight, but was persuaded that a four could be made at little more cost, and with all the advantages of smoothness and silence that no twin could provide. The advocate of the four, and its designer, was 18-year old draughtsman Stanley Edge, who was invited to do all the design work at Austin's country home, well away from the factory. He studied a number of contemporary light cars and was influenced by the PEUGEOT Quadrilette as much as any, employing the same design of 4-cylinder water-cooled engine, A-frame chassis

1909 Austin (ii) 18/24hp limousine, by Barker.
NATIONAL MOTOR MUSEUM

1921 Austin (ii) Twenty tourer.
P.M.A.HULL

1923 Austin (ii) Twelve 2-seater.
NICK BALDWIN

and transverse-leaf front suspension, with quarter-elliptics at the rear. An advanced feature for such a small car, and one not shared with the Peugeot, was a 4-wheel braking system. This was uncoupled, the rear brakes being operated by the pedal and the front by the hand lever. Effective use of the brakes required some skill, as did the clutch which was the trickiest and most sensitive of any contemporary light car – pedal travel was measured in millimetres.

The Seven was far from an ideal light car, yet it was ahead of its rivals, and very good value at £165 for a tourer capable of carrying two adults and two children. After 100 had been made with the original 696cc engine, capacity went up to 747cc in the Spring of 1923, and remained at that size for the rest of the Seven's life. The design was steadily improved over 17 years, the more important milestones

1925 Austin (ii) Seven Chummy tourer.
NATIONAL MOTOR MUSEUM

NICK BALDWIN

AUSTIN, HERBERT (1866–1941)
The name of Herbert Austin is associated with two famous British makes, Wolseley and his own Austin. Like that of his contemporary William Morris, his name became synonymous with the popular British car, though Austin always had a slight edge over his rival, encapsulated in the slogan 'You Buy a Car but you Invest in an Austin'.

Herbert Austin was born on a farm at Little Missenden in Buckinghamshire and when he was four years old his father took up the post of bailliff to Earl Fitzwilliam at Wentworth Woodhouse in Yorkshire. This was nearly forty years

before a later Earl became associated with motors, making the Sheffield-Simplex car and Ner-A-Car motorcycle. Austin was educated at the village school and then at Rotherham Grammar School, and seemed destined for railway engineering apprenticeship, like Henry Royce and W.O. Bentley. However a meeting with an uncle who had visited Australia convinced the 18-year old Austin that his future lay on the other side of the world, and in 1884 uncle and nephew set out for Melbourne. At first he worked with his uncle, but after two years he joined the Wolseley Sheep Shearing Machine Co. which had just been set up in Sydney by another Englishman, Frederick York Wolseley.

Austin already had a good reputation as an engineer, having studied hard at night school in Melbourne, and he suggested many valuable improvements to Wolseley's sheep shearing machines. In October 1889 Wolseley and Austin moved back to England and set up a factory in Birmingham. Austin soon found that some subcontractors were supplying very poor quality parts, which were damaging the reputation of Wolseley's products. He sorted this out by increasing the proportion of components made in-house, and also diversified into bicycle parts. He was made manager in 1892, and supervised the move to a larger factory at Aston, Birmingham, in 1895. By then he was becoming interested in the motor car, having visited the Paris Salon in 1895. At this event he was greatly impressed by the Léon Bollée 3-wheeled voiturette. During the winter of 1895/6 he built a car of his own, along Bollée lines but with a horizontally-opposed 2-cylinder engine in place of the French car's single. It was a most unusual design, with combustion taking place in a single chamber separate from the pistons, whence the gases were taken by ribbed tubes to the cylinders. Ignition was by hot tube, but an advanced feature was the use of overhead valves, the inlet valves mechanically operated as well. It probably did not work very well, and no records survive of its trials. Austin was probably reluctant to manufacture it anyway because of possible legal action from the Coventry Bollée company.

During 1896 he built another car, as different from the first as it could be. Also a 3-wheeler, it had its single wheel at the front, and a 2-cylinder engine of more conventional layout. The first car had been built away from the Sheep Shearing company's works, but the directors looked more favourably on the second, especially after it had been well-received at the National Cycle Show in December 1896. They actually issued a catalogue of 'The Wolseley Autocar No.1', though only the one car was made. It was later fitted with a single-cylinder engine, and in it Austin made his first long-distance journey, from Birmingham to Rhyl and back. He built his first 4-wheeler in 1899, and a creditable performance in the Thousand Miles Trial held in the Spring of 1900 brought orders for replicas. Few, if any, were delivered by the Sheep Shearing Machine Co., as a new company was formed, with backing from Vickers. Austin had made contact with this large engineering and armaments firm through his friend, the American Hiram Percy Maxim who was a director of Vickers. Austin had supplied some components for Maxim's steam-powered aeroplane.

In February 1901 Vickers bought the car-making interests from the Wolseley Sheep Shearing Machine Co. for £12,400 in cash plus 67.5% second debentures of £100 each to the company and 33 of these debentures to Austin. The Sheep Shearing Machine Co. was free to carry on any business except that of making motorcars, and was still active in the 1920s, with Herbert Austin as chairman. Austin's contract with Vickers ran for five years from 1 April 1901, but he was tactfully asked to resign four months before the expiry of the contract, the main reason being Vickers' dissatisfaction with Austin's stubborn championship of the horizontal engine. Before he resigned he bought a disused printing works at Longbridge, outside Birmingham, and formed his own company, the Austin Motor Co. Ltd in December 1905. Curiously, in view of his split with Vickers, they were of thoroughly conventional design with vertical engines. He was one of the first car makers to establish showrooms in major cities. The London premises in Oxford Street had a repair service, hire car facilities and a club room. He had good relations with his staff, and organised an annual subscription dinner which was attended by about 20% of the Longbridge workforce.

Like many car makers, Austin had a very profitable war, though any financial success was overshadowed by the death of his only son, Vernon. He had no one to succeed him and eventually groomed Leonard Lord as his heir. He was knighted in 1917 for his company's contribution to the war effort, and from 1918 to 1925 was Conservative MP for a district of Birmingham. However, politics did not appeal to him and he never made a speech in the House of Commons. By 1920 the company was in serious difficulties, due to the slow selling of the 20hp model, and his major creditors, the Midland Bank and the Eagle Star Insurance Co., put in new managers with whom Austin clashed bitterly. He attempted to sell his company to General Motors, but without success.

Feeling unwelcome at Longbridge, Austin spent an increasing amount of time at Lickey Grange, his country house with 200 acres of parkland. There he set to work with an 18-year old draughtsman, Stanley Edge, to design a small car which would bring motoring within the reach of a much wider public than hitherto. It seems that at first he favoured a flat-twin engine such as that used in the Rover Eight, but Edge wisely insisted that only a four would distance the car from the cyclecars which dominated the bottom end of the car market at the time. The Austin Seven, as it became known, was built in some secrecy in a corner of the Longbridge factory, and was launched at London's Claridges Hotel in July 1922. Within two years it had almost killed off the cyclecars, and seriously damaged the sales of motorcycles and sidecars. The Austin Motor Co. was rising again, and by 1934 it was Britain's largest car manufacturer, though not for long. Austin seldom matched the output of his rival William Morris, nor did he make so much money, but he was very successful in export markets. Between 1929 and 1933 the British share in world car exports rose from 7 to 25%, much of the rise being due to Austin.

With the approach of World War II, Austin became chairman of the Shadow Aero Engine Committee, which organised large-scale production of Bristol aero engines, and later complete aircraft, in 'shadow' factories built with government aid. He was created Baron Austin of Longbridge in 1936,

1932 Austin (ii) 16/6 Henley saloon.
NATIONAL MOTOR MUSEUM

1939 Austin (ii) 12 Ascot saloon.
NATIONAL MOTOR MUSEUM

1951 Austin (ii) A40 Devon saloon.
NATIONAL MOTOR MUSEUM

although he was slightly uneasy with the title, having no social pretensions. Though into his seventies, he took great interest in the day-to-day work of the factory; he was described as chairman, managing director, production manager, chief engineer, and plant engineer rolled into one, being involved in everything 12 hours a day, seven days a week. It was too punishing a schedule, and he had to resign from the chairmanship of the Shadow Aero Engine Committee shortly after the outbreak of war. He died in May 1941.

Austin married an Australian, Ellen Dron, in 1887. They had a son, Vernon, who was killed on the Western Front in 1916, and a daughter, Zoë, who, as Zoë Lambert, was the co-author of a biography of her father.

NG

Further Reading
Lord Austin, the Man, Zoë E. Lambert and R.J. Wyatt, Sidgwick & Jackson, 1968.

1961 Austin (ii) A40 Mark 2 hatchback.
NATIONAL MOTOR MUSEUM

being an electric starter in 1924, a stronger camshaft and coupled brakes in 1930, a 4-speed gearbox in 1933, synchromesh on the two upper ratios in 1934, and on second as well in 1935. The chassis was lengthened in 1931 to give accommodation for four adults. A great variety of body styles was offered over the years in addition to the original tourer, which soon became known as the Chummy. Metal and fabric saloons, the latter made by Gordon England, were introduced in 1926, and a 2-seater tourer in 1927. William Lyons made some 3500 Swallow saloon and 2-seater bodies on the Seven from 1927 to 1932. Numerous sports models were made, starting with the factory version in 1924, and continuing through various designs by Gordon England, Boyd Carpenter, Burghley, and others. The factory offered the supercharged Ulster, of which a few were sold from 1927 to 1930, and two sports models, the 65 or Nippy and the 75 or Speedy, from 1933 to 1936. The latter had shallower doors, a pointed tail and higher gearing. They were not particularly fast (75mph/120km/h) but provided enjoyable motoring for those who wanted to look sporty; about 600 were sold.

Although having what one historian described as 'unpredictable road holding and indescribable brakes', the Seven was raced extensively and successfully over many years. Its successes began with a Brooklands handicap in March 1923 (the driver was Austin's son-in-law Arthur Waite), and continued through a series of supercharged cars from 1925 to 1930, and culminating with the twin-ohc single seaters of 1936–1939 whose engines gave 116bhp at 8000rpm. Delivery vans were offered from 1923, and there were also military Sevens used as scout cars and machine gun carriers. The Seven was made under licence in France as the ROSENGART from 1928 to 1939, in Germany as the DIXI (later BMW-DIXI) from 1928 to 1932, and in America as the AMERICAN AUSTIN (later Bantam) from 1930 to 1941. It also inspired to some extent the Japanese DATSUN of 1933, although this was not a direct copy, as has sometimes been alleged. The 747cc engine survived in RELIANT 3-wheeled cars until 1962. The last of some 375,000 Sevens was delivered in March 1939.

Austin in the 1930s
In the 1920s Austin relied on three models, the Seven which was an unchallenged best-seller in its field, the Twelve which was as reliable for the makers as it was for its owners, and a good, if unspectacular, model for the chauffeur-driven sector in the Twenty. The next decade saw a much more complex range, with overlapping between old and new models, and between 4- and 6-cylinder cars of about the same size. The best seller was the Ten Four introduced in May 1932 and made until 1947. It had a 3-bearing 21bhp engine of 1125cc and a 4-speed gearbox. Originally

made only as a 4-door saloon, it was available with cabriolet, tourer and roadster bodies from 1933. Synchromesh came in 1934, and the bodies were restyled for 1935, and again for 1937 and 1939, by which time a saloon was again the only offering. As with the larger Austins of the 1930s, the Ten's body styles were named after English towns and villages – among the better-known examples were the Sherborne, Lichfield and Cambridge saloons, the Eton 2-seater and Ripley sports tourer, although the regular tourer was simply called the Open Road. Total production of Tens up to 1939 was 161,584, easily outselling rival tens from Morris, Standard or Wolseley.

The faithful old Twelve Four was continued up to 1935, and was joined by the 1525cc Light Twelve Four made from 1933 to 1936. The arrival of this model led some people to refer to the older car as the Heavy Twelve Four, though this was never an official name. The Light Twelve Four originally shared the same body as the Light Twelve Six, a 1496cc 4-bearing six which was less reliable than the fours. It was improved by the adoption of a larger 1711cc engine in 1934, and there was even a sports model, with lowered frame, high-compression engine and sloping, chromed radiator grille. This was made as a tourer and sports saloon, and had its 4-cylinder equivalent in the Ripley sports tourer. The saloon bodies were made by Ambi–Budd in Germany, and were the same as those used by Adler.

The larger Austins were all sixes, and had generally similar styling. The 3400cc Twenty was the oldest, dating back to 1927 when it supplemented and then replaced the 4-cylinder Twenty. It was made up to 1938, with the usual improvements – coil ignition in 1930, synchromesh in 1934, Girling brakes in 1936. 5053 were made. Of similar appearance were the 2249cc Sixteen and 2511cc Eighteen, which received the same improvements and styling changes as the Twenty. About 50 of these cars were fitted with the Hayes automatic transmission in 1935–36.

For 1937 the smaller Austins were modernised, with engines moved forward, sloping radiators and all-steel bodies with integral luggage boots. These were the Ten Cambridge, Twelve Four Ascot and Fourteen Goodwood saloons. They were joined in 1938 by a similarly-styled Eighteen and in 1939 by the 28hp, a 4016cc successor to the Twenty, of which only 290 were made. The same styling was seen on the Big Seven of 1938–39, an attempt to update the Seven with a 900cc engine and 2- or 4-door saloon bodies. It had the same chassis and suspension as the regular Seven, so was rather old fashioned, despite its appearance. Described by the late Michael Sedgwick as 'an infelicitous attempt to bridge the gap between the Seven and the Ten; there are better Austins', it nevertheless sold 23,514 examples.

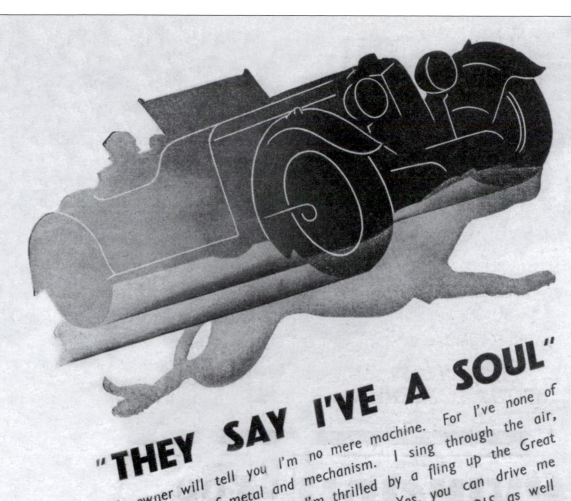

"THEY SAY I'VE A SOUL"

My owner will tell you I'm no mere machine. For I've none of the deadness of metal and mechanism. I sing through the air, alive and responsive, and I'm thrilled by a fling up the Great North Road at 70, hour after hour. Yes, you can drive me at 4,000 r.p.m. indefinitely because my oil COOLS as well as lubricates the engine. Stored in a cooling tank away from the heat, over 2 gallons per minute pass through my entire engine. Illustrated particulars and name of nearest Agent from Aston Martin Ltd., Feltham, Middlesex. 'Phone Feltham 218.

12-70 H.P. "Le Mans Mark II" 2/4 Seater model on 8' 7" Chassis £610
12-70 H.P. "Le Mans Mark II" 4 Seater model on 10' 0" special Chassis £640
12-70 H.P. "Le Mans Mark II" Sports Saloon on 10' 0" Chassis £700
12-80 H.P. "Ulster" 2 Seater 100 m.p.h. model on 8' 7" Chassis £750

ASTON ✈ MARTIN
"lithe as a panther"

Sole Distributors for London Area : GORDON WATNEY & CO., LTD., 31, BROOK STREET, W.1. 'Phone: Mayfair 026?

1958 Austin (ii) Princess IV saloon.
NICK GEORGANO

The last pre-World War II Austins were again completely restyled, with pointed radiator grilles, alligator bonnets and semi-unitary construction incorporating an integral floor. Place names were out now, and the new models were known simply as the Eight, Ten and Twelve. The Eight used the same engine as the Big Seven, the Ten had the 1125cc unit of previous Tens, and the Twelve, which was introduced a week before war broke out, had the 1525cc engine of the old Light Twelve Four. Very few were made prewar, but the Eight sold some 20,000 units, and its tourer model was made in large numbers for military use between 1939 and 1944.

Austin remained profitable throughout the 1930s, and the 1933 share issue was oversubscribed eight times. In 1936 Sir Herbert Austin became Baron Austin of Longbridge, and two years later the dynamic but ruthless Leonard Lord (1896–1967) joined the board. He became chairman on the death of Lord Austin in May 1941.

Export or Die
As in the first conflict, Austin produced enormous quantities of military material during World War II, including 108,000 cars and utilities, mostly Eights and Tens, 82,500 larger trucks, and several thousand airframes and complete aircraft (Stirling, Battle, Hurricane and Lancaster). These were made at a new factory at Cofton Hackett which was used 30 years later for the manufacture of the Maxi engine.

The postwar car range was announced in September 1944, well before the end of hostilities, although production did not start immediately. Like most of their contemporaries, the Austins looked like the 1939/40 models, but an important newcomer was the Sixteen. This had a new 2199cc ohv engine, the first to be used in an Austin car, in the chassis and body of the Twelve. This was revived, along with the Eight and Ten. Although its acceleration was not sparkling, the Sixteen could exceed 75mph (120km/h), and combined with traditional British appointments such as an opening windscreen, sliding roof and leather upholstery, made for an attractive car. It was the most popular Austin on export markets, which assumed much greater importance to British industry than before the war. 'Export or die' was the Government's slogan, and firms which could not show a good performance in foreign markets were denied their allocation of steel.

Austin had no fears on this score. Of 5394 cars sold abroad between June and December 1945, 3197 were Austins, and in the early months of 1946 their share of the export market was still over 50 per cent.

The Sixteen was made up to 1949 (35,434 built), and its engine survived in the restyled Hampshire and Hereford saloons up to 1954, and in the FX3 and FX4 taxicabs until 1973. The first all-new postwar Austins were the Sheerline and Princess, large and relatively expensive cars in the idiom of the prewar Twenty. The Sheerline had razor-edge styling previously associated with Rolls-Royce and Bentley, while the Princess' more rounded saloon bodies were made by Vanden Plas. Both cars had 3993cc ohc 6-cylinder engines from Austin's 5-ton truck, coil independent front suspension and hydraulic brakes. Considering their prices, £1277 for the Sheerline and £2101 for the Princess, the big Austins sold well, approximately 9000 Sheerlines and 1910 Princesses. The long-wheelbase version of the latter was rebadged Vanden Plas in 1959 and made up to 1968. A number of these are still in use with hire companies and funeral directors.

The Eight, Ten and Twelve were made up to the end of 1947 when they were replaced by a single model, the 1200cc ohv A40. Made as the Dorset 2-door or Devon 4-door saloons, the A40 brightened up the postwar scene as they were among the first British cars to come in pastel shades of fawn, green and blue instead of the austerity black of their predecessors. They were quite lively performers, too, with a top speed of 70mph (112km/h). Most of the 354,000 made were Devons, and well over 50 per cent were exported, including quite a number to the United States, where small family cars were virtually unknown. In 1952 the A40 was restyled and given hydraulic brakes as the Somerset, and for 1955 it received a completely new slab-sided body as the Cambridge.

The 1948 London Motor Show saw two new Austins: the A70 Hampshire saloon replaced the Sixteen, using the same engine in an A40-type chassis with A40 body styling, but the A90 Atlantic convertible was quite new in appearance and in the Austin range. Aimed deliberately at the American market, it had an all-enveloping body with waterfall motif running down the centre of the bonnet, and three headlamps. The engine was a large four of 2660cc and although it could reach 90mph (144km/h) its short wheelbase made handling somewhat dangerous. For all its American features such as power-operated top and steering column gearchange, the Atlantic did not sell well on the American market. It lacked the cuteness of the A40 and was too small and too expensive to compete with traditional native convertibles by the likes of Ford and Buick. In 1950 a 2-door saloon version appeared, with a lower axle ratio and better low-speed acceleration. Nearly 8000 Atlantics were made between 1949 and 1952. Its most important legacy was its engine, which was used in the first Austin-Healey sports cars.

Since the disappearance of the Eight in November 1947 Austin had no really small car, but this was rectified at the 1951 Motor Show with the appearance of the A30. Known for a time as the Seven to capitalise on the fame of Austin's prewar baby, the A30 had an 803cc 4-cylinder ohv engine. It was the first small car to have stressed-skin unitary construction and a hypoid rear axle. Although it was only 136in (3452mm) long, it was made as a 4-door saloon, in addition to a 2-door (from 1953) and an estate car (from 1955). It had full hydraulic brakes as fitted to the later A40s, and the 803cc engine was more powerful than the 918cc side-valve unit of the rival Morris Minor.

The 1952 Austin-Morris merger which gave birth to the British Motor Corporation led to the Austin engine being used in the Minor from late 1952. For 1957 the engine was enlarged to 948cc; thus equipped, the Austin became the A35 and the Morris, the Minor 1000. The A35 had the same bodies as its predecessor with a larger rear-window. Smaller wheels were compensated by higher overall gearing. It was successful in saloon car racing and its engine was used in the Austin-Healey Sprite. In 1958 the A35 was replaced by a new car bearing the familiar designation A40. This had a Pininfarina-styled 2-door saloon body, and a 3-door hatchback which was a pioneer of this layout. The engine was the A35's, replaced in 1962 by a 1098cc unit. More than 342,000 were made up to 1967.

Among the larger Austins, the A40 Cambridge became the 1489cc A50 and A55 in 1957, and in 1959 the Cambridge was given a new Pininfarina-styled body which it shared with the Morris Oxford, MG Magnette 111, Riley 4/68 and Wolseley 15/60. Further up the scale was the A90 Westminster saloon, with a 2639cc 6-cylinder engine and styling resembling an enlarged Cambridge. In 1959 it, too, was restyled by Pininfarina and given a 2912cc engine to become the A110. Like the smaller cars it was badge-engineered as the Wolseley 6-110 and Vanden Plas 3-litre.

The Issigonis Era
Leonard Lord feared that the Suez crisis of 1956 would lead to long-term and severe fuel shortages in Europe, and invited Alec Issigonis, who he had met when the latter was working for Morris in the 1930s, to design a completely new small car. In fact fuel never became as scarce as Lord feared, but Issigonis' baby was to become one of the best-known cars of the century. It outlived both its promoter and designer, and production lasted into the 21st Century. In order to fit the maximum passenger space into the shortest possible wheelbase, Issigonis mounted the engine transversely, driving the front wheels though a 4-speed gearbox located in the sump. Suspension was independent all round, by an ingenious system of rubber blocks in compression. This was developed in conjunction with Alex Moulton and Dunlop, who made the compression units. The engine was just about the only part of the car which was not new, being the A30 unit enlarged to 848cc.

The first prototypes ran in October 1957, and less than two years later, in August 1959, the car was launched, several thousand having been already built so that dealers would have sufficient stock. The Austin version was called the Seven, and the Morris, the Mini Minor. The only difference lay in the colours offered and in the wavy grille bars of the Austin. The name Seven never caught on, and soon they were universally known as Minis. Top speed of the first 33bhp models was only 70mph (112km/h), but the Mini's excellent handling soon attracted the attention of tuning specialists. At first they worked on completed cars with little or no help from the makers, but in September 1961 came the Mini Cooper, tuned by racing car builder John Cooper with BMC's blessing, and sold as part of the Mini range. The engine was enlarged to 997cc and tuned to give 65bhp with twin SU carburettors, and top speed was now 85mph (137km/h).

In 1962 the Mini Cooper began its rallying career under the new head of BMC's Competition Department, Stuart Turner. With drivers such as Rauno Aaltonen, Paddy Hopkirk and Timo Makinen the Mini Coopers won the 1962 Tulip, Swedish, German and Route du Nord rallies. They became more competitive in 1963, with the 1071cc Cooper S which was followed by the 1275cc version, with 75bhp and 100mph (161km/h). The years 1964 to 1967 saw a remarkable string of successes for the Coopers, including the Monte Carlo in 1964, 1965 and

1979 Austin (ii) Maxi 1750 HL hatchback.
NATIONAL MOTOR MUSEUM

1989 Austin (ii) Maestro Special hatchback.
ROVER GROUP

1982 Austin (ii) Metro 1.3S hatchback.
NICK GEORGANO

1967. They were the moral victors in 1966 as well, finishing 1–2–3, only to be disqualified because their headlamp dipping system was non-standard. They also won 16 other major rallies in these years, and in 1965 Aaltonen won the European Rally Championship. Minis were also prominent in saloon car racing; Sir John Whitmore won the British Saloon Car Championship in a tuned Mini (pre-Cooper) in 1961, John Love followed this with a Cooper in 1962, and in 1964 Warwick Banks took the European Saloon Car Racing Championship. In an Australian 500 Mile Race for saloon cars Minis took the first ten places. From 1968 the Mini Cooper was less competitive, due to the arrival of the twin-cam Ford Escorts, though they continued to compete in club events for a number of years. Production of the Mini Cooper ran from 1961 to 1967 (44,859 made), and of the Cooper S from 1963 to 1971 (191,242 made). In 1970 the Mini was given marque status of its own, and the rest of its history is covered under MINI.

1972 Austin (iv) Apache saloon.
NICK GEORGANO

Meanwhile the Issigonis principle of transverse engine and front drive was being extended to larger cars. In 1963 came the Austin 1100, a year after the Morris version. Both were essentially enlarged Minis, with 1098cc engines, Hydrolastic suspension which interlinked front and rear wheels, and disc brakes at the front. 2- and 4-door saloons were offered, with an estate car coming in 1966, and from 1967 a 1275cc engine turned the car into the Austin 1300. They were made up to 1973, together with Morris, MG, Riley, Vanden Plas and Wolseley versions. Total production of the Austins was about 1,119,800, and of all the variants about 2.1 million. The replacement was the Allegro which had a similar engine layout in a new, more rounded, bodyshell, with Hydragas suspension. There were five engine sizes, from 998 to 1748cc, the latter being used in the twin carburettor 1750TC, capable of 100mph (161km/h). The Allegro proved a grave disappointment to British Leyland, for although it was 5.6in longer and 3in wider than the 1300 it had less interior and boot space, and with the smallest engine it was slower than both its predecessor and the Morris Marina with the same engine. The quartic steering wheel, shaped like a television screen, did not prove popular, and was dropped after two years. It was made up to 1982, total sales being 642,350, less than a third of the total sales of all the 1100/1300s. Historian Jonathan Wood said that the Allegro's failure marked the start of the decline of the British motor industry as a volume producer.

Next up the scale in the transverse-engined cars was the 1800, which was powered by a detuned 1798cc MGB engine in a wide 6-light saloon hull, and was also badged as a Morris and a Wolseley. This was made from 1968 to 1975, being joined in 1972 by the 2200 which had a new 2227cc 6-cylinder engine derived from the 4-cylinder Maxi. The next development of this line was the curious wedge-shaped 18/22, powered by the same engines and made as an Austin for 1975 and renamed PRINCESS from 1976 onwards. In its last incarnation the design became an Austin again; the Ambassador (1982–1984) had a restyled 5-door hatchback body and a choice of 1695 or 1994cc engines. Sized between the 1300 and 1800, and outliving them both, was the Maxi, a 5-door hatchback powered by a single-ohc 1485cc engine, with a 5-speed gearbox. Larger engines of 1748 and 1994cc followed, the latter only offered in the Maxi's final season of 1981. An unusual hybrid made from 1968 to 1971 was the 3-litre. This used the 2912cc 6-cylinder engine from the MGC mounted longitudinally and driving the rear wheels, in a bodyshell derived from that of the 1800, and with all-independent self-levelling suspension. Only 9992 were made.

In 1983 the Allegro gave way to the Maestro, which also took over the role of the Maxi. Like this car it was a 5-door hatchback with the 1275cc A Series engine or 1598cc single-ohc O Series. It was joined a year later by the Montego, essentially a Maestro with a 4-door saloon body on a longer wheelbase. Engine options were the same as for the Maestro, with the addition of a 1994cc unit in carburettor or fuel injection forms. More powerful versions were badged as MGs. Meanwhile for 1981 came British Leyland's answer to the Ford Fiesta, the Austin Mini Metro, soon abbreviated to Metro. This was a 3-door hatchback which shared the Allegro's Hydragas suspension and came initially with three engine options, 998 and 1275cc in two degrees of tune, the most powerful being the 72 bhp 1.3S. Later, more powerful MG Metros were made, the peak being reached by the 250–410 bhp 6R4 Group B rally car. The Metro sold very well, though it was not as profitable to make as the Maestro and Montego. The millionth Metro was delivered in October 1986, by which time a 5-door hatchback had joined the

range, and a 5-speed gearbox arrived, not before time, in May 1990. By then the Metro was no longer an Austin but a Rover. It carried the name Rover Metro until 1994 when it became the Rover 100.

The 10 millionth Austin was made in September 1985, but little over four years later the name was effectively dead. Maestros and Montegos were given Rover badges from the end of 1989, and the Metro officially became a Rover in May 1990.
NG

Further Reading
The Austin, 1905–1952, R.J. Wyatt, David & Charles, 1981.
Complete Catalogue of Austin cars since 1945, Anders Clausager, Bay View Books, 1992.
The Austin Seven, Chris Harvey, Haynes, 1985.

AUSTIN (iii) (AUS) 1949–1974

1949–1956 Austin Motor Co. of Australia Ltd, West Melbourne, Victoria.
1957–1968 British Motor Corporation Australia, Zetland, New South Wales.
1968–1974 Leyland Motor Corporation Australia, Zetland, New South Wales.

As Herbert Austin first collaborated with F.Y. Wolseley in Australia to develop a sheep-shearing machine, it is fitting that unique Austins were made in Australia. Soon after World War II the Austin Co. purchased the Ruskin Body Works, the sole remaining operation of the former Tarrant group, then being liquidated. That facility enabled tourer and car-type utility (pick-up) bodies to be built for the popular A40. The B.M.C. amalgamation meant consolidation, in 1957, at the new state-of-the-art plant built on the former Victoria Park racecourse earlier purchased by Lord Nuffield. Its process for corrosion protection and painting by rotation of the body while immersed was an industry pinnacle. The first wholly-manufactured type was WOLSELEY 1500-based, the Austin twin being named Lancer. It was restyled with tail fins in 1959. Australian production Farina-line A60 Cambridge, with a larger bore giving 1622cc, gave greater performance in a car of similar price to the Holden, 15in wheels being retained for better ground clearance. In 1962 the Freeway revision had a full width grille and the Australian-made Blue Streak engine – named after a joint British-Australian rocket testing program. It was a 6-cylinder version of the B-series, with 2433cc, driving through a 3-speed manual gearbox, with a Borg Warner 35 automatic as an option. The front-wheel drive models were sold under one marque in Australia so, as the Mini and 1100 were MORRIS, the 1800 was an Austin. Australian initiatives were a utility (pick-up) with a low floor, having a 1800 x 1200mm clear area, and the development of an optional automatic transmission, incorporating a local Borg Warner unit controlled by a dash-mounted selector, prompted by demand from clientele being offered automatics on competing makes. Australia was the source of the cast housings which were supplied to the UK for some time. In 1970 the X6 appeared, an Austin 1800 development fitted with a transverse 6-cylinder 2227cc ohc E-series engine. Revised styling included extended bonnet and luggage trunk on the longer wheelbase, while a base-line Tasman and deluxe Kimberley, with two carburettors were offered. The last car with the Austin name was made in 1974 when the LEYLAND P76 replaced it in production.
MG

AUSTIN (iv) (ZA) 1971–1978

Leyland Car Division, Blackheath, Cape Province.
Leyland's South African branch made Minis, Jaguars and Rovers, but also some individual designs. The best-known of these was the Austin Apache, a 1300 with a fresh body styled by Michelotti which had a built-out boot in place of the fastback. This design was also made in Spain as the AUTHI Victoria. A 6-cylinder Morris Marina was also made at Blackheath.
NG

AUSTIN-HEALEY (GB) 1952–1971

1952 Donald Healey Motor Co. Ltd, Warwick.
1953–1970 Austin Motor Co. Ltd, Longbridge, Birmingham.
1970–1971 Austin-Morris Division, British Leyland Motor Corp. Ltd, Abingdon, Berkshire.
In the early 1950s Donald Healey planned a new sports car which could be built in larger numbers than the limited-production Riley-engined cars he was then making. For an engine he favoured the 2660cc 4-cylinder unit of the Austin Atlantic, and installed it in a box-section frame with coil-and-wishbone independent

1954 Austin-Healey 100/4 sports car.
NATIONAL MOTOR MUSEUM

front suspension. He called it the Healey Hundred in view of its anticipated top speed of 100mph (161km/h).

The simple alloy-panelled 2-seater body had exceptionally eye-catching lines. It certainly caught the eye of Sir Leonard Lord, head of the recently-formed British Motor Corporation, when it was shown at the 1952 London Motor Show. Seeing it as a car which might succeed on the American market where the Atlantic had failed, Lord snapped up the design, concluding a deal with Healey before the Show had ended whereby the car would be made by Austin and sold as the Austin-Healey 100. New badges were quickly made, and the car which had been entered at the Show as a Healey left it ten days later as an Austin-Healey.

Lord arranged for the bodies to be made by Jensen at West Bromwich, and the Austin-Healey was assembled there, using engines brought from Austin's Longbridge factory. The bodies were now mostly of steel, only the bonnet and boot being made of alloy. This continued until 1957, when all Austin-Healey production was transferred to the MG factory at Abingdon. The 100 was an immediate success, and output soon reached Leonard Lord's hoped for figure of 100 per week, once production began in the summer of 1953. The car made its racing debut at Le Mans that year, finishing 2nd and 3rd in class, and 12th and 14th overall.

At the end of 1954 a special competition version called the 100S was announced. This had a 132bhp alloy-head engine, 4-speed gearbox plus overdrive in place of the three plus overdrive of the standard 100, and disc brakes all round. Jensen produced a light alloy body shell with a smaller grille. Only 55 of the 100S were made, and nearly all went for export. The standard 100 was given four speeds in August 1955, but the first major change came in 1956 when the 2639cc 6-cylinder C engine from the Austin A90 Westminster was installed in the Austin-Healey to make the 100-6. The wheelbase was lengthened by 2in to allow for two children's seats behind the driver and passenger, though a 2-seater 100-6 was also available. In 1959 the engine was enlarged to 2912cc and the car renamed the Austin-Healey 3000.

With the 3000, BMC had an ideal rallying car, and from 1960 to 1964 they achieved numerous successes, their best years being 1960 and 1961. The leading drivers were the Morley twins, Donald and Eric, Pat Moss (Stirling's sister), and Ann Wisdom, with support from Bill Shephard and John Gott and, from 1963,

Timo Makinen. Among their successes were 1st and 3rd in the 1960 Marathon de la Route, 2nd in the Alpine, and 2nd and 3rd in the RAC. Pat Moss and Ann Wisdom won their second ladies' championship (their first was in 1958 with the 100-6), and were chosen as Drivers of the Year by the Guild of Motoring Writers. The Morleys won the Alpine in 1961 and 1962, and Makinen won the GT class in the 1963 Monte Carlo, but by then the Mini-Coopers were beginning to establish themselves, and fewer successes came to the big Healeys. However, Rauno Aaltonen won the 1964 Marathon de la Route.

In racing, the big Healeys were not so prominent, though the works 100S cars finished 1–2–3 in their class at Sebring, and 1–2 in the Mille Miglia, both in 1955. Three 100-6s won the team prize at Sebring in 1958, but in most major events the Healeys were outclassed by the 3-litre Ferraris. BMC concentrated their racing efforts on the Sprite. The 3000 remained in production until 1968 with few changes, most of which were concerned with increasing power. The final 3000 Mark IIIs gave 150bhp. The majority of all the 3000s had 2+2 seating, and on the Mark III (1963–1968) it was the only body style available. A total of 41,534 3000s were made, together with 14,436 100-6s and 14,012 of the original 100. The big Healey was mourned by many enthusiasts when it was discontinued, but its heavy steering and bumpy ride were old-fashioned by the late 1960s. It had always been popular on the US market, but many changes would have been needed to make it conform with the new safety regulations. In 1968 Donald Healey built three prototypes of the 4000, which used a twin-cam version of the 3909cc Rolls-Royce R engine supplied for the Vanden Plas Princess R, in a lengthened 3000 chassis, but sadly it was not chosen for production. At least two companies have made replicas in recent years, HALDANE of the 100 and HMC of the 3000.

The Sprite

In 1956 Lord asked Donald Healey to produce a small sports car in the tradition of the MG Midget. This appeared two years later as a unitary construction 2-seater powered by a tuned version of the 948cc A engine as used in the Austin A35. The bonnet and wings opened up to give excellent access to the engine and front suspension, and the headlamps projected from the low bonnet, giving the car its distinctive appearance which earned it the name 'frogeye'. The Sprite was mainly

1963 Austin-Healey 3000 sports, Spa–Sofia–Liège Rally.
NATIONAL MOTOR MUSEUM

1958 Austin-Healey Sprite sports car.
NATIONAL MOTOR MUSEUM

1970 Austin-Healey Sprite V sports car.
NATIONAL MOTOR MUSEUM

the work of Donald Healey's son Geoffrey, aided by chassis engineer Barrie Bilbie. The independent front suspension came from the A35, while the rack-and-pinion steering was borrowed from the Morris Minor. The original Sprite was capable of 84mph (135km/h), and at £678 was excellent value. When it appeared, the only competition came from the 2-cylinder Berkeley, but in 1962 the Triumph Spitfire appeared as a more serious rival, and ultimately outsold the Sprite.

Within a year or two Sprite conversion kits appeared, raising power from 45 to 60 or 70bhp, while body modifications included a streamlined front end and a fastback coupé top. Some of these tuned Sprites could exceed 100mph (260km/h), while Graham Hill drove a specially-prepared example at 132.17mph (212.66km/h) on a Belgian motorway. The Sprite's racing career got under way in 1959 with a 1–2–3 class win at Sebring and a class 6th in the Targa Florio. In 1960 and 1961 the Sprites won class victories in many events including Sebring, Le Mans, and the Brands Hatch TT. Leading drivers were Walt Hansgen, Bruce McLaren, Pat and

Stirling Moss. Despite the presence of Innes Ireland and Steve McQueen in the team, the Sprite had poor seasons in 1963 and 1964, but 1965 was better, with 1–2 at Sebring, 1st at Le Mans and the Nurburgring and 2nd in the Targa Florio. These were all class victories, but in the Brands Hatch 1000 Miles a Sprite finished 2nd overall to an MGB. The Sprite continued to do well up to 1968, and their last success as team cars was 1–2–3 at Sebring in March 1969. The new British Leyland Competition Department did not enter Sprites later in the year, and closed down completely in the summer of 1970.

In May 1961 the original Sprite was replaced by the Mk II which had front disc brakes and a more conventional bonnet in which the 'frogeyes' were replaced by headlamps mounted normally at the front of the wings. A month later MG brought out their version of the Sprite, for which the name Midget was revived. It differed only in the grill and a chrome bar down the side of the body. For 1963 the 1098cc Mini Cooper engine was used in the 'Spridgets' as they were nicknamed. The Sprite III (1964–66) was similar, but had wind-up windows and the rear semi-elliptic springs replaced the quarter-elliptics. A detuned 1275cc Mini Cooper S engine came on the Mk IV (1966–68), while the Sprite V had black sills and Rostyle wheels.

In December 1970 the agreement between British Leyland and Donald Healey came to an end, so the last 1129 Sprite Vs were badged simply as Austin Sprites. The final one was delivered in July 1971, but the MG Midget was continued until the end of 1979. Total production of the 'frogeye' was 38,999, and of all Spridgets 316,899. Like the big Healey, the Sprite attracted the replica builders, in particular the FROGEYE company on the Isle of Wight.

NG

Further Reading
The Austin Healey, Donald Healey and Tommy Wisdom, Cassell, 1960.
The Big Healeys, a Collector's Guide, Graham Robson, MRP, 1981.
Sprites and Midgets, a Collector's Guide, Eric Dimmock, MRP, 1981.

AUSTRAL (AUS) 1913
Austral Cycle & Motor Works, Caulfield, Victoria.
The passing fashion for cycle-cars was followed by the maker of Austral motor-cycles, with its offering, which had an 8hp 947cc Peugeot vee-twin engine with automatic inlet valves. A friction drive system was employed, transmission being completed by belts to the rear wheels. Friction drive was then common, but its Chater-Lea front-wheel brakes would have then been most unusual, particularly on a minimum vehicle.

MG

AUSTRALIAN SIX (AUS) 1919–1926
Australian Motors Ltd, Ashfield, New South Wales.
The first examples were AMERICAN SIX, imported by F.H. Gordon & Co. and fitted with new badges. In a large new factory at Ashfield, assembly with greater local content, including a radiator with a classic Grecian temple form, was carried out. Mechanically of US origin, with a 23hp Rutenber engine of 3772cc, driving via a Grant-Lees 3-speed gearbox, it had a wheelbase of 122in (3098mm). Artillery and disc wheels were available. Despite good initial prospects, failure of many engines led to the discovery that they were not up to contract standard, needing to be stripped and rebuilt before fitting to cars. This cost burden effectively destroyed the budgeted profit margin and caused the company's 1922 financial collapse. The assets were purchased by Harkness & Hillier of Fivedock, and a revised model, with a 26hp 3816cc Ansted ohv engine appeared, being built in small numbers until 1926. It is thought that as many as 1000 units were produced, making it the most prolific Australian type prior to World War II.

MG

AUSTRALIS (AUS) 1901–1905
Australis Motors, Leichardt, New South Wales.
Cycling and engineering came together at the works of G.W. & G. Wood when the manufacture of Leichardt cycles was established. An attraction to the new form of power soon developed, as was evident when their shop was named the Austral Gas Engine Works. Experiments were made, in conjunction with a pioneering motorist, Charles Highland, to power cycles, but success was not achieved until 1897 – with a motor bicycle using a De Dion-Bouton engine. It seems that both Highland and the Woods made further motor-tricycles and motor-quads before a small Australis car, with a single-cylinder water-cooled 3hp engine to De Dion-

Bouton pattern arrived in 1901. Apart from its rims and tyres, it was wholly made by the Wood firm, which offered engines suitable for cycles and motors, cooling fans, and a carburettor of its own design. By this time the Australis Motors title had been adopted, and surviving engines have that name cast into their crankcases. In 1905 a 4-seater tonneau vehicle from Australis was sighted.

MG

AUSTRO (A) 1913–1914
Fritz Huckel, Neutitschein.

This was a rare example of an Austrian-built cyclecar. It was powered by a 5/7PS V-twin NSU engine, followed by a V-twin by Laurin & Klement, with 4-speed gearbox and final drive by double chains. Front suspension was on Morgan lines, being independent by sliding pillars. In 1914 Huckel made a larger car with 14hp 4-cylinder engine and shaft drive. Austro cyclecars did well in competitions such as the Semmering hill climb. After the war Huckel, who was also a hat maker, produced a few more cyclecars under the name GNOM. This was a Czech car as Neutitschein (renamed Novy Jicin) was in the newly created republic of Czechoslovakia.

NG

AUSTRO-DAIMLER (A) 1899–1934
1899–1902 Österreichische Daimler Motoren Gesellschaft Bierenz, Fisher & Co., Wiener-Neustadt.
1902–1910 Österreichische Daimler Motoren GmbH, Wiener-Neustadt.
1910–1928 Österreichische Daimler Motoren AG, Wiener-Neustadt.
1928–1934 Austro-Daimler-Puch AG, Wiener-Neustadt.
1934 Steyr-Daimler-Puch AG, Wiener-Neustadt.

The Austrian branch of the German DAIMLER (i) company was set up by Eduard Fischer, managing director of the engineering firm Bierenz Fischer, to make Daimlers under licence. A preliminary run of 100 cars was planned, virtually identical to the Phoenix made at Cannstatt. In 1901 Paul Daimler (1869–1945), son of the founder Gottlieb (1834–1900) became technical director of Austro-Daimler, and a few of his PD-Wagen were made in Austria. They were smaller than the Daimlers, with 9hp 2-cylinder engines and chain drive. Paul left the Austrian company in 1905, and was succeeded by Ferdinand Porsche (1875–1951) who remained at Wiener-Neustadt until 1923. The Austrian company became financially independent of the German one in 1906. Emile Jellinek (1853–1918), who had given the name of his elder daughter Mercedes to the products of German Daimler, set up an Austrian company, Österreichische Automobile Gesellschaft, to sell a car which he ordered from Austro-Daimler and sold under the name of his younger daughter Maja. It was a conventional car with a 4520cc 24/28PS T-head 4-cylinder engine, 4-speed gearbox, and a choice of shaft or chain drive. Jellinek ordered 600 Maja cars for sale in France, but it seems that fewer were actually delivered. In 1909 the Maja was renamed Austro-Daimler 28/36PS and in improved form was made up to 1914. Other Austro-Daimler models included the 18/22, 23/30 and 27/60PS. A team of 28/36s was entered in the 1909 Prince Henry Trial and performed sufficiently well for Porsche to design what he called a proper car for the 1910 Trial. This was a much more advanced design, with a 5714cc 4-cylinder engine, and inclined overhead valves operated by a shaft-driven single ohc. The specification included twin magnetos and light steel pistons. Final drive was by chains, which was perhaps old-fashioned by 1910, but Porsche was afraid that a shaft and bevel rear axle might not be strong enough. The cars were fitted with striking tulip-shaped 4-seater bodies designed by Ernst Neumann-Neander who was a pioneer in aerodynamic shapes. Five cars were entered in the 1910 Prince Henry Trial, those driven by Porsche, Eduard Fischer and Count Heinrich Schonfeld finishing 1st, 2nd and 3rd. Two others finished in the first ten, the marque winning nine of the twelve cups for which they were eligible. The design went into production in 1911, now with shaft drive. They were the most powerful cars made by Austro-Daimler, though not the largest. Thus, with the Vauxhall Prince Henry and Hispano-Suiza Alfonso, they are considered among the first real sports cars, obtaining their power from ingenious design rather than sheer size. The ohc-engine developed 95bhp from 5.7-litres, while the largest side-valve engine in the range produced only 60bhp from nearly 7-litres. About 200 Prince Henrys were made between 1911 and 1914, mostly with open 4-seater bodies. Many went to the United States and to England, where they were marketed as Austrian-Daimlers. Ties with the German company were completely severed in 1911, and Neumann-Neander designed a new badge featuring the two-headed eagle, heraldic device of the Imperial family which

1900 Austro-Daimler tonneau.
NATIONAL MOTOR MUSEUM

1909 Austro-Daimler 6.5-litre Prince Henry tourer.
NATIONAL MOTOR MUSEUM

1920 Austro-Daimler 15/35PS tourer.
NATIONAL MOTOR MUSEUM

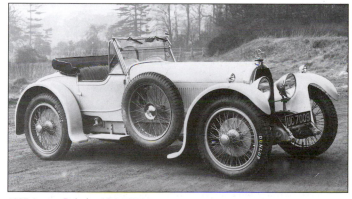
1927 Austro-Daimler ADR 19/100 sports car.
NATIONAL MOTOR MUSEUM

1920 Austro-Fiat tourer.
NATIONAL MOTOR MUSEUM

symbolised the double monarchy, Austria and Hungary. Permission was granted personally by the Emperor Franz-Joseph. Porsche-designed smaller cars, the 2210cc 9/30PS and 3560cc 14/32PS, swept the board in the Austrian Alpine Trials of 1911 and 1912. These were part of the regular range made up to 1914, along with the 4520cc 18/36PS, 5714cc 22/80 PS (Prince Henry) and 6900cc 27/60PS. Just before the outbreak of war a smaller car appeared, the 2009cc 6/25PS, which was revived after the war. A larger 4-cylinder side-valve car, the 3300cc 15/35PS, joined the 6/25PS in 1920, but in 1921 came a more important design, the 4420cc 6-cylinder AD617 with single ohc. This was the work of Porsche and his younger assistant Karl Rabe (1895–1968) who Porsche promoted over the heads of older men, and who designed all the larger Austro-Daimlers for the rest of the marque's existence. The other postwar design was entirely Porsche's, the very advanced Sascha racing voiturette. It was named after Count Sascha Kolowrat, a colourful sportsman who had taken part in a prewar Alpine Trial with a pet pig in the rear seat of his Laurin & Klement. The Sascha had a 4-cylinder twin-ohc engine which developed 45bhp from only 1090cc. It could be used on the road, or stripped as a racing car, like the Brescia Bugatti. Three ran in the 1922 Targa Florio, two in the 1100cc class and one whose bored-out engine put it in the larger class. The small Saschas won their class easily, and the larger was driven into 6th place by Alfred Neubauer, later to become director of the Mercedes-Benz racing programme. Successful though they were, few Saschas were sold to the public, and the directors objected to so much being spent on racing. The death of works driver Fritz Kuhr in a 2-litre Sascha at Monza in 1923 was the final blow to the racing programme. Porsche left to join Mercedes-Benz, for whom he was to design the legendary SS and SSK models. Meanwhile Rabe improved the AD617 by adding 4-wheel brakes on the ADV of 1924 to 1927. He also designed a smaller 6-cylinder car, the 2540cc ADM I (1923–1924), which was enlarged to 2613cc in the ADM II (1924–1927) and to 2994cc in the ADM 3-litre (1926–1928). The ADMII and 3-litre were made in touring and sports form, the latter being capable of 90mph (145km/h). In 1927 Rabe broke new ground with the ADR. This used the same 2994cc engine as the ADM, mounted in a completely new chassis which consisted of a tubular backbone enclosing the propeller shaft, forked at the front to carry the engine. There were typically continental swinging half axles at front and rear, with suspension by transverse leaf springs. The ADR came in two models, the 70bhp long wheelbase touring chassis, and the 100bhp long- or short-wheelbase sporting chassis. About 2400 were made from 1927 to 1931, and sporting versions had many successes, especially in the hands of Hans Stuck. The last Austro-Daimler passenger cars were the 3614cc 6-cylinder Bergmeister (Mountain Master) and 4624cc straight-8 ADR8. The Bergmeister engine gave 120bhp and a top speed of 90mph (145km/h) with a light body, while the 100bhp ADR8 chassis generally carried more formal bodies. However, company politics

prevented either from realising their potential, and not more than 50 were made of each. The ADR8 ceased production in 1933, while the Bergmeister lasted a year longer. Austro-Daimler had merged with PUCH in 1928 to form Austro-Daimler–Puchwerke AG, and in 1929 they began an association with Austria's largest car builder, STEYR. This led to full amalgamation in 1934 as Steyr–Daimler–Puch AG. As both companies had the same bankers, and were to some extent competitors, one had to go, and Austro-Daimler were the victims. Though production ended in 1934, some chassis were not bodied until 1937. The name survived on some 6x4 military vehicles up to 1942, though these were made in the Steyr factory.
NG

AUSTRO-FIAT (A) 1907–1936
1907–1921 Österreichische Fiat AG, Vienna.
1921–1936 Österreichische Automobilfabrik AG, Vienna.
This company was founded in 1907 for importing Italian-built Fiats into Austria, and in 1911 manufacture began, of the Tipo 1 and 2, both with 4-cylinder monobloc engines of 1.8 and 2.6-litres, respectively. Austro-Fiat also built vans and chain-driven trucks, the latter not entirely of Fiat design. In 1921 came the first car of Austrian design, known as the A.F. Model C.1. This had a 2.5-litre 4-cylinder engine with 4-speed separate gearbox, front-wheel brakes and a Germanic vee-radiator. It was made in small numbers up to 1928, when it was replaced by a smaller car, the 1.3-litre Typ 1001 which had swing-axle rear suspension as used by Austro-Daimler and Steyr. This is not surprising as A.F. had become associated with Austro-Daimler in 1925. When Austro-Daimler merged with Steyr in 1934 the Typ 1001 became redundant, being very close in size and price to the smaller Steyrs. The last 1001s, which looked not unlike the Lancia Augusta, were made in 1936, but its makers were by no means finished with motor vehicles. Commercial vehicle production continued, the products being renamed O.A.F. after World War II. There were strong links with the German truck and bus maker M.A.N., and after 1975 O.A.F.s were similar to M.A.N.s, though still carrying their own badges.
NG

AUSTRO-GRADE (A) 1923–1927
Austro-Grade Automobilfabrik AG, Klosterneuburg.
This was similar to the German-built GRADE cyclecar, with 800cc 2-stroke engine and friction transmission, and a chassisless boat-type aluminium body. Towards the end of the make's life a 4-seater version was launched, but it did not have time to prove itself.
HON

AUSTRO-RUMPLER (A) 1920–1922
Austro-Rumpler-Werke, Vienna.
This was a tiny cyclecar with seating for one person and powered by a 3/10PS engine. There was apparently no connection with the advanced cars made in Germany by Edmund Rumpler.
HON

AUTECH (i) (GB) 1980s
Autech Classic Cars, Bromsgrove, West Midlands.
This company, which specialised in classic Jaguars, was one of a plethora of concerns producing Jaguar C-Type replicas in Britain during the 1980s. Unlike most, the bodywork was replicated entirely in aluminium. Jaguar XK engines of 3.4- or 3.8-litres were used.
CR

AUTECH (ii) (J/I) 1989–1991
Autech Japan Inc., Kanagawa.
Autech is a company closely affiliated with Nissan and its stock-intrade was modifying a wide variety of Nissan cars, including styling kits and disabled conversions. It went out on a limb in 1989 with the launch of the Autech Stelvio AZ1, an extraordinary 2+2 coupé designed and built by Zagato of Italy. It was based on a Nissan Leopard platform with a front-mounted twin-turbocharged 3-litre engine developing 280bhp. Its angular bodywork featured bizarre humps in the front wings housing the rear-view mirrors. The company planned to build 203 examples at a price equivalent to £58,000.
CR

AUTHI (E) 1966–1976

Automóviles de Turismo Hispano Ingleses, Landaben, Navarra.

This firm built English MORRIS and AUSTIN cars under licence, starting with Morris 1100, MG 1100 and Morris Countryman, followed by Mini 850, 1000 and 1275C, and the Victoria, a special Austin only built in Spain and South Africa, based on the Austin 1100 and 1300. These cars sold very well but were not of the same quality as cars built in England. The Mini 1275C used an MG 1300cc engine. In 1976 the state-owned Seat was obliged to take over the factory, building there some SEAT models and the only LANCIA Beta Coupé and HPE cars prepared outside Italy. The next owner, VOLKSWAGEN, used the plant to produce the Polo. In 1999 this plant was one of the most modern in Europe, with very high quality standards.

VCM

AUTOAR (RA) 1950–1962

Automotores Argentinos, Buenos Aires.

Production of utility vehicles with 2199cc Jeep engines and transmissions started in 1950. The 2-door saloon, launched in 1951 had the same mechanical components. Piero Dusio, creator of the famed CISITALIA cars, made in Italy and then in Argentina, was one of the sponsors of Autoar. Later in the 1950s the saloon was discontinued and only station-wagon and pickup versions were offered. The station wagon had two engine options: Jeep or Fiat 1900cc. From 1960 onwards, NSU Prinz cars were also made under licence by Autoar. The last year Autoar vehicles were made was 1961, when 204 units were produced. NSU production stopped in 1962, after 2228 had been made.

ACT

AUTOBARN see GECKO

AUTOBIANCHI see BIANCHI

AUTOBLEU (F) 1953–1957

Automobiles Autobleu, Paris.

Autobleu began in business by supplying components for improving the appearance of the Renault 4CV, moving on to complete rebodying of the 4CV. Spring 1953 saw a 2-door coupé with wrap-around rear window styled by Ghia. These sold in small numbers, but were hampered by their price, more than double that of a regular 4CV saloon. Unlike ALPINE, Autobleu did not modify the Renault's engine to improve performance. A convertible styled and built by Chapron was announced in 1955, when Autobleu made a single example of a coupé based on the larger, front-engined Renault Fregate. The body was styled and built by Boano.

NG

AUTO-BUG (US) 1909–1910

The Auto-Bug Co., Norwalk, Ohio.

In appearance and power unit, the Auto-Bug was a typical high-wheel buggy with 22hp 2-cylinder engine under the seat. What made it unusual was the drive system; the rear axle was stationary, and drive was by bearing-mounted sleeves on which the wheels turned. Four models were listed, a runabout, surrey, touring and delivery van, all priced at $850. Production has been estimated at 38 cars, the last leaving the factory in June 1910. Company superintendent Arthur E. Skadden then made the NORWALK car in the same factory.

NG

AUTO BUGGY see A.B.C. (i) and SUCCESS

AUTOCAR (US) 1900–1912

The Autocar Co., Ardmore, Pennsylvania.

The Autocar name has been famous on trucks for more than 90 years, but originated on cars made by the former Pittsburgh Motor Vehicle Co. (see PITTSBURGH (i)). With the move to Ardmore in April 1900 came a change of name; the first Autocar was a 2-seater runabout with 3hp single-cylinder engine and chain drive. By the end of the year 27 had been made, and next year's production was well up, at 163 cars. These had 6hp 2-cylinder engines and shaft drive. It is thought that they were America's first shaft-driven cars with more than one cylinder. Early Autocars had left-hand tiller steering, and, when wheel steering was introduced on the 1905 model, the wheel remained on the left, very unusual for American cars

1990 Autech (ii) AZ1 coupé Zagato.
NICK GEORGANO

1955 Autobleu 4CV coupé.
NATIONAL MOTOR MUSEUM

1902 Autocar Type VI 8 ½hp runabout.
NATIONAL MOTOR MUSEUM

at that date, though it became much more widespread after Henry Ford adopted it on the Model T. Autocar, however, went over to right-hand steering in 1906. The Autocar grew in vehicle size and production over the next few years; 1905 models had gearchange, clutch, spark advance and retard, and accelerator all located under the steering column. The first four, a 16/20hp tonneau came in 1905, and by 1908 the range was topped by a large 60hp six at $6500–7000, though as this was advertised as a 10- or 16-passenger limousine it sounds more like a bus. Though listed with other Autocars, this may have been a product of the AUTO CAR Company of Buffalo, who did list a 10-seater in 1907. Commercial vehicles were introduced in 1907 and soon came to outnumber cars. Production of the latter fell from a peak of 823 in 1907 to 611 in 1911. Although that year's catalogue spoke of 'continued interest in the manufacture of pleasure cars', the 1912 models were the last, and there were very few of them. They were conventional 30hp

1911 Autocar Type XXIV 30hp tourer.
JOHN A. CONDE

1920 Autocrat 10/12hp 2-seater.
NICK BALDWIN

4-cylinder tourers. Autocar trucks became widely known, the company being independent until 1953 when they were taken over by White. In 1981 White was acquired by Volvo, but Autocar continued as the custom-built heavy division of VolvoWhite.

NG

AUTO CAR (US) 1907; 1911

Auto Car Equipment Co., Buffalo, New York.

Mainly builders of commercial vehicles, this company announced an enormous 60hp 6-cylinder limousine with accommodation for up to 10 passengers. Few were made, and the company concentrated on commercials up to 1911, by which time their name had been changed to Atterbury. They offered another 10-seater, this time a touring car, and again it lasted only one season. Atterbury trucks, however, were made up to 1935.

NG

AUTO CLASSICS INTERNATIONAL (US) c.1994–1996

Auto Classics International, Tempe, Arizona and Hawaiian Gardens, California.

The ACI Rennsport 550 was a replica of the Porsche 550 Spyder racing car. It used a round tube space-frame with 1600cc to 2400cc Volkswagen engines. Standard suspension was VW, with optional custom-fabricated parts. They were available in kit or assembled form. ACI moved from Arizona to California in 1995. This kit was later sold by VINTAGE SPYDERS.

HP

AUTO CONVERSIONS BY FRANK (US) c.1996

Auto Conversions by Frank, Santa Maria, California.

The sole model for this company was a rebody kit for Chrysler LeBarons that made them look like Mercedes 500 SLs. Sold in kit and assembled form.

HP

AUTO CRAFT NORTHWEST (US) c.1967

Auto Craft Northwest, Portland, Oregon.

Auto Craft sold a dune buggy body and a VW-based sports car kit. The latter was called a Mk III and appeared to be a FIBERFAB Avenger.

HP

AUTOCRAT (GB) 1913–1926

Autocrat Light Car Co., Birmingham.

The Autocrat began life as a cyclecar powered by an air-cooled V-twin Peugeot engine, followed quickly by a water-cooled JAP, also a V-twin. The Peugeot was mounted with its cylinders fore and aft and the crankshaft transverse, as on the early G.N., but the JAP was mounted in the usual way, with the crankshaft in line with the frame. Both models had bullnose radiators, that on the air-cooled car being a dummy. Only the first car had chain final drive, the JAP-engined version having chain-drive to the gearbox and shaft-drive to the rear axle. Later in 1913 a 1098cc 4-cylinder Chapuis–Dornier engine was offered, and for 1914 the twin was dropped. Drive was now by shaft to the 3-speed gearbox, and the bullnose radiator had been replaced by a flat one. A 1340cc Coventry–Simplex engine was listed for 1915, and it seems that some cars were made well into World War I, as was not unusual with light cars. The people behind the company were both women, Ivy Rogers and a Miss Howell.

Postwar Autocrats were made in a different factory, but still in the Balsall Heath area of Birmingham. They bought their engines from a variety of sources, including Hotchkiss, Anzani, Meadows and Dorman. The latter company supplied 240 of their 1529cc engines, with both overhead and side valves, and Meadows provided 30 1496cc ohv units. Some quite luxurious bodies were offered, including a coupé-phaeton with detachable hard top. At £875 in 1920, it was one of the most expensive light cars on the market. Electric starting and saloon bodies were available by 1923, but production from 1924 to 1926 appears to have been on a very small scale. The company was taken over by CALTHORPE in 1926, but they were in trouble themselves, and the Autocrat factory was closed in the same year. Only one Autocrat is known to survive.

NG

Further Reading
'The Autocrat–aristocrat of light cars', M. Worthington-Williams, *The Automobile,* November 1991.

AUTO CUB (US) 1956

Randall Products, Hampton, New Hampshire.

For those who valued low cost over any considerations of comfort or performance, the Auto Cub fitted the bill. Its single-seater plywood body was like a soapbox on wheels, steering was by tiller and the rear-mounted Briggs & Stratton or Clinton engine gave only 1.6bhp. Overall length was only 51in. Even at the amazingly low price of $170, few buyers were tempted.

NG

AUTOCULT (GB) 1983–1985

Autocult, Dunbar, East Lothian.

Scottish kit cars are a rare breed, and the Tigress perhaps showed why. It was a curvaceous VW Beetle-based 2+2 coupé that looked more than a little unhappy. Its glassfibre bodywork featured Countach-style forward-hinging doors with winding Beetle windows. Very few were made.

CR

AUTOCYCLE (US) 1906–1907

Vandegrift Automobile Co., Philadelphia, Pennsylvania.

This was a most unusual car, one of that select breed which had its four wheels arranged in diamond pattern rather than at the four corners of the frame. The side wheels were smaller than those at front and rear, and were not unlike the stabilisers used to help young cyclists. Indeed it was said that 'the balance wheels carry little or no weight under normal conditions'. The engine was an air-cooled 6hp twin driving the rear wheel by belt. Among the backers of the company were Henry G. Morris and Pedro Salom, who had been pioneers of the electric taxicab (*see* MORRIS & SALOM).

NG

AUTO CYCLECAR *see* TIGER

AUTO DESIGN OF CALIFORNIA (US) c.1980–1985

Auto Design of California, San José, California.

The Jaguar XK-120 has been replicated by many companies, but Auto Design was one of the first, and certainly made the most variations. One was a custom chassis to take 4-cylinder Ford Pinto running gear. Another adapted the body to a Toyota pick-up truck chassis. The least likely version utilised a stretched VW Beetle chassis, which hardly seemed appropriate. They also made a conversion for 1979 – on Mustangs (the Munich) with Mercedes SL-style grille and trim. The Britannia was a styling kit that made a Cadillac Seville or Eldorado resemble a Rolls-Royce from the front. They also made a replica of a 1932 Ford Woody wagon that used Ford running gear.

HP

AUTO-DYNAMIC (US) 1900–1902

The Auto-Dynamic Co., New York, New York.

This company, which made its own batteries, built electric cars in several body styles, including a 4-seater trap, brougham, hansom cab and delivery wagon.

NG

AUTODYNAMICS (US) c.1963–1972

Autodynamics, Marblehead, Massachusetts.

In addition to turning out hundreds of Formula Vee race cars, Autodynamics' boss Ray Caldwell found time to make street cars as well. The Deserter dune buggies (also sold by Alex Dearborn) were very popular. They added a sports car kit called the Hustler in 1967. It looked like a mildly restyled Lotus Elan (Autodynamcis sold Elan replacement panels as well) grafted to a VW Beetle floorpan. It was a well engineered kit and VW, Porsche and Corvair engines could be installed. It was sold only in kit form.

HP

AUTOETTE (i) (US) 1912–1913

Manistee Auto Co., Manistee, Michigan.

This was one of America's first cyclecars. It was also one of the smallest, with a 400cc single-cylinder engine rated at only 4.9hp. Transmission was by friction discs, with vee-belt final drive. The 72in (1827mm) wheelbase 2-seater roadster cost $300. The car was sometimes referred to as the Manistee.

NG

AUTO-ETTE (ii) (US) 1913

Auto-Ette Co., Chrisman, Illinois.

This was another cyclecar, which overlapped the car from Manistee by a year. This possibly explains the slight difference in spelling. It was a larger car, with 9hp 2-cylinder Spacke engine, shaft drive and a 96in (2436mm) wheelbase.

NG

AUTOETTE (iii) (US) 1952–1957

Autoette Electric Car Co., Long Beach, California.

This was one of several makes of basic electric transport, little more than a road-going golf cart. The 2-seater open 3-wheeler had limited accommodation for shopping behind the seats. Long Beach was a suitable factory location, with its large population of retired people.

NG

AUTOGEAR (i) (GB) 1922

Foster Engineering Co. Ltd, Letchworth, Hertfordshire.

This was a conventional light car powered by a 7hp flat-twin engine and with friction transmission. It was sometimes known as the Foster to avoid confusion with the other Autogear being made in Leeds, while another name used for the car was Accelera.

NG

AUTOGEAR (ii) (GB) 1922–1923

Autogears, Leeds, Yorkshire.

This appeared a few months after the FOSTER (i), but it was a much less conventional machine, being related to the STANHOPE 3-wheeler. Like this car, it had belt drive to the single front wheel, but used a Blackburne V-twin engine in place of the Stanhope's V-twin JAP. The Stanhope became the Bramham in 1923, and both it

and the Autogear were supposed to be made in Ireland under the name Leprachan. The Autogear's manufacturers were given as McLysaght & Douglas of Dublin, while the Stanhope was sold by W.E.S. Gilmour, also of Dublin. Perhaps he sold both makes.

NG

AUTOGNOM (D) 1907

Deutsche Motorfahrzeugfabrik GmbH, Berlin.

This car was shown at both Paris and Berlin motor shows in 1907, but it is unlikely that production began.

HON

AUTOKIT (US) c.1971–1985

Autokit, Alameda, California.

The Invader GT was a low, striking kit car based on VW running gear. Among its unusual features were clear plastic gull-wing doors. Built and designed by Bruce Weeks, it sold in large numbers and was also built in Spain. Although there were at least four models, they all looked very similar. The Invader project was later acquired by KAYLOR ENERGY PRODUCTS.

HP

AUTO LÉGER (F) 1904–1907

Autos Léger V. Crepet, Lyons.

The Auto Léger (literally Light Car) was made in very limited numbers, though each of the three cars was different. The most dramatic was the first whose bonnet and mudguards were shaped in the form of the head and wings of a dragon, said to terrify pedestrians. The creature held the radiator in its claws, and its wings served as mudguards. Made of bronze, the bonnet was so heavy that three men were needed to lift it. Powered by a 9hp 2-cylinder engine with 3-speed gearbox and shaft drive, it was built with a tonneau body, later converted to a light truck in which form it was actually exhibited at the 1904 Paris Salon. More conventional were a chain-driven 2-seater and a shaft-driven 4-seater sold to a doctor. All had 9hp 2-cylinder engines made in the workshop. M. Crepet's workshop was very small; together with his partner M. Toussant, he had a staff of four men and an apprentice. The partners soon returned to the silk business from which they came.

NG

AUTOLETTE (NL) 1905–1906

S. Bingham & Co., Rotterdam.

Brothers Seymour and Daniál George moved to Rotterdam from England in 1871 and founded a firm for renting covers in the harbours there. From 1890 they assembled bicycles and, later, motorcycles under the tradename 'Eenhoorn' (unicorn). In 1905 they put a third wheel on a motorcycle, and a tricar with the name 'Autolette' was born. It had a 4hp single-cylinder air-cooled 2-stroke engine, followed in 1906 by 5hp and 7hp engines in a four-wheeler voiturette. After a series of chain-driven cars with either 12, 16 or 24hp engines, production quietly ceased in 1907. The firm imported Oldsmobile cars for a while around 1903.

FBV

AUTO-LUX (I) 1937

Auto-Lux SpA, Milan.

This was a light electric 3-wheeler built by a group of electrical firms. Exhibited at the 1937 Milan Show it never went into production, but the company did commercialise a 3-wheeled electric delivery van from 1945 to 1950.

NG

AUTOMATIC (i) see STURTEVANT

AUTOMATIC (ii) (US) 1921

Automatic Electric Transportation Co., Buffalo, New York.

This was a neat-looking little electric 2-seater on a short wheelbase of 65in (1650mm), with overall length being only 95in (2411mm). Much smaller than the average American electric car, and with a top speed of only 18mph (29km/h), it was expensive at $1200, and few were sold. Also made was a delivery van on a slightly longer chassis; the company also made industrial trucks and sold out to the well-known Walker Vehicle Co. of Chicago in 1927.

NG

AUTOMECCA (US) 1973–1978

AutoMecca, Tujunga, California.

The Brubaker Box was put into production by this company in kit or completed form. Renamed the Roamer Sport Van, it sold in small numbers until the company reorganised in 1977 and moved to Chatsworth, California. Roamers were built to customer specification and an off-road racing version, the Baja Box, was also offered. Possibly as many as 1500 Roamers were built.

HP

AUTO MILAN see LE MANS

AUTOMIRAGE (I) 1974–c.1987

Automirage srl, Rastignano, Bologna.

The main business of this operation was production of beach buggies, sold under the names Mirage, Moon and Pirana. From 1975 it also offered the Pickwick, a curious Fiat 126-based buggy-style leisure vehicle with open-topped glassfibre bodywork. The following year arrived the Mirage 3, a very small 3-wheeled cyclecar with a 50cc Morini single-cylinder engine mounted in the tail and driving the single rear wheel by chain. A larger model called the 250 (later the IV) arrived in 1981, boasting either a BCB 125cc single-cylinder or 251cc 2-cylinder engine. It could come as a 4-wheeler or as 3-wheeler with a single front wheel.

CR

AUTO-MIXTE (B) 1906–1911

SA l'Auto-Mixte, Herstal, Liège.

This company built petrol-electric vehicles of PIEPER design, using conventional 4-cylinder engines combined with a dynamo and electric motor. Two sizes of engine were listed in 1907, a 3768cc 20/24CV and a 6133cc 30CV, and in 1909 Auto-Mixte exhibited a chassis powered by a Daimler-Knight sleeve-valve engine. They were expensive, and few passenger cars were sold. Most Auto-Mixte vehicles were commercials, including a 34-seater bus delivered to London in 1910. The French G.E.M. petrol-electric car is believed to have been built under Auto-Mixte licence. In 1912 the name of the commercials was changed to Pescatore, and one Pescatore car was built, probably on a truck chassis. From 1919 the factory was used for production of Gillet motorcycles.

NG

AUTOMOBILE (US) 1899–1900

The Automobile Manufacturing Co., Baltimore, Maryland.

This was a 2-seater steam car with a more solid appearance than most of its contemporaries, wheel steering and a Renault-type bonnet. It had two double-acting cylinders and a flash boiler.

NG

AUTOMOBILE ATLANTA (US) c.1994

Automobile Atlanta, Atlanta, Georgia.

The Porsche 914 received a face lift from this kit company, which gave it a semi-Porsche 904 look.

HP

AUTOMOBILE CONSTRUCTION (i) **(US)** 1901–1902

Automobile Construction Co., Milwaukee, Wisconsin.

Company manager Hermann C. Mueller offered to make cars to the client's design, from parts supplied either by the client or by himself. Prices were from $350. In 1909 Mueller offered a high-wheeler under his own name.

NG

AUTOMOBILE CONSTRUCTION (ii) **(US)** 1914

Automobile Construction & Engineering Co., Philadelphia, Pennsylvania.

Another firm offering cars to client's orders, this company was aimed more at dealers than private owners. Components included a 4-cylinder Continental engine, 3-speed gearbox and shaft drive. These, together with a 'first class body', were offered for $675. The engine was set exceptionally far back in the chassis.

NG

AUTOMOBILE VOITURETTE see GASMOBILE

AUTOMOBILETTE (F) 1911–1924

1911–1915 Coignet et Ducruzel, Billancourt, Seine.

1919–1924 Constructions d'Automobile de Bellevue, Bellevue, Seine-et-Oise.

The Automobilette was one of the better-known French cyclecars, and closely resembled its rival the BEDELIA. In fact the prewar models differed mainly in having the luxury of doors, denied to the Bedelia owner. Otherwise both cars had tandem seating for two, with the driver in the rear seat, although Automobilette also offered a monocar. The engine was a 6/8hp twin and final drive was by belts. The chassis was underslung with the semi-elliptic springs inverted, as on the American Underslung, and the car had a bullnose radiator.

1914 models offered the choice of a 6hp Anzani twin or 10hp Automobilette four, still with belt drive, but in the summer of 1914 came a proper light car with the 4-cylinder engine, shaft drive and side-by-side seating. The same layout was seen on the postwar Automobilette, though proprietary engines were used, a 1095cc Ruby or 1243cc Altos. These cars were made at a new factory at the top of a hill, which was said to account for the Automobilette's good hill climbing powers. They were sometimes known as C.A.B. Automobilettes.

NG

AUTOMOBILI INTERMECCANICA (I/US/CDN) 1960 to date

This colourful company was founded by native Hungarian Frank Reisner, who had designed racing cars for Giannini in Italy. He and his wife Paula started a company in Turin selling speed equipment, and in 1960 built a series of Formula Junior racing cars. Their first street car was the IMP, which was short for Intermeccanica-Puch. It was an aluminium-bodied coupé based on Steyr-Daimler-Puch 500cc running gear, and 21 were built. The next project, the APOLLO GT, was more complex. It was a Buick-powered sports car for other companies to market and sell. In 1965 they built a prototype called the Veltro, which was based on an English Ford engine. They also built a prototype Ford Mustang station wagon for Bob CUMBERFORD. Their next project was a Ford V8 powered sports car called the GRIFFITH which failed after a short production run, but continued as the ITALIA and OMEGA. Around 500 had been built by 1970. The FITCH Phoenix, a Corvair-based sports car, was built in prototype form but planned production was doomed when Chevrolet cancelled the Corvair. Another short-run project was the MURENA sports station wagon, which used a 7000cc Ford V8 engine. In 1971, a facelifted Omega called the INDRA was built for Opel dealers in Europe, but production was halted after 125 copies. Another short-run project was the SQUIRE, a Ford-powered Jaguar SS-100 replica. In 1975, Reisner moved the company to California where he intended to produce more Indras. However, this did not work out and Intermeccanica switched to building a Porsche Speedster replica with fibreglass bodies and VW running gear. They were sold in partial and fully assembled forms. Reisner sold his interest in the Porsche replica operation to Tony Baumgartner, and after about 600 were built, the project was sold to CLASSIC MOTOR CARRIAGES. In 1980, Intermeccanica built a 4-seater neoclassic kit car called the LaCrosse that was based on a 5700cc Ford V8. It differed from most neoclassics by not having full running boards and, initially, in being designed for CHECKER running gear. In 1982, Intermeccanica moved to Canada, where they built a replica of the 1959 Porsche Convertible D called the Roadster RS. Although the company was officially Canadian at that point, final assembly was done in Ferndale, Washington. The Roadster RS was very successful and on later models the VW floorpan was replaced with a tube frame. Options included wide mudguard flares, a hardtop, and Porsche 911 running gear. Company leadership passed to Henry Reisner, son of the founders. Intermeccanica later built a prototype of a VW Kubelwagen replica, but it had not been produced as of 1999.

HP

AUTOMOTETTE (F) 1898–1899

Compagnie Francaises des Cycles Automobiles, Paris.

This was a 3-wheeled 2-seater voiturette powered by a 3½hp single-cylinder engine driving the rear wheel by belt. Not unlike a Léon Bollée in appearance, it was sold in England by the Automobile Association Ltd of Holland Park, London, who listed it as a British car. The makers also offered a 4-seater model which was apparently not sold in England.

NG

AUTOMOTIVE CONCEPT AND DESIGN (US) 1993 to date
Automotive Concept and Design, Phoenix, Arizona.
The Scorpion was a graceful kit body that fitted the Pontiac Fiero chassis. It was very popular and distribution was picked up by PISA, who sold Fiero bodies from a number of manufacturers.
HP

AUTOMOTIVE DESIGNS MONZETTA (US) c.1990 to date
Automotive Designs by Scotty, Klamath Falls, Oregon.
This kit was a simple restyling job on a 1975 Chevrolet Monza sedan. The kit added a fastback top, more aggressive grille, wheel flares and side scoops. It was available in kit or assembled form.
HP

AUTOMOTIVE REFLECTIONS (US) c.1984
Automotive Reflections, Williamsburg, Virginia.
This company sold and assembled kits from other manufacturers, including the MAGNUM GT, the Corsair MG-TD replica, the Esquire 1929 Mercedes, and an SS-100.
HP

AUTOMOTO (F) 1901–1907
Chavanet, Gros, Picard et Cie, St Étienne.
SA de Constructions Mécanique de la Loire, St Étienne
This motor-cycle firm began car manufacture with a light voiturette not unlike a De Dion Bouton in appearance, with *vis-à-vis* seating, tiller steering and tubular frame. It was powered by two 2hp air-cooled engines driving the rear axle by a 2-speed gearbox. In 1902 it was available in England in kit form for £97 10 shillings (£97.50). Later cars had 4-cylinder engines of 12, 20, 30 and 40hp, front mounted behind Mercedes-type radiators, with double-chain final drive. The 1904 24hp model had a capacity of 5.7 litres, and the largest 40/45hp of 1907 was of more than 7 litres. From 1904 they were sold in England under the name Automotor. The SVELTE was produced by the same company.
NG

AUTOMOTOR (US) 1901–1904
The Automotor Co., Springfield, Massachusetts.
This company evolved from the Springfield Cornice Works which had built the METEOR (i), and the 1901 Automotor was virtually identical to the 1900 Meteor. Both had a front-mounted single-cylinder De Dion or Aster engine and single-chain drive. The Automotor's aluminium 2-seater body was supplied by the Springfield Metal Body Company. By 1903 the Automotor had grown up into a 4-seater rear-entrance tonneau powered by a 16/20hp 4-cylinder engine with double-chain drive. This was priced at $3000, compared with $850 for the single-cylinder runabout.
NG

AUTONIQUE (US) c.1985
Autonique Division of Unifoam Products Inc., Thief River Falls, Minnesota.
This simple kit transformed the looks of the lowly Ford Pinto with a tall tail spoiler and a long, pointed nose. They were sold only in kit form, and included instructions for installing a V8 engine.
HP

AUTO PRATIQUE (F) 1912–1913
Sté l'Auto Pratique, Paris.
This was a typical cyclecar powered by a 5hp single-cylinder engine, but it was unusual for a car of that size in having shaft drive.
NG

AUTO RED BUG see RED BUG

AUTORETTE (F) 1913–1914
Guerry et Bourguingnon, Paris.
This was one of many ephemeral French cyclecars, powered by a 1100cc 2-cylinder engine.
NG

1901 Automoto voiturette.
NATIONAL MOTOR MUSEUM

AUTO SANDAL (J) 1954
Japan Auto Sandal Motors, Tokyo.
One of a number of short-lived Japanese light cars of the 1950s, the Auto Sandal had a rear-mounted 5½ hp single-cylinder engine, 3-speed gearbox and a 2-seater body.
NG

AUTO SIMPLETTE (F) 1912–1913
Pierre Pestourie, Paris.
This was one of two miniature cyclecars for children exhibited at the 1912 Paris Salon, the other being the BABY AUTO. The Auto Simplette was the more radical of the two, having a tiny 2-stroke engine driving a 2-foot 2-bladed propeller inside a wire cage at the rear of the vehicle. Top speed was only 5mph (8km/h), and the engine was said to be governed so that the car would not exceed this speed even when running downhill, though how this was achieved with a propeller-driven vehicle was not explained. The only brake on what *The Cyclecar* called 'this curious little toy' was a shoe acting on one of the solid rear tyres. The maker, Pierre Pestourie, may have been concerned with the later PESTOURIE ET PLANCHON cyclecar.
NG

AUTOSPEED (US) c.1994 to date
Autospeed Motorcars Corp., Orange, California.
Autospeed made a variety of kit cars, including 289 and 427 Cobra replicas, two variations on the Porsche Speedster, and a VW-based small-scale replica of the Hummer, called the Halfvee. They also briefly built a Ferrari Daytona replica based on the McBURNIE kit.
HP

AUTO SPORT PERFORMANCE PRODUCTS (US) 1994 to date
Auto Sport Performance Products, Tempe, Arizona.
Auto Sport bought their Cobra kit car project from NORTH AMERICAN FIBERGLASS and then added other models to their line. In addition to Street 289, 289 FIA and 427 Cobra replicas, they sold two GT-40 replicas built on Pontiac Fiero chassis. They resembled the Mk I and Mk II versions, and were sold in kit or assembled form.
HP

AUTOTRAK see COBRETTI

AUTOTRI see KELSEY

AUTO TRI-CAR (US) 1914
A.E. Osborn, New York, New York.
Osborn had built a 3-wheeler in 1906 for his own use, and in 1914 he offered a development of this at $250 with single-cylinder engine and $350–400 with 2-cylinder engine. Both power units were made by Prugh, and drove by 2-speed planetary transmission and roller chain to the single front wheel. Body styles were a tandem or side-by-side 2-seater, surrey or light delivery van.
NG

1959 Auto Union (i) 1000SP coupé.
NICK BALDWIN

1960 Auto Union (i) 1000S saloon.
NICK BALDWIN

AUTOTRIX (GB) 1911–1914
Edmunds & Wadden, Weybridge, Surrey.
This was a 3-wheeled cyclecar offered in two sizes, the smaller with a 4hp single-cylinder JAP engine and belt drive, the larger with a 9hp 2-cylinder engine, also by JAP, a Chater-Lea gearbox and chain drive. For those who preferred water-cooling, a 6hp Fafnir engine was available in the larger chassis.
NG

AUTOTUNE (GB) 1984 to date
Autotune Ltd, Rishton, Lancashire.
Autotune's first road car project was the Aristocat. Although not a true replica, it clearly evoked the style and presence of the Jaguar XK140 drophead coupé. It was significantly wider because of the width of the donor Jaguar XJ6 subframes and axles. Anthony Taylor conceived it for historic replica racing, with a huge space frame chassis and Jaguar mechanicals all round. A fixed head model from 1991 matched the original XK140 dimensions. The 1990 Gemini revived the shape of the FALCON Mk2 bodyshell of the 1950s, with a space frame chassis designed to accept anything from Ford Escort to Rover V8 engines. Autotune also developed

a replica of the McLaren M1 racing car, using a space frame chassis which duplicated the original, including Ford or Chevrolet small-block V8 engines sited amidships. Most were used on the circuit, but there were road versions as well.
CR

AUTO UNION (i) (D) 1958–1962
Auto Union AG, Ingolstadt.
The Auto Union combine was founded in 1932, as an amalgamation of four makes, AUDI, DKW, HORCH and WANDERER. The name was applied to the rear-engine racing cars built in the Horch factory and raced with great success from 1934 to 1939, but only one production car was marketed solely as an Auto Union. This was the 1000SP, a convertible powered by a 981cc 3-cylinder DKW engine. It was given a different name to distinguish it from the more mundane DKW saloons, but essentially it was, as the late Michael Sedgwick said 'a DKW dressed up by Baur to look like a mini Thunderbird'. Front disc brakes were provided in the car's last season, 1962. Total production was 6640. The DKW saloons also carried the name Auto Union 1000 from 1957 to 1963.
NG

AUTO UNION (ii) (RA) 1959–1969
Industria Argentina Santa Fe S.A., Santa Fe.
The Argentine Auto Union was a copy of the German automobile of the same name. At first, only the Auto Union 1000 4-door saloon was made, powered by a 3-cylinder, 2-stroke 980cc engine. Then came the 'Combi DKW Auto Union', and a sporty coupé designed by Fissore but powered by the same 980cc engine. Production of the Auto Union 1000 totalled 21,797 units, and that of the Fissore sports version reached 700 units.
ACT

AUTO VAPEUR (F) 1905–1906
Sté l'Auto Vapeur, Paris.
This was one of a number of short-lived steam cars which appeared around 1904 to 1906, hoping to gain some of the SERPOLLET market, but as this more famous make had only three years to go, they had little success. The Auto Vapeur

had a multi-tube boiler and 4-cylinder horizontally-opposed engine mounted in the centre of the frame. Final drive was by shaft. Others in the same class were the FIDELIA and WEYHER ET RICHMOND.

NG

AUTOVIA (GB) 1936–1938

Autovia Cars Ltd, Coventry.

Autovia Cars was formed by RILEY to build a luxury car in a higher price bracket than any existing model, using a development of Riley's V8 engine, enlarged to 2849cc and giving 90bhp, in a long frame with underslung worm drive. Most had Armstrong-Siddeley 4-speed pre-selector gearboxes, but some of the later ones had all-synchromesh 4-speed units. A new factory was acquired and among the directors were Victor Riley and designer Charles Van Eugen, formerly of Lea-Francis. They were certainly ambitious and even imitated Rolls-Royce in having a chauffeurs' school. Two body styles were offered, a 4-light sports saloon and a 6-light limousine, built by Arthur Mulliner, though at least one was bodied by Windover. At £975 for the saloon and £995 for the limousine the Autovia was overpriced, and probably would have struggled in the market place anyway. As it was, Riley's receivership in February 1938 (before the Nuffield takeover) spelt the end for Autovia. About 35 were made. There is a club for the make, quite separate from any Riley club.

NG

Further Reading
'The Autovia', M. Worthington-Williams, *The Automobile*, September, 1986.

AUTO-ZAGAIA (P) 1988–c.1990

This was a local Portuguese Porsche 356 Speedster replica produced by a Porsche racing driver called Nunez and his son, licensed from APAL in Belgium and produced by the Volkswagen concessionaire in Lisbon. It was later called the Classico.

CR

AUTOZODIACO (I) c.1971–1978

Autozodiaco was one of Italy's leading beach buggy manufacturers and one of its buggies – the Damaca – had the distinction of being styled by Tom Tjaarda, author of the De Tomaso Pantera. In 1974 it diversified into microcars with the Charly, a sympathetically-styled 3-wheeled microcar with angular plastic bodywork. It was powered by a 49cc Minarelli 2-stroke engine. Production passed to ALL CARS in 1978.

CR

AUTRAM (F) 1924

Listed only for one year, the Autram was larger than most ephemeral French makes, having a 2951cc 4-cylinder engine. The design also featured a 4-speed gearbox and front-wheel brakes.

NG

AUVERLAND (F) 1984 to date

Auverland SA, St-Germain-Laval.

Auverland took over the defunct COURNIL factory in 1984, producing essentially the same 4x4 models initially. Two model ranges were offered. First was the familiar SCII, available in short- and long-wheelbases and Renault petrol/diesel and Peugeot diesel engines. The other model was the A series, a version restyled by Benoît Contreau with more comfortable suspension and some plastic bodywork. Again there were short- and long-wheelbases and a choice of SOFIM diesel or Fiat petrol engines. After 1988 the A series was renamed the A2 and was joined by the A3, a redesigned 4x4 model, again in two wheelbase lengths and with a wide choice of bodywork. The motive power came from a Peugeot 1.9-litre diesel (later also 2.1-litre diesel and 1.6-litre petrol units). A 2-wheel drive model was added in 1991 and a longer-wheelbase version called the A4 was launched in 1998. In 1996 Auverland diversified with the launch of the A5, a microcar designed for the French *sans permis* class. It had a small polyester hatchback body for two passengers. Suspension was all-independent by MacPherson struts and coil springs, and front disc brakes were fitted. The motive power came from a rear-mounted Lombardini 505cc twin-cylinder diesel, and drove the rear wheels via an automatic gearbox. Auverland's current range consists of the A3, A4 and A5, while under the name Sovamag it has also made a range of military vehicles since 1988.

CR

1937 Autovia V8 saloon.
NATIONAL MOTOR MUSEUM

1920 A.V. Monocar.
NATIONAL MOTOR MUSEUM

A.V. (GB) 1919–1924

1919–1923 Ward & Avey Ltd, Teddington, Middlesex.
1923–1924 A.V. Motors Ltd, Teddington, Middlesex.

Messrs Ward and Avey bought the rights to the prewar CARDEN Monocar and began to build it in the former Carden factory. Rear-mounted 5 and 8hp JAP engines were mostly used, though some examples had Blackburne or MAG power units. The bodies were made of plywood, mahogany or compressed paper, and were supplied by the Thames Valley Pattern Works. Several hundred of these were made, and also about 50 of the Bi-car, which had tandem seating for two, JAP or Blackburne engines and Sturmey-Archer gearboxes. For 1921 the Bi-car had side-by-side seating and was renamed the Runabout. The Monocar was dropped after 1922 and the Runabout was the only model offered up to 1924, after which the company said that they were making cars to special order only. It is most unlikely that any A.V.s were built after 1924, though the company remained in business for many years. At first they were Jowett agents, and after Jowett's demise they turned to selling Rootes Group products.

NG

AVA (GB) 1986–1987; 1990–1991

1986–1987 AVA Cars, Frome, Somerset.
1990–1991 AVA Cars, Bristol.

The AVA K1 kit-built convertible was designed by Nick Topliss and its main claim to fame was a professed Cd figure of just 0.295. The K1 was based around the Ford Escort Mk3, which fitted into subframes in a stainless steel chassis tub. The glassfibre body came in one piece and featured shallow doors. The project was sold to a German company, but it reappeared briefly in the UK in 1990.

CR

1984 Avanti II coupé.
AVANTI MOTOR CORP

AVALON (GB) 1990–1992
Avalon Automotive, Stocksbridge, Sheffield, Yorkshire.
Originally this project was displayed as a styling exercise under the name Curtana, but it eventually became a definitive production proposition as the Avalon S30 (later 250LE). It was a strikingly-styled open-topped mid-engined sports car based on Ford Escort parts, using a space frame chassis and glassfibre body. A coupé version was planned but it is doubtful if even one of the intended 250 production run was actually completed.
CR

AVANTE (GB) 1982–1986
Avante Cars, Stoke-on-Trent, Staffordshire.
This VW Beetle-based kit car had quite sophisticated styling by Melvyn Kay. Beetle engines were usual, but water-cooled fours like the Golf GTI would also fit. Mk2 versions from 1983 were longer, taller and gained more space in the engine bay and interior (2+2), as well as sharper front-end treatment and rear three-quarter windows.
CR

AVANTI (US) 1965–1991
1965–1985 Avanti Motor Corp., South Bend, Indiana.
1986–1987 The New Avanti Motor Corp., South Bend, Indiana.
1987–1988 The New Avanti Motor Corp., Youngstown, Ohio.
1988–1991 Avanti Automotive Corp., Youngstown, Ohio.
When STUDEBAKER ended production of their striking Avanti coupé in 1965 two former dealers, Nathan Altman and Leo Newman, bought the rights and a part of the Studebaker factory to continue production. As the original Studebaker V8 engine was no longer available, they used Chevrolet Corvette V8s of 5360cc up to 1969 when it was joined by an optional 5735cc. This was standardised from 1971 to 1973, when capacity went up to 6555cc. Because of the different engine, the front of the frame was tilted up slightly compared with the Studebaker Avanti, but this merely levelled the car, as the original had a forward tilt. However the frame, suspension and fibreglass body (supplied by Molded Fiberglass of Ashtabula, Ohio, who also made Corvette bodies) were essentially the same as on the original. They called their car Avanti II, and built 45 cars in their first season. They reached the 100 mark in 1968, and sold around 100–125 a year through the 1970s. Sales peaked at 287 in 1984. The Avanti II was not highly-priced for a hand-built car,

costing $8145 in 1972, compared with $13,500 for an Excalibur. In October 1982 the company was sold to Stephen Blake, who dropped the II from the name the following year, and in 1985 introduced a convertible to join the coupé. 228 convertibles were made. Avanti changed hands again in April 1986, becoming the New Avanti Motor Corporation. No cars were made in 1986. New owner Michael Kelly, a 36-year old Texas ethanol baron, introduced a long-wheelbase coupé in 1988 when Avanti moved to Youngstown, Ohio. Shortly afterwards he sold it to John Cafaro who renamed the company again, now as Avanti Automotive Corporation. The long wheelbase coupé was discontinued but the regular coupé and convertible were continued, and 97 examples of a 4-door sedan were made in 1990. The engine was still the Corvette's, now of 4998cc. There were also two prototypes, a Luxury Touring Sedan on a 123in (3122mm) wheelbase and a limousine on an enormous 174in (4416mm) wheelbase. Avanti production ended in 1991, though it was rumoured that partially-completed cars remained in the factory, and were possibly built up to customer's order for several years after that. Official production figures from 1987 to 1991 were 190 coupés, 58 long-wheelbase coupés, 228 convertibles, and 97 sedans.
NG

Further Reading
'Avanti II: Nat Altman can make a car that you will love', Richard M. Langworth, *Automobile Quarterly*, Vol.10, No.3.

AVERAGE MAN'S RUNABOUT (US) 1906
Adams Automobile Co., Hiawatha, Kansas.
George Adams gave an unusual name to his 2-seater car, but otherwise there was nothing very original about it. The engine was a horizontally-opposed 10hp twin, and the car had friction transmission and single-chain drive. It was offered for sale only in 1906, though Adams made a few more cars from 1907 to 1909 for his personal use only.
NG

AVERIES (GB) 1911–1915
Averies-Ponette Ltd, Englefield Green, Surrey.
The first car to carry this name was the French-built LA PONETTE single-cylinder cyclecar imported by John Averies and sold either as the Averies or Averies-Ponette. Early in 1913 he offered a light car with 1050cc 8/10hp 4-cylinder engine, 3-speed gearbox and shaft drive. This was said to have been based on the Rolling

made by Paul DUPRESSOIR and was probably a Rolling bodied in England, or possibly imported as a complete car.

NG

AVERLY (F) 1900–1901
G. Averly, Lyons.
Georges Averly was a pioneer of electric traction, having built an electric tramway which linked the railway station with the exhibition site at the 1894 Lyon Exposition. He made a few electric cars around the turn of the century, but their details are not known, even by the leading historian of Lyons cars, Lucien Loreille.

NG

AVIA (GB) 1961
Armat Ltd, West Kingsdown, Sevenoaks, Kent.
This was a very short-lived coupé which used Triumph Herald power combined with a 2+2 seater fibreglass coupé body. A price of £655 was quoted, but the car never went on sale.

NG

AVIETTE (GB) 1914–1916
Hurlin & Co., Hackney, London.
This was one of the most primitive of the cyclecars, having a 4hp single-cylinder JAP engine, chain drive to a variable pulley on the countershaft, and final drive by a single belt to the offside rear wheel. Steering was by the outmoded centre pivot system and the boat-shaped body, which could be had in single- or 2-seater form, was made of hickory slats. At least the Aviette was cheap; £55 would buy you a single-seater and £65 a 2-seater. The company also made the larger HURLINCAR and sold components for the home assembly of cyclecars.

NG

AVIONETTE see GAUTHIER

AVIOR (B) 1946–1947
This was a handsome-looking sports car in the prewar idiom, with flowing wings and disc wheels, powered by a 70bhp 1930cc 4-cylinder engine of unspecified origin, though it was said to be British-made. Suspension was independent all round, by rubber at the rear. Coupé and saloon versions were announced, but it is not known if any were built. Possibly the 2-seater sports was the only Avior to see the light of day.

NG

AVIS (A) 1921–1928
1921–1924 Technische Werkstatten GmbH, Vienna.
1924–1928 Avis Flugzeug-und Automobilwerke GmbH, Vienna.
This former aircraft firm turned to cars after the manufacture of aeroplanes was banned in Germany and Austria. Their cars were neat-looking light vehicles with 4/20PS 2-cylinder engines, and were made with a variety of bodies including a coupé de ville which could be used as a taxicab.

HON

AVOLETTE (F) 1955–1959
Sté Air Tourist, Paris.
The Avolette was a small, open 3-wheeler based on BRUTSCH designs, using Ydral, Sachs or Maico engines from 125 to 250cc. All were single-cylinder units, and final drive was by chain to the rear wheel. In 1957 Lambretta engines of 125 and 150cc were used. In 1958 an associated company, the Société France Jet, announced another Brutsch design, the V2N 4-wheeler with 175cc Ydral engine, which they sold under the name France Jet. Like the 3-wheelers, it had no doors, but an improved version for 1959 had doors and a 280cc AMC engine. This was exported to America.

NG

AVON (i) (GB) 1903–1912
Avon Motor Manufacturing Co. Ltd, Keynsham, Bristol.
An early attempt to bridge the gap between motorcycle and conventional car, the nucleus of the Avon Trimobile was their own single-cylinder water-cooled engine, graduating from 4hp through 4½hp and 5hp to an eventual 6hp RAC

1903 Avon Trimobile 2-seater.
NICK BALDWIN

rating (98 × 114 mm). This was rear-mounted, with a 3-speed gearbox, on strong bridge girders within a motorcycle-type tubular frame, although wheel steering was employed for the single front wheel. Chain final drive was used. In the absence of road springs the commodious 2-person seat was mounted on large coil springs, a refinement absent from the light delivery van version. The price increased from 80 guineas (£84) to 95 guineas (£99.75) in 1905, and a front-engined, 4-wheeler was then also offered at 106 guineas (£111.30), with conventional leaf suspension. London agents were appointed (Otto-Bennett Motor Co., Snow Hill), but sales remained mainly local and gradually petered out completely.

DF

AVON (ii) see CHALLENGER

AVON (iii) see PHOENIX (ii)

AVRO (GB) 1919–1920
A.V. Roe & Co. Ltd, Manchester.
Alliott Verdon-Roe's Avro aircraft company was one of the major suppliers of combat aeroplanes during World War I, and, like so many others, turned to the motor industry to keep at least some of the workforce in employment. They made Avrolite bodies for Model T Fords, and announced their own car in 1919. This had an integral construction body/chassis with a light timber framework panelled in aluminium. A variety of engines was tried in several experimental cars, including a 1330cc four, a single-cylinder 2-stroke and a 5-cylinder radial. It was said that a Model T engine was used in one prototype, which is not surprising, considering Avro's bodybuilding links with Ford, and that Ford's Trafford Park factory was not far away from the Avro premises. However, it is unlikely that any of these cars actually reached the market place. The same can be said for Verdon-Roe's 2-wheeled monocars, which were intended to provide more civilised and weatherproof transport than a motor cycle. He made at least two, one with a Barr & Stroud 2-stroke engine in 1923, and another with 350cc Villiers engine in 1927. They were probably inspired by the HARPER RUNABOUT, which was made in the Avro factory from 1921 to 1926.

NG

A.V.T (GB) 1995 to date
Alternative Vehicles Technology, Hatch Beauchamp, Somerset.
The A.V.T. 100E was claimed to be the first British kit-form electric car. In style it resembled a Renault Espace, although the glassfibre bodywork was smaller and had only two doors plus a hatchback. The square section steel chassis incorporated most mechanical components from the Rover 100, including the front subframe, suspension, steering, brakes and transmission (with semi-automatic clutch). A front-mounted series-wound 14.66 kilowatt motor was standard, though a disc motor was optional. A top speed of 100mph (160km/h) was claimed, with a range of up to 80 miles (128km).

CR

1920 Avro saloon.
NICK BALDWIN

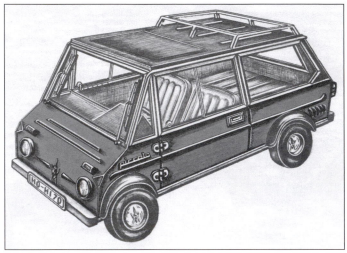

c.1972 A.W.S. (ii) 250K Piccolo city car.
NICK BALDWIN

AVX (US) 1997 to date
This was a modified Pontiac Firebird whose front-end styling somewhat resembled that of the Avanti. Engines were a choice of 3.4-litre V6 (from 1993-95 donor cars), 3.8-litre V6 (from 1995 to date donor cars) or 5.7-litre V8. A choice of 5- or 6-speed manual or 4-speed automatic transmissions was offered, and the bodies were hardtop coupé, T-top coupé or convertible.
NG

A.W. (PL) 1939
Zaklady Przemyslowe 'Bielany' SA, Warsaw.
In 1937 Anton Wieckowski, the owner of an important company which supplied sheet metal to POLSKI FIAT, decided to enter car manufacture himself. With engineers hired from PZInz, makers of the Polski Fiat, he produced a prototype in 1938. It had a central backbone frame and a 4-cylinder side-valve engine of 1300cc developing 32bhp. A 40bhp ohv unit was planned as well. A 4-speed

gearbox was used, and the prototype had an open wooden body; the production car was intended to have an aerodynamic 2-door steel saloon body. A factory was prepared at Warka, near Warsaw, and production planned to start in 1941. Wieckowski had received an order from the Polish Army for 1000 light cross country vehicles. About 50 per cent of the factory equipment had been delivered when the German invasion put an end to the plans. The prototype was destroyed in 1944, and after the war the company was nationalised.
RP

A.W.E. (GB) 1990–c.1996
Alan Wilkinson Engineering, Yeovil, Somerset.
This small traditional-style roadster was a cost-effective kit based on a Triumph Herald/Vitesse chassis, modified by siting the engine further back and having some leaves removed from the rear suspension. The doorless body was plastic and there was a choice of cycle or full wings. The plastic radiator surround, headlamp rims and screen supports could be chromed.
CR

A.W.S. (i) (D) 1949–1951
Autowerke Salzgitter, Salzgitter.
The main business of this company was refurbishing Jeeps and fitting them with station wagon bodies. However, a very original 2-stroke 4-cylinder radial diesel engine designed by Ludwig Elsbett was tried on a station wagon body. Only a few prototypes were made.
HON

A.W.S. (ii) (D) 1971–1974
Automobilwerk Shjopper GmbH, Berlin-Rudow.
This company developed the Piccolo, a small 4-seater city car whose body frame was a skeleton of square steel tubes and special angular brackets. This was covered with plasticised sheet metal panels, making body repairs simple and economical. It was powered by a 247cc 2-stroke Goggomobil engine. About 1400 were made, but such small cars were really out of fashion in the 1970s.
HON

AXONA (F) 1920
This was an obscure cyclecar powered by a 3hp 2-cylinder engine of 662cc.
NG

AYERS (US) c.1985
Ron Ayers Classic Cars, Simpsonville, South Carolina.
This Cobra replica stood out from the rest by using MG Midget doors and windshield for better weather protection, and lockable handles. Most Ayers-built cars had mild engines and automatic transmissions for an emphasis on practicality. They were sold in kit or assembled form.
HP

AYRESPEED (GB) 1994 to date
Ayrespeed, London.
Motoring journalist Iain Ayre (who had previously launched cars under the BROOKLAND name) was behind the Ayrespeed Six, a replica of the Jaguar XK120. Roadgoing versions were offered, but competition use was more readily envisaged.
CR

A.Z. TEC *see* AUTECH (ii)

BABCOCK (i) (US) 1906–1912

Babcock Electric Carriage Co., Buffalo, New York.

Frank A. Babcock had been manager of the Buffalo Electric Carriage Company, makers of the BUFFALO (ii). The first Babcocks were similar to the Buffalos, made in four models of stanhope and runabout using the maker's own batteries. Babcock drove one of these the 100 miles from New York to Philadelphia on a single charge, claiming a world record at the time. For 1907 the Babcock range was extended to six models, including the traditional coupé typical of the American electric. Open and closed cars were made up to 1912, one of which was a roadster with a bonnet, giving the appearance of a petrol car. In 1912 Frank Babcock merged his company with the Clark Motor Company, also of Buffalo, which had experimented with an electric car but had not marketed it. The new firm was called the Buffalo Electric Vehicle Company, and continued production in the same factory until 1915.

NG

BABCOCK (ii) (US) 1909–1913

H.H. Babcock Co., Watertown, New York.

This company was an old-established maker of horse-drawn carriages with a 60-year history, when they built an experimental car in 1908. After a year of testing it went on the market as the Model A, a high-wheeler with 18hp 2-cylinder engine. These were made in 1910 also, and were joined by a conventional tourer with 35hp 4-cylinder engine. The high-wheeler was dropped after 1910, and the Babcocks of the three remaining years of the car's life were tourers with 32, 35 or 40hp engines, with a limousine listed for 1911 only. After 1913 the company built bodies, mostly for trucks and ambulances during World War I.

NG

BABY see FOURNIER (ii)

BABY AUTO (F) 1912–1913

This was a tiny cyclecar intended for children. It was powered by a 1.5hp air-cooled engine under a bonnet, and driving by shaft to the rear axle. It could be started from the seat, by a leather strap attached to a shaft which was linked by sprocket and chain to the crankshaft. Its cost was less than FFr 40, but *The Cyclecar's* correspondent was unimpressed with this or its propeller-driven rival the AUTO SIMPLETTE, remarking 'What their introduction signifies, we are at a loss to understand'.

NG

BABY BLAKE (GB) 1922

E.G. Blake, Croydon, Surrey.

This was an unconventional cyclecar powered by two 2-stroke engines, each with friction discs instead of flywheels, running in opposite directions. A third disc movable between the two gave an infinitely variable drive. A price of £150 was quoted, but very few were sold.

NG

BABY-BROUSSE (CI) 1963–1979

Ateliers et Forges de l'Ébrié, Abidjan.

An ex-patriate Frenchman, Maurice Delignon, was the first person to commercialise a utility car based on the Citroën 2CV chassis, in the style later adopted by the Méhari. Its rigidly flat bodywork was produced in a mixture of steel, aluminium and wood. The same company also developed a Renault 4-based prototype but this did not enter production. In 1969 Citroën acquired the licence to the Baby-Brousse and, by the time production ended in 1979, over 31,000 had been built. Production also took place in Iran from 1970 and at the Citroën factory in Chile between 1972 and 1976; the Chilean version was known as the Yagan.

CR

BABY DAWFIELD see D.P.L.

BABY MOOSE see see CECO

B.A.C. (GB) 1921–1923

British Automotive Co. Ltd, Chelsea, London.

1921 B.A.C. 9.5hp 2-seater.
M.J.WORTHINGTON-WILLIAMS

This was a light car whose prototype was based on the MATHIS, though production cars used Belgian-designed and British-built Peters engines in two sizes, 1207cc 9.5hp and 1498cc 10.8hp. They were 4-cylinder side-valve units, and attempts to convert them to ohv were apparently unsuccessful. The gearbox was a 4-speed Meadows, and final drive was by shaft. Body styles included a 2-seater with dickey and a 4-seater. Probably no more than 20 were made. One of the employees was W.G.Watson, later well-known for his work with INVICTA and LAGONDA.

NG

BACCHUS see ASP

BACHELLE (US) 1900–1903

1900–1903 Otto von Bachelle, Chicago, Illinois.
1903 Bachelle Automobile Co., Chicago, Illinois.

Otto von Bachelle was an electrical engineer who built a small number of cars powered by two separate motors driving the rear wheels. A battery charge was sufficient for 35 miles, not a high figure then or now. Bachelle's formation of a company seemed to be his undoing, for it did not survive 1903. He later worked for E.R. Thomas, maker of the THOMAS Flyer.

NG

BACON (US) 1919–1920

Bacon Motors Corp., New Castle, Pennsylvania.

Frank Bacon built a few cars in Nebraska in 1901, and in 1919 he tried again with a roadster powered by a 35hp Herschell-Spillman engine. A week after the corporation was formed in December 1919 he was killed in a road accident, and although his partners said that they would proceed with manufacture, predicting a daily output of 25 cars by October 1920, little more was heard of the Bacon.

NG

BADAL (IND) 1975–1981

Sunrise Auto Industries Ltd, Bangalore.

This was a bulky-looking 3-wheeler with single front wheel and three doors, two on the nearside and one on the offside. The engine was an Italian-made single-cylinder 2-stroke of only 198cc, mounted at the rear and driving through a 4-speed constant-mesh gearbox. Hydraulic brakes acted on the rear wheels only. Top speed was 47mph (75km/h). In 1981 it was replaced by a 4-wheeler called the Sail, but this was short-lived. 1982 saw the Sail (Sunrise Auto Industries Ltd) Dolphin, a 2-door 4-wheeler closely based on the RELIANT Kitten. This remained in production until 1994, latterly under the marque name SIPANI.

NG

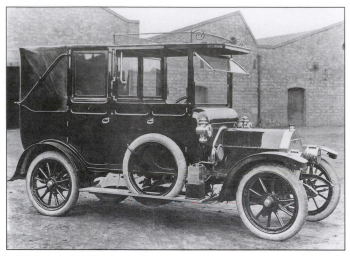

c.1912 Baguley 15/20hp landaulet.
NATIONAL MOTOR MUSEUM

BADEN (US) 1916–1919

Baden, Missouri.

Little is known about this car, made in a suburb of St Louis. They had 4-cylinder engines made in a local foundry, and were built to customers' order, with no advertising or press announcements. It seems that they were of poor quality and unreliable; one car broke four crankshafts in a year. Nevertheless between 30 and 50 Badens were sold.

NG

BADGER (i) *see* F.W.D.

BADGER (ii) (US) 1910–1911

Badger Motor Car Co., Columbus, Wisconsin.

The Badger was made in one model, powered by a 30hp 4-cylinder Northway engine, and offered in tonneau, tourer and roadster forms, at a uniform price of $1500. It lasted for only two seasons, and in 1911 the price of the tourer and roadster was lowered to $1250. The cars were not entirely satisfactory, the Los Angeles agency complaining that the engines were too small. After 237 cars had been made, the company was liquidated, and the factory sold to the Columbus Canning Company.

NG

BADMINTON (F/GB) 1907–1908

Badminton Motors Ltd, Willesden, London.

The first chassis of the car, sold in England as the Badminton, was made in France. One of the designers, a M. Teste, was said to be a well-known racing driver; possibly he was connected with the TESTE ET MORET. The cars were bodied at the Willesden factory, which had formerly been occupied by the British Fiat agency, but it is not certain if complete cars were made there. Two 4-cylinder engines were listed, a 14/20hp of 2.8-litres and a 20hp of 3.4-litres. At least two Badmintons were said to have been sold to China.

NG

BADSEY (GB/ZA/USA) 1978 to date

1981–1983 Bill Badsey, South Africa.

1983 to date Bill Badsey Racing USA, Ventura, Calfornia.

Bill Badsey's first car project was the 1978 Eagle, an attractively-styled targa-topped sports coupé based on BMC 1100 components. However, the Eagle never reached production in Britain (where it was conceived), as in 1979 Badsey emigrated to his native South Africa, where he built the Bullet in 1981. This was an extraordinary three-wheeler, boldly claimed to be capable of reaching 200mph. A very sturdy chassis housed much of the rear end of a Suzuki motorcycle, though the GSX1100 (or 1300cc six-cylinder) engine was sited up front, between the passenger's knees, driving the rear wheel by means of a lengthy chain. Entry was gained by flopping forward a canopy on gas struts. Badsey continued to offer the Bullet from his new California base, and engine choices now encompassed Yamaha Venture, Suzuki GSX and 1.2-litre turbocharged engines with up to 200bhp. A more modest three-wheeler arrived in the form of the Fun Machine. Based on a ladder-type chassis with sizeable outriggers, the Fun Machine used a 552cc DOHC Yamaha Vision motorbike engine mounted just behind the front axle line. It powered the single rear wheel via shaft drive. The driver sat astride the engine and steered via a pair of handlebars to a conventional rack. Front suspension was by lower track control arms, upper rocking arms and coil/spring damper units plus an anti-roll bar, while at the rear a Yamaha Venture swinging arm was used in conjunction with double coil/spring dampers. Badsey went on to make electric go-peds and boats.

CR

BAER (D) 1921–1924

Paul Baer Motorenfabrik GmbH, Berlin.

Founded in 1908 to make engines which were supplied to a number of car makers, this company tried to enter the manufacture of complete cars after World War I. Their product used a 770cc 2-cylinder 2-stroke engine, but few were made.

HON

BAGULEY (GB) 1911–1921

Baguley Cars Ltd, Burton-on-Trent, Staffordshire.

Ernest Edward Baguley was a locomotive engineer who founded the RYKNIELD Engine Co. (later Motor Co.) at Burton-on-Trent in 1903. Burton was, and still is, a centre of the brewing industry, and Baguley was financed by A. Clay, a director of the Bass brewery. Ryknield trucks were widely used by Bass and other Burton breweries. After a spell with B.S.A. for whom he designed their first 4-cylinder cars, Baguley returned to Burton and began to make cars under his own name in the former Ryknield factory. Designed on similar lines to those of the B.S.A., the Baguley was a conventional car with 3306cc 15/20hp 4-cylinder side-valve engine, 4-speed gearbox and worm drive. It was made with open 2- or 5-seater bodies and as a limousine. There was also a Colonial tourer with higher ground clearance. Only 84 Baguley cars were made up to World War I, though two smaller cars were made in the same factory, the ACE (ii) and SALMON. The Baguley was revived briefly after the war as the AE 20/25hp. An extra 3mm of bore gave a capacity of 3530cc, but otherwise the design was unchanged. It had little appeal in the postwar market, and only four or five were made.

NG

Further Reading

M. Worthington-Williams, *The Automobile*, September 1994.

BAILEY (i) (US) 1906–1910

1906–1907 Bailey-Perkins Motor Co., Springfield, Massachusetts.

1907–1910 Bailey Automobile Co., Springfield, Massachusetts.

Bertram Bailey financed production of a car designed by the brothers Julian and James Perkins, who had built their prototype under their own name in 1906. It was a very unusual car, with a 22hp 4-cylinder 2-stroke rotary engine. A more powerful model with 30/35hp engine was announced in 1908. It was unusually tall, with running boards two feet above the ground, so it is hardly surprising that sales were few.

NG

BAILEY (ii) (US) 1907–1916

S.R. Bailey & Co., Amesbury, Massachusetts.

S.R. Bailey was an old-established coachbuilder in a district where there were several, including the better-known Biddle & Smart and Judkins. In 1907 they brought out an electric car which they called the Queen Victoria Phaeton. A range of 80–100 miles per charge was claimed, and the makers said that it was the first designed specifically for the Edison battery. The Phaeton was made with little change from 1907 to 1915, and was joined by other models such as roadsters for two or four passengers, and a cabriolet. Unusually for an American electric car, it was never offered as a closed coupé. Prices were high, at up to $3300 for a 4-seater roadster.

NG

BAILEY-KLAPP *see* ELCO

BAILEY & LAMBERT (GB) 1903–1905

Bailey & Lambert Ltd, London.

This company sold a light car powered by a 6½hp single-cylinder De Dion-Bouton engine. It may have been largely or entirely the product of LACOSTE ET BATTMANN, like so many other contemporary light cars. It was sold as the B & L Wonder in 1903, and as the Pelham in 1904/05.

NG

BAILLEAU (F) 1901–c.1914

A. Bailleau, Longjumeau, Seine-et-Oise.

The Bailleau voiturette was launched at the Paris Salon in December 1901. It was a light 2-seater powered by a 2¾hp single–cylinder De Dion-Bouton engine mounted under the seat. With water-cooled cylinder head the price was the equivalent of £96, full water-cooling costing a further £8. The car had a tubular frame, wheel steering and a dummy bonnet which served as a tool chest. M. Bailleau made a speciality of converting quadricycles to voiturettes, and, said *The Motor Car Journal*, '…he has received so many orders for conversions that an immediate extension of his works has been rendered necessary'. By 1904 the cars had front-mounted engines of 6 or 9hp, still by De Dion, and shaft drive. A 16hp 4-cylinder car appeared in 1906 and in 1911 the range consisted of a 6hp single, 6hp twin and 10/12hp four. Production seems to have petered out soon afterwards, but may have survived until the outbreak of World War I in 1914.

NG

BAILLE-LEMAIRE (F) 1898–1902

Constructeurs Baille-Lemaire, Crosnes, Seine-et-Oise.

This company made a variety of products ranging from steel tubes and headlamps to opera glasses, and built a few cars from time to time. Their first was entered in the tourist class of the 1898 Paris–Amsterdam–Paris race. Described as a Baille-Lemaire carriage, it had an 8hp vertical 2-cylinder engine with air-cooled cylinders and water-cooled heads, and belt final drive. Its successors were on the same lines.

NG

BAILLEREAU (F) 1908

Little is known about this make, which was listed in 1908 only as a shaft-driven voiturette powered by a large single-cylinder engine.

NG

BAILLEUL (F) 1904–1905

Louis Bailleul, Levallois-Perret, Seine.

Listed for one season only, this was a medium-sized car powered by a 14/16hp 4-cylinder engine.

NG

BAINES (GB) 1900

Baines Ltd, Gainsborough, Lincolnshire.

Baines were established as bicycle makers in 1886, and in 1900 announced a light 'cycle-built' car powered by a 2¼ hp De Dion-Bouton engine, with steel tube frame and belt drive. It was designed by F.L. Baines who had worked with R.M. Wright on GODIVA and STONEBOW cars. A price of £100 was quoted, but production never started.

NG

BAJA (A) 1920–1925

1920–1921 N. von Jacabffy GmbH, Vienna.
1921 Bartsch & Frankmann, Vienna.
1921–1924 Baja Cyclecar Co., Vienna.
1924–1925 Fiscgamender Werke AG, Vienna.

Designed by Max Bartsch, this cyclecar was available as a single- or 2-seater, powered by a 460cc Hiero single-cylinder engine mounted at the rear and driving the right rear wheel by chain. In 1922 a 602cc 2/8PS water-cooled engine was substituted. A 790cc 2-cylinder engine was also offered. The body was of self-supporting chassisless construction, which made for a very light vehicle.

HON

1914 Bailey (ii) electric roadster.
NATIONAL MOTOR MUSEUM

c.1906 Bailleau 2-seater.
NATIONAL MOTOR MUSEUM

BAJAJ (IND) 1959 to date

Bajaj can trace its origins back to 1945 and it began importing Piaggio 3-wheelers into India as early as 1948. It won a licence to build these from 1959, as well as scooters. Its main three-wheeled output was miniature trucks and rickshaws, and it also produced the German Tempo 3-wheeled truck. It made a new break with the Tempo Trax range of rugged off-road utility vehicles. Power came from a 2.4-litre ACT turbodiesel engine developing 88bhp and a wide range of body styles was available, from double-cab to 4-door convertible. The resemblance to a Mercedes G-Wagen was not overly cheeky, as many of the mechanical components derived from Mercedes. Subsequent versions came with a variety of bodywork, including a 6-door limousine and glassfibre-bodied Matador. Both 2- and 4-wheel drive systems could be fitted. Other than scooters, in 1998 the only passenger cars being made were the Autorickshaw 3-wheeler and the Trax range.

CR

BAKER (i) (US) 1897–1899; 1902

1899 National Machine Co., Hartford, Connecticut.
1902 Worcester Cycle Co., Worcester, Massachusetts.

Herbert C. Baker planned to build motor carriages and marine engines in the plant of the Mather Electric Company at Hartford, backed by English capital. Nothing seems to have emerged from this idea, but in 1899 he announced that he was making a 3-cylinder car in the plant of the National Machine Co., also in Hartford. It is not certain that any cars were made there, but in 1902 he cropped up again in Worcester where he did complete at least two cars, still with 3-cylinder engines.

NG

BAKER (ii) (US) 1899–1916

1899–1915 Baker Motor Vehicle Co., Cleveland, Ohio.
1915–1916 Baker, Rauch & Lang Co., Cleveland, Ohio.

The Baker was one of the best-known electric cars in America, helped by the energy and enthusiasm of its inventor, Walter C. Baker. He helped Henry Morris and Pedro Salom with their Electrobat cars made in Philadelphia in 1893, and then set up the American Ball Bearing Co. in Cleveland in 1898. The same year he established the Baker Motor Vehicle Co. with the help of his father-in-law Rollin C. White, best known for his WHITE cars and trucks, and also for the ROLLIN car in the 1920s.

The first Baker electric was a simple tiller-steered 2-seater runabout selling for $850. An early customer was the electrical engineer, Thomas Edison, who bought one as his first car. The runabout and the better-equipped Phaeton Stanhope were the only models until 1904, when the range expanded to four styles, including the curiously-named Physician's Chapalete. By 1907 no fewer than fourteen models were listed, from a Stanhope on a 68in (1726mm) wheelbase to an Inside Drive Coupé on a 92in (2335mm) wheelbase. The most expensive model was the Extension Front Brougham, whose driver sat high up behind the passengers as in a hansom cab, which sold for $4000. Annual production reached 400 in 1905 and doubled to 800 the following year, making Baker the biggest producer of electrics in the world. Only in about 1913 were they overtaken by DETROIT. Trucks were introduced in 1907 and were made in several sizes up to 5 tons. In 1910 shaft drive was introduced on some models; the runabouts had bonnets giving them the appearance of petrol cars. Among prominent owners of Baker electrics were the King of Siam, 'Diamond Jim' Brady, and Mrs William Howard Taft, wife of the President of the United States. By 1914 Baker were losing sales to Detroit and other companies, and the following year they merged with another Cleveland electric car maker, RAUCH & LANG. Baker cars were made only into the 1916 season, while Rauch & Lang lasted until 1920 in Cleveland, and for several more years at Chicopee Falls, Massachusetts. As Baker, Rauch & Lang they also made the OWEN MAGNETIC car, the chassis in the Baker factory, the bodies by R & L. Baker continued to make electric industrial trucks, while R & L under the name Raulang made bodies for a variety of middle-sized car makers, including Biddle, Franklin, Jordan, Lexington, Reo, Stanley, and Wills Sainte Claire. Walter Baker joined the board of Peerless in 1919.

NG

BAKER (iii) (US) 1917–1924

Baker Steam Motor Car & Manufacturing Co., Pueblo and Denver, Colorado.
The Baker Steam Car was more fancy than fact, although touring cars and a roadster were produced, as well as a steam truck, mostly in the early 1920s. After the production of steam vehicles had been halted, Baker boilers, designed by Dr Hartley O. Baker, were used successfully as replacements on Stanley cars.

KM

BAKER-BELL (US) 1913

Baker-Bell Motor Co., Philadelphia, Pennsylvania.
This company made a small 2-seater roadster called the Hummingbird. It had a 22.5hp 4-cylinder engine and cost $675. It was only made for one season, but a delivery van on the same chassis lasted into 1914. Baker-Bell were also agents for the Commerce truck, and were probably more active as dealers than as manufacturers.

NG

BAKER & DALE (GB) 1913

Baker & Dale Ltd, Southbourne, Hampshire.
Designed by T.A. Hubert, the Baker & Dale cyclecar had a 2-cylinder engine and long belt drive, also a semi-circular steering wheel said to be a feature of other cyclecars designed by Mr Hubert. Less than a month after the announcement of the Baker & Dale, *The Cyclecar* announced another car of his design, a tandem 2-seater powered by a single-cylinder Buckingham engine. This appeared to have a conventional steering wheel.

NG

BALASHI (US) 1999

Balashi Autoworks & Carriage, Lantana, Florida.
The Balashi was a Lamborghini Countach replica based on Pontiac Fiero running gear. They also sold a Lambo golf car body.

HP

BALATON (H) 1955

Székesfehérvári Motorjavító Vállalat, Székesfehérvár.
The Székesfehérvár Motor Repair Company, headquarters of the Hungarian microcar project under the umbrella of the Ministry of Metallurgy and Engineering created two bubblecars in 1955: the ALBA REGIA and the Balaton. The latter was named after the biggest lake in Hungary. It was designed by József Zappel, but its suspension, with the arms held by rubber tags, was the idea of Ernő Rubik, Hungarian aeroplane designer and father of the inventor of the Rubik cube. All other mechanical parts were shared with the Alba Regia. The second difference was the body: the roof and the doors of the Balaton formed one unit and had to be pushed backwards to gain access to the cabin. It was made in aeroplane fashion again.

PN

Further Reading
'Hungarian Microcars, part II', *Classic Car Mart*, December 1996.

BALBO (I) 1953

Carrozzeria Balbo, Turin.
Alfonso Balbo set up a coachbuilding firm as early as 1914 and after World War II it applied itself in a rather different direction with a microcar prototype. The Balbo B400 was presented at the 1953 Turin Motor Show as a small 2-seater roll-top coupé. Its 398cc 14.9bhp 2-stroke twin-cylinder engine was rear-mounted in unit with the gearbox and differential. A prominent styling feature was an American-style chrome 'jet-intake' ornament on the nose. It did nothing that the Fiat Topolino was not already doing, and never passed the prototype stage.

CR

BALBOA (US) 1924–1925

Balboa Motors Corp., Fullerton, California.
The Balboa was a car ahead of its time, both mechanically and in its sleek design, and, although widely promoted on a local basis, never managed to proceed beyond three prototypes. Designed by William H. Radford, chief engineer of the corporation, the initial pilot model was completed in early 1924. The Balboa was equipped with a straight-8 supercharged engine, designed by him, producing 100bhp. The engine had been designed by Radford during the engineer's earlier association with the Kessler Motor Co. of Detroit, Michigan. It contained two 2¼ in diameter rotary transfer valves extending the length of the engine on each side of the base of its cylinders. Tru-arc disc wheels and 4-wheel hydraulic brakes were also used. The wheelbase measured 131in (3325mm), and the car was debuted in March 1924 at the Ambassador Hotel in Los Angeles, California. Problems with the engine resulted in a replacement with a Continental 8-cylinder L-head engine. Ultimately, a second car – a Brougham – was completed, plus a bare chassis, the latter with a 127in (3223mm) wheelbase. The three prototypes had been constructed in a former wire plant in an area of orange groves, and prices for the car were listed from $2900 for the first unit completed – a touring car – and up. Difficulties with the modified Kessler engine and alleged stock manipulation ended the Balboa shortly following its final exhibition at Santa Ana, California, in March 1925.

KM

BALDELLI (I) 1972

Baldelli, Sicily.
In 1972 this Sicilian company showed the Murena, an odd-looking twin-headlamp coupé. It had a tubular sub-structure and light alloy bodywork and could be fitted with 1300 or 1600cc engines. Intended production never materialised.

CR

BALDI (I) c.1973–c.1976

G.A.M.C., San Remo.
Going under the delightful name of Baldi Frog, this Italian microcar was as aesthetically unpleasing as its name suggested. It used Fiat 500 mechanicals and a tall estate-type plastic body. As an alternative to Fiat 2-cylinder rear-mounted power, 125cc and 302cc engines were also offered. Baldi's other model was the Sahara 4, a Renault 4-based plastic-bodied leisure vehicle that closely resembled the Renault Rodeo.

CR

BALDNER (US) 1900–1903

1900–1902 Baldner Brothers, Xenia, Ohio.
1902–1903 Baldner Motor Vehicle Co., Xenia, Ohio.
Jacob Baldner had worked with Charles Duryea in Peoria, Illinois, on early DURYEA (i) cars before he built a prototype tiller-steered 2-cylinder 2-seater buggy with his brother Fred. After forming their Motor Vehicle Company they launched a wheel-steered model with 8hp 3-cylinder engine, and for 1903 a more ambitious 20hp 3-cylinder 4-seater tonneau. Apparently they had difficulty in balancing the engine, and discontinued production late in 1903, after only nine cars had been made. Fred was later connected with the XENIA cyclecar, while Jacob was unwise enough to sue Henry Ford over a transmission design. The case lasted until the mid-1920s, when Jacob lost, after doubtless paying enormous legal fees.
NG

BALDWIN (i) (US) 1899–1901

Baldwin Automobile Co., Providence, Rhode Island.
L.F.N. Baldwin built a steam van for a local department store in 1896, and three years later he completed a 4-seater steam car with vertical 2-cylinder engine, single-chain drive and typical spidery appearance. This was to be built by the Baldwin Automobile Co. but there is no evidence that production extended beyond the one car. He then built the BALDWIN (ii) in Pennsylvania.
NG

BALDWIN (ii) (US) 1899–1901

Baldwin Automobile Manufacturing Co., Connellsville, Pennsylvania.
This was L.F.N. Baldwin's venture in Pennsylvania, and was not much more successful than the one in Rhode Island. The car was similar to the earlier one, though the body seated only two passengers. Not more than 12 cars were delivered, one surprisingly finding its way to Hawaii where it was bought by Queen Liliuokalani. After several reorganisations, Baldwin returned to Providence, where he took on agencies for White and Stanley steam cars.
NG

BALDWIN-MOTION (US) 1967 to date

Motion Performance Inc., Baldwin, Long Island, New York.
Chevrolet performance parts were the primary business for this company when owner/designer Joel Rosen partnered with dealership Baldwin Chevrolet to sell high-performance versions of Chevrolet passenger cars. Starting with a new Corvette, they added a bonnet scoop, vents, and plexiglass-covered headlights to produce the Phase III GT. The three versions (SS-350, SS-454, and SS-427) were based on engine size. They were sold in fully assembled form or the individual components could be purchased separately. In 1971 Baldwin-Motion added a complete Mako Shark body kit that replicated the Chevrolet show car of the same name. They also sold modified Camaros, Chevelles and very quick V8-powered Vegas. Although the last new Baldwin-Motion car was built in 1974, Motion continued to sell fibreglass body kits and performance parts.
HP

BALL (US) 1902–1903

Miami Cycle & Manufacturing Co., Middletown, Ohio.
Charles A. Ball had built a steam car as early as 1868, in Paterson, New Jersey, but local prejudice prevented his using it for long. By 1902 the climate for cars was more favourable, and Ball built a large steam car in Middletown, Ohio. Called the Ramapaugh after an Indian tribe, it was one of the biggest cars of its day, with an engine developing a claimed 60hp, a weight of over 2 tons and an 8-seater touring body. Petrol capacity was 24 gallons and water capacity 68 gallons. A fatal accident to a small boy forced Ball to leave town in April 1902, and he returned east where he sold the car to New York's Waldorf Astoria Hotel. He then built two more, similar in design and size to the Ramapaugh, which he sold for $10,000 each. These were probably built for him by the New York Gear Works. Suggestions that they were made in Middletown are less credible, in view of the bad reputation the fatal accident had earned him there.
NG

c.1925 Ballot 2LTS 2-seater by Compton.
NATIONAL MOTOR MUSEUM

1925 Ballot 2LTS fabric saloon.
NICK GEORGANO/NATIONAL MOTOR MUSEUM

BALLARD (US) 1901–1902

H.C. Ballard & Son, Oshkosh, Wisconsin.
Gunsmith A.W. Ballard (1845–1922) built his first car in 1894, a 2-cylinder buggy with engine over the rear axle which was driven by chain. Another was sold to a local doctor shortly afterwards, and in February 1901 a company was formed to make a 4-seater dos-à-dos with engine located, as before, at the rear and driving the rear axle by chain. Probably few were made, and there were no further references to the Ballard car after 1902.
NG

BALLOT (F) 1921–1932

Éts Ballot SA, Paris.
Ernest Ballot was a marine engineer who founded a company to make marine engines in 1906. He soon extended his range to power units for cars and commercial vehicles; among his customers were important firms such as Delage, La Licorne and Mass. The company was re-formed in 1910 as Établissements Ballot SA, directors including two prominent car makers, Adolphe CLEMENT-BAYARD and Fernand CHARRON. Some complete taxicabs were made, but the first Ballot cars did not appear until after World War I, during which Hispano-Suiza V8 aero-engines were made. The company earned fame with racing cars whose engines were as different from the pedestrian prewar side-valve units as can be imagined. Designed by Ernest Henry, the father of the twin-ohc layout, they were 4.9- and then 3-litre straight-8s which competed at Indianapolis in 1919 and in the French Grands Prix in 1920 and 1921. A twin-cam four also ran in the 1921 Grand Prix, and its engine formed the basis of the first road-going Ballot, the 2LS, which had a capacity of 1994cc and four valves per cylinder. Announced in 1921 it was made as a 2-seater sports car or 3-seater cloverleaf and was, inevitably, very expensive. On the British market it cost £1350, compared with £795 for the single-camshaft 2LT which joined it and eventually took over. Top speed was 93mph (150km/h). Not more than 100 were made, up to 1924, by which time production was concentrated on the

Conduite Intérieure quatre places
Licence Weymann
sur châssis 8 cylindres long

1930 Ballot RH3 4-seater coupé.
NATIONAL MOTOR MUSEUM

single-ohc models. The few lucky purchasers of the 2LS were very enthusiastic. An English owner, J. Lucas-Scudamore, writing in *The Autocar* in 1924 said '...the Ballot, in my opinion, is the most wonderful car in the world, and I defy anyone to produce a car which would not have collapsed long ago....under the terrible gruelling to which I have subjected this one'. However, he added that he would not recommend it to any old or nervous person! The expensive 2LS could never have reached a wide market, and in order to broaden their sales Ballot asked Henry to design a cheaper car with a single-ohc. He felt this was beneath his dignity, and left to join Sunbeam-Talbot-Darracq.

Designed by Fernand Vadier, the 2LT had the same cylinder dimensions as the 2LS, but a single camshaft and two valves per cylinder. Output was 48bhp, compared with 75bhp for the 2LS. The 2LT was a more tractable car, as well as more reasonably priced, and was suitable for touring as well as sports bodies. It had a 4-speed gearbox, and 4-wheel brakes (with Dewandre vacuum servo from 1925). From 1924 the engine could be supplied in high-performance form, with hemispherical combustion chambers and inclined valves, this car being known as the 2LTS. Power was about 60bhp. About 1500 2LTs were made, and 500 of the 2LTS. When the 2LTS was announced, quality 2-litre cars tended to have more than four cylinders, so the 2LT6 was launched at the 1926 Paris Salon. It never went into production, and for 1928 Ballot moved from a six to a straight-8, the 2618cc RH. This proved to be underpowered, and the engine was hastily bored out to give 2874cc, and finally to 3050cc on the 105bhp RH3 listed from 1929 to 1932. The 6- and 8-cylinder engines were not designed in house by Vadier but by a Unic engineer, Marzloff. Apparently Vadier and Marzloff never even met, an unsatisfactory situation as Vadier designed the chassis. The RH3 was a good-looking car on a 130in (3300mm) or 142in (3604mm) wheelbase, and eminently suited to elegant coachwork by firms like Figoni and Vanvooren. The single-ohc was gear-driven, unlike the shaft drive on the 2LT series, Dewandre servo brakes were standard, and the last models had constant-mesh gears. However, sales were disappointing (about 580 of all straight-8s from 1927 onwards), and Ballot was in decline. Ernest had been dismissed by Pierre Forgeot who headed the board, and the company was taken over by HISPANO-SUIZA in 1930. They gave more power to the RH3 chassis by installing their own 4580cc 6-cylinder engine. This car was marketed at first as the Ballot HS26 (Hispano-Suiza 26CV), and in the autumn of 1931 was renamed the Hispano-Suiza Junior. It lasted only to 1933, when the factory was turned over to the manufacture of diesel engines.

NG

Further Reading
'Ernest Ballot, a look at a Defaced Monument', Griffith Borgeson,
Automobile Quarterly, Vol. 15, No.2.
'Ballot's Production Era', Griffith Borgeson,
Automobile Quarterly, Vol. 20, No.2.
The 2-litre and 8-cylinder Ballots, Paul Frere, Profile Publications, 1967.

BALZER (US) 1894–1900
1894–1898 Stephen M. Balzer, Bronx, New York.
1898–1900 Balzer Motor Carriage Co., Bronx, New York.
Stephen Balzer was probably the first man to use a rotary engine in a motor car. His prototype of 1894, which still exists in the Smithsonian Institution

in Washington, DC, had a 10hp 3-cylinder rotary engine mounted vertically, revolving round a fixed horizontal crankshaft and driving one rear wheel by gearing. There were three forward speeds but no reverse, not a serious problem as the whole car was less than 6ft long. Balzer built three cars before he formed a company in 1898, and promised to build 100 more. How many he did make is uncertain, but is likely to have been much less than that. He also experimented with a 5-cylinder rotary engine, and this was used in the 1906 CAREY, also built in the Bronx.

NG

BAMA (F) 1921–1922
Charles Barrelier, Asnieres, Seine.
This was a very light 3-wheeled cyclecar resembling a bath chair, powered by a rear-mounted 285cc flat-twin engine. Final drive, surprisingly for so small a car, was by shaft to a differential-equipped rear axle. Top speed was a heady 22mph (35km/h).

NG

BAMBI (i) (E) 1954
Manufacturas Mecanicas Aleu SA, Barcelona.
The short-lived product of a firm better known for motorcycles, which were made from 1953 to about 1960, the Bambi was a very light 3-wheeler with doorless open 2-seater body, and 125cc single-cylinder Hispano-Villiers engine driving the rear wheel by chain. It weighed only 320lb (145kg), and top speed was 45mph (75km/h).

NG

BAMBI (ii) (RA) 1961
Fabrica de Automotores Utilitarios Saicf, Buenos Aires.
A member of the board of Fabrica de Automotores utilitarios Saicf visited West Germany in 1958 and contacted Elektromaschinenbau Fulda GmbH, makers of the FULDAMOBIL microcar. A licence was granted for Fuldamobil production in Argentina, under the Bambi name. Saloon and pick-up versions of the Bambi powered by Sachs 200cc 10.2bhp engines were produced. It was estimated that first year production would be 800 units. In fact, only 480 vehicles were produced.

ACT

BAMBY (GB) 1983–1985
Alan Evans, Hull, Humberside.
A microcar enthusiast called Alan Evans was inspired by his acquisition of a PEEL P50 to create a modern equivalent. Like the Peel, the Bamby was a single-seater glassfibre-bodied 3-wheeler with a 49cc engine. Braking was by hydraulic discs on the front wheels, there was handlebar steering (later a conventional wheel) and the transmission was a 3-speed automatic. It weighed only 235lb (107kg) and could return 100mpg. Early examples had a single gull-wing door, later changed to a conventionally hinged door. The engine was progressively upgraded from a 49cc Minarelli to Yamaha, then Suzuki moped units. An initial production rate of 20 per month proved over-optimistic, and the Bamby was too expensive at £1389 plus tax to score much success with its target market of 16-year olds and housewives. Probably around 50 Bambys were made.

CR

B&B see ISDERA

B&B COBRA (US) 1999 to date
B&B Cobra Manufacturing, Granby, Missouri.
B&B duplicated the 427 Cobra on a steel tube frame with Ford Mustang II suspension. Sold in kit and fully assembled form.

HP

B&S see E.W.M.

BANDINI (I) 1947–1963
Autocostruzione Bandini, Forli.
Bandini was one of the many small Italian constructors which flourished in the early postwar period. The first car, which appeared in 1947, used a tuned Fiat 500 engine in a tubular frame, made from small diameter tubes, and was

sufficiently successful to lead to Bandini making small numbers of similar cars. By 1952 Bandini was concentrating on the 750cc class with a Fiat-derived engine of 759cc (59×63.5mm) with twin overhead camshafts. Front suspension was by coil springs and double wishbones, and although Fiat's influence was apparent through the design, the number of actual Fiat parts was small; as an instance, the transmission castings were Fiat but the internals were Bandini.

When the Italians discovered that they had no answer to British manufacturers in the 500cc Formula Three, they instigated their own 750cc national 'Formula Three'. Bandini made a number of dual purpose cars which could be run in the Italian 'F3' and, by the addition of lights and mudguards, could become sports cars, and these enjoyed some success in the early 1950s.

Bandini tried to break in the American market, but in common with others who used Fiat-based 750cc engines, he discovered he could not compete with Crosley-based specials. Bandini therefore offered cars fitted with Crosley engines and they were competitive throughout the 1950s.

Bandini soldiered on until 1961 when he produced a front-engined Formula Junior which was obsolete even when the first drawings were made. The marque more or less ended there, but there was a later attempt to revive with a pretty, mid-engined, 750cc car which arrived when everybody else had lost interest in the class.

ML

BANDIT (GB) 1995–1997
Concept Car Company, Oxford.
One could hardly fail to have an opinion about the styling of the Bandit, which was described by the manufacturer as 'radically different'. Launched at the 1995 Frankfurt Motor Show, it was an extraordinary open-topped 4-seater with a sculptural feel that blended sports, buggy and hot rod styles. It used a space frame chassis and composite bodywork and a Rover 1.4-litre K-series engine, though 1.5-litre Peugeot diesels were also offered. Soft and hard tops, as well as detachable doors, were optional, and cars were supplied either in kit form or complete.

CR

BANGERT (US) c.1954–1963
Bangert, Los Angeles, California.
Noel Bangert built a number of kit car bodies that were popular with racers as well as street car builders. His first was a simple cigar-shaped sports car with cycle mudguards, but his most popular model was a full-width enclosed kit. It sat on a tubular Bangert frame that used prewar Ford suspension, a shortened American sedan or the Kurtis 500KK kit car chassis. This body had an oval grill, various headlight options and cut-back mudguard openings like a Ferrari 250 Testarossa. The last Bangert body appeared in the late 1950s and was popular with Bonneville top-speed racers. It had side indentations like then-current Corvettes, with a Ferrari-like nose and tail. Bangert sold the moulds for his bodies to John Treverbaugh in 1959, who sold them to Tom Bednar in 1960. Bednar advertised them for sale in 1963.

HP

BANKER (US) 1905
A.C. Banker Co., Chicago, Illinois.
Billed as 'A Chicago Car for Chicago People', the Banker was a conventional 4-seater tonneau powered by a 4.6-litre 4-cylinder engine with shaft drive. The body was of wood construction at $2250 or aluminium at $2500, while a limousine in either material cost $3000. Evidently not many Chicago people bought Bankers, for the make did not survive into 1906.

NG

BANKER JUVENILE ELECTRIC (US) 1905
Banker Brothers Co., Pittsburgh, Pennsylvania.
The Banker brothers were successful car dealers who dabbled in manufacture of cars for their own use, from 1895 onwards. The only model they put on sale was a light 2-seater electric runabout for children powered by a 1.5hp Westinghouse motor. Top speed was about 11mph (19km/h), though this could be governed to a lower speed if parents thought it desirable. The price was $600.

NG

BANNER BOY BUCKBOARD (US) 1958
Banner Welder Inc., Milwaukee, Wisconsin.
While most replicars recalled grand classics, the maker of the Banner Boy Buckboard chose the ultra-simple BRIGGS & STRATTON buckboard for inspiration. They even used a Briggs & Stratton 2.75hp single-cylinder air-cooled engine. Unlike the original, drive was not to a fifth wheel but to the right rear-wheel by centrifugal clutch and V-belt.

NG

BANTAM (i) (GB) 1913
Slack & Harrison Ltd, Kegworth, Leicestershire.
The Bantam differed little from many other cyclecars, having an 8hp V-twin Precision engine, with belt and variable pulley transmission and chain final drive.

NG

BANTAM (ii) (US) 1914
Bantam Motor Co., Boston, Massachusetts.
This was an attractive-looking cyclecar with a 14hp air-cooled V-twin engine under a Renault-type bonnet. Wire wheels and flared wings completed a sporty appearance. Transmission was by friction discs and final drive by chain. For a factory the makers rented a corner of the LENOX Motor Company's service facilities, and Bantam production was minimal.

NG

BANTAM (iii) see AMERICAN AUSTIN

BAR HARBOR (US) 1900–1902
Boston Automobile Co., Bar Harbor, Maine.
The fashionable summer resort of Bar Harbor might seem an unlikely location for a car factory, but the owners said 'Each summer brings just the class of people to the town who can afford to indulge in the automobile luxury'. The car was a light steamer made in 2- and 4-seater models selling for $700 and $1000 respectively. Orders came from far and wide, including two from Lancashire, England and one (a single-seater) from Bombay, India. Nevertheless the company failed by 1902. The cars were originally called Standards, then Bostons, before the Bar Harbor name was adopted in February 1901.

NG

BARADAT-ESTEVE (E) 1922
Cortina Baradat y Esteve, Barcelona.
This was a conventional-looking car powered by a most unusual engine, a 4-piston Torus unit in which the pistons worked in an annular cylinder or circular tube, transmitting power to a crankshaft in the centre of the tube. The engine was designed for aircraft, and was said to deliver 110bhp at 16,000rpm, from a capacity of only 2-litres. However, as with the later Wankel engine, one had to use an equivalence factor to calculate capacity, as the cylinder was so completely different from that of a conventional engine. Suspension was unconventional too, by longitudinal coils running parallel with the chassis frame, as in the Citroën 2CV. The car was designed by the brothers Claudio and Carlos Baradat Guille, and financed by Federico Esteve Anglada. The small factory belonged to Esteve and his partner Senor Cortina who held the agency for Austin, Maxwell, and Moon cars, and later MGs. It is said that 12 Baradat-Esteve cars were made, but this figure probably includes some other cars, including an Austin, in which the engines were used as test beds.

NG

BARBARINO (US) 1924–1925
Barbarino Motor Car Corp., New York, New York.
Salvatore Barbarino was an automobile designer and engineer, who took over assets of the defunct RICHELIEU company in 1923 and set out to market a small car of his own design. The Barbarino, of which an estimated ten were completed, was a high-grade product, including a 4-cylinder Le Roi engine of Barbarino's design. Four–wheel brakes, a high, rounded radiator, wheelbase of 110 in (2792mm) and bodies built to the customer's order, by Churpurdy Auto Coach of New York City, completed the basic specifications.

KM

1901 Bardon 5hp spyder.
NATIONAL MOTOR MUSEUM

BARCAR (GB) 1904–1906
Phoenix Motor Co., Southport, Lancashire.
The Barcar had a vertical 10hp 3-cylinder engine in which the middle cylinder had a larger bore than the other two, working off the exhaust gases of its smaller neighbours. This engine was enclosed with clutch and transmission in an aluminium base bolted to the chassis. The name was derived from those of the two sponsors, W.H. Barrett and C.C. Cardell who had previously made the PHOENIX (ii). The Phoenix company later made motor boat engines at Altrincham, Cheshire.
NG

BARCHETTA (GB) 1993–1996
Simpatico, The Dove Company Ltd, East Dereham, Norfolk.
In between designing the McLaren F1 and the Jaguar XJR-15, Peter Stevens penned the Barchetta 595, a car that betrayed his passion for the Fiat 500. Based on a Fiat 126 floorpan, it was a finely proportioned little doorless GRP/Kevlar tub looking like a topless Fiat 500 with fat wheelarches. Kits were rather expensive for a chassis-less body, but quality was high, thanks to The Dove Company, which had been responsible for the plastics in the Jaguar XJ220. Only around 12 Barchettas were made.
CR

BARCLAY (GB) 1933
Barclay Motors Ltd, Aston, Birmingham.
The Barclay project was unusual in that the makers planned to make a family saloon at a time when such cars were already the preserve of the major mass producers. It was an assembled car with 1122cc Coventry-Climax engine (as used in the 10hp Crossley which it slightly resembled), Moss gearbox, Spicer joints and an ENV spiral bevel rear axle. A pre-selector was an alternative to the 4-speed synchromesh gearbox. It was described as having good road-holding and a brisk performance, despite a high axle ratio of 4.6:1. The 4-door saloon body was made by Jensen, and the car was 'intended to appeal primarily to lady drivers', but it did not get beyond the prototype stage.
NG

BARDON (F) 1899–1903
1899–1901 SA des Automobiles et Traction (système Bardon), Puteaux, Seine.
1901–1903 Automobiles Bardon, Puteaux, Seine.
Louis Bardon's cars used horizontal opposed-piston engines of Gobron-Brillie type, with two pistons, crankshafts and flywheels per cylinder. The crankshafts meshed with a transverse shaft which engaged with a differential shaft to provide three speeds. Final drive was by double-chains. The first Bardon had a 4/5hp single-cylinder engine mounted under the floor, supplemented by a front-mounted 10hp twin in 1901. In that year he merged with the Gaillardet company, makers of proprietary engines and the DOCTORESSE car. Bardons

were made in Frederic Gaillardet's factory, at least for some of the company's life. Financial backing came from Pierre de la Ville le Roulx, who was also involved with WESTINGHOUSE. Bardon also made commercial vehicles which survived the cars by one year. There was no production from 1905 to 1906 when his factory was acquired by Georges Richard for the manufacture of UNIC cars. A majority shareholding in Richard's company was held by Baron Henri de Rothschild who owned the land on which the Bardon factory was built.
NG

BARISON (I) 1923–1925
Fabbrica Automobili Barison, Livorno.
Designed by Silvio Barison, this was a short-lived car powered by a 2474cc 4-cylinder rotary valve engine developing 55bhp. Only 25 were made before financial difficulties brought about the end of the firm.
NG

BARNARD (GB) 1921–1922
A. Ward, St Mark's Engineering Co., London.
The Barnard was made in touring and sports models, both powered by 1169cc air-cooled 4-cylinder Henderson motorcycle engines which were possibly war surplus units. A 3-speed gearbox without reverse transmitted power to a chain-driven rear axle. A dummy bullnose radiator characterised the cars, and sporting models had a long straight-through exhaust pipe running the length of the body.
NG

BARNES (i) (GB) 1904–1906
1904–1905 George A. Barnes, Lewisham, London.
1905–1906 George A. Barnes, Deptford, London.
Although he never seems to have formed a company, George Barnes made a number of tricars with 5hp engines mounted ahead of the front wheels and driving the single rear wheel by a long chain or V-belt. The price was 58 guineas (£60.90). When he was at the Deptford address he was described in trade directories as a motor car maker, and justified this by advertising a 4-wheeled light car powered by a 12hp 4-cylinder engine, available in 2- or 4-seater forms. This was announced in January 1906, but does not seem to have lasted out the year. He also made tricars with 6, 8 or 12hp engines.
NG

BARNES (ii) (US) 1907–1910
Barnes Manufacturing Co., Sandusky, Ohio.
This company launched two cars in 1907, the Barnes and the SERVITOR. The latter lasted only one year, but the Barnes was made until at least 1910, possibly up to 1912. It was a roadster with 4-cylinder air-cooled engine. It is possible that the man behind it was H.C. Barnes who took over the ANHUT Motor Car Co. in 1910.
NG

BARNHART (US) 1905
Warren Automobile Co., Warren, Pennsylvania.
H. F. Barnhart built his first car in 1897 when he was in dental school, and another in 1899, both in association with his father-in-law C. D. Betts. In 1905 he put a car on the market, a large tourer with 44hp 4-cylinder engine and an automatic control in which one or more cylinders could be cut out, a forerunner of Cadillac's unsuccessful 4–6–8 system of the 1980s. The $3500 Barnhart lasted only one year, after which its maker returned exclusively to dentistry. It was alternatively called the Warren, after its home town.
NG

BAROQUE see KNUDSEN

BAROSSO (I) 1923–1924
Officine Barosso, Novara.
The Barosso was a small cyclecar powered by a 495cc single-cylinder engine. A pedal-operated gearchange gave two forward speeds and one reverse, and final drive was by chain.
NG

BARRETT (GB) c.1948–c.1960

Based in Bath, Barrett made a number of invalid tricycles, starting with conventional tiller-steered vehicles powered by 250cc single-cylinder Villiers engines with 3-speed gearboxes. The Model 41 of 1949 was intended for 'patients up to 20 stone living in hilly districts'. In the mid-1950s the Model 58 Barrett Minor had a fully-enclosed fibreglass coupé body intended for small persons with short arm reach. This was followed by the Model 60 Barrett Midget for patients up to 4ft 6in tall, also with a fibreglass body but it was a convertible with a canvas hood.

NG

BARRÉ (F) 1899–1930

1899–1908 Gaston Barré, Niort, Deux-Sevres.
1908–1923 G. Barré et Cie, Niort, Deux-Sevres.
1923–1927 Barré et Lamberthon, Niort, Deux-Sevres.
1927–1930 SA des Automobiles Barré, Niort, Deux-Sevres.

The Barré was one of those regional French firms which never achieved great fame outside their own area, yet made sound and reliable vehicles for thirty years. At the 1899 Paris Salon they showed a 3-seater light car, one seat for 'a child or light person' facing the other two, with a 4hp Gaillardet engine, 2-speed transmission and belt final drive. They used mostly proprietary engines, 1901 models having 4hp single-cylinder De Dion-Bouton, 2-cylinder Aster, and 4-cylinder Buchet engines. In 1903 these were used in tubular chassis for the small model, and armoured wood frames for the larger. They had 3-speed gearboxes with direct drive on top, and shaft drive. Apart from the engines and tyres, the whole car was made in-house, including bodies. These were the usual 2-seater, 4-seater rear-entrance tonneau, and a limousine. Barré began exporting cars early, and by 1903 had shipped cars to the Transvaal, India, and Indo-China.

Gaston Barré did not form a company until 1908, when about 50 people were making several models, from an 8hp with De Dion-Bouton or Ballot 2-cylinder engine, a 9hp with large De Dion-Bouton single, to a 12/16hp 4-cylinder Ballot-engined tourer. In 1912 seven models were listed, from 8/10hp to 24/30hp, all with 4-cylinder monobloc engines and shaft drive. Bodies were still made in-house, and this probably lasted for the whole of the marque's lifetime. For power units Barré relied on Ballot, as they did in the 1920s. By then their range had slimmed down, being confined to fours of 1131 to 2813cc. Front wheel brakes were available on the 1692cc torpedo sport in 1924. Production dwindled in the later 1920s, and probably no Barrés were made after 1930, though the marque was listed up to 1932. The range then consisted of three 4-cylinder models, the 8/10hp B5, 10/18hp BS and 12/24hp AS2.

NG

Further Reading
'Les Fins Voitures du Barré', M. Worthington-Williams, *The Automobile*, April 1999.

BARREIROS (E) 1951–1969

Barreiros Diesel, Madrid.

Founded in 1951, Eduardo Barreiros first produced a number of trucks and, especially, diesel engines, which were much needed in Spain. In 1963 he signed a contract with CHRYSLER to build the Dodge Dart in Spain as the Barreiros Dart, the largest Spanish postwar car. A special Spanish version called the 3700 GT had rectangular headlamps, a different radiator grill and a 4-speed gearbox, as well as disc brakes on all wheels. From 1966 the SIMCA 1000 was also produced in Madrid. In 1969 the Barreiros brothers had to leave the company, which passed to the Chrysler European Division. Later, the same factory built the Simca 1200 and Chrysler 150 and 180. In 1978 the company was sold to the emerging Peugeot-Citroën Group, which built the TALBOT 150/180, Horizon and Samba models at Madrid, and in 1999 was still producing PEUGEOT models. The truck division was sold to Renault.

VCM

BARRELLIER (F) 1919

This manufacturer of 3-wheeled invalid cars for war-wounded also offered a single- or 2-seater 3-wheeler for general sale. It had a horizontal twin engine under the seat, driving through a 2-speed gearbox and worm final drive. The chassis was tubular, with bicycle-type forks for the single front wheel. Low-pressure balloon tyres were used.

NG

1903 Barré 10hp tonneau.
NICK GEORGANO

1924 Barré 10/12hp tourer.
NATIONAL MOTOR MUSEUM

BARRIE *see* BELL (ii)

BARRINGTON (GB) 1932–1936

Barrington Motors Ltd, Sheffield.

A keen and competitive rider of Scott 2-stroke motorcycles in his early years, Barrington Budd was inspired to design a 3-cylinder 2-stroke car engine, which he completed in 1929. Having tested this form for more than two years in an old Austin Seven, he then produced a prototype car, fitted with a 2/4-seater open body of amateur construction utilising aluminium panelling over a light ash frame. This chassis frame was specially produced by Rubery Owen and many fitments were of his own maufacture. This gave excellent service, but the 782cc engine was deemed insufficient to carry full 4-seater coachwork and the second prototype was of over 900cc. This was to be known as the Nimble Nine, but Holbrooks Coachworks refused to supply the fashionable 2-door saloon body ordered by Budd unless payment was made in advance, and it was run only in chassis form. After 1936 no further activity was undertaken though strenuous efforts were made to sell the design to AUSTIN, CITROËN and others. Budd used the first car successfully up to World War II, covering over 100,000 miles.

DF

BARRIQUAND ET SCHMITT (F) 1905

Based at Neuilly-sur-Seine, this company made a short-lived large 4-cylinder car with 4-litre ohv engine and shaft drive. There may have been a connection

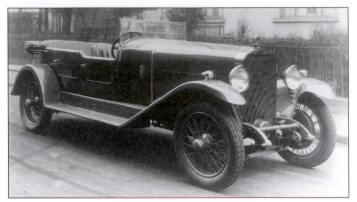

1925 Barron-Vialle sports tourer by Gordon England.
BRIAN DEMAUS

with Barriquand et Marre who made engines which were supplied to several car makers including Eudelin, Le Gui and Withers.

NG

BARRON-VIALLE (F) 1923–1929

1923 Sté des Automobiles Six, Strasbourg.
1924–1929 Barron, Vialle et Cie, Lyons.

This was a high-quality car made by former Berliet engineer A. Barron and body builder Antoine Vialle. They made trucks in Lyons up to 1920 when they turned to the more profitable business of railway carriage repairs. Three years later they returned to road vehicles by taking over a car which had been made at Strasbourg for one year under the name Six. This was designed by the Gadoux brothers, who were also responsible for the OMEGA SIX, and had a 2077cc 6-cylinder single-ohc engine. They continued the name Six for a year, then used their own more distinctive names for their high-quality car. During the summer of 1924 they added an eight with the same cylinder dimensions, 70 × 90mm, with a capacity of 2770cc. An additional model was the Super Six Sport, which used the 8-cylinder engine in the smaller chassis. Barron left the company in 1925, as did the Gadoux brothers in 1926, but Vialle continued production for a further three years. The same basic designs of 6- and 8-cylinder engines were made, later work being by Emile Lachanary who had come from S.L.I.M., another Lyons firm. In 1928 and 1929, capacity rose to 2.4- and 3.2-litres. Production was small, not more than 50 or 60 cars per year, but they had agents in Switzerland, Belgium, Italy, and Britain. Engines and chassis were made in-house, but bodies were bought from outside suppliers. In 1929 Vialle ended production, and moved to Arondon, Isere, where he resumed the manufacture of commercial vehicles. This lasted to 1937, when his factory became a camp for refugees from the Spanish Civil War.

NG

BARROWS (US) 1895–1899

Barrows Vehicle Co., New York, New York.

Charles H. Barrows designed a battery-powered car with two front wheels close together, separated only by the battery. This power unit could be attached to various bodies for one to four passengers, making what the builders called 'practically a mechanical horse'. The prototype was made by Barrows at Willimantic, Connecticut, but production cars were made in New York City, though Barrows also tried to interest the Lengert Co. of Philadelphia. Some vehicles were also made by the New England Electric Vehicle Co., an offshoot of the Electric Vehicle Co. of Hartford, Connecticut, makers of the COLUMBIA (i).

NG

BARTHEL (US) 1903–1904

Barthel Motor Co., Detroit, Michigan.

Oliver Barthel was a consulting engineer who had worked with Charles Brady King on his first car of 1896, and was later associated with Henry Ford in building racing cars. When Ford and Barthel lost their jobs with the Detroit Automobile Co. they both turned to making cars under their own names. Only two Barthels were made, 14hp 2-cylinder cars, while Ford was rather more successful.

NG

BARTHOLOMEW see GLIDE

BARTLETT (CDN) 1914–1917

1914–1916 Canadian Bartlett Automobile Co. Ltd, Toronto, Ontario.
1916–1917 Canadian Bartlett Automobile Co. Ltd, Stratford, Ontario.

Designed by R.C. Bartlett, this car had two unusual features, 4-wheel brakes, the first seen on a Canadian car, and a double frame, one for the running gear and engine, the other supporting the body. Between them there were four air bags which cushioned the upper frame from road shocks. This was particularly necessary as the wheels had solid tyres, which Bartlett favoured because of the short life of pneumatics. These tyres were made by the Bartlett company, and were supposed to last the life of the car. Suspension and brakes apart, the Bartlett was quite conventional, using imported American engines, Northway for the first seven cars, then Continental and Farmer, with LeRoi powering most of the 600 cars made. Body styles were a 5-seater tourer ($995), 2-seater roadster ($665) and a light truck. The double frame was dropped on later cars, the air bags simply connecting the upper frame and axles. Shortage of American components due to World War I forced Bartlett into bankruptcy in late 1917, but he continued as an active inventor into the 1970s. At least one tourer survives.

NG

BARTON (US) 1903

Barton Boiler Co., Chicago, Illinois.

This boiler company offered to build 'special steam tonneau cars', and at least two were sold, using Barton's flash boiler, a Mason 2-cylinder slide-valve engine and Burnell paraffin burner.

NG

B.A.S. (GB) 1993

B.A.S. Developments.

The B.A.S. 308 debuted at the 1993 Stoneleigh Kit Car Show, and was a Ferrari 308 replica. It used Ford Scorpio components in a space frame chassis and was powered by a mid-mounted Rover V8 engine.

CR

BASSETT (GB) 1899–1901

Bassett Motor Syndicate, London.

The prototype Bassett (which still exists) was built in 1899, but a new car 'on which the Bassett Motor Syndicate has been working for some time', was shown at London's Agricultural Hall Exhibition in May 1901. It was a 4-seater powered by a 4hp Schwanemeyer engine mounted below the rear seat, with 2-speed gearbox. The engine, transmission and rear axle were contained in a single aluminium oil chamber. Little was heard of it after its announcement.

NG

BASSON'S STAR (US) 1956

Basson's Industries Corp., Bronx, New York.

This was a 3-wheeler with single front wheel and a stylish fibreglass 2-seater body, powered by a single-cylinder 2-stroke Ilo engine. It was designed and promoted by Gil d'Andrea.

NG

BASTEAU (F) c.1912

Leopold Basteau, Challans, Vendée.

Basteau, who had worked with Gustav Eiffel, made two or three light 2-seater cars in an electrical factory.

NG

BASTIN (B) 1907–1909

Ateliers Bastin, Liège.

Joseph Bastin made a small number of touring cars with 4-cylinder engines, shaft drive and round radiators in the Delaunay-Belleville style. Later he took on agencies for foreign cars, particularly D.F.P. In 1912 he founded a new company at Angleur-Streupas to make trucks.

NG

BAT (GB) 1903–1909
Bat Motor Manufacturing Co. Ltd, Penge, Surrey.
Sometimes incorrectly rendered B.A.T., this company owed its name to its founder, Samuel Robert Batson who capitalised on his name with the slogan 'Best After Tests'. Most Bats were tricars, originally on bicycle lines, with a wicker passenger seat over the front axle. Engines were 3 or 6hp single-cylinder units mounted low in the centre of the frame. By 1904 more car-like models were made, with a chair-type seat for the driver instead of the usual saddle, and a semi-enclosed wooden body for the passenger. The engine was a 6hp 2-cylinder Fafnir. In 1909 Bat introduced the Carcycle, which resembled a motorcycle and sidecar, but with four wheels, the front ones being steered by handlebar.
NG

BATES (US) 1903–1905
Bates Automobile Co., Lansing, Michigan.
M.F. Bates built the first internal combustion engine in Michigan in 1889, and founded the Bates & Edmonds Motor Co. to manufacture them. He turned to cars in 1903 with a 16hp 2-cylinder tourer, following this with one using an 18hp 3-cylinder engine in 1905. Despite the optimistic slogan 'Buy a Bates and Keep Your Dates', production ended that year. The site of the Bates factory is now the home of the R.E. Olds Museum.
NG

BATEUP see AUSCAR

BATTEN (GB) 1935–1938
Beckenham Motor Co. Ltd, Beckenham, Kent.
One of the lesser-known Anglo-American Sports Hybrids, the Batten used a shortened Ford chassis of the 1932–33 period, with a current V8 engine boosted from 80 to 97bhp. The frame was underslung and shortened by 16in (406mm), being also 8.5in (216mm) narrower at the rear. With a weight of only 2182lb (942kg) performance was spectacular, with a top speed of over 100mph (160km/h). Most Battens used Ford-type transverse suspension, but one or two had ifs. The first cars had stark door-less 2-seater bodies, but later examples had more civilised sports tourer drophead coachwork. In 1937 a new model appeared which was the only one to break away completely from Ford styling. It had a very low 2-seater body, cycle-type wings, a sloping grill and headlamps faired into the bonnet sides. Top speed was 118mph (190km/h). Probably no more than one was made, and overall production of Battens did not exceed ten.
NG

BAUCHET (F) 1901–1903
SA des Moteurs H. Bauchet, Rethel, Ardennes.
The Bauchet was powered by a front-mounted 5/7hp vertical twin engine, with 4-speed gearbox and shaft drive. It was fitted with a 4-seater tonneau body.
NG

BAUDIER (F) 1900–1901
G. Baudier, Paris.
Similar to the contemporary Renault in appearance, the Baudier was a light voiturette powered by a 3hp water-cooled De Dion-Bouton engine. Like the Renault, it had shaft drive.
NG

BAUDOUIN (B) 1904–1906
S.A. de Construction Mécanique et d'Automobiles, Brussels.
This company formerly made the DECHAMPS, and in January 1904 introduced a new car called Baudouin, at which time the Dechamps name was dropped. The Baudouin was made in two 4-cylinder models, of 15 and 25hp, with early examples of single-ohc. The chassis was of armoured wood or steel. In 1904 and 1905 the same factory (located at 38 boulevard Baudouin, hence the car's name) made the DIRECT car designed by Robert Goldschmidt.
NG

BAUGHAN (GB) 1920–1929
1920–1921 Baughan Motors, Harrow, Middlesex.
1921–1929 Baughan Motors, Stroud, Gloucestershire.

1936 Batten V8 drophead coupé, one of a kind, built for Lord Plunkett.
NATIONAL MOTOR MUSEUM

1923 Baughan cyclecar.
NICK GEORGANO

Henry Baughan was a talented engineer who had previously worked with De Havillands and some early aircraft techniques were used in his cyclecars. The first of these bore the Middlesex registration MD 264, which was retained through several reincarnations and remains on the car in its last form to this day. Originally a Blackburne engine and Sturmey-Archer gearbox were fitted; it now has a JAP 1000cc V-twin with a Morris Oxford gearbox and dynastarter. Four other cars were sold and a tiny 'works' flatbed truck was also made. More success attended motorcycle manufacture and the firm diversified into general engineering work, turning later to rubber and plastics.
DF

B.A.W. see SCHURICHT

BAY STATE (i) (US) 1907–1908
Bay State Automobile Co., Boston, Massachusetts.
The first car to carry the name of the State of Massachusetts was a conventional large 7-seater tourer powered by a 40hp 4-cylinder engine. For 1908 a 5-seater runabout was added to the range, but the make did not survive long into the year.
NG

BAY STATE (ii) (US) 1922–1926
R.H. Long Co., Framingham, Massachusetts.
R.H. Long was a shoe manufacturer and an aspiring politician who was twice defeated in his run for Governor of Massachusetts by Calvin Coolidge, who was shortly to become President of the United States. Prominent in the civic and social life of Framingham, he decided to embark on the manufacture of automobiles in 1921, with production several months later. His Bay State car would be a success in a relatively small way, with a workforce of 400 employees turning out several hundred cars per year. The Bay State had pleasing lines designed by Herbert C. Snow, formerly an engineer with Peerless, Willys-Overland and Winton, and was otherwise a fully-assembled car with a Continental 6-cylinder engine, its Model 6R used in the 1922 line of cars and the updated

1923 Bay State (ii) sedan.
JOHN A. CONDE

1925 Bayliss-Thomas 11.9hp 2-seater.
NATIONAL MOTOR MUSEUM

1913 Beacon V-twin cyclecar.
NATIONAL MOTOR MUSEUM

8R in 1923 and 1924. A full line of both open- and closed-body styles were available, with prices ranging from $1095 to $2395 for the 6-cylinder offerings of 1923 to 1925. The cars were distributed primarily in Massachusetts and neighbouring Connecticut, Manchester, New Hampshire, and Brooklyn, New York. Production peaked in Bay State's first year, but fell sharply in 1924. In 1925 an eight was introduced, to be built in addition to the 6-cylinder line. This used a Lycoming engine, but by 1925 production had dropped to 50 cars, including both sixes and eights. The company struggled into 1926, although by this time production had ended and the few cars sold, although updated, were in reality leftover units. The Bay State factory, however, remained active in the production of the Luxor taxicab, a product of M.P. Müller's taxi empire centred in Hagerstown, Maryland, the space having been rented from Long in 1924. In addition to the Luxor cab, the stillborn STANDISH car was built in the same

factory, as were the first units of Müller's Elysee truck. R.H. Long subsequently established the R.H. Long Motor Sales Co. as a distributor of Cadillacs, which, as a GM dealership, still survives.
KM
Further Reading
'The Long Road to Success? Richard Long and his Bay State automobile', Beverly Rae Kimes, *Automobile Quarterly*, Vol. 28, No. 3.

BAYARD, BAYARD-CLEMENT *see* CLEMENT-BAYARD

BAYLEY *see* LIPSCOMB

BAYLISS-THOMAS (GB) 1922–1929
Excelsior Motor Co. Ltd, Tyseley, Birmingham.
Bayliss, Thomas & Co. was founded in Coventry in 1874 to make bicycles under the name Excelsior. Motorcycles followed in 1896 and long outlasted the cars. In 1913 they made the world's largest single-cylinder motorcycle engine, displacing 850cc. A new company was formed in Birmingham in April 1920 under the name Excelsior Motor Co. Ltd, and a car was planned. As there was already the well-known Belgian Excelsior car they used the original name, Bayliss-Thomas. It was a conventional light car powered by a 1498cc 4-cylinder Coventry-Simplex engine, with their own 3-speed gearbox. In addition to the usual open 2- and 4-seater bodies, they offered a sliding-door saloon made by Bowden of brake fame, and a doorless aluminium-bodied long-tailed sports model.

The 10.8 was soon joined by the 8.9hp Junior, powered by a 1074cc engine said to have been made in-house, but probably a Meadows unit. The 3-speed gearbox was also by Meadows, and the worm rear axle by Wrigley. From 1924 they turned exclusively to Meadows for their engines, using several sizes of both side-valve and ohv units from the 1247cc 9.8 to the 1795cc 13/30. Only the latter had a 4-speed gearbox, but all had Moss spiral bevel rear axles. Front-wheel brakes were adopted in 1927. About 500 Meadows engines were supplied, and in the mid-1920s the factory had a capacity of 40 cars a week, though they never achieved this figure. The Bayliss-Thomas was listed up to 1931, but production probably did not last beyond 1929. It is thought that about 1000 cars were made altogether. Excelsior motorcycles were made up to 1964, when the company name was Excelsior-Britax, makers of seat belts and other components.
NG
Further Reading
'The Bayliss-Thomas Story', M. Worthington-Williams, *The Automobile*, January 1990.

BAYONET (AUS) 1913
James A. Munro & Co., Melbourne, Victoria and Sydney, New South Wales.
Clearly a relabelled, but unidentified French type, the Bayonet was offered in models powered by 4-cylinder Ballot side-valve engines of 9hp (1131cc), 11hp (1590cc) on a 108in (2738mm) wheelbase, 14hp (2292cc) on a 115in (2921mm) wheelbase, and 22hp (4082cc). Other features in common were Claudel carburettor, Bosch magneto, cone clutch, 3-speed gearbox and wire wheels. Munro bodies were fitted and the Bayonet was competitively priced but faded when supply was curtailed due to the outbreak of war.
MG

B.B. *see* BEBE

B.B.C. *see* BERETTA

B.C.K. *see* KLINE KAR

B.D.A.C. *see* BUCKMOBILE

BEACH BOYS RACING (US) c.1990–1992
Beach Boys Racing, Venice, California.
The 'ugly duckling' Porsche 914 was the target for this company that sold tuning and bodywork modifications. Their Monterey model was a 914 with the roll-bar top removed and a slope-nose front end added. Flares covered wide

wheels and the suspension was massaged. Modified Porsche 6-cylinder engines were optional, and body modifications could be carried out in fibreglass or metal.

HP

BEACON (GB) 1912–1914

1912 Beacon Hill Motor Works, Hindhead, Surrey.
1912–1913 Beacon Engineering Co., Hindhead, Surrey.
1913–1914 Beacon Motors Ltd, Liphook, Surrey.
The Beacon was a fairly typical cyclecar apart from the offering of a cane body as an alternative to the metal panelled wood frame. The prototype used a V-twin JAP engine with friction transmission and chain drive, while the production model of 1913/14 had a 1093cc French-built Griffon engine, also a V-twin, with shaft drive to a 3-speed gearbox on the rear axle.

NG

BEAL (US) 1981–1983

Great American Coachworks, North Hollywood, California.
This was a replicar in the style of the Duesenberg J, featuring a large phaeton body with dual sidemounts. The chassis and engine were by General Motors and the radiator was crowned by an emblem similar to that of the Duesenberg.

NG

BEAN (GB) 1919–1929

1919–1926 A. Harper Sons & Bean Ltd, Tipton, Dudley, Worcestershire.
1926–1929 Bean Cars Ltd, Tipton, Dudley, Worcestershire.
A. Harper Sons & Bean was a well-known Midlands firm, founded in 1908 though its history dated back into the 19th century. They supplied nearly half Britain's car makers with castings, deliveries running at 500 tons per week. After World War I they decided to become car makers themselves, and took over the design of the 11.9hp PERRY. It was obviously a prewar design, having been launched in October 1914, and Bean were at a disadvantage from the start in offering an engine with a cast-iron fixed cylinder head bolted to an aluminium crankcase, with a separate gearbox mounted on its own subframe. The capacity was 1796cc. There were ambitious plans to mass produce the car, known as the Bean Twelve, using two factories, a former munitions works at Tipton for assembly and a former shell factory at Dudley for bodywork. Plans called for 50,000 cars per year within a few years, but this was never achieved. July 1920 saw a peak of 505 cars made, and in 1921/22 about 80–100 were delivered each week. Harper Bean were members of a consortium which included SWIFT and VULCAN, the Sheffield steel makers Hadfields, radiator makers Gallay, and Marles steering. They hoped to achieve efficient quantity production by standardisation of parts, but this never came about.

Despite production of about 2000 cars in 1920, overspending led to Harper Bean being wound up at the end of the year. It was not until a year later that they were reorganised and able to restart production. The Twelve was continued until 1927, with about 10,000 being made, and was supplemented in 1924 by the 2384cc Fourteen on similar lines, though it had unit construction of engine and gearbox. It became the 14/40 in 1927, having the same engine size but with Ricardo-designed combustion chambers and a reversion to a separate gearbox. About 4000 were made up to 1928. In 1926 Bean brought out their first six, but not having the capital to make their own engine, they bought the 2692cc ohv engine from Meadows. Designated the 18/50 it also had a Meadows gearbox in unit with the engine.

Harper Bean was taken over by their steel suppliers, Hadfields, in 1926, possibly in settlement of unpaid bills for steel. This fresh injection of capital led to two new models, the 2297cc 4-cylinder 14/40 and the 3.8-litre Imperial Six. The latter had a Bean-built engine with Ricardo head and was intended mainly for colonial use. The Australian explorer Francis Birtles drove one from England to India, but it performed badly and the model was never put into production. The new 14/40 was generally known as the Hadfield-Bean to signify the company's new ownership. It was quite modern-looking, with wire wheels (on the 14/70 sports models), a slight vee to the radiator and fabric saloon as well as tourer bodies. The 14/70 had Dewandre vacuum servo assisted brakes. However, the engine was not reliable and not many were sold. The 'old' 14/40 was a better car, but was very old-fashioned by 1928 when it was dropped. Hadfields decided to concentrate on a range of commercial vehicles, and the last Bean cars were made in 1929. Two years later the commercials had gone as well.

1922 Bean 11.9hp tourer.
JONATHAN WOOD

1927 Bean 18/50hp saloon.
JONATHAN WOOD

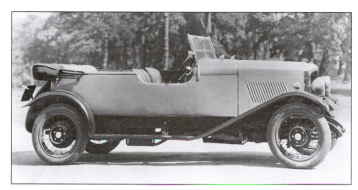
1929 Hadfield-Bean 14/70hp sports tourer.
JONATHAN WOOD

One section of the company survived as Beans Industries Ltd, and had further car involvement when they built the Thunderbolt Land Speed Record car for George Eyston in 1937. Much later, as Beans Engineering which had been part of British Leyland, they acquired the RELIANT Motor Co., though they sold it again to a consortium headed by former Jaguar executive Jonathan Heynes in 1996.

NG

Further Reading
'Bean – The Giant That Never Grew', John Mullins,
The Automobile, October and November 1983.

BEAN-CHAMBERLAIN *see* HUDSON

BEARCAT (US) 1955–1956

American Buckboard Corp., Los Angeles, California.
Like the Banner Boy Buckboard, this was a revival of the Briggs & Stratton Flyer concept of buckboard, with direct drive from a 2-cylinder air-cooled motorcycle engine to a fifth wheel at the rear. The price was under $1000.

NG

1923 Beardmore 2-litre sports car.
NATIONAL MOTOR MUSEUM

1988 Beauford convertible.
BEAUFORD CARS

BEARDMORE (GB) 1919–1928

Beardmore Motors Ltd, Glasgow.

William Beardmore & Co. Ltd was one of Scotland's largest steel producers in the late 19th century, and also built battleships at their yards at Dalmuir. Sir William Beardmore (later created Lord Invernairn) was the largest shareholder in ARROL-JOHNSTON from 1902. His firm supplied chassis to Arrol-Johnston (and other car makers), and he kept an interest in the company up to its demise in 1929. Beardmore made aero-engines and 650 complete aircraft during World War I, and in 1919 they launched their own cars. It was an ambitious range, of three different cars each made in a different factory. The 1486cc 11.4hp was to be made in a former fuse factory at Anniesland, Glasgow, the 2413cc Fifteen in Arrol-Johnston's former Underwood works at Paisley, and the 4-litre Thirty at Coatbridge. Very few of the latter were made, and the Fifteen was better-known as a taxicab than as a private car. Both these models had side-valve engines, but the 11.4 had a skew-gear shaft-driven single-ohc unit derived from that used in the unsuccessful Arrol-Johnston Victory. This was unsatisfactory at first, chewing up timing gears, and was replaced by a 1656cc side-valve unit, but for 1921 a modified ohc engine, enlarged to the same size as the side-valve unit, was back. All engines, and indeed most of the cars, were made at Paisley.

The skew gear gave way to chain drive in 1923, and the engine was increased in size to 1962cc in 1924. A single-seater powered by this engine and driven by Cyril Paul broke the Shelsley Walsh hill climb record in 1924. The following year the bore was reduced, giving a capacity of 1880cc, as the original block had been stretched to the limit. 1925 was the last year for the ohc models, but a 2391cc side-valve 16/40 was made in small numbers up to 1929. It used the same engine as Beardmore's taxicab, which was better known. At least 6000 taxis had been made by 1928, compared with perhaps 500 of all types of car.

Vehicle production ended in Scotland in 1929, but taxis were continued in a London factory which had been the service centre for Beardmore cars. This lasted up to 1967.

NG

Further Reading
'Twas a Famous Victory', Kenneth Hurst, *The Automobile,* October 1991.

BEARDSLEY (US) 1914–1917

1914–1915 Beardsley Electric Co., Los Angeles, California.
1915–1917 Beardsley Electric Co., Culver City, California .

One of the few electric cars to be made in California, the Beardsley was made by Volney S. Beardsley who had been president of the Auto Vehicle Co., makers of the TOURIST (i), and then had a dealership for the COLUMBUS Electric. The Beardsley brougham and victoria were typical electrics in appearance, but an unusual model was the 2-seater roadster whose long bonnet, rounded tail and wire wheels enabled it to compete in appearance with any petrol-engined roadster. The cars took part in several long-distance demonstrations, including a run of 1500 miles in 14 consecutive days on one battery charge per day, averaging a daily 107.5 miles. The driver was Beardsley's wife, and all ten observers were women. 'A California car that does California proud' said company advertising, and in 1915 they moved to larger premises at Culver City, where 40 employees worked. However, World War I caused a shortage of parts, and this, combined with the dwindling popularity of the electric car, led to the Beardsley's demise during 1917, after 661 cars had been made. The company was absorbed into the Moreland Motor Truck Co., whose head Watt Moreland had been a Beardsley vice-president since 1914. Moreland trucks were made until 1941.

NG

BÉATRIX (F) 1907

M. Tisserand, Paris.

The Béatrix was listed in three sizes, 15/18, 24/30, and 30/40hp, though given its short life, not all may have been made. The most advanced feature of the Béatrix was the monobloc casting of the 6-cylinder engines, at a time when sixes were comparatively rare, and most such engines had the cylinders cast in pairs.

NG

BEATTIE (NZ) 1997 to date

Formtool Engineering Ltd, Auckland, North Island.

A dual-purpose track racing/road car built by Stephen Beattie, its lines were reminiscent of late 1960s Lola and Lotus sports racers. With a tubular space frame, of 84in (2140mm) wheelbase, which was augmented by stressed alloy floors and sills, the suspension was by coil-damper units on a wishbone independent front end and well-located Ford Escort rear axle. Rack and pinion steering, 15in Minilite wheels and a fibreglass body were other features. Optional engines were a Ford Cortina 2-litre ohc unit giving 180bhp, with disc/drumbrakes for the road, or a Toyota 2-litre twin ohc camshaft-type providing 200bhp, in conjunction with disc brakes all round, for competition use.

MG

BEAUDET (F) 1993–1997

Franck Beaudet, St André de Cubzac.

Electrical engineer Franck Beaudet produced the Beaudet 1, a 1930s traditional-style convertible. It used a Peugeot 505 2.0-litre engine and Opel Ascona running gear in a specially-conceived chassis.

CR

BEAUFORD (GB) 1985 to date

Beauford Cars, Upholland, Lancashire.

Unlike so many neo-classics, the Beauford became an institution in its own right. The first cars intriguingly used a Mini bodyshell mounted on a big ladder chassis, surrounded by flowing wings and preceded by a very long bonnet. The definitive Beauford was a plastic-bodied two-door open tourer. Beaufords used Ford Cortina mechanicals, with options of Ford 4/V6, Nissan straight-6 or Rover V8 engines. Optional body styles included 4-door saloon and 4-door tourer styles, also available in 'long body' form, with the front bulkhead moved forward to free up extra legroom for its main clientele – wedding hire companies. Over 1000 had been built by 1998.

CR

BEAUFORT (D/GB) 1901–1906

The Beaufort Motor Co., Baden.

The very English-sounding Beaufort was largely a German car, some being made by the ARGUS company in Baden. The company was capitalised and registered in England, the cars being sold from premises near Baker Street in

c.1902 Beaufort tonneau.
NATIONAL MOTOR MUSEUM

London. Some may have been assembled or bodied there. One of the men behind the Beaufort was Oliver Stanton who had taught King Edward VII (when Prince of Wales) to ride a bicycle and drive a car.

The first Beaufort had a single-cylinder Bergmann engine and belt drive, but this gave way to shaft drive by November 1902, when models of 6 and 9hp (single-cylinder), 12 and 18hp (2-cylinders), and 14 and 24hp (4-cylinders) were listed, 'made in the works at Baden'. Later models included a 28/32hp four and a 30hp six. Commercial vehicles were also listed, including a 12hp 2-cylinder taxicab chassis and a heavy forward-control truck, which may well have been a make other than Argus.

NG

BEAUJANGLE (GB) 1972–1973
Beaujangle Enterprises, Manchester.
After making cheap Ford T-bucket shells, this company produced the Can-Am, based on an American kit car design, supposedly inspired by US Can-Am racers. The basis was a VW floorpan shortened by 5in (127mm), with suspension modifications to improve handling. Six were made, though the design was very briefly revived by a company called Lemazone in 1985.

CR

BEAUMONT (F) 1913
Made in the Avenue de la Grande Armée, Paris, the Beaumont was listed in two models, both fours, of 1724 and 2720cc. The name was also used for a model of the ACADIAN.

NG

BEAVER (i) (US) 1912
Beaver State Motor Co., Gresham, Oregon.
The Beaver was built by P.A. Combs of Portland, Oregon, former vice-president of an auto supply company in that city. A corporation was formed for the further

manufacture of the car, which featured a 6-cylinder 45hp engine. Its builder believed it to be the first pleasure car in the United States equipped with the Daimler-Lanchester worm drive, gears having been imported from Coventry. No further cars were made, but the corporation survived as a maker of sewer pipes, metal castings, rail car wheels, cement mixers, and petrol engines.

KM

BEAVER (ii) (GB) 1984–1985;1991
1984–1985 Kit Cars International, Barnsley, Yorkshire.
1991 Beaver Coach Works, South Woodham Ferrers, Essex.
Richard Oakes was named as the designer of this dull-looking estate-type kit car, designed around a Ford Escort windscreen, doors and mechanicals. The glassfibre body was mounted on a steel chassis.

CR

B.E.B. (D) 1922–1923
Busse Elektromobil-Bau KG, Magdeburg.
This was one of several electrically-powered cyclecars to appear after World War I. It seated two people.

HON

BÉBÉ; B.B. (F) 1912–1915
Hubert Barraud, Monlucon.
The Bébé was a light car made in four models, a 2 seater with single-cylinder Anzani or Buchet engines, and a 2- or 4-seater with 8/10hp 4-cylinder Chapuis-Dornier engine. They had 4-speed friction transmissions and shaft drive. 1915 models had conventional 3-speed gearboxes. Hubert Barraud had quite a substantial factory, but it is believed that no more than 100 cars were made in all. The trademark was 'B.B.' and the cars sometimes went under that name.

NG

139

BECCARIA

1913 Bédélia V-twin built for the Cyclecar Grand Prix.
NATIONAL MOTOR MUSEUM

BECCARIA (I) 1911–1916
B. Beccaria, Turin.
Beccaria was a well-known metal forging firm who made Italy's first channel-steel frames, and supplied frames to FIAT and STORERO among others. They made a small number of cars under their own name, though these may have been FLORIOs, as there were links between the two companies.
NG

BECCLES ROBOTICS (GB) 1988
The Beccles Robotics BT7 was a flared-arch Austin-Healey replica launched at the Newark Kit Car Show in 1988, but no more was heard of it.
CR

BECHEREAU (F) 1924–1925
Louis Bechereau, Paris.
Bechereau made a small number of light sports cars powered by a 1194cc twin-ohc Salmson engine, with Lancia-type ifs and streamlined body.
NG

BECK (i) **(F)** 1920–1922
Automobiles Beck, Lyons.
This was a light car powered by a 1499cc 4-cylinder single-ohc engine which developed a remarkable 32bhp, with 3-speed gearbox on the rear axle. Its most unusual feature was independent suspension of all four wheels by coils. The semi-streamlined bodies were fronted by a handsome vee-radiator. Only two prototypes were made. The backer and originator of the design was Charles Beck-Maillard, but most of the work was by Jean François, who later worked for Delahaye.
NG

BECK (ii) **(US)** 1982 to date
Beck Developments, Upland, California.
Chuck Beck had an extensive background in road racing and kit manufacture when he started this company. He had previously built the Stripper for CORSAIR cars and other dune buggies. Beck spent years developing his first sports car, a replica of the Porsche 550 Spyder using VW or Porsche running gear. It was very successful, and although kits were manufactured in California, assembled cars were farmed out to a factory in Brazil. Beck also sold Brazilian Porsche Speedster and Super 90 Cabriolet replicas. Beck purchased the VIP Ferrari Testarossa kit project, but had not produced any as of 1998. Another Beck project was the Shogun, a tiny Ford Festiva with a 200hp Ford SHO Taurus engine wedged under the hatchback. Beck also added a replica of the 'knobbly' bodied Lister sports-racer that could take Jaguar or Corvette engines. In 1996 Beck sold the Porsche project to THUNDER RANCH and stopped selling kits, but in 1998 they resumed production of the Lister replicas.
HP

BECKMANN (D) 1900–1926
Otto Beckmann & Cie Erste Schlesische Velociped und Automobilfabrik, Breslau.
Though car production lasted for 26 years, the Beckmann was little known outside its location in Eastern Germany, and in exports to Eastern Europe. As the name indicates, they were bicycle makers (since 1882) before car production began in 1900. The first car was a voiturette powered by a single-cylinder De Dion-Bouton engine, and this was followed by 2- and 4-cylinder cars using proprietary engines from France. From 1904 Beckmann made their own engines, and a great variety of different models was made, with 2-, 4- and 6-cylinders. The 4-cylinder 40PS four of 1907 had a capacity of 8600cc. Beckmann cars took part in the Herkomer Trials in 1906 and 1907.
Only a few cars were made after World War I. The 8/24 and 10/30PS 4-cylinder models were made, followed by an 8/32 and a 12/40PS which had engines by Basse & Selve. In 1926 the works were taken over by OPEL who found them a useful way of supplying their Eastern markets.
HON

BECOGNÉE (F) 1930
This was a light sports car powered by a 746cc side-valve V-twin JAP engine with shaft drive. The prototype, which was probably the only Becognée made, had a doorless open 2-seater body, but a hardtop was planned, also the use of an ohv engine, and eventually a 4-cylinder model. However, the Depression was a bad time to launch a new sports car, and the Becognée had no successors.
NG

BÉDÉLIA (F) 1910–1925
1910–1916 Bourbeau et Devaux, Paris.
1920–1925 Mahieux et Cie, Levallois-Perret, Seine.
The Bédélia was the first of the new breed of cyclecar which was to multiply so extensively between around 1912 and the outbreak of World War I. In 1908 18-year old engineering student Robert Bourbeau built a very light 4-wheeler with an ash frame and two seats in tandem. It was powered by a motorcycle engine which drove through a 2-speed belt drive, and steering was by cable and bobbin to a centre pivot front axle, the whole axle turning with the wheels. Front suspension was by a single centrally mounted coil spring. The driver sat at the rear, but both passengers had to play their part; to change gear the driver used a lever to bend the rear springs slightly, which had the effect of moving the axle forward and thereby slackening the belts. The passenger then moved the belts from one pulley to another by means of a stick. Bourbeau confessed in an interview that the machine was not designed but just grew. It sounds an improbable recipe for success, but Bourbeau was encouraged by his friend Henri Devaux who provided sufficient capital to establish a small factory which began to turn out the cyclecars during 1910.

140

Engine options were three sizes of single-cylinder, from 3½ to 5½hp, and a 10hp V-twin. The design changed little up to 1914, apart from the addition of some creature comforts such as a hood. Some models had running boards, and disc wheels were available, these being used on the car with which Bourbeau won the 1913 Cyclecar Grand Prix at Amiens. One of the first customers had been a doctor who used his Bédélia as an ambulance, though how his patient coped with the belt shifting was not explained. Bédélias were used for the same purpose during the war, but by then the driver could control the gear-changing himself. In 1920 Bourbeau and Devaux sold their business to a former distributor, M. Binet, who had cars built for him by Mahieux et Cie. They were more conventional, with side-by-side seating and a 3-speed gearbox. Among the engines offered was a 990cc V-twin Train.

NG

BEDFORD (GB) 1904
Wilson Bros, Bedford.
Wilson Brothers were electrical engineers who announced a three-model range of cars which did not survive the year 1904. They were a 6hp single-cylinder 2-seater with armoured wood frame and solid tyres, a 10hp twin, and a 16hp four with pneumatic tyres. The latter had a Roi-des-Belges tourer body by Vedrine of Paris. They do not seem to have made any more cars, but by the 1920s they had merged with another Bedford firm, C. E. Humphries, who sold spares for the London-built METEORITE. The Bedford name was sometimes used for BUICKs bodied in England, though these more usually went under the name Bedford-Buick.

NG

BEDOUIN (GB) 1985–1987
Central Vehicle Conversions (R.W. Services), Ravenstone, Leicestershire.
The Bedouin was a kit-built utility car, the British equivalent of a Citroën Méhari. It used an unmodified 2CV/Dyane/Ami floorpan to which was bolted to a boxy, fully-enclosed estate-type body. Early bodies were made mostly of plywood, but later ones used more glassfibre.

CR

BEE (US) c.1979
Bee Engineering, Westminster, California.
The 720-B town coupé was a tiny sedan powered by an 8hp electric motor. Top speed was 40mph with a range of 40 to 60 miles.

HP

BEEBE (US) 1905–1906
Western Motor Truck & Vehicle Co., Chicago, Illinois.
This company began experimenting with vehicles about the turn of the century, and may have sold a few cars under the name Western. In 1905 they launched the Beebe Model E, a $1250 tourer powered by a 30hp 2-cylinder 2-stroke Wats engine, with friction drive and a pedal-operated starter. The 1906 model was called the Issue No.3 and had a smaller engine of 14hp with a 2-seater body. The price was lower too, at $650, but the company went out of business the same year. Despite the maker's name, they produced only one truck, in 1906. There was another Chicago truck maker called Western, active from 1917 to 1923, but it is not thought that there was any connection with the makers of the Beebe.

NG

BEECHCRAFT (US) 1946
Beechcraft Aircraft Co., Wichita, Kansas.
This celebrated aircraft manufacturer built a hybrid power car called the Plainsman. It used an aircraft engine to power four electric motors that were positioned at each wheel. It was a fastback sedan with an aluminium body and frame. Only two prototypes were built as the projected price was too high.

HP

BEESTON (GB) 1899
Beeston Motor Cycle Co., Coventry.
This company was well-known for their tricycles and quadricycles. At the 1899 National Cycle Show they exhibited a light car with a 3½hp engine under the seat, and gear drive.

NG

B.E.F. (D) 1907–1913
Berliner Elektromobilfabrik GmbH, Berlin.
This was an electric 3-wheeler designed by Victor Harhorn. The 4hp motor was mounted above, and drove the single front wheel by vertical shaft to the hub. Harhorn also designed the more sophisticated GEHA, with the motor incorporated in the hub.

HON

BEGG (NZ) 1964–1975
George Begg Machinery, Drummond, South Island.
Produced by an engineering concern in a country town, the Begg competition cars, powered by a 4.7-litre Chevrolet V8 engines, came to the attention of the public in 1967 and a Begg-Chevrolet sports car took the New Zealand speed record at 177mph (285km/h) in 1968. The FM series racing cars, of monocoque contsruction, were prominent in Formula 5000 competition and smaller models with 1600cc Ford engies were also manufactured.

MG

BEGGS (US) 1919–1923
Beggs Motor Car Co., Kansas City, Missouri.
The Beggs entered the automobile business in 1919, previously having been specialists in elaborately hand-carved bodies for circus wagons and carousel merry-go-rounds. The Beggs car was a typical assembled car of its time, using Continental 7R and 8R engines. Production was confined to open models through 1920 and, although a coupé and a sedan were offered by 1921, production was almost entirely targeted to touring cars, these priced at $1175 through 1922 and increased to $1495 in 1923, its final year of activity. Total Beggs production reached at least 200 units and possibly as many as 250.

KM

BÉGOT ET MAZURIÉ; BÉGOT ET CAIL (F) 1899–1902
1899–1900 Bégot et Mazurié, Rheims.
1900–1902 Bégot et Cail, Rheims.
Bégot et Mazurié were general engineers who made a few light cars with 4hp single-cylinder engines of 642cc, similar to a De Dion-Bouton, but with some differences. They were mounted in the front of the frame, and final drive was by double-chains. In 1900 the company name was changed to Bégot et Cail; Cail were locomotive makers who also built the large 6-wheeled BORDEREL-CAIL car. These Bégot et Cails were offered with either 5hp single-cylinder De Dion-Bouton-type or 7hp 904cc V-twin engines of their own make. They had 4-speed gearboxes and double-chain drive. The 1900 V-twin had a 4-seater dos-à-dos body, but in 1901 all four seats faced forward. Steering was by vertical tiller. The surviving Bégot et Mazurié has wheel steering and an inclined column, but this is almost certainly a later modification.

NG

BÉHAR (F) 1984–1985
Alain Béhar, Toulouse.
Inspired by seeing a Brazilian Lafer, Alain Béhar produced his own Beetle-based 1930s-style roadster in France. It looked rather like a British Spartan, though its VW engine was rear-mounted. He succeeded in obtaining government aid to develop a production model with the stipulation that it should be built on a Renault chassis with a front-mounted engine.

CR

BEIJING (CHI) 1958 to date
1958–1966 Beijing Auto Works, Beijing Municipality.
1966–1976 Beijing Dongfanghong Auto Works, Beijing Municipality.
1976 to date Beijing Auto Works, Beijing Municipality.
Together with the auto works in Changchun, Nanjing and Shanghai, the Beijing factory is one of the first four factories which produced automobiles in China. In 1958, during the period of the Great Leap Forward, the Beijing First Auto Accessories Factory Workshop introduced its first motor car, the JINGGANGSHAN, soon followed by the Beijing CB4, a V8-engined convertible and limousine. There was only one convertible, used for parade services, registered in September 1958, as 1-06227.

1978 Beijing BJ-212 4x4 utility.
BEIJING AUTO WORKS

1934 Belga Rise 3.8-litre saloon by Vesters et Neirinck.
NICK GEORGANO

The limousine appeared in two versions, the second version restyled. The Chinese five stars disappeared from the front end, replaced by a badge. Only five of these cars, which looked like a contemporary American limousine of flamboyant design, seem to have been produced. A smaller car followed in 1960, a clear twin of the Russian Volga saloon, named DONGFANGHONG. In 1961 the first all-wheel drive was introduced, to replace the old jeeps and Russian GAZ all-wheel drives in the People's Liberation Army. It was a small jeep-size vehicle called Beijing BJ210, a year later succeeded by the bigger, well-known Beijing BJ212, which became the standard 4 × 4 in China in the last four decades of the 20th century. A motor car, called the Beijing BJ750, using the same 4-cylinder 2445cc engine as the BJ212 (clearly a copy of the Russian UAZ engine) was made from 1973 to 1975. This Beijing was also not very successful, with only 90 units being built, as the government gave priority to the Shanghai limousines of the same size. An experimental version with a wankel engine (BJ751) is worth mentioning, and there were also some tests with a 6-cylinder engine. In 1988 the car was revived, and three units were made with a Beijing Jeep Cherokee engine, the BJ752. The front and rear end were reshaped, and the Beijing United Auto and Motor Corporation badge, to which the Beijing Auto Works at that time belonged, was put on the font. Beijing Auto Works were able to use the Cherokee engine as, from 1983, this factory was partner in a joint venture with American Motors, which produced Chinese BJ212 and American Cherokees together.

In 1996 and in 1998 Beijing Auto Works made a batch of 4-door estate cars, named Beijing BJ6470 Qishi, which was in fact an earlier Mazda 929 estate. The vehicle was made at the request of several Beijing taxi companies, the price was 99,000Y ($10,000). There were two engine sizes: 2.0- and 2.2-litre.
EVIS

BEISEL (US) 1914
Beisel Motorette Co., Monroe, Michigan.
The Beisel Motorette was a cyclecar powered by a 1560cc 4-cylinder Prugh engine, with friction transmission and belt final drive. In April 1914 the National United Service Company of Detroit contracted to sell two years' output of Motorettes, but production ended the same year.
NG

BEKKA (F) 1906–1907
Barclay et Knudsen, Paris.
This short-lived car derived its name from the initials of the makers (B.K.). Two models were listed, a 12/16 and an 18/24hp, both 4-cylinder, with chain drive.
NG

B.E.L. see STERLING

BEL-MOTORS (F) 1974–1980
Sté Bel-Motors International, Les Sables d'Olonne, Vendée.
The Veloto C-10 3-wheeled microcar was the first design of M.J. Bellier. It used a 49cc Motobécane engine to drive the rear wheels via an automatic transmission. The spindly wheels were suspended by rubber and the bodywork was in glassfibre. A further model in 1979 was the C-10S, a fully-enclosed microcar with all-independent suspension, while the last microcar product was the C12 (or Minoto) of 1980 (later built by AROLA). Meanwhile M. Bellier formed his own new enterprise, BELLIER.
CR

BELARO (i) (GB) 1993 to date
Lakeside Carriage Co., Redditch, Worcestershire.
Belaro was one of the first British companies to use the Pontiac Fiero as the basis for a glassfibre kit body, and its Berlinetta was an American designed Ferrari Testarossa look-alike modified for British consumption. The body kit cost £2000 in 1996. Another model was the S.P.M. 286, a Ferrari 308 GTB look-alike, also based on a Fiero chassis, taken over from a Gloucestershire company.
CR

BELARO (ii) (US) c.1994
Tom Bellaw, Altamonte, California; British American Motorcars, Kissimmee, Florida.
Expatriate Brits Roy and Tony Morris bought the Belaro kit project from Tom Bellaw and simplified it for easier assembly. It was a Ferrari-inspired rebody for the Pontiac Fiero, and they were available in kit or assembled form.
HP

BELCAR see BRUTSCH

BELDEN (US) 1907–1911
Belden Motor Car Co., Pittsburgh, Pennsylvania.
E.H. Belden ran the Belden Transmission Company before he began manufacture of complete cars. These were initially a 30hp four, of which only a prototype was made in 1907, followed by 40/50 and 40/60hp sixes made in tourer, roadster, and town car models, and selling for high prices of $4800 to $6000. Plans called for 100 cars to be made in 1909, but Belden probably did not achieve anywhere near this figure, as in September he admitted that he had completed his *first* 6-cylinder car.
NG

BELGA (B) 1920–1921
Automobiles Belga, Marchienne-Zone.
Originally called the Nile et Brunel, the Belga was a conventional light car powered by a 1592cc 4-cylinder Ballot engine. 2- and 4-seater bodies were offered, and the car had a handsome vee-radiator. Designed by Brunel and Van Caubergh, its only unusual feature was its friction transmission giving 10 forward speeds. Unfortunately this did not work very well as the driven disc wore out quickly, giving the equivalent of clutch slip.
NG

BELGA RISE (B) 1928–1937
Sté Belge des Automobiles Sizaire, Brussels.
This company was formed to manufacture cars of SIZAIRE FRÈRES design, and began at about the same time that French production ended. It was founded by Georges Sizaire and the company's Belgian agent Richard Thielen. Like the French cars, the Belga Rise had a Rolls-Royce-type radiator, but carrried the badge Belga Rise licence Sizaire. A variety of engines was used, initially 6-cylinder Willys-Knight, but also Hotchkiss AM80, and straight-8s by Minerva,

Continental and Talbot. Surprisingly for a design famous for all-round independent suspension, the Belga Rise acquired a rigid rear axle from 1932. Gearboxes were conventional 3-speed or 4-speed Cotal pre-selectors. In 1936 Belga Rise completed 35 6-wheeled reconnaissance cars for the Belgian Army. At least one car survives, a Talbot-engined saloon in the Autoworld Museum in Brussels.

NG

BELGICA (B) 1899–1909

1899–1902 Sté des Cycles et Automobiles Belgica, Brussels.
1902–1906 SA Franco-Belge de Construction Automobiles, Brussels.
1906–1909 Usines de Saventhem SA, Saventhem.

The Sté des Cycles Belgica was founded in 1885, and prospered greatly through supplying large numbers of folding bicycles to the Belgian Army. Its chairman Louis Mettewie turned to cars in 1899, showing electric cars alongside his bicycles at that year's Brussels Exposition. In 1901 the first petrol-engined Belgica appeared, an 8hp 2-cylinder light car with bodywork by De Ruyter Demissine. This was followed by two single-cylinder models, three twins and a four, all with chain drive, designed by French-born Georges Desson. In July 1902 the company name changed, thanks to a large injection of French capital, the new organisation having offices in Paris as well as Brussels. The 1903 20hp four had an electric clutch, but otherwise Belgicas developed along conventional lines, with shaft drive introduced in 1905 and the first 6-cylinder engine in 1907. By 1906 production had expanded beyond the capacity of the Brussels factory, and a move was made to Saventhem, where Belgica merged with the Usines de Saventhem who made cars under the name US Brevets MATHIEU. The factory made cars, trucks, buses, fire engines and marine engines; the smaller Brussels factory was retained for component manufacture. The president of the new company was the Baron van Zuylen de Nyefelt, a founder of the Automobile Club de France. In 1908 the Belgica range consisted of three 4-cylinder cars, the Type K 14/16hp, the Type H 20/24hp and the Type G 30/40hp, together with the Type G6, a 6-cylinder 40/60hp of 10,300cc. Belgicas were of high quality, with aluminium and bronze components and dual ignition on many of the models. Unfortunately, this was reflected in high prices, and in 1909 they could no longer compete. The factory was taken over by EXCELSIOR (i).

NG

BELL (i) (GB) 1905–1926

1905–1914 Bell Brothers, Ravensthorpe, Yorkshire.
1920–1926 Cooperative Wholesale Society, Alexandra Park, Manchester.

The Bell brothers ran the Calder Ironworks at Ravensthorpe and in 1905 launched a car designed by Edwin Humphries. It had an 8/10hp 2-cylinder engine and 3-speed gearbox, and was described as 'heavier than usual for this class of vehicle'. It was followed by larger cars with 4-cylinder engines, of 16, 20, 24 and 30hp. The 16hp was popular as a taxicab, but Bell production was small, and they were seldom sold outside their home county. In 1919 they planned to revive the 16, 20 and 30hp models, but the designs were bought up by the Cooperative Wholesale Society (the Co-op) who put them into production in a factory in Manchester. Most of the output was of commercial vehicles, but a few 16hp cars were made for Co-op officials, and possibly for sale to customers. Two models with Dorman engines were listed, a 4-litre 25hp in 1922 and a 2.6-litre 15.9hp in 1923. These were sometimes known as CWS-Bell, and were listed up to 1926, though it is unlikely that any were made as late as that.

NG

BELL (ii) (US) 1915–1922

Bell Motor Car Co., York, Pennsylvania.

The Bell was described by *Motor* as 'a 4-cylinder car with many attractions', but it was a very conventional assembled product, with engines initially by G.B.& S, and Continental, though they standardised on a larger 36hp Herschell-Spillman from 1920. This pushed the price up from $775 when the car was announced to $1395 for a roadster and $1500 for a tourer. In 1918 they moved into the factory just vacated by the PULLMAN company. In 1921 Charles E. Riess organised Riess Motors Inc. to take over Bell production and rename the car the Riess-Royal, but this fell through and the Bell name was retained until production ended some time in 1922. Just 63 cars were made that year, out of a total of 1933. Bell had a number of African-American dealers, which was unusual at that time.

NG

1905 Belgica limousine.
NATIONAL MOTOR MUSEUM

1908 Bell (i) 20hp tourer.
NATIONAL MOTOR MUSEUM

BELL (iii) (CDN) 1916–1918

The Barrie Carriage Co., Barrie, Ontario.

This carriage company was founded in 1903, and in 1915 its head Simon Dyment decided to enter the car business by assembling the American BELL (ii). The first cars were delivered in 1916, initially made entirely from imported components, though later upholstery and tops were made in the Barrie workshops, and Lycoming engines were used. Between 20 and 40 cars were made, but poor workmanship, inexperienced staff and wartime shortages brought the operation to an end in May 1918.

NG

BELL (iv) (GB) 1920

W.G.Bell, Rochester, Kent.

This was a 3-wheeled cyclecar with single front wheel, powered by a Precision engine. The planned price was between £120 and £150, but production never started.

NG

BELL (v) (F) 1924–1925

Cyclecars Bell, Choisy-le-Roi, Seine.

The makers of the French Bell were being too modest in calling their car a cyclecar, for it had a 4-cylinder engine and shaft drive. The engine was an air-cooled ohv 1095cc flat-4 designed by Vaslin, who was also responsible for the ALMA, and M. Bellais. There were plans to sell the car in Britain under this name at the very low price of £95. However, nothing came of this. As the Bell,

1920 Bellanger Type A1 tourer.
NATIONAL MOTOR MUSEUM

1901 Belle 8hp tourer.
NATIONAL MOTOR MUSEUM

the design was short-lived, for it was taken up by MAJOLA, and in modified form appeared on the Majola stand at the 1926 Paris Salon as the Type GV. It was offered up to 1928, but probably few were made.

NG

BELLANGER (F) 1912–1925

Sté des Automobiles Bellanger, Neuilly-sur-Seine.

These cars were made by Robert Bellanger (1884–1966) who began his motor trade career in 1906 by selling Delaunay-Belleville and Westinghouse cars in Paris. In 1912 he began production of a medium-sized car powered by 2.6- or 3.3-litre 4-cylinder English DAIMLER sleeve-valve engines. This was followed by a 2-litre, as used in the BSA Stoneleigh, and a 6.3-litre six which in England powered the Daimler 38hp. They had cone clutches, Riley detachable wire wheels, and imposing bullnose radiators. Their slogan was 'Son capot est d'argent et son silence est d'or' ('her bonnet is silver and her silence is golden'). During World War I Bellanger expanded into aircraft, armoured cars, and farm equipment, and also bought the SA des Chantiers Naval de l'Ouest at St Malo, which made a variety of sea and river craft. After the war he continued this business, while other companies he owned made tools, cycle components, and semi-diesel engines for marine and industrial work. Doubtless profits from these activities helped finance car production, which in 1919 concentrated on a conventional car powered by a 3181cc 4-cylinder side-valve American Briscoe engine, with wooden wheels. About 2000 of this model, the A1, were made, some being used as taxicabs in Paris. They still had the large bullnose radiators, which were also seen on the larger Bellangers. Made in much smaller numbers, these were designed by ex-Spyker engineer Valentin Laviolette who had made experimental front-drive cars just before and just after World War I. His designs

for Bellanger had 4253cc 4-cylinder or 6362cc V8 engines with transverse horizontal valves, cantilever rear suspension, and uncoupled four-wheel brakes. The V8 also had double-elliptic front springs. The 4-cylinder chassis could be had with a 2-seater sports body, rather incongruous on such a large chassis of only moderate performance. Bellanger production seems to have ended around 1923, though some lists carry the name to 1925. In that year the factory was sold to PEUGEOT, who sold it on to ROSENGART three years later. The Bellanger name was not quite finished, though, for in 1928 DE DION-BOUTON equipped some of their 1.3-litre Model JPs with vee-radiators and marketed them under the name Bellanger Model B1. Quite why they thought this would improve sales is uncertain, and the venture lasted less than a year. Robert Bellanger later went into politics and spent his retirement restoring a ruined 11th century Provençal chateau, using a Jeep-like vehicle of his own construction made from components from various Bellanger cars.

NG

BELLE (CH/GB) 1901–1903

E.J. Coles & Co., Upper Holloway, London.

The Belle had a 6hp single-cylinder engine mounted under a short bonnet and inclined forwards. Transmission was by belt to a countershaft which meshed with an intermediate shaft to give three forward speeds, final drive being by chains. It had wheel steering which, unusually, was mounted in the centre of the frame, so that the car could be driven from either the left or the right, though really only comfortably if the driver were seated in the middle. Behind him was a rear-entrance tonneau body. The origin of the Belle is uncertain; Mr Coles was described as 'putting on the market' the Belle car, which might or might not mean that he made it, and there have been suggestions that it was of Swiss origin. By 1904 he was no longer offering the Belle, but was selling the Swiss WYSS (later BERNA). At the Crystal Palace Show in February 1903 Coles exhibited cars of 6, 10 and 22hp (make unspecified) in addition to the Belle, now rated at 8hp. It was said that a Belle was the first car to be driven onto a London stage (Alhambra, Leicester Square, in 1901).

NG

BELLEFONTAINE (US) 1908

Bellefontaine Automobile Co., Bellefontaine, Ohio.

The Bellefontaine succeeded the TRAVELER (i) which, in turn, was a development of the ZENT. Slightly larger than the Traveler, it had a 32hp 4-cylinder engine and shaft drive. The only body style offered was a 5-seater tourer at US$2500. It was sold for one season only, after which the company functioned as a garage and agency for other makes. However, in 1917 they merged with the Economy Motor Co. of Tiffin, Ohio, makers of the ECONOMY (ii).

NG

BELLIER (F) 1980 to date

1980–1990 Sté J. Bellier, Les Sables d'Olonne, Vendée.

1990 to date Sté J. Bellier (Automobiles Bellier), Talmont Saint-Hilaire.

The designer of the BEL-MOTORS Veloto, M. Bellier, formed a new company in 1980 to make his 2-seater microcar which he called the Formule 85. It was powered by a rear-mounted 50cc Motobécane engine with automatic transmission, although Sachs 125cc and diesel 325cc engines later became available as well. In 1986 a new range of cars was launched with the names XLD, GTD and VX, with a choice of Lombardini 325cc or 500cc engines. In 1994 a new VX minicar range was launched with a convertible appearance that echoed the Renault Clio. 2- and 4-seater versions were offered with 502cc twin-cylinder diesel engines developing either 5.4bhp or 12.5bhp. Despite its long standing, Bellier was always one of the minor players in the French voiturette market.

CR

BELMOBILE (US) 1912

Bell Motor Car Co., Detroit, Michigan.

The Belmobile Model A (in fact the only model they made) was a 2-seater roadster with a surprisingly long bonnet considering that it housed a 2-cylinder engine. Rated at 20hp, it was combined with a 2-speed gearbox and shaft drive. Introduced at the Detroit Automobile Show in January 1912, the Belmobile did not last out the year.

NG

BELMONT (i) (US) 1909–1910

1909–1910 Belmont Motor Vehicle Co., Castleton-on-Hudson, New York.
1910 Belmont Automobile Co., New Haven, Connecticut.

The Belmont was a conventional car with 30hp 4-cylinder engine and shaft drive, offered as a 4-seater tonneau or 5-seater tourer, both priced at $1650. Despite changes of company name and location, very few cars were made. One of the original backers was Dr C. Baxter Tiley, who also made the TILEY at Essex, Connecticut.

NG

BELMONT (ii) (US) 1916

Belmont Electric Automobile Co., Wyandotte, Michigan.

This company offered two models of electric car, a 4-seater limousine and a 6-seater limousine, as well as a light delivery vehicle. Production was very limited.

NG

BELMONT (iii) (US) 1917

Belmont Motor Co., Toledo, Ohio.

The Belmont Six was announced in March 1917, with a Buda engine, Hotchkiss drive and a price of $1750. Probably no more than two prototypes were made.

NG

BELSIZE (GB) 1897–1925

1897–1902 Marshall & Co., Manchester.
1903–1906 Belsize Motor & Engineering Co. Ltd, Manchester.
1906–1925 Belsize Motors Ltd, Manchester.

This car took its name from the Belsize Works, formerly a bicycle factory, where Marshall & Co. began making cars in 1897. These were based on the French HURTU, which in turn was a close replica of the BENZ. Some, though from photographic evidence not all, Marshalls had a tubular radiator at the front which was absent on the Hurtu and Benz. A Marshall won a Gold Medal at the Agricultural Hall Show in 1899, and one ran in the 1900 Thousand Miles Trial. A new design appeared in 1901, a shaft-driven 4-seater tonneau powered by a 12hp 2-cylinder Buchet engine. It was the first car to be called a Belsize, though this was a model name, the car being described as Marshall's 'Belsize'. The company was reformed as the Belsize Motor Car & Engineering Co. Ltd in 1903, and was reformed again with considerably more capital in 1906.

The twin was joined by a 20hp 3-cylinder car with dashboard radiator, and by 1906 the Belsize range included 18/24hp models with both three and four cylinders, a large 30/40hp four and an advanced 24/30hp six of 5880cc with overhead valves. This was made until 1908 and was joined by two larger sixes, the 7774cc 40hp and 11,724cc 60hp. More typical were the 1943cc 10/12hp made from 1912 to 1916 and 2543cc 14/16hp, made from 1909 to 1913. The 10/12, in particular, was one of the better Edwardian small cars, with side-valve engine, unit construction of engine and gearbox, and worm-drive rear axle. Belsize were also well-known for commercial vehicles at this time, from taxicabs to charabancs and fire engines powered by enormous engines of 14¹/₂-litres. In 1914 the works employed 1200 men and was turning out an average of 50 vehicles per week.

Belsize began the 1920s with a single model, the 2798cc 15hp, a rather old-fashioned design with fixed cylinder head, a well-made but dull car. It was joined in late 1921 by something completely different, the Belsize-Bradshaw light car powered by a 1294cc oil-cooled V-twin designed by Granville Bradshaw who had been responsible for the air-cooled flat-twin A.B.C., the Skootamota, and engines for numerous motorcycles. In fact, only the crankcase was cooled by the oil, which also lubricated the gearbox, multi-plate clutch, and steering box, the cylinder heads being air-cooled. The engines were made for Belsize by Dorman, and gained a reputation for overheating and difficult starting. Estimates of production range from 750 to about 1500, made from 1922 to 1924. For 1925 a 1250cc water-cooled four replaced the Bradshaw design, and there was also a new larger car in the shape of the 1696cc 14/30 six. This had overhead valves, a 4-speed gearbox and 4-wheel brakes. Few of these were made as the company was in the hands of a receiver, and the companion 2496cc 20/40 straight-8, priced at £1050, probably hardly emerged from the prototype stage.

NG

c.1982 Bellier F85 50cc microcar.
NICK GEORGANO

c.1990 Bellier XLD 325cc diesel microcar.
NICK GEORGANO

1900 Belsize dog cart (sold under the name of Marshall).
NATIONAL MOTOR MUSEUM

Further Reading
'The Belsize from Manchester', M. Worthington-Williams,
The Automobile, February 1984.
'The Car with the oil-cooled engine', Malcolm Jeal,
The Automobile, October 1989.

1903 Belsize 12/16hp tourer.
NATIONAL MOTOR MUSEUM

1909 Belsize 14/16hp tourer.
NATIONAL MOTOR MUSEUM

1921 Belsize 15.9hp tourer.
NATIONAL MOTOR MUSEUM

BEN HUR (US) 1917–1918
Ben Hur Motor Co., Willoughby, Ohio.

The Ben Hur was backed by L.L. Allen and designed by B.P. Bagby, neither very eye-catching names, so they chose that of the famous novel (and film) for their car. It was a good-looking torpedo tourer with wire wheels and a slightly pointed radiator. The engine was a 29hp 6-cylinder Buda, and three body styles were offered: 4-seater roadster, 7-seater tourer, and 7-seater touring sedan. By February 1918 between 30 and 40 cars had been delivered, but the company was in receivership three months later. Bagby then designed the Kay See (later the HIGHLANDER).

NG

BENBAR (AUS) 1912; B. & B. 1913
Bennett & Barkell Ltd, Sydney, New South Wales.

In line with the rage then for cyclecars, Bennett & Barkell, a motorcycle manufacturer, entered the fray. Built on a tubular chassis, the Benbar was powered by a 2-cylinder 8hp air-cooled Chater-Lea engine transmitting via a 3-speed gearbox and belt drive. There were cycle guards and an all-steel body with leather upholstery while a speed of 40mph was claimed. The company followed up in 1913 with the B. & B. cyclecar, also powered by a 2-cylinder Chater-Lea engine, with dual ignition, producing 14.7hp. A leather faced clutch, 3-speed gearbox and an overhead worm rear axle conveyed the drive. Its wheelbase measured 78in (1981mm) and it weighed 306kg. Possibly there was only one of each type made.

MG

BENDIX (i) (US) 1908–1909
The Bendix Co., Chicago, Illinois; Logansport, Indiana.

Vincent Bendix (1882–1945) was sales manager for the HOLSMAN Company, one of the best-known makers of high-wheelers, and when he set up on his own, his car was also a high-wheeler. It differed from most of the breed in having a 4-cylinder engine of 20/24hp, later increased to 30hp. It featured a double-disc friction transmission, which could also be used for braking. Final drive was by chains. The Chicago factory made the TRIUMPH (ii) which Bendix continued, as well as adding another make of his own, the DUPLEX (ii). About 7000 of the Bendix and Duplex were made up to 1909, but in 1910 Vincent Bendix joined F.A. AMES at Owensboro, Kentucky. He later achieved great fame and fortune in making magnetos, generators, braking systems, and washing machines.

NG

BENDIX (ii) (US) 1932–1934
Steel Wheel Corp., (Bendix Aviation Corp.), Elkhart, Indiana.

In 1934 Bendix developed a prototype automobile to study the feasibility of putting it into production. It was developed in secrecy under the phantom name of the Steel Wheel Corp. Designed by Al Ney, it had a Continental six engine and a proposed monocoque chassis made of Duramold, a wood-based composite. The prototype had a conventional steel chassis and the fully independent suspension was mounted in large blocks of rubber for very little movement. An aluminium body was added and the prototype was taken to Europe to show it off. No one was impressed and production was shelved.

HP

Further Reading
'FWD Bendix', Mike Lamm, *Special-Interest Autos*, Nov/Dec 1971.

BENELLI *see* BERETTA and F.A.M.

BENHAM (US) 1914
Benham Manufacturing Co., Detroit, Michigan.

In January 1914 George Benham bought the assets of the S. & M. company and built a slightly modified S. & M. under his own name. It was a handsome car, offered in roadster, tourer, and town car models, powered by a 6-cylinder Continental engine. Only 19 cars were made before the company was dissolved. The name survives in a very short street where the car was made, north of East Grand Boulevard (home of Packard).

NG

BENJAMIN; BENOVA (F) 1921–1931
Maurice Jeanson, Asnières, Seine.

The Benjamin was a typical light car which, although it had a 4-cylinder engine and shaft drive, just managed to keep within the cyclecar class (350kg overall weight). The engine was a 750cc side-valve unit of Jeanson's own manufacture, originated by Lemaître et Gerard, and early cars had a 3-speed transaxle with no differential. Like the Austin Seven, suspension was by transverse leaf spring at the front and quarter-elliptics at the rear. By 1923 there was a long-chassis model which could carry 4-seater tourer, saloon, and light truck bodies, and a single-ohc sports engine gave 62mph (100km/h) in a 2-seater. In 1924 Benjamin announced a true cyclecar in the shape of the P2. This had a 525cc vertical-twin 2-stroke engine mounted in the rear of a boat-shaped perimeter frame. Though the prototype won its class in the 1923 Tour de France, it was not a commercial success, and Benjamin hastily returned to 4-strokes, though they did list a 630cc 3-cylinder rear-engined car for 1925. Their larger cars now had Chapuis-Dornier or Ruby engines of 945 and 1095cc, the latter with overhead valves. Front-wheel brakes appeared on the last Benjamins which were shown at the 1926 Paris Salon.

The make reappeared in 1927 as the Benova (New Benjamin in Latin) which was made with the Chapuis-Dornier engine and also with a small straight-8 of 1502cc by S.C.A.P. This was made up to at least 1929, but the fours, in four sizes from 945cc to 2.1-litres, were listed up to 1931.
NG

BENNER (US) 1908–1909
Benner Motor Car Co., New York, New York.
The Benner Six was powered by 25/30hp ohv 6-cylinder engine designed and built by R.P. Benner who had been a machinist for more than eight years. Body styles were 2-seater runabout, 3-seater roadster, and 4-seater tourabout. Although he only had a small factory, at 1677 Broadway, he made about 200 cars, all of which were sold in the New York area, without showrooms or dealers.
NG

1925 Benjamin 7/22CV tourer.
NATIONAL MOTOR MUSEUM

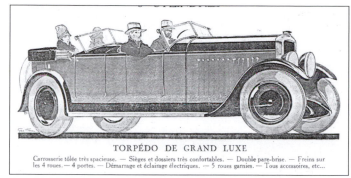
1928 Benova Type G 8-cylinder torpedo tourer.
NATIONAL MOTOR MUSEUM

NATIONAL MOTOR MUSEUM

BENDIX, VINCENT (1882–1945)
Vincent Bendix was born in Moline, Illinois, on 12 August 1882, the son of the Reverend John Bendix, a Methodist minister. He was only 16 when he went to New York to make his fortune. Working for a supply firm in the bicycle trade, he made improvements on chains and sprockets, and established contacts throughout the bicycle industry.

In 1901 he went to work for Glenn Curtiss who was then building the Torpedo motorcycle, leaving in 1904 to become general sales manager for the Holsman high-wheeler. He eventually started a new venture to make his own motor buggies, and the Bendix car was produced for him by the

Triumph Motor Co. of Cragin, Illinois. Starting in 1907, about 7000 were sold in around 18 months, although he maybe did not reap much financial benefit from this experience, for in 1909 he was working for Charles Foster in Chicago as a Cadillac salesman. A year later he was signed up as southern sales manager by the Haynes Automobile Co.

After seeing the Ames car at the Chicago motor show in 1910 and on a trip to the factory in Kentucky, he landed a contract to develop a new model and handle its marketing and sales.

The electric self-starter was still a very new device when he invented a self-disengaging starter drive, his first patent application being filed in 1912, but in 1913 the Eclipse Machine Co. of Elmira, New York, began production of the Bendix drive starter, and by 1940 they had made more than 60 million of them.

He became a director of the Parrett Tractor Co. of Delaware in 1918 and helped arrange its merger with the Hicks Tractor Co. in 1921, becoming president of the new company.

In 1923 Bendix bought the US manufacturing rights to the Perrot 4-wheel-brake patents and organised the Perrot Brake Co. in South Bend, Indiana. His reputation was more than nationwide, and 'he starts 'em and he stops 'em' became part of America's automotive folklore.

In 1929 he was elected chairman of Bendix-Cowdrey Brake Tester, Inc., and served as chairman of General Instrument Corp. He became a director of Bragg-Kliesrath Corp. in 1930 and was head of the Stromberg Carburetor Co. in 1931. He founded Bendix-Westinghouse to produce compressed-air brakes and power steering and started Bendix Aviation Corp. During the 1930s Bendix bought the rights to the Weiss constant velocity universal joint, organised the Bendix Corp. as a holding for his industrial interests, and put Bragg-Kliesrath, Eclipse Machine, and the Perrot Brake Co. into the holding as well. However, he sold majority control of the Bendix Corp. to General Motors. In 1942 he resigned from Bendix Aviation Corp., and two years later founded Bendix Helicopter Inc.

He died from a coronary thrombosis in New York on 27 March 1945.
JPN

1920 Bentley 3-litre all-weather tourer by Harrison.
NATIONAL MOTOR MUSEUM

BENNET (US) 1972 to date
Bennet Automotive, Hayward, California.
Although they specialised in Cobra replicas, Bennet also assembled kits from other manufacturers and sold kit car parts. The Bennet replicas have tube frames, and independent rear suspension was added in the 1990s.
HP

BENNETT (US) c.1983
Bennett Motorcars, Inc., Lakeland, Florida.
The Witton Tiger was the obvious inspiration of the Alden kit car built by Alden Bennett. The body was similar to a Tiger except for stainless-steel outside exhaust pipes poking out of the bonnet like an Excalibur. It used a steel tube chassis with Ford Pinto or Mustang II running gear and 4-, 6-, or 8-cylinder Ford engines.
HP

BENOIS ET DAMAS (F) 1903–1904
Benois et Damas, Neuilly-sur-Seine.
This company made a small number of 8hp 2-cylinder and 12hp 4-cylinder cars, both with shaft drive. The factory was part-owned by Adolphe Clement, and may have made the Sphinx engines used in CLEMENT-BAYARD, GLADIATOR, and TALBOT (i) cars.
NG

BENSON (US) 1901
Benson Automobile Co., Cleveland, Ohio.
This company was formed to take over the steam car activities of the EASTMAN Automobile Company. The Eastman design was slightly modified to become the Benson, and about 12 were made before the end of 1901.
NG

BENTALL (GB) 1906–1913
E.H. Bentall & Co. Ltd, Maldon, Essex.
Bentall were agricultural engineers with a history dating back to 1797, and are still in business today. They began small-scale production of cars in 1906, starting with two twins, of 9 and 11hp, and a 16/20hp 4-cylinder car. These had over-square engine dimensions (100 × 95mm), which put them at a disadvantage in a tax system whereby the rate was decided on the bore alone. Nevertheless, quite a number were sold, mostly to farmers who were familiar with Bentall's reputation in the agricultural field, though some went abroad. One of the last, a 1912 16/20 cabriolet, was bought by the MP for Maldon. The Delaunay-Belleville-like round radiators were made in France, and the cars were supplied in chassis form only. Most bodies came from W.F. Thorn of Islington, Munnions of Chelmsford, and Adams of Colchester. About 100 Bentalls were made, of which one survives today.
NG

Further Reading
'From Ploughshares to Cars – and Back Again', M. Worthington-Williams, *The Automobile,* August 1987.

BENTEL (i) (US) 1900–1901
The Theodore F. Bentel Co. Ltd, Pittsburgh, Pennsylvania.
A prominent bicycle dealer, Theodore Bentel designed a steam car which would be especially suited to the heavy roads and steep hills of Western Pennsylvania. A few cars were built, but technical details are lacking.
NG

BENTEL (ii) (US) 1916–1919
George R. Bentel, Los Angeles, California.
George Bentel was the Los Angeles MERCER distributor, who began to customise cars for his clients, eliminating running boards and providing disc wheels in brass or nickel finish, which could be fitted over standard wire or wood wheels. When World War I brought supplies of new cars to an end, Bentel customised old ones, selling them for as much as $10,000. Among the chassis he worked on were JORDAN and SIMPLEX. The coming of peace and the availability of new cars killed the demand for Bentel's creations.
NG

BENTLEY (GB) 1919 to date
1919–1931 Bentley Motors Ltd, Cricklewood, London.
1933–1935 Bentley Motors (1931) Ltd, Derby.
1946–1971 Bentley Motors (1931) Ltd, Crewe, Cheshire.
1971 to date Rolls-Royce Motor Cars Ltd, Crewe, Cheshire.

After World War I, W.O. Bentley returned to the partnership which he shared with his brother, H.M. Bentley, the main business of which was selling imported D.F.P.s. However, his ambition was to make a car bearing his own name, and to this end he formed Bentley Motors Ltd in August 1919. Nominal share capital was £200,000, but cash in the bank was only £18,575. Bentley Motors was under-capitalised from the start, and this situation did not improve for the rest of the company's 12-year life. A mortgage had to be taken out to build the factory in Cricklewood, so it was hardly surprising that it took two years for the first car to reach a customer.

The first prototypes were made at New Street Mews, off Baker Street in central London, in a property belonging to J.H. Easter, who had trimmed the bodies of the D.F.P.s. Bentley's right-hand man in designing the new car was Frank Burgess, a former works driver and designer for Humber, who had been responsible for the twin-ohc engines used in that company's 1914 Tourist Trophy racing cars. These, in turn, owed much to the pioneering twin-cam engine designed by Ernest Henry for the 1912 Peugeot GP cars. Burgess brought a TT Humber to Bentley Motors, and there were clear similarities in the designs, though the Bentley unit had only a single-ohc, shaft driven from the front of the crankshaft. Like the Peugeot, there were four valves per cylinder. The stroke was unusually long, dimensions being 80 × 149mm, giving a capacity of 2996cc. The car was called the 3-litre Bentley, the first time a British car had been described in terms of litres rather than horsepower. The cylinder head was non-detachable, a feature of all Cricklewood Bentleys. The rest of the car was conventional enough, with a 4-speed gearbox controlled by a right-hand gear lever, semi-elliptic leaf springs all round, and brakes on the rear wheels only (until 1924).

The new car was announced in *The Autocar* in May 1919, before any had been built, and even before Bentley Motors was formed. There was an illustration by the magazine's resident artist, F. Gordon Crosby, who had followed Bentley's ideas as to what the car should look like. However, the pointed radiator and winged 'B' were Crosby's own work. The radiator was more pointed than in the actual car, closer to that of the D.F.P. A chassis was ready for London's first postwar Motor Show in October 1919, but the engine was a dummy with no crankshaft. By Christmas an engine was running at New Street Mews (causing protests from the irate matron of a nearby nursing home), and deliveries were promised for June 1920. However, development work took longer than expected, and the first car was not delivered until September 1921.

With a chassis price of £1050 it was one of the most expensive cars on the British market, yet sales built up quite encouragingly, from 21 in 1921 to 122 in 1922, 204 in 1923, and 402 in 1924. The standard 4-seater tourer body was made by Vanden Plas, whose premises were close to Cricklewood, and many other body styles were built by custom coachbuilders, from stark 2-seaters to heavy landaulets. W.O. never anticipated that his cars would carry formal bodies, but the customers had to be satisfied, and a longer chassis was listed from 1923. Three basic types of 3-litre were made, usually described by the colour of their badge. They can be summarised as follows:

Blue Label – The standard model with 117.5in (2982mm) wheelbase, made from 1921 to 1929, together with a 130in (3300mm) wheelbase made from 1923 to 1929.

Red Label – The 117.5in (2982mm) chassis with higher compression ratio (5.3:1) made from 1924 to 1929.

Green Label – Extra short wheelbase, 108in (2741mm), with 6.3:1 compression ratio. Guaranteed 100mph (160km/h) top speed. Made from 1924 to 1926.

Describing the 3-litre models by their badge colours became a tradition, but there were no hard and fast rules. In fact, a customer could have whatever colour badge he wanted, to match the colour of the coachwork. Some yellow and maroon badges were seen. Production of all 3-litres totalled 1622.

By the mid-1920s Bentley was already thought of as the archetypal British sports car, with the mystique which it has had ever since. Racing successes at Le Mans (five victories between 1924 and 1930) ensured that the layman knew more about it than any other sporting make, and the glamour of owners such as actresses Beatrice Lillie and Gertrude Lawrence, not to mention Prince George (later the Duke of Kent) and the 'Bentley Boys' headed by Woolf Barnato, kept the tabloid press interested.

The popularity of heavy coachwork led Bentley to plan a larger car, initially with a 4½-litre 6-cylinder engine. A prototype was extensively tested in France in 1925, where a chance encounter with the prototype Rolls-Royce Phantom I

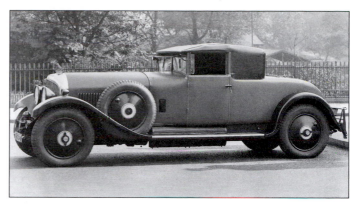

1927 Bentley 6½-litre coupé.
NATIONAL MOTOR MUSEUM

1937 Bentley 4¼ -litre saloon by Park Ward.
NATIONAL MOTOR MUSEUM

convinced Bentley that an even larger engine was needed. The 6-cylinder ended up with a capacity of 6597cc, being known as the 6½-litre. It went into production in 1925, and was made in three wheelbases, 132 (3350mm), 144 (3655mm), and 150in (3807mm). The longest made for an enormous car, 200in (5076mm) long, as large as a Rolls Phantom 1 or Daimler 45hp, and it carried very fine formal coachwork. A sporting version of the 6½-litre with higher cr and twin SU carburetters was known as the Speed Six. Total production of the 6½-litre, which lasted up to 1930, was 545, of which 182 were Speed Sixes. In 1930 came the largest Bentley, an enlarged 6½-litre whose capacity went up to 7983cc. Known as the 8-litre, it had a lower frame with outset rear springs, and a new gearbox. Output was 200 or 225bhp according to cr, and the 8-litre had a remarkable performance, being capable of 100mph (160km/h) so long as the body was not too heavy. Unfortunately, its introduction in October 1930, coincided with a low ebb in the company's fortunes, not helped by the Depression. Only 67 of the planned 100 8-litre chassis were sold by the company while it was still independent, the remaining 33 being completed under the direction of the receiver. The last was delivered in December 1932, though completed earlier; 35 8-litres were on the short (142in/3604mm) wheelbase, and 65 on the long (156in/3960mm).

On the sporting side Bentley decided that more power was needed from the 4-cylinder engine, and in 1927 brought out the 4½-litre, which had the same cylinder dimensions as the 6½. With a capacity of 4398cc and output of 110bhp, the 4½ could exceed 90mph (145km/h) with a light sporting body, and replicas of the Le Mans cars could do 100mph (160km/h). Two wheelbases were available, 117.5 (2982mm) and 130in (3300mm). The Le Mans cars had the shorter chassis, and at first it was expected that most sales would be of these, as the carriage trade was catered for by the 6½- litre. However, more customers ordered the longer chassis which carried quite formal coachwork. The nearest to standard coachwork on the 4½ was the 4-seater open tourer by Vanden Plas, which they also built on the 3- and 6½-litre chassis. Among providers of saloon and coupé bodies were Hooper, Maythorn, Gurney Nutting, H.J. Mulliner, and Windover. The 4½-litre was in production from the summer of 1927 until June 1931, and few changes were thought necessary. In 1929 a plate clutch replaced the former cone variety, and the heavier crankshaft fitted to the supercharged models was used on all 4½s from mid-1929.

1948 Bentley Mark VI 4¼-litre saloon.
NATIONAL MOTOR MUSEUM

1963 Bentley S3 Continental saloon by Park Ward.
NATIONAL MOTOR MUSEUM

The most important variation was the controversial supercharged model, or 'Blower 4½' as it is usually known. This came about because Sir Henry Birkin, who had won at Le Mans in 1928 with a standard 4½, realised that more power would be needed if Bentley were to repeat the performance in 1929. A 4½-litre belonging to Bernard Rubin was taken to Birkin's workshops at Welwyn Garden City (owned by Dorothy Paget) and fitted with a Roots-type supercharger designed by Amherst Villiers, then Britain's leading expert on forced induction. The blower more than doubled the power, from 110 to 240bhp. However, there is some mystery about the early work on the Blower Bentley, and it is likely that initial work took place at Cricklewood. W.O.'s well-known dislike of supercharging ('it would pervert its design and corrupt its performance,' he said) meant that extensive work on supercharging would not be welcome at Cricklewood. The competition cars were prepared at Welwyn, but the run of 50 production blown cars was made at Cricklewood as they were favoured by Woolf Barnato who was financing the company. For long distance racing W.O. was proved right, for the 1929 and 1930 Le Mans races were won by unblown Speed Sixes, while Birkin's Blower 4½ set a new lap record in 1930 and then retired. The Blower Bentley was catalogued for 1929, to meet Le Mans rules that at least 50 cars had to be made to allow entry to the race. No more than the 50 were built, (plus five 'Birkin' cars) and they are among the most sought-after Bentleys today. Just over half, 26 cars, were fitted with Vanden Plas open 4-seater bodies, the other carrying a variety of coachwork from open 2-seaters to saloons. Overall production of the 4½-litre was 665.

The last Cricklewood Bentley was the 4-litre, built as an emergency measure to provide a cheaper car than the 8-litre. Unlike all the earlier cars, it did not have an ohc engine but an inlet-over-exhaust layout designed by Sir Harry Ricardo. Capacity was 3915cc and output about 120bhp. Unfortunately the chassis, based on that of the 8-litre, was too heavy to allow for reasonable performance. 'A basically sound engine was fitted to a grossly overweight chassis intended for a car with twice the engine capacity and 80% more power' (Michael Hay in *Bentley, the Factory Cars*). This, coupled with the departure from the traditional overhead camshaft, has led the 4-litre to be despised by many Bentley enthusiasts. Just 50 were made.

NICK BALDWIN

BENTLEY, W.O. (1888–1971)

It is a coincidence of motoring history that the men behind two of Britain's best-known cars, Henry Royce and Walter Owen Bentley, should have begun their careers as railway engineering apprentices, Royce with the Great Northern Railway at Peterborough, and Bentley in the same company's shops at Doncaster. The parallel ends there, though, for while Royce came from a very poor background and had to cut short his apprenticeship because his aunt could no longer support him, Bentley's family were comfortably off. His father was a businessman and the family lived in Avenue Road, St John's Wood, in London. He was educated at Clifton College, like his five brothers, leaving at 16 to join the GNR, where he worked under Henry Ivatt, designer of the 4-4-2 Atlantic locomotives. Having originally despised the motorcar as a 'disgraceful vehicle that splashed people with mud', Bentley soon found

more pleasure in motorcycles and cars than in railways. He raced a 5hp Rex motorcycle at Brooklands in 1909 and bought his first car, a second-hand Riley V-twin in 1910. He worked as a General Assistant at the National Motor Cab Co. in Hammersmith (which later made the K.R.C. light car), then in 1912 joined his brother Henry, always known as 'H.M.' just as he was known as 'W.O.', in selling D.F.P. cars. He improved their performance with the use of lighter pistons made of 88 per cent aluminium and 12 per cent copper. The Bentley-improved D.F.P.s won several races at Brooklands, and, with a new Bentley-designed camshaft, took Class B records in 1913 and 1914. He covered the 'flying mile' at 89.7mph (144.3km/h) – a creditable speed for a 2-litre car. The Bentley brothers persuaded D.F.P. to adopt aluminium pistons in a production car, which they sold as the 12/40, though few were made as they were launched less than a month before the outbreak of World War I.

During the war Bentley worked for the Technical Board of the Royal Naval Air Service, improving the French Clerget rotary engine, where his experience with aluminium pistons was of great value. The modified Clerget engines were called BR1 and BR2 (Bentley Rotary), and were made by Gwynne and Humber.

After the war 'W.O.' returned to the partnership of Bentley & Bentley, but soon gave all his attention to Bentley Motors, whose first car was announced in May 1919. Always short of capital, Bentley approached the millionaire sportsman Woolf Barnato for help in 1925. This resulted in a virtual take-over by Barnato, who held 109,400 £1 preference shares and 114,000 one shilling ordinary shares in the reformed company, of which he was chairman. By contrast, Bentley had 6000 and 3000 shares, respectively, though 'H.M.' and a few other people had some shares as well. 'H.M.' was not happy with the new regime, and soon resigned, but 'W.O.' got on well with Barnato, who never overruled him on engineering and racing matters. As 'W.O.' said: 'He looked on me as an engineer first, a racing manager second, and a businessman third – a poor third'.

Bankruptcy and New Ownership

Bentley Motors was under-capitalised from the start, and would probably have failed in 1925 without the support of the millionaire sportsman Woolf Barnato. His support came at the expense of W.O. losing control of his company, for Barnato held a large proportion of the shares of the reorganised company. By June 1931 the company's debts were so large that it could not continue trading. Barnato was unable or unwilling to extend his support. A receiver was called in, and it was thought that NAPIER, with which Bentley had had discussions about a new car, would be the new owners. However, they were outbid by a mysterious organisation called the British Central Equitable Trust Ltd. Several days passed before even Bentley himself learnt that the Trust represented ROLLS-ROYCE. A new company was formed, Bentley Motors (1931) Ltd, which was a wholly-owned subsidiary of Rolls-Royce, and W.O. found himself an employee with little say in the design of the new car. Increasingly unhappy, he left to join LAGONDA in 1935. The Cricklewood factory was sold to Addressograph Multigraph Ltd in October 1932, and was later sold to Smiths Instruments Ltd, who continued there until the early 1980s, when the factory was demolished to make way for a trading estate.

The new Bentley was announced in the summer of 1933. Known as the 3½-litre, it had a modified Rolls-Royce 20/25 engine in a new chassis which had been designed for a 2½-litre Rolls that never went into production. The 3669cc pushrod ohv engine had a higher compression ratio than when it was used in the 20/25, twin carburettors, and improved cylinder head design. Output was about 105bhp, 20bhp more than in the Rolls. The chassis was conventional, with semi-elliptic springs all round, and brakes were assisted by an engine-driven servo. The 4-speed gearbox had synchromesh on the two upper ratios. Following Rolls-Royce tradition, the 3½ was supplied as a chassis only, but the makers recommended a number of styles which were made in small runs by the coachbuilders. This cut costs and reduced waiting time for delivery. The best-known of these recommended bodies were the 4-door saloon by Park Ward and open tourer by Vanden Plas.

The new 'Rolls Bentley' as the popular press dubbed it, was a much smoother and more comfortable car than those from Cricklewood, and very little slower

1977 Bentley Corniche convertible and T series saloon.
NATIONAL MOTOR MUSEUM

than a 4½ over twisting roads. It may have disappointed the purists who worshipped the vintage Bentleys with their outside gearchange and burbling exhausts, but most people were delighted with the 3½. Even W.O. himself said 'Taking all things into consideration, I would rather own this Bentley than any other car produced under that name', while enthusiasts such as Raymond Mays, Sir Malcolm Campbell, George Eyston, and Woolf Barnato were happy customers. Motor industry figures who favoured the new car included R. Gordon Sutherland of Aston Martin, Leonard Lord of Austin, Archie Frazer Nash, and David Brown. As with the vintage Bentleys, the performance of the 3½ was hampered by increasingly heavy coachwork, and in 1936 more power was obtained from the 4257cc engine used in the Rolls-Royce 25/30.

Barnato was one of the colourful team of drivers known as the Bentley Boys, who did so much to promote the company's name during the1920s, especially with their string of five Le Mans victories. Mostly younger than 'W.O.', and much richer, they made his role a curious one: 'I was part father confessor, part schoolmaster, who was always happy to climb down from the rostrum and join in any classroom foolery'. Nevertheless, they accepted his discipline on the race track, if only because they knew that there were many contenders for a place in the team.

Bentley was regarded as a fair employer, but one who would brook no slackness or mistreatment of his tools. There was a legend that if there was an apprentice doing anything very wrong, he would stop and look at the offender, and that look was so penetrating that he would never grow any taller. If the offence was very bad indeed, 'W.O.' would not only stop, but he would take his pipe out of his mouth as well, and the look was so severe that the offender would shrivel up and be dwarfed forever.

In June 1931 Barbato withdrew his support, allowing Bentley Motors to go into liquidation. Though his fortune had been badly hit by the Wall Street Crash, he undoubtedly could have net the mortgages amounting to £65,000, but was probably dissuaded by his financial advisers, who had no sympathy with cars, and particularly with motor racing. In his autobiography Bentley showed remarkably little bitterness over this decision, which brought about the end of his independent company. He hoped that Bentley Motors might be taken over by Napier, and indeed plans were made for a Napier-Bentley luxury sports car. However, at the last minute Napier were outbid by a mysterious group called the British Central Equitable Trust, of which newspapers said that 'nothing is known of its intentions, nor is any director of the Trust apparently identified with motor-manufacturing interests'. It was only a few days later, and then not in a formal statement but through remarks overheard by Mrs Bentley at a cocktail party, that 'W.O.' learnt that the trust was a front for Rolls-Royce.

Bentley was retained as an employee by Rolls-Royce, but had little say in design matters, and became increasingly unhappy with his position. When his contract came up for renewal in 1935 he resigned, joining Lagonda, which had just changed hands. Its new owner, Alan Good, announced that the company was going to build the best car in the world, and that Bentley had two years in which to do it. The result was the V12, which appeared at the 1937 London Motor Show, although 'W.O.' also had a hand in improving the 6-cylinder cars. He was aided by a number of former Rolls-Royce staff who he had lured away from Derby, in particular Stuart Tresilian, who persuaded him to use a short stroke for the V12. He was also responsible for the 2-litre dohc engine which powered the postwar Lagonda, and which attracted David Brown to buy up Lagonda so that he could use the engine in the Aston Martin DB2. Brown decided not to retain Bentley's services; 'I was told that he would sit in a car for an hour or so, puffing his pipe, and then say "We must raise the dashboard one inch", only to have it put back the way it was later'.

Bentley later developed a dohc 3-litre engine for Armstrong-Siddeley, but they decided that they could perfectly well design an engine for themselves, and rejected Bentley's design on the grounds of a noisy camshaft drive. In his retirement he was a revered figure to the Bentley Drivers' Club, welcoming many gatherings of the vintage cars at his home in Surrey.

Bentley was married three times. His first wife, Leonie, died shortly after World War I. He then married Poppy (marriage dissolved 1932), and finally, in 1934, Margaret Robert Hutton, with whom he enjoyed a very happy marriage. She survived him by 18 years, dying in 1989 at the age of nearly 98. He had no children.

NG

Further Reading
The Cars in My Life, W.O.Bentley, Hutchinson, 1961.
W.O. Bentley, Engineer, Donald Bastow, Haynes, 1978.

1992 Bentley Continental R coupé.
NATIONAL MOTOR MUSEUM

Performance was about the same as the early 3½s, 90mph (145km/h) with reasonable coachwork. In 1938 the 4¼ was given an overdrive top gear with the new Autobahnen in mind. This meant that at 90mph (145km/h) the engine was turning at about 1500rpm less than with the ordinary top gear. Production of the 4¼-litre was 1234, slightly more than that of the 3½, which found 1177 customers.

The final pre-World War II Bentley was the Mark V which borrowed coil ifs from the Rolls-Royce Wraith, and had synchromesh on second gear as well as the higher ratios. Introduced in the summer of 1939, it was killed by the war. Nineteen chassis were completed, though not all were bodied, together with 11 experimental cars of Mk V type. These included the Corniche streamlined saloon and the 'Scalded Cat' which was fitted with a 5.6-litre straight-8 engine similar to that in the Rolls-Royce Phantom IVs. In addition, six incomplete chassis were put into storage, and used to provide spare parts.

Postwar Success and Decline

From 1946 onwards Bentley came ever closer to Rolls-Royce in design and styling, and the name was near to extinction in the early 1980s, before company policy favoured a more distinctive image which has lasted up to the present. The Mk VI announced in the Spring of 1946 shared with the Rolls-Royce Silver Wraith a 4257cc engine, similar in size to the prewar unit, but with inlet-over-exhaust valve layout. There were a few differences between the engines; the Bentley had a high-lift camshaft and twin carburettors. While the Silver Wraith was still offered in chassis form only, the Bentley had a standard 4-door saloon body made by Pressed Steel at Oxford, and finished at the Rolls factory at Crewe. Although numerous custom styles were made on the Mk VI chassis, about 80 per cent carried the standard steel body. This was also used by Rolls from 1949 on their Silver Dawn model. From mid-1951 the engine was enlarged to 4566cc, and the R-type Bentley (1952–55) had a larger luggage boot and optional automatic transmission on the later cars.

In 1952 the R-type Continental fast-back coupé was introduced as a catalogued model, with body by H.J. Mulliner. It was developed from the ordinary R-type by Ivan Evernden and styled by J.P. Blatchley, both of Rolls-Royce. Most of the 208 R-type Continentals had the beautiful Mulliner bodies, but some were bodied by Abbott (coupé) or Park Ward (convertible). In April 1955 the R-type/Silver Dawn was replaced by the S-type/Silver Cloud which had a 4887cc engine in a new Pressed Steel saloon body. There was now

no difference between the Bentley and Rolls-Royce versions apart from the radiator, for which Rolls buyers paid £130 more. The Continental was continued in the S-type, as a Mulliner coupé or Park Ward coupé and convertible. By 1959 the 6-cylinder engine, which dated back to the Rolls-Royce Twenty of 1922, had reached the limits of its development, yet more power was needed if Rolls-Royce was to keep up with the larger American cars. The answer was a completely new V8 engine of 6230cc, the largest used in a Bentley since the demise of the 8-litre. Yet it weighed 10lbs lighter than the six, thanks to the light alloy block, and with the same body as the S1, the new S2 was 15mph (24km/h) faster. Introduced in 1959, the engine remained largely unchanged until 1970, when it was enlarged to 6750cc. Twin headlamps arrived on the S3 of 1962, and special models were still available, such as the Continental coupé or convertible by H.J. Mulliner and Park Ward, who had merged in 1961, and the Mulliner Flying Spur 4-door saloon. After the introduction of the S3 there was no longer any difference in engine specification between the Continental and the regular models. The last Continental chassis was delivered to the coachbuilders on 29 November 1965, and was not received by the customer until January 1966, four months after the model had been officially replaced by the T Series.

In October 1965 all Bentley and Rolls-Royce saloons gave way to a new, integral-construction 4-door saloon with self-levelling independent suspension all round. This was sold as the Bentley T Series and Rolls-Royce Silver Shadow. There were no body styles peculiar to the Bentley, though there were some variations on the standard saloon with both radiators. These included a James Young 2-door saloon, and a 2-door saloon and convertible by H.J. Mulliner/ Park Ward which were renamed Corniche in 1971. The T Series years were lean ones for the Bentley marque, with a very small proportion wearing Bentley radiators. In the early postwar years the Mk VI outsold the Silver Dawn and coachbuilt Silver Wraith by three to one, but in the 1970s fewer than 10 per cent of Rolls-Royce sales were Bentleys, and in 1980 the figure dropped to 4 per cent. It seemed hardly economic to perpetuate the name, but instead of dropping Bentley, Rolls-Royce directors, led by Peter Ward, decided to give it greater individuality.

A Bentley Revival

In 1980 the T Series/Silver Shadow was replaced by a new car with freshly styled body designed by Austrian-born Fritz Feller. They were a little longer, wider and lower, with 30 per cent more glass area. The Bentley version was called the

Mulsanne after one of the straight stretches on the Le Mans circuit where the Bentley Boys had distinguished themselves more than 50 years before. The Spring of 1982 saw the first high-performance model which was to distance the Bentley image from Rolls-Royce. This was the Mulsanne Turbo which used a Garrett AiResearch turbocharger to give a boost in power of around 50 per cent, from 200 to 300bhp. Top speed was limited to 135mph (217km/h) by a sensor which restricted turbo boost, but acceleration from 0 to 60mph (0-96km/h) took only 7.5 seconds, no mean feat for a car weighing 4950lbs. The Turbo's body was similar to that of the Mulsanne, but it could be easily identified by the painted radiator shell, the same colour as the rest of the body, instead of in silver. The makers were adamant that the Turbo would never carry a Rolls-Royce radiator, and it has been calculated that if it did, an additional 35bhp would be needed to obtain the same performance, because of the drag imposed by the square radiator shell.

In 1985 the Turbo was joined by an improved model, the Turbo R with modified suspension and larger tyres. The range was completed by a lower priced Bentley, the Eight with mesh grille and less luxurious interior. Its price in 1984 was £49,497, or £5943 less than a Mulsanne and £12,246 less than a Mulsanne Turbo. In September 1992 the Eight and Mulsanne S were replaced by the Brooklands which featured a new bonnet and green badge harking back to the vintage Green Label models. This remained the 'base' model Bentley until 1998. The sporting image of Bentley brought about a dramatic increase in sales. In 1986, when the group sold 2603 cars the ratio between Rolls and Bentley was 60:40, and in 1991, with lower overall sales of 1731, the ratio was approximately 50:50. A few years later the proportion was 60:40 in favour of Bentley. In 1991 a new and more distinctive coupé joined the saloons. The Continental R was a 2-door 4-seater coupé styled by Ken Greenley and John Heffernan, and was derived from a concept car of 1985 called Project 90. The engine was slightly tweaked to give 333bhp, and a 4-speed General Motors automatic gearbox replaced the 3-speeder of previous models, though all Rolls and Bentleys received the 4-speed box in the Spring of 1992. A convertible version of the Continental, the Azure, styled and built by Pininfarina, appeared in 1995, while the previous year had seen another convertible, the Java concept car which was planned to have a smaller engine. 1996 saw a short-wheelbase Continental T with output boosted to 410bhp.

In the Spring of 1998 the Rolls-Royce Silver Seraph was announced with BMW V12 engine; the Bentley version was called the Arnage and used a turbocharged 4398cc BMW V8 giving 354bhp and 5-speed automatic transmission in the same body shell. Alongside this, the Azure convertible was continued with the old 389bhp 6750cc V8, as well as the Continental S coupé and 426bhp T coupé. They were joined in autumn 1998 by the SC (Sedanca Coupé). This had a fixed rear portion of the body and output raised to 408bhp. For 2000 the 6750cc V8 was available in the Arnage bodyshell, with a Red Label badge. The BMW-powered Arnage was named the Green Label, both names recalling 1920s 3-litre Bentleys.

New Ownership
In June 1998 Rolls-Royce Motors was bought from Vickers by Volkswagen in a surprise bid after it had been expected that it would be acquired by BMW. The supply of BMW engines for Bentley and Rolls-Royce cars seemed in doubt, but two months later the two German firms reached an agreement whereby VW would retain control of Rolls until the end of 2002, when it would pass to BMW. Bentley will remain in VW hands. VW ownership led to several projected new Bentleys totally different from existing models. The 1999 Geneva Show saw the Hunaudières concept car with 4-wheel drive and mid-mounted 64-valve W16 engine displacing 8litres and developing 623bhp. It was suggested that the car signalled Ferdinand Piech's determination to see the Bentley name back at Le Mans, but opinion was divided as to whether the supercar would be built for sale. Shortly afterwards it was announced that the Bentley name might appear on a V12 off-roader built on an extended version of the forthcoming VW Transporter.

NG

Further Reading
W.O. Bentley, Engineer, Donald Bastow, Haynes, 1978.
The Cars in my Life, W.O. Bentley, Hutchinson, 1961.
Bentley, the Silent Sports Car 1931–1941, Michael Ellman-Brown, Dalton Watson, 1989.
Bentleys Past and Present, A.F. Rivers Fletcher, Gentry Books, 1982.

1995 Bentley Turbo R saloon.
ROLLS-ROYCE MOTOR CARS

From Cricklewood to Crewe, Michael Frostick, Osprey 1980 (particularly useful on the financial background).
Bentley, Fifty Years of the Marque, Johnnie Green, Dalton Watson, 1969.
The Vintage Bentley 1919–1931, Michael Hay, Dalton Watson, 1986.
All the Pre-war Bentleys, as new, Stanley Sedgwick, Bentley Drivers' Club 1976 (Production figures of prewar Bentleys, so often disputed, are taken from this book, in which the author says 'The summary of production cars supersedes all previous editions... and must, I think, stand unchallenged for all time.')
Bentley, the Cars from Crewe, Rodney Steel, Dalton Watson, 1988.
The Bentley Bedside Book, Hugh Young (compiler), Bentley Drivers' Club, 1961 (not definitive, but a fascinating pot-pourri of reminiscences and little-known facts).

BENZ (D) 1885–1926
1885–1899 Benz & Cie, Rheinische Gasmotorenfabrik, Mannheim.
1899–1911 Benz & Cie, Rheinische Gasmotorenfabrik AG, Mannheim.
1911–1926 Benz & Cie, Rheinische Automobil- und Motorenfabrik AG, Mannheim.
Among all the claims about the maker of the world's first motorcar, there can be little doubt that the first petrol-engined car to run successfully and to lead to production within a few years was that of Karl Benz (1844–1929). In the early 1880s Benz was running a small company making stationary engines. While his partners Kaspar Rose and Friedrich Esslinger concentrated on the profitable side of the business, Benz became increasingly absorbed in the challenge of making a suitable engine to power a road vehicle. The stationary engines were 2-strokes running on coal gas, but Benz decided that petrol was the better fuel for a much smaller engine, and that it should be a 4-stroke. His first engine had a 954cc horizontal single cylinder, and developed 0.75bhp at 400rpm. This was slow compared with the engine of his rival Gottlieb Daimler, which turned at 750rpm, but Benz always favoured slow running engines, claiming that they were less likely to shake themselves to pieces. Even in 1900 Benz engines were no faster than 700rpm, when a De Dion-Bouton turned at more than twice that speed. Benz's ignition was advanced, being by battery and coil, whereas Daimler used the hot tube system, but there was no radiator – the water was just allowed to boil away. The Benz engine was mounted in a light tubular frame, and transmission was by a flat leather belt to a countershaft, final drive being by double-chains to the rear wheels. The first car had no system for changing gear, but the belt could be moved from a free pulley on the countershaft to a fixed one, to give the action of a clutch. The unsprung single wheel was at the front because, like many pioneers, Benz could not design a steering layout for two front wheels, being ignorant of the Ackermann system.

The 3-wheeler was ready by the autumn of 1885, but there is no record of when it made its first run. These were held within Benz premises to start with, and probably no trials on public roads took place until early 1886. He received a patent on 29 January 1886, but the first mention in the local press did not occur until 4 June. A month later the correspondent of the *Neue Badische Landeszeitung* was able to record that he had ridden in the car. It seems to have performed quite well, and Benz built a second car, similar in design, but with a

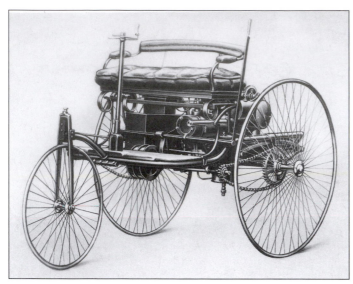

1886 Benz 3-wheeler.
NATIONAL MOTOR MUSEUM

1903 Benz Parsifal 8/10PS phaeton.
NATIONAL MOTOR MUSEUM

1910 Benz 100PS Prince Henry tourer.
NATIONAL MOTOR MUSEUM

full-elliptic spring for the front wheel, followed by a third which had a number of important improvements. These included a larger engine of 1045cc developing 1.5bhp at 500rpm, a 2-speed transmission by belt and pulleys, and wooden spoke instead of wire wheels. This Modell 3 was the first Benz to go into production, about 25 being made from 1888 to 1894. Larger engines of 1660 and 1990cc were fitted to the later cars.

Production and Exports

At first Benz found it very difficult to sell his cars. The idea of a horseless carriage was so novel that hardly anybody was prepared to buy one. He might never have become established as a manufacturer had he not shown a car at the Munich Engineering Exhibition in September 1888. He found only one buyer but he was an influential one. Emile Roger had been selling Benz gas engines in France for several years, and thought that a car would be an attention-getting addition to his line. He exhibited the car under his own name, and later took out a licence to assemble Benz cars in Paris. Frenchmen were more adventurous than the conservative citizens of Mannheim, and of the 69 cars made up to the end of 1893 (these included 4-wheelers) 42 were sold in France, 15 in Germany, and 12 in other countries. In 1890 two new partners replaced Rose and Esslinger; Friedrich von Fisher and Julius Ganss were more sympathetic to the motorcar, but also had a sound commercial approach which was an essential foil to Benz's idealistic character.

In 1893 the first Benz 4-wheeler appeared. This was the Viktoria, powered by a 1745cc engine developing 3bhp, the general layout of engine and transmission being similar to that of the 3-wheelers. Engine size was gradually increased, to 1990cc in 1894, 2650cc in 1895, and 2925cc in 1898. The first Viktorias were 2-seaters, but a 4-seater *vis-à-vis* was soon available, followed by a 4-seater with all seats facing forwards, a landaulette, and a 6-seater phaeton. Delivery vans and buses were also built on the Viktoria chassis. As a companion to the heavy and expensive Viktoria, Benz brought out the Velo in 1894. This was a lighter machine, selling for between DM2000 and DM2800, compared with DM3800-6000 for the Viktoria. The Velo's 1045cc engine developed 1.5bhp to start with, but by 1900 had risen to 3bhp with no increase in capacity. The Velo had wire wheels and only two seats, but otherwise the layout was similar to the Viktoria, with horizontal rear-mounted engine and belt and pulley transmission. A 3-seater called the Comfortable was available from 1896.

The arrival of the Velo saw a great increase in Benz sales. From 129 cars (of all models) in 1895, they rose to 181 in 1896, 256 in 1897, and 603 by 1900. The 1896 figure was greater than the combined production of all cars in Great Britain and the United States. Up to the turn of the century the Benz was the world's best-known car, and there were a number of imitators. Among these were the HURTU in France, the ARNOLD, MARSHALL, LIVER, and STAR(i) in Britain, all based on the Velo, while the American MUELLER-BENZ from Chicago and the Columbus, Ohio-built Benz Spirit were derived from the Viktoria. In 1899 a flat-twin engine of 1710cc, known as the Contra-Motor, was introduced, and like the singles was gradually increased to 2690, 2940, and finally 3720cc. The appearance of Benz cars hardly changed from 1894 to 1900, but in 1900 some cars gained a small dummy front bonnet, implying the presence of a front-mounted engine in the modern fashion. In fact Benz cars were seriously outdated by 1900, and this was reflected in sales, which dropped from that year's high point of 603 to 385 in 1901 and 226 in 1902. There is an interesting parallel with Henry Ford, who also built the world's best-known car and stubbornly refused to update it even when sales began to fall.

In desperation Fischer and Ganss called in two designers, Georg Diehl and French-born Marius Barbarou, to design new models with front-mounted vertical engines. Barbarou's car was called the Benz-Parsifal and came in several sizes, from a 952cc single to a 5880cc four. Most had shaft drive, though the largest was chain driven. Though more up-to-date, the Parsifals did not perform well, and sales dropped to 172 in 1903; Barbarou lost his job as chief engineer and returned to France to work for DELAUNAY-BELLEVILLE. Benz had designed a new 4-cylinder engine before he left, and was asked back to put this into a modified Parsifal chassis. However, in 1906 he made a final break with his company, founding another one with his two sons Eugen and Richard, BENZ SÖHNE.

From 1908 design was in the hands of Hans Nibel (1880–1934) who had joined Benz from the Munich Technical High School in 1904. Nibel was a racing driver as well as a designer, and remained with Benz until after the merger with Mercedes in 1926. His cars were conventional, well-built machines with 4-cylinder engines and shaft or chain drive, appealing to the more conservative buyer than Mercedes. Their positions were similar to those of Daimler and Rolls-Royce in Britain. A keen Benz owner was Prince Henry of Prussia, who founded the Trials named after him, though his brother Kaiser Wilhelm II preferred Mercedes. Among other royal or noble Benz owners were Kings Oscar II and Gustav V of Sweden, Prince Charles Anton of Hohenzollern, and

NICK BALDWIN

BENZ, KARL (1844 – 1929)

The Benz family had been blacksmiths in the Black Forest village of Pffenrot for generations. Karl's father, Johann-Georg (1809–1846) broke the tradition by becoming a stoker and then a driver for the newly-opened Karlsruhe-Heidelberg railway in 1842. Two years later Karl was born, and two years after that Johann-Georg died of pneumonia following a railway accident. His young widow struggled to put Karl through the Karlsruhe Lyzeum, where he developed interests in photography and clocks. He earned money by travelling the Black Forest taking phtographs of anyone willing to pay him, also repairing their clocks.

After four years at the Karlsruhe Polytechnikum, young Benz had a series of rather unsatisfactory jobs, first in the locomotive works, then making scales and building bridges, before setting up his own machinists shop in Mannheim in 1872. There he made bending and metal-forming devices, and began to experiment with a 2-stroke engine. After a year of trying, he managed to get it to run on New Year's Eve, 1879. With the help of the bank and business partners he set up Gasmotorenfabrik Mannheim in October 1882. Benz was soon taken up by the challenge of making a self-propelled vehicle, and as was to happen with Gottlieb Daimler, Henry Royce, and many other motorcar pioneers, his ideas infuriated his partners, who thought the idea a dead-end and a waste of time. In January 1883 he resigned from the company, but soon found other partners who looked more favourably on the vehicle idea, though the main purpose of their company was to manufacture stationary gas engines. Benz & Cie, Rheinische Gasmotorenfabrik was registered on 1st December 1883, and the engines were soon finding a gratifying number of customers.

The stationary engines worked on the 2-stroke principle and were fuelled by gas, but when Benz began to plan his first car, he chose a 4-stroke design and benzin fuel. This was more volatile than gas and could be stored more easily on a light vehicle. Details of the first and subsequent Benz cars are given in the main entry on the make.

Work on the first car was very much a family effort, with Karl's wife, Bertha, pedalling furiously on her sewing machine to charge the battery, and 12-year-old son Richard helping out. It was Bertha who made the world's first inter-city journey in, or rather on, a motorcar. Wanting to visit her mother in Pforzheim, about 50 miles from Mannheim, she considered taking the train, but her elder son, 15-year old Eugen, argued that they should use the second car, which needed proving over a long distance. Rising before dawn on an August day in 1888, Bertha and her two sons crept out of the house, leaving Karl a note to assure him that they were not abandoning him for ever, pushed the car sufficiently far from the house so as not to wake her husband, and started off. The first steep hill presented a problem, as the single-speed car could not cope with three passengers. Richard, being the lightest, stayed at the tiller, while his mother and brother pushed, this being repeated on all subsequent hills. When the engine coughed to a stop because of a blocked fuel line, the resourceful Bertha cleared it with a hat pin, and when an ignition wire short-circuited, she made an insulator from a garter. A shoemaker provided new leather for the brake block, and they reached Pforzheim before nightfall. When Bertha cabled her husband to announce their safe arrival, he was delighted and proud of both wife and car, but he insisted that she remove the driving trains and send them back to Mannheim by train, as he needed them for the third car he was preparing for the Munich Engineering Exposition in September. His family had to stay in Pforzheim until he had obtained a spare pair of chains. Eugen told his father that he really must do something about the the hill-climbing, and a low gear was provided for the third car.

The car was well-received at Munich, and Benz won a gold medal, but only one customer came forward. This was Emile Roger, who was to provide Benz with most of his business in the early years (see ROGER). Benz has also been described as 'almost endearingly unworldly', and he certainly infuriated some of his associates. One feels that Bertha was impatient with his tinkering, which is why she made that famous journey, though she was unfailingly loyal in the early years of their marriage, when his pursuit of his ideas meant less bread on the family table. His partners on the gas engine business, Max Rose and Friedrich Esslinger, left him in May 1890, and were replaced by two local merchants, Friedrich von Fischer and Julius Ganss, who managed the stationary engine side of the business and gave Benz a fairly free hand with the cars. By 1900 the company was the most successful car maker in the world, with more than 2000 cars sold, as well as about 2200 stationary engines. However, the basic designs were not keeping up with the times, and as the 58-year-old Benz refused to modernise, Ganss called in a 33-year-old designer, Georg Diehl, to produce a car with front-mounted vertical engine and shaft drive. Announced in September 1902, it was not a success, which must have pleased Benz, but Ganss did not give up. He hired another designer, French-born Marius Barbarou, who produced parallel designs to those of Diehl. Benz felt slighted by their rivalry, in which he was barely involved at all, and resigned as a director in April 1903. He returned as a consultant thirteen months later, but was apparently not consulted very much, and in 1906 he left for good, forming a new company with his sons, Eugen and Richard, C. Benz Sohne. He did not play an active part in this company, though he lived for a further 23 years. His last important public appearance was in 1925 when, with Bertha by his side, he drove his original 3-wheeler in a parade of ancient vehicles in Munich. He died in April 1929.

Karl Benz married Bertha Ringer in 1872. They had five children: Eugen, Richard, Clara, Thilde, and Ellen.

NB. There has been some controversy over the spelling of Benz's christian name. Apparently he preferred Carl, but his birth certificate shows Karl, and this is the form favoured by Daimler-Benz.

NG

Further Reading
Three-Pointed Star, David Scott-Moncrieff, Cassell, 1966.
The Star and the Laurel, Beverly Rae Kimes, Mercedes Benz of North America, 1986.
Mercedes-Benz Personenwagen, Werner Oswald, Motorbuch Verlag, 1986.

1926 Benz 16/50PS saloon.
HANS-OTTO NEUBAUER

1952 Beretta BBC saloon.
GRAHAM GOULD

Grand Duke Maximilian of Baden. Between 1908 and 1914 Benz cars varied greatly in size, from the 1570cc 6/14PS to the 9850cc 37/70PS. There were 25 different sizes of 4-cylinder engine made during these years, and two sixes, the 21/50PS and 25/65PS which were introduced in 1914 and 1915, respectively. In addition, there were two exceptionally large models powered by airship engines, made in very small numbers. These were the 10,087cc 39/100PS and the 21,495cc 82/200PS. The latter was the largest-engined car ever offered for sale. It had chain drive, whereas the 39/100PS was shaft driven. A chassis cost 36,000 marks, compared with 19,000 marks for the 8430cc 33/75PS. Benz production grew encouragingly during the years up to 1914, reaching 1340 in 1910, and rising to 3093 in 1912. This was more than Mercedes were making, and in addition Benz were active in the fields of commercial vehicles and aero engines.

The Postwar Years
Economic conditions were very bad in Germany in the early postwar years, with materials, especially tyres, in very short supply. Benz, like several other car makers, sold their cars without tyres, leaving the customer to do the best he could to get his vehicle shod. Nevertheless Benz made 988 cars in 1919, of four prewar models, the 8/20PS, 14/30PS, 18/45PS and 25/55PS. The first new model was the 6/18PS with 1570cc single-ohc engine. It was the only ohc Benz engine, and although it was an attractive small car with a sports version, the 6/45PS, it was only made up to 1921. Several larger sixes were made in the 1920s, up to the 7-litre 27/70PS, and car production rose to 2260 in 1925. A completely unconventional car was the *Tropfenwagen* (tear drop car) inspired by Edmond RUMPLER's streamlined rear-engined car which appeared at the 1921 Berlin Show. The Tropfenwagen was built originally as a Grand Prix racing car with 2-litre twin-ohc 6-cylinder engine mounted behind the driver but ahead of the rear axle, in the classic mid-engined position favoured by designers of sports and racing cars from the 1960s onwards. Only three GP cars were made, and a handful of sports cars, one of which was sold to Benito Mussolini.

By 1925 Benz was in serious financial difficulties, brought about by speculation in their shares by the financier Jakob Schapiro. After pressure from the Benz financial director Wilhelm Kissel, most of the shares ended up with the Deutsche Bank who also owned a large number of Daimler shares. This paved the way for a merger which had been under discussion since 1919. Benz and Mercedes cars shared a stand at the 1925 Berlin Show, and the full merger took place on 1 July 1926, the new company being called Daimler-Benz AG and its products, MERCEDES-BENZ. The board included three brilliant engineers, Hans Nibel from Benz, Ferdinand Porsche, and Friedrich Nallinger from Daimler. Two Benz models appeared with Mercedes-Benz badges, the 10/30PS and 16/50PS, but were made for one season only. Among the provisions of the merger were pensions to Karl and Bertha Benz. Karl died in 1929 at the age of 84, and Bertha was 95 when she died in 1944.

NG

Further Reading
Three-Pointed Star, David Scott-Moncrieff, Cassell, 1966.
The Star and the Laurel, Beverly Rae Kimes,
Mercedes-Benz of North America, 1986.
Mercedes-Benz Personenwagen 1886–1986, Werner Oswald,
Motor Buch Verlag, 1986.

BENZ SÖHNE (D) 1906–1926
C. Benz Söhne, Ladenberg am Neckar.
When Karl Benz and his sons Eugen and Richard made their final split with the company Karl had founded, they set up another at Ladenberg, not far from Mannheim, and began to make cars under the name C. Benz Söhne (Benz Sons). In fact Richard remained at Mannheim until 1908, when he joined his father and elder brother. The first Benz Söhne cars were quite small, of 8/12PS and 10/18PS. The latter became the 10/22PS (2608cc), and there was also a 3565cc 14/42PS, but output was very small, probably not more than 100 cars in their 20-year life. In 1913 they experimented with the Henriod rotary-valve engine, but it was not put into a production car. After World War I the 8/25PS and 14/42PS were made up to 1926, when the factory turned to making components for Daimler-Benz. This it continues to do today, in a factory not greatly changed since 1907, and still in the hands of the Benz family.
NG

BERARD (F) 1900–1901
C. Berard, Marseilles.
Berard was an engineer who made about 20 cars with 2-cylinder engines of his own design.
NG

BERETTA (I) 1949–1952
Beretta, Gardone Valtrompia, Brescia.
Famous for armaments since the 16th century, Beretta considered car manufacture to keep their workforce busy after the slump in demand for guns at the end of World War II. The Beretta BBC had a 750cc V-twin engine of Beretta's own design driving the front wheels, a 4-speed gearbox, and all-independent suspension by coils at the front and swing axles at the rear. The body was an all-enveloping 2-door saloon. Three prototypes were made, of which one survives.
NG

BERG (US) 1903–1905
1903–1904 Berg Automobile Co., Cleveland, Ohio.
1904–1905 Worthington Automobile Co., New York, New York .
Hart O. Berg admired the European style of car so much that he openly admitted that the car bearing his name would be 'of foreign type' and 'almost an exact copy of the Panhard'. The first Bergs came in two sizes, 8hp 2-cylinder and 15hp 4-cylinder, both with gilled-tube radiators and chain drive. In 1904 Berg launched another car, the EUCLID, named after Cleveland's Euclid Avenue, and later that year he sold out to the Worthington Automobile Co. of New York who made an up-dated Berg with larger 4-cylinder engines of 24hp, honeycomb radiators, and shaft drive. Robert Jardine, designer of the Berg and Euclid, later designed another Cleveland car, the ROYAL TOURIST, while Hart Berg became a financial supporter of the Wright brothers.
NG

BERGANTIN (RA) 1960–1962

Industrias Kaiser Argentina, Santa Isabel, Cordoba.

In 1959 Mr James McCloud, president of IKA (Industrias Kaiser Argentina), wanted to build a European-style car with Jeep mechanical components, which were already being manufactured in Argentina. This was called Project X-60. He went to Europe where ALFA-ROMEO agreed to sell him all the necessary dies to make the Alfa-Romeo 1900 saloon, which had just been discontinued. The result was the Bergantin, an Alfa look-alike with a 2480cc Jeep engine and other Jeep components such as the rear axle. Production started on 10 March 1960 and the last unit was made on 21 February 1962. A total of 4796 Bergantin cars in Standard, De Luxe and Taxi versions were made.

ACT

BERGDOLL (US) 1910–1913

Louis J. Bergdoll Motor Co., Philadelphia, Pennsylvania.

The Bergdolls were a prominent Philadelphia family who built a high-quality car in a fine seven-storey factory in downtown Philadelphia. Two 4-cylinder models were made, of 30 and 40hp, and as many as nine body styles were listed in 1911. The 1912 Model 40 had a self-starter. However, the Bergdolls were not astute on the business side, and the company went into receivership in March 1913. A few more cars were assembled in a small factory on the family estate on West Chester Pike.

NG

BERGÉ (F) 1923

M. Caillat, Pré St Gervais, Seine.

This was a conventional light car powered by 7/10 and 10/12CV 4-cylinder engines of Fivet manufacture, or a 12CV 4-cylinder Janvier. They had wire or disc wheels, and three body styles were offered, all open models with 2, 3, or 4 seats. A sporting model had a pointed tail.

NG

BERGER (D) 1901–1902

Chemnitzer Motorwagen-Fabrik Bruno Berger & Co., Chemnitz.

This company made a small number of cars on Benz lines, not surprising as Bruno Berger had been a former employee of Benz.

HON

BERGMANN (i) see LILIPUT and ORIENT EXPRESS

BERGMANN (ii); BERGMANN-METALLURGIQUE (D) 1907–1922

Bergmann Elektrizitätswerke AG, Berlin-Reinickendorf; Berlin-Halensee.

Sigmund Bergmann was born in Germany in 1851 and emigrated to America where he was in partnership with Thomas Edison. The companies they founded eventually merged to form General Electric. In 1891 he returned to Germany and set up in business in Berlin, making switches, meters, electric motors, and other equipment. Production of electric vehicles, both passenger and goods carrying, began in 1907, under the trade name Fulgura. A few petrol-engined cars may have been made in 1908, but more important was the licence production of the Belgian METALLURGIQUE from 1909 onwards. Marketed as Bergmann-Metallurgique they had mainly Belgian-built components and Vanden Plas bodies to start with, but later a higher proportion of German-made components were used, together with coachwork from German firms. The largest Bergmann-Metallurgique was the 7320cc 29/70PS which the Belgians knew as the 38/90CV, but there were also smaller models, the 1560cc 6/18PS and the 3565cc 14/40PS.

After World War I only one model was made, now called simply Bergmann, although it was a Metallurgique design. This was the 2.6-litre 10/30PS, made in Belgium as the 14CV. After 1922 Bergmann made only electric commercial vehicles, which were built in large numbers up to 1939, and were widely used by the German Post Office.

Between the wars Bergmann came under the control of another large electrical organisation which at one time made cars, SIEMENS-SCHUCKERT, and is today active in Berlin in the manufacture of telecommunication equipment, electric motors, transformers, postal franking machines, and other items.

HON

1908 Bergmann (ii) Fulgura electric landaulet
NICK BALDWIN

BERKELEY (i) (GB) 1956–1961

Berkeley Cars Ltd, Biggleswade, Bedfordshire.

Berkeley was Britain's leading caravan maker in the 1950s, and it pioneered the use of fibreglass in their construction. Lawrence 'Lawrie' Bond was a maverick designer who believed in small-engined, light cars and front-wheel drive. They united to make the Berkeley sports car.

The Berkeley B60 of 1956 had fibreglass unitary construction (a world first), all independent suspension and a 322cc air-cooled, 2-stroke, 2-cylinder Anzani engine which drove via chains to the front wheels. It was called the B60 because its top speed was 60mph (96km/h). Before long, it was replaced by the Excelsior-powered B65, but production was suspended when the Austin-Healey Sprite arrived in 1958.

When production resumed there were two distinct strands. The most popular was the T60, a 3-wheeled version of the B65. It had no rival and it was true to the original concept. Around 2500 were made in a year which contrasts to the approx. 2000 4-wheelers made, 1956–61.

The revised 4-wheeled cars were the B90 (492cc 3-cylinder Excelsior) which came as a 2- or 4-seater. The B95 and B105 had 4-stroke 692cc Royal Enfield 'Constellation' parallel twin engines and, since the B105 had 50bhp in a car which weighed less than 800lb, it achieved some competition success.

Berkeley commissioned John Tojeiro to design a conventional sports car, the Bandit, to rival the Sprite. It was shown in 1961, had Ford Anglia running gear, and was being prepared for production when recession hit the caravan business and the parent company collapsed.

In the late 1980s the Bandit was briefly revived in New Zealand as the Ibis Berkeley while, in Britain, a number of T60 copies were made.

MJL

BERKELEY (ii) (GB) 1991 to date

1991–1996 Berkeley Motor Co., Syston, Leicestershire.

1996 to date Berkeley Developments, Langley Hill, Nottinghamshire.

Berkeley Developments was formed in 1970 to restore original Berkeleys and the original body moulds were eventually used to make new shells. In 1991 a new company was formed and by 1993 production of complete T60 replicas had begun, using newly engineered ladder chassis or folded aluminium panels bonded to the glassfibre body. The standard power was Mini (in a Mini front subframe), various motorcycle units (like the original T60) or Citroen 2CV. Bandini and Camerotta models were available. Eventually a four-wheeler Mini-powered Berkeley replica was produced.

CR

BERKSHIRE (US) 1905–1912

1905–1907 Berkshire Motor Co., Pittsfield, Massachusetts.

1907–1908 Berkshire Automobile Co., Pittsfield, Massachusetts.

1908–1909 Berkshire Motor Car Co., Pittsfield, Massachusetts.

1909–1912 Berkshire Auto-Car Co., Pittsfield, Massachusetts.

1912 Belcher Engineering Co., Cambridge, Massachusetts.

1905 Berliet tourer at Coupe du Salon.
NATIONAL MOTOR MUSEUM

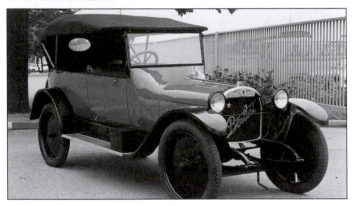

1920 Berliet Type VL tourer.
NATIONAL MOTOR MUSEUM

The Berkshire gained its name from the Berkshire Hills, close to its home town of Pittsfield, where the cars were tested. Several sizes of Herschell-Spillman engine were used, an 18hp in 1905 and then 20, 30 and 50hp fours, and a 50hp six in 1906. Later they standardised on a 35hp four. Early models used a patented transmission designed to prevent stripping of gears, but it was not a success. There were frequent financial crises, as indicated by the number of changes of company name. In 1912 the Belcher Engineering Co. bought up a stock of Berkshire parts but only managed to assemble three cars. The STILSON car shared the Berkshire's factory and at least one director. It is possible that the 6-cylinder Berkshire assembled by Belcher in 1912 may have used Stilson parts, though this make was last listed in 1909. Total Berkshire production was 150 cars and one truck.

NG

BERLIET (F) 1895–1939

Automobiles M. Berliet, Lyons.

The Berliet was the most important and longest-lived make of car from Lyons, itself France's second most significant car-making city, after Paris. Marius Berliet (1866–1949) came from a family of silk weavers, and showed his mechanical talent by designing a machine for cutting ribbon in 1893. The following year he began work on his first car, but it was not completed until 1895. It had a single-cylinder horizontal engine and seated two in tandem, this layout chosen because Berliet's workshop had a narrow door. He was not going to make Henry Ford's mistake of making a car too wide, and having to demolish the doorframe before it could be got out. The first car was not very successful, but a local industrialist saw potential in it, and asked Berliet to make another, this time with a 2-cylinder engine and side-by-side seating. It was completed at the beginning of 1898, and, though pleased with it, the customer gave it back to Berliet so that he could use it as a basis for a production car.

Berliet bought a small workshop in 1899 and, with only three employees, began manufacture of a car with rear-mounted 1204cc horizontal engine which could be removed as a complete unit, 4-speed gearbox and left-hand drive wheel steering. Space was so limited that the cars were completed on the pavement

outside the works. Six cars were built in 1899, and the following year Berliet moved to considerably larger premises. He issued his first catalogue in 1900. The 1901 Berliets were greatly improved, with front-mounted 2 and 4-cylinder engines, double-chain drive, and rear-entrance tonneau bodies. The 12hp 4-cylinder car was used by T.C. Pullinger as a basis for the car he designed for SUNBEAM. In 1902 Berliet expanded still further when he bought up the premises of AUDIBERT-LAVIROTTE, pioneer Lyons car maker who had rejected Berliet when he suggested partnership in 1897. This expansion was financed by a local businessman named Giraud. By 1903 the business was large enough to justify an agency in Paris, which was managed by Emile Lavirotte. Later he would represent the company in Moscow.

By 1905 Berliet had 250 employees and turned out 300 cars. They were on Mercedes lines and had 4-cylinder engines of 12, 20, and 40hp, with mechanically-operated inlet valves, honeycomb radiators, and pressed steel frames. Luxurious open and closed bodies were provided, and Berliet were among the top rank of French car makers.

The American Connection

In 1905 Berliet was visited by Albert J. Pitkin, president of the American Locomotive Company. This was a large organisation, controlling some of the most important builders of locomotives in the United States. Wanting to get into car production, Pitkin bought a licence to make Berliet cars at Providence, Rhode Island (see AMERICAN BERLIET). The licence brought $100,000 to Berliet and enabled him to expand still further. The new factory made commercial vehicles as well as cars, and these were to outlive car production by more than 40 years. Indeed, present-day Renault heavy trucks are made in Berliet's factories at Venissieux, outside Lyons.

Berliet cars were made in a wide variety up to 1914. At the bottom of the range was a 904cc vertical twin, followed by fours of 1½- and 2-litres, while the largest cars were an 8.6-litre 60hp and an 11.3-litre 80hp. A petrol-electric Berliet-Mixte was listed for 1908 only. By 1912 even the largest models had shaft drive, and a 4.4-litre 20/25hp had an L-head engine, which layout gradually replaced the T-head previously used. In 1914 there were five models, all with monobloc 4-cylinder L-head engines, from a 1.6-litre 12hp to a 6.3-litre 40hp. About 3000 cars per year were made, putting Berliet in fourth place among French car firms, after Renault, Peugeot and Darracq. They were sold all over the world, as far afield as Russia, Brazil, Java, the Phillipines and Australia.

Wartime Prosperity, Postwar Developments

As soon as World War I broke out Marius Berliet stopped car production and threw himself and his firm into the war effort. Their major contribution was the CBA 4-ton truck, of which 25,000 were made, but they also made Renault tanks and 75mm shells. It was to make all this material that Berliet built their Venissieux factory on a 400-hectare site. For his postwar programme Berliet decided on a one-model policy for both cars and trucks. The car was called the VB, and had a 3.3-litre 4-cylinder engine in unit with a 3-speed gearbox and with fixed disc wheels with detachable rims. The design owed much to the Dodge Four, an example of which Berliet had bought and dismantled. He planned an output of 100 cars per day, but seldom exceeded 15. Many of the VB's components were made of inferior steel, and claims under guarantee poured in. More than 400 rear axles alone had to be replaced. This was a disaster for Berliet and soon wiped out the profits he had made during the war. Truck sales were slow as well, because of the large number of war surplus vehicles which could be bought for half the price of a new CBA. Berliet had to be bailed out by the banks, losing control of his company. However, by 1929 he had won it back.

The unlucky VB was succeeded in 1921 by the VL, a similar design but a better-built car which laid the foundations of success later in the decade. In 1923 it became the VI, with smaller bore which put it into the 12CV tax class instead of 15CV. As the VF it was made until 1925, available with front-wheel brakes, but by this time there were two new models with ohv engines, 4-speed gearboxes, and detachable wire wheels. These were the 1160cc VH and 3958cc VK. The latter had aluminium pistons, and with a dual-cowl torpedo body was a really handsome car. A return to 6-cylinder models was made in 1927, of which the bestseller was the 1812cc side-valve VH. Combined with good commercial vehicle sales, this restored the Berliet company to prosperity and enabled Marius to regain control from the banks. He was now 62 years old and was very much the autocrat, as Ettore Bugatti was at Molsheim.

From the mid-1920s he became increasingly interested in producer gas units, known in France as *gazogènes*. He acquired a licence to make the charcoal-fuelled

Imbert *gazogène*, then modified it to work by burning wood, so avoiding the necessity of reducing the wood to charcoal first. This *gazobois* system was offered on several models of Berliet truck and on some cars. In 1935 there was a 3.3-litre 4-cylinder car using the saloon body of the contemporary Dauphine, with the *gazobois* unit in a large and ugly container in place of the luggage boot. It could cruise at 53mph (85km/h), with a top speed of 62mph (100km/h). Two took part in the Rallye des Carburants Nationaux. However, few were sold, because the public was not familiar with the system, and were put off by the ungainly appearance and loss of luggage space. The contemporary Panhard *gazogène* cars sold no better.

During the 1930s Berliet concentrated increasingly on commercial vehicles, including some of the first French-built diesel trucks and buses. By 1939 there were 12 truck models but only two cars. The most important passenger cars of the 1930s were the 944 (9CV, 4-cylinder, 4-speed), and the 1144 (11CV, 4-cylinder, 4-speed), though there was a lesser-known 943 with 3-speed gearbox. In the summer of 1934 the 11CV was given rack-and-pinion steering and transverse-leaf independent front suspension, being renamed the Dauphine. The 9CV followed suit in the summer of 1935. These models were made up to 1938 with a variety of attractive open and closed bodywork, saloons, coupés, cabriolets and roadsters. The Dauphines were competing against the Peugeot 401/402 and Renault Vivaquatre, but were more expensive than either, an inevitable consequence of being made in smaller numbers. Berliet car production averaged 3000 or less per year in the 1930s. The last passenger car was the Dauphine 39 which went into production in March 1939. Handsome though they were, the Dauphines were due for replacement by then, but Berliet could not afford to tool up for a new body. They therefore bought the streamlined 6-light 402B saloon from Peugeot which was mounted on a Dauphine chassis lengthened by 16in. From the rear to the scuttle it was identical to the Peugeot, but had its own pointed radiator grille and exposed headlights in place of the Peugeot's which were located behind the grille. The old 1990cc Dauphine engine was used, and though it had the advantage of a 4-speed gearbox, at 34,900 francs (36,000 from June 1939) it cost about 15 per cent more than the Peugeot. It is unlikely that many would have been sold even had World War II not intervened, but, as it was, no more than 200 found customers. The last 15 were completed by the Geneva agents in 1946. The traditionally-styled 11CV Dauphine was also made for the 1939 season, under the name Super Dauphine.

Like Louis Renault, Marius Berliet was imprisoned in 1944 for having made trucks for the Nazis, but he was soon released. He died in 1949, aged 83. After the war Berliet concentrated on commercial vehicles which they made in great variety and considerable numbers. They merged with Citroën in 1967 and were acquired by Renault in 1974. Gradually Renault badging took over from Berliet, though the latter designs survived for nearly 20 years after the take-over.

NG

Further Reading
Marius Berliet, l'Inflexible, Saint Loup, Presse de la Cité, 1962.
'Berliet, Lucien Loreille', *l'Album du Fanatique,* November 1969–March 1970.

BERNA (CH) 1902–1911

1902–1904 Joseph Wyss, Berne.
1904–1906 J. Wyss, Schweizerische Automobilfabrik Berna, Olten.
1906–1907 Motorwerke Berna AG, vorm. J. Wyss, Olten.
1908–1911 Berna Commercial Motor Ltd, Olten.

Joseph Wyss, a locksmith and mechanic, built his first Berna car in 1902. Its single-cylinder engine of 785cc, delivering 5.2bhp, was placed under the rear seats of the 'Ideal' *vis-à-vis* voiturette. The engine and chassis were clearly influenced by the successful De Dion-Bouton models. The 2-speed gearbox was fitted to the De Dion-type rear axle and could be operated without the need of a clutch. No reverse gear was provided but top speed was a respectable 24mph. In 1903 Wyss presented the new Berna 'Unicum' with a new engine of 8bhp mounted in the front part of the tubular chassis. It was advertised with tonneau, *vis-à-vis*, phaeton and spider bodies with 2–4 seats. Nine cars of this type were built and some exported to England. With expansion, the premises in Berne became too small, and Wyss moved to Olten in late 1904 where the production of a commercial vehicle with 2 tons payload was taken up.

At least one prototype of a 2-cylinder passenger car was completed in 1905. The T-head engine was mounted in a conventional tubular chassis with separate

1933 Berliet 944 roadster.
FONDATION DE L'AUTOMOBILE M. BERLIET

1939 Berliet Dauphine saloon.
NATIONAL MOTOR MUSEUM

gearbox and shaft drive. Ernst Marti was hired as a technician and designer. He accompanied Wyss and the works foreman Egg on a visit to London, and liking the city, he decided not to return to Switzerland for some time. In 1906 the enterprise needed more capital and was re-formed into a shareholders' company. The first 4-cylinder 35/40hp truck was exhibited at the London show, but business did not develop as expected and Joseph Wyss retired. A young man, Locher, 22 years of age, was appointed as manager. He decided to drop the commercial vehicles and again concentrate on passenger cars. He hired Doutre, a French engineer, who was responsible for the design. When the first of the new cars was finished he invited his wife and brother-in-law on a pleasure trip to Paris. At that time the safe of the company was said to have been empty except for two copper coins. After having delivered six of the new 14/16 PS or 20/22 PS chassis with shaft drive and a T-head 4-cylinder monobloc engine of 2270cc or 2798cc only, the company went into liquidation. What remained was bought by the British financial group Hudson Consolidated. Ernst Marti returned from England and became managing director, a position he held until his retirement in 1952. He once again turned to commercial vehicles but there were also trials with small 2-stroke engines and around 1911 at least one more passenger car was completed, possibly using parts remaining from the Doutre experiment. Berna, which became number two in production of commercial vehicles in Switzerland, was taken over by SAURER in 1929 and continued to build heavy trucks and buses until 1972.

FH

Further Reading
'Biography Ernst Marti', Ferdinand Hediger,
Automobil Revue, 28 January 1971.
Berna 1904–1954, Berna PR.

1896 Bersey electric Victoria. The Brighton Run car that went by train.
NATIONAL MOTOR MUSEUM

BERNARDET (F) 1946–1950

Automobiles Bernardet, Châtillon-sous-Bagneux, Seine.

The Bernardet brothers were leading makers of sidecars between 1922 and 1946, and also made scooters from 1949 to 1955. Their venture into car building was a substantial 3-seater roadster powered by a 798cc side-valve flat-four engine driving the front wheels. Other features of this advanced little car included rack-and-pinion steering, all-independent suspension, and a 4-speed synchromesh gearbox. Capacity rose to 848cc in 1947 and in 1949 a 746cc 4-cylinder 2-stroke engine was used. Designed by Marcel Violet of SIMA VIOLET fame, this was mounted transversely, anticipating the Mini by ten years. The Bernardets could not get government sanction to make their car, as the Renault 4CV had been chosen as the only permitted sub-1-litre 4-cylinder car. Only three prototypes were made.

NG

BERNARDI (i) (I) 1899–1901

Societa Italiana Bernardi, Padua.

Enrico Bernardi (1841–1919) was Professor of Hydraulic and Agricultural Machinery at the University of Padua. In 1882 he made a tiny single-cylinder petrol engine which he used to drive a sewing machine. Capacity was 122cc and output 0.024bhp at 200rpm. Two years later he installed it in a tricycle for his 4-year old son who used it for carrying sand and stones, arousing great envy among his friends. This was more than a year before Karl Benz tested his first car, and though Bernardi's tricycle was never intended to be more than a toy, he deserves credit for a pioneering machine. In 1892 he built a larger 3-wheeler with 624cc horizontal engine for carrying adults, and a version of this was made in small numbers by MIARI E GIUSTI from 1896 to 1899. When they discontinued production Bernardi made a few more under his own name. They were offered with engines of 2½, 4½ and 6hp, but manufacture ended in June 1901.

NG

BERNARDI (ii) see BLAKELY

BERRET (F) 1899–1903

Sté Cannoise d'Automobiles, Cannes.

One of very few makes of car from the French Riviera, the Berret was built in prototype form in 1895. Like its successors, it had a 3-cylinder engine. Only seven production cars were made, between 1899 and 1903.

NG

BERSEY (GB) 1895–1899

W.C. Bersey, London.

Walter Bersey was an electrical engineer who built an electric bus in 1888, but his first passenger cars were not made until 1895. They resembled motorised horse carriages, and may well have been so. The bodies were by Arthur Mulliner of Northampton and power was provided by twin motors, a 2-speed gearbox with clutch (unusual in an electric), and chain final drive. Three of these carriages ran in the London–Brighton Emancipation Run in November 1896, though it was widely rumoured that they completed the journey by train. This was finally confirmed by Walter Bersey in a speech to the Veteran Car Club in 1935. More famous than his private cars were Bersey's taxis, of which 75 ran in London between the end of 1897 and June 1900. They had bodies by either Mulliner or the Gloucester Railway Carriage & Waggon Company. No Bersey private carriage is known to survive, but a taxi can be seen in the National Motor Museum at Beaulieu. Bersey himself turned to petrol, selling Delahaye and Darracq cars. He also compiled *The Motor Car Red Book* for a number of years.

NG

BERTOLDO see MARCA TRE SPADE

BERTOLET (US) 1908–1910

1908–1909 Dr J.M. Bertolet, Reading, Pennsylvania.
1909–1910 Bertolet Motor Car Co., Reading, Pennsylvania.

Dr Bertolet built a number of cars before he incorporated his company. They were conventional touring cars with a 40hp 4-cylinder engine, the only unusual feature being a body which could be converted from 5-seater tourer to 2-seater runabout by removing the rear seats to reveal a deck 'when a more sporting effect is desired'. They did not survive 1910, though a few may have been completed from parts into 1911.

NG

BERTONI (I) 1948

Bertoni, Lodi, Lombardia.

Typical of many immediate postwar microcars, the Bertoni was a quite pretty doorless 2-seater roadster designed by a motorcycle racer. Its rear-mounted engine was a 4bhp 125cc Vespa unit, complete with a 3-speed Vespa transmission. Probably only one car was ever built.

CR

BERTRAND (i) (F) 1901–1902

Bertrand et Cie, Paris.

This short-lived company offered light cars in two sizes, with 4hp De Dion-Bouton or 6hp Aster engines: 2- or 4-seater bodies were available, and final drive was by single-chain. Though made in small numbers, one travelled as far afield as Russia, where it won its class in the 1901 Moscow–St Petersburg Trial. One Bertrand survives today in France.

NG

BERTRAND (ii) (F) 1921–1924

M. Bertrand, Poitiers.

The Bertrand cyclecar used a 903cc 4-cylinder Ruby engine with 3-speed gearbox, shaft drive to a countershaft and final drive by belts. Sports models used a 970cc Ruby or 1098cc ohv CIME engine. Several competed successfully in races and hill climbs and a few were exported to Spain and Portugal. About 30 Bertrands were made.

NG

BERWICK (US) 1904

Berwick Auto Car Co., Grand Rapids, Michigan.

The short-lived Berwick electric runabout was a tiller-steered 2-seater with a claimed top speed of no more than 15mph (24km/h). It was stylishly finished with an abundance of brasswork, black body, and red running gear.

NG

BESASIE (US) c.1993

Besasie Automobile Company Inc., Milwaukee, Wisconsin.

The Baci was a neoclassic car based on Ford Thunderbird running gear. It had a unique shape with flowing mudguards and sloped tail, but with a small dorsal fin and a steeply sloped body-coloured grill. Roadster and convertible body styles were offered. It used a tubular steel space-frame chassis that added 10in (254mm) to the Ford length, while the engine was relocated 20in (508mm) further aft. They were sold in fully assembled form.

HP

BESST (AUS) 1924
May's Motor Works, Adelaide, South Australia.
A typical assembled car of its time, the Besst used US components. The engine was a 4-cylinder 19.6hp Lycoming of 3155cc with a Zenith carburettor and an Eismann magneto, while the gearbox was a 3-speed Muncie. The rear axle was fully floating, electrics were Dyneto and Houk wire wheels were standard fitting on the 116in (2947mm) wheelbase car. A Richards 'King of the Road' touring body was highlighted, being equipped with many items usually available only at extra cost. It seems that the Besst was essentially the CROW-ELKHART model L, although the time-lag could indicate that the chassis were clearance stock. Six cars are known to have been built.

MG

BEST (i) (US) 1898–1899
Best Manufacturing Co., San Leandro, California.
Best was one of the most prominent names among makers of steam traction engines which were widely used in farming and in the logging industry of the North West United States. In 1898 Daniel Best built a large touring car with seats for eight passengers, powered by a 7hp 2-cylinder engine, with friction clutch and chain drive. Top speed was 20mph (32km/h), though this was reduced to 18mph (29km/h) when the full complement of eight passengers was aboard. Best planned manufacture of this enormous car, but it never took place, nor did that of a smaller 2-seater runabout he completed in 1899. The Best factory was sold to the Holt tractor company in 1914, and later passed to Caterpillar, who used it until 1982.

NG

BEST (ii) (F) 1921
The Courbevoie-built Best was a conventional touring car powered by a 1944cc 4-cylinder Janvier engine.

NG

BEVERLEY-BARNES (GB) 1923–1931
1923–1928 Lenaerts & Dolphens, Barnes, London.
1928–1931 Beverley Works Ltd, Barnes, London.
This car owed its name to the Beverley Brook which runs through the south-western London suburb of Barnes. The factory was formerly occupied by the makers of the EAGLE (vii) cyclecar. A light car called the Nova was to have been made there in the summer of 1914; there is a tantalising link between this and the Belgian NOVA, an equally short-lived venture directed by Florimond Lenaerts, as the company which took over the premises was Lenaerts & Dolphens, headed by a Count Lenaerts and two other Belgians, M. Dolphens and M. Flamand. Was Florimond the Count's son?

The company made Le Rhone aero-engines during the World War I, with a largely Belgian workforce, and then engaged in machining work for a number of car makers, the best known of which was BENTLEY. This lasted until Bentley were able to set up their own machine shop in 1926, thanks to finance from Woolf Barnato. Three years before that the partners decided to make cars themselves, though this was always a sideline. Their first, the 24/80, had a 3994cc single-ohc straight-8 engine developing 90bhp. It was a large car, on a 150in (3807mm) wheelbase, and had a radiator almost identical to that of Rolls-Royce. With a Vanden Plas body it cost £1150. Surprisingly for a firm which supplied Bentley, the Beverley engine was rough and lacking in power (perhaps it never reached the claimed 90bhp). To remedy this a larger engine of 4826cc was brought out in October 1924, this being called the 30/90. Only two of these were made, together with one with an even larger engine of 5445cc, which was shown at Olympia in 1927 with a 7-seater cabriolet body by Labourdette. Together with seven 24/80s, this brought the total of the large Beverley-Barnes to just ten.

The 24/80 was dropped in 1926 and a new smaller straight-8 was announced, the 2442cc 18. Only one of these was made, and in 1928 came a new engine design derived from the 18 but enlarged to 2736cc and with chain-driven

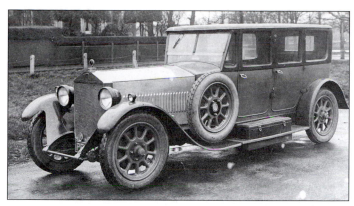

1924 Beverley Barnes 24/80 saloon.
NATIONAL MOTOR MUSEUM

twin-ohcs and inclined valves. Capacity went up to 2956cc in 1929. With twin carburettors and lower lines with cycle-type wings and wire wheels, the 22/90 Beverley (no longer Beverley-Barnes) was an attractive car, but the times were against it. Probably no more than two were made; one, with a 4-door sports saloon body by Harrington, was shown at Olympia in 1929 and 1930. Beverley later supplied some of the engines to Sir Dennistoun Burney for his BURNEY STREAMLINE cars, and also assembled about 12 low-chassis 4½-litre units for INVICTA. They were probably still doing some work for Bentley, as a former employee remembers people from Rolls-Royce coming down to Barnes and destroying Bentley cylinder blocks (presumably for the 4-litre) after the RR takeover of Bentley. Known production of Beverley-Barnes and Beverley is 14 cars (of which two survive). One was built as an ambulance but used by glaziers for carrying large glass panels. Seven other 'possibles' have been suggested, several in chassis form only.

NG

Further Reading
'Beverley Barnes – the Anglo-Belgian Enigma', M. Worthington-Williams, *The Automobile*, May 1983.

BEVERLY (US) 1904
Upton Machine Co., Beverly, Massachusetts.
The Beverly was the successor to the last UPTON (i), with its 4-cylinder engine increased from 16 to 22hp, and the gilled-tube radiator replaced by a honeycomb. Its most unusual feature was that the headlamps turned with the steering. At $4000 it was an expensive car, and it did not outlast the year 1904. In September 1905 the Upton Machine Co. was reorganised as the Beverly Machine Co., and produced transmissions up to 1908 when the factory was sold to the CAMERON Car Co.

NG

BEYSTER-DETROIT (US) 1910–1911
Beyster-Detroit Motor Car Co., Detroit, Michigan.
The principal products of this company were light delivery vans, but a few runabouts were also made. These used the HUPMOBILE 20 engine, and must have been quite similar to this better-known Detroit product.

NG

B.F. (D) 1922–1926
Bolle-Fiedler Automobilwerke GmbH, Berlin.
The B.F.'s engine was unusual in two respects, in having 3-cylinders and being a 2-stroke. Capacity was 1026cc, putting it in the light car class, and examples of the make competed successfully in various races and hill climbs.

HON

B.G.S. (F) 1898–1906
Sté des Voitures et Accumulateurs Bouquet, Garçin et Schivre, Neuilly, Seine.
Prominent makers of electric vehicles, B.G.S. offered a wide range at the turn of the century: dogcarts, phaetons, and several sizes of commercial vehicle. They entered a car in the 1899 Paris–Ostend race, but it retired due to an accident. In 1900, a specially-equipped car driven by M. Bouquet covered 163

1909 Bianchi 20/30hp tourer.
NATIONAL MOTOR MUSEUM

1930 Bianchi S5 saloon.
NATIONAL MOTOR MUSEUM

1960 Bianchina 500 cabriolet.
NATIONAL MOTOR MUSEUM

miles (262km) on a single charge, beating by 68 miles (110km) the previous record set by a KRIEGER. Most of the car was taken up with batteries which weighed 1260kgs. Like regular B.G.S. models, its motor was mounted behind the front axle, driving a countershaft, final drive being by chains. From about 1904 the cars were more generally known as Garçin or Garçin-Renault. They had shaft drive and the appearance of petrol-engined cars. B.G.S. also made some cars for sale by CRÉANCHE.

NG

BGW (US) c.1982 to date
Bohemian Glass Works Ltd, Milwaukee, Wisconsin.
The Volkswagen Beetle was never the same after BGW started making body kits in the early 1980s. The Speedster changed it into a convertible with a hint of Porsche Speedster. Other kits made the VW look like a miniature 1940 Willys coupé, a panel truck, and a 1936–1940 Ford opera coupé. The Speedster could be outfitted with wide wheel flares and spoilers, and rumble seats were optional on all models. In the early 1990s, they changed their name to Spectre/BGW. They also offered a frame kit to adapt their bodies to V8 or Pinto power.

HP

BIANCHI; AUTOBIANCHI (I) 1899–1939; 1957–1987
1899–1905 Edoardo Bianchi, Milan.
1905–1939 Fabbrica Automobili e Velocipede Edoardo Bianchi, Milan.
1957–1968 Autobianchi Spa, Milan.
1968–1987 Fiat Spa (Sezione Autobianchi), Milan.
Although they were never widely known outside Italy, Bianchi cars and commercial vehicles sold in considerable numbers in their homeland. In the 1920s they were generally third in the production league, after Fiat and Lancia and ahead of Alfa Romeo and O.M. The origins of the marque date back to 1885 when 20-year old Edoardo Bianchi set up a small cycle works in Milan. He prospered in the cycling boom of the 1890s, and like many others began experiments with motor tricycles towards the end of the decade. These had De Dion-Bouton engines, as did his first four-wheeler. Made in 1899, this had a tubular frame and single-cylinder engine, and was followed by other prototypes with single- or 2-cylinder engines. Voiturette production was sporadic, and the company did not become established as a car maker until 1905. The previous year they had been joined by Antonio Merosi, later to become famous as the designer of the Alfa Romeo RL series. His designs for Bianchi were strongly influenced by Mercedes, with large 4-cylinder T-head engines, multi-disc clutches, 4-speed gearboxes, and chain drive. The 1905 models were the 4½-litre 16/22hp and 7.4-litre 24/40hp, later joined by the 8-litre 40/50hp and the enormous 11.4-litre Tipo E 90hp.

In 1907 Bianchi opened a new factory dedicated to car production, leaving the original one for bicycles and motorcycles. By 1909 Bianchi cars were beginning to penetrate foreign markets, with sales offices in Paris, London, Vienna, Zürich, Berlin, New York, and Buenos Aires. The smaller models had shaft drive by 1908, though chains were continued on the larger until 1916, being almost the last chain-driven passenger cars in the world. A more modern model for 1908 was the Tipo G with 2.9-litre L-head monobloc 4-cylinder engine, joined by 2.1- and 4.4-litre cars, also with shaft drive. In 1910 Bianchi sold 450 cars, which put them in second place behind Fiat, who sold 1698. A variety of 4-cylinder cars was made up to 1914, designed by Antonio Santoni who replaced Merosi in 1909. The smallest was the 1244cc Tipo S sold in England as the 10/12hp and available in one body style only, and one colour (grey-green body and black wings). Larger models included the 2120cc 12/18hp, and 7960cc 40/50. In 1914 this was renamed the 42/60 and in 1915 the 42/70. The sporting model of this had wire wheels and a Mercedes-like vee-radiator. Electric lighting and starting were optional on home market cars and standard on export models. The 3306cc Tipo B, introduced in 1915, had electric lighting as standard. Bianchi set up their own coachwork department in 1913, and thereafter most of the cars had factory bodies, though some sold in England were bodied by British firms.

After the war Bianchi concentrated on one model, the 1693cc Tipo 12, a conventional car with fixed cylinder head. It became the Tipo 16 in 1923, now with detachable head, and was joined by the 1953cc ohv Tipo 18. Four-wheel brakes arrived in 1925, on the 1287cc Tipo S4. This was Bianchi's most important inter-war car, a rival for Fiat's Tipo 509, though made in far smaller numbers. About 6600 were made of the S4 and its successor the S5, between 1925 and 1934, less than 10 per cent of Fiat's output. The S4 was made with a variety of bodies, open and closed, becoming the S5 in 1928 when coil ignition replaced the magneto. The last S5s, made in 1932–34, had larger engines of 1452cc and gearboxes in unit with the engine.

In 1928 Bianchi broke new ground with the S8, a 2731cc pushrod ohv straight-8 with dry sump lubrication and mechanical pump feed. Like the contemporary straight-8 BALLOT it was good looking, but lacked the performance to go with its appearance. Capacity went up to 2906cc in 1930, and in 1933 there was a short-wheelbase version, the S8bis, capable of 84mph (135km/h). In 1934 the S5 gave way to the S9, which had the same size engine but with five-bearings for the crankshaft instead of three, and new styling. It gained hydraulic brakes and synchromesh in 1936, but was no match for the Lancia Aprilia or Fiat 1500. Only 360 S9s were made in 1939, the last year for Bianchi passenger cars.

Revival under Fiat
The Bianchi name survived on bicycles, motorcycles, and commercial vehicles, and a few prototype cars were made in 1950. In 1955 Milanese industrialist Ferrucio Quintavalle organised a new company involving Bianchi, Fiat, and tyre makers Pirelli. It was called Autobianchi SpA and continued the manufacture

1937 Bianchi S9 saloon.
NATIONAL MOTOR MUSEUM

of trucks, while motorcycles were made by a separate company, Edoardo Bianchi SpA. Two years later came the first car to bear the Autobianchi name. Called the Bianchina, it was a 2-seater coupé using the chassis, engine and transmission of the 2-cylinder Fiat 500, with a more attractive body. It was joined later by a 4-seater saloon, estate car, and delivery van. In 1958 Giuseppe Bianchi, Edoardo's son, sold the family holdings in Autobianchi to Fiat, and in 1963 Fiat gained full control.

The Bianchina remained in production throughout the 1960s, and in 1969 the Autobianchi factory took over manufacture of the Fiat 500 estate car, the Giardinera. The factory was at Desio, in the suburbs of Milan, which Bianchi had built in 1939 for motorcycle manufacture. Fiat also made overdrive gearboxes there. From the 1960s onwards Autobianchi's role was to act as a testing ground for new ideas before they were put into mass production by Fiat. In 1964 came the Autobianchi Primula with transverse Fiat 1100D engine driving the front wheels. Made as a saloon, sports coupé, and estate car, the Primula was the first car from the Fiat empire to have rack-and-pinion steering. Five years after it was introduced, Fiat brought out the best-selling 128, which incorporated many of the ideas tried out in the Primula. Autobianchi's next new model was the A112, a front-drive 2-door saloon which anticipated the Fiat 127. Introduced in 1969, it was made up to 1987. Originally powered by a detuned 903cc 42bhp engine as used in the Fiat 850, later A112s received a 965cc 48bhp unit and an Abarth-tuned 1050cc developing 70bhp. Apart from the short-lived A111 of 1970, Bianchi's equivalent of the Fiat 124, the A112 was the sole Autobianchi model up to its demise in 1987. It sold steadily with little change apart from minor restyling, and was popular for its handling and cheeky styling which it shared with the INNOCENTI Mini. More than a million had been sold by 1983, and the final production figure was 1,255,000. It was replaced by the Lancia Y10, which still carried the Autobianchi name in some markets.

NG

BI-AUTOGO *see* SCRIPPS-BOOTH

1965 Autobianchi Primula saloon.
NICK GEORGANO/NATIONAL MOTOR MUSEUM

1971 Autobianchi A112 saloon .
NATIONAL MOTOR MUSEUM

1918 Biddle Model K roadster.
NATIONAL MOTOR MUSEUM

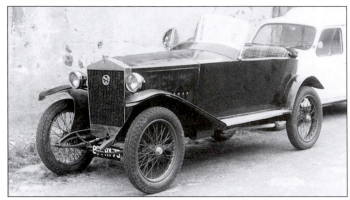

1923 Bignan Type AL sports car.
NATIONAL MOTOR MUSEUM

1925 Bignan 2-litre tourer.
NATIONAL MOTOR MUSEUM

BIDDLE (US) 1915–1923

1915–1921 Biddle Motor Car Co., Philadelphia, Pennsylvania.
1921–1923 Biddle-Crane Motor Car Co., New York, New York.

The Biddle was introduced as a car with the panache that would find favour with a clientele who wanted something different and distinctive, without it being in any way freakish in appearance. Toward this goal, the car achieved a niche of its own in the luxury car market with a stunning design and a pointed radiator similar to that of the Mercedes. Mechanically, it differed little from any other assembled car on the contemporary market, its power plant being a Buda 4-cylinder L-head engine developing 40bhp at 2000rpm, and a wheelbase of 121in (3071mm). Although wood artillery wheels were standard, the greater majority of Biddles produced were equipped with wire wheels, which emphasised the lithe appearance and, in point of fact, the Biddle was largely regarded as a car for the boulevard rather than for open-road touring. Coachwork was almost entirely fashioned by in-house builders and a good percentage of the cars were delivered with designs ordered by the purchaser. In 1920 new management took

over Biddle after perhaps 500 cars had been completed, but less than a year later, in 1921, the company was taken over by a group headed by F.L. Crane. The Biddle offered an option of a 4-cylinder Duesenberg engine as early as 1918, and although the Rochester-Duesenberg four was theoretically available until the end of production, the greater number of cars were completed with the Buda power plant. Relatively few cars were produced after 1920, these carrying prices in the $3500 to $5000 price bracket. Production ended during 1922, the last Biddle cars being sold in 1923 and marketed as 1923 models.

KM

Further Reading
'A Little on the Biddle', Beverly Rae Kimes,
Automobile Quarterly, Vol. 11, No. 3.

BIDDLE-MURRAY (US) 1905–1907

Biddle-Murray Manufacturing Co., Oak Park, Illinois.

This company was organised in Chicago for car manufacture and apparently some cars were made, though details of their design and price are not known. When the company was closed in March 1907 on the petition of creditors it was stated that they had made automobiles in a small way. They also made at least one forward-control truck.

NG

BIENE (D) 1923

M.F.C. Zimmermann, Berlin.

The Biene (bee) was one of several makes of cyclecar to use the flat-twin BMW motorcycle engine. It had friction disc transmsission.

HON

BIFORT (GB) 1914–1915

Bifort Motor Co., Fareham, Hampshire.

Founded by a Mr White, the Bifort company made a light car with imported engine and chassis. The 1327cc 10.4hp 4-cylinder engine came from Belgium and the chassis from Maubeuge in Northern France, probably supplied by S.U.P. The bodies were made at the works. The Bifort was said to be popular with naval officers, but few were made because of the outbreak of World War I. White later formed Duple Motor Bodies at Hornsey, North London, in 1919, initially making bodies convertible from car to van (hence the name, from duplex, or dual purpose). They later became famous for bus bodies at Hendon, Middlesex, and are still in business today as Hestair Duple at Blackpool.

NG

BIGNAN (F) 1918–1930

Automobiles Bignan, Courbevoie, Seine.

A wide variety of cars carried the name of Jacques Bignan, yet the only ones that he seems to have made himself were the 2-litre touring and sports models of 1922 to 1930. Bignan started in business in 1911 by making 1½-litre 4-cylinder side-valve engines in partnership with Lucien Picker, who later made Picker-Janvier engines. The first car to bear the Bignan name had a 3480cc 4-cylinder side-valve engine in a chassis made by De La Fournaise. The car was assembled in the GREGOIRE (i) factory and was sold in England by Malcolm Campbell under the name Gregoire-Campbell. In 1921 the stroke was reduced from 92 to 85mm to bring the car within the 3-litre class for competitions. Brakes were on the rear wheels only at first, but later servo-assisted Perrot four-wheel brakes were fitted. Most were bodied as tourers (they served as official cars in the 1920 Tour de France cycle race) but some had coupé de ville bodies. Unusually for the time, they carried a three year guarantee.

Bignan entered three cars with 1.4-litre side-valve engines in the 1920 GP de Voiturettes at Le Mans, but it is not certain that this model was sold for road use. He also developed with Nemorin Causan a 3-litre ohc four which produced a remarkable 96bhp, but this again was used only in competitions.

In 1922 Bignan opened a factory at Courbevoie with enough space to make complete cars. Two models were launched that year, the 11CV single-ohc 2-litre (1978cc) and a 1097cc 4-cylinder sports car which was in fact a SALMSON AL3, at first distinguished only by the removal of the Salmson badge, though later models carried the wide, square Bignan radiator. Bignan also went badge-engineering with the E.H.P., whose 1.2-litre 8CV S.C.A.P.-engined car carried a Bignan radiator. Other models of the complex Bignan range used 1590cc side-valve Ballot or 1690cc single-ohc S.C.A.P. engines. The more original 11CV had a 4-speed gearbox and Hallot servo-assisted brakes. Only the front wheels had brake drums, those at the rear being operated by a transmission brake which was a large drum behind the gearbox. This system was also used on the contemporary CHENARD-WALCKER. The standard engine developed 50bhp, but the competition engine, which was catalogued, used desmodromic valves to develop 70bhp. Historian Serge Pozzoli thinks that no more than eight were sold to the public. From 1924 these positively closed valves gave way to the conventional system, but there were four valves per cylinder. They had many successes in racing, and a saloon won the 1924 Monte Carlo Rally. In 1926 the 11CV was redesigned with an 8-valve engine incorporating twin oil pumps. This gave 60bhp and was available on wheelbases of 120 and 132in (3046 and 3350mm), the latter suitable for formal closed bodywork. Weymann bodies were popular on Bignans. Other bodies were by C.G.A., owners of E.H.P.

In 1926 Automobiles Bignan collapsed, being rescued by the Société La Cigogne. Jacques Bignan was not part of this new venture, though he continued to interest himself in the Monte Carlo rally, winning it in 1928 in a Fiat 509. The 11CV was made up to 1930, joined by two models using S.C.A.P. straight-8 engines of 1808 and 2340cc. The later models went under the name Bignan-MOP.

NG

BIJ 'T VUUR (NL) 1902–1905
C. Bij 't Vuur, Arnhem.
In 1901 C. Bij 't Vuur joined a rally through Holland with a self-built car with a 6hp single-cylinder Aster engine with electrical ignition. In general the car looked like a French Darracq, but Bij 't Vuur built the chassis himself, and his brother delivered the bodies. A second car with a stronger 6½hp engine was on display at the fourth automobile exhibition, the RAI in Amsterdam in 1904. The following year 9hp and 12hp engines were available; as well as the Aster engine, Dion-Bouton and Panhard engines. The customer had finally to choose between the French Buchet engine or the Germain engine from Belgium. After receiving an order to manufacture a series of three buses, the firm became bankrupt before the buses were ready. Someone else completed them and after a short time they were exported to England. The Bij 't Vuur company never came back; they probably built about 25 cars in all.

FBV

BIJOU (GB) 1901–1904
Protector Lamp & Lighting Co. Ltd, Eccles, Manchester.
This light car had a 5hp single-cylinder horizontal engine, with chain drive to a countershaft on which was mounted the speed-change mechanism. Two chain wheels were alternately engaged by internally expanding clutches. There were two clutch pedals, one for each speed; there was no reverse. The car could be started by a handle from the driver's seat. The makers also delivered a fire engine, powered by a 7hp 2-cylinder engine, to Eccles Fire Brigade in 1901.

NG

BIKINI (I) 1965
This curious beach-cum-utility car was composed of a basic tubular frame and scant glassfibre body panels. The doorless body could seat four persons and featured a large fold-flat windscreen and bug-eye headlamps. A Fiat 500 Giardiniera engine was mounted at the front driving the front wheels, and the suspension was derived from the Mini.

CR

BILLARD (F) 1922–1925
E. Billard, Villeneuve-le Guyard, Yonne.
Billard made very small cyclecars, one with a 2hp engine and single-seater body, the other a 4hp 2-seater.

NG

BILLIKEN (US) 1914
Milwaukee Cyclecar Co., Milwaukee, Wisconsin.
The Billiken cyclecar used a 1.6-litre 12hp 4-cylinder engine, epicyclic gearbox, and shaft drive. Production must have been small, as by June 1914 they were planning a move to Sacramento, California, but the company failed before this

could happen. The Billiken mascot was a small Buddha-like figure which was offered as an accessory on any make of car.

NG

BILLINGS (GB) 1900
E.D. Billings, Coventry.
The Billings 2-seater voiturette had a 2hp De Dion-Bouton single-cylinder engine, front mounted with no bonnet to cover it. Tiller steering was not unusual in a car of this type, but it had the advanced feature of shaft drive. An alternative name was Burns, as it was to have been sold by J. Burns of London.

NG

BILLY FOUR (US) 1910
McNabb Iron Works, Atlanta, Georgia.
The Billy Four was an attractive-looking 2-seater roadster with 20hp 4-cylinder engine, epicyclic gearbox, and shaft drive. The Model 1 was priced at $500, but there was no Model 2.

NG

BILMAR (GB) 1971–1972
Bilmar, Portland, Dorset.
Although notably wider than the Lotus Seven and having larger headlamps and a different tail treatment, the Bilmar Buccaneer echoed the Seven's style quite closely. Alloy body panels fitted over a space frame chassis designed for a Triumph Spitfire engine, gearbox and front suspension, and a Ford Corsair rear axle. Only 11 were made.

CR

BIMEL (US) 1916–1917
Bimel Buggy Co., Sidney, Ohio.
The Bimel appears to have been the continuation of the Elco, which was to have been built by the Elwood Iron Works of Elwood, Indiana which went bankrupt before the car reached the market-place. The rights to the Elco were then acquired by the Bimel Works of Signey, Ohio, previously the Bimel Buggy Works, but which had become the manufacturer of automobile wheels. In 1916 the small generic roadster and touring cars bearing the Elco badge had been introduced. However, the venture failed a year later and it is believed that the remaining unsold cars were marketed with the Bimel badge. Plans for a 6-cylinder Bimel to replace the 4-cylinder model were under way, but presumably the project never reached the prototype stage. The plans called for a Caille engine, built by the Caille Perfection Motor Co. of Detroit, Michigan, widely known as a manufacturer of marine engines, slot machines and other gambling equipment.

KM

1901 Bijou 5hp 2-seater.
NATIONAL MOTOR MUSEUM

165

1969 Biota Mark I sports car.
NATIONAL MOTOR MUSEUM

1921 Birmingham sedan.
NICK BALDWIN

BINNEY & BURNHAM (US) 1902

Binney & Burnham, Boston, Massachusetts.
Partners James L. Binney and John Appleton Burnham built a number of heavy steam cars, including a folding front seat 4-seater, and a touring car with accommodation for eight passengers, or six with plenty of space for luggage. The engine was a 2-cylinder unit, and the boiler supplied pressure at 150psi. When the partnership was dissolved in January 1903, John Burnham joined Frederick Lyman to make a petrol car which they called the LYMAN & BURNHAM.
NG

BIOTA (GB) 1969–1976

1969–1970 Houghton Coldwell, Thurcroft, Yorkshire.
1970–1976 Houghton Coldwell, Dinnington, Yorkshire.
The Biota Mini-based sports car boasted a proper space frame chassis, Mini front subframe and Mini trailing arm/coil sprung rear. Its unusual doorless glassfibre body incorporated a distinctive roll-over bar and a large bonnet bulge to accommodate the tall Mini engine. As it weighed only 8cwt, performance was a strong suit, bolstered by success at hill climbs. The 1972 Mk2 had a De Dion rear end and a bigger cockpit. Around 35 Biotas were made in all.
CR

BIRCH (US) 1916–1923

Birch Motor Cars Inc., Chicago, Illinois.
The Birch was a mail-order car which was advertised primarily in pulp magazines or monthly journals such as *Popular Mechanics*. The company and its manner of selling cars was similar to its Chicago contemporary, the BUSH. The centre of operations was the Birch Motor College, a technical institute, students of which served as assemblers of some of the Birch operations. The cars were put together by such other automobile companies as the CROW-ELKHART of Elkhart,

Indiana, and SENECA of Fostoria, Ohio, and engines for both the 4- and 6-cylinder lines of Birch included Beaver, Herschell-Spillman, Lycoming, Le Roi, and Supreme. Like the Bush, Birch Motor College students were urged, as a part of their training, to sell the cars with the incentive of obtaining their own Birch car, by selling a certain number of them. With this, they were also provided with the Birch agencies in their community.
KM

BIRCHALL see McCOY

BIRCHFIELD (GB) 1985 to date

C.V. Shapecraft, Northampton.
Since the Birchfield Sports was productionised by an ex-Panther employee, Clive Smart, it is not surprising that it resembled a PANTHER J72. The bodywork was created by hand in aluminium and all the curved areas were shaped by hand in several pieces. The chassis was a very strong space frame with a massive central spine, and it used Jaguar XJ6 mechanicals. This was the most expensive kit car ever sold in Britain when it was launched in 1985. Some 22 cars had been made by 1998, when the car remained available to special order.
CR

BIRD (US) c.1966–1980

Bird Automotive, Omaha, Nebraska.
Fred Schwester built the 'Super Bird' Ford Model T hot rod kit. It included a box-tube frame and would accept any Chevrolet V8 engine. They were sold in kit or assembled form.
HP

BIRKIN (ZA) 1982 to date

Birkin International, Pinetown, KZN, South Africa.
Started by John Watson in 1982, the Birkin was very much inspired by the Lotus Super Seven. The company started off building cars for a Lotus dealer called Status Cars, launching the first car at the 1983 South African Grand Prix. As per the original Lotus, the construction consisted of a spaceframe chassis with aluminium body panels and glassfibre wings and nose (though, later on, carbon fibre wings were also offered as an option). The front suspension used Ford components, while at the rear an independent set-up was developed as an alternative to the original live rear axle, which was derived from Toyota. Engines were usually Ford – offered with carburettors or Birkin designed fuel injection – though many other engine installations were offered, including Mazda rotary, Toyota twin cam, Cosworth BDR and Opel. In 1986 a new factory and assembly line was set up to produce about five cars per month, and by 1988 Birkin celebrated its 200th vehicle. Birkin also built Ray Formula Fords at the rate of 400 per year. They also did some engineering work on the BROOKE ME190. Despite legal moves by Caterham Cars, Birkin in 1999 continued to produce almost precise replicas of the Lotus Seven Series 3 under the name Birkin S3.
CR

BIRMINGHAM (US) 1921–1922

Birmingham No-Axle Motor Corp., Jamestown, New York.
The Birmingham car was an attempt to change automotive design by featuring 4-wheel independent suspension by means of transverse semi-elliptic springs instead of conventional axles. A Haskelite fabric-covered sedan body further separated the car from conventional designs on other American cars of the period. A Continental 7R 6-cylinder L-head engine was fitted to the Birmingham which had a wheelbase of 124in (3147mm). Despite such arduous testing as driving pilot models over a series of railroad ties, the Birmingham failed after approximately 20 cars had been completed. The axleless principle of the car was subsequently used on the unsuccessful CANADIAN SIX and the general lines of the Birmingham were continued on the PARKER cars of Montreal which otherwise employed conventional suspension.
KM

BISCAYNE (RA) 1998 to date

Osvaldo Bessia, Buenos Aires.
The Biscayne Roadster was an AC Cobra replica made in the area of the Aeropuerto Internacional de Don Torcuato. The car was fitted with a fibreglass

body and powered by a Ford V8-302 engine, developing 285bhp. It had a Tremac transmission with overdrive.

ACT

BISCUTER (E) 1953–1960

Autonacional SA, Barcelona.

When Gabriel Voisin displayed his Biscooter ultra-basic front-wheel drive economy car at the 1950 Paris Salon, it was greeted with a fairly lukewarm reception. Intended production did not begin in France, but instead a licence was granted to Damien Casanova's Autonacional operation in Spain. Of the two prototypes Voisin had created (one in 1950 and one in 1951), it was the earlier one that was chosen as the production car, whose name was changed to Biscuter by the Barcelona-based firm Autonacional, as the one to make in series.

The Spanish firm gave the rather sparsely-bodied, doorless, almost baroque 2-seater rather more of a body, and swapped the Gnome-et-Rhône 125cc engine for a 9bhp 197cc Hispano Villiers single-cylinder unit, still mounted up front. The chassis remained an aluminium monocoque, a Voisin hallmark. The transmission was a 3-speed unit, and braking acted on the differential at the front and was by drums at the rear. Weighing only 528lbs, the Biscuter was claimed to achieve 48mph (76km/h) – a figure guaranteed by the Argentinian racing driver Fangio – and to return 57mpg. After a June 1953 launch, the first production cars were made towards the end of the year. The basic model was an open 2-seater which came to be something of a definitive form of city transport in Spain. Other body options soon appeared: a coupé with fully-enclosed glassfibre bodywork and a 4-seater estate were both offered. As these appeared, the models were named the 200R (open), 200C (estate), and 200F (coupé). There was even a Voisin-designed extended-wheelbase open 4-seater in 1955, but this remained a prototype. By the time Biscuter was withdrawn from sale in 1960, between 15,000 and 20,000 had been sold, making it one of the most successful microcars ever made. Production was also scheduled in India, Morocco, Israel, Ireland, and Argentina.

There is a curious adjunct to the story, for in 1984 an industrial group presented a modern microcar design called the Biscuter 2000. It had angular doorless open bodywork that unfortunately looked like a golf cart, and it was to be powered by 50cc petrol or 360cc diesel engines. The financial implications of manufacturing the car prevented a production run.

CR

BITTER (D) 1973–c.1992

Bitter & Co. KG, Schwelm.

Erich Bitter specialised in limited edition and often sporting versions of Opel cars. His first, the Diplomat CD, was a 2-door coupé based on the 5.4-litre Opel Diplomat V8, with automatic transmission, power steering, power disc brakes and a De Dion rear axle. Bitter made 463 of these up to 1979, when a new model appeared, based this time on the 3-litre 6-cylinder fuel injected Opel Senator. Options included a 5-speed manual gearbox and interior trim in Chinese buffalo hide. In 1990 he brought out an Omega-based car, the Type 3, with saloon, coupé, or convertible bodies and a choice of 177 or 204bhp engines, the latter with 24-valves. At the 1991 Frankfurt Show, alongside the Type 3s, Bitter showed the Trasco, a mid-engined supercar with an unspecified engine. The car was said to be in the early stages of development, but never proceeded beyond a prototype. Production of the other models ended shortly after that.

NG

BIZZARRINI (i) (I) 1965–1969

Prototipi Bizzarrini Srl, Livorno.

In 1962, the former Alfa Romeo and Ferrari engineer, Giotto Bizzarrini, established a company to act as a subcontractor to the motor industry. Among his products was the Lamborghini V12 engine and chassis for Iso. In 1965 Bizzarrini was allowed to make the Strada 5300, a 2-seat lightweight version of the Iso Grifo A3C with a 365bhp 5.4-litre Chevrolet engine.

It was intended to be a road/competition car, but fell between two stools. It was made in small numbers until 1969 and, in the USA, was sold as the Bizzarrini GT America.

Bizzarrini's second car, the Europa introduced in 1967, resembled a scaled-down Strada. It had a fibreglass body, a steel platform chassis with 4-wheel disc brakes, independent suspension by coil springs and double wishbones, and an

c.1951 Biscuter 200 microcar .
NATIONAL MOTOR MUSEUM

1920 Bjering 2-seater.
NATIONAL MOTOR MUSEUM

unmodified 110bhp 1.9-litre Opel engine. It was claimed to be capable of 127mph, but there were few takers and the Europas hastened the marque's decline.

Before Bizzarrini closed his car operation in 1969, he built the P538 (aka Spyder), an unsuccessful mid-engined sports racer. A road version, the Varedo, was made for Iso in 1972, but did not reach production.

MJL

BIZZARRINI (ii) (US) 1990 to date

Disegno di Bizzarrini, Tustin, California.

This was an ambitious project to reintroduce the Bizzarrini name with a low-volume, high-priced sportscar. The Bizzarrini BZ-2001 was a prototype built in 1992 using a design by Giotto Bizzarrini with backing from Barry Watkins in California. The first car was built on Ferrari Testarossa running gear. Disignio di Bizzarrini was set up to produce the car on a limited basis, with long range plans of building their own chassis and V12 engine. They also intended to do design and development for other companies. The first run of BZ-2001 specials, which would use any drivetrain the buyers wanted, were to sell for $250,000 each.

HP

BJERING (N) 1918–1920

H.C. Bjering, Gjovik.

A/S Raufoss Ammunisjonsfabrikker, Raufoss.

H.C. Bjering made a small number of distinctive cars in which driver and passenger sat in tandem, with the driver behind, as on the early BEDELIA. The first five had wooden bodies and an air-cooled V4 engine between passenger and driver. They were used by country police, the arrested man being placed in front where the driver could keep an eye on him. In winter they could be fitted with skis in place of the front wheels. The last two Bjerings were made by an ammunitions company, who still retain one of them. They were considerably redesigned, with metal bodies and an in-line 4-cylinder engine at the rear, behind the back wheels.

NG

1930 Blackhawk (ii) Model L8 tourer.
NICK BALDWIN

B.J.S (GB) 1987
B.J.S. Motors, Mansfield, Nottinghamshire.
The B.J.S. Mistral was an abysmal plastic-bodied 2+2 gull-wing coupé based on Ford Cortina parts, with styling supposedly inspired by the Lamborghini Countach. A good indication of its quality was that one customer got stuck inside the one and only car ever seen, at the 1987 Belle Vue kit car show.
CR

BLACK (i) (US) 1893; 1896–1900
1896–1899 C.H. Black Manufacturing Co., Indianapolis, Indiana.
1899–1900 Indianapolis Automobile & Vehicle Co., Indianapolis, Indiana.
Charles Black was a blacksmith and wagon maker who drove a friend's Benz in 1891 and was fired with the idea of making a car of his own. This was completed two years later, and was on Benz lines, with a single cylinder-engine and horizontal flywheel, which was pulled to start the engine. In 1896 Black secured sufficient finance to begin manufacture, and turned out a small number of cars, very much on Benz lines. His 'physician's phaeton' of 1899 was a near replica of the Benz Viktoria, though practically all parts were made in Indianapolis. In 1900 he returned to full time carriage building, though another company, trading as the Indiana Motor & Vehicle Co., continued Black's cars into 1901, selling them as the Indiana.
NG

BLACK (ii) (US) 1903–1909
Black Manufacturing Co., Chicago, Illinois.
The Black Co. made mainly high-wheelers powered by 10hp 2-cylinder air-cooled engines, and using chain drive and solid rubber tyres. In 1908 they sold a number of the 4-cylinder cars made by Crow Motor Co. under the name of BLACK CROW.
NG

BLACK BARON (E) 1996–1998
Rolf Menke, Alicante.
The German Rolf Menke built (in Spain) a special, on a Beetle chassis, called the Dreamster (a contraction of the words *Dream*car and Road*ster*), a 2-seater with plastic body and different Volkswagen engines from 44bhp up to the 150bhp of the Golf Gti. Doors and a folding roof were only available as extras, and about 20 cars were finally built.
VCM

BLACKBURN (i) (GB) 1919–1925
Blackburn Aeroplane & Motor Co. Ltd, Leeds, Yorkshire.
This famous Yorkshire aircraft firm, like so many others, ventured into car manufacture after World War 1, when war-time contracts ended and the aircraft market virtually disappeared. Rather surprisingly, however, they produced a very conservative car when other aircraft manufacturers were adapting aviation experience to the road. The engine of the Blackburn was a big 4-cylinder Coventry-Simplex of 3160cc, its cylinders cast in pairs, although a monobloc was introduced for 1922. The gearbox was separate, and a cone clutch was used. The radiator was a copy of the Rolls-Royce, a common practice of the time. Blackburn also made bodies for other car makers.
NG

BLACKBURN (ii) (US) 1920–1921
Blackburn Automotive Co., Houston, Texas.
This was an improved Model T Ford with power raised from 20 to 23bhp, and a conventional sliding gear transmission substituted for the T's epicyclic. The only body style, a 5-seater tourer, was priced at US$400. Possibly as many as 500 were sold.
NG

BLACK CROW (US) 1910–1911
1910 Black Manufacturing Co, Chicago, Illinois.
1911 Crow Motor Car Co., Elkhart, Indiana.
The Black Crow, previously a model designation by BLACK (ii), became a make in its own right in 1910. The company built several models, two of which retained the high-wheeler design. In 1911 the name changed to Crow.
KM

BLACK DIAMOND *see* BUCKMOBILE

BLACKHAWK (i) (US) 1903
Clark Mfg Co., Moline, Illinois.
After six years of building experimental cars, W.E. Clark announced his Blackhawk runabout. It was offered with single- or 2-cylinder engines, in the same chassis and with the same epicyclic gearbox and single-chain drive. Steering was by tiller and there was no weather protection. The single-cylinder runabout was priced at $750 and the 2-cylinder phaeton at $850. Not more than 50 Blackhawks were made, and the make survived less than a year. In 1906 Clark tried again with the DEERE-CLARK.
NG

BLACKHAWK (ii) (US) 1929–1930
Stutz Motor Car Co. of America, Indianapolis, Indiana.
The model designation of Blackhawk had previously applied to the Stutz Model BB of 1928, which had used the name in the two words 'Black' and 'Hawk'. It was launched in 1929 as a cheaper companion car to the larger Stutz and was regarded as a make in its own right rather than a model. It could be had with either an ohc-6 or as a straight-8, developing 85bhp and 95bhp at 3200rpm respectively. Mounted on a 127¹/₂in (3236mm) wheelbase, a complete line of open and closed models – some with custom coachwork – was offered. Prices for the Blackhawk with factory coachwork ranged from $1995 to $2785. Production figures were disappointing with 1310 sold in the boom year and only 280 in 1930, a victim of the 1929 Crash.
KM

BLACKJACK (GB) 1996 to date
Blackjack Cars, Helston, Cornwall.
For all Richard Oakes' celebrated designs (such as the Nova, Midas and Deltayn Pegasus), the Blackjack Avion was the first that he actually productionised himself. This was a handsome 3-wheeled cyclecar using a Citroen 2CV engine mounted in a steel tube subframe, a rear subframe accepting a single swinging arm. The coil spring front suspension was based on Citroën components. The doorless open body was in glassfibre, with optional weather gear.
CR

BLACK PRINCE (GB) 1920
Black Prince Motors Ltd, Barnard Castle, Co. Durham.
The Black Prince was a very light cyclecar powered by a 2³/₄hp Union air-cooled 2-stroke engine. It had a 2-speed belt transmission and was made mostly of wood, both body and chassis. A version with two coupled engines was also made. At least two Black Princes survive today.
NG

BLAKE (GB) 1900–1903
1900–1901 F.C. Blake & Co., Hammersmith, London.
1901–1903 F.C. Blake & Co., Kew, Surrey.
Blake was a manufacturer of engines for use in other cars, including PRITCHETT & GOLD, and also in light locomotives and launches. In 1900 he built a *vis-à-vis* with 7hp 4-cylinder horizontal engine, and the following year a rear-entrance

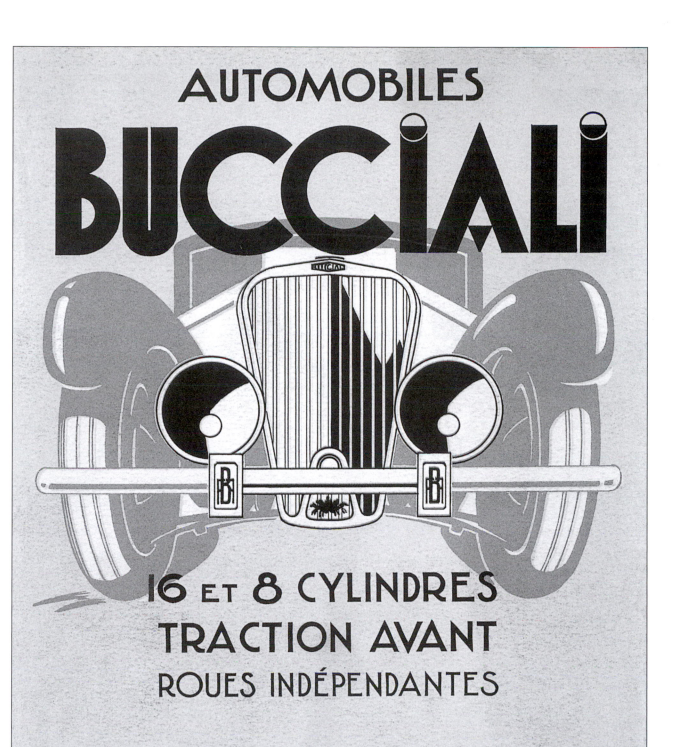

1980 Blakely Bernardi roadster.
ELLIOTT KAHN

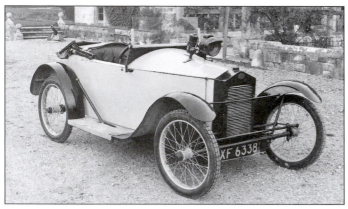

1921 Blériot-Whippet 8.9hp 2-seater.
NATIONAL MOTOR MUSEUM

tonneau with two 4hp 2-cylinder engines under a long bonnet, the top of which was almost entirely covered by the radiator. He moved to Kew in September 1901, and possibly built no cars there, though engine manufacture continued at least until 1904.

NG

BLAKELY (US) c.1972–1987

Blakely Auto Works, Love Park, Illinois; Princeton, Wisconsin.
Started by Dick Blakely, their first kit car was a Lotus 7-style roadster called the Bantam using Ford Pinto running gear with a steel tube frame. In 1975 they added a more civilised version with doors and a nicer interior called the Bearcat. It was also longer, heavier and more like a Morgan in character. In 1980 Blakely was bought by Art Herchenberger who moved the company to Princeton, Wisconsin. A restyled version of the Bearcat called the Bernardi was introduced. It had a chrome grill with horizontal slats borrowed from the Oldsmobile Cutlass. The Bearcat and Bernardi offered V6 Ford engines in addition to the Mazda rotaries and Pinto 4-cylinder engines that had been standard in Blakely kits. In the 1980s the Bantam was renamed the Hawk and the Bernardi was offered in fully assembled form. In 1985 the company changed its name to Bernardi Auto Works. The Blakely/Bernardi kits were very popular and many sold.

HP

BLENHEIM (NZ) 1915

Wairau Cycle & Motor Works, Blenheim, South Island.
C.J. Bateman, who had produced the Blenheim motorcycle in 1913, joined the fashion for cyclecars when he showed his example in 1915, which was powered by a 2.5hp J.A.P. engine and employed belt drive to the rear wheels. It was then claimed to be the smallest practical car in the nation and able to travel 120 miles on one gallon (4.55 litres) of fuel.

MG

BLÉRIOT (F) 1921–1922

Blériot Aéronautique, Suresnes, Seine.
This company was founded in 1909 by Louis Blériot who gained everlasting fame on 25 July 1909 when he became the first man to fly the Channel, in a monoplane of his own construction. Aeroplane production became very important during World War I when a British factory was set up at Addlestone, Surrey, to make both Blériot and Spad aircraft (see BLÉRIOT-WHIPPET). The Suresnes factory made a small number of cyclecars with 8/10hp 2-cylinder 2-stroke engines and shaft drive.

NG

BLÉRIOT-WHIPPET (GB) 1920–1927

Air Navigation & Engineering Co. Ltd, Addlestone, Surrey.
The A.N.E.C. built Blériot and Spad aircraft during World War I, and to keep the factory going after the war they took up a cyclecar designed by George Herbert Jones and W.D. Marchant. The most interesting aspect of this was the Zenith-Gradua belt transmission, an infinitely variable system using vee-belts and movable pulleys. This had been used on motorcycles made by Zenith, for which the two men worked. The cyclecar was named Blériot-Whippet, after the aircraft, and there was no other connection with the more ephemeral French cyclecar of the same name, despite the claim by *The Autocar* that the latter was the French edition of the Blériot-Whippet. Jones & Marchant's prototype used a JAP V-twin engine, but the production Blériot-Whippet had an air-cooled Blackburne V-twin. Jones and Marchant soon improved this unit, with roller bearing big ends. The cars had ash frames and 2-seater bodies made in tourer and sports versions. Jones left to work with Granville Bradshaw in 1921, but the cars were steadily developed, gaining chain drive and then shaft drive. However, they could not compete with cars such as the Austin Seven, and production ended in 1927. ERIC LONGDEN cars were also made in the factory which was later used by Weymann, making fabric bodies for cars, followed by bus bodies. This lasted until 1965 when it was acquired by Plessey.

NG

BLISS (US) 1906

E.W. Bliss Co., Brooklyn, New York.
This company was a well-known builder of heavy presses and drop-forging machinery, also torpedos for the US Navy, who entered the car market with a high-priced touring car powered by a 30hp 4-cylinder T-head engine with integral flywheel and fan and double-chain drive. Chrome and nickel steel were extensively used in the car. The tourer was priced at US$5000, but other bodies could be ordered at higher prices still. Bliss built only 10 cars before deciding that he had had enough of the automobile business.

NG

B.L.M. (US) 1906–1907

Breese, Lawrence & Moulton Motor Car & Equipment Co.,
Brooklyn, New York.
Sidney Breese and Charles Lawrence built an experimental racing car in 1905, when they were barely out of their teens. They priced this at US$12,000 and quickly realised that it was not a practical proposition. After Andrew Moulton joined the team they announced the Pirate Runabout; this used a 24hp French-built Mutel engine, had shaft drive, and a stark 2-seater body. Advertised as 'The Greatest Runabout in the World', and capable of 70mph (112km/h) with the right gearing, it was priced at $3500. They also advertised a landaulette at $4500, but very few of either model were made. Lawrence and Moulton later built the L.M. car in Paris, though it is thought that they only made two, one for each of them.

NG

BLODGETT (US) 1922

Blodgett Engineering & Tool Co., Detroit, Michigan.
The Blodgett company were established makers of tools, jigs, dies, and special machinery for the auto industry, who decided to enter the field of complete cars with a tourer powered by a 6-cylinder Continental engine. It had disc wheels and was quite good-looking, but never went into production. The planned sedan and coupé were probably never built.

NG

BLOMSTROM (US) 1902–1903; 1907–1908
1902–1903 C.H. Blomstrom, Detroit, Michigan.
1907–1908 Blomstrom Manufacturing Co., Detroit, Michigan.
C.H. Blomstrom built experimental cars in 1897 and 1899, and in 1902 went into production with a small single-cylinder runabout. He built 25 of these, then formed the C.H. Blomstrom Motor Co. to make a car called the QUEEN. In August 1906 he formed a new company and used his name again on the car. The Blomstrom 30 was more ambitious than the previous Blomstrom or the Queen, having a 30hp 4-cylinder engine, shaft drive and tourer or runabout bodies. For 1908 horsepower was upped to 35, though doubtless the same size engine was used. Blomstrom announced that he would make 200 cars that year, 175 tourers and 25 runabouts, but whether this number were actually completed is uncertain. Later in 1908 he was making the GYROSCOPE, and later still, he was associated with the FRONTMOBILE and REX (iii).
NG

BLOOD (US) 1903; 1905–1906
1903 Michigan Automobile Co. Ltd, Kalamazoo, Michigan.
1905–1906 Blood Brothers Auto & Machine Co., Kalamazoo, Michigan.
The first car designed by the bicycle making brothers Maurice E. and Charles C. Blood was a very small tiller-steered 2-seater with a wheelbase of only 48in (1218mm). Much of its construction was derived from bicycle practice, and in 1904 the brothers decided to go for something larger, on a 54in (1371mm) wheelbase. This and subsequent cars were called MICHIGAN (i). In 1905 they parted company with their backers, the Fuller brothers, and resumed the Blood name on a line of touring cars with 12 or 16hp 2-cylinder engines. These lasted only into 1906, while the Michigan, made by the Fullers but of very similar design to the Blood, lasted a year longer.
NG

BLOOMQUIST (US) 1959
Gordon Bloomquist, Jamestown, New York.
A modified Kaiser frame and an ALMQUIST Sabre body were the basis of this prototype that never made it into production. A Kaiser 6-cylinder was the proposed engine.
HP

BLUE & GOLD (US) 1912–1913
A Automobile Co., Sacramento, California.
Taking its name from the California state colours, this was an ambitious project to mass produce reasonably-priced cars, but very few were completed. These included a four at US$1150 and a six at US$2100, both with 3-speed gearboxes. In 1914 the curiously-named A Automobile Company planned to build a car called the Richmond in Richmond, California, but nothing came of this.
NG

BLUE RAY (US) c.1992 to date
Blue Ray GT Engineering, The Woodlands, Texas;
GT Engineering, The Woodlands, Texas.
Company owner Jim Simpson collected rare sportscars, and in his collection were two Lancia-Nardi show cars named the Blue Ray I and Blue Ray II. He used some styling cues from them to produce his own exotic convertible sports car, using Mazda 929 running gear, called the Blue Ray III. It used a monocoque chassis with fabricated suspension and sold for a pricey $197,000. Blue Ray also sold a Datsun 240Z rebody that looked like a Ferrari 250 GTO and a Mazda Miata (MX5) rebody that resembled a miniature Ferrari Daytona Spyder. They also sold several Brazilian-built Porsche replicas as well as an English Lancia Stratos replica. In 1998 they relocated to Langley, Washington, under the name of SIMPSON DESIGN AND DEVELOPMENT.
HP

BLUMBERG (US) 1915–1922
Blumberg Motor Manufacturing Co., Orange, Texas.
These cars used 4-cylinder and V8 engines designed by Hamilton Blumberg and made, like the rest of the car, chassis and bodies, in their own factory. They were said to run so cool that no fan or radiator grill was needed. They had Renault-

c.1978 B.M.A. (ii) Brio 47cc microcar.
NICK GEORGANO

style dashboard radiators, apart from a prototype wire-wheeled roadster of 1919 which had a conventional front-mounted radiator. In 1918 they began manufacture of the Blumberg Steady Pull farm tractor; more of these were made than of the cars, production surviving up to 1924.
NG

B.M.A. (i) (GB) 1952–1957
1952 Battery Manufacturing Association, Hove, Sussex.
1952–1953 B.M.A. & Electrical Equipment Co., Hove, Sussex.
1952–1953 Gates & Pearson Ltd, Hove, Sussex.
1954–1957 Electric Motors (Hove) Ltd, Hove, Sussex.
Electric cars never made much mark in Britain, unlike France and Germany where the idea gained ground in the petrol-starved era around the war. The B.M.A. Hazelcar was a rare exception. Named after R.E. Hazeldine of Hazeldine Motors, it had a very compact 2-seater open aluminium body. Power came from a specially designed 1½ or 2hp electric motor and nine 6V batteries with a double reduction duplex chain drive via a 4-speed gearbox and switch-operated reverse. Speeds up to 20mph (32km/h) and a range of up to 60 miles (96km) were quoted but, at £535, it was too expensive to have any impact. A van version was also offered, but only six electric Hazelcars were ever built, plus a final one fitted with a Ford Eight engine.
CR

B.M.A (ii) (I) 1971–1994
B.M.A., Alfonsine, Ravenna.
The first microcar produced by B.M.A. was the Amica, a 3-wheeler powered by engines of between 50 and 223cc. Its plastic bodywork boasted gull-wing doors. The 1978 Brio was a bizarrely-shaped single-seater 3-wheeler, resembling a slice of cheese on wheels. A 47cc Sachs engine sat in the tail driving the right rear wheel only. A slightly larger model was the Nuova Amica of 1980, available as a 3- or 4-wheeler and with a choice of petrol or 360cc diesel engines. After the Brio left production in 1986, the two Amica models remained B.M.A.'s mainstay.
CR

BMB AUTOMOTIVE (US) c.1980
BMB Automotive, San Diego, California.
The Survivor was a 4-seat dune buggy that was designed to mount an electric winch so it could be pulled over inhospitable terrain.
HP

B.M.C. SPORTS (US) c.1952
British Motor Car Co., San Francisco, California.
This was an early project of Kjell Qvale, who later became a principal importer of English cars to the US and the owner of Jensen. The B.M.C. used a GLASSPAR-built fibreglass body on an English Singer chassis. The Singer 1500cc engine was fitted with twin Solex carburettors.
HP

B.M.W.

1932 BMW DA4 3/15PS saloon.
NATIONAL MOTOR MUSEUM

1934 BMW 315 cabriolet.
NATIONAL MOTOR MUSEUM

B.M.W. (i) **(D)** 1928 to date

1928–1939 Bayerische Motoren Werke, Eisenach; Munich.

1952 to date Bayerische Motoren Werke AG, Munich.

One of Germany's most charismatic makes had a long apprenticeship in aero-engines and motorcycles before cars were thought of. The ancestor of the present company was the Bayerische Flugzeugwerke (Bavarian Aeroplane Works) which was formed through the amalgamation of two other aero-engine makers in 1916. The name was changed to Bayerische Motoren Werke the following year. Among the leading architects of the new group were the Italian-born Austrian banker Camillo Castiglione and a young flying officer, Franz-Joseph Popp, who later became managing director of BMW and father-in-law of the British racing driver Dick Seaman.

Forbidden to make aero-engines after World War I, BMW branched out into other fields, notably engines for motorcycles and heavy trucks. In 1923 they built their first motorcycle, two features of which – the horizontally-opposed cylinders and shaft drive – are still characteristics of BMW motorcycles today. The engines were used in a few small German cars, such as the B.Z., the MAJA (ii), the 2-wheeled MAUSER Einspurwagen, and 3-wheeled WESNIGK. BMW themselves built one or two prototypes using their flat-twin engine, but did not proceed with them, and when they did turn to cars, it was to a foreign design.

In October 1928 BMW bought up the DIXI Werke of Eisenach who were making three lines of car, a 1.6-litre four, a 2.3-litre six, and an Austin Seven under licence. They did not bother with the larger models, but they continued the Austin Seven, or Dixi 3/15PS. They were called DA1 by the factory, standing for Dixi Austin or Deutsche Ausfuhring (German Workmanship). This was to distinguish them from the first 100 cars which were imported complete from England. From 1 January 1929 they were badged as BMWs, though some surviving cars carry both BMW and Dixi badges. The Dixi name was retained until July 1929, when a new model called the DA2 3/16PS appeared. This had a different radiator from the Austin design, coupled four-wheel brakes, and a wider body without running boards. Six body styles were offered, the closed saloons being all steel by Ambi Budd of Berlin. In 1929 came the BMW Wartburg (DA3) sports model with pointed-tail 2-seater body, and in 1931 the DA4 saloon in which four passengers could be accommodated for the first time. Up to the Spring of 1932, 25,356 Dixi and BMW 3/15 cars had been made.

Goodbye to the Austin Seven

On 1 March 1932 BMW cancelled their agreement with Austin, although it still had some time to run, as they wanted to move up-market with a design of their own. This appeared at the end of March as the 3/20PS Typ AM (Auto Munchen). It was little larger in engine capacity (782cc) or overall length, but it had pushrod overhead valves and a completely new central backbone frame, with rear suspension by transverse leaf springs and swing axles. There were also swing axles at the front, an unsatisfactory feature carried over from the DA4. Saloon, cabriolet, and roadster bodies were made in the Daimler-Benz body factory at Sindelfingen. There were close links between BMW and Daimler-Benz at this time; several directors sat on the boards of both firms, and many dealers sold both makes. This was quite convenient when BMW made smaller cars which complemented the Mercedes-Benz range, less so when they

Fritz Fiedler (in the hat) with Albert Kalkert.
NATIONAL MOTOR MUSEUM

FIEDLER, FRITZ (1899–1972)

Born in Austria on 9 January 1899, Fritz Fiedler attended local schools and later studied engineering in Vienna and Munich. He worked for AGA in Berlin from 1920 to 1923, then joined Stoewer, helping Bernhard Stoewer with the design of the F-6 6/30PS model. He also designed the engines for the 8-cylinder 1997cc S-8 and 2462cc S-10 Superior.

He was chief engineer of Horch from 1930 to 1932, leaving on the formation of Auto Union to join BMW as chief engineer for automobiles. His first design replaced the last of the Austin-licenced models. He personally did all the chassis design up to 1941.

After World War II, H.J. Aldington invited him to join AFN at Isleworth, to design a new-generation Frazer Nash sports car. He worked with both AFN and the Bristol Aeroplane Co., until 1950, when he returned to Germany and signed up with Adam Opel AG. But a year later, he returned to BMW as technical director and member of the board.

He was responsible for the 503 and 507, and the small 600 and 700 models. He personally directed the engineering of the 1963 1500 and its derivatives, the 1800, 2002, 2000ti, and so on.

After his official retirement on 1 January 1964, he remained a consultant to BMW until 1968. He died on 8 July 1972.

JPN

1936 BMW 319/1 sports car.
NATIONAL MOTOR MUSEUM

grew up to rival the cars from Stuttgart. From 1933 BMW came to rely mainly on Ambi Budd for saloon bodies and Autenrieth and Reutter for cabriolets. The next stage in BMW development was the Typ 303, which went into production in the Spring of 1933. This had a small 6-cylinder engine with the same cylinder dimensions as the 3/20, giving a capacity of 1173cc. The frame was tubular (not a backbone), in which the side and cross members were welded into a very rigid ladder construction at a time when most manufacturers were still using rivetted or bolted chassis construction. The swing axles were replaced by rigid ones, with transverse-leaf independent front suspension. The bonnet was fronted by the pointed grille called the 'nierenformig' (kidney shape) which, in much modified form, is still an identifying feature of BMW cars today. Among the 303's modern features were rack-and-pinion steering and hydraulic brakes. Top speed was just over 62mph (100km/h). There was also a companion Typ 309 which used the 3/20 4-cylinder engine, slightly enlarged to 845cc, in similar bodies to the 303, from which it could be distinguished by the absence of bumpers. 2300 303s were made (1933–34) and 6000 309s (1934–36).

In 1934 the 303 grew up into the 1490cc Typ 315 which developed 34bhp in standard form, and 40bhp in triple-carburettor sports form. This was the first BMW to show the influence of Fritz Fiedler who had previously been with STOEWER and HORCH. He was to play a very important part in BMW design up to his retirement in 1964. The sports version of the 315 was known as the 315/1. It had an attractive 2-seater body with spatted rear wheels, and was capable of 75mph (120km/h). The performance of these cars in the 1934 Alpine Trial so impressed H.J. Aldington of Frazer Nash that he decided to import them to Britain, offering them and later BMW models in slightly Anglicised form under the name Frazer Nash BMW.

With a 1911cc engine (45bhp standard, 55bhp sports), the 315 became the 319. Body styles were generally similar to those of the 303 and 315. The 303 was dropped in 1934 after a production run of 2300, and the 315 in 1937 after 9765 had been made.

The 1936 Berlin Show saw an important new BMW, the 326 which was the company's first 4-door saloon. With a 1971cc 50bhp engine it had a good performance with a top speed of 72mph (116km/h). Styling was more streamlined than on previous BMWs, with a thinner radiator grille which characterised all models up to 1940. The chassis was entirely new, being a box section frame with torsion bar suspension at the rear. More than two thirds of the 15,936 cars made

1939 BMW 327/80 cabriolet.
NATIONAL MOTOR MUSEUM

had 4-door saloon bodies by Ambi Budd, but there were about 5000 2- and 4-door cabriolets by Autenrieth, and 641 chassis were supplied for special coachwork. The 326 remained in production well into World War II, and new cars were still being delivered up to May 1941, though only for military or essential civilian use.

There were several derivations of the 326. The 320 (1936–38) was a cheaper 2-door saloon on a shorter wheelbase, which used the 326 frame in conjunction with semi-elliptic rear suspension. The 321 (1939–41), the same car as the 320 with rear-hinged doors and the 326's suspension. The 327 (1937–41), an attractive 2-seater coupé and convertible. With the 80bhp engine of the 328, it was known as the 327/28 in Germany, or 327/80 in England. The 329 (1936–37) was the old 1911cc 319 with the later style of grille and body shape. The 335 (1939–41) was a scaled up 326 with 3485cc 6-cylinder engine; body styles were 4-door saloon and cabriolet.

The most sporting prewar BMW was the 328, which had the same cylinder block as the 326 with a completely new head incorporating hemispherical combustion chambers and cross pushrods. Only one camshaft was used, operating the inlet valves in the usual way, while horizontal pushrods ran across the cylinder head to operate the exhaust valves. This gave the advantages of twin-

1957 BMW 600 saloon.
NATIONAL MOTOR MUSEUM

1958 BMW 507 sports car.
NATIONAL MOTOR MUSEUM

ohcs at less complexity and expense. Power was raised from 50 to 80bhp. The twin-tube frame was similar to that of the 319/1, and the body was a neat 2-seater with a 326-style grille flanked by headlamps which were partially-faired into the front wings. The rear wheels were enclosed in spats, but these were usually left off for competitions and even for everyday driving. Top speed of a standard 328 in touring trim was 96mph (155km/h), but Sammy Davis covered 102.16 miles (164.51km) in the hour at Brooklands in a prototype with lightweight body and aero windscreen. Modified cars with high-compression engines and improved porting and valves could exceed 118mph (190km/h), a remarkable speed for a 2-litre car in the 1930s. The 328 was not particularly expensive, selling for RM7400, only RM100 more than a 326 cabriolet. A total of 462 production 328s were made between 1937 and 1939, as well as some competition cars for the 1940 Mille Miglia. These had more streamlined bodies than the standard 328, and were prototypes for the 328's successor which was never built, though the early postwar Frazer Nash was of somewhat similar appearance. The 328's cross-head engine was used in several postwar sports cars including VERITAS, AC Ace, BRISTOL, and FRAZER NASH.

The Postwar Scene

BMW faced severe problems after the war, with their Munich factory in ruins and their Eisenach factory in the Eastern zone of Germany. Cars soon began to emerge from Eisenach, the 321 saloon being made from 1945 to 1950, and the 327 cabriolet and coupé from 1948 to 1956. From January 1952 the 327 was sold under the name EMW (Eisenacher Motoren Werke) as the West German company objected to the confusion of two cars from different political zones carrying the same name. Motorcycle production was resumed at Munich in 1948, but no cars appeared for another four years. A small 2-seater coupé powered by a 600cc flat-twin motorcycle engine was considered, but BMW director Hanns Grewenig thought that this would lower the company image for upmarket cars, and the 331 was only made as a single prototype. (It still exists, in a museum in Malmo, Sweden.)

BMW did not have the funds to develop a brand-new postwar car, and the 501 which was launched at the 1951 Frankfurt Show was something of a compromise. It used the 326 engine and transmission in a new, part-tubular chassis with a rather bulbous 6-light saloon body. At 1340kg it was heavier than the 326, and with only 65bhp performance was not very exciting. It was not until the arrival of the 100bhp 2580cc V8 in the 502 in 1954 that performance became really satisfactory for a car of that class and price. As BMW lacked body-building facilities at first, the early 501 saloon bodies were made by Baur of Stuttgart who also built cabriolets from the 1970s. No production 501s reached the public until November 1952, and they were made until 1958, with a production run of 8936. From 1955 a 2077cc engine was used.

The V8-engined 502 was a better car, with servo brakes on the deluxe models and discs at the front on some of the later cars, to curb the 109mph (175km/h) top speed. The 502 was made up to 1963, latterly with a 140bhp 3168cc engine. It outsold its rival, the Mercedes-Benz 300, with delivery of 13,044 cars. All the factory-bodied cars were saloons, but some 2- and 4-door cabriolets were made by Baur and Autenrieth on 501 and 502 chassis.

Three other production cars used the V8 engine, as well as the 505 long-wheelbase limousine, of which only two were built. The production cars were the 503 convertible and coupé, the 507 2-seater sports car, and the 3200CS coupé. The 503 was a 2+2 seater with styling by Count Albrecht Goertz, of which 413 were made between May 1956 and March 1959. It was seen by the makers as a rival to the Mercedes-Benz 300S, which was somewhat more expensive, but the 503 never had the charisma of the Stuttgart car. Better known than the 503 was the 507, also Goertz-styled, which had a shorter wheelbase and a 150bhp high compression version of the 3168cc V8 engine giving the 2-seater a top speed of 137mph (220km/h). Unlike the other V8s it was available with an optional 5-speed gearbox. It attracted a lot of attention at the 1955 Frankfurt Show, but did not sell very well, probably because of the counter-attraction of the glamorous and faster Mercedes-Benz 300SL, whose sales were helped by its racing successes. A total of 252 507s were sold, customers including the Kings of Greece and Morocco, and Prince Rainier of Monaco.

The 3200CS was a Bertone-styled replacement for the 503, with engine boosted to 160bhp. 538 were made between February 1962 and September 1965.

The Isetta years

Despite Hanns Grewenig's misgivings about making small cars, in 1955 BMW decided to supplement the slow sales of the 501 and 502 with a really cheap car. The Italian ISO company had recently introduced the Isetta 'bubble car' powered by a 236cc 2-cylinder 2-stroke engine, and BMW acquired the licence to make the cars at Munich. They made minor changes to the styling and replaced the Italian engine with their own 245cc single-cylinder 4-stroke, as used in their R27 motorcycle. From February 1956 a 298cc engine was available, but more than half the Isettas sold had the smaller engine as there were driving licence concessions for sub-250cc cars. The BMW-Isetta was sold in Britain, and later made there, with a single rear wheel, so that it could be driven with a motor cycle licence and carry a lower road tax. Total production of Isettas by BMW between 1955 and 1962 was 161,360.

In August 1957 BMW brought out a 4-seater development of the Isetta. The 600 had two doors, the swing-up front one as on the Isetta, and a door on the near side for passengers. The engine was a 582cc flat twin from the R67 motorcycle giving 20bhp and a top speed of 62mph (100km/h). About 35,000 600s were made between 1957 and 1959.

The final development of the rear-engined 2-cylinder theme was the 700, made as a convertible, coupé, and saloon from 1960 to 1965. This was much more car-like than the 600, with styling by Michelotti. The 697cc flat-twin engine gave 30bhp, but twin carburettor sports models (700CS) developed 40bhp and could exceed 84mph (135km/h). The 700 was the first postwar BMW to be raced, gaining 22 international class wins between 1960 and 1965. Grand Prix driver Jackie Ickx began his racing career with a 700 in 1963. 188,121 700s were made.

A New Era

In the autumn of 1959 BMW faced financial disaster. The big saloons had never sold in the numbers expected, and although Isetta production was very high, the makers earned very little profit on each one. To make matters worse, motorcycle sales dropped disastrously, from 29,699 in 1954 to only 5400 in 1957. In 1959 the chairman of the BMW board, Dr Hans Feith, who was also a director of the Deutsche Bank, proposed a merger with Daimler-Benz, but this was strongly opposed by both shareholders and dealers. Helped by a DM30 million loan from truck makers MAN, BMW managed to beat off the Daimler take-over,

1965 BMW 1800 saloon(*left*) and 2000CS coupé (*right*).
NATIONAL MOTOR MUSEUM

and later the Quandt Group, headed by the brothers Herbert and Harold Quandt, became major shareholders.

The 700 was put into production under the new regime, but the pressing need was for an up-to-date full-size car. Working under Alex von Falkenhausen, a small team designed a remarkable 4-cylinder 1499cc engine with chain-driven ohc, an unusual feature for a mass-production car in 1961. The same basic engine block was used for the 1600, 1800, and 2000, and even the 500bhp turbocharged 2-litre engines used in Group 5 saloon car racing. Other features of the 1500 were unitary construction 4-door saloon bodies, independent suspension all round, and disc brakes on the front wheels. It was a very advanced package for a popularly-priced saloon. When it was shown at the 1961 Frankfurt Show the recommended price was DM8500, but this had risen to DM9485 by the time cars began to reach customers in the summer of 1962. This was still cheaper than the Mercedes-Benz 190, and buyers preferred the BMW's more sporting handling.

The 1500 was the start of a large family of 4-cylinder BMW saloons. It was joined in 1964 by the 1573cc 1600 and 1773cc 1800 and in 1966 by the 1990cc 2000. Both these were available in twin-carburettor high-performance form, carrying the suffix TI (Touring Internationale). The most powerful was the 1800 TI/SA (Sonderausfuhrung). This was called the Tisa by the racing fraternity, and was only sold to holders of competition licences. The engine developed a basic 130bhp, much more with tuning, and a 5-speed gearbox was standard. Only 200 were made, from the end of 1964 to autumn 1965. The 2000 was also made as a coupé (2000C/CS) with Karmann body, being the ancestor of a long line of BMW coupés.

In 1966 came the 1600-2, later simply 1602, which used the 1573cc engine in a 2-door saloon on a shorter wheelbase than the 1500/1800/2000 family of 4-door saloons. The engine developed 85bhp, later raised to 105bhp in the 1600TI. It gave rise to another line, of which the best known was the 2002; this had the 2000 engine in the 1602 body, and was also made as a cabriolet by Baur and a 3-door hatchback called the Touring. These styles were also available with the 1600 engine. The 2002 was made from 1968 to 1976, and within these years there were several high-performance versions. The 2000ti had twin dual-choke Weber carburettors and 120bhp, while the 2002tii had Kugelfischer fuel injection and gave 130bhp. 5-speed gearboxes were available, and top speed was around 118mph (190km/h). Fastest and rarest of the family was the Turbo, made from 1973 to 1974 only. It was Europe's first turbocharged road car, but was not without faults as there was an unavoidable lag before the turbocharger came into action, and when it did it gave a pronounced kick. Also its reliability was not up to usual BMW standards, and fuel consumption was very high. But it was certainly fast, with a top speed of 130mph (210km/h). Sales were hit by the fuel crisis, which made such aggressive cars seem anti-social. One feature

of the car was the word Turbo written in reverse on the front bumper, which was thought to be threatening to other motorists who read it in their rear-view mirror. Only 1672 Turbos were made, compared with 38,703 of the 2002tii, and 348,988 of the 2002. These figures show how the new generation of 4-cylinder cars had helped BMW to become a major producer. From less than 10,000 per year at the beginning of the 1960s, sales reached over 74,000 in 1966 and 221,298 in 1975. BMW production was exceeded only by Volkswagen, Opel, and Ford, and yet the marque retained a cachet which put it well ahead of these mass producers.

In 1968 BMW brought out the first six of the new era. This was the 2500/2800, whose engines were essentially the fours with two extra cylinders; like the smaller engines these were slanted at 30 degrees to ensure a low bonnet line. The bodies were new 4-door saloons and the specification included disc brakes all round, power steering, and optional automatic gearboxes. In addition to the saloons there was the 2800CS 4-seater coupé, ancestor of the 6 Series coupés made up to 1989. In 1971 the 6-cylinder engines were enlarged to 1985 and 3295cc, and mounted in the 3.0S and 3.3L saloons and 3.0CS and CSi coupés. These were made until 1975 and took BMW into competition with the large Mercedes-Benz saloons and coupés. However, they were expensive for what they offered, a 3.3L saloon costing as much as a V8-engined Mercedes-Benz 450SE. The coupés were made in competition form as the famous 'Batmobiles', with large wings above the boot lid to keep the 350bhp cars on the ground. They had many successes in European Touring Car Championship events between 1973 and 1976.

An interim model was the 4-cylinder 5 Series, made from 1972 to 1981. This used the 1800 and 2000 engines in new 4-door saloon bodies made in the GLAS factory at Dingolfing, which BMW bought in 1966. They had also briefly made two Glas models with BMW badging, the 4-cylinder 1600GT and V8 2300. In the mid-70s the BMW range began to emerge in the form it still has today, the 3 Series of 2-door saloons with 1600, 1800, and 2000 engines, the 5 Series with 6-cylinder 2500, 2800, and 3000 engines, the 6 Series coupés with a variety of 6-cylinder engines from 2800 to 3400, and the 7 Series of large saloons with power steering as standard and the same engines as the 6 Series (728, 730, 733i). In addition there was the 520 six which used an all-new 1990cc engine. In 1977 this engine went into the 3 Series in two sizes, the 1990cc in the 320-6 and the fuel-injected 2315cc in the 323i. The 3 Series was restyled in 1983 when a 4-door saloon became available for the first time, and was also offered as a cabriolet by Baur. This had a roll-bar, but in 1985 BMW brought out their own fully-convertible cabriolet, the 325i. Another model in the 325i range was a 4x4 saloon, (325iX introduced in 1985) and the 3 Series also included a 2443cc 6-cylinder diesel engine. An estate car (Touring) was launched in 1988.

1980 BMW M.1 coupé.
NATIONAL MOTOR MUSEUM

1990 BMW Z.1 sports car.
BMW

1992 BMW 320i convertible.
BMW

The 5 Series was restyled in 1981 and was made in nine different versions with four engine sizes from 1990 to 3430cc. The 6 Series coupés were little changed in the 1980s, being offered in three engine sizes, 2788cc in the 628CSi, 3430cc in the 635Csi, and 3453cc in the M635CSi. The latter was a 24-valve twin-ohc unit developing 255bhp and with a top speed of 158mph (255km/h). In 1989 they gave way to the restyled 8 Series, the 850i with 3430cc 24-valve six or the new 4988cc V12 also offered in the 7 Series saloons. This gave 300bhp and had a separate Motronic engine management system for each bank of cylinders, so that even with one bank out of action the car could be driven at 124mph (200km/h).

The 7 Series was completely restyled and updated in the autumn of 1986, with 2986 or 3430cc sixes or, from 1987, the V12. This put BMW in the luxury car class, up against Mercedes-Benz, whose own V12 did not arrive until 1991. By 1999 BMW had made more than 100,000 V12 engines, of which 75,000 went into the 7 series saloons and 23,000 into the 8 Series coupés. The V12 used in modified form in the McLaren F1 supercar and in the Rolls-Royce Silver Seraph. The 1999 V12 engine developed 326bhp from 5379cc. In the 1990s BMW continued its four main series, 3, 5, 7, and 8, with major restyling of the 3 Series in November 1990 and 'evolutionary' restyling in February 1998. The 1990 series (factory code E36) was made as a 4-door saloon, cabriolet, and estate with four engines available, two fours and two sixes, from the 1596cc 316i to the 2494cc 325i. Initially the cabriolet and estate retained the old styling, but were later brought into line with the saloon, while a coupé arrived in 1992. The more modestly restyled E46 series of 1998 was reminiscent of the current 5 Series, and offered five engines from a 118bhp 1895cc four in the 318 to a 2793cc 193bhp six in the 328, including a 1951cc diesel four in the 320D. The 5 and 7 series also evolved during the 1990s.

A new model quite separate from the traditional series was the Z1, a 2-seater sports car which was originally a concept car to test new ideas, but went into production from June 1989 to June 1991. It had a tub chassis of galvanised steel to which were attached thermoplastic body panels. The doors slid vertically into the sills, making for easier access when parked in a tight space. The Z1 was powered by a 325i engine giving a top speed of 143mph (230km/h). Although sold in the UK, it was never made with right-hand drive. Only 8093 were built. A more widespread sports car was the Z3 made in a new plant at Spartanburg, South Carolina, from 1996. Like the Z1 it was a 2-seater, but with conventional doors and construction. At first only 4-cylinder engines of 1793 or 1895cc were available, which hardly gave performance to measure up to its looks, but later it received 2793 and 3201cc sixes, the latter being part of the M Series and giving 321bhp an a top speed of 155mph (250km/h). A larger-engined car in the Z Series was the Z8 roadster powered by the M5's 400bhp 5-litre V8, with styling cues from the 507 of the 1950s.

The M Series

In 1972 a separate company called BMW Motor Sport GmbH was formed to handle the company's sporting activities. They produced a concept car called the Turbo, a gull-wing coupé powered by a mid-mounted 2002 Turbo engine. It was purely a design study with no plans for production, but in 1977 the idea was revived when BMW was looking for a high-performance car for road and track to replace the CSL. It was originally coded the E26, but became known as the M1 as it was the first complete car to emerge from the Motor Sport division. Although it bore a striking resemblance to the Turbo, it had conventional rather than gull-wing doors, and the engine was mounted longitudinally rather than transversely. The 3453cc six gave 277bhp, and was mated with a 5-speed ZF transaxle. This was the 'basic' road car, but for Group Four racing a 470bhp engine was planned.

To be eligible for Group Four a minimum of 400 road cars had to be built, and BMW looked to Lamborghini to do this, as they had done a lot of work on the prototype. However, the Italian firm could not undertake the contract, so the fibreglass bodies and steel frames were built by Ital Design in Turin and then taken to Baur in Stuttgart who mounted the engines and fitted the bodies. A total of 456 M1s were made, and they paved the way for a series of M models which were derived from regular production Series. These included the M635CSi coupé, three generations of M3, three of the M5, and the most powerful model of the Z3 roadster. The 1998 M3 saloon had a 321bhp six as used in the Z3M, giving the 4-door saloon a top speed of 155mph (250km/h). The M3 engine was also available in the coupé and cabriolet models. A restyled M3 for 2000 used a 340bhp 3.4-litre engine. More dramatic still was the 1999 M5, whose 32-valve 4941cc V8 gave 400bhp at 6500rpm, with a top speed of 155mph (250km/h). In the summer of 1998 it was estimated that 100,000 M models had been made. From 1994 the M3 was made alongside other 3 Series in the main BMW factory, but the M5 was still assembled by BMW Motor Sport.

In 1999 BMW entered a new market with the X5, a high ground clearance 4x4 to challenge the Range Rover. Made in the North Carolina factory, it was available with five engine options, two sixes, two V8s and a turbo diesel. There were also plans for a smaller 4x4 using 3 Series running gear.

In the corporate field, BMW acquired a significant involvement in the British motor industry when they purchased ROVER in 1994. Four years later they began supplying V8 and V12 engines to ROLLS-ROYCE, but their anticipated take-over of the British firm was frustrated by VOLKSWAGEN. However, it was agreed that rights to the Rolls-Royce name would pass to BMW in January 2003. Rover was sold to the Phoenix consortium in spring 2000.

NG

Further Reading
BMW from 1928 – The Complete Story, Werner Oswald and Jeremy Walton, Haynes, 1982.
BMW Automobile 1952 bis heute, Halwart Schrader, Schrader Verlag, 1993.
BMW since 1945, Richard Busenkell, Patrick Stephens, 1981.
Unbeatable BMW, Jeremy Walton, Osprey, 1979 (the sporting side).
BMW M-Series, Alan Henry, Crowood Auto Classics, 1994.
'BMW beginnings: Dixi DA-1', Duanna Carling,
Automobile Quarterly, Vol. 29, No. 4.
Automobile Quarterly, Vol. 36, No. 4 (Edition devoted to BMW).
'328: BMW's first legend', Gavin Farmer,
Automobile Quarterly, Vol. 37, No. 4.

B.M.W. (ii) **(US)** c.1948–c. 1970
Boulevard Machine Works, Los Angeles, California.
This company produced electric minicars and golfmobiles for a number of years, and in 1966 introduced a larger electric roadster with two motors and eight 3-cell batteries giving a claimed maximum speed of 70mph.

NG

B.M.W. (iii) **(ZA)** 1968 to date
1968–1974 Euro Republic Automobile Distributors Pty Ltd, Pretoria.
1975 to date BMW (South Africa) Pty Ltd, Rosslyn.
The first South African-built BMWs were individual to that country, combining the chassis/body of the GLAS 1700 with BMW's 1800 and 2000 4-cylinder engines. These were made up to 1975, after which regular BMW's very similar to those made at Munich were built. In 1998 only the 3 Series was assembled locally.

NG

B.N. (I) 1924–1925
Bianchi e Negro, Turin.
Looking like a scaled down Lancia Lambda, the B.N. (white and black) was a light car powered by a 960cc 4-cylinder ohv engine made in touring and sports versions. The latter was capable of 65mph (105km/h).

NG

1999 BMW Z3 roadster.
BMW

1999 BMW 7 Series saloon.
BMW

B.N.C. (F) 1923–1931
Bollack, Netter et Cie, Levallois-Perret, Seine.
After AMILCAR and SALMSON the B.N.C. was the best-known small French sports car of the 1920s. The original design was first marketed as the JACQUES MULLER from 1920 to 1922, when Muller sold out to the Bollack brothers and Netter. Under his own name Muller made 2- and 4-cylinder cars, but it was only the four that interested the new owners. It used an 892cc 4-cylinder side-valve engine made by S.C.A.P., to which B.N.C. added ohv Ruby engines of 750 or 970cc. Touring, sports and delivery van models were made, and the cars sold well in export markets as well as at home. Most exports went to Belgium and Spain, but some were sold in England. Closed bodies became available in 1925. These included a delightful little 2-seater coupé called the Supercab.

The 970cc Ruby engine powered B.N.C.'s first sports models, but in 1925 more serious sports cars appeared, powered by 1100cc S.C.A.P., 1088cc Ruby DS or 1097cc Ruby K engines. The latter developed 60bhp and gave the car a top speed of 100mph (160km/h). At the end of 1925 a vertically mounted Cozette supercharger could be had, making the B.N.C. the first catalogued supercharged French car. The supercharged short chassis was named the Montlhery, the same without supercharger was the Monza, and the long chassis was the Miramas, all named after racing venues where B.N.C. had done well.

In 1927 the B.N.C. received a sloping radiator and a frame underslung at the rear, which gave it a much lower appearance. Touring models, which included 4-door saloons, generally had the vertical radiator, though the firm was small enough to meet special orders, which makes generalisations dangerous. For example, though most superchargers were Cozettes, the Zoller was seen on some B.N.C.s as well. Three vertical radiator 4-seater sports tourers were made with 1496cc Meadows 4ED engines, one of which ran at Le Mans in 1929.

Lucien Bollack left the company in 1928 to set up a business importing Lycoming engines. This tempted him to build a car under his own name (see LUCIEN BOLLACK). His place at the head of the firm was taken by Charles de Ricou, a colourful character who had been an entrepreneur in Indo-China and had tried to run an aerial postal service. He continued the smaller B.N.C.s, but also went empire building. He bought up the stock of LOMBARD parts and assembled a few cars which he sold under the B.N.C. name, using a B.N.C. radiator. He also bought the rights to the A.E.R.-Mercier pneumatic suspension,

B.N.C.

1924 B.N.C. sports car.
NATIONAL MOTOR MUSEUM

1929 B.N.C. Monza sports car
NATIONAL MOTOR MUSEUM

and exhibited a handsome coupé called the A.E.R on the B.N.C. stand at the 1930 Paris Salon. It used a 6-cylinder Citroën engine, but de Ricou planned that production models should use engines from ROLLAND-PILAIN, another company he had bought. He also tried to launch a range of large American-style cars powered by 4- or 4.9-litre Lycoming engines and using frames bought from DELAUNAY-BELLEVILLE and A.E.R suspension. No more than six of these Aigles were made. All this was too much for a relatively small firm at the time of the Depression, and the whole empire collapsed in 1931, bringing down Rolland-Pilain as well. However, racing driver and garage owner André Sirejols bought up the stock of chassis and S.C.A.P. and Ruby engines, and assembled a few of the small sports cars up to 1939.

NG

Further Reading
'BNC ou l'Épopée Cyclecariste Jacques Potherat',
l'Album du Fanatique, June 1969–February 1970.

BOBBI-KAR (US) 1945–1947
Bobbi Motor Car Corp., San Diego, California.
This economy car looked a lot like a Crosley and was built in coupé, sedan, and station wagon form. They had fibreglass bodies and 1060cc 4-cylinder engines. The coupé engine was mounted in the rear, but the others had front-mounted engines. In 1947 Bobbi-Kar relocated to Birmingham, Alabama, reorganised and changed the company name to KELLER.

HP

BOBBY ALBA *see* ALBA (ii)

BOCAR (US) 1958–1962
Bocar Manufacturing Co., Denver, Colorado.
BOb CARnes built his first Chevrolet-powered sportscar to compete in hill-climbs and road racing. The XP-4 was their first production model and it had a light tubular space frame with VW/Porsche front suspension, Chevrolet drum brakes and a live axle at the back. With a stunning fibreglass body, a 4600cc

Chevrolet V8 and a short 90in (2284mm) wheelbase, it was a hot performer. The similar XP-5 that followed had better Buick 'Alfin' drum brakes. Bocars were sold in body only, kit and fully assembled form for street and racing use. The XP-6 was an experimental model with a 104in (2640mm) wheelbase and a 450hp Chevrolet with a crank-driven Potvin supercharger on the front breathing through a modified Rochester fuel injection system. It had Kurtis-style live axles at both ends. The XP-7 was a production model that was similar to the XP-6, but with VW front suspension and an optional supercharger. The last Bocar was the Stiletto, which had a streamlined body that looked like a cross between a Lotus 11 and a Bonneville streamliner. It had the XP-6 chassis with live axles and a supercharged Chevrolet engine. Only a few Stilettos were made before a fire destroyed the factory in 1962.

HP

BODOR (CDN) 1986–1987
Abraham Bodor, Brantford.
Presented at the Toronto Motor Show, Volvo specialist Abraham Bodor's sports car resembled a lowered Morgan. It was unusual in having steel bodywork rather than glassfibre, and featured a low-set roll-over bar. The mechanical side derived from Volvo.

CR

BOHANNA STABLES *see* NYMPH

BOISSAYE (F) 1904
Automobiles Boissaye, Paris.
Although it lasted less than one year, the Boissaye company advertised a wide range of cars from 12 to 45hp, all using 4-cylinder Mutel engines.

NG

BOISSELOT (US) 1901
Boisselot Automobile & Special Gasoline Motor Co., Jersey City, New Jersey.
Boisselot offered a 0.25hp single-cylinder engine which could be used to motorise a bicycle, and also two models of car, the Pearl 2-seater with a 3hp engine, and the 6hp La Boisselot for three or four passengers. Prices were $600 and $1200 respectively. There were plans to build a car for the 1901 Buffalo Endurance Run, to be powered by two of their motors, and they also offered motors in various sizes for other car manufacturers.

NG

BOITEL (F) 1946–1949
Automobiles Boitel, Paris.
The first Boitel minicar had a 400cc 2-cylinder 2-stroke engine mounted behind the driver but ahead of the rear axle, in the position made fashionable on racing and sports cars from the late 1950s. For the 1948 Paris Salon the body was restyled, wire wheels gave way to discs, and the engine was a 589cc DKW, also a 2-cylinder 2-stroke. The extra power boosted speed from 47 to 56mph (75 to 90km/h), but did not help sales, which were minimal.

NG

BOLIDE (i) (F) 1899–1907
1899–1905 Léon Lefebvre et Cie, Paris.
1905–1907 Sté l'Auto Reparation, Paris .
The Bolide was designed by Léon Lefebvre who had started in the motor business as early as 1896 with the LEO (i). This had a horizontal-twin Pygmée engine, and Lefebvre followed this layout with the first cars made under his own name. In 1900 he listed three models, an 8hp twin of 2090cc, a 16hp twin of 5298cc, and a 40hp four of 11,693cc, the latter intended mainly for racing. Before building these cars in France he sold a licence to the Belgian SNOECK company, who made them up to 1902. Drive was originally by a wide belt, replaced by chain in 1901. In 1902 Lefebvre changed direction altogether, making a range of conventional cars of which the smallest used an 8hpDe Dion-Bouton engine, with Aster and Tony Huber in the larger 2- and 4-cylinder cars. In 1905 he left the company to make cars under the name PRIMA. Bolides were continued by a new company, the Société l'Auto Reparation, in three models, a 12hp monobloc four, a 22hp four and a 35hp six, all shaft driven.

NG

BOLIDE (ii) **(US)** 1969–1970

Bolide Motor Car Corp., Huntington, New York.

This project was a joint development of Jack Griffith (who had masterminded the Griffith/TVR/Ford combination) and Borg-Warner. The B-W Marbon Division had been developing a moulded plastic car body/chassis in the 1960s that became the AMT Piranha. The Bolide Can Am 1 appears to have been a development of that project. The version shown at the New York Auto Show in 1969 bore a strong family resemblance and had the same Corvair engine, although the Can Am 1 was to have been fitted later with a 7000cc Ford V8 with a new rear drive system developed by Borg-Warner. It does not appear to have made it into production. Bolide also proposed a sports-utility vehicle with 4-wheel drive and a Jeep V6 engine.

HP

BOLLÉE *see* AMÉDÉE BOLLÉE and LÉON BOLLÉE

BOLSOVER (GB) 1907–1909

Bolsover Bros Ltd, Eaglescliffe, Co. Durham.

The Bolsover steam car was said to be the result of eleven years' experience in adapting steam to the propulsion of automobiles. It was a 2-seater with 3-cylinder poppet valve engine under the bonnet and a semi-flash boiler under the seat. A 4-cylinder engine was mentioned in advertising. It had shaft drive direct from the crankshaft to the rear axle. Paraffin fuel was used and the frame was of armoured ash wood.

NG

BOLTE (US) 1901

T.H. Bolte, Kearney, Nebraska.

Thomas H. Bolte was a bicycle dealer who made a small runabout powered by an 8hp single-cylinder engine, with belt drive to the countershaft and final drive by single-chain. Suspension was by full-elliptic springs all round. He planned to form a company, and quoted a price of US$600, but production never started.

NG

BOLWELL (AUS) 1964–1982

Bolwell Cars Pty Ltd, Mordialloc, Victoria.

Like some other specialist producers, Bolwell began with sports specials but commercial activity in kit cars commenced in 1964 with the Mk IV, suitable for 4-cylinder engines. The Mk V coupé was intended for 6-cylinder Holden components and only one Mk VI mid-engined competition car was made. The 1967 Mk VII became popular due to its attractive lines. Its backbone chassis and integral fibreglass body accepted Holden mechanicals and 450 were sold until 1972 when tighter design rules militated against kit cars.

In 1969 the world-class Nagari (Mk VIII) arrived, only as a complete car, weighing 916kg and powered by a 4953cc Ford V8 giving 221bhp. Built on a 90in (2286mm) wheelbase, it was a fibreglass coupé built on a backbone chassis 11in (267mm) deep. Major components were Ford with coil spring and damper units all round and Austin 1800 rack and pinion steering. Ventilating 14in alloy wheels of Bolwell design were fitted with 185 radial tyres. In 1972 a roadster was shown, the same year when an lhd car was built for appraisal in the United States. Sales were encouraging during 1973 but slumped badly in 1974. The decision to withdraw from car production was taken by the year's end. It was a great disappointment, as export sales to South Africa had also been in prospect but thwarted, as in the United States, by more stringent design rules. Campbell and Graeme Bolwell were fibreglass specialists and sportscar enthusiasts; Graeme had worked at Lotus when the Europa was being developed. 140 examples (including 13 roadsters) of the Nagari (an Aboriginal word for 'flowing') were produced up to 1975 when work was concentrated on industrial fibreglass.

The strong attraction to cars remained, however, resulting in the release of the clubman-type Ikara ('throwing stick') in 1979. Built on a space frame with fibreglass bodywork, it was fitted with a 1588cc VW Golf power pack behind the seats and the running gear was derived from the Holden-Isuzu Gemini. It had disc brakes all round and weighed only 650kg. However, it received but a luke-warm response, only ten being sold, but a 1985 report stated that the project had been sold to Greece. Such was the deep impression made by the

1969 Bolwell Nagari coupé.
NATIONAL MOTOR MUSEUM

Nagari that two attempts were later made by others to revive production. Bolwell Fibreglass continued with commercial work.

MG

BOMBARDIER (CDN) 1996 to date

Bombardier Inc., Sherbrooke, Quebec.

The Bombardier Neighbourhood Electric Vehicle was aimed at resorts, golfers and short-distance drivers. Six 12V lead–acid batteries powered a 4kW electric motor, and a maximum range of 37 miles (60km) and a top speed of 25mph (40km/h) were quoted. The two-passenger NEV was very short and, while the roof was fixed, doors were an optional extra. After first being released in 1996, production began in 1997 by a huge multinational company whose creator had previously invented the snow 'ski-doo'; it had also made the Volkswagen Iltis 4x4 under licence in the 1980s.

CR

BON-CAR (GB) 1905–1907

Edinburgh & Leith Engineering Co., Leith.

This was a steam car of which details are sparse, and which may never have emerged from the prototype form. It was also known as the Bonne-Car.

NG

BONALLACK (GB) 1951–1952

Bonallack and Sons Ltd, Forest Gate, London E7.

Produced by a commercial body builder, the Bonallack Minnow was a very small 3-wheeler with the single wheel at the rear. The chassis consisted of two light-alloy box sections braced with crossmembers, and the front suspension was independent by coil springs. At the rear, a pivoted alloy subframe carried the coil-sprung single wheel. The Excelsior Talisman 250cc 2-cylinder 2-stroke engine was rear-mounted. The simple open bodywork was made of aluminium sheet and featured a single headlamp. But at £468 including tax it was too expensive and too crude to make any impact.

CR

BOND (i) **(GB)** 1922–1928

F.W. Bond & Co. Ltd, Brighouse, Yorkshire.

There were two distinct phases in the life of this little-known Yorkshire car. At first medium-sized assembled cars were built using a 2306cc 14.3hp 4-cylinder Tylor engine, followed in 1924 by two sizes of Continental, a 2121cc ohv four called the 14/40 and a 3181cc side-valve six, the 23.4hp. Both used other American components including a Brown-Lipe gearbox and Timken axles. These were made in very small numbers until 1927 when Bond replaced them with a low-slung 2-seater sports car not unlike a Frazer Nash in appearance. Only three of these were made, one with a 1496cc 4-cylinder Anzani, and two with Meadows units of the same capacity.

Bond also designed the CHIC for production in Australia by Chic Cars Ltd of Adelaide.

NG

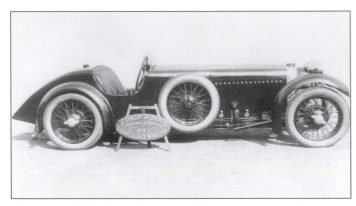

1927 Bond (i) 1½-litre Super Sports by Jarvis.
NATIONAL MOTOR MUSEUM

1954 Bond (ii) Mark C 3-wheeler on return from Monte Carlo.
NATIONAL MOTOR MUSEUM

1958 Bond (ii) Mark E 3-wheeler.
NICK GEORGANO

1966 Bond (ii) Equipe GT coupé.
NATIONAL MOTOR MUSEUM

BOND (ii) (GB) 1948–1974

1948–1964 Sharp's Commercials Ltd, Preston, Lancashire.
1965–1970 Bond Cars Ltd, Preston, Lancashire.
1971–1974 Reliant Motor Co. Ltd, Tamworth, Staffordshire.

Lawrie Bond (1907–1974) had built several 500cc racing cars using stressed-skin construction, when he announced his 3-wheeler using the same construction in May 1948. It was powered by a 122cc single-cylinder Villiers engine mounted over the front wheel which it drove via a 3-speed gearbox (without reverse) and single-chain. The open 2-seater body had no doors, and there was no rear suspension apart from the tyres. When the Bond Minicar went into production in August 1948 the engine capacity had risen to 197cc, still by Villiers, and the body had been restyled. It was gradually refined over the next 17 years, gaining in 1952 an optional electric starter to replace the kick starter under the bonnet, front wheel brakes and bonded rubber rear suspension in 1953, a reverse gear in 1957, and from 1959 a 246cc Villiers engine and 4-speed gearbox. Bodies became wider, with separate front wings on the Mk C in late 1951 and full-width on the Mk E in 1956. The Bond Minicar was the longest-lived and most successful of Britain's minimal motoring cars, and when production ended in 1964, 24,484 had been made. In 1965 came a replacement for the Minicar in the shape of the 875 which had a rear-mounted Hillman Imp engine, and fibreglass monocoque 4-seater saloon body. It was a rival to the RELIANT 3-wheeler, and when Reliant took over Bond in 1970 it was an immediate casualty. Production of the 875 was 3431 cars.

Before the Minicar's demise, Bond had entered the 4-wheeler market with the Equipe. This was a fibreglass 4-seater GT coupé on a Triumph Herald chassis, with the Spitfire's 1147cc twin-carburettor engine. The fibreglass body shell had the Herald's steel doors and scuttle. From 1967 a 1296cc engine was used, and in the same year there was a larger model, the Equipe 2-litre. This was powered by the 1991cc Triumph Vitesse 6-cylinder engine and had a restyled body, still with steel doors and scuttle. A convertible was available from October 1968, as was the later type of Vitesse rear suspension. Like the 875, the Equipe was a victim of the Reliant take-over. 4388 were made, of which 1432 were the 2-litre. Reliant sold the Preston factory and launched a new 3-wheeler which, being a different type of car, was not a rival to their own 3-wheelers. The Bond Bug was a radical-looking coupé, closed, but without doors, and with an almost vertical Kamm-type sawn-off tail. Styled by Tom Karen of Ogle, the fibreglass body was available in only one colour, tangerine, and the Bug was usually photographed with 'mini-skirted dolly birds', to emphasise that it was a fun car aimed at the young, part of the 'swinging London' image. It used Reliant's 700cc alloy engine (750cc from 1973) which gave it a 75mph (120km/h) top speed. 1620 were made up to 1974, and the concept was revived in 4-wheeler form in 1992 by Mike Webster, who sold it under the name WMC BUG.

NG

Further Reading
Lawrie Bond, the Man and the Marque, Nick Wotherspoon, Bookmarque Publishing, 1993.

BONET I DALMAU (E) 1889–1890

Bonet i Dalmau, Barcelona.

The very first Spanish car was a 3-wheeler, with single wheel at the rear, and a Daimler single-cylinder engine of only 1hp. It was too light to drive well, but was the first attempt in the country. Francesc Bonet i Dalmau was the owner of a well-known textile company, and he also designed a 4-wheeler, but due to problems with the differential he abandoned the project.

VCM

BONIQUET *see* J.B.R.

BONITO (GB) 1981–1987

1981–1983 A.C.M. Ltd, Poole, Dorset.
1983–1984 A.E.D. International, Torpoint, Cornwall.
1984–1985 Bonito Performance Centres, Torpoint, Cornwall.
1985–1987 Seraph Cars, Bristol, Avon.

The Bonito began life with America's leading kit car company FIBERFAB before licensed production was taken up in Germany by a company with the same name. This was a Ford GT40-ish coupé on a VW Beetle floorpan. A company called A.C.M. imported it to Britain from 1981, then manufactured it, still with a Ford Taunus P6 windscreen and Opel Rekord rear screen. A.E.D. then developed a convertible version, and the project passed to Seraph Cars in 1985, which made a proper backbone space frame chassis for it, based around Cortina front suspension, a live rear axle and front-mounted Ford 4-cylinder or V6 engines, or a Rover V8.

CR

BONNÉVILLE (F) 1897–c.1900
L. Bonnéville, Toulouse.

Bonnéville was a bicycle maker who built a small number of cars with rear-mounted De Dion-Bouton engines, tiller steering, and tubular frames. He also had cycle factories at Biarritz and Villeneuve-sur-Lot, but it is not thought that cars were made there.

NG

BONNY DAYS see GALOPIN

BONS (E) 1902
José Bons, Barcelona.

Well-known car components firm, including complete engines, José Bons Damians decided to produce a 4-cylinder car with 24hp and shaft drive in 1902. It is not known how many cars were sold.

VCM

BORBÁLA (H) 1986–1990
Tóth Lajos, Budapest.

Lajos Tóth, a fan of specialist cars dreamt about offering Hungarians the chance to own something similar to a Lotus Seven. The only suitable donor was the Lada so he took a 1500 model and used its engine, gearbox, and suspension in a tubular-framed construction. A plastics company saw a marketing opportunity in the car and helped Tóth to complete the first Borbála. By the time it was ready the company was in financial difficulties and that meant the end for the Borbála.

PN

BORBEIN (US) 1904–1909
H.F. Borbein & Co., St Louis, Missouri.

H.F. Borbein built an electric runabout in 1900, but it was not commercialised. In 1901 he joined the BRECHT Automobile Company, which made electric and steam cars, but by 1903 was concentrating on offering components and cars without engines. Borbein changed the company name to his own in October 1903 and continued the kit car policy with a variety of models. For example, the No.26 was a large steel-framed chassis 'furnished ready for power...with or without upholstering'. Borbein continued this business at least until August 1907, when the business was in receivership, though he was advertising as late as 1909.

NG

BORCHARDING (D) 1925
Borcharding GmbH, Berlin.

This 2-seater 3-wheeler was quite a latecomer in the German cyclecar stakes, and had little chance of success.

HON

BORDEREL-CAIL (F) 1905–c.1908
Sté Cail, Denain, Nord.

The Société Cail were pioneer locomotive builders who made one of northern France's first locomotives in 1846. They were associated with the BEGOT ET CAIL car in 1900, and in 1905 built a large 6-wheeled limousine designed by F. Gros. Powered by a 15/18hp 4-cylinder engine, this drove on the centre axle, while both front and rear wheels steered. A similar car with a more powerful engine of 25/30hp was shown at the 1906 Paris Salon, and a conventional 4-wheeled car with 30hp 4-cylinder monobloc engine was launched in 1907.

NG

BORGWARD (i) (D) 1939–1961
1939–1949 Carl F.W. Borgward Automobile-und Motoren-Werke, Bremen.
1949–1961 Carl F.W. Borgward GmbH, Bremen.

1970 Bond (ii) Bug 700ES coupé.
NATIONAL MOTOR MUSEUM

1905 Borderel-Cail 15/18hp limousine.
NATIONAL MOTOR MUSEUM

Although Carl Borgward (1890–1963) had been associated with cars and commercial vehicles since the 1920s (see GOLIATH and HANSA) no car bore his name until 1939, when the Hansa 2000 was renamed Borgward 2000. The slightly larger 2300 which was launched in October 1939 always carried the Borgward name, and was made until 1942.

After World War II Borgward brought out a new car to which he gave the model name Hansa. Its 1498cc 4-cylinder ohv engine was two thirds of the 1939 6-cylinder 2300, but in appearance it was quite new, with a slab-sided 2-door saloon body which was the first of its kind from a German manufacturer. The backbone frame was carried on from the prewar design, but a platform replaced the outriggers of the older model. The all-independent suspension was unchanged. Launched at the 1949 Geneva Show, the Borgward Hansa attracted a lot of attention as it was the first all-new German car. Production was slow to start, only 1148 cars being delivered during 1949, but it went on to sell 22,504 units before it was replaced by the slightly larger-engined 1800. A 4-door saloon joined the range in 1950, and there was also an estate car and a cabriolet. The latter was a 4-seater and was built for Borgward by Hebmüller. Borgward also built their own 2+2 cabriolet on a shorter wheelbase with a more powerful twin-carburettor engine. A 4-speed gearbox with synchromesh on the two upper ratios was standard equipment, but from 1950 Borgward offered the Hansamatic automatic transmission for an extra DM520. The 1800 (1952–54) had a 1758cc engine in the same chassis and body styles, and from 1953 there was also a diesel version. Production of the 1800 was 11,337, of which 3226 were diesels.

In June 1954 Borgward replaced the 1800 with the car by which he is best remembered, the Isabella. This was a unitary construction 2-door saloon powered by a 1493cc ohv engine. The gearbox was the 4-speed all-synchromesh

1939 Borgward 2300 cabriolet.
NATIONAL MOTOR MUSEUM

1952 Borgward Hansa convertible.
NATIONAL MOTOR MUSEUM

unit fitted to the later 1800s, and the old transverse leaf front suspension was replaced by coils and wishbones. Styling was much crisper than on the previous Borgwards, and the Isabella won many friends in Germany and abroad. Top speed was 78mph (120km/h), and in the high-performance TS version, 90mph (144km/h). The TS had a more distinctive exterior trim with dual colour scheme and a flash down the side of the body. Of the 202,862 Isabellas made, about 40 per cent were of the TS model. In addition to the saloons there was an estate car and a 2-seater coupé. A few convertibles by Deutsch were also made.

The Isabella had a successful career in saloon car racing, winning its class in the 1956 Production Car Race at Silverstone, and at Spa and the Gran Premio Argentino in 1957. Bill Blydenstein was the most successful tuner of Isabellas, his own car having a successful record up to 1961 when he won the Spa Touring Car Race outright against opposition from newer Alfa Romeo, Riley and Volvo cars.

In 1952 Borgward added a larger car to his range in order to compete with the Mercedes Benz 220 and Opel Kapitan. The 2400 had an 80bhp 2337cc 6-cylinder engine with hemispherical combustion chambers, while its coil independent front suspension anticipated that of the Isabella. The full-width body seated six, and had a sloping back which may have put off the conservative citizens at which it was aimed. For them a more conventional booted saloon was added in March 1953, priced at DM15,450 compared with DM12,950 for the more streamlined model. The 2400 also anticipated the Isabella in its unitary construction; the lateral reinforcements on the floor also acted as heating ducts. A 3-speed gearbox was standard, but the Hansamatic transmission was also available. Problems with this have been cited as the reason for the poor sales of the 2400, but it is more likely that the market was too small, and already well catered for by BMW, Mercedes-Benz, and Opel. Only 1132 were made, and 356 of the second series with 100bhp 2240cc engine. This was discontinued in 1958 and no large Borgwards were made until 1960 when the 2.3-litre appeared. This had the 2240cc engine in a new 4-light saloon body with optional air suspension. Transmission was by a 4-speed all-synchromesh gearbox or a Hobbs 4-speed automatic. About 2500 were made between July 1960 and August 1961 when Borgward ended all car production. The LLOYD Arabella de Luxe was

NATIONAL MOTOR MUSEUM

BORGWARD, CARL FRIEDRICH WILHELM (1890–1963)

The son of a coal merchant, Carl Friedrich Wilhelm Borgward was born on 10 November 1890, in the Altonci section of Hamburg. He was trained as a mechanic and worked his way through college to an engineering degree in 1919. He became a partner in the important-sounding Bremer Reifenindustrie, which was in fact a small tyre factory with no more than 24 workers. Borgward bought new machines and began to make sheet-metal parts and automotive radiators, phasing out the tyre production.

In 1923 he reorganised the company as Bremer Kühlerfabrik Borgward

GmbH, with his partner Wilhelm Tecklenborg (1882–1948). Their biggest customer was the Hansa-Lloyd Werke.

The Blitzkarren of 1924 was their first complete vehicle, a 3-wheeler with a cargo box in the middle, a single front wheel, and a bicycle saddle for the driver at the back. The 2.2hp DKW engine was mounted alongside the cargo box, with belt drive to the left rear wheel.

The Goliath, introduced in 1926, was a 3-wheeled delivery vehicle, but had a front axle under the cargo box. It had a steering wheel, but the rear end was pure motorcycle, with two saddles.

In 1927 Borgward took over Karosseriefabrik Louis Gaertner, and the following year he consolidated his interests as Goliath-Werke Borgward GmbH. For some time he had been buying shares in Hansa Automobilwerke AG of Varel in Oldenburg, and by 1929 he held a controlling interest in the company. Also in 1929 he bought control of his biggest customer, Hansa-Lloyd Werke AG. These acquisitions were merged into a new corporation, Hansa-Lloyd & Goliath Werke, Borgward & Tecklenborg, Bremen. That cumbersome title was simplified in 1938, becoming Carl F. W. Borgward GmbH.

The Borgward factories were 80 per cent destroyed in World War II, but the business was rebuilt in record time, and some 2700 vehicles were produced from 1945 to mid-year 1948.

Borgward was an industrial leader of inexorable energy. He did delegate responsibility and authority, but his interest in the details of product engineering and design never waned. He was a frequent (perhaps meddlesome) visitor in the styling studio and the drawing office; he paid less attention to the accountants and the balance sheet, and between November 1960 and February 1961, Borgward went bankrupt.

He retired and lived quietly in Bremen until his death on 28 July 1963. He had one son, Kurt, from his first marriage, and two sons, Claus and Peter, and a daughter Monik from his second. Claus had a career with Volkswagen, but the others had nothing to do with automobiles.

JPN

marketed as a Borgward in 1960 and 1961, while the Isabella was assembled in small numbers up to 1966 by a company which bought up a large stock of parts.

NG

Further Reading
'Borgward', Jerry Sloniger, *Automobile Quarterly*, Vol. 6, No. 3.

BORGWARD (ii) (RA) 1960–1965
Dinborg, Industrias Argentinas Automotrices SA, Cordoba.
A joint study between government-owned DINFIA and Borgward Argentina SA, led to the creation of Dinborg, aimed at the production of Borgward cars and commercial vehicles. Production started in 1960, just a few months before the collapse of the BORGWARD group in Germany. The Borgward Isabella with 1493cc 4-cylinder engine developing 64bhp and closed 2-door saloon body was made. Total production of Argentine Borgwards was 2295 units.

ACT

BORGWARD (iii) (MEX) 1967–1970
Fabrica Nacional de Automoviles SA, Monterrey.
This company revived the 2240cc 6-cylinder Borgward saloon and manufactured it for three years. The only difference between the Mexican and German cars was that the former had coil rear suspension in place of the air suspension of the Bremen product.

NG

BORIE *see* AMILCAR

BORITTIER (F) 1899
This was a light belt-driven 2-seater voiturette powered by a rear-mounted De Dion-Bouton engine. It was built at Mayet, Sarthe.

NG

BORLAND (US) 1912–1916
1912–1914 Borland-Grannis Co., Chicago, Illinois.
1914–1916 Borland Grannis Co., Saginaw, Michigan.
Formerly know as the IDEAL (ii), made by the Ideal Electric Vehicle Company, this electric car appeared under the Borland name for the first time at the 1912 Chicago Automobile Show. Only one body style was offered that year, a brougham on a 92in (2335mm) wheelbase, with chain or shaft drive. In 1913 the range widened, to include a roadster and a coupé on the short wheelbase, and a landaulette and limousine on a 123in (3122mm) wheelbase. These had Renault-style bonnets and were much grander-looking than the average electric car. They were also much more expensive than the smaller Borlands, costing US$5500, about double that of a coupé or roadster. In 1914 Borland combined with ARGO (i) and BROC to form the American Electric Vehicle Company, though the Borland name was continued for two more seasons. Production moved to Saginaw shortly after the amalgamation.

NG

BOSCHETTI *see* BUGANTIC

BOSELLI (I) 1952
This was a very short-lived 3-wheeled microcar, dubbed the Libulella (dragonfly), powered by a 6bhp 160cc Mondial 2-stroke engine. It was based on a design conceived in Austria as the LIBELLE.

CR

BOSLEY MK.I (US) 1955
Richard Bosley, Ohio.
One of the great 'might-have-been' stories. Richard Bosley built this one-off car with an eye to building a production version later. It had a steel tube frame and a hulking Cunningham-modified Chrysler 'Hemi' V8. The fibreglass body was probably one of the most beautiful ever made and yet Bosley, a horticulturist, had never studied design or engineering! It was featured in every major car magazine in America. Bosley later traded it for a Corvette that was to be the prototype chassis for a line of street cars called the Bosley Interstate. A prototype was shown in 1966, but production never got off the ground.

HP

1954 Borgward (i) Isabella saloon.
NATIONAL MOTOR MUSEUM

1961 Borgward (ii) 2.3-litre saloon.
NATIONAL MOTOR MUSEUM

BOSS (US) 1897–1909
Boss Knitting Machine Works, Reading, Pennsylvania.
Sometimes referred to as the Eck after its builder James L. Eck, the Boss was made over a longer period than most steamers, though it never became widely known. Eck built his first steam car in 1892, and went into production five years later with a 7hp 2-cylinder car made with 2-seater runabout or 4-seater *dos-à-dos* bodies. The running gear was carried on an unsprung sub-frame. Power quoted went up to 8hp in 1905 and 10hp in 1907, but the wheelbase remained at a short 75in (1904mm) up to the end. Cars were never more than a sideline to Eck's knitting machine business, and he built only 22 cars in thirteen years.

NG

B.O.S.S. (US) 1911
The B.O.S.S. Co., Detroit, Michigan.
This company derived its name from those of the four partners, Frank A. Bowen, John A. Olson, Frank A. Smith, and Franklin Stratton. The car was designed by Stratton, and had a 35hp 4-cylinder engine and body convertible from passenger to delivery vehicle. Production was very limited.

NG

BOSSAERT (F) 1959–1964
Carrosserie Gété, Méteren.
M. Bossaert produced a coupé based on the Citroën DS with its wheelbase shortened by 18½in (470mm). The design was by Pietro Frua and, while it retained the front end virtually unaltered, the rear end was in notchback form. The bodies were manufactured by Italsuisse, and later Bossaert entered into a partnership with the coachbuilder Gété. A convertible version was offered, as well as a restyled coupé under the name Stelvio.

CR

BOSTON-AMESBURY (US) 1902–1903
Boston & Amesbury Manufacturing Co., Amesbury, Massachusetts.
This company showed its first car at the Mechanics' Fair in Boston in November

1922 Bour-Davis Model 21S, tourer and roadster.
KEITH MARVIN

1902. It had an 8hp 2-cylinder engine and a folding front seat for two additional passengers and left-hand steering, unusual at that time. A 16hp car was also listed, but there is no proof that it was made.

NG

BOSTON HIGH WHEEL (US) 1907
Boston High Wheel Auto Manufacturing Co., Boston, Massachusetts.
Most high-wheelers were made in the Middle West, and Boston proved unfertile ground for this car. It was quite typical of its kind, with 12hp 2-cylinder engine, large-diameter wheels (44in at the front, 48in at the rear), and solid tyres. The transmission was by an expanding/contracting sheave system with belts.

NG

BOTY'S (F) 1907
This was a light voiturette powered by a 6.2hp single-cylinder engine. It was listed in 1907 only. A neat-looking 2-seater ran in the 1907 Coupe des Voiturettes, finishing 16th out of 31 entrants.

NG

BOUFFORT (F) 1957–1961
Victor Bouffort, Paris.
Aeronautical engineer Victor Bouffort created a whole series of prototypes, none of which ever came to production. He was also the inventor of the suitcase-scooter. His first car was the City-Car of 1952, an extremely small 3-wheeler of ovoid appearance, with a rear-mounted engine and single front headlamp. Next came a low-slung doorless roadster based on the Peugeot 403, first seen in 1957. Two years later came another city car, the Transville. Extremely short (85in/2150mm long), it featured a canopy that hinged forward for entry. Finally in 1961 came the 3-wheeled Enville, a single-seater microcar which, like Bouffort's other city cars, had a Sachs engine. Bouffort later helped design the Minima, a Citroën-sponsored city show car with a Citroën Dyane engine, seen at the 1973 Paris Salon.

CR

BOUHEY (F) 1898–c.1902
Sté des Usines Bouhey, Paris.
The Usines Bouhey were said to have made Pygmée engines as early as 1896, while they entered an electric phaeton in the 1898 Concours de Fiacres in Paris. They were making 10/12hp 2-cylinder petrol cars in the early years of the century, several of which were listed for sale second-hand in English papers in the years 1904 to 1908.

NG

BOUILLOT-HELSEL (GB) 1983
Bouillot-Helsel, Jersey.
This painstaking, sumptuous and very up-market replica of the Jaguar E-Type roadster was presented at the 1983 London Motorfair. It carried an exorbitant price tag and was very short-lived.

CR

BOULET (F) 1902–1903
Boulet et Cie, Paris.
The Boulet quadricycle was listed with single-cylinder Aster engines of 4, 6, or 8hp, rear-mounted and driving by belts. A 6hp model, described as 'a somewhat terrifying quadricycle' ran in the 1903 Paris–Madrid race.

NG

BOUND (GB) 1920
Bound Brothers, Southampton.
This was a single-seater cyclecar powered by a 3½hp Precision engine with friction transmission. It was exceptionally narrow – only 26in (660mm) wide.

NG

BOUR-DAVIS (US) 1916–1922
1916–1917 Bour-Davis Motor Car Co., Detroit, Michigan.
1919–1922 Louisiana Motor Car Co., Shreveport, Louisiana.
The Bour-Davis appeared on the American automotive scene with an assembled product which differed from its peers by a slightly slanted and pointed radiator. Its initial production was limited and in 1918 the company was taken over by the Shadbourne Brothers of Chicago, Illinois, with a factory at Frankfort, Indiana, in which the Shadbourne concern was trying to promote a car called the Shad-Wyck. Although the Shad-Wyck never materialised despite considerable promotion, the Bour-Davis limped through the year with a meagre handful of less than 25 cars completed. The company was reorganised in 1919, centring its operations in Shreveport and, from the start, was touted as being designed especially with southern road conditions (which were awful) in mind. In this metamorphosis, which proved to be its final attempt, the car appeared without its previous V-shaped radiator but with the radiator placed slightly ahead of the front axle. Another selling point, emphasised in its literature and advertising, was the continuation of the leather front seat over the seat's top and down to the rear floor for the enlightenment of the rear seat passengers on the touring car, Bour-Davis' only model with the roadster. The Bour-Davis used a Continental 9N 6-cylinder engine. Production of the Bour-Davis in its second coming peaked in 1920 with an estimated 250 units, far below its earlier sales in the north. In 1923 Bour-Davis was taken over by J.M. Ponder and the Ponder Motor Manufacturing Company, but the planned continuation of the car failed to materialise aside from one prototype, in reality probably a leftover Bour-Davis with a different radiator badge and hubcaps.

KM

BOURASSA (CDN) 1899–1926
H.E. Bourassa, Montreal, Quebec.
Henri-Emile Bourassa came from a family of skilled cabinet makers, but turned to mechanical things at an early age. A link with fame, though he would not have realised it at the time, was his friendship with Louis Chevrolet who lived with him for eight months after his arrival in Canada from Switzerland. Bourassa completed his first car in 1899, and for the next 26 years he built various one-off cars to special order. These ranged from runabouts to a heavy seven-passenger tourer, and he also designed two cars for the LEDOUX Carriage Company in 1914.

His last car, the Bourassa Six, had a side-valve engine and transmission of his own design in a RICKENBACKER chassis. It was completed in 1926, but he could not find a company to put it into production, and after six years he had the car demolished.

NG

BOURGEOIS-MAGNIN (F) 1920
Bourgeois et Magnin, Mâcon, Saône et Loire.
Little is known about this make except that two models, of 6 and 12hp, and seating between two and six passengers, were listed in the *Annuaire Générale de l'Automobile* in 1920.

NG

Modèles 1939

1922 Bow-V-Car 10hp 2-seater.
NATIONAL MOTOR MUSEUM

BOURGUIGNONNE (F) 1899–1901

Chesnay, de Falletans et Cie, Dijon.

The Bourguignonne voiturette was powered by a 3hp single-cylinder Gaillardet engine which was nominally air-cooled, but when it showed signs of overheating a spray of water could be activated onto the cooling fins. The car had wheel steering and four speeds, operated by fast-and-loose pulleys.

NG

BOURSAUD (F) 1897–1899

Usines Boursaud, Baignes, Charente.

The Boursaud was powered by a single-cylinder De Dion-Bouton engine mounted at the rear, driving through a 2-speed Bozier gearbox without reverse. The body was a *vis-à-vis*, and only three cars were made.

NG

BOVY-DHEYNE (B) 1902–c.1910

Ateliers de Construction Albert Bovy, Molenbeeke-St Jean, Brussels.

Usines Bovy was founded in 1888 to make bicycles. The first Bovy-Dheyne cars (occasionally called Dheyne-Bovy) were made in 1902, but it was not until 1904 that serious production began. From the start their use as commercial vehicles was considered, with bodies that could be converted from tourers to goods vehicles. They were also popular as taxicabs. A 1906 model had a 2280cc 12CV 2-cylinder engine with 3-speed gearbox and armoured wood frame. This was also available as a forward-control truck, and within a few years truck production had completely eclipsed that of passenger cars. In 1929 Bovy merged with another truck maker, Brossel, who had recently acquired former car maker PIPE. They merged their acquisitions and as Bovy-Pipe the name survived up to 1950. Bovy motorcycles were also made up to 1932.

NG

BOW-V-CAR (GB) 1922–1923

1922 The Plycar Co. Ltd, Upper Norwood, London.
1922–1923 The Plycar Co. Ltd, Luton, Bedfordshire.

This cyclecar was the second venture of Charles Beauvais, his first being the C.F.B. It was an unusual design, having an integral plywood body and chassis, and was powered by a rear-mounted 10hp air-cooled V-twin Precision engine driving through a Juckes 3-speed gearbox and chain to the rear axle. Steering was by wire and bobbin. An ingenious touch was the porthole in the side of the bonnet to admit light from the side lamps to illuminate the dashboard. Very few were made, and Beauvais achieved no real fame until he became a stylist for Avon Coachworks where he designed the striking Avon Standards.

NG

BOWEN (i) (GB) 1905–1906

J. Bowen, Didsbury, Manchester.

James Bowen began experimenting with cars in 1902 or 1903, and in 1905 had one ready for exhibition. Its first appearance was at the Manchester Show in February 1906. It was a single-cylinder 6hp light car with a 3-speed gearbox giving direct-drive on top, and shaft final drive. With a Rover automatic carburettor it was priced at £150. At the end of 1906 Bowen left Manchester for Edinburgh, and the business was sold to J.N. Aitken who made bicycles and motorcycles under the name Ladas.

NG

BOWEN (ii) (GB) 1906–1908

Bowen & Co., London.

Although the London-built Bowen was contemporary with the Manchester one, and the same class of car, there was no connection between the two. The London car had a 9hp vertical-twin engine, 3-speed gearbox, and shaft drive. Several body styles were offered, including a delivery van. The 2-seater cost £175. The whole car, including the engine, was made at the Mount Pleasant factory of Bowen & Co. who were originally brass founders, the company dating back to 1808.

NG

BOWMAN (US) 1921–1922

Bowman Motor Car Co., Covington, Kentucky.

The short-lived Bowman was a small car of a 108in (2741mm) wheelbase and, aside from the 4-cylinder engine which the company itself manufactured, was in every way an assembled car. Production was not large and body styles were limited to a 2-seater roadster and a touring car.

KM

BOWSER (GB) 1922–1923

E. Bowser, Leeds, Yorkshire.

Edward Bowser made a small number of light cars powered by the 1021cc 9hp flat-twin Koh-I-Noor engine made in Glasgow by Hugh Kennedy who used it in his own ROB ROY light car. The Bowser had a 3-speed gearbox, shaft drive, and a 2-seater body. It was expensive at £300 (reduced to £225 in 1922). In the 1930s Bowser made two styles of sidecar, a Super Sports, and a streamlined saloon.

NG

BOXER (GB) 1986–1987

Created by Ian Shearer, earlier responsible for the NIMBUS, the Boxer Sprint was a roofless, screenless sports car that was designed for either road or race use. Like the Nimbus, it was powered by a mid-mounted Mini engine and used a glassfibre monocoque. Probably only one prototype was built.

CR

BOYER (F) c.1899–1906

Boyer et Cie, Suresnes, Seine; Puteaux, Seine.

Noé Boyer was a director of the Phebus branch of the Clement-Gladiator and Humber bicycle company, hence the use of the Phebus name on Aster and De Dion-Bouton-powered tricycles, and later on the PHEBUS-ASTER voiturette. It is uncertain when the name Boyer was first used on a car, though one competed in the 1899 Paris–Rambouillet Race. By 1901 they were making conventional voiturettes with front-mounted single-cylinder Aster or 2-cylinder Buchet engines. De Dion-Bouton and Meteore engines were also used. The cars had tubular frames and chain drive, with the water tank for the frontal radiator located at the rear of the frame. In 1901 a Boyer was said to have been driven from Paris to Barcelona without a breakdown; a remarkable feat, if true.

In 1902 Boyers were sold in England under the name York, but this was discontinued because of quality problems. By 1903 larger cars with 4-cylinder engines were made, with side-valves in an L-head, armoured wood frames, and chain drive. From about 1905 Boyer cars were made in the PRUNEL factory at Puteaux, from where other marques such as GNOME, GRACILE, and J.P. issued. It is possible that some of these may have been Boyers or Prunels. The last cars sold under the Boyer name were three fours and a six shown at the 1906 Paris Salon.

NG

BOZIER (F) 1906–1915

Sté des Automobiles Bozier, Puteaux, Seine.

The origins of this company date back to 1898 when it was founded at Neuilly, moving to Puteaux in 1901. They made tricycles, gearboxes, and other components, and also possibly a few electric cars. Their first petrol car appeared in 1906; it had a 4½hp single-cylinder De Dion-Bouton engine, a Bozier-made 3-speed gearbox and shaft drive. It was unusual in that the crankshaft was set at 45 degrees to the front axle, the crown wheel was offset, and there was no differential. It was also known as the Mistral.

In 1908 the range was extended to an 8hp twin and 4-cylinder models of 10, 14, and 24hp, all of conventional design. The twin used a monobloc of Bozier's own manufacture, as did a 763cc single-cylinder voiturette of 1911. That year there was also a 1846cc four with a single-ohc, described as the first 4-cylinder engine made by Bozier, so presumably the earlier engines were proprietary units, probably De Dion-Bouton. It had full-pressure lubrication.

The company continued to make quite advanced 4-cylinder cars in 1.7-, 2-, 2.4-, and 3.6-litre models up to 1914. They had overhead valves to 1913, then for 1914 reverted to side valves. The two larger models were available in Colonial form, with higher ground clearance. Only the 1.7-litre 8hp was listed for 1915, production ceasing at the end of that year. Though Boziers were listed after World War I, it is unlikely that any were made.

NG

B.P.D. (GB) 1913

Brown, Paine & Dowland Ltd, Shoreham, Sussex.

This was a typical cyclecar powered by an 8hp air-cooled V-twin J.A.P. engine, with 2-speed gearbox and final drive by long belts running more than half the length of the frame. *The Cyclecar* said they were 'very struck with this machine' when they inspected a prototype in March 1913, but nothing more seems to have been heard of it.

NG

B.R.A. (GB) 1981 to date

1981–1993 Beribo Replica Automobiles, Doncaster, Yorkshire.
1995–1996 Rodney Rushton, Cheriton Bishop, Exeter.
1996–1998 B.R.A. Engineering, Holywell, Flintshire.
1998 to date B.R.A. Motor Works, Flint, Flintshire.

Restoration experts John Berry and Peter Ibbotson formed B.R.A. to produce an AC Cobra replica, though unusually it was moulded from an original 289 narrow-arch model. The first examples incorporated a front spoiler, aero screens, squared wheel arches and a bigger interior, but more accurate replicas followed. MGB mechanicals sat in a steel multi-tube chassis with double wishbone front suspension and a leaf sprung live rear axle. A V8 version was also offered from 1982. A 427 replica followed in 1984, boasting Jaguar suspension in a platform chassis designed by Gerry Hawkridge (later of TRANSFORMER). Rover V8 engines were the recommended power units, though American V8s were possible. The 427 project was eventually sold to a German firm. The J-Type of 1984 was a cycle-winged 2-seater inspired by the 1930s MG Midget, with MGB suspension and a choice of MG or Ford engines, while the P-Type was the same car with flowing wings. Out of character was a Mini Moke replica for Fiat Panda parts, with a steel body and tubular chassis, and a 4x4 option, but only one was built. B.R.A.'s final model was the 1992 CX3 trike, a Honda CX V-twin motorbike-engined Morgan-style barrel-back car. Manufacture of the trike passed to a Welsh firm, which, in 1998, also presented a Citroën 2CV-powered version, called the CV3. The original Doncaster partners retired in 1993 but the P-Type project was passed on to Rodney Rushton in 1995. The A.C. 289 replica ended up with TYLER.

CR

BRABHAM (AUS) 1986

Hi-Tech Car Co., Smithfield, New South Wales.

The name of World Championship racing driver Jack Brabham is very well known to enthusiasts and was attached to the British-built racing cars he drove. It had also been used on a performance version of the HOLDEN Torana in the late 1960s, but in 1985 it was being applied to a high-performance sports coupé developed by Cliff Trefry and Bob and Wal Hadley. This design group had previously built the TRIAD which, although it did not attain production status,

1901 Boyer coupé.
NATIONAL MOTOR MUSEUM

1902 Bradbury (i) 4½hp voiturette.
M.J.WORTHINGTON-WILLIAMS

attracted the attention of Sir Jack and a group of promoters. Applying the expertise honed on that project, a composite unitary structure which would accept unstressed fibreglass panels, was finalised. A Holden 5-litre V8 engine driving through either a 5-speed manual or a 4-speed automatic transmission, all independent suspension, rack and pinion steering and ventilated disc brakes, were specified. At 75in (1900mm) the body was very wide, and featured flush glass, a targa top and provision for a simple change from rhd to lhd. After a year of effort it became obvious that sufficient backing to begin production would not be forthcoming and the project was reluctantly allowed to lapse.

MG

BRADBURY (i) **(GB)** 1901–1902

Bradbury Bros, Croydon, Surrey.

The first car to be made in Croydon, the Bradbury was a 2-seater voiturette powered by a 4hp single-cylinder engine of the company's own manufacture. It had a 2-speed gearbox and chain drive. Few were made as the company's main business was the manufacture of batteries and electrical equipment such as voltmeters, contact breakers, and sparking plugs. They also imported a few Pinart engines from Belgium.

NG

BRADBURY (ii) **(GB)** 1904–c.1906

Bradbury & Co. Ltd, Oldham, Lancashire.

Well-known motorcycle makers from 1902 to 1925, Bradbury offered a tricar with various bodies. The largest was the Governess, which could accommodate

1897 Georges Richard (Brasier) 8hp wagonette.
NATIONAL MOTOR MUSEUM

two adults and two children, access to the front seats being by a door. A commercial version was also made. The engine was a 4½hp single-cylinder motorcycle unit. It is not certain for how long the Bradbury Tricar was made, but as the tricar boom was almost over by 1906 it is unlikely to have lasted beyond this date.
NG

BRADEN RIVER ENGINEERING (US) c.1996 to date
Braden River Engineering, Bradenton, Florida.
This Jaguar XKE replica kit was very accurate in appearance, even though it was based on 1979–85 Mazda RX-7 running gear. Engines up to 400hp were available. They were sold in kit and fully assembled form.
HP

BRADLEY (i) (US) 1920–1921
Bradley Motor Car Co., Cicero, Illinois.
The short-lived Bradley was typical of the undistinguished assembled cars that proliferated on the American automotive scene during the late 'teens and 1920s. A Lycoming engine was used and the 4-cylinder Bradley was augmented by a 6-cylinder car in 1921. A 5-seater touring car was the only body style built and production was an estimated 200 to 250 cars before the company ceased trading.
KM

BRADLEY (ii) (US) 1971–1981
Bradley Automotive, Minneapolis, Minnesota.
One of the great rags-to-riches-to-rags stories in kit car history, Bradley burst on the scene with a simple, inexpensive kit called the Bradley GT. Based on the same VW Beetle floorpan and running gear that most kits used at that time, it had low sides so no doors were needed, and clear plexiglass side windows that folded up for entrance. It was available in basic and pre-assembled form. According to company figures, over 5000 were sold. In 1980 the Bradley GT-II was added to the line. It was more civilised, with gull-wing doors and more room than the GT. However, it was harder to build and more expensive, so it did not sell as well. It was also offered in electric-powered form as the GTE. In 1980 Bradley bought several kits from other manufacturers to add to their line. The MGT was a MG-TD replica on a VW pan and the Baron was a copy of the Fiberfab Gazelle. They also bought a shortened 1957 Thunderbird replica from VEEBIRDS that fitted on a VW floorpan. The best new kit was an attractive neoclassic called the Marlene. Due to a variety of business problems, Bradley closed down in 1981. However, the Bradley GT was picked up by SUN RAY PRODUCTS, and the Marlene was passed on to CLASSIC ROADSTERS.
HP

BRADLEY (iii) (GB) 1992–1996
Bradley Motor Company, Whalley, Lancashire.
Strongly reminiscent of the FALCON Mk1 bodyshell, the Bradley S61 originally used Ford Ten components, but a chassis for Ford Escort parts was developed. There was also a completely different steel tube chassis designed to accept a Rover V8 engine.
CR

BRADWELL (GB) 1914
Bradwell & Co., Folkestone, Kent.
The Bradwell Monocar was a very light single-seater cyclecar powered by a 3½hp engine which could be started from the seat. It had belt final drive and cost a modest £65.
NG

BRAMHAM see STANHOPE

BRAMWELL (US) 1904–1905
Springfield Automobile Co., Springfield, Ohio.
This car was made by the father-and-son team, W.C.and C.C. Bramwell, after they had severed their partnership with John T. Robinson. They took their 8hp light car design which had been made as the BRAMWELL-ROBINSON, to Springfield where it went into production as the SPRINGFIELD (i). After they took control of the Springfield Automobile Company, they changed the name of the car to their own, and made it into early 1905, when the venture failed. The Bramwell runabout had a single-cylinder engine under the seat, epicyclic gearbox, and chain drive. The frame was made of laminated wood armoured with steel, and the car cost $800, $50 less than when it was made by Bramwell-Robinson.
NG

BRAMWELL-ROBINSON (US) 1899–1902
John T. Robinson & Co., Hyde Park, Massachusetts.
John Robinson made paper box machinery and provided financial support for W.C. Bramwell and his son, C.C. Bramwell, to make a light car. The Bramwell-Robinson Sociable was a 3-wheeler powered by an air-cooled single-cylinder engine of only 3hp, mounted under the seat and driving the single rear wheel by chain. Three were tested at the turn of the century, leading to a production run of 25. The Bramwells then turned to four-wheelers, making two models in 1901 and 1902, the 5hp Model A and 8hp Model B, both 2-seater runabouts. By this time they had parted company with Robinson, who went on to build a large 4-cylinder called the ROBINSON (i), later POPE-ROBINSON.
NG

BRANDT (F) 1948–1950
Brandt, Draveil, Seine-et-Oise.
Previously involved with armaments manufacture, Jules Brandt stunned visitors to the 1948 Paris Motor Show on the presentation of the Brandt Reine 1950. In almost all respects it rewrote the motoring rulebook. Its main design principle was 'everything forward', so it had a front-mounted engine and front-wheel drive. The remarkable drivetrain occupied only 4 per cent of the car's total volume: this was a 2-stroke 780cc 4-cylinder engine, with an extra four charging cylinders. In each of the engine's main cylinders there were two pistons mounted in a horizontally opposed position. There were oscillating plates with ball joints for the connecting rods and main shaft. A remarkable 75bhp was claimed for this powerplant. Another innovation was the fact that the epicyclic gearbox and magnetic clutch were mounted in situ with the engine, in a transverse position, and provided six forward gears. The suspension was all-independent by transverse parallel arms with rubber springing, and the braking was by dual-circuit hydraulically-operated drums. The wheels were of light alloy and all four of them steered. The curious yet aerodynamic bodywork lacked any side doors: instead access was provided both front and rear, for four passengers sitting either side of a gangway. Sadly the Reine 1950 was never commercialised.
CR

BRASIE (US) 1914–1916

Brasie Motor Car Co., Minneapolis, Minnesota.

Frank R. Brasie had built the Twin City truck when he decided to go into the cyclecar business, using a design by J.M. Michaelson who was making a few cyclecars under his own name. The Brasie had a water-cooled 12hp 4-cylinder engine, unlike the MICHAELSON, which was air-cooled, and was made in three models, the Messenger 2- and 4-seater roadsters and the Packet delivery van. They had friction transmission and belt drive. In 1916 the company name was changed to the Packet Motor Car Manufacturing Co., and the vehicles were renamed Packet too, but by then they were nearly all delivery vans. This venture lasted only into 1917.

NG

BRASIER including GEORGES RICHARD, RICHARD-BRASIER, and CHAIGNEAU-BRASIER (F) 1897–1930

1897–1905 Sté des Anciens Éts George Richard, Ivry-Port, Seine.
1905–1926 Sté des Automobiles Brasier, Ivry-Port, Seine.
1927–1930 Sté Chaigneau-Brasier, Ivry-Port, Seine.

The Richard company was founded in Paris in about 1850, to make photographic and optical equipment and, later, bicycles. The SA Georges Richard was founded in 1893 by Georges and his brother Max who mentioned cars in their prospectus, though they did not actually make any until 1897. Then they offered a Benz-like car with belt drive and three forward speeds. This was joined by a smaller car based on the Belgian VIVINUS. In 1901 Henri Brasier left MORS to join Georges Richard. Though the Vivinus-derived cars were continued for more than a year, Brasier started a new regime of larger cars on Panhard lines, with 2- or 4-cylinder engines in four models, from 10 to 40hp. At first they were chain driven, with tubular frames on the smaller cars, but by 1904 all frames were of pressed steel. In that year there were two twins and three fours, of which the largest, the 40hp, was still chain driven, the others all using shaft drive. There was also a 5½hp single-cylinder voiturette sold in England in 1903 as the Pony Richard, which was probably the last survivor of the Vivinus regime. Output was 624 cars in 1904, when the company gained the first of its two victories in the Gordon Bennett race. Léon Théry drove a specially built 9.9-litre 80hp chain-driven car, and in 1905 he won again, this time with an 11.2-litre 90hp car. Despite Brasier's guiding hand, the cars were not generally called Richard-Brasier until the 1904 season, and in October that year Georges Richard left, to form his own company which made cars under the name UNIC.

The Brasier range was all shaft-driven from 1906, but the cars remained quite conservative, with exposed valve gear and pair-cast cylinders until 1912, when a more modern light car with 11.1hp monobloc 4-cylinder engine appeared. The larger Brasiers had 4-cylinder engines up to 5878cc (35/50hp), and sixes up to 7680cc (50/70hp). Curiously, in 1911 and 1912 they offered a 1526cc 10/12hp 2-cylinder light car. Henri Brasier's policy of making increasingly expensive cars, which he pursued from 1906 to 1908, brought the company to the brink of bankruptcy, and the situation was not helped by the fact that there were no more racing successes to impress wealthy enthusiasts. However, increasing attention to smaller cars brought about a recovery. Output from May 1909 to April 1910 was 628 cars, and in the same period 1910/11 795 cars were made. In the calendar year 1911 969 cars were made, at an average price only half of that in 1907. From 1905 to 1908 some Brasiers were made in Turin under the name FIDES.

Like that of so many famous old names, the Brasier story in the 1920s was one of slow decline. They began with a 3402cc 18/30hp side-valve four of no particular distinction, joined in 1922 by a smaller four with 2063cc ohv engine and front-wheel brakes. This had quite a good turn of speed; two tourers ran in the second Le Mans 24 Hour Race in 1924, finishing 7th and 8th.

In 1926 the company was bought by the Chaigneau family who were bicycle makers. They changed the name to Chaigneau-Brasier and brought out the TD-4, a 9CV 4-cylinder light car made in tourer and 2-door saloon models. This unremarkable car did not find many buyers, even though one covered 11,200 miles in North Africa in eight days. In 1928 they made a dramatic move upmarket with a front-wheel drive coupé powered by a 3490cc single-ohc straight-8 engine. It is unlikely that they had enough funds to develop such a complex design properly, and from 1929 the economic climate was against new luxury cars. Few, if any, straight-8s were sold, and in 1930 the company was reorganised by GEORGES IRAT. By the end of the year the factory had been sold to DELAHAYE.

NG

1903 Richard Brasier tonneau.
NATIONAL MOTOR MUSEUM

c.1906 Brasier tonneau.
NATIONAL MOTOR MUSEUM

1910 Brasier 12/18hp tonneau.
NATIONAL MOTOR MUSEUM

BRASINCA (BR) 1964 to date

Brasinca, São Paulo.

Founded in 1949, Brasinca started building bus bodies. Later on, they started furnishing bodies for FNM and other Brazilian makers, until 1963, when Brasinca presented their own caravans. They were the first Brazilian caravans. Shortly afterwards they started work on what was called project Boulevard, a sports car version of the Aero-Willys. But Willys lost interest and Brasinca developed their own sports car, the GT 4200, with Chevrolet mechanical components. The 6-cylinder engine was modified with three SU carburettors. The GT 4200 was presented at the São Paulo Salon in 1964. Seventy-five of these sports cars were made, all of them coupés. Thirty-five of them were supplied in kit form. GT production stopped in 1965 because the Brazilian economy was in difficulties and component prices were continually rising. The GT 4200 project was sold to Sociedad Tecnica de Veiculos, SVT, that changed the vehicle's name to UIRAPURU. The Uirapuru was shown at the 1966 Brazilian Auto Show, where the convertible version was unveiled. Brasinca continued making components for other Brazilian motor-vehicle manufacturers. They returned to complete vehicles in 1984, trying to fill specific market niches with the Passo Fino and Manga Larga station wagons. These large vehicles were superseded by other station wagons and trucks like the Quarto de Milha and Andaluz.

ACT

BRAUN (A) 1900–1907
1900–1901 August Braun, Eerstr Oesterreichische Motorfahrzeugfabrik, Vienna.
1901–1907 August Braun & Co., Vienna.
August Braun was a pioneer Austrian car maker. His first design was based on the French Victoria Combination or PARISIENNE, with a 4hp single-cylinder De Dion-Bouton engine driving the front wheels, and centre pivot steering. He later made conventional cars powered by a 4hp engine of his own design. At the beginning his partner was Wilhelm Stift, later associated with CELERITAS and GRAF & STIFT cars.

NG

BRAVO (i) (F) 1900
N. H. Bravo, Clichy, Seine.
This short-lived manufacturer made 6-seater wagonettes powered by 5 or 8hp engines of his own manufacture.

NG

BRAVO (ii) (D) 1921
Union Kleinauto-Werke, Mannheim.
After making trucks during World War I, this company turned to light cars. A 4/10PS 2-cylinder car was made, and also a four, but production was only on a small scale. The company also made the RABAG-BUGATTI and built bodies for other firms.

HON

BRAZIER (US) 1902–1903
H. Bartol Brazier, Philadelphia, Pennsylvania.
French-born Brazier made a heavy wagonette powered by an 18hp 2-cylinder engine. It seated six passengers, those in the rear seats facing inwards. He never incorporated a company and made cars on a custom basis, to order only. As well as the wagonette, he listed phaetons and surreys at prices from US$2550 to US$3400.

NG

B.R.B. (GB) 1921
B.R.B. Engineering Co., Hornsey, London.
This was a cyclecar powered by an 8hp V-twin JAP engine, with friction transmission and chain drive. A price of £200 was quoted for a 2-seater, but very few were made.

NG

BRECHT (US) 1901–1903
Brecht Automobile Co., St. Louis, Missouri.
This company was a branch of the Brecht Butcher's Supply Company, owned by the Brecht brothers, Gus, Frank, and Charles. Their manager was H.F. Borbein who bought the company in October 1903 and changed the name to BORBEIN. Brecht cars were made in steam and electric form, the former being called Rushmobiles. They had 6hp 2-cylinder non-condensing engines and were available in four body styles, as well as a delivery van. The electrics were very similar in appearance to the steamers, and were available with solid or pneumatic tyres. In 1903 Brecht offered engineless cars, 'ready for power', and Borbein continued this business when he took over.

NG

BREESE (F) 1911
Robert Breese, Paris.
American-born Robert Potter Breese made a light sporting car powered by 4-cylinder Ballot or Fivet engines. About 65 were made, of which one survives in the United States. In 1919, by now a Lieutenant in the US Aviation Service, Breese built a midget car using many aircraft parts and powered by a 2-cylinder Harley-Davidson engine. This was purely for his own amusement, though he later sold the car to a French duke.

NG

BREEZE see DE TAMBLE

BREGUET (F) 1907; 1942
1907 Atelier Breguet, Paris.
1942 Sté des Ateliers d'Aviation Louis Breguet, Toulouse.
Although separated by 35, years these very different cars were linked by Louis Breguet who became one of France's best known aircraft builders. In 1907 he announced two models of 6-cylinder car, of 30 and 50hp. They were also known as Sixcyl Breguet. Breguet soon turned to aircraft, but returned to cars during the acute petrol shortage of World War II, when he joined the ranks of electric car makers. His was a 2-seater coupé on a 78in (1980mm) wheelbase with Paris-Rhone motor mounted at the rear of the central frame chassis, the body being on outriggers. The tyres were remoulds as new ones were not obtainable. Top speed was 30mph (48km/h), and range 65 miles.

NG

BREMAC (US) 1932
Bremac Motor Corp., Sidney, Ohio.
An experimental automobile, the Bremac featured an 80hp 8-cylinder engine mounted at the rear of the chassis. A 5-seater sedan was the only body style planned. The Bremac differed from other experimental cars of the era in having no chassis frame or propeller shaft. The car was a failure.

KM

BREMEN (US) c.1969–1988
Bremen Sport Equipment, Bremen, Indiana.
Also known as ARX Industries and B.S.C. Corp.
The Sterling (Nova) was one of the most popular kits of the 1970s, and Bremen responded with a variation called the Sebring. Bremen president Al Hildebrand had been a Sebring distributor and made the changes he thought it needed. Although the general lines remained, including the lift-up cockpit top, the nose was shortened and the headlights put under retractable covers. The side and tail layout were different as well. It was based on the VW floorpan, although Bremen also offered a V6 powered version with a tube frame and 4-wheel disc brakes. The ultimate Sebring had a turbocharged 3800cc V6. Another Bremen product was the Creighton, a Pinto or Mustang II-based neoclassic kit car that looked like a 1930s American convertible. Their other models were the Mini Mark, a small, inexpensive neoclassic based on VW running gear, and a dune buggy with a Ford Model T nose called the Citation. This buggy grew into a full-length version called the Maxi-Taxi. All were available in kit or assembled form. Bremen also imported the Puma, Ventura, Adamo, Glaspac Cobra, and Lafer kits from Brazil.

HP

BREMS (DK) 1900–1904
A.L. Brems, Viborg.
The Brems brothers Aage and Jacob were bicycle builders who spent some time at the Eisenach factory where the WARTBURG (i) was made. Their first car, with 3.8hp air-cooled 2-cylinder engine, was quite similar to the Wartburg, which in turn was based on the DECAUVILLE Voiturelle. The first car, like the Wartburg/Decauville, had no rear suspension, but this was rectified on later Brems cars, of which only eight were made altogether. Each was of different design, several with single-cylinder engines and the last a 2-cylinder again.

NG

BRENNABOR (D) 1908–1933
Gebr. Reichstein Brennabor-Werke, Brandenburg.
Founded in 1871 by Carl Reichstein (1847–1931) this company was well-known for bicycles and motorcycles (made from 1901 to 1914) when they started car production in 1908. They began with a 3-wheeler, the Brennaborette with single front wheel and 452cc single-cylinder Fafnir engine which drove the rear axle by chain. In 1909 they built their first 4-wheeler, with 904cc 2-cylinder Fafnir engine and shaft drive. 4-cylinder engines of their own design followed, though they also bought engines from STOEWER. Several different models were made up to 1914, including the 1328cc 5/12PS Typ B, 1592cc 6/18PS Typ L4, and 2476cc 10/28PS Typ F8. They were all of conventional design, with side-valves in an L-head, and monobloc casting, though early examples of the F8 were pair-cast. A popular model introduced in 1914 was the 1453cc M3 with 3-seater body. Brennabors sold well in England, where they were marketed under the name Brenna.

After the war the company concentrated on a single model to start with, the 2091cc side-valve 8/24PS Typ P. This was made up to 1927 (from 1926 as the Type PW), and was joined in 1922 by the Typ S with 1569cc ohv engine. This was followed by the Typ R with the same cylinder dimensions but with side inlet and overhead exhaust valves. Made up to 1928, it was Brennabor's best-selling model, with about 20,000 delivered in its four-year lifetime. Brennabor was a serious producer in the 1920s, being second only to Opel. Their peak years were 1927 and 1928, when they made about 100 cars per day, as well as light commercial vehicles. Eduard Reichstein, son of founder Carl, spent some time in America and was very impressed by the mass production methods of General Motors. From 1922 to 1928 Brennabor joined HANSA LLOYD and NAG in the GDA (Gemeinschaft Deutsche Automobilfabriken) group.

In 1928 they turned to larger cars, the 2547cc 10/45PS 6-cylinder Typs AK and AL, and 3080cc 12/55PS, followed by the 2460cc Juwel 6 and 3417cc straight-8 Juwel 8. The latter was not a success, even though it was the cheapest German-built straight-8, and only about 100 were sold. Smaller 4-cylinder cars were made as well, but Brennabor were in difficulties in the early 1930s. A prototype front-wheel drive saloon with 10/45PS 6-cylinder engine did not get into production, but its development cost the firm a lot of money. In 1931 they brought out their smallest car for many years, the 995cc side-valve Typ C with transverse front suspension, which was a competitor for the 1-litre Opel, but they sold only about 2000 cars in three seasons. Alongside it in 1933 they offered two sixes, the 1957cc Typ E and 2460cc Typ F, the latter a development of the Juwel 6, but only about 200 were made of both types. All car production ceased by the end of 1933, though the company continued to make bicycles and prams (with which they had started in 1871) until World War II, when they turned to armaments. The factory was destroyed by bombing towards the end of the war.
HON/NG

BRENNAN (US) 1902–1908
Brennan Motor Manufacturing Co., Syracuse, New York.
Brennan were mainly engine builders who supplied power units to a number of car manufacturers, including SELDEN. However, they made complete cars from time to time, the earliest dating from 1902. In 1907 they were overstocked with engines and produced a few more 4-cylinder cars. They then returned solely to engine manufacture until 1913 when, for one season, they listed a range of 2-, 3-, and 5-ton trucks.
NG

BRESCIANA see S.M.B.

BREW-HATCHER (US) 1904–1905
The Brew-Hatcher Co., Cleveland, Ohio.
William A. Hatcher was employed by Winton and the Ohio Automobile Co. where he had worked on the Model F Packard. In about 1903 he and Francis O. Brew started a components supply company, launching their first car in January 1904. It had a 16hp horizontally-opposed twin engine and a rear-entrance tonneau body. In 1905 the same model was offered, but on a longer wheelbase, which allowed for a side-entrance tonneau, and there was also an 18/24hp 4-cylinder tourer. Car manufacture ended in Autumn 1905 when Brew retired to join the Internal Revenue Service (Income Tax). The car was sometimes known as the B & H.
NG

1911 Brennabor 10hp 2-seater.
NICK GEORGANO/NATIONAL MOTOR MUSEUM

1925 Brennabor Typ R 6/25PS tourer.
NATIONAL MOTOR MUSEUM

1932 Brennabor Typ C 4/20PS saloon.
NATIONAL MOTOR MUSEUM

BREWSTER (US) 1916–1925; 1934–1936
1916–1925 Brewster & Co., Long Island City, New York.
1934–1936 Springfield Manufacturing Co., Springfield, Massachusetts.
Between 1915 and 1925 the venerable firm of Brewster & Co., carriage builders and makers of custom-built car bodies, produced an expensive and meticulously built automobile in a variety of open and closed models. Powered by a 4-cylinder Knight sleeve-valve engine of its own design, these compact town-carriage types of cars were widely sought after by the wealthy who did not want the ostentation of a large custom-built car. These Brewsters could be readily identified by their round radiator grille, which had been designed to represent the Delaunay-Belleville car, of which Brewster had the American franchise until World War I curtailed further shipment. The Brewster steering-wheel position could be placed on either side subject to the choice of the customer and many of the town

c.1916 Brewster 26hp limousine.
NICK GEORGANO/NATIONAL MOTOR MUSEUM

1934 Brewster-Ford town car.
NATIONAL MOTOR MUSEUM

1900 Brierre 3½hp tonneau.
NATIONAL MOTOR MUSEUM

cars, which made up the majority of the cars, carried patent-leather bumpers. Brewster was absorbed by Rolls-Royce (US) in 1925.

The Brewster reappeared in 1934 in a series of open and closed bodies mounted on Ford V8, Buick and other standard chassis and carried heart-shaped grilles, flared wings and split-bumpers. Approximately 120 of the later Brewsters were completed and identified on their hubcaps with Brewster & Co., Long Island City, N.Y.

KM

Further Reading
'Brewster: when modesty was the best policy', Beverly Rae Kimes, *Automobile Quarterly*, Vol. 7, No. 3.

BRICKLIN (CDN) 1974–1975

Bricklin Vehicle Corp., St Johns, New Brunswick.

There are uncanny parallels between Malcolm Bricklin's sports car and the De Lorean – only that the Bricklin SV-1 safety car arrived five years before John Z De Lorean's. Bricklin – already famous for importing the Subaru 360 into the States – persuaded the Canadian government to fund his project to the tune of $23 million, building a new factory in an area in need of employment. Just like De Lorean, production cars suffered from poorly engineered gull-wing doors and quality problems, and within a year the whole project had collapsed, since each car reputedly cost twice as much to build as the asking price. Gull-wing doors apart, the SV-1 was notably safety-conscious, with a large impact-resistant front bumper and interior safety features. Bright 'safety colours' were impregnated into the acrylic/glassfibre bodyshell, which was characterfully styled. The suspension derived from the AMC Javelin and 1974 cars had AMC 5.9-litre V8 engines; 1975 models switched to Ford V8 power and transmission. Of the 2897 cars built, 144 had manual transmission. Malcolm Bricklin went on to import Fiats and Yugos into the USA.

CR

BRIDGEWATER (GB) 1905–1908

Bridgewater Motor Co. Ltd, Eastover, Bridgewater, Somerset.

This company grew out of Harry Carver's Cycle Works, founded in 1887, and from around 1900 carried on repairs of motorcycles and cars, becoming agents for De Dion-Bouton and MMC cars in 1902. They built their first car in 1905. They were assembled vehicles with chassis by Malicet et Blin and engines by Ballot or White & Poppe. The former were of 16/20 or 24/30hp, and the latter 12 and 14hp. All were 4-cylinder T-head units. Bodies were by the local firm Raworth & Co. Bridgewater production ran to no more than 11 or 12 cars, mostly sold locally. The company then returned to selling a variety of makes of car, their association with Austin lasting for 40 years. They turned to selling Renaults in 1980, and closed down in 1994.

NG

Further Reading
The Bridgewater Motor Car, Rod Fitzhugh, Avalon Press, Coventry, 1995.

BRIERRE (F) 1900–1901

E.J. Brierre, Paris.

The Brierre was a light voiturette powered by a rear-mounted 3.5hp single-cylinder De Dion-Bouton engine, with water-cooled cylinder head and air-cooled block. Final drive was direct by gear to the rear axle. The 2-seater wood-framed body was panelled in aluminium. Brierre, who also made motorcycles and quadricycles, in 1901 became the Paris agent for COTTEREAU. Instead of his own voiturette, he turned to manufacture under licence of a Cottereau with front-mounted 7hp V-twin engine, this business lasting until 1903.

NG

BRIEST-ARMAND (F) 1897–1898

Eugene Briest et Frères, Nantes.

After experimenting with a steam tricycle, Eugene Briest built a number of cars powered by single-cylinder horizontal petrol engines, with bodies for two, four, or six passengers. At least one ran on alcohol fuel and competed in the alcohol fuel trials of 1899.

NG

BRIGGS-DETROITER *see* DETROITER

BRIGGS & STRATTON (US) 1919–1924

Briggs & Stratton Co., Milwaukee, Wisconsin.

In 1918 accessory manufacturer Briggs & Stratton bought the rights to the Motor Wheel, which had been made by the A.O. Smith Co. as the SMITH FLYER. This was a 4-wheeled buckboard with a cycle-type wheel at each corner and six wooden slats for a frame. There were no springs as the slats were considered sufficiently flexible to give a fairly comfortable ride. At the rear was a 2.5hp

1905 Brillié 20/24hp tourer.
NATIONAL MOTOR MUSEUM

single-cylinder air-cooled engine mounted on a wheel which was let down on the road. The engine was started first, and care had to be taken with the throttle; too little and the engine stalled, too much and you burnt the tread off the tyre. Despite its primitive specification the buckboard was quite popular, and several hundred were sold at $200 each. A vehicle of similar design, though 10in longer and with its two seats in tandem, was sold under the name CORONA (iv) in 1922, and may have been made by Briggs & Stratton.

In 1924 Briggs & Stratton sold the rights to the Automotive Electric Service Co. of Newark, New Jersey, who made petrol and electric versions under the name RED BUG.

Briggs & Stratton continued to make a wide range of motors, especially for outboard attachments for boats and for lawn mowers, in which field they are still active. Their only other automotive product was an experimental 6-wheeled petrol-electric car of 1979, in which a 694cc engine drove a generator to charge the battery pack.

NG

BRIGHTWHEEL (GB) 1986–1989
Brightwheel Replicas, Christchurch, Dorset.
Ken Cook's Brightwheel assumed the ex-SHELDONHURST Cobra replica and called it the Viper. That meant it inherited the option of Ford Granada suspension and drive trains or Jaguar running gear and a Rover V8 engine. There was also a budget Ford Cortina-based Viper 4. A final effort was the CR6 Stinger of 1988, a Countach replica. After the company failed, the Viper was revived by COBRETTI, although Ken Cook continued to operate as CLASSIC REPLICAS.

CR

BRILLIÉ (F) 1904–1908
Sté des Automobiles Eugène Brillié, Le Havre.
Born in 1863, Eugène Brillié was in partnership with Gustave Gobron in the manufacture of GOBRON-BRILLIÉ cars from 1898 to 1903, when he set up his own business. Though based in Paris, all his vehicles were made for him by the

Schneider armaments and engineering firm at Le Havre. Cars were always secondary to trucks and buses; the company became famous as the first suppliers of motor buses to the city of Paris. Two models of passenger car were listed from 1904, the 20/24hp Type G and 35/45hp Type H, the latter sharing an engine with the Paris buses. The engines were of inlet-over-exhaust layout, and the specification included 4-speed gearboxes and shaft drive. In February 1908 the Brillié company went into liquidation, and no more cars were made, though Schneider continued to make buses under their own name.

NG

BRISCOE (US) 1914–1921
Briscoe Motor Corp., Jackson, Michigan.
Benjamin Briscoe (1869–1945) was an important figure in the US motor industry for some time before he began to make cars under his own name. In 1886 he founded the Briscoe Manufacturing Co. which, among other contracts, supplied radiators and sheet metal parts to Oldsmobile. In 1904 he joined Jonathan Maxwell in making the MAXWELL-BRISCOE, which he incorporated in the unsuccessful United States Motor Co. combine in 1910. On his own again in 1913 he formed Briscoe Frères in Paris with his brother Frank (1875–1954). They built a cyclecar called the AJAX (iii) which they made in modified form in Jackson, Michigan as the ARGO (ii).

In January 1914 he launched the Briscoe car, a conventional light car with 2.5-litre 4-cylinder side-valve engine, available as a 3-seater cloverleaf roadster or 5-seater tourer. Its only unusual feature was the single cyclops-eye headlamp mounted above the radiator. This idea, also used by GARFORD, was not successful, as a single headlamp was against the law in many states. It lasted through the 1914 and 1915 seasons, after which the Briscoe became completely conventional in appearance. A Ferro V8 engine was offered in 1916, about the same size as the fours and in the same wheelbase, though at a cost of an additional $200. It was not continued for 1917, when there was a new 24hp air-cooled four. 1919 was Briscoe's best year, with 10,237 cars sold, but the next two years saw sales drop to 6120 and 4175. Late in 1921 Briscoe sold the company to Clarence A. Earl who made cars of similar design, though more powerful,

1915 Briscoe Model B Cloverleaf roadster.
NATIONAL MOTOR MUSEUM

1906 Bristol (i) 16/20hp tourer.
NATIONAL MOTOR MUSEUM

under his own name up to 1923. Before leaving his firm Briscoe supplied a number of 4-cylinder engines to BELLANGER, but after 1921 he played no further part in the auto industry.

From 1916 to 1921 Briscoes were made in Canada by the Canadian Briscoe Motor Co. Ltd in the former Brockville-Atlas factory. Production was considerably lower than in the US, about 1000 cars annually.

NG

BRISSONET (i) (F) 1934–1935
Éts Brissonet, Neuilly, Seine.
This was a very small single-seater which resembled a child's car powered by a 175cc single-cylinder engine mounted behind the driver. It weighed only 120kg and had a top speed of 20mph (32km/h). After the war Brissonet made scooters and, in 1953, a 3-wheeler called the Speed, a name also applied, most inappropriately, to the prewar car.

NG

BRISSONET (ii) (F) 1953
Éts Brissonet, Neuilly, Seine.
Having successfully commercialised the Speed scooter, Brissonet branched out into microcars with the Soucoupe Roulante at the 1953 Paris Salon. It was an absolutely tiny doorless open 3-wheeler, weighing only 150kg, and was powered by a 200cc 2-stroke engine with a 3-speed gearbox. The project remained stillborn.

CR

BRISSONNEAU & LOTZ (F) 1957–1958
Brissoneau & Lotz, Paris.
This locomotive builder also turned its hand to coachbuilding in the mid-1950s. The nearest it came to a production car was a smart 2/3-seater open sports car

based on the platform of a Renault 4CV. It used plastic bodywork. In 1959 the company was contracted by Renault to build its Floride.

CR

BRISTOL (i) (GB) 1902–1908
1902–1904 Bristol Motor Co., Bristol.
1904–1908 Bristol Motor Co. Ltd, Bristol.
Unlike many modest early motor manufacturers, Bristols designed and constructed most parts of their cars themselves. The engineering expertise was provided by William Appleton, who had previously had a works in Weston-super-Mare, whilst the admininstrative side was handled by Arthur Johnson. The first model was a 2-cylinder 10hp, based on the contemporary Daimler, but the Bristol Industrial Museum retains a 4-cylinder 1906 16/20 tourer of 3053cc. Only 20 cars were sold before Johnson transferred to the Bristol Carriage and Wagon Works and the business closed. Though he formed a successor Bristol Motor Co. in 1924, this company did not attempt manufacture and developed agencies for other makes instead.

DF

BRISTOL (ii) (US) 1903–1904
Bristol Motor Car Co., Bristol, Connecticut.
This was a 2-seater runabout powered by an 8hp single-cylinder air-cooled engine, driving through an epicyclic gearbox. Production began in March 1903, but by May the makers had merged with the American Hardware Corp. of New Britain, Connecticut, who were to launch the CORBIN in 1905. The Bristol's designer Frederick Manross may have continued production into 1904, but that year he joined Frederick Law to establish a company to make the LAW car.

NG

BRISTOL (iii) (GB) 1946 to date
1946–1960 Bristol Aeroplane Co. Ltd, Filton, Bristol.
1960 to date Bristol Cars Ltd, Filton, Bristol.
The Bristol Aeroplane Co. was Britain's oldest aircraft firm, founded in 1910. During World War II they built many famous designs, including the Blenheim and Beaufighter, names which were used on several models of Bristol car, and after the war the enormous Brabazon and widely-used Britannia air liners. The company came into car manufacture through Don Aldington, who was working for Bristol and whose brother, H.J. Aldington, was head of FRAZER NASH. 'H.J.' had a high regard for the BMW 328 engine and its designer Fritz Fiedler, and had sold a number of 328s and other BMW models in England under the name Frazer Nash-BMW. In 1945 the brothers decided that the BMW engine should be used in two new British cars, a luxury sporting saloon called the Frazer Nash Bristol, and an open sports car called the Frazer Nash. When the first Bristol appeared in September 1946 it had lost the Frazer Nash part of its name, and was more of a coupé than a saloon. Its styling resembled a BMW 327 with more rounded lines that had benefited from wind tunnel testing. The 1971cc engine, with Fiedler's ingenious cross-shaft head avoiding the need for twin camshafts developed 85bhp with three carburettors, though some of the earlier examples had less powerful single-carb units. The first engine was bench-tested in May 1946, and a complete car was running by July. Though some were made in the latter half of 1946, including two drophead coupés, the 400, as it was called, did not make a public debut until the Geneva Show in March 1947. The price in England was a hefty £2724, more than a 3.5-litre Jaguar, but enough customers were happy to pay over the odds for Bristol's combination of quality and individuality, a situation which has continued up to the present day.

The production 400 was made only as a 2-door coupé, though in addition to the two dropheads, 'specials' included some estate cars. These were aimed at the avoidance of Purchase Tax, a device also used by other quality British carmakers such as Alvis and Lea-Francis. A total of 474 400s were made between 1947 and 1950, but in 1948 it was joined by the 401. This had a longer and more streamlined coupé body whose styling was based on a Superleggera Touring of Milan design, though refined by Dudley Hobbs working with Bristol's wind tunnel. The 401 used the chassis and running gear of the 400. Announced at the same time was the 402, a drophead version of which only 23 were made, compared with 611 coupés. In 1953 the 401 was replaced by the 403, similar in appearance, but with a new crankshaft and camshaft, and with larger valves

1953 Bristol (iii) 403 saloon.
NATIONAL MOTOR MUSEUM

which gave 100bhp. It was a considerable improvement over the 401, but competition from other makes, in particular Jaguar, hampered sales, and only 281 were delivered up to 1955.

An addition to the range in 1953 was the 404, a 2-seater coupé built on the shorter chassis used for the ARNOLT-BRISTOL. Its rectangular hollow grill marked the end of the BMW-derived grilles, and it was a handsome car with a 110mph (177km/h) top speed, but at twice the price of a Jaguar XK140 it was hardly a bargain, and only 52 were sold. The hollow grille was also seen on the 405 (1954–58) which was the only 4-door saloon that Bristol has ever made. A Laycock de Normanville overdrive was standard, and the 405 was the first Bristol to have an opening boot. It acquired front disc brakes in 1958. 308 were made, including 43 2-door dropheads by Abbott.

New Engines, New Owners

In 1958 the familiar 1971cc engine was enlarged to 2216cc in the 406 saloon, but a much more significant change came with the 407 in 1963. At the end of 1959 a 3650cc twin-ohc engine was ready, but funds were not available for it to be put into production. Instead, Bristol tuned to an American unit, the 5130cc 250bhp V8 Chrysler. This was mated to a 3-speed Torqueflite automatic gearbox, and coil independent front suspension replaced the traditional BMW transverse springs. The 407's body was similar to that of the 406, a rather angular 2-door saloon.

In 1960 the Bristol Aeroplane Company merged with Hawker-Siddeley, which meant that they acquired car makers ARMSTRONG-SIDDELEY. There were plans to make a cheaper Bristol in larger numbers, but these were opposed by Sir George White, grandson of the aeroplane company's founder, and by Anthony Crook, ex-RAF pilot and a 1950s racing driver who sometimes out-drove Stirling Moss and Tony Brooks, and who was Bristol's London distributor. Together they formed a new company, Bristol Cars Ltd. White retired after a serious accident in 1969, and four years later Crook bought his shares to become sole owner, which he remains today.

Some body panels were made in London by Park Royal Vehicles of Acton around 1962–3, but the arrangement was not satisfactory, and since then the whole car has been built at Bristol, apart from the engine and transmission.

1950 Bristol (iii) 400 coupé.
NATIONAL MOTOR MUSEUM

1988 Bristol (iii) Beaufighter turbocharged convertible.
BRISTOL CARS

1907 Britannia (i) 24/40hp limousine.
NATIONAL MOTOR MUSEUM

Since the arrival of the 407, the Bristol story has been one of gradual evolution, with no dramatic new models. The size of the Chrysler engine was enlarged to 5211cc on the 409 (1966–7), to 6277cc on the 411 (1970–74), and to 6556cc on the 411 Mk II (1974–76). Among many improvements were power steering from 1966, dual-circuit brakes from 1968, and an optional turbocharger from 1978. Bodies have always been 2-door saloons, but in 1975 came a Targa-top convertible styled by Zagato, the 412. This was joined in 1976 by the 603, a completely restyled saloon. Bristols were given names for the first time in the 1980s, the Targa convertible becoming the Beaufighter (Beaufort without the Targa top), and the saloons the Britannia and (with turbocharger) the Brigand.

An improved Britannia, the Blenheim, came in 1993, and became the Blenheim 2 in 1998 and Blenheim 3 in 1999. Engine capacity was slightly down at 5898cc, dictated by the availability of the Chrysler unit, and the Torqueflite transmission now had four speeds, but the same design of box-section chassis, with steel frame supporting an aluminium body, followed many years of Bristol tradition. Production figures are not disclosed, but are believed to be less than 100 per year. Bristol has no need to advertise, and they have not taken a stand at a motor show since 1984.

NG

Further Reading
Bristol Cars and Engines, L.J.K. Setright, Motor Racing Publications, 1974.
Bristol – the Quiet Survivor, Charles Oxley, Charles Oxley, 1989.
Bristol, an Illustrated History, Charles Oxley, Crowood Press, 1990.
A Private Car. An account of the Bristol, L.J.K. Setright, Palawan Press, 1999.

BRIT (GB) 1902–1905
1902–1903 Hunt's Steam Sawmills & Carriage Accessories, Bridport, Dorset.
1903–1905 EA Chard & Co., Bridport, Dorset.
John Hunt obtained engineering experience in Bedminster, Bristol, before coming to Bridport. He considerably modified an early Daimler wagonette, constructing his own 2-cylinder replacement engine, as well as more obvious alterations, such as improved steering and a much larger radiator. The success of this effort caused him to offer complete vehicles to his own designs, named after the local river, but it was soon found that there was a steadier business in the manufacture of engines only. Brit marine engines were marketed successfully for many years.
DF

BRITANNIA (i) (GB) 1896–1899; 1906–1908
1896–1899 Britannia Electric Carriage Syndicate Ltd, Colchester, Essex.
1906–1908 Britannia Engineering Co. Ltd, Colchester, Essex.
Both Britannia companies were part of the Britannia Lathe & Oil Engine Co. Ltd, which had been founded in 1871. The electric cars closely resembled horse-drawn vehicles, body styles being landaus or barouches, with flowing lines. During their second phase of manufacture, Britannia made conventional petrol-engined cars with 12/18hp and 24/40hp 4-cylinder engines, and one 6-cylinder model with a 30/45hp engine.
NG

BRITANNIA (ii) (GB) 1913–1914
Britannia Engineering Co. Ltd, Nottingham.
The Britannia cyclecar was offered with an air-cooled 2-cylinder 2-stroke engine, but other engines could be fitted to the customer's choice. It had a 4-speed gearbox with belt final drive. The price was a modest £85.
NG

BRITANNIA (iii) (GB) 1957–1960
Britannia Cars Ltd, Ashwell, Hertfordshire.
Acland Geddes was a wealthy enthusiast who dreamed of making his own cars. In 1957 he commissioned John Tojeiro to design a GT car, a class which was then still novel in Britain.

The Britannia GT had a tubular chassis with all-independent suspension, a Raymond Mays-converted Ford Zephyr engine producing about 110bhp, and a pretty, but not exceptional, fibreglass body. To give Britannia provenance, Tojeiro designed cars for the new Formula Junior racing class.

The Britannia GT might have found a niche had it been offered as a knock-down kit and so escaped purchase tax. According to John Tojeiro, the entire project lacked direction and planning and when the Britannia GT came to the market in 1958 it cost £2400.

This was more than £400 above the price of a Jaguar XK150 so it is no surprise that Britannia folded in 1960 having made no more than six cars, not all of which were completed.
MJL

BRITISH (GB) 1905–1907
British Motor & Engineering Co. Ltd, London and Caversham, Reading, Berkshire.
The inappropriately named British car was based on imported parts, the engine deriving from the German FAFNIR concern. Initial productions were the Model 'A', a 6hp 2-cylinder and the Model 'B', a 4-cylinder rated at 10/12hp. Advanced features included a steering-column gearchange and a starting mechanism operated from the driving position, though the latter was mechanical, by means of a crankhandle connected to the engine by chain, rather than the electrical devices favoured later. Plans for expansion were not supported by adequate sales and production ceased after two seasons.
DF

BRITISH COACHWORKS (US) c.1980–1986
British Coach Works, Arnold, Pennsylvania.
The MG-TD was the visual target of this kit manufacturer. They made a rear-engined version to fit Volkswagen running gear and a front-engined model for Pinto drivetrains.
HP

BRITISH EAGLE see HODGSON

BRITISH ENSIGN (GB) 1919–1923
British Ensign Motors Ltd, Willesden, London.
Ensign Motors Ltd was founded in 1913 to market the ENSIGN, which was probably an imported car and also went under the name British Ensign. An Ensign truck was launched in December 1914 and made until 1923. In 1919, like Leyland, British Ensign decided to enter the luxury car market. They brought in Edward H. Gillett who had designed some steam vans and buses at the turn of the century. His design for British Ensign, known as the EP6, was a large and expensive car powered by a 6792cc 6-cylinder engine with pair-cast cylinders and single-ohc. It bore some resemblance to the Hispano-Suiza H6, but unlike the French design had a detachable cylinder head. The 3-speed gearbox was in unit with the engine, and final drive was by spiral bevel. It appeared at the London Motor Show at Olympia in 1919 as a chassis, under the name Ensign, but a year later it had been renamed British Ensign and was shown both in chassis form and with H.J. Mulliner pullman limousine body. It appeared again in 1921 when a price of £2325 was quoted for a complete car.

It was shown again in 1922, but with a different name, radiator and transmission. Called the Crown Ensign, it had a pointed radiator and the Entz magnetic transmission also used on the OWEN MAGNETIC. The Crown name came from an American, J.L. Crown, who had acquired the Entz patents, selling them

1920 British Ensign EP6 tourer.
NATIONAL MOTOR MUSEUM

to the Magnetic Motors Corp. of Chicago (see DEERING MAGNETIC) as well
as to Ensign and, later, to the Magnetic Car Co. of Chelsea (see MAGNETIC).
The EP6 was not made after 1923, and probably no more than 12 cars were
made.

In 1922 British Ensign launched a smaller assembled car called the Ensign
Twelve. It had a 1795cc Meadows engine and was made in 2- and 4-seater models.
At £465 it was expensive for what it offered, and only 37 were made. All Ensign
production had ended by late 1923, though the company entered the car field
again in 1926 with the £100 GILLETT.

NG

Further Reading
'Flying the Flag – the story of the British Ensign', M.J.Worthington-Williams,
The Automobile, January 1995.

BRITISH LION (GB) 1903–1904
British Lion Co., Leicester.
This company supplied a variety of components apart from engines, which they
said were easily available from other sources. Items they did provide included
artillery wheels, a bucket-seat body, live axles, tanks, bonnets, 3-speed + reverse
gearboxes, and, presumably chassis frames, though the latter did not appear in
their advertising. As the firm advertised that their components were available in
large quantities, they were apparently aiming at the trade rather than at kit car
builders.

NG

BRITISH SALMSON (GB) 1934–1939
British Salmson Aero Engines Ltd, Raynes Park, London.
This firm was established in 1930, taking over from the French-controlled
Moteurs Salmson with British capital provided by the Martineau family.
They hoped to supply engines for the light aircraft industry, but although some
were bought by British Klemm, and at least one powered a Cierva Autogiro,
they needed alternative work, and in 1934 began to make the SALMSON S4C
under licence from the French firm. The British Salmson had the same 1471cc
twin-ohc 4-cylinder engine but offered synchromesh on 3rd and top speeds of
the 4-speed gearbox which was not available on the French car, and bodies were
strictly English in style and manufacture, saloons and tourers by Ranalah and
Newns. The standard 12/55 engine gave 55bhp and a 70mph (112km/h) top
speed, but with the 70bhp twin-carburettor 12/70, it was good for 80mph
(130km/h). Production of all S4Cs was about 350.

In 1937 the S4C was replaced by the S4D, with the engine enlarged to 1596cc,
although heavier bodies meant that performance was no better than the S4C

1936 British Salmson S4C 12hp saloon.
NICK BALDWIN

1938 British Salmson 20/90 sports car.
NICK GEORGANO/NATIONAL MOTOR MUSEUM

12/55. On the first S4Ds the engine was bored out to give 1730cc, but this was
dangerously near the block's limit, and most of the c.75 S4Ds made had the
smaller engine. Bodies were a curved back 6-light saloon and a drophead, and
the S4D shared the transverse-leaf ifs and hydraulic brakes of the French
Salmsons. The last British Salmson had no French counterpart; the 20/90 had a
twin-ohc 6-cylinder engine of 2580cc giving 90bhp and a top speed in excess of
90mph (145km/h). The first cars had Bendix brakes, later replaced by Lockheed

1911 Briton (i) 10hp 2-seater.
NATIONAL MOTOR MUSEUM

c.1915 Broc electric coupé.
NATIONAL MOTOR MUSEUM

hydraulics. Though only 12 20/90s were made, there were four body styles, 2-seater sports with slab-tank or sloping rear ends, a drophead, and a 2-door sports saloon. The last was delivered in 1939, but 4-cylinder production ended in 1938, the company finding that it was more profitable to import French Salmsons. They remained active in general engineering, and from 1950 to 1952 they made the 31cc Cyclaid engine for motorising bicycles. The factory was later used for jam manufacture, and British Salmson moved to Glasgow where they made printing presses.

NG

BRITOMOBILE (GB)

American steam car imported into GB, probably Locomobile.

NG

BRITON (i) (GB) 1909–1928

1909–1912 Briton Motor Co. Ltd, Wolverhampton, Staffordshire.
1912–1928 Briton Motor Co. (1912) Ltd, Wolverhampton, Staffordshire.
The Briton was developed from the Starling, a small car made by the Star Cycle Co. Ltd which was a wholly-owned subsidiary of Star Engineering Ltd, makers of the STAR (i). In 1909 the Cycle Co. changed its name to Briton, and the 2-cylinder Starling was continued under the new name, together with a 10hp four. Briton was run by Edward Lisle Jr, son of Edward Lisle Sr who had founded

the Star company and was still Chairman and Managing Director. The twin was dropped in 1911, and in 1913 Briton introduced a new 10hp 4-cylinder model with a capacity of 1750cc. In 1912 Briton production was moved from the Star factory to premises of its own, also in Wolverhampton.

Like so many other car makers, Briton flourished during World War I with military contracts. They entered the postwar market with two models of 4-cylinder light car, the 1373cc 9.8hp and 1743cc 10/12hp. They were expensive for their size, and in 1922 the company went into liquidation. It was bought by C.A. Weight who continued the two models up to 1928. After he discontinued the cars, he took on the agency for Caterpillar Tractors. About 600 cars were made under the Weight regime out of an estimated total of 1400 for all postwar production.

NG

BRITON (ii) see KESTREL and E.W.M.

BRIXIA-ZÜST see ZÜST

B.R.M. (GB) 1991

Mangoletsi, Cheshire.
One of the most famous names in motor racing history was set to become a road car manufacturer in the early 1990s, although ultimately economic circumstances persuaded them otherwise. The then owners of the B.R.M. name, Rubery Owen, teamed up with engineering firm Mangoletsi and ex-Zakspeed F1 engineer Paul Brown to design a new car for Group C racing and for road use. A new 3.5-litre V12 engine was designed by Terry Hoyle (lately of Cosworth Engineering), claimed to produce 400bhp, and a second twin-supercharged 4.0-litre V12 was designed for racing. Plans were revealed to enter production at a rate of 50–100 cars a year, starting from 1993, at a price of £200,000, and scale models were shown. Nothing further was heard of the project.

CR

BROADBEST (GB) 1987–1988

Broadbest, Poole, Dorset.
To Broadbest goes the doubtful honour of building the world's first driveable Lamborghini Countach replica, developed from the VENOM, with a space frame chassis engineered by G.T.D. Called the Primo, Rover V8 engines and Renault 30 transaxles were fitted.

CR

BROADWAY (GB) 1913

Broadway Cyclecar Co., Coventry.
This was a simple cyclecar powered by a German-made 8hp air-cooled V-twin Fafnir engine. It had two speeds and belt final drive. Steering was by wire cable and bobbin, and the price was a modest £80.

NG

BROC (US) 1909–1916

1909–1910 Broc Carriage & Wagon Co., Cleveland, Ohio.
1910–1914 Broc Electric Vehicle Co., Cleveland, Ohio.
1914–1916 Broc Electric Vehicle Co., Saginaw, Michigan.
The Broc Carriage & Wagon Co. began building bodies in 1904 and five years later launched a range of four electric cars: two coupés, a stanhope, and a victoria. They were quite typical of American electrics of the period; the Model 19 roadster of 1911 had a bonnet giving the appearance of a petrol car, but this was also featured by several other manufacturers. There was a considerable improvement in appearance between 1912 and 1914 when even the coupé had lower and more rounded lines. Brocs were offered with a choice of wheel or tiller steering and chain or shaft drive. In 1914 Broc merged with ARGO (i) and BORLAND to form the American Electric Car Co. Production was transferred to Saginaw, but the Broc name was continued for two years more.

NG

BROCK (CDN) 1921

Brock Motors Ltd, Amherstberg, Ontario.
The Brock had its origins in the plans of baker and car salesman William Riley Stansell to build a car in the former AMHERST factory. He incorporated a company

called Stansell Motors Ltd, but before any cars were built it had been reorganised by the shareholders as Brock Motors, with Stansell relegated to the position of manager. Only one Brock Six was completed, a conventional tourer powered by a 55bhp Continental engine. Stansell then moved to London, Ontario, where he made the LONDON SIX.

NG

BROCKLEBANK (GB) 1927–1929

Brocklebank & Richards Ltd, Birmingham.

Described as 'Birmingham's answer to the US challenge', the Brocklebank was planned by Major John Brocklebank and designed by R.W. Richards. Both men were enthusiasts for the flexible American 6-cylinder engine, and Richards had worked at the Essex factory in Detroit in the early 1920s. Admittedly the Essex at that time was a four, but he would have been familiar with the 6-cylinder Hudson made by the parent firm, and Brocklebank was a Hudson owner. The pushrod ohv engine Richards designed was smaller than any American six, having a capacity of 2051cc. Axles and 3-speed gearbox were made by Warner in the US, and the rather angular 4-door saloon body came from P.W. Watson & Sons Ltd of Lowestoft, Suffolk. An advanced feature was the use of Lockheed hydraulic brakes.

The company was formed and a specification published in 1925, but the Brocklebank's first appearance at a show was in October 1927. Production began earlier that year, and quite a number were sold in Australia and New Zealand. A repeat order for 100 cars was reported from those countries in June 1927. At the 1928 Olympia Show more attractive bodies were exhibited, an aluminium-panelled saloon by Gordon England and a fabric saloon by Weymann. Open 2- and 4/5- seater models were also listed, but it is not known how many were made. The company failed during 1929; Sir Herbert Austin considered buying the factory but thought the price asked by the liquidators was too high. Spares were bought by Smith's Garage of Birmingham who ordered one Meadows 6-cylinder engine, indicating that they contemplated restarting manufacture. However this never happened. Estimates of Brocklebank production vary between 350 and 600.

NG

Further Reading
'The Brocklebank Six', M.J.Worthington-Williams, *The Automobile*, December 1994.

BROCKMORE (GB) 1993–1994

Brockmore Classic Replicas, Brierley Hill, West Midlands.
This was the production version of a Triumph TR2/TR3 replica first seen in prototype form in 1991 from a company called Grand Illusions. It was offered as a Ford-based kit (Cortina front suspension and Sierra rear suspension), or as a conversion of the Triumph Spitfire.

CR

BROCKVILLE; BROCKVILLE ATLAS (CDN) 1911–1914

1911 Carriage Factories Ltd, Brockville, Ontario.
1912–1914 Brockville Atlas Auto Co. Ltd, Brockville, Ontario.
The Brockville was made by a company that had originated as the Canada Carriage Co. before the turn of the century. In 1909 it was taken over by Carriage Factories Ltd, and Canada Carriage's owner Thomas J. Storey found himself with an under-used factory. Deciding to enter the car business he began with the Brockville 30 which was really an EVERITT, assembled from parts supplied by the TUDHOPE factory at Orillia, Ontario, who were also making the Everitt.

After about 80 Brockville 30s had been assembled, Storey and his son Fred launched a car of their own design which they called the Brockville Atlas in view of the fact that its 4-cylinder engine was made by the Atlas Engine Works of Indianapolis. In fact most of the car's chassis and mechanical parts were imported too, but the bodies were built in the former carriage factory. Touring, roadster, and landaulette styles were available. In 1914, following the death of the man who was responsible for building the wooden bodies, the Storeys turned to steel construction, but this was unsuccessful, as was the new model powered by a 6-cylinder Rutenber engine. Production ceased at the end of 1914, after about 300 Brockville Atlases had been made. The factory was later used for the manufacture of the Canadian Briscoe.

NG

1927 Brocklebank 15hp saloon.
NATIONAL MOTOR MUSEUM

BROGAN (US) 1946–1951

B&B Specialty Co., Rossmoyne, Ohio.
A series of extremely small passenger and commercial vehicles was made under the Brogan name just after the war. All were 3-wheelers, some with a single front wheel and others with a single rear, and both 2- and 4-seater versions were offered, the latter with the name Broganette. A small Onan 2-cylinder air-cooled 10bhp engine was rear-mounted and a clutchless transmission was used. Some early models were sold under the name B&B Three Wheel.

CR

BROLGA (AUS) 1969

Kemproof Industrial Plastics, Dee Why, New South Wales.
Designed and built by Nick Gracc, this sports coupé was notable for its very low overall height of 37in (940mm). A mid-engine layout coupled a 1498cc Ford Cortina GT engine to a reversed Volkswagen transaxle. Its seating was set so far forward that the pedals were ahead of the front axle line, a feature also contributed to by a wheelbase of only 82in (2082mm). Of eye-catching form with a sharp nose to an almost horizontal rear window and a Kamm-inspired tail, the body was mounted on a rigid box form structure incorporating roll-over bars. It featured gull-wing doors and one-piece lift-up front and rear sections. The Brolga is Australia's only crane, noted for graceful dance routines.

MG

BROMPTON (GB) 1921

The London-built Brompton cyclecar was unusual in having front-wheel drive and independent suspension by coils on all four wheels. It was powered by a MAG V-twin engine.

NG

BROOK (US) 1920–1921

Spacke Machine Tool Co., Indianapolis, Indiana.
The Brook was the renamed cycle car which had been marketed as the SPACKE in 1919. The 2-cylinder Brook was available only in its 2-seater All-Weather model which had an interesting name considering the Brook was sold without either doors or a roof. Probably under 25 cars of its Model S-21 were completed in 1921 when the car was taken over by the Peters Motor Corporation of Pleasantville, New Jersey.

KM

BROOKE (i) (GB) 1901–1913

J.W. Brooke & Co. Ltd, Lowestoft, Suffolk.
This company was founded in 1875 under the Brooke name, though an earlier business on the same site dated from 1866. They were millwrights, boiler makers, and iron and brass founders, and were also celebrated for their marine engines. Their first car was tested in 1901 and put on the market early the following year.

c.1903 Brooke (i) 14hp tonneau.
NATIONAL MOTOR MUSEUM

1902 Brooks (i) 8hp 4-seater.
NATIONAL MOTOR MUSEUM

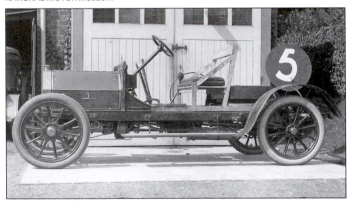

c.1908 Brooks & Woollan 15.9hp.
NATIONAL MOTOR MUSEUM

It had a 10hp 3-cylinder vertical engine derived from a marine unit mounted transversely under a small bonnet. It drove by chains to an all-chain gearbox, and final drive was also by chains. In 1903 it was joined by a new model with longitudinal 14hp engine, also of three cylinders, which drove by shaft to the all-chain gearbox. These early cars had a bowl in the centre of the steering wheel to hold small articles such as goggles and gloves. A more conventional range came in 1905, with 4-cylinder engines of 15/20 and 35hp and conventional sliding gearboxes. By this time cars accounted for about 75 per cent of Brooke's business, the rest coming from marine engines. Brooke's first 6-cylinder car, and their first shaft-driven model, was announced in the summer of 1906. It was of 25/30hp and 4784cc, and was joined by a 6592cc 40hp six in 1907; thereafter all Brooke cars had six cylinders. Production dwindled after about 1908, though *The Autocar* listed the cars up to 1910 and some lists carried them until 1913. A most unusual car powered by a Brooke engine was the 'swan car' built by R. N. Mathewson, an

Englishman resident in Calcutta, in 1909. The chassis and body, which featured a swan's beak which opened and shut with a hissing sound, and could even be made to eject a stream of water, were made in India, and the car then shipped to Lowestoft for the 6-cylinder engine to be fitted. This car survives today, together with a junior version for children.

NG

BROOKE (ii) (GB) 1991 to date

1991–1993 Brooke Motor Co., Norwich, Norfolk.
1993–1996 Brooke Cars, Loddon, Norfolk.
1996 to date Brooke Kensington, Bicester, Oxfordshire.

Toby Sutton launched the Brooke 245 in 1991, a Grand Prix-style car which, in kit form, cost £2000. It was based on Renault 5 parts using a front-mounted engine and steel tube/box chassis. It looked like a single-seater, but a section of the evocative rear hump could be removed, turning the glassfibre car into a tandem 2-seater. With the ME190 of 1994 the concept matured: the seating was now side by side and the engine was now mounted amidships. The powerplant was a tuned 16-valve Vauxhall Cavalier 2-litre unit, developing nearly 190bhp (ME stood for mid-engine, 190 indicated the power output). The space frame chassis had double wishbone and coil spring suspension all round and the transmission was a Renault 5-speed manual. The ME190 proved popular as a fully-built car in Japan but remained available in kit form in Britain.

CR

BROOKLAND (GB) 1993–1994

The Brookland Motor Co., London.

Kit car journalist Iain Ayre made the Brookland Swallow, a 1960s-style trike based on Mini parts. The steel chassis was strong, and there was space for four passengers, but this meant the car was overweight and so never reached production. Shortly after announcing the Speed Six, a Jaguar XK120 replica, the company was forced to change its name to AYRESPEED.

CR

BROOKLANDS see (GB) SAFIR

BROOKS (i) (GB) 1902

Brooks Motor Co. Ltd, Foleshill, Coventry.

Described as a 'light motor phaeton', the Brooks was available with 2- or 4-seater bodies, and was powered by an 8 or 12hp vertical twin Belgian-built Pinart engine. Transmission was by a Brooks-designed 3-speed gearbox and final drive was by shaft to a live rear axle. The Brooks was also offered with a 10cwt delivery van body.

NG

BROOKS (ii) (CDN) 1923–1929

Brooks Steam Motors Ltd, Stratford, Ontario.

The Brooks Steam Car was the second most popular steam car in America during the 1920s, some 180 units comprising the total output of the company. Excepting the lone prototype touring car of 1923, all Brooks cars were fabric-covered 4-door sedans featuring a 2-cylinder engine similar to that of the Stanley. Oland J. Brooks, an American who headed the enterprise, also formed two taxicab companies in Stratford and Toronto which were served exclusively by Brooks Steamers. Priced at CDN$3885 initially, the figure was reduced to CDN$2885 in 1927, the year the company was placed in receivership. In 1929 remaining Brooks cars were auctioned off at CDN$150 to CDN$400 apiece.

KM

BROOKS & WOOLLAN (GB) 1907–1910

Brooks & Woollan, Caversham, Reading, Berkshire.

This firm advertised a bespoke car construction service, using proprietary parts to suit the taste and pocket of the customer. Woolland claimed 'many years experience' in motor manufacture and was held in high regard by Bernard Secretan, a surgeon at the Royal Berkshire Hospital, who claimed to have made the first climb of Porlock Hill in a small car with a 7hp White and Poppe-engined Swift in 1906. In 1908 Secretan commissioned a 15.9hp White and Poppe-engined car with initially a 2-seater Victoria body, which gave great satisfaction on overseas tours and also ran in stripped form at Brooklands. Despite such success there were few other takers, notwithstanding the Greek soubriquet of 'Doru' and the slogan 'Swift and Silent as the Spear'. The firm developed instead their coachbuilding activities, particularly on the larger De Dion Bouton chassis, and later prospered as Caversham Motors Ltd.

DF

BROOKVILLE ROADSTERS (US) c.1988–1994
Brookville Roadsters Inc., Brookville, Ohio.
This all-steel reproduction of the Ford Model A roadster was sold in kit form with a custom frame, General Motors steering, and was set up for a Chevrolet 5700cc engine.

HP

BROOMSTICK (GB) 1993 to date
Broomstick Cars Ltd, Leighton Buzzard, Bedfordshire.
The Broomstick BS120 was a fairly accurate glassfibre replica of the Jaguar XK120, made by a commercial vehicle engineering and restoration firm. The ladder chassis duplicated the original Jaguar chassis quite closely, and there were all-XJ mechanicals. An alternative body style was offered in the form of a different front end featuring recessed cowled headlamps that were reminiscent of the C-Type Jaguar.

CR

BROTHERHOOD (GB) 1904–1907
1904–1906 Brotherhood-Crocker Motors Ltd, West Norwood, London.
1906–1907 Brotherhood-Crocker Motors Ltd, Sheffield, Yorkshire.
The Brotherhood was designed by Percy Richardson, formerly of DAIMLER (ii), and made by a subsidiary of the large engineering firm, Peter Brotherhood, which had been formed in 1867. Their main factory was on the South Bank of the Thames near Westminster Bridge, and it is likely that the car's components were made there and assembled at West Norwood. The directors were Stanley Brotherhood and Jonathan Crocker, and a major shareholder was the Yorkshire landowner and coal magnate Earl Fitzwilliam. The car was a high-quality product with 12/16hp pair-cast 4-cylinder engine and double-chain drive. It was succeeded in 1905 by a larger car with 20hp engine and only two pedals, the functions of brake and clutch being combined in one. The accelerator worked in an arc rather than an up-and-down movement.

Not long after production of the 20hp started, the parent company sold their London premises, which became the site of County Hall, and moved to Peterborough where they still exist today, now under American ownership. They could not obtain planning permission for a car factory at Peterborough, but Earl Fitzwilliam suggested a move to Sheffield. 'We make the steel in Sheffield; why are the cars made in London, Birmingham and Coventry?' he asked. He spent £10,990 on the erection of a factory at Tinsley on the eastern outskirts of Sheffield, and it was completed in July 1906. Although the Brotherhoods no longer had any connection with the cars, the company continued to trade under the Brotherhood-Crocker name, with Percy Richardson still in charge of design, up to late 1907. In November of that year a new car was announced under the name SHEFFIELD SIMPLEX; it bore little resemblance to the Brotherhood, though Richardson remained as chief designer.

NG

Further Reading
Cars From Sheffield, Stephen Myers, Sheffield City Libraries, 1986.

BROUGH SUPERIOR (GB) 1935–1939
Brough Superior Cars Ltd, Nottingham.
Brough Superior is more familiar for its motorcycles and it was advertised as 'The Rolls-Royce of Motorcycles'. George Brough put around a story that he had Rolls-Royce's permission to use its name, but the phrase was in inverted commas because it was a quote from a journalist.

Despite their reputation, Brough's motorcycles were assemblages of proprietary components, plus a distinctive fuel tank and a large dash of showmanship. Every original project which Brough undertook was stillborn.

Brough Superior cars were also assemblages. Starting in 1935, Brough bought Hudson chassis for £85 and had the coachbuilder, Atcherly, fit a 4-seat drophead body for £125. The cars featured such items as automatic chassis lubrication and built-in jacks, but claims that the engines were tuned should be treated with scepticism.

1905 Brotherhood 20hp tourer, Percy Richardson at the wheel.
NATIONAL MOTOR MUSEUM

1935 Brough Superior 4.2-litre drophead coupé.
NATIONAL MOTOR MUSEUM

Brough 4-litre cars, made 1935–6, had the 4168cc straight-8 Hudson engine. Railton, which also used the engine, objected and Brough had to take the Hudson Six, with its 3455cc 6-cylinder engine and shorter chassis. The Brough 3.5-litres was available with a Centric supercharger, when 99mph was claimed. There was also a lighter model, with a sports body, called the Alpine. About 70 Hudson-powered cars were made.

In 1938 came the larger Brough XII with a Charlesworth body, a 4387cc Lincoln V12 engine and a chassis designed by Brough. It was handsome, but heavy, slow and expensive. Only one was made.

After 1939 Brough turned to precision engineering.

MJL

BROUHOT (F) 1898–1911
Brouhot et Cie, Vierzon, Cher.
Charles Brouhot started an agricultural engineering business towards the end of the 19th century, making threshing machines and stationary engines which could run on petrol, paraffin or alcohol. In 1898 he set up a separate automobile division, making a car with a 3hp single-cylinder engine mounted horizontally at the rear, hot-tube ignition, tubular frame, and a 3-speed gearbox with spur gear drive to the rear axle. This was quickly replaced by an improved model with 2-cylinder engine quoted as of either 5 or 7hp, electric ignition, four forward speeds and 2- or 4-seater bodywork. This was shown at the Salon du Cycle in Paris in 1898. The engine was moved to the front on the 1902 7hp single-cylinder voiturette, and in 1903 larger cars with 10hp twin and 15 and 20hp 4-cylinder engines and double-chain drive were made. There was also a 40hp 8013cc racing car built for the Paris–Madrid race, which may have been a one-off. It crashed near Angouleme, killing the mechanic as well as a soldier and a young man among the spectators. Brouhot never raced again.

Coil ignition gave way to Simms-Bosch magneto on most models in 1905, when there were five engine sizes offered, from 15hp (3306cc) to 40hp (8013cc). An even larger model was offered in 1906, the 60hp of 10,560cc, but very few of these were sold because of their high price. Brouhots were cars of top quality, rivals to the products of De Dietrich or Delaunay-Belleville, though not so well known.

1907 Brouhot tourer by Barker.
NATIONAL MOTOR MUSEUM

1904 Brown (i) 6hp 2-seater.
NATIONAL MOTOR MUSEUM

One customer was the King of Portugal who bought a limousine. They were sold on the UK market under the names Club and Smart. Forward-control commercials were added to the range in 1906, and 1908 saw a curious voiturette powered by a single-cylinder 9hp engine with transverse crankshaft and final drive by belt. This did not please traditional Brouhot customers, though it was included in the catalogue until the end of car production in 1911. More attractive was the final model, a 15hp four of 1942cc with monobloc engine and shaft drive. By this date some of the larger Brouhots were also shaft driven.

Car production ended in 1911, probably because they were becoming harder to sell in the face of competition from larger makes, and Brouhot wanted to concentrate on the agricultural side of the business, to which cars had always been secondary. They became bankrupt in 1914 because of the failure of an Argentine associate, and were taken over by the Société Française de Vierzon Matériel Agricole, who made steam traction engines from 1915 and agricultural tractors under the name SFV up to 1959.

NG

Further Reading
'De la Batteuse à l'Auto – Brouhot de Vierzon', J-R Dulier,
l'Album du Fanatique, September–November 1977.

BROWN (i) (GB) 1900–1913

Brown Bros Ltd, London.
Brown Brothers were famous motor factors, selling a great variety of accessories and components of all kinds for cars, motorcycles, and bicycles. Founded in 1888 it became a limited company in 1897 and two years later they offered motor tricycles and a light steam car. This was the American WHITNEY (i) which they sold under the name Brown-Whitney. In 1901 they began to offer cars under the Brown name, though the origin of these is uncertain, as were most subsequent Browns. Certainly they had no manufacturing premises in their large emporium in Great Eastern Street. Some cars were made by STAR (i) with bodies by Salmons. They were shaft-driven light cars with 3-speed gearboxes

and automatic-inlet-valve Aster engines in 6hp single- or 8hp 2-cylinder models. The catalogue stated that almost any kind of engine could be fitted. A surviving 18/20hp of 1905 has a 4-cylinder Brotherhood-Crocker engine, and the 1906 Brown 12/16hp was powered by a Forman engine. At the 1906 Olympia Show there were three fours, of 18/20, 20/22, and 24hp, and a 40hp six, though 2-cylinder models were still listed in 1908, one being a large brake with solid tyres. Also in 1908 Brown launched a new make, the ALBRUNA, which represented the smaller end of the range, while Browns were larger. In the last year that they were listed, there was a 20/22hp four and a 35hp six. The Albruna survived into 1912, and motorcycles were continued up to 1929, the postwar ones being sold under the name Vindec. Brown Brothers were still issuing their famous catalogues in 1998.

NG

BROWN (ii) (US) 1914

Brown Cyclecar Co., Asbury Park, New Jersey.
This company made two models, a typical cyclecar powered by a 10hp 2-cylinder Spacke engine and belt drive, and the Monmouth Raceabout. This had a 20hp 4-cylinder engine and shaft drive. Bankruptcy followed the company's formation in less than 12 months.

NG

BROWN (iii) (US) 1916

Brown Carriage Co., Cincinnati, Ohio.
This carriage company made a late entry into the automobile business, offering a conventional tourer powered by a 4-cylinder Le Roi engine.

NG

BROWNIE (US) 1916

J.O. Carter, Hannibal, Missouri.
This was simply the CARTERMOBILE (i) renamed, with a reduction in price from US$985 to US$735. This did not seem to help the rather undistinguished car to sell any better, and although Carter claimed late in 1916 that his car was being made by the Carter Manufacturing Co. in Detroit, nothing more was heard of the project.

NG

BROWNIEKAR (US) 1908–1911

Omar Motor Co., Newark, New Jersey.
This was a very small 2-seater roadster on a 66in (1676mm) wheelbase powered by a 3hp single-cylinder engine which gave it a top speed of 10mph (16km/h). It was described as 'a toy designed for harmless sport and amusement of the young folks' and it was claimed that it could be operated by any intelligent child of 8 years or more. The price was a modest $150. It was designed by William H. Birdsall, chief engineer of the MORA company. The maker's name Omar, was a convenient anagram of Mora.

NG

BRUBAKER BOX (US) 1972

The Brubaker Group, Los Angeles, California.
Although originally intended as a kit car, the Brubaker Box was produced as a fully assembled vehicle. It was an advanced mini-van design that used a Volkswagen Beetle floorpan and running gear. Designed by industrial designer Curtis Brubaker, it received tremendous publicity and much public interest. It was spacious and more civilised than most kit cars. Unfortunately, VW would not sell new chassis without bodies, so Brubaker had to buy new cars and sell the bodywork to repair shops before adding his shell. Although the Box showed great promise, the price ended up being too high and only three were built. The project was sold to AUTOMECCA.

HP

BRULE-PONSARD (F) 1900–1901

H. Brule et Cie, Paris.
This was a 2-wheeled *avant-train* unit which provided a self-contained method of motorising horse-drawn vehicles. It was powered by a 4.5hp Rozer et Mazurier 3-cylinder engine, in which the exhaust gases from two cylinders actuated the third at lower pressure. This system was also used in the COMPOUND car.

NG

1904 Brush (i) Brushmobile 6hp 2-seater.
NATIONAL MOTOR MUSEUM

BRUNAU-WEIDMANN (CH) 1907
Automobilfabrik J. Weidmann & Co., Brunau, Zurich.
J. Weidmann had produced parts and clutches for other companies' cars for some time, before building the first commercial vehicles under his own name in 1905. Two years later he displayed two advanced 'Alpina' passenger cars at the Zürich Automobile Exhibition. The 14/18PS with monobloc 4-cylinder engine and shaft drive had an attractive coupé de ville body, while the equally attractive limousine of basically similar design had the 20/24 PS engine. Weidmann seriously considered taking part in the Peking–Paris race of 1907 and prepared a tourer, but ultimately did not start. In 1908 he ceased production of his own vehicles and instead produced the FISCHER and later the HELIOS cars under contract.
FH

BRUNN (US) 1906–1911
Brunn Carriage Manufacturing Co., Buffalo, New York.
Founded in the middle of the 19th century by Henry Brunn, this respected carriage maker built a few electric cars. The 1906 models were marketed by James McNaughton, also of Buffalo, while a 1910 car was sold as the Clark Electric. The famous automobile coachbuilder, Hermann Brunn & Co., was founded in 1908 by a nephew of Henry Brunn.
NG

BRUNNER (US) 1910
Brunner Motor Car Co., Buffalo, New York.
This company was mainly a maker of delivery vans with 16hp 2-cylinder engines, epicyclic gearboxes and shaft drive. A touring car was also available on the same chassis. An unusual feature of the Brunner design was a separate silencer for each cylinder.
NG

BRUNSWICK (US) 1916–1917
Brunswick Motor Car Co., Newark, New Jersey.
In general appearance the Brunswick was a conventional 5-seater tourer powered by a 4-cylinder Wisconsin engine. Closer inspection revealed such luxury items as a Waltham clock in both front and rear compartments, and cabinets in the rear for sandwiches, thermos flasks, and other requisites for a civilised picnic. However, the price of US$1950 was too low for a profit to be made, and probably no more than prototypes of the Brunswick were made.
NG

BRUSH (i) (GB) 1902–1904
1902–1904 Brush Electrical Engineering Co. Ltd, Lambeth, London.
1904 Brush Electrical Engineering Co. Ltd, Loughborough, Leicestershire.
Founded in 1880 as the Anglo-American Brush Electric Light Corp., this company changed its name to Brush Electrical Engineering in 1889. Their headquarters were at Loughborough, but cars were made initially at the London branch. Brush held the agency for the French SAGE car, and the first Brushes were not unlike the French product, having 10hp 2-cylinder Abeille engines, Sage 3-speed gearboxes, and chain drive. Larger cars with 4-cylinder 12, 16, and 20hp engines followed in 1903, and were made up to September 1904. Meanwhile a completely different design was made at Loughborough. Sometimes called the Brushmobile, it had a 5 or 6hp horizontal single-cylinder engine with single-chain drive and coil springs all round. It was in fact, a Vauxhall with a different bonnet; some were made in the Vauxhall factory, which at that time was at Wandsworth, in south west London. After 1904 Brush made no more passenger cars, though they continued with heavy commercial vehicle chassis at Loughborough up to 1910, and a subsidiary, Brush Coachworks Ltd, made a large number of bus and coach bodies up to 1952. Brush returned to commercial vehicles in 1946 with a range of 3- and 4-wheeled battery electric vans and milk floats, which were made up to 1968.
NG

c.1908 Brush (ii) 12hp runabout.
NATIONAL MOTOR MUSEUM

1957 Brütsch Rollera 49cc 3-wheeler.
NATIONAL MOTOR MUSEUM

1958 Brütsch V2N 2-seater.
NATIONAL MOTOR MUSEUM

BRUSH (ii) (US) 1907–1913

Brush Runabout Co., Detroit, Michigan.

This was a popular 2-seater runabout designed by Alanson Partridge Brush (1878–1952) who had designed the engine of the first single-cylinder Cadillac, and manufactured by Frank Briscoe in his radiator factory in Detroit. It had a 6hp single-cylinder engine, wooden frame and axles (oak, hickory, and maple) and coil springs all round. Among unusual features of the original Runabout were counter-clockwise rotation of the engine, left hand drive, solid tyres, and a curious friction clutch which was said to eliminate the need for a gearbox. It was hastily replaced by a 2-speed epicyclic transmission for 1908, and the solid tyres were supplemented by pneumatics in 1908 and only available to special order after 1910. A Brush with a 2-cylinder engine, longer wheelbase, and dickey seat was seen at the 1908 New York Auto Show, but does not seem to have gone into production. A 4-seater and a closed coupé appeared in 1910 and delivery vans were also made.

In 1909 Briscoe built a new factory for manufacture of the Brush, which he said would be the largest in the automobile business. Production jumped from about 2000 in 1909 to 10,000 a year later. In 1910 Frank's brother Benjamin Briscoe formed the United States Motor Corp. as a reply to Billy Durant's General Motors. It was a vast and unwieldy conglomerate, with six car makers and about 130 component firms. Of the car makers, only Brush and Maxwell were profitable, but funds were switched around between the various divisions of the corporation which did not help Brush. Also the market for single-cylinder cars was dwindling. A basic 2-seater called the Liberty-Brush was introduced in 1912, and was the only model for 1913. At $350 it was very cheap, but production did not last out the year 1913. A.P. Brush, meanwhile, had left the company to join Oakland, for which he designed a 2-cylinder engine, also with counter-clockwise rotation. He later set up a consultancy with his brother William, and made many useful contributions to car design, including the double transverse rear suspension used on the Marmon 34, Monroe, Saxon-Duplex, and Elgin, and the Z-section frame in which the running boards stiffened the main frame.

NG

Further Reading

'The Brush Runabout: Everyman's Car', James Zordich, *Automobile Quarterly*, Vol. 24, No. 3.

BRÜTSCH (D) 1951–1958

Egon Brütsch Fahrzeugbau, Stuttgart.

Brütsch built a number of prototype small cars, but none saw series production. His first, the Brütsch 1200, had a fibreglass 2-seater body with Ford Taunus 12M running gear, while the most unusual was the Mopetta or Rollera single-seater 3-wheeler. Powered by a 49cc single-cylinder engine driving one of the rear wheels, it was only 67in (1700mm) long and weighed 134lb (61kg). It was probably the smallest car ever made. In 1957 Georg von Opel, a member of the OPEL family though not connected with the firm, planned to make it under the name Opelit, but nothing came of this. Brütsch's 3-wheeled designs went into production in France as the AVOLETTE and in Switzerland as the BELCAR.

HON

BRYAN (US) 1918–1923

Bryan Steam Motors, Peru, Indiana.

Bryan Steam Motors was headed by George A. Bryan, a pioneer in modern steam engineering who formed his manufacturing company with the main purpose of building steam vehicles. A steam truck and steam tractor showed considerable promise but never got beyond the testing stage. All told, he also completed six cars all differing from each other in appearance, but proving successful. Five of these prototypes were almost certainly touring cars, although a sixth may have been a closed brougham which was sketched on a 1921 Bryan brochure. Bryan later concentrated his efforts on gas and oil burners for use in domestic heating.

KM

B.S. *see* E.W.M.

B.S.A. (GB) 1907–1926; 1929–1940

1907–1924 Birmingham Small Arms Co. Ltd, Birmingham.
1923–1926; 1933–1936 Birmingham Small Arms Co. Ltd, Coventry.
1929–1940 B.S.A Cycles Ltd, Birmingham.

Although the Birmingham Small Arms Co. was formed as a limited company in 1861, its origins date back to more than 160 years earlier. When King William III complained that he had to go to Holland to buy satisfactory weapons, the MP for Warwick, Sir Richard Newdegate, secured a Royal contract for leading Birmingham gunsmiths to produced 200 muskets at 17 shillings (85p) each.

In the late 19th century B.S.A.'s main activity was the manufacture of machine guns, shotguns, and rifles, to which they added bicycles in 1880. Apart from a gap between 1888 and 1893, B.S.A. cycles were made continuously until about 1982, although owned by Raleigh Industries from 1956. Their first involvement with cars came in 1900 when they made components for ROOTS & VENABLES in their factory at Small Heath, Birmingham. When car manufacture was planned they bought a former government arms factory at Sparkbrook, choosing as manager Colonel E.E. Baguley who had been with RYKNIELD. Under him was Leslie Wilson who later became secretary of the Midland Automobile Club, whose famous Shelsley Walsh hill climb he organised from 1913 to 1958. Baguley's car was a conventional 4-cylinder design, with L-head cylinders cast in pairs and shaft drive. About 150 were made of this 18/23hp model from 1907 to 1910, and it was joined by a smaller 14/18hp (later 15/20hp) and a larger T-head 25/33hp which was based on the 40hp ITALA. In December 1910 B.S.A. took over DAIMLER (ii) which led to the replacement of the Baguley and Itala designs by a single model with 13.9hp Knight sleeve-valve 4-cylinder engine, 3-speed worm-drive transaxle and pressed steel tourer body. With different radiator this was also sold by Siddeley-Deasy as the STONELEIGH. Production lasted into 1915.

After World War I, B.S.A. sold two distinct lines of car. In 1921 they brought out a light car powered by a 1075cc V-twin engine made by the British Hotchkiss factory in Coventry, with 3-speed gearbox, overhead worm drive, and 2-seater body. Electric starting was unusual in a car of this size. It was made up to 1925, and production was between 4000 and 5000. In 1923 these 10hp twins were joined by three models of sleeve-valve car which were, in fact, small Daimlers, and were made by Daimler with B.S.A. radiators. Other distinguishing features were quarter-elliptic springing and disc wheels. There were two fours of 1444cc and a small six of 1540cc. Production figures are not known, but certainly fewer were made than of the V-twins. They were discontinued in mid-1926, and no more cars carried the B.S.A. name until 1929.

B.S.A. had begun motorcycle manufacture in 1910, and by the late 1920s they were the largest motorcycle producers in Britain, if not in the world. It was from the motorcycle factory at Small Heath that the new car emerged. It was a 3-wheeler designed by F.W. Hulse and used a 1021cc V-twin engine based on the Hotchkiss design but made by B.S.A., who had acquired the rights from Morris after he had bought up the British Hotchkiss company. Unusually for its date the engine drove the front wheels, which were independently sprung by double transverse leaf springs. Made in Family and Sports models, it had a lower performance than the Morgan, but was more comfortable and easier to drive. The bodies were made by BSA themselves and also by Carbodies and Avon. A larger engine of 1075cc was used from 1933; 2- and 4-cylinder 3-wheelers were made up to 1936, about 5200 twins and 1700 fours. A smaller number of 4-wheelers were also made using the same engines, about 100 twins and 300 fours, though no 4-wheelers at all were made in 1934.

A new 4-wheeler came in 1935; called the Scout, it was made initially as a 2-seater sports, with the same 1075cc 4-cylinder engine as the previous T9, but with lower lines and sweep panel dual-tone colour scheme, as seen on the De Luxe 3-wheelers. For 1936 the Scout acquired a larger engine of 1203cc and a variety of bodies to supplement the Sports – these included a 4-seater sports and a fixed-head coupé. For 1938, on the Series 6 Scout, there was also a drophead coupé and a 2-door sports saloon. The Series 6 also had a longer wheelbase and steel spoked wheels in place of wire. The engine gained an extra main bearing, and it was credited with 70mph (113 km/h). Production of all Scouts was 3003, and they were made up to the outbreak of World War II.

1933 saw a quite separate range of B.S.A. cars. Called the 10hp and the Light Six they were really Lanchesters and were made in that company's Coventry factory which it shared with Daimler. The Ten had a 1185cc 4-cylinder side-valve engine and mechanical brakes instead of the Lanchester's ohv unit and hydraulic

c.1922 Bryan sedan.
NATIONAL MOTOR MUSEUM

c.1912 B.S.A. tourer.
NATIONAL MOTOR MUSEUM

1923 B.S.A. 11hp tourer.
NATIONAL MOTOR MUSEUM

1932 B.S.A. Family 3-wheeler.
NICK GEORGANO

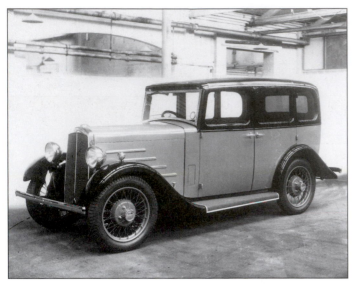

1934 B.S.A. 10hp De Luxe saloon.
NATIONAL MOTOR MUSEUM

brakes, but it shared the fluid flywheel of the Lanchester. At £230 for a 6-light saloon, the 10hp B.S.A. was the cheapest car ever offered with a fluid flywheel. The standard saloon bodies were made by Pressed Steel, but a variety of coachbuilt bodies was also available. The 4-light saloon by Holbrook was called the Varsity when offered by B.S.A., but was also seen on Standard and Vauxhall chassis, when it was known as the Dorchester and Suffolk, respectively. Capacity went up to 1298cc for 1936, when the Ten shared the vee-radiator grille of the Light Six. This was also a badge-engineered Lanchester of 1378cc, but unlike the Ten it had an ohv engine. A variety of body styles was offered, paralleling the Lanchester range in most cases, though prices were around £65 lower. These crypto-Lanchesters were phased out after 1936 when the Coventry firm moved to larger models.

B.S.A. did not resume car production after the war, though they built a prototype 3-wheeler in 1960 called the Ladybird, powered by a Triumph Tigress engine. During the 1950s B.S.A. bought up a number of well-known motorcycle firms including Ariel, New Hudson, Sunbeam, and Triumph, as well as continuing their own 2-wheelers which were made up to 1973. In July of that year B.S.A.'s assets were acquired by the Norton-Villers Group, and the name was revived in 1980 for a range of light motorcycles made at Garrets Green, Birmingham.

NG

Further Reading
Lost Causes of Motoring, Lord Montagu of Beaulieu, Cassell & Co., 1960.
'The B.S.A. Scout', Graham Skillen, *The Automobile*, August 1985.
'B.S.A. Cars', M. Worthington-Williams, *The Automobile,* March 1996.

B.T.C. (GB) 1921–1922
British Transmission Co. Ltd, London.
This company was mainly a component supplier, but they also offered complete cars and trucks. Among the former were a cyclecar powered by a 9hp air-cooled flat-twin Kennedy engine, and an 11.9hp four with independent front suspension by transverse leaves. At least one of the latter was built.

NG

BUAT (F) 1900–1905
Automobiles Leon Buat, Senlis, Oise.
This company showed a voiturette powered by a 3.5hp De Dion-Bouton engine at the 1900 Paris Salon, but three years later they standardised on Aster engines for their range of five cars. These were single-cylinder models of 6.5 and 9hp, a 12hp twin, and 16 and 24hp 4-cylinder cars. They were not very individual in appearance, the smaller cars having De Dion-type bonnets while the larger resembled Peugeots. In 1905 Buat offered a six car range, from 8 to 30hp.

NG

BUBU *see* MITSUOKA

BUC (F) 1922–1927
Bucciali Frères, Courbevoie, Seine.
Of Corsican descent, the Bucciali brothers were born in Arras and grew up in Boulogne-sur-Mer.

The first Buc was a 2-passenger roadster built in 1922 and powered by a prewar Ballot 4J 4-cylinder 1989cc engine. Paul Albert Bucciali (1887–1981) began to design it in 1917, with a conventional ladder-type frame and parallel semi-elliptic springs on both front and rear axles, 3-speed gearbox, and brakes on the rear wheels only. With his brother Angelo (1889–1946) he formed a company to make sports and racing cars. Angelo was the president and business manager, while Paul designed and built the cars.

By November 1922 the Bucciali brothers had a new product ready, the AB-1 voiturette powered by a parallel-twin 1340cc water-cooled 2-stroke engine with a common combustion chamber and a ball-bearing crankshaft, designed by Marcel Violet. It delivered 39hp at 4500rpm. The car also had 4-wheel brakes and a 4-speed gearbox with overdrive fourth. At least three AB-1s were built in 1922–23.

Marcel Violet provided Bucciali with a V4 2-stroke 1462cc engine delivering 52hp at 3800rpm. In 1923–24 it was installed in an AB-1 bis chassis with a 2-passenger lightweight body, an AB-2 chassis with a 4-passenger body, and AB-4 sports roadster.

In 1924 the 4-Spéciale appeared, a racing model powered by a 4-stroke 1479cc single-ohc CIME 4-cylinder engine with a Cozette supercharger, producing 65hp. The prototype was built in 1924, and two other 4-Spéciales were completed in 1925. Tipping the scales at 720kg, it was too heavy to be successful in racing.

Up to 1925 the Bucciali brothers were mainly interested in selling their designs, whole or in part, to the industry, and they attracted some interest, but no solid contracts. As a company, Buc was not paying its way; they had to produce and sell more cars.

Initially, Paul Bucciali thought in terms of a sports car with a V4 2-stroke engine. The AB-5 was planned as a production car, with a Violet-designed stepped-bore 1308cc V4, but they had no assurance of a steady supply of engines, and it was shelved before the prototype was completed.

The project was renamed AB-4-5, and materialised with a 1587cc SCAP single-ohc 4-cylinder engine in a 112in (2843) wheelbase chassis with a 4-speed gearbox and 4-wheel brakes. From 1925 to 1927 the Bucciali brothers made at least 100 such chassis. Most of them carrying coach or saloon bodies, but also some cabriolets, torpedoes, and delivery vans.

In 1926 they obtained a 6-cylinder 1490cc single-ohc engine with twin Solex carburettors and a 7-bearing crankshaft, designed by Némorin Causan. It delivered 70hp at 5000rpm, and was mounted in an AB-4-5 chassis for testing. Known as the AB-6, it was slated for production, but the touring version was never built. It was pre-empted by Paul Bucciali's newfound enthusiasm for front-wheel drive. He had seen the racing performance of the Tractas, but never made contact with J. A. Grégoire.

Instead he turned to Edmond Massip, an engineer who had been on the Latil engineering staff when the 4-wheel drive trucks were designed and also had experience in passenger-car and commercial-vehicle design from UNIC.

The first chassis drawn up by Massip and Paul Bucciali had a 4-cylinder 1709cc SCAP engine with pushrod-operated overhead valves, installed with the flywheel at the front end, with a 3-speed gearbox bolted to the clutch housing, and a short shaft-connection to the final drive unit, with enclosed double-jointed drive shafts. That front suspension set-up, with parallel semi-elliptic leaf springs, was the idea of Dmitri Sensaud de Lavaud, a friend of Edmond Massip.

Massip's collaboration with Bucciali did not last long, but Sensaud de Lavaud maintained contact after Bucciali adopted his symmetrical steering linkage and independent rear suspension with enclosed rubber springs. He also tried – with little success – to convince Bucciali of the advantages of his electric brakes and patented swashplate transmission.

The 10CV prototype was fitted with a faux-cabriolet body and exhibited at the Salon de Paris in October 1926, alongside another front-wheel drive Buc chassis with a straight-8 2396cc SCAP engine, and a similar driveline. Neither ever progressed beyond the prototype stage, but they served to start the Bucciali brothers on a new course. In 1928 they stopped calling their cars Buc. From then on, they were named BUCCIALI.

JPN

BUCCIALI (F) 1928–1933

1928–1930 Bucciali Frères, Courbevoie, Seine.
1930–1933 SA des Automobiles Bucciali, Neuilly-Sur-Seine.

The 10CV and 11CV BUC TAV-6 prototypes from 1926 marked the technical starting point for the Bucciali cars. During 1927 Paul Albert Bucciali redesigned Edmond Massip's front-wheel drive layout and revised the suspension systems. He moved the engines forward in the chassis, putting the power flow from the crankshaft first through the final-drive reduction gears, turning the rotation 90 degrees, and fitting a transverse 3- or 4-speed gearbox. He revised the front suspension, replacing the parallel semi-elliptics with a transverse leaf spring, and double-jointed driveshafts turning inside tapered tubes.

A new chassis incorporating these changes was displayed at the Paris Salon in 1927 with a 2443cc L-head CIME engine and a 4-speed gearbox.

The TAV-6s from 1926 were used as experimental cars, and the 4-cylinder chassis was rebuilt with a 1488cc CIME engine and Sensaud de Lavaud's swashplate-and-ratchet-drive transmission, but the friction losses in the drive train were too great for the little engine. This car also served to test the electric brakes, and was on the Bucciali stand in the Paris Salon of October 1928. Both TAV-6 cars were broken up in 1929.

Paul Bucciali now figured that his cars ought to be big and powerful, and placed an order for 8-cylinder engines with Continental Motors. The TAV-8 was first shown as a 4-passenger torpedo at the Paris Salon in 1929, powered by an L-head 4398cc Continental straight-8 engine. It delivered only 85hp at 3000rpm, but it was quiet, reliable, and not expensive. Bucciali put it in a narrow cradle which could be pulled out for engine work (or exchange). The transverse gearbox had constant mesh on second and third, with dogclutch engagement.

Bucciali went to the New York Auto Show in January 1930 with a new car called the TAV-30, essentially the same as the TAV-8, powered by a 5217cc L-head Continental engine. The objective was not really to sell cars in America, but to get the US industry to sign up for licences to the Bucciali patents. It appears that a chassis and a licence were sold to Peerless. The TAV was built on a 130in (3300mm) wheelbase, and the chassis was priced at FFr170,000. Saoutchik built a cabriolet on the TAV-30 chassis. No more than three TAV-30 chassis were made, however.

Always looking for more power, Bucciali purchased three old 6-cylinder 3920cc long-stroke, 1924-model Mercedes engines with Roots-type blowers, providing 100hp at 3100rpm. It appears that one such engine was installed in a front-wheel drive chassis, but the other two were sold without being mounted in Bucciali cars.

The biggest mystery about Bucciali cars was the 'Double-Huit', first displayed as a prototype at the Paris Salon in October 1930. The exhibited engine was a mock-up of a pure Bucciali design, which looked like a U16, with a single vertical cylinder block. In the blueprints the bores were drilled at 22 degrees 30 minutes from vertical, making a theoretically perfect 45 degree V16.

Bucciali also held a patent for combining two vertical 8-inline engines with two crankshafts, into a 16-cylinder power unit, which led to rumours that the 'Double-Huit' consisted of two Continental engines with a Bucciali crankcase. No more than 155hp was claimed from the 7600cc engine, but the chassis was listed at FFr220,000.

The company left Courbevoie in 1930, and moved its headquarters into new premises at Neuilly, but the workshops were moved into rented premises near Angers, where prototype construction continued.

In 1931 Bucciali bought three 4890cc 125hp V12 sleeve-valve engines from VOISIN, and concocted a new model, the TAV-12. Two chassis equipped with this engine were built in 1931–32, and a third was sent to Saoutchik for coachwork. The TAV-12 Berline Saoutchik, built on a 146in (3706mm) wheelbase, appeared at the Paris Salon in 1932. The TAV-12 had the transverse 3-speed gearbox in combination with a 2-speed (dual-crown-wheel) final drive.

In 1932 a 5275cc L-head straight-8 Lycoming engine was mounted in a TAV-30 chassis and the final Bucciali was a Lycoming-powered TAV-30 assembled at Angers in the autumn of 1933. Experimental work continued for some time, and in 1936 Bucciali made a new car with a rear-wheel drive chassis and a 2000cc 6-cylinder Mathis engine, the styling directly derived from the TAV-30.

The Bucciali brothers then closed the motor company and formed an enterprise to exploit their patents – The Société de Mécanique et des Brevets Bucciali.

Between 1935 and 1940 Paul Bucciali designed military vehicles, none of which won the approval of the Department of Defence, but some of which presaged postwar designs produced by other manufacturers, such as the Panhard EBR 8-wheeler armoured car.

JPN

1932 Bucciali TAV-12 saloon.
NICK BALDWIN

Further Reading
'The Elusive Bucciali', Griffith Borgeson,
Automobile Quarterly, Vol. 17, No. 4.

BUCHANAN (i) (AUS) 1956–1961

N. H. Buchanan Motor Co. Pty Ltd, Lidcombe, New South Wales.

Nat Buchanan, a racing driver and radio maker, was keen to build a car using the new wonder material, fibreglass. In 1956 he revealed a sports coupé employing English Ford components such as a hot Consul engine giving 71bhp, although the Zephyr Six engine was listed. However, the front suspension was transverse leaf, the wheelbase was 91in (2311mm) and it weighed 815kg, but to his disappointment it sparked no interest. The work with fibreglass continued and a sports body mould was made using, as a pattern, one of the Kangaroo Stable's Aston Martin DB 3S cars. The resulting shell was aimed at the replacement market, being made to fit a range of cars such as the Austin A40, MG, Singer, etc, and it was eagerly received by sports drivers who appreciated the benefits of reduced weight. A chassis kit was also offered to accept Holden components.

Nat still wanted to produce his own car, and he sold the after-market business to J. & S. Fibreglass after 108 units had been sold; more were added later to make it Australia's most prolific conversion sports body. He then applied himself to the design and production of the Buchanan Cobra, which appeared in 1958. A neat roadster, it made use of Standard Ten mechanicals installed in a chassis made by the Pressed Metal Corporation and there was talk of Standard dealers handling sales. On a wheelbase of 90in (2286mm), it weighed 816kg, so that the 44hp twin carburettor engine provided a satisfying performance. The failure of this promising programme was blamed on the arrival of the Austin-Healey Sprite but, in reality, it was the unavailability of mechanical components which killed it, after the Standard Ten had been superseded by the Triumph Herald. During this period of delay, the Cobra project was taken over by the Pressed Metal Corporation. About 20 examples are known to have been made. J. & S. bought the moulds and sold some bodies for customer fitting.

MG

BUCHANAN (ii) (US) c.1984

Buchanan Automotive Technology, Carpenteria, California.

The Tryker was a 3-wheeled kit car that used a motorcycle engine driving the front wheels through a Honda Accord transmission. Honda suspension was also used, mounted on a steel perimeter frame. The body was sheet aluminium and had a neoclassic look with vertical radiator grill and cycle-type front mudguards. Trykers were only sold in kit form.

HP

BUCHET (F) 1911–1930

1911–1918 Sté Buchet, Levallois-Perret, Seine.
1919–1930 Gaston Sailly, Moteurs et Automobiles Buchet, Billancourt, Seine.

The Société Buchet was founded in 1888 to manufacture Elie Victor Buchet's invention of an electric arc lamp. They turned to engines in 1899, making full overhead conversions of the inlet-over-exhaust valve De Dion-Bouton engine, as well as their own proprietary units. Over the next ten years these were supplied to a variety of car manufacturers, including Boyer, Chainless, and Reyrol. In 1902 there was an enormous Buchet tricycle, probably a one-off, powered by a 4245cc 2-cylinder engine, with no gearbox or differential. They had interests in aviation too, supplying the engines for Santos Dumont's airship in 1901 and making a V8 aero-engine in 1906. Their first complete 4-wheeler was a taxi offered

c.1922 Buchet 10/18hp tourer.
M.J.WORTHINGTON-WILLIAMS

in 1910, and a year later they brought out a 12/20hp car with 2176cc 4-cylinder monobloc engine, 3-speed gearbox, and bevel drive. It was followed by smaller cars of 1.1 and 1.5 litres. The former was exported to England in chassis form and bodied by Hollingdrake of Southport who sold it under the name ASCOT in 1914 and 1915.

In 1919 Buchet was bought by Gaston Sailly who moved into a new factory at Billancourt. A range of very conventional cars was offered, mostly fours of 1131 and 1460cc, though there was also a 1730cc six from 1928 to 1930. The larger four (Type B2) gained an additional 2mm in the bore in 1923, raising capacity to 1551cc, and front-wheel brakes on the B4 in 1924. With overhead valves it became the B5. A choice of Solex or Zenith carburettors and Saga or Lavalette magnetos was offered. Bodies were tourers, saloons, and coupés. Though Buchets were never known for their performance, they were attractive looking, with wire wheels and a curved radiator not unlike that of the B.N.C. They were unable to compete with the mass producers, and like Hurtu, Barré, Motobloc, and so many others they failed to survive into the 1930s.

NG

BUCKBOARD (i) (US) 1904
H. S. Moore, Cleveland, Ohio.
This car was described by *The Automobile Review* as the cheapest machine on the market, but they did not quote a price or give details. It was presumably similar to the Orient Buckboard made by WALTHAM (ii). H.S. Moore also made the STAR (ii).

NG

BUCKBOARD (ii) (US) 1956
Don Bruce, Bronx, New York.
This design for a modern cyclecar used a 4CV Renault frame powered by an Ariel 'Square 4' motorcycle engine. The rakish 2-seater body was formed from marine plywood bulkheads and planked with mahogany strips. The engine was in the rear and poked up through the body. Designer Don Bruce sold plans and brochures showing how to build your own version on a number of US and European frames.

HP

BUCKEYE (i) *see* PEOPLE'S

BUCKEYE (ii) (US) 1903
Motor Storage & Manufacturing Co., Chillicothe, Ohio.
Powered by a 12hp 4-cylinder engine, this was a surrey-type vehicle with conventional front seat and two cross benches at the rear facing each other. Total seating capacity was eight. After one year the makers turned to a new car called the LOGAN (i).

NG

BUCKEYE (iii) (US) 1911
Buckeye Wagon Co., Dayton, Ohio.
This maker of horse-drawn wagons added a high-wheel motor buggy to their range for one year only.

NG

BUCKINGHAM (i) (GB) 1913–1923
1913–1915 Buckingham Engine Works, Coventry.
1922–1923 Buckingham Engineering Co. Ltd, Coventry.
Announced in December 1912, J.F.Buckingham's cyclecar was originally called the Chota (Hindustani for 'small'). It had a 6/8hp 746cc single-cylinder ohv engine of Buckingham's own design and manufacture, unusual at a time when most cyclecars used proprietary engines from firms like J.A.P. or Precision. Final drive was by belt. An extraordinary low-slung single-seater with tapered wooden prow and the same engine was announced in May 1913; it was said to have been built for attacking Brooklands records, but was also offered for sale. During 1913 Buckingham added a 1492cc V-twin with slightly staggered cylinders, and in September he changed the Chota's name to his own. By early 1914, 15 cars a week were being made at the Spon Street factory. Engines were also supplied to other cyclecar manufacturers, including Duo and H.C.E.

During World War I Buckingham achieved fame as the inventor of the incendiary bullet for anti-Zeppelin work. In 1920 he brought out his postwar cyclecar, with the prewar 2-cylinder engine, 2-speed gearbox and belt drive. The 2-seater body was by Charlesworth. Very few were made until the Alvis company started manufacture in their Holyhead Road factory. Transmission was now by conventional Moss 3-speed gearbox and shaft drive. However, like all cyclecars, the Buckingham suffered badly from the introduction of the Austin Seven, and Alvis discontinued it in 1923. Probably no more than 30 were made by Alvis.

NG

BUCKINGHAM (ii) (AUS) 1933–1934
Buckingham & Ward Motors Pty Ltd, Footscray, Victoria.
The first Australian car effort by this firm was the 1931 Hamard, with a 6-cylinder 25hp ohv engine and a wheelbase of 130in (3302mm). As the nation was then in the depths of the Depression, it was no surprise that nothing more was heard. The Buckingham 60 of 1933 was a more moderate concept, attuned to those times. Its 4-cylinder 22hp ohv engine displaced 2808cc, had 3-speeds and the wheelbase was 110in (2794mm). It was announced that a consortium of producers had been arranged to supply every component for the all-Australian car. A companion range of commercials named Ward, up to 1.5 tonnes capacity, was also projected.

At the 1933 Melbourne Motor Show a display gave prominence to locally made engine castings and chassis frame. A saloon, with a Whiteman Elite body, was on the road later in the year and a coupé, with an Egan body, was on view at the 1934 Motor Show. Although having all the marks of a serious venture, the prevailing conditions of social distress weighed against success and it quietly faded. Not deterred, its promoters kept their goal in view and were again contenders, as Pengana Motor Industries, prior to World War II, when the Government was making encouraging noises about local car production.

MG

BUCKLAND (GB) 1985 to date
Dick Buckland, Llanwern, Gwent.
Dick Buckland was a Morgan trike owner who decided that he could improve on the formula. His B3 had a strong Zintec steel backbone with front double wishbone suspension, a Ford Escort engine, drive to the single rear wheel via an Escort gearbox and specially-made propshaft to a sprocket and chain. The glassfibre main body tub hinged upwards for mechanical access. Only one car was made each year.

CR

BUCKLE (AUS) 1955–1961
Buckle Motors Pty Ltd, Sydney, New South Wales.
As Bill Buckle gained increasing influence over the direction of the car retailing firm founded by his father, his inclination was towards production because he had been impressed with the possibilities opened up by fibreglass. In 1955 he revealed his first effort, a roadster employing many Ford Zephyr Six components, but it remained a prototype. It served as a basis for further development, which resulted in the 1957 appearance of the Buckle 2.5-litre coupé, built on a 94in (2387mm) wheelbase and weighing 890kg. Although still using mainly Zephyr components, by then from the Mk 2, the front suspension was by transverse leaf. Twin carburettors and a locally made

overdrive unit, to complement the 3-speed gearbox, were available, as was an imported Raymond Mays cylinder head for ultimate power. Despite the careful development work, which resulted in a product of a high standard for a fibreglass car of that time, the project resulted in financial loss. It was terminated after about 20 cars were made and when the volume of fibreglass work built up for the Australian production of the GOGGOMOBIL. A modified Mini, the Buckle Mini-Monaco appeared in 1966, with a fibreglass roof extending back from a more raked windscreen and having a more reclining driving position.

MG

BUCKLER (GB) 1947–1962

1947–1954 Bucklers, Reading, Berkshire.
1954–1958 Buckler Cars Ltd, Reading, Berkshire.
1961–1962 Buckler Cars, Reading, Berkshire, Crowthorne, Berkshire.
1961–1962 Buckler Engineering Ltd, Crowthorne, Berkshire.

Derek Buckler's hero was Henry Ford because Ford had brought motoring within the reach of almost everyone. This inspired Buckler to attempt to bring motor sport within the reach of the common man. From his engineering works, in 1947, appeared the Buckler Mk V – he did not want people to think it was a first effort. The Mk V was remarkable for two things: it was only the second spaceframe design ever – Cisitalia was the first – and it was the world's first kit car of the modern era.

At a time when cars on the home market were virtually unobtainable, Buckler gave people the chance to turn a wreck into a sports car. Buckler could provide all the components except for the body but, if someone arrived at the works with a complete car that was presentable, he was given a Buckler badge.

Bucklers were used as road cars on weekdays and, at weekends, in rallies, trials, hill climbs and, even, races. After 1952 this type of activity declined as cars became more freely available.

The company's work was to the highest quality and rivals such as Lotus used Buckler close-ratio gears and Buckler was entrusted with the building of the frame of the first Brabham racing car.

Buckler made around 500 cars to a dozen designs of spaceframe and not all were registered as a Buckler. The nearest to a production car was the Ninety, made from 1954. It was a dual-purpose road/racing car with a low, slippery body, but it was no match for cars like Cooper and Lotus.

Buckler declined during the 1950s. It was caught between more glamorous, if more expensive, cars like Lotus, and special suppliers offering cheaper, inferior, products.

Then karting arrived in Britain in 1959 and it was motor sport for the common man. Buckler karts were initially very successful but Derek Buckler was in declining health and he sold the company in 1962.

That was the year that the kit car market suddenly collapsed and the demise of the company coincided with its founder's death.

MJL

BUCKLES (US) 1914

T.E. Buckles, Manchester, Oklahoma.

The Buckles cyclecar was typical of its type, with 10hp air-cooled 2-cylinder Spacke engine, friction transmission, and belt final drive. However, it probably never reached the production stage, though a price of $350 was suggested. No company was ever formed for its manufacture.

NG

BUCKMOBILE (US) 1903–1905

1903–1904 Buckmobile Co., Utica, New York.
1904–1905 Black Diamond Automobile Co., Utica, New York.

This was a light 2-seater roadster powered by a 10hp 2-cylinder engine mounted under the seat, with chain final drive. A choice of air- or water-cooling was offered. It was designed by William H. Birdsall who was later responsible for the BROWNIEKAR, MORA, and REGAS. In October 1904 the Buckmobile company merged with the Black Diamond Automobile Co. who moved production to a different factory. The 1904–5 Buckmobiles had slightly longer wheelbases and engines quoted as 15hp. Not more than 40 were made in all before the factory was sold in August 1905.

NG

1949 Buckler 1172cc sports car at Brunton hill climb.
NATIONAL MOTOR MUSEUM

1957 Buckler DD2, with Coventry-Climax 1100cc engine.
NATIONAL MOTOR MUSEUM

BUEL (US) 1897–1903

Buel Machine Works, Woburn, Massachusetts.

James Frederick Buel's machine works had been founded by his father in 1857, and made drill presses and freight elevators. In 1897 he began to build steam cars for friends and local customers; apart from boilers and tyres, the whole car was made at his works. Prices were around $500–600, and output was no more than one car per year.

NG

BUFAG (D) 1923

Hellmuth Butenuth, Dortmund.

Butenuth built a small tandem-seated 3-wheeler using 2-stroke engines of 2.5 or 5PS driving the single rear wheel. The chassis was made of rectangular section steel tubes. A production run of more than 100 was claimed, but this is doubtful as proper production cannot be verified. Probably only a few examples saw the light of day. After World War II Butenuth made trucks in Berlin under the name Econom.

HON

BUFFALO (i) (US) 1900–1902

Buffalo Automobile & Auto-Bi Co., Buffalo, New York.

This company was formed by Erwin Ross Thomas who had built bicycles for a number of years, and gave the names Auto-Tri and Auto-Two to the motorised versions. His cars were made in two models, the 3.5hp Buffalo Junior and 6hp Buffalo Senior, both with single-cylinder engines. In 1903 the E.R. Thomas Motor Co. which had made engines only, took over the Thomas Auto-Bi Co., and the cars were henceforth known as Thomas, of which the Thomas Flyer, which won the 1908 New York–Paris Race, was the most famous.

NG

BUFFALO

BUFFALO (ii) (US) 1901–1906; 1912–1915
1901–1906 Buffalo Electric Carriage Co., Buffalo, New York.
1912–1915 Buffalo Electric Vehicle Co., Buffalo, New York.
This company built a wide range of electric vehicles, from typical light runabouts, stanhopes, and golf breaks to a large 4-seater touring car with batteries ahead of the passengers under a small bonnet and beneath the seats. Priced at $5000 it was listed for 1903 only. After 1906 the company was taken over by F.A. Babcock who renamed the products after himself. This lasted for six years, after which he merged with the Clark Automobile Co. and the Buffalo Automobile Station Co. to make Babcock Electrics again. These had Renault-style bonnets and were offered in roadster, brougham, and coupé forms. Sales were hit by the waning popularity of electrics and the company closed in 1915.

NG

BUFFUM (US) 1901–1907
The H.H. Buffum Co., Abington, Massachusetts.
A maker of both cars and motor boats, Buffum built tourers with 20hp horizontal 4-cylinder engines and chain-and-gear transmissions from 1901 to 1903. They were said to be preparing to make 50 cars in 1903, but for 1904 they turned to a more conventional design, with 28hp vertical 4-cylinder engine, sliding gear transmission and double-chain final drive. Also in 1904 they built an enormous racing car with two horizontal fours coupled together to make a flat eight, and coil springs to all four wheels. This was catalogued under the name Buffum Greyhound. It was the first 8-cylinder car offered for sale in America, though how many customers they found is not known; possibly only one was made. For 1906 they again offered an eight, this time a V8 with the same cylinder dimensions as the HEWITT, so perhaps it was the same engine. It was a French-designed Antoinette.

NG

BUFORI (AUS) 1990–1995
Bufori Motor Car Co., Merrylands, New South Wales.
The Madison kit car, for fitting to the Volkswagen platform, was offered in Australia and attracted the attention of Gerry Khouri, who purchased the design rights and revised it with increased dimensions and the adoption of carbon fibre/kevlar for body construction. In 1991 an enlarged 4-seater, the V6i, was developed to accept a front-mounted 3.8-litre Holden Commodore engine, and this was revised in 1994 with coil spring front suspension. The Madison Mk 2 also appeared that year, featuring greater interior space, a 2-litre Subaru engine mated to the Volkswagen transaxle, 4-wheel disc brakes and an optional automatic transmission.

MG

BUGANTIC (F) 1982 to date
Michel Boschetti, Gorbio.
Produced in an area not far from the Italian border, the Bugantic was a replica of the 1927 Bugatti Type 35B offered in kit form or fully-assembled. Its mechanical basis was the Volkswagen Beetle, including its rear-mounted engine, and the bodywork was in glassfibre. In 1988 a Bugatti 55 replica was added, motorised by either Ford or Opel engines. As interest in the Bugatti replicas faded, the Bugatti project was passed on in 1997 to Philippe Calderon, while Boschetti turned to producing a Porsche 550 Spyder replica called the Salinas (the name of the town where James Dean died at the wheel of a 550 Spyder).

CR

BUGATTI (i) (D;F) 1909–1956
Automobiles E. Bugatti, Molsheim, Bas Rhin.
No make of car has earned such a charismatic reputation on such a small output (about 7800) as Bugatti. Noisy, firmly sprung, and challenging to drive, they have attracted a devoted following all over the world. There are currently Bugatti clubs in five countries.

After making a tricycle and a 4-cylinder car in his native Italy, Ettore Bugatti worked for De Dietrich, Mathis, and Deutz in Germany, and it was during his time with the latter firm that he built the car which was to be the ancestor of all production Bugattis. Completed in the cellar of his house in Cologne, it had a 1208cc 4-cylinder engine whose overhead valves were operated by curved, exposed tappets as on the Deutz cars which Bugatti was working on. The rest of the car

BUGATTI, ETTORE (1881–1947)
If anyone deserved the title 'Le Patron' it was Ettore Bugatti, who ruled his fiefdom at Molsheim in an almost feudal manner, dominating his factory in the best tradition of the English squire. He was born a long way from Alsace, in Milan where he was christened Ettore Arco Isidoro. His father Carlo (1856–1940) was a talented designer of furniture, examples of which are still preserved in a number of museums. He was running a small furniture factory in Milan at the time of Ettore's birth. His younger son Rembrandt (1885–1916) became a successful sculptor and while Ettore turned his back on art to pursue things mechanical , he was more of an artist than most car designers. Jean-Albert Grégoire said of him 'Bugatti was an artist pure and simple; his only scientific knowledge stemmed from ever growing experience, plus a natural mechanical bent supported by the gift of observation'.

Little is known of Ettore's schooling, except that he attended Milan's School of Fine Arts, but at the age of 17 he became an apprentice at bicycle makers Prinetti & Stucchi. Not content with riding one of their De Dion-Bouton-powered tricycles, he added a second engine, and began winning races with it. In 1899 he built a quadricycle with four engines, two ahead of the rear axle and two behind it. He admitted that this was not a great success, and in 1900/01 he built a conventional car with 3054cc 4-cylinder engine and chain drive. He was financed by the brothers the Counts Gulinelli, and the car received high praise in the Gazzetta dello Sport, though the fact that the article was written by a friend of Bugatti's may have coloured the report a little. 'Yesterday's boy' – he is only 19 – has disappeared. Today he is the esteemed constructor of a model which has received a high degree of perfection'.

The article spoke of a 'vast establishment' in which Bugatti's cars would be made in large numbers, but he was soon 'poached' by the Baron de Dietrich who owned a large industrial concern in Alsace. Thus began the first of Bugatti's three ventures working for other car makers which, as Griffith Borgeson pointed out, meant 'that he was going to school at last. With his charm and his luck he succeeded in landing in situations in which he was qualified neither by training nor by experience. Put very simply, his employers had the honour of financing his experiments until he was ready to stand on his own'.

Bugatti built five designs for De Dietrich, according to his own recollection, including an extraordinary racing car in which the driver sat behind the rear axle, and which was excluded from the 1903 Paris–Madrid race on the grounds of poor visibility. It was later rebuilt with a high driving position. Apparently none of these cars was very reliable, and in 1905 Bugatti was dismissed by the Baron, who doubtless wished he had left the young Italian in Milan. He next worked for, or rather with, Émile Mathis for whom he built about 15 cars under the name Hermés. These, too, seem to have been unreliable, and Mathis later wrote to Bugatti asking if

210

he could not use some of the Hermés parts in manufacture of Deutz cars, as the Hermés were unsaleable.

Ettore built a prototype for Deutz in 1907, and they were sufficiently impressed to engage him as their designer on 1st September 1907. They were the first to show the distinctive design which would characterise Bugatti cars in the years to come. In particular, they had single overhead camshafts with large valves operated by short curved tappets. His contract with Deutz allowed him to do other work on the outside, so he was not 'moonlighting' as some have suggested, when he began work on a small car in the cellar of his house. There has been much speculation about his reasons for choosing such a small engine (1207cc); also, because of the similarity between Bugatti's Type 10 and the 1908 Isotta-Fraschini racing voiturette there have been suggestions that he designed the latter. However the European industry generally was moving towards smaller monobloc engines and away from the behemoths of the past few years, so Bugatti was really keeping up with fashion. As for the Isotta Fraschini, there is no evidence of any input from Bugatti; however he may easily have seen one, perhaps belonging to Émile Mathis who acquired and studied any promising designs.

Ettore is said to have been encouraged to manufacture his little car by the admiration of the famous aviator Louis Blériot, who inspected it in September 1909. He acquired part of a disused dye works at Molsheim, about 13 miles west of Strasbourg, and moved there with his family at Christmas 1909. Five cars were made there in 1910, according to Bugatti's right-hand man Ernest Friderich, of similar design to the Type 10, but with a larger bore giving a capacity of 1327cc. The rest of the story of the cars is given in the accompanying columns, but what of the man?

The successful reception of the original car of 1901 and consequent offer of work by De Dietrich undoubtedly influenced Bugatti to a very great extent. The fact that he had no formal technical training made him rely on instant judgement in many design decisions, and instant success fed a natural egoism. To quote the Bugatti expert Hugh Conway, 'Clearly highly intelligent, with strong spatial abilities, he was quick to pick up design concepts or features which could be appreciated visually. Conversely the study of his work shows no ready appreciation of scientific or thermodynamic principles, which explains a too-long retention of techniques demonstrably unsatisfactory'. He opposed Friderich on the adoption of front-wheel brakes, and his son Jean on ifs.

Like the stylist Harley Earl, his genius lay in spotting good ideas that had been worked out by his trained engineers. Among those whom he relied on were Zürich Polytechnic-trained Felix Kortz (up to his death in 1927), engine man Édouard Bertrand, chassis engineer Antonio Pichetto and his architect Henri Muller who made all the stress calculations on the railcars. From about 1930 he came to rely increasingly on his son Jean, who took his place as leader of the team, while being also a talented stylist.

Bugatti seems to have been popular with his workforce, most of whom he knew by their Christian names. He would tour the factory daily, often on horseback for he was a passionate horseman, keeping a large stable in the compound which combined the atmosphere of factory and country estate. Like W.O. Bentley and Henry Royce he was very impatient with anyone using tools incorrectly, or not working hard enough. There was hardly any industrial unrest at Molsheim until 1936 when communist-inspired strikes swept France and did not spare the Bugatti factory. Ettore was so bewildered and hurt by this that he left Molsheim in the charge of Jean, and went to live in Paris. He did not, however, surrender control; Jean visited him once or twice a week to report to Le Patron. Jean's death while testing a car in August 1939 affected him deeply, and while he worked during the war on new designs, of boats and machine tools as well as cars, in Paris and Bordeaux, he never returned to Molsheim. He died on 21st August 1947, a few weeks short of his 66th birthday.

Bugatti married, in 1902, Barbara Maria Bolzoni, by whom he had four children, L'Ebé (1903–1980) named after his initials, E.B., Lidia (1907–1972), Jean (1909–1939) and Roland (1922–1977). Barbara died in 1944 and in 1946 he married Geneviève Delcuze by whom he had two children, Thérèse b.1943 and Michel b.1946.

NG

1910 Bugatti (i) Type 13 2-seater.
NATIONAL MOTOR MUSEUM

1922 Bugatti (i) Brescia 2-seater by Compton and Hermon.
NATIONAL MOTOR MUSEUM

1925 Bugatti (i) Type 30 4-seater sports car.
NATIONAL MOTOR MUSEUM

Further Reading
L'Épopée Bugatti, L'Ebé Bugatti, Éditions de la Table Ronde, 1966.
Bugatti, le Pur Sang des Automobiles, H.G. Conway, Haynes, 1987.
Bugatti, the Dynamics of Mythology, Griffith Borgeson, Osprey, 1981.
Bugatti, the Man and the Marque, Jonathan Wood, Crowood, 1992.

1929 Bugatti (i) Type 41 Royale 2-door saloon by Weymann.
NATIONAL MOTOR MUSEUM

1927 Bugatti (i) Type 40 2-seater by Jarvis.
NATIONAL MOTOR MUSEUM

was conventional, with a 4-speed gearbox separate from the engine and semi-elliptic springs front and rear. It was Bugatti's 10th design, including the work he had done for other firms, so he called it the Type 10.

Bugatti resigned from Deutz towards the end of 1909, and in December he rented a disused dye works at Molsheim in Alsace. This was German territory at the time, so the Bugatti was a German car up to the end of World War I. Here he began to make a car very similar to the Type 10, though a bore enlarged by 3mm gave a capacity of 1327cc. He called it the Type 13 (there is no record of Types 11 and 12). The first was delivered to a customer in the Spring of 1910, but only four more were made that year, according to the reminiscences of Bugatti's partner, Ernest Friderich. However, 75 were delivered in 1911, and 175 in 1913. At first the car did not excite a great deal of attention. When *The Autocar* reported on the 1910 Paris Salon, their correspondent said that 'a little Bugatti and a little Bedelia seemed most delightful looking runabouts. In these, two people can sit one in front of the other', so he cannot have looked very closely at the Bugatti. The grouping together of the jewel-like Bugatti with the crude, belt-driven

Bedelia would be enough to cause apoplexy among Bugatti-fanciers of a later era. It was streets ahead of any contemporary small car, particularly in its precise steering and lightness of control. The pioneer vintage car enthusiast Cecil Clutton wrote of a Type 13, 'It is essentially to be controlled with fingers and toes rather than hands and feet. The gear lever is flicked rather than pushed or pulled'.

The 1912 catalogue listed three models, the Type 13 on a 74.8in (1898mm) wheelbase, the Type 15 (94.6in 2401mm) and the Type 17 (115in/2919mm). In the 1913 catalogue (for 1914 models) the longer wheelbase cars were numbered Types 22 and 23. They had improved engines and reversed quarter-elliptic springs, and the famous Bugatti oval radiator was used for the first time, replacing the squared-off radiator topof previous models. Bugatti did not make his own coachwork until 1923; most of the prewar cars were bodied by Widerkher of Colmar who were later tocarry the better-known name of Gangloff, bodying Bugattis up to 1939. Other coachbuilders who worked on the early Bugattis were Durr of Colmar and Fossier of Strasbourg.

In addition to the Type 13 family, Bugatti made six examples of a much larger car with 5024cc 4-cylinder engine which had three valves per cylinder, two inlet and one exhaust. He was to use this layout on aero engines and all 8-cylinder car engines up to the Type 50. Final drive was by chains, the only example of this on a Bugatti, though one was converted to shaft drive for the 1914 Indianapolis 500 Mile Race. The 5-litre car was called the Type 18, and the first sale was made in 1912. The best-known Type 18 was the Labourdette-bodied 2-seater which was bought by the air ace Roland Garros in 1913, which came to England after his death, and was raced at Brooklands under the name Black Bess. This survives today, (chassis no.474) together with another with pointed tail racing body (chassis no.471), and chassis no.715 in the French Musée Nationale de l'Automobile at Mulhouse. About 345 Bugattis were made in all before the outbreak of World War I.

In 1911 Bugatti built a small car with 855cc 4-cylinder engine and a curious transmission in which two concentric propeller shafts provided the two forward speeds. Apparently he had no intention of manufacturing this design. After Wanderer in Germany had turned it down he offered it to Peugeot who made it as the famous Bebe Peugeot, selling 3095 between 1912 and 1914.

New Nationality

In 1918 the Bugatti changed nationality. The territory of Alsace, which had been lost to Germany after the Franco-Prussian War of 1870–71, became French once more. Ettore had strong links with France and had spent the war years in Paris where he supervised the design of aero-engines. The most famous of these was the 16-cylinder double-bank 500hp engine which was made by Duesenberg Motors of Elizabeth, New Jersey. Returning to Molsheim, he exhumed the three 16-valve engines which had been built for the 1914 Coupe des Voitures Légères, and which had been buried for safety during the war. Three cars ran at the 1920 Coupe des Voiturettes at Le Mans, victory going to Friderich. The following year brought Bugatti their greatest triumph to date, when the 16-valve cars took the first four places in the Italian Voiturette GP at Brescia. From this the Type 13 became known as the Brescia, and this name has been applied loosely to the longer Types 22 and 23 as well. Strictly speaking, the only car which should be called a Brescia is the 74.8in (1898mm) model with plain-bearing engine up to 1921, and ball bearings thereafter. The longer cars, which had plain bearings up to 1923 or so, should be called Brescia Modifié. Just to complicate matters, some Full Brescia engines were mounted in the 94.6in (2401mm) chassis, as the longer wheelbase helped road holding. Engine dimensions on the first models of 1920 were 66 × 100mm (1368cc), growing to 68 × 100mm (1453cc) and finally in 1924 to 69 × 100mm (1496cc). The Brescia Modifié carried a wide variety of coachwork, 3-seater clover leaf, 4-seater tourers, fixed and drophead coupés and a few 4-door saloons. The Brescia and Brescia Modifié were discontinued in 1926, after about 2000 had been made. They were the only Bugattis to be made under foreign licences, by CROSSLEY in England, RABAG in Germany and DIATTO in Italy. Rabag (Rheinische Automobilebau AG) was formed specifically to make Bugattis, producing no other models, but for Crossley and Diatto the ventures were small sidelines to their general production. Not more than 25 cars were made by any of these firms. Crossley were too busy on their own cars to allow much space or finance for the Bugatti, while Rabag merged with Aga in 1925, the new group going bankrupt soon afterwards.

Eight cylinders

At the 1921 Paris and London Shows Bugatti displayed a chassis with a 3-litre straight-8 engine. Like other Bugattis this had a single-ohc, and the cylinders had three valves, as on the prewar Type 18. The gearbox was mounted on the rear axle. Front wheel brakes were featured, though they were not connected up, the whole car being incomplete. Eventually it ran and was fitted with a body, but Bugatti could not afford to put it into production. It was numbered Type 28.

The following year a smaller 2-litre straight-8 appeared which did go into production. This Type 30 had a conventionally-located gearbox, and the front wheels were hydraulically braked by a specially-designed master cylinder. The rear brakes were cable operated. The first four Type 30s carried racing bodies with cowled radiators and pointed tails. De Viscaya finished 2nd in the 1922 French GP at Strasbourg. For the 1923 French GP at Tours, Bugatti used roller-bearing engines and very unusual all-enveloping bodies nicknamed 'tanks'. These were the first bodies to be made at Molsheim; by 1928 he had a fully-fledged bodyshop, making closed bodies as well, though Gangloff remained an important supplier of coachwork. The touring Type 30 sold well for an expensive car, about 600 finding customers between 1923 and January 1926. Most were fitted with open 4-seater coachwork. The hydraulic brakes proved troublesome, with leaking from the master cylinder, and later Type 30s had cable operated brakes at the front as well as the rear. In comparison with later Bugattis, the Type 30 has come in for quite a lot of criticism, but it was well thought of when new. The eminent journalist Charles Faroux, who must have driven practically every quality car of his day, wrote to Ettore Bugatti '...you have sold me a motorcar which is absolutely unbeatable. I cannot imagine anything which could give more joy than this experience with my 2-litre Bugatti'.

A successor to the Type 30, with gearbox integral with the rear axle, was planned under the type number 33, but it was never built, and the production successor was the Type 38, made from January 1926 to November 1928. This used a 1990cc engine based on that of the 35A in a lengthened 30 chassis with cable brakes almost identical to those of the racing cars. The engine was not powerful enough for a sporting tourer of the late 1920s, and after 385 had been made (about 50 with superchargers), the 38 was replaced by the Type 44. This had a 2991cc engine on similar lines to the 39s, but with more refinements and giving a top speed of around 80mph (130km/h). The wheelbase was the same as that of the 38 (123in/3122mm), and the 44 was made with a variety of bodies, open and closed. A growing proportion of these came from Bugatti's own coachworks.

1928 Bugatti (i) Type 44 cabriolet by Van Vooren.
NATIONAL MOTOR MUSEUM

1932 Bugatti (i) Type 55 roadster.
NATIONAL MOTOR MUSEUM

Motor Sport described the Type 44 as 'the first serious attempt at a Bugatti touring car.' In July 1930 it was succeeded by the Type 49, with the engine enlarged to 3257cc, and there was a quieter gearbox. A fan was used for the first time on an 8-cylinder Bugatti. The 49 was an interim model between the 44 and the twin-cam Type 57, and is regarded by many knowledgeable Bugatti enthusiasts as the finest of all touring models from Molsheim, its shorter wheelbase and consequent lower weight giving it better handling than the 57. Production of the 49 was 470 cars, while the 44 accounted for 1095. This was the largest production of any Bugatti model, apart from the 16-valve Brescias in their various forms.

Pur Sang – the Type 35

If any one model can be said to have established the Bugatti reputation, it must be the Type 35. This was the replacement for the Type 30 and 32 'tank' for Grand Prix racing, and made its first appearance at the 1924 French GP at Lyons. The engine was the same size and basic design as the Type 30, but it had five crankshaft bearings instead of three, and better lubrication. The gearbox was similar to the Brescia's, but carried on cross tubes. In place of the Type 30's hydraulic front brakes, the Type 35's were mechanical all round, with servo assistance at the front. The wheels were of cast light alloy, and the body a classically simple 2-seater headed by the Bugatti horseshoe in its purest form.

There were numerous variations on the Type 35 theme, some supercharged and with engines that varied in size from 1492cc (Type 39 unsupercharged, 39A supercharged) to 2262cc (Type 35B supercharged, 35T unsupercharged). In its various forms the Type 35 was the most successful competition car of the 1920s. In 1926 alone they won 12 major events, taking first three places in three of them. Bugatti took the manufacturers' championship that year, or Championship of the World as it was called at the time. About 340 Types 35/39 were made between 1924 and 1931, a remarkable figure for what was essentially a racing car, though some were used on the road.

The other racing Bugatti of the 1920s was the Type 37, a 1496cc 4-cylinder replacement for the Brescia. This had a Type 35 chassis and the 3-valve-per-cylinder

1938 Bugatti (i) Type 57SC coupé by Corsica.
NATIONAL MOTOR MUSEUM

layout of the straight-8 engines. The body was similar in shape to that of the Type 35, but the smaller car could easily be distinguished by its narrower radiator and wire wheels in place of cast alloy spokes. It was appreciably cheaper than the 8-cylinder cars – British prices in 1927 were £525 for a Type 37, £675 for a Type 35A and £1100 for a Type 35. Probably more 37s were used on the road than 35s, though both models were seen with sketchy wings and lights, and a few 37s were fitted with lightweight closed bodies. They were widely used in racing and hill climbs by amateurs, but did not figure in major events.

The Type 43 can be regarded as a road-going version of the 35, having the blown 2262cc engine of the 35B in a shortened 38 chassis, and the 35's characteristic cast alloy wheels. The standard body was a Bugatti-built close-coupled 4-seater with only one door. The European correspondent of *The Autocar* described the 43 as 'having all the characteristics of a racing car, indeed it is a racing car with a touring body'. Its top speed was 100mph (160km/h) and 0-62mph (0-100km/h) took just over 12 seconds. The 43 was the only road-going Bugatti to have a full roller-bearing crankshaft. A total of 160 were made between 1927 and 1931.

'Ettore's Morris Cowley'
While the Type 37 replaced the sporting Brescia, Bugatti needed a reasonably priced touring car to follow on from the Brescia Modifié. This appeared in mid-1926 as the Type 40. The engine was the same 1496cc 3-valve unit used in the Type 37, while the chassis was a shortened version of the 38, with similar axles and gearbox. The most familiar body was a Molsheim-built close-coupled 4-seater tourer, though the chassis was available to outside coachbuilders as well.

Because of its comparatively modest performance (top speed around 75mph (120km/h)) and low price (£365 in 1929), the Type 40 was nickname 'Ettore's Morris Cowley', but it was still a typical Bugatti in its handling. About 830 were made between 1926 and 1932, including a batch of 50 Type 40As made in 1930. These had the 72mm bore cylinders of the Type 49, giving a capacity of 1623cc, dual ignition, and were mostly fitted with American-style roadster bodies with a dickey seat and a hatch for golf clubs. The Type 40 had no successors in the 1930s, subsequent Bugattis all having 8-cylinder engines.

La Royale, Ettore's Greatest Folly
The years 1925–30 were the best that Automobiles Bugatti enjoyed. Car sales were

good, racing successes were at their peak and in 1926 there was the promise of an important contract from the French Air Force for a 16-cylinder double-bank aero-engine. As it happened the contract never materialised, but one bank of the engine formed the basis of the Type 41, variously known as La Royale or the Golden Bug. Ettore had been fascinated with the challenge of a super car to outdo all others as early as 1913, when he outlined his ambition in a letter to a friend. By 1926 the engine was available and the times seemed right, with world prosperity riding high and his own company making good profits.

As used in the prototype, the straight-8 engine had dimensions of 125 × 150mm, giving a capacity of 14,726cc and a claimed output of 300bhp at only 1700rpm. This figure was given by W.F. Bradley when he first described the car for *The Autocar*, and is undoubtedly exaggerated. 200bhp is a more reasonable figure. The engine design was fairly typical of Bugatti practice, with a single-ohc and three valves per cylinder. Ignition was dual, by battery and magneto. The engine weighed 350kg, and the crankshaft alone, 100kg. This provided enough inertia to make a flywheel unnecessary. However, a short drive shaft led to a light flywheel below the front seat, behind which was the clutch. The 3-speed gearbox was in unit with the rear axle, second gear being direct and third an overdrive.

The chassis of this enormous car had a wheelbase of 187in (4746mm), and the body of the prototype was a 7-seater tourer taken from a Packard. It was completed in 1926 and subsequently received four different bodies, including the Coupé Napoleon coupé de ville which it carries today. Numerous myths arose about the Type 41, starting with its names. Golden Bug was an unofficial one coined by Bradley and was said to hint at gold in its construction or at least in the mascot, but this was not so. It is more likely that it was chosen to imply great wealth and perhaps to upstage the Rolls-Royce Silver Ghost. Ettore preferred the name La Royale, as he doubtless hoped for royal buyers, though none materialised. The names of Kings Alfonso of Spain, Carol of Rumania, and Zog of Albania have been linked with the Royale, but so far as is known none of them even inspected the car, let alone bought one.

Only six Royales were completed, the 'production' version having a shorter stroke of 130mm giving 12,763cc, and a wheelbase of 169in (4289mm). Details of all six are as follows:

Chassis number	Bodies	Original Owner	Present Owner (at 31/12/98)
41 100 (prototype)	1. 7-passenger tourer from Packard	Bugatti family	Musée Nationale de l'Automobile, Mulhouse
	2. Coupé by Bugatti		
	3. Saloon by Bugatti		
	4. Coupé by Weymann		
	5. Coupé de ville by Bugatti		
41 111	1. Roadster by Bugatti	Armand Esders	General William Lyon, USA
	2. Coupé de ville by Henri Binder		
41 121	Cabriolet by Ludwig Weinberger	Dr Josef Fuchs	Henry Ford Museum, Dearborn, Michigan
41 131	Limousine by Park Ward	Capt C.W. Foster	Musée Nationale de l'Automobile, Mulhouse
41 141	2-door saloon by Kellner	Bugatti family	Secki Gushi, Japan
41 150	Berline de voyage by Bugatti	Bugatti family	Blackhawk Collection, USA

Dates of manufacture are not given, as it is not certain whether all the components were made at one time, or finished in response to eventual demand. It is likely that all the engines were completed together, as were 25 others which were used in railcars. Although announced in 1926, no Royale was sold until 1932, and three were never sold, remaining the property of the Bugatti family up to the 1950s.

As a commercial enterprise the Royale was a disaster, but Bugatti made the best of the situation by selling the unused engines to the SNCF (French Railways) for use in high-speed railcars. They proved so popular that a further 136 engines were built between 1933 and 1939, with 79 complete railcars. Three types were produced, the 'light' type of 400hp (two engines), the 'double' with four engines and 800hp with a single trailer, and a triple with trailer front and back. Bodies were by Gangloff and the cars were assembled in the Bugatti factory. Ettore built extensions to the factory dedicated to railcar production, and transferred workers from car production as well as taking on extra labour.

Touring and sports Bugattis in the 1930s

By 1929 Bugatti must have realised that he would never sell many Royales, so he introduced a smaller luxury car, the 5360cc Type 46. This was similar in layout to the Royale, and even used the same stroke of 130mm, though the bore was drastically reduced to 81mm. As in the Royale, the 3-speed gearbox was on the rear axle. The chassis was long enough to take handsome 4-door saloon bodies, and a top speed of 93mph (150km/h) was possible with a high rear axle ratio. The 46 was launched in the autumn of 1929, and was made up to about 1936. Some of their last chassis were not sold until after World War II. About 400 were made, including about 20 supercharged models called the Type 46S.

Another large luxury car which supplemented the Type 46 was the Type 50, significant as it was the first production Bugatti to have a twin-cam engine. The chassis was a shorter version of the 46, with similar transmission, but the engine was a new 4942cc straight-8 with two inclined valves per cylinder in place of the three vertical valves of previous Bugatti practice. This supercharged engine developed close to 200bhp, as much as a Royale of nearly three times the capacity, giving a top speed of 108mph (175km/h). The Type 50 had a reputation for difficult handling, and the British importer Colonel Sorel would not sell them. Of the 65 made, only one was delivered to a British customer. The 50 was conceived as a more sporting car than the 46, most bodies being 2-door coupés or cabriolets, though there was a 50T with the 46's 137.9in (3500mm) wheelbase, on which some 4-door saloons were built. The Type 50 engine was used in the Type 53 4-wheel drive racing car and in the Type 54 GP car.

The twin-cam theme was continued in a smaller sports car, the Type 55 which used the supercharged 2262cc engine from the Type 51 GP car in the chassis of the Type 54. The standard body was a beautiful 2-seater with long, sweeping wings, designed by Ettore's son Jean. Although only a 2-seater, it was the obvious

successor to the Type 43, and had a higher performance. Top speed was 112mph (180km/h). A price of £1200 in 1932, rising to £1350 the following year, restricted sales, and only 38 were made. Most carried Jean's factory-built body, though about four closed coupés were made, as well as a few custom styles.

The influence of Jean Bugatti was increasingly evident in the 1930s, and it was due to his pressure on his father that the twin-cam engine was introduced. He also argued in favour of independent front suspension, but was overruled. The car which bore his stamp more than any other was the Type 57, the last production Bugatti. Introduced in 1934, its engine had the same dimensions as the Type 49, giving 3257cc, but had twin-ohcs driven by a train of gears from the rear of the crankshaft, unlike the Types 50 and 51 which were driven from the front. The prototype had a smaller engine of 2864cc and independent front suspension by transverse springs, but when Ettore heard about this heresy he ordered them to be replaced forthwith by the conventional beam axle. Brakes were mechanical, replaced by hydraulics in 1938. The bodies were styled by Jean, the saloons being made at Molsheim and the open ones by Gangloff at Colmar. Chassis were also available for custom coachbuilders to work on, these including Graber, Letourneur et Marchand, Saoutchik, and James Young.

The 57 was intended as a Grand Tourer rather than a sports car, though competition models were made, and gave Bugatti his only Le Mans victories, in 1937 and 1939. From 1936 it was the only Bugatti in production, and this one-model policy was undoubtedly more successful than the complicated series of the expensive Types 46, 50, and 55 made earlier in the decade. More sporting versions came in 1936/37 with the 57S and 57SC. They had lowered chassis on which the rear axle beam passed through the frame, magneto ignition, and dry sump lubrication. They were the only Bugattis to have vee-radiators, by which they could be distinguished easily from the touring Type 57s. They were also 12.6in (320mm) shorter in wheelbase. These engines developed 170bhp, and when supercharged (57SC), over 200bhp. The supercharger was also available on the standard 57 chassis, in which form it was known as the 57C.

Total production of the Type 57 was 684, made up as shown in the table below:

Type 57	unsupercharged	130in wheelbase	1934–1939	546 made
Type 57C	supercharged	130in wheelbase	1935–1939	96 made
Type 57S	unsupercharged	117.4in wheelbase	1936–1938	
Type 57SC	supercharged	117.4in wheelbase	1936–1938	42* made

* Some 57S were converted into 57SC specification after they were delivered, so an exact breakdown between the two models cannot be given. An SC with a light 2-seater body was capable of 124mph (200km/h), making it the fastest road-going Bugatti and one of the fastest prewar cars in the world.

The Last Bugattis

Jean was killed in August 1939 while testing a Type 57C. This and the outbreak of World War II less than a month later put paid to the 57's successor that he was working on. Numbered the Type 64, it had the 57's engine in a Duralumin chassis in which the rear axle passed through an aperture in the frame, in the manner of the 57S. The one prototype had a Cotal electric gearbox, though there were plans to use either an Armstrong-Siddeley pre-selector or a Daimler fluid flywheel. The body was a 2-door coupé and the radiator had a vee shape not unlike that of the 57S. Plans to install a 4.5-litre engine never materialised.

During and just after the war Ettore worked on several designs, including the Type 68, a baby car powered by a twin-cam 16-valve 4-cylinder engine of only 370cc, which turned at the very high speed of 9000 to 12,000rpm, and the Type 73, a 1488cc 4-cylinder car to be made as a coupé with 8-valve single-cam engine or a supercharged racing car (Type 73C) with two camshafts and 16 valves. Only one Type 68 was completed, and no more than four Type 73s, which were made in the La Licorne factory in Paris, which Bugatti had bought. One, shown at the 1947 Salon, had a coupé body by Pourtout. The 73C got no further than a single engine.

Ettore died in August 1947, and the development of a postwar car fell to his younger son Roland and factory manager Pierre Marco. In 1951 they brought out an updated Type 57 called the Type 101. The engine was basically similar to the 57, but it had a downdraft Weber carburettor in place of the Stromberg, and a Cotal gearbox. The bodies were new, all-enveloping designs made by Gangloff. Two cars were shown at the 1951 Paris Salon amid optimistic forecasts

1991 Bugatti (iii) EB110 coupé.
NATIONAL MOTOR MUSEUM

1999 Bugatti (iii) EB218 saloon.
BUGATTI

1909 Buggy Car high-wheeler.
NICK BALDWIN

from the press as well as from the makers, but at a price of three million francs, double that of a Delahaye 135, it was a non-starter. Only six Type 101s were made. The marque made its final Salon appearance in 1952. Four years later came the Type 251, a Grand Prix car with transverse 2432cc straight-8 engine mounted behind the driver. It handled disastrously and never completed a race. At the same time a roadster with twin-cam 1.5-litre 4-cylinder engine, the Type 252, was briefly tested but never developed properly.

In 1963 Bugatti was bought up by Hispano-Suiza, once great car makers themselves, but by then into diesel and aircraft engines. They were later absorbed by SNECMA, the French nationalised aerospace industries combine, and the factory continues to be busy making aircraft components today.

NG

Further Reading
Bugatti – le Pur Sang des Automobiles, H.G. Conway, Foulis, 4th edition, 1987.
Bugatti – the Man and the Marque, Jonathan Wood, Crowood Press, 1992.
Bugatti by Borgeson, Griffith Borgeson, Osprey, 1981.
57 – the Last French Bugatti, Barrie Price, Veloce Publishing, 1992.

BUGATTI (ii) (GB) 1981–1982
Bugatti Cars Ltd., London.
Quite how this company justified its use of the famous Molsheim manufacturer's name remains a mystery, for this was an entirely unremarkable replica of the Bugatti Type 35. It was exhibited at the 1981 London Motorfair but disappeared soon after.

CR

BUGATTI (iii) (I) 1991–1995/1998 to date
1991–1995 Bugatti Automobili SpA, Campogalliano, Modena.
1998 to date Bugatti, Volkswagen Group, Wolfsburg.
Of all the attempts to revive the Bugatti name in postwar years, the extraordinary efforts of Romano Artioli came closest to succeeding. The plan was grand: a state-of-the-art factory was built in northern Italy, industry greats were hired (including Paolo Stanzani as technical director and Marcello Gandini as designer) and a brand new V12 engine was created from scratch. The new Bugatti EB110 was to be a superlative mid-engined supercar, the sort of car which Ettore would have been making if he were still alive. The EB110 name was chosen as a composite of Ettore Bugatti's initials and the fact that the car was to be launched on the 110th anniversary of his birth. The aluminium-bodied Bugatti's styling (created by an Italian architect) was dramatic but controversial. Mechanically the Bugatti was highly advanced. Its centrepiece was a V12 engine fitted with no less than four turbochargers and 60 valves, developing 553bhp. There was a 6-speed gearbox mated to a 4-wheel drive system, and Bugatti claimed a top speed of 212mph (341km/h), stating that this was the fastest road car in the world, only beaten by its lightweight SS model with a 611bhp engine and up to 221mph (356km/h). In the end, Artioli simply became too ambitious. First he bought Lotus from General Motors in 1993, then he commissioned ItalDesign to build a new 4-door super saloon called the EB112, but ItalDesign stopped work on the project, claiming lack of payment. The plant closed in September 1995 with $60 million of debts. A total of 139 cars had been built (some sources say considerably fewer), including one for Michael Schumacher. In 1998 the Bugatti name was bought by Volkswagen, which showed an enormous ItalDesign EB118 coupé concept study at the 1998 Paris Motor Show, with an 18-cylinder 6.3-litre engine developing 555bhp. This was followed at the 1999 Geneva Motor Show by a 4-door saloon EB218 model, which was destined to enter production under Volkswagen's auspices.

CR

BUGATTI-GULINELLI (I) 1901–1902
Officine Gulinelli, Ferrara.
In 1900 the brothers Counts Gulinelli agreed to finance the 19-year old Ettore Bugatti in the manufacture of a car he had designed. It had a 3054cc 4-cylinder engine, 2-seater body and chain drive. It won a Gold Medal at the International Breeding and Sport Exhibition in Milan in May 1901, on which occasion *La Gazetta dello Sport* remarked that it had 'a simple and most potent motor capable of exacting daily service and of very great speed if necessary'. The same magazine said that Bugatti and the Gulinellis would start a vast establishment in Milan for the building of motorcars, but instead Bugatti was lured away to Alsace by the Baron DE DIETRICH.

NG

BUGETTA (US) 1969 to date
Bugetta Inc., Costa Mesa, California.
Well-known race car fabricator Jerry Eisert built a line of highly sophisticated sports cars that resembled dune buggies. Although they looked like buggies, these Bugettas had an aluminium monocoque chassis with fabricated double-A-arm front suspension and rear-mounted Corvair, VW, Renault, or Porsche engines. There were three tops so the Bugetta could be configured as a mini pick-up truck, fastback sports car or touring car. About 50 were built. Eisert also built a one-off sports car with a mid-engined Ford V8 as a show car for Autolite

spark plugs. It had a fibreglass body and automatic transmission. Although production plans were discussed, it remained a one-off. Eisert continued to build show and race cars for major manufacturers.

HP

BUGGY CAR (US) 1908–1909

The Buggy Car Co., Cincinnati, Ohio.
This company purchased the assets of the Postal Auto & Engine Co. of New Bedford, Indiana, which had made POSTAL high-wheelers since 1906. The Buggy Car was also a high-wheeler, powered by a horizontally-opposed 2-cylinder engine offered in two sizes, 12.5 and 16/18hp. A choice of friction disc or epicyclic transmission was offered, and final drive was by double-chains.

NG

BUGMOBILE (US) 1908–1909

Bugmobile Co. of America, Chicago, Illinois.
The unfortunately named Bugmobile was a high-wheeler powered by a 12hp 2-cylinder horizontally-opposed engine with a conventional sliding gearbox and final drive by steel cables. The 1908 Model A had a 68in (1726mm) wheelbase and the Model B one of 76in (1929mm). The same wheelbase was quoted for the Model C of 1909, with an engine uprated to 15hp.

NG

BUICK (US) 1903 to date

Buick Motor Co., Flint, Michigan.
The Buick has had a long-standing claim on the hearts of American car owners, holding the upper middle-class ground of high quality yet unostentatious cars. For nearly 100 years it has lived up to its slogan 'When Better Automobiles are Built, Buick Will Build Them'.

David Dunbar Buick had toyed with the idea of making a car during his time with the Buick Auto Vim & Power Co. and Buick Manufacturing Co., makers of engines chiefly for marine use, between 1901 and 1903. He built at least one car, aided by Walter Marr, who left to make his own car in Elgin, Illinois, the MARR Touring Runabout. After a fire had destroyed his factory and stock of parts in August 1904 Marr returned to Buick as chief engineer. By this time Buick was running the Buick Motor Co. which had been financed by the Briscoe brothers who later made their own cars (BRISCOE and MAXWELL-BRISCOE), though, finding that Buick did not share their dynamic approach to business, they soon sold the company to James H. Whiting, manager of one of the largest wagon makers in Flint, Michigan.

The Buick Motor Co. made stationary engines with overhead valves, the Buick Valve-in-Head Motor whose design had been variously credited to Walter Marr, David Buick, and his assistant Eugene Richard. It was the company's staple product up to 1904, and Whiting was happy for the company to remain an engine maker only. However, Buick and Marr pressed him to consider the manufacture of complete cars, and in the Spring of 1904 he agreed. Some experimental cars had been made in the latter half of 1903, but little is known of them, though presumably they used the Valve-in-Head Motor. Claims that 16 were made in 1903 cannot be substantiated. The first properly attested Buick car ran in July 1904; it used a horizontally-opposed 2-cylinder engine of 16hp (2605cc) which was mounted under the seat and drove the rear axle by an epicyclic transmission and single-chain. The first sale took place in August 1904, to Dr H.H. Hills of Flint. (Henry Ford's first car sale was also to a doctor). His car had a side-entrance tourer body, and may have been the first car rebodied.

By the end of 1904, 37 cars had been sold, all of them 4-seater tourers priced at $950 or $1200. Though the same size engine was used, there was an increase in output from 16 to 22hp, which coincided with the higher price. All 1904 Buicks were called Model B, though two very similar 1905 Model Cs were completed before the end of the year. Development of these cars had used up nearly all of James Whiting's capital, and the company might have gone under had the directors not invited the attention of William Crapo Durant. The man who was later to set up General Motors was not very interested in cars in 1904, but he agreed to ride in a Buick and was sufficiently impressed to purchase the majority of stock, and transfer production to one of his buggy factories at Jackson, Michigan. However, this was only an assembly plant, the engines and transmissions still being made at Flint, and bodies by Whiting's Flint Wagon Works.

1906 Buick Model F tourer.
NATIONAL MOTOR MUSEUM

1909 Buick Model 10 toy tonneau.
NATIONAL MOTOR MUSEUM

With Durant's capital, Buick became successful for the first time. In 1905, 750 cars were built, all Model Cs. This was similar to the Model B, with the option of a Cape Cart Top for weather protection. Production rose to 1400 cars in 1906 and 4641 in 1907, in which year Buick was second to Ford in the US production league. It was also the year in which a front-engined 4-cylinder car was introduced. These Models D, S, H, and K used a 4180cc engine with side-valves in a T-head, the only departure from overhead valves in Buick's history. Roadster and tourer models were made, most with conventional 3-speed gearboxes, though the Model S roadster retained the epicyclic transmission which was also used on the 2-cylinder Buicks, which were made up to the end of the 1911 season.

In 1908 came the popular Model 10 which is often credited with ensuring the success of Buick, for it was a happy combination of performance, reliability and good looks. Most Model 10s were finished in 'Buick grey' which was an off-white colour, and the cars were often referred to as the little white Buicks. The 2702cc 4-cylinder engine had square dimensions (95.25 × 95.25mm), and transmission was epicyclic, with high gear being operated by a lever on the right side, and low gear by a pedal. The only body style for 1908 was a 3-seater with a small dickey seat which sold for $900. In 1909 additional styles were offered, including a 4-seater tourabout and, later in the season, a toy tonneau which had non-detachable body with doors to the rear seats. 8100 Model 10s were made in 1909, out of a total of 14,606 Buicks. David Buick left the company in 1908, later being involved in two other car companies, LORRAINE (ii) and DUNBAR.

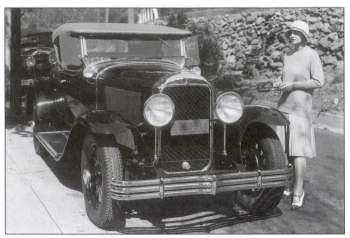

1929 Buick Master Six roadster.
NATIONAL MOTOR MUSEUM

NICK BALDWIN

BUICK, DAVID DUNBAR (1854–1929)

David Dunbar Buick gave his name to one of America's most respected marques, yet he played relatively little part in the company, and left before it had achieved much renown. He was born in Abroath, Scotland, the son of a joiner who moved with his family to Detroit when David was two. At the age of fifteen he went to work for the Alexander Manufacturing Co., a maker of plumbing fixtures, eventually becoming foreman. When the company failed in 1882, he and school friend William Sherwood took over, reforming it as Buick & Sherwood. They made a success of it, and Buick had a number of patents to his credit, the most important of which was a method of applying porcelain to cast-iron baths and sinks, thus giving the world the enamel bath which was soon taken for granted. At about the same time he became interested in the internal combustion engine, and began to spend more time tinkering with this than on his business. As George Dammann, author of *Seventy Years of Buick*, wrote 'He was an inventor of far above average talent, but as a businessman he was a complete flop'. Sadly, this was to be demonstrated over and over again in his career.

In 1901 he sold his interest in the plumbing business, realising $100,000 which he invested in the Buick Auto Vim & Power Co., formed to make engines mainly for farm and marine use. He fitted one of these to a car, but little is known about it. By 1902 the Auto Vim company was failing, due to erratic production and non-delivery of orders. Buick formed a new company called the Buick Manufacturing Co. to make an ohv engine, but again there were problems with meeting orders, and again the company failed. Salvation came from the Briscoe brothers, but on condition that they had full financial

Foreign ventures

Two involvements with foreign countries began at about this time. In 1908 an agreement was signed with the McLaughlin Carriage Co. of Oshawa, Ontario, whereby Buick supplied engines and running gear to the Canadian company who mounted their own bodies, selling the cars under the McLAUGHLIN name. This arrangement lasted for 15 years, after which the name was changed to McLaughlin-Buick, and differences between the Canadian and American products became very slight. After World War II the cars were simply Canadian-built carbon copies of the US Buick.

The first European venture came in 1909 when assembly began in London of the Bedford-Buick. Like the Canadian cars, these had engines and chassis from Flint, with locally-made bodies, mostly by Grosvenor who later became Vauxhall's preferred coachbuilder. The Bedford-Buick name survived to about 1920.

Twins and Sixes

The last 2-cylinder Buick was not introduced until 1910, and had a run of little over a year. The Model 14 had the smallest engine of any Buick, at 2080cc, mounted under the bonnet, unlike the earlier 2-cylinder cars which carried their engines under the front seat. It was a strange mixture of the old and the new, for control. The company was reformed as the Buick Motor Co, a title it retains to this day. The Briscoes soon became disillusioned, though, with the slow output of engines, and withdrew their support.

Next it was the turn of buggy maker James H. Whiting, who moved the company to Flint, Michigan. In 1904 Billy Durant bought a controlling interest, and at last production of cars began to get going. However, as the Buick Motor Co. flourished, there was less room in the organisation for its founder. Buick was constantly making suggestions to the engineers, who were mostly Durant's men. They complained that if they implemented even half his suggestions, the production line would be stopped more often than it was running. Buick was also keen on selling his engines to other car makers. This did not please Durant at all, and in 1908 Buick left, with a personal gift of $100,000 from Durant who probably thought it was money well spent.

Buick turned to oil speculation in California. Other people made fortunes in this field, but Buick lost a substantial part of his $100,000, and returned to Michigan where he formed a company with his son Tom to make carburettors. After a few years this failed, and in 1921 he became associated with a car again, heading a group which reformed the Lorraine Motors Corp. of Grand Rapids, Michigan. Their new car was to have had a Buick-designed ohv engine, but only a prototype was made. He next turned up in Walden, New York, in 1922, where he was involved with a car for which he chose his middle name, Dunbar. The David Dunbar Buick Corp. was to be capitalised at $5 million, but nothing like that sum was raised. Only one car was completed, a roadster with a 6-cylinder Continental engine, and there was speculation that the company was formed to sell stock rather than to make cars. Possibly the unworldly Buick was unaware of this, or perhaps he needed the money.

Out of a job again, Buick invested what little money he had left in real estate in Florida. Again, this was a money spinner for many, but not for Buick who returned to Detroit in 1927, virtually broke. Aged 72, he took a job as an instructor at the Detroit School of Trades, but was not up to it for long, being transferred to the reception desk. Outside, countless Buicks rolled by, but their original creator toiled away unnoticed. He could never afford to retire, nor to buy a Buick. However, he was not downhearted. When interviewed in 1928, he said 'The failure is the man who stays down when he falls…instead of jumping up and figuring what he's going to do tomorrow. That's what success is, looking ahead tomorrow.' Sadly, there were not to be many tomorrows for David Dunbar Buick. He died in March 1929, eleven months after that interview.

Buick was married twice, to Caroline who died in 1912, and by whom he had four children, Tom, Winton, Mabel and Frances, and a few years later to Margaret who survived him and by whom he had a daughter.

NG

Further Reading
The Buick, a Complete History, Terry Dunham and Lawrence Gustin, Automobile Quarterly Publications, 1980.

the transmission was by sliding gear, not epicyclic as one might have expected, yet final drive was by chains. Also known as the Buggyabout, the Model 14 was aimed at the economy-minded and cost only $550 compared with $1000 for the larger 2-cylinder Model F, and up to $2750 for the top 4-cylinder cars. Only 3300 were built, and Buick never ventured into the cheap car market again.

The regular Buicks of the 1911–14 era were conventional fours of 2703, 3293, and 5211cc, with Delco electric lighting and starting being standard on all models by 1914. After experimenting with a V6 engine in 1912 they brought out a conventional 6-cylinder engine in 1914. As used in the Model B-55 it was a pair-cast unit of 5424cc developing 48bhp. Innovations on this model and other 1914 Buicks were left-hand steering and a centrally-mounted gear lever. A tourer was the only style available with the 6-cylinder engine to start with, but a roadster was added in 1916.

Another experimental model, made in 1915, was a V12 intended as a competitor for the Packard Twin Six. Only one was made, and it still existed in 1949, owned by Walter D. Marr, son of Buick's erstwhile partner. 1916 saw Buick's first sedan, available with a smaller six of 3670cc, and also record production of 124,834 cars. This put Buick in third place, behind Ford and Willys Overland, and they continued to hold third or fourth places for most years up to the mid-1920s. The four was dropped after 1918, and all Buicks had 6-cylinder engines until August 1921 when a new 2786cc four, the Model 22, was introduced as a 1922 model. This was made until 1924, after which no more 4-cylinder Buicks were made until 1980, when GM's X-cars appeared.

No major changes were made to Buicks until the 1924 season when front-wheel brakes and detachable cylinder heads were adopted, and the rounded radiator shell gave way to an angular shape, not unlike a Packard. This led Packard to plagiarise the well-known Buick slogan 'When prettier automobiles are built Packard will build them'.

The four was replaced by a new Standard Six of 3130cc for the 1925 season. This and the 4178cc Master Six made up the range for the next four years. 1929 was the year of the 'pregnant Buick', so called because of the bulging body sides which were supposed to be a styling attraction, but did not go down well with the public. A more acceptable development of 1929 was the offering of 43 colour options on all models, not just the De Luxe range. The Packard-like radiator

1941 Buick Century Model 66-S sedanette.
NATIONAL MOTOR MUSEUM

1961 Buick Skylark convertible.
NATIONAL MOTOR MUSEUM

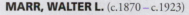

MARR, WALTER L. (c.1870 – c.1923)

Walter L. Marr was born about 1870 in Lexington, a small sawmill town in Michigan and got his first job in 1887 in a factory that built marine steam engines for boats and yachts sailing on the Great Lakes. The company's superintendent designed a single-cylinder gasoline engine which went into production in 1888, giving him a solid background in engine work.

He left in 1896 to set up his own business in Detroit, making bicycles. He also designed and built a gasoline engine which he installed in a farm wagon, and a motor tricycle. He established the W. L. Marr Auto-Car Co. in Detroit in 1902, intending to build light cars with single-cylinder horizontal engines mounted below the seat and with chain drive to the rear axle. However, in 1903 he teamed up with David Buick and designed an overhead-valve flat-twin engine for the Buick car.

He also designed the flat-twin engine for Buick's Model F. Buick's first 4-cylinder engine was developed by the Janney Motor Co. of Jackson, Michigan, which was controlled by W. C. Durant. When Durant took charge of Buick, merging it with Janney, Marr, along with Durant's chief draftsman, Enos A. de Waters, redesigned this engine with overhead valves, and in this form it went into Buick's Model 10 of 1908.

By this time Marr had the official title of chief engineer of Buick, and would no doubt have had a long career in Flint, had he not been a victim of ill-health. He left Buick in 1913 and settled on Signal Mountain near Chattanooga, Tennessee, but continued to send new engine designs to Flint. Before leaving he had designed a V6 engine, and in 1914 proposed a V12, but although Buick built these engines and tested them, in the lab and on the road, they never put them into production.

For many years, Enos de Waters sent him Buick test cars for approval and invited suggestions for improvement. Marr's career (and perhaps his life) ended about 1923.

JPN

Walter Marr (right) with David Buick in a 1904 Buick.
NICK BALDWIN

1972 Buick Riviera coupé.
NATIONAL MOTOR MUSEUM

gave way to a simpler, curved style, and engine capacities went up to 3918 and 5072cc. For 1930 Buick launched a cheaper line of car which they christened MARQUETTE, but it lasted only one year.

For 1931 Buick took a major decision to replace the sixes with an all-straight-8 range. There were four models, the Series 50, 60, 80, and 90, with three sizes of engine, 3616cc in the 50, 4467cc in the 60, and 5650cc in the 80 and 90, which

NATIONAL MOTOR MUSEUM

MITCHELL, BILL (1912–88)

William LeRoy Mitchell was born on 2 July 1912 in Cleveland, Ohio. His family moved to Greenville, Pennsylvania, where Bill's father became a Buick dealer. Bill's dad would bring home Mercers and Auburns and other trade-ins, and it wasn't long before young Bill began drawing cars in grade school.

When he reached his early teens, his parents divorced, and Bill's mother moved to New York City, where she worked for the Barron Collier advertising agency. When Bill turned 15, she got him a summer job there as an office boy. On weekends he'd check out Manhattan's auto row, especially the import- and luxury-car showrooms: Hispano-Suiza, Alfa, Mercedes, Rolls-Royce, and Isotta-Fraschini.

Bill also befriended the three car-crazy young sons of his boss, particularly Sam Collier, who was Mitchell's age. When the father, Barron Collier, discovered Bill's talent for drawing automobiles, he set him up as an apprentice in the agency's art department.

After high school in 1929, Bill attended Carnegie Tech. and studied industrial design. Then in the summer of 1931, again working at the Collier agency, he took evening courses at New York's Art Students League. It was during this period that Bill became involved with the Collier Brothers' amateur auto-racing adventures on Long Island.

Now, instead of haunting auto row on weekends, Mitchell would hop into his Ford roadster and roar out to Pocantico Hills, near Tarrytown, New York, where the Collier Brothers had bulldozed a dirt track on their father's property. They called their track Sleepy Hollow Ring, after the famous Nurburgring circuit in Germany. These were wealthy kids who'd gone from early go-karts to Austin- and Willys-powered racing specials, then to MGs and Bugattis and Auburn speedsters. Mitchell occasionally raced with them, but that wasn't his forte. More often he sketched the action. Mitchell also created the charging Bentley logo for ARCA, the Colliers' hobby organisation (ARCA stood for Automobile Racing Club of America, which later became SCCA, the Sports Car Club of America).

An acquaintance arranged for Bill to send his racing sketches to GM Art & Colour. Harley Earl liked the young man's style and hired him on 10 December 1935. Mitchell was 23, and the two designers soon developed a father/son relationship. They were similar in temperament and had abiding interests in car design, clothes, and motor sports.

Mitchell aspired to become Buick's design chief. In 1937, Earl went one better and appointed him head of the Cadillac studio. Here his first major design was a smaller Cadillac, the 1938 60-Special sedan. The 60-S had a coupé trunk, no running boards and windows framed in thin chrome channels. Its body led to the GM Torpedo C-body of 1940.

Bill married his high-school sweetheart, Jane, and fathered two daughters. He spent World War II in the Navy, in Washington illustrating training manuals. After the war, he returned to the Cadillac studio, and four years later Harley Earl chose him to manage Earl's private industrial-design firm. When Mitchell came back to GM again in 1953, Earl elevated him to director of styling. And when Earl retired in December 1958, Mitchell, his hand-picked successor, took his place.

Mitchell's first cars as vice president – actually created before he took office – were GM's 1959 models. These resulted from a minor revolt against Earl's styling philosophy, a revolt that Mitchell led. The '59s departed from Earl's traditional format by being more linear, cleaner and less 'chromey'. Whereas Earl favoured heavy ornamentation, tall hoods, massive bumpers, and differed in their wheelbases. In various forms these engines served Buick well for the next 22 years. Another improvement on the 1931 Buicks was a synchromesh gearbox, which was standard on all but the Series 50. The following year it was standardised across the range.

Depression and Recovery

Like all other American car makers, Buick was hard-hit by the Depression, sales dropping from a peak of 266,753 in 1926 to a paltry 40,620 in 1933. That year saw restyled Buicks, with a sloping vee-grill and skirted bumpers, while the Division was given a boost by the transfer from the AC Spark Plug Co. of Harlow H. Curtice. He would guide Buick's fortunes until 1948. His first action was to call for a new model which would be of Chevrolet size but a Buick in character. This was the Series 40 which joined the range in 1934. It had a 93bhp 3818cc engine in a 117.1in (2972mm) wheelbase and was a good performer with a top speed of more than 80mph (130km/h). All 1934 Buicks had 'knee action' independent front suspension, while 1936 saw completely fresh styling supervised by Harley Earl, and the Fisher Turret Top all-steel body.

Names replaced series numbers from the 1935 season; the 40 became the Special, the 50 the Super, the 60 the Century, and the 90 the Limited. In 1936 the Super was renamed Roadmaster. The calendar year 1936 saw 179,553 Buicks sold (4.8 per cent of the US industry's total), and 1937 was even better, with 227,038 (5.8 per cent). The 1937 range of 4064 and 5247cc eights covered everything from a Special sedan at $855 to a Limited limousine on a 138in (3503mm) wheelbase at $2342. The three millionth Buick was delivered on 25 October 1936.

1938 Buicks had coil suspension all round and Dynaflow engines. These were the same size as before, but domed high-compression pistons boosted power

1978 Buick Century Limited sedan.
NATIONAL MOTOR MUSEUM

from 100 to 108bhp in the smaller engine, and from 130 to 141bhp in the larger. A Century convertible was timed at 102.93mph (165.75km/h). The main changes for 1939 were steering column gearchange on all models, and new styling with a waterfall grill and partially-recessed headlamps. By 1941 these were fully flush with the front wings, as on most American cars. There were few engineering changes up to the 1942 models, introduced on 3 October 1941, but production was halted on 2 February 1942, after 94,442 had been made. The previous year's production had reached record levels, 310,955 cars in 1940 and 316,251 in 1941. An unusual venture was the commissioning of a line of custom bodies from the high-class coachbuilders, Brunn of Buffalo, New York. Built on the Limited chassis, these were mostly traditional styles such as town car, landau brougham, and landaulette. The proposal did not please GM's Cadillac Division who regarded the top end of the market as traditionally theirs, and they brought pressure to stop the Buick/Brunn link. Because of the very small market for such cars it is unlikely that many would have been sold anyway, but in fact only two or three of each style were made. A number of Buick chassis were sold each year to European coachbuilders, including Carlton and Thrupp & Maberly in England, Nordberg in Sweden, and several Swiss firms.

As with most other American cars, the first postwar Buicks were similar to the 1942 models, with very slight restyling. They had the advantage that the 1942s were advanced anyway, with wings faired into the doors, so they sold well from their introduction in October 1945. The Limited series was not revived, leaving the Special, Super, and Roadmaster to carry the Buick banner. The first important change came in 1948 with the option of Dynaflow automatic transmission on the Roadmaster. Within two years 85 per cent of all Buicks sold would have Dynaflow. In July 1949 Buick launched the Riviera, a 2-door coupé with no B-pillar behind the door. This style became known as the hardtop convertible, or simply hardtop, and was copied by most American manufacturers, and by several in Europe as well. The Riviera was the first truly new body design by General Motors since World War II. At first the Riviera was available only in the Roadmaster series, but in 1950 the style became part of the Super range as well. Confusingly, the Riviera name was also given to a 4-door sedan which was no hardtop, but merely a lengthened and deluxe version of the regular sedan. A pillarless 4-door sedan, an extension of the original Riviera theme, was available from 1955, and in 1957 there was a pillarless station wagon. The Riviera name was kept alive on a few Buick models in the early 1960s, but it was no longer a distinctive car. Then for 1963, came a new Riviera, in no way related to the earlier car but aimed at the Thunderbird market.

Buick had a record production year in 1949, with 398,482 cars built for 7.7 per cent of the total industry. Buick remained in fourth place, behind Chevrolet, Ford, and Plymouth, and they were to hold this position for several years, beating Plymouth into third place from 1954 to 1956. They celebrated their 50th anniversary in 1953 with a brand new 5276cc V8 engine. This was only the fourth major change in engine design in the company's history, and was the first radical engine innovation since the straight-8 of 1931. The new engine was available in the Super series (164bhp with synchromesh, 170bhp with automatic), and 188bhp in the Roadmaster series. The Special used the 4315cc straight-8 in the 1953 models, but the following year saw an all-V8 range.

marque identifiers like portholes, fins, and rockets, Mitchell's touch was more delicate. He put the emphasis on shape and form.

Mitchell's outstanding designs included such cars as the 1963 and 1966 Buick Rivieras, the split-window 1963 Corvette and the '68 Stingray, the 1960 and 1965 Corvairs, 1967 Olds Toronado and Cadillac Eldorado, all of GM's 1965 models, most early Pontiac Bonnevilles, the 1968 Pontiac GTO, and the 1970/71/72 Camaro and Firebird.

Mitchell surrounded himself with what came to be known as his 'Young Turks', a group of dynamic, talented designers who headed the studios and produced the actual designs. The Young Turks consisted of Dave Holls, Stan Wilen, Irv Rybicki, Stan Parker, Paul Gillan, Jack Humbert, and Chuck Jordan.

Late in his GM career, Mitchell developed the 'sheer look', with such exponents as the 1976 Cadillac Seville and 1977 Chevrolet Caprice. He also created the controversial, Rolls-Royce-inspired, 1980 Seville. One of his final designs was the stillborn, retro-styled 'Phantom' show coupé of 1977, a car that his boss, Howard Kehrl, hid from the GM board of directors.

Mitchell was a loud, colourful, often profane, domineering man who could break the tension in a studio with humour — a quip or a witty remark. Unlike Earl, he rarely fired anyone. Like Earl, though, he made a concerted effort to lead the auto industry in styling, and nearly always succeeded. Mitchell became active in motor racing during his vice presidency and defied GM's establishment by racing his Sting Ray privately. He had no Sloan-like patron to come to his rescue, and he survived by a combination of cajolery and bullying. He made plenty of enemies but managed to keep them at bay.

When Bill Mitchell retired in 1977, his hand-picked successor, Chuck Jordan, was passed over, probably because GM's higher-ups thought Jordan too much like Mitchell. Instead, they elected Irv Rybicki as Mitchell's successor.

In retirement, Mitchell opened his own industrial design firm. He took up painting, restored his vintage cars, and rode his 50-odd custom and high-performance motorcycles, usually wearing helmets and driving suits in colours to match the bikes. In the early 1980s, Bill developed heart problems and underwent bypass surgery. He closed his office in 1984 and passed away on 12 September 1988.

ML

The other novelty of 1953 was the Skylark, a limited production convertible in the Roadmaster series with Kelsey Hayes wire wheels, distinctive body trim, and a full complement of luxury features such as the Continental kit which included an exterior spare wheel in its own cover behind the boot. An individual touch was the provision of the owner's signature under a lucite cover on the steering wheel hub. Stylist Ned Nickles lowered the windscreen by four inches. Naturally it used the most powerful Roadmaster engine, but though it looked sporty, it did not have European sports car handling, and attracted fewer buyers than Buick hoped. At $4596 it cost more than $1000 over the price of a regular Roadmaster convertible, and only 1690 of the 1953 Skylarks were sold. Buick tried again the following year, with more dramatic styling and a shorter wheelbase, but the 1954 Skylark sold only 836 units and, hardly surprisingly, there were no 1955s.

Compacts and Personal Cars

Buick styling and sales went through a disappointing period in the late 1950s, with heavy, ponderous lines on the 1958 cars, and wedge-shaped fins on the 1959s. Sales dropped alarmingly, from 535,364 in 1956 to 407,231 in 1957, 257,124 in 1958 and 232,579 in 1959. Even 1960's figure of 307,804 was disappointing compared with others in the American industry which enjoyed a boom year. Buick's place in the production league fell to ninth, their lowest since 1905. Then, in the space of two years, Buick produced two important new models which helped to reinstate them as leading and innovative manufacturers. The first was the Special, an all-new compact car powered by a 155bhp 3523cc all-aluminium V8 engine. The wheelbase was 11in (279mm) shorter than any other Buick at 112in (2843mm), and tyres were 50mm smaller on 330mm rims. The striking sculptured side styling was shared with larger Buicks, with some differences at the rear, but somehow looked better on the smaller car. Four body styles were offered, sedan, coupé, convertible, and station wagon. For the convertible the Skylark name was revived; it had a different grill and rear panels from the other Specials, and a 185bhp engine.

The aluminium V8 was joined for 1962 by a 3245cc V6 which was also used by Oldsmobile in their F-85 compact car from 1964. From that year Buick used a cast-iron block V8 in the Special as well as the V6. The aluminium-engine design was sold to Rover in 1968, being used in several of their larger cars as well as in most Range Rovers. It was also seen in the MGB GT V8 and the Morgan Plus 8. The V6 was used in the Special and Sklylark, with increases in engine size, up to the 1972 season, and it was revived, with a capacity of 3785cc, in the Skylark hatchback coupé of 1975.

Buick's other important innovation of the 1960s was the new Riviera coupé, a 4-seater personal car aimed at the Ford Thunderbird market. It was designed in a GM Special Production Studio headed by Ned Nickles. The new car might have ended up as part of the Oldsmobile or Pontiac line-up, or even as a revived La Salle, but with support from GM's head of styling, Bill Mitchell, it went to Buick. The crisp styling was quite unlike any other 1963 Buick (Bill Mitchell told Nickles he envisaged something between a Rolls-Royce and a Ferrari) but the engine was the standard 325bhp 6570cc V8 as used in the Electra and Le Sabre models. For an extra US$50 though, the purchaser could have an engine bored out to give 6964cc and an extra 15bhp. The big Riviera was continued to 1976, from 1970 having a 7456cc engine. The model was then down-sized in line with other GM cars; the name survived into the late 1980s, and was revived for another personal coupé in 1992.

Smaller Cars and Front-Wheel Drive

Up to the mid-1970s the full-sized Buicks followed the American pattern of ever larger and more powerful engines, the largest had a capacity of 7456cc and was made from 1970 to 1976. However, emission controls reduced power over the same period from 370 to 205bhp. Front disc brakes were available as an option from 1972 on all but the economy Skylarks. These were really intermediate size rather than compact, but in 1973 Buick gained a genuine compact in the Apollo on a 111in (2817mm) wheelbase. It used a Chevrolet Nova body shell and the option of a 4096cc Chevrolet in-line six or a 5735cc Buick V8. In 1975 came the sub-compact Skyhawk hatchback coupé which shared a body with the Chevrolet Monza, though its engine was a new 110bhp 3785cc V6.

The oil crisis of 1973/4 forced GM to the decision that its full-sized car must be down-sized. Names such as Le Sabre and Riviera were retained, but from 1977 engine sizes and wheelbases shrank, and by 1980 the largest V8 was of 5735cc and gave a mere 160bhp. 1979 saw an all-new front-drive Riviera which shared a chassis with the Cadillac Eldorado and Oldsmobile Toronado. It had

1996 Buick Park Avenue sedan.
NICK GEORGANO

independent suspension all round and the option of four wheel disc brakes. Engines were a turbocharged 3785cc V6 or 5735cc V8. More engine options were available in 1981, including a 4129cc V6, 5030cc V8, and 5735cc V8 diesel.

During the early 1980s the Buick range became increasingly aligned with other makes. Thus the Skyhawk introduced in 1982 was a J-car sharing a bodyshell with Cadillac's Cimarron, Chevrolet's Cavalier, Oldsmobile's Firenza, and Pontiac's Sunbird. Engines were mostly common to the other models as well, though from 1984 Buick and Pontiac offered a 1835cc turbocharged engine which gave 150bhp, nearly double the power of the normally-aspirated engine of the same size. Next in size was the Skylark X-car introduced for 1980, a sister car to the Chevrolet Citation, Olds Omega, and Pontiac Phoenix. The J and X cars had front-wheel drive, and this spread up the range, to reach the intermediate Century for 1982 and full-sized Electra for 1984. The Regal intermediate coupé went front-drive in 1987, leaving the Electra and Le Sabre station wagons as the only rear-drive Buicks. Confusingly, the sedans bearing these names had front-drive. The station wagons had 5030cc V8 engines, but otherwise the largest power unit used by Buick was a 3785cc V6 (150 or 165bhp) in the Century, Le Sabre, and Electra sedans, and the Riviera and Reatta coupés. The latter was a new model for 1988, a 2-seater coupé on a shortened Riviera platform, with a top speed of 118mph (190km/h). At $25,000 it was the year's top price Buick. It was conceived as a 'halo' car, enhancing the corporate image and luring into the showrooms customers who might then buy a cheaper car in the Buick range. They were assembled at the Reatta Craft Center in Lansing, Michigan, but sales never reached the Center's capacity of 25,000 cars per year. Little over 20,500 were made between October 1987 and May 1991, when the Reatta was discontinued. A convertible Reatta arrived for 1990, together with a new luxury front-drive sedan with 3785cc V6 engine, the Park Avenue. A supercharged version was planned for 1992, while 1991 saw a return to the big, rear-drive theme called the Roadmaster. A sister to Chevrolet's Caprice, it had a 5702cc V8 engine and was made in sedan and station wagon forms. The latter were the roomiest cars on the American market, with 87 cubic feet of load space. At $21,445 it was $2940 cheaper than the smaller front-drive Park Avenue. Made at Arlington, Texas, the Roadmaster was continued until 1996.

In Spring 1994 Buick brought out a new Riviera with totally fresh styling by Bill Porter, derived from the Lucerne concept car and quite unlike any other Buick. It had modern independent rear suspension with semi-trailing arms, toe-control links, coil springs, and anti-roll bar, and was powered by the 3785cc supercharged V6 engine first seen in the 1992 Park Avenue Ultra sedan. It was made up to November 1998, now with 243bhp. Since the disappearance of the Roadmaster, Buick has had an all-front drive range, and apart from the Riviera all have been 4-door sedans. In 1999 the entry model, the Century, had a 162bhp 3135cc V6 and the more expensive Regal Le Sabre and Park Avenue had the 3785cc V6 in 208 or, with supercharger, 243bhp forms.

NG

Further Reading
Seventy Years of Buick, George Dammann, Crestline Publishing, 1973.
The Buick, a Complete History, Terry B. Dunham and Lawrence R. Gustin, Automobile Quarterly Publications, 1980.

1936 Buick 8

223

1910 Burg 30hp tourer.
JIM BURG

BUKH & GRY (DK) 1904–1905
Bukh & Gry, Horve.
This was a light car powered by a 10/12hp 2-cylinder engine and friction transmission.
NG

BULANT (AUS) 1971
Bulant Motors Pty Ltd, Annangrove, New South Wales.
Being located adjacent to the Amaroo Raceway, it was no surprise that Brian Rawlings should have been building clubman and competition cars for some time before developing a road car, the Bulanti, a mid-engined Mini-based fibreglass coupé. Although of the same dimensions as the Mini, it was of totally different construction, and built on a fabricated steel frame which accepted the Mini sub-frames. Of low build, at 40in (1016mm) high, it weighed 1177lb (535kg). The Bulant name derived from the bull-ant, which is notorious for its sting. When construction proved to be more complex and less economic than envisaged, the project was allowed to lapse after three cars were made.
MG

BULGARI (GB) 1990–1991
Jewellery tycoon Gianni Bulgari placed an advertisement in the press in 1990 for drivetrain and component suppliers for a new high-performance luxury car. Later details and pictures emerged, showing a peculiar-looking 2-door coupé with seating for three in the front and two in the rear. A running prototype apparently used Vauxhall 2-litre twin-cam power and 4-wheel drive. Lotus assessed the Bulgari but nothing more was heard of the project.
CR

BULLOCK (i) (AUS) 1901–1902
Bullock Cycle & Motor Works, Adelaide, South Australia.
John Bullock had done well selling bicycles and became enthusiastic about the prospects presented by motors. In 1901 a light 2-seater vehicle appeared, and this was referred to as a quadricycle, despite having a steering wheel and side by side seating. It was powered by a 2.75hp air-cooled motor and was claimed to be capable of 12.5mph. In 1902 a motorcar was made with a 4hp water-cooled, De Dion-Bouton engine and a 2-speed transmission. This attracted praise for being an excellent conveyance, in which travel was undertaken to many district shows for exhibition. It seems unlikely that sales resulted as motorcars soon gave way to Bullock motorcycles which were marketed for several years through his chain of cycle stores.
MG

BULLOCK (ii) (GB) 1972–1973
Bullock, Shepperton, Middlesex.
This singularly inelegant 2-seater sports kit car consisted of a glassfibre body mounted on a pre-drilled box section chassis for Ford Anglia parts. The Bullock B1 had bulbous headlamp pods to clear the front suspension but the B2 employed Triumph Herald suspension that obviated the need for these pods. About three dozen Bullocks were sold.
CR

BULLY (D) 1933
Bully Fahrzeugbau, Berlin.
The Bully was a 3-wheeled 2-seater coupé powered by a 200cc single-cylinder engine driving the single rear wheel by chain. A few cars had 600cc engines, but production in any case was very limited.
HON

BÜNGER (DK) 1947–1949
De Forende Automobilfabrikker, Odense.
Engineer Borge Bünger created a 3-wheeled 'people's car' with the help of a coachbuilding company. The front end looked conventional, with a sloping coupé rear over the single rear wheel. A front-mounted 600cc Ilo 2-cylinder 19bhp engine was fitted, and a top speed of 56mph (90km/h) was claimed. Three people could be fitted in the rather cramped interior. No production run ensued.
CR

BURDICK (US) 1909
Burdick Motor Co., Eau Claire, Wisconsin.
Ralph Burdick was a successful manufacturer of small 2-stroke marine engines when he decided to enter the motor business. This he did with an enormous 7-seater tourer on a 142in (3604mm) wheelbase, powered by a 9668cc 6-cylinder Continental engine. Only one was built, priced at $7000, but it is not certain if Burdick ever found a buyer for it. A planned Greyhound model (presumably a roadster) was never built.
NG

BURG (US) 1910–1913
L. Burg Carriage Co., Dallas City, Illinois.
This company made buggies in Weaver, Iowa, from about 1870 to 1900 when the plant was destroyed by fire and the company moved to Dallas City. After experimenting with a high-wheeler in 1907, Louis Burg adopted a conventional lay-out for the car he launched in 1910. It had a 30hp Rutenber 4-cylinder engine and was made in three styles, 5-seater tourer, 5-seater roadster, and 3-seater runabout, all priced at $1750. For 1910 they added a larger 6-cylinder model, rated at 50hp and priced at $2400 for a 7-seater tourer. This was the only offering for 1913, the engine now quoted as 60hp. It has been suggested that the move to six cylinders brought about the downfall of the Burg car. They ceased production in 1913, after about 50 had been made. Burg continued as buggy makers until 1919, when falling demand forced them to close. The factory later became a dance hall and, later still, a frozen food factory.
NG

BURGERS (NL) 1898–1906
Eerste Nederlandsche Rijwielenfabriek, Deventer.
The successful Eerste Nederlandsche Rijwielfabriek (First Dutch Bicycle Factory) at Deventer was established in 1869 by Hendricus Burgers. Less well-known is his career as a car manufacturer. In 1899 he published advertisements for a 1-ton lorry and a light vehicle at the price of DG2100. Burgers also delivered De Dion engines, so it is logical that he used these engines himself in his production vehicles.
  At the Amsterdam exhibition of 1900 Burgers had a 3-wheeled vehicle on display with his own engine. Earlier he had used Minerva and Fafnir engines too, and in later years he used De Dion engines again. In 1907 Burgers had English STAR and STUART cars on display at the RAI exhibition, but as a not so successful importer. In 1952 they tried to start the production under licence of the German BRÜTSCH, but, just like in Germany, it was a disaster. The firm became bankrupt in 1961, and the name of Burgers went to the Amersfoort firm Pon.
FBV

BURGETT & WEST (US) 1899
C.E. Burgett-William S. West, Middleburg, New York.
The Burgett & West or West & Burgett, depending on which of their descendants is approached, was intended for production but never progressed beyond its pilot model. This was a 2-cylinder steam car constructed by C.E. Burgett, a machinist, and William S. West, operator of a Middleburg laundry. Using gasoline

1930 Burney Streamline saloon.
NATIONAL MOTOR MUSEUM

for fuel, drive was by a single chain to the rear axle. The car was operated for several years and believed to have been scrapped.

KM

BURKE (GB) 1906–1907

Burke Engineering Co. Ltd, Clonmel, Tipperary.

The first car to be made in what later became the Irish Republic, the Burke used a 24/30hp French-built engine, though the chassis and gearbox were of their own manufacture. Final drive was by chains. They said that they only bought in parts which they were unable to make themselves. The Burke made its appearance at the first Irish Motor Show in January 1907, and was still listed in 1908. The company were also agents for the ASTAHL car.

NG

BURLAT (F) 1905–1907

Sté des Moteurs Rotatifs Burlat Frères, Lyons.

Four Burlat brothers were involved in their car, but it seems that the youngest, Antoine, was the designer. His engine was a 12/16hp rotary unit with four cylinders and a capacity of 2798cc. It was mounted vertically under a very low bonnet in which the starting handle was located in the centre of the round radiator. The car had a conventional 4-speed gearbox and shaft drive. Burlat built his engine in 1904, and in 1905 with his brothers bought a large factory in the Lyons suburb of Villeurbanne for manufacture of the cars. A 4/5 seater tourer was exhibited in front of the Paris Salon in December 1905, and three more cars were completed. Apparently there were serious problems with overheating. Even so, Burlat sold a licence to a Coventry firm to build his engines for sale in Great Britain and its colonies, but only for use in taxis and aeroplanes! Burlat formed a separate company for the manufacture of commercial vehicles, the first of which was completed in 1906. It was a 2-ton lorry and used the car's engine but running on naphthalene rather than petrol. He planned to make 5-ton forward-control lorries with 8-cylinder rotary engines, but probably the 2-tonner was the only one completed. From 1907 to 1914 he made a number of aero-engines where the rotary layout was the norm rather than the eccentricity which it was for road vehicles. He was later involved in the design of the Sans Secousse models for COTTIN-DESGOUTTES.

NG

BURLINGTON (GB) 1981–1992

1981–1988 Burlington Motor Spares, Southam, Warwickshire.
1988–1989 The Burlington Motor Company, Northampton.
1989–1992 Burlington Design Group, Northampton.

Haydn Davis built his Burlington SS in traditional style around the wings and nose cone of the Morgan. A Triumph Herald/Vitesse chassis sat underneath it, though the engine was moved rearwards and the suspension modified. The doorless body was a metal-and-glassfibre-jointed plywood main tub clad in aluminium. A purpose-designed chassis became available from 1982 for Morris Marina/MGB/Ford Escort drive trains. The project was sold off to a company called DORIAN in 1986. Meanwhile, the Arrow (again Herald-based) introduced the idea of a 'plans-built' car to Britain: customers made the aluminium-skinned plywood body tub themselves. The Arrow had cycle wings, but the later Berretta had flowing glassfibre wings. The Chieftain (a Willys Jeep replica) was another aluminium-and-plywood plans-built car on a Herald or Spitfire chassis, while the Centurion was a design by the American company QUINCY-LYNN.

CR

BURLY (US) c.1993

Burly Industries, Mendon, Utah.

Custom VW Beetles were the speciality of this kit car manufacturer. The Buffel was a custom rear body that fitted onto a chopped Beetle. It looked like an early European special body with a coupé top and enclosed rear wheels. A 'Woody' body with real wood trim on a station wagon-style rear end combined with their 1937 or 1940 Ford-style bonnet made a stylish surfboard carrier.

HP

BURNEY (GB) 1930–1933

Streamline Cars Ltd, Maidenhead, Berkshire.

The most radical car to be made in Britain between the wars, the Burney Streamline was the work of Sir Charles Dennistoun Burney (1888–1968) who, as well as being a successful businessman and Conservative MP, was a tireless inventor. A great supporter of streamlining, he was put in charge of building the R.100 airship at Howden, Yorkshire, where among his fellow workers were author Neville Shute and bouncing-bomb inventor Barnes Wallis. He built his first car at

225

Howden in 1928/9. It had a spaceframe of Duralumin alloy covered with fabric, and the rear-mounted engine was a 1481cc front-drive Alvis unit turned back to front. Suspension was all-independent by transverse springs, and brakes were hydraulic. Top speed was over 80mph (129km/h).

Aided by some wealthy friends, including textile heir Stephen Courtauld, who bought one of his cars, Burney formed Streamline Cars Ltd and took part of the premises at Maidenhead which also housed the remnants of G.W.K. and the British IMPERIA. Burney admitted many years later that it was quite unsuited for anything other than prototype work, but nevertheless he issued a lavish catalogue and built 12 cars there. Like the prototype, they had fabric-covered spaceframe bodies and independent suspension all round. Three different types of engine were used, the 2956cc straight-8 Beverley-Barnes (nine cars), 3190cc Armstrong-Siddeley 20 (two cars) and 4389cc straight-8 Lycoming (one car). With the latter the radiator was behind the engine, while with the other units it was mounted ahead. Top speed was said to be 75mph (121km/h) with the 6-cylinder engines, and 85mph (137km/h) with the eight. However, a weight distribution of 70 per cent on the rear axle did not make for good handling. The Amalgamated Press' *Motoring Encyclopaedia*, which normally reported uncritically on cars, observed '...the shifting of the centre of gravity towards the rear is likely to have less desirable effects on the car's stability'. Three styles of front end were offered, a rounded front with headlamps faired into it, a conventional pointed dummy radiator and a bonnetless front in the style of modern MPVs. The Burney's unusual appearance naturally attracted plenty of attention, which was increased when the Prince of Wales acquired one in July 1931.

Burney tried to interest a number of major manufacturers in his designs, including Standard and Riley, but the firm that showed the most interest was Rolls-Royce. Ernest Hives, then head of the experimental department, tested a Burney in December 1931, and was impressed with its speed and silence. 'I would not like to have the responsibility of turning it down', he reported to Sir Henry Royce. However, turned down it was, for one cannot imagine the company making a rear-engined Rolls-Royce. Nor would they agree to Burney's request that they should supply him with components, hardly surprising as they never supplied any items to other manufacturers.

Burney's last fling was to take the Lycoming-engined car to Detroit in an attempt to interest the major car makers there. The press was enthusiastic, the manufacturers were not. No more cars were made at Maidenhead, but Burney sold a licence to Crossley who fitted their own 1990cc 6-cylinder engine in a modified design. The streamlined shape and independent suspension were still there, but the radiator was at the front, necessitating complicated plumbing, with two separate tanks front and rear. Only 25 Crossley-Burneys were made; two survive, but none of the Burney Streamlines. Burney himself went on to design aerial gliding bombs, gun-fired rockets, and sonar apparatus for detecting fish.

NG

Further Reading
Lost Causes of Motoring, Lord Montagu of Beaulieu, Cassell, 1960.
'A Pioneer who was too far ahead of his time', John Price Williams, *The Daily Telegraph*, 9 May 1998.

BURNS (i) *see* BILLINGS

BURNS (ii) (US) 1908–1912
Burns Bros, Havre de Grace, Maryland.
The Burns was a high-wheeler, and like many others was built by a former maker of carriages and buggies. In its original form it had a 16hp 2-cylinder air-cooled engine, friction transmission and double-chain drive. As well as the traditional open buggy, it could be had with a fully-enclosed Transformable Coupé body. An 18/20hp 4-cylinder engine was also available for 1910, but lasted only one year. Smaller wheels were used on the last models of 1912, in an attempt to get away from the buggy appearance, but cars were abandoned that year. Perhaps the problem was that Maryland was a long way from the traditional Mid-West markets for high-wheelers.

NG

BURROWES (US) 1904–1908
E.T. Burrowes Co., Portland, Maine.

Cars were never more than a sideline for this company, which was a leading manufacturer of house screens. Two distinct types of car were made, a light chain-driven runabout with single-cylinder engine under the seat in 1904/05, and a conventional shaft-driven tourer with 4-cylinder engine, in 1908. Not more than eight cars were made in all.

NG

BURROWS (US) 1914–1915
Burrows Cyclecar Co., Ripley, New York.
This was a typical cyclecar powered by a 9hp 2-cylinder air-cooled Mack engine, with friction transmission and final drive by long belts. At 106in (2690mm) the wheelbase was long for a cyclecar. Tandem seating was used on the 1914 model, while for 1915 the side-by-side pattern was adopted. Neither this nor a price reduction from $375 to $295 helped sales.

NG

BURTIS MOTORWORKS (US) 1999 to date
Burtis Motorworks, Yonkers, New York.
Cobra replicas in several flavours were the speciality here. Body styles included 289, 427, 289FIA and 427SC types. There were several suspension options including live rear axles and IRS. Engine choices were Chevrolet, Ford and Chrysler small-blocks. It was sold in kit and assembled form.

HP

BURY (US) 1926–1927
Charles W. Bury, New York, New York.
Probably no more than a single Bury was completed. This midget car with a 73 inch (1853mm) wheelbase was, in its builder's mind, the shape of things to come in economical motoring, much along the lines of the Austin Seven which had been debuted in 1922 and had since met with phenomenal success in England. The 2-passenger roadster was fitted with a Continental H2 4-cylinder engine but efforts in financing and obtaining a factory site, both unsuccessful, doomed the Bury before it got beyond the single prototype.

KM

BUSH (US) 1916–1925
Bush Motor Co., Chicago, Illinois.
The Bush, like its Chicago counterpart, the BIRCH, was literally a car without a factory. John H. Bush decided to sell cars by mail-order exclusively and toward this goal he struck up a deal with several plain-Jane assembled car manufacturers to ship cars directly from their factories to the purchaser who would have paid for the car in advance. Among the companies supplying Bush cars to their buyers were Piedmont, Norwalk, Pullman, Sphinx, Crow-Elkhart and Huffman, which simply attached a Bush badge and related nomenclature on cars as needed. Bush – again like Birch – ran small advertisements in such magazines as *Popular Mechanics* and, during the new car famine of World War I, noting that a new Bush car was readily available 'if you actually need it', adding that 'our cars are being produced under full authorisation of the US Government War Industries at Washington, DC' although one wonders how. 'If you need a car' the ad continued, 'write to us', adding 'Don't write if you can get on without it. If you are accessible to transportation which you can use – don't buy a car now. We want to place our cars where they can accomplish the most good, especially until the end of the war.' It was a curious form of salesmanship but it worked to some extent and, after the war, Bush continued in business for seven years. Bush also founded Bush College in Chicago, a training school in auto mechanics and sales which, upon graduation, the students would be given a Bush car at cost and the right to sell franchises for the car. The Bush offered a variety of both open and closed models, 4-cylinder cars powered by a Lycoming K engine and the sixes by a Continental 7R. A pickup truck was also available. Probably several hundred Bush-badged cars were sold in the firm's nine-year existence, all supplied by other manufacturers.

KM

BUSSON (F) 1907–1908
Voiturettes Busson, Paris.
This company made a small number of 7/9hp 2-cylinder voiturettes in 1908, but were more active in selling other firms' products. The 1907 Busson-Dedyn

1934 Butz 400cc chassis.
NATIONAL MOTOR MUSEUM

was a 30hp NAGANT, while they also sold the small 6-cylinder DE BAZALAIRE as the Busson-Bazalaire.

NG

BUSY BEE (GB) 1922–1923
Joseph Mills, Mansfield, Nottinghamshire.
This was a light 3-wheeled monocar powered by a 5hp single-cylinder Stag engine, with 2-speed gearbox and chain drive. It was built to order only.

NG

BUTLER (US) 1982–1997
Butler Racing, Goleta, California.
Ron Butler was an employee at Shelby American when they were racing Cobras, and later made components for ARNTZ. When Arntz went out of business, Butler ended up with the production jigs and moulds and put the Arntz kit back into production. He made few changes in the basic design until he sold the project in 1998 to G&S MOTORSPORTS.

HP

BUTTERFIELD (GB) 1961–1963
Butterfield Engineering, Nazing, Essex.
To the Butterfield Musketeer goes the honour of being the world's first Mini-based kit car. It was oddly styled, with a long nose that titled forward for engine access and bulbous lines in glassfibre. Into a multi-tubular chassis could be fitted either an 848cc or 998cc Mini engine. An up-market specification included a rev counter and optional adjustable dampers. Its high price (almost twice as much as a Mini) consigned it to an early grave.

CR

BUTTEROSI (F) 1919–1924
Sté Nouvelle des Automobiles Butterosi, Boulogne-sur-Seine.
In his book *French Vintage Cars*, John Bolster began his entry on this make 'Some people think all vintage cars were good, which only proves that they have never owned a Butterosi!' There may be some truth in this unkind comment, for it seems to have been an undistinguished small car powered by a 1327cc side-valve 4-cylinder engine, though it did have unit construction of engine and 4-speed gearbox and a combined magneto and dynamo. Body styles were 2-seater, 4-seater tourer and an ugly 6-light saloon whose appearance was not helped by Michelin disc wheels. The wire-wheeled 2-seater was better looking.

The Butterosi was shown at the Paris and London Shows in 1919, and was heavily advertised in the British press, including many national dailies, but after an appearance at the Scottish Show in January 1920, little more was heard of it, though it was carried by some lists up to 1924.

NG

Further Reading
'The Butterosi; Fragments on Forgotten Makes No.87', Bill Boddy,
Motor Sport, November 1987.

BUTZ (D) 1934
Bungartz & Co., Munich.
This was an attempt to enter the people's car market with a small 4-wheeler powered by a rear-mounted 400cc 2-cylinder engine. It was unusual in having independent suspension all round. The body was a 2-seater coupé, and the Butz could be supplied with a 2-wheeled trailer in matching colours for carrying luggage.

HON

B.W.R. (F) 1996 to date
B.W.R., Villemur sur Tarn.
This was an A.C. Cobra 427 replica, fully homologated for sale in France. Three versions were marketed: a luxury model, a competition model, and a pure race car. Tuned Rover 3.9- or 5.0-litre V8 engines were fitted.

CR

BYERS (US) 1955–1960
Byers Manufacturing, El Segundo, California.
Jim Byers only built two models of body shells for kit cars, but they were both excellent designs. He had co-operated with Dick Jones on the METEOR kit cars in 1953–55, but when Jones moved to Colorado, Byers restyled the design and marketed it as the SR-100 because it was designed to fit a 100in (2538mm) wheelbase chassis. However, it could be shortened if needed. This body received rave reviews and was very popular on street cars. Byers added the CR-90 for competition use on a 90in (2284mm) wheelbase. It had a strong Italian flair and an optional headrest. In 1960 Byers sold his moulds to VICTRESS Manufacturing who continued to sell them until 1961 when they sold their kit car line to LA DAWRI. La Dawri later passed the moulds on to KELLISON, who dropped the CR-90 but carried the SR-100 until the late 1960s.

HP

B&Z (US) 1961–c.1981
B&Z Electric Car Co., Long Beach, California.
One of the most successful and long-lived electric cars ever made was the Electra King. The boxy glassfibre-bodied microcar was built virtually unchanged for around 20 years. Both 3-wheeled and 4-wheeled models were built, the former with a single front wheel. A series-wound dc electric motor fed around 1bhp to one of the rear wheels via chain and a 3-speed transmission. More powerful (2bhp and 3.5bhp) versions were later added, and there was a choice of tiller or steering wheel, and foot or hand controls. The most popular version had two seats, but there was a 4-seater with a Surrey-type roof and a rearward-facing rear seat.

CR

B.Z. (D) 1925
Bootswerft Zeppelinhafen GmbH, Pottsdam-Wildpark.
This was one of a number of small cars to use the 494cc flat-twin BMW motorcycle engine. It had an aluminium body.

HON

B-Z-T (US) 1915
B-Z-T Cyclecar Co., Owego, New York.
This was a late entry into the cyclecar market, and though it was more refined than some, it failed to sell. It had a 12/15hp air-cooled 2-cylinder engine, friction transmission and, unusually for a cyclecar, shaft drive. The name came from the three men behind the project, C.K. Ball, W.H. Zeh, and D.N. Thompson.

NG

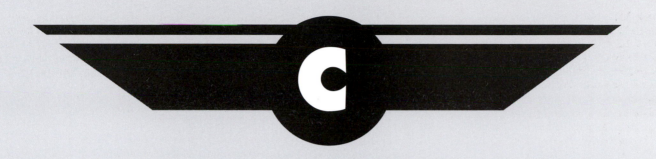

CABAN (F) 1926–1932

Yves Giraud-Cabantous, Boulogne-sur-Seine.

Giraud-Cabantous was a racing driver who had several successes at the wheel of Salmsons before setting up as a manufacturer. All his cars used 1097cc Ruby 4-cylinder engines in a chassis of his own construction. At first he used the 30bhp Ruby Type OC, but from 1928 the more powerful 38bhp OS was employed. Some cars of 1931 and 1932 had the 43bhp K engine, while one or two racing Cabans had supercharged K engines, which gave 60bhp and a top speed of 105mph (170km/h). Only 28 Cabans were made in all, of which 19 were sports or racing cars, six were saloons and three cabriolets. After ending car manufacture, Giraud-Cabantous had a successful career at the wheel of Chenard-Walcker, Delahaye, and Talbot cars.

NG

CADILLAC (US) 1902 to date

1902–1905 Cadillac Automobile Co., Detroit, Michigan.
1905 to date Cadillac Motor Car Co., Detroit, Michigan.

For many years the Cadillac was the ultimate symbol of personal success to the average American, although it originated as a low-price car with many similarities to the first Ford. This is hardly surprising, given the history of the two companies.

The celebrated engineer, Henry M. Leland (1843–1932) was running a successful business, Leland & Falconer, making engines and transmissions. Among his customers was OLDSMOBILE, but when R.E. Olds turned down his latest engine on grounds of cost, and also because retooling for it would cause an unacceptable delay, Leland had to look elsewhere for business. He had been invited by the directors of the ailing Henry Ford Co. to advise them on the liquidation of their firm, but instead he suggested that his engine would go well in their car, and that a new company should be formed for its manufacture. For a name they chose that of the French explorer Antoine de la Mothe Cadillac (1656–1730) who had discovered Detroit early in the eighteenth Century. The Cadillac Automobile Co. was formed on 22 August 1902, and the first Cadillac car was completed on 17 October. It was retrospectively called, like the contemporary Ford, the Model A, although Cadillac did not use the 'A' designation in 1903. It was typical of American design at that time, with a single-cylinder horizontal engine under the seat, 2-speed epicyclic transmission and single-chain drive to the rear axle. The 2-seater was priced at $750, but a rear-entrance tonneau could be had for an extra $100. The car looked very similar to the Model A Ford, made by the Ford Motor Co. which Henry started after leaving his previous concern, but this had a 2-cylinder engine, and did not appear until June 1903.

In January 1903 the Cadillac was displayed at the New York Automobile Show. It was fortunate in having a successful salesman, William E. Metzger, later the 'M' of the E.M.F. car company, who took 2286 orders before the week was out. Production did not start until March, but by the year's end 2497 Cadillacs had been made. This figure is according to historian Walter McCall, but Gary Hoonsbeen, working from surviving invoice books, quotes 1652, although he admits the invoice list may not be complete. The 1904 figure was 2418, not helped by a disastrous fire in April which interrupted production for four weeks. The first model, now called Model A, was continued for 1904, joined by Model B which used the same engine but had a different appearance thanks to a dummy bonnet. This implied that the car had a front-mounted engine, although in fact it was in its usual place under the seat. The bonnet offered a small amount of luggage.

A genuine front-engined car, with four cylinders, arrived for 1905 in the shape of the Model D. With a capacity of 4932cc and a $2800 price tag, the Model D marked a significant move up-market for Cadillac, although it was still well below the true luxury cars such as Winton, Thomas and Locomobile, which sold for $5000 or more. Cadillac made 3712 cars in 1905, of which 156 were Model Ds, and the rest single-cylinder cars. In October 1905 the Cadillac Automobile Co. was merged with Leland & Falconer who made their engines; the new company was called the Cadillac Motor Co., a title it still holds today. Henry M. Leland was general manager.

In 1907 he began importing the famous Johanssen gauges from Sweden. Invented by Carl Edward Johanssen, the 'Jo Block' gauges eventually made possible the complete interchangeability of parts which Leland saw as essential to the motor industry. His ideas were put to a dramatic test in 1908 when the British Cadillac importer, Frederick S. Bennett, took three single-cylinder

1929 Caban 6CV cabriolet.
NATIONAL MOTOR MUSEUM

1920 Cadillac V8 Opera coupé.
NATIONAL MOTOR MUSEUM

runabouts to Brooklands where they were completely taken apart. The 2163 components were then thoroughly mixed up and piled in three heaps. The cars were then reassembled, started and ran perfectly. This feat won for Cadillac the Thomas Dewar Trophy, awarded annually since 1904 to the manufacturer who had made the most significant advance in motor engineering. Cadillac was the first US company to win the trophy, which they were awarded again in 1913 for their Delco combined electric lighting and starting.

New Models and a New Owner

A very important year for Cadillac was 1909. The single-cylinder cars which had done so much to establish the company were dropped, as were the existing fours. About 16,000 singles had been made. Their replacement was a single model, the 3702cc 4-cylinder Thirty. This up-to-date design was available with three body styles, roadster, demi-tonneau and tourer, and was priced at a reasonable $1400 ($1600 in 1910 when the limousine cost $3000). It sold a record 5903 during its first year. The other big development of 1909 was that William C. Durant, who had founded General Motors the previous year, bought Cadillac for $5.6 million. He wisely allowed the Lelands, Henry and his son Wilfred, to remain in charge, Henry becoming president and general manager.

The Thirty was made without major change up to 1912, and in that year came the important step of using the Delco electric lighting and starting system. Invented by Charles F. Kettering (1876–1958) of the Dayton Engineering Laboratories Co. (hence the name Delco), the starter was a miniature dynamo actuated by the battery. It was so powerful that a chassis carrying 12 men could be propelled solely by the starter motor. Once it had done its work of starting the engine (it was geared to the flywheel) it reverted to its role as a dynamo, supplying electric current for the ignition and lighting, and charging the battery. This ancestor of all modern systems immediately put Cadillac ahead of all other makes in sophistication and convenience. Within a year most makers of quality cars were scrambling to catch up.

1929 Cadillac V8 transformable town cabriolet.
NATIONAL MOTOR MUSEUM

1938 Cadillac V16 formal sedan.
NATIONAL MOTOR MUSEUM

The name Thirty was dropped on the 1912 models because, with a capacity increased to 4690cc in 1911, the output was well above 30hp. Prices were up somewhat as well, although the cars were still excellent value, with a basic price of $1800, rising to $3250 for a 7-seater limousine. For 1913 capacity went up to 5994cc, and power to 48bhp. Production was well up on previous years, at 12,708 in 1912 and 17,284 in 1913.

In 1914 a 2-speed rear axle was introduced which, combined with a 3-speed gearbox, gave six forward speeds. However, the AUSTIN Automobile Co. of Grand Rapids, Michigan, already held a patent on this, and, threatened with legal action, Cadillac quietly dropped the device the following year. A more lasting innovation for 1914 was the adoption of lhd. In September 1914 Cadillac announced their 1915 Model 51. Externally similar to the 1914 models, it differed radically under the bonnet by having a V8 engine. Cadillac were not the first to make a V8 (De Dion-Bouton had been building them in small quantities since 1910), but they were the first manufacturer to standardise the layout and to make it in large numbers. They have offered a V8 every year for the past 85 years.

The Model 51's engine was a 90 degree V8 of 5145cc which developed 70bhp at 2400rpm. Side-valves were actuated by a single camshaft in the neck of the vee. Designed by Scottish-born D. McCall White under the supervision of the Lelands, the V8 propelled the car at speeds up to 65mph (105km/h). Nine body styles were available, at prices from $1975 to $3600. Just over 13,000 cars were sold in the first year, a remarkable figure for a new and untried design. Cadillac soon had their imitators as they had done with the electric starter. Within a few years more than 20 US manufacturers were offering V8-powered cars.

Few changes were made to the V8 over the next four years, apart from an increase in power to 77bhp, thanks to a new carburettor. On the personal front, the Lelands left in 1917 after a disagreement with Durant about wartime production. The patriotic Lelands wanted to made Liberty aero engines, but Durant insisted that car production should continue. As overall boss of General Motors he had his own way but the Lelands were soon making aero engines in the new Lincoln factory, which would later make cars under the same name.

After its acquisition by Henry Ford in 1922, Lincoln would become a serious rival to Cadillac in the high price field. In fact Durant's policy was not unpatriotic, for thousands of Cadillacs served in the war as staff cars for senior officers, in the British, Canadian and French armies, as well as with the US forces. The V8 engines were also used in crawler tractors and balloon winches.

Detachable cylinder heads arrived on the 1918 models, and front-wheel brakes in 1924, but the V8 evolved only gradually up to 1928, when there was major restyling. Between 1920 and 1930 Cadillac prices rose, and with many custom bodies on offer the make's prestige rose too, but it did not become pre-eminent until the really exclusive makes such as Duesenberg, Locomobile and Pierce-Arrow disappeared in the 1930s. Among the leading coachbuilders working on Cadillac chassis were Fleetwood, Judkins, Uppercu (the New York distributors), and the Don Lee studios of Los Angeles. The chief stylist for Don Lee was Harley J. Earl (1893–1969), who joined Cadillac in 1927 and was put in charge of the La Salle project, the junior line of Cadillac which was launched that year.

The new Cadillacs were called the Series 341, from their engine capacity of 341cu in (5587cc). They were sold in two distinct price classes, standard with Fisher bodies at $3295 to $3950, and custom with Fleetwood bodies at $4095 to $6200. Fleetwood now belonged to General Motors, and practically all their work was on Cadillac and La Salle chassis. In 1930 seven styles were offered in the Fisher line, and 37 by Fleetwood. Fisher was a mass producer, also owned by GM. As might be expected, there were few styling changes for 1929, but an important innovation was the synchromesh gearbox, the world's first use of the now universal system.

Cadillac's sales had climbed dramatically in the 1920s, from 19,628 in the 1920 model year to 56,038 in the 1928 model year, made up of 40,000

NICK BALDWIN

LELAND, HENRY (1843–1932)

One of the greatest American engineers, Henry Leland was a generation older than most of the men he Inspired, the founders of the industry like Ransom Olds and Henry Ford. He was born on a Vermont farm in 1843, the eighth child of Leander and Zilpha Leland who were of pioneer stock; Leander's ancestors had arrived in Massachusetts in 1652. He started work at the age of fourteen in the Crompton-Knowles Loom Works at Worcester, Massachusetts, where a mechanic made one of the great mistakes of history by observing to young Henry, 'Thou'll never be a mechanic, lad'. His apprenticeship at Crompton-Knowles over, he joined the Springfield Armoury, making rifles for the Civil War, then joined the Colt Revolver Works in Hartford, Connecticut. Probably the best-equipped machine shop in the world, it was at Colt that the concept of interchangeable parts became a practical reality, leading to mass production.

After two years at Colt Leland joined Brown & Sharpe at Providence, Rhode Island, which had produced the world's first practical hand

1959 Cadillac 62 sedan.
NATIONAL MOTOR MUSEUM

micrometer and the first universal milling machine. There, men worked to tolerances as close as four millionths of an inch, and Leland was in his element, soon contributing inventions of his own, including a hair clipper and the world's first universal grinding machine, which appeared in 1876. When Brown & Sharpe decided to expand their sales westwards, Leland was their natural choice, This took him to Detroit, where at last he was able to realise his ambition and start his own firm. This was in partnership with Robert C. Faulconer, a wealthy lumber man, and an associate from Brown & Sharpe, Charles Norton. They were joined by Leland's son Wilfred, who shared his father's mechanical skills, and abandoned a medical career to become an engineer. Leland, Faulconer & Norton was founded in September 1890; their work included tool and lathe grinders, milling machines and gear cutters, while they also acted as consultants to the industry. They developed gear-set making machinery for the Pope and Pierce bicycle companies, which brought them considerable revenue. By 1896 they had a foundry for high-grade casting work, and began to make steam engines, many of which were used in Detroit's tramcars. They also made internal combustion engines for marine use, which naturally led them into the infant car industry.

Their first customer was Ransom Eli Olds to whom they supplied transmissions and single-cylinder engines for the Curved Dash. The Dodge brothers also provided engines of identical design, but they gave less power because they were less precisely machined than the Leland engine. Henry Leland was not happy working for Ransom Olds, who was more concerned with getting cars on the road than in precision engineering. He was attracted by the Henry Ford Co. which seemed to have potential, even though its founder had spent so much time on racing cars that only a single prototype road car had been built. Henry left in March 1902 and Leland was invited by his directors to value the machinery for liquidation of the firm. Instead, he offered to reorganise it and so, at the age of nearly sixty, he was in at the foundation of another great American marque. A new name had to be found as Henry Ford was no longer involved, and they chose Cadillac, after the French explorer Antoine de la Mothe Cadillac who had established a trading post at Detroit in 1701. Leland & Faulconer naturally provided the single-cylinder engines, and also transmissions and steering gear. The first car was supplied to the Centaur Motor Vehicle Co. of Buffalo, New York (who made electric cars of their own) on 5th March 1903.

Leland's obsession with precision and interchangeability stood Cadillac in good stead through the time that he was with the firm This was demonstrated during the famous Standardisation Test at Brooklands in 1908 when three Cadillacs were completely dismanted, the parts scrambled and then the cars were re-assembled successfully. He was instrumental in adopting Charles F. Kettering's Delco electric starter on 1912 Cadillacs, and in the V8 engine which was announced in September 1914.

The previous month war had broken out in Europe, and Leland was one of those who believed that America should help in supplying material to the Allies, in particular, aero engines. He asked Billy Durant, head of General Motors of which Cadillac was a part, if the new Cadillac body plant could be used for manufacture of the Liberty engine, but Durant refused. Furious, Henry Leland and Wilfred left Cadillac and founded their own company to make the engines. Henry was a great admirer of Abraham Lincoln, and would have joined Lincoln's army at the beginning of the Civil War had he not been too young, so he chose the name Lincoln for his new company. They made 6500 engines up to January 1919, then turned to a new car, which also carried the Lincoln name. Also a luxury V8, it was in many ways an improved Cadillac. Due to inability to obtain the necessary further financing, Lincoln went into receivership in 1922, and was acquired by Henry Ford for a bargain $8 million. The Lelands remained with the company, but Ford's promise of lack of interference was not borne out in practice. Henry Ford had promised the spend two hours a day sorting out any problems which might arise, but he never saw the Lelands at all. After five months they both left. Leland was now 79 but continued to be active in local affairs. He had always been interested in social welfare and civic matters and had organised the Detroit Citizens League, of which he was president for many years. He was given honorary degrees of Doctor of Engineering by the Universities of Michigan (1920) and Vermont (1923). He died on 26th March 1932, aged 89. Wilfred became a mining engineer after leaving Ford.

NG

Further Reading
Automobile Design – Great Designers and their Work,
Ed. R. Barker and A. Harding, David & Charles, 1970.

1980 Cadillac Seville Elegante sedan.
NATIONAL MOTOR MUSEUM

Cadillacs and 16,038 La Salles. These were record figures which would not be beaten until 1941.

For 1930 the V8 engine was increased in size to 5785cc and in power to 95bhp, but it was overshadowed by the impressive and innovative V16 which was launched in January 1930. This had been under development for more than three years, and was Cadillac's challenge for the top of the luxury market. Designed by Owen M. Nacker, the engine was basically two straight-8 ohv engines on a common crankshaft, angled at a narrow 45 degrees. Each bank had its own fuel and exhaust system. Among the engine's refinements were hydraulic valve adjusters which were exceptionally silent. It was said that at idling speed nothing could be heard apart from the spark of the contact points. The V16's capacity was 7420cc and output 165bhp. Top speed was 78–90mph (125–145km/h) according to the coachwork fitted. This came in no fewer than 54 styles, a bewildering array from sporty roadsters, convertibles and coupés to formal limousines and town cars. They were all semi-custom designs built by

Fleetwood, prices starting at $5350 for a roadster, and rising to $9700 for a town brougham. In addition the V16 chassis was supplied to other firms including Murphy, Waterhouse and, in France, Saoutchik, for full customs. The V16 was built and serviced to a higher standard than other Cadillacs; dealers were required to provide the factory with weekly and monthly owner reaction and service reports on each V16 delivered.

Sales of the V16 began encouragingly, with 2887 finding customers in the 1930 model year, but in 1931 only 364 were sold. From 1932 to the end of production in 1940, only a further 1152 sales were recorded. The Depression accounted in part for this decline, but also there was the factor experienced by other makers of expensive cars, that much of the demand was satisfied in the first year, and customers were not likely to make annual changes of a car costing up to $9000. Also, V16 sales were hit by the arrival in the autumn of 1930 of the V12. This was a similar design of engine and chassis, but with a capacity of 6030cc (135bhp). The wheelbase was 8in shorter than the V16's, and there were fewer body styles, but prices were lower, at $3795 to $4345 for the Fisher-bodied range, and $3945 to $4995 with Fleetwood bodies. It is difficult to explain the difference in prices between the V12 and V16, as the smaller engines would not have been much cheaper to manufacture, and the bodies would have cost about the same. Probably the V12 was simply more realistically priced, and sales were correspondingly higher, at 5725 in 1930–31. V16 prices were subsequently reduced, a Fisher-bodied sedan costing $4595 in 1932. The 1934 V16s had ifs, like the smaller Cadillacs, and styling followed 1930s trends with skirted mudguards and narrow radiator grilles, although it was always distinct from that of the V8.

The V12s and V16s were made up to the end of the 1937 season, when the V12 was dropped and a new side-valve V16 launched for 1938. Known as the Series 90, this had a much wider angle between the banks of cylinders (135 degrees), and monobloc construction. Square dimensions of 82.5 x 82.5mm gave a capacity of 7062cc (185bhp). Twelve semi-custom body styles by Fleetwood were offered, at prices from $5140 to $7175. Only 514 were sold in three seasons, 1938 to 1940. It was the last production 16-cylinder car in the world,

NICK BALDWIN

KETTERING, CHARLES FRANKLIN (1876–1958)

Charles Franklin Kettering was born on a farm near Loudonville, Ohio, on 29 August 1876. He earned his first $14 by reaping a field of wheat, and spent the money on a telephone, with which he began to experiment.

After working for a period as a village school teacher he entered Ohio State

University and studied mechanical engineering, graduating in 1900. He held a position with Star Telephone Co. of Ashland, Ohio, before joining the National Cash Register Co. of Dayton, Ohio, in 1904, where he met Edward A. Deeds, who was then general manager. In 1907, pooling their resources, they resigned from National (later NCR), and founded Dayton Engineering Laboratories. These laboratories would eventually form the core of General Motors Research Laboratories.

He had long had ideas about an improved ignition system for internal combustion engines, which he now developed. Also in 1907 he demonstrated a complete system, with coil, battery, and distributor with integrated breaker points and spark advance, to Ernest E. Sweet of Cadillac, who adopted it in 1908. Kettering and Deeds started a manufacturing branch of the Dayton Engineering Laboratories, trading under the Delco name.

Following the death of his friend, Byron J. Carter, maker of the friction-driven CARTERCAR, through injuries sustained in an accident with a starting handle, he began working on an electric starter. Other told him it could not be done, for a motor and battery capable of turning the engine would be prohibitively large and heavy. However, looking back on his work with cash registers, he recalled how small were the motors which opened till drawers. This was possible because the motors only had to operate for less than a second, and he reasoned that, as an automotive starter would only be required to run for a matter of a few seconds, it could not only be quite small, but would also be able to draw enough power from the car's service battery.

Working at the Robbins & Meyers factory in Springfield, Ohio, and using a 3/4hp motor, with a system of chains and sprocket wheels, he experimented with starting a 4-cylinder Cadillac engine using a 6-volt battery from G.W.Lowrey & Co, using the same armature to serve as both generator and starter– charging at 6 volts, with a discharge of 24volts for starting. The firest test took place on Christmas Eve, 1910, with field coils made by the Acme Wire Co. The Cadillac installation was completed on 17 February 1911, and was followed by a series of tests by Cadillac themselves before the first order was placed.

although it is believed that Cadillac studied proposals for another V16 in the 1960s.

V8s up to World War II

The Series 341 V8 engine was enlarged to 5785cc in 1930, and continued with little change up to 1936, when it was replaced by a new lightweight monobloc unit made in two sizes, 5376cc in the Series 50 and 5670cc in the Series 60 and 75. The Series 60 was a smaller and less expensive Cadillac designed to compete with the new Packard 120 in the medium priced class. Only three body styles were available, sedan, coupé and convertible, at prices from $1645 to $1725. In 1936 Cadillac sales doubled to 25,884 and all models had hydraulic brakes. Other improvements of the decade included ride control in 1932, no-draught ventilation in 1933, Dubonnet style ifs in 1934 and 'turret top' all-steel bodies in 1935.

The Series 60 was continued up to 1938 when it was joined by a striking new model, the 60 Special. Styled by William L. Mitchell, who Harley Earl had promoted to head of the Cadillac studio, the 60 Special had a profound influence on American car design. The roof was 3in lower than on other Cadillacs, the window area was 32 per cent greater than on other 60s, the boot was longer and more completely faired into the bodywork, and there were no running boards. The overall effect was almost that of a 4-door convertible with the top up. It was the first GM design to dispense with running boards, starting a trend which had spread to most American cars by 1941. The 60 Special was not cheap, at $2090, but it sold better than any other Cadillac model, 3703 units in its first year. Apart from annual grille changes it was made in the same form up to the end of the 1941 season. A total of 17,900 were made, and the name was retained by Cadillac for its most distinctive 4-door sedans up to the 1970s.

All 1938 Cadillacs had steering column gear change as standard, a year ahead of other GM cars. The V8 line in 1938 included the regular 60 in sedan and convertible forms, the intermediate Series 65 and the top of the line Series 75. This was made in several body styles, but after the war the title 75 was applied exclusively to the long wheelbase limousines, a tradition which lasted until 1976.

1989 Cadillac Fleetwood Sixty Special sedan.
GENERAL MOTORS

For 1939 the 60 was replaced by the 61 which shared body shells with Buick, La Salle, Oldsmobile, and Pontiac, an example of the standardisation which has continued with growing force up to the present. The La Salle was dropped after the 1940 season, but Cadillac offered a wide range of five models for 1941, when the options included air-conditioning and Hydramatic automatic transmission. The 60 Special, 61, 62, and 63 rode on a 126in (3200mm) wheelbase, and the 75 wheelbase was 136in (3454mm). Longest of all 1941 Cadillacs was the new Series 67 on a 139in (3528mm) wheelbase. Its 6-window body was shared with the Buick Limited. Although longer than the 75, the 67 had a less luxurious interior and was about $400 cheaper. For the first time since 1926, all Cadillacs used the same engine.

Cadillac sold 66,130 cars in 1941, a record for the marque. The 1942 season ended abruptly on 4 February, when all passenger car production gave way to military needs. Cadillac's contribution to the war effort consisted mainly of light tanks and components for Allison aero engines. The 1942 models were launched in September 1941, and 16,511 were made in the following five months. The main differences on the 1942 models were heavier grilles, wings that extended into the front doors, and a higher proportion of fastback bodies. About 60 per cent of customers, double the 1941 figure, opted for Hydramatic transmission.

Cadillac's Greatest Years

The 20 years after World War II saw Cadillac at the height of its prestige, even if they had nothing to offer as grand and exclusive as the V16. Of their rivals, Packard faded away in the 1950s, and Lincoln always had a somewhat staid air. It might have been favoured by the White House, but the successful businessman or Hollywood star preferred a Cadillac. Particularly in convertible form, ownership of a Cadillac showed that you had made it. There was a popular play and film called '*The Solid Gold Cadillac*'; somehow '*Solid Gold Lincoln*' would not have sounded right at all.

The first postwar cars came off the line at Cadillac's Detroit plant on 17 October 1945, and only 1142 cars were made up to the end of the year. The company had more than 100,000 orders, so long waiting lists were inevitable. Because of this, production took priority over innovation, and up to 1948 Cadillac showed little change over the 1942 models. But this was no different from most other US car makers. In 1946, 29,194 cars were delivered, and the following year 61,926, the second best year ever.

For 1948 most Cadillac bodies were completely restyled, with lower, wider grilles and small tail fins. Within a few years these became a feature of most American cars, reaching their climax on the 1959 Cadillacs. The only model not to have the new styling was the 75 limousine, which retained its 1942 appearance until the 1950 season. The 1949 Cadillacs were little changed in appearance, but under the bonnet there was an all-new short-stroke ohv V8 engine of 5424cc. It was more compact and lighter than the 5670cc side-valve unit it replaced, but developed 160bhp, 10bhp more than its larger capacity predecessor. With various improvements this engine lasted through the 1967 model year, by which time it had been bored out to more than 7 litres, and gave 340bhp. Milestones of 1949 included record sales of 92,554 cars in the model year, and the completion of the one millionth Cadillac on 25 November. It had taken the company 47 years to make its first million cars; the second million would take less than nine years.

1990 Cadillac Allante convertible.
NATIONAL MOTOR MUSEUM

Fastback coupés disappeared from the 1950s range when Cadillacs had a heavier look which characterised them for several years. Briggs Cunningham entered a virtually stock Series 61 coupé in the 1950 Le Mans 24 Hour Race, finishing in tenth place, one place ahead of another Cadillac which carried an enormous boat-shaped body which earned it the nickname 'Le Monstre'. Cadillac V8 engines were fitted to a number of Allard J2 sports cars, one of which finished third in the 1950 Le Mans race.

Engine size and power output rose gradually in the 1950s, reaching 5980cc (265bhp) in 1956, 6391cc (345bhp) in 1959 and 7030cc (340bhp) in 1964. Hydramatic drive was increasingly popular, and from 1951 only the 75 limousine was still offered with a manual gearbox. It was dropped even on the 75 after 1955, and all Cadillacs had automatic transmission until the advent of the small Cimarron in 1980.

A striking new model for 1953 was the Eldorado convertible. This began life as a show car for GM's Motorama, but unlike most of its kind it was put into production. It was basically a Series 62 convertible, but had a wrap-around windscreen, a slight cut-away to the doors and a flush-fitting metal cover which completely concealed the top when it was lowered. Unlike other Cadillacs it had wire wheels, while the interior was very luxurious. The cost of all this was $7750, compared with $4130 for a regular 62 convertible.

Cadillac sold 532 Eldorados in their first year, and 2150 in 1954. By then they were less distinctive as the whole range now had wrap-around windscreens, and the top no longer disappeared completely. The price was down to $5738. 1955 Eldorados had the pointed fins which would appear on Cadillacs for 1958, and their own 270bhp engine, 20bhp more powerful than that used in other models. Eldorado convertibles were made up to 1976.

An even more expensive and exclusive car was the Eldorado Brougham of 1957. Also based on a Motorama show car, this was a pillarless hard-top with every imaginable comfort and power assistance. The main chassis feature which distinguished it from all other Cadillacs was its air suspension. This employed an air 'spring' at each wheel, comprising a domed air chamber, rubber diaphragm, and pistons. Fed by a central air compressor, the domes were continually adjusted for load and road conditions via valves and solenoids. Unfortunately the air domes leaked and cars were frequently returned to dealers. Many owners chose to abandon the system in favour of conventional coil springs. The Eldo Brougham cost a staggering $13,074 (Lincoln's exclusive Continental Mk II cost only $10,000), which limited sales to 400 in 1957 and 304 in 1958. The really exclusive Brougham was not made after that, although the name survived on a less distinctive car up to the end of the 1960 season.

Although now America's top luxury cars, Cadillacs were not made in modest numbers. The dramatic growth in production during the 1950s and 1960s was a tribute to the purchasing power of large numbers of Americans. Output reached six figures for the first time in 1950 (103,857); by 1955 it was 140,777, and in the 1964 model year, when the three millionth Cadillac was made, 165,959 cars were delivered. Improvements in the 1960s were gradual rather than spectacular, with engine size rising to 7735cc in 1968 and 8193cc in 1970. This was the largest Cadillac engine ever made, exceeding the mighty V16, and was also the largest engine of any postwar American car. It was made until downsizing began in 1977. A new box-section perimeter frame replaced the

X-braced frame in 1965 when styling was also new, with a simpler grille and negligible fins.

Front-Wheel Drive

A spectacular new model joined the Cadillac range for 1967. The Fleetwood Eldorado coupé was an entry in the personal car market occupied by Buick's Invicta and Oldsmobile's Tornado. Like its Oldsmobile cousin introduced in 1966, the new Eldorado had front-wheel drive, which had not been seen on a production American car since the Cord 810 of 1937. The Cadillac was the first design to combine front drive, variable ratio steering and automatic level control as standard equipment. The engine was the 7030cc V8 modified for front drive. The Hydramatic transmission was mounted alongside the engine, and was directly connected to the differential which drove the front axle. The Fleetwood Eldorado was built on its own assembly line, and had a wheelbase of 120in (3045mm), shorter than any other 1967 Cadillac.

The first generation front-wheel drive Eldorado was made with little change for four years, apart from increases of engine size in line with other Cadillacs. Eldorado production reached 89,653 up to 1970, a second generation model coming for 1971. This was made as a convertible as well as a coupé, but was a larger and heavier car with lower performance. The convertible was dropped in 1976, part of the general American trend against open cars which would, however, be reversed only a few years later. It was a sad day, and truly the end of an era, when the last convertible Cadillac came off the lines on 21 April 1976. It was kept by the makers for their own historical collection, but 199 identical 'last' convertibles were built, and became instant collectors' items.

In 1977 the massive 8193cc engine was reduced to 6966cc, and because of emission controls, progressively detuned to 183bhp, less than a 5.4-litre engine gave in 1952. The next generation Eldorado was a much smaller car, 1100lb lighter and on a wheelbase 12.5in (317mm) shorter. The engine was of 5735cc, available in diesel as well as petrol form. The new Eldorado shared its chassis with Buick's Riviera and Oldsmobile's Tornado, and the styling was similar to those cars too, although not identical.

The Shrinking Cadillac – 1976 to the Present

In the 1970s the Cadillac Division of GM had to face the unwelcome fact that the energy crisis had put an end to the really large-engined 'gas guzzling' car which had been their staple product. Their first response to this was the Seville, a compact-sized 4-door sedan launched in 1975. It was powered by a 5735cc V8 engine available in petrol or diesel form, and was 35in (888mm) shorter than the regular-sized Sedan de Ville. The chassis was similar to the X-cars of Buick (Apollo), Chevrolet (Nova), Oldsmobile (Omega), and Pontiac (Ventura), but the body had a distinctive razor-edge styling which made the car instantly recognisable. Although smaller than other Cadillacs, it was not cheaper, being seen as a prestige car competing in the BMW/Jaguar/Mercedes-Benz market. The price was $12,479, while the full-sized Cadillacs cost between $8197 and $10,414, apart from the luxurious 75 limousine which sold in very small numbers for $14,557.

The first generation Seville was made up to 1979, only as a 4-door sedan, although several custom coachworks built 2-door coupé and convertible conversions. 1980 saw a new Seville with front-wheel drive and razor-edged fastback styling which recalled Hooper's work on Rolls-Royces in the 1950s. The regular engine was the 5735cc diesel, making the Seville America's first car to standardise a diesel engine. The engine was made by Oldsmobile, which supplied all GM's diesels, while the new Seville body came from an assembly plant at Linden, New Jersey, which also built Eldorado, Buick Riviera and Oldsmobile Tornado bodies.

Cadillac entered the 1980s encouraged by record production of 381,113 cars made the previous year. There were more models in the range; apart from the Seville and Eldorado there were standard sized coupés and sedans in the De Ville and Fleetwood Brougham series, and the top of the line limousine. This was no longer called a Series 75 but the Fleetwood limousine, made in 7- or 8-seater versions. The De Ville and Fleetwood Brougham were shorter than before, but still traditional designs in having rear-wheel drive and separate chassis frames.

1981 saw two important innovations, the V8-6-4 engine and the sub-compact Cimarron sedan. The engine had an electronic control system which actuated four, six or eight cylinders according to the driving requirements at any given moment. Selection of the number of cylinders was completely automatic. Intended as an aid to fuel economy, the V8-6-4 had a capacity of 6030cc, and was available in all Cadillacs except the Cimarron and Seville. The V8-6-4

2000 Cadillac Seville STS sedan.
GENERAL MOTORS

proved troublesome, and for 1982 was available only in the Fleetwood limousine. It was dropped altogether when Cadillac launched an all-new 4080cc V8 used in some 1982 models and all 1983s. For 1981 and 1982 only, Cadillacs could be had with a Buick-built 4130cc V6.

The Cimarron was the smallest-engined Cadillac since before 1910, and the first 4-cylinder since 1914. In fact it was merely one of the General Motors J-cars, sharing body shell and engine with the Chevrolet Cavalier, Buick Skyhawk, and Oldsmobile Firenza. The 1842cc 4-cylinder engine was mounted transversely and drove the front wheels. The standard gearbox was a 4-speed manual (Cadillac's first since 1955), but a 3-speed automatic was available as an option. The Cadillac Division did not seem too happy about adding this small car to its range, and promoted it as the 'Cimarron by Cadillac'. The Cadillac name did not appear anywhere on the car. The Cimarron (named after a Texas river) was made up to 1990, latterly with a 2838cc V6, while the manual gearbox had five speeds.

The larger Cadillacs were considerably changed when the De Ville became part of GM's C range, sharing a body shell with the Buick Electra and Oldsmobile 98 Regency. Engines were to some extent individual to each marque, Cadillac having a 4087cc transverse V8 developing 132bhp. The De Ville was made alongside the conventional Fleetwood Brougham. The last year for the long wheelbase Fleetwood limousine was 1987. By then it had the 4080cc V8 mounted transversely and driving the front wheels. It was essentially a De Ville lengthened by the specialists Hess & Eisenhardt, whose connection with Cadillac went back many years with the building of hearse and ambulance bodies. Convertibles returned to the Cadillac range in 1984, on the Eldorado which was also made in coupé form.

Although they were better trimmed and more luxurious than other GM marques, the Cadillac of the mid-1980s lacked the individuality and distinction of former years. To put this right, a new car was launched in 1986 which shared no body panels with other GM products, although the engine and transmission were those of the Eldorado and the chassis was a shortened Eldorado frame. Named the Allante, it was a 2-seater styled by Pininfarina in Turin. The frames were flown out to Turin where the bodies were built in a plant separate from Pininfarina's other activities. The complete cars were then flown back to Detroit in specially-equipped Boeing 747s for drive train installation and final finishing. This operation was dubbed 'the longest production line in the world' and undoubtedly contributed to the Allante's high cost. At $54,000 it was twice the price of an Eldorado, and for 1989 it was increased to $57,183, although

there was a larger engine of 4474cc. Each Allante was supplied with a convertible top and a hard-top. The latter was made of aluminium and could easily be carried by two people and fixed over the folding convertible top in less than a minute. Cadillac hoped to sell 4000 Allantes in 1987, but only managed 1651, although 1987 was better at 2569. There were serious problems with quality control on early Allantes, such as leaks, squeaks and rattles, horns that did not work and heaters that worked too well, which seriously damaged the car's reputation. For 1993 the Allante received the new 32-valve Northstar V8 engine allied to a 4-speed automatic transmission, but that was the last year for the distinctive Cadillac.

The Eldorado and Seville received new styling for 1992, although they were not so distinct from each other as before. The high-performance versions, the STS (Seville Touring Sedan) and ETC (Eldorado Touring Coupé) used a new 4572cc twin-ohc all-aluminium Northstar V8 engine for 1993. A big new rear-drive Fleetwood was announced for 1993, a cousin to the Chevrolet Caprice and Buick's reborn Roadmaster. However, these echos of the traditional American car had only a short life. On 27 November 1996 the last Fleetwood left the production line at Arlington, Texas, along with the Roadmaster, Caprice and Chevrolet Impala SS.

This was the end for the 5735cc V8, later Cadillacs mostly having the 4572cc Northstar. The exception was the Catera introduced in 1994. This was basically a rebadged Opel Omega with German-built 2962cc V6 engine and was intended to give Cadillac an entry into the younger market occupied by Lexus and BMW. Another totally new field for the marque was the large 4x4. Launched in August 1998, the Escalade was a cousin to the Chevrolet Tahoe, and a rival to Lincoln's Navigator. The regular Cadillacs for 1999 were the Seville and De Ville sedans and Eldorado 2-door coupé.

A dramatic new Cadillac planned for a 2002 introduction is the Evoq, which originated as a concept car at the 1999 Detroit Show. A rear-drive 2-seater roadster powered by a supercharged version of the Northstar V8 engine, reduced to 4228cc, it will share a platform with the next Chevrolet Corvette, and will be built alongside it at Bowling Green, Kentucky.

NG

Further Reading
Cadillac and La Salle, Walter McCall, Crestline Publishing, 1982.
Cadillac, Maurice D. Hendry, E.P. Dutton, 1973.
Standard of the World, Maurice D. Hendry,
Automobile Quarterly Publications.

1920 Caffort 10hp 3-wheeled landaulet.
NICK BALDWIN

1920 Calcott 11.9hp 2-seater. (The Calcott brothers in the car.)
NATIONAL MOTOR MUSEUM

CADIX (F) 1920–1923
Automobiles Jean Jannel, Cadix-Martinville, Vosges.
Built in the Vosges district, far from traditional centres of car manufacture, the Cadix was a conventionally assembled car using 4-cylinder Ballot engines in two sizes, 1590 and 2292cc. Two body styles were offered, a 2- and a 4-seater, both open. Regional manufacturers usually relied on local customers rather than national, but it seems there were not enough in the Vosges, and Jean Jannel closed his business after four years of trading.
NG

C.A.E./CARSON *see* CORSE

CAESAR *see* SCACCHI

CAFFORT (F) 1920–1922
Sté des Anciens Éts Caffort, Paris.
The Caffort was an unusual car whose two front wheels were mounted so close together that it had the superficial appearance of a 3-wheeler. This avoided the need for a differential, a device used on a number of rear-driven cars such as the M.B. (i) and Isetta, but the Caffort was the only such design with front-wheel drive. The 1-litre flat-twin engine lived alongside the driver and drove through a 3-speed gearbox and bevel gears. Cafforts were more often seen as taxis and delivery vans than as passenger cars. The company had made marine engines in Marseilles for several years before setting up car manufacture in Paris.
NG

CAIL-BORDEREL *see* BORDEREL-CAIL

CALCOTT (GB) 1913–1926
Calcott Bros Ltd, Coventry.
The Calcott was a good quality light car which, like its alphabetical neighbour the Calthorpe, sold quite well until defeated by the big guns such as Morris and Standard. The company originated as Calcott & West in 1886, making bicycles and roller skates. The partners were William and James Calcott and Enoch West, who subsequently made PROGRESS and WEST-ASTER cars. A limited company was formed in 1896, making bicycles which were sold to other firms to offer under their own names. Motorcycles followed in 1904 and were made until 1915, but two years before that the first Calcott car was launched. This had a 10.5hp 4-cylinder side-valve engine of 1460cc designed by Arthur Alderson who came from Singer, and after World War I would design cars for Lea-Francis. The radiator was quite similar to that of Standard. Calcott had no coachwork department, bodies being made for them by Hollick & Pratt, Cross & Ellis, Charlesworth, and Tom Pass. The London store Harrods offered a sporty cloverleaf, possibly made by them.
The 10.5hp Calcott was made up to 1917, latterly being supplied mostly to the army. It was revived after the war with a slightly larger stroke, as the 11.9hp (1644cc), and a longer wheelbase, although the 10.5hp was brought back in 1922, later becoming the 10/15, and available with 4-seater coachwork. The first Calcott with detachable cylinder head and 4-wheel brakes was introduced in 1923. This was of 13.9hp (2120cc), later designated 12/24. Unfortunately it developed a very bad reputation for broken rear axles.
Calcott's finances, so encouraging immediately after the war when they paid a 40 per cent dividend, were less satisfactory by 1925. Prices rose at first, then were drastically cut, that of the 11.9 dropping by £100 in 1923, but they probably made no profit at the lower figure. The introduction of a 6-cylinder model for 1925 was not the best move in the circumstances. The 2565cc 16/50 cost £495 as a tourer or £650 as a saloon, £150 more than the 12/24 with the same body. The cost of tooling up for the new model bankrupted the company and very few Light Sixes were sold. The factory, built in 1896 and now a listed building, was taken over by Singer in 1926, although voluntary liquidation was not completed until 1927. Total Calcott production was about 2500, of which fewer than 20 survive today.
NG
Further Reading
'A Casualty of Mass Production', M. Worthington-Williams.
The Automobile, March 1989.

CALDWELL-VALE (AUS) 1913
Caldwell-Vale Motor Tractor Co. Ltd, Auburn, New South Wales.
Felix Caldwell of South Australia had focused on 4-wheel drive when his brother, Norman, suggested that it was essential for farm tractors. He designed a motor-plough which showed sufficient promise for a new company to be proposed in 1909. Apparently there was insufficient response but a 7-tonne, 80hp unit was built as a road tractor and this attracted attention when used to haul a 7-trailer road train for an entertainment troupe. The project moved to Sydney and a company was formed in conjunction with the locomotive builder, Henry Vale & Sons, to build road tractors with 4-wheel drive and power-assisted steering. A car, with a 4-cylinder, 4310cc 32hp engine and 4-speed gearbox, using the 4-wheel drive in conjunction with 4-wheel steering, was built in 1913 and, after tests on sand hills at Botany, went to work on a Queensland property. Road tractors were the priority until the firm was voluntarily liquidated in 1916 following legal action.
MG

CALEDONIAN (GB) 1899–1906
Caledonian Motor Car & Cycle Co., Aberdeen.
This company assembled a limited number of cars to special order, using De Dion-Bouton or Daimler engines. In 1908 they were agents for Peugeot and Standard, with no mention of car production. A different make, also called Caledonian, made a few taxicabs at Granton in 1912–14.
NG

CALIFORNIA (i) **(US)** 1900–1902
California Automobile Co., San Francisco, California.
This US West Coast company offered steam, petrol and electric cars at prices from $500 to $3000, which were said to be markedly lower than those of comparable cars from the East Coast. How many were actually made is uncertain; a published photograph of a 1902 runabout is identical to an Henriod. Possibly

California had acquired a licence to build Henriods, but it is more likely that they used the photograph to indicate the style of car they would like to build. Some petrol cars went under the name Ryder, after their designer Bainbridge Ryder. In 1902 the company was reorganised to make steam cars only, which were called Calimobiles. These were listed as a $900 runabout and $1600 tourer, together with a 9-seater stagecoach, of which at least three were built. This venture did not last beyond 1903.

NG

CALIFORNIA (ii) (US) 1910

California Automobile Co., Los Angeles, California.

This company continued the production of 2- and 4-cylinder TOURIST cars, formerly made by the Auto Vehicle Co. To these they added a line of fours bearing the California name, of 30, 40 and 50hp. They announced that combined production in 1910 of both Tourist and California cars would be 150, but how many of these were Californias is not known. From 1914 to 1917 they made the BEARDSLEY Electric.

NG

CALIFORNIA (iii) (US) 1913

California Cyclecar Co., Los Angeles, California.

'At last America has a real cyclecar', trumpeted the British *Cyclecar* magazine in June 1913, although the California was not, in fact, the first. Designed by L.E. French, it had a typical cyclecar specification, with 10hp air-cooled twin engine, friction transmission and double vee-belt drive. Mr French fixed a price of $395, but the California never went into production under that name. Instead, he found new backers and built an almost identical car under the name LOS ANGELES.

NG

CALIFORNIA (iv) (US) 1923–c.1924

Leach Motor Car Co., Los Angeles, California.

The California was a 4-cylinder automobile intended to be a smaller companion car to the massive and expensive Leach 6-cylinder cars, which had found a dedicated clientele of stars and starlets of the contemporary silent film screen. Its ohv engine had been designed by Harry A. Miller who had designed the not altogether successful 100hp engine introduced in 1921 as the Leach 999. The California was debuted in Oakland, California in early 1923 at the Ulrey-Noteware Agency which also handled sales for the Leach and exhibited in the agency's showroom while Leach, then beset with financial problems, struggled to remain afloat in the automobile industry. The California display car has been described as a 5-seater touring model. The Leach 6-cylinder car was phased out later in 1923 and, whereas California Motors, Inc., which had been formed earlier that year, appears to have survived into 1925, further production of the California seems doubtful.

KM

CALIFORNIA ACE (US) c.1994 to date

C-F Enterprises Ltd, Long Beach, California.

The Cal Ace was a fibreglass body kit for the MGB with vaguely A.C. Ace 2.6 overtones. Sold only in kit form with instructions for installing V6 and Rover engines.

HP

CALIFORNIA COMMUTER see AERO VISIONS

CALIFORNIA COMPONENT CARS (US) c.1980–1984

California Component Cars Inc., Oakland, California.

In addition to building the British Sterling (neé Nova) kit, this company also made a restyled Sterling called the Sovran. The lower section of the body was strengthened, and the headlights were changed to an electrically operated pop-up design. Variations in bonnet scoops were offered, but the most obvious changes from the Sterling were the squared-off wheel openings.

HP

CALIFORNIA CUSTOM COACH (US) c.1984–1988

California Custom Coach Inc., Pasadena, California.

1995 Callaway C7 coupé.
HAROLD PACE

The Auburn Speedster was a popular classic to replicate in kit form, and that is exactly what this company did. They based their kit on a Ford chassis and running gear. It could be purchased in kit or completely assembled form. California Custom Coach also made a stretched 4-door Corvette for 'Vette lovers with a family.

HP

CALIFORNIA TOURING COACH CO. (US) c.1982

California Touring Coach Co., Newark, California.

The Panzer was a kit car that mounted a fibreglass replica of a Porsche 935 or 935RSR body onto a Volkswagen Beetle chassis. Either VW or Porsche motors could be ordered.

HP

CALIFORNIAN SIX (US) 1920

California Motor Corp., Los Angeles, California.

The Californian Six barely managed to make it off the drawing board despite seductive advance advertising and generous coverage by an enthusiastic automotive press. The Californian Six was an assembled car equipped with a Beaver 6-cylinder engine, wire wheels with rear-mounted spare and a long 7-seater phaeton body mounted on a 134in (3400mm) wheelbase. Introduced in May 1920 in the showrooms of the Gates-Kelly Automotive Co. of Los Angeles, it was promoted as having been designed for the requirements of the Western motorist, whatever that meant. The pilot model, unfortunately, turned out to be the last as well as the venture's entire production with the exception of two additional chassis, left unbodied when the corporation failed.

KM

CALIMOBILE see CALIFORNIA (i)

CALL (US) 1911

Call Motor Car Co., New York, New York.

Little is known about this make, which was not recorded in the automotive press. Evidence of its existence comes from a tax assessor's handbook, which listed a 25hp Model H and 28hp Models O, R, and S.

NG

CALLAWAY (US) 1984 to date

Callaway Cars Inc., Old Lyme, Connecticut.

After selling turbocharger kits, Reeves Callaway started building limited-edition cars for major manufacturers. His first job was making 36 turbocharged versions of Alfa Romeo GTV/6 sedans. In 1985 he developed his first twin-turbocharged Corvette, the C4. It produced 345hp and was good for 178mph (286km/h), which prompted Chevrolet to offer Callaway conversions as factory options with full warranties. Callaway designed the Aston Martin Virage V8 engine in 1989. By 1990 a Callaway Corvette model called the Sledgehammer produced 880hp and was clocked at 254.76mph (409.91km/h). In 1993, the Super Speedster was added to the line. It was a Corvette with a cut-down windscreen and twin rear headrests. It packed a 700hp turbocharged Corvette ZR-1 engine and sold for $300,000. They then developed a line of normally

c.1908 Calthorpe tourer.
NATIONAL MOTOR MUSEUM

1920 Calthorpe Sporting Four 10hp tourer.
NATIONAL MOTOR MUSEUM

aspirated cars called Supernaturals. This included the C6 Corvette, the C8 Camaro and the C9 Impala SS. All had over 400hp engines. In 1995, a vastly reworked Corvette called the C7 LM was developed for the street and racing. It had a rounded, more aerodynamic nose with covered headlights and a new tail with a pedestal-type spoiler. With 435hp it was good for 182mph (293km/h) in the street version, and 193mph (311km/h) in the 475hp race car. A contract with Range Rover resulted in 220 C11 Limited Edition Range Rovers with 245hp engines and special black paint schemes. In 1998 they introduced the C12, a Corvette-based sports car with an all-original body. It had a top speed of 190mph (306km/h) and was raced as well as sold for street use.

HP

CALLISTA (F) 1950–1952
Société Callista, Paris.
Made by Messieurs Monge and Rowe, the Callista was a small car using Dyna-Panhard components and available in two body styles, the Ranalagh roadster and Coupe des Alpes convertible. The latter body was made by Callista, while the Ranalagh was the work of Dijon-Tourisme who later made the RAFALE. Towards the end of 1952 the Callista distributor, Raymond Gaillard, formed a new company, ARISTA. The Ranalagh became the Arista Le Mans.

NG

CALORIC (US) 1903–1904
Chicago Motocycle Co., Chicago, Illinois.
This company was formed in 1898 and announced an ambitious plan to make petrol, steam, and electric vehicles. They concentrated on repair work to start with, and it was not until 1902 that a car appeared at all. Called the Chicago, it had a 2-cylinder petrol engine, but by 1903 it had been renamed Caloric. Two 2-cylinder models were listed for 1903, of 4.5 and 6.5hp. The starting procedure involved heating the cylinder head with a torch until it was red hot, so the makers said! Perhaps this was a form of hot tube ignition. For 1904 a 9hp

3-cylinder was offered as well, with a coupé body as high as it was long. In August 1904 the company announced that they were returning to repair work and making marine engines. However, in 1905 they made a few examples of the FOSTLER car.

NG

CALPINE (NL) 1979–1983
Calpine B.V., Utrecht, The Netherlands.
This car's name suggests that it was intended to be a replica of the Alpine-Renault A110 Berlinette, and this was indeed the manufacturer's proud claim in its sales literature. Somewhat bizarrely, however, the Calpine's fibreglass body was not moulded from an Alpine, but rather from the Berlinette's arch rival, a Matra-Bonnet Djet. Unlike the Alpine or Matra, the Calpine used a Volkswagen engine instead of a Renault unit, and had true 2+2 seating. The Calpine used a standard length VW Beetle platform, necessitating the Djet body's rear wheels to be moved back a few inches. Very few Calpine kit cars were sold, although the car's moulds are still known to exist with a Matra specialist in northern Holland.

CR

CALTHORPE (GB) 1905–1926
Calthorpe Motor Co. Ltd, Birmingham.
One of the better-quality British light cars, the Calthorpe sprang, like so many other Midlands makes, from the cycle industry. In the 1890s George W. Hands set up a bicycle business called Hands & Cake, changing the name in 1897 to the Bard Cycle Manufacturing Co. Ltd. Four years later this became the Minstrel Cycle Co., and in 1905 the Minstrel & Rea Cycle Co., the Rea being a cheaper bicycle named after a local river.

Meanwhile he had entered the car business with a 10hp 4-cylinder shaft-driven light car which made its appearance at London's Agricultural Hall Show in February 1905. Few 10s were made, and by July it had been enlarged to the 12/14 with a White & Poppe engine, which was made for three years. It was joined in 1907 by a bigger car still, the 28/40, also White & Poppe powered.

In 1906 Calthorpe became a limited company and manufacture was moved from the bicycle factory to new premises at Bordesley Green, Birmingham, where it remained for the rest of its life. The Minstrel & Rea Cycle Co. introduced motorcycles in 1909, later changing its name to the Calthorpe Motor Cycle Co. Ltd, which survived to 1938, outliving the cars by 12 years. Calthorpe bought up another Birmingham car maker, MOBILE (ii) in 1907. Mobile's manager, Louis Antweiler, joined Calthorpe and stayed as a director until the firm closed. For 1908 Calthorpe turned to Alpha as their engine supplier, with a 16/20hp 4-cylinder car which had a handsome rounded bonnet. There was also a smaller 12/14hp used for taxi work as well as passenger cars.

Calthorpe was one of the few British firms to enter Continental races in the years up to 1914; along with Sunbeam and Vauxhall they contested the *Coupe de l'Auto* with modified versions of their production cars, although with no great success. In November 1913 their most important model, the 9.5hp Calthorpe Minor, appeared. The design had appeared earlier in the year, with round radiator and without the name Minor. The definitive rectangular radiatored Minor was a light car using a 1094cc 4-cylinder side-valve engine of their own manufacture, and 3-speed gearbox. Bodies were mostly made by Mulliners of Birmingham, and were of a higher quality than the average light car. Yet at £168 for a 2-seater they cost less than rival products from Calcott, Morris or Singer. In 1917 Calthorpe purchased Mulliners, whose factory was next door to theirs, taking possession of the premises once government contracts were completed. Calthorpe's war effort was devoted to the manufacture of mines and grenades.

Calthorpe returned to car production in 1919 with the 10.5hp, slightly enlarged to 1260cc, and soon the weekly output reached 42 cars. Body styles included drophead and fixed-head coupés, and polished aluminium 2- and 4-seater sporting bodies. These could be had with higher performance engines, comprising Ricardo alloy pistons and high-lift camshafts. However, prices were considerably higher than those of rivals such as Morris, and by 1923 sales could not justify an output of more than 40 cars per week. George Hands left in 1921 to make a car under his own name, but this survived for only three years before he returned to Calthorpe. He brought with him the design of a 1991cc six with shaft-driven single-ohc, which was offered from 1925 as the Calthorpe Six Type

C. Very few were made, and it is possible that there was only one, branded a Hands in 1924 and a Calthorpe in 1925–26. The old 9.5 was still made, now with 4-speed gearbox and called the 10/15hp, and there was also a 1496cc 12/20 designed by Cecil Davidson. However, none of these could save the company, and the Bordesley Green factory closed abruptly towards the end of 1924. Hands tried to keep the business going, announcing the formation of a new company, although nothing seems to have come of this. Calthorpe had a stand at the 1925 Motor Show, where three cars were shown including the Six, but they were old stock. The business was offered as a going concern in 1926, but attracted no buyers, and in April the factory was sold off in two lots. A company called Calthorpe Motor Spares Ltd was formed in June, but although it advertised 10/15 and 12/20 cars up to 1928, none were made. Like Whitlock, the Calthorpe name was a long time a-dying. Some lists carried it as late as 1931, and the *Motoring Encyclopedia* of 1932 spoke of it as a current make, illustrating its entry with what was obviously a 12/20 of about 1925. Fewer than 10 Calthorpes are thought to survive today.

NG

Further Reading
'The Enterprising Calthorpe', Bill Boddy, *The Automobile,* October 1985.

CALVERT (US) 1927
Calvert Motor Associates, Baltimore, Maryland.
The Calvert was planned as a small 6-cylinder car which was designed for the low-priced market which included such economy-priced automobiles as the Chevrolet, Star, and the recently introduced Whippet. The Calvert failed to get into actual production although a few prototypes – a roadster and touring cars – were completed. Prices were announced at $795 and $825. With a model designation of Duplex Three, the cars were fitted with a 6-cylinder Continental L-head engine with a bore and stroke of 2¹/₂ × 5 inches, both types with a weight of 1660lb (755kg), a 105in (2665mm) wheelbase, and disc wheels.

KM

CALVY (GB) 1983–1986; 1990–1992
1983–1986 Calvy Motor Car Co. Ltd, Southend, Essex.
1990–1992 Calvy Car Co., Warley, West Midlands.
Calvy started life as NG agents and the first Mitchel was a direct copy of the NG TC. Legal action forced a MkII redesign with a new ladder chassis instead of the NG's cruciform type, a squarer front end, and doors. The mechanical basis was MGB, though Rover V8 power became an option.

CR

CAM (F) 1972–1973
Conversion Automobile Moderne, Chassagny.
Run by Gérard Maurin and Claude Crétin, this company specialised in a single-seater autocross vehicle called the Offroad and a buggy called the Punch-Buggy up until 1972. Then it turned its attention to a fun car kit based on the Renault 4, an open-topped doorless plastic machine with quad headlamps.

CR

CAMAT (P) c.1987–c.1996
Comp. Ind. Montagem de Automoveis, Porto.
The Camat Douro was an MG TD replica based on VW Beetle components, sold complete and in kit form.. A special chassis for a front-mounted Ford engine was reportedly being developed, and this was also to go under a second model, a sports car inspired by the classic Talbot.

CR

CAMBER/MAYA (GB) 1966–1969
1966–1967 Checkpoint Engineering Ltd, Rye, Sussex.
1967–1969 W. West (Engineers) Ltd, Rye, Sussex.
Derek Bishop (who had previously made the HERON Europa) and George Holmes made their first Mini-based GT in Greenwich in 1966, but the project quickly moved to Holmes' Camber Sands workshop (hence the name). The construction was of a tubular steel frame, Mini subframes and fibreglass body mouldings reinforced with steel. After six cars were made, a revised version with raised headlamps was sold under the name Maya GT in 1967 but Holmes' death in a road accident sealed its fate after a further six had been made.

CR

1968 Camber Maya GT coupé.
NICK GEORGANO/NATIONAL MOTOR MUSEUM

1900 Cambier 8hp 'petit omnibus.'
NATIONAL MOTOR MUSEUM

CAMBIANO (US) c.1993
Cambiano Motor Co., Charlotte, North Carolina.
The Ferrari 365GTB4 Daytona coupé was the inspiration for this replica. Other American Daytona replicas used Corvette running gear, but this one rode on a steel tube ladder frame with Ford Thunderbird suspension at both ends (irs at the back). Turbocharged Ford V6 and 5000cc V8 engines were used. They were sold in kit or turnkey form.

HP

CAMBIER (F) 1897–c.1905
Éts Cambier, Lille, Nord.
This company specialised in air-compressing equipment for some time before it became interested in cars. The first of these were rear-engined machines on Benz lines, some of which were made under licence at Malines in Belgium. This factory also made a front-engined light car with chaindrive. In 1897 the Lille factory made a coach with a 30hp 3-cylinder horizontal engine, for service in Algeria. This was almost certainly a one-off, and by 1900 they were making cars with 2-cylinder horizontal engines of 5 and 8hp. Body styles included a closed 'petit omnibus' on the 8hp chassis. Also advertised in 1900 were vehicles with 3- and 4-cylinder engines; the latter were possibly commercial vehicles, for the company became well-known for these, including buses and fire engines. In 1901 Cambier made cars under licence from Eugene Mathieu, a Frenchman who made cars in Belgium under his own name from 1902 to 1906. Those made by Cambier included a 6hp belt-drive voiturette and chain-driven cars of 8 and 12hp. In 1902 Cambiers were modernised, with front-mounted engines and shaft drive. Cars of 8 and 12hp were made until the end of production two or three years later.

NG

1920 Cambro 192cc 3-wheeler.
NATIONAL MOTOR MUSEUM

1904 Cameron 9hp 2-seater.
NICK GEORGANO

1910 Cameron 36hp tourer.
NICK BALDWIN

CAMBRO (GB) 1920–1921

Central Aircraft Co. Ltd, Northolt, Middlesex.

One could hardly imagine a more minimal car than the Cambro, designed by F.J. Camm, founder editor of *Practical Motorist* magazine and G.A. Broomfield. Resembling a child's pedal car, it was a 3-wheeler powered by a Johnson flat-twin 2-stroke engine of only 192cc, which drove the single rear wheel directly by chain, with no gears, although there was a free-wheel device to assist manhandling. The driver was frequently called on to manhandle his machine as there was no reverse gear. At least it was light, weighing only 165lbs. It was a single seater, leading *The Light Car & Cycle Car* to observe rather naively '... perhaps for that reason it would not be acceptable to the family man.' The price was £82 19s (£82.95). The Cambro was listed for only two years, and it is not known how many were made, although a photograph shows three lined up in front of the factory.

NG

CAMELOT CLASSICS (US) c.1980

Camelot Classics, Ventura, California.

The Phariance was neoclassic, built to replicate the look of the Hispano Suiza tulipwood speedster. It had a wooden body built of hickory, Honduran mahogany, and brass.

HP

CAMERON (US) 1903–1920

1903–1904 United Motor Co., Pawtucket, Rhode Island.
1904–1906 James Brown Machine Corp., Pawtucket, Rhode Island.
1906–1908 Cameron Car Co., Brockton, Massachusetts.
1908–1913 Cameron Car Co., Beverly, Massachusetts and New London, Connecticut.
1913–1914 Cameron Car Co., West Haven, Connecticut.
1919–1920 Cameron Car Co., Stamford, Connecticut.

Few car manufacturers can have had so many addresses, seven in 17 years, and this does not include a plant in Alma, Michigan devote solely to trucks. The brothers Everitt S. and Forrest F. Cameron had been involved with two steam cars, the ECLIPSE (i) and the TAUNTON (i), before they began car manufacture under their own name. The first Cameron had a 6hp single-cylinder air-cooled engine, and unusually for the period having shaft drive. They were made in the factory of the James W. Brown Textile Machine Co. (founded in 1829) but marketed by the United Motor Co. Then Brown, an ex-mayor of Pawtucket, insisted on his company being listed as the maker, although the cars were Camerons, not Browns. When the Brown company was taken over in 1906 by people uninterested in car making the Camerons moved to Brockton, but did not turn out any cars until the end of the year, when the 1907 models were announced. These had 16 and 24hp 4-cylinder engines and gearboxes on the rear axle, a feature that was to distinguish Camerons until the end. A need for more factory space led them to move to Beverly in 1908, where they occupied the factory in which the UPTON had been made. The first 6-cylinder Cameron, a 30/36hp made at New London, was introduced in 1909. More than 600 cars were made in 1911, their best year. In 1913 all production was concentrated in a former piano factory at West Haven, but because of the move no cars were made that year, the few '1913 Camerons' being left over from the 1912 season.

For 1914 water-cooling was adopted for the first time, and the cars had pointed vee-radiators. As they were active in the export field, Cameron were badly hit by World War I, and declared bankruptcy at the end of 1914. Part of the factory was leased to the Euclid Motor Car Co. for manufacture of the EUCLID (iii) cyclecar, a venture in which Everitt Cameron had a hand. No Camerons were made until 1919, when the brothers announced a new car from Stamford. Advertised with air- or water-cooling, about 120 were made in 1919 and 1920, after which the Camerons finally gave up making their own cars. Forrest moved to Cleveland where he attempted to launch a new small car, but failed, and was involved in the design of the MARSH (ii) and POMEROY cars. Everitt concentrated on the design and manufacture of marine and aero engines.

NG

Further Reading
The Cameron Story, William T. Cameron, International Society for Vehicle Preservation, 1990.

CAMILLO (E) c.1940–1947

José Maria Camps, Barcelona.

This company was chiefly a maker of electric platform and works trucks, but it made a few passenger cars and vans during a period of acute fuel shortage in Spain.

NG

CAMPAGNA (CDN) 1997 to date

Campagna Motorsport, Plessisville, Quebec.

High performance 3-wheelers achieved a certain popularity in the 1990s and perhaps the most extreme was the Campagna T-Rex. It was a mid-engined trike using a steel tube chassis and dramatic glassfibre bodywork. The 1.1-litre 4-cylinder motorcycle engine (developing 155bhp) and 5-speed sequential gearbox enabled a top speed of 130mph (209 km/h) and 0–60mph (0-96 km/h) in 4.3 seconds.

HP

CAMPBELL (i) (AUS) 1901–1912

Campbell's Cycle Works, Hobart, Tasmania.

Noted racing cyclist Archie Campbell built a *dos-à-dos* 4-seater steamer of 7hp, powered by a cylinder on each side of the vehicle, and which was driven by chains. The boiler was located under the seats and steering was by tiller.

AUTOMOBILES

COTTEREAU
& Cie

René
Vincent
05.

DIJON

Transverse front and rear semi-elliptic springs, bicycle-type wheels, and a prominent front condenser were fitted. In about 1906 he made a second car, with an internal-combustion engine fuelled by naphtha. His third vehicle, probably of about 1912, was a light electric 2-seater which was the only one to attract a buyer. He also offered his motor-bicycles in the early period.

MG

CAMPBELL (ii) (US) 1918–1919
Campbell Motor Car Co., Kingston, New York.
The Campbell was successor to the EMERSON and continued the basic Emerson design, a light car with a 4-cylinder engine and a 110in (2792mm) wheelbase. A touring car was the only model made and relatively few cars were completed.

KM

CAMPEADOR *see* ARTES

CAMPERO (E) 1973–1975
Master Diso, Barcelona.
Based on the SIMCA 1200, the Campero had a fibreglass body that could be completely removed. It looked like the Citroën Mehari and was distributed by a Chrysler dealer in Barcelona.

VCM

CAMPION (GB) 1913
Campion Cycle Co. Ltd, Nottingham.
This was a typical cyclecar powered by an 8hp V-twin J.A.P. engine, with friction transmission and final drive by belts. The makers were much better known for their motorcycles, which were built from 1901 to 1925.

NG

CANADA CARS *see* GALT

CANADIAN (CDN) 1921
Colonial Motors Ltd, Walkerville, Ontario.
Colonial Motors was backed by Earl G. Gunn, formerly of Packard, who was responsible for the car's design, and particularly for the ifs by superimposed double transverse leaf springs linked by king pin support arms at each end. This had been used on the PARENTI, which was just going off the market when the Canadian was announced. This system was also used in modified form on the BIRMINGHAM and WRIGHT (iii). Otherwise the Canadian was a conventional tourer powered by a Continental 6-cylinder engine and fronted by a handsome vee-radiator. Gunn never obtained adequate finance, and probably only one Canadian was made.

NG

CANADIAN BABY CAR (CDN) 1914
Montreal, Quebec.
One of Canada's few cyclecars, this was also known as the C.B.C. It was offered with a choice of J.A.P., De Luxe or Wizard engines, and common to all were an epicyclic transmission and final drive by vee-belts. A price of CDN$495 was quoted, but the Canadian Baby never went into production.

NG

CANADIAN CROW (CDN) 1915–1918
Canadian Crow Motor Co. Ltd, Mount Brydges, Ontario.
This was a Canadian-built CROW-ELKHART but was much less successful than its American counterpart. The men behind the company were merchants and farmers with no experience of the motor industry, although they had reasonable financial backing. The cars were at first assembled from American components, although bodies were always Canadian-built. Gradually items such as springs and axles were also made at Mount Brydges, but full manufacture was never achieved. About 100 tourers and five clover leaf roadsters were completed in 1916, but very few after that, and bankruptcy was declared early in 1918.

NG

CANADIAN MOTOR SYNDICATE (CDN) 1897–1899;
CANADIAN MOTORS (CDN) 1900–1902
1897–1898 Canadian Motor Syndicate, Toronto, Ontario.
1899 Still Motor Co. Ltd, Toronto, Ontario.
1900–1902 Canadian Motors Ltd, Toronto, Ontario.
These companies were linked by the designs of British-born inventor William J. Still. He began experimenting with electric vehicles in 1891, although his first ideas were for rail cars. In 1893 he built an electric car (Canada's first) for a Toronto patent lawyer, Frederick Featherstonhaugh. This was named after the customer rather than the inventor, but Still's reputation spread, and in 1897 a group of investors formed the Canadian Motor Syndicate to build vehicles designed by Still. The first was a 3-wheeled electric delivery tricycle, the second a 3-wheeled car with wicker seat which was virtually the delivery tricycle turned round, with the single wheel at the rear, and the third a *dos-à-dos*, with 6hp petrol engine, which was controlled by a single lever. Pushed forward it gave forward speed, pulled back gave reverse and it also acted as a steering tiller. Still soon abandoned this and formed the Still Motor Co. to make electrics exclusively. These included the delivery tricycle, an improved version of the 3-wheeled car, a 4-seater dog-cart, the Ivanhoe 2-seater buggy and a large delivery van.

By the beginning of 1900 Still had run out of capital, but was rescued by a British-financed group called Canadian Motors Ltd. They offered the previous Still designs under their own name, and lined them up outside their factory for a group photograph. It seems likely that at this stage no more than one had been made of each model. CML added two more designs, a 4-seater victoria and a Tally-Ho, a charabanc for 15 passengers. Still's 4-seater dog-cart was named the Oxford. Some of these cars were sold in London by Shippey Bros, who took to mounting their own bodies and eventually made so much of the vehicle that it was not worth CML carrying on. Their vehicles were not selling well in Canada either, and CML closed down in 1902. However, the following year a new company, Canada Cycle & Motor Co., was formed to make a new electric car called the IVANHOE.

NG

CANADIAN REPLICAR (CDN) 1980–c.1988
Canadian Replicar, Campbellford, Ontario.
This company produced an Auburn Speedster replica to the usual formula, with a GM 5.0-litre V8 engine. From 1985 it also offered an MG TD replica.

CR

CANADIAN STANDARD (CDN) 1913
Canadian Standard Auto & Tractor Co., Moose Jaw, Saskatchewan.
This company was formed in November 1912 by an American, A.R. Walton, helped by local businessmen who hoped to create an auto industry in their small prairie city. Walton moved machinery from Fort Wayne, Indiana, where he had been building a truck, to Moose Jaw, and planned a 4-cylinder tourer to sell for about CDN$2000. A few prototypes were made in 1913 before the locals withdrew their support, and nothing more was heard of Walton's project. There seems to have been no link in design or personnel with the MOOSE JAW STANDARD built in the city four years later.

NG

CANAM CLASSIC CARS (US) c.1992
CanAm Classic Cars, Minneapolis, Minnesota.
This small company made a Ferrari Testarossa replica that fitted Pontiac Trans-Am and Chevrolet Camaro chassis. They were available in kit or turnkey form.

HP

CANDA (US) 1900–1902
Canda Manufacturing Co., Carteret, New Jersey.
Canda began with a 2-seater quadricycle of De Dion-Bouton type, joined by a tricycle and, in 1901, by a side by side 2-seater Stanhope and Spider Runabout. The tricycles and quads were powered by 1.75hp single-cylinder engines, while the larger cars had two 2.5hp single-cylinder engines, giving speeds up to 15mph (24km/h).

NG

C&C (US) c.1994

C&C Service & Performance Centers, Pocono Summit, Pennsylvania.
The Lamborghini Countach was replicated by C&C with a tube frame and Chevrolet V8 power. Both 5700cc and 7400cc engines were offered, along with fabricated suspension. They were sold in kit and assembled form.

HP

C. & H. (GB) 1913

Corfield & Hurle Ltd, Stamford Hill, London.
This was a 3-wheeled cyclecar offered in two models, with 704cc 6hp Fafnir or 964cc 8hp Precision engines. Both had Chater-Lea 3-speed gearboxes and chain final drive to the single rear wheel.

NG

CANDY APPLE (GB) 1994 to date

Candy Apple Cars, Danbury, Essex.
The Finale was a fibreglass coupé rebody of the Pontiac Fiero, built by ex-racing driver Peter Ashdown, with the mouldings done by Eurosport. The styling (incorporating Vauxhall headlamps and rear hatch) and its ease of build made it a popular kit, especially in export markets. With alternative nose and rear styling the model was also available as the Fino.

CR

CANNOISE *see* BERRET

CANNON (i) **(US)** 1902–1906

Burtt Manufacturing Co., Kalamazoo, Michigan.
This car was made by two machinists: Frank Burtt gave his name to the company, and Warren B. Cannon to the cars. They began with a 7hp single-cylinder runabout and 15hp 2-cylinder tonneau, progressing in 1905 to 24hp 2-cylinder and 50hp 4-cylinder cars. Transmissions were epicyclic or sliding gear; these, like the engines, were made in the Burtt factory. However, by 1906 they mostly made friction clutches for other manufacturers, and Kalamazoo stationary engines. There was no connection with the Cannon steamer, a one-off racer made by George Cannon in Cambridge, Massachusetts.

NG

CANNON (ii) **GB** 1953–c.1970

M.R.B. Cannon, Gover Hill, Tonbridge, Kent
The trial cars built by Mike Cannon were among the few of their kind made for commercial sale. Working single handed, Cannon made about 120 cars between 1953 and the end of 1966. Most were delivered in kit form, and used Ford 10 engines. From 1967 he made them to special order only at the rate of one or two per year, as the market was saturated and the cars did not wear out.

NG

CANSTEL (AUS) 1970–1989

Specialised Fibreglass Mouldings, Taren Point, New South Wales.
G.S. Motor Bodies Pty Ltd, Carlton, New South Wales.
A clubman-type designed by Allan McCann and Graham Steele, the Canstel was first offered as a kit for fitting to a Triumph Herald chassis. As the Heralds became scarce, the 1972 Mk 2 was a revised chassis designed to accept Herald components. However, tightened design rules brought it to an end after 39 had been made. The Mk 3 of 1978 was sold as a complete car by Terry O'Neill of G.S., with Mazda rotary and Toyota Celica engines. In 1988 engines for unleaded fuel were fitted, by which time a further 55 examples had been produced.

MG

CANTA *see* WAAIJENBERG

CANTERBURY (GB) 1903–1906

Canterbury Motor Co., Canterbury, Kent.
This small company assembled cars from various well-known component suppliers. In 1903 they listed two models, a 6hp 2-seater with single-cylinder De Dion-Bouton engine, 3-speed gearbox and shaft drive, and a 12hp 4-seater tonneau with 2-cylinder Aster engine and chain drive. In 1906 a few larger cars were assembled, using 16/20hp 4-cylinder White & Poppe engines.

NG

1904 Canterbury 8hp 2-seater.
MICHAEL WORTHINGTON-WILLIAMS

CANTONO (I) 1900–1911

1900–1905 E. Cantono, Rome.
1906–1911 Società Anonima FRAM, Genoa.
The invention of an Italian army officer, Captain Eugenio Cantono, this was a 2-wheeled electric fore-carriage which could be used to motorise horse-drawn carriages to give them a new lease of life. The batteries were mounted over the axle, and the motors gave independent drive to each wheel. The carriage part was modified so that band brakes could be applied to the rear wheels. Cantono's designs were sold in France from 1902 by the Compagnie des Voitures Électriques of St Ouen, and in America by the Cantono Electric Tractor Co. of Marion, New Jersey, from 1904 to 1907. It was described by an American journalist as 'a ponderous creation'. In 1906 the name of the parent company was changed to FRAM (Fabbrica Rotabili Avantreni Motori), and the factory moved to Genoa.
The 1906 range consisted of the Tipo A for attachment to private carriages, the Tipo B for use with commercial vehicles, and the Tipo Turismo which was supplied as a complete vehicle. On later models the motors and batteries were covered by a bonnet, giving more of the appearance of a petrol car. In 1906 a FRAM with a 2-cylinder petrol engine was announced, and in 1908 a licence was taken out by a German firm, Deutsche Elektromobil GmbH of Düsseldorf. Commercial vehicles assumed greater prominence from about 1909, and were the sole offerings from 1911 to 1913 when the parent company closed down. Development contined for a further two years in France, where the designs were made by De Dion-Bouton. A number of FRAMs were used for refuse collection in Paris.

NG

CAP (B) 1914

The Cap light car had an air-cooled V-twin J.A.P. engine and a tandem 2-seater body. One source says that it was designed in England but built in Belgium, another that it was probably of entirely English origin.

NG

CAPEL (GB) 1900–1901

Creek Street Engineering Co. Ltd, Deptford, London.
This was a light 3-seater voiturette with a single seat facing the driver and passenger, powered by a 4hp 2-cylinder engine located under the driver's seat. It was designed by Herbert Capel of the Clarkson & Capel Steam Car Syndicate (see CLARKSON), but he died in January 1901 before the car was completed. Manufacture was taken up by the Creek Street Engineering Co., but few cars were made.

NG

CAPITOL (US) 1902

Capitol Automobile Co., Washington DC.
This was a 2-seater steam car with opulent curves which the designer called a steam chariot. He claimed that he built it in 1889, but did not try to market it until 1902, at a price of $1200. Apparently only the one car was ever made, and it still exists.

NG

1908 Car De Luxe Model B 50hp tourer.
JOHN A. CONDE

c.1914 Carden monocar.
NICK GEORGANO

CAPRICORN (GB) 1985
Capricorn, Wakefield, Yorkshire.
This was a very short-lived kit car in the style of the Willys Jeep, based on Mini parts.
CR

CAPRICORNIA (AUS) 1957–1959
Ludgate Automotive Developments, Adelaide, South Australia.
When Lea-Francis Cars withdrew from production in 1953, its Chief Engineer, Albert Ludgate, joined the Adelaide firm of J.A. Lawton & Sons. However, his enthusiasm for performance cars and a contact with a former Queenslander persuaded him to design and build a duplex tube chassis frame, to accept Holden components for a sports car. Its wheelbase was 91in (2311mm) and it weighed 713kg. Taking its name from the Tropic of Capricorn region, the first of the series was fitted with an English R.G.S. fibreglass body. Other bodies were fitted; one with a BUCHANAN body and a Repco Highpower cylinder head enjoyed a long and successful competition career, later under the name Ricardian. Capricornia Junior go-karts and T.Q. midget racing cars were also constructed.
MG

CAPRONI see CEMSA

CAPS (US) 1902–1905
Caps Bros Manufacturing Co., Kansas City, Missouri.
The Caps brothers manufactured printing machines and made a few cars for their neighbours, starting with a 14hp 2-cylinder 2-seater in 1902, and progressing to some cars with tonneau bodies. In 1905 a group of bankers formed the Farmer's Auto-Motor Co. to manufacture Caps cars, but before production could start they decided that the KANSAS CITY was a better proposition. J.C. Caps stayed on to supervise production of the new car.
NG

C.A.R. (i) (I) 1906
Cantieri Automobilistici Riuniti, Palermo, Sicily.
This company announced ambitious plans to make touring and racing cars, light cars, voiturettes, goods vehicles, omnibuses, motor boats and engines from 7 to 120hp. Little is known about the actual vehicles made. Apart from the even more shadowy Olivieri, which was just a name in a directory, C.A.R. is the only known Sicilian car maker.
NG

C.A.R. (ii) see COSMOS

C.A.R. (iii) see G.A.R.

C.A.R. (iv) (US) c.1982–1984
Classic Auto Reproductions, Babylon, New York.
Early Fords were the staple of this kit car company. The Special A was a 1929 Model A replica, and was available in Roadster or Dual Cowl Phaeton Limousine form. The Special T was a 1957 Thunderbird replica. Both were based on Ford Pinto or Mustang II running gear, and were available in kit or turnkey form.
HP

CAR DE LUXE (US) 1906–1909
1906–1907 De Luxe Motor Car Co., Toledo, Ohio.
1908–1909 De Luxe Motor Car Co., Detroit, Michigan.
This car lived up to its name, for it was a high-quality and expensive machine. The 1907 Model A had a 50hp 4-cylinder engine and was priced at $4750 for a 7-seater tourer. Originally located in the former YALE (i) factory in Toledo, the company moved to Detroit in 1908, where a limousine/landaulette at $5000 was added to the range. The 1909 models were quoted as 50/60hp and included a 7-seater limousine at $6250. Before the move to Detroit, De Luxe president Nathan M. Kaufman merged his company with that of C.H. Blomstrom who made the BLOMSTROM and QUEEN cars. The De Luxe factory was later used for manufacture of the FLANDERS.
NG

CAR SYSTÈME (F) 1981–1989
Construction Automobile Redonnaise, Redon.
Founded by Gérald Maillard and Patrick Faucher, this enterprise produced a shortened 'beach car' version of the Renault 4 with only two seats, no doors and a soft top. A Renault 6-based version was also available, as well as a 4-seater model. The model was known as the Car Système JP4, and several hundred were built. In 1989 the company turned to making Renault 5 convertibles.
CR

CARCANO (I) 1898–1901
This maker of motorcycle engines exhibited a 3hp voiturette at the 1901 Milan Show. Its only claim to fame is that Carlo Maserati, one of the six celebrated brothers, was involved in its design.
NG

CARDEN; NEW CARDEN (GB) 1913–1925
1913–1914 Carden Engineering Co. Ltd, Farnham, Surrey.
1914–1916 Carden Engineering Co. Ltd, Teddington, Middlesex.
1919–1922 Carden Engineering Co. Ltd, Ascot, Berkshire.
1922–1925 Arnott & Harrison Ltd, Willesden, London.
John Valentine Carden was a prolific inventor who was interested in ultra-light aircraft and cross-country vehicles as well as cars. He built his first cyclecars at his private workshop in Farnham; various designs were tried including a tandem 2-seater, but the first model which he offered for sale was a single seater. Making its public appearance at Brooklands in April 1913, it had a low-slung monocoque body of ash planks and was powered by a 481cc 4hp single-cylinder

J.A.P. engine mounted at the rear and driving forward by roller chain to a cone clutch on the rear axle. There was only one forward speed and no reverse. With an overall ratio of 4:1 Carden lapped Brooklands at over 46mph (75km/h), but production versions were to have a ratio of 5:1. Front suspension was by a single coil spring, and steering was by centre pivot. Carden offered replicas at £55, forming Carden Engineering for manufacture with backing from G.C. Holzapfel. They moved into larger premises at Teddington in February 1914. There a new model with V-twin engine of 654cc and 2-speed gearbox was made, priced at £70, or in De Luxe form for £80. The basic single-cylinder model was also still made.

By 1916 Carden had sold his monocar design to Ward & Avey Ltd, who took over the Teddington works. It was still listed as a Carden in *Light Cars & Cyclecars of 1916*, but in 1919 it reappeared as the A.V. Carden designed another cyclecar which he sold to Edward A. Tamplin who marketed it under his own name.

In 1919, at new premises at Ascot, Carden launched another design, this time a side by side 2-seater with rear-mounted horizontal-twin 2-stroke engine of 707cc. The cylinders were arranged side by side rather than horizontally opposed, with the heads pointing to the rear, and driving the rear axle through a 2-speed gearbox. The price was originally a round £100, but rose to £134 in 1921. Carden left the firm that year, to pursue an engineering career including the Carden-Loyd tracked load carrier which was built by Vickers. He inherited a baronetcy in 1932, and died in an air crash in 1935.

The Carden company was bought by Arnott & Harrison, who marked the change of ownership by renaming the car New Carden. They gave it a dummy bonnet which made it look more substantial, but the engine and transmission were unchanged. The price was 138 guineas (£144.90), not good value when just over £20 more would buy an Austin Seven with a more reliable 4-cylinder engine. Prices were reduced for 1924, to £100 for the family model and £110 for the sports. For 1925 they offered a more expensive car called the Sheret, after its designer A.H. Sheret. It had chain instead of spur gear drive, three forward speeds instead of two, and a 3-seater body. Few were made, and all production ended at Willesden in 1925.

NG

CARDIAC (CDN) c.1992–c.1995
Cardiac Cobra Sportscars Ltd, North Vancouver, British Columbia.
This was one of innumerable A.C. Cobra replicas. Conventionally, it used a cross-braced chassis with Ford Mustang front and Jaguar rear suspension and any small or big-block V8 engine. As well as glassfibre bodies, aluminium was an option.

CR

CARDINET (F) 1900–1906
Compagnie Française des Voitures Electromobiles, Paris.
A wide range of electric vehicles was made under the Cardinet name. The first models carried their batteries under the frame, but from 1901 onwards they were hidden within the body, giving a neater appearance. Open and closed town carriages were made, including a landaulette with front-wheel drive, and a hansom cab with two motors driving the rear wheels.

NG

CARDWAY (US) 1923–1924
Frederick Cardway, New York, New York.
Colonel Frederick Cardway was formerly associated with both Packard and Pierce-Arrow in their export division and the Cardway, an undistinguished car both in design and its variety of standard components, appeared as a touring car equipped with right-hand steering with the export market in mind. Production never got underway with only four touring cars completed during 1923. At least one and probably two more followed in 1924, their only difference being the model of Continental 6-cylinder engine fitted, a 6Y for the 1923 quartet and the 7U for 1924. One of the cars was exported to Australia but the fate of the remaining four or five is unknown. One of the Cardways survives, owned by a Canadian collector.

KM

1920 Carden 7hp cyclecar.
MICHAEL WORTHINGTON-WILLIAMS

1924 New Carden family tourer.
MICHAEL WORTHINGTON-WILLIAMS

1923 Cardway tourer.
KEITH MARVIN

1902 Carlton (i) tonneau.
MALCOLM JEAL

CAREY (US) 1906
Carey Motor Co., New York, New York.
The Carey was one of that select band of cars to use rotary engines, in this case a 10hp 5-cylinder Balzer unit with vertical crankshaft. Made in the Bronx, close to Balzer's works, it was exhibited in 2-seater form at the Automobile Club of America Show in 1906, but probably very few were made or sold.
NG

CARHARTT (US) 1911–1912
Carhartt Automobile Co., Detroit, Michigan.
Hamilton Carhartt was stretching a point when he boasted of '28 years of manufacturing success culminates in the Carhartt car', for his manufacturing expertise had been gained in making overalls, not cars. He advertised two models of 4-cylinder car, the Junior 25hp and Four 35hp, the latter with six different body styles. They varied from a runabout to a limousine yet all were priced identically at $2250. For 1912 Carhartt offered a four rated at 50hp, priced at $2500 to $3500.
NG

CARIBBEAN (GB) 1976–1983
Reef Engineering, Lichfield, Staffordshire.
Designed by an ex-Reliant chief engineer called John Crosthwaite, the Caribbean Cub and Cob used Reliant mechanicals (Kitten/Fox). Most were sold to Barbados and the Seychelles but kits were also offered in the UK. The Cub was a doorless 4-seater beach car with a lockable boot, the Cob was a 2-seater pickup which also boasted doors.
CR

CARISMA (GB) 1990–1996
1990–1992 Carisma Engineering, Sandy, Bedfordshire.
1992–1993 Scorhill Motors, Walton-on-Thames, Surrey.
1993–1996 Scorhill Motor Co., Chertsey, Surrey.
Carisma stated that its Century was not a replica of the SS100. Rather, it was a pastiche of rather awkward proportions. The ladder chassis was designed to accept Ford Cortina mechanicals with a steel bulkhead, fibreglass main body and aluminium engine side panels, and a 4-seater was optional. The Century's makers disappeared in 1992 but it was resurrected by SCORHILL as the Century 2-seater and Manhattan 4-seater.
CR

CARLETTE (GB) 1913
Holstein Garage, Weybridge, Surrey.
The Carlette cyclecar was powered by an 8hp V-twin J.A.P. engine which drove by rubber belt to a countershaft. This could be swung to and fro with a travel

of 50mm to give variable gearing, and was controlled by a small wheel placed outside the body on the off-side. Final drive, also by belt, was to the off-side rear wheel only. Double belt drive could be provided '. . . which we should certainly prefer', commented *The Cyclecar*. The prototype that they tested had a very simple body without lights or wings.
NG

CARLETTI (I) 1998 to date
Carletti SpA, Donato, Biella.
Cleverly using modified styling elements of the Opel Corsa, the Carletti Top 500 microcar measured only 117in (2970mm) long. Powered by a front-mounted 5.4bhp Lombardini 505cc diesel engine, it also used a variable automatic transmission and front disc brakes. The main structure was in steel with body panels in plastic; the rear section of the 2-seater was designed to fold away for open-air motoring.
CR

CARLSON (US) 1904
Carlson Motor Vehicle Co., Brooklyn, New York.
Former manager of the New York repair department for the WINTON Carriage Co., Charles A. Carlson set up on his own to make cars, commerical vehicles and engines. Only one model of passenger car was made, a 20hp runabout on the same 90in (2284mm) chassis as the firm's light truck. Carlson then made commercials exclusively, up to 1910.
NG

CARLTON (i) (GB) 1901–1902
Carlton Motor Co., Coventry.
This company briefly offered three models of light car, powered by Aster engines of 8hp (single-cylinder), 12hp (2-cylinder) and 24hp (4-cylinder).
NG

CARLTON (ii) *see* MARLBOROUGH

CARLTON (iii) (GB) 1983 to date
1983–1986 Carlton Mouldings, Barnsley, South Yorkshire.
1986 to date Carlton Automotive, Barnsley, South Yorkshire.
The Carlton Commando came at a time when the Dutton Sierra was Britain's best-selling kit car and aimed to beat it on size, chunky looks, giant cabin and practical Ford Cortina basis. There were estate, 'sports truck' (pick-up), and flat bed options, plus a 6-wheeler. Some 450 were sold in all. The 1985 Carrera was a 4-seater coupé that looked somewhat like a Jaguar E-Type. Initially it was sold as a Ford Cortina based coupé, but Rover V8 powered and Jaguar based options followed. Carlton also took over the M.C. Acer and developed a BMW M1-style coupé prototype that never reached production.
CR

CARMIER (F) 1927
Sté Commerciale des Automobiles Carmier, Paris.
The Carmier was a conventional-looking light sports car, unusual in its 1100cc flat-four air-cooled engine. It had a 3-speed gearbox and shaft drive to a fully floating rear axle.
NG

CAR-NATION (US) 1912–1915
American Voiturette Co., Detroit, Michigan.
The Car-Nation was large for a cyclecar, having an 18hp 4-cylinder engine and conventional 3-speed gearbox. Three models were offered, a tandem 2-seater, a side by side 2-seater and a 4-seater tourer. In late 1913 American Voiturette's president, Charles S. Shaffer bought the KEETON company, who were making a large 6-cylinder car, which would indicate that he did not have complete faith in light cars. By the end of 1914 the company was in receivership, and although it was stated that 600 Car-Nations and 100 Keetons would be assembled under receivership, probably far fewer were.
NG

CAROLUS; CAROLETTE *see* KNOLLNER

CARON (F) 1900–1901
Caron et Compagnie, Paris.
The Caron was a voiturette powered by a 5hp 2-cylinder air-cooled engine. This was mounted at the front of the car, and power was transmitted via a 3-speed gearbox and propeller shaft to a live rear axle. This was a very advanced feature for a light car at this time.

NG

CAROSELLI (US) 1997 to date
Caroselli Design, El Segundo, California.
The Rodster was a unique kit car with hot-rod flair based on the Chevrolet S-10 Blazer sports-utility vehicle. The top was removed, and rounded front and rear mudguards were added. Two noses were offered, one with an oval opening and the other was a replica of a Ford hot rod.

HP

CAROUSEL (ZA) Mid–1980s
Carousel Engineering CC, Stanger.
Presenting its 1929 Mercedes SSK replica as the 'Springbok Sports Kar', this was a typical SSK reproduction. Two types were offered, one on a VW Beetle chassis and the other with its own front-engined chassis designed for Ford Cortina parts and a choice of leaf spring or coil spring rear suspension. The bodywork was in glassfibre. Another model was an Aston Martin V8 lookalike using Ford Cortina suspension and a 3-litre Ford V6 engine in a ladder frame.

CR

CARPEVIAM (GB) 1903–c.1905
Charles Peacock & Co. Ltd, London.
The origins of the Carpeviam are uncertain as Charles Peacock was a selling agent rather than a manufacturer. The car was a light 3-wheeler with 3.5hp single-cylinder engine driving the single rear wheel by chain via a 2-speed gearbox. Steering was by tiller. It was built on tricar lines although the two seats were side by side. The price was from £99, and a canopy for hot weather was an optional extra at £3.50. A suggestion for the unusual name was that it was a corruption of the Latin 'Carpe diem' ('seize the day').

NG

CARR REPLICAS (ZA) 1990s
Carr Replicas, Rivonia.
Roy Carr's replica of the Ferrari Daytona Spider was called the CR12. It utilised virtually all its necessary components from the Jaguar XJ, mounted in a tubular steel space frame chassis. Engine choices encompassed Jaguar V12 or any proprietary V8. Cars were supplied in kit form or fully-built.

CR

CARRIAGE-MOBILE *see* SUMMIT (i)

CARRICO *see* DE TAMBLE

CARROLL (i) **(US)** 1911–1912
Carroll Motor Car Co., Strasbourg, Pennsylvania.
Despite considerable fanfare on a local basis, only one Carroll car was ever completed. Initially shown in 1911, this unit was completed in 1912. It featured a Continental 4-cylinder engine which developed 40hp. Plans for two lines of cars, 4- and 6-cylinder models, were announced in the automotive press in 1913 but were never built.

KM

CARROLL (ii) **(US)** 1921–1922
Carroll Automobile Co., Lorain, Ohio.
Few Carrolls were built and all were stereotyped exclusively into one open model, a 5-seater touring car, for although a roadster was offered in the 1922 line-up, it presumably never reached the prototype stage. The cars had a distinctive appearance with a radiator positioned behind the front axle. Although a Rochester 6-cylinder engine was initially announced for the Carroll, this never materialised and such Carrolls that were completed were powered by a Beaver, also a 6-cylinder engine. The Carroll had a California (fixed) top, disc wheels,

1922 Carroll (ii) 6-cylinder California Top tourer.
KEITH MARVIN

1921 Carrow 11.9hp 2-seater.
MICHAEL WORTHINGTON-WILLIAMS

front and rear bumpers, and various other accoutrements which 'came with the car'. It was priced at $3985. A story surrounding the Carroll reported that a trainload of Carrolls that had been consigned for West Coast distribution, had been shipped without anti-freeze in winter weather and, upon arrival, were all discovered to have their engine blocks cracked. Whether the legend is true has never been proven, but Carroll production failed to reach 200 cars before the company failed.

KM

CARROW (GB) 1920–1923
1920–1921 Whitley Bay Motor Co., Newcastle upon Tyne.
1921–1923 Carrow Cars Ltd, Hanwell, Middlesex.
The Carrow was a substantial light car powered by a 1820cc 4-cylinder Dorman engine in unit with a 3-speed gearbox, with shaft drive to a spiral bevel rear axle. Chassis records indicate that only the first 12 cars used the Dorman engine, after which the power unit is listed as a Carrow. This was almost certainly a Belgian Peters unit of the same capacity as the Dorman, and in fact the Carrow bore a very close resemblance to the Belgian P.M. car. It is likely the Carrow was assembled from components imported from P.M., or that these components were made under licence. The link is confirmed by two directors of P.M., Pierre Malherbe and Pierre Mullejans joining the Carrow board in 1921, the same year that the move to Hanwell was made. Three body styles were shown at the 1921 Olympia Show, open 2- and 4-seaters and a saloon. A coupé was also listed in advertising, but most of the Carrows made had open 2-seater bodies, judging by surviving photographs. The bodies were said to be made in-house, but may have been imported. Carrow did not exhibit at Olympia again; in October 1923 Carrow ceased trading and a month later P.M. became majority shareholders. Only one Carrow is thought to survive today.

NG

Further Reading
'Mining Motors', M. Worthington-Williams, *The Automobile*, April 1997.

CARS & CONCEPTS (US) c.1985
Cars & Concepts, Brighton, Michigan.
This company built convertible conversions for American car manufacturers, and also sold a run of specially modified Lincolns called the Mark VII GTC.

1920 Carter (iii) 11.9hp 2-seater.
IVAN HOFFMAN

1908 Carter Twin Engine tourer.
KEITH MARVIN

This was a Lincoln Mk VII with suspension upgrades from Jack Roush Performance and Ford. Although handling was improved, a standard 5000cc V8 was used. C&C added wider wheels with performance tyres and aerodynamic body panels along the sides. They were only sold in black and white. The Mark VII GTC was only sold through Lincoln dealers and the price was an expensive $38,686 in 1985.

HP

CARTEL (GB) 1983
Cartel Ltd, Woking, Surrey.
Better known for its range of body styling kits and vehicle conversions, Cartel attempted to produce its own car in 1983, the T.I.G.E.R. (Turbo Intercooled Ground Effect Roadster). Conceived by designer Chris Humberstone, and boasting ground effect technology by Ken Tyrrell, it was a dramatically styled wedge-shaped sports car. The styling was dominated by a forward-hinging canopy, ultra-low nose and large air dams front and rear. A Renault 2.7-litre V6 engine was mounted amidships and could be fitted with optional twin turbochargers. Cartel announced ambitious production plans: chassis would be made in Britain and shipped to the USA for completion at up to 200 units per year, but Cartel stuck with its body kit business.

CR

CARTER (i) (US) 1901
Michigan Automobile Co., Grand Rapids, Michigan.
This was a light steamer with automatic burner, priced at $1000. It was designed by Byron J. Carter who later built the CARTERCAR.
NG

CARTER (ii) (GB) 1913
S. Carter, Selly Oak, Birmingham.
Unusually for so small a car, the Carter cyclecar was powered by a 4-cylinder engine of only 6.2hp, and had shaft drive. Only a prototype was built.
NG

CARTER (iii) (AUS) 1916–1924
H.C. Carter, North Unley, South Australia.
Although he built cars and stationary engines, Clifton Carter operated on a personal basis rather than forming a company. His first effort was a belt-drive cyclecar built on a wooden chassis and powered by a 7hp engine. An 11hp car was also registered in 1916 and a similarly powered roadster, for his own use, followed in 1917. An 8.7hp car had been produced by 1920 when two cars of 11.9hp were exhibited at the first Adelaide Motor Show. Their 4-cylinder, 1525cc ohv engines were of monobloc construction with Dixie magnetos and Zephyr carburettors. Cone clutches, 3-speed gearboxes, quarter-elliptic springs and 710 × 80mm tyres were also featured, while their wheelbase measurements were 103 and 109in (2616 and 2768mm).

A further belt-drive cyclecar, a sturdy example built on a duplex tube chassis frame and powered by an 8hp air-cooled ohv engine, was completed in 1922, but that was Carter's final effort at car making. An interesting aside is that his mother was a cousin of Charles W. Nash, the US car maker, whose father went to the United States from Adelaide.
MG

CARTER (iv) (GB) 1967
Carter Engineering Co. Ltd, Tamworth, Staffordshire.
Alister Carter announced production of his Carter Coaster in spring 1967. It was a very small (98in/2500mm long) 2-door saloon with an electric motor supplied by four 12V 40A batteries. It did not proceed beyond the prototype stage.
CR

CARTER STEAM CAR (US) 1920–1921
Richard Carter Automobile Co., Gulfport, Mississippi.
The paraffin-powered Carter had a 2-cylinder engine and was available only as a 5-seater touring car with a price of $2350. Like most steamers of the period, the Carter resembled a conventional petrol car. Production is not certain, but may have reached an output of 25 cars.
KM

CARTER TWIN ENGINE (US) 1907–1908
Carter Motor Car Co., Hyattsville, Maryland.
Designed by Howard A. Carter, this car had two 4-cylinder engines mounted side by side under the bonnet, each with its own radiator, ignition and exhaust. One was sufficiently powerful to get you home if the other failed, although they could also be used together. With a 5-seater tourer body, the Carter cost $5000. Maybe this was justified by the complexity of the two engines, but customers preferred to trust to one. Very few were sold, and in 1909 Howard's brother, Gary A. Carter, took over the factory to make the WASHINGTON (i).
NG

CARTER'S CONVERSIONS (US) c.1992–c.1994
Carter's Conversions, Imlay City, Minnesota.
This company made a variety of kits, including replicas of the 427 Cobra, Lamborghini Countach (Rambo), Ferrari F-40 (Modena), and Dino 246 (Roma). The Cobra had a tube frame with Ford or Chevrolet V8 power, while the others used Pontiac Fiero running gear. All were availablein kit or turnkey form.
HP

CARTERCAR (US) 1905–1915
1905–1906 The Motorcar Co., Jackson, Michigan.
1906–1908 The Motorcar Co., Detroit, Michigan.
1908–1915 The Cartercar Co., Pontiac, Michigan.
This was the work of Byron J. Carter (1863–1908), who had offered the CARTER (i) steam car in 1901, and had then incorporated the JACKSON Automobile Co. In 1905 he set up his own company, rather unimaginatively called The Motorcar Co., to make cars whose main feature was friction drive. 'No clutch to slip, no gears to strip', was one of his claims. Initially they were offered in two single-cylinder models, 6.5 and 7.5hp, and a 10hp twin, the latter being progressively enlarged up to 1909, when the largest was quoted as a 22/24hp. In 1906, 101 cars were made and 325 in 1908. The change of name to Cartercar Co. coincided with the purchase of the factory of the Pontiac Spring & Wagon Co., makers of the PONTIAC (i). Byron Carter died of pneumonia in April 1908, and in October 1909 the company was bought by Billy Durant to become part of General Motors. From 1910 all Cartercars had 4-cylinder engines, a 25 and 35hp in 1910, growing in size to the 45hp Model S of 1912, on a 122in (3100mm) wheelbase. Closed coupés and sedans were offered as well as open cars from 1912, and friction drive was featured up to the end in May 1915. Durant had lost control of GM in 1910 and did not regain it until September 1915, by which time it was too late to save the Cartercar, even if he had wanted to. He later admitted that it had been a mistake to buy the make just to be able to offer a friction-drive car. The Cartercar plant was used for OAKLAND production. About 25 Cartercars survive today.

NG

Further Reading
'A few why's worth considering, being a narrative on the Cartercar', Beverly Rae Kimes, *Automobile Quarterly*, Vol. XII, No.2.

CARTERET (F) 1922
Automobiles Carteret, Courbevoie, Seine.
Made by Louis Vienne, who was also responsible for the OCTO, the Carteret was a neat-looking cyclecar powered by a 904cc Ruby 4-cylinder engine. Transmission was through a friction system by cones, in which top gear was direct through the full engagement of the conical faces. Made under Domecq-Cazeaux patents, this system proved fragile and unreliable, and damaged sales of the Carteret, which was otherwise a well-equipped and reasonably priced car. A sports model with more powerful engine and streamlined body was offered, but may never have been built.

NG

CARTERMOBILE (US) 1921–1922
Washington, D.C. and Hyattsville, Maryland.
The Cartermobile, unsuccessfully designed for the low-priced market, failed to get beyond a handful of prototypes including open models and, possibly, two closed examples. The Cartermobile was fitted with a Herschell-Spillman 7000 4-cylinder L-head engine, had a wheelbase of 112in (2843mm) and a price of $895 for the touring car. Headquarters were in Washington; the factory at Hyattsville, Maryland.

KM

CAS (CS) 1921
Ceska Automobilová Spolecnost, Praha.
CAS appeared at the Prague motor exhibition in 1921. The Rechziegel brothers, both machine engineers, began to construct and produce motor cycles and scooters. One year later, their first 4-wheel 2-seater cyclecar was built. The CAS cyclecar with a steel frame was powered by the Coventry Victor 689cc air-cooled flat-twin engine placed in front. Later some domestic Walter twin-cylinders were used.

MSH

CASALINI (I) 1969 to date
Costruzioni Meccaniche Caslini srl, Piacenza.
This moped, scooter and trike manufacturer produced the amusingly-named Sulky 3-wheeler, a very small 2-seater powered by a 50cc or 60cc engine. Unusually it had all-steel bodywork of very straight lines, mounted on a tubular chassis. It gained the option of four wheels in 1980 (in which form it was known

c.1980 Casalini Sulky 49cc microcar.
NATIONAL MOTOR MUSEUM

as the Bretta or David) and a Break estate body style. 80cc and 125cc engines were also offered, and there was another model called the Kore, also available with three or four wheels. With sales of 1000 per year, Casalini long outlived other Italian microcar makers. From 1996 an additional offering was the Sulky yDea, a conventional 4-wheeled small car powered by a 500cc Lombardini (or 583cc Mitsubishi) diesel twin, and having MacPherson front and semi-independent rear suspension, plus variable automatic transmission. By 1998, some 30,000 passenger cars had been made.

CR

CASE (i) (CDN) 1906–1909
Howard Case & Co., Lethbridge Motor Car Co., Lethbridge, Alberta.
The first car to be built commercially on the Prairies, this was designed by Howard A. Case and had a 20/24hp air-cooled 4-cylinder engine with friction transmission and chain final drive. The specification included Fawkes airless tyres, presumably solids, which were pretty old-fashioned for passenger cars by 1906. Only small numbers were made, priced at CDN$2000. There was no connection with the better-known American Case.

NG

CASE (ii) (US) 1910–1927
The J. I. Case Threshing Machine Co., Racine, Wisconsin.
The Case was a conventional car made by one of America's best known makers of threshing machines, steam traction engines, and agricultural tractors. Car production began in 1911, when they purchased the factory of the recently-defunct PIERCE-RACINE company. In fact, the 40hp 4-cylinder Case was a Pierce-Racine renamed, but smaller fours of 25 and 30hp were added later. The engines were made in house, but many other components were bought in, such as transmissions from Brown-Lipe, rear axles from Weston-Mott and carburettors from Rayfield. Peak production was reached in 1915, with 2630 cars made. They were widely distributed through the large dealer network for traction engines and petrol tractors.
In 1918 the fours were replaced by a 6-cylinder engine made by Continental, who supplied all Case's engines for the next nine years. The engine was rated at 29.4hp (3.9 litres) and this was gradually increased to 31.5hp (5.3 litres) by 1923. Usually only one size was offered each year, but in some years, such as 1923, an overlap between models made two sizes available, the 3957cc 8R and the 5327cc 6T. In 1922 a smaller 3670cc Continental 7R was available, but output declined during the 1920s. Output fell from 1936 in 1920 to 636 in 1926, while in the make's last year only 187 cars were delivered. The cars, like the agricultural vehicles and equipment, carried an eagle emblem modelled on 'Old Abe', the famous mascot of the Wisconsin Regiment, from 1861 to 1881.

NG

Further Reading
'Case in point: Car from Racine', Thomas S. LaMarre, *Automobile Quarterly*, Vol.31, No.3.

1922 Castle Three 10hp 3-wheeler.
NATIONAL MOTOR MUSEUM

1902 Castro 14hp limousine.
JOAQUIN CIURO GABARRO

CASSELL (GB) 1900–1903

Central Motor Co., Glasgow.
This was an assembled car using 2- or 4-cylinder engines by Aster or De Dion-Bouton. A Cassell with 25hp 4-cylinder engine was entered in the 1903 Thousand Mile Trial.

NG

CASTLE THREE (GB) 1919–1922

Castle Motor Co. Ltd, Kidderminster, Worcestershire.
The Castle Motor Co. was owned by the brothers Stanley and Loughton Goodwin, who made shells, gun carriage hubs, and aero-engine components during World War I. Like so many others, they hoped to cater for the postwar demand for popular cars, their choice being a 3-wheeler with single wheel at the rear. They aimed to 'Rolls-Royce the Morgan' and to that end the engine had 4 cylinders, which was unusual when nearly all rival 3-wheelers relied on 2-cylinder power. The first 12 cars had 1094cc Dorman units, after which they turned to the Belgian-made 1207cc Peters. Transmission was by epicyclic gears, and the rear wheel was driven by shaft. The epicyclic transmission was listed through the car's life, but at least some of the later cars, including one of the

two known survivors, had proprietary 3-speed gearboxes. The Castle Three was a quality small car, and this was reflected in the 2300 orders which were taken at the 1919 Olympia Show. However, production was slow to start, and only about 350 were delivered in all, before the Goodwins sold their works to a local carpet firm. A prototype 4-wheeler, the Castle Four, never went into production.

NG

Further Reading
'The Castle Three – Fragments on Forgotten Makes, No.15', W. Boddy, *Motor Sport*, November 1960.

CASTRO (E) 1901–1904

J. Castro Sociedad en Comandita, Barcelona.
Juan Castro was one of the creditors when the LA CUADRA company failed, and seeing a future for the motorcar he took over manufacture of the existing La Cuadra 2-cylinder chain-driven cars. Their designer was the Swiss engineer Marc Birkigt, who soon produced a more up-to-date car, with 10hp 2-cylinder engine and shaft drive, followed in 1903 by a 14hp T-head 4-cylinder shaft-driven car. However, finances were shaky and in June 1904 Castro's company was taken over by a group of businessmen headed by Damien Mateu. He realised that Castro had a valuable asset in the talented Birkigt, so he retained him as chief designer for the new company, and honoured him by including his nationality in the company's name, La Hispano-Suiza (Spanish-Swiss) Fabrica de Automoviles, the car being the celebrated HISPANO-SUIZA.

NG

C.A.T. (F) 1911

Construction Automobiles Tarnaise, Rabastens, Tarn.
Probably the only car to be made in the remote, mountainous region of Tarn, the C.A.T. was an 8hp 4-cylinder 2-seater, made in open and coupé form. Its top speed was only 30mph (48km/h), but the makers made a virtue of this by stating that a low speed avoided excessive tyre wear.

NG

CATERHAM (GB) 1973 to date

1973–1987 Caterham Cars Ltd, Caterham, Surrey.
1987 to date Caterham Cars Ltd, Caterham, Surrey & Dartford, Kent..
Caterham Cars took over production of the Lotus Seven in May 1973. After only 38 of the S4 type, it switched to the purer, older S3 in 1974. Ford 1300 or

252

1600 engines were offered alongside the 126bhp Lotus Big Valve Twin Cam. As supplies of Lotus engines dried up, Vegantune Twin Cam engines were fitted from 1981 but the definitive Caterham Sevens were those fitted with tuned Ford engines: Caterham offered the Sprint (with 110bhp) and the Supersprint (135bhp). A Morris Ital live rear axle replaced the Escort unit in 1980 and a De Dion rear suspension option was introduced in 1985.

An even more powerful Seven emerged in 1984 when Cosworth supplied engines developing 150–170bhp, in which form the cars were known as the HPC and a driving test had to be taken before Caterham would supply a car. A Vauxhall 2-litre-powered HPC (with 175bhp) arrived in 1991, just before Caterham started fitting Rover K-series engines as standard. These started with the 1.4-litre engine (103–128bhp) but moved up to 1.6- and 1.8-litres. All models gained 4-wheel disc brakes in 1988, impact protection in 1990, Bilstein suspension in 1991 and a 6-speed transmission option in 1995. The fastest Sevens of all were the J.P.E. (Jonathan Palmer Evolution) – an ultra-lightweight version with a 250bhp BTCC Vauxhall engine – and the Superlight R, a stripped-out model using a heavily modified 190bhp Rover 1.8-litre engine. With more power again was the R500 of 2000, with a 230bhp Rover engine developed by Minster Race Engines..

A new chapter was written in 1996 when production began of the 21. This was another 2-seater sports car but with enveloping bodywork (in fibreglass or aluminium) and opening doors and boot. The design was by Iain Robertson, mounted over a slightly modified Seven chassis.

CR

CAUSAN (F) 1923–1924
Automobiles Causan, Levallois-Perret, Seine.
This was a very small cyclecar powered by a single-cylinder 2-stroke engine of only 350cc, designed by the great engineer Nemorin Causan, who had been responsible for early Delage engines and had also worked for Bignan, La Licorne, La Perle, and Vernandi. It had a 2-speed gearbox and, surprisingly for so small a car, shaft drive. In 1924 the name was changed to D'AUX and production moved to Rheims.

NG

CAVAC (US) 1910–1911
Small Motor Car Co., Detroit, Michigan.
On paper the Cavac roadster seemed an attractive proposition, with a 24hp monobloc 4-cylinder engine mounted in an underslung frame, giving it a very low and racy appearance. All the engine's moving parts were enclosed. The makers had ambitious plans for manufacture in Detroit and Winnipeg, but beyond a few prototypes, nothing more was heard of the Cavac.

NG

CAVALIER (US) 1926
Cavalier Motor Associates, Baltimore, Maryland.
Heralded as 'The first of the Pony Cars', the Cavalier was a car which pioneered an arrangement by which it could be used as a roadster, phaeton, coupé or sedan by the simple expedient of adding or removing panels and parts, the idea being that the car could be tailored to the occasion. Aside from its novelty, the car was as generic as a car could be, powered by a 4-cylinder ohv engine developing 32hp and a 98in (2487mm) wheelbase. Its price was set at $595 'a.g.d.' (at your garage door). The four-in-one idea was that of the car's promoter, Norton L. Dods, who had earlier marketed the Vernon car, named after Mount Vernon, New York, where the Cavalier prototype was also built. Despite its novelty, production of the Cavalier ended with its lone prototype.

KM

CAVALLO (GB) 1983–1985
Cavallo Cars, Leeds, Yorkshire.
The Cavallo Estivo was one of the more promising British kits of the early 1980s: a sharply styled convertible with four seats and a large boot. The choice of donor vehicle was all wrong, though; into the box section steel chassis went humble BMC 1100/1300 mechanicals. It was marketed as a kit car but was withdrawn to re-engineer it as a fully-built vehicle. It never re-emerged.

CR

1983 Caterham Super Seven.
CATERHAM CARS

1996 Caterham Super Seven Road-Sport 2-seater sports car.
NATIONAL MOTOR MUSEUM

1999 Caterham 21 2-seater sports car.
CATERHAM CARS

1926 Cavalier Four 2-seater.
KEITH MARVIN

1904 Cavendish 9hp tonneau.
STEPHEN MYERS

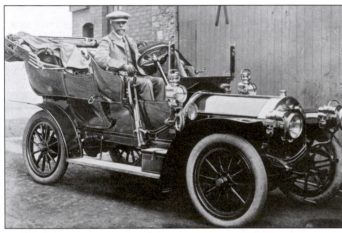

1907 C.C.C. 18/22hp tourer.
NATIONAL MOTOR MUSEUM

CAVENDISH (GB) 1903–1905
Sheffield Motor Co., Sheffield, Yorkshire.
The Cavendish is something of a mystery make as although the Sheffield Motor Co. had quite large premises near the centre of the city, they were not suitable for manufacture. At least seven cars were registered in the district, with engines of 6, 9 and 10hp. Two of the 6hp models were powered by De Dion-Bouton engines.
NG

C.B. (US) 1917–1918
Carter Brothers Motor Car Co., Hyattsville, Maryland.
The brothers Gary and Howard Carter built the WASHINGTON (i) from 1909 to 1912, and were subsequently involved with the HARVARD and MONARCH (vi) before relaunching three models of the latter under the name C.B. A four, a V8 and a V12 were listed, but probably no more than a few prototypes were made. The brothers' final venture was the CARTERMOBILE.
NG

C.B.A. (E) 1982–1985
Cia Balear de Automoviles, Palma de Mallorca.
The Swede Thomas Wadström founded this company on the Balearic island of Mallorca, offering three different bodies of vintage design using Citroën 2CV platforms. The Condesa, Duquesa and pick-up had polyester bodies with a lot of nice brass detailing. The cars were the mascot of the Balear Tourist Board and sold to several countries. In 1985 the company wanted to expand into building electric cars, but the death of the founder in 1986 prevented this. In 1987 there was an attempt to revive the company on the Canary Islands calling it CCA, but this was not successful.
VCM

C.C. (GB) 1991 to date
Car Craft, Lytham, Lancashire.
This company began with a characterful rebody for a Fiat 126, sold under the name C.C. Zero. A simple steel tube chassis was designed to house the engine, gearbox, running gear and most other parts from the 126, while the tiny body used aluminium main panels and fibreglass nose and wings in a traditional/fun car fusion. To make way for C.C.'s next project, the Cyclone, the Zero was taken over in 1995 by Zero Engineering of London. The Cyclone was 'a Lotus Seven for the 1990s': a transverse mid-mounted Vauxhall engine, space frame chassis, pro-race suspension and a low, doorless, lightweight fibreglass body incorporating a fixed roll-over bar.
CR

C.C.A. *see* C.B.A.

C.C.C. (GB) 1906–1907
Chassis Construction Co. Ltd, Taunton, Somerset.
An associate company of C. Allen & Sons Ltd, engineers, C.C.C. advertised a range of chassis in complete or componenet form for local coachbuilders and assemblers. The advertised engines were T-head BALLOT, ranging from 8hp single-cylinder to a 4-cylinder of 110 × 130mm bore and stroke, designated the 20/30. Most chassis parts were imported from MALICET ET BLIN. One of their few customers was the BRIDGEWATER Motor Co., who built a small number of various 4-cylinder models. An attempt to market a taxicab to London hackney regulations was also unsuccessful.
DF

CC INDUSTRIES (US) c.1994–c.1996
CC Industries, Sawyer, Minnesota.
Although they started out selling restoration parts for older Corvettes, this company added a kit replica of the 1957 Corvette called the Concept 57. It used a special tube frame with a mixture of Ford and Chevrolet parts.
HP

C.C.R. (F) 1922–1923
This Parisian-built cyclecar was offered in three models, one with $2\frac{1}{2}$ hp Villiers engine and two speeds, and two with $3\frac{1}{2}$hp Train engine and three speeds. The latter was available with wood or steel chassis. The steel version, known as the B2, was renamed SANTAX when it appeared at the 1923 Paris Salon.
NG

C.D. (F) 1962–1965
Automobiles Charles Deutsch, Paris.
For 25 years aerodynamicist Charles Deutsch enjoyed a fruitful partnership with René Bonnet as the D in the French racing marque D.B. (Bonnet being the B). In 1961 D.B. was dissolved, Bonnet departing to develop his own range of Renault-powered sports car, while Deutsch remained loyal to air-cooled Panhard engines. Deutsch's first solo model was the 1962 C.D.-Panhard Coach, a slippery 701cc fibreglass coupé marketed by Panhard and distributed through its extensive French dealer network. A competition version of the front-wheel drive Coach gained the 1962 Le Mans Index of Performance, while the following year C.D. campaigned a DKW-powered coupé at Le Mans. Production of the C.D.-Panhard Coach ceased when Deutsch changed his competition allegiance to Grac and Peugeot. C.D.'s final two years saw a concentration on motor sport only with a number of wind-cheating Le Mans racers using Peugeot 204 engines. C.D. abandoned racing in late 1967, and Deutsch went on to become France's Minister for Transport in the early 1970s.
CR

C. DE L. (US) 1913
C. de L. Engineering Works, Nutley, New Jersey.
This obscure car was listed in two models, a 3.2-litre 20/30hp and a 7-litre 30/60hp, both with 4-cylinder engines. They advertised that the pistons could be 'single or double acting at the pleasure of the operator', whatever that meant. Single or double acting are terms more usually applied to steam engines.
NG

C. DE S. *see* COGNET DE SEYNES

C.D.M. (GB) 1983

This company displayed a prototype for a car that was adaptable from three to four wheels (called Triune and Pharos respectively), but the design never reached production.

CR

CECO (US) 1914–1915

Continental Engine Co., Minneapolis, Minnesota (1914),
and Chicago, Illinois (1914–1915).

This was a cyclecar originally called the CONTINENTAL (iv), powered by a 12hp 4-cylinder air-cooled engine, with friction transmission. Roadster, tandem 2-seater and delivery van models were offered at prices ranging from $350 to $395. When the company moved to Chicago, one of the partners, John Pfeffer, stayed behind to make a cyclecar of his own, the BABY MOOSE.

NG

CEDRE (F) 1975–1987

1975–1979 Sté Seve-Cedre, Sainte Croix Volvestre, Ariège.
1979–1987 Cedre sarl, Sainte Croix Volvestre, Ariège.

Engineer François Guerbet showed an electric microcar called the Mini 1 or Soubrette as early as 1974. The Midinette prototype appeared the following year, although production did not begin until 1979. The Midinette was powered by a 1.2kW motor, capable of a top speed of 31mph (50 km/h) and a range of 37 miles (60km). It was ultra-basic transport, being a single-seater sheltered autocycle with sliding Perspex doors and an angular polyester body. Suspension was by rubber blocks. The standard version was a 3-wheeler but there was a most unusual 5-wheeled model called the 5x5 Solaire. Cedre stuck with electric power while most French microcar firms adopted petrol and diesel engines and the market reacted by ignoring the Cedre.

CR

CEGGA (CH) 1960–1970

Automobiles Cegga, Aigle.

The brothers Claude and Georges Gachnang founded the make in 1960. Their first car was a modified AC-BRISTOL, which took part in the 1960 Le Mans 24-hour race, finishing in 22nd position despite having run out of road and losing two hours in restarting. The modifications were on the chassis, suspension, and engine and a new body was made. Then various sports, sports-racing, and Formula 1 cars making use of FERRARI, MASERATI, and COOPER engines and components were completed. The Cegga was successfully raced in hill climbs and smaller races. When Georges Gachnang suffered a bad accident in the 1970 Faucille hill climb, activities were terminated.

FH

CEIRANO (i) (I) 1901–1904

1901–1903 Fratelli Ceirano, Turin.
1903–1904 G.G. Fratelli Ceirano, Turin.

Giovanni Batista Ceirano was the eldest of three brothers, all of whom had extensive involvement with the Italian car industry. In 1880 he opened a bicycle shop in Turin where he made cycles under the name Welleyes, using this name for his first car built in 1899. Designed by Aristide Faccioli, it was a rear-engined single-cylinder 2-seater with belt drive. The design was acquired by the newly formed FIAT group who put a modified version into production as the first FIAT. Finding himself with a factory but no car Ceirano began to make another design on Renault lines, with front-mounted single-cylinder Aster or Dion engines and shaft drive. In 1903 Faccioli, who had joined FIAT, returned to Ceirano, for whom he designed a 4-cylinder car. In 1904 Giovanni Batista's younger brother who was called simply Giovanni (1865–1948), left to form his own company to make the JUNIOR (i), and from 1906 the S.C.A.T. The elder brother reorganised his company as S.T.A.R., to make the RAPID (ii).

NG

1901 Ceirano (i) 5hp tonneau.
NATIONAL MOTOR MUSEUM

1926 Ceirano (ii) Tipo150 tourer.
NATIONAL MOTOR MUSEUM

CEIRANO (ii) (I) 1919–1931

1919–1924 Giovanni Ceirano Fabbrica Automobili, Turin.
1924–1931 Stà Ceirano Automobili Torino, Turin.

Giovanni Ceirano and his son Ernesto sold their interest in S.C.A.T. in 1917, and two years later they launched their own make, the second to bear the name Ceirano. The first model was the 16/20, with 2.3-litre 4-cylinder engine, followed by the 2950cc Corsa. These were made until 1924 when the Ceiranos bought back an interest in S.C.A.T. They discontinued the larger S.C.A.T. models and launched a new small car which was built in the S.C.A.T. factory. The Ceirano Tipo 150 was an attractive car with 1460cc side-valve engine, 4-speed gearbox and brakes on all four wheels. The tourer body was very like a scaled-down Lancia Lambda, although unlike Lancia the Ceirano had a conventional chassis. The sporting model was called the 150S and had an ohv engine. Both models were sold in England by Newton & Bennett Ltd under the name Newton-Ceirano. In 1926 there was a short-lived 2.3-litre Tipo 230 which was not sold outside Italy. In the late 1920s Ceirano concentrated increasingly on commercial vehicles, although for 1930 they launched a new Tipo 150S with ifs, and the appearance of a Lancia Artena, which survived barely a year. Trucks and buses were made up to the late 1930s, latterly by S.P.A.

NG

1904 Celer 8hp 2-seater.
NICK GEORGANO/NATIONAL MOTOR MUSEUM

1903 Celeritas 2-cylinder roadster.
HANS-OTTO NEUBAUER

CEL (H) 1987 to date

Cél Lézing Kft, Budapest.

In 1987 Mátyás Borlóy, director of HiCox, a repair shop in Budapest created a city car. It was based on the Trabant and Mathias. There was hope that it would be the next generation Trabant, but it never happened. When Borlóy sought help to prepare the car for technical examination he met László Rekettye at Ikarus. Rekettye raced and tuned rally cars in the 1960s and 1970s. Later he built buggies, so he was quite familiar with special cars. He also participated in the TECOPLAN Leo project.

Borlóy, Rekettye, and a mutual friend got together and decided that their next project should be something in the lines of the Lotus 7. To secure the financial background they asked the help of Tamás Vadas, director of Cél Lézing, distributor of, among other things, OLTCIT cars.

Vadas suggested a 4-seater 'Lotus', but it turned out to be a ridiculous idea. His next suggestion was to create Jeep-alikes as it was obvious that an off-roader craze was on the way. But Jeeps weren't available in Hungary, so work on an UAZ-based Jeep started in 1990. A year later the finished article was exhibited at the Budapest International Autoshow. Four more were built before Vadas lost interest and stopped the work. The cars have been gathering dust ever since.

PN

CELER (GB) 1904

The Celer Motor Car Co., Nottingham.

The only evidence for this company is a surviving car, which carries the maker's nameplate on the engine. The engine was an 8hp vertical twin with automatic inlet valves, and transmission was by a 3-speed gearbox and shaft drive.

NG

CELERITAS (A) 1901–1903

Automobilfabrik Celeritas, Vienna.

This company was founded by Willy Stift, who had financed August BRAUN's company and would later join the Graf brothers in the manufacture of the GRAF & STIFT. The Celeritas was a voiturette with 12hp 2-cylinder Buchet engine and 5-speed gearbox.

NG

CELTIC (i) **(GB)** 1904–1908

1904–1907 Bradford Motor Car Co., Bradford, Yorkshire.

1907–1908 Thornton Engineering Co., Bradford, Yorkshire.

These cars were of conventional design with 4-cylinder engines and shaft drive. They were hand made, only eight cars leaving the factory in five years. Four used Aster engines, three White & Poppe and one Mutel; all were sold locally. The Thornton Engineering Co. later sold the Teco car, which was an imported BAILLEUL.

NG

CELTIC (ii) **(F)** 1908–1913

Marcel Caplet, Le Havre.

Caplet had made 3-cylinder engines which he sold under the name Triplex at least as early as 1906. However, his cars had 4-cylinder engines. In 1912–13 he was offering three models of 12hp car.

NG

CELTIC (iii) **(F)** 1927–1929

Compagnie Générale de Voitures à Paris, Paris.

This Celtic was a small car with 4-cylinder engine, originally of 700cc, later enlarged to 1085cc. It was made by a large taxicab operator who also made a bigger car, the CLASSIC (ii), which was mostly, if not exclusively, seen as a taxi. The Celtic was probably their attempt to cater for the passenger car market, but made little impact.

NG

CEMSA (I) 1946–1950

Caproni Electromeccanica Saronno, Cameri.

This advanced car was made by a branch of the large Caproni group, one of Italy's major aircraft builders, which had also controlled ISOTTA-FRASCHINI since 1933. The Cemsa was intended to be a small family saloon to complement the large rear-engined Isotta-Fraschini Tipo 8C. Designed by Franco Fessia, who had been responsible for the Fiat Topolino, it shared some of the Fiat's features, such as an engine ahead of the front axle. However, in the Cemsa, the engine was a flat-four of 1093cc and drove the front wheels. It had a pressed-steel platform-type chassis and coil independent suspension all round. Two bodies were offered, a 4-door saloon and a 2-door convertible.

The Cemsa's career was dogged by political considerations, as the Caproni group had been a strong supporter of Mussolini, and were therefore out of favour with the largely left-wing postwar Italian government. However, it is by no means certain that it could have succeeded in a market dominated by Fiat. It appeared at several motor shows in Italy, France, and Switzerland between 1947 and 1949, but production never started. The design was taken up by MINERVA in 1953, but the Belgian firm was in no position to mass produce cars, and nothing materialised. However, the design did not die, for in 1960 it was adopted by LANCIA, who made it with only slight changes as the Flavia. It is a tribute to the advanced thinking behind it that a 14-year old design was quite acceptable in 1960, and indeed remained in production at Lancia until 1975.

NG

CENIA (F) 1900

Central Automobile, Neuilly, Seine.

This was a 2-seater voiturette powered by a single-cylinder 3½ hp Aster engine, with 2-speed gearbox and shaft drive.

NG

CENTAUR (i) **(GB)** 1900–1901

Centaur Cycle Co. Ltd, Coventry.

Powered by a front-mounted 4.5hp single-cylinder engine, the Centaur had a 4-seater *dos-à-dos* dog-cart style of body. Transmission was by a Benz-like system of fast and loose pulleys.

NG

CENTAUR (ii) (US) 1902–1903

Centaur Motor Vehicle Co., Buffalo, New York.

This company offered both petrol and electric cars, the former being 5 or 6hp runabouts and tourers at $700–800, the latter a runabout at $850. It seemed keener to promote its electric cars, saying 'The shrewdest dealers are pushing electrics', but sold few of either kind. After discontinuing its own cars, it became agents for Cadillac and Yale.

NG

CENTAUR (iii) GB 1974–1978

Concept Developments, Market Harborough, Leicestershire.

This was a development of the rear-engined Adams Probe with glass fibre/plywood monocoque sandwich construction and Hillman Imp mechanicals. Under different management it became the Pulsar in 1978.

NG

CENTAUR (iv) (US) c.1985

Centaur Car Company, Garden Grove, California.

This kit car company built a replica of the Lotus Super 7 called the Centaur 7. It had a monocoque steel chassis and was adaptable to a wide range of engines, although the Mazda rotary was recommended.

HP

CENTAUR MOTOR CORP (US) c.1980–1985

Centaur Motor Corp., Milwaukee, Wisconsin.

The company that made this large neoclassic car was not related to the other Centaur that made a Lotus 7-type vehicle in California. The Milwaukee-built Centaur neoclassic resembled a Mercedes 500K with a beak-like grill. The fibreglass body clothed a General Motors drivetrain and suspension. Luxury features included air conditioning, cruise control, solid wood dash, leather interior, a rumble seat and a full stereo system. Price for a turnkey car was $44,900 in 1985.

HP

CENTAURUS (BR) 1962

Automoveis e Motores Centaurus SA, Campinas.

The Centaurus as depicted in this company's publicity leaflets, was an ugly but sporty open 5-seater, with an aluminium body built on a wooden structure. Interestingly, it was a fitted with two 2-stroke horizontally opposed 2-cylinder engines of 800cc each. It was claimed that the car could be propelled by both engines running at the same time or with only one doing the work. It was claimed that with both engines running the Centaurus could reach 88mph (140 km/h). With only one of the 30bhp engines at work, top speed was 63mph (100 km/h). Apparently, only one prototype was made.

ACT

CENTRAL (i) (US) 1903

Central Automobile Co., Cleveland, Ohio.

This company exhibited a car with horizontally-opposed twin engine, epicyclic gearbox and single-chain drive at the 1903 Chicago Auto Show, but that was its sole appearance. One feature, shared with several cars, was a tilting steering wheel to accommodate portly drivers.

NG

CENTRAL (ii) (US) 1906

Central Automobile Co., Providence, Rhode Island.

This company planned to build cars with rotary steam engines, and had imported several such units from Europe for use in prototypes. They planned to make 10hp runabouts at $800 and 20hp tourers at $1200–1500, building 100 the first year, but the company did not last out the year 1906.

NG

CENTURI see TEILHOL

c.1978 Centaur (iii) coupé.
NICK GEORGANO

1902 Century (i) 5hp Tandem.
NATIONAL MOTOR MUSEUM

CENTURY (i) (GB) 1899–1907

1899–1901 Century Engineering & Motor Co. Ltd, Altrincham, Cheshire.
1901–1904 Century Engineering & Motor Co. Ltd, Willesden, London.
1904–1907 Century Engineering Co. Ltd, Willesden, London.

The first Century vehicles were made by Ralph Jackson, who had started in business in 1885 as a cycle maker. In 1899 he brought out the Century Tandem, a tricar powered by a 2.25hp single-cylinder engine. It had wheel steering at a time when most tricars still had handlebars. He made tricars for a number of years, from 1901 under the name EAGLE (i), although similar designs made in London were still called Century. In May 1901 Century moved to London, coming under the control of Sydney Begbie, who was the first importer of Aster engines into England. Jackson moved back to Altrincham where he started making Eagles. In 1903 Begbie launched the first Century cars, with 8 or 12hp 2-cylinder Aster engines, French transmissions and English-built chassis and bodies. There was also a larger model with 22hp 4-cylinder Mutel engine. The tandems used De Dion-Bouton (3.5hp), Aster and M.M.C. (both 5hp) engines. For 1905 they were improved as the New Century Tandem with 2-cylinder engines and double radiators, one on each side of the rear wheel. They also offered a 16hp 4-cylinder car called the Princess.

NG

CENTURY (ii) (US) 1900–1903

Century Motor Vehicle Co., Syracuse, New York.

This company began the new century well by announcing steam and electric cars, followed by one with a petrol engine in 1902. The company claimed to have made more than 60 steamers and electrics by November 1901. Some of the steamers were exported to England where they were sold under the name Ophir. They had 2-cylinder engines and were unusual in having a steeply sloping shaft drive from engine to rear axle; most steamers of the period used chain drive. The petrol-engined car had a 7hp single-cylinder engine and a 4-seater *dos-à-dos* body. It was known as the Century Tourist, although this name was also used by H. Ward Leonard for cars he was building in 1901. The company announced in December 1902 that it was discontinuing steam cars, and all production ended during 1903.

NG

1969 C.G. roadster.
NATIONAL MOTOR MUSEUM

CENTURY (iii) **(US)** 1912–1915
1912–1914 Century Electric Motor Car Co., Detroit, Michigan.
1914–1915 Century Manufacturing Co., Detroit, Michigan.
This was an electric car distinguished from its contemporaries by having an underslung frame. A roadster was offered in 1912, but otherwise bodies were the usual broughams. Steering was by tiller and there was a choice of solid or pneumatic tyres. The speed controller gave six speeds, and the series-wound Westinghouse motor was geared directly to the rear axle.
NG

CENTURY (iv) **(GB)** 1928–1929
Century Cars Ltd, London.
This was a short-lived light car, which probably never progressed beyond the prototype stage. It was powered by a 7hp 4-cylinder engine, originally quoted with dimensions identical to those of the Austin Seven, 56 x 76mm, 747cc. However, it cannot have been an Austin as it was a 2-stroke. Later announcements gave dimensions of 49.2 × 85mm (646cc), so perhaps the larger figures were a mistake. A 5-bearing crankshaft was unusual on so small an engine. A photograph shows it with an open 2-seater body which the *Light Car & Cyclecar* described as purely experimental 'on production cars both chummy and fabric saloon bodies will be fitted'. They also said that those responsible for the design were negotiating to produce the car in the near future on a quantity basis. Drawings were published of a chummy 2-seater, to sell at £100, and a 2-door saloon, but these may well never have been made.
NG

CENTURY TOURIST *see* WARD LEONARD

CERES (US) 1983
This was a promising 3-wheeled coupé powered by a rear-mounted Daihatsu 3-cylinder engine. Ten prototypes were constructed before the designer balked at the investment required to productionise it.
CR

CERTUS (i) **(GB)** 1907–1908
Certus Gearless Co. Ltd, London.
This car seems to have been built to demonstrate the principle of friction drive rather than as a serious commercial proposition; 2- and 4-cylinder cars were made, the latter with a 3-litre Aster engine.
NG

CERTUS (ii) **(D)** 1928–1929
Diercks & Wroblewski GmbH, Offenburg.
This coachbuilding firm had a short-lived venture into making complete cars. They offered models using S.C.A.P. engines in four sizes; 7/32, 8/45, 6/60 and 8/80PS, in chassis and bodies of their own construction. The economic crisis prevented serious production.
HON

CÉSAR (F) 1906
David, Boudène & Compagnie, Paris.
Two models of César were offered, a 7hp single-cylinder and a 10hp 4-cylinder. David, Boudène & Compagnie were the agents, as the cars were made for them by Doriot & Flandrin, who made cars under their own name as well, later becoming the better-known D.F.P.
NG

CEYC (E) 1922–1928
Central Electrotécnico y de Comunicaciones, Madrid and Bilbao.
This car was unusual in that it was designed and built by the Spanish War Ministry, a light car prepared for military communications, and using a valveless 4-cylinder 792cc 2-stroke engine with only two combustion chambers. It was presented to the Military in 1923, and one year later to the general public at the Barcelona Motor Show. CEYC commissioned the company Euskalduna in Bilbao to build up this model for the general public, keeping the name of CEYC for the military version. At the 1926 show both makes were presented on individual stands, but they were the same cars. Later models were capable of nearly 70mph (113 km/h). Euskalduna also developed its own cars, with a larger engine, designed by the same person responsible of the CEYC; only a few were built.
VCM

C.F. (US) 1907–1909
Cornish-Friedberg Motor Car Co., Chicago, Illinois.
This was a very conventional car, powered by a 35hp 4-cylinder engine, made in tourer and roadster forms. The company was under-capitalised, and lasted less than two years. In 1909, one of the partners, Louis Friedberg, announced a new car called the Chicago Forty. The specification was identical to that of the C.F., and he was probably trying to sell off existing cars.
NG

C.F.B. (GB) 1920–1921
C.F.B. Car Syndicate Ltd, Upper Norwood, London.
The grand-sounding C.F.B. Car Syndicate may have made no more than one car; certainly there was no serious production. It was a cyclecar powered by a 1078cc 9hp air-cooled V-twin Precision engine, driving through a friction transmission in which the driven disc slid up and down a cone, rather than across the face of another disc, as was more usual. From the disc, transmission was by bevel gears to a countershaft, and then by belts to the rear wheels. The frame was made of reinforced ash. The initials were those of Charles F. Beauvais who made another cyclecar, the BOW-V-CAR in the same district, and later became well-known as the stylist for Avon bodies which transformed the appearance of Crossley and Standard cars in the 1930s.
NG

C.F.L. (GB) 1913
F. Clayton & Co., Blackheath, London.
The C.F.L. was a simple cyclecar powered by an air-cooled flat twin engine, with final drive by belts. It was priced at £105, but production was minimal.
NG

C.G. (F) 1966–1974
Carrosserie Chappe Frères et Gessalin, Brie-Comte-Robert, Seine-et-Marne.
Having been coachbuilders since the 1950s, the C.G. marque was born at the 1966 Paris Salon, where it displayed the Spider 1000. This was a pretty glassfibre-bodied convertible sports car using Simca 1000 parts, including the 40bhp 944cc engine in the tail. Feeble performance led to more powerful versions, including the 1.1-litre, 49bhp 1000S and 85bhp 1200S from 1968. From 1972 the Simca Rallye engine was offered in the C.G. 1300, with power outputs of between 82bhp and 95bhp, or more with a supercharger. C.G.s were also offered in removable hardtop and fixed coupé styles. Because of its strong competition links with Simca, C.G. cars were sold in France through the Chrysler dealer network, enabling reasonably strong sales (101 units in 1972, for example).
CR

CGC (AUS) 1988 to date

Classic Glass Cars, Virginia, South Australia.

Builders of this Cobra replica, Dominic and Enzi Cocci, availed themselves of the expertise of Australian Technology in Adelaide during its development. Built on a 4-rail chassis of 90 or 94in (2286 or 2388mm) wheelbase, using Jaguar suspension and brakes front and rear, the 5-litre Ford V8 engine was the prime choice but Chevrolet, Holden or Leyland Australia V8s of between 4.4 and 7 litres, were compatible.

MG

C.G.E. (F) 1941–1946

Compagnie Général Électrique, Paris.

This was the most attractive-looking of the wartime electric cars made in France. It was designed and built by Jean Grégoire, who had designed the AMILCAR Compound, and used a number of elements from that car, including the cast aluminium frame. It had a normal range of 55 miles, but in September 1942 Grégoire covered 158 miles between Paris and Tours on a single charge. Production of the C.G.E. was permitted by the German occupying authorities on condition that the majority were exported to Germany. Although two cars per week were made for nearly two years, so far as is known, none left France. One was offered to the director of a biscuit factory in return for his weight in biscuits, and everyone was happy with the transaction. Like the other French electrics, the C.G.E. barely survived the end of the war. A coupé was shown at the 1946 Paris Show, but no production followed.

NG

C.G.V. (F) 1901–1906

Charron, Girardot et Voigt, Puteaux, Seine.

This company was formed by three successful racing drivers who had all driven for Panhard, Fernand Charron (1866–1928), Léonce Girardot (1864–1922) and Émile Voigt. Charron and Girardot had been in partnership since 1897 in l'Agence Générale de l'Automobile, a successful Panhard dealership which prospered by charging a premium of 15–30 per cent for early delivery. Voigt joined them shortly afterwards, and in 1901 they launched their first car. It was on Panhard lines, as one might have expected, although as one of the shortcomings of the Panhard was a high centre of gravity, the C.G.V. was distinctly lower. The radiator was mounted lower than on the Panhard, ahead of a coal-scuttle type bonnet and just above the dumb irons. It had a 3306cc 15/20hp 4-cylinder engine with automatic inlet valves, 4-speed gearbox and chain drive. A transverse leaf spring at the rear was another improvement over the Panhard. Although the 15/20 was exhibited in 1901, no deliveries were made until the following year. The engine was little changed during 1902, although they soon dropped automatic inlet valves on their larger engines, retaining them only on their smallest model, an 8hp twin. By 1905 all models had mechanically-operated inlet valves. The range was expanded in 1902 to include a 40hp of 8616cc. They now had a competitor for the largest Panhard. C.G.V. showed the world's first straight-8 at the 1902 Paris Salon. It had what were described as 'eight 5hp cylinders arranged in sets of four', in other words, presumably two of the 20hp engines in tandem. The engine was considered to be so flexible that no gearbox was provided. It attracted great crowds at the Salon, but did not go into production, although it was catalogued as the Type G.

Two years after its introduction, C.G.V. could boast a very aristocratic clientele, including the King of Portugal, eight French princes and, in England, the Duchess of Devonshire and Earl of Carnarvon. The make was represented in England from the end of 1902, and during 1902–03 it was imported into America by Smith & Mabley, who sold it as the American C.G.V. They even assembled it for a short while, this work taking place at the Rome Locomotive Works, Rome, New York, with bodies provided by J.M. Quimby & Sons of Newark, New Jersey. Only seven cars were made at Rome, priced at the high figure of $5500 each. By 1905 the range had been extended to cover big T-head 4-cylinder cars of 4.9-, 6.2- and 9.8-litres, still with armoured wood frames. In 1906 an even larger car, the 12.9-litre 75/90hp which required a geared down starting handle, was introduced. The engine was the same size as those in the 1905 Gordon Bennett racing cars. One was supplied to an American customer as a *berline de voyage* with built-in lavatory.

Production rose steadily, from 76 cars in 1902 to 196 in 1903 and 265 in 1905. In November 1906 the London financier Davison Dalziel formed a British

1902 C.G.V. 8-cylinder roadster.
NATIONAL MOTOR MUSEUM

1906 C.G.V. 30hp tourer.
NATIONAL MOTOR MUSEUM

company, Automobiles Charron Ltd. Although the company was legally British, much of the stock was French-owned. However, the partnership was breaking up; Girardot left to sponsor the G.E.M. petrol-electric car, while Voigt joined the still independent American C.G.V. operation in New York. Only Charron remained, as works manager at Puteaux, and the cars were renamed CHARRON for 1907. He only stayed a further year, leaving in 1908 to join CLÉMENT-BAYARD, having recently married Adolphe Clément's daughter.

NG

CHABOCHE (F) 1901–1906

E. Chaboche, Paris.

Although it was only marketed for six seasons, the Chaboche was France's second most important make of steam car, after Serpollet. In 1901 they offered a 4-seater *vis-à-vis* with rear-mounted boiler and 6hp horizontal engine mounted in the centre of the chassis, and a 6-seater brake with 12hp centrally mounted engine and boiler at the front of the frame in the manner of a steam lorry. This was later developed into a range of commercial vehicles, while 1903 passenger cars had 12 or 20hp engines, still centrally mounted, and flash boilers at the rear. Final drive was by chain. Body styles included coupé de ville and limousine. The 1905 models were more conventional in appearance, with a 30hp vertical engine front-mounted under a bonnet. Chaboche dropped passenger cars in 1906 to concentrate on commercial vehicles, which were continued up to about 1910.

NG

C.H.A.D. (GB) 1996 to date

1996–1998 Claydon Hamilton Automotive Design, Maldon, Essex.

1998 to date C.H. Automotive, Bristol, Avon.

The Supersport 4 was predominantly the work of Tony Claydon, an ex-racing driver and designer of the Tara 2 prototype that almost went into production as

259

1907 Chadwick Great Six tourer.
NATIONAL MOTOR MUSEUM

an Aston Martin. This was a 4-seater coupé vaguely reminiscent of a Nissan 300ZX, using a steel chassis and fibreglass body, and sold mostly in kit form. The major components derived from the Ford Sierra (a 4 × 4 Cosworth option was even available) and Ford 4-cylinder or various V8 engines could be installed. A split between the founders of the company led to a redesigned version called the SS4, later known as the Cerity R.

CR

CHADWICK (US) 1904–1916

1904–1907 Fairmount Engineering Co., Philadelphia, Pennsylvania.
1907–1916 Chadwick Engineering Works, Pottstown, Pennsylvania.
Lee Sherman Chadwick (1875–1958) invented an advanced laundry machine in 1899, and later worked for the Boston Ball Bearing Co., putting the failing firm into profit. He built two experimental cars there, then moved to the SEARCHMONT company in Philadelphia, for which he designed a 2-cylinder car. He was working on a four in 1903 when Searchmont went under; he bought a wagon load of parts and assembled them into a car which was the first Chadwick. After one or two had been made in a small workshop at Chester, Pennsylvania, he moved into an old stable in Philadelphia, which he named the Fairmount Engineering Co. The first production Chadwicks emerged from this factory in 1904; they had 32hp 4-cylinder engines and chain drive, costing $4000 with a 7-seater tourer body. They were continued into 1905, when 25 were made, and into 1906 when they were joined by a larger 40/45hp car selling for $5000. Chadwick production was always very small; 30 cars were made in 1906, and their best year ever was 1908 when 38 cars were delivered.

In 1906 Chadwick developed his masterpiece, which was put on the market for 1907. The Chadwick Great Six had an 11,583cc 6-cylinder engine with ohv and copper water jackets that developed 75bhp at only 1100rpm. With a light runabout body, top speed was over 80mph (130km/h). The driving chains were enclosed in aluminium cases. The Great Sixes were mostly made in a new factory that Chadwick had bought at Pottstown and which opened in March 1907. He chose this location because of its proximity to the Light Foundry Co., on which he relied for many components. Chadwick cars did well in competitions, and in order to increase the amount of mixture which could be admitted to the cylinders due to limited valve area, works driver Willy Haupt tried a compressor which forced in the mixture at a greater pressure than that of the atmosphere. This was the world's first supercharger, although the word was not used at the time. It gave the Chadwicks a great advantage in sprints and hill climbs, although it was not so successful in racing. Contrary to some reports, it was offered on production Chadwicks, as a $375 extra, but how many private customers took up the offer is not known. Prices were high anyway – $5500 for a tourer and $6500 for the short wheelbase semi-racer.

Chadwick's success did not last for long. In 1910 the Light Foundry Co. ended its agreement because of Chadwick's slow payment, and he was faced with the expensive prospect of setting up his own foundry. He wanted to spend more

money on improving the car, which was now called the Perfected Great Chadwick Six, but his backers disagreed, and in 1911 he left to pursue other interests. He worked for the Perfection Stove Co., but his labour of love was the Chadwick Road Guide. Production continued at Pottstown, styles including a limousine and landaulette as well as the open models, but output declined year by year from 1911. Although the same engine was used, the name Great Chadwick Six was dropped after 1913, the cars just being called Model 19. In the final year of 1916, only seven cars were delivered.

NG

Further Reading
'Chadwick – Remember the Name', Beverly Rae Kimes,
Automobile Quarterly, Vol. 9, No.2.

CHAIGNEAU (F) 1926

Automobiles Chaigneau, Paris.
Under the imposing name Chaigneau Speciale Grand Sport, this company advertised two models of light car, a 6CV of 1093cc and a slightly larger 7CV with lowered chassis. They had 3-speed gearboxes, and the 6CV was available with torpedo, sports or saloon bodies, the 7CV only in sporting form. Maximum speeds ranged from 56mph (90km/h) for the 6CV saloon to 72mph (115km/h) for the 7CV sports. In 1927 M. Chaigneau joined forces with BRASIER to make the Chaigneau-Brasier, a car in the same class as the Speciale Grand Sport, though with different sizes of engine.

NG

CHAIGNEAU-BRASIER see BRASIER

CHAIKA see GAZ

CHAINLESS (F) 1900–1903

S.A. des Voitures Légères 'Chainless', Paris.
In an early example of 'Franglais', the makers of this car chose a name to indicate that it used shaft drive. The first models used 8 or 12hp 2-cylinder Buchet engines, and looked very like the contemporary De Dion-Bouton. In 1903 a 24hp 4-cylinder model was added to the range. The company did not seem to have total faith in shaft drive, for in 1900-01 they also offered chain-driven cars under the name Knowles-Chain.

NG

CHALFANT (US) 1905–1912

Chalfant Gasoline Motor Car Co., Lenover, Pennsylvania.
The first Chalfants had 22hp 2-cylinder engines, epicyclic gearboxes and double-chain drive. The standard body was a 5-seater tourer, although they said that a runabout was also available. In about 1908 a 4-cylinder model was offered, and production continued fitfully until 1912. No more than 50 Chalfants were made in seven years.

NG

CHALLENGE see MARCUS

CHALLENGER (GB) 1985 to date

1985–1987 Triple C Car Care Clinic, St Austell, Cornwall.
1987–1993 Triple C Challenger, Corby, Northamptonshire.
1993 Reiver Motor Car Co., Newtown St Boswells, Roxburghshire.
1993 to date Avon Coachworks, Bath, Avon.
There was evidently a market for a credible Jaguar E-Type Roadster replica in the 1980s. The Challenger was the first such attempt but initially it used Cortina parts, so authenticity suffered. It grew closer to the original specification after a Jaguar-based chassis was launched in 1986, with optional Rover V8 or Ford V6 power. A lightweight E-Type replica was launched in 1991, a year before the project moved to Scotland. A further model, also launched in 1991, was the Malibu (alternatively known as the Tiger or Marathon), a Ford-based estate car kit resembling a Mitsubishi Shogun and offered in 2- and 4-wheel drive forms, while Challenger also briefly made the NG TF. The Scottish firm that took over the Challenger also made the Ecosse (a wide-arch E-Type) and an A.C. 428 replica, but it is unlikely that any such kits were sold.

CR

CHALMERS; CHALMERS-DETROIT (US) 1908–1924

Chalmers Motor Car Co., Detroit, Michigan.

The Chalmers-Detroit was the successor to the Thomas-Detroit which had been in production since 1906, and would become one of the more popular American cars between 1912 and 1919. Headed by Hugh Chalmers who had been vice-president of the National Cash Register Co., the Chalmers-Detroit was a medium-priced 4-cylinder car, available as a roadster and a touring car at $1500 and a limousine at $2500. In 1911 the Chalmers-Detroit became the Chalmers and offered two series of 4-cylinder cars in both open and closed models priced from $1500 to $3000, self-starters being included as standard equipment. A 6-cylinder series was introduced in 1913 and the 4-cylinder cars were continued, although they were dropped from the 1915 models and the sixes would be used exclusively until the end of production. Chalmers production peaked in 1916 with more than 21,000 cars completed and, in 1917, an L-head engine replaced the earlier ohv type.

Approximately 20,000 Chalmers cars left the factory during the war years of 1917 and 1918. Production of 10,000 cars in 1919 was followed in 1920 with a slight drop in sales of 9,800 units. By this time, presumably subscribing to the safety in numbers theory, Hugh Chalmers, always the salesman, agreed to lease his plants to Maxwell, being the Chalmers' major competitor in the marketplace. Hugh Chalmers' reasoning was that leasing the Chalmers plants would allow Chalmers to get the benefit of Maxwell's tooling and manufacturing equipment and at the same time use his promotion expertise to promote the sales of both makes. Despite his intentions, the plan was not overly successful since, at this time, many makes of cars were in severe financial difficulties due to over-expansion during the war effort. The situation affected most other automobile companies, though some suffered less.

In an attempt to boost production and resulting sales, Walter P. Chrysler was called in to try and reorganise Maxwell. Chrysler was planning to organise his own corporation and in 1922 Chalmers was taken over by Maxwell which had become a Chrysler subsidiary. The last Chalmers cars featured Lockheed hydraulic brakes with 1923 production less than 1000. These were Chalmers' last cars and the unsold units were marketed early in the following year as 1924 models. The Chalmers was supplanted in the Chrysler Corporation by the newly launched Chrysler Six which, through 1925, used the Maxwell as its 4-cylinder companion car. In 1926 the Maxwell became the Chrysler Four.

KM

CHAMBERS (GB) 1904–1927

1904–1907 Chambers & Co., Belfast.
1907–1927 Chambers Motors Ltd, Belfast.

The Chambers is arguably the most important car to have been made in Northern Ireland. It may not have had the flamboyance and controversy of the De Lorean but it lasted much longer and contributed more to the economy of Ulster. The engineering business of Chambers & Co. opened in 1897, and made a speciality of a machine for wiring the corks into lemonade bottles. The entry into the motor business came through Jack Chambers who worked for the Vauxhall Iron Works and designed for them the first 5hp VAUXHALL car, launched in 1903. On returning to Belfast, he designed a small car which had much in common with the Vauxhall, horizontal engine, although a twin rather than a single, epicyclic gearbox and coil suspension. Rated at 7hp, it was marketed as the Downshire until February 1905, when the name was changed to Chambers. Twins were made up to 1910, in 8, 10 and 10/12hp models, and a horizontal four was tried in 1908. It proved unreliable and was replaced by a 12/14hp vertical four bought in from Coventry Climax. This was not used for long as Chambers preferred to make their own engines.

These were monobloc fours of 2052cc (11/15hp) and 2370ccc (12/16hp), which powered all Chambers vehicles, cars, lorries, and ambulances, up to 1924. They retained the rear axle-mounted epicyclic gearbox up to 1920. Nearly all bodywork was made in-house, using seasoned Irish oak. Several combination cars were made, with interchangeable goods and passenger bodies.

Chambers flourished during the war, making ambulances and 18lb shell cases, but problems soon arose after the armistice. The adoption of electric lighting and starting proved costly, as with limited production they could not place large orders, and the moulders' strike of 1921 interrupted the supply of castings from Coventry. They could not afford to develop a new engine with detachable cylinder heads, yet the market demanded them, so in 1924, after considering the 6-cylinder 2-stroke Wege engine from Australia, they turned to Meadows

1909 Chalmers 30hp roadster.
NATIONAL MOTOR MUSEUM

1916 Chalmers Model 6-40 Californian Top tourer.
NATIONAL MOTOR MUSEUM

1924 Chambers 18hp saloon.
NATIONAL MOTOR MUSEUM

who supplied two engines, the 4-cylinder 2121cc EH and the 6-cylinder 2692cc EN. They also supplied gearboxes. Only two fours and nine sixes were made before Chambers abandoned car production in 1927. For some years most of their work had been rebodying their own cars as commercial vehicles with lengthened wheelbases, and also rebodying Karrier chassis, for which they were agents. Part of the works was let to the Belfast Omnibus Co. About 500 Chambers cars were made, of which the last, an 18/48hp six saloon, survives today in the Ulster Folk Museum.

NG

Further Reading
'Chambers – The All-Irish Car', M. Worthington-Williams, *The Automobile,* March 1983.

1952 Champion (iv) 400 coupé.
NATIONAL MOTOR MUSEUM

1902 Champrobert 8½hp petrol-electric tonneau.
NATIONAL MOTOR MUSEUM

CHAMBON (F) 1912–1914

Auguste Chambon, Lyons.

Auguste Chambon trained as a civil engineer, and early in the twentieth century he was running a factory in Lyons making gearboxes, differentials and his own patented specialist machinery. He became a car maker in 1912, offering a medium-sized touring car powered by a 2154cc long-stroke engine (70×140mm). This was almost certainly of LUC COURT manufacture, this company also being located in Lyons, and making an engine of the same dimensions. The 4-speed gearbox was mounted on the rear axle. Chambon made about 20 of these tourers, as well as a one-off for a local doctor. This had two 4-cylinder engines mounted side by side; even with a 6-seater tourer body, it could reach 68mph (110km/h). Chambon car production ended with the outbreak of World War I; after the war he made some agricultural tractors, and in 1925 merged with the makers of the Rhony'x motorcycle.

NG

CHAMELEON see ENTERPRISE

CHAMEROY (F) 1907–1911

Automobiles Chameroy, Le Vesinet, Seine-et-Oise.

This company was better-known for its non-skid tyres than for its cars. These were light cars and voiturettes with single, 2- or 4-cylinder engines and variable belt drive without recourse to gearbox or differential.

NG

CHAMPION (i) see FAMOUS

CHAMPION (ii) (US) 1916

Champion Auto Equipment Co., Wabash, Indiana.

The Champion was a conventional looking car made in 2-seater and tourer form and powered by a 3080cc 4-cylinder side-valve engine rated at 36hp. Its only unusual feature was an automatic tyre inflator which could be operated while the car was in motion. Introduced at the 1916 Chicago Automobile Show, the Champion did not make it into 1917, although apparently 167 cars were built in 1916.

NG

CHAMPION (iii) (US) 1917–1924

1917–1923 Direct Drive Motor Co., Pottstown, Pennsylvania.
1923–1924 Champion Motors Corp., Philadelphia, Pennsylvania.

Originally sold under the name Direct Drive, early models drove through gearing on the rear wheel rims. Later cars had conventional drive. Two nearly identical versions were available, the Tourist with a Lycoming 4-cylinder engine, and the Special with a 4-cylinder Herschell-Spillman. The only external differences were in the radiator shape, the Tourist carrying a Packard shape while the Special had one resembling the Rolls-Royce. Production, such as it was, consisted of a touring car or phaeton, priced at $1050 to $1195. It is doubtful that total production in the company's eight years exceeded 50 cars and the production probably ended during the early part of 1923. However, the company was technically extant when Willys-Overland announced a 'mystery model' in the autumn of 1923, which turned out to be a close-coupled 4-door club sedan in its popular Series '91' line-up and which was christened the Champion. The model went into production and sold reasonably well. In May 1924, however, Willys-Overland received an angry letter from Champion Motors which took umbrage at Overland's use of the name 'Champion'. The letter went on to say that Champion Motors' production had been closed down for most of the preceding year but that it had been planning to market as many as 3000 cars during the 1924 calendar year which, it claimed, had been stifled by the Overland's use of the Champion name. This was most unlikely and it is assumed that the Champion name, being absent from automotive rosters by mid–1923, implied that the car had gone out of business. Willys-Overland immediately ordered its dealers and distributors to expunge the Champion name from any sales literature. Nothing further was heard of the matter in the automotive press, or elsewhere, and it may be assumed that the matter was settled out of court. Champion Motors went out of business shortly afterwards.

KM

CHAMPION (iv) (D) 1948–1954

1948–1950 Hermann Holbein, Herrlingen.
1951–1952 Champion Automobil GmbH, Paderborn.
1952–1954 Rheinische Automobilfabrik Hennhofer & Co., Ludwigshafen.
1954 Rheinische Automobilwerke Thorndal & Co., Ludwigshafen.

Hermann Holbein was a former BMW engineer and racing driver who built his first prototype in 1946. It was a tiny 2-seater roadster, about 72in (1827mm) long and powered by a rear-mounted 200cc Triumph motorcycle engine. It had a central tubular frame and, unlike all later Champions, separate cycle-type wings. The first production car, made from 1948 to 1950, had a 250cc 6PS Triumph single-cylinder or a 10PS 2-cylinder engine, also mounted at the rear of a tubular frame but with all-enveloping 2-seater roadster body. About 400 of these were made, and were followed by the 400, with 400cc Ilo or 450cc Heinkel engines and coupé bodies by Drauz. These were made at Paderborn from March 1951 to the end of 1952, production totalling 2052 cars.

Manufacture then moved to Ludwigshafen where two different companies were involved in making the 400 coupé and, from 1954 to 1956, the 500G estate car. Hennhofer & Co made 1941 coupés, and Thorndal 284 coupés and 20 estate cars. In 1955 production was taken over by the motorcycle makers MaiCo, who made the estate, and also saloon and convertible models, under the name MAICO-CHAMPION.

NG/HON

CHAMPROBERT (F) 1902–1905

De Champrobert & Compagnie, Sté de Constructions Électro-Mécaniques, Levallois-Perret, Seine.

This car was unusual in its combination of a small engine, an 8hp single-cylinder De Dion-Bouton, with petrol-electric drive which gave five forward speeds and one reverse. The front-mounted engine was connected directly to a dynamo which provided current to a controller and then to an electric motor next to the rear axle, which it drove directly by spur wheel gearing. From 1903 to 1905 the car was known as the Electrogénia. Larger engines were used on these, a 12hp De Dion-Bouton or 16hp Aster.

NG

1929 Chandler Eight saloon.
NATIONAL MOTOR MUSEUM

CHANDLER (US) 1913–1929

1913–1926 Chandler Motor Car Co., Cleveland, Ohio.
1927–1929 Chandler-Cleveland Corp., Cleveland, Ohio.

For most of its 17 years in business, the Chandler was one of the most popular middle-priced cars in the United States. The company was formed in 1913 by a group of men, former officials of the Lozier Motor Co., and its radiator shape confirmed that association. Its first cars, constituting its 1914 line, with production of nearly 3000 units, a harbinger for sales to follow. Production increased annually and would reach more than 20,000 cars in its banner year of 1926. The car owed its popularity to numerous improvements over the years, coupled with an ambitious and successful advertising and promotion campaign. Chandler regularly advertised in such prestigious magazines as the *National Geographic*, emphasising both its standard models plus those with sporting treatment such as its successful Dispatch touring car of the early 1920s. This differed from the standard offering with its wire wheels, individual step plates in lieu of a conventional running-board, a trunk with nickeled strips at the rear of the bodies to prevent scratching, and bevelled glass wind wings. A successful endurance run up Pike's Peak gave rise to Chandler's Pike's Peak Engine; its adoption of a constant mesh transmission and one-shot chassis lubrication were rigorously promoted, the car's individuality emphasised by its radiator treatment, initiated on the 1927 models, which included three vertical nickeled strips against the core, similar to the false front on the contemporary Franklin. Chandler, in 1919, introduced a lower-priced companion car, the Cleveland, ostensibly an independent make which added to its success in the marketplace. The Cleveland was discontinued at the end of 1926 and the Chandler Motor Car Co. became the Chandler-Cleveland Corp. to the end of its days. In 1927 an 8-cylinder series was added to the existing six. Chandler was bought by the Hupp Motor Car Corp. at the end of 1928. Hupp planned to introduce a companion line of cars to augment the existing Hupmobile series. Whether further plans had been made for this move is not known but the Stock Market Crash of 29 October 1929 and the resulting Depression ended it.

KM

Further Reading
'Chandler: Built to master a mountain . . . and more', John F. Katz,
Automobile Quarterly, Vol. XXIV, No. 4 and Vol. XXV, No.3.

1922 Chandler Six tourer.
NATIONAL MOTOR MUSEUM

CHANG'AN (CHI) 1990 to date

Chang'an Auto Corporation (1990) Chongqing Municipality.
Chang'an-Suzuki Auto Corporation (1993), Chongqing Municipality.

The Chang'an Machinery Works, a military ordnance factory in the city of Chongqing, at that time part of the Sichuan province, assembled a Jeep CJ5 in 1958 as Changjiang no. 46. In 1982 this works started the licence production of Suzuki ST 9½-ton minitrucks, followed by the first Suzuki Alto motorcar (model 1985) in 1990. They were sold as Chang'an Alto SC 7080, and were soon assembled in several other factories all over China: in Jilin, in Xi'an, and in Xiangtan. Production numbers raised to 50,000 units at the end of the 1990s. The Canadian Suzuki Swift version was trial produced under the name Chang'an SC 7100 Alto II and the newer Zen version as Chang'an Alto SC 7090. In 1993 a second factory was built in Chongqing to produce Altos, owned by the Chang'an-Suzuki Auto Corporation. Suzuki has a 35 per cent holding in this corporation, and Norinco, North China (Beifan) Industry Corporation, China's most important weapon production and trade company, has 65 per cent.

EVIS

263

1994 Changcheng CC 6470 saloon.
ERIK VAN INGEN SCHENAU

1991 Changjian JZK 6420 saloon.
ERIK VAN INGEN SCHENAU

CHANGCHENG (CHI) 1994–1996
Changcheng Auto Industrial Corp., Baoding City, Hebei Province.
The Changcheng ('Great Wall') factory made, in very small quantities (about 100 per annum), some small and medium size buses, 1½-ton small trucks, and a motor car, called the Changcheng CC 6470. The car was a Ford Taunus lookalike, with a length of 185in (4700mm). Some, surprisingly, showed the single English word 'Great' on the rear end.

EVIS

CHANGJIAN (CHI) 1991 to date
Jiaozuo Bus Works, Mengxian County, Henan Province.
Under-powered mini cars, of the Changjian JZK6420 type, using a Chinese 2-cylinder engine, were very popular as cheap taxis in the 1990s in Central China, as in the city of Xi'an. The cars were made of glassfibre reinforced plastic in very small series, which allowed the factory to make many different body styles; at least seven are known. Some vehicles used the designation Changjian (which means 'Large Sword') JZK 1010S. The factory also made some minibuses.

EVIS

CHANNON (GB) 1903–1907
E. Channon & Sons Carriage & Motor Works,
Dorchester and Weymouth, Dorset.
A successful carriage builder, Edward Channon developed agencies for other makes as well as offering complete vehicles under his own name. The only model advertised was a 10hp 2-cylinder, somewhat similar to the contemporary DARRACQ, with smart 4-seater open bodywork as standard. Bore and stroke were given as 4 × 5in, giving approximately 2.1-litres capacity, and it was claimed to be of 'English manufacture throughout'. The feature of the design given greatest prominence was automatic ignition advance and retard. The price quoted in 1905 was 225 guineas (£236.25) complete with tools. Channon retained an enduring curiosity for innovation and flew his own aircraft in 1908.

DF

CHAPEAUX (F) 1940–1941
Voitures E. Chapeaux, Lyons.
Émile Chapeaux was an electrical engineer who made four cars to individual order. Three were based on older chassis, Amilcar, Salmson and Mathis respectively, although with Chapeaux's own coachwork, batteries, and running gear. The first, ordered by a Red Cross official, was a coupé, the second and third, for a company director and a lawyer, were 2-door saloons. The fourth, ordered by a jeweller, was an original design, a low-slung 3-wheeler with single rear wheel. Chapeaux had to discontinue his 'production' at the end of 1941 because of shortage of raw materials, particularly lead for batteries. His cars were made in the Ultima motorcycle factory and then at the coachbuilders, Declerieux.
In 1968 he announced a 3-wheeled electric town car, of which 20 were to be built for a hire company, but they never materialised.

NG

CHAPMAN (US) 1899–1901
Belknap Motor Co., Portland, Maine.
W.H. Chapman was an electrician employed by the Belknap company who built a very light electric car powered by two 0.5hp motors, one geared to each rear wheel. The car rode on bicycle wheels and the inventor said that it could carry one passenger normally, and two on smooth roads. The 2-seater was called the auto-buggy, but other body styles were offered, although it is not known if they were built.

NG

CHAPUIS-DORNIER (F) c.1920
This well-known maker of proprietary engines is sometimes listed as a manufacturer of complete cars on the strength of second-hand examples listed in magazines. These may have been other makes using Chapuis-Dornier engines as there is no known published evidence of complete cars.

NG

CHARADE (F) 1989–1991
1989–1990 Charade Automobiles S.A., Clermont-Ferrand.
1990–1991 Charade Automobiles S.A., Brassac les Mines.
Both coupé and convertible versions of the Charade Monza sports car were built. The company turned to either Peugeot (1.9-litre) or VW (1.8-litre) for its powerplant, offering 130–160bhp engines mounted centrally in the coupé. However in the convertible the 70–130bhp VW 1.5-litre or Peugeot 1.4/1.9-litre engines were located in the front and drove the front wheels. The bodywork, which featured scissor-type doors, was made in South-East Asia. Kits and complete cars were sold.

CR

CHARENTAISE (F) 1899
Pougnaud et Brothier, Ruffec, Charente.
This was a 2-seater voiturette powered by a front-mounted 2.25hp single-cylinder engine.

NG

CHARETTE see INTERNATIONAL (i)

CHARGER see EMBEESEA

CHARLATTE see HRUBON

CHARLES RICHARD (F) 1901–1902
Sté des Moteurs et Autos Charles Richard, Troyes, Aube.
Two engines were offered in the Charles Richard light car, a 4hp single or an 8hp 2-cylinder. They could run on alcohol fuel as well as petrol. Final drive was by belt. Cars and light lorries competed in the Northern Alcohol Trials of 1901 and 1902.

NG

CHARLES TOWN-ABOUT (US) 1958–1959

Stinson Aircraft Tool & Engineering Corp., San Diego, California.
Named after its sponsor, Dr Charles Graves, various prototypes of an electric coupé were built by an aircraft company. The definitive version closely resembled a Volkswagen Karmann-Ghia coupé, with 1957 De Soto rear fins and lights. The glassfibre bodywork sat on a tubular aluminium frame. Two 3.2 horsepower electric motors were fitted, one for each rear wheel, powering the car for a reported range of up to 80 miles (128 km) at speeds of up to 58mph (93 km/h).

CR

CHARLEY (AUS) 1911–1914

Charley Cars Ltd, Malvern, Victoria.
When J.J. Charley retired from farming, he was aware of the difficult conditions for cars in rural areas. His solution to this problem was the introduction of a most complex drive and suspension system which consisted of the wheels being attached to long swinging arms, leading at the front and trailing at the rear; springing was by bell cranks and long coil springs located each side between front and rear wheels. As the drive was by bevel gears and shafts running inside the arms, it could be built as rear-, front- or 4-wheel drive. A demonstration car was built and taken to Europe when Berliet showed some interest; that firm tested the concept and made chassis available for further examples. One, fitted with a body by Damyon Bros, was sold to New Zealand but despite a number of orders being lodged by pastoral firms, the project failed due to internal dissention, some directors having another agenda. The high cost of the intricate system, involving 15 bevel gears for a 4-wheel drive, would, however, have counted against commercial success.

MG

CHARLON (F) 1905–1906

Société des Automobiles Charlon, Argenteuil, Seine-et-Oise.
This company offered a single-cylinder 9hp 2-seater with belt drive, a 12hp 2-cylinder, and three fours from 16/20 to 40/50hp. They were largely conventional in design, the largest using chain drive, the others being shaft driven apart from the 9hp. They also advertised commercial vehicle chassis.

NG

CHARRON (F) 1907–1930

Automobiles Charron Ltd, Puteaux, Seine.
After the partnership which had made the C.G.V. broke up in November 1906, and the company was recapitalised in London, the cars were renamed Charron. Fernand Charron only stayed with the firm which bore his name for a short time, leaving in 1908 to join CLEMENT-BAYARD. For 1907 the Charron range was similar to that of C.G.V. in 1906, including a massive 75hp with over–square dimensions of 180×160mm, (16,277cc), but for 1908 the monsters were dropped, the largest Charron being the 6782cc 30hp which was offered with chain or shaft drive. All others were shaft driven, and at the bottom of the range was a 1205cc 8hp vertical twin. It was the first Charron to have a dashboard radiator in Renault style, this feature being extended across the range for 1909. There were new engines in 1909 as well, with L-heads in place of the previous T-heads. The 8hp was used as a taxicab in London as well as in Paris, and was made under licence in Bohemia by PRAGA.

Charron brought out its first six for 1910, the 3617cc 30hp, which was well received by the public, and remained in the range until 1913. A curious anachronism of 1909 was the chain-driven 2411cc 12hp, although larger chain drives from the C.G.V. era remained in the catalogues until 1912. An important new model appeared for 1914, the 845cc 4-cylinder Charronette, an attractive small car in the Calthorpe Minor and Singer Ten class, which made more impact on the British market than the larger Charrons had done. After the war its engine was enlarged to 1057cc and the radiator was moved to the front, as it was on the bigger Charrons. These were undistinguished cars, of 2411 and 3402cc; the former was dropped in 1921 but the larger, known as the PGM, survived in the catalogue up to 1927, by which time Charron was virtually out of business. Front-wheel brakes arrived for 1925, and a 2771cc six was announced the same year. Valves were now overhead on all models. The last new model was a small six of 1806cc which, with a light car powered by a slightly enlarged version of the Charronette's engine, made up the range in their final year.

NG

c.1911 Charron 15hp landaulet.
NATIONAL MOTOR MUSEUM

1914 Charron Charronette 10hp 2-seater.
NICK GEORGANO

1921 Charron-Laycock 10.5hp coupé.
NATIONAL MOTOR MUSEUM

CHARRON-LAYCOCK (GB) 1919–1926

W.S. Laycock Ltd, Sheffield, Yorkshire.
The link between the French Charron company and Sheffield-based W.S. Laycock was provided by the financier Davidson Dalziel, who had formed Automobiles Charron Ltd in 1906 (see C.G.V.), and who became chairman of W.S. Laycock Ltd in 1916 on the death of the founder William Samuel Laycock. The company was very busy on munitions work during the war, but Dalziel looked to the postwar years when imported cars would be penalised by the McKenna duties imposed by the Government. In 1919 he signed an agreement with Laycock that they would build the 17.9hp Charron at Sheffield, but this never came about. Instead, a British-designed small car, the work of W.F. Milward (later works manager for HAMPTON), went into production under the name Charron-Laycock. It was probably of French origin, although there was no equivalent model made at Puteaux, for all the original drawings were in metric figures. It had a 1372cc 4-cylinder side-valve engine with detachable head and shaft drive to a spiral bevel rear axle. Capacity was raised to 1460cc in 1920, and the slightly vee'd radiator of the prototypes was changed to a flat shape, but

CHARTER OAK

c.1994 Chatenet Châtelaine SLB2 microcar.
NICK GEORGANO

1914 Chater-Lea cyclecar.
NICK GEORGANO

otherwise the Charron-Laycock was little altered during the seven years of its life. It was a high-quality small car but this was reflected in its price, £625 for a 2-seater in 1920, and £725 for a coupé. Although Laycock reduced the prices over the next few years, this was in line with the rest of the industry, and the Charron-Laycock remained expensive for its size. Most of the bodies were made by Laycock, although some saloons were made by Mulliner and drophead coupés by Vanden Plas.

W.S. Laycock Ltd went into receivership in December 1920, and although car production continued, the directors may have felt that this was a liability, even though the Charron-Laycock had a good reputation. In 1925 they sold rights to the car to the Birmingham Railway Carriage & Wagon Co., although spares were taken over by Gower & Lee, which effectively became the manufacturers. Few cars were made by them, however, and although the Charron-Laycock was carried by some guides up to 1928, production had ended two years before. About 500 are thought to have been made, of which only three are known to have survived.

NG

Further Reading
'Charron-Laycock', M. Worthington-Williams,
The Automobile, April 1991.
Cars from Sheffield, Stephen Myers, Sheffield City Libraries, 1986.

CHARTER OAK (US) 1917
Eastern Motors Syndicate, New Britain, Connecticut.
This grandly-named company planned to make a touring car powered by a 6-cylinder Herschell-Spillman engine and priced at $5000. This seems a very high figure for what was a very ordinary car, and only one was completed. The name came from the oak tree in which the royal colonial charter of 1662 had been hidden.

NG

CHASE (US) 1907–1912
Chase Motor Truck Co., Syracuse, New York.

As its name implies, this company was mainly concerned with making trucks and its passenger vehicles were based on the trucks. They had air-cooled 3-cylinder 2-stroke engines, chain drive and solid tyres. The Model F Surrey or Pleasure Car had a 4-seater body with no doors at front or rear, the rear seats being removable to form a light truck. After cars were dropped in 1912, 4-cylinder trucks were continued up to about 1917.

NG

CHATEL-JEANNIN (D) 1902–1903
Compagnie de Construction d'Automobiles Chatel-Jeannin, Mulhouse, Alsace.
This Alsatian car had a 7hp single-cylinder horizontal engine with two flywheels placed close together, the connecting rod head being between them. Engine, 2-speed gearbox, and differential were all enclosed in an aluminium casing on the rear axle from which no mechanical parts were visible. Access was by a panel in the casing, which could be removed for maintenance. The chassis was tubular, and the body comprised two basket-work armchair seats. Chatel-Jeannin also made a 4-seater tonneau, in which the 12hp 2-cylinder engine was under the driver's seat, transmission being by double chains to the rear axle. The claimed top speed of 50mph (80km/h) seems distinctly optimistic.

NG

CHATENET (F) 1985 to date
Automobiles Chatenet et Cie, Pierre-Buffière.
One of France's many *sans permis voiturette* manufacturers, Chatenet could trace its automotive history back to 1974, when it showed its first Formula Vee racing car. In the 1980s it turned to producing the La Châtelaine, which was styled by Gérard Godefroy, the same man who designed the Venturi sportscar. This was one of the better-equipped *voiturettes* of its time and had the distinct advantage of a 3-year guarantee. It was powered by a front-mounted 325cc Lombardini diesel or a 654cc Ruggerini. In 1991, when it opened a new factory to cope with demand, it was producing 1000 cars per year. 1994 saw an all-new model line-up based around the Stella, with very handsome styling and seating for either two or four passengers. This model had a 505cc Lombardini diesel engine and automatic transmission. A new model was promised for 1999.

CR

CHATER-LEA (GB) 1907–1908;1913–1922
Chater-Lea Ltd, London.
This company was better known for its motorcycles and components made from 1900 to 1935, than for cars, although these were made in two phases, The Carette, introduced in 1907, was a 2-seater powered by a 6hp air-cooled V-twin Sarolea engine mounted amidships on the off-side, with chain drive to one rear wheel. It was still offered in 1908, at the low price of 95 guineas (£99.75), but Chater-Lea made no serious efforts at production. In 1913 they announced a shaft-driven light car powered by an 8hp 4-cylinder engine, which was continued into the 1920s. Nearly all components were made in Chater-Lea's large nine-storey factory in Banner Street in the City of London.

NG

CHATHAM (CDN) 1906–1909
Chatham Motor Car Co. Ltd, Chatham, Ontario.
The first Chathams were powered by 20/22hp air-cooled flat-twin Reeves engines, and may have been largely imported cars. They had epicyclic gearboxes and shaft drive. By the summer of 1907 the makers had turned to water-cooling, offering a conventional car with vertical 4-cylinder engine of 25hp. The tourer bodies were supplied by William Gray & Sons Ltd, also of Chatham, which later made the GRAY-DORT car.

Early in 1908 the Chatham company was sued by a Detroit parts supplier, presumably for some infringement of patents, although the exact details are not known. The assets were auctioned and the company reorganised to make a larger 4-cylinder car of 30hp. Production of these lasted to the end of 1908 or early 1909. About 75 to 100 4-cylinder Chathams were made. In 1910 the factory was bought by the ANHUT Motor Car Co. of Detroit, although Anhut cars ware never made there.

NG

1969 Checker Marathon sedan.
NATIONAL MOTOR MUSEUM

CHATSWORTH (GB) c.1903–c.1908

This is a shadowy make whose origins are uncertain. A 9hp Chatsworth competed in the 1903 Derby & District Auto Club hill climb, and in 1907 Joseph Briddon of Bakewell was listed as the maker of the Chatsworth bicycle. These references would imply a Derbyshire origin for the car, together with the proximity of Chatsworth House, seat of the Dukes of Devonshire. However, *Porter's Motor Trade Directory* for 1908 lists a George W. Pyne of 118 Chatsworth Road, Clapton, North East London, as the maker of the Chatsworth car. Possibly the two cars were unconnected.

NG

CHAUSSON *see* C.H.S.

CHAUTAUQUA (US) 1914

Chautauqua Cyclecar Co., Jamestown, New York.

Powered by a 12hp 2-cylinder Spacke air-cooled engine, this was a typical cyclecar with only two unusual features; its 56in (1422mm) tread, standard for larger cars but wide for a cyclecar, and the steering column-mounted gear change. The Chautauqua's maker, H.J. Newman, planned a 4-cylinder model, but was out of business before this could be made.

NG

CHAVANET *see* AUTOMOTO

CHECKER (US) 1922–1982

Checker Motors Corp., Kalamazoo, Michigan.

The Checker automobile was a by-product of the Checker Cab, the latter one of the most prolific and prominent of all taxicabs produced in the United States. The Checker was initially the Model C-44 taxicab of the 1921 offerings by the Commonwealth Motor Car Co. of Joliet, Illinois. That year 126 were completed, before Commonwealth was acquired by the Markin Body Co. of Chicago which started building the cab under the Checker badge. Probably the first passenger car built by Checker – and this on special order – was a roadster, built in 1924 for the Automobile Blue Book Association for its road inspection team. By 1923 3000 Checker cabs were in service but a few custom-built sedans and limousines were constructed on a one-off basis. Although the Checkers of the 1920s used Buda 4-cylinder engines, these would be replaced by Continental sixes by 1930. In the lean Depression years of 1931 and 1932 the company built its Utility model, straight-8 sedan which could be, and was, used

for private use and priced at $1795. A few custom limousines were also built on special order using Checker's larger chassis, notably a bullet-proofed car for Sam Insull of Chicago.

In 1959 Checker seriously targeted its cars toward the passenger car market with its Superba sedan, practically identical to its taxicab and featuring high doors, jump seats and rugged construction. The Superba was supplanted by the updated, though similar, Marathon, which would continue until the demise of the company. Power of the Checker cars was by a 3.7-litre Continental six until 1965 when it was replaced by Chevrolet sixes or V8s. Meanwhile, a station wagon and 8-door, 12-seater limousine had been added to the existing sedan. Production remained around 5000 cars per year throughout the years. In 1981 an automatic transmission was introduced. By this time available engines included a 3.8-litre V6, a V8 of 4.4- and 4.5-litres, and a 5.6-litre V8 GM diesel. Checker ceased operations on 8 July 1982.

KM

Further Reading
'The checkered history of the Cab from Kalamazoo', John A Heilig, *Automobile Quaterly*, Vol.30, No.2.

CHEETAH (i) (US) 1963–1965

Bill Thomas, Anaheim, California.

Although intended to be a 'homologation special', the Cheetah was built in small numbers despite overwhelming odds. Bill Thomas was famous for building racing Corvettes and Chevrolet II sedans when the idea of a Chevrolet-based sports car to challenge the Cobras was born. Chevrolet originally intended to support the construction of 100 street cars so they could be raced as GT cars. However, during the development period the number required rose to 1000 units and Chevrolet backed out. They were compact, lightweight coupés with tube chassis designed by top race car fabricator Don Edmunds. Less than 30 complete cars were sold, in both street and race trim. Power came from Chevrolet 5300cc V8s with modified fuel injection systems. Race Cheetahs had 520hp, weighed 1510lbs and had a top speed of over 200mph (320km/h), but the chassis and drum brakes were not up to the power. Although all were built as coupés, one had the top cut off to alleviate extreme cockpit heat. The prototype of the street version, the Super Cheetah, which was to have had a 7000cc engine and a longer wheelbase, was never completed. All Thomas Cheetahs were sold in completed form, but kit replicas have been made by several companies, including ALLIED INDUSTRIES and C-R CHEETAH RACE CARS.

HP

1922 Chelsea(iii) electric coupé.
NATIONAL MOTOR MUSEUM

1904 Chenard-Walcker 14CV tonneau.
NATIONAL MOTOR MUSEUM

c.1913 Chenard-Walcker 12/18hp or 16/20hp coupé.
NATIONAL MOTOR MUSEUM

1924 Chenard Walcker 2-litre saloon.
NATIONAL MOTOR MUSEUM

CHEETAH (ii) **(GB)** 1983–1986

1983–1984 Cheetah Cars, Newcastle, Tyne & Wear.
1984–1986 Cheetah Cars, Chester-le-Street, Co. Durham.
Cheetah occupied the very bottom rung of the British kit car industry with poor quality, ill-conceived products, typified by its first effort, the Mirach. This was supposedly inspired by the Lamborghini Miura, and used a hotch-potch of parts (including an Alfasud mid-engine and Ford Cortina hubs and steering). The Mirach 2 was launched a matter of months afterwards, looking closer to the Miura but still of poor quality. Next Cheetah produced an AC Cobra replica called the Viper, whose lack of accuracy was laughable. Cheetah also offered the Shamal, an odd-looking coupé intended for Lancia, Alfa Romeo or Ford engines, the barchetta-style SV (a race-orientated car based on Alfasud or Lancia Beta parts) and a Ford GT40 replica.
CR

CHEETAH (iii) **(NZ)** 1989–1996

Cheetah Cars, Auckland, North Island.
With styling along Jaguar E-type lines, the Cheetah made use of Holden Kingswood mechanical components, although the Ford V8 could, alternatively, be fitted. The wide Holden track was retained, resulting in the roadster being 6in wider than the E-type, but it allowed the Holden rear window to be used as a windscreen. At 1996 production stood at nine examples.
MG

CHELMSFORD see CLARKSON

CHELSEA (i) see WELCH

CHELSEA (ii) **(US)** 1914

Chelsea Manufacturing Co., Newark, New Jersey.
Although the makers called it a cyclecar, this was in the light car class, with 12hp 4-cylinder water-cooled engine, conventional gearbox, and shaft drive. The company announced that it would make 500 cars in 1914, but actual output was probably much smaller.
NG

CHELSEA (iii) **(GB)** 1922

Wandsworth Engineering Works, Wandsworth, London.
The year 1922 was very late for the introduction of an electric car in Britain, and, predictably, the Chelsea Electric had a very short life. It was a 2-seater coupé with a conventional bonnet which gave it the appearance of a petrol car. The B.T.H. motor was mounted just ahead of the rear axle, and the batteries of 44 cells partly over the rear axle and partly under the bonnet. The price was £700, but few, if any, were sold.
NG

CHENARD-WALCKER (F) 1900–1946

1900–1906 Chenard, Walcker et Compagnie, Asnières, Seine.
1906–1946 SA des Anciens Établissements Chenard et Walcker, Gennevilliers, Seine.
Ernest Chenard (1861–1922) was a bicycle manufacturer who started in business at Asnières in 1883. In 1898 he was joined by Henri Walcker (1877–1912) to form a company which made motor tricycles of De Dion-Bouton type. In 1900 they progressed to their first car; it had an 1160cc vertical twin engine of their own manufacture, four forward speeds and a curious transmission incorporating a double back axle. The drive was taken by two half shafts independently of a dead beam axle. The shafts drove internally-toothed gear wheels on the hubs, similar to the system seen on Milnes-Daimler commercial vehicles. This design was used by Chenard-Walcker until the 1920s, although a cheaper car was offered with a conventional axle, and in 1904 there was a short-lived 12hp twin with chain drive. Chassis were of armoured wood until 1907, and pressed steel thereafter.

The business prospered, and in 1905 they turned out 400 cars as well as marine engines up to 80hp. In March 1906 the partners became a Société Anonyme (public company) with help from the Banque Centrale Française, and with the additional capital built a new factory at Gennevilliers, a Paris suburb close to their former home at Asnières. They were to stay there for the rest of the company's

1938 Chenard-Walcker Aigle 22 saloon.
NATIONAL MOTOR MUSEUM

life. Also in 1906 they adopted the eagle radiator badge, which was a characteristic for many years and gave rise to the Aigle (eagle) models in the 1930s. Only 4-cylinder cars were made after 1905, the smallest for the home market being the 3021cc 14/16, although a short-stroke 2.6-litres was made exclusively for export to Britain. However, 1907 saw a 942cc single-cylinder voiturette, which was made up to 1910. Annual production was about 1200 cars in 1910, rising to 1500 three years later, when Chenard-Walcker were the ninth largest car makers in France.

Up to 1910, the engines had side-valves in a T-head, but these gave way to the more modern L-head design in the 2.1-litre P type, and the older layout was soon dropped. Monobloc engines with full pressure lubrication were adopted in 1912, and the company's first 6-cylinder car, of 4.5-litres capacity, made its appearance in 1913. At the outbreak of war the range consisted of the six and three fours, of 2-, 2.6-, and 3-litres capacity.

Only the 3-litre (3016cc) Model UU was revived in 1919, although it was joined in 1920 by the 2648cc 12CV and the 1952cc 2-litre Model TT in 1922. Ernest Chenard died in 1922, being succeeded by his son Lucien (1896–1971), although the company was largely owned by outside interests, the Donnay family and Georges Stein, who was Lucien's brother in law. The early postwar Chenards were old-fashioned, with separate gearboxes and foot-operated transmission brakes, but in 1922 Henri Toutée (1884–1943), who had been hired by Henri Walcker in 1906, designed a new 3-litre car with single-ohc 4-cylinder engine and Hallot servo-assisted brakes. These were unusual in that they acted on the front wheels and transmission, but there were no brake drums on the rear wheels. As well as being a fine touring car this model was raced quite extensively, having the distinction of winning the first 24-hour race at Le Mans. The drivers were two Chenard engineers, René Léonard and André Lagache. A 4-litre straight-8 joined the 3-litre cars at Le Mans in 1924, but did not finish the race; very few, if any, were sold to the public. Touring Chenards of the mid- 1920s

1933 Chenard Walcker Aigle 4 saloon.
NATIONAL MOTOR MUSEUM

were side-valve versions of the 2- and 3-litre sporting cars, with plug covers which gave them the appearance of ohv units. Smaller cars of 1496cc were made from 1922, joined in 1928 by a 1286cc. There were also the remarkable little tank bodied sports cars, with 1100cc pushrod ohv engines which had many racing successes and were sold in small numbers to private owners.

By 1925 Chenard et Walcker were turning out 100 cars per day, making them the fourth largest car makers in France. They had several links with other firms, including SÉNÉCHAL, whose small sports cars were made from 1922 to 1927 by a Chenard subsidiary, the Société Industrielle et Commerciale de Gennevilliers. They also made A.E.M. front-drive electric delivery vans, and in 1927 joined a consortium with DELAHAYE. There were plans to bring UNIC into the group

1904 Chenu 24hp tourer.
MALCOLM JEAL

c.1912 Cheswold 15.9hp tourer.
NATIONAL MOTOR MUSEUM

as well, but Unic turned down the invitation. The Delahaye partnership lasted until 1931 and produced a series of cars under both names, and which were very similar in appearance. The smallest of the Chenards was the 8CV Z2 with 1286cc side-valve engine, and there were also fours of 1730 and 2979cc (the old 3-litre). The first 6-cylinder Chenard since 1914 had a 2877cc inlet-over-exhaust valve engine, which was made by Delahaye and used in their own cars. Another Delahaye six used by Chenard was the 3471cc of 1931. One might have expected the 4-cylinder Chenard engines to be used by Delahaye, but this was not the case. However, Delahaye did adopt Chenard's ribbon radiator from 1928 onwards. In 1931 Chenard supplied some engines to Ariès, to which company Henri Toutée had moved in 1927, although he returned to Chenard in the 1930s.

The alliance with Delahaye ended in September 1931, which seemed to be a good thing for both companies, for Delahaye began their line of sports cars which gave them a totally new identity, while Chenard-Walcker became more adventurous in design. The first sign of this was the adoption of transverse leaf ifs for 1934, followed by a front-wheel drive car designed by Jean Grégoire. This was called the Super Aigle 4, and was available with two engine sizes, 2180cc (Type P) and 2500cc (Type N). These engines were also used in rear-driven cars with similar styling, the 4S and 4N. There was a smaller rear-drive car, the 1630cc Aiglon. One of the drawbacks of the front-drive cars was their close resemblance to the conventional models. Apart from the absence of running boards, there was little to distinguish a Super Aigle 4 from an Aigle 4S, yet it was 1400 francs more expensive. The Super Aigles also suffered from being introduced at the same time (1934) as the front-drive Citroëns which had ohv

engines and all-steel bodies and were 8000 francs less expensive. About 1000 of the first series Super Aigles were made, followed by 300 of the second series (1936), which had Cotal gearboxes.

Another innovation was a 3580cc V8 which was used in the Aigle 8, made from 1934 to 1937. Externally this resembled the Aigle 4N, with the same wheelbase and body styles, although the range of these was not so wide. Prices, however, were some 15,000 francs higher. All Chenards gained ohvs for 1936, but in that year the company was taken over by Chausson, the large body-building concern, and this spelt the end of individuality for the Chenard-Walcker. The 1938 models had Chausson bodies which were identical to those supplied to Matford, while two of the three models had non-Chenard engines – the Aigle 20 was powered by the 11CV Citroën engine and the Aigle 8 by a 3622cc Ford V8. Only the Aigle 22 still had the 2180cc ohv Chenard engine, and even this had gone by the 1939 season. The last Aigle 22 and Aigle 8 saloons could only be distinguished from Matfords by their radiator grilles, although the convertibles had pillarless Vutotal windscreens made under Labourdette patents, which the Matford did not have. The smaller cars had Bendix brakes, while the Aigle 8 had dual-circuit hydraulics. These models were made up to the outbreak of World War II, and a few were assembled in 1946. From 1947 Chenard-Walcker concentrated on a light forward-control van powered by a Peugeot engine, and from October 1950 these carried Peugeot badges.

Note:
There has been some confusion of the cars' names, Chenard-Walcker or Chenard et Walcker. The first company name was Chenard, Walcker et Compagnie, so there was no dispute until 1906 when the public company Société Anonyme des Anciens Établissements Chenard et Walcker (public company of the former Chenard and Walcker business) was formed. The company was now Chenard et Walcker, and the cars were sometimes called by this name as well, although there was no hard and fast rule.

NG

Further Reading
'The Rise and Fall of Chenard-Walcker', Jan Norbye,
The Automobile, November 1996.
Toutes le Voitures Françaises 1935, René Bellu, Herme-Vilo, 1984.
Toutes le Voitures Françaises 1939, René Bellu, Edita-Vilo, 1982.
Chenard-Walcker-FAR, Claude Rouxel and Jacques Dorizon,
Histoire et Collections, 1998.

CHENU (F) c.1903–c.1907
Automobiles Chenu, Paris.
Chenu showed a range of cars at the 1903 Paris Salon, including a light shaft-driven chassis with 9hp single-cylinder or 12hp 2-cylinder engines, and a heavy chain-driven chassis for 12, 20, 30 or 40hp 4-cylinder engines. A car advertised second-hand several years later had a 40hp De Dion-Bouton engine, but it is not certain that all the Chenus were De Dion-powered. In 1906 they advertised cars of 14, 20, 50, 90, and 100hp, but probably only the smaller were built. The company later made aero engines.
NG

CHESIL (GB) 1988 to date
1988–1991 Street Beetle, Christchurch, Dorset.
1991 to date Chesil Speedsters, Burton Bradstock, Dorset.
This Porsche 356 Speedster replica began life with Street Beetle. Quality was the watchword in all areas and the Chesil quickly established a reputation as probably the best 356 replica around. The fibreglass body had a tubular steel sub-chassis to fit on a shortened VW floorpan. There was also an interesting optional stripped-out model with a head fairing from 1994 (called the Speedster SE) and a fixed hardtop model. The company also developed a Porsche 550 Spyder replica.
CR

CHESWOLD (GB) 1911–1915
E.W. Jackson & Son Ltd, Doncaster, Yorkshire.
The Jackson company was established in 1904 as general engineers, and ventured into car production with a design by M.C. Inman Hunter who had previously been chief designer for ADAMS-HEWITT. The Cheswold car, named after a local stream, had a 2612cc 15.9hp 4-cylinder engine with separately

cast cylinders, 4-speed gearbox, and worm-drive rear axle. This was made by Wrigley, but the engine and gearbox were made in-house. The radiator was dashboard mounted, in Renault style. Only one model of Cheswold was offered in the five years of its life, an open tourer, though some were bodied as ambulances.

NG

CHEVENET (F) 1935–1936
M. Chevenet, Lyons.
This was a 4-seater 3-wheeler powered by a 500cc motorcycle engine driving the single rear wheel through a 3-speed gearbox. As well as the open 4-seater, the Chevenet was made as a cabriolet and a saloon. Sales were modest, and limited to the Lyons district.

NG

CHEVROLET (i) (US) 1912 to date
Chevrolet Motor Co., Detroit, Michigan.
The Chevrolet marque came into existence because William C. Durant, who had founded General Motors in 1908 and lost it to bankers two years later, wanted to regain control, for which he needed new cars and new companies. He organised the LITTLE Motor Car Co. in Flint, Michigan, to make a cheap car which would earn money quickly. For his larger car he chose the name Chevrolet, from the racing driver Louis Chevrolet (1878–1941), who was already well-known to the American public through his exploits with Buick racing cars. He was a clever practical engineer as well as a skilled driver, but he was not a designer, so he invited his friend Étienne Planche to join him and Durant. Planche had worked for the WALTER (i) Automobile Co. in New York, where he had met Chevrolet, and designed the first MERCER.

The design he came up with was called the Chevrolet Classic Six. It had a 4900cc 6-cylinder T-head engine and 3-speed gearbox, and was made in one body style only, a 5-seater tourer. Its most distinctive feature was a handsome German silver domed vee-radiator, possibly reflecting Chevrolet's European background. The price was $2150, a little above that of the new Cadillac 30, and in the same class as the 50hp Speedwell, Haynes Model Y and other upper middle class cars. It was a large car; its engine capacity was larger than any Chevrolet until 1958, and few Chevrolets have ever had a wheelbase longer than the 120in (3050mm) of the Classic Six.

The Chevrolet Motor Car Co. was incorporated on 3 November 1911, but production did not get under way until late the following year. Durant did well to sell just under 3000 of a fairly expensive car in little over two months. An electric starter replaced the compressed air system on the 1913 Classic Six, which sold 5987 units in the year, but Durant realised that he needed a cheaper car if sales were to take off. He therefore improved the Little Six, renamed it the Chevrolet Light Six and priced it at $1475, to sell alongside the $2500 Classic Six. The last season for this big Chevrolet was 1914; a much more important development that year was the introduction of a truly low-priced car, the Series H Four. This had a Mason ohv engine of 2786cc and was available in two styles, a 2-seater roadster called the Royal Mail at $750 and a 5-seater tourer called the Baby Grand at $875. Louis Chevrolet was unhappy at his name being used on a cheap car, and resigned in October 1913 to pursue his own career making the successful FRONTENAC racing cars. Planche also left to join DORT.

The 1914 Chevrolet range was unique in that three different valve layouts were used in a single year, T-head on the Classic Six, L-head on the Light Six and pushrod ohv on the Four. The sixes were dropped for 1916, when the Series H Four was joined by a very important newcomer, the 490. This was named for its price in dollars. They only reached this figure by cutting out electric lighting and starting, but Durant was determined to match, if not undercut, Ford's prices. He did not succeed, for within two months of the 490's introduction Ford reduced the price of the basic Model T to $440. However, the 490, which used the same Mason engine as the Model H, sold well for it offered a conventional transmission and had more modern lines than the T. It was, however, very utilitarian, being finished in a dull black, without a trace of brightwork. About 18,000 were sold in 1916 and 57,692 in 1917, unimpressive compared with Ford's 622,351, but good enough to keep Durant happy. The H Series, renamed F Series for 1916, was continued on a slightly longer wheelbase, but production was never as high as that of the 490. As the FA, it acquired a larger engine of 3670cc in 1918, and was continued as a larger companion to the 490 up to 1922. The engine was made by Northway of Detroit, which GM had acquired in 1909,

1922 Chevrolet (i) FB tourer.
NATIONAL MOTOR MUSEUM

1931 Chevrolet (i) Series AE Six sedan.
NATIONAL MOTOR MUSEUM

1938 Chevrolet (i) Master De Luxe 2-door sedan.
NICK GEORGANO/NATIONAL MOTOR MUSEUM

1946 Chevrolet Aero Fleetline coupé.
NICK GEORGANO

1953 Chevrolet (i) Corvette.
NATIONAL MOTOR MUSEUM

rather than Mason who continued to make the 490's engine. Mason was also responsible for a new departure in late 1917, a 55bhp 4691cc V8 which went into the D Series tourer. It was a late entry into the V8 field, for at least 17 other US manufacturers had already followed Cadillac's lead, and although reasonably priced at $1285, the V8 did not sell well. In the 1918 model year 2710 were sold, and about 70 as 1919 models, most of them delivered before the end of 1918.

Billy Durant lost control of General Motors for the second time in November 1920, when he was forced to resign as the price of having his personal debts paid by the du Pont family and the J.P. Morgan bank. The new president, Pierre S. du Pont, considered dropping the Chevrolet, but was dissuaded by vice-president Alfred P. Sloan. It was a fortunate decision for General Motors, for within ten years Chevrolet was to become the Corporation's top selling car, and to oust mighty Ford from their place at the head of the American production league.

The Copper-cooled Experiment

In 1923 Chevrolet launched one of their few flops. The copper-cooled engine, really air-cooled, was so called because it had thick U-shaped copper plates mounted vertically on the cylinders. It was designed by Charles F. Kettering of Delco ignition fame, all development work being carried out at his laboratories at Dayton, Ohio. Its attractions were that it had fewer parts, less weight, a higher output for its size than a water-cooled unit, and could not boil in summer or freeze in winter. The 2212cc engine (Chevrolet's smallest until the 1976 Chevette) developed 22bhp, only 4bhp less than the 2802cc engine used in the 490. The downside was that it overheated badly, and its power dropped drastically when the engine was hot. Chevrolet planned to make 1000 copper-cooled cars per month, rising to 50,000 per month by October 1923, and the eventual phasing out of the water-cooled engine. In fact, only 759 were ever built, of which 239 were scrapped before they left the factory, and of the 500 which reached the dealers only about 100 found private buyers, the rest being kept as demonstrators. Some of the engines were used as stationary power units in Chevrolet factories; a handful of these survive, as do two complete cars. Chevrolet would not try air-cooling again until the controversial Corvair of the 1960s.

The Superior and the Stove Bolt Six

The 490 remained in production until 1922, and apart from a bad period in

NICK BALDWIN

CHEVROLET, LOUIS (1878–1941)

Louis Joseph Chevrolet was born on Christmas Day 1878 at La Chaux de Fonds in Switzerland. The family was of French origin, and the name is believed to have been derived from chevre à lait, meaning milk goat. When he was ten years old the family moved back to France, to the wine-producing Beaune district where young Louis invented a new wine pump for filling the vats with juice from the press. He then went to work in a bicycle repair shop and became a successful racing cyclist. Like many others he moved easily from the cycle to the car world, and from 1896 onwards took jobs at several well-known car makers such as Mors, Darracq, Hotchkiss and De Dion-Bouton.

In 1900 Chevrolet crossed the Atlantic, and entered the US via Canada where he worked as a chauffeur for six months, before joining the American branch of De Dion Bouton. Ever restless, he moved on to the Fiat importers, Hollander & Tangeman, for whom he drove large cars of 90 and 110hp, winning a number of races. From 1906 to 1907 he worked for the E.W. Bless Co., who made the expensive Bless car, moving from there to Buick in 1907. This was a fateful move, for he met Billy Durant who hired him as a consultant on the new car that Durant planned to launch, after his first departure from General Motors in 1911. Durant wasn't too impressed with Chevrolet as a racing driver, for he did have a habit of breaking cars (the Buick he drove in the first Indianapolis 500 Mile Race in 1911 retired with a broken crankshaft), but he admired his technical expertise. It is not certain whether Chevrolet had begun work on a car design before he met Durant, or if the idea was Billy's from the start. Although he was a clever practical engineer, Chevrolet had no formal training, so he called on his old friend and fellow-countryman Etienne Planche to do the actual design work on the car which became the Chevrolet Classic Six.

Although Chevrolet and Planche had promised a 'French-type light car' the vehicle they came up with was more typically American and by no means light. Sales were not bad for a $2150 car, but Durant needed a mass-market car, and commissioned a new smaller 4-cylinder car, the Model H. This did not please Chevrolet, who was proud of his name and did not want to see it on a cheap car. There was increasing friction between himself and Durant, not least over smoking habits. Durant felt that an executive of an up-and-coming car company should smoke cigars, if anything, and was irritated by the cheap cigarette which was constantly hanging on Chevrolet's lips, Parisian style. Durant's other associates such as William Little and A.B.C. Hardy came from higher social backgrounds than Chevrolet who, apparently, had no pretensions and was satisfied to be himself, 'a rough-hewn and tough racing car driver and engineer'. When Durant raised the cigarette question, Chevrolet is said to have exploded "I sold you my car and I sold you my name, but I'm not going to sell myself to you".

The upshot of this disharmony was that Chevrolet left the company in October 1913, selling his stock which was not worth much at the time, but would have made him a millionaire had he hung onto it. The following year Chevrolet organised a company of his own, but his name belonged to Durant, so he called it the Frontenac Motor Corp. This company built racing cars, both 4- and 8-cylinder models, which were highly successful in board track racing, and provided most of the competition for Duesenbergs and Millers from 1916 until the early 1920s. Louis drove them to many victories, but it was his younger brother Gaston who won the Indianapolis 500 in 1920, followed by Tommy Milton's victory in 1921. From 1922 to 1934 Louis made and sold special cylinder heads for Model T Fords, which were sold under the name Fronty-Ford. They were invincible on the dirt tracks, less so at Indianapolis where the more expensive Millers held sway. However they ran steadily there, L.L. Corum's car finishing 5th in 1923. A Fronty-Ford was driven at Indy by Alfred Moss, Stirling's father, in 1924. Louis Chevrolet never much money from his Frontenacs, but he was prouder of them than of the millions of cars which carried his name.

In the early 1920s Chevrolet was also chief engineer to the American Motors Corp of Plainfield, New Jersey, makers of the American (vi). All cars were tested by Chevrolet before delivery, and carried a badge inscribed OK Chevrolet. He also did some design work on marine and aircraft engines, and was in demand as a consulting engineer until shortly before his death in 1941.

He married Suzanne Treyvoux in 1905.

NG

Further Reading
Chevrolet, 1911–1985, Richard M. Langworth and Jan P. Norbye, Publications International, 1984.
Chevrolet, a History from 1911, Beverly Rae Kimes and Robert C. Ackerson, Automobile Quarterly Publications, 1984.

1961 Chevrolet (i) Corvair Coupé.
NATIONAL MOTOR MUSEUM

1920–21, caused by public anxiety in the wake of Durant's problems, Chevrolet sales held up well. Sloan decided not to compete with Ford head on, but to aim a little higher, giving the comforts and refinements which the ageing Model T could not offer. The 490's successor was the Superior, which had a more modern appearance, with a higher bonnet line and drum-type headlamps. The engine was the same as the 490's, and was continued up to the end of the 1928 season. By then the original 28bhp had been raised to 35bhp. The noisy bevel rear axle was redesigned on the 1925 models, which also featured a variety of colours in the new Duco cellulose finish. From January 1924 Chevrolet's fortunes were guided by Danish-born William S. Knudsen (1879–1948), who had been Ford's general manager, and was in charge of manufacturing Eagle boats during World War I. Under his guidance Chevrolet soon recovered from the copper-cooled disaster. The larger FB was dropped after 1922 as it was too close to Oakland and Oldsmobile in price, leaving Chevrolet to pursue a one-model policy for many years. Annual sales were 415,814 in 1923, dipped to 262,100 in 1924, then rose to 444,671 in 1925 and 588,962 in 1926. Chevrolet's position in relation to Ford was very interesting – in 1924 Ford outsold Chevrolet by more than six to one, in 1925, four to one and in 1926 less than three to one. Then in 1927, the year when Ford factories were closed down for six months due to the changeover from Model T to Model A, Chevrolet shot up into first place, with sales of 1,749,988. Ford took the lead again in 1929 and 1930, but thereafter practically every year up to the present day has seen Chevrolet in the lead, and never lower than second. By 1928, in addition to the main factory at Flint, Chevrolet had assembly plants in eight other cities, from Tarrytown, New York (the former Maxwell-Briscoe plant) to Oakland, California. A Canadian plant at Oshawa, Ontario, opened in 1916.

The 1928 Chevrolets, named the National series, had larger engines and front-wheel brakes, but they were completely superseded for 1929 with the introduction of Chevrolet's first 6-cylinder engine since 1915. Nicknamed the 'Cast Iron Wonder' for its use of iron pistons when the majority of the industry was turning to aluminium, it had a capacity of 3180cc and developed 46bhp. Another nickname was 'Stovebolt Six', from the slotted bolts which held on the cylinder head. This simple ohv engine did not attract a lot of attention at the time, nor did it deserve to. As historian Richard M. Langworth wrote, 'It was not a high-quality power unit. Every part of it had been designed to be just good enough and no more'. Yet it was made, with various improvements and occasional enlargements, for more than thirty years. It powered every Chevrolet car made from 1929 to 1954, more than 18.5 million, as well as nearly 5 million light trucks.

For several years Chevrolet used different names for each year's models; the 1928s were Nationals, 1929 Internationals, and the names for 1930, 1931 and 1932 were Universal, Independence and Confederate. In 1933 a cheaper six was called the Standard, so the regular model became the Master Six, and this name was continued up to 1942. Knudsen kept his eye on Ford during the 1930s, particularly after the arrival of the V8 in 1932. His Confederate Six of that year offered synchromesh, free wheeling, and a power increase to 60bhp, as well as being one of the best-looking Chevrolets made. Stylist Dave Holls said 'In 1932 every car was a jewel', and that went for Chevrolet just as much as for Cadillac.

New lines, with skirted wings and a slight vee to the radiator were introduced in 1933. Two sizes of engine were offered, 2986cc on the Standard Six and 3389cc on the Master Six.

Dubonnet-type ifs arrived on the 1934 models, giving them a strong advantage over Ford who would struggle on with their transverse leaves until 1948. Chevrolet scored another point over Ford by introducing hydraulic brakes for 1936. Fisher's 'Turret Top' steel roof came in with the 1935 Master Six.

Chevrolet was now confidently in the lead of the production race. Between 1931 and 1959, the only years in which Ford beat them were 1935, and then by only 140,000 cars, and the quite unrepresentative year 1945, when the whole industry was struggling to change over from wartime production. There were not many mechanical changes in the seven years up to America's entry into World War II, although capacity went up to 3548cc (85bhp) on the 1937 engines which had four bearings instead of three. However, styling progressed greatly, with a Cadillac-inspired divided grille for 1939, while by 1941 Chevrolet had eliminated running boards, and had a horizontal grille and faired-in headlamps. New body styles included Chevrolet's first station wagon in 1939, a convertible with power-operated top (America's first in the low-price field), and a fast-back 2-door coupé in 1942. This Fleetline Aerosedan was the ancestor of many postwar fastback Chevrolets, including 4-door sedans.

Chevrolet made no passenger cars between 30 January 1942 and 3 October 1945. The start up was three months later than Ford's, which explains Chevrolet's low figure of 12,776 cars delivered that year, compared with Ford's 34,439. The 1946 Chevrolets were little changed from the 1942s, but now carried the name Stylemaster and Fleetmaster, the latter being the more expensive line. The Fleetline Aerosedan proved very popular, selling nearly 160,000 in 1947, out of a total of 695,986. Chevrolets were little changed until the 1949 season when, in common with most US car makers, they brought out their first new postwar models. These had completely fresh styling, with all-enveloping bodies in both fastback and notchback models. The station wagon still had a lot of wood in its construction, but before the end of 1949 this had given way to an all-steel design. Under the bonnet was still the old Stovebolt Six which gave 90bhp – not particularly exciting. However, the horsepower race was still a few years off, and no one bought a Chevrolet for high performance. Capacity went up to 3850cc in 1953, giving 115bhp. Styling evolved only slowly up to 1955, although there were novelties such as the Bel Air hard-top convertible of 1950, the year in which Powerglide 2-speed automatic transmission was introduced as a $159 optional extra on the De Luxe series only.

New Engine, New Styling

For 1955 Chevrolet brought out a brand-new V8 engine, although the old six was still available. Designed by Ed Cole, the new engine was an over-square design (95.25 x 76.2mm) of 4342cc developing 162bhp, with a 180bhp power pack available at extra cost. Styling was new too, with a horizontal 'eggcrate' grille inspired by Ferrari, a wraparound windscreen and a dip in the body line

NICK BALDWIN

KNUDSEN, WILLIAM S. (1878 – 1948)
Born Signius Wilhelm Poul Knudsen in Copenhagen on 25 March 1879, William S. Knudsen was to achieve fame in World War II for running what President F.D.Roosevelt so felicitously called 'the arsenal of democracy'.

Having been turned down by the Danish navy he sailed to the USA in 1900 at the age of 21.. He worked in the Seabury shipyards at Morris Heights, New Jersey, and when they closed he found a job in the Erie Railroad shop at Salamanca, New York, repairing locomotive boilers. While visiting Buffalo on behalf of his brother in Copenhagen, who imported bicycles made there at the John R. Keim Mills, he was offered, and took, a job there. John R. Keim also made steam engines for Foster in the UK, and they soon had an order for brake drums from the Olds Motor Works, as well as orders from Ford for sheet metal parts such as silencers, wings, and fuel tanks. In 1911 Henry Ford bought the John R. Keim Mills, and Knudsen had to organise Model T assembly at Buffalo, introducing several innovative techniques, and pioneering spray-painting of the body exteriors.

In 1913 Ford brought Knudsen to Dearborn and put him in charge of setting up 27 regional assembly plants.

In 1917 he organised the production of Eagle boats for the US Navy at Ford's River Rouge plant, using methods unheard of in the shipbuilding industry (such as making the hulls in three sections, each one being brought to structural completion before being riveted together).

Following an inspection tour of the Ford plants in the UK, Knudsen went on to make arrangement for setting up Ford assembly plants in Spain and Denmark. He left the Ford Motor Co. on 1 April 1921 in protest against henry Ford undermining his authority, and joined Ireland & Matthews metalworking as general manager. David Ireland introduced him to Charles Stewart Mott, Vice President of General Motors, who in turn introduced him to Alfred P. Sloan, which led Knudsen, on 23 February 1922, to a General Motors staff position at a salary of $30,000. Within months he was assigned to Chevrolet and his salary was raised to S$50,000. He was made president of Chevrolet on 15 January 1924, a position that also made him a General Motors vice president. At that time Ford was outselling Chevrolet in the North American market by more than six to one. At a dealer convention in Chicago, Knudsen stood up and shouted, in his thick Scandinavian accent, 'I vant vun for vun!' Three years later he had his wish come true.

On 16 October 1933 Knudsen became Executive Vice President of General Motors, in charge of all car, truck, body, and accessory operations, and he was elected President of GM in May 1937, when Alfred Sloan became Chairman.

On Monday 27 May 1940 Knudsen was called to a meeting at the White House, and this ultimately led to him serving on the Council of National Defense, in charge of the manufacture of tanks, engines, aeroplanes and other arms and military goods. He was granted leave of absence from GM and his name was taken off the payroll. His position was formalized on 7 January 1941 when he was named Director-General of the Office of Production Management. He was not only running a purchasing department of 25,000 prime suppliers and 120,000 sub-contractors, but also dealing with matters of plant construction, methods and tooling, and coordinating the flow of materials, right through to the day of delivery, for the US Army, the US Navy, and the Lend-Lease programme. In 1942 his title changed to Director of War Production. He received the Distinguished Service Medal in May 1944, with an additional Oak Leaf Cluster in May 1945. From 1 September 1944 to 1 June 1945 he served as Director of Air Technical Command. He re-joined General Motors on 2 July 1945, and flew to Europe a few days later to survey damage to GM property and to make plans for renewed production. Soon the assembly plants of Belgium and Denmark were humming again, and Adam Opel AG was rebuilt. Back in Detroit he was too old to fit in with the new GM hierarchy, and he retired, dying there on 27 April 1948.

He married Clara Elizabeth Euler in 1911. They had a son, Semon (see Pontiac), and three daughters, Clara, Elna, and Martha.

JPN

that had been seen on the Buick Skylark. They were the most striking new cars of the 1955 season, and took Chevrolet to a record 1,830,028 sales in the calendar year. The 1956 models were little changed, although the 'eggcrate' grill gave way to a wider and more conventional design. Power was increased to 140bhp in the six and 205bhp in the V8 (225bhp with the Corvette's 4-barrel carburettor). Chevrolet was now a car to be reckoned with in the performance field, with a 0-60mph (0-100km/h) time of around 10 seconds.

The 1957 Chevrolets were even more powerful, with a 4637cc fuel injection engine which gave 283bhp, one horsepower for every cubic inch of its capacity. The smaller 4342cc V8 was still available, as was the 3850cc six, called the Blue Flame since 1953, but it was the big fuel injection engine which captured public attention. Combined with striking body styles, it made the 1957 Chevrolet an outstanding car and a favourite among Chevrolet collectors today. The bodies were, in fact, face-lifted rather than new, as Chevrolet wanted to get a third year of life out of the 1955 shell, but striking colour schemes combined with a redesigned grille and rear end made them seem reasonably different. Studio head Clare McKickan said, 'We did everything we could to change those cars, within the ground rules that we were stuck with'.

The 1958 Chevrolet did have all-new bodies, with four headlamps and dramatic inward canted wings at the rear. This theme was carried still further in the 1959 bodies, which were all new again, with bat-wing fins and horizontal cat's-eye tail lights. The 1958 bodies were replaced after one year because the '59s were shared with certain models of Buick, Oldsmobile, and Pontiac. The fins were more restrained in 1960, and dropped altogether on the 1961 cars. A bigger V8 of 5703cc (315bhp) was available in 1958. Three years later this had been joined by an even more powerful option, a 6703cc giving 360bhp.

The Corvette

Before continuing the development of the regular Chevrolets, we must look at the Corvette, which has been continously developed up to the present day. The idea behind the Corvette came from GM's head of design, Harley Earl, a sports car enthusiast who wished GM had something to offer comparable to the Jaguar XK120. It originated as a dream car to be shown at GM's Motorama in 1953, and used a stock Chevrolet frame shortened by 13in (330mm) to 102in (2590mm), and the engine moved back in the frame by 178mm. This meant that the driver could touch a rear wheel from his seat. The engine was a stock 3850cc Chevrolet six, with power raised from 115 to 150bhp, and transmission was a 2-speed Powergilde automatic, which seemed pretty incongruous on a sports car. The body was in fibreglass, the first use of this material in a quantity-produced car. Three show cars were built, a roadster called the Corvette, a fastback coupé called the Corvair, and a station wagon called the Nomad. The last two remained prototypes, although both names would be used for other Chevrolets later on, but the Corvette was so enthusiastically received by the public at the show that it was put into limited production.

The first cars came off the line at Flint on 10 June 1953, and 315 had been built by the end of the year. Most went to GM executives, although a few were sold to the public at $3550, nearly double the price of any other Chevrolet. The average buyer was put off by crudities such as Plexiglas side curtains and the absence of door handles. To gain access you had to thrust your hand through an open window and slide an interior door release. In 1954 Corvette production was transferred to St Louis, Missouri, and 3640 were made. They did not sell well, and dealers had many left on their hands. It seemed as if the Corvette was a mistake, and there were many in GM who wanted it scrapped. Only 700 were sold in 1955, but for 1956 Chevrolet's new V8 engine was dropped into the Corvette and it was offered with manual transmission, wind-up windows and sculptured body sides. At last it was a serious sports car, with a 118mph (190km/h) top speed, rising to 132mph (212km/h) with the fuel-injected 1957 engine, which put it into Jaguar XK140 territory. Sales immediately improved, reaching 6397 in 1957.

The real success of the Corvette was due to Belgian-born, Russian-educated Zora Arkus-Duntov who worked on the engine and suspension over the next few years, so that by 1962 the 5358cc V8 was giving 380bhp. Production passed the 10,000 mark in 1960, the first year in which the Corvette made a profit for Chevrolet. Its basic lines changed little until 1963, but a removable hard-top was available from 1956 and quad headlamps were featured from 1958. A 4-speed manual gearbox, the first in an American car for many years, was optional from 1957, although the 3-speeder was standard, and the 2-speed automatic was still available.

1982 Chevrolet Cavalier Station wagon.
NATIONAL MOTOR MUSEUM

1989 Chevrolet Beretta GTU coupé.
GENERAL MOTORS

In 1963 came the Sting Ray, which apart from the engine, was a completely new car. The body was restyled and in addition to the roadster there was a striking split-window fastback coupé which outsold the open car. Handling was improved by independent suspension all round, with coil springs at the front and transverse leaf spring and lower wishbones at the rear. The wheelbase was shorter by 4in (102mm), and the track 2in (50mm) narrower. Weight distribution was 48/52, compared with 53/47 for the previous Corvette. The most powerful engine option gave 360bhp, and a top speed of 145mph (235km/h). Although the 3-speed gearbox and automatic were still offered, 83.5 per cent of 1963 Corvette customers chose the 4-speed box, and this proportion increased over the next few years, only to drop when the heavier and larger Stingray came in 1969.

The 1963 Sting Ray was certainly popular, selling over 21,000 cars, compared with the best figure of 14,500 for any previous year. Notable milestones included introduction of disc brakes in 1965, when engine capacity went up to 6490cc. In keeping with the horsepower race, 1966 Sting Rays had 6997cc engines delivering 425bhp. With the 3.08:1 rear axle, theoretical top speed was now 170mph (275km/h). Most powerful of all was the L88 competition engine of 1967–68, which developed a formidable 560bhp.

The Sting Ray name disappeared in 1968 when a restyled Corvette appeared. Designed by Dave Holls, this was based on an experimental car called the Mako Shark 11. It was 7in (180mm) longer, mostly in overhang at the front, and 25kg heavier. The Stingray name (now one word) was revived for the 1969 models which had wider wheels, a stiffer frame, and more room for passengers. These new Corvettes sold very well, 28,566 in 1968 and 38,762 in 1969, although a sign of the times was that coupés outsold roadsters by five to one. Engines in the 1968–70 cars were of 5358 and 6997cc, but in 1971 a 7440cc was offered. This was in fact less powerful than the 7-litre unit, and its size was necessary in view of increasingly strict emission controls. By 1976, when the Corvette achieved record sales of 46,558, the largest engine was the 5358cc, giving only 165 or 205bhp. Chevrolet kept sales high by changing its image from a sports car to a fashionable machine for the upwardly-mobile professional.

Few changes were made to the Corvette until 1983, by which time its familiar shape had become a classic, or just old-fashioned, depending on your point of view. Corvette sales reached a high of 53,807 in 1979, when 113kg were trimmed off the weight, and the front airdam and spoiler were revised. The last of the Holls-designed Corvettes were the 1982 models. These retained the 5358cc engine, now offered with electronic fuel injection, and had, at last, exterior access to the luggage compartment. Their successors, the sixth generation Corvettes, were announced in mid–1983 as 1984 models (officially there were no 1983 models). Production was moved from St Louis to Bowling Green, Kentucky. They were completely restyled with a lower roof line which made them look larger, although they were actually almost 9in (224mm) shorter. The aerodynamic lines were aided by a 64 degree slope to the windscreen. The frame was a Lotus-like backbone chassis welded to an upper birdcage for added strength. The convertible, dropped in 1975, returned to the range in 1986, engineered by the American Sunroof Corp. which also aided GM with the convertible versions of the J-cars.

The next big step in Corvette development was the LT-5 engine, which was new for 1989. This had the same capacity, 5735cc, as the previous engine, but

MICHAEL LAMM

JORDAN, CHUCK (b.1927)

Charles Morrell Jordan grew up near Whittier, California, east of Los Angeles. At age 12, Chuck learned to drive his father's 12-speed Moreland farm truck, which led to his lifelong love for wheeled contraptions of all sorts.

In school and at home, Chuck spent much of his time doodling trucks and cars. His mother and grandmother encouraged him and, on Sundays, at church, Chuck's grandmother would bring along a pad and pencil so he could draw... 'to keep me quiet', he says.

By the time he left high school, Chuck knew he wanted to design cars. He enrolled at MIT and earned a degree in mechanical engineering, taking summer courses at the Chouinard Institute of Art in Los Angeles.

In 1947, at age 19, Chuck won the General Motors Fisher Body Craftsman's Guild auto-design competition. The prize was a $4000 scholarship plus a four-day trip to Detroit. Here he toured GM's research and styling facilities and met Harley Earl. Earl's assistant, Howard O'Leary, told Jordan to 'come back and see us when you graduate'.

Chuck started at GM Styling in 1949 in a truck studio. Here he created, among other things, the flush-sided, trendsetting pickup that went into production as the 1955 Chevrolet Cameo Carrier. The Korean War intervened, but he returned to GM in July 1953 and was soon promoted to chief designer of a special-projects studio. Harley Earl asked Jordan, then 27, to design an articulated twin-diesel crawler tractor for GM's Euclid Division and the streamlined Aerotrain for GM's Electromotive Division.

At that point, Bill Mitchell took Chuck aside and gave him a piece of advice. 'Listen, kid', Mitchell told Jordan, 'if you want to get anyplace around here, you've got to get into cars'. Much as he liked trucks and heavy equipment, Jordan knew Mitchell was right. He subsequently became chief designer of an advanced studio and spearheaded the design the Buick Centurion showcar for the 1956 GM Motorama.

In October 1957, Jordan found himself head of the Cadillac studio, where he completed the 1959 Cadillac and the 1960 facelift. His first all-new Cadillac was the linear, elegant 1961 model.

In 1962, Jordan became Bill Mitchell's assistant in charge of exterior design. He subsequently played a major role in shaping two of his favorite designs, the 1966 Oldsmobile Toronado and 1967 Cadillac Eldorado.

Then in 1967, Mitchell sent Jordan to Opel in Germany as director of design. Over the next three years, Jordan turned Opel from a farmer's car into a sophisticated European contender with models like the Manta, Ascona, Rekord II and the Opel CD showcar.

When he returned to the U.S. in 1970, Jordan shared exterior design responsibilities with Irv Rybicki. Tough times followed, especially with the growing emphasis on downsizing and meeting new government regulations. But times would get even tougher for Jordan.

In 1977, when Mitchell retired, most observers felt that Jordan would follow him into the vice presidency. Mitchell himself wanted Jordan to succeed him. However, during his days at Opel and partly in the States, too, Jordan had gotten a reputation for feistiness. He had a quick temper. His flare-ups were always for the good of the design, but he managed to make enemies in high places. So when Mitchell retired, Irv Rybicki became GM's next vice president of design, and Jordan became Rybicki's second in command.

Jordan was devastated. Due to differences in design philosophy, Jordan and Rybicki were nearly always at odds. These were difficult days for both men and, as it turned out, it was not a memorable era in GM design history.

When he was finally elected to the top spot in October 1986, Jordan realized he'd have only six years before he, too, retired. He was determined to make that time count.

Jordan immediately revived GM's showcar tradition and promptly produced one for each division. The idea was to show the public and the corporation the new direction Jordan had in mind. He considers the more significant of these image and concept cars the Cadillac Voyage, the Chevrolet Sting Ray III, California Camaro, Pontiac Banshee, Olds Vision, Buick Bolero, GM Ultralite and the HX-3 hybrid van.

In terms of production cars, Chuck's legacy includes the 1992 Cadillac STS and Eldorado, 1992 Pontiac Bonneville, 1993 1/2 Camaro/Firebird, 1994 Chevrolet S-10 trucks, 1995 Buick Riviera, 1995 Oldsmobile Aurora and the 1996 Cavalier/Sunfire.

But he also laid a few eggs. The rebodied 1991 Chevrolet Caprice didn't sell nearly so well as the Mitchell version, and the futuristic "dustbuster minivans," which began with the Pontiac Trans Sport concept van, were also less than successful.

Jordan always fought passionately for creative automobile design. He admits to being a tough, uncompromising design leader and has said that his devotion to the design itself sometimes affected his personal relationships. Even so, most agree that he brought excitement and appeal back to the design of GM cars and trucks.

When Jordan turned 65 in 1992, most insiders believed that the vice presidency would pass to his top assistant, Jerry P. Palmer. The only other person in contention was Wayne Cherry. Cherry had spent most of his career overseas, so relatively few people in this country knew him. Palmer, on the other hand, had a high profile as the longtime chief designer of Camaros and Corvettes.

Chuck Jordan retired on 31 October, 1992. Two weeks later, word came down that Cherry would be GM's next design v.p. Palmer got the No.2 spot.

Jordan lives with his wife, Sally, in Southern California, where he consults, writes and enjoys his Ferraris. His son, Mark, works as a top designer for Mazda in nearby Irvine, California.

ML

1980 Chevrolet Corvette Stingray.
NATIONAL MOTOR MUSEUM

was a completely new design, with smaller bore and longer stroke, twin camshafts for each bank of cylinders, and four valves per cylinder. Developed by Lotus, which had recently been acquired by GM, the LT-5 deveploed 385bhp yet still complied with all emission regulations.

The LT-5 engine was installed on the Corvette ZR-1, which also featured Selective Ride Control (optional on lesser Corvettes) and a 6-speed manual transmission which shifted automatically at light throttle openings (below 35 per cent) and low speeds (12–20mph (20–30km/h)). The ZR-1 was a limited edition Corvette, and sales did not exceed 15 per cent of all 27,000 sold in 1991. It was made up to 1995, alongside the less powerful LT-1 models. Although their engines had only two valves per cylinder, improved breathing enabled them to give 300bhp, and their price was little more than half the $64,000 asked for the ZR-1. The fifth generation Corvette appeared in 1997, with new 339bhp engine, still of 5735cc, and a restyled body. A convertible vewrsion was available from 1999. An all-new Corvette was planned for 2002, to share a platform with the Cadillac Evoq.

The Corvair

In the autumn of 1959 Chevrolet launched their entry into the compact car stakes, alongside Ford's Falcon and Plymouth's Valiant. The Falcon was strictly conventional, the Valiant unusual in its slanted engine, but the Corvair broke all the rules as understood by American engineers at the time. The engine was an air-cooled flat-6 mounted at the rear, chassis and body were of unitary construction, and suspension was independent all round, by coils at the front and swing axles at the rear. Not since the 1948 Tucker, which sold only 49 units, had the American public been offered such a radical design, yet they bought 250,000 Corvettes in its first year. The 2288cc engine developed 80bhp and gave a top speed of 85mph (135km/h). The original body styles were a 4-door sedan and 2-door coupé, the latter available in sporty Monza form from May 1960. The Monza had bucket seats and many extra luxuries, later becoming the best selling of the Corvairs. A station wagon joined the range for 1961, but did not sell very well and was dropped two years later. In its place came the Monza convertible which established the Corvair as an enthusiast's car. With the optional 4-speed gearbox and a turbocharged 150bhp engine, a Monza Spider was a real challenge on a winding road compared to an MGA or a Triumph TR. The turbocharger, so widespread today, had never been used in a car before, so Chevrolet engineers were breaking new ground when they installed one in the Monza Spider. The Thompon Valve turbocharger was also used in the contemporary Oldsmobile F-85 Jetfire.

Much has been written about the Corvair's dangerous handling, reaching its peak in the book, *Unsafe at Any Speed*, published in November 1965 by the lawyer and safety crusader Ralph Nader, who did not even hold a driving licence. The Corvair did tend to understeer, but not excessively so long as correct tyre pressures were maintained. Despite several well-publicised lawsuits in the wake of Nader's book, it would not be correct to say that bad publicity killed off the Corvair. As early as May 1965, when Nader was still at his typewriter, word went down the line at GM to stop any further development on the Corvair, just to do enough to satisfy Federal smog and safety requirements. The speciality market, in which the Corvair found itself by 1965, although Chevrolet had intended it to be a regular family car, was being conquered by the Ford Mustang. This had the great advantage that its wide engine compartment could accommodate any size of V8, whereas the Corvair flat-6 could not be enlarged without a complete redesign, and when a 4637cc V8 was tried the handling was so terrible that the idea was quickly forgotten.

Corvair sales slumped badly from 1965, dropping from just over 204,000 to 73,360 in one year, and for 1967 Chevrolet introduced the Camaro, a direct rival for the Mustang, which proved very successful. There was really no place in the line up for the Corvair, and production was run down, from 18,000 in 1967 to only 3103 in 1969, before the last was made in April that year. Some special models of the Corvair were made and sold under separate names; these included the LOST CAUSE and YENKO STINGER.

New Models in the 1960s, Smaller Models in the 1970s

The Chevrolet range became increasingly complex in the 1960s, contrasting with their previous one-model policy. In 1962 the Corvair was supplemented by the Chevy II. This was a direct answer to Ford's Falcon, being a front-engined semi-compact on a 110in (2794mm) wheelbase, with a choice of 2507cc 4-cylinder or 3180cc 6-cylinder engines, and the usual range of sedan and station wagon bodies, also a hard-top and a convertible in the top Nova series. For 1964 Chevrolet bridged the gap between the Chevy II and the full-size Biscayne and Impala with the Chevelle, a more stylish and upmarket car than the Chevy II, with 3180cc 6-cylinder or 4637cc V8 engines. The good-looking Chevelle was a best seller in the 1960s, with 338,286 sales in its first year, 351,272 in 1966, and 369,106 in 1967. The best-selling model of the Chevelle was the upmarket

Malibu, while the most expensive was the high-performance Chevelle SS. The Chevelle was the first Chevrolet to use GM's perimeter-type frame, which was standardised on the full-size cars in 1965. In contrast, the Chevy II had integral construction.

The full-size Chevrolets grew in size and performance in the 1960s. From 1963 to 1968 they came in three ranges, Biscayne, Bel Air, and Impala. A luxury version of the latter was the Caprice Sport Sedan of 1965, which became a separate range from 1966 onwards. In that year the biggest V8 in the Impala (shared with the Corvette), was the 427 (cu in) of 6997cc which gave 425bhp and propelled an Impala SS coupé from 0 to 60mph (0–100km/h) in just over six seconds. The biggest engine ever used in a Chevrolet was the 454 of 7440cc, introduced in 1970 to keep power up in the wake of emission controls. However, at 390bhp it was less powerful than the 427. The top prestige model, and no mean performer either, was the Monte Carlo coupé on the Chevelle chassis, powered by the 454 engine.

In September 1966 came the Camaro, a 'pony car' aimed directly at the highly successful Ford Mustang. Like its rival it used largely off the shelf components, many of them coming from the Chevy II. The body was new, a close-coupled 4-seater in coupé or convertible form. Like the Mustang, the Camaro was designed to appeal to several different markets and therefore came with a choice of five engines, from a relatively tame 3770cc six to a 6490cc V8 developing 375bhp. The 5735cc V8 was specially developed for the Camaro, and soon spread to other Chevrolet models, becoming the most popular of all GM's V8s.

Camaros did well in Trans-Am and NASCAR racing, and continued to shine in stock and modified car events for many years. The most powerful model sold to the public was the Z28 with 4949cc V8 engine developing over 300bhp. It also had heavy duty suspension, power assisted disc brakes on the front wheels, and special broad stripes painted on the bonnet. These extras cost about $750 over the basic price of $2700, but the Z28 sold better than Chevrolet expected. Only 602 were sold in 1967, but 7199 found buyers in 1968 and 19,014 in 1969.

The Camaro was restyled as a '1970½' model, introduced in February 1970. More distinctive than its predecessors, it had a vee-grille and fastback roof line. Styling was by Bill Mitchell, who had made his debut with GM with the Cadillac Sixty Special in 1938. There was only one body style, a coupé, as convertibles were losing popularity. The basic lines of this second generation Camaro remained unchanged until 1981, although the grille sloped backwards from 1974 onwards. The third generation, new for the 1982 season, had a

MICHAEL LAMM

RYBICKI, IRVIN (b.1921)

If he'd had his druthers, Irvin W. Rybicki would have ended up not a car designer but a baseball player. He was born in Detroit on 16 September, 1921, one of three children. His father worked for a Detroit inter-urban railway. His family was very close, and he remembered being spanked only once as a child. He'd stolen 26¢ from his father. 'I'll never forget it', he said, 'because I could see the hurt in my dad's eyes'.

As a teenager, Irv became deeply involved with sports. In high school, he joined the track, tennis, golf, swimming and baseball teams. His greatest love was and still is baseball. At one time, he played on three teams in three different leagues three times a week every spring, summer and fall. He was too small to play professionally, but he played for fun for years after he married, until his wife finally asked him to stop and pay attention to his family.

Rybicki's interest in cars grew out of an early interest in airplanes. At 12 or 13, he dreamed of being a pilot. When Irv was 17, his uncle bought a new, black, 1938 Cadillac 60-Special. Irv was working in his uncle's grocery store at that time, and when his uncle pulled up in the Cadillac, Irv and his cousin, Scotty, ran out and jumped into the front seat. 'I looked around', recalled Irv, 'and I thought to myself, "Holy Christ, is this a beautiful car!" And I thought, "If somebody can make a car look this good, maybe I can do it even better." It inspired me. So I started sketching cars, and from that day on I never stopped. I forgot about airplanes entirely'.

By age 19, Rybicki had put together an informal portfolio, which his dad – unbeknownst to Irv – showed to Jules Andrade at GM Art & Colour. Andrade interviewed Irv but told him immediately that they weren't hiring. It was 1938, the year of recession in the Depression, and Art & Colour was laying people off. But Andrade did put Irv on a list for future consideration. Irv continued to work in his uncle's grocery, kept playing baseball and filled notebooks with car designs.

In 1942, he was drafted and became a sergeant in the tank corps. The firing of cannons left him temporarily deaf. He received a medical discharge in 1943 and went home. 'It was a disaster for me', he recounted. 'I had one helluva time living with that'.

He began studying art at the Meisinger School in Detroit, where he learned perspective and airbrushing. He also took a job at the GM Proving Grounds in Milford, Michigan. An engineer there noticed his futuristic car drawings pinned to the office walls and suggested that Irv think about the Harley Earl school. He enrolled in 1946.

Of the 15 students who started the class that year, only he and Carl Renner finished. After graduation, Rybicki went into Bill Mitchell's Cadillac studio, where he remained for five years. He then spent five more years in Art Ross's Oldsmobile studio, five years with Paul Gillan's Pontiac design group, and finally back to Oldsmobile, where he took over as chief designer in May 1957.

One of his proudest accomplishments during that period was the creation of the 1959 Olds front end. He and his good friend, Jack N. Humbert, designed it together, each working independently at home. The design took shape over the telephone. Rybicki said that he and Humbert "talked" the front end onto paper. Harley Earl was so taken with the Olds frontal theme that he asked Ned Nickles to adapt it to the 1960 Corvair.

In 1977, General Motors elected Irv Rybicki vice president of design. He replaced Bill Mitchell, whose choice for the job had been Chuck Jordan. Mitchell was shocked by the choice, Jordan was devastated, but no one was more surprised than Rybicki. GM's executive committee simply did not want another volatile, unpredictable, autocratic designer. Jordan, they felt, was too much in the mold of Earl and Mitchell.

Rybicki ran GM Design Staff without histrionics and in a businesslike manner, which management liked. Ironically, he selected Jordan as his design director--his second in command. The two never saw eye to eye and fought constantly, albeit quietly. Designs done on Rybicki's watch were adequate but uninspired. Nothing stood out as industry-leading or cutting-edge in the way that Earl and Mitchell had led. It's true that Rybicki's vice presidency coincided with one of the toughest and lowest periods in American automaking. Perhaps no one could have done much better. But the Rybicki years – 1977 to 1984 – are still talked about as the nadir of GM design.

When Rybicki retired, he moved to Florida and never looked back.

ML

1999 Chevrolet Camaro coupé.
GENERAL MOTORS

radically redesigned body styled by Jerry Palmer with a family resemblance to the 1984 Corvette. Although it looked long and low, it was 18in (460mm) shorter and its weight was cut by about 990lb (450kg) to 2495lb (1134kg). Engine options were a 2471cc four, 3752 V6 and V8s of 4375 and 4998cc. The fourth generation Camaro was launched in December 1992, no longer with the 4-cylinder engine but with a 3350cc V6 and 5665cc V8. A 3791cc V6 was available from 1995, and the smaller V6 was dropped in 1996.

At the beginning of the 1970s the smallest Chevrolet was the Nova, formerly the Chevy II, with 4, 6 or 8-cylinder engines from 2507 to 5030cc, but for 1971 it was undercut by a new subcompact, the Vega. This all-new car in the Ford Pinto class had a 2294cc single-ohc 4-cylinder aluminium block engine, and came in four body styles, 2-door sedan, hatchback coupé, station wagon, and delivery van. It sold 400,000 units in its first year, but its popularity soon waned as the public discovered severe rust problems, while the engine was unreliable. Annual sales dropped to around 100,000 by the middle of the decade, and the Vega was replaced in 1977 by the Chevette. Two sporty Vegas were the Monza introduced in 1975, a Mitchell-styled car which had overtones of the Ferrari GTC/4, and the Cosworth Vega. This had an engine reworked by Cosworth Engineering in England, with a 16-valve head and a shorter stroke to bring it into the under 2-litre racing class. Sadly its performace was not up to enthusiasts' expectations, and only 3508 were made, in 1975 and 1976. The Monza, which shared a body with the Buick Skylark, survived the demise of its parent Vega, and was made until 1980.

The larger Chevrolets were sharply downsized for 1977, the Impala losing 11in (280mm) in overall length, 45in(1140mm) in wheelbase and 550lb (250kg) in weight. A 4096cc six was now the standard engine, with optional V8s of 4998 or 5735cc. Although not so fast, the new Impalas and Monte Carlos had much better fuel consumption, and could still carry six adults in comfort. In 1980 they lost another 99lb (45kg), and the straight-6 was replaced by a 3752cc V6. Those who wanted a V8 had a choice of 4375 or 4998cc units, although the station wagon could still be had with a 5735cc Oldsmobile V8 or a diesel of the same size.

International Connections
Up to the end of the 1970s the Chevrolet was as American as apple pie, but soon they were not only sharing models with other countries, but an increasing number of Chevrolet-badged cars were actually made abroad. The first example of this trend was the Chevette, one of the T-cars made in Brazil, in England as the Vauxhall Chevette, in Germany as the Opel Kadett, in Australia as the Holden Gemini, and in Japan as the Isuzu Gemini. It came in two engine sizes, 1373cc and 1599cc, and was originally made only as a 3-door hatchback – a five-door

1976 Chevrolet (i) Chevette hatchback.
NATIONAL MOTOR MUSEUM

model was added for 1978. Sales were slow to start with, as the American public was not accustomed to such small cars, and the fuel crisis of 1973–74 was receding a couple of years later. However, by the early 1980s Chevettes were selling around 200,000 per year, adequate even by Chevrolet's standards. The smaller engine was dropped after 1977, but a 1818cc diesel was available from 1981. The Chevette gave way to Japanese-made designs after 1987. These were the 993cc 3-cylinder Suzuki Swift, sold as the Chevrolet Sprint from 1984, the 1971cc 4-cylinder Isuzu Gemini (Chevrolet Spectrum) and 1587cc Toyota Corolla, sold as the Chevrolet Nova. This was actually made in the United States, by a company jointly owned by GM and Toyota, called New United Motor Manufacturing Co., of Fremont, California. From 1989 the imports were handled by a subdivison of Chevrolet marketing under its own name, GEO, but this was brought to an end in 1996 and the three Geo models, Metro (formerly Chevrolet Sprint), Prizm (Nova), and Tracker (Suzuki Samurai) became Chevrolets again.

The other international car was the Cavalier, introduced for 1982 with a transverely-mounted 1842cc 4-cylinder engine driving the front wheels, and made as a 4-door sedan or 2-door coupé. It was also made by other GM divisions, as the Buick Skyhawk, Cadillac Cimarron, Oldsmobile Firenza, and Pontiac Sunbird. Foreign versions were the Vauxhall Cavalier, Opel Ascona and Holden Camira. A convertible was made for 1983, Chevrolet's first open car since 1976, and for 1984 capacity was increased to 1989cc. The 1985 Z24 coupé came with a 2834cc V6 as standard. The Cavalier was a great success with American buyers – sales exceeded 270,000 for the 1982 model year, rising to more than 462,000

1999 Chevrolet Corvette convertible.
GENERAL MOTORS

1978 Chevrolet (iii) Opala coupé.
NATIONAL MOTOR MUSEUM

for 1984. With several restylings, it was still made in 1999, in sedan and coupé forms, with 2190cc 116bhp 8-valve, or 2392cc 151bhp 16-valve engines.

Larger Chevrolets also went over to front drive in the 1980s. The long-lived Nova gave way in 1979 to the Citation, one of GM's X-car family with choices of 2471cc 4-cylinder or 2835cc V6, both transversely mounted, and sedan or coupé bodies. For 1982 Chevrolet brought out another front-drive car in the same class as the Citation. This was the Celebrity, an A-class car, which shared a body shell with the Buick Century, Oldsmobile Cira, and Pontiac 6000. The same engine options as in the Citation were offered, with the addition of a 4294cc V6 diesel. The Citation and Celebrity were offered together until 1985, after which the older car was withdrawn. In 1987 Chevrolet launched two new models which were unusual in that they were exclusive to Chevrolet, with no equivalents from other GM divisions. Made at a dedicated plant at Wilmington, Delaware, the Corsica sedan and Beretta coupé were aimed at the quality small car market which had been heavily penetrated by European and Japanese products. Although their engines were the familiar 1991cc 4 and 2835cc V6, they had attractive modern lines and sold well; 225,000 sold in the calendar year 1987, although production did not start until March. A Beretta convertible was introduced in 1990. They were made up to 1997. A new range for 1989 was the Lumina, one size up from the Beretta/Corsica, and made in sedan, coupé or 8-seater MPV forms. The latter was almost identical to the Pontiac Trans Sport. Engines were the 2474cc four or 3108cc V6. For 1991 a twin-cam 200bhp V6 enlarged to 3392cc was available in the Z34 Lumina sedan.

At the top of the range were the classic rear-drive Caprice sedan and Monte Carlo coupé with 4300cc V6 and 5001cc V8 engines. The Caprice was completely restyled for 1990, a bulbous, curvaceous tribute to middle America's love affair with large rear-drive cars. A cousin to the Buick Roadmaster, it was nearly 216in (5482mm)long, and 3in (76mm) wider than the old Caprice. However, its shape gave it a drag coefficient of only 0.33, compared with 0.41 for its predecessor. The standard engine was the 5001cc V8, replaced in 1994 by a 4342cc V8.

There was also a high-performance Caprice variant, the Impala SS, with the Corvette LT-1's 5735cc engine. The Caprice/Impala was made up to the end of 1996 when GM abandoned the large, rear-drive theme, probably for good, although they were mourned by policemen and taxi drivers, for whom special Caprices had been made, as well as by conservative 60+ drivers.

The demise of the Caprice left Chevrolet with an all-front drive and transverse engine range, apart from the Corvette and Camaro. In addition to the Metro, Prizm and Cavalier, in 1999 there was the Alero coupé and sedan, similar to the Oldsmobile Alero but using the Chevrolet name for the export market, the mid-sized Malibu and large Impala.

NG

Further Reading
Chevrolet, A History from 1911, Beverley Rae Kimes and Robert C. Ackerson, Automobile Quarterly Publications, 1984.
Chevrolet 1911–1985, Richard M. Langworth and Jan P. Norbye, Publications International Ltd, 1985.
Camaro! From Challenger to Champion, Gary L. Witzenborg, Automobile Quarterly Publications.
Corvette: America's star-spangled sports car, Karl E. Ludvigsen, Automobile Quarterly Publications.

CHEVROLET (ii) (RA) 1962 to date
General Motors Argentina S.A., Buenos Aires.
General Motors Argentina S.A. was created in 1925. At first they only sold Chevrolets imported from the USA but not long afterwards, other GM makes were also distributed. Cars were assembled in Buenos Aires at a rate of 1,250 units per month. Commercial vehicle production started in 1960 and, in 1962, a local version of the Chevy II with 6-cylinder pushrod engine was presented. Early ones, officially designated Chevrolet 400, had an engine capacity of 3179cc, but later on, the Chevrolet Super was offered, with 3769cc engine. The smaller engine soldiered on in the Chevrolet Special. In 1967 the Chevrolet Super Sport was offered too, with 4097cc, 150bhp engine, but clothed in the same 4-door sedan body. This Chevrolet range, plus some local Opel variants, continued until 1978, when the factory was closed down. However, production of Brava and Silverado pick-ups was resumed almost immediately, and in 1981 the Opel K180, very similar to the Brazilian Chevette, was introduced. The Kadett 1.8 was produced until 1996. The Monza 2.0GL was produced from 1994 to 1997 and the Omega GLS 2.2 was produced only in 1995 and 1996. The Corsa and the Vectra were both introduced in 1994 and were still in production in 1999. The Omega was reintroduced in 1998. Introduced in 1998, were the Astra 4-door saloon and station wagon.

ACT

CHEVROLET (iii) (BR) 1964 to date
G.M. do Brasil SA, São Caetano do Sul.
Twenty-five Chevrolets a day were assembled at the President Wilson Street plant, in São Paulo, from 1925 onwards. However, not until 1954 were truck cabs made locally, and the first local Chevrolet engine was produced in 1958. The first true Brazilian passenger vehicle made by G.M. was the C-141, a station wagon with high ground clearance suitable for bad roads. Its 4.3-litre 6-cylinder engine was a direct descendant of the original 1929 cast-iron Chevrolet 6, and the last of this series to be made anywhere in the world. In 1969 the Opala series of sedans and coupés of mixed Chevrolet and Opel Rekord lineage were presented; engines were either 2.5-litre fours or 3.8-litre sixes. The latter was enlarged to 4.1-litres and developed 140bhp for 1972. The Opala line was continued until 1982. By then, the expensive Diplomat version had four speeds and air conditioning as standard. G.M. do Brasil was first with the Chevette (T-car) in 1974: engine was a 1.4-litre 5-bearing four with cogged-belt ohc. Initially only drum brakes were fitted; front disc brakes arrived on the 1976 models. In 1988 came the 1.6-litre option, and the twin barrel carburettor. Also, a diesel-engine version was produced. In its 1988 form, the Chevette lasted until 1992, when the last units were sold. In the meantime, in 1985, the Monza, with 1.8-litre engine had been born. It was succeeded by the Mega in 1997.

The Corsa sedan with 1.6-litre engine came in 1994. In 1999, the Corsa was produced in 2 and 4-door versions, with 1-litre or 1.6-litre petrol engines or 1.7-litre diesel engines. The Vectra, a 4-door sedan with a 2-litre engine, was introduced in 1994 and was still being produced in 1999. The Astra sedan, in

2-door form with a 2-litre engine, started to be produced in Brazil in late 1998, being exported to Argentina, one of Brazil's partners in the Mercosur, a common-market also formed by Uruguay and Paraguay. Sometimes Brazilian Chevrolets have other, less probable connections. For example, in 1996 General Motors kicked off a joint-venture to assemble Chevrolet Blazer off-road vehicles in Yelabuga, in the north of Tatarstan, one of the most industrialised of the republics of the Russian Federation. The venture used Brazilian-made car kits while seeking to increase the amount of locally-produced components.

ACT

CHEVROLET (iv) (ZA) 1968–1983

General Motors South Africa (Pty) Ltd, Port Elizabeth.

The South African branch of GM had their own make, the RANGER (iv), but also made other variations on Holden, Opel, and Vauxhall designs under the Chevrolet name. These included Vauxhall Viva/Firenzas with 2494cc Chevrolet engines, and large sedans powered by V8 engines which were essentially Holdens, but sold under the names Kommando, Constantia, and De Ville. These came with a choice of manual or automatic transmission. In 1978 came the Opel Ascona-derived Chevair, and the Nomad, a Chevrolet-powered light 4 × 4. The 1981 range consisted of the Chevair, the Rekord with 4-cylinder Opel or Chevrolet engines, the Holden-derived Commodore, and a 4.1-litre version of the Opel Senator. In 1983 GM of South Africa discontinued the Chevrolet name, and turned to the asssembly of Opels.

NG

CHEVRON (i) (GB) 1965 to date

A.D. Bennett & Co. Ltd, Salford, Lancashire.

The main force behind Chevron was Derek Bennett, who first made a reputation for himself as a midget car racer on speedway tracks in northern England in the 1950's. Derek built several Bennett Specials, for the 750 and 1172 formulae, and for Formula Junior, and prepared cars for others. The breakthrough came in 1965 with the Clubmans car, the Chevron B1, powered by a Ford 1500cc engine. Just two were made, but they were immensely successful in racing. It is often assumed that the 'B' stood for Bennett, but actually it stood for John Bridges, a long-time Bennett supporter who entered cars under the banner of 'Red Rose Motors'.

The following year saw four production Clubmans cars (B2) and the first mid-engined GT, the twin-cam Ford engined 1598cc Chevron B3. This featured a fully-triangulated spaceframe made from round, square and oval tubing, with monocoque sills and bulkheads, which made for a particularly strong cockpit area, while the pretty fibreglass body was aerodynamically efficient. With only slight modifications, the body was to feature on all Chevron GT cars for the next few years and it has become a clssic. Over the next two years the GT concept was developed through the B4 (a one-off, with a 1991cc BMW engine), B5 (a one-off with a 1938cc BRM V8 engine) and the B6, which was available with either a Ford or a BMW unit. One only of the Ford (1598cc twin-cam) was produced, but five of the BMW version were made. All of these cars won first time out.

By the time the B8 appeared in 1968, only 18 Chevrons of any description had been made. This splendid little GT car, which was highly successful in Group 4 racing, but could also be driven on the road, would establish Chevron and 44 examples would be made, 35 of them with BMW engines. Within five years Chevron had leapt from being the maker of two Clubmans cars to becoming an important constructor making its mark in Formula Three, Formula B (Atlantic) and Formula Two while also introducing the B16 in GT and Spyder versions. The B16 was designed solely to race and, among other successes, it won the European 2-litre Sports Car series.

When Derek Bennett died after a hang gliding accident in March 1978, however, Chevron went into rapid decline largely because his sisters, who inherited his shares, would not, or could not, provide sufficient investment. The company name has since been sold several times, largely to acquire the right to make spares though, occasionally, there have been attempts to revive Chevron in motor racing. The current owner of the name built a prototype B8R with a 2-litre Warrior engine, an Alfa Romeo transaxle and a leather interior. It was capable of over 150mph. For various reasons, plans to put it in production with Type Approval were shelved.

MJL

Further Reading
Chevron – The Derek Bennett Story, Gordon David, Patrick Stephens.

CHEVRON (ii) (GB) 1990 to date

Chevron Cars, Piddletrenthide, Dorset.

Chevron, the celebrated sports/GT racing manufacturer of the 1960s, revived its classic B16, the European Sports Car Championship winning racer of 1969. It followed the original layout closely, including a semi-space frame and monocoque centre section, aluminium sills and floorpan, non-stressed glassfibre coupé body, and coil-over-damper double wishbones up front and wishbone-and-radius-arms at the rear. A modern engine was chosen in the 215bhp 2.0-litre Cosworth, or alternatively Renault GTA/A610 or Toyota 16V. The Renault GTA also donated its transmission. Options included Kevlar bodywork, air conditioning and a racing version. Chevron then relaunched its 1968 B8 model (44 of which had been made originally) as a road or race car in 1992. Initially, complete turn-key cars were sold at prices from around £40,000 although kit versions became available in 1994. The original mid-mounted BMW engine was swapped for a choice of Alfa Romeo or Ford twin cam 16-valve engines, mated to an Alfa 33 transaxle, and a top speed of up to 170mph (273km/h) was claimed. The cars were actually built by Scott Ellis Racing. The Pick Me Up of 1994 marked a complete change of direction, being an Austin Metro-based utility car sold as a budget kit. Under the boxy glassfibre-and-aluminium body sat a substantial steel tube chassis, body options encompassing a flatbed, soft top and 2- or 4-seaters.

CR

CHEVRON (iii) (NZ) 1991–1997

Chevron Engineering, Auckland, North Island.

A clubman-type vehicle made by Evan Fray, the Chevron used the Vauxhall Viva front suspension and rear axle on a ladder frame of 38mm diameter tube. A wide range of engines, from 1600cc Ford or Toyota to 4.4-litre Leyland Australia or 5-litre Ford V8s were fitted. A popular clubman, 218 had been produced by 1996 and examples had been exported to Australia, New Guinea and Japan.

MG

CHEYENNE (F) 1992–c.1996

Automobiles Cheyenne, Sambris.

In style the Cheyenne vaguely resembled a Willys Jeep and was designed to perform a combined utility-recreational role. It used a 1.0-litre Peugeot engine (from 1995 a 1.2-litre Renault Twingo unit) driving the front wheels only, mounted in a galvanised steel chassis. The very basic bodywork was in glassfibre, with a roll-over cage and optional doors.

CR

CHI & THE GANG (TAIWAN) Mid–1990s

Chi & The Gang, Taiwan.

The R390 Spyder was a sports car sold in kit and turn-key form in Taiwan. Its Ferrari-esque open bodywork was available in glassfibre or carbon-fibre. Double wishbone suspension was employed all round in a space frame chassis, and engine options encompassed 2-litre Cosworth turbo up to Chevrolet 5.7-litre V8 (up to 500bhp was quoted).

CR

CHIC (AUS) 1923–1926

Chic Cars Ltd, Adelaide, South Australia.

The concept of Clarence Chick, this was an assembled car using British components, the prototype having been made by F.W. Bond in Yorkshire. The engine and gearbox were by Meadows while a Lucas magneto, Zenith carburettor, Gallay radiator, Rubery-Owen frame, Woodhead springs, and C.A.V. electrics were used. Front-wheel brakes were available, as was the choice of disc or Sankey artillery wheels. Two sizes were made, a 14/40hp, 4-cylinder on a 118in (2997mm) wheelbase and a 6-cylinder 18/48hp on a 128in (3251mm) chassis; roadster, tourer, and saloon bodies by T.J. Richards & Sons being fitted. During its currency it was stated that the chassis were built at Wolverhampton but, later, MONARCH of Birmingham was the nominated supplier. More than 40 had been sold by the time of receivership in 1926.

MG

1925 Chiribiri Tipo Milano 10.4hp saloon.
NATIONAL MOTOR MUSEUM

CHICAGO (i) (US) 1895–1899
Chicago Motor Vehicle Co., Harvey, Illinois.
The main products of this company were horse-drawn carriages, despite their name, but they offered to equip any of their vehicles with a 'double-cylinder hydro-carbon motor'. It is not known how many were so equipped, although one was entered in the 1895 *Chicago Times-Herald* Race. The company continued in business after the turn of the century making commercial vehicles, but went bankrupt in late 1904.
NG

CHICAGO (ii) (US) 1902
Chicago Motocycle Co., Chicago, Illinois.
This company announced a car powered by a curious engine that was said to be able to run on hot air as well as petrol or paraffin fuel. Instead of a water jacket to cool the cylinders, it had an asbestos jacket to conserve the heat. Starting required the application of a torch to the cylinder head. Whether it ever ran is uncertain, but for 1903 the car's name was changed to CALORIC.
NG

CHICAGO (iii) (US) 1905–1907
Chicago Automobile Mfg Co., Chicago, Illinois.
This was a late entry into the steam car market, powered by a 25/30hp V4 engine, with 2-speed transmission and shaft drive and a 5-seater tourer body. Starting time from cold was claimed to be 2 minutes, but this would seem to be highly optimistic as it is only 30 seconds longer than the sophisticated Doble of the 1920s. With a *Roi des Belges* body, the price was $2500.
NG

CHICAGO (iv) (US) 1913–1916
Chicago Electric Motor Co., Chicago, Illinois.
The Chicago Electric was a fairly typical electric car offered mostly in closed form, although there was a cabrio-roadster in the 1915 range. The broughams were described as 'front drive' and 'rear drive', but the former did not have drive to the front wheels, merely a driver's controls in one of the front seats, whereas in the rear-drive brougham the driver sat in a rear seat and peered over the shoulders of the passengers in front. The appearance of the car was characterised by a domed roof over the door, to allow easy entrance for those wearing high hats. This was also seen on some Pierce Arrows.

An attraction at the 1914 Chicago Automobile Show was a brougham heavily endowed with brocade, silk and the crossed keys of St Peter in gold, worked into the cloth. The doors carried the Papal Crest, for the car was to be a gift from a group of Catholic laymen in Chicago to Pope Pius X. Its fate is a mystery, for there is no record of its arrival at the Vatican.
NG

CHICAGO MOTOR BUGGY (US) 1908
Chicago Motor Buggy Co., Chicago, Illinois.
This was a typical high-wheeler with 15hp 2-cylinder air-cooled engine. It was unfortunate that the BLACK company was also making a car called the Chicago Motor Buggy, and their's was cheaper. This Chicago did not last more than one season.
NG

CHICAGOAN (US) 1952–1953
Triplex Industries Ltd, Blue Island, Illinois.
This fibreglass-bodied 2-seat roadster was based on Ford running gear coupled with a Willys 6 or a V8, and was sold in kit or fully assembled form. In 1954 its name was changed to TRIPLEX.
HP

CHICK ENTERPRISES (US) 1994 to date
Chick Enterprises, Butler, New Jersey.
Due to the popularity of the 1988 Francis Ford Coppola film *Tucker, the Man and the Dream*, there was a wave of interest in Tucker cars. Chick DeLorenzo was a kit car builder who owned an original Tucker. He also worked with Coppola on the film and was able to pull a set of moulds from Coppola's car when it was being restored. He sold a basic kit that fitted Ford, Lincoln, and Chevrolet chassis, with bodies made by EXOTIC ENTERPRISES.
HP

CHIEF (i) (US) 1908
Chief Manufacturing Co., Buffalo, New York.
This was a 2-seater runabout with a 10/12hp air-cooled 2-cylinder 2-stroke engine, with friction transmission and single-chain drive. It was priced at $600, but few were made.
NG

CHIEF (ii) (US) 1911
Chief Motor Car Co., Detroit, Michigan.
The second car to bear the name Chief lasted no longer than the first, but it was more distinctive, having a V8 engine three years before Cadillac announced theirs. The 5-seater tourer body could be converted to a light delivery truck. Probably only a prototype was made.
NG

CHILTERN (GB) 1919–1920
Vulcan Motor & Engineering Co. Ltd, Dunstable, Bedfordshire.
This was a medium-sized tourer powered by a 1.8-litre 4-cylinder Dorman KNO engine. The company name hints at links with the VULCAN (i), and it is believed that Vulcan chassis were delivered to Dunstable to be fitted with different radiators and locally-made bodywork. The similarity of mounting gearbox and torque tube also indicated that the Chiltern was Vulcan-based. Possibly as many as 100 were made.
NG

CHIMERA *see* A.D.

CHIMO (CDN) 1980–c.1988
1980–1985 Customotive Inc., St Laurent, Quebec.
1985 Customotive Inc., Ottawa, Ontario.
1985–c.1988 Image Inc., Smiths Falls, Ontario.
This was an originally-styled coupé, and at the time the only glassfibre car being made in Canada. Almost inevitably it was based on a VW Beetle floorpan, with VW, Ford V6 or Mazda rotary power options, and its angular fastback bodywork made use of a Chevette windscreen.
CR

CHIRIBIRI (I) 1913–1927
Chiribiri & Co., Turin.
Born in Venice, Antonio Chiribiri worked for Florentia, Isotta-Fraschini, and Zust before setting up on his own in 1910. At first he made aero engines, but entered the car business at the request of Count Gustavo Brunetta d'Usseaux. The light cars were called SIVA, after the Hindu goddess Shiva, but after about 100 had been made the Count lost interest, and Chiribiri started making them under his own name. They had 8/10hp 4-cylinder monobloc engines, alloy pistons, and worm drive. In 1915, with an enlarged bore, they became the 10/12hp. As Chiribiri was increasingly involved with war work, he sold the components to Alfredo Gallanzi, who made the car under the name ARDITA.

In 1919 Chiribiri brought out a new design, the Normale with 1592cc 4-cylinder side-valve engine, reduced to 1499cc in 1922 to bring it within the 1.5-litre class for competitions. Touring models with this engine were the Roma,

Monza, and Milano, and the twin-ohc sports models were the Monza Normale and Monza Corsa. The latter was supercharged and only three were made. One was Tazio Nuvolari's first racing car, while the others were driven by Antonio Chiribiri's sons. Chiribiris were exported to France and Britain, but production was never large. In 1927 the company went into liquidation, the factory being taken over by Lancia.

NG

CHIYODA (J) c.1932–1935
Tokyo Gas & Electric Engineering Co., Tokyo.
This company built trucks from 1918 under the name T.G.E., renaming them Chiyoda in 1931. The name was that of the Imperial Household's location, and celebrated the delivery of a truck to the Household. Most Chiyodas were trucks, but a small number of passenger cars were built for government officials and senior army officers. They had 6-cylinder engines of about 4-litres capacity, and were made as tourers or sedans. The Model H was a sedan similar in appearance to the 1935 Pontiac, and the Model HS was a 6-wheeled open tourer for seven passengers.

NG

CHOTA see BUCKINGHAM

CHRISTCHURCH CAMPBELL (GB) 1921–1922
J. Campbell Ltd, Christchurch, Hampshire.
This was a light car powered by a 1436cc 10.8hp Coventry-Simplex 4-cylinder side-valve engine with Meadows gearbox. The chassis was priced at £395, and an open 2-seater at £495, very high figures for what was an undistinguished assembled car. No more than six were made, together with a final model which used a tuned 11.9hp Dorman engine.

NG

CHRISTIANE HUIT (F) 1927–1929
Automobiles Christiane Huit, Rennes, Île-et-Vilaine.
Designed and built by A. Andrieux, the Christiane Huit was, as one would gather from its name, an 8-cylinder car, although the first chassis used a Citroën B2 engine converted to ohvs. This was replaced by a 1980cc single-ohc 32-valve straight-8 engine built by Andrieux. Twin Cozette carburettors were used, and the car had a top speed of 90–93mph (145–150km/h) with a 4-seater sports body in which the rear seats were staggered. Andrieux competed in a number of local hill climbs and sprints and finished creditably in the 1927 Targa Florio (run that year in Brittany). He then built a lighter car, shorter and strictly a 2-seater, with disc brakes. He intended to make cars with similar engines in 2-, 2.5- and 3-litre sizes, but postponed his plans because of the Depression, and never revived them.

NG

CHRISTIE (US) 1904–1911
1904–1905 Christie Iron Works, New York, New York.
1905–1907 Direct Action Motor Car Co., New York, New York.
1908–1911 Walter Christie Automobile Co., New York, New York.
J. Walter Christie, the first serious American exponent of front-wheel drive was a prominent contender in early auto racing, initially as a participant at Daytona-Ormond Beach, Florida in 1904 and notably as the first American contender in the French Grand Prix three years later at the wheel of an updated much heavier racing car. In 1905 he began work on a 50hp front-drive car which, completed in 1906, was fitted with a body by Healey and with a price tag of $6500. This was ostensibly the prototype for others to come. They never came and shortly after its completion, his Direct Action Motor Car Company failed. After forming a new company, Christie decided to build a front-drive taxicab. Four of these were initially planned as pilot models, three of which were completed for service in New York City. Plagued by necessary finances, Christie turned his attention toward the conversion of fire apparatus from horse-drawn to self-propelled vehicles. Continuing his front-wheel drive principle, he invented a tractor which, when attached to the front of horse-driven steamers, aerials and ladder trucks, was able to pull them to the scene of fires or other related emergencies under its own power. In 1911 Christie formed the Front Drive Motor Co. in Hoboken, New Jersey, where for several years countless horses were put out to pasture as from 600 to 800 pieces of fire apparatus were converted to self-propelled status. Christie died in 1944.

KM

1906 Christie 50hp tourer.
KEITH MARVIN

1926 Chrysler (i) 70 roadster.
NICK GEORGANO/NATIONAL MOTOR MUSEUM

Further Reading
'The Front-wheel Drives of John Walter Christie, Inventor', Stan Grayson, *Automobile Quarterly*, Vol. XIV, No.3.

CHRITON (GB) 1904
Chriton Automobile Co., Saltburn-by-the-Sea, Yorkshire.
Several models were advertised by this company located on the North Yorkshire coast, from a 10hp 4-cylinder shaft drive 2-seater to a 24hp four and 30hp six, with higher powered cars made to order. The 10hp was certainly built, as one competed in the 600 Mile Small Car Trials held in August 1904. The larger cars may well have existed only on paper.

NG

CHRYSLER (i) (US) 1924 to date
Chrysler Corporation, Detroit, Michigan.
Walter Chrysler had plenty of experience in the motor industry before he launched the car bearing his own name, having been president of the Buick Division of General Motors, and the saviour of Willys Overland and Maxwell-Chalmers. The first Chrysler car grew out of his involvement with the latter firm, for he saw that there was a gap in the market for an up-to-date car with above average performance which could be made in sufficient numbers to keep the price low. There was no one at Maxwell who could produce such a design, nor did he have the qualifications himself, so he called in a team of three talented engineers who had caught his attention when he was at Willys Overland. They were Carl Breer (1883–1970), Owen Skelton (1886–1969) and Fred Zeder (1886–1951). In 1921 they formed their own design consultancy, ZSB Engineering. Chrysler called them 'The Three Musketeers' and put them to work in a vacant part of Willys' Elizabeth, New Jersey factory. They refined a design that they had already worked on while at Willys; the larger version was bought by Billy Durant and marketed as the FLINT, while the smaller became the basis for the new Chrysler.

1934 Chrysler (i) Airflow sedan.
LANCE HENNINGSEN

1952 Chrysler (i) Custom Imperial sedan.
NATIONAL MOTOR MUSEUM

The car they came up with had a 3301cc side-valve 6-cylinder engine with a 4.7:1 cr, higher than the US average at the time, which was closer to 4:1. Other features were aluminium pistons, an oil filter, full pressure lubrication, and hydraulic 4-wheel brakes. The engine developed 68bhp, so it was not unreasonable to call »it the Chrysler 70, a title which was continued until 1927. Nine body styles were offered, styled by Oliver Clark, formerly with Studebaker, at prices from $1335 for a 5-seater tourer to $3725 for a town car.

Because the new car was still a prototype, Chrysler was refused permission for a stand at the New York Auto Show in January 1924. Instead he exhibited it in the lobby of the Hotel Commodore, headquarters hotel for the show, where it attracted more attention than it would have done among countless other cars at the show. Hundreds of orders were placed, which encouraged the bankers to

let Chrysler have the money he needed to start production. The Chalmers was dropped, and the new Chryslers came down the line a few months after the launch at the Hotel Commodore. Sales during the first year were a very encouraging 32,000.

There were several important developments during 1925. In June the Maxwell Motor Corp. was reorganised as the Chrysler Corp., and for the following year the Maxwell Four was revamped and renamed the Chrysler 58. After a year of using Fisher bodies, Chrysler bought the Kercheval body plant in Detroit, which became their own bodyworks. Also in 1925 Chrysler Canada was formed, assembling cars in the former Maxwell factory at Windsor, Ontario, and production of marine engines began in Detroit, a business which is still carried on today.

From the start the Chrysler 70 had a performance well above average, with a top speed of 70–75mph 112–120km/h), and the name soon began to figure in competitions. As well as having numerous successes in hill climbs in the US, Chrysler was the only major US manufacturer to enter cars at Le Mans before World War II; their best performance was in 1928, when two roadsters finished third and fourth, beaten only by a Bentley and a Stutz, both much more expensive cars.

Chrysler offered a three-car range for 1926, the 3044cc 4-cylinder Model F-58, the 3582cc 6-cylinder Model G-70 and the 4719cc 6-cylinder Series E-80, to which the name Imperial was given. This was used for senior models in the Chrysler range up to 1954, when it became a make in its own right for 20 years. Styling features of the 1926–30 Imperials were the Vauxhall-like bonnet flutes, which brought an unsuccessful suit for patent infringement from the British firm. The Imperial took Chrysler into a higher price bracket, up to $5475 for the 7-seater town car, where they were competing with Lincoln and Cadillac, but sales were very good at 48,254 for the 1927 model year. Overall, Chrysler sold 182,195 cars in 1927, putting them in seventh place among US car makers. The 1927 figure was not exceeded until 1965. No other new company became so successful so quickly, but they did have the great advantage of a large dealer network, nearly 4000, inherited from Maxwell and Chalmers. They soon set up other foreign operations to follow that in Canada; S.A. Chrysler opened in Antwerp, Belgium in 1926, and Chrysler Motors Ltd at Kew, near London, in 1927. Several Kew-assembled cars were fitted with British-built bodies, and in the 1930s Plymouths and DeSotos were sold in the UK as Chryslers, as the British public were not familiar with these American marques.

In contrast to the upmarket Imperial, Chrysler moved into a lower price bracket with his acquisition in 1928 of Dodge Brothers which made medium-priced cars, and then into Ford/Chevrolet territory when he launched the Plymouth in 1928. The 4-cylinder Chrysler was sold under the Plymouth name from 1929 onwards, which explains why Chrysler sales dropped to only 92,034 in what was a boom year for the industry as a whole. If the Plymouth figures were added, the total was 185,626.

For 1930 4-speed gearboxes were introduced, but they were not really necessary with the flexible 6-cylinder engine, and they were dropped for the following season. Major changes were seen in 1931, with a new pointed radiator grille styled after that of the Cord L-29, and four new straight-8 engines. Three of these were for the medium-priced cars, of 3938, 4273 and 4622cc, and the fourth was a massive 6306cc unit for the new Series CG Imperial. With a 145in (3683mm) wheelbase, it was one of the largest cars made in the United States at the time. Four styles of factory bodywork were available, as well as four 'semi-customs' from Le Baron. Chassis were also supplied to various custom coachbuilders for individual bodies to be built. With 125bhp, a CG with a reasonably light body could reach 95mph (155km/h). Low and sleek, with a slightly sloping radiator set well back, the CGs were among the best looking cars of their day, and were not particularly expensive. Prices for factory bodied cars ran from $2745 to $3145, and for the semi-customs, from $3150 to $3575. The contemporary Lincoln V8 cost from $4600 to $7400. The CG was succeeded by the generally similar CL for 1932 and 1933. Total production of this most classic of Chryslers was 3599, of which only 271 were CLs, such was the effect of the Depression on sales of luxury cars.

The Airflow

In 1934 Chrysler introduced one of the best-known cars in motoring history. The inspiration for the revolutionary car came from Carl Breer, although the other two musketeers, Skelton and Zeder, were active in its development, and styling was by Oliver Clark. The idea for a streamlined car came to Breer in 1927, when

NICK BALDWIN

CHRYSLER, WALTER (1875–1940)

Walter Percy Chrysler was born in Wamego, Kansas, on April 2nd 1875, the son of locomotive driver Henry Chrysler and Anna Maria Breymann. Though the Chrysler family had lived in America since the late eighteenth century, they were of German origin, the name being originally Greisler. As a boy he worked selling from door to door calling cards and silverware that he ordered from a mail order catalogue, and also dairy produce from the family cows. When he was 17 he joined his brother Ed on the Union Pacific Railroad, starting as a cleaner at four cents an hour. After an apprenticeship and many changes of job he became, at the age of 30 superintendent of motive power for the Chicago Great Western Railroad with the princely salary of $200 a week.

Three years later he bought his first car. It was no ordinary car, but a brand-new Locomobile tourer, one of America's finest automobiles, priced at $5000. He had only $700 in the bank, and had to borrow the rest from a friend who was, conveniently, the second vice-president of the Continental National Bank. He learnt to drive it on the way home from the Chicago Auto Show and then completely dismantled it to see how it worked. This was the start of Chrysler's move away from railway engineering towards that of the automobile.

In 1912, when he was working for the Pittsburgh branch of the American Locomotive Co. (Alco) which made cars at their Providence, Rhode Island, factory, he was invited to become works manager for Buick. This came about because a director of Alco, James Jackson Storrow was also interim president of General Motors. Chrysler's $6000 salary was half what Alco had been prepared to offer him, but within a year he was earning well over $12,000, and by 1916 Durant had offered him the presidency of Buick, worth $500,000 ($120,000 in salary plus stock certificates) . The contract was for three years, and as soon as Chrysler could extricate himself he did, as there had been constant clashes over Durant's interference with the way Chrysler wanted to run the company.

At the end of 1919, at the age of only 44, Chrysler was planning to retire, but was approached by the board of Willys Overland to reorganise the ailing Toledo company. Reluctant to take the job, he asked for the unheard of salary of $1 million a year for a two-year contract. Willys Overland agreed, and by the expiry of his contract he had significantly reduced the company's debt. One of his actions was to halve John North Willys' $150,000 annual salary, which may have been the reason why Willis sold his $200,000 Pasadena home to Chrysler in April 1921. He now had reputation as a 'miracle company doctor'. and was invited to do the same job for Maxwell-Chalmers. He accepted even before his contract with Willys was up, and for a while juggled both jobs. He had already met the met the men he called his 'three musketeers', Fred Zeder, Owen Skelton and Carl Breer; in 1920 they left Studebaker and joined Chrysler at Willys-Overland. The design which he hope to use for a new Willys Six was bought by Billy Durant, who marketed it as the Flint Six, but Chrysler simply set his friends to design a smaller and better car which appeared in January 1924 as the Chrysler 70. Eighteen months later the former Maxwell Motor Co. became the Chrysler Corp. Within a few years what had been an average-sized car company became one of the 'Big Three'. This was achieved not only by the success of the Chrysler marque itself, but by acquisitions and the launch of new marques. 1928 was the busiest year of Chrysler's life, for he bought the Dodge Brothers Co. from bankers Dillon Read for $170 million, and launched two new marques, De Soto and Plymouth, all in the space of two months. In recognition of this *Time* magazine chose Chrysler as their Man of the Year for 1929. Soon afterward he attracted further publicity by erecting the Chrysler Building in New York. Completed in April 1930, the 77-floor structure, designed by William van Alen, was the city's tallest building, though for less than two years before it was outstripped by the Empire State Building in 1931. Chrysler personally supervised much of the design, including the Chrysler radiator caps with wings linked by a frieze of abstracted car wheels.

In 1935 Walter Chrysler stepped down from the presidency of the Chrysler Corp in favour of Kaufman T. Keller, assuming the less demanding role of chairman of the board. He held this post until his death on August 18th 1940.

He married, in 1901, Della Forker, by whom he had four children: Thelma who married Byron Foy, president of the De Soto Division, Bernice who married Colonel Edgar Garbisch, Walter Junior who ran his own air conditioning firm as well as being a Chrysler executive, and Jack who joined the firm as a machinist and later became an executive with, like his brother, a suite of offices in the Chrysler Building.

NG

Further Reading
'Walter P. Chrysler, an American Workman', Karla A. Rosenbusch, *Automobile Quarterly*, Vol.32, No.4.
'One for All and All for One, Chrysler's Three Engineers', Karla A. Rosenbusch, *Automobile Quarterly*, Vol. 37, No.3.

1957 Chrysler (i) New Yorker sedan.
NATIONAL MOTOR MUSEUM

1964 Chrysler (i) New Yorker sedan.
NATIONAL MOTOR MUSEUM

1986 Chrysler (i) 5th Avenue sedan.
CHRYSLER

he saw a flight of Air Force fighters so streamlined that he mistook them for geese. He decided that traditional features such as the vertical radiator and windscreen, separate lamps and wings must go if a car was to penetrate the air well. Over the following six years several prototypes were built, one with a rear engine. This made the car tail heavy, so the production Airflow had a front-mounted engine, set much further ahead than in conventional cars. It was located over the front axle instead of behind it, one third ahead of the axle. The engine was tilted 5 degrees towards the rear, to lower the clutch and gearbox. All passengers sat within the wheelbase, and the frame was a light, cage-like steel girder network which carried the body panels. Unlike most American cars, the Airflow used no wood whatsoever in its construction. There was spacious accommodation for three passengers on each of the front and rear seats. Just about the only part of the Airflow that was not radically new was the engine. There were familiar Chrysler eights in three sizes, 4900cc in the Series CU, 5301cc in the Series CV Imperial, and 6306cc in the Series CX Custom Imperial.

The Airflows were launched in January 1934, but production did not start until April. Such a delay was very damaging, for customers became impatient and cancelled their orders, while it gave competitors time to suggest criticisms which could not be refuted by experience. Carl Breer said 'We had a lot of fallacies to combat, and no cars to combat them with'. However, plenty of complaints from customers came in when the cars did reach the market, mostly arising from faulty building. Probably the first 3000 Airflows did suffer from quality control problems, and by the time these had been put right the damage was done. And then there was the Airflow's appearance, which was too radical for many buyers. Only 11,292 were sold in 1934, of which the enormous Custom Imperial accounted for a mere 67. The single model of conventional Chrysler, the CA/CB six, sold 25,252 units, and kept the company in profit.

For 1935 they hastily brought out the Airstream, a revised conventional car in 6- and 8-cylinder models, while making the Airflow look a little less radical by giving it an Airstream-like prow. This did not help sales, rather the reverse, for only 7751 Airflows were bought in 1935, 5911 in 1936 and 4391 in 1937, the model's last year. The Airflow may have seemed a disaster at the time, but its influence was enormous. All-enveloping bodies and forward mounting of engines became the norm in the late 1940s, while streamlining was adopted by Lincoln and others in the 1930s. Abroad, the Airflow shape was copied in places as far afield as Britain with the Singer Airstream, France with the Peugeot 402, Sweden with the Volvo PV36 and Japan with the Toyota AA.

New Men, New Models
The 1935 Airstreams were styled by Ray Dietrich, who came from Le Baron and headed Chrysler's exterior design staff up to the end of 1938. Oliver Clark remained in overall charge of the styling department which was called, as at General Motors, the Art & Colour Section. Also in 1935 Walter Chrysler handed over the company presidency to his right-hand man Kaufman T. Keller. He was described as 'like Chrysler, an erstwhile railroad man, and a hearty two-

NICK GEORGANO

KELLER, KAUFMAN T (1885–1966)
The man who succeeded Walter Chrysler at the helm of the Chrysler Corp was in some ways very like his former boss. He was described as 'Like Chrysler, an erstwhile railroad man, and a hearty two-fisted and go-getting automotive executive as well'. Kaufman Thuma Keller was born in Mount Joy, Pennsylvania on 27 November 1885 and educated in local grade schools and business school at Lancaster, Pennsylvania. After spending two years in England as secretary to an author and lecturer he was hired by Henry L Barton, works manager at the Westinghouse locomotive factory at East Pittsburgh in 1906. He spent two years studying every department, then in 1909 became assistant to the superintendent of the car engine department of Westinghouse. After a year he followed the usual pattern of moving around to better himself, spending time at Detroit Metal Products, Metzger, Hudson and Maxwell. In 1911 he joined General Motors central office staff, working mainly on Cadillac. It was there that he met Walter Chrysler who later hired him as master mechanic at Buick in 1917.

fisted go-getting automotive executive as well'. He was cautiously conservative as well, and after the Airflow debacle he was not going to allow any excesses from the styling department. This was possibly the reason for Ray Dietrich's short stay.

The demise of the Airflow in 1937 saw the end of the big 6306cc straight-8, and the largest engine of the late 1930s was a 135bhp 5301cc straight-8 which powered the Saratoga, New Yorker and Imperial series. Six-cylinder models bore the names Royal, Windsor and Traveler. Technical changes in the later 1930s included ifs and hypoid rear axles in 1937, steering column gearchange in 1939 and fluid drive semi-automatic transmission which was standard on the 1939 Custom Imperial and optional on the other eights. From 1941 it was standard on all the eights, but manual remained the only transmission on the sixes until 1946.

Although the great majority of Chryslers had standard factory bodies, dealers could place special orders for various custom styles with the Derham Body Company of Rosemont, Pennsylvania. These were only available on the Imperial chassis, and numbers were very low; 16 in 1937, 11 in 1938, 7 in 1939, and one each in 1940 and 1941. One of the 1939 orders was for a 7-passenger convertible town car built for the visit to the US of King George VI and Queen Elizabeth. A somewhat similar, but smaller, car was built in Chrysler's Canadian factory on a 6-cylinder Royal chassis for the Canadian part of the King and Queen's tour.

In 1941 Chrysler brought out their first station wagon, using a steel roof and body covered with white ash framing and mahogany veneer panels over metal doors. Several other US manufacturers were getting into the station wagon market at the time, but the Chryslers were unusual in having rounded backs instead of the square, van-like shape of their contemporaries. This was the first indication of a move away from the station wagon's commercial image towards its acceptability as a passenger car. The 6- and 9-passenger wagons were named the Town & Country models, after a well-known upmarket monthly magazine.

1986 Chrysler (i) LeBaron convertible.
CHRYSLER

1990 Chrysler (i) LeBaron coupé.
CHRYSLER

Keller stayed with General Motors for some time, being manufacturing manager of Chevrolet until 1924 when he was made vice-president and general manager of GM of Canada Ltd. In 1926 he joined Chrysler, as vie-president in charge of manufacturing, becoming a director in 1927 and vice-president and general manager of Dodge in 1928. Within 90 days of taking over at Dodge he had raised productivity to the point where less than half the available floor space was needed.

When Walter Chrysler retired Keller took over as president, a post that he held until 1950. He was a deeply conservative man, and his influence on Chrysler styling was somewhat negative. The debacle of the Airflow made him very suspicious of radical ideas. Under his direction no one was encouraged to be an innovator and indeed he seems to have been rather frosty to stylists in general. He told Alex Tremulis, 'Sometimes you stylists think like engineers, and that makes sense. . .' While it cannot be proved that he disagreed with stylist Ray Dietrich, the latter left Chrysler at the end of 1938. After the war Keller was not in favour of lowering the roof line, being a hat wearer and a great believer in headroom. In an address to the Stanford University School of Business in the summer of 1948, he said 'Many of you Californians may have outgrown the habit, but there are parts of the country containing millions of people, where both the men and the ladies are in the habit of getting behind the wheel, or in the back seat, wearing hats.' When he saw some of the new offerings from rivals, he remarked 'We build cars to sit in, not to piss over.'

The result of this attitude was that the 1949 Chrysler group cars were fairly undistinguished, particularly in comparison with the all-new Fords. Sales began to drop and Keller knew that he must overcome his prejudices to keep in the marketplace. He hired the innovative Virgil Exner whose first project was the K-310, a concept coupé with body built in Italy by Ghia. Keller was, surprisingly, very keen on this car (the K stood for Keller) and wanted to put it into production , but projections showed that it would be unrealistically expensive. Keller stepped up to become chairman of the board at the end of 1950, which meant that he had less day-to-day control of the company. In April 1956 he retired and devoted himself to civic projects.
NG

Only 1998 Town & Country wagons were made in the 1941 and 1942 models, but after the war, the wood framing and panelling idea was revived, not for station wagons but for a whole range of cars. The 1946 brochure showed five body styles, a roadster, a brougham, a 2-door club coupé, a 4-door sedan and a convertible. Of these, the roadster was never built, and only one brougham and seven club coupés saw the light of day. The sedan and the convertible were put into production, the former on the 6-cylinder Windsor chassis and the latter on the 8-cylinder New Yorker chassis. Unlike some postwar station wagons, which had wood veneer strips on metal panels, the Town & Country had structured wood framing made of white ash with shaped plywood panels, while the interior was well furnished with leather and Hylander wool. This hand work was reflected in the price, which was $2366 for the sedan compared with $1561 for a regular steel sedan, and $2742 for the convertible, a premium of $549 over the ordinary convertible. The 1946 and early 1947 sedans had steel roof racks, but late 1947 and all 1948 sedans had beautifully made wooden racks.

As with most American cars, Chryslers were little changed during the three years 1946–48. The Town & Country models attracted a great deal of attention, and even if Chrysler made little profit on them, their publicity value was excellent. For 1949 all Chryslers were restyled, and only the 8-cylinder convertible was made in the Town & Country style, exactly 1000 being produced. For 1950 a hard-top coupé was the only model, selling for $4002 when an all-steel Newport hard-top cost $3103. Even at these prices, the later Town & Country models had fewer wood embellishments than the 1946–48 models, and for 1951 Chrysler abandoned the hard-top for a series of Town & Country station wagons, which had a decreasing amount of wood in their construction. A total of 14,301 of the 'genuine' Town & Country models was made between 1946 and 1950.

The Power Race Begins

Up to 1951 there was little engineering novelty at Chrysler, the company relying on two engines, a 4106cc six in the Royal and Windsor, and a 5301cc eight in the Saratoga and New Yorker. Then for 1951, came a trendsetting new engine,

2000 Chrysler (i) PT Cruiser sedan.
CHRYSLER

the famous hemi, a 5426cc ohv V8 with hemispherical combustion chambers, which developed 180bhp. In one leap Chrysler had overtaken all their competitors, for while Cadillac, Oldsmobile, and Studebaker were all making V8s, they did not have hemispherical combustion chambers, which gave better breathing and more power per litre. Unfortunately these engines were heavier and more expensive to make, as they needed two sets of rocker shafts, rocker arms and pushrods per cylinder. The hemi engine has been compared to the Airflow in that it was an important trendsetter but lost money for its makers. However, it sold much better than the Airflow, and was made for eight years before giving way to a polyspherical chamber in 1959. Soon after that Chrysler went over to a wedge-shaped chamber like everyone else.

The effect of the hemi head on the industry was to spark off the horsepower race. The 1951 Chrysler had 20bhp more than was delivered by Cadillac from the same capacity, so they responded with a 190bhp for 1952 and 210bhp for 1953. By 1955 the Chrysler was giving 300bhp, still from 5426cc, and the following year a capacity increase to 5800cc boosted output to 340bhp. From then until 1960 Chryslers were generally the most powerful cars in the United States, although in 1958 Lincolns and Mercurys had 400 to Chrysler's 390bhp. The Chrysler hemi engines were used by a number of other makes such as Allard (ii), Cunningham (ii), and Facel Vega. At the other end of the scale the old side-valve six was continued until 1955, when it gave way to a 4932cc 188bhp V8 used in the lower-priced Windsors and New Yorkers.

The most important Chrysler for 1955 was the 300, intended as a 'personal car', although not so different from the regular models, as was Ford's Thunderbird. The 300 used the New Yorker as a base, and was a 2-door hard-top with the divided grille of the Imperial, and a natural leather interior exclusive to the 300. The engine had twin 4-barrel carburettors and developed 300bhp, hence the name. The 1956 model was the 300B, the first of the 'letter cars' in the 300 series. They were never intended to be big sellers, sales for 1955 being 1725 and for 1956, 1102. They were taken up enthusiastically by stock racers, and in 1955 won 32 of the 52 NASCAR races.

Like all 1957 Chryslers, the 300C was styled by Virgil Exner, and had a more aggressive appearance to go with its 375bhp 6424cc engine. Most powerful of the letter series was the 300H of 1962, which, with the optional performance pack gave 405bhp from 6768cc, and had a top speed of 135mph (217km/h). These cars were made in even smaller numbers than the original 300s, only 558 of the 300H and 400 of its successor, the 300J. The last of the letter cars was the 300L, but it had lost the sporting image, and there was not much to distinguish

it from other Chrysler models. In 1954 the Imperial became a separate marque within the Chrysler Group, in the same way that DeSoto, Dodge, and Plymouth were. For its history up to 1975, see IMPERIAL (vii).

Chrysler had made an experimental gas turbine car in 1954, and ten years later built a series of 50 turbine-powered 4-seater hard-tops using Ghia bodies and Plymouth running gear. These were loaned to selected individuals to be driven under all conditions, then returned to the factory. Apart from a few which went to museums, all the turbine cars were broken up when the tests were completed. No production resulted, any more than it did from gas turbine experiments by Rover, Renault and Fiat, but at least Chrysler made more than any of the European companies.

Throughout the 1960s and early 1970s, Chryslers were large cars with V8 engines up to 7210cc, and all with automatic transmissions. Between 1956 and 1965 these were controlled by push buttons, a feature unique to the Chrysler Corp. It was only abandoned when the US governemt insisted that all cars should have standardised controls.

Smaller Cars and Front-wheel Drive

Chrysler was the first US manufacturer to give up the convertible, in 1970, but also the first to revive the style, in 1982, when it came back into favour. The first move towards smaller cars came in 1975 with the introduction of the Cordoba, an upmarket Dodge Charger with 6555cc engine, but shorter and lighter than any other models. It was Chrysler's best seller that year, at 150,105. By 1979 the biggest engine was down to 5899cc, and the same year saw 6-cylinder engines back in the range for the first time since 1955. With a capacity of 3687cc, they were used in the LeBaron station wagon and Newport sedan, which rode on wheelbases of 113in (2862mm) and 119in (3010mm) respectively. From 1981 to 1983 the name Imperial was revived for a luxury coupé to compete with the Cadillac Seville. Powered by a 5211cc V8 it featured electronic fuel injection and a digital instrument panel.

A further move towards smaller cars came in 1982 with the LeBaron made in sedan, coupé or convertible models. This had a 2212cc Chrysler or 2556cc Mitsubishi 4-cylinder engine, mounted transversely and driving the front wheels. Equivalent cars in other Chrysler Corporation ranges were the Dodge Aries and Plymouth Reliant, and the models were collectively known as the K cars. For 1984 came a sporty coupé version of the K car, badged as the Chrysler Laser or Dodge Daytona. These had optional turbochargers which boosted the 2212cc engine's output from 84 to 140bhp. As in the other K-cars, a 5-speed manual gearbox was an alternative to the 3-speed automatic. The small car theme was extended with the H cars, introduced in mid–1984. These had the same engine options as the LeBarons, but were slightly larger, with sedan bodies of notchback shape which were actually 5-door hatchbacks. Known as the Chrysler LeBaron GTS and Dodge Lancer, they were aimed at the market cornered by imports such as the Honda Accord. These small cars proved a life-saver for Chrysler, which suffered very serious financial problems in 1978. This led them to sell off their branches in Britain, France and Spain. Former Ford president Lee Iacocca became president of Chrysler in 1978, and worked wonders to turn the company round and into profit by 1983. In 1984 Chrysler

MICHAEL LAMM

GALE, THOMAS C. (born 1943)

Thomas C. Gale was born on 18 June, 1943 in Flint, Michigan and also grew up there. His father worked for Buick as an experimental engineer.

Tom decided in high school that he wanted to become an auto designer, but his counselors weren't aware of any design colleges. They recommended he take up mechanical engineering instead. Or architecture. After exploring on his own, Tom decided to go to Michigan State University to major in industrial design, with minors in engineering and physics. After his undergraduate work, Gale took a master's degree in design and later an MBA as well, all at MSU.

After college, Gale found work with GM's AC Spark Plug Division. While still at AC, Tom had the option of moving on within GM or going to Chrysler as an engineer. In 1967, he decided to go to Chrysler as an advanced body engineer, figuring he could always move from engineering into design but not vice-versa.

Gale worked in Chrysler engineering until 1971, then got assigned to the design office and became a designer. After a stint as a senior designer, he left design for two years (1976–77) to work as a senior analyst in Chrysler's product planning office but then returned to design. Gale became Chrysler's director of interior design in 1981, director of exterior design the next year and v.p. of design in 1985. By 1991 he'd been put in charge of all aspects of Chrysler's minivans in addition to design, and in 1993 he became v.p. of product design and international operations. In 1996, he also took over product development.

Gale's background in engineering, design, product planning and management makes him unique in the annals of design administration. No one has ever brought so much interdisciplinary expertise to a car company before.

With the merger of Chrysler and Daimler-Benz, Tom has been mentioned for even greater responsibilities, especially in light of Chrysler's decade of styling successes. He launched cab-forward design with the 1988 Lamborghini Portofino, 1989 Chrysler Millennium and Eagle Optima showcars. Also designed under his watch were the Dodge Viper, Plymouth Prowler, Dodge Durango SUV, plus a number of showstopping concept vehicles like the retro Chrysler Atlantic and Jeepster. All this bodes well for the legitimacy of US auto and truck design in general – not just at Chrysler but in all three major American car companies.

ML

took a 15.6 per cent stake in the Italian sports car maker, Maserati. This bore fruit in 1985 with the Chrysler-Maserati TC, a convertible derived from the LeBaron but with a shorter wheelbase, and 2-seater body, using the standard 2212cc 4-cylinder engine with a twin-ohc 16-valve head designed by the Italian company. With turbocharger this gave 200bhp. Announced in 1985 it did not go into production until 1988 and did not live up to its promise, having disappointing handling. It cost around $30,000, compared with $19,666 for the most expensive LeBaron convertible. Later models had the 2998cc V6 Mitsubishi engine and automatic transmission in place of the 5-speed manual of the original car. Production was phased out early in 1991, after 7,300 had been made.

The big rear-drive New Yorker was continued through the 1980s, selling 100,000 units as late as 1987, but was finally dropped at the end of 1989, leaving Chrysler with an all front-drive range. Turbochargers were dropped from the LeBaron series for 1992, and the name was seen only on convertibles in 1995 and 1996, after which it disappeared altogether. A most important new range appeared in 1993, the LH with 'cab forward' styling which involved a shortened nose and large cabin area. Engine options were 3302 or 3518cc V6s, the latter with 24 valves and ohcs. They were mounted longitudinally, which made for considerable front overhang, but the overall effect was to make the LH America's most distinctive sedan. The first in the series was the Concorde, with sister cars in other divisions being the Dodge Intrepid and Eagle Vision. They were joined for 1994 by the longer and more luxurious New Yorker and LHS. The latter cost over $30,000. Other models in the 1995 line-up included the Sebring coupé, a luxury edition of the Dodge Avenger and based on the Mitsubishi Galant floorpan. It was made at the Diamond Star plant at Normal, Illinois, which Chrysler set up jointly with Mitsubishi in 1989. A smaller car in the 'cab forward' family was the Cirrus sedan with 2497cc ohc V6 engine, sold in Europe as the Stratus. These made up the 1998 Chrysler range, together with the Town & Country MPV which had been made in various models since 1984, and was sold in Europe under the Voyager name. In fact, European market Voyagers were made at the Steyr-Puch factory in Austria. Other cars sold in Europe as Chryslers were the Neon (a Plymouth in the US) and Viper sports car (Dodge in the US). Of all American car makers, Chrysler had the best record of bringing concept cars to production. These included the Dodge Viper and Plymouth Prowler, and in 1999, the Chrysler PT Cruiser, a retro-styled 4-door sedan based on Neon running gear. First seen as the 2-door Pronto Cruizer concept at the 1998 Geneva Show, it was ready for production a year later. Shorter than the Neon, it was larger inside than the Ford Focus or VW Golf. It was powered by the Neon's 1996cc 16-valve engine, with a 2.4-litre option to come later.

Chrysler made a number of acquisitions and mergers from 1987, when they bought American Motors from Renault for $600 million, mainly to obtain the valuable Jeep business. Also in 1987 they bought Lamborghini, selling it on to the Indonesian Mega Tech group in 1993. The most important development was the merger with Mercedes-Benz which took place in May 1998. The German firm had the larger share (57 per cent) in the £24 billion group, which was the fifth largest car maker in the world, judged on their combined 1997 production figures.

NG

Further Reading
Seventy Years of Chrysler, George Dammann, Crestline Publishing, 1974.
Automobile Quarterly, Vol. 32 No.4, (whole issue devoted to Chrysler).
'One for All and All for One; Chrysler's Three Engineers',
Karla A. Rosenbusch, *Automobile Quarterly*, Vol. 37, No.3.

CHRYSLER (ii) (AUS) 1957–1980

Chrysler Australia Ltd, Keswick, South Australia.
Chrysler Australia Ltd, Tonsley Park, South Australia.

Chrysler's Australian operation began in 1951, built on the former T.J. Richards' bodybuilding firm, and commenced by producing the PLYMOUTH, also as DE SOTO and DODGE clones. The 1957 revision, with a full-width grille and tail fins, was the Chrysler Royal only. In 1959 a 5050cc V8 was added and this continued until 1964, after the sixes had been replaced by the Valiant. The 1962 Plymouth Valiant was a Chrysler in Australia and its acceptance prompted the building of a new factory, with local models gradually diverging from home market models.

1966 Chrysler (ii) Valiant Premium sedan.
NATIONAL MOTOR MUSEUM

1977 Chrysler (iv) Sunbeam LS hatchback.
NATIONAL MOTOR MUSEUM

1946 C.H.S. 330cc 2-seater.
NICK BALDWIN

Completion of a foundry complex at Lonsdale allowed production of the Australian 6-cylinder 'hemi' engine in 1970. A new body shell in 1971 removed any similarities with overseas models and Valiant became a make, with the Chrysler name then being applied to prestige versions. The French 180 model arrived in 1975 but this had a longer nose to accommodate the optional local 6-cylinder motor and was named Centura. In accordance with overall Chrysler-Mitsubishi arrangements then in place, Australia produced the Sigma, with its 'balance-shaft' engine, as a Chrysler. The energy crisis of that period favoured the Sigma at the expense of the full-sized types and this led to the 1980 take-over by Mitsubishi.

MG

CHRYSLER (iii) (F) 1970–1979

Chrysler France SA, Poissy, Seine-et-Oise.

Chrysler's involvement with the French industry stemmed from its minority interest in SIMCA in 1958, leading to control by 1963. Various models of Simca were made up to 1981, but in 1970 there appeared a car made in the Simca

factory but badged as the Chrysler 160 and 180. Designed jointly in Britain and France, and originally intended to carry a Humber badge, it was a 4-door saloon with a choice of three single-ohc 4-cylinder engines of 1639, 1812 and (from 1973) 1981cc engines, with McPherson strut ifs and coils at the rear. The 1.6-litre (160) had disc brakes at the front only, and was confined to the French market. With the larger engines, discs were provided all round and the 2-litre model came with automatic transmission only. From 1977, when a diesel engine was also available, production was transferred to Chrysler's Spanish factory. Two years later, all Chrysler's European operations were sold to PEUGEOT, which continued some models under the Talbot name. The 180 was made for a short time in Spain as a Talbot.

NG

CHRYSLER (iv) (GB) 1976–1979

Chrysler UK Ltd, Ryton-on-Dunsmore, Coventry and Linwood, Glasgow.

Chrysler acquired a majority holding in the Rootes Group in 1964, but existing HILLMAN and HUMBER models were continued under their former names until 1976. Then the Humber name was dropped, and the Hillman Hunter and Avenger became Chryslers, although without any significant mechanical change. The first distinctive model appeared for 1978; the Chrysler Sunbeam was a 3-door hatchback based on a shortened Avenger frame, powered by single-ohc 4-cylinder engines of 928, 1295 or 1598cc. The smallest was a stretched Hillman Imp unit; the largest could be had in limited production Ti form, with twin Weber carburettors. Made at Linwood, in the factory opened for production of the Hillman Imp, it was rebadged as a Talbot for 1980, when more powerful models were made including the exciting Sunbeam-Lotus, and dropped in 1981. Also produced in Britain (at Coventry) were the French-designed front-drive Alpine and Horizon (see SIMCA and TALBOT (iii)).

NG

C.H.S. (F) 1945–1946

Sté Anonyme des Usines Chausson, Asnières, Seine.

Chausson were radiator makers who supplied more than 80 per cent of all radiators for French vehicles before World War I, and who very successfully turned to bus manufacture in 1947. Just after the war they considered entry into the microcar market with an open, doorless 2-seater powered by a 330cc single-cylinder 2-stroke engine driving the front wheels. It had independent suspension all round. Two prototypes were made with this engine, and one with a 550cc twin, a larger version of which was used in a Chenard-Walcker forward-control van. If the C.H.S. had gone into production it would have been called a Chenard-Walcker, as this company had been owned by Chausson since 1936. After Chausson abandoned the idea, there were plans for it to be made in England by Delaney-Gallay who were also radiator makers, but these came to nothing. Reportedly Austin also showed an interest.

NG

CHURCH-FIELD (US) 1912–1913

Church-Field Motor Co., Sibley, Michigan.

Austin Church and H. George Field combined to form this company to make electric cars. The design was unusual in several ways, having an underslung frame and a 2-speed epicyclic transmission that provided a total of 20 speeds. Two models were listed, a coupé and a roadster, the latter with a top speed of about 30mph (50km/h). They were launched at the Detroit Automobile Show in January 1912, but the plant was closed in September 1913. A few cars may have been assembled from parts in hand, but in 1915 Church-Field's remaining assets were sold for $600, less than 25 per cent of the price of one coupé.

NG

CHURCH GREEN (GB) 1997 to date

Church Green Engineering, East Knoyle, Dorset.

This company had a significant hand in several specialist car projects, including the GOZZY, and created bespoke bodywork for various classic cars including Ferrari and Porsche. However the first car it produced under its own name was a replica of the Lotus Eleven. Unlike the original Lotus, this was designed to use the chassis and all mechanicals of a Lotus or Caterham Seven. The bodywork was exquisitely reproduced in fibreglass.

CR

CHRYSLER

CHRYSLER
MOTORS LTD
KEW GARDENS
SURREY

62
72
80

NATIONAL MOTOR MUSEUM

1910 Cino Model A 40hp tourer.
NICK BALDWIN

CHURCH PNEUMATIC (US) 1913–1914
Church Motor Car Co., Chicago, Illinois.
This company claimed to build a car without most of the components considered essential by other car makers. These included gearbox, clutch, carburettor, gear lever, timing gears, sleeves, and inlet and exhaust valves. All these were replaced by the Church Pneumatic System, which the company would explain in literature sent free on request, but they did not apparently do so to the press. A price of $2500 was fixed for a large tourer on a 132in (3353mm) wheelbase, and at least one photograph was published, but whether the car shown conformed to the strange description advertised, is not known.
NG

CHURCHILL *see* HALLAMSHIRE

CICOSTAR (F) 1980–1984
C.I.C.O. SA, Limoges, Haute-Vienne.
This was an unusually smart, rounded monobox microcar with a rear-mounted engine. It was available in two forms: a 47cc Sachs 3-wheeler or a 49.9cc Motobécane 4-wheeler, both having automatic transmission and independent front suspension. A larger and more angular 50cc or 125cc 4-wheeler, the Matic, was offered from late 1980.
CR

C.I.D. (F) 1912–1914
Constructions Industrielles Dijonnaises, Dijon.
This company was a reorganisation of the former COTTEREAU et Compagnie, which was the leading make in Dijon. As C.I.D. two lines of car were made. The Baby was a light car powered by a 8hp single-cylinder Buchet engine, with 4-speed friction transmission and front suspension by single transverse spring. The same design was sold under the name EMERAUDE, although this had ordinary semi-elliptic front suspension. The other line of C.I.D. was a larger car with a rotary-valve engine made in three sizes, 14, 16 and 22hp.
NG

CIEM (CH) 1902–1905
Compagnie de l'Industrie Eléctrique et Mécanique CIEM, Geneva.
The Thury-Nussberg early steam tricycle of 1877, which was notable for its high top speed of 25mph (40km/h), was built in the workshops of CIEM, Geneva. Apart from various electric equipment, from 1901 CIEM built electric-motors and internal-combustion engines for cars built by other companies. At the Paris Salon in late 1902, CIEM presented an electric town car. Not satisfied with the noisy petrol engine nor with the limited operational radius of electromobiles, CIEM in 1903 launched two models with a combined system. The 8hp model had a V2 engine, and the 16/24hp model a V4 engine, which were coupled with a dynamo and the rear wheels were driven by electro motors. In 1905 two new engines were developed – a vertical twin 8/12hp of 2077cc and a 4-cylinder with L-head 16/24hp of 4562cc capacity. These *voitures mixtes,* as well as an electromobile, were also displayed at the Paris Show. Charles Stewart Rolls was seriously interested in placing a substantial order and taking over the sole agency for Great Britain. For various reasons, including a delay in delivery of the example car, the plans did not materialise. From 1906 onwards CIEM manufactured cars under the brand name STELLA.
FH

CIEMME (I) 1985–c.1988
Ciemme, Bologna.
The Italian ARO importer developed a couple of more stylish models based on the Romanian off-roader. The first was oddly called the TV Grizzly and was based on the Aro 240, but with longer, taller bodywork, an American-style grill, and a VM 2.4-litre 100bhp turbodiesel engine. Next came the Scorpion, a sporty-style pick-up with gull-wing doors. It used either Renault 1.4-litre petrol or VW 1.6-litre diesel/turbodiesel engines.
CR

C.I.M.E.M (I) 1951–1955
C.I.M.E.M., Milan.
The Girino was a tiny doorless open 3-wheeler. In its tail sat a Vespa single-cylinder 4.5bhp engine and 3-speed gearbox driving the swinging rear wheel. It weighed 200kg and could travel at up to 32mph (51km/h). A further prototype, the Motospyder, arrived in 1955 with a 125cc engine.
CR

CINCINNATI (US) 1903–1904
Cincinnati Automobile Co., Cincinnati, Ohio.
The Cincinnati steam car was similar in specification to most of its contemporaries, with a 10hp single-cylinder engine under the seat, driving the rear axle by single-chain, and tiller steering. It differed in its appearance, which was lower and more rakish than the norm, due to a longer wheelbase. This did not seem to help sales, and production lasted little more than a year.
NG

CINGOLANI (I) 1952
Ezio Cingolani, Recanati, Ancona.
This minute but rather handsome 3-wheeled micro coupé used the mechanical elements of a Vespa scooter. That included a 125cc 3bhp single-cylinder engine and 3-speed gearbox. Its aluminium bodywork kept weight down to a mere 119kg, giving it exceptional economy. A production run did not ensue.
CR

CINO (US) 1910–1913
Haberer & Co., Cincinnati, Ohio.
The Haberer company was described as one of the most important carriage builders in Cincinnati. In 1910 it brought out a conventional car powered by a 40hp 4-cylinder engine, made in tourer and roadster models. This was joined in 1912 by a 60hp six, which was continued alongside a 50hp four for 1913. The Cino might have had a bright future, but the spring flooding of the Ohio River inundated the factory and made it impossible to continue manufacture.
NG

C.I.P. (I) 1922–1924
Cyclecar Italiana Petromilli, Turin.
Designed by Constantino Petromilli, this was a light car powered by a 1075cc 4-cylinder ohv engine.
NG

CIPHER *see* STEVENS

CIRCLEVILLE (US) 1914
Circleville Automobile Co., Circleville, Ohio.
This company planned to make a cyclecar powered by an engine patented by Walker Lee Crouch. It was unusual for a cyclecar to be offered with electric lighting and starting, features that made it good value at $425, but apparently few were made.
NG

CISITALIA (i) **(I)** 1946–1965

Cisitalia SpA, Turin.

In 1939, Piero Dusio, a former soccer star, established Consorzio Industriale Sportiva Italia (Cisitalia) to make and sell a range of sports equipment. Cisitalia spent the War years making military uniforms, and also a fortune. After the war, in 1946, Cisitalia offered a Fiat-powered single-seater racing car at a reasonable price. These were followed by open and coupé 2-seat competition cars and, in 1947, road cars were marketed.

The 202 Gran Sport was available as a coupé or cabriolet and, like its sisters, it had a spaceframe chassis – Cisitalia was the first to sell them. Apart from the spaceframe, everything else on the chassis was Fiat 1100, although the engine was tuned to give 66bhp. What set it apart was the Pinin Farina body which was hailed as a masterpiece. It was not, however, enough to disguise the fact that the Cisitalia was a Fiat special which would barely reach 99mph (160km/h) yet cost twice as much as a Jaguar XK120.

Dusio had over-reached himself on all fronts – he had commissioned a grand prix car from the Porsche studio – and, in 1949, he moved his business to Argentina. In Argentina, Dusio made cars based on the Willys Jeep, but bearing the Cisitalia name.

In Italy, Carlo Abarth, who had worked on the Cisitalia Grand Prix car, began to make cars based on the Cisitalia 202 and they founded a separate tradition. An Italian consortium revived Cisitalia and, by 1952, 170, 202 Gran Sports had been made.

In 1952 the firm offered a new coupé with a fairly basic chassis, a De Dion rear axle, and a 160bhp 2.8-litre 4-cylinder B.P.M. marine engine. It was claimed to do 134mph (216km/h), but found few takers. Cisitalia then turned to making customised Fiats until it finally folded in 1965.

MJL

Further Reading

'Cisitalia', Stanley Nowak, *Automobile Quarterly*, Vol.VIII, No.2.

CISITALIA (ii) **(RA)** 1951–1965

Cisitalia Argentina, San Fernando, Buenos Aires.

In 1949 Piero Dusio transferred his operations from Italy to Argentina, where he involved himself with the Autoar project. In 1951 he founded Cisitalia Argentina, announcing they would make 'sports and fast touring cars, backed by Fiat-Concord'. However, Cisitalia stressed that their cars would be quite different from Fiat production units. Cisitalia was also associated with Abarth.

The Cisitalia Abarth was powered by a modified Fiat 850cc engine which developed 54bhp. There were coupé and spyder versions of this small 2-seater sports car. A top speed of 100mph (160km/h) was claimed for the coupé.

Interestingly, a station wagon and a van were also produced by Cisitalia, powered by a Fiat 4-cylinder 767cc engine developing 35bhp.

No production figures were released, but for many years a good number of the little Cisitalia sports cars were seen on the roads of Argentina.

ACT

CITERIA (NL) 1958–1959

Citeria NV, Den Haag.

This promising small hardtop convertible sadly never made production, principally because its creator, Puck van Beekum, had to serve a prison sentence after trying to forge cheques. The Citeria featured a pretty glassfibre 2-door body with a soft top or detachable hard top. It used a BMW 600 30bhp twin-cylinder engine and 4-speed gearbox mounted in the tail of its tubular steel chassis. Since the Citeria weighed only 1100lb (500kg), a top speed of 84mph (135km/h) was achieved at its well-publicised Zandvoort launch, attended by Stirling Moss. It was too expensive to succeed, especially against the similar BMW 700 launched around the same time.

CR

CITO (D) 1905–1909

1905–1907 Cito Fahrradwerke AG, Cologne-Klettenberg.

1907–1909 Cito-Werke AG, Cologne-Klettenberg.

Cito was a manufacturer of bicycles and motorcycles, turning to cars in 1905 with the Citomobil, using OMNIMOBIL components. The following year new models appeared with 6/10PS 2-cylinder Aster and 10/16 or 15/24PS 4-cylinder Fafnir engines. However, production was limited, and in 1909 the car branch was closed down.

HON

1946 Cisitalia (i) coupé by Pinin Farina.
NATIONAL MOTOR MUSEUM

1963 Cisitalia (i) 850cc convertible.
NATIONAL MOTOR MUSEUM

CITROËN (i) **(F)** 1919 to date

1919–1924 André Citroën, Ingénieur-Constructeur, Paris.

1924–1968 S.A. André Citroën, Paris.

1968–1976 Automobiles Citroën, Citroën S. A., Paris.

1976–1979 Automobiles Citroën, Peugeot S. A., Paris.

1979 to date Automobiles Citroën, Peugeot S. A., Neuilly-sur-Seine.

When the Citroën Type A 10CV prototype was shown to the public with a price tag of FF 6995, in a borrowed showroom on the Champs-Élysées on 28 May 1919, French car buyers stepped into a new world. Here, for the first time was a complete car, ready for immediate use, including coachwork, toolkit, spare wheel, electric starting and lighting, offered at approximately one-third of what an equivalent vehicle cost in 1914, Citroën received 16,000 orders within two weeks.

Jules Salomon and his friend, Edmond Moyet, who worked together at Le Zèbre before the war, created the Citroën Type A. The engine was Moyets work, an L-head 1327cc 4-cylinder unit delivering 18hp at 2100rpm. Designed for low stress levels and long service life with only two main bearings, Type A ran reliably and economically, with an average fuel consumption of 7.5 litres per 100km, and had a top speed of 40mph (65km/h). It had left hand drive, simple controls, and Michelin's new (patented in 1914) pressed-steel disc wheels. It was produced with a choice of two wheelbases and four body styles: 3- or 4 passenger torpedo, 3- or 4-passenger saloon, coupé de ville, and delivery van.

The first delivery to a private customer was made on 4 July 1919. For several months production was only 30 cars a day, but a total of 24,033 Type A cars were built from 1919 to 1921. Citroën moved fast on several fronts at the same time, preparing a model range in perpetual evolution, expansion of the industrial base, and fresh initiatives in promotion and marketing. Louis Guillot became technical director of Citroën, a title which made him André Citroën's closest

1921 Citroën 10CV Torpedo.
NATIONAL MOTOR MUSEUM

1924 Citroën 5CV cloverleaf 3-seater.
NATIONAL MOTOR MUSEUM

1925 Citroën B2 11.4hp saloon.
NATIONAL MOTOR MUSEUM

technical advisor. He was an engineering graduate of the École des Arts le Métiers, who had been an aircraft engineer with the Morane Brothers. Henri Dufresne was a toolmaker for Mors when he first met André Citroën in 1909. He left Paris two years later to become chief engineer of Martini, returning in 1913 when offered the position as chief engineer of Mors, but Citroën hired him away in 1914 to get his help in laying out the munitions plant. He stayed on, and in 1918–19 started a methods office for Citroën's car production.

Citroën produced 2810 cars in 1919 and 12,244 in 1920. Output climbed to 21,000 units in 1922, 32,700 in 1923 and 55,400 in 1924. In 1919 André Citroën engaged Lucien Rosengart as a special director of financing. One of Rosengart's

first recommendations was to raise retail prices across the board, and the base price of Type A shot up to FFr11,000 which was still not much more than half the price of any comparable French car.

Rosengart also set up a credit organisation, SADIF, which was not restricted to assisting Citroën's dealer organisation, but open to collaboration with agents of all makes. At Rosengart's initiative, Citroën also started a taxicab company in Paris, which not only put thousands of cars most visibly on the streets, but also got people to ride in Citroën cars, broadening the ranks of potential customers. Rosengart left Citroën in 1923 by mutual agreement.

The 10CV B2 was essentially a replacement for Type A. It was exactly the same type of car, with the engine enlarged to 1452cc and 20hp at 2100rpm, and with available body styles including landaulette and fixed-head coupé, plus the Caddy, a boat-tailed roadster with a 22hp engine. The B2 proved longer-lived than its predecessor, 90,241 units, including 300 Caddys being built from 1921 until the end of 1925.

The lowest-price end of the market puzzled André Citroën. Where was the limit and how big was that segment, hitherto the preserve of cyclecars? The Citroën 5CV, shown at the Paris Salon in 1921 with production beginning in 1922, would give the answers. Salomon and Moyet had been preparing it for some time, originally planning a 750cc single-cylinder engine, tested in both air-cooled and water-cooled versions, but Moyet ended up with a water-cooled 856cc L-head 4-cylinder unit rated at 11hp. To cut costs, it had a two-bearing crankshaft, thermosyphon cooling, and no fan. The chassis was simpler and lighter than on the B2, with a 92.5in (2348mm) wheelbase, but bodies were styled to make it look like a baby B2.

To produce the 5CV, Citroën rented the former Clément-Bayard factory at Levallois, originally erected in 1893 for Cycles Clément. For the first time in France, the marketing was slanted towards feminine clientèle, which paid off handsomely. Prices for the 5CV cabriolet started at FFr10,700 in 1922, rising no further than FFr14,000 by 1926. The arrival of the Trèfle in 1924 (a torpedo with three seats in cloverleaf formation) boosted the 5CV sales curve at a critical moment, and the Levallois plant was soon turning out 250 cars a day. Sales of the Trèfle exceeded 10,000 units a year until the end of production in May 1926. Total 5CV production reached 80,232 units.

An engineer himself, André Citroën knew that the product (and its price) was the key to success, and never skimped on spending for its planning and development. But there were setbacks. In 1922, Guillot became troubled by tuberculosis and could no longer work regular hours, but kept his title and salary, though his responsibilities were shared out. Citroën also had to cope with Moyet's departure in 1922. He left because he wanted to make sports cars, and his first Amilcar was a sort of hot-rod 5CV.

Maurice Norroy, a graduate of the École Centrale des Arts et Manufactures, with experience from Nardon in Nancy and Chanard at Rueil, joined Citroën in 1923 at an executive level. Paul Laubard, who held an engineering diploma from the Institut Industriel du Nord, was on Citroën's engineering staff from 1923 to 1931, but left engineering to become a businessman. Salomon found an able assistant in Georges Sallot, who came to Citroën in 1923 and worked on the evolution of the B2, before preparing the B12 and the B14.

André Citroën incorporated his enterprise as a Société Anonyme on 24 July 1924, and hired J. Paul Vavon to be his technical director. Guillot was assigned to the selection of engineering staff personnel, but still had André Citroën's ear. In 1926 it was Guillot who hired Maurice Brogly away from Renault to become head of Citroën's drawing office (replacing Salomon, who had been dismissed). In 1923 the Quai de Javel plant was reorganised and a moving assembly line installed, it was only 49m long, but daily output increased from 150 cars to 250. Competition in the 10CV market forced Citroën to add more refinements to the B2, which became B10 in June 1924. In its 18-month production span, 17,259 cars of B10 specification were built.

In 1924 Citroën purchased a licence for steel-body construction from the Budd Company and began erecting a steel-stamping plant with 250 presses at St Ouen-Gare. A year later, Citroën took over the Société des Automobiles Mors, with offices in Rue du Théatre, off Rue de Commerce, within walking distance of the Quai de Javel. Without fanfare, André Citroën also began to buy up all the real estate surrounding the Quai de Javel factory, providing space for expansion, simultaneously investing in property of the greatest potential value. A new plant was put up at Clichy, including a foundry, press shops, and a facility for making rubber parts. The Grenelle plant came on stream in time to produce front and rear axle assemblies for the B14, and engine production was transferred to Rue Gutenberg, on the east side of the Javel Complex, its first product being the C4 engine in 1929. In 1929 Citroën finally bought the title to the Levallois plant which had been leased since 1921.

The 1925 B12 was a 10CV model created by Salomon and Sallot, introducing steel bodies and 4-wheel brakes to Citroën's customers, based on the B2, it had a reinforced chassis frame and a new front suspension. Within two years, Citroën produced 38,381 of them. The B12 was replaced by the B14, which was really André Citroën's idea of a luxury car, held closely within the dimensions of its predecessor.

There was not much of Salomon in the B14 but a lot of Sallot. The new 9CV 1539cc L-head engine, however, was the work of Henri Jouffret, who had designed a 16-cylinder aircraft engine for Peugeot in 1921. With its reinforced 2-bearing crankshaft, it was a tough, reliable power unit, delivering 22hp at 2300rpm. The chassis resembled Chrysler's, and body styles also reflected Chrysler influence. Citroën produced 50,526 cars of B14 specification from 1926 to 1927 including a B14F coach with a two-tone paint job, plus 59,391 cars of B14G type from 1927 to 1928.

To compensate for the increasing absences of the ailing Guillot, Henri Dufresne was named Assistant Technical Director of Citroën in 1930, but Jouffret left in 1931 to join Chenard-Walcker, and Michelat returned to Delage in 1932. Guillot died in February 1933, and was replaced by Maurice Norroy.

In 1931 André Citroen purchased a licence for Chrysler's floating power engine-mounting patents, and its principles were adapted to the C4G (1932 model), and soon afterwards, the C6G. The C6 was essentially the same vehicle as the C4 with a 6-cylinder version of the same engine (on a 4-bearing crankshaft). The C4 was produced from October 1929 until October 1932, reaching a total of 243,912 units, including approximately 45,000 vans. C6 production was matched to much lower demand and totalled approximately 35,000 cars.

The next generation of cars became collectively known under the nickname 'Rosalie' from a series of specially prepared roadsters which set long-distance speed records at Montlery, sponsored by Société des Huiles Yacco. Appearing in July 1933, the first one to figure in Yacco publicity as Petite Rosalie had a standard 8A chassis with a semi-streamlined racing body. The 8CV, first shown at the Paris Salon in October 1932, replaced the C4 and had a new 1452cc L-head 4-cylinder engine with a Désaxe crankshaft and Floating Power mounting system, peak output was 32hp at 3200rpm. The car had a 106.3in (2698mm) wheelbase and was 167in (4238mm) long overall; the saloon weighing 1165kg. Citroën produced only the saloons, but implemented a clever scheme for series production of coaches, coupés and cabriolets by outside bodywork manufacturers, notably Sical, Manessius, and Million Guillet.

The 10CV was practically identical to the 8CV, except for a bigger (1767cc) version of the same engine, rated at 36hp. The 15CV was a replacement for the C6, with an improved 2560cc engine rated at 56hp, and a beefed-up frame. Like the 8CV, the 10 and 15CV models had 3-speed gearboxes – unlike the 8CV, they featured free-wheeling as standard.

All three Rosalie types went into production in October 1932, and were discontinued in May 1934. During their short life, they were restyled once, becoming 8B,10B and 15B and the final 226 15CV cars had torsion-bar ifs. There was a short-wheelbase 10CV saloon named 10AL, which was also fitted with the 6-cylinder engine to make a lively 15AL.

The production record reveals that the public preferred torque to economy, since 35,596 10CV cars were made, compared with only 8,000 8CV cars. At the same time, Citroën built 4,469 15A and 2300 15AL cars, followed by a total of 8,400 15B and 15BL cars produced between May and September 1934.

La Traction

André Citroëns infatuation with front-wheel drive had two principal sources. One was the racing successes of the Tracta cars and conversations with J. A. Grégoire; the other was a prototype he had been shown in the Budd factory on a visit to America in 1931, accompanied by Henri Dufresne.

The Budd prototype was smaller than most US-built cars of its time, and considerably lower. The unit-construction steel body had been developed by Joseph Ledwinka. The engine was an aluminium V8 designed by William Taylor (formerly of the Scripps Motor Co., and Kermath Marine Engine Co.), and the front-wheel drive chassis was drawn up by William J. Muller, former Chief Engineer of Ruxton.

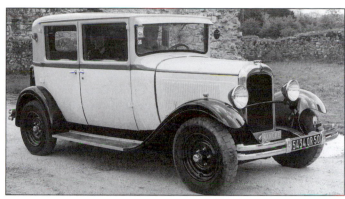

1929 Citroën C4 saloon.
NATIONAL MOTOR MUSEUM

1930 Citroën Six 20CV tourer.
NATIONAL MOTOR MUSEUM

1948 Citroën 11 Légère Berline.
NATIONAL MOTOR MUSEUM

1954 Citroën 15-Six Familiale.
NATIONAL MOTOR MUSEUM

1953 Citroën 11 Normale saloon.
NATIONAL MOTOR MUSEUM

Soon, André Citroën had a fairly precise mental picture of the next car his factories would produce, but it was such a radically different concept that he did not trust Maurice Brogly and his staff with the task of engineering it. Brogly had no higher technical education and his thinking was steeped in Renault practice. Months went by while André Citroën hesitated. He stopped hesitating when an ex-Voisin engineer, André Lefèbvre, called for an interview. He had himself been working on front-wheel drive projects for some time. Lefèbvre joined Citroën in March 1933 to take charge of the entire front-wheel drive programme. He had no title and reported to no one except André Citroën. He was given a separate office, away from the official engineering department and drawing offices, where he could work with a few of his own assistants.

The task was enormous, for it would be a new car from the ground up, sharing nothing at all with existing models. Maurice Sainturat, who had signed up with Citroën in May 1932, was put in charge of engine design, and set about creating a 4-cylinder iron block with wet liners, and pushrod-operated ohvs. Maurice Julien, a mining engineer who had joined Citroën in 1928, designed the ifs, Lefèbvre laid out the driveline himself, along the same general lines as the Adler, but with the important distinction of placing the gearbox in front of the final drive unit, so as to move the engine's centre of gravity closer to the front wheels.

Body engineering was handled in close contact with the Budd Co. Raoul Cuinet, Chief Body Engineer and Pierre Franchiset, Body Draughtsman, had a hectic time, crossing the Atlantic back and forth with models and blueprints.

André Citroën did not approach any of the established coachbuilders or stylists in connection with the Traction. He went outside, hiring a sculptor who had not previously done any automotive work: Flaminio Bertoni. His design was an outstanding success, Lefèbvre's group could not long continue to work on a production model programme in complete isolation. The first communications with the engineering staff were handled by Roger Prudhomme, Test Engineer and head of the prototype construction shop. Later, liaison was made directly under the pressure of time. Everything for the Traction was given priority, and by some near-miracle, the 7CV made its public debut on 7 March 1934. The car had gone from the idea stage to production model in a record short time of only 65 weeks.

Regrettably, it had not had the benefit of proper testing and development. Testing had not been neglected – André Citroën even turned over a huge area of his estate at La Ferté-Vidame to make proving grounds, where tests could be conducted privately and in secret. This project just needed more testing than an orthodox car. It was not planned that way, but the initial customers were made to do a lot of it.

Charles Houdin was Manufacturing Director of Citroën in 1933, with 'Casimir' Kazimierczak as his assistant. They had the task of revamping the plant for the Traction. André Citroën had been almost physically sick with envy when Louis Renault staged a huge inaugural reception for the multi-level factory built on the Ile de Séguin in the Seine, linked by bridges to the main plant at Billancourt.

A major retooling of the Javel plant was necessary to accommodate the special needs of the Traction, but André Citroën had a personal compulsion to outdo Renault, and ordered a general clearing of a central area big enough to put up a new main assembly hall, 300m long, 56m wide, and 25m high, with bridge-type travelling cranes and overhead conveyors. Amazingly this was accomplished without ever disturbing current production, then running at an average of 400 cars a day. Production of the Traction 7A–priced at FFr18,000– began on 10 April 1934, at a rate of 100 cars a day, passing to 200 cars a day by the end of April, and reaching 300 on 10 May.

All over France, cars were returned to the dealers with engine mountings torn apart, failed universal joints, broken gearboxes, and cracks in the body structure. André Citroën had some nasty moments of doubt as to his choice of front-wheel drive, and had hurried conferences with Georges Broulhiet, Maurice Sizaire, and Jean Andreau to reassure himself. He also consulted with J. A. Grégoire on constant-velocity universal joints. The Floating Power, which worked so well on the C4 and the Rosalie models, was not equally suitable for front-wheel drive. Paul Daubarède, a graduate of the École Centrale at Lyon who had put Floating Power on the Citroën C4, now had to adapt the engine mounting system to a front-wheel drive installation not in a frame or sub-frame but in a unit-construction body.

André Citroën even called in Pierre Lemaire, Professor of Acoustics and Vibrations, and Director of the École Centrale at Lyon to help his former pupil. Lemaire had in fact lectured in American universities in 1925–26 on the vibration forces of engines and engine-mounting geometry, laying down the principles on which R.K. Lee of Chrysler based his patents. The result was a more refined system called Pausodyne.

Improvements were introduced at a fast pace. Citroën made 7000 cars of 7A specification from March to June 1934, followed by the 7B, with a 1529cc engine of 35hp at 3200rpm. For the 7B, Citroën added cabriolet and faux-cabriolet (i.e. coupé) body styles, and over 20,000 7B cars were made. A 1628cc version of the same engine was mounted in the 7C, delivering 36hp at 3800rpm, which arrived before the end of 1934. A bigger model, the 11A, went into production in August 1934. The styling was near-identical, but the bodies differed in width and length, and the 11A had a 46hp 1911cc engine. The 11A hit the market with a price tag of FFr25,000 when the 10B was selling at FFr25,250 and the 15BL at FFr27,250. The 1911cc engine had originally appeared in the 7S L/A short-chassis sports model, made only in a small series of 1500 cars from June to October 1934, when it was renamed 11AL . For the 11A, Citroën also offered a long-wheelbase Familiale six-light saloon body.

André Citroën was all set for rapidly phasing out all the older models and devoting the full factory capacity to front-wheel drive cars, but the transition was not well planned.

Citroën had 57 models in 1933 and 76 in 1934, with so many permutations of chassis and body styles, that 7 to 15 different bodies were available for each type of chassis. There was no interchangeability of parts between any car in the Traction family and any older model. The cost of rebuilding the Javel factory, the quality problems of the earliest Traction models and the slow build-up of the production rates contributed to the worsening of Citroën's financial situation.

The company was declared bankrupt on 21 December 1934. Michelin, as the biggest creditor, agreed to take it over. The 32 year-old Pierre Michelin was named

1954 Citroën 2CV saloon.
NATIONAL MOTOR MUSEUM

Chairman of Citroën, with Pierre Boulanger as Managing Director. André no longer had an office, nor a title. One day, running into the founder, in a corridor, Pierre Michelin told him: 'Monsieur Citroën, leave us alone. There is nothing for you to do here'.

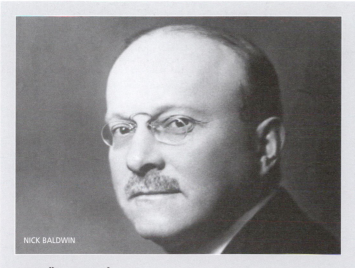

NICK BALDWIN

CITROËN, ANDRÉ (1878–1935)

André Gustave Citroën was born in Paris on 5 February 1878, the son of an Amsterdam diamond merchant, Levi Bernard Citroën and his wife, the former Masza Emilia Kleinman. His mother died shortly after his birth, and his father took his own life in 1884, after a business swindle. André was educated by relatives, and graduated from the École Polytechnique in 1901. Shortly afterwards, on a visit to his mother's family in Poland, he met an uncle who was an inventor and showed him a patented gear system with double helical teeth. This appealed greatly to André, who set up a small factory at St. Denis to make industrial gears on his uncle's lines. He also sold licences for the system to Skoda and the Bergheimische Stahl of Remscheid in the Rühr.

Initially production was based on the wooden chevron design brought from Poland, which would later become the basis of the Citroën trademark. As production increased, more machines were purchased, and by 1910 annual sales had reached one million francs. Among their applications was the steering gear for the Titanic. At a time when business was slack Citroën's company made 500 engines for Sizaire-Naudin. Citroën was related to a director of Mörs, and sat informally on the Mörs board from about 1907.

In December that year there was a proposal to close the company down, but Citroën opposed this, and became managing director in 1911, helping the firm to recovery. At the same time he built a new factory on the Quai Grenelle in Paris, and his company became Societé Anon. Des Engrenages Citroën in 1913, with a capital of 3 million francs.

He was called up for military service in August 1914, and was soon aware of the shortage of ammunition. A friend arranged a meeting with Albert Thomas, the minister for arms production, and Citroën made the bold claim that he could supply 20,000 shrapnel-filled shells every day, starting in six months. It was a highly speculative plan, with no proof that he could deliver. The City of Paris placed a 12,000 square metre site at his disposal, on the left bank of the Seine. It was mostly vacant land, partly used for the unauthorised growing of soup vegetables, with a small idle steel works. Citroën secured a 99-year lease on the site, but did not have the funds to erect a factory. However these were forthcoming through his family connections with the diamond trade, in particular a M. Eknayan who had helped with the salvation of Mörs. Ground was broken towards the end of 1914, and production began in July 1915 at a daily rate of 10,000 shells, increased to the target figure of 20,000 a few months later. During 1917 the plant had a workforce of 12,000 and a daily output of 50,000 shells. When the war ended, Citroën had delivered more than 23 million shells.

Before the end of hostilities Citroën decided to become a car manufacturer. He was not an engineer, but contacted Louis Dufresne who had an existing design for a 3.8-litre sleeve valve-engined car which he was anxious to produce. Just before the contract was signed, Citroën had a change of heart. He contacted another designer, Jules Salomon to design a popular car which would appeal to the masses. Dufresne's original sleeve valve car later became the first Voisin.

During the 1920s Citroën made a lot of money, but he also spent a lot, on publicity stunts such as illuminating the Eiffel Tower from top to bottom with the name Citroën, on a château at La Ferté-Vidame, whose vast grounds later accommodated Citroën's test track, on a yacht and gambling at Deauville. He was also obsessed with rivalry with Louis Renault, and the competition forced both men to develop new products at an accelerating pace. This pushed SA André Citroën further and further into debt. In December 1934 a large number of creditors forced the company into bankruptcy; a government commission took control, which later passed to Michelin. His sudden fall seriously affected his health, both mentally and physically. His stomach ulcers developed into a tumour which could not be removed surgically, and he died in a Paris hospital on 3 July 1935.

Citroen married, in 1914, Georgina Bingen (1896–1955). They had two sons, Bernard (b.1917) who like his father graduated from the École Polytechnique but did not join the family firm, and Maxim (b.1919) and a daughter, Jacqueline, who married the Comte de Saint-Sauveur.

JPN/NG

Further Reading
André Citroën, the Man and the Motor Cars,
John Reynolds, Wrens Park Publishing, 1999.

1959 Citroën DS19 saloon.
NATIONAL MOTOR MUSEUM

Michelin did not agree with the plan to stop production of all older models to make front-wheel drive cars only and ordered that separate assembly be kept running as long as needed. A certain amount of cross-breeding took place. The 7UA was an 8CV chassis with the 1628cc 7B engine, and the 11UA was the 10CV vehicle with the 1911cc 11A engine. The 7UA and 11UA were produced from January 1935 to July 1938, in numbers of 7,260 and 7,400 units respectively. British versions were made with Meadows engines, David Brown gearboxes, Salisbury Axles and Sankey frames. Pierre Michelin was killed in a road accident on 29 December 1937, and Pierre Boulanger was promoted to President of Citroën.

Pierre Boulanger had been with Michelin since 1922 and was used to running a big business without an organisation chart. He never regularised André Lefèbvre's position–everyone in the company just knew he was the engineering boss. But Boulanger killed the 22CV prestige-car project. Prototypes had been shown at the Paris Salon in 1934, with more daring styling, and a V8 engine made up by combining two 1911cc blocks.

Development of the 7C and 11A were top priorities, and Georges Sallot designed a rack and pinion steering gear which replaced the Gemmer worm and roller steering in 1936, and a new rear axle with revised suspension.

The original body shell had a solid rear panel, with a circular depression for the spare wheel. Luggage was loaded on and off through the folding rear seat. Beginning in 1936, a bottom-hinged trunk lid carrying the spare wheel was adopted.

The 11A, 22AL and 11N (for Normale) became 11B in January 1937, with the 1911cc engine delivering 46hp at 3800rpm, enough to raise the top speed to 65mph (105km/h). A 56hp performance engine became available in March 1939. The assembly lines stopped for the 7C in June 1941, 11B in July 1941 and 11BL in November 1941. The count for the 7C came to 69,500 cars, and for all the 11 models, 152,465 cars.

Maurice Sainturat designed a 6-cylinder engine by adding two cylinders to the 1911cc unit, and putting the crankshaft in four main bearings. The 15-Six, distinguished by its longer bonnet, went into production in April 1938, and with Normale and Familiale saloon bodies. The 2867cc ohv engine delivered 77hp at 3800rpm on a 6.3:1 compression ratio, giving the car a top speed of 80mph (130 km/h). Approximately 2000 15-Six cars were built up to 1940.

The 2CV

The 2CV was Boulanger's idea–nothing precise in technical terms, but he divined a future market for motorised minimal-cost rural transport; a combined family/utility vehicle with considerable off-road capability. An engineer, Chataigner was put to work on defining the concept, with targets for weight, cost and performance levels. What Boulanger told Lefèbvre was that he wanted him to work on specifications for a vehicle that would carry two persons and a 110lb (50kg) sack of potatoes at a speed of 37mph (60 km/h) with a fuel consumption of less than 3l/100km.

The initial design was prepared in 1935–36, and the first prototype was made in 1937. Roger Prudhomme was then in charge of prototype construction. Lefèbvre drew up the chassis, with centrally mounted transverse torsion bars, longitudinal wires, and cranks, covered by French Patent no. 837,667, dated 18 November 1938. Edmond Moyet, who had left Amilcar and returned to Citroën in 1936, designed a water-cooled flat-twin engine and Alphonse Forceau designed a three-speed gearbox for it.

Lefèbvre made lightness the number one objective, which led to the use of Duralinox for most of the body panels. The front wings were sheet steel stampings, but the wheels were magnesium. The 1937 prototype weighed less than 880lb (400kg), ran at 31mph (50 km/h) with four persons and 110lb (50kg) of luggage, consuming approximately 5l/100km. 200 test cars were built at the Levallois plant in 1939. Boulanger wanted to sell the car with a retail price of FFr5000, but in 1939 Pierre Bercot's cost-accounting determined that its cost would be 40 per cent higher than calculated. The extensive use of expensive light alloys did not tally with Boulanger's insistence on the use of low-cost materials, and the whole project was placed in question.

In January 1941 Walter Becchia left Talbot and signed up with Citroën as an engine designer. He changed the specifications to air-cooling and chose a two-piece crankshaft with one-piece conrods. Lefèbvre revised the chassis, adopting a pair of horizontal coil springs serving both front and rear wheels, as invented by Mercier, an aeronautical engineer from Liore & Olivier. The very soft, long-travel suspension gave a shock-free ride on the worst surfaces but little resistance to body roll on curves, and even if the wheels were not farm-tractor size, the car would go over unmade tracks, even across fields and through forests on rough paths.

Caneau, Muratet and Steck designed a new body in 1943. The alloy sheets for the bonnet were corrugated to give extra strength and avoid vibration. The roof was fabric, and the seats were simple tubular structures with canvas. A new prototype was made in 1944 and it became a full-scale new-car programme.

Postwar production of the 11B began in June 1945, with the addition of the 15-Six in February 1946. The 11BN was not back in production until March 1947. Their replacement models were still in the concept stage, as all efforts were concentrated on the 2CV. The 2CV was unveiled at the Paris Salon by Pierre Boulanger on 6 October 1948, before Vincent Auriol, President of the French Republic. The car was seen by 1,300,000 visitors. Their reaction: astonishment. The press found it laughable–with one exception: Robert Braunschweig of Switzerland, who predicted a brilliant future for the car.

Production did not start as planned in 1949, but got under way in 1950, when the waiting list was so long that the factory would have to work to capacity for the next six years to fill the orders on hand. The original 375cc engine put out 9hp at 3500rpm and gave the car a top speed of 33.8mph (54.5 km/h). The owners did not complain about a lack of speed. They were overwhelmed by the car's qualities–the ride comfort, the spaciousness, and the economy. At first, it was reserved for the home market. Its first international showing took place in Geneva in March 1952 signalling the start of exports. Assembly of the right-hand drive 2CV began at Slough in 1953.

An optional 12hp 425cc engine was added in 1954, with a centrifugal clutch, disengaging below 1000rpm. On the 1956 models, rear window area was doubled, and a year later, a metal trunk lid was fitted in place of the canvas cover. Production increased to 107,250 units in 1957, and for the next decade varied from 126,000 to 168,000 cars a year.

Pierre Boulanger did not live to see the success of the 2CV, for he was killed at the wheel of his 15-Six H, with a 4-speed gearbox, on 11 November 1950. One of the Michelin family's most trusted executives, Robert Puiseux, assumed the Citroën Presidency, though he continued to spend most of his time with the tyre company at Clermont Ferrand. Day-to-day operations were handled by Pierre Bercot, who was given a seat on the board. Bercot trained as a lawyer, studied economics, and joined Citroën in 1937. Bercot threw full priority behind the big-car project while down-playing the development of the 2CV itself, though very keen on adding up-market variations, which he saw as the start of filling the gap in the centre of the Citroën model range. But the company was living on credit. Production volume was only one-half of what was needed to break even.

In July 1952, the 11B and the 15-Six body shells were given a built-in trunk, and in 1955 the 11B engine was fitted with a new cylinder head, raising output to 60hp at 4000rpm–and top speed to 75mph (120km/h). In 1954–55, 3062 15-Six cars were made with air/oil rear suspension and automatic level control.

The DS19

André Lefèbvre and Flaminio Bertoni had been toying with plans for a successor model to the 11B and 15-Six since 1938.

The car Lefèbvre had on the drawing board in 1950 was a streamliner with a fuel-injected flat-six engine, fully automatic transmission, four-wheel disc brakes with an anti-lock system, power steering, and steered headlamps. The chassis had a clever all-independent torsion-bar suspension with automatic level control. That system was discarded in favour of a unique air/oil suspension, for which a separate plant was set up at Asnières in 1953, with high-precision machines and the shops sealed against dust.

Citroën held patents on hydraulic suspension going back to 1944, and Paul Mages (with his assistants Meignan and Dascotte) developed a new system which provided very low-frequency ride rates and automatic level control, included in the same central hydraulic system that also provided power brakes, power steering, clutch operation and gearshift servos. Lefèbvre had to give up his hopes for an automatic transmission, but a 4-speed gearbox with semi-automatic shifts was tested in a T-45 truck in 1949, and later in the 15-Six. Eventually it became clear that the flat-six would not be ready for the schedule Puiseux had set for the programme (too low on specific power, too many cooling problems, and so on).

Bertoni's elegant body profile did not need changing, for shifting the engine inside the wheelbase opened up free space for the hydraulic reservoir, accessories, and the spare wheel. Citroën had built its own little wind tunnel at La Ferté-Vidame for aerodynamic testing, and the car did indeed qualify as a low-drag streamliner. The body engineering task fell to Franchiset and Estaque. André Estaque had joined Citroën in 1944 and had worked in the body methods department since 1946. The body structure of the DS19 was a steel platform with a bulkhead and support elements reaching no higher than the window sills, the doors had frameless windows, and the roof was a plastic insert. The steel body

1967 Citroën Ami 6 saloon.
NATIONAL MOTOR MUSEUM

1968 Citroën 1 Dyane saloon.
NATIONAL MOTOR MUSEUM

c.1975 Citroën Mehari utility.
NICK GEORGANO

1978 Citroën CX estate car.
NICK GEORGANO

1973 Citroën SM coupé.

panels were not stress-bearing and simply bolted on. Only the engine was carried over from the previous Citroëns. Instead of Lefèbvre's flat six, the DS19 had the familiar 75bhp 1911cc 11D 4-cylinder engine.

The DS19 made its bow at the Paris Salon in October 1955, and in the first 45 minutes after opening, Citroën took orders for 749 cars at a price of FF930,000 each. At the end of the first day, 12,000 orders had been booked. No more than 69 cars were completed before the end of 1955, however, followed by 10,859 in 1956 and 28,592 in 1957. A variant of the new model, ID19 was presented in Paris in September 1956. It differed from the DS19 in having non-assisted steering, normal clutch and gearshift, a 66hp 1911cc engine, and lower-grade trim and equipment, yet it was priced at FFr925,000, compared with FFr682,500 for the 11B Traction. Production of the Traction ended in July 1957.

Production of the ID19 began in May 1957, but only 5655 units had been built by year-end. In 1958, a total of 26,951 ID19s were produced. Estate cars, business and ambulance versions of the ID19 were introduced in October 1958, along with the DS19 Prestige which had a partition behind the front seats and a two-way radio-telephone.

Robert Puiseux retired in 1958 and on 3 July 1958, Pierre Bercot was appointed President of Citroën, with Antoine Brueder as Managing Director. In July 1958, André Lefèbvre retired due to health problems and Jean Cadiou was named administrative head of Citroën's car engineering. He appointed Georges Sallot as head of the drawing office, with a young associate, Hubert Seznec. Major product responsibilities were also given to Forceau, Grosseau, Estaque and Alléra.

Throughout this upheaval, Citroën maintained a flow of new models. The 2CV 4 × 4 Sahara was added in 1958. It had a second power train in the rear, i.e. two 12hp 425cc engines, one driving the front wheels and the other the rear wheels. It proved to give 45 per cent gradeability in the sand dunes. The 2CV got wider tyres and better heating in 1959, and a facelifted front end in 1960. A new instrument panel with a fuel gauge was fitted in 1962, along with twin electrical wipers (earlier models had a wiper only on the driver's side, driven off the speedometer cable).

For 1961 the 425cc 2CV engine was uprated to 13.5hp, and top speed climbed to 53mph (85km/h). The 1963 425cc engine was uprated to 18hp, raising top speed to 59mph (95km/h). All 1965 model 2CV cars were fitted with hydraulic dampers on the rear wheels, and export models were equipped with constant velocity universal joints.

Bercot thought there was a market for a bigger, stylish and more powerful car on the 2CV platform, which led to the Ami-6. Albert Grosseau was head of small-car engineering when it was developed. He had joined Citroën's Service Department in 1952 and was transferred to the Design Office in 1958, succeeding

Sallot, who retired as head of all production-model car engineering in 1966. He immediately began preliminary studies for a DS replacement.

The Ami-6 made its debut on 24 April 1961, with the most controversial styling, and a 22hp 602cc version of the flat twin. Bercot was betting on heavy demand for the car, and had set up a completely new assembly plant for it at Rennes-la Janais. But it was finished behind schedule, so the first series of Ami-6 cars were built in the Panhard factory at Ivry. Ami-6 sales never lived up to Bercot's expectations.

Bercot had long wanted an alliance with another French car company, but state-owned Renault was 'the enemy' and not a possible partner. He put out feelers to H.T. Pigozzi about an alliance with Simca, but their talks were broken off when Agnelli (FIAT) sold their Simca holdings to Chrysler in 1962. By 1963 Bercot was making advances to Peugeot, and a tentative agreement for industrial co-operation, joint purchasing and research, was signed in November 1963. But in the Spring of 1966, Maurice Jordan went to the Montreal Trade Fair, where he met Pierre Dreyfus of Renault. They talked a lot, and Jordan dropped Citroën for a new plan of collaboration with Renault. Bercot was stuck in a blind alley. He tried to diversify into trucks and buses by taking majority control of Berliet, which proved a further drain on Citroën's (and Michelin's) finances. In 1966 and 1968 the French Government bailed out Citroën with low-interest loans totalling $60m. Over the weekend of 21-22 September 1968, after about six months of talks, the details of an alliance between Citroën and Fiat were negotiated by François Michelin and Gianni 'l'Avvocato' Agnelli. Full ownership of Citroën was placed in a joint holding. Pardevi (Société de Participation et de Développment Industriel) was established on 21 December 1968, in which Michelin held 51 per cent and Fiat 49 per cent.

Collaboration on new products began quickly, with the twinning of the programmes for the successor models to the Citroën DS and Lancia Flavia/Flaminia. What became the CX and Gamma started out with common platforms and body structures, but ended up without sharing anything. The two cultures could not be combined. Other points of conflict arose. Fiat's management wanted more integration, while Citroën's leaders sought greater independence. Fiat wanted Citroën to abandon the small-car market entirely, while building on Citroën's strength in the upper price brackets where Fiat was weak, to generate higher profits for the alliance. The eventual split of the alliance hinged upon the arrival of new Citroën models and the company's return to profits.

The GS, M-35, GSA, and SM

The idea of the GS was to make a very modern, compact car with unique qualities, such as ride comfort, by using air/oil suspension, and economy by putting two 2CV engines together to make an air-cooled flat-four. The architect of the GS was Alain Roché who had joined Citroën's Technical Methods Department in 1955 and became a member of Estaque's Body-Engineering group in 1957.

The GS body was an all-steel shell with detachable front wings, and smooth, non-controversial styling by Robert Opron and Jean Giret. Giret had been an industrial designer with Arthur Martin (home appliances) before he started with Citroën as a modeller and free-hand artist. Opron came from Simca to Citroën in 1962 and was named Director of Styling in June 1964.

The 55bhp 1015cc GS engine with a belt-driven ohc on each side, was designed by Jean Dupin who had worked under Becchia and Moyet for years, and was rewarded by being put in charge of all air-cooled engine development in 1972. Becchia retired in 1968 and Moyet died at the wheel of his car one evening in 1967, just after leaving his office, the car still in the garage. The GS went into production at Rennes-la Janais in August 1970, and 12,620 units were built by the end of the year. For the first time, the plant's full capacity was to be utilised. GS output climbed from 158,675 cars in 1971 to 195,138 in 1972 and 223,067 in 1973.

NATIONAL MOTOR MUSEUM

BUDD, EDWARD G. (1870–1946)

Edward G Budd and his partner Joe Ledwinka are perhaps among the most underrated people to shape the motor industry in the 20th century. Whilst everyone is aware of the impact of Ford on car making, few seem to know of the – perhaps even more important – impact of these two men. The system of making cars from pressed and welded sheet steel now determines the economics of the mass production car industry worldwide. All the fundamental and most expensive elements of a modern car plant; press shop, body plant and paint shop owe their existence to the technologies introduced by Budd and Ledwinka. Investments in these technologies and the returns on these investments through car sales determine whether a car manufacturer is profitable or not. While the high investments in engine and transmission plants can be spread over large sections of a model range and several model generations and can even be sold to competitors, the body determines the look of a car and has to be suitably different for each car model.

Edward Gowan Budd was born in Smyrna, Delaware on 28 December 1870. He was apprenticed to the Smyrna Iron Works, after which he moved to Philadelphia. He studied at the University of Pennsylvania, became interested in the possibilities of pressed metal as opposed to cast metal and, when a friend received funding to make pressed steel pulleys, joined his American Pulley Co. In 1902 one of the firm's customers, Hale & Kilburn offered him twice his salary to come and work for them and develop pressed parts to replace existing cast metal components. Thus Budd came to play a key role in the decline of the once invincible cast iron industry, by replacing many of its products with superior pressed steel. Most of Hale & Kilburn's output went to the railroad rolling stock industry – Budd's first move into vehicle engineering and railway rolling stock remained one of the Budd company's core product areas.

One of the first firms to recognise the potential of the new technology in car bodies was Hupmobile. They approached Hale & Kilburn and Budd was made responsible for helping Hupmobile develop the body for its model 32 of 1912. The bodies for this first all-steel production car were shipped to Hupmobile in Detroit for paint and trim. The absence of wood allowed much higher baking temperatures to be used in the paint drying ovens.

This removed a major bottle-neck from the body production process. Car bodies could take several weeks to dry, particularly in the case of some lighter colours with lower pigment content. These could now be dried in only one day. In addition, it removed the not uncommon danger of the timber frame of a body catching fire during the drying process.

This initial success prompted Budd to resign from Hale & Kilburn and set up his own company for the development of all-steel bodies. He took with him Joseph Ledwinka – a relative of Tatra's Hans Ledwinka – as chief engineer and many Budd patents are in fact in his name. Having established the basic technology for making pressed and welded steel bodies, considerable resources were still needed to make the process feasible for series production. Early attempts at welding the pressings led to many distortions in the bodies until suitable body-framing jigs were developed. Many other techniques now commonplace in car body-building were developed by Budd at this time, although even today, the actual use of much of this technology remains somewhat of a 'black art' in the industry.

The breakthrough came with the first volume application, the new car launched by the Dodge brothers, after they left Ford. Dodge Brothers ordered some 5,000 all-steel open tourer bodies in 1914, followed by a further 50,000 in 1915. Budd and Dodge developed a close buyer-supplier relationship reminiscent of the close links now credited to the Japanese keiretsu system. Dodge did not use the innovation in body technology much in its advertising, but nevertheless other car manufacturers soon followed its lead. By the early 1920s Buick, Oakland, Willys-Overland, Studebaker, luxury car maker Wills Sainte Claire and even Ford had become customers.

From these early US successes, the technology spread. André Citroën visited Budd in 1923 and was the first to bring Budd all steel technology to Europe. He claimed that the new system allowed Citroën to increase daily output from between 30 and 50 to between 400 and 500. Budd's patents were framed in such a way that few dared adopt the technology without involving Budd. Among those few was Renault, but others called in teams of Budd engineers to set up the system. Among early licencees in Europe were Morris, Fiat, Simca, Peugeot and Volvo. Joint ventures were set up in Germany and the UK to support the new technology locally.

The next step was even more important. Budd, Ledwinka and others soon realised that it was now possible to phase out the separate chassis and move to a full unibody or monocoque construction. Early experiments with monocoque construction, such as the 1899 Latil, 1923 Voisin GP and Lancia Lambda predated Budd, but his technology now made it feasible to make them in large numbers. With this came the rise in popularity of closed bodies to enhance structural rigidity. The first cars using this technology in mass production were the landmark Citroën Traction Avant of 1934 and the Opel Olympia of 1937. Ironically, Detroit was among the last to adopt all-steel welded unibody construction and phase out the chassis, though by the 1990s few mass produced cars worldwide were made any other way.

Even after Budd's death in 1946, his company retained the spirit of innovation and rather than sticking doggedly with steel alone it has developed expertise in alternative body materials, most notably aluminium and sheet moulding composite (SMC). During the 1990s The Budd Company combined with the German Thyssen group to form Thyssen-Budd, one of the world's leading suppliers of automotive body systems in steel, aluminium or plastic composites.

PN

Further Reading
'The All-Steel World of Edward Budd', Stan Grayson, *Automobile Quarterly*, Vol.16, No.4.

1980 Citroën GS saloon.
NICK GEORGANO

1980 Citroën Visa 4-door hatchback.
NATIONAL MOTOR MUSEUM

The smaller cars evolved in a pattern of predictability mingled with surprises. In the spring of 1965, the 2CV cars assembled in Belgium could be ordered with an optional 28bhp 602cc flat-twin. Bercot wanted to modernise the 2CV, giving it a new style without changing its character, and brought out the better-equipped, more civilised Dyane in August 1967, with styling by Louis Bionier of Panhard, and a choice of 435cc and 602cc flat-twins. That year 2CV sales dropped from 168,384 to 98,685 units.

Bercot wanted to phase out the base 2CV, but it did not work. People preferred the lower-priced older model, whose production exceeded 121,000 units in both 1970 and 1971, compared with figures of 96,546 and 97,091 for the Dyane. Both were produced at Levallois until 1982 when the Dyane was discontinued after a run of 1,443,500 units.

Another variant on the 2CV platform was the Mehari, a recreational vehicle with an all-plastic (Cycolac) open body, introduced in 1969. It was built in small series of 10,000 to 12,000 units a year up to 1984, beginning at Nanterre and Rennes, but transferred to Forest, Belgium and Vigo, Spain in 1970. A Méhari 4 × 4 with a 7-speed gearbox was introduced in 1981.

The Ami-6 was restyled (toned down) for 1969 and renamed Ami-8. From 1973 to 1976 it was also built as an Ami Super , with the 1015cc flat-four from the GS.

The M-35 was a coupé version of the Ami-series, appearing in November 1969, with a single-rotor Wankel engine. At the instigation of Jacques Nougarou, head of technical research, and other engineers, Citroën's management became interested in the Wankel engine, and in June 1964, representatives of Citroën and NSU met in Geneva to form a joint venture, Société d'Étude Comobil, to plan a rotary-engined car. A second joint venture, Comotor S.A. was organised on 9 May 1967, to manufacture Wankel engines for Citroën and NSU products, and supply Wankel engines to outside clients. In 1968 Comotor moved into a

small factory at Altforweiler in the Saar, Germany. The M-35 engine was based on the power unit of the NSU Spider and delivered 49bhp at 5500rpm. A field-test fleet of 500 cars was planned, but less than 300 were actually put on the road.

A twin-rotor version based on the NSU Ro-80 engine had been in preparation for two years when Michel Audinet was put in charge of Wankel engine development in the Citroën laboratories. In 1973–74 Citroën built a small series of GS Bi-rotor cars for testing and evaluation, but production was postponed due to the fuel crisis.

Changes on the DS19 and ID19 models were mostly under the skin. Engines for the 1961 model DS19 put out 83bhp, the ID remaining at 66bhp. A DS19 cabriolet, designed by Citroën and built by Chapron, was added to the range in 1961. The front end was 'cleaned up' for the 1963 models, which gained approximately 6mph (10km/h) in top speed.

André de Bladis became Chief Engineer of Citroën's power-unit design staff after Becchia's retirement. Born in 1925, he held diplomas from the École des Arts et Métiers in Paris and the École des Moteurs at Rueil. He led the design of new 4-cylinder 84bhp 1985cc and 100bhp 2175cc engines with 5-bearing crankshafts, which were mounted in the 1966 DS19 and DS21; the ID19 received a 78bhp version of the 1985cc engine.

The DS20 replaced the DS19 for 1968, with a 103bhp 1985cc engine, which also went into the ID20. A year later, the D Special and D Super replaced the ID19 and ID20. The 1970 DS21 was given a 5-speed gearbox as standard (optional on the D Super). The DS23 appeared as a 1972 model, with a 2347cc engine, delivering 110bhp in carburettor form and 130bhp with D-Jetronic fuel injection.

The SM came into being as a pure experiment. Pierre Bercot was worried that, except for small, low-powered cars, Citroën was practically alone in building front-wheel drive models. A nagging doubt that other manufacturers were right and Citroën wrong, was plaguing him. One day in 1963 he called in Jacques Né and asked him if there was a limit to the amount of power that could be put on the road through the front wheels.

After testing DS-based experimental cars with up to 380hp, Né reported that Citroën had the know-how for building front-wheel drive cars with any amount of power. The research programme was then turned towards application, which resulted in the production of the SM.

Maserati supplied the 180bhp 2760cc V6 engine, and Opron and Giret styled a modern coupé body for the modified DS chassis. It was approved, and an initial production run began at the Javel Plant in March 1970.

No customer orders were taken until October 1970, however. Over a four-year span, Citroën produced 12,290 SM cars, including the final 199 units which were assembled by Ligier at Abrest near Vichy in 1975. And on 22 May 1975, Citroën placed Officine Alfieri Maserati in liquidation and transferred its Modena-based personnel back to Paris.

The corporate set-up was changed in 1968, with Citroën S.A. being formed as a holding under the presidency of Pierre Bercot, with two operating divisions, S.A. Automobiles Citroën for manufacturing and Société Commerciale Citroën for sales. Claude Alain Sarre was named president of S.A. Automobiles Citroën, with Raymond Ravenel as managing director. Then aged 41, Sarre had been with Citroën since 1956, holding a succession of sales positions. Ravenel was an engineer with diplomas from the Arts et Métiers of Angers and Lille who had joined Citroën in 1949, working on timing studies, tooling, training and personnel assignments.

Sarre managed to cut Citroën's operating losses in half, but the company still reported a staggering $11.5million deficit in 1969. It was to get worse, for Citroën lost $80million in 1970. Sarre was quickly dismissed, and replaced by Raymond Ravenel while Bercot went into retirement in 1971.

It was not just the GS that changed Citroën's financial picture, for the 2CV/Dyane/Ami 8 family made its contribution along with the D-series. Citroën made a $5million profit in 1972. These figures – and a downtrend in Fiat's own fortunes – meant that Fiat lost the upper hand in their conflict, but even earlier, the executives of both Peugeot and Renault, worried about the risk of Citroën coming under Italian control, had filed a petition to block a full Fiat-Citroën merger with Charles de Gaulle's minister for industry, François-Xavier Ortoli. The President of the Republic, still in his 'Quebec Libre' frame of mind, declared 'collaboration yes, dictatorship no'. PARDEVI was dissolved by common agreement on 24 June 1973, and Michelin recovered Fiat's shares for a $50million cheque.

7
4 CYL.

11
4 CYL.

22
8 CYL.

CITROËN
TRACTION AVANT

1981 Citroën CX saloon.
NATIONAL MOTOR MUSEUM

1983 Citroën BX 4-door hatchback.
NATIONAL MOTOR MUSEUM

1989 Citroën AX GT hatchback.
NATIONAL MOTOR MUSEUM

In June 1974 François Michelin asked for a meeting with François Gauthier, President of Peugeot, to discuss the Citroën problem. Secret negotiations were carried on for many months, and the government proposed to pay $86million to Peugeot for taking over Citroën.

On 6 December 1974 they decided to merge Citroën and Peugeot to form an automobile group of international dimensions. Peugeot was to acquire 90 per cent of Citroën's shares on a tight time schedule. Panhard-Levassor was integrated with the Peugeot organisation, and Berliet was divorced from Citroën and sold to Renault. Automobiles Peugeot and Automobiles Citroën were established on 12 May 1976 as fully-owned subsidiaries of Peugeot SA.

CX

The brief for the successor model to the D-series demanded new architecture (getting the engine out of the passenger compartment) and a lower profile with more modern styling. An in-line 4-cylinder engine made in three sizes was accommodated transversely, driving the front wheels. The central hydraulic system mixed elements of the GS and SM suspension, steering and brakes. It became a long (183.4in/4655mm) car on a 112in (2843mm) wheelbase, with strong family resemblance to both the GS and the SM.

Albert Grosseau was in overall charge of the CX programme, Pierre Cordier developed the engines for transverse installation, tilted 30 degrees forward, and André Barthélémy was the principal chassis engineer. Opron and Giret provided the styling, with André Estaque as head of body engineering, discarding D-series principles for an elaboration on the GS type of structure,

The CX went into production at Aulnay-sous-Bois, a highly automated and robotised factory, in September 1974, and quickly reached a daily rate of 440 units, although the planned capacity was 900 units a day. The entire Javel works was scheduled for demolition. The city of Paris repurchased the site for FFr37.5 billion in 1974, although car production went on until 1977, and Citroën used the offices until 1979. When the operations closed, a total of 3,227,105 cars had been built at the Quai de Javel.

The final production figure for the D-series, ending in May 1975, was 1,456,718 cars. When Raymond Ravenel retired, George Taylor was named President of Automobiles Citroën on 8 December 1974. He was born in Rumania in 1921, the son of an English father and French mother, and was only 20 when he collected his diploma from the Hautes Études Commerciales in Paris. He had served his previous career in various manufacturing and executive positions with Peugeot.

The long-wheelbase (122in/3095mm) CX Prestige went into production in July 1975, and a CX estate car followed in October 1975. A diesel engine, derived from the 1965-model vans became optional in January 1976. The CX 2400 GTi with electronic fuel injection arrived in May 1977, delivering 128bhp at 3600rpm. Introduced in July 1979, the CX Reflex and CX Athena were powered by new Peugeot-built 1995cc ohc engines, signalling the coming integration of engine production. The 95bhp CX 25 turbo diesel went into production in April 1984.

Sales of the CX tapered off from an average of 60,000 cars a year to 45,000 between 1980 and 1988, when Citroën introduced the X range. The CX saloon was discontinued in April 1989, but the CX estate car was kept in production by Heuliez until 1991, reaching a combined total of 1,571,746 units.

Rationalisation of the Model Programme

Peugeot's management, headed by Jean-Paul Parayre, was eager to centralise the product planning and engineering functions for the two makes, which meant eliminating several Citroën models and replacing them with Peugeot-based cars.

The 2CV was the most obvious target for the axe. Actually, Ravenel and his executives had decided as early as 1972 to stop building the 2CV, but the date was repeatedly pushed back because the car was still in demand. At the Slough plant, 2CV production had ended in 1959, although the factory remained open, building other models. The British Citroën subsidiary, however, decided to create its own 'Bijou' type of 2CV, using the same platform and mechanical elements, with a modern 4-passenger coupé body designed by Peter Kirwan-Taylor. It was a fibreglass-reinforced plastic body produced by Whitson & Co. In 1960–61, a total of 213 Bijou cars were built and sold.

In 1982, Citroën was still turning out the 2CV at a daily rate of 500 cars at Levallois, and had no fixed date for its demise. It was phased out in the face of diminishing demand, and the Levallois plant was closed on 29 February 1988. Production of the 2CV continued at Jiangualde, Portugal, until April 1991. The final production figure for the 2CV was 5,069,821 cars, the majority (2,846,470) assembled at Levallois.

The Ami-8 was discontinued in 1978, but the GS lived on. A bigger (1222cc) 58bhp engine became standard in 1976, and the car was renamed GSA in 1979, when the displacement was increased to 1299cc and output to 65bhp at 5500rpm. Options, including a 5-speed gearbox and C-Matic, were added for the GSA, which was produced up to 1986. The final production total for the GS/GSA was 2,466,757 cars.

The first of the Peugeot-Citroën cross-breeds was the 1976 Citroën LN, which combined the 602cc air-cooled flat-twin with the platform and body of the Peugeot 104 Z, assembled at Aulnaysous-Bois at a daily rate of 250 units. Two years later it became available with a water-cooled 4-cylinder 1124cc Peugeot engine. The Peugeot 104 platform also served for the Citroën Visa, which arrived in 1978, sharing the LN power trains, with new exterior sheet metal giving it a Citroën look. It was assembled at the Rennes-la Janais plant.

A 64hp 1219cc 4-cylinder engine became optional in the Visa in 1980. The Visa had a facelift in 1981, and an 80bhp 1360cc engine powered the Visa GT. Launched in July 1982, the 60bhp 1769cc Visa diesel went into production in March 1984. Cumulative production of the Visa reached 965,000 units in

1990 Citroën XM saloon.
CITROËN

1984, by which time its assembly had spread to Aulnay-sous-Bois and Vigo, Spain. Its replacement was the AX, arriving in October 1986, though the Visa remained in production until 1988, with a run of 1,614,000 cars.

A low-cost version of the Visa was prepared for production in Rumania as the OLTCIT, beginning late in 1981, with a special 652cc air-cooled flat-twin. The contract was signed in December 1976, and the Craiova plant was built for a capacity of 130,000 cars a year but never turned out more than 30,000 a year.

The integration with Peugeot caused a major upheaval in personnel on both sides. Albert Grosseau was named PSA Group Technical Director in 1976, and five years later he was moved laterally to serve as the PSA Group's Director of Research and Scientific Affairs. Michel Durin, long-time director of Citroën's General Methods Department, took over as PSA Group Technical Director.

Jacques Lombard became head of Citroën's Product Planning Office in 1978. A mining engineer who joined Peugeot in 1953, he succeeded George Taylor as President of Automobiles Citroën in January 1979, with Xavier Karcher as Managing Director. Karcher came to Peugeot in 1956 from the École des Arts et Manufactures, and worked in the design and experimental departments at La Garenne from 1958 to 1967, holding a succession of executive positions since then.

François Rollier, a top executive who had taken over the Citroën S.A. presidency from Pierre Bercot in 1971, was pushed out in 1976, when the holding was assimilated into Peugeot S.A.

André de Bladis was transferred to the PSA Group vehicle design staff at La Garenne in November 1980 and retired in 1987. Jacques Desbois from Peugeot was named Director of Citroën Product Engineering in 1980. He had served as Chief Mechanical Engineer at Sochaux in the 1960s and 1970s and as Director of Engineering for Talbot in 1979–80.

Jacques Né, who had worked on urban-car projects for Citroën subsequent to the SM assignment, was transferred to La Garenne in 1976 and became project manager for the Eco 2000 project (a low-pollution, low-consumption recyclable prototype) but retired in 1985.

Hubert Alcera went to work for Ligier after the end of the SM development in 1970, but returned to Citroën in 1974 and was assigned to the military vehicles department of Panhard-Levassor in 1981. Robert Opron went to Renault in 1975, and Jean Giret retired in 1978 after styling the Visa. In 1982 Citroën split the

styling department in two: a near-term production-car studio at Velizy under the direction of Carl Olsen, and an advanced studio at Sophia-Antipolis under Trevor Fiore.

Planning for the Citroën BX began in 1977, with an enlarged GSA platform, air/oil suspension, and transversely mounted 4-cylinder Peugeot engines. Body design was contracted to Bertone on the strength of sketches and a scale-model by Marcello Gandini. The BX went into production at the Rennes - la Janais plant in September 1982, the saloon being 166.5in (4226mm) long with a 104.5in (2652mm) wheelbase. Jacques Chevreton was chief body engineer for the BX, and specified a lot of plastic components, including the tailgate, bumpers and grill, while reducing the number of steel pressings to 334 (compared with 531 on their GSA). The engines were 72hp 1360cc and 90hp 1580cc units. The 65hp 1905cc BX diesel arrived in September 1983, followed by the BX 19 GT (105hp at 5600rpm) in July 1984. A BX estate car was added in June 1985, and the GTi 16S with its 160hp 16-valve 1905cc engine followed in July 1987. A 90hp 1769cc turbo diesel became available in March 1988, and the BX 4 × 4 came on the market in January 1989.

The Citroën AX which went into production in June 1986 was a very different type of car from the 2CV, but it inherited the entry-level position in the model line-up. The new series PSA Group engines found their first application in the AX, in sizes of 954cc with 45bhp; 1024cc with 55bhp; and 1360cc with 105bhp. The chassis layout followed the pattern of the Peugeot 205, but on a smaller scale. Carl Ülsen directed the styling, and Paul Giraud was chief body engineer. The Aulnay-sous-Bois plant was tooled to produce 1000 AX cars a day. The 95hp 1294cc AX Sport was added and a 75bhp 1360cc AX 4 × 4 followed in October 1992. The one-millionth AX was built on 17 January 1990, and the two-millionth AX on 21 September 1993.

The XM was planned as a successor to the CX but more than that, it would be made big enough to accommodate the PRV V6 engine as well as the 4-cylinder power units from the CX. It was intended for a production life of 10 to 12 years in 4-door saloon and estate car forms.

Styling proposals were invited at the beginning of 1984. By that time, Trevor Fiore had left Citroën and the advanced studio at Sophia-Aiytipocis was closed, its functions transferred to the ex-Chrysler design centre at Carrière, which

1996 Citroën Saxo 1.6i VTS hatchback.
NATIONAL MOTOR MUSEUM

2000 Citroën Synergie MPV.
NATIONAL MOTOR MUSEUM

submitted several concept sketches. Carl Ülsen proposed one design, and the young Californian, Dan Abramson, recently transferred to Velizy from the Chrysler-UK studio at Whitley, made another. Bertone submitted a set of sketches by Marc Deschamps, with a mixture of soft and crisp lines, which Xavier Karcher preferred. Bertone was asked to provide a 1/5th scale model, which was approved in September 1984. Carl Ülsen resigned in protest, and Art Blakeslee, who had worked under Elwood P. Engel at Chrysler in Detroit before taking over the studio at Whitley, was named Director of Citroën styling.

The Rennes - la Janais factory was expensively remodelled and heavily robotised, with a daily capacity of 450 XM cars. Production began at Rennes in 1988. Assembly of the XM estate car was contracted out to Heuliez, who started production in September 1991. The engine options included 110bhp and 112bhp versions of the 1998cc 4-cylinder XU series, the 170bhp 2975cc 90 V6, an 83bhp 2138cc XUD diesel, and a 110bhp 2088cc XUD turbo diesel. A 200bhp V6 became available in October 1991, and the 145bhp 1998cc turbo CT was added in December 1991.

For approximately 18 months, under the effect of novelty, the XM sales curve was rising, but it went into a dive in 1991, and the daily production rate was throttled to a mere 45 cars. A facelift in 1994 proved of no avail, nor did new engine options for 1995 boost the demand. A 135bhp 16-valve 1998cc unit replaced the 110- and 122bhp versions, and a 130bhp 2446cc turbo diesel was added.

The PSA Group had been slow to formulate a successor to the GSA, for its planning – led by Luc Epron, ex-Peugeot engineer and Citroën's top marketing executive – did not begin until GSA production had been halted. It was defined as a smaller and more modern version of the BX, and Art Blakeslee gave the styling assignment to Donato Coco, a talented young Italian industrial designer whose earlier work had been in non-automotive areas. He drew the first ZX sketches in 1986. Production of the ZX began in March 1991 at Aulnay-sous-Bois. Breaking the traditions of the GS and BX, its suspension was pure Peugeot, with coil springs for all four wheels.

By the end of 1991 it was also assembled at Poissy and Vigo, Spain, at a combined rate of 1450 cars a day. The LX coupé was added in September 1992, and the LX estate car followed in November 1993.

Regis Baudier, a Peugeot engineer who had been transferred to Talbot (ex -Chrysler France) in 1980, was named head of Citroën's Product Engineering Department in 1989, with Jean-Claude Leclercq as Manager of the drawing office. He put Jean Heinrich in charge of developing the AX into the more refined Saxo and started planning a successor for the BX. Heinrich had been Plant Manager at Altforweiler from 1970 to 1975, spent three years in international planning and was then Director of the Rémery engine plant.

The Saxo looked bigger and was heavier than the AX which it replaced in November 1995. It was based on the Peugeot 106 platform, and the engine options included a 2587cc 90bhp 8-valve unit, a 1587cc 120bhp 16-valve unit, and a 58bhp 1527cc diesel.

The BX successor was named Xantia and was unveiled at the Geneva Salon in March 1993. Jean Heinrich had been named Project Manager in 1989. The main changes were an elaboration on the XM Hydractive suspension to include electronic anti-roll control, and a slick new look. Although Bertone got some credit for the styling, it was in fact Dan Abramson's work, from the Velizy studio. The engines were off-the-shelf PSA Group power units: 112bhp 1761cc 16-valve, 135bhp 1998cc 16-valve, 150bhp turbo CT Activa, and 110bhp 2088cc turbo diesel VSX. A 170bhp V6 24 Activa became optional (with ZF automatic transmission) in 1994. The Xantia estate car went into production in May 1995, and the Xantia was facelifted in December 1996.

The Citroën Xsara which replaced the ZX in 1997 was essentially the same car mechanically, but with a whole new look created by Giles Taylor under Art Blakeslee's supervision. The 4-door saloon was the sole model for almost a year, the coupé and estate car following in 1998. The Xsara Picasso Minivan on the saloon platform went into production at mid-year 1999.

In the year 2000, Citroën finally had the most coherent line-up since 1931 – and much broader in scope, variety, and price range.

JPN

Further Reading
Quai de Javel-Quai André Citroën, 1919–1973, Pierre Dumont, EPA, Paris, 1973.
La Tragedie d'André Citroën, Sylvain Neiner.
André Citroën, Jacques Wolgensinger, Hammarion, Paris, 1991.
Citroën Histoire et les Secrets de son Bureau d'Études, Roger Brioult, Edifiée, Fontainebleu, 1987.
Avant Traction. Le Grand Livre , Olivier de Senes, EPA, Paris, 1993.
L'histoire d'André Citroën, Charles Nocherand, Editions Christian, Paris, 1979.
SM Citroën, Jan P. Norbye, Automilia, Milano, 1991.
André Citroën: The man and the Motorcars, John Reynolds, 1998.

CITROËN (ii) (RA) 1960 to date

Citroën Argentina S.A., Buenos Aires.

Late in 1958, the local firm Staud y Cia. started a joint study with Société Anonyme André Citroën, leading to the plan to start producing Citroën vehicles in Argentina. Thus Citroën Argentina S.A. was born, producing the 2CV model from 1960. The 3CV was introduced in 1969, the Ami 8 in 1970 and the Mehari in 1971. The 2CV, 3CV, and Mehari proved very popular in Argentina, because of their low initial cost and ease of maintenance. However, in later years they started to be considered too crude. Their production petered out at the beginning of the 1980s, when the Visa had already been introduced (in 1981).

In 1999, Citroën Argentina S.A. was producing the ZX, Xantia SX, Berlingo Multispace and Xsara SX models.

ACT

CITY MOBILE (GB) 1984

City Mobile Ltd, Fairwarp, Sussex.

Leaning 3-wheelers have been a consistent but obscure part of motoring life, but no design ever came as close to production as Dr Edmund Jephcott's City Mobile Micro. Its enclosed body was styled by Richard Oakes and was made of glassfibre with one side door only. It was intended as a commuter car, and was claimed to have better stability than 4-wheeled cars. The patented tilting mechanism was, at first, mechanically operated by pedals but later modified to a damped pendulum system because of weight factors. The engine was a mid-mounted 350cc snowmobile unit and transmission was by an automatic gearbox and clutch to the rear wheels. The prototype was displayed on the Design Council's Drive Forward exhibition at the 1984 Birmingham Motor Show but, despite much press coverage, Jephcott never got a backer to put the car into production, although there was some interest from Honda.

CR

CITY & SUBURBAN (US/GB) 1901–1905

City & Suburban Electric Carriage Co. Ltd, London.

This company was agent for the American COLUMBIA (i), of which it sold a variety of models from a light 2-seater to heavy landaulettes and shooting brakes. Most of the bodies were of British manufacture, which made the City & Suburban an Anglo-American product. One of its first customers was Queen Alexandra, who bought a 2-seater 'victoriette' for travel around the grounds of Sandringham in 1901. This car is now in the National Motor Museum at Beaulieu. Two years later another royal customer was the Prince of Wales (later King George V), who bought a town brougham. The cheapest model in 1903 was the Niagara runabout for doctors, which sold for £250. Its name came from that of the former skating rink in Westminster which was the company's headquarters. It also had a large building 'comprising several floors' at Denman Street, off Piccadilly Circus. Early in 1903 the company announced a petrol-electric car which owed nothing to Columbia. It was a Daimler (ii) with 5.5hp 2-cylinder engine driving electric motors in the rear wheels. In heavy traffic the petrol engine could be switched off, and it would run for several miles on its batteries. It did not go into production. From 1904 some City & Suburbans, following Columbia's example, adopted wheel steering, but the make did not survive beyond 1905.

NG

CITY EL see MINI EL

CITYCOM (DK/D) 1987 to date

1987–1996 CityCom A/S, Randers.
1996 to date CityCom Elektromobile GmbH, Aub.

This Danish electric car design was certainly the most popular electric car of recent years. Launched as the Mini-El, objections from Austin Rover forced a name-change to City-El. The design was a very compact and basic 3-wheeler. A front-mounted 2.5 or 3.6kW electric motor (fed by three 12V batteries) powered the right-hand rear wheel only via a belt. A range of 30 miles (48km) was quoted, with a top speed of only 25–30mph (40–48km/h). In construction, there was an acrylic sandwich tub with hinging upper bodywork to allow entry, plus a roll-over bar, built over an aluminium-and-steel chassis. Three distinct body styles were offered: enclosed, half-open and fully-open, all with seating for one adult plus a rear-facing child behind. The car's exposure was boosted by the appearance of a batch at the 1992 Barcelona Olympic Games. After the Danish operation believed it had saturated its market, it passed the City-El on to a German company. Over 5000 had been supplied by 1997.

CR

CIVELLI DE BOSCH (F) 1906–1909

Civelli de Bosch et Compagnie, Paris.

This company showed an 8/10hp 2-cylinder light car at the 1906 Paris Salon, following it with a 16/25hp 4-cylinder and a 40/50hp 6-cylinder, all with shaft drive.

NG

CIZETA (I) 1988–1995

1988–1991 Cizeta Moroder Motors srl, Modena.
1991–1995 Cizeta Automobili SpA, Modena.

Conceived in a 'boom' era when supercars were in the ascendant, the Cizeta was originally called the Cizeta-Moroder after the founder (ex-Lamborghini engineer Claudio Zampolli) and the initial finance provider (music producer Giorgio Moroder). Stylistically, it strongly resembled the Lamborghini Diablo, perhaps not surprising since Marcello Gandini designed both cars. The Cizeta made its mark because of its mid-mounted engine: a V16 unit of 6.0-litre capacity, with 64 valves and 519bhp. The car was soon renamed V16T to signify the engine and transmission layout, the 5-speed transaxle being mounted at right-angles to

1902 City and Suburban Grand Victoria.
NATIONAL MOTOR MUSEUM

1989 Cizeta Moroder V16 coupé.
CIZETA

the engine. The extremely wide 2-seater coupé bodywork was in aluminium – rather worryingly, never tested in a wind tunnel – and sat over a steel chassis with aluminium and carbon-fibre strengthening, plus all-independent suspension. A light redesign occurred in 1992, but its very high price and a lack of customers – it is thought that no more than 12 were built in all – consigned it to its grave.

CR

C.K. see A.S.D.

CK3 DESIGN (US) 1997 to date

CK3 Design, Las Vegas, Nevada.
This company bought the NICE CAR COMPANY in 1997 and resumed production of their 1967 Corvette Sting Ray replica.

HP

CLAEYS-FLANDRIA (B) 1953–1954/1979–1980

Claeys-Flandria S.A., Zedelgem.

At the 1954 Brussels Motor Show a dumpy little economy car was shown to celebrate the 60th anniversary of the Belgian Flandria motorcycle factory. It used a rear-mounted 250cc or 400cc Ilo engine and a 3-speed gearbox. The dumpy coupé bodywork could seat 2+2 passengers. However, no production run began. In 1979 the motorcycle company again assaulted the microcar market with the Mobilcar. It was offered in two versions: a 3-wheeled saloon and a 4-wheeled convertible. Both had a 50cc air-cooled 3bhp engine and coil spring suspension. It was just as short-lived as the earlier project.

CR

1974 Clan (i) Crusader coupé.
NICK GEORGANO/NATIONAL MOTOR MUSEUM

1902 Clarendon Favourite tourer.
NATIONAL MOTOR MUSEUM

CLA-HOLME (US) 1922

Cla-Holme Motor Car Co., Denver, Colorado.
This was a 4-wheel-drive roadster powered by a 6-cylinder engine, either by Falls or Continental, according to different sources. The transmission offered eight forward speeds. Only one prototype was made.

NG

CLAN (i) (GB) 1971–1974

Clan Motor Co. Ltd, Washington, County Durham.
The Clan Crusader was a small GT coupé with a fibreglass monocoque and a rear-mounted Sunbeam Stiletto engine. It was designed by Lotus engineers, Paul Haussauer, Brian Luff (later of Status cars), and John Frayling and they formed a company which received a government grant to establish a factory in Washington, County Durham. Production began in 1971.

The design was widely admired although, at £1400, it was expensive for its performance (99mph (160km/h), 0-62mph (0-100km/h) in 12 seconds) and, before long, the Crusader was offered in kit form. The introduction of VAT in 1973 damaged the kit car market while the uncertainty in the wake of the OPEC oil crisis, killed many kit makers, Clan included.

Production ended in 1974 after 315 cars had been made. There were several attempts to revive the project, including a government-backed attempt in 1984 in Belfast. Several kit cars inspired by the Clan have also been made.

MJL

CLAN (ii) (GB) 1984

Despite the De Lorean saga, the Northern Irish authorities gave backing to an attempt to revive the Clan Crusader in Belfast in 1984. The revived Crusader had wider wheel arches than the original, and retractable headlights. Power came from a Hillman Imp engine, in production for industrial use, while the Clan 'Clover' used Alfasud running gear.

The company was soon in financial trouble and its fate was sealed when allegations appeared in the press that second hand parts had been sold as new. The project folded after about 40 cars had been made.

CR

CLAPP (US) 1898–1900

1898 New Haven Chair Co., New Haven, Connecticut.
1900 Clapp Motor Vehicle Co., Jersey City, New Jersey.
After gaining automotive experience with the Duryea brothers on their early vehicles, Henry Clapp moved to New Haven where he built a 4-seater car using a 6hp 2-cylinder engine in a buggy frame. He had ambitious plans for manufacture, and hoped to secure the recently vacated premises of the New Haven Chair Co. However, the factory was not suitable nor could it be made suitable, although they had built bicycles which were at least closer to cars than chairs. His next venture was in Jersey City, where again he had ambitious plans that never came to fruition.

NG

CLARENCE (GB) 1919

C.W. Harrison, Northwich, Cheshire.
Announced only three months after the Armistice, the Clarence was a 3-wheeler but differed from most of its kind in having a 10hp 4-cylinder engine. Transmission was by friction discs and final drive by chain to the single rear wheel. *The Light Car & Cyclecar* illustrated its announcement of the Clarence with drawings and a photograph of a half-scale model, so it is possible that a full-size car was never completed.

NG

CLARENDON (GB) 1902–1904

Clarendon Motor Car & Bicycle Co. Ltd, Earlsdon, Coventry.
This company was founded to make a light 2-seater car with 7hp single-cylinder engine and shaft drive. By 1904 it had debts of £2500, and never recovered. Liquidation took place in 1906, but car production had ceased before then.

NG

CLARIN MUSTAD (N/F) 1916–1917; 1935

1916–1917; 1935 Mustad & Son, Oslo.
1917 Clarin Mustad, Duclair, Seine-Inférieure.
Built by Hans Clarin Horiïd Mustad was a rare example of a 6-wheeled passenger car, and what is more it was a 6 × 4, with both rear axles driven. The prototype had a limousine body, but an open tourer was planned. A 4-cylinder engine was originally used, replaced in 1917 by a 7050cc 6-cylinder unit giving 85bhp and a top speed of nearly 60mph (100km/h). Both engines were built in Mustad's workshops, while the bodies were made by O. Sørensen, also of Oslo. After initial development work in Norway, Mustad moved to France where he hoped there would be more customers. Possibly no cars were made at Duclair, and certainly none of the ambulances, trucks and buses that he planned. Back in Norway, Mustad made various experimental vehicles, including, in 1935, a neat-looking single-seater coupé in which Fiat components were used. The prototype 6-wheeler, rebodied and re-engined in 1927, assisted in the evacuation of Oslo in 1940, and survives today in the city's Norsk Teknisk Museum.

NG

CLARK (i) (US) 1900–1909

Edward S. Clark Steam Automobiles, Boston, Massachusetts.
Edward Clark began making steam boilers in 1895, and started experiments with steam cars about five years later. His first cars were light, even flimsy looking, with folding passenger seats ahead of the driver, and single-chain drive. By 1904 he was offering a substantial-looking vehicle with horizontally opposed 4-cylinder engine under the seat and boiler ahead, under the rear-facing passenger seat. An old-fashioned note was struck by the vertical steering column. Clark steamers from 1905 were more up-to-date, with sloping steering columns, large bonnets fronted by a condenser which looked just like a radiator, and substantial side-entrance tourer bodies. At a top price of $5000 they were very expensive, when the comparable White cost $2500–2700. By 1909 Clark had dropped his price to $2750 for a rakish-looking 4-seater roadster. Very few Clark steamers were sold, and car making seems to have been a sideline from his main business of making components, and general repair and painting work on cars of all kinds. He never even bothered to incorporate a company for car manufacture. From 1910 to 1912 he made a few petrol-engined trucks with 2-stroke engines.

NG

1917 Clarin-Mustad 6-wheeled saloon.
MICHAEL WORTHINGTON-WILLIAMS

CLARK (ii) **(GB)** 1901

Charles Clark & Sons, Retford, Nottinghamshire.

This was a light 4-wheeler powered by a 2.75hp De Dion-Bouton engine, converted from a De Dion tricycle. Production never started.

NG

CLARK (iii) **(US)** 1903–1905

A.F. Clark & Co., Philadelphia, Pennsylvania.

This company was formed to make electric passenger cars and trucks, as well as batteries, motors, and controllers. In addition to a 4-seater electric car it made a petrol-electric with a 7hp engine that charged the batteries at 35-amps, 'and 45 to 48 amps when speeding along at 30mph (48km/h).' The standard battery electrics had a top speed of 20mph (30km/h). Few were made of either type, and Clark later made unsuccessful attempts to manufacture electric cars in Toledo, Ohio, and Buffalo, New York.

NG

CLARK (iv) **(NZ)** 1904–1906

H.S. Clark, Hawke's Bay, North Island.

In 1903 Clark imported two engines from the USA; a single-cylinder and a flat-twin. He installed them in vehicles of his own construction; designing and building the chassis, mechanicals and bodywork. By 1906 when both had been completed, the single was sold and he retained the twin for his own use.

MG

CLARK (v) **(US)** 1910–1912

Clark Motor Car Co., Shelbyville, Indiana.

This Clark was a conventional car with 4-cylinder engine made in touring and roadster forms. The engines, described as 30hp and 40hp in 1910–11, and as 30/40hp in 1912, were by Rutenber. The company was reorganised following bankruptcy in June 1912, but soon after that it was acquired by Maurice Wolfe who had made the WOLFE and WILCOX at Minneapolis. He assembled a few Clarks from parts on hand, then moved his operation to Piqua, Ohio, where he made the METEOR (vii).

NG

CLARK (vi) **(US)** 1910–1911

Fergason Motor Co., Lansing, Michigan.

Made by Frank Clark, who had formerly built the CLARKMOBILE, and machine shop owner Claude Fergason, this was a larger car with a 14hp 2-cylinder engine, also horizontally-opposed, and solid tyres. After a year of business, Clark turned to commercial vehicles, forming the Clark Power Wagon Co., but this lasted only a year.

NG

CLARK-HATFIELD (US) 1908–1909

Clark-Hatfield Automobile Co., Oshkosh, Wisconsin.

This product of a former buggy maker was a typical high-wheeler powered by a 14hp 2-cylinder engine. Its only unusual feature was that the friction transmission was mounted ahead of the engine rather than behind, which must have required a very long final drive chain. After a year of car making, the company turned to truck bodies under the name J.L. Clark Manufacturing Co.

NG

CLARKE-CARTER *see* CUTTING

CLARKMOBILE (US) 1903–1904

The Clarkmobile Co., Lansing, Michigan.

This was a light 2-seater runabout powered by a 7hp single-cylinder engine mounted under the seat. Unusual in so small a car was shaft drive. Its maker, Frank Clark, claimed 'our car has been thoroughly tested for two years', but ended production at the end of 1904. He returned to the car business six years later with the CLARK (v).

NG

CLARKSON (GB) 1899–1902

1899–1902 Clarkson & Capel Steam Car Syndicate Ltd, Dalston, London.
1902–1903 Clarkson Ltd, Chelmsford, Essex.

Thomas Clarkson was better-known as a maker of steam commercial vehicles, particularly buses, than of passenger cars, although he built some unusual designs.

1990 Classic Motor Carriages Tiffany coupé.
CLASSIC MOTOR CARRIAGES

The first, made in partnership with Herbert Capel who designed a petrol car sold under his own name, was a massive barouche whose body was suspended by C-springs on an underframe which carried all the machinery. The engine was a compound vertical unit using paraffin fuel, and was mounted at the rear of the frame, below the driver who sat behind his passengers in hansom cab style. The condenser was at the front. Exhibited at the Automobile Club's Show at Richmond in June 1899, it was almost certainly a one-off, as was a light steam victoria converted from a horse-drawn carriage, seen at the same show.

In 1902 Clarkson moved to Chelmsford and made a few steam cars powered by 12hp 2-cylinder engines. They were usually known as Chelmsfords, and most had bodies of the station bus variety, with inward facing seats. Few were made, and Clarkson concentrated on steam buses. At its peak his fleet in London alone numbered 173 vehicles. He stayed in business until the mid-1920s.

NG

CLASSIC (i) (US) 1916–1917

Classic Motor Car Co., Chicago, Illinois.
There was nothing particularly classic about this car, which was a conventional design using a 20hp 4-cylinder Lycoming engine, offered as a 5-seater tourer or 3-seater cloverleaf roadster. Production ended in 1917 because of component shortages brought about by World War I, but in 1920 plans were announced for a revival of the make at Lake Geneva, Wisconsin. A Classic Four and Classic Six were to have been made, but the project did not get off the ground.

NG

CLASSIC (ii) (F) 1924–1928

Compagnie Générale de Voitures à Paris, Paris.
This was a conventional medium-sized car, powered by a 1846cc 4-cylinder Chapuis-Dornier engine, with the option of a 1593cc sleeve-valve unit. The makers were well-known taxicab operators and it seems that the majority of Classics were bodied as taxis or light trucks, although a landaulette and a tourer were shown at the 1926 Paris Salon. The pointed radiator and disc wheels gave the taxi a close resemblance to the Citroën B2. The company also made the smaller CELTIC (iii) and sold its design to LEON MAX.

NG

CLASSIC AUTOMOTIVE REPRODUCTIONS (GB) 1983–84

Classic Automotive Reproductions, Bridlington, East Yorkshire.
This firm built a wide variety of replicas on a bespoke basis: Cobras 289 and 427, Mercedes SSK, a V8-powered Lamborghini Countach, Jaguar D-Type, Lola, and Ferrari Testa Rossa.

CR

CLASSIC CARS OF COVENTRY see VIKING

CLASSIC COACHCRAFT (US) c.1985

Classic Coachcraft, San Diego, California.
Corvette running gear was the basis for this Ferrari Daytona replica kit. Roadster and coupé versions were available.

HP

CLASSIC CONNECTION (US) c.1985

Classic Connection, Boca Raton, Florida.
This kit car was a replica of the 1954 Corvette. It used a Chevrolet V6 or V8 engine.

HP

CLASSIC ENGLISH RACING AUTOMOBILES (GB) 1990s

One of many such companies, Classic E.R.A. produced an aluminium bodied Jaguar C-Type replica using Jaguar MkII or all-torsion bar suspension. A D-Type replica was also marketed.

CR

CLASSIC FACTORY (US) c.1985

Classic Factory, Pamona, California.
This company built replicas of classic cars including the Mercedes 500K, the Auburn Speedster and Phaeton and the Cord 812. All were designed around Ford running gear and were sold in kit or fully assembled form.

HP

CLASSIC GLASS (US) c.1993–1995

Classic Glass, Clinton, Michigan.
A 'Pro-Street' version of the 1963 Corvette was sold by this kit car company. It used a tube frame with Ford suspension and was intended for Chevrolet V8 engines. 'Pro-street' cars, popular in the United States, looked and ran like dragsters but were legal for street use. Hence the massive drag slicks and skinny front wheels that this model had.

HP

CLASSIC ILLUSIONS (US) c.1985

Classic Illusions, Duarte, California.
Replicas of classic cars were the speciality of this kit car manufacturer. Their line included replicas of the Mercedes 500K and the 1954 Corvette. The Mercedes replica was based on Ford running gear, while the Corvette used mid-sized General Motors components.

HP

CLASSIC IMAGES (GB) 1992

Classic Images, Purton, Swindon, Wiltshire.
This firm made the AWR, a Rover V8-powered 1930s style roadster, and the MSR3, an unfinished Renault 5-powered trike.

CR

CLASSIC INTERNATIONAL (US) c.1992–1993

Classic International, Fargo, North Dakota.
This kit car company built replicas of Cobras, but they were more attracted to Mercedes designs. They sold replicas of the 300SL Gullwing, the 540K and 300 SLR. Running gear was based on Ford Mustang components.

HP

CLASSIC MOTOR CARRIAGES (US) 1973–1996

Classic Motor Carriages, Miami, Florida; Innovative Street Machines, Classic Auto Replicas, C.A.R.S., Auto Resolution, Champion Auto Works, and GGL.
This large kit manufacturer built a wide variety of kits. They made replicas of Cobras, Porsche Speedsters, 1933 Ford Victorias, 1934 Fords, MD-TDs, and Bugattis. They also made a line of neoclassics including the Gazelle, Tiffany, and Royale. The Gazelle, an inexpensive VW or Ford Pinto-based kit with vaguely Mercedes lines, became one of the best selling kits of all time. They bought industry giant FIBERFAB which expanded their line even farther. They were shut down in 1996 by the legal authorities of the State of Florida.

HP

CLASSIC MOTORS INTERNATIONAL (US) c.1979

Classic Motors International, Mishikawa, Indiana; Legend Classics, South Bend, Indiana; Carrera Motorsports International Inc., Hickory, North Carolina.
CMI made an extremely accurate replica of the 1953–57 Porsche 550 Spyder racing car. Many of the body and trim parts would interchange with the original, but the

powerplant choices were Porsche 356 or 912 engines. They were sold in assembled form, and there were three models based on trim and mechanical specification. The S was the base model, the Cabriolet added a top, side curtains and other luxury items, and the Carrera came with 4-wheel disc brakes and a hotter 912 engine.

HP

CLASSIC REPLICARS *see* RAWLSON

CLASSIC REPLICAS (GB) 1989 to date
Classic Replicas, Bournemouth, Hampshire.
Ken Cook's BRIGHTWHEEL operation ceased trading in 1989 buthe continued to produce kit cars under the Classic Replicas badge. Models included the Viper Cobra replica and a Mini Moke replica called the Cub (later known as the Mule). In 1992 Classic Replicas assumed control of D.M.S. and its products, including the Venom budget Cobra replica and Bullit.

CR

CLASSIC REPRODUCTIONS *see* SANDWOOD

CLASSIC ROADSTERS (US) 1979 to date
Classic Roadsters, Fargo, North Dakota.
One of the larger American kit car manufacturers, they had an impressive line-up that sold well. The Duchess was an MG-TD replica based on VW mechanicals, while the Saxon replicated the Austin-Healey 3000. It used a tube frame with V8 or V6 engines. A modified Saxon with wheel flares to cover wider tyres was dubbed the Sebring. Replicas of the Mercedes 500K followed, as well as a neoclassic called the Marlene that had been built by BRADLEY. They added an SS-100 replica called the Duke in 1982. It was built on Ford or General Motors running gear. Of course, they also had a Cobra replica. They closed in 1993 but reopened with new management. AKA Performance Classics.

HP

CLASSIC SPORTS CARS (i) (US) c.1985–1990
Classic Sports Cars, Holly Hill, Florida.
This kit car company started out with an MG-TD replica called the Daytona MIGI and a quasi-Bugatti replica called the Moya. These were available as VW or Chevrolet Chevette-based kits. In 1988 they bought two models from other companies. These were replicas of the 1953 Corvette and 1955 Thunderbird. AKA Daytona Automotive Fiberglass, Daytona Auto and Kit Car World.

HP

CLASSIC SPORTS CARS (ii) (GB) 1986–1989
Classic Sports Cars, Ringwood, Hampshire.
Ferrari 250 GTO replicas were a controversial breed, often beleaguered by lawsuits from Ferrari. This was one of the better ones, based on an American idea, and used the Datsun 240/260Z as a basis. The mechanicals, glass and electrics of the Z were retained, while customers had the choice of sticking with Datsun's interior or going for a replica set-up.

CR

CLASSICO *see* AUTO-ZAGAIA

CLAUDE DELAGE (F) 1926
Claude Delage, Clichy, Seine.
Claude Delage was unrelated to the famous Louis, and his cars were much less glamorous. Two models were offered, conventional tourers powered by 1685cc Ballot or 1843cc 4-cylinder Sergant engines. They had 4-speed gearboxes, shaft drive and a top speed of around 37mph (60km/h). Claude Delage also offered a motorcycle in 1925, but this seems to have been as short-lived as his cars.

NG

CLAUZET (F) 1956–1959
Clauzet, Reims.
Clauzet's first attempt at rebodying a Citroën 2CV came in 1956 when it showed a classically-styled coupé body for the 2CV chassis. At the 1959 Paris Salon, Clauzet presented an extraordinarily ugly 4-seater coupé using a Citroën 2CV

1928 Claveau 9CV saloon.
NICK BALDWIN

engine. The bodywork was metal but the roof featured a Plexiglass panel.

CR

CLAVEAU (F) 1926–1934; 1946–1956
Automobiles Claveau, Paris.
Born in 1892, Emile Claveau was one of the most persistent inventors in the motoring field, designing a wide variety of cars over a 30-year period, although he made few sales, if any. He must clearly have had an alternative source of income, but its nature is unknown. He first came to public attention in 1926, when he announced a highly unconventional light car powered by a rear-mounted 1100cc flat-four engine in a monocoque frame with Lancia Lambda-type all-independent suspension. He called it the Autobloc, and took a stand at the Brussels Show in December. His next show appearance was at Paris in October 1927, when he exhibited the Autobloc in 1100 and 1477cc forms, and also a streamlined saloon with the larger engine. He advertised his cars in the English language *French Automobile & Allied Trades Exporter*, promoting the Autobloc as 'a rational car, light and powerful', and claiming top speeds of 75mph (120km/h) for the Standard model and 85mph (140km/h) for the Special model. At the 1928 Salon he showed these cars again, and also a 4CV powered by a 577cc vertical twin 2-stroke engine. There was a Claveau stand at the 1929 Salon but it was empty as the car had been damaged in an accident a few days earlier.

In 1930 Claveau changed tack completely, going over to front engines driving the front wheels. His power unit was now a 750cc 2-stroke V-twin, and the car again featured all-independent suspension and monocoque construction. As well as a coupé, this one was offered as a light delivery van which Claveau said would be built in England and sold for £110. Needless to say neither this nor any of the cars were sold, indeed the van may never have been built, as only a drawing was used to illustrate it. A number of other front-drive cars were made up to 1934, and for at least one, the 1123cc Type C, Claveau quoted a price of 13,900 francs.

Claveau next surfaced at the 1946 Salon, where he exhibited a most advanced design, the Descartes saloon. At that show he had only an engine and a model of the car, but in 1947 a complete car was ready. Its engine was a 2292cc V8 with single ohc to each bank of cylinders, a 5-speed all-synchromesh gearbox, driving the front wheels, all-round independent suspension and monocoque construction. The body was a spacious 4-door streamlined saloon with a drag coefficient of only 0.34, and a top speed of over 93mph (150km/h) was claimed. The Descartes was exhibited at the Paris and Geneva Shows up to 1948, and a brochure was issued, but as with his prewar designs Claveau was not able to put it into production. He had no facilities for manufacture in any quantity, but hoped to sell the design to someone who had. His final Salon appearance came in 1955 when he showed the Claveau 56, a 2-door saloon powered by a 996cc 3-cylinder DKW engine, again with front-wheel drive. More aerodynamic than the Descartes, its drag coefficient was only 0.23. Claveau stressed that the German engine was only used in the prototype because it was of convenient size and was suited to front-wheel drive. When the design was taken up by a French

1899 Clément-Panhard voiturette.
NATIONAL MOTOR MUSEUM

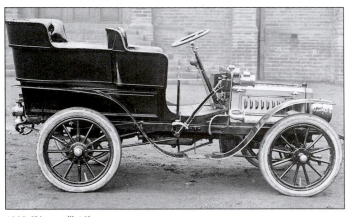

1903 Clément(i) 16hp tonneau.
NATIONAL MOTOR MUSEUM

1905 Clément-Bayard tourer.
NATIONAL MOTOR MUSEUM

manufacturer, a French engine would be used, but there were no more firms clamouring to make the Claveau 56 than for any of his earlier designs.

NG

Further Reading
'Two of a Kind, Gallic Motor Engineers', M. Worthington-Williams,
The Automobile, August 1997.
Toutes les Voitures Françaises 1947, René Bellu,
Histoires et Collections, Paris, 1996.
'Les Automobiles Claveau', Serge Pozzoli and Jacques Rousseau,
l'Album du Fanatique.

C.L.C. (F) 1911–1913

Cockborne, Lehurchet et da Costa, Paris.
Two small cars were offered under this name, a 6hp single-cylinder, and a 10hp 4-cylinder announced in 1912. Both engines were 2-stroke.

NG

CLECO (GB) 1936–1940

Cleco Electric Industries Ltd, Leicester.
Founded in 1936, Cleco specialised in battery electric vehicles, mostly factory and platform trucks, although some road-going vehicles of the milk float variety were made. Their car was a tiny saloon on a 78in (1981mm) wheelbase which had the appearance of a stunted Volkswagen Beetle. A range of about 55 miles was claimed, but this could only be achieved at an average speed of 15mph (23km/h). Its price of £375 would have bought three Morris Eights, so it is hardly surprising that only six were sold. Cleco continued electric van production up to 1957.

NG

C.L.E.M. (F) 1912–1914

1912–1914 Compagnie Lyonnaise d'Études Mécaniques, Lyons.
1914 Sté des Voiturettes Clem, G. Gineste-Lacaze et Compagnie, Lyons.
This car was made by Compagnie Lyonnaise d'Études Mécaniques, hence the initials, although the cars were also known by the name Clem, after the first customer, Mme Clemence Servoz, who was to become the maker's mother-in-law. The designer and manufacturer was a former test driver for LA BUIRE, Gaston Bouvier, who assembled the small car using a 1130cc 4-cylinder Fondu engine, Dupressoir chassis and gearbox, Alix radiator and 2-seater bodies by a small local firm. Bouvier employed no more than 20 men, as the work was assembly rather than manufacture, but he was able to turn out about 12 cars per month. In February 1914 he left to join the textile industry, and a new company was formed which added a slightly larger car with 1320cc engine, which could carry 4-seater bodywork.

NG

NICK BALDWIN

CLÉMENT-BAYARD, ADOLPHE (1855–1928)

Together with Alexandre Darracq, Clément-Bayard was one the greatest entrepreneurs of the French cycle and early motor industry. He was born Adolphe Clément at Pierrefond in the Oise district, and lost both parents at an early age. Educated at Compiégne and then at Crépy-en Valois, he wanted to enter the École des Arts et Métiers, training ground of so many motor men, but his teacher sent him to be apprenticed to a grocer. To say the least this was uncongenial to young Adolphe; sweeping the shop before being allowed the privilege of weighing out prunes and pasta was, he said 'insupportable' He soon became an apprentice locksmith, learnt how to work in wood, and made himself a primitive wood-frame bicycle. In 1872 he set out to find his fortune on this machine, with all his worldy goods on his back. He found work in a general machine shop at Tours, then went to Bordeaux and finally to Lyons where he was employed in a bicycle factory. At last he had found his calling.

CLÉMENT (i); CLÉMENT-BAYARD (F) 1898–1922

1898–1903 Clément et Compagnie, Levallois-Perret, Seine.
1903–1922 Sté Anonyme des Établissements Clément-Bayard,
Levallois-Perret, Seine; Mezières.

These cars were made by one of the greatest figures in the early French motor industry, Adolphe Clément (1855–1928). Having made a fortune in the bicycle and pneumatic tyre industries (see biography), Clément entered the motor trade through his involvement with GLADIATOR and in 1897 joined the board of PANHARD ET LEVASSOR, becoming chairman in 1900. This led to the first car to bear his name, the Clément-Panhard which was introduced at the Paris Salon in December 1898. Designed by Commandant Krebs of Panhard, it had a rear-mounted 763cc 3.5hp inclined single-cylinder engine with automatic inlet valve and hot-tube ignition. Tubular extensions from the body sides extended forward to a steering head from which the front wheels were steered from a centre pivot. Surprisingly the steering was controlled by a wheel rather than a tiller. It was in several ways an an archaic design, yet it sold in reasonable numbers. A reverse gear was provided during 1899 and in 1901 a 3-seater *vis-à-vis* was added to the 2-seater. At the same time power was increased to 4.5hp and electric ignition supplemented the hot tube system; either could be used at the driver's choice. About 200 were imported into Scotland by James STIRLING, and sold under the names Stirling-Panhard or Clément-Stirling.

Although carrying the Panhard name, the Clément-Panhard was not made by them but by Clément in his own factory at Levallois-Perret, where he was also making a light voiturette with 2.5hp De Dion-Bouton engine geared to the rear axle. To complete his range Clément imported COLUMBIA (i) electric cars from the United States, and which he fitted with French bodies and sold under the name Electromotion. In 1900 the Levallois works employed 400 men, while he had another factory at Mezières near the Belgian border, which made components for bicycles and cars, and from which Panhard was also supplied with components. By the end of 1901 Cléments were front-engined light cars designed by Marius Barbarou; they had 7hp single-cylinder, 8hp twin and 12hp 4-cylinder engines and shaft drive. For 1903 the range was extended to include 16hp 4-cylinder models, with mechanically-operated overhead inlet valves.

c.1912 Clément-Bayard 2-seater.
NATIONAL MOTOR MUSEUM

Cléments and Gladiators were being made in the same factory – the main difference was that Gladiators were chain-driven, while Cléments had shaft drive. In October 1903 Clement resigned from the boards of both Gladiator and Panhard, and as cars bearing the Clément name were still being made in the Gladiator factory, he chose a new name for his cars, Clément-Bayard (sometimes Bayard-Clément), after the Chevalier Bayard who had saved Mezieres from the Duc de Nassau in 1521.

Clément-Bayard cars were sold in England by the British Automobile Commercial Syndicate, backed by the Earl of Shrewsbury and Talbot, and managed by Danny Weigel. In 1903 a factory was built at Ladbroke Grove in West London. At first

In 1878 he moved to Paris, and with his savings and some borrowed money he bought a small bicycle works. His business prospered and he was soon able to buy a large stadium where novices could learn to ride a bicycle. This was very important at the beginning of the cycle boom, when thousands wanted to take up the sport, but had no idea of how to ride. Clément himself made his name as a racing cyclist, and took the first step towards becoming a tycoon when, in 1891, he bought the French rights for the English Dunlop pneumatic tyre. In a few years these patents were worth £100,000. In 1894 he sold his holdings and the Clément bicycle name to a group of English businessmen, Harvey du Cros, Martin Rucker, H.J. Lawson and E.T. Hooley. The latter two did not have the best of reputations, and both were to serve jail sentences for fraud later, but Clement received his money and promptly invested it in more land for factory buildings .He bought land which almost surrounded the Panhard factory, and also put up a large factory in the suburb of Levallois-Perret. Here he made not complete cycles but components which he sold to a vast number of small constructors across France. In 1895 he had bought a factory at Mezières, in the Ardennes close to the Belgian border, where he also made bicycle parts. This factory was not part of the deal with the English syndicate, and Clément also retained a stake in the new Clément-Gladiator-Humber company. Gladiator was the name of a bicycle company formed in 1891 by Alexandre Darracq and Jean Aucoc, and Humber was the French branch of the famous British cycle maker.

Clément entered the car business in 1897 with a little rear-engined car called the Clément-Gladiator, followed by a Clément-De Dion in 1898. More significant than these was his place on the board of Panhard et Levassor. In January 1899 the company ceased to pay royalties to Émile Levassor's widow on the grounds that a new engine was being used. She sued the company with the support of Rene Panhard, but lost the case and this cost Panhard his chairmanship of the board, which went to Clément. By 1900 he was making the Clément-Panhard car and also the Clément-De Dion, but in January 1903, to avoid a conflict of interest, he resigned from the board of

Panhard et Levassor, and in October from Clément-Gladiator, though that company continued to use his name.

Also in 1903 he added the suffix Bayard to both his own name and that of his cars. This came from his Mezières connection, for in the centre of the town was a statue to the Chevalier Bayard, *le chevalier sans peur et sans reproche*, the 16th century hero who had saved Mezières from the Duc de Nassau in 1521. He called the cars Voitures Bayard (A. Clément, constructeur), or Bayard-Clément for short, but they were also known as Clément-Bayard. The company prospered over the next few years, and Clément sold a licence for manufacture in Italy by Diatto. Clément cars were made in London under the name Talbot from 1903, but Adolph Clément ended his connection with the British company in 1907. In 1909 he ordered the building of an airship powered by two Clément-Bayard engines of 220bhp each. Her hoped to sell it to the French Army, but they rejected the idea, and eventually he found a buyer in the British War Office who paid him £16,000 for it, though they did not make much use of it.. He also made a number of other aero engines which were found, long after the war, in boxes that had never been opened, despite being marked 'extremely urgent'

At the outbreak of World War I Adolph Clément-Bayard was nearly sixty. He had made more money than he needed, and decided to retire to the large villa, 'Le Paradis' which he had built a few years earlier at l'Esterel. He had an enjoyable retirement, brought to an end when he had a fatal heart attack while at the wheel of his car in 1928.

He had two children, Albert who worked for his father and was killed while practising for the 1907 French Grand Prix, and a daughter who married rival car maker Fernand Charron.

NG

Further Reading
'Clément-Bayard', Jean-Robert Dulier,
l'Album du Fanatique, October 1975-March 1976.

1913 Clement(ii) 16/20hp all-weather tourer.
NATIONAL MOTOR MUSEUM

c.1929 Clément-Rochelle chassis.
NATIONAL MOTOR MUSEUM

the cars made there were almost identical to the French product, and were known as Clément-Talbots. Later they became plain TALBOTs, although the company name remained Clément-Talbot Ltd until 1938, long after Adolphe and his cars had departed from the scene.

Clément was one of the largest car makers in Europe in 1904, with an output of some 1200 vehicles. The Levallois factory employed 1500 men, with a further 400 working at Mezières. The two factories made all parts except tyres. The machinery at Levallois was mostly American. The 1904 Clément-Bayard range consisted of five models, all shaft-driven, a 6hp single, 7hp twin and fours of 14, 20 and 27hp. Racing cars with engines up to 100hp (16,786cc) were made, and competed with some success in Gordon Bennett and, from 1906, Grand Prix races. Adolphe Clément's son Albert was killed in practice for the 1907 Grand Prix, and after the 1908 season his father gave up interest in racing. The 1906 touring car range was more extensive than ever, consisting of six models, from a 1361cc 8hp twin to two large chain-driven fours of 6330cc (35/45hp) and 9232cc (50hp). In that year Clément sold a licence to DIATTO in Turin for the manufacture of several 2- and 4-cylinder models which were marketed up to 1910. Adolphe Clément was a director of Diatto from 1906 to 1909.

In 1908 an important new model was introduced. This was the 1590cc 10/12hp 4-cylinder with monobloc engine and dashboard radiator, a feature which was to be typical of Clément-Bayards up to 1914. The last year for the big chain-driven 35/45 and 50/60hp cars was 1911, and thereafter the whole range had shaft drive and dashboard radiators. Commercial vehicles were also made, including light vans from 1903 and heavier trucks from 1906. Taxicabs were a speciality; in 1909 there were 456 Clément-Bayard cabs in Paris, where they were second in popularity to Renault.

In 1911 three models of 6-cylinder car were introduced, of 15, 20, and 30hp,

and in 1912 there was a 20hp 4-cylinder with Knight sleeve-valve engine. These did not last long, and the 1914 range consisted entirely of fours, from a 1356cc 8hp to a 6838cc 30hp. The smaller cars made up the bulk of the business; they could only be bought ready bodied, whereas those of 12hp and above could be had in chassis form. 1500 cars were made in 1913, which meant that Clément was no longer among the industry leaders (Peugeot made about 5000 and Renault 4700 that year), but they were still among the top dozen French car makers. In 1915 they broke with tradition and gave the 8hp car a frontal radiator, although it was not greatly changed mechanically.

Adolphe Clément-Bayard retired in 1914, and doubtless the absence of his dynamic personality was partly responsible for the firm's decline in the 1920s. The 8hp was revived in 1919, joined by a new 2601cc 12hp, but they were undistinguished cars and few were made. The Mezières factory was sold soon after World War I, and in 1922 Citroën took over the premises at Levallois.

NG

Further Reading
'Clément Bayard', Jean-Robert Dulier,
l'Album du Fanatique, October 1975–March 1976.

CLEMENT (ii) **(GB)** 1908–1914

Clement Motor Co. Ltd, Coventry.
When Clement-Talbot Ltd was formed in 1903 to make cars of Clément (i) design in England, the generally similar GLADIATOR was imported by E.H. Lancaster. In 1907 the name Clement All British Motor Co. was adopted, and from 1908 they were made in Britain, at the SWIFT (i) factory in Coventry. They were almost identical to Swifts, except for their radiators of Talbot shape, longer wheelbases and higher prices. A 10/12hp twin and fours of 14/18 and 18/28hp were made, and two larger models were listed, 23/35 and 35/45hp, whose specifications were identical to those of French-built Gladiators. It is thought that they were imported rather than built at Coventry. A similar range was offered for 1909 and 1910; all the Clements at the 1910 Olympia Show had bodies by Salmon. All British Clements for 1911 were Swift-built, the large 30/40hp being described as a French Clement, that is a Gladiator not a Clément-Bayard. By 1913 the twin had been dropped, and there were only two fours in the Clement range, the 12/14 and 14/18hp, which were almost identical to the 12 and 15hp Swifts. For 1914 a new 16/20hp Clement was introduced which did not correspond exactly with any Swift model, although it was generally similar in design.

NG

CLÉMENT-ROCHELLE **(F)** 1928–1930

Clément et Rochelle, Clamart, Seine.
This was an attractive-looking small sports car powered by a 1097cc 4-cylinder ohv Ruby engine, available in three versions, the 30bhp D, 35bhp DS and 50bhp K, the latter with Cozette No.6 supercharger which gave it a top speed of 87–90mph (140–145km/h), depending on which bodywork was used. The lightest body was a doorless sports car, although Clément-Rochelle never entered any competitions with this model; they were simply interested in making a high-performance road car. Other bodies were a cabriolet, faux-cabriolet (coupé), and 2-door saloon. Suspension was independent all-round, by transverse leaf springs. At the front, stub axles slid on a pair of guides, rather like a double version of the Morgan system. Swing axles were used at the rear. About 100 Clément-Rochelles were made.

NG

CLÉMENT-TALBOT *see* TALBOT (i)

CLENET **(US)** 1976–1986

Clenet Coachworks, Santa Barbara, California.
This hand-built touring car launched the 'neoclassic' fad that was popular in the US. These were cars styled with a 1930s look, but were not a replica of any specific car. It was the brainchild of Alain Clenet, an expatriate Frenchman who had worked with Dick Teague at American Motors. The Clenet Series I (1976–79) was built on a Lincoln Continental chassis and the cockpit area was a cut-down MG Midget hull with MG doors and windshield. The Lincoln V8 was used along with an automatic transmission. With a 120in (3045mm) wheelbase and a 2-seat body, the bonnet was very long with sweeping running boards to

1980 Clenet Series I roadster.

complete the classic look. Dashboards were black walnut, air conditioning was standard and Connolly leather was used on the luxury interior. These were very popular despite their high price ($27,500 in 1976). A 4-seater Cabriolet model (Series II) was added in 1979. Demand was high, and by 1981 the price had risen to $83,500. The Series III models (1982–84) were built on a longer wheelbase with a unibody chassis. In 1985 and 1986, Clenet added a hardtop model to the roadster and cabriolet line. By 1986 Alain Clenet had sold the company and it moved to Carpinteria, California under the ownership of Alfred DiMora. The company closed its doors at the end of 1986, although in 1998 there was an effort to revive the company on a small scale. All Clenets were sold in fully assembled form although their neoclassic concept was widely copiedby the kit car market.

HP

CLESSE (F) 1907–1908

Clesse et Compagnie, Levallois-Perret, Seine.

The Clesse was announced in 1907 as a voiturette with 6.2hp single-cylinder engine and friction drive. In 1908 a 2.8-litre 4-cylinder car was listed by this short-lived firm.

NG

CLEVELAND (i) *see* SPERRY

CLEVELAND (ii) **(US)** 1902–1904

Cleveland Automobile Co., Cleveland, Ohio.

This company was founded by A.L. Moore, who had sold the Cleveland Machine Screw Co., makers of the SPERRY Electric to the American Bicycle Co., and wanted to enter the petrol car business. His range for 1902 consisted of a 2-seater roadster with single-cylinder engine, and a 4-seater tourer with 15hp 2-cylinder engine. These were continued into 1903, and for 1904 a 20hp 4-cylinder tourer replaced the twin, and the single-cylinder models were still made. All had chain drive.

NG

CLEVELAND (iii) **(US)** 1905–1909

Cleveland Motor Car Co., Cleveland, Ohio.

No sooner had A.L. Moore's Cleveland Automobile Co. gone out of business than another firm sprang up in the city. Its car was a descendant of the METEOR (v), which was built by the Federal Manuacturing Co. of Cleveland for sale by the

1981 Clenet Series II cabriolet.

1906 Cleveland(iii) Model H tourer.

Worthington Co. in New York. The first Cleveland had a 4-cylinder 20hp engine, offered with runabout body on a 91in (2311mm) wheelbase, joined for 1906 by a 30/35hp tourer or double phaeton on a 104in (2642mm) wheelbase. Prices were high, at $3500 for the double phaeton, and rose to $5000 for a 30/35hp

1924 Cleveland(vi) Model 42 roadster.
JOHN A. CONDE

1906 Climax (i) 20/22hp tourer.
NATIONAL MOTOR MUSEUM

limousine in 1907, and the same price for a 40/45hp in 1908. These prices were too high for what was on offer, and production ended in 1909 after about 1000 cars had been made. An unusual feature of the Cleveland was that the rear axle half shafts could be slid out simply by removing the hub caps.

NG

CLEVELAND (iv) **(US)** 1909–1910
Cleveland Electric Vehicle Co., Cleveland, Ohio.
This company was formed with the intention of making electric taxicabs, but when the production car appeared it was a passenger car made in three forms – runabout, victoria and coupé, at prices from $2250 to $2800. They had 3.5hp motors and six forward speeds. They were designed by Raymond B. Doty, a descendant of Edward Doty, who arrived in America on the *Mayflower* in 1620, and from whom the Editor of this Encyclopedia is also descended.

NG

CLEVELAND (v) **(US)** 1914
Cleveland Cyclecar Co., Cleveland, Ohio.
Promoted as 'The Aristocrat of Cyclecars' or 'The Peer of Cyclecars', this car had experienced men behind it; Company chief W.E. Burnes came from Garford and Stearns, while designer Robert Clark came from England, where he had worked for Daimler and Humber, and when in the US had been an employee of Columbia and Stearns. The car itself showed little sign of this distinguished background, having a 16hp 4-cylinder engine, friction transmission and belt final drive. Priced at $395 for a 2-seater roadster, it survived less than a year.

NG

CLEVELAND (vi) **(US)** 1919–1926
Cleveland Automobile Co., Cleveland, Ohio.

The Cleveland was, to all intents and purposes, an independent make of car although, in reality, it had been set up as a companion car to the popular CHANDLER, also built in Cleveland, Ohio. The Cleveland was lower-priced than the Chandler, had a shorter wheelbase, and a smaller and less powerful Chandler-built 6-cylinder ohv engine. Featuring a full line of both open and closed models, Cleveland cars were priced from $895 to $1625. An estimated 50,000 Clevelands were sold during its eight years of production. In 1927 the Cleveland appeared as the Chandler Standard Six.

KM

CLIFT see SINCLAIR

CLIMAX (i) **(GB)** 1905–1909
Climax Motor Co., Coventry.
The Climax was an assembled car using engines from Aster or White & Poppe, 3-speed gearboxes and shaft drive. The 1905 models used a 10/12hp Aster 2-cylinder engine, 15hp W&P 3-cylinder or 16 and 20hp fours, both from Aster. For 1906 only fours were offered, a 14hp W&P and a 16 or 22hp Aster. In 1907 a 20hp 6-cylinder W&P-powered car was offered. Rolls-Royce-type radiators were used on the first Climax cars, but later models were flat topped.

NG

CLIMAX (ii) **(US)** 1906–1911
Climax Electric Works, New Salem, Massachusetts.
For its first two years this company operated out of a henhouse belonging to Levi W. Flagg, who was in partnership with William E. Taft, former builder of the TAFT steamer. The company planned to make an electric car, but then turned to petrol, offering a roadster powered by an 18hp 2-cylinder engine for $500, or in kit form, for only $290. Friction transmission was not unusual, but a centrally mounted steering column was, preceding the McLaren F1 by nearly 90 years. In 1908 they moved out of the henhouse into a purpose-built factory, but bankruptcy ensued in 1911. A new company, which may have operated alongside the Climax Electric Works, was the T & F Cyclecar Co. which supplied components to cyclecar manufacturers. This business survived at least into 1915.

NG

CLIMBER (US) 1919–1924
Climber Motor Corp., Little Rock, Arkansas.
The Climber was the most significant car to be built in Arkansas and was organised for sales targeted toward the southern American marketplace, primarily in its home state of Arkansas plus Mississippi, Oklahoma and Tennessee. A number of dealerships were opened. Climber offered 4-cylinder and 6-cylinder series, both powered by Herschell-Spillman engines and initially with a price range of $1385 and $3250 for the 4-cylinder roadster and the 6-cylinder sedan respectively. The Climber was also sold in light truck form with an estimated 75 to 100 completed. Total production of Climber passenger cars has been estimated at 200 to 225.

KM

CLINT YOUNG see C.Y. PRODUCTIONS

CLINTON (CDN) 1911–1912
Clinton Motor Car Co. Ltd, Clinton, Ontario.
This company was a descendant of the Clinton Thresher Co., whose factory was burned down in 1908 and was rebuilt three years later for making cars and trucks. The Clinton car was made as a large tourer, roadster or combination car that could be converted from passenger to goods carrying. Power came from a 4-cylinder engine, probably of the company's own manufacture. It boasted that its car had no foreign input, but had 'Canadian design, Canadian capital, Canadian workmen'. Not more than eight passenger cars were made, and an unknown number of combination cars and trucks. The company went out of business by November 1912.

NG

CLINTON E. WOODS (US) 1897–1901
1897–1900 Clinton E. Woods, Chicago, Illinois.
1901 Woods-Waring Co., Chicago, Illinois.

Clinton Woods was a pioneer designer of electric cars. He built a prototype in 1897, and the Fisher Equipment Co. made 60 cars of Woods' design in 1898. The following year he became works superintendent of the Woods Motor Vehicle Co., but left in early 1901 to form Woods-Waring. A variety of designs was offered, including a stanhope, brougham, hansom cab and delivery van, but the company failed by the end of the year. Woods Motor Vehicle Co. continued in business until 1918.

NG

CLIPPER (US) 1955–1956

Studebaker-Packard Corp., Detroit, Michigan.

For the 1956 season PACKARD decided to market its lower priced Clippers as a separate make, in an attempt to distance them from the senior Packards which it wanted to identify as a luxury make to rival Cadillac and Lincoln. This decision came from company president James J. Nance, who thought that the policy of promoting cheaper models had been 'bleeding the Packard name white'. Clippers were made in three models, De Luxe, Super, and Custom, all using the 5768cc V8, which gave 240bhp in the De Luxe and Super lines, and 275bhp in the Custom. Body styles were a 4-door sedan and 2-door hard-top, and styling was very close to that of the senior Packards. For the 1957 season the Clipper was reabsorbed into the Packard range, and in fact used a Studebaker body shell. Total output of the 'independent' Clippers was 18,482, well above the 10,353 senior Packards made in the 1956 season.

NG

CLOUGHLEY (US) 1901–1903

1901–1902 Cloughley Automobile Manufacturing Co., Cherryvale, Kansas.
1903 Cloughley Motor Vehicle Co., Parsons, Kansas.

Robert H. Cloughley built his first steam car in 1896, and tried to use it in a taxi service, but found few customers. In 1901 he built another steamer and set up a company to manufacture it, but achieved only one sale. Early in 1903 he moved to Parsons where he started another company to make petrol cars in addition to steamers. They shared the same body style, a high 4-seater surrey (without a fringe on top, or any form of weather protection) and final drive by single chain. The 8hp 2-cylinder steamer was priced at $1200, the 9 and 12hp 2-cylinder petrol models at $1500. The company did not survive the year 1903, and Cloughley later earned his living as a painter.

NG

CLOUMOBIL (D) 1906–1908

Automobilbauerei Clou Alfred Karfunkel, Berlin-Charlottenburg.

This company made two distinct types of car, an electric 3-wheeler driving on the single front wheel, and a small car powered by a 4-cylinder petrol engine.

HON

CLOYD (US) 1911

Cloyd Auto Co., Nashville, Tennessee.

Percival C. Cloyd was a car repairer who decided to be a car maker as well. His design was a conventional one, with 40hp 4-cylinder engine, 3-speed gearbox and shaft drive. Body styles were a runabout and roadster on a 110in (2791mm) wheelbase and a tourer on 123in (3121mm). Very few were made.

NG

CLUA (E) 1948–1958

Construcciones Metálicas Clua, Barcelona.

This company was a motorcycle manufacturer. For a short time from 1952 they produced a fibreglass 2-seater powered by a 497cc 2-cylinder 4-stroke engine. In all about 100 were made.

NG

CLUB (i) see BROUHOT

CLUB (ii) (D) 1922–1924

Club Automobilefabrik GmbH, Berlin-Charlottenburg.

Only one model was offered by this short-lived make, a 2-seater powered by a 1.3-litre 4-cylinder Atos engine. It had wire wheels and a Rolls-Royce type radiator.

HON

1956 Clipper Custom 4-cylinder sedan.
NICK BALDWIN

1958 Clua sports coupé.
NICK GEORGANO

CLUB CAR (US) 1910–1911

Club Car Co., New York, New York.

This company was a co-operative which supplied cars only to members of the club. They were actually built by Merchant & Evans of Philadelphia, with 40/50hp 4-cylinder engines from the American & British Manufacturing Co. of Bridgeport, Connecticut, and bodies from Biddle & Smart of Amesbury, Massachusetts. Several styles were offered, from a runabout at $2800 to a limousine or landaulette at $3750. The club organisers were New York bankers (another group with a similar scheme made the ORSON), but membership was so low that very few cars were delivered. Merchant & Evans sold off the remaining Club Cars under the name Devon.

NG

CLULEY (GB) 1921–1928

Clarke, Cluley & Co., Coventry.

The makers of the Cluley car were established in 1890 as a general engineering firm, soon turning to bicycles and, in 1903 to textile machinery. The following year they announced a tricar, the Globe Cymocar, but it did not go into serious production. They prospered with armaments work during World War I and, like so many companies, found themselves with a workforce too large for the much reduced volume of civilian business. This led them to car manufacture – a prototype light car designed by Cecil Bayliss, (ex-PERRY), with possible input from Arthur Alderson (ex-LEA-FRANCIS), was built in 1920, and was ready for production two years later. It had a 1328cc 4-cylinder side-valve engine of Cluley's own manufacture with monobloc casting of cylinders, and a 3-speed gearbox in unit with it. Slightly larger engines of 1460 and 1644cc were introduced in 1922 and 1923, joined by a 1790cc unit, which had pair-cast cylinders. A short-lived six called the 16/40 was listed for 1924 only; it had the archaic feature of a separate gearbox. Brakes were on the rear wheels only, and had the unusual design of two sets of drums, mounted concentrically, each with its own set of aluminium shoes. At £575 it was expensive and few were sold.

Taking its place at the top of the range in 1925 was another four, the 14/30 at a more modest £395. This had a 1944cc Meadows engine, and was joined in

1924 Cluley 10/20hp Chummy tourer.
NATIONAL MOTOR MUSEUM

1904 Clyde 7hp 2-seater.
NATIONAL MOTOR MUSEUM

1927 by the ohv 2120cc 14/50. The smaller 1460cc 10/20 acccounted for most of the 3,000 Cluleys made, but it was dropped after 1926. The 14/30 and 14/50 were continued into 1928, but then Clarke, Cluley returned exclusively to textile machinery. There was a downturn in this business as well, and in 1933 they had only 17 employees, but subcontract work for Rolls-Royce from 1934 proved their salvation, and another war saw them working on Rolls-Royce Merlin aero engines. The Coventry factory was destroyed in an air raid, but a new factory was built at Kenilworth, where they are still active today.

NG

Further Reading
'From Coventry to Kenilworth', M. Worthington-Williams,
The Automobile, April 1984.

CLYDE (GB) 1901–1930

1901–1904 Clyde Cycle & Motor Car Co. Ltd, Leicester.
1905–1907 G.H. Wait, Leicester.
1908–1930 G.H. Wait & Co. Ltd, Leicester.
George Henry Wait was a pioneer cyclist who set up in Leicester as a cycle maker in 1890. He was dabbling in four wheelers as early as 1899, when he advertised the Clyde Pennington Victoria, an unwise involvement with the notorious

Edward J. PENNINGTON, as well as an M.M.C. tricycle. The first car of his own make appeared in 1901, having a front-mounted 3.5hp Simms engine, with 2-speed gearbox and belt drive to a countershaft which was geared to the rear axle. For 1902 a 5hp Aster or 6hp De Dion-Bouton engine was used, and by 1905 power was provided by 8hp White & Poppe or 12hp Aster engines. Motorcycles were also made from the turn of the century; a Clyde is said to have given Winston Churchill his first motorcycle ride, although whether he owned one is not so certain.

The original firm was wound up in 1905, the assets being disposed of including 25 bicycles, 60 motorcycle frames, 12 motorcycles and one 2-cylinder car. This would indicate that cars were always a minority in George Wait's activities. By the time production ended he is said to have made only 245 cars and 25 commercial vehicles, but 470 motorcycles and about 4,000 bicycles. He concentrated on garage work from 1906, although cars were made from time to time. The only known surviving Clydes date from 1906 and 1908 – the former has a 12/14hp 3-cylinder White & Poppe engine, and the latter a 8/10hp 2-cylinder Aster engine. Most of the few Clydes made up to 1914 used either Aster or W & P engines.

A few Clydes were made in the 1920s, but Wait's main business was in agencies for various makes, including Humber. Models listed included 2-cylinder cars of 995 and 1003cc, said to be of Wait's own manufacture, and various fours of 1196, 1496, and 1550cc, which were almost certainly proprietary units. George Wait drove his 1906 12/14 until well into his 80s, taking part in Veteran Car Club events in the 1950s.

NG

CLYMER (US) 1908

Durable Motor Car Co., St Louis, Missouri.
This was a short-lived high-wheeler powered by a 12hp 2-cylinder engine, with solid tyres and offered in four body styles. The cars were guaranteed for a year, more than the life of the company as it turned out.

NG

CLYNO (GB) 1922–1930

1922–1929 Clyno Engineering (1922) Ltd, Wolverhampton, Staffordshire.
1929–1930 RH Collier & Co. Ltd, Birmingham.
The Clyno name was coined by cousins Frank and Alwyn Smith from Thrapston, Northamptonshire, for the variable-width belt drive pulleys which they marketed to give a form of gearing for early single-speed motorcycles. Progressing to the manufacture of complete motorcycles, at first from proprietary parts, they developed a popular lightweight 2-stroke. World War I saw a great expansion in the company's facilities, with a major contract for the supply of V-twin motorcycle combinations for the Motor Machine Gun Service.

Prototype light cars were constructed in 1913 and 1919, but the firm was always undercapitalised and suffered a severe set-back when financiers Thomas de la Rue & Co. withdrew their backing. The re-formed company of 1922 brought in George Stanley to head a design team for a new light car, of generally conventional specification with a Coventry-Climax engine of 1368cc. The price of £250 was competitive for this pleasant, lively and reliable model, which quickly gained an excellent reputation. Demand was such that motorcycle production was suspended for the next year. In 1924 an 11.9hp was first announced, with Clyno-built instead of merely Clyno-assembled engine. Exports were looked after by the introduction of a 'Colonial' model, but this can hardly have been cost-effective as, although of similar design and appearance to the home-market version, it differed slightly in practically every detail. A promising and attractive wire-wheeled sports model also appeared, but was dropped quite soon due to demand for the standard product. The 2-bearing 10.8hp engine, as ever with 'Clyno' deceptively cast on the valve chest, was changed from ball to white-metal mains, and the price was cut to £198. Sales Manager Harry Cocker continued to back up his aggressive marketing with competition successes, particularly in trials such as the MCC classics.

For 1925 4-wheel brakes became an option and the range of body styles increased. De luxe versions were always 'Royal' and customarily finished in an appropriate blue. For 1926 4-wheel brakes were standardised, which necessitated a longer chassis frame and revised suspension. Production of the 10.8hp leaped to 11,149 for the year, bringing the firm into third place behind Austin and Morris. The 12hp car at last became available, at first with Coventry-Climax engine but later, as planned with Clyno's own. Cracks in the fabric, however, were starting to appear. As motoring writer John Stanford succinctly put it, Clyno built good cars badly and there were reports of inaccurately machined camshafts, unfaced fabric transmission joint spiders and so on. One reason adduced for the variable quality of assembly was the policy of employing numbers of first-year apprentices, reducing wages costs virtually to a nominal level, and then sacking and replacing them, regardless of ability, when their experience qualified them for higher pay rates. From 1927, the heavier engines of the 12/28 and later 12/35 cars, with wider and longer chassis and more sophisticated bodywork, stifled the liveliness and lightness of control for which the earlier cars were renowned. Worse problems stemmed from the increase in unsprung weight of both front and rear axles following the adoption of larger brakes. This not only adversely affected comfort and handling but also reliability, putting an increased strain on the basically unchanged transmission components. A move to expanded premises at Bushbury Park, replacing the cramped Pelham Street works, was unfelicitously timed to coincide with a downturn in sales.

In late 1927 the A.G. Booth-designed 'Nine' was announced, although as a modest 8.3hp it defeated itself from the start for those who expected that the nomenclature indicated a 28 per cent power increase over an Austin Seven. Hailed as the first Clyno with coil ignition, in fact the 1928 run used a Lucas GB4 magneto. As with all 1928 and later models, the radiator shell was of a new shape, in retrospect less attractive but cheaper to produce, whilst to cut costs and still look fashionable an interior-quality maroon leathercloth cladding was standardised for both saloons and tourers. The only apparent advantage of the 'De Luxe' saloon was sliding rear windows. The Coventry-Climax side-valve was durable and dependable, but besides the shoddy bodywork the car had a somewhat ponderous and archaic air and sales never remotely approached expectations. The 'Century' model was so named in honour of an attempt to bring down the price to £100, though in fact the complete car never retailed below £112.10.0. To make even this possible, equipment was skimped to an unacceptable level. Only three small lights were supplied and even the familiar blue enamel backing to the radiator badge was eliminated. This version stuck so direly in agents' showrooms that in the end most were unprofitably returned to Bushbury for upgrading. In the trade it was nicknamed the 'Cemetery'. A.J.S. had been linked to Clyno through having a major bodywork contract for the larger models in succession to Mulliners, whilst waiting for the Bushbury factory to be commissioned, but their later 'Nine' was in most respects dissimilar to Clyno's effort.

Ever anxious to keep in fashion, a side-valve Straight Eight prototype was made. Still fitted with rather temporary bodywork, this was retained by an ex-employee who used it in Devon for many years. There were also plans for a 6-cylinder model and a prototype was rumoured to still exist in Winchester after World War II.

Clyno was already in retreat when the 1929 recession arrived. The receiver's faith in the help they might get from their largest distributor, Rootes Bros of London, was misplaced and the decision to close down was taken in September of that year. The buyer was Alfred Herbert Ltd, who retained the premises and sold the other assets to RH Collier & Co. They sold a few more cars, including some 12/35's under construction which they completed from their stock of parts. They retained the spares and sold on the name, goodwill and some machinery to a group who formed a new Clyno Engineering Co. in Birmingham. This firm concentrated on niche markets for specialist equipment, such as camera gantries for the film industry, and had nothing to do with motors. Despite the production of some 40,000 cars in little over 7 years, the name quickly dropped from the public eye.

DF

1923 Clyno 10.8hp 2-seater.
NATIONAL MOTOR MUSEUM

1926 Clyno 10.8hp saloon.
NATIONAL MOTOR MUSEUM

1928 Clyno Twelve 2-seater.
NATIONAL MOTOR MUSEUM

C.M. *see* MOCHET

C.M.N. (I) 1919–1923

1919–1920 Costruzioni Meccaniche Nazionali SA, Milan-Pontedera.
1920–1923 Officine Meccaniche Toscana di Pontedera, Milan-Pontedera.
This company was active in aviation and general engineering during World War I, and turned to car manufacture in 1919 to keep its workforce busy. Its car was a conventional and rather dated design with 2.3-litre 4-cylinder and 2.9-litre 6-cylinder side-valve engines. More interesting was the 2-litre Tipo Sport of 1922

with ohvs. The company's best claim to fame was that the young Enzo Ferrari worked for it as a tester during 1919–20, and left to join Alfa Romeo.

NG

CMV (E) 1944–1945

Construcciones Móviles SA de Valencia, Valencia.
The engineer Ernest Rodriguez Iranzo, involved in DAVID, NACIONAL PESCARA, and other Spanish cars, developed an electric car with batteries and 3hp engine on the rear. The engine was in unit with the differential, with two

propeller shafts driving the front wheels. This was a modern one-box design, designed for use as taxi. On the same base a small delivery van was developed. These cars were shown at the Valencia Fair in 1945 and at the Madrid Fair in 1946, where the Government took test drives.

VCM

C.N. (GB) 1985 to date
Christopher Neil Sportscars, Northwich, Cheshire.
Of the several attempts to replicate the classic Lotus Elan, Christopher Neil Sportscars of Cheshire was better qualified than most, being a leading Lotus specialist. Using restoration expertise, a reproduction backbone chassis was offered with a near-replica fibreglass body, interior and running gear, under the name C.N. Sprint. As an alternative to Elan components, a more modern power train could be fitted in the form of the Ford CVH engine, mated to a Ford Cortina or Sierra gearbox and Triumph front hubs.

CR

COACHSMITHS (US) c.1990
Coachsmiths, Mabelvale, Arizona.
The Blackstone Town Coupé was a neoclassic kit car based on a Chevrolet Monza or Pontiac Sunbird. Using the cockpit area of the donor car, it added a long bonnet, chrome grill and long, sweeping mudguards with side-mounted spares. The chassis was stretched to a 137in (3477mm) wheelbase and Chevrolet Malibu suspension was used. It was sold in kit or assembled form. Coachsmiths also made a rebody kit for the Pontiac Firebird called the Icon that gave it a pseudo-Ferrari Testarossa look.

HP

COACHWORKS OF YESTERYEAR (US) c.1992
Coachworks of Yesteryear, Cocoa, Florida.
Vintage pick-up trucks were an unusual speciality for a kit car company, but a replica of the 1936 Ford pick-up was the only product for this Florida firm. They were available in kit or assembled form, and fitted an original Ford chassis or their own steel tube frame. Power was from Ford or GM V8s.

HP

COADOU-FLEURY (F) 1921–c.1935
Marcel Coadou, Trébeurden, Cotes du Nord.
Marcel Coadou, a captain in the French Air Force reserve and director of the flying school at Saint-Michel en Greves, started with a small cyclecar with aluminium monocoque frame, 850cc 4-cylinder Ruby engine, 2-speed epicyclic gearbox and shaft drive. Top speed was a creditable 43mph (70km/h). In 1927 he replaced the Ruby engine with that of a Citroën B2 which he endowed with ohvs. In view of the extra power (30bhp in place of 20), he gave his car front-wheel brakes. The body was more streamlined and the flared wings of the original were replaced by ailerons behind each wheel. In 1929 he reverted to wings, of the cycle type, and made his car into a coupé, following this with a 2-door saloon. Coadou took out patents for his designs in Germany and Britain as well as in France, and hoped to find a backer who would put the car into production. The final version of what was basically the same car, although drastically modified, had an aerodynamic coupé body with an aircraft-type sliding cockpit and wire wheels in place of the discs used on all previous versions. This car, known as the Aerolithe, survives today.

NG

COAST TO COAST (US) c.1988
Coast to Coast Auto Styling, Camp Hill, Pennsylvania.
Their TR Fiero kit car adapted Ferrari Testarossa-like body panels to the Pontiac Fiero. The lines were not close enough to be considered a replica, but they had an Italian flavour. Sold in kit or fully assembled form.

HP

COATES-GOSHEN (US) 1908–1910
Coates-Goshen Automobile Co., Goshen, New York.
Joseph Saunders Coates was a sulky-racing enthusiast, and ran the Miller Cart Co. in Goshen which manufactured high-quality sulkies. He built an experimental

car in this factory in 1905, and three years later was able to go into production with the Coates-Goshen car. Like his sulkies, it was a high quality product, with 25 or 32hp 4-cylinder engine and a frame dropped at the scuttle to give a lower entrance. They were made in runabout, town car and baby tonneau models, the latter being a 4-seater tourer. For 1910 larger engines of 45 and 60hp were offered, the latter on a 140in (3556mm) wheelbase, selling for $4200. After 32 cars had been made the factory burnt down and Coates was unable to continue his business. From 1912 to 1914 he made the Coates Tricar, a 3-wheeled delivery van, thereafter concentrating on the design of horse-racing tracks. He persevered with this into his late 80s.

NG

Further Reading
'Something went wrong in the Land of O'Goshen: The failed Promise of the Coates-Goshen', Spencer Murray, *Automobile Quarterly*, Vol.31, No.3.

COATS (US) 1921–1923
1921–1922 Coats Steam Car Co., Columbus, Ohio.
1922–1923 Y.F. Stewart Motor Manufacturing Co., Bowling Green, Ohio.
The Coats, a 3-cylinder steam car designed by George A. Coats, was introduced in early 1921. It was announced that the car would be available as a touring car – the prototype of which had been built – a roadster and a sedan, all to sell for $1085. Despite announcements of Columbus as the hub of its manufacturing activities, no more prototypes followed until 1922, by which time the Coats had moved its operations to the Y.F. Stewart Motor Manufacturing Co. of Bowling Green, Ohio. By the time the car was finally placed on the market, there were insufficient finances left for actual production which turned out to be the completion of the several touring cars which had been under construction as additional prototypes. The car, frequently and erroneously listed as Coats-Stewart or Stewart-Coats, dates from the latter days of the company's existence and refers to the factory in which it was to have been built.

KM

COBRETTE (US) c.1998
Group Five Ltd, Mesa, Arizona.
A Cobra replica kit with a difference, this one had a stretched body that bolted to a stock 1968–82 Corvette chassis. Engines and running gear were Chevrolet.

HP

COBRETTI (GB) 1990 to date
1990–1992 Cobretti Engineering, Sutton, Surrey.
1992–1993 Cobretti Engineering, Wallington, Surrey.
1993 to date Autotrak, Wallington, Surrey.
Cobretti Engineering used to be BRIGHTWHEEL agents, so when the Brightwheel Viper ceased to be available, Cobretti restarted manufacture. Three versions were on offer: the Viper 4 (Ford Cortina or later Sierra/Granada basis), Viper V8 (Jaguar basis with Rover/American V8 power), and V12 (Jaguar running gear and engine). All suffered from out-sized front wheel arches to accept full-width Jaguar axles, though narrow arches were optional on Jaguar-based cars. This design was revived under the name Autotrak Cobretti.

CR

COCHOT (F) 1899–1901
G. Cochot, Paris.
Cochot's voiturettes were made in two forms, a tandem 2-seater steered from the rear seat, and a side by side 2-seater. Both used a 2.5hp single-cylinder engine of Cochot's own manufacture, which was geared to the rear axle. Cochot later made the larger LUTECE 4-cylinder car.

NG

COCK (NL) 1968
Cock NV, Assen.
Established in 1958, Cock built the Little Tyrant 3-wheeled truck until 1974, but its only attempt at a passenger car was the Cockpitt, presented at the 1968 Amsterdam Show. This was a very small city car with all-flat panelwork powered by either a single-cylinder petrol engine or an electric motor.

CR

COCKERELL (D) 1924–1927

Friederich Gockerell, Munich.

Although the maker of these cars spelled his name *Gockerell*, the cars themselves were known as *Cockerells*. Friederich Gockerell (1889–1965) was better known for the unconventional Megola motorcycles with 5-cylinder radial engine mounted in the front wheel, than for his cars. The first of these was a neat-looking 2-seater powered by a 905cc 4-cylinder 2-stroke engine with the unusual feature, for that date, of separately cast cylinders. His next car, completed in 1926, also used a 2-stroke engine, but with two cylinders and a capacity of 1056cc. This had front-wheel drive, and 4-wheel brakes, but these were uncoupled, the pedal operating on the front wheels and the handbrake on the rear. At least three of these were made, and Gockerell hoped to obtain finance to make a series of 100, but this never happened. He fitted a 1086cc 6-cylinder 2-stroke to one of his cars, with which he had some success in competitions, and planned a straight-8 2-stroke which was probably never built. In 1926 he also built five prototypes of the Cockmobil, a 3-wheeler which used the front wheel and power unit from the Megola motorcycle, with 2-seater or light van bodies. He continued his inventions up to his death. An interesting project was a 4-seater with rear-mounted turbine engine projected in 1946.

NG

COEY (US) 1901–1902; 1913–1917

1901–1902 C.A. Coey & Co., Chicago, Illinois.

1913–1917 Coey Motor Co., Chicago, Illinois.

Charles A. Coey's first car-building venture involved electric and petrol runabouts, the latter with 5hp 2-stroke engines. How many were made is not certain, but at least ten electrics were completed, as in 1902 he was offering to hire these out. He also formed the C.A. Coey School of Motoring, and became the Chicago agent for the THOMAS Flyer. These activities kept him busy until he decided to become a car manufacturer again. The Coey Flyer was a large car with 4- or 6-cylinder engines, the latter of 6.3-litres and on a 128in (3251mm) wheelbase. He supplemented the Flyer range with two smaller cars, the 9hp 2-cylinder Coey Junior and 12hp 4-cylinder Coey Bear. In 1914 the Junior was upgraded and renamed C-A-C. In 1916 the Coey company was absorbed by the Wonder Motor Truck Co., which continued a smaller Flyer for one year.

NG

COGGSWELL (US) 1910–1911

Coggswell Motor Co., Grand Rapids, Michigan.

This company seemed more interested in boasting of the local content of its car, '. . .designed by a Grand Rapids man, assembled by Grand Rapids workmen, and carrying a Grand Rapids name. . .' than of the car's design. This was advanced, for the 35hp 4-cylinder engine had a single-ohc and valves inclined at 45 degrees. Dual ignition was provided. However, neither of these features nor local pride could help the company, which folded after only pilot models of the car had been made.

NG

COGNET DE SEYNES (F) 1912–1926

Automobiles Cognet de Seynes, Lyons.

Like several other car companies (such as Rolls-Royce, De Dion-Bouton), this company was formed by the partnership between a wealthy enthusiast and a talented engineer. The backer was Edouard de Seynes (1882–1957) and the engineer Victor Cognet who had invented a constant-mesh gearbox which he made in a small workshop in Lyons. They built one or two prototypes of a small car before 1912 when they went into production. It had a 1122cc 4-cylinder side-valve engine in unit with a 3-speed gearbox; with the propeller shaft and rear axle they were enclosed in an oil-filled cylindrical sump, on the same lines as the SIMPLICIA. The lower friction provided by this system enabled the little engine to propel a substantial 4-seater tourer at speeds up to 35mph (56km/h). The tourer seems to have been the only body style available in prewar days, although de Seynes had an aluminium 2-seater built for his own use in 1914.

One car was completed as late as 1916, but the company otherwise made components for Anzani aero engines. In 1920 new owners took over, and the cars became known as C de S. They hoped to make 300 cars per year, including a 6-cylinder model, but nothing came of this, the new owners soon departed and de Seynes regained control. He continued production on the more modest

1913 Coey 'Bear' light car.
NATIONAL MOTOR MUSEUM

1923 Cognet de Seynes tourer.
NATIONAL MOTOR MUSEUM

scale of about 20–30 cars per year. The postwar cars were not greatly changed mechanically, apart from a longer wheelbase and full electric equipment, but their appearance was typical of the early 1920s, with disc wheels and a slight vee to the radiator. Two body styles were now available; the tourer and a 3-seater cloverleaf similar to that on the Citroën 5CV, and a saloon was added later. The company closed in 1926 owing to competition from the mass producers. Sales had been mostly local, although one Cognet de Seynes got as far as Hankow in China. Edouard de Seynes joined Rochet-Schneider as commercial director, and was also a driving examiner. Two of his cars are known to survive.

NG

COHENDET (F) 1898–1914

André Cohendet et Compagnie, Paris.

Cohendet were important suppliers of components to a number of car makers, including DECAUVILLE, but a few complete cars were listed under their name from time to time. In 1898 a 3hp quadricycle and a light car with 2-cylinder air-cooled engine were reported, and two years later they announced their intention of bringing out steam and electric cars as well as petrol cars. In 1901 they advertised a 700cc single-cylinder engine for sale to other manufacturers. Contemporary advertisements showed medium-sized cars on conventional lines.

1912 Colby 30hp underslung chassis.
NICK BALDWIN

1923 Cole Aero Eight tourer.
NATIONAL MOTOR MUSEUM

Both 2- and 4-cylinder Cohendets with 3-speed gearboxes and shaft drive were on show at the 1903 Paris Salon. A 12hp was still listed in 1905, but thereafter Cohendet concentrated on subcontract work until 1910, when a voiturette with a 703cc single-cylinder engine and chain drive was announced, under the name l'Américaine. This was named after C.R. Goodwin, an American resident in Paris. It was marketed up to the outbreak of World War I, being joined for 1914 by a 1.5-litre 4-cylinder car, also with chain drive. Cohendet were better-known for commercial vehicles.

NG

COLANI (D) 1964–1968
Lutz Colani, Berlin.
Lutz Colani was primarily a stylist who briefly offered a kit car with a 2-seater roadster or coupé body, to take Volkswagen components.

HON

COLBURN (US) 1906–1911
Colburn Automobile Co., Denver, Colorado.
One of the more successful cars to be built in Colorado, the Colburn was generally conventional, being made with several sizes of 4-cylinder engine from a 25hp in 1906 to a 40/45hp from 1909 to 1910. Apart from making a roadster capable of more than 60mph (100km/h), Colburn was famous for its unusual model names. These included the 1906 Rex Alta (Latin for 'King of the Heights') and 1907 Skyscraper, both referring to the cars' ability in the mountains. In 1909 Colburn introduced a dashboard radiator, with Renault-style bonnet ahead of it. The company was founded by Judge E.A. Colburn, a wealthy mine owner from Cripple Creek, Colorado.

NG

COLBY (US) 1911–1914
Colby Motor Co., Mason City, Iowa.
William Colby was in partnership with David W. Henry, who had made the HENRY car at Muskegon, Michigan. They launched a conventional car with a 40hp 4-cylinder Excelsior engine, and had completed 100 of them by the spring of 1911. The 1912 Model L, launched in August 1911, had a smaller engine of 30hp and underslung frames, and was offered in tourer, roadster and coupé forms. The 40 with conventional frame was continued. In December 1911 the Colby company merged with the National Cooperative Farm Machinery Co. of Davenport, Iowa. William Colby was retained as president but Henry was made redundant, and later built the OMAHA in Nebraska. The merger seemed to be good for business, for 1912 was Colby's best year, with 203 cars made. 1913 Colbys had 4- and 6-cylinder Continental engines. The company was sold again in October 1913, and this time William Colby was out. The new owners, Standard Motor Co., planned to build a $3 million factory at Minneapolis, but nothing came of this, and hardly any cars were made in 1914. It was reported that the company was losing $1000 a day, and was only kept alive by regular donations from a wealthy 74-year old widow. When her son put a stop to this, Colby was bankrupt. An estimated 550 cars had been made in all.

NG

COLDA (F) 1921–1922
Automobiles Colda, Paris.
This was a short-lived medium-sized car powered by a 1843cc Sergant engine.

NG

COLDWELL (GB) 1967–1969
Coldwell Engineering and Racing Ltd, Sheffield, Yorkshire.
This was a successful attempt to make a road and race GT car with mid-mounted Mini power. Around six cars were produced and the design formed the basis of a string of 2-litre sports-racing cars from 1970.

CR

COLE (US) 1909–1925
Cole Carriage Co.; Cole Motor Co., Indianapolis, Indiana.
Early Cole cars were high-wheelers with 14hp air-cooled flat-twin engines. In 1910 a 30hp in-line four was introduced, with pair-cast cylinders, dual ignition, a core clutch and 3-speed gearbox, and shaft drive. It had pair-cast cylinders, a 3-speed gearbox, shaft drive, and dual ignition. Electric lighting and starting were standardised in 1913, when a 50hp four and a 60hp six of 7.3 litres were added to the range. The latter was priced at up to $4250 for a 7-seater berline limousine. Left-hand steering and coil ignition were adopted in March 1914. The 4-cylinder engines were made by Cole, but from 1914 the six was built for them by Northway. In March 1915 Cole announced a V8 with 5676cc Northway engine. The fours and sixes were dropped, and the V8 was the sole engine offered by Cole for the rest of the make's life. From 1918 the car was known as the Cole Aero Eight. 1916 was their peak year, with 5160 cars delivered, though some sources claim 6225 in 1919. In the early 1920s Coles were noted for their unusual bodies, closed models having octagonal rear quarter windows. Some of these bodies were made by Willoughby. They also had unusual names, 'tourosine' and 'sportosine' for touring and supposedly sporting limousines, and 'brouette' for a small brougham. Cole was also early in its adoption, in 1924, of balloon tyres: 'Did you ever go ballooning on a Cole?' became their slogan. Westinghouse air springs were another feature of the last Coles. Sales fell in the 1920s, and Joseph Cole decided to liquidate (while the company was still solvent) in 1925, when only 607 Coles were made.

NG

COLE-WIEDEMAN (GB) 1905–1906
William Cole & Co. Ltd, Hammersmith, London.
This was a tourer powered by a 14hp 4-cylinder White & Poppe engine, with shaft final drive. A larger four and a 20/24hp six were also listed, but it is not known if they were actually built.

NG

COLEMAN (US) 1933, 1935
Coleman Motors, Littleton, Colorado.
Coleman Motors was prominent in the manufacture of 4-wheel drive trucks from 1923 into the 1950s and then for conversions until the company failed in 1986. The two cars completed were an attempt to enter the automotive marketplace. Toward this goal, the initial prototype car was built in 1933, featuring slab sides and devoid of conventional mudguards, a design which would become the norm in

automobile design 30 years hence. The power for this pilot model was a Ford V8 engine, mounted under the sharply-arched front axle, which placed it ahead of conventional auto design at the time. A Ford transmission, rear axle assembly, and wheels were likewise incorporated into the Coleman design. Plans to produce the car at $1000 each failed to materialise, probably due to its then-radical design and also the serious economic situation at the time. However, two years later a second prototype was completed with similar lines based on a 1935 Ford V8 two-door sedan but, like the initial attempt, the project was abandoned.

KM

COLIBRI (D) 1908–1911
Norddeutsche Automobilwerke GmbH, Hamelin.

The first Colibri car had an 860cc 2-cylinder engine, and was succeeded in 1910 by a 1360cc monobloc 4-cylinder model. This was succeeded in 1911 by a slightly larger car called the SPERBER. The Colibri was sometimes listed under the initials of the manufacturer, NAW. Its home town was made famous in the poem, *The Pied Piper of Hamelin*.

HON

COLIN (F) 1932–1934
Automobiles Colin, Gennevilliers, Seine.

The Colin was mainly made as a racing car in 350 and 500cc forms, competing successfully in the Bol d'Or events in the Bois de Boulogne. They were also fitted with sketchy road equipment, and the 500cc model was offered for sale in 1933. It had a vertical-twin engine and coil ifs. In September 1934 the Colin brothers announced a larger car powered by a 1097cc Ruby DS 4-cylinder engine, but this never went into production. A prototype with roadster body was built, and a companion closed car was listed, but probably never built.

NG

COLLET (F) 1969–1970
Michel Collet SA, Paris.

Inspired by racing go-karts and a drive in a contemporary Marcadier Barquette, Michel Collet set about producing an exclusive 2-seater sportscar of his own design. The resulting Collet MC1 of 1969 sported a wedge-shaped glassfibre body clothing an elaborate tubular frame structure, with the primary running gear borrowed from a Renault 8, including the rear-mounted 1.3-litre Gordini engine. The targa-top MC1 weighed in at a mere 700kg, giving a theoretical maximum speed of 124mph (228km/h). Despite its promising on-paper potential, only one MC1 was ever produced. By the late 1990s Michel Collet was sculpturing motoring art from his Parisian workshop.

CR

COLLINET (US) 1920–1921
1920–1921 Collins Motors Inc., Huntington, New York.
1921 Collins Motors Inc., Garden City, New York.

The Collinet was probably the only car which was built as a model of the Collins car, ostensibly produced by Albert H. Collins, erstwhile builder of the Kalamazoo-based WOLVERINE but which, under the Collins badge, failed to build anything more than a pilot model. The Collinet with a 2-seater speedster body was identical in every way to Collins' earlier Wolverine, with a 132in (3350mm) wheelbase and 4-cylinder Wisconsin engine. This car was exhibited at the New York Auto Salon in November 1920. The car carried an astounding price tag of $5500 with further production to be 'on special order' with prices to run between $5000 and $6500. Despite continued plans for the Collinet, it is doubtful that any further production was attempted.

KM

COLLINS (US) 1919–1921
1919–1921 Collins Motors Inc., Huntington, New York.
1921 Collins Motors Inc., Garden City, New York.

Albert H. Collins had headed the moribund WOLVERINE Motors Inc., of Kalamazoo, Michigan, which had built two or three sporting cars, one carrying a Rochester-Duesenberg 4-cylinder engine, before going out of business. Collins had a grandiose plan to manufacture a full complement of 'quality' automobiles which would combine utility, economy and sporting lines and announced a car for the 1920 model year which never appeared. By mid-year work had begun on

c.1908 Colibri 8PS tonneau.
NICK GEORGANO/NATIONAL MOTOR MUSEUM

1901 Colliot 4½hp tonneau.
NICK GEORGANO

an expensive speedster which would sell for $5500 but, upon completion, the car was given a badge of its own – the Collinet – and presumably any Collins cars existed only in press releases.

KM

COLLIOT (F) 1900–1901
Deliry et Fils, Soissons, Aine.

This company made a light car with 2-seater or 4-seater rear-entrance tonneau body, powered by a 4.5hp transversely-mounted V-twin engine. A surviving example has a single-cylinder De Dion-Bouton engine, and this may have been an option offered by the makers, or substituted at a later date. Transmission was by a 4-speed gearbox and chain drive.

NG

COLOMBE (F) 1920–1925
Automobiles Colombe, Colombes, Seine.

Two quite distinct designs were offered by this firm. The first was an assembled car using Model T Ford engine and transmission, with French-built bodies, but in 1923 they introduced a tiny 3-wheeler with air-cooled single-cylinder 345cc

1921/2 Colonial(v) roadster.
KEITH MARVIN

engine, friction transmission and chain drive to the single front wheel. Instead of conventional forks, this was supported by a tube on one side only, to which was mounted a sturdy leaf spring. The two seats were slightly staggered, and there was also a delivery van version.
NG

COLOMBO (I) 1922–1924
Officine Meccananiche Colombo, Milan.
Primarily a maker of aero engines, this company exhibited a 3-wheeled delivery van at the 1922 Milan Show, then turned to a light car powered by a 1300cc 4-cylinder engine with single-ohc.
NG

COLONIAL (i) (US) 1912
Colonial Electric Car Co., Detroit, Michigan.
The Colonial electric car appeared at the height of popularity for this type of vehicle, but failed to make a mark, probably because there were already several well-established electrics, particularly the Detroit made in the same city. The Colonial was a 5-seater brougham in which a cut-glass vase and a vanity case were standard equipment. A 3-seater coupé was announced at the same time, but remained a prototype. Rumours that the company might be sold to General Motors were unfounded. One of the partners in Colonial, William E. Storms, later made the STORMS electric cyclecar.
NG

COLONIAL (ii) (US) 1917–1921
Colonial Automobile Co., Indianapolis, Indiana.
Few of these assembled cars were produced. Mostly touring models, they were powered by a 6-cylinder ohv engine. The wheelbase was 116in (2944mm) and prices started at $995.
KM

COLONIAL (iii) (US) 1920
Mechanical Development Corp., San Francisco, California.
Although only one of the West Coast Colonial cars was built, it is important as being the first car completed – at least in the United States – with 4-wheel hydraulic brakes, appearing even before the similarly equipped Duesenberg and Kenworthy. The car had a straight-8 engine with a bore and stroke of 63 × 114mm (2840cc) which developed 60bhp. Besides a unique hard-top

touring body, readily convertible into a closed car, it featured disc wheels with two side-mounted spares. The prototype probably cost $30,000 to construct, but production models, which were to follow, were to have sold for $1800.
KM

COLONIAL (iv) see SHAW (i)

COLONIAL (v) (US) 1921–1922
Colonial Motors Co., Boston, Massachusetts.
The Colonial was a disc-wheeled attractive sporting-type of car which the prospectus claimed would be produced 'in excess of 100 units in its first year' of production. Probably less than ten units – if that – ever got on the road. With a high, rounded radiator and a 130in (3299mm) wheelbase, the Colonial was powered by a 6-cylinder Beaver engine, with an 88 × 133mm (4850cc) bore and stroke. Three open models plus a coupé were planned, but probably only the open models were ever made.
KM

COLT (i) (US) 1907
Colt Runabout Co., Yonkers, New York.
This was a light roadster powered by a 40hp 6-cylinder engine made in the works of William S. Howard, in space rented by the Colt's manufacturer William Mason Turner. He called it the 'Mile A Minute' runabout, probably a realistic title in view of the car's large engine and light weight of 816kg. Alas, even at a modest price of $1500, the Colt did not appeal to many buyers, and the price was probably too low to allow Turner any profit. His company closed within the year of its opening. Estimates of production vary between two and 'less than a hundred'. Howard, who had made several cars in and around Yonkers previously, made a few Colt-like sixes in 1908.
NG

COLT (ii) (US) c.1958
Colt Manufacturing Company, Milwaukee, Wisconsin.
A 375cc Wisconsin engine powered this tiny economy car. It had a fibreglass body with small fins and automatic transmission.
HP

COLT (iii) see MITSUBISHI (i)

COLTMAN (GB) 1907–1920

H. Coltman & Sons, Loughborough, Leicestershire.

This was a conventional tourer powered by a 3704cc 20hp 4-cylinder engine, with dual ignition, 4-speed gearbox and shaft drive. It had a round radiator which resembled that of a Delaunay-Belleville. Priced at £320, it was listed by *The Motor Car Red Book* up to 1913, although press references are scant apart from the notice of its introduction in November 1907. However, two chassis were said to have been made in 1920.

NG

COLUMBIA (i) (US) 1897–1913

1897–1899 Pope Manufacturing Co., Hartford, Connecticut.
1899 Columbia Automobile Co., Hartford, Connecticut.
1900 Columbia & Electric Vehicle Co., Hartford, Connecticut.
1901–1909 Electric Vehicle Co., Hartford, Connecticut.
1909–1913 Columbia Motor Car Co., Hartford, Connecticut.

The history of the Columbia is complex, being linked to the ambitions of Colonel Albert Augustus Pope (1843–1909), whose aim was to dominate the vehicle industry, as Billy Durant tried to do later. A veteran of the American Civil War, Pope began making bicycles in 1877, and by 1899 he had formed the American Bicycle Co., a conglomerate which controlled some 45 manufacturers. He was a businessman rather than an engineer, and had his vehicles designed for him by employees. One of these was Hiram Percy Maxim, son of the inventor of the machine gun. In fact, Pope had ordered the building of one or two experimental cars, both petrol and electric, before the arrival of Maxim in 1897, but production did not begin until Maxim took control of design. From 1898 onwards he came up with a whole range of electric vehicles, from a light 2-seater runabout to a 12-seater omnibus. He and Pope favoured electricity because batteries could be charged from the ordinary type of electric light stations to be found in all towns of any size. Pope, however, hedged his bets by making some petrol-engined cars from 1899.

Meanwhile the Electric Vehicle Co. of Elizabethport, New Jersey, headed by Isaac L. Rice, acquired from MORRIS & SALOM the rights to the Electrobat front-drive taxicab. No sooner had he done so than financier William Collins Whitney bought up the Electric Vehicle Co. with the intention of making 2000 cabs for use in America's major cities. He merged his activities with those of Colonel Pope, the idea being that Electric Vehicle would make the cabs, and Pope's Columbia Automobile Co. the passenger cars, both electric and petrol. The former Electrobat taxicab was redesigned to have front-wheel steering and rear-wheel drive. Whitney's plans for 2,000 cabs were realised, but the venture was not profitable for Pope. However, he had other irons in the fire, including purchase, in 1900, of the RIKER Electric Vehicle Co., which gave him an entrée into the heavy truck field. From 1903 trucks of Riker design were made under the Columbia name.

Hiram Maxim left Pope in 1902, and design of a new series of petrol cars was given to Frederick A. Law. The 1903 Columbia range consisted of 20 varieties of electric vehicle and one 12/14hp 2-cylinder petrol car. The following year this was joined by a 30/35hp 4-cylinder car, selling at $4000–5000. By 1907 there were seven petrol models and the electric range was reduced to eight. The last year for the electric was 1911, when only two models were listed. Petrol cars were continued to 1913, including, in 1912 and 1913, one powered by a 38hp 4-cylinder Knight sleeve-valve engine. Ironically, in view of Colonel Pope's earlier empire building, the Columbia fell victim to another grandiose scheme, Benjamin Briscoe's United States Motor Co. Colonel Pope had left the Electric Vehicle Co in 1903 to form POPE-HARTFORD. His later ventures included POPE-TOLEDO, POPE-ROBINSON, POPE-TRIBUNE, and POPE WAVERLEY.

NG

COLUMBIA (ii) (US) 1914

American Cyclecar Co., Seattle, Washington.

This was a typical cyclecar with friction transmission and belt final drive. Somewhat more unusual was the use of ohvs in its 2-cylinder engine. It seems that constant changes in the design delayed manufacture for too long, and the cyclecar boom was over before the Columbia could reach the market.

NG

c.1899 Columbia (i) electric demi-coach.
NICK GEORGANO

1904 Columbia (i) Mk XLII tonneau.
NATIONAL MOTOR MUSEUM

1920 Columbia (iv) Six sedan.
NATIONAL MOTOR MUSEUM

COLUMBIA (iii); COLUMBIAN (US) 1914–1917

Columbia Electric Vehicle Co., Detroit, Michigan.

Formed as Columbia Electric Vehicle Co. in February 1914, this company rapidly changed their name to Columbian, to avoid confusion with the Hartford-based Columbia, although in fact that firm was already out of business. The cars were typical of electric practice, but their curved lines gave them a better appearance than many. A 2-seater runabout and 3-seater couplette were listed for 1914–15, with a heavier-looking 4-seater brougham added for 1916. At $785 in 1914 the

1908 Columbus (ii) 10hp motor buggy.
NICK BALDWIN

1912 Columbus (ii) electric coupé.
NICK BALDWIN

1908 Comet(i) 25hp roadster.
NATIONAL MOTOR MUSEUM

runabout was very reasonably priced, but this was too low to make a profit, and by 1916 the same car cost $1175.

NG

COLUMBIA (iv) (US) 1916–1924
Columbia Motors Co., Detroit, Michigan.
The Columbia was low-priced assembled car which used well-known propriety units and attracted a lot of buyers. Two models were offered, powered by Continental sixes. As many as 6000 were sold in 1923, mostly the roadster, at $995. Columbia purchased the LIBERTY in 1923, but both makes failed in 1924. The Columbia used thermostatically-controlled radiator shutters as early as 1920, one of the earliest cars to do so.

KM

COLUMBUS (i) see IMPERIAL (ii)

COLUMBUS (ii) (US) 1903–1915
1903–1914 Columbus Buggy Co., Columbus, Ohio.
1914–1915 New Columbus Buggy Co., Columbus, Ohio.
In business since the 1860s, the Columbus Buggy Co. was one of the largest makers of horse-drawn vehicles in America. While many such firms entered the self-propelled field with a high-wheel motor buggy, Columbus made electric vehicles to start with, although they added a high wheeler in 1907. For three years they made only one style of electric, a folding-top runabout, but in 1906 added a station wagon, surrey, and closed coupé. Several designs of open and closed electrics were continued to 1915.

The high-wheeler, powered by a 10hp 2-cylinder air-cooled engine, and with rope drive, was made from 1907 to 1908 only, and in 1909 it became a larger, more conventional car called the FIRESTONE-COLUMBUS, named for the company president Clinton D. Firestone.

In 1914 the company was reorganised, control passing to a group of Buffalo businessmen including Charles A. Finnegan of the E.R. THOMAS Co. There were rumours that the Thomas Flyer might be built in Ohio, but this did not happen. In May 1915 the factory was sold, ending production of both Columbus electrics and Firestone-Columbus petrol cars.

NG

COMAHUE (RA) 1968–1980s
These were specialist coupés and estates based on the 3.8-litre I.K.A. Torino, with engines tuned to give 200bhp. They had a 4-speed gearbox and servo-assisted disk/drum brakes.

NG

COMET (i) (US) 1906–1908
1906–1907 Occidental Motor Car Co., San Jose, California.
1907–1908 Hall Auto Repair Co.; Hall Automobile Co., San Francisco, California.
Elbert Hall's Comet was an advanced roadster powered by a 3293cc 4-cylinder ohv engine of Hall's own design. The first car was built in the works of the Occidental Car Co., which shared premises with the makers of the SUNSET. When Occidental closed down in 1907, Hall moved to San Francisco where he made six more Comets. It is believed that they were all 2-seater roadsters, and they had considerable successes in local races. In 1909 and 1910 he built two more cars to special order, one with a 6-cylinder engine and one with a V8. The latter was bought by George W. Scott, with whose company secretary, Bert C. Scott, Hall went into partnership to build Hall-Scott engines at Berkeley, California. These were widely used in trucks, buses, railcars and aircraft.

NG

COMET (ii) (CDN) 1907–1908
Comet Motor Co., Montreal, Quebec.
If any car could have succeeded it ought to have been the Comet, for the makers had wealthy and influential backers, and the car was well-engineered using high quality imported components. The engine was a 24hp 4-cylinder unit bought from CLÉMENT-BAYARD and is believed to be the same engine that the French firm sold to DIATTO. An English-built Hele-Shaw clutch was used, the lamps and radiator were American, and the tourer and landaulette bodies locally built. Unfortunately all this did not come cheap, and the Comet was priced at CDN$5000. A Comet achieved some fame when it was used to carry the Prince of Wales (later King George V) during a visit to Montreal.

Larger engines were announced for 1908; a 40hp four and a six which was soon dropped. The 24hp was continued, now at CDN$4000, and was listed for the 1909 season, although it is unlikely that any were built in 1909. Estimates of production vary between 50 and 200. The company stayed in business selling high-quality American cars, eventually standardising on Packard.

NG

COMET (iii) (US) 1914–1915
1914 Economy Cyclecar Co., Indianapolis, Indiana.
1915 Comet Cyclecar Co., Indianapolis, Indiana.
This was a belt-driven cyclecar seating two passengers in tandem, powered by a 10hp air-cooled 2-cylinder Spacke engine. Production possibly did not exceed the original batch of 25 cars. The first name, Economy Cyclecar Co., was dropped

1921 Comet (v) production line.
NICK BALDWIN

when the makers discovered the existence of the ECONOMYCAR in Providence, Rhode Island.

NG

COMET (iv) (US) 1914

Continental Motors Corp., Buffalo, New York.
This was a very short-lived conventional car powered by a 25hp 4-cylinder engine, and sold in two models, a roadster at $750 and a tourer at $950. The makers had no connection with the well-known Continental Motors Corp. of Michigan, which supplied engines to many car makers.

NG

COMET (v) (US) 1917–1922

Comet Automobile Co., Decatur, Illinois.
Initially using Lewis and then Continental 6-cylinder engines, the Comet was a typical assembled car of its time, existing longer than most of its contemporaries, during which time several hundred were produced. The Comet sold on a domestic basis, primarily in the midwest, as well as being exported, mainly to Belgium. A 4-cylinder line was projected in 1921, but few cars were completed and production of the sixes ended in 1921, the 1922 cars simply being left-over cars built the preceding year. The final cars were sold following several receiverships.

KM

COMET (vi) (GB) 1921

Preston Autocar Co. Ltd, London.
This was a light sporting car powered by a 10hp 4-cylinder engine, with 4-speed gearbox and shaft drive. The only photographs show a spartan 2-seater body devoid of doors or bonnet. The factory location is not known, but it is unlikely to have been in the West Central district of London, which was more probably an office.

NG

COMET (vii) (GB) 1935–1937

Comet Car & Engineering Co. Ltd, Croydon, Surrey.
The 1930s were not propitious years to launch a small car in direct competition with the mass-producers, and it is hardly surprising that the Comet progressed no further than the prototype stage. It had a 1201cc 4-cylinder ohv engine

1922 Commander Six tourer.
KEITH MARVIN

developing 46bhp, a 4-speed gearbox and ifs. Four body styles were offered, 2- and 4-seater sports, saloon and drophead coupé. The latter two were made by Abbott. Whether all of these styles were actually built is not known. Prices ranged from £435 to £465.

NG

COMET (viii) (US) 1946–1948

General Developing Co., Ridgewood, New York.
This 3-wheeler had a plastic 2-seat body and wire wheels. It supposedly got over 100mpg from a 4¹/₂hp air-cooled engine.

HP

COMET (ix) (US) c.1951

Comet Manufacturing Co., Sacramento, California
This tiny roadster was sold in kit or assembled form. Comet were well-known for their successful line of midget racing cars and this was merely a street version. A 6hp engine propelled it to 40mph (64km/h) and returned 60mpg.

HP

COMET (x) see SN1

1989 Commuter Triton electric 3-wheeler.
NATIONAL MOTOR MUSEUM

1906 Compound 16hp tourer.
NATIONAL MOTOR MUSEUM

COMMANDER (US) 1922

Commander Motors Corp., Chicago, Illinois.

Commander was to have been a car to replace the OGREN of Milwaukee, and to sell in the same price range – $5000 and up – which was not hard to believe as the lone Commander prototype was in reality a rebadged Ogren touring car. The Ogren had reached hard times and, in an effort to maintain the car, Hugo Ogren set up the Commander Motors Corp., with headquarters on New York City's Wall Street and an envisioned new factory in the Chicago area, but with temporary production in the Ogren's Milwaukee factory. To promote the Commander, Ogren rebadged an Ogren touring car adding the Whyte Motor Control, an arrangement in which all dash instruments were located in a container within the radius of the steering wheel. Ogren's efforts to launch the Commander were futile and the Commander Motors Corp. was terminated, with the Ogren Motor Co. in Milwaukee failing shortly thereafter.

KM

COMMERCE (US) 1922

Commerce Motor Truck Co., Detroit, Michigan.

Commerce was a well-known truck and bus manufacturer, in business from 1911 to 1932, latterly as part of the Garford-Relay group. For one year they offered a 10-seater tourer which was really more of a small bus, although described as a passenger car. It was powered by a Continental 9A 6-cylinder engine, and priced at $2350.

NG

COMMODORE (US) 1921–1922

Commodore Motors Corp., New York City, New York.

The first Commodore was an expensive six with Continental engine, on a long wheelbase of 133in (3365mm), and with prices from $4000 to $5200. Presumably this proved difficult to sell, for the 1922 Commodore had a 4-cylinder Wisconsin engine, with the same wheelbase, but prices down to $2950–3500. Production of both models was very small.

NG

COMMONWEALTH (i) (US) 1903–1904

Coburn & Co., Boston, Massachusetts.

Powered by a single-cylinder engine mounted at the front under a Renault-style bonnet, the Commonwealth was offered in 2-seater and 4-seater versions. Final drive was by chain. Only one prototype is known to have been built.

NG

COMMONWEALTH (ii) (US) 1917–1922

Commonwealth Motors Co., Joliet, Illinois.

The Commonwealth was the continuation of the PARTIN-PALMER following the reorganisation of that company resulting in six years production of a 4-cylinder assembled car using both Herschell-Spillman and Lycoming engines, plus a 6-cylinder offering – 'The Victory Six' – available only during 1919. Through the first four years of its existence only open cars comprised Commonwealth's offerings, these were augmented in 1921 by the Model C-44 sedan and a taxicab, also a C-44 model, the latter given the designation of Checker. In November 1921 Commonwealth merged with the Markin Body Corp., and at this time all body options were dropped in favour of the taxi which was rebadged Checker. At the time of the merger, Commonwealth's 1922 line, limited to the taxi, had begun producing cabs, the few which were completed being the only Checkers to carry the Commonwealth nomenclature.

KM

COMMONWEALTH (iii) (US) 1980–1982

The Commonwealth Custom Coach Builders Inc., Lake Grene, New York.

The Commonwealth Custom A12-1 was a sports car with a customised FIBERFAB Avenger body and a GM V6 engine with ZF 5-speed transaxle. They were sold in turn-key form to buyers' specifications.

HP

COMMUTER (US) 1979–c. 1982

Commuter Vehicles Inc., Sebring, Florida.

This 2-seater hatchback electric coupé was previously the SEBRING VANGUARD. The company added a bigger van/estate car model, still with hydraulic drum brakes and a beam axle. Range was 50 miles at a cruising speed of 35mph (56km/h).

NG

COMPOSITE AUTO (US) 1991 to date

Composite Auto Inc., Concord, Massachusetts.

Vantage Motorsports, Cambridge, Massachusetts.

The MGA came in for a high-tech re-creation from this company. Buyers could opt for a sandblasted and rebuilt MGA chassis or a lightweight frame made of fibreglass, Kevlar, carbon fibre and Nomex honeycomb coring that cut 300lbs off the original MGA weight. The engine was a Toyota twin cam 1600cc engine with dual Mikuni carburettors, a 5-speed transmission, and fully independent Toyota suspension. They were sold in kit or assembled form.

HP

COMPOUND (US) 1904–1908

Eisenhuth Horseless Vehicle Co., Middletown, Connecticut.

Eagle Motor Car Co., Middletown, Connecticut.

John W. Eisenhuth built an experimental car at Newark, New Jersey in 1898, but did not proceed to manufacture. Around the turn of the century he met D.F. Graham, who had designed the Graham-Fox compound engine. This was a 3-cylinder unit in which the centre cylinder worked solely on the pressure of the exhaust gases from the other two cylinders. 'Why waste this pressure down the silencer?', Graham asked. A car was exhibited under the Graham-Fox name at the 1903 New York Automobile Show. Then Eisenhuth acquired the factory of the aborted Keating company at Middletown, Connecticut, and put cars into production under the name Compound. They were of conventional appearance, with the 3-cylinder engine under a bonnet, 3-speed gearboxes and shaft drive. One model was offered for 1904, a 20hp, and for 1905 there were two, a 12/15 and a 24/28hp, which was possibly the 20hp renamed. Contrary to the general rule, wheelbases shrank over the years rather than growing, from 100in (2540mm) in 1904 to 81 or 96in (2070 or 2438mm), although in 1907 there was one large model, a 40hp 7-seater tourer on a 115in (2921mm) wheelbase. At some time during the Compound's lifetime, the company name was changed to Eagle, and it is possible that some of the later cars went under the Eagle name. This was because John Eisenhuth's name was not a good advertisement, owing to his financial manipulations.

NG

COMUTA-CAR (US) c.1983
Aerospace Engineering & Manufacturing, Sebring, Florida.
This tiny 'commuter car' was available as a sport coupé or sport van powered by the buyer's choice of petrol, diesel or hybrid electric propulsion. The Comuta-Car had an aluminium frame, roll cage and a Cycolac plastic body. Built on an ultra-short wheelbase with 10in wheels, its angular styling looked decidedly utilitarian. They were sold in kit or assembled form.

HP

CONAN (GB) 1986–1988
Conan Cars, Manchester, Lancashire.
This attempt at a Countach replica looked fairly accurate but the space frame chassis was awkwardly engineered (it was supposedly based on a Lotus Esprit backbone), while the fibreglass body panels (reputedly taken from a genuine Lamborghini) were of very poor quality. The selection of mid-mounted Rover V8 power and VW Beetle transmission – and even a VW Beetle engine option – lacked any credibility and the name (Conan Terminator) was highly dubious.

CR

CONCEPT (GB) 1973–1977
Concept Developments, Market Harborough, Leicestershire.
In 1969, Dennis Adams designed the PROBE 15, the world's lowest ever car at just 29in high. In 1970, Peter Timpson acquired a Probe 15 bodyshell, widened it and added a pair of Perspex windows that doubled up as doors. The car height went up (to 37in), but so did its practicality. The Hillman Imp basis remained, and the body was a tough fibreglass-and-plywood monocoque with box sections and steel tube reinforcement. Some 26 examples were built. A 2+2 Centaur Mk II was developed but the project quickly passed on to PULSAR. A completely different model, the Condor roadster, was stillborn.

CR

CONCEPT AUTOMOBILES (US) c.1988–1992
Concept Automobiles Inc., Las Vegas, Nevada.
The GCT was a Lamborghini Countach replica with a sturdy steel tube space frame and fabricated suspension. Powered by Chevrolet V8 engines, it was a more serious (and costly) alternative to the usual crop of Fiero-based Lamborghini replicas.

HP

CONCEPT DESIGN (US) c.1983–1992
Concept Design, Arroyo Grande, California.
The Tahoe T was a new direction for the classic Model T hot rod kit. Instead of a big V8 engine, these used Kawasaki, Honda, Suzuki or Yamaha motorcycle engines mounted in the front. They had 4-wheel disc brakes and independent suspension.

HP

CONCORD (US) c.1896–1898
Concord Motor Coach Co., Concord, New Hampshire.
This was a light steam car with single-chain drive made by Dr Adrian H. Hoyt. As many as 11 cars may have been completed.

NG

CONCORDE (U) 1965
Montevideo.
The Concorde is a Uruguayan mystery, as apparently no cars were ever completed by the factory, although in 1965 components and a production line were shown to the press by a trio of entrepreneurs: Pedro Walter Garrido Breno, Walter Cesar Cuadra Badano and Fernando Perdomo Avellaneda. They had joined forces to produce a 700cc 2-cylinder car under the 'Concorde 700' name. They said it would be wholly made in Uruguay, except for the bearings, carburettor and spark plugs. In 1966 they were still announcing the car, saying two prototypes had been made and that they had components to build five more cars. However, nothing was ever heard of them again after that. When interviewed many years later, they were reluctant to talk about the matter.

ACT

CONCOURS MOTORS (US) c.1994
Concours Motors, Ramona, California.
The Concours Peerless was a handsome neoclassic built on a modified Lincoln-Mercury chassis with Ford V8 power. Sold in kit and fully assembled form.

HP

CONDÉCOURT (F) 1988–c.1995
Carrosserie de Condécourt, Condécourt.
Francois Fontaine's Jeepy was an open-topped leisure vehicle based on the Renault 4, although R5 engines could be fitted if required. 2- and 4-seater models were offered with either front or 4-wheel drive, and both kits and complete cars could be bought.

CR

CONDOR (i) (GB) 1913
Condor Motor Co., Coventry.
This company was mainly a maker of proprietary engines for motorcycles and cyclecars, but they offered complete motorcycles from 1907 to 1914. In 1913 they built a most unusual cyclecar powered by one of their 4hp air-cooled single-cylinder engines. This was mounted on the offside, half way down the frame, and drove a wheel mounted in the same position on the opposite side. There were single wheels at the front and rear, both of which steered. The effect was that of a Sunbeam-Mabley deprived of one of its wheels. It was said to have been built to the designs and specifications of a customer, and it is not known if Condor built any others like it.

NG

CONDOR (ii) (CH) 1922
Condor SA, Cycles & Motorcycles, Courfaivre, Berne.
Condor is one of the oldest and most respected names in the manufacture of cycles and motorcycles in Switzerland. In 1922 the company tentatively launched a 10hp light car with MAG 4-cylinder side-valve engines of 1130cc. The 2-seater torpedo with shaft drive and disc wheels was very similar to the contemporary Citroën 5CV. Its top speed was 44mph (70km/h) and a consumption of seven litres per 60 miles was considered worthy of promotion. Only five cars were built before the venture was dropped.

FH

CONDOR (iii) (B) 1946
Altona, Antwerp.
This company began making 3-wheeled commercial vehicles in 1938 and produced a prototype for a sports car following World War II. It is believed that very few, if any, were made.

CR

CONDOR (iv) (D) 1957–1958
Fahrzeugwerke Weidner, Schwabisch-Hall.
This was the name given to the Hans Trippel-designed light car sold in France as the MARATHON. It had a 677cc 3-cylinder 2-stroke Heinkel engine, 4-speed gearbox and a fibreglass coupé body. Weidner took out the licence to make it, and about 200 were built before lack of capital and a good distribution network brought the project to an end.

HON

1951 Connaught L2 sports car at Brands Hatch 1956.
NATIONAL MOTOR MUSEUM

CONDOR (v) (AUS) 1979–1988

Revolution Fibreglass Pty Ltd, Bayswater, Victoria.
A fibreglass Dino 246-inspired coupé for mounting on the Volkswagen platform, the Condor was based on the Kelmark from the USA but was altered sufficiently to conform with Australian design rules by Bill Kain, Gordon Peters and John Dixon. The Mazda 12A rotary engine was the performance choice but 1600cc Ford and Mitsubishi units were favoured and the cars were available in either kit form or complete. A 1981 development was a lengthened 4-seater version and the programme was sold in 1988. Since then nothing more has been heard.

MG

CONE (GB) 1914

Cone Car Co., Leyton, Essex.
This was a cyclecar powered by a 4.5hp single-cylinder air-cooled engine, with friction transmission by cones, hence its name.

NG

CONNAUGHT (GB) 1949–1953

1949–1951 Continental Cars Ltd, Send, Surrey.
1951–1953 Continental Engineering Ltd, Send, Surrey.
Continental Cars was founded in 1945 by two ex-RAF fliers, Rodney Clarke and Mike Oliver, to sell and prepare high performance cars. New cars were scarce, but some chassis were available and Continental Cars made its own cars, based on a standard Lea-Francis 14hp chassis.

Oliver was a gifted engine tuner and, with an aluminium body by Leacraft of Egham, performance was excellent. Two models were offered, the L1 and the more powerful L2. There were no takers for the L1, but six L2s were made. The first was bought by Kenneth MacAlpine, a wealthy amateur racer. MacAlpine was already a customer of Continental Cars and he became Connaught's patron.

When Lea-Francis introduced torsion bar ifs in 1949, the L2 became the L3, but the handling was inferior and only two were completed. A stripped down version, the L3/SR, was intended for racing in America, but it was slow, expensive and poorly made and only three were sold. Production officially ended in 1953.

Connaught's real success was its formula cars, which were superbly made and handled well, but were always under-powered. In 1955 at Syracuse Tony Brooks beat a strong field to give Britain its first grand prix win for more than 30 years. Connaught, always short of money, folded in 1957.

MJL

CONOVER (US) 1907–1912

Conover Motor Co., Paterson, New Jersey.
Designed by Edwin K. Conover, this car was built for him by the Watson Machine Co., also of Paterson. It was a large and expensive car powered by a 35/40hp 4-cylinder Rutenber engine, with shaft drive and a tourer body, the rear of which could be removed to make a 'high power runabout'. The price was $3475, but the makers earned no profit at this figure. It was estimated that to recover the Watson company's expenses the cars would have to have been priced at $9000, in which case even fewer than the actual figure of 25 would have been sold. The Watson Machine Co. is still in business today at the same address, making wire rope machinery.

NG

CONRAD (US) 1900–1903

Conrad Motor Carriage Co., Buffalo, New York.
This company began by making light steam cars with tiller steering and single-chain drive. In 1902 no fewer than seven styles were offered, at prices from $750 to $1200. For 1903 a reduced range of steamers was joined by a line of petrol cars with 8, 9, and 12hp 2-cylinder engines, also with single-chain drive but wheel-steered. The company was wound up at the end of 1903, but one model was revived the following year as the LACKAWANNA.

NG

CONRERO (I) 1951–1961

Virgilio Conrero, Moncalieri, Turin.
Virgilio Conrero was already an established engine tuner before he created his own sports car marque, initially building Formula Junior racing cars with Michelotti bodywork. He also essayed road cars, mostly based on Alfa Romeo, with suitably enhanced outputs, although he later favoured OSCA engines.

CR

CONSTANTIN (F) 1951–1957

Constantin, Paris.
Constantin specialised in tuning postwar Peugeot models. From the early 1950s it built a handful of Peugeot 203-based sports cars and racers, campaigning the latter with mixed results at Le Mans. Heavily modified Peugeot 203-based 2-door coupés were Constantin's most popular models, however.

CR

CONSTANTINESCO (F) 1926–1928

Constantinesco Torque Converter Ltd, Paris.
Rumanian-born George Constantinesco became a naturalised British subject in 1916, and earned considerable fame and fortune through his invention of the synchronised machine-gun, which could fire bullets through the revolving propeller blades of a fighter aircraft. 50,000 synchronised gears were supplied. In 1922 he began to work on a unique form of torque converter which would do away with gear changing. It involved a swinging pendulum whose rate of swing varied according to the resistance imposed by the output shaft from the road wheels. The input from the engine was via a connecting rod from the crankshaft, as the system was housed between the two cylinders. The engine was a 494cc vertical twin 2-stroke. Although resident for most of his life in England, and making his torque converter in London, Constantinesco had the rest of the car built in Paris. A few open 2-seaters were made, priced at £250, and a saloon listed at £370. A car was shown at the 1926 Paris Salon, and although the Constantinesco was never seen at Olympia, an advertisement said that 'a number of these wonderful cars are on show in London at Devonshire House, Piccadilly'.

NG

CONSULIER (US) 1988 to date

Consulier Automotive, Riviera Beach, Florida.
Mosler Automotive, Riviera Beach, Florida.
This ultra-high performance car used the latest racing technology. An all-composite monocoque chassis carried fabricated suspension with Chrysler disc brakes. The front suspension was of rocker-arm type with inboard coil-over springs. The original engine was a turbocharged Shelby-modified Chrysler 4-cylinder rated at up to 224bhp. With a total of under 2000lbs, it was very fast and was highly successful in club-level racing. The LX model had air conditioning, electric windows, leather interior, and other comfort items, while the sportier GTP Sport model was stripped to save weight. They should have sold like hot cakes except for two things – the high price ($63,000 for the LX) and bland bodywork that looked like a doorstop with a roof. Later, the Consulier was offered in kit form as well. During the 1990s, the company changed its name to Mosler Automotive (after founder Warren Mosler) and stretched the chassis to make room for a modified Chevrolet V8 bolted to a Porsche 4-speed transaxle. With 446hp the new Mosler Intruder was very fast

(0–60mph (0–100km/h) in 4.16 seconds), but the assembled price was up to $98,500. It was still available in kit form as well.

HP

CONTE (D) 1979
Herzog Stahlbau, Kreiftel, nr. Frankfurt.
This was an amphibious car powered by a Ford V6 engine in 2.3- or 2.6-litre sizes. It had independent suspension all round and a 10-speed all-synchromesh gearbox. At DM65,000 it was very expensive, and only one prototype was made.

HON

CONTEMPORARY CLASSICS (US) c.1979–1995
Contemporary Classic Motor Car Co., Mamaroneck, New York.
This company built some of the best kit Cobra replicas, using Jaguar XKE suspension front and rear. Founder Peter Bayer had owned and raced a number of authentic Cobras. In 1986 they added a Cobra Daytona Coupé replica based on the same Jaguar-based frame. By 1994 they had adapted a Ferrari 250 California Spyder replica, called the Contemporary GT Roadster, to fit a stretched version of their frame as well.

HP

CONTINENTAL (i) (US) 1907
Continental Motor Car Co., Chicago, Illinois.
Only one model was made by this company, a 2-seater roadster powered by a 12hp 2-cylinder engine offered in air- or water-cooled forms, epicyclic gearbox and shaft drive. It had a completely circular radiator with the name in script filling the space in the centre.

NG

CONTINENTAL (ii) (US) 1907–1908
1907–1908 University Automobile Co., New Haven, Connecticut.
1908 Continental Automobile Co., New Haven, Connecticut.
This was a heavy-looking car listed with three 4-cylinder engines, 25, 30, and 35hp. Body styles were the Model A Runabout at $2400, Model B Tonneau at $2700 and Model C Touring at $3000. It was described as 'the first foreign-designed car built in America at a moderate price', although evidence of foreign design was not given.

NG

CONTINENTAL (iii) (US) 1910–1914
Indiana Motor & Manufacturing Co., Franklin, Indiana.
This Continental was a conventional car with 4-cylinder engines of 35 and 40hp, offered with torpedo, runabout or tourer bodies. Closed models were never listed. High-quality appointments such as machine-buffed leather upholstery and a mahogany dashboard were not enough to save the make, which was severely undercapitalised. In 1912 it was reorganised by Frank N. Martindale and Frank M. Millikan, and for 1914 the car was offered under the rather clumsy name of Martindale & Millikan. That was its last season.

NG

CONTINENTAL (iv) see CECO

CONTINENTAL (v) see MOOSE JAW STANDARD

CONTINENTAL (vi) (US) 1933–1934
Continental Automobile Co., Grand Rapids, Michigan.
The Continental Automobile Co. was a division of the Continental Motors Corp., the nation's most prolific supplier of engines to the American automobile industry. The company was formed explicitly to pick up the pieces of the DeVaux-Hall Motor Corp. and the DEVAUX car which had failed at the beginning of 1932. The company continued the car through 1932 as the DeVaux-Continental. In 1933 the DeVaux-Continental re-emerged as the Continental, to all intents and purposes a DeVaux with updated cosmetic treatment. Three models were offered under the Continental badge, the Beacon – a 4-cylinder car with prices from $355; the Flyer – a six with a price range of $450 to $535, and the Ace, selling for $725 to $816. The Continental was considered a good car and a good bargain – the Beacon being the lowest-priced automobile offered in

c.1992 Consulier LX coupé.
HAROLD PACE

1933 Continental(vi) Beacon 2-door sedan.
KEITH MARVIN

the United States with the sole exception of the American Austin. But Continental appeared at an economically bad time, 1933 being the nadir of the Great Depression, and its total sales for the year were a low 3,310. The Beacon was the only Continental continued into 1934, and phased out with less than 1,000 cars produced. The Continental was also sold in Canada under the Frontenac badge, the Beacon and Flyer being assembled at the plant of Dominion Motors at Leaside, Ontario and the Ace being imported and rebadged before sale.

KM

CONTINENTAL (vii) (US) 1955–1957
Ford Motor Co., Continental Division, Dearborn, Michigan.
The Continental Mk II was built in response to Lincoln dealers who were asking for a new car to replace the much-loved V12 Continentals which had been made from 1940 to 1948. Market research indicated that there were between 250,000 and 300,000 families in the United States whose disposable incomes would justify spending $10,000 on a car. At the time the most expensive domestically made car was the Cadillac 75 Imperial Sedan at $5643, so for Ford to offer a car at approaching twice that figure was a gamble from the start.

A separate division was set up under 26-year old William Clay Ford, Henry II's younger brother. Several designs were considered and that by John Reinhart was chosen. It was a low and wide 4-seater coupé with no family resemblance to the Lincoln, very important if the Continental was to be seen as a high-prestige make in its own right. Bodies were not made by Ford's usual suppliers, but by Mitchell-Bentley of Ionia, Michigan. The engine was Lincoln's new 6030cc V8 developing 285bhp. Output would have been higher if plans to use fuel injection had been adopted, but the budget would not allow this. The Continental Mk II was launched in June 1955 as a 1956 model, and priced at $9695. Public response was disappointing. Of the survey's 250,000 families who could have afforded a Continental Mk II, only 1325 actually signed up. Few changes were made for 1957, although power was upped to 300bhp. Production ended on 13 May that year. The total number sold was 2989, to which can be added 23 prototypes for an overall figure of 3012. Among the prototypes was a convertible by Derham which went to Mrs William Clay Ford.

1956 Continental(vii) Mk II coupé.
NATIONAL MOTOR MUSEUM

1910 Cooper(i) 20hp limousine by Sanders of Hitchin.
NATIONAL MOTOR MUSEUM

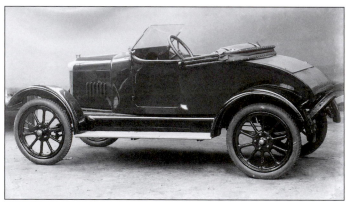

1923 Cooper(ii) 11hp 2-seater.
NATIONAL MOTOR MUSEUM

The Continental name was retained as a separate marque for 1958, but it shared Lincoln styling, and for 1959 was absorbed into the Lincoln range. A separate Continental range was relaunched in 1968, but it was never as distinctive as the massive Mk II, and is described under LINCOLN (vi).

NG

CONVAIR (GB) 1958–59

Corvair Developments, Leytonstone, London.

This company was one step up from the usual glassfibre sports car shell maker of the time, also offering its own twin-tube steel chassis designed for BMC A-series components. The Mk1 shell was a typical open glassfibre affair, although there was an option hardtop, with gull-wing doors.

CR

CONVAIRCAR (US) 1947

Consolidated-Vultee Aircraft Corp., San Diego, California.

This was one of many postwar 'flying car' projects (see AEROCAR). It used a small fibreglass car body with a Crosley engine for power on land and a set of wings with a Lycoming engine that could be attached for flying. Although it was successfully flight tested, the prototype crashed when it ran out of fuel and the project was dropped.

HP

CONY (J) 1961–1966

Aichi Machinery Industry Co. Ltd, Nagoya.

A product of a former aircraft company, the Cony was first seen in 1946 as a 3-wheeled light commercial vehicle. Four-wheelers were added in the 1950s, and for 1961 the company launched a passenger version. Known as the Model 360, it was a 4-seater 2-door saloon powered by a rear-mounted 359cc 2-cylinder engine giving 18bhp. An estate car version was added later, but production was always small compared with commercial vehicles. In 1965 Aichi was absorbed into the Nissan group, and production of Cony cars and commercials ended the following year.

NG

COOK (I) 1900

Officine Pastore e Racca, Turin.

Designed by a lawyer, Marcello Racca, this was a small car powered by a 3.5hp single-cylinder Aster engine, with 2-speed gearbox, belt drive and tiller steering. The reason for the English-sounding name is not known.

NG

COOPER (i) (GB) 1909–1910

Cooper Steam Digger Co. Ltd, King's Lynn, Norfolk.

This company was founded in 1894 to make a large traction engine, designed by Tom Cooper, with three digging teeth on a shaft at the rear. It was intended for ploughing, but was less successful than the more familiar two-engine system with a cable-drawn plough crossing the field between them. Not more than 12 Cooper Steam Diggers were made, although a few traction engines for the road were made as well. A new line of business was clearly needed, and this was provided through Cambridge graduate W.M. Pryor who became joint managing director in 1904, bringing fresh capital and a contact with Ralph Lucas, the inventor of the Lucas Valveless 2-stroke engine. He placed an order for 50 engines of his design to be made by Cooper, but Tom Cooper was unable to complete these, so Lucas took his design to David Brown Ltd in Huddersfield, where cars were made under the name VALVELESS. However, the idea of making motorcars appealed to Cooper, and he designed a 2-cylinder 2-stroke piston-valve engine which he fitted to a car in 1909. It had chain drive to the gearbox and further chain drive to the rear wheels. The production Cooper, which was ready for the 1909 Olympia Show, had a 3260cc 4-cylinder engine, also a 2-stroke with piston valves, shaft drive to the 3-speed gearbox and to the rear wheels. An auxiliary gearbox close to the rear axle gave a total of six forward speeds.

Only six Coopers were made, each differing in detail from the other. One had a longer wheelbase to accommodate a large limousine body. A tourer survives today, and is kept by the Cooper Roller Bearing Co. Ltd, descendants of Tom Cooper's company.

NG

COOPER (ii) (GB) 1919–1923

1919–1920 Cooper Car Co., Bedford.
1922–1923 Cooper Car Co. Ltd, Coventry.

E. Cooper's first car had a 3-cylinder air-cooled ohv engine of 1493cc, said to be of American origin. It was purely experimental, and only one was made. In 1922, with backing from theatre and garage owner S.H. Newsome, Cooper set up a company in Coventry to make a more conventional light car powered by a 1368cc Coventry-Climax 4-cylinder side-valve engine, Moss gearbox, and Wrigley rear axle. Several body styles were offered, from a 2-seater at £235 to a coupé at £300, but few cars were completed. Newsome drove a variant of the Cooper powered by a Janvier engine and called a Warwick at Brooklands, and was later seen in rallies at the wheel of Jaguars.

NG

COOPER (iii) (GB) 1947–1951

Cooper Car Co. Ltd, Surbiton, Surrey.

Father and son, Charles and John Cooper, were enthusiastic supporters of the post-World War II 500cc racing movement. They took the front suspension of two scrap Fiat 500 Topolini, separated them by a simple ladder frame and put a motorcycle engine behind the driver.

Cooper became a substantial maker of 500cc racing cars by using ingenuity at a time when materials were restricted. Scrap yards provided aluminium for the cast wheels, the integral brake drums were sawn from the cylinder liners of marine diesel engines, Morrison air raid shelters provided the steel for the suspension castles, and so on.

The first Cooper sports car was a 2-seat version of the 500cc car, but with a Triumph engine and an enveloping body. This remained a prototype, but Cooper made around two dozen chassis (in three batches, 1948, 1950, and 1952) which could be used as the basis for either a road or a competition car. All these cars were front-engined versions of the basic 500cc chassis and engines included MG, Ford, Vauxhall, Rover, and Lea-Francis.

Some 500cc single-seater chassis were also adapted by special builders to serve as the basis for front-engined sports cars. Most Cooper-Bristol Formula 2 cars of 1952/3 were converted to sports cars – and were converted back to single-seaters when that became financially expedient.

No subsequent Cooper sports car could be passed off as a dual-purpose machine *by intent,* although the Cooper-Jaguar of Col Michael Head (father of Patrick) was used for Continental touring. In 1959, Cooper experimented with a Climax-powered Renault Dauphine and, from there, it was but a short step to the Mini Cooper.

MJL

COOPER (iv) (CDN) 1986–c.1988

Cooper Coach Craft, Missisauga, Ontario.

This was a locally assembled Canadian version of the Californian Daytona, a replica of the Ferrari Daytona Spider.

CR

COOTIE *see* CUSTER

COPYCATS/PROTEUS (GB) 1982 to date

1982–1987 Copycats Ltd, Bolton, Lancashire.
1987–1991 Proteus Reproductions, Bolton, Lancashire.
1991 to date Proteus Cars, Bolton, Lancashire.

With its delightful Jaguar C-Type replica, Copycats soon established itself as probably the leading classic Jaguar replicator. There were two types: a very expensive aluminium-bodied replica for Jaguar Mk II parts (and therefore a live rear axle), or a fibreglass body for Jaguar XJ6 parts, which was easier to finish, some 2in wider and boasted irs. Both versions could be bought fully built as well as in kit form. Jaguar D-Type and XKSS replicas followed in 1987, the year when the company changed its name to Proteus. Bodyshells were available in long- or short-nose forms, with single door or dual doors, and with a fixed or detachable rear fin. Proteus also made an exacting replica of the Mercedes-Benz 300SLR racer and the Norseman vintage van replica, while its most recent Jaguar replica was the P90, an extraordinary copy of the XJ13 racer, using a V12 mid-mounted engine. A fully enclosed version was built in 1996.

CR

COQ (F) 1920

Robert de Coquereamont, Rouen, Seine Inférieure.

This was a short-lived cyclecar which probably did not pass the prototype stage. It was powered by a 2-stroke engine driving through a 4-speed gearbox, with a torpedo body. Electric lighting and starting were provided, features not always found on minimal cars at the beginning of the 1920s.

NG

CORAT (I) 1946

At the 1946 Turin Motor Show a small coupé was shown under the name Corat MV2 Lupetta (meaning wolf cub). It had a narrow rigid rear axle to which the 250cc 5.5bhp single-cylinder 4-stroke engine was linked.

CR

1949 Cooper(iii) prototype sports car (Vauxhall Twelve engine).
NATIONAL MOTOR MUSEUM

1910 Corbin Cannonball 6-cylinder speedster.
NATIONAL MOTOR MUSEUM

CORBETT (US) c.1988–1994

Corbette Motor Cars, Archbald, Pennsylvania and Santa Barbara, California.

Former aerospace engineer Adrian Corbett started in the kit car business with a VW-based Lamborghini Countach replica. It was sold in kit and turnkey form. However, it was not successful and by 1992 he had moved his new business, Corbett Automotive Design, to Lampoc, California and introduced a radical new car called the Patriot. It was a low-slung aerodynamic shape with no resemblance to anything else on the market. It was based on the Pontiac Fiero and was available in kit or fully assembled form. At $85,000, it is doubtful many turn-key cars were sold.

HP

CORBIN (i) (US) 1905–1912

Corbin Motor Vehicle Co., New Britain, Connecticut.

Corbin was a wholly owned subsidiary of the American Hardware Corp., which is still in business today. Philip Corbin had made a few cars at Bristol, Connecticut under the name BRISTOL, and launched the Corbin car in 1905. Two models were made, both with 4-cylinder air-cooled engines, the 16/20hp Model D and 24/30hp Model C. Cooling was by two fans set above the cylinders. Air-cooling was used up to 1910, but water-cooled engines were introduced in 1908. The later Corbins were quite substantial cars, the largest being the Model 40 7-passenger limousine on a 120in (3048mm) wheelbase, priced at $4000. Corbins were characterised by a distinctive peak to the radiator shell which was carried through to the bonnet. It seems that car manufacture depended on the enthusiasm of Philip Corbin, and his retirement brought about the end of the Corbin car.

NG

Further Reading
'Corbin: An American abroad', Jonathan A. Stein,
Automobile Quarterly, Vol.29, No.2.

1930 Cord L-29 phaeton.
NICK GEORGANO/NATIONAL MOTOR MUSEUM

CORBIN (ii) **(US)** c.1998 to date
Corbin-Pacific Inc., Hollister, California.
The Corbin Sparrow was a 3-wheeled electric car with a teardrop-shaped enclosed body. It used a 15kw electric motor with 13 lead-acid batteries. It was expected to sell for $13,000. A model with V-twin petrol engine was planned, giving a top speed of 150mph (241km/h).
HP

CORBITT (US) 1907–1914
Corbitt Automobile Co., Henderson, North Carolina.
Richard Corbitt made buggies from the 1890s, and moved into automobiles in 1907 with what was essentially a motorised buggy. It was a high-wheeler with 2-cylinder engine, single-chain drive and the simplest of piano-box bodies without wings. He added the latter in 1908, and by the end of 1909 had built about 100 high-wheelers. For 1910 he turned to conventional cars with 18/20hp 2-cylinder engines, following these with a 30hp four for 1912. A 30/35hp four followed in 1913, and the final year of car production saw a slightly smaller engine of 26hp, although on the same wheelbase and with the same body styles as in the previous three years. All Corbitt bodies were open models. Car production was abandoned because of the growing demand for Corbitt trucks, which had been made since 1910. Although never a large producer by the standards of International or Mack, Corbitt was a respected name in the truck field for more than forty years; they supplied the US Army with 6x6 trucks in World War II, and were in the business up to 1958.
NG

CORD (US) 1929–1931; 1935–1937
Auburn Automobile Co., Auburn, Indiana.
'The Cord L-29 created more attention and produced fewer sales than any other $3000 car in history except one, its successor'. This comment by American historian Beverly Rae Kimes sums up very well the cars of Errett Lobban Cord. The only cars to bear his name, the front-drive Cords were the third automotive ventures of the energetic entrepreneur from California, who had already taken over AUBURN and DUESENBERG, setting them both on a path to fame which they would never have achieved without him.

Cord was attracted to the principle of front-wheel drive through seeing Miller cars racing at Indianapolis, and in 1927 he purchased the patents and manufacturing rights to the Miller design. These needed substantial alterations before they were suitable for road use, and Cord hired Cornelius van Ranst, who had designed another front-drive racing car, to do the job. Harry Miller and racing driver Leon Duray were also brought in as consultants. The engine they chose for the new car was a modified version of the 4891cc Lycoming straight-8 used in Auburns, turned round and driving forward to the 3-speed gearbox and a hypoid differential to the front wheels. After a prototype had shaken its doors off when Cord drove it over rough ground, the chassis was cross-braced between the main side members, the first time an American chassis had been strengthened in this way. The bodies were designed by John Oswald and Alan Leamy, the latter being responsible for the vee-radiator grill which set off the Cord's low lines so well, and which was closely copied by Chrysler for their 1931 models.

Christened the L-29 after the year of its introduction, the Cord was launched in September 1929 with four body styles, sedan, convertible sedan, convertible coupé and brougham, at prices from $3095 to $3295. There were also a few

NICK BALDWIN

BUEHRIG, GORDON (1904–1990)
Gordon Miller Buehrig was born on 18 June 1904, grew up in Mason City, Illinois and attended Bradley Polytechnic in Peoria. He launched his career in 1924 as an apprentice with the Gotfredson Body Company in Detroit.

Buehrig never seemed to stay in any one place very long. In 1926, he went to New York and took a job with LeBaron. When Briggs bought LeBaron, Buehrig returned to Detroit and worked briefly for Packard in 1927; then joined Harley Earl's growing Art & Colour section in 1928, switching to Stutz later that year. In 1929, when a job with Duesenberg popped up, Buehrig grabbed it and found himself, at age 25, that company's chief and only body designer.

At Duesenberg, Buehrig answered mostly to president Harold Ames and occasionally to E.L. Cord himself. Just how many different body designs Buehrig created for Duesenberg over the next three years even he couldn't estimate. In his book, Rolling Sculpture, he did say that about half of all Duesenberg bodies produced were his designs. The other half came from various coachbuilders. Buehrig also designed the 'Duesenbird' hood ornament.

In 1930, Buehrig hired Phil Derham of the Philadelphia coachbuilding family to be his body engineer. And in 1932, designer Herb Newport also joined Duesenberg. Buehrig and Newport worked together briefly, but in 1933 Buehrig returned to GM Art & Colour for most of that year.

When Buehrig got to GM, Harley Earl was staging one of his famous design competitions. The prize: a trip to the Century of Progress World Fair in Chicago. Earl named five team leaders: Buehrig, Tom Hibbard, Jules Agramonte, Jack Morgan and Frank Hershey. Just before the contest, Earl delivered a lecture about the aesthetic importance of the 'face' of a car and how designers ought always to emphasize the front end.

Buehrig took issue and argued that it was the body shape, not the face, that was the most important element in a design. With his contest model, Buehrig wanted to show Earl how unimportant the face could be, so he conceived a faceless car--a coffin-nosed, pontoon-fendered, fastback sedan with hidden headlights and without a conventional grill. He intentionally made the front as featureless as he could.

His design did have a few horizontal louvers low on the prow, but the

1936 Cord 810 sedan.
NATIONAL MOTOR MUSEUM

cooling system consisted of two small outside radiators set between the fenders and the sides of the tapering hood. Buehrig's design finished dead last in the contest, and Jack Morgan's team won the trip to Chicago.

Late in 1933, while Buehrig was still with GM, he got together with Harold Ames to discuss the possibility of designing a 'small Duesenberg' in the vein of the LaSalle, Lincoln Zephyr and Packard One Twenty. Senior Duesenbergs weren't selling at all well during the Depression.

Buehrig left GM, returned to Duesenberg and showed Ames his GM contest model. Ames liked it, thought it would make a wonderful baby Duesenberg and commissioned Weymann to build a running metal prototype on an Auburn chassis. This prototype, finished toward the end of Feb. 1934, had all the hallmarks of the 1936 Cord 810. Thus Buehrig's GM contest model became one of the great classics of all time.

While at Duesenberg, Buehrig also updated Al Leamy's 1932 Auburn speedster, transforming it into the 1935–36 Auburn 851 speedster. After Auburn-Cord-Duesenberg's demise, Buehrig opened a design office for the Budd Company (1936–38) and designed a VW-sized car for Budd called the Wowser. After World War II, he became co-manager of Raymond Loewy's South Bend Studebaker studio (with Virgil Exner). In 1948, while still with Loewy, Buehrig created the futuristic but ill-fated Tasco sport fastback.

In 1949, he joined Ford, where he served as a body designer, product planner and research engineer. Among his engineering patents were the T-top and the center-mounted fuel filler. He also contributed to the 1956 Continental Mark II. Buehrig retired in 1965 and taught at Art Center College of Design in Los Angeles. Gordon Buehrig passed away at his home in Grosse Pointe Woods, Michigan in early 1990.

ML

custom town cars and a speedster by Murphy. The L-29 was widely acclaimed by the motoring press, and not only in the US. It won several Concours d'Élégance in European cities such as Monte Carlo, Berlin and Prague, and was hailed by American *MoTor* magazine as 'The first really new automobile design to appear on the market for many years'. Cord hoped to sell 5000, following them with a similar number of the L-30 for 1930, L-31 for 1931 and so on. In fact, only 1819 were sold in 1929, and 5010 altogether. There was no L-30, as the L-29 remained in production until 31 December 1931. L-29 sales were badly hit by the Wall Street Crash which took place less than two months after its launch. The conservative American public was very wary also of anything so revolutionary as front-wheel drive. They bought even fewer of the RUXTON, which was the only other front-wheel drive car on the US market at the time. In 1931 prices were dropped to $2395–2995, and the cylinders were bored out by 3.175mm to give a larger capacity of 4934cc. The last 157 cars were called 1932 models, although none was built that year.

The next car to bear the Cord name was launched in November 1935, although development began more than two years before. The Depression had hit Duesenberg sales very hard, as even those who could afford America's most expensive car felt it was not in the best of taste to do so. Cord, therefore, planned to make a 'baby Duesenberg' to sell for around $2000, and commissioned his chief body designer Gordon Buehrig, to produce something startlingly new. Buehrig came up with a streamlined and quite distinctive shape, with a grill which wrapped around the front of the bonnet, and extended half way down the bonnet sides. Two radiators were mounted in the airstream between the wings and the bonnet, and the headlamps retracted into the wings. The body was a six-window sedan without running boards.

In 1934 it was decided that the new car should be a Cord rather than a Duesenberg, and that in the tradition of the L-29, it should have front-wheel drive. Buehrig restyled the body with four windows instead of six, and the twin radiators were replaced by a conventional single one behind the grill, which now extended to the scuttle on each side. There were four body styles, the

1964 Cord 810 Sportsman.
NATIONAL MOTOR MUSEUM

Westchester and Beverly sedans (identical except for upholstery pattern), 2- and 4-seater convertibles called Sportsman and Phaeton. Its engine was a 4730cc V8 designed and built for the car by Lycoming. With 125bhp, it gave the Cord a top speed of 92mph (148km/h). The 4-speed gearbox was controlled by an electro-vacuum pre-selector which was operated by a tiny lever and gate on the steering column. Really rapid changes were not possible with this system, and the Cord's acceleration was not outstanding – 0 to 60mph (0-100km/h) in 20.1 seconds (*The Autocar* Road Test, 29 May 1936).

The new Cord, named the 810, made its appearance at the Chicago and New York Shows in November 1935. The show regulations stipulated that a minimum of 100 cars should be completed before a model could be exhibited, but all Cord could come up with was eleven. Even these were non-runners, with wooden transmissions. However, he was not thrown out, and by the time the doors closed on the two shows he had 3600 firm orders, and interest shown by a further 7639 possible customers. Cord's salesmen promised delivery by New Year's Day 1936, but the first production car did not even leave the factory before 15 February. The delay was fatal, for many customers cancelled their orders, some through impatience, others because they were alarmed by rumours about transmission problems in the new cars. The Cord 810 was an expensive car; at $1995 to $2145, it cost around $500 more than the Cadillac Sixty, and getting on for four times as much as a Ford V8. As with its predecessor, it attracted tremendous publicity at home and abroad, and four cars, three sedans and a convertible, were chosen as the official cars at the 1936 Indianapolis 500 Mile Race, although the actual pace car was a Packard 120. Several Indy drivers chose Cords for their personal transport, as did films stars Tom Mix and Jean Harlow, who had hers painted and upholstered to match her platinum blonde hair. Among many compliments which the car received, Gordon Buehrig's favourite was 'It didn't look like an automobile. Somehow it looked like a beautiful thing that had been born and just grew up on the highway'.

Because of the production delays, sales of the 810 were disappointing – only 1174 in the calendar year 1936. Cord introduced two important changes for 1937 on the Model 812; a supercharger which boosted power from 125 to 190bhp, and a longer wheelbased Custom series. These were only available in the closed models, and answered criticisms of lack of leg room for rear seat passengers. They also had larger luggage boots which somewhat spoilt the clean lines of the original sedan. The Custom Berline had a glass division, although one cannot imagine that many Cord owners employed chauffeurs, as the pleasure of driving oneself was one of the joys of the car. The 812s were more expensive than their predecessors, at $2445 to $2645 for the short-wheelbase models, and $2960 to $3060 for the Custom series. Only 1146 were sold in the US before production ended in August 1937. Just under 3000 had been made; US sales were 2320, with the balance being exports for which no figures are available. The state-by-state breakdown is interesting; from a high of 353 in California and 303 in New York, down to three in Nevada, two in North Dakota and one in Arkansas. Even this beat Vermont, whose cautious citizens bought not a single Cord 810 or 812. A good proportion, about 1000, have survived worldwide. The body shells had a second lease of life when they were bought by GRAHAM, who used them in their rear-drive Hollywood models of 1939–40, and also made them for HUPMOBILE for their Skylark.

Although his automotive activities ended in 1937, E.L. Cord was far from finished as a businessman. He turned to real estate on the West Coast, started an all-music radio station and made a fortune in uranium in the 1950s. He became a senator for the state of Nevada, and died in 1974, aged 79.

NG

Further Reading
The Classic Cord, Dan R. Post, Motor Classic Bookhouse, Arcadia, California, 1952.
Errett Lobban Cord – His Empire, His Motor Cars: Auburn, Cord Duesenberg', Griffith Borgeson, Automobile Quarterly Publications.

CORD 810 (US) 1964–1966
Cord Automobile Company, Tulsa, Oklahoma.
The 1936–37 Cord was replicated in 8/10 (hence the name) scale by this company. Company president Glenn Pray retained original Cord stylist Gordon Buehrig to design the down-sized 810, and a Corvair engine and transaxle were moved forward to provide front-wheel drive like the original. The body was made of Royalex, a sturdy plastic. Unlike the original Cord, these replicas were only offered in convertible form. Less than 100 cars were built before they closed their doors, although somewhat similar mini-Cords were built by SAMCO.

HP

CORMERY (F) 1901
H. Cormery, Billancourt, Seine.
Like the Sunbeam-Mabley, the Cormery light car had a diamond pattern wheel arrangement.

NG

CORNELIAN (US) 1914–1915
Blood Brothers Machine Co., Kalamazoo; Allegan, Michigan.
The Blood brothers had already made a car under their own name from 1902 to 1906, and in 1914 they returned to the auto business, this time with a cyclecar which they called the Cornelian. It had a 1688cc 13hp 4-cylinder Sterling engine, shaftdrive and, very unusual for the time, integral construction and irs. Introduced at the New York Automobile Show in January 1914, it was priced at $435. An encouraging number of orders led the brothers to move from Kalamazoo to a new factory at Allegan, which they occupied in March 1915. A Cornelian gained a lot of publicity when Louis Chevrolet drove one in the 1915 Indianapolis 500 Mile Race, the smallest-engined car to race there. However, this did not help sales, and Cornelian production ended in October 1915, after about 100 had been made.

NG

CORNELY (F) 1972–1974
Cornely, Malakoff.
This VW Beetle-based sports fun car was presented at the Racing Car Show in 1972 by Lem Design as the Moana. It was designed by Yvan Labat and realised by Roger Matigot. The design was productionised in 1973 by Cornely. It featured styling that was vaguely reminiscent of the Matra M530, with a fixed rear section and roll-up sides to allow entry.

CR

CORNILLEAU (F) 1912–1914
Automobiles Cornilleau, Asnières, Seine.
This company produced three models, an 8/10hp with 770cc 2-stroke engine, and two fours, a 10hp 1469cc and a 12hp 2296cc, both with 4-stroke engines. All Cornilleaus were shaft-driven.

NG

CORNILLEAU STE BEUVE (F) 1904–1909
Cornilleau et Ste Beuve, Paris.
Also known as the C.S.B., this car was originally made in 8 and 16hp versions, and from 1906 in 14, 18 and 20/30hp models. They were all shaft-driven, but an unusual feature was that of variable lift inlet valves. The 20/30hp was built for sale by STRAKER-SQUIRE in England, and this design was later made in England by Straker-Squire.

NG

CORNISH CLASSIC CARS (GB) 1985–1986

1985–1986 Cornish Classic Cars, Blackwater, Truro, Cornwall.
1986 Cornish Classic Cars, Corsham, Wiltshire.
Two models were offered by this Cornish-based kit car company: a Citroën
2CV-based Edwardian-style 4-seater called the Parisienne, and the Osprey, a
Mercedes SSK replica designed for Ford Cortina mechanical parts.

CR

CORNISH-FRIEDBERG *see* C.F.

CORNU (F) 1905–1908

Paul Cornu, Lisieux, Calvados.
Paul Cornu's voiturette was powered by two single-cylinder Buchet engines,
each driving a rear wheel by a long belt. It had a light tubular frame. Maximum
speed was nearly 50mph (80km/h). The inventive M. Cornu also built a twin-
rotor helicopter powered by an Antoinette V8 engine.

NG

CORONA (i) **(D)** 1904–1909

Corona Fahrradwerke und Metallindustrie AG, Brandenburg/Havel.
Like so many others this company progressed from bicycles to motorcycles
(in 1903) and then to cars a year later. They began with the Coronamobil, a
3-wheeler with single-front wheel behind which was mounted on a single-cylinder
Fafnir engine with chain-drive to the rear wheels. The 2-seater body was suspended
at the rear by C-springs. In 1905 they brought out a 4-wheeler with 6/8PS
single-cylinder engine and friction drive made under MAURER licence. In fact
the Corona looked very like a Maurer. Later they made a larger car with 9/11PS
2-cylinder engine, also under licence from Maurer.

HON

CORONA (ii) **(F)** 1920

Automobiles Corona, Paris.
This was a mysterious make on a par with the British-built OWEN (i), although
its 'life' was much shorter. Its specification, as described in *The Autocar* in March
1920, was impressive, including a 7238cc V12 engine with ohvs operated by
two camshafts in the base chamber, an aluminium crankcase and dry sump
lubrication. Designed by G. Michaux, it was to be sold with a 5-year guarantee,
and at the end of 60,000 miles the makers undertook to completely overhaul the
car, at a cost of £200. The chassis price was £3000. However, no road tests or
photographs were ever published, and no French historian has heard of it.

NG

CORONA (iii) **(GB)** 1920–1923

Meteor Manufacturing Co. Ltd, Tollington Park, London.
The British-built Corona was a light car with no particular features, although
the makers seemed to use a different engine for each year of manufacture. When
announced it had a 1459cc 4-cylinder engine, enlarged to 1526cc in 1921, while
for 1922 a 2-cylinder unit of 998cc was adopted. Some of these engines
may have been by Bovier, while for 1923 the Corona was powered by a 1246cc
4-cylinder Coventry-Climax. The twin cost £250, but the fours were all on the
expensive side, £475 in 1920 and 1921, and £300–425 in 1923.

NG

CORONET (i) **(GB)** 1904–1906

Coronet Motor Co. Ltd, Coventry.
This company was founded in 1903 to make motorcycles, although few, if any,
of these seem to have been made. Car production began in 1904 under the
supervision of chief engineer Walter Iden, son of George Iden who had designed
several cars for M.M.C. Two Coronets were made at first, an 8hp single and a
16hp 4-cylinder car with the unusual firing order of 1-2-3-4. They were said to
be of all-British manufacture except for the radiator, ignition coil and springs,
which were imported from France. For 1905 two 4-cylinder cars were made, a
12hp with gilled tube radiator and a 16/20hp with honeycomb radiator.
Both had shaft drive and rear-entrance tonneau bodies. The company was
chronically under-financed, for even when it started it was underscribed by
almost £7000 on nominal capital of £20,000. It failed in 1906, and the factory
was taken over by Humber.

NG

1907 Cornilleau Ste Beuve tourer.
NATIONAL MOTOR MUSEUM

1905 Coronet(i) 16hp tonneau.
NATIONAL MOTOR MUSEUM

1958 Coronet(ii) 3-wheeler.
NICK GEORGANO/NATIONAL MOTOR MUSEUM

CORONET (ii) **(GB)** 1957–1960

Coronet Cars Ltd, Denham, Buckinghamshire.
The Coronet represented an attempt to offer full-size car refinements in a
microcar package. It was an open 2 or 3-seater with a single rear wheel, in front
of which its 328cc Excelsior twin-cylinder 18bhp engine was fitted. The bodywork
was made in fibreglass by the coachbuilders, James Whitson & Co., who also
made and assembled most of the rest of the car. The Coronet's chassis employed
suspension and steering components from the Standard 8. Probably around 250
were made.

CR

CORRE (i) *see* LA LICORNE

CORRE (ii) **(F)** 1908–1914

J. Corre et Compagnie, Rueil, Seine et Oise.
J. Corre was one of several car makers who left the firm they had founded to seek
pastures new. Better-known examples were Karl Benz, August Horch, and
Ransom Olds. Corre left his company, Société des Automobiles Corre, at about
the time when the name La Licorne was taking over from Corre, so presumably

1919 Cosmos Light Car.
NATIONAL MOTOR MUSEUM

the new regime did not object to his using his own name for his new company, although he also called the cars Le Cor or J.C. They were small cars with 4-cylinder engines, not unlike the La Licornes which were being made at the same time. The 1912–13 range consisted of three models, a 1459cc 8hp, 1725cc 10hp, and 2120cc 12hp.

NG

CORREJA (US) 1909–1914

Vandewater & Co., Elizabeth, New Jersey.

A conventional 4-cylinder car made initially in 4- and 7-seater models with engines of 30 and 50hp, the Correja was offered as a 35hp runabout for the 1911 season. After this the makers reverted to a fuller line of 35hp 4- and 60hp 6-cylinder cars, ending up with a 34hp six for 1914. Their best year was 1911, when 120 cars were sold. It seems that the return to a multi-model range for 1912 was the Vandewater's undoing; few cars were made after 1911, and the company was declared bankrupt in February 1914.

NG

CORRY (GB) 1983–1985

1983–1985 Corry Car Co., Lisburn, County Antrim.

1985 Corry Cars, Ballynahinch, County Down.

When the famous Welsh sports car maker DAVRIAN disappeared, a Northern Irish businessman called Will Corry bought up the remains. He asked Tony Stevens (who was earlier responsible for the STEVENS Cipher) to redesign the bodywork. Its main role was as a competition car, and the mid-engined sports coupé notched up a few successes in minor rallies but sales of road cars were few.

CR

CORSAIR (US) c.1980–1986

Corsair Products, Ontario, California.

In addition to a Volkswagen-based MG-TD replica, Corsair built a very unusual dune buggy called the Stripper. It used a tube frame and fibreglass tub for off-roading, but for street use or inclement weather it included a basic fibreglass coupé body that could be lifted on and off when needed. There is no relationship to the Corsair neoclassic kit built by the ROARING 20s MOTOR CAR CO.

HP

CORSE (GB) 1986 to date

1986–1988 Handmade Cars, Bushey, Hertfordshire.

1989–1991 Litton Cars, Skipton, North Yorkshire.

1992 to date Carson Automotive Engineering, Skipton, North Yorkshire.

This began life under the name Allora, and was a fairly accurate Lancia Stratos replica offered in kit form. Mechanically it derived most of its parts from the Lancia Beta. Revived as the Litton Corse, and subsequently as the Carson Corse, it had a totally revised chassis with custom-made suspension, a semi-monocoque chassis, and various Lancia, Renault, Rover 800, Ferrari, Vauxhall or Alfa Romeo engine options.

CR

CORSON (US) c.1990–1996

Corson Motorcar Co., Phoenix, Arizona.

Although this company specialised in installing Chevrolet V8 engines into Pontiac Fieros, they also made two Fiero-based kit cars. The Corson GT coupé resembled a Ferrari Berlinetta Boxer, and the Corson Spyder was a convertible version of the same shape. Corson built these kits with up to 440hp engines and they were available in kit or assembled form.

HP

CORY (US) 1907

Cory Automobile Co., Auburn, Indiana.

The Cory was a very small car with 4hp single-cylinder 2-stroke engine, with friction transmission, priced at US$300. Its wheelbase was only 63in (1600mm). Introduced in February 1907, it did not survive the year.

NG

C.O.S. (US) 1907

Carl Oscar Scholbach Breslau.

This small company is reported to have two models, a 14PS four and a 20PS six, but further details are not known.

NG

COSMOPOLITAN (US) 1907–1910

D.W. Haydock Motor Car Manufacturing Co., St Louis, Missouri.

The prototype of this car, called the Haydock Front Drive, was a high-wheeler with round radiator and drive from a 5hp single-cylinder engine by single-chain to the front axle. Production models retained the front engine location, unusual for high-wheelers, which generally had their engines under the seat, but drove by chain to the rear wheels. For 1908 a 10/12hp 2-cylinder engine was used for three models, for 2, 3, and 4 passengers. Engine power rose over the next two years, to 14hp for 1909 and 18hp for 1910.

NG

COSMOS; C.A.R. (GB) 1919–1920

Cosmos Engineering Co. Ltd, Bristol.

This was a most unusual light car powered by a 3-cylinder air-cooled ohv radial engine of 1206cc, designed by Roy Fedden (1885–1973), who had been responsible for the prewar STRAKER-SQUIRE. Transmission was by a 3-speed gearbox and shaft drive to a differential-less rear axle. Suspension was by the Adams system (also used by DOUGLAS (i)) in which centrally mounted coil springs were connected to the axles by long arms with bell crank levers. In 1920 the Bristol Aeroplane Co. showed an interest in the design, and an output of 200 cars per week, to sell at 200 guineas (£210), was forecast, but cancellation of the project put an end to hopes of Cosmos production. However, they acquired the services of Roy Fedden who designed many successful aero engines for them. He left Bristol in 1942, and designed another advanced car powered by a rear-mounted sleeve-valve radial engine. A prototype saloon was built in 1946.

NG

COSTE (F) 1993 to date

Coste Engineering, Pineuilh.

Jacques Alain Coste built his M6 Turbo prototype in 1993 and was persuaded to enter production. This was a coupé with a removable roof, and was inspired by the Ferrari P4 racer. Into a tubular chassis went a Renault V6 engine, mounted centrally, with optional turbocharging. The first model, which closely resembled the Ferrari and was called the C1, was joined by the C2 in 1996. Unfortunately, it looked rather less like a P4 and was fitted with a Ford 2.3-litre 4-cylinder engine, but it was substantially cheaper than the C1. Both kits and compete cars were sold.

CR

COSTIN (GB) 1970–1972

Costin Automotive Racing Products Ltd, Little Staughton, Bedfordshire.

Aircraft aerodynamicist turned automotive engineer Frank Costin's name was very well-known for his work with Lotus, Vanwall, Marcos, and various racing car projects but there was an attempt to make a sports car under his own name.

The Costin Amigo was an ambitious project, which was born at Costin's base in North Wales but actually manufactured at an aerodrome, and subsequently a more modern factory, both near Luton. This was because the mechanical basis was from nearby Vauxhall, the 2.3-litre engine and modified suspension coming from the VX4/90 model. The chassis was an evolution of Costin's familiar plywood monocoque, with a wooden rear end structure and aerodynamically-designed fibreglass main body panels. The design was widely admired for its strength, handling balance and performance (135mph (217km/h) top speed, 0-60mph (96km/h) in 7.2 seconds), but its price – £3326 – consigned it to an early fate with only seven cars constructed. One car had competed in the 1971 Le Mans. Frank Costin's name subsequently appeared on the T.M.C. COSTIN sports car and an abortive single-seater commuter car built in Wales.

CR

COTAY (US) 1920–1921

Coffyn-Taylor Motor Co., New York, New York.

The Cotay was something of a curio in the American automobile panorama of the early 1920s, being rather a cross between a conventional 2-seater roadster and a cycle car, the craze for the latter, so prevalent in the 'teens, moribund by 1920. The Cotay name was an amalgam of Frank Coffyn and James B. Taylor Jr, two former pilots who drew Everett Cameron, designer of the CAMERON car, into a partnership to market a small car which would have sufficient public appeal stateside, combined with brisk export sales, to become successful in the marketplace. Cameron built a 4-cylinder air-cooled engine and production of the car began in the Stafford, Connecticut plant of the Liberty Manufacturing Co., which was engaged in the Liberty Light Car, also with a Cameron engine, which failed to get into production. The Cotay was a 2-seater roadster constructed of a wooden frame and disc wheels made of glued-together plywood slices, a body of an aluminium skin on a wooden frame and otherwise a conventional design. It featured a 3-speed transmission, a 105in (2665mm) wheelbase, aluminium step plates, and 18bhp. The Cotay was shown in London in conjunction with the London Motor Show of 1920.

However, the Cotay failed to attract the American buyer and what it claimed to offer was overshadowed by what the public felt it had not. A shipment of 25 Cotays, fitted with right-hand steering, was sent to its English concessionaire, Bramco Ltd of Coventry, where it failed to attract the British buyers. In 1921 the Cotay was phased out of production.

KM

COTE (F) 1900; 1908–1913

Sté des Automobiles et Moteurs Cote, Saint-Dizier, Haut Marne (1900); Pantine, Seine (1908–1913).

The first car offered under the Cote name was a voiturette powered by a 3hp 2-cylinder horizontal engine, with spur-gear drive and tiller steering. Few were made, and the name was next heard of in 1908 when cars with 2- and 4-cylinder 2-stroke engines were offered. Apart from the engines they were conventional in design. Six models were listed in 1912, from 4 to 18hp, but only two in 1913, the last year of production, a 1.1-litre 8/17CV and a 2.1-litre 16/28CV.

NG

COTTA (US) 1901–1903

1901 Charles E. Cotta, Lanark, Illinois.
1902 Love Manufacturing Co., Rockford, Illinois.
1903 Cotta Automobile Co., Rockford, Illinois.

Charles Cotta's light steam car looked much like its many contemporaries, but was unique in having drive to the front wheels as well as the rear. Both axles steered as well. The 6hp 2-cylinder engine was mounted in the centre of the frame, and power was transmitted to all four wheels by chains. Cotta built the first car in his father's nursery at Lanark, following this with four cars built for him by the Love company in Rockford. In January 1903 he founded his own company, and announced production of 10 cars for that year. It is not known if they were all made, and in November he sold his patents to the Four Wheel Drive Wagon Co. of Milwaukee, Wisconsin which made petrol-engined trucks from 1904 to 1907.

NG

1972 Costin Amigo coupé.
NATIONAL MOTOR MUSEUM

1921 Cotay roadster.
NATIONAL MOTOR MUSEUM

1911 Cote at start of Coupe des Voitures Légères.
NATIONAL MOTOR MUSEUM

COTTEREAU (F) 1898–1910

Cottereau et Compagnie, Dijon.

This company was founded in 1891 by the brothers Louis and Henri Cottereau. Bicycles were made exclusively up to 1898 when a light car powered by a 5hp (1272cc) air-cooled V-twin engine, 3-speed gearbox and single-chain drive was launched. The cars merited the title voiturette but as this word had been appropriated by Léon Bollée, the Cottereaus called theirs a voiturine. Steering was by handlebar, replaced by a wheel in 1900, when the engine was enlarged to 9hp (1884cc). A Benz-like car with 3.5hp single-cylinder engine was offered in 1900, but Cottereau customers preferred the more refined twins, and few were sold. Five models of Cottereau were offered for 1901, three twins of 5, 7, and 9hp, a 5hp single-cylinder called the Selecta, and a 10hp four.

From 1901 to 1903 the 7hp Cottereau was made under licence by E.J. BRIERRE, who was the Paris agent for the Dijon firm. In 1902 the 5 and 7hp 2-cylinder voiturines had water-cooled cylinder heads. The smaller had single-chain drive, while the 7hp used twin chains. Both had an unusual camshaft brake in which

c.1906 Cottereau 2-seater.
NATIONAL MOTOR MUSEUM

1907 Cottin-Desgouttes tourer in Criterium de la France.
NATIONAL MOTOR MUSEUM

1911 Cottin-Desgouttes 60hp roadster.
NATIONAL MOTOR MUSEUM

the operation of a pedal brought into effect a different cam profile which closed all the valves, thus acting as a brake on the engine, a system also used on the 1904 8hp Rover. The largest of the 1902 Cottereaus was a chain-driven 16hp 2-litre four. Cottereau made a complex range at this time, from a 5hp single called the Populaire in England, to a 9hp vertical twin, a 10/12hp 3-cylinder model and a 16hp four. In 1905 there were three 3-cylinder models, the 1786cc 10/12, 2550cc 12hp and 15/18hp, the latter of the same size but offered with a choice

of shaft or chain drive. Cottereau was a comparatively large firm at this time, with 350 employees who made practically all of the cars, chassis and bodies, in the factory, although some frames were bought in from Arbel. Motorcycles were made from 1905 to 1909.

The 1906 range was the widest yet, from an 8hp single-cylinder with tubular chassis and single-chain drive, which could also be had with armoured wood frame and double-chain or shaft drive, through a 9hp twin, the 10/12, 12 and 15/18hp 3-cylinder cars and a 24hp four. Cottereaus were characterised by Hotchkiss-like round radiators. The firm adopted the pretentious badge of a torch accompanied by the words *In hoc signo vinces* ('in this sign I conquer') used by the Emperor Constantine. The French historian J.R. Dulier observed that customers for the smaller cars did not understand Latin, while those who might have bought a larger Cottereau were unimpressed with such pretension. Sales declined inexorably from 1908, despite a varied range which included a 26hp four with pair-cast cylinders in 1907 and a 9hp chain-driven single-cylinder light car in 1910. Before the end of that year Cottereau was bought by the Constructions Industrielle Dijonaise, which launched a new range of cars under the name C.I.D.

NG

Further Reading
'Cottereau et ses Voiturines', Jean-Rober Dulier, *l'Album du Fanatique*.

COTTIN-DESGOUTTES (F) 1905–1931

1905–1906 Sté des Automobiles Pierre Desgouttes et Compagnie, Lyons.
1906–1931 Automobiles Cottin et Desgouttes, Lyons.
Pierre Desgouttes began his motor industry career with AUDIBERT-LAVIROTTE, and when that company was taken over by BERLIET in 1902 he joined the larger firm, for which he helped in the design of the 10hp model which became the basis for the SUNBEAM. Failing to get on with Marius Berliet, he left in 1904 and set up his own company for the manufacture of a large chain-driven car powered by a 6330cc 24/40hp pair-cast 4-cylinder engine. Slightly cheaper than the Berliet, it was favourably received at the 1905 Paris Salon. Three other models were announced, of 12, 18/22 and 50/70hp, but probably the 24/40 was the only Desgouttes to be completed.

A leading shareholder was Cyrille Cottin, who came from a rich textile family, and at the end of January 1906 the name of company and car was changed to Cottin-Desgouttes. It is probable that output of cars under the Desgouttes name was limited to the two Salon cars, a bare chassis, and a limousine. Under the new name three models were made in 1906, the 24/40 being joined by the 3770cc 18/22 and 10,220cc 50/70hp which Desgouttes had announced the previous year. Sporting successes, particularly in sprints and hill climbs, attracted a growing clientele, and by 1910 the firm had 300 employees. The range was extended at both ends; 1907 saw a 2412cc 12/14hp, and 1909 a 1538cc 12hp which was the first shaft-driven Cottin-Desgouttes. Chain drive was continued on the larger models up to 1914. The big 50/70 with oversquare cylinder dimensions (150 × 140mm) was dropped after 1908, but an even larger engine of 10,613cc (130 × 200mm) was made from 1911 to 1914, variously called the 60hp or 45/70hp. Pair-cast 6-cylinder engines of 20 and 45hp appeared in 1909, and the first monobloc four was the 1846cc 12hp of 1911. Cottin-Desgouttes were exported quite widely, especially to Great Britain and Australia. In 1913 450 cars were made; a respectable figure, although dwarfed by the 3000 from Desgouttes' former partner, Berliet.

Cottin-Desgouttes had made commercial vehicles, particularly *cars alpins* or charabancs for mountain excursions, since 1907, and a considerable number of trucks were turned out during World War I. Commercial chassis were continued after the war, together with four larger models of passenger car designed on essentially prewar lines. These were the 3216cc 14/16, 4071cc 18/20, 5026cc 25/35 and 7238cc 32hp, the latter a monster on a 141in (3600mm) wheelbase with twin rear wheels. Very few were made. In 1922 these dinosaurs gave way to a more modern design, the 2613cc ohv M-type with 5-bearing crankshaft (the larger earlier cars only had three), light alloy pistons and twin sparking plugs per cylinder. Coupled 4-wheel brakes were provided. In 1923 it was joined by a larger car with the same cylinder dimensions and six cylinders, giving a capacity of 3920cc. This was made as the M6 Léger for light sporting bodies and a top speed of 80mph (130km/h), and the M6 Long for formal coachwork. The M models were the last designs of Pierre Desgouttes, who was replaced in 1922 by another ex-Berliet engineer, Paul Joseph. He was responsible for the competition model M de Course, with long-stroke (83 × 138mm) 4-cylinder engine of 2986cc with twin horizontal plugs and three valves per cylinder, two inlet and one exhaust. They had underslung frames, and floorpans which completely enclosed the engine and transmission. No more than 20 of these were sold, but they were very successful in competitions, winning the 1924 Grand Prix de Tourisme. The 1925 GP de Tourisme cars had streamlined saloon bodies made, like most of the open bodies, by Ottin. The last of the M de Course cars was made in 1928.

Production in the mid–1920s was running at around 35 vehicles per month, of which perhaps a third were commercial chassis. The 1926 Salon saw a new model, the Sans Secousses (without shocks) designed by Paul Joseph and Antoine Burlat who had made rotary-engined cars under his own name 20 years before. This used the 2613cc M or 2986cc M de Course engines in a new chassis, low slung and with transverse leaf independent suspension all round. Those at the front took the place of the axle. The rear brake drums were mounted inboard, close to the differential. Bodies were mostly saloons and cabriolets by Ottin, although Vanden Plas and others also worked on the Sans Secousse chassis. Several different sizes of engine were offered, from a 1683cc side-valve four to a 3548cc six. The four was made by C.I.M.E., the first proprietary unit used by Cottin. The 1930 models had hydraulic brakes and synchromesh on the two top speeds. They were advanced and good-looking cars, but the sands of time were running out for Cottin-Desgouttes. They struggled to compete with larger American cars such as Chrysler and Nash, which cost no more. Cyrille Cottin considered a merger with fellow Lyons car makers Rochet-Schneider, and also with Citroën, Delahaye, and Rosengart, but nothing came of these plans. Car production ended in the summer of 1931, but a new company was formed to dispose of 10 million francs worth of stock, so a new Cottin-Desgouttes could still be bought in 1932. A prototype with 2343cc straight-8 S.C.A.P. engine and coupé body was built in 1931, and commercial chassis, some with American Lycoming straight-8 engines, were made up to 1934. The factory was divided up, part becoming a school for engineering apprentices and part a showroom for Unic trucks. From 1937 it was used for manufacture of Isobloc coaches. Cyrille Cottin died in 1942 and Pierre Desgouttes in 1955.

NG

Further Reading
'Cottin-Desgouttes', Lucien Loreille, *l'Album du Fanatique*.

COTTON (GB/AUS) 1911
Cotton Motor Car Co., Ltd, Brisbane, Queensland.
Alfred Cotton controlled a large area of pastoral land across northern Australia and was aware of the need for a vehicle which could cope with journeys over inhospitable terrain such as sand-hills, bogs, and river fords. His answer was to patent an engine-driven winch mounted between the front dumb-irons. The powered cross-shaft could also have a pulley fitted to drive machines. Entitled 'Multi-in-parvo' (much in a little), the type was built under contract by Rennie & Prosser in Glasgow, Scotland. The engine was a 16/24hp ohv White & Poppe; the car weighed 1323kg and it had a very good ground clearance. It was successfully demonstrated when a 4900-mile journey was made through outback Queensland. Possibly as many as 15 examples were sold. In 1914 Alfred's son, Sidney, built a cyclecar with variable pulley transmission, prior to his war service; during his war service he invented the 'Sidcot' flying suit.

MG

COUDERT *see* LURQUIN-COUDERT

COUNTACH COMPANY (GB) 1993
This obscure Countach LP400 replica used Chevrolet/Ford V8 or Renault V6 power, and was marketed in various kit-built stages as the Gandini and Stanzani.
CR

COUNTESS *see* KINGFISHER

COUNTRY CLASSICS (US) c.1994
Country Classics, Erhard, Minnesota.
This company built a replica kit of the 1963–67 Corvette Sting Ray coupé called the CSR637. It used a tube frame with 1984–87 Corvette suspension and a Chevrolet V8 engine.
HP

1925 Cottin-Desgouttes 3-litre tourer.
NATIONAL MOTOR MUSEUM

1926 Cottin-Desgouttes Sans Secousses saloon.
NATIONAL MOTOR MUSEUM

COUNTRY CLIMBER (GB) 1992
This box-shaped plans-built jeep was shown at 1992 Scottish Kitcar Show.
CR

COUNTRY CLUB (US) 1903–1904
Country Club Car Co., Boston, Massachusetts.
Despite its grand name, the Country Club was a fairly ordinary car, powered by a 16hp horizontal twin engine with 4-seater rear-entrance tonneau body. Its most unusual feature was operation of the 3-speed gearbox by compressed air from one of the cylinders. Only a few examples of this $2500 car were made.
NG

COUNTY (GB) 1907
Halifax Motor Car Co., Halifax, Yorkshire.
This was a medium-sized 4-cylinder tourer made in very small numbers by a well-known garage.
NG

COURIER (i) (US) 1904–1905
Sandusky Automobile Co., Sandusky, Ohio.
This was a larger companion car to the SANDUSKY, having a 7hp engine and 70in (1780mm) wheelbase against the 5hp and 65in (1650mm) of the smaller

1910 Courier(iii) 20hp roadster.
NATIONAL MOTOR MUSEUM

1920 Coventry-Premier 3-wheeler.
NICK BALDWIN

c.1922 Coventry-Premier 10hp 2-seater.
NATIONAL MOTOR MUSEUM

car. It also had a sliding gear transmission, while the Sandusky used the epicyclic system. Both had single-chain drive and 2-seater runabout bodies, although the Courier was offered with a 4-seater tonneau on the 8hp Model F of 1905. Courier production may have totalled 225 cars.

NG

COURIER (ii) (F/GB) 1906–1908

Euston Motor Co. Ltd, London.

This car was assembled from French-made components, and some may have been imported fully assembled, although the 16/20hp chassis was described as all-British. Three models were listed in 1906, an 8/10hp 2-cylinder and two fours of 18/24 and 24/30hp, the latter two having engines by Gnome. A 25hp six was listed for 1908. The firm was also responsible for the WASP (i), but this was sold from a different address.

NG

COURIER (iii) (US) 1910–1912

Courier Car Co., Dayton, Ohio.

This company was a subsidiary of STODDARD-DAYTON, formed in order to make a cheaper car which would not detract from the reputation of the parent company's product, rather as the Marquette was formed by Buick and the Blackhawk by Stutz. The first Courier had a 20hp 4-cylinder engine and was made in roadster and tourer forms, selling for $1050 and $1200 respectively. Stoddard-Daytons sold that year for between $1600 and $2800. For 1911 a 25hp engine was used, with a longer wheelbase. The 1912 models were called Courier Clermonts and output was now quoted at 30hp. No closed body styles were offered in the Courier range. In 1912 Stoddard-Dayton became part of the United States Motor Co., and Courier was naturally included in the combine. The collapse of U.S. Motors caused the demise of both makes.

NG

COURIER (iv) (US) 1922–1923

Courier Motor Co., Sandusky, Ohio.

The Courier was the successor to the MAIBOHM car which failed in the summer of 1922. Powered by a 6-cylinder Falls engine and with a choice of three open and two closed body types and priced from $1295 to $1995, it was a good-looking car, featuring cycle mudguards and small pseudo-lanterns as cowl lights. Sales were disappointing despite an export market to Australia and New Zealand. Fewer than 400 Couriers found buyers before the company failed after an existence of less than a year.

KM

COURNIL (F) 1960–1984

1960–1977 Cournil, Aurillac, Cantal.
1977–1981 Sté Gevarm, Saint-Germain Laval.
1981–1984 S.I.M.A. SA, Saint-Germain, Laval.

Bernard Cournil opened a Hotchkiss dealership after World War II and began modifying the Jeeps to his own tastes, with both Hotchkiss and Ferguson diesel engines, reinforced chassis and modified bodywork. Eventually the authorities insisted that these were cars in their own right, requiring type approval, and so the 'Tracteur Cournil' marque was born. Initial sales were confined mostly to farmers, but the marque gained a wider reputation. In 1965 Cournil was forced to change engines, since Ferguson no longer made diesels. After briefly trying Indénor, Cournil settled on Leyland and later still Saviem, before deferring again to Peugeot and Renault diesels and Renault petrol units by the 1980s. About 1000 cars had been made by 1970. In 1982 a model restyled by Benoît Contreau was presented, boasting polyester bumpers, softer suspension and Fiat petrol of SOFIM diesel/turbodiesel engines. The marque was reborn in 1984 under the name AUVERLAND.

CR

COUSY (F) 1955

Automobiles Cousy, Castillon-la-Bataille, Gironde.

The Cousy was a simple plastic-bodied sports car designed for either circuit or road use. It tipped the scales at a featherweight 360kg, with a choice of rear-mounted 500cc BMW or Panhard Dyna engines fitted into a tubular chassis.

CR

COUVERCHEL see C.V.R.

COVENTRY CARS (ZA) 1990s

Coventry Cars, Pietermaritzburg.

The Coventry Classic was a Lotus 7 lookalike that was, however, longer, wider and taller than the original. It was powered by locally-built Ford 1600 Kent engines. This company also offered the British ROTRAX and a Jeep CJ lookalike with Ford 2 or 3-litre engines.

CR

COVENTRY PREMIER (GB) 1914–1923

Coventry Premier Ltd, Coventry.

The origins of this company dated back to 1876 when a bicycle maker, Hillman & Herbert, was founded in Coventry. One of the partners was William Hillman who later made the HILLMAN car. The company later became Hillman, Herbert & Cooper Ltd, and in 1892 the Premier Cycle Co. Ltd. Motorcycles were taken up in 1908 and a cyclecar was built from 1912 to 1914 (see PREMIER (iii)). In November 1914 the name was changed to Coventry Premier, and works manager G.W.A. Brown (formerly with TALBOT (i)) designed an advanced small 4-cylinder car which did not go into production because of the war, although prototypes were tested throughout the next four years. When peace came it was decided that a 3-wheeler was what the market wanted, so Brown's design was abandoned, replaced by a 3-wheeler with 1056cc V-twin engine, shaft drive to the rear-mounted gearbox and enclosed chain final drive. In 1921 Coventry Premier was bought up by SINGER (i), which developed a 4-wheeled replacement for the 3-wheeler. This was introduced in September 1921, and stocks of the 3-wheeler were gradually sold off. It used the same V-twin engine and gearbox mounted on the rear axle. About 500 3-wheelers and 1200 4-wheelers were sold. For 1923 a cheaper version of the Singer Ten was badged as a Coventry Premier, and the next season the name was dropped. However, it survived on Singer-made bicycles up to the late 1920s.

NG

COVENTRY VICTOR (GB) 1926–1938

Coventry Victor Motor Co. Ltd, Coventry.

The forerunner of this company was founded in 1904 as Morton & Weaver, the name being changed to Coventry Victor in 1911. Horizontally-opposed engines were made, one powering an aeroplane designed and built by partner W.A. Weaver. Called the Weaver Ornithoplane, it was the first monoplane to fly in Britain, in 1906. Engines were supplied to several motorcycle makers as well as two foreign car builders, JEECY-VEA in Belgium and C.A.S. in Czechoslovakia. Their best British customer was GRAHAME-WHITE. In 1919 they launched a motorcycle powered by a 688cc flat-twin engine, and this unit went into a prototype light car which never saw production. Motor cycles were made up to 1930, and in 1926 came the Coventry Victor 3-wheeler powered by the same 688cc flat-twin, with 2-speed gearbox and chain drive. Most were made as open 2-seaters but an Avon-built coupé was added in 1929. For 1932 the 3-wheeler was restyled by C.F. Beauvais as the Luxury Sports with two-tone paint scheme, vee-windscreen and radiator and more flowing lines. The bodies were built by Avon, for whom Beauvais also styled Standards. The engine was enlarged to 749cc, but the smaller engine and plainer styling could still be had at £75, for those who did not wish to pay the £110 price tag of the Luxury Sports. Ohvs were available on the Luxury Sports, which had a 3-speed gearbox as standard. Production lasted to 1938, with larger engines of 850 or 998cc available on the later models.

In 1949 Coventry Victor considered re-entering the car market with a small saloon, codenamed Venus, powered by a 747cc flat-four engine. Only prototypes were made. The company continued to make horizontally-opposed engines, diesels from the 1950s, which had many applications including powering lifeboats and as auxiliary engines for yachts and fishing vessels. They also did a lot of subcontracted engineering work, among which was manufacture of the Martin V8 engine used in the DEEP SANDERSON prototype, which subsequently became the MONICA. The founder, W.A. Weaver, ran the company until his death in 1970, when it was reorganised by his son as A.N. Weaver (Coventry Victor) Ltd.

NG

COVERT (US) 1902–1907

1902–1904 Byron V. Covert & Co., Lockport, New York.
1904–1907 Covert Motor Vehicle Co., Lockport, New York.

1935 Coventry Victor Luxury Sports 3-wheeler.
NATIONAL MOTOR MUSEUM

1991 Covin Speedster 2-seater sports car.
MICK SPENCER

Byron Covert planned to make a steam car, but his first production machine was a petrol-engined runabout with 3hp single-cylinder engine and chain drive. It was very small, with a 62in (1575mm) wheelbase and weighing only 350lbs (160kg). For 1903 he replaced chain-drive with gear-drive from the rear axle-mounted gearbox, and quoted power went up to 5hp. A 24hp 4-cylinder tourer at $2250 was offered in 1904 and 1905, but for the last two years of the firm, only the runabout was listed, now with a 6.5hp engine and 72in (1830mm) wheelbase.

NG

COVIN (GB/IRE) 1984 to date

1984–1992 Covin Performance Mouldings, South Woodham Ferrers, Essex.
1992–1995 D.J. Sportscars, Harlow, Essex.
1995–1998 Grand Performance Cars, Luton, Bedfordshire.
1998 to date Grand Performance Cars, Ireland.

A VW Beetle based replica of the Porsche 911 may sound execrable, but there was a big demand for it and Porsche itself was sufficiently put-out to demand a redesign. The Turbo Coupé was the result, but it still looked close enough to fool many people. A cabriolet version was soon added. There was a choice of a Beetle floorpan or a purpose-made chassis, and of VW engines or water-cooled units such as the Ford Escort. A Rinspeed-style droop-snoot option was also popular. Covin also developed its own Porsche Speedster replica (available from 1989), and offered its own chassis that was designed to accept, most unusually, VW Variant mechanicals. There was also an abortive McLaren M6 replica.

CR

COVINGTON (US) 1961

Henry Covington, St Petersburg, Florida.

Starting with a Renault 4CV and a knowledge of aerodynamics, Henry Covington built a radically low (42.5in) 2-seat sports car with fully enclosed wheels and a cockpit top that hinged up for egress. Named the El Tiburon (Spanish for shark), it used aerodynamic theory based on the work of Dr Augustus Raspet. In 1961, Covington announced his intention of producing body shells for customers.

HP

1914 Cowey 10/12hp 2-seater.
NATIONAL MOTOR MUSEUM

COVINI (I) 1978–c.1990
Ferruccio Covini Automobili, Castel San Giovanni (PC).
The first product of this company was the T-44 Soleado, a very squarish 4 × 4 off-road vehicle that used VM turbodiesel engines of 2.0- or 2.4- litres capacity, with rigid axles and leaf springs at either end. In contrast, the Sirio GT of 1980 was a handsome mid-engined 2-seater coupé that, surprisingly, also used an air-cooled VM diesel engine; a turbodiesel version with 125bhp arrived the following year. Alternatively, a Lancia Gamma 2.0- or 2.5-litre engine could be fitted. The 5-speed gearbox also came from Lancia, and there was all-independent suspension and servo-assisted disc brakes all round. 14 Sirios were made in 1981. A further model, the Leonesse, was in preparation in 1982, but this V8 or straight-6 turbodiesel-powered car apparently never saw the light of day. Covini was still in existence in 1990 with the coupé model (now renamed C88) and a new 3.7-litre 6-cylinder turbodiesel coupé called the T40.
CR

COWEY (GB) 1910–1915
Cowey Engineering Co. Ltd, Kew Gardens, Surrey.
This company exhibited two cars at the 1910 Olympia Show to demonstrate its pneumatic suspension system, in which four cylinders of compressed air took the place of springs. It incorporated a self-levelling device, as used in more sophisticated form 45 years later in the Citroën DS19. The cars, which were powered by De Dion-Bouton engines of 10 and 20hp, had solid tyres, to demonstrate the efficacy of the compressed air system. They were experimental but three years later Cowey offered for sale a light car using the same system. It had a 10hp 4-cylinder Chapuis-Dornier engine, a Morris-like bullnose radiator and friction drive in which a flywheel with conical facing acted as the driving disc. It was priced at £300.
NG

COX (i) (GB) 1914
Cox Brass Manufacturing Co., Glasgow.
This was probably an imported make as the Cox company were described as handling the car for Great Britain and elsewhere. It had a 4-cylinder engine with detachable head, 3-speed gearbox with direct drive on top, and acetylene lighting. The price was £230. Electric lighting and starting was available, but, as *The Motor Trader* reported 'presumably this will cost more'. A Cox was driven from Glasgow to London in 11¾ hours with only six gear changes.
NG

COX (ii) *see* G.T.M.

COYOTE (US) 1908–1909
Pacific Motor & Automobile Co., Redondo, California.
The Coyote Special was made only as a rakish 2-seater roadster with a very long bonnet, necessary as it housed a straight-8 engine. The crankshaft and crankcase were made by Pacific, but many other engine components, as well as springs, axles and wheels, came from FRANKLIN. A top speed of 75mph (120km/h) is likely to have been exaggerated. Only two Coyote Specials were built.
NG

C.P.C. (GB) 1993–1995
1993–1994 A.J. Performance Cars, Bruntingthorpe, Leicestershire.
1994–1995 Classic Performance Cars, Wales.
An ex-employee of DEON, Tony Butler, set up as A.J.P. and created a Ferrari P4 replica called the AJ4S that was very similar to Deon's P4. Shortly after, A.J.P. left its Leicestershire address for a site in Wales and was renamed Classic Performance Cars. There was also the CPC3, a replica of the Ferrari P3, which differed from the later Ferrari only by its squarer rear end.
CR

C.P.T. (US) 1906
Chicago Pneumatic Tool Co., Chicago, Illinois.
This company was a well-known maker of air compressors and pneumatic tools. In 1906 it completed a batch of 50 2-seater runabouts solely for the use of its travellers. They had 22hp 2-cylinder engines and solid tyres. From 1910 to 1918 C.P.T. made delivery vans and trucks sold under the names Duntley and Little Giant.
NG

C-R CHEETAH (US) 1994 to date
C-R Cheetah Race Cars, Phoenix, Arizona.
Robert Auxier had been restoring Corvettes for some time when he decided to build a high-quality, accurate replica of the Bill Thomas CHEETAH. With help from original Cheetah designer Don Edmunds, he recreated the tube frame and Chevrolet V8 running gear of the originals. They were sold in kit or fully assembled form.
HP

CRAIG-DORWALD (GB) 1902–c.1912
Putney Motor Co., Putney, London.
This company was better known for marine engines than for cars. In 1904 they built an 18.3-litre 150bhp V12 engine, probably the world's first 12-cylinder unit. It was originally intended for a Russian airship, and was later put into a yacht in Hong Kong. Cars were made to special order, and were individually designed and built. The first was a light car with single-cylinder engine and single speed, made in 1902, followed by a 10hp 2-cylinder commercial traveller's car in 1903. Other models used 8hp single, 18hp twin and 24hp or 50hp 4-cylinder engines. The latter powered a worm drive chassis with only one forward speed, fitted with a sumptuous barouche body for the Earl of Norbury. Total output was not more than 12 cars. Craig-Dorwald also sold the imported MAYFAIR (i) in 1906–07. As Ailsa Craig Ltd, they continued in the marine engine business for many years.
NG
Further Reading
'Fragments on Forgotten Makes, No.17: The Craig-Dorwald', Bill Boddy, *Motor Sport*, October 1961.
'Craig-Dorwald and Ailsa Craig cars', Maurice Harrison, *The Veteran & Vintage Magazine*.

CRAIG-HUNT (US) 1920
Craig-Hunt Motors, Indianapolis, Indiana.
Craig-Hunt, as a manufacturer of automobiles, turned out to be more of an idea than an actuality. Previously a specialist firm building speed parts, a 16-valve engine conversion and a special Peugeot-type racing body for Model T Fords, the Craig-Hunt company had been in business since 1915. In 1920 it decided to concentrate on its own car, closely modelled on Ford lines, but featuring a conventional transmission. Considerable full-page magazine advertising marked its promotional efforts, occasionally illustrated by a sketch of the car which looked remarkably like a Model T Ford. The Craig-Hunt failed to achieve serious production.
KM

CRAIG-TOLEDO (US) 1907
Craig-Toledo Motor Co., Toledo, Ohio.
This car gained its name from the city of manufacture and the Craig shipbuilding family who financed it. The prototype was built in Dundee, Michigan under the name Maumee, but production began in Toledo in January 1907. It was powered

by a 40hp 4-cylinder engine and was made only as a 3-seater roadster, selling at the high price of $4000. A 3-point suspension was its most unusual feature. The company planned to build 100 cars during 1907, but as they were bankrupt by June, certainly far fewer were made. Eight remained on hand at the time of the bankruptcy.

NG

CRAINE (AUS) 1908

Thomas Craine Carriage Works, South Melbourne, Victoria.

Aware of US enthusiasm for the high-wheeled motor buggy, Craine's offering was aimed to tempt horse users to change to motors. It had a Phillips water-cooled flat-twin motor of 12/14hp, which drove through a 3-speed gearbox, differential and chain final drive. Ball bearing axles, solid rubber tyres and a brake, which disconnected the drive, were other features. There is no indication that it attracted horse folk to motoring.

MG

CRAMPIN-SCOTT (GB) 1900–1901

Crampin, Scott & Co., London.

This car was powered by a 6hp horizontal single-cylinder engine and had a 2-speed gearbox. A reverse gear was extra. Maximum speed was no more than 12mph (19km/h).

NG

CRANE (US) 1912–1915

1912–1915 Crane Motor Car Co., Bayonne, New Jersey.
1915 Crane Motor Car Co., New Brunswick, New Jersey.

The Crane was one of the most expensive, if not the most expensive, automobiles built in the United States during its three year existence, with a chassis price of $8000. The car paid considerable attention to existing automobile designs by Henry Middlebrook Crane, a noted engineer who had designed a number of trophy-winning speedboats, which were built by the Crane & Whitman Co. with which he was associated. Following experimentation with a number of designs used by several quality cars, the Crane-Whitman Co. became the Crane Motor Car Co. targeted exclusively for automobile production.

The Crane featured a 6-cylinder L-head engine developing 110bhp, a wheelbase of 136in (3452mm) and available only in chassis form with coachwork by top quality speciality houses. About 40 Cranes, depicted as the Model 3 series, were completed by late 1914 when the Crane Co. was purchased by the Simplex Automobile Co. of New Brunswick, New Jersey, a move ostensibly designed by Simplex to acquire the services of Crane who moved his operation to New Brunswick and built a few more Cranes – these designated Model 4. Here he perfected an improved design which resulted in the car known as the Simplex-Model 5, Simplex-Crane, or the more widely known Crane-Simplex which built up to 500 cars before closing down for the war effort in 1917. (See CRANE-SIMPLEX.)

KM

CRANE & BREED (US) 1912

Crane & Breed Manufacturing Co., Cincinnati, Ohio.

This was a carriage maker founded in 1850 who built an experimental electric runabout in 1902 and commenced series production of ambulances and hearses in 1909. For the year 1912 only, they offered a series of passenger cars in eight body styles, from a tourer at $3000 to a landaulette-limousine at $4500. They used the same 48hp 6-cylinder engines as the professional cars, and rode on a long wheelbase of 152in (3860mm). Presumably it was not a profitable venture as the cars were not offered for 1913. Crane & Breed continued to make professional cars up to 1924, using their own bodies on 6-cylinder WINTON chassis.

NG

CRANE-SIMPLEX (US) 1915–1924

1915–1919 Simplex Automobile Co. Inc., New Brunswick, New Jersey.
1920–1924 Crane-Simplex Co. of New York Inc.,
Long Island City, New York.

The Crane-Simplex, more properly Simplex, Model 5 or Simplex-Crane, was the lineal successor to the Model 3 Crane automobile and was first produced after the Crane Motor Car Co., of New Brunswick, New Jersey was purchased by

1918 Crane-Simplex sedan.
NATIONAL MOTOR MUSEUM

Simplex in 1915. Designed by engineer Henry Crane, erstwhile head of the Crane Co., who was made a vice president of Simplex, the new model exemplified the American luxury car, its chassis priced at $5000, and custom coachwork provided by a stable of the country's most highly regarded body specialists, among them Brewster, Demarest, Holbrook, Kimball, and Quinby. The Crane-Simplex was a large car and an impressive one, an L-head six with a 4³/₈ × 6¹/₄ in bore and stroke with 8795cc capacity and 110bhp. The 2-ton chassis carried a wheelbase of 143in (3629mm). By the autumn of 1917 the company, needed for the war effort, terminated production of the car, by which time the chassis price had risen to US$7500. An estimated 475 to 500 cars were on the road. An interesting sidelight in the design of the car was the availability of various types of radiator shapes besides the Crane-Simplex standard, high-rounded 'cathedral type' similar to that of the contemporary Fiat. The cars were built with great precision and a number of them were subsequently modernised by being redesigned and rebuilt by such companies as Brewster and LeBaron. Notably, too, many of the cars were maintained by their original owners for more than 20 years without any modernisation whatsoever. In 1920 the assets of the company were acquired by Emlen S. Hare who had also acquired those of both the Locomobile and Mercer and from whom Henry Crane obtained the assets and subsequently full ownership of the Crane-Simplex, and who set up a new company at Long Island City to continue its manufacture. The new line of cars differed little from prewar cars with the exception of an increase in the chassis price which was set at a massive $10,000. Very few of these cars found buyers and the main activities of the reorganised company were in providing a rebuilding service for existing cars as well as a repair depot for them. The Crane-Simplex was highly regarded in the fine luxury car market taking its place alongside the Locomobile 48, American Rolls-Royce, and custom-bodied Cunningham, and the few other cars in the similar price bracket.

KM

CRAWFORD (US) 1904–1923

Crawford Automobile Co., Hagerstown, Maryland.

Crawford began as a builder of bicycles and his company was acquired in 1905 by Matthias P. Möller, head of the Möller Pipe Organ Co., which would ultimately become the largest builder of organs in the country. The automobile was, however, a separate company and production of Crawford cars never exceeded the 275 cars completed during 1910. A handful of trucks were also built by the company over the years. Chain drive was employed in 1907 with transaxles featured in the 1911–1914 models. Later Crawfords featured disc-covered artillery wheels and 6-cylinder Continental engines in 60 and 70bhp forms. In 1922 the make experimented with a radically designed military-fendered, brass-plated sporting model it called the Dagmar after Möller's daughter. In 1923 only a

1904 Cremorne 12hp steam limousine.
NATIONAL MOTOR MUSEUM

1914 Crescent (iv) Ohio tourer.
NICK BALDWIN

single Crawford was made (for the superintendent of the organ company) and simultaneously all passenger car operations were focused on the production of the DAGMAR as a make in its own right.
KM

CRAWSHAY-WILLIAMS (GB) 1904–1906
Crawshay-Williams Ltd, Ashtead, Surrey.
This company was formed in November 1904 and made cars for less than two years. They had Simms engines of 14/16 and 20/24hp and double-chain drive, being generally similar in appearance to the Mercedes.
NG

CRÉANCHE (F) 1899–1906
Sté L. Créanche, Courbevoie, Seine.
This company entered the car field with a voiturette powered by a 4hp De Dion-Bouton engine mounted on a movable fore-train. This could be moved forwards or backwards to give variable tension to a belt that connected the engine to a countershaft at the rear of the car. In 1900 they sold under their own name light electric cars made for them by B.G.S. Créanche cars grew in size and became more conventional with the passing of the years. At the 1904 Paris Salon they showed five cars, from 8 to 30hp, the latter being quite a substantial chain-driven tourer. The smaller models used De Dion-Bouton engines and shaft drive. Prices ran from 4200 francs for the 10hp to 12,000 francs for a 30hp side-entrance tourer with fixed top. The 1906 range was reduced to four models, and the largest was a 16hp four.
NG

CREATIVE CARS (US) 1996 to date
Creative Cars, Ore City, Texas.

This Texas-based kit car company built replicas of the Ferrari Testarossa, 512TR and F40 in addition to the 427 Cobra, Mercedes 500SL, and Lamborghini Countach. The Cobra had a tube frame while the 500SL was based on a Chrysler LeBaron, but the others built on Pontiac Fiero chassis. They also sold a conversion kit for installing 8150cc Cadillac V8 engines into Fieros.
HP

CREATIVE COACH (US) c.1995
Creative Coach, California.
This kit company developed a prototype of a Lamborghini Diablo replica called the Lambada. They supposedly also made a replica Mercedes 500SL that fitted on a Chrysler LeBaron chassis, and a Corvette stretch limousine.
HP

CREIGHTON (US) c.1991
Dick Creighton, Glendate, Arizona.
The Mariah was a radically reworked Bradley GT-II kit car with an Oldsmobile 3800cc V6 engine. The VW frame and suspension were upgraded with Oldsmobile parts and disc brakes. The body received a new tail and headlight treatment, as well as large radiator intakes on the sides. Creighton offered to build similar cars for $25,000 to $40,000. Kits were not offered.
HP

CREMORNE (GB) 1903–1904
Cremorne Motor Manufacturing Co. Ltd, Chelsea, London.
The Cremorne was one of the lesser-known British steam cars and was offered in two models, of 6.5 and 12hp, with vertical 2-cylinder engines and steam generated at 220psi. Final drive was by chain, and both open and closed bodywork was available. A 1-ton truck was also offered and in 1906 a 36-seater bus with 20hp 4-cylinder engine was listed.
NG

CRENDON REPLICAS (GB) 1994 to date
Crendon Replicas, Brill, Aylesbury, Buckinghamshire.
Although a latecomer to the Cobra replication scene, the CR 427 leant towards authenticity by having a twin round tube chassis and straight dashboard, then veered away again by incorporating a central bulkhead. It had the usual Jaguar running gear, plus Ford or Chevrolet small or big block V8 power options.
CR

CRESCENT (i) (US) 1905
Crescent Automobile & Supply Co., St Louis, Missouri.
Although the firm claimed that it would make a speciality of racing cars designed by company president O.H. Van Kleck, the only Crescents to see the light of day were 2-cylinder tourer and roadster models, selling at $950 and $885 respectively.
NG

CRESCENT (ii) (US) 1907–1908
Crescent Motor Car Co., Detroit, Michigan; Constantine, Michigan; Goshen, Indiana.
This company was formed to take over production of the RELIANCE touring car and the MARVEL roadster, two Detroit firms that had recently given up car manufacture. Before any cars were made Crescent was taken over by the Constantine Motor Car Co. who would build a new design of car. This was never made either, and in November 1908 it was reported that a new home had been found in a former soap factory in Goshen, Indiana. By the beginning of 1909 there was no more news of the Crescent, although a few prototypes were possibly built in one of the three locations.
NG

CRESCENT (iii) (GB) 1911–1915
1911–1913 Crescent Motors Ltd, Walsall, Staffordshire.
1913–1915 Crescent Motors Ltd, Birmingham.
The Crescent was a neat-looking cyclecar powered by a 964cc 7/9hp J.A.P. air-cooled V-twin engine with friction disc transmission and belt drive. After the move to Birmingham a water-cooled Blumfield V-twin was adopted, and final drive was by chain. They seemed to be popular with lady cyclecarists, and in April

1913 it was reported that at least three Crescents were operated by lady drivers in the West Midlands.

NG

CRESCENT (iv) (US) 1913–1914
Crescent Motor Co., Carthage, Ohio.

This Crescent was a continuation of the OHIO (i) and was made in the same factory. The new company was organised by Ralph Northway, who had recently sold his engine company to General Motors, and would later make cars and trucks under his own name at Natick, Massachusetts. Two models were made under the Crescent name, the former Ohio with 4.4-litre 4-cylinder engine and the Royal, a larger car with 7.4-litre 6-cylinder Northway engine. Both were made in touring form only, and few were made of either as the company was out of business before the end of 1914.

NG

CRESPELLE (F) 1906–1923
Automobiles F. Crespelle, Paris.

This company began by making small sporting cars which did particularly well at hill climbs such as Gaillon. They used single-cylinder proprietary engines with very long strokes, such as an Aster (106 x 192mm) and a De Dion-Bouton (100 × 280mm). Later they built more conventional cars with 4-cylinder engines but continued to engage in sport. A 14CV Type H finished third in the 1912 San Sebastian Rally. On the eve of war in 1914 they offered five 4-cylinder models, from the 1460cc 7CV to the 3617cc 18CV with 4-speed gearbox. All engines were probably bought in; the 7CV could well have been a Chapuis-Dornier, while another model used the 2983cc long-stroke Janvier engine.

The postwar Crespelles appeared in 1920 and used Sergant engines in three sizes, 1590, 2116, and 2410cc. The smallest had a 3-speed gearbox, the other two, 4-speeds. They had disc wheels and body styles included a tourer and a saloon. Crespelle had an eye on the export market, and their stand at the 1920 Brussels Salon was twice the size of that of Citroën. This did not prevent the company closing down in 1923.

NG

Further Reading
'Autos Crespelle Alexis', *La Vie de l'Auto*, 10 November 1988.

CRESTMOBILE (US) 1901–1905
Crest Manufacturing Co., Cambridge, Massachusetts.

This company began by making engines and other components, and early in 1901 launched their Crestmobile Model A. It was a very simple runabout with a 2hp single-cylinder air-cooled engine mounted ahead of a straight dash, with chain drive to the rear wheels and tiller steering. Later in the year they added the Model B with 3.5hp engine and the Model C with 5hp engine under a small bonnet. Shaft drive was adopted in 1903 when the company claimed to have made 1000 cars. In 1904 the engine was quoted at 8.5hp, while a 15hp 2-cylinder model was exhibited in 1904 and 1905. In the latter year Crest was absorbed into the ALDEN-SAMPSON company who sold left-over Crestmobiles into 1906 and possibly 1907. The 1904 Crestmobile was sold in England by O'Halloran Brothers as the O.H.B.

NG

CREWFORD (GB) 1920–1921
Crewford Garage, London.

Like the AEROFORD the Crewford was based on the Model T Ford, using the standard engine and transmission in a lowered chassis. The polished aluminium 2- or 4-seater bodies gave the cars a distinctive appearance, aided by a choice of bullnose or Rolls-Royce type radiators.

NG

CRICKET (US) 1913–1914
Cricket Cyclecar Co., Detroit, Michigan.

The Cricket was a typical cyclecar powered by a 9hp V-twin engine by Motor Products of Detroit. Less usual, although not unknown, was the location of the engine, beside the driver on the offside, a feature used as late as 1954 on the GORDON (iii). Final drive was by belt. The Cricket was designed by an Englishman, Anthony New, who was said to have made a cyclecar in London in

c.1912 Crespelle roadster.
NATIONAL MOTOR MUSEUM

1901 Crestmobile 5hp runabout.
NATIONAL MOTOR MUSEUM

c.1921 Crewford saloon.
NATIONAL MOTOR MUSEUM

1912, although the identity of this is not known. Late in 1914 the makers sold out to Motor Products who built the engine, and Cricket manufacture was discontinued.

NG

1941 Crosley convertible coupé.
NICK BALDWIN

CRIPPS (GB) 1913
Cripps Cycle Co., Forest Gate, London N.
Bicycle-makers Cripps built a prototype cyclecar powered by a 7hp V-twin JAP engine, with 3-speed gearbox and final drive by chain. A somewhat unusual feature, although not unknown at the time, was a starter operated by pulling a chain on the dashboard. A price of £95 was quoted, but very few were made.
NG

CRITCHLEY-NORRIS (GB) 1906–1908
Critchley-Norris Motor Co. Ltd, Bamber Bridge, Preston, Lancashire.
This company was better-known for bus chassis than for cars. They were designed by J.S. Critchley who had been with DAIMLER and had designed the first CROSSLEY. Both car and bus chassis by Critchley-Norris used 40hp 4-cylinder Crossley engines, with 4-speed gearboxes and chain drive. Critchley also designed the front-drive PULLCAR which was made in the same factory.
NG

CROFTON (US) 1959–1961
Crofton Marine Engine Co., San Diego, California.
The rights to the CROSLEY engine were purchased by this company, who primarily sold it as a stationary engine. They also resurrected the Crosley Farm-O-Road midget jeep and called it the Bug.
HP

CROISSANT (F) 1920–1922
S.A. des Anciens Éts V. Couverchel, H. Croissant et Compagnie, Paris.
The first Croissant was a cyclecar, but the company soon offered a larger tourer powered by a 1690cc 4-cylinder single-ohc S.C.A.P. engine, with 4-speed gearbox. They also advertised an 8-cylinder model, which probably used two of the fours coupled together, as the cylinder dimensions (70 × 110mm) were identical. Whether this was built is not known, and few Croissants of any kind were completed. One of the partners, V. Couverchel, may have been connected with the C.V.R. made before World War I.
NG

CROMPTON (i) (US) 1902–1905
Crompton Motor Carriage Co., Worcester, Massachusetts.
When the makers of the Crompton Loom decided to enter the car field, they considered steam and electric power. They soon abandoned the latter, and built an unusual steamer with 24 separate fire-tube boilers mounted in two groups on each side of the 4-cylinder horizontal engine. Drive was by vertical shaft to the rear axle. The body was a 2-seater, and the curved dash gave it some resemblance to the Oldsmobile. The Crompton was well received at the 1903 Boston Automobile Show, but a factory fire in May 1905 ended production.
NG

CROMPTON (ii) (GB) 1914
Crompton Engineering Co., Hendon, Middlesex.
Sometimes known as the T.D.C. after its designer T.D. Crompton, this cyclecar was available as a monocar or 2-seater. They were powered by J.A.P. engines of 5/6hp or 8hp, both being available in either model. A welded steel body gave the car a very clean appearance.
NG

CROSBY (US) c.1982–1990
Crosby Metal Products, Ontario, California.
In addition to assembling and modifying many MANTA kit cars for customers, Crosby also made an original design kit car called the Crosby Fun 1+1. It was a narrow car that fitted on a VW Beetle chassis. The driver and passenger sat in tandem fashion in the narrow cockpit and the wheels had cycle-type mudguards. A 'sports car' nose and high tail wing completed the racer image. Their Manta conversions included installing V8 engines into the Montage and a radical, turn-key Manta conversion called the Can Am. It included a racing-type chassis with fabricated suspension, a ZF transaxle and a modified Chevrolet V8
HP

CROSLEY (US) 1939–1952
Crosley Motors Inc., Cincinnati, Ohio.
Probably the most advanced automobile manufacturer in America during the post-World War II years was Crosley. Owned by Powel Crosley, Jr, they pioneered the construction of quality small cars to an indifferent nation raised on high speed and cheap petrol. Crosley was a self-made millionaire whose companies sold more radios than anyone in the world, manufactured refridgerators and owned a professional baseball team. But his first love was the automobile business despite the fact that it would cost him money, not make it. The first Crosley had its public debut at the 1939 New York World's Fair. Powered by an air-cooled 15hp Waukesha twin that was developed from an orchard sprayer motor, the little car had an 80in (2030mm) wheelbase. Convertible coupé, sedan and station wagon bodies were offered. The first models had numerous problems, but they were ironed out by the time production ceased in 1942 due to the US's entry into World War II. During the war Crosley bought the rights to a lightweight 4-cylinder stationary engine with a fixed head and a copper-brazed sheet metal block called the Cobra. This high-revving 717cc ohc engine powered the next generation of Crosley cars. Vehicle production resumed in 1946 with new larger models. With the other auto manufacturers unable to meet demand, Crosleys were popular and over 28,000 were sold in 1948 alone. However, by 1949 full-size cars were back into full production at roughly the same price as the Crosley, and the Cobra engine proved to have corrosion problems. It was replaced with the CIBA engine, a revamped Cobra with a cast iron block assembly and integral head. In 1949 Crosley became the first company in the world to adopt 4-wheel disc brakes. The same year Crosley introduced the Hotshot, a tiny, doorless sports car that was highly successful in racing, winning the Index of Performance at Sebring in 1951. A fancier version with doors called the Super Sports followed, but sales continued to slip and Crosley ceased automotive operations in 1952.
HP

Further Reading
'The forgotten Man's Car – Crosley of Cincinnati', Stan Grayson, *Automobile Quarterly*, Vol.XVI, No.1.

CROSSLAND STEAM CAR (US) 1919–1923
Crossland-Pfaff Engineering Laboratories, Chicago, Illinois.
The Crossland Steam car was an on-again off-again affair which began when automobile engineer Harry Crossland Pfaff started designing a kerosene-fuelled steam car which he felt might dominate the steam car market, steamers apparently enjoying a renaissance at the time, most of them later discovered to exist as lone prototypes or representing stock speculations in the field. Interest in the rebirth of the steam car was reaching its peak when the Crossland was exhibited at the Congress Hotel in Chicago during Auto Show week in January 1923 – a stunning 5-seater phaeton priced at $1985. The Crossland featured a polished aluminium body and disc wheels and it was claimed to have only 29 moving parts, 16 of which were in its 2-cylinder engine. The exhibition car attracted considerable attention – but not enough for such a car's survival in a competitive market – and the Crossland faded from the automotive scene before a half dozen cars had been completed and sold.
KM

CROSSLEY (GB) 1904–1937

1904–1910 Crossley Brothers Ltd, Gorton, Manchester.
1910–1937 Crossley Motors Ltd, Gorton, Manchester.

The brothers William and Frank Crossley set up in business as makers of stationary gas engines in 1866, acquiring the British patents from Otto & Langen. They supplied engines to a wide variety of businesses, although not to breweries because of their teetotal principles. Their involvement in motor vehicles came about because London car dealers Charles Jarrott and William Letts wanted a high class British-made car to sell alongside their imported Oldsmobiles. There is a parallel here with Charles Rolls looking for a car from another Manchester firm, although Henry Royce was in a smaller way of business than the Crossley brothers. Jarrott and Letts already had a design in the shape of a large 4-cylinder car on Mercedes lines which had been prepared for them by Daimler's former works manager J.S. Critchley. It had a 22hp 4760cc T-head engine, choice of magneto or coil ignition, 4-speed gearbox, and double-chain drive. The Crossleys agreed to make it, using Belgian chassis frames, but otherwise all components made in their factory. After the end of 1906 they made their own chassis as well. Having completed his design work Critchley did not stay with Crossley but set up as an engineering consultant in London, although he kept his connection with the North through his involvement with the CRITCHLEY-NORRIS and PULLCAR.

The 22hp Crossley, sometimes called the Crossley-Critchley, was joined in 1906 by a larger car of 40hp and 6970cc on similar lines, although it had a water-cooled transmission brake as seen on contemporary FIATs. Charles Jarrott used one of these to set new records for the journey from London to Monte Carlo. Shaft drive appeared on the 1907 models, as did the first Crossley radiator with green Maltese cross, although chain drive devotees were given the option of their system from May 1907. It was finally dropped in 1909, when the 40hp was joined by two smaller cars, the 2411cc 12/14hp and the 4116cc 20/25hp. The latter engine was to last Crossley until 1925, and powered the famous R.F.C.-type 25/30, of which thousands were made for the Services during World War I. After the armistice, when the Crossleys and their drivers were demobilised, many gave sterling service as charabancs and country buses. From 1909 to 1912 the 12/14 was fitted with Allen-Liversidge front wheel brakes, but these were not satisfactory. They were uncoupled, and the footbrake on the front wheels and the handbrake on the rear had to be applied simultaneously and with equal pressure if they were to work properly.

In 1910 Crossley Motors was formed as a separate company from the gas engine business, and at the same time they acquired the retail business of Jarrott & Letts which had started them off in car manufacture. The 40hp was dropped after 1912, and the 12/14 grew to 2612cc thanks to a 10mm increase in stroke, being known henceforth as the 15.9hp. The sporting model was known as the Shelsley and looked very handsome with bullnose radiator and wire wheels. In 1913 three prototypes were built of a 10hp quality light car, which might have proved a serious rival to Calthorpe and Singer, but the war prevented further development.

Crossley were quick to get back into car production after World War I, delivering 25/30s from February 1919 onwards. The engine was enlarged to 4536cc, and had aluminium pistons, but otherwise they were substantially the same as the R.F.C.-type 20/25, although they had Shelsley-type rounded radiators. In 1921 the 25/30 was joined by the smaller 19.6hp of 3705cc. This was more modern in having a detachable cylinder head, although it still had a transmission brake. A sports version, the 20/70, with slipper-type pistons, knock-off wire wheels and lightweight polished aluminium body appeared in 1923. Despite having side-valves, it was good for 75mph (120km/h), and had a good sporting record. Perrot servo-assisted four wheel brakes were optional from 1924.

The 25/30 and 19.6 became very popular with royalty, both at home and abroad. While King George V remained mostly loyal to his Daimlers for official use, his sons the Prince of Wales and Duke of York (later Kings Edward VIII and George VI) both used fleets of Crossleys on tours of India, Australia and South America. George V had a special 6-wheeled shooting car with 19.6hp engine and Hooper body for use at Sandringham. Foreign monarchs who favoured Crossleys included King Alfonso XIII of Spain, the King of Siam and Crown Prince Hirohito of Japan.

Crossley had a number of involvements with other makes during the 1920s, not all of which were helpful to their finances. A proposed merger with AVRO

1906 Crossley 22/28hp tourer.
NATIONAL MOTOR MUSEUM

c.1914 Crossley 20/25hp tourer.
NATIONAL MOTOR MUSEUM

1929 Crossley 15.7hp coupé.
NATIONAL MOTOR MUSEUM

in 1919 never really got off the ground, but in November 1921 Sir William Letts announced an agreement with BUGATTI under which the Type 22 would be made at Gorton. In fact, it was assembled from imported components, but some changes were made; in particular the width of the gears was increased, making for longer life, and the rear axle shaft was increased in diameter. The journalist Edgar Duffield thought that the Crossley version 'seemed to lack some of the sting of the Molsheim production', but he did find it smoother and quieter. It was also cheaper, but Crossley did not persevere with the Bugatti for long. Production did not exceed 25 cars.

Meanwhile Letts had also looked westward in order to obtain a low-priced line of cars rather than make them themselves. Willys-Overland-Crossley Ltd was formed in 1920, and various models from the WILLYS range were assembled in a separate factory at Heaton Chapel, Manchester. Most were identical to their American counterparts, but the Overland 13.9hp used an 1802cc Morris Oxford

1936 Crossley Regis 10hp saloon.
NATIONAL MOTOR MUSEUM

1929 Crossley Canberra 20.9hp limousine.
NATIONAL MOTOR MUSEUM

engine in order to reduce the horsepower tax. Also made at Heaton Chapel was the Willys-based Manchester truck, and, from 1931 to 1933, the final A.J.S. cars. The factory was closed in 1933; never a success, it accounted for much of the £285,000 loss suffered by Crossley in 1926.

From 1923 to 1928 Crossley made a more popular-sized car, the 2388cc Fourteen. Distinguished by its flat radiator when the larger Crossleys had rounded ones, it was well-made but unexciting. The best *The Autocar* could say about it was that it was a sensible car. Nevertheless 5600 were made, compared with only 1100 of the 19.6. The 1925 Olympia Show saw a very important new model for Crossley; the 18/50 was the company's first 6-cylinder car, and the first to have ohvs. Capacity was 2692cc, enlarged to 3198cc in 1928 to cope with the heavy bodies which were sometimes inflicted on it. Crossley had their own body department, and only a few chassis were supplied to outside coachbuilders. The largest body on the Super Six was the Canberra limousine on a long wheelbase. A smaller companion six, the 1991cc 15.7hp, appeared in 1928, and this was built up to 1934. Like the 20/70 it was made in sporting form, called the Shelsley, with twin-carburettor engine which gave a top speed of 77mph (124km/h). The

engine was supplied to LAGONDA for their 16/80 from 1933 to 1935. The Shelsley, and indeed all the 2-litre Crossleys, were very well-made and long-lived. One example has covered well over 220,000 miles (354,000km) in the hands of the same owner since 1961.

From 1931 the 15.7 and 20.9hp Crossley Sixes had twin-top 4-speed gearboxes, and were known as Silver and Golden Crossleys. The long-wheelbase limousine was still known as the Canberra. The 15.7 was continued to 1934, the larger six, nominally, to 1937, although very few were made latterly. Bus manufacture was becoming increasingly important for Crossley, and on the car side an entry into the popular car field came with the Ten launched in 1932. This was the first Crossley to use a proprietary engine, a 1122cc F-head Coventry-Climax which was insufficiently powerful to cope with the heavy bodies provided, mostly 4-door saloons called Torquay or Buxton. For 1935 it was restyled by Charles Beauvais of Avon Coachwork. Called the Regis, it had a double dropped frame with more attractive lines but no improvement in performance. To rectify this Crossley added the Regis Six, which used the same chassis and body powered by a 1476cc six also by Coventry-Climax and similar to the unit supplied to TRIUMPH for their Gloria Six. About 2000 Tens were made and 600 Regis Sixes before Crossley decided to call it a day and concentrate on commercial vehicles. The last passenger cars were a handful of 3-litre sixes with Regis styling which may have been made as late as 1937, but were probably supplied only to directors of the firm.

A curious venture which cannot have helped the balance sheet was the Crossley-Burney of 1934. This was a BURNEY Streamline saloon with a 2-litre Crossley engine at the rear. They were made at Gorton to Burney designs, and apart from the Crossley radiator looked very like the cars that had been made at Maidenhead a few years earlier. They found little favour, and only 25 were made, but this is more than twice as many as Sir Dennistoun Burney had achieved.

Bus and trolleybus manufacture continued after World War II, in a new factory at Stockport, but a merger with A.E.C. in 1948 led to Crossleys becoming badge-engineered versions of the A.E.C., and production ended in 1956.
NG

Further Reading
Lost Causes of Motoring, Lord Montagu of Beaulieu, Cassell, London, 1960.

THE THREE-LITRE CROSSLEY

ALW 654

BY APPOINTMENT

BY APPOINTMENT

THE CROSSLEY has always been accepted as one of the world's finest cars, and the Three-Litre is the finest car even Crossley's have built.

The Three-Litre Crossley with self-changing, pre-selective gearbox is essentially modern in design and incorporates many new features all proven, all sound. This car is not merely a sports model. Certainly it has a superlative performance and attains an easy 75 m.p.h., accelerating with lightning smoothness. But more important still, it combines with its exceptional performance a luxurious comfort for passengers and driver. Riding in this Crossley is like riding on air.

The specification is worthy of a close study. A trial run can be easily arranged. The Three-Litre Crossley is a car to see now, a car to drive, a car to own.

1922 Crouch(ii) 2-seater.
NATIONAL MOTOR MUSEUM

1900 Crowden dog cart.
NATIONAL MOTOR MUSEUM

1917 Crow-Elkhart Model 33 cloverleaf roadster.
NICK BALDWIN

CROSVILLE (GB) 1906–1908

Crosville Motor Co. Ltd, Chester.

Crosville cars were designed by the Frenchman Georges Ville, who also made cars under his own name, and three of them were made in France by Morane of Paris. These were two tourers and a coupé de ville, with 20hp 4-cylinder engines. Only one car, a 50hp tourer with Hotchkiss-like round radiator, was made entirely in England. Crosville later became very successful bus and coach operators.

NG

CROUAN (F) 1897–1904

Sté des Moteurs et Automobiles Crouan, Paris.

The first Crouan had a rear-mounted 10hp 2-cylinder engine, but by 1900 two models were being made with several advanced features. They were a 5hp single-cylinder voiturette with automatic advance and retard of ignition, and a 16hp 2-cylinder car with similar automatic ignition and a 'pneumatic transmission'. The 1901 5hp had a small 'spyder' seat behind the front seats, and five forward speeds, although whether these were via a conventional sliding gearbox or a belt system is not certain. Five speeds were still advertised in 1903, when there were two models, a 6.5hp twin and 16hp four, both being front-mounted horizontally-opposed units.

NG

CROUCH (i) (US) 1894–1900

1894–1899 Pierce & Crouch, New Brighton, Pennsylvania.
1899–1900 Crouch Automobile Manufacturing & Transportation Co., New Brighton, Pennsylvania.

W. Lee Crouch built his first car in 1894, a simple 2-seater wire-wheeled runabout whose springs formed the side member of the frame, in the manner of the later curved dash Oldsmobile. Two years later he was commissioned by Dr Carlos C. Booth to make a car to take part in the New York City to Irvington, NY race organised by *Cosmopolitan* magazine. Called the Booth-Crouch, it had a 3hp single-cylinder engine and a heavier appearance than the 1894 car, due to its artillery wheels. It was unsuccessful in the race (as were most of the other competitors).

Crouch then announced his intention to make engines rather than complete cars, but he was back in the field in 1899 with a steam car powered by an 8hp V-twin engine, with a boiler providing superheated steam at a working pressure of 275psi.

NG

CROUCH (ii) (GB) 1912–1928

Crouch Cars Ltd, Coventry.

John Walter Fisher Crouch had experience with the Daimler and Deasy companies before setting up his own car making business in 1912. His first product was the Carette, a 3-wheeler powered by a 740cc V-twin engine of his own manufacture, mounted behind the seats. Practically the whole car was made in-house, including the armoured ash frame and metal panelled bodies. The cylinders were arranged fore and aft so the crankshaft was transverse, and drove via chain to a 3-speed gearbox, and thence by chain to the single rear wheel. Introduced in early 1912, it was joined by a 4-wheeled version in November, built on similar lines but with a larger engine of 906cc and a curious rear axle in which the shafts and the outer casing revolved together, being carried by ball bearings. Capacity went up again to 994cc in 1913 and to 1018cc in 1914.

The 4-wheeler was revived with little change after the war, engine capacity soon rising to 1115cc. For 1922 a completely new Crouch was announced. Called the 8/18, it had a 1248cc front-mounted engine, still a V-twin, shaft drive and a pressed-steel frame. The next step towards conformity came in November 1922 when a 1496cc 4-cylinder Anzani engine was featured on the 12/24 model. This was available with various 2- and 4-seater body styles, and was a well-built light car, although not cheap at £335 for a 2-seater and £395 for a pointed-tail sports car capable of 60mph (96km/h). Production was running at 15 cars per week in 1925, by which time the 2-cylinder models had been dropped. London sales were handled by Alfred Moss, father of Stirling, who had a number of successes at Brooklands. A cheaper model was the 10, powered by a 1196cc Dorman engine, of which about 60 were made in 1923 and 1924. Two body styles were offered, the Economic 4-seater at £225 and Climatic 2-seater at £235. The last Crouch was the 11/27, with 1368cc Coventry Climax engine, and available as a saloon in addition to open models. It was made alongside the 12/30 until manufacture ended in 1928. There was nothing wrong with the Crouch, but, as Calcott, Calthorpe, Clyno and others were to find out, competition from the major manufacturers was too great. Approximate production figures were 800 for the 12/30 and 100 for the 11/27. In all, about 2500 Crouches were made. John Crouch returned to Daimler where he had started out, joined by his son who worked on the postwar DB18 models, and became director of bus sales in the 1960s.

NG

Further Reading
'Quickly off the Mark – the Crouch', M. Worthington-Williams, *The Automobile*, September 1984.

CROW (i); CROW-ELKHART (US) 1911–1925
1911–1916 Crow Motor Car, Elkhart, Indiana.
1916–1923 Crow-Elkhart Motor Car Co, Elkhart, Indiana.
1923–1925 Century Motor Co, Elkhart, Indiana.
The Crow was acontinuation of the Black Crow under a new name, and during 1911 the name was changed again to Crow-Elkhart. It was a very conventional design, made in various sizes of 4-cylinder engines from 20 to 40hp, with two sizes of 6-cylinder model being added in 1913. Most of the engines were bought from outside suppliers, which included Atlas, Gray, Herschell-Spillman, Lycoming, and Rutenber. However an in-house ohv four was offered in 1918. Most Crow-Elkharts wre fairly plain in appearance, with artillery wheels, but the 1917/18 Model 33 cloverleaf roadster was an attractive design, with wire wheels and a vee radiator.

The Elkhart factory had a capacity of 30 cars per day, but never made anything like that number, the peak year was 1917 when 3800 cars were made. Some cars were supplied to BUSH of Detroit to sell under their own name. The Crow family were eased out of the business in 1919, but the new owners could not help sliding sales. Crow-Elkhart was in receivership in early 1922, and in 1923 were taken over by a subsidiary, Century Motors, which made the Morriss-London for export to England. The last official year of production for Crow-Elkhart was 1923, when 236 cars were made, but a few more may have been assembled from parts on hand up to 1925. The last models had 3153cc 4-cylinder Lycoming or 4078cc 6-cylinder Herschell-Spillman engines.

NG

CROW (ii) *see* CANADIAN CROW

CROWDEN (GB) 1898–1901
Charles T. Crowden, Leamington Spa, Warwickshire.
Charles Crowden had been works manager of the Great Horseless Carriage Company in Coventry. His own vehicles were largely experimental, and none was produced commercially, although he did sell a few fire engines which were conversions of horse-drawn appliances to steam power. His cars included a steam brake and a 10hp petrol-engined dog-cart, which he built to test the merits of the two power systems. In 1900 he built another petrol car, with 5hp single-cylinder horizontal engine and three speeds by belt and pulley drive. This car still exists in the Museum of British Road Transport at Coventry. He supplied a steam fire engine to the Norwich Union Fire Insurance Co. at Worcester, and a petrol-engined engine to his local fire brigade at Leamington Spa in 1902. After 1904 Crowden retired to Ramsgate, Kent.

NG

CROWDUS (US) 1899–1902
Crowdus Automobile Co., Chicago, Illinois.
Introduced at the end of 1899, the Crowdus was a simple electric runabout with tubular frame and wooden wheels. Steering was by tiller, which also controlled acceleration and braking. The Crowdus Automobile Co. was not incorporated until 1901, and a year later the make was dead, despite the promise of a car which would cover 100 miles on one charge.

NG

CROWDY (GB) 1909–1912
1909–1911 Crowdy Ltd, London.
1911–1912 Crowdy Ltd, Northfield, Birmingham.
A.E. Crowdy had been Wolseley's sales manager for Lancashire, and in October 1909 he acquired the assets of the WEIGEL Motor Co. whose premises were in Olaf Street, just off Latimer Road, North Kensington. He showed three cars at the Olympia Show a month after his purchase. These were two conventional cars of

1910 Crowdy 20/30hp enclosed landaulet.
NATIONAL MOTOR MUSEUM

Weigel design with 4-cylinder engines of 20/30 and 30/40hp, and the third with a 12/14hp Hewitt piston-valve engine (also used on the DAVY which shared a stand with Crowdy) and dashboard radiator. He also listed a 29.4hp six with Hewitt engine. The Weigel-type cars, which may have been Weigels renamed, had front-mounted radiators. Crowdy offered a 3-year guarantee, and availability of parts for five years. Sadly, the company did not last that long.

The same range was listed for 1912, but in the autumn of 1911 Crowdy had moved to Northfield, near Birmingham, where he rented a former roller skating rink. As Trevor Picken, author of *The Story of Hampton Cars*, wrote 'Surely Crowdy must have been the only British car manufacturer to build his cars on a surface of maple wood which rested on a layer of felt supported upon a seasoned pine base'.

Despite these delights, the company went into receivership in February 1912, and it is not certain how many cars were made at Northfield. The new owners used Crowdy Ltd to take over a private venture which used the name Hampton Engineering Co. In February 1913, they launched the first of the HAMPTON cars.

NG

Further Reading
The Story of Hampton Cars, Trevor Picken, Hampton Cars, 1997.

CROWN (i) (GB) 1903
Crown Car Co. Ltd, London.
This company made, or possibly only sold, a very light 3-wheeler with 5hp engine mounted over the single front wheel. It weighed only 224 lbs, and sold for the very modest price of £80.

NG

CROWN (ii) (US) 1905–1907
Detroit Auto Vehicle Co., Detroit, Michigan.
This Crown was offered in two models of passenger car, as well as a delivery van. The cars had 12hp 2-cylinder or 24hp 4-cylinder engines, with bodies being 2-seater runabout or 4-seater tourer. Transmission was by friction discs on the runabout and epicyclic gears on the tourer, with final drive being by shaft on both models. In 1906 a new 2-cylinder car, of 22/24hp, whose engine was designed by ex-Cadillac engineer Edward T. Ross, appeared. His car was sometimes called the Detroit, to distance it from the Crowns which apparently did not have a good reputation. The whole of the 1907 production was bought by John North Willys, but the Detroit Auto Vehicle Co. closed down at the end of the year.

NG

CROWN (iii) (US) 1908–1910
Crown Motor Vehicle Co., Amesbury, Massachusetts.
This was a typical high-wheeler with horizontally-opposed 2-cylinder engine and chain drive. It was made for the Crown Motor Vehicle Co. by Graves & Congdon, who took over complete control after Crown's president W.A. Shafer resigned in 1910. The last models were sometimes known as Graves & Congdons.

NG

c.1920 Crown Magnetic tourer.
NATIONAL MOTOR MUSEUM

1904 Croxted 8/10hp 2-seater.
NICK BALDWIN

1910 Croxton-Keeton French 30 Suburban tourer.
NICK BALDWIN

CROWN (iv) **(US)** 1913–1914

Crown Motor Car Co., Louisville, Kentucky.
The fourth make to bear the Crown name was a cyclecar powered by a 1.7-litre 4-cylinder engine, with friction transmission and shaft drive. It was made by members of the Lambert family, at least one of whom, B.F. Lambert, had been involved with the Buckeye Manufacturing Co., makers of the LAMBERT. This survived for 12 years, but the Crown's lifespan scarcely covered two years. The Lamberts moved to New Albany, Indiana, where they made the even shorter-lived HERCULES (iii).
NG

CROWN ENSIGN *see* BRITISH ENSIGN

CROWN MAGNETIC (US/GB) 1920

Owen Magnetic Automobile Co., Wilkes-Barre, Pennsylvania.
The Crown Magnetic was an attempt to market a rebadged version of the OWEN MAGNETIC automobile in Britain. In 1920, exporter J.L. Crown ordered 500 Owen Magnetic chassis to be shipped to England, where they would be offered for sale through LeGrice Elers Ltd, of London, with coachwork to customer order. As with the Owen Magnetic, the most noteworthy feature was the Entz electro-magnetic transmission. As Owen Magnetic was unable to fulfill the order, very few, perhaps around 20, Crown Magnetics were ever completed. Crown later collaborated with Ensign Motors Ltd in the CROWN-ENSIGN, another application of the Entz transmission.
KF

CROWTHER; CROWTHER-DURYEA (US) 1915–1917

1915–1916 Crowther Motor Co., Philadelphia, Pennsylvania.
1916–1917 Crowther-Duryea Motor Co., Rochester, New York.
The Crowther was a light car with 23hp 4-cylinder engine, sold by Henry Crowther and made for him by the Cresson-Morris Co. of Philadelphia. It used Charles E. Duryea's patent transmission by twin grooved rollers which engaged with the rims of the rear wheels. Cresson-Morris were also making the DURYEA (ii) cyclecar; in 1916 Henry Crowther engaged Charles Duryea to work for him. Production of the cyclecar came to an end and the Crowther became the Crowther-Duryea, although it only lasted for a year. Early in 1917 it was announced that 100 cars were being assembled; these were probably the only Crowther-Duryeas to be made.
NG

CROXTED (GB) 1904–1905

Croxted Motor & Engineering Co. Ltd, Herne Hill, London.
Croxted's first car was a 2-seater with 8hp 2-cylinder Aster engine and shaft drive. It was of conventional design, and *The Automotor Journal* observed 'The chassis does not differ materially from others of the live axle type. . .'. It had a De Dion-type bonnet with the radiator below it. For 1905 two 4-cylinder cars were made, of 14 and 20hp, with conventionally-placed honeycomb radiators.
NG

CROXTON; CROXTON-KEETON (US) 1909–1914

1909–1910 Croxton-Keeton Motor Co., Massilon, Ohio.
1910–1911 Croxton Motor Co., Cleveland, Ohio.
1912–1914 Croxton Motor Co., Washington, Pennsylvania.
Herbert A. Croxton (1872–1940) and Forrest M. Keeton (1874–1944) both had motor industry experience when they joined forces in 1909. Croxton had built the JEWEL (i) and Keeton had been associated with the POPE-TOLEDO and DE LUXE cars. They built two lines of car under the Croxton-Keeton name, the 'German' and the 'French'. The former, based on the Jewel, had a Rutenber engine and frontal radiator, and derived its name from a resemblance to the Mercedes, while the 'French' had a Renault-type dashboard radiator and all seating between the axles. Neither was made under the Croxton-Keeton name for long, as the partners quarrelled in the summer of 1910, and Keeton moved to Detroit to make a car bearing his name alone. Croxton continued the line at Cleveland, calling them the German 40 and 48 and the French 30 and 38.

Although the 'French' cars were smaller, there was little difference in price, and indeed the 'French Taxi' was the most expensive of the 1911 Croxtons, at $3300. In March 1911 Croxton merged with another Cleveland firm, ROYAL TOURIST, but the merger lasted only for a few months. The two ranges were continued in 1912, when a 44hp French Six was added.

Croxton built a new factory at Washington, Pennsylvania, but few cars were built there, and all production ended early in 1914. The factory was used briefly for the manufacture of the UNIVERSAL (i) light car.
NG

C.R.S. (GB) 1960–1961

C.R.S. Auto Engineers Ltd, Footscray, Kent.
Rather like L.M.B., this company offered a box-section chassis for various proprietary fibreglass shells, usually the E.B. Debonair. Ford E93A parts were used.
CR

1952 C.S.C. sports car.
NATIONAL MOTOR MUSEUM

CRUISER (US) 1917–1919

Cruiser Motor Car Co., Madison, Wisconsin.

The Cruiser was more of an experiment than a viable motor car which, with the exception of its novelty approach, was the typical assembled automobile of its time, manufactured practically 'from the ground up' of standard, proven components by various companies specialising in various fields such as engines, wheels, frames, radiators, etc. It was only available as a roadster and touring car and the roadster took the spotlight in making the Cruiser different from all others with its Special Camping model, which targeted its market toward would-be campers or those anticipating lengthy trips into rural areas or sparsely settled places. Toward this end the Special Camping Roadster was ambitious in its equipment which included seats transformable into beds, chairs, ice-box, tent, stove and a spartan array of cooking utensils. Nor was that all. The car also offered a rudimentary water closet operated by portable plumbing with hot and cold running water, the water held in four large storage compartments, two on each running board. Prices were $1075 for both the unadorned roadster and touring car plus $100 for the roadster's camping extras. It may have been ahead of its time as it failed to attract buyers, although as it was wartime, several of the camping roadsters were tested by the US Army. Although production continued following the Armistice, the Cruiser failed to capture public fancy and production ended in the early fall of 1919.

KM

CRUSADER (US) 1914–1915

Crusader Motor Car Co., Joliet, Illinois.

This light car was a refinement of the DAYTON (iii) cyclecar, using the same 18hp 4-cylinder engine of the last Dayton, but with a 3-speed gearbox and shaft drive. A price was never fixed, and probably only pilot models of the Crusader were made.

NG

CRYPTO (GB) 1904–1905

Crypto Engineering Co., London.

This company assembled a small number of cars using a 2-cylinder Tony Huber engine in a Dupressoir chassis.

NG

CRYSTAL CITY (US) 1914

Troll & Manning (Corning Motor Car Co.), Corning, New York.

Raymond Troll and Charles Manning built a cyclecar which they named Crystal City after the name given to their town because it was the home of the famous Corning glass company. Their car had an 18hp 4-cylinder Farmer engine with conventional 3-speed gearbox and shaft drive. Their 'factory' was located in a small garage, and the planned output of 25 cars in 1914 may never have been achieved. In the summer of that year they styled themselves the Corning Motor Car Co.

NG

CS+2 *see* STIMSON

C.S.A. *see* MOSS

C.S.C. (GB) 1952–1955

Wrigley Motors (Gainsborough Engineering Co. Ltd), Middleton, Manchester.

The aerodynamic C.S.C. sports car never really passed the prototype stage but was well thought-out. Its tubular chassis had all-independent suspension by wishbones and transverse leaf springs. The engine fitted to the prototype was a 647cc B.S.A. vertical twin motorcycle unit, driving through a B.S.A. 4-speed gearbox to the rear wheels via chain. Production cars were to have 750cc Royal Enfield engines with Albion 3-speed transmissions, and the top speed was quoted at 75mph (120km/h). By 1955 C.S.C. had developed a chassis for Austin A30 components, fitted with a Rochdale fibreglass body.

CR

CSONKA (H) 1899–1912

János Csonka, Budapest.

János (John) Csonka was a pioneer among Hungarian car builders. His clever solutions (he co-invented the carburettor) and skills had a great impact on early Hungarian motoring.

He was born in 1852 to a rural blacksmith family. His father taught him the necessary skills, but the young Csonka wanted to learn more, so he moved to Budapest where he was employed by the Hungarian Railways. Then he wandered through Europe where, among other things he studied internal combustion engines.

c.1920 Cubitt 16/20hp tourer.
NATIONAL MOTOR MUSEUM

1925 Cubitt Model K 16/20hp 2-seater.
NATIONAL MOTOR MUSEUM

On his return, he applied for a workshop foreman job at the Budapest Technical University, which he duly got. In that workshop he created the first Hungarian-made internal combustion engine and other stationary engines. His work attracted the attention of one of the biggest Hungarian heavy industrial companies, Ganz. Ganz patented Csonka's inventions internationally, but they failed to do so in the case of the carburettor which Csonka and one of his colleagues Donát Bánki created during the spring of 1893.

In 1900 the Hungarian Post decided to equip some of their postmen with motorised tricycles. Two of these were designed by Csonka and built by Ganz. Five years later Csonka designed the winning proposals for postal vans which were built by RABA and RÖCK.

Small series of these postal vans, some of them were equipped with limousine bodies, were made in the following years. These vehicles were the first Hungarian-designed and built cars.

After a few one-off passenger cars constructed to special orders, Csonka turned his attention to small cars. In 1909 he introduced his first model, which was the first Hungarian-built car equipped with a cardan shaft. It was powered by a 1-cylinder 4bhp engine, and some of them were still in use 25 years later!

In 1911 Csonka introduced a 8bhp water-cooled small car. The most interesting feature was the block construction: the engine, gearbox, transmission and brakes formed one unit. 14 were made, 12 were bought by the Post, one formed the basis of the MAG small cars, and the last one was bought by a local doctor.

A year later big industrial companies which wanted to enter into the automotive manufacturing business but feared Csonka's talent, insisted that he either remain at the University and focus on teaching or set up his own company to make cars. Csonka remained at the University and that spelled the end of his car-making activities. In 1924 he retired and set up his own firm where he built stationary engines. He died in 1939.

PN

C.T.D. (P) 1989–1990
Journalist José Calema founded C.T.D. to make a very small monocoque plastic economy car, in collaboration with a group of disabled people. The prototype used a 1.8bhp Zündapp engine.
CR

CTX (US)
CTX Motorcars Inc., Brenham, Texas.
The AC Cobra came in for yet another clone job by this company. Starting with a body and chassis from EVERETT-MORRISON, CTX added their own custom irs based on Corvette pieces. Engines were usually Ford, ranging from a turbocharged SVO 4-cylinder to a 460in (11,675mm) V8. All were sold in fully assembled form.
HP

CUB (i) (US) 1914
Szekely Cyclecar Co., Richmond, Virginia.
This was a typical cyclecar powered by a De Luxe air-cooled V-twin engine, with tubular frame and belt drive. It was built by two graduates of the University of Berlin who were recent immigrants to the United States, Otto Szekely and Charles Berthal.
NG

CUB (ii) see ANDERSEN

CUBITT (GB) 1919–1925
Cubitt's Engineering Co. Ltd, Aylesbury, Buckinghamshire.
The Cubitt car was made by a subsidiary of Holland, Hannen & Cubitt Ltd, the famous builders founded by Thomas Cubitt in 1815. They were responsible for much of the housing in Bloomsbury and Belgravia, as well as for Osborne House in the Isle of Wight, and the new east wing of Buckingham Palace. By the time they built the Cenotaph in Whitehall in 1920, their subsidiary was already engaged in car production. They aimed to make an American-type car in large numbers, and chose a 2815cc 4-cylinder side-valve engine of monobloc construction, with detachable cylinder head. The massive gearbox was mounted separately from the engine and had the un-American feature of right-hand change. The rear axle was also massively-built, with overhead worm drive. This contributed to the car's high build which led to rolling on corners. Bodywork, initially tourers only, but later 2-seaters and saloons were offered, came from a factory across the road which had formerly housed the IRIS company.

Cubitt sales never reached the anticipated 100 per week, peaking at about 60 in 1921, although this figure was not maintained for long. The price had risen from £298 at its announcement in April 1919 to £442 in mid-1920, and the high appearance and rolling gait did not endear it to many customers. However, the Cubitt found some favour in Australia, where its high ground clearance was appreciated.

In 1922 S.F. Edge, the famous ex-NAPIER publicist and now managing director of A.C., took control of Cubitt. One result of this was that engines of Anzani design were made by Cubitt for A.C., and also some bodies. Edge brought in J.S. Napier (no connection with the car-building Napier company) from ARROL-JOHNSTON to redesign the car. He made no drastic changes, retaining the same engine and gearbox but using an underslung worm-drive rear axle, and replacing the cantilever rear springs with long semi-elliptics. Aluminium pistons and lighter connecting rods helped performance and the cars looked lower and more attractive. However, the price went up to £475 for a tourer, and sales continued to fall. For 1925 the Cubitt was restyled again, the Model K having a squared-off radiator in place of the previous rounded radiator, and prices were dropped to £335, although there was also an L4 with open-drive limousine or landaulette coachwork at £500–525. Cubitt went into voluntary liquidation in 1925 after about 3000 cars had been made. Four are known to survive in England, and several more in Australia.
NG

Further Reading
'Built by Builders – the Cubitt', M. Worthington-Williams, *The Automobile*, October 1987.

CUBSTER (US) 1949

Osborn Wheel Co., Doylestown, Pennsylvania.

This early kit car was powered by a 6.6hp engine with a chain drive.

HP

CUDELL (D) 1898–1908

1898–1900 Cudell & Co., Motorenfahrzeugfabrik, Aachen.

1900–1902 AG für Motor und Fahrzeugbau vorm. Cudell & Co., Aachen.

1902–1905 Cudell Motor Compagnie GmbH, Aachen.

1905–1908 Cudell Motoren-Gesellschaft GmbH, Berlin.

This company began by making De Dion-Bouton tricycles under licence, followed by the 3.5hp De Dion voiturette. Max Cudell made further models of De Dion type up to 1904 when he brought out completely new cars designed by Karl Slevogt. The 4-cylinder engine was an advanced design with 5-bearing crankshaft and ohvs. At least two sizes were made, a 16/20PS and a 35/40PS, the latter with a capacity of 6100cc. The Berlin branch, headed by Paul Cudell, made very few cars. In later years the company made motor boat engines and also the Cudell carburettor.

HON

CULEBRA (US) c.1991–1995

Culebra International Ltd, San Luis Obispo, California.

This kit car company made two models. The Corvette Culebra adapted Ferrari Testarossa-style side strakes, nose and tail to the 1984 and up Corvette. The Diavalo was a Ferrari F-40 replica based on the Pontiac Fiero chassis. There were two versions of the Diavalo, the most expensive of which required lowering the roof line and laying the windshield back at a steeper angle. Sold in kit and assembled form.

HP

CULMEN (F) c.1909

Sté des Moteurs à Gaz et d'Industrie Automobiles Otto, Paris.

Culmen was the name given to a range of cars made by the company which also made F.L. and OTTO cars. Three models were offered, one with a 9hp 1125cc single-cylinder engine of Otto manufacture, and two fours by Chapuis-Dornier, the 1460cc 8hp and 1725cc 10hp. The 9hp was considerably cheaper than the others, at 2500 francs for the chassis, compared with 3750 and 3950 francs for the fours. They all had 3-speed gearboxes, shaft drive, and an identical wheelbase of 88.5in (2246mm). Three body styles were offered, open 2- and 4-seaters, and a coupé.

KB

CULVER (i) (US) 1905

Practical Automobile Corp., Aurora, Illinois.

Designed by Dr D.D. Culver as the ideal car for a physician, this turned out to be a conventional high-wheeler powered by a 6hp 2-cylinder engine, epicyclic transmission, and double-chain drive. The steering column tilted for ease of entry, useful for a doctor making frequent house calls. Culver never managed to get his car into production.

NG

CULVER (ii) (US) 1916–1917

Culver Manufacturing Co., Culver City, California.

This was a very light 2-seater built for youngsters, and powered by a 4hp single-cylinder engine made by Culver Manufacturing Co. It was priced at $225.

NG

CUMBERFORD (US) c.1966; 1981–1984

Cumberford, Stamford, Connecticut and Austin, Texas.

In 1966 stylist Robert Cumberford and writer Barney Clark produced a one-off Ford Mustang with a station wagon body built in Italy by Frank Reisner. This was intended to be followed by volume sales, but no more were built. In 1981 Cumberford brought out the Cumberford Martinique, a retro-styled roadster he built with his brother James. It had a BMW 3200cc 6-cylinder engine and a cast aluminium chassis. The 1930s-styled body was aluminium with Kevlar mudguards trimmed in mahogany veneer. When it was announced in 1982, the expected price was to be in the $125,000 range. However, financing fell through

1899 Cudell De Dion 3hp *vis-à-vis*.
NATIONAL MOTOR MUSEUM

1914 Cumbria cyclecar.
GOWAN COULTHARD

and the project was moved to Texas while the search for another backer continued. Although Robert Cumberford continued development of the Martinique, only a few cars were completed.

HP

CUMBRIA (GB) 1913–1914

Cumbria Motors Ltd, Cockermouth, Cumberland.

The only known car maker in the county of Cumberland (although the Pratchitt steam wagon was made at Carlisle), the Cumbria was unusual in being offered as a single-seater, or monocar, in addition to the familiar 2-seater cyclecar form. The monocar was powered by a 6/8hp air-cooled V-twin J.A.P. engine with belt final drive, while the 2-seater had an 8/10hp engine, also by J.A.P., and chain drive. In 1914 there was also an 8.3hp 4-cylinder light car with shaft drive.

NG

CUMMIKAR *see* RONTEIX

CUNDALL (GB) 1902

R. Cundall & Sons Ltd, Shipley, Yorkshire.

Cundall were known as makers of stationary oil engines, and in January 1902 they announced a car powered by one of their 2-cylinder horizontal engines. It developed 7bhp at 850rpm. The number made is uncertain, but the Cundall car did not survive into 1903.

NG

CUNNINGHAM (i) (US) 1907–1936

James Cunningham Son & Co. Inc., Rochester, New York.

The venerable firm of James Cunningham Son & Co. was founded in 1838 and by 1900 was regarded as a manufacturer of carriages, buggies, sleighs and cutters. It was about this time that the company experimented with self-propelled vehicles by building an experimental electric car. No further prototypes followed in this regard until 1907 when, after building three more experimental electric-powered runabouts, plans were drawn up for a range of petrol-powered automobiles, the first of these appearing in 1910, hard on the heels of a petrol-powered

1915 Cunningham (i) Model S limousine.
NICK BALDWIN

c.1927 Cunningham (i) Series V-6 tourer.
KEITH MARVIN

1929 Cunningham (i) Series V-7 town car.
KEITH MARVIN

funeral car, the first of a complete range of hearses and ambulances for which Cunningham would be renowned. The first Cunninghams were fitted with both 4- and 6-cylinder engines by Buffalo and Continental, but shortly an in-house 4-cylinder engine replaced them, this developing 40bhp. Production was small and the 4-cylinder engine was used through 1914. For 1916 a Cunningham 8-cylinder engine developing 100bhp at 2400rpm was introduced on a longer chassis and the 4-cylinder power plant was discontinued. By this time Cunningham ambulances and funeral cars were unashamedly built along luxurious lines and high performances with prices to match and the decision was made to concentrate exclusively on the V8-engined 'V' series which would be continued for the remainder of passenger car production. By 1920 the car had reached the pinnacle of its development, tailored to an affluent clientele with a chassis price of $4800 and standard coachwork priced as high as $9000 and, with custom treatment, as high as $12,000. The company built the cars a few at a time, constantly improving the basic V8 power plant and listing the succeeding series as V-1 to V-9 at the end of the company's production, rather than dating the cars. The company had ended its carriage building in 1915 and

instead of marketing the product through distributors and dealers, sold the passenger cars through hospital officials and funeral directors who were using Cunningham ambulances and hearses. The Cunningham occupied an exclusive niche in the luxury car market and much of its success was due to repeat orders by its customers. The car was generally regarded as a car of quiet elegance and its advertising was limited to the more exclusive and conservative periodicals.

At the peak of its production, an annual figure of 375 units overall has been noted, 185 being passenger cars, the remainder being relegated to the ambulance and funeral car customers, the cars being available on both 132in (3350mm) and 142in (3553mm) chassis.

The last Cunningham automobiles were completed in 1931 but sales extended into 1933, the cars marketed during 1932 and 1933 being regarded as models for those years. The Cunningham chassis was last used for funeral coaches in 1934 and for 1935 the company produced a limited number of town car bodies for Ford V8 chassis, similar to the Brewster-Fords of the same period. Funeral car coachwork for 1935 and 1936 saw these bodies mated to Oldsmobile, Packard, and Cadillac chassis, production being concluded during the latter year although the town car Ford ended in 1937.

KM

Further Reading
'Cunninghams for the Carriage Trade', *Automobile Quarterly*, Vol.III, No.4.

CUNNINGHAM (ii) (US) 1951–1956

B.S. Cunningham Co., West Palm Beach, Florida.

Although principally known for his racing cars, Briggs Cunningham's small company also built America's first great postwar sports car. They had to build 25 street cars to be considered a manufacturer so they could enter LeMans, and this presented quite a problem for a small 35-person organisation. Their first car, the C-1, was a dual-purpose street-and-race car with a Cadillac V8 and a 3-speed transmission. It had a 105in (2665mm) wheelbase and a heavy frame with Ford-based front suspension and a De Dion system in the rear. The sole C-1 was a prototype for the C-2R race cars that followed, which used Chrysler Hemi V8s but were otherwise the same. The C-1 was used on the street and as a practice car for the racing team. The next street car was the C-3, which was intended for street use only. The first one was bodied in Florida and looked like a C-2 with a fixed hard-top, but it was too expensive to build so it remained a one-off. Production C-3s had a 107in (2715mm) wheelbase and were fitted with stylish convertible or coupé bodies in Italy by Vignale. They looked like large versions of the bodies Vignale was making for Ferraris of that period. The C-3 used a standard 225hp Chrysler Hemi with automatic or 3-speed manual transmissions, although full-race 310hp engines were optional. Weight was a hefty 3500lb (1591kg) and rear suspension was by a live axle. At $10,000, the C-3 was the most expensive American car of the time, and only 26 chassis were built. When Cunningham shut down, there were a number of chassis still at Vignale awaiting their bodies. These were sold bare and bodied by later owners in a variety of styles.

HP

Further Reading
'Briggs Cunningham and the Cars he built', Eric Nielssen, *Automobile Quarterly*, Vol. II, No.4.

CUNNINGHAM (iii) (US) 1997 to date

The Cunningham Company, Lime Rock, Connecticut.

The 1952 Cunningham C-4R had been a very successful racing car, and this company built a replica of it. Financing was from Briggs Cunningham III, son of the man who built the originals. They were pretty accurate reproductions, with aluminium bodies, 5430cc Chrysler 'hemis' and a very high price tag. Buyers could stay original or opt for more modern running gear. They were only sold in fully assembled form.

HP

CUPELLE *see* LACOSTE et BATTMANN

CURSOR (GB) 1985–1987

Replicar Ltd, Dunkirk, Faversham, Kent.

Alan Hatswell's REPLICAR, purveyors of kit-form replicas of Bugattis, Jaguars and Ferraris, launched its 'revolutionary micro vehicle' under the Cursor name

1952 Cunningham (ii) Vignale coupé.
NATIONAL MOTOR MUSEUM

in 1985. Designed as fun transport for 16-year olds who were not yet permitted to drive cars, it was an odd-looking single-seater 3-wheeler coupé described as a 'GT hatchback convertible'. It had a fibreglass body with a canvas roof on a tubular steel chassis and a mid-mounted 49cc Suzuki CS50 moped engine. A top speed of 30mph was offset by a fuel consumption of about 90mpg. After about 50 had been made, a 2-seater version followed with a more powerful Suzuki CP50 engine and gull-wing doors fitted. The final ten or so of the 50 2-seaters built had Honda Vision moped engines. Most of the later models were exported to Austria. The project was sold on to a firm in Belgium, but production there apparently never began.

CR

CURTANA see AVALON

CURTIS (US) 1920–1921
Curtis Motor Car Co., Little Rock, Arkansas.
The Curtis automobile was the result of a 'vision' by former Little Rock Mayor Charles E. Taylor that there was no reason why a good car could not be manufactured in the South, thus avoiding the unnecessary expenses of shipping, taxes, etc. And if the idea had been a logical one, Little Rock would have been home to another car besides the already established CLIMBER. In any event, the idea was far over-extended before a Curtis could be completed, calling for both 6- and 4-cylinder cars, trucks, tractors, and a window on the export market. Where the few completed Curtis cars were built is uncertain, but almost assuredly not in Little Rock. Although plans for a factory there were announced, no factory appeared. Most of the completed cars were 6-cylinder touring models with a Continental 7R engine and disc wheels, otherwise similar to numerous other cars of the period. The four was powered by a Herschell-Spillman Model 700 power plant and differed from the six in its wheels which were of the artillery wood type. Shortly before Christmas 1920, a large advertisement appeared in the local press with the headlines 'Twenty-Five Curtis Automobiles for Christmas Presents', the following copy announcing the cars could be bought on a first-come-first-served basis for $1690 or $400 off the list price of the six. The reason for this discount did not appear in the advertisement, although it appears to have been a nice way of saying that the Curtis enterprise was closing down. The number

c.1985 Pre-Cursor.
REPLICAR

c.1986 Cursor P-Type
REPLICAR

359

1922 C.W.S. (i) 3-wheeler.
NICK BALDWIN

of cars bearing the Curtis badge has never been determined. Automobile Industries claimed 30; other sources anywhere between 45 to 60. Doubtlessly a number of Little Rockers found a Curtis under their Christmas trees. Where the cars were assembled remains a mystery.

KM

CURTIS-WRIGHT (US) 1958–1984
Curtis-Wright, Wood Ridge, New Jersey.
Although aircraft were the primary concern at Curtis-Wright, they also dabbled in ground transportation. In 1959 they experimented with a hover car, but their major accomplishment was the development of the first American rotary engine for automotive use. They designed the engine in 1958 after seeing an experimental rotary on a visit to NSU, from whom they later took out the licence for American rotary production. Their first prototype was built in 1958, a single-rotor design of 984cc. By 1962 they had developed it sufficiently for Chrysler to show interest and they installed one into a Dodge Dart. Ford tried one in a Galaxy, but both declined to proceed. In 1965 a twin-rotor, 185hp version was installed in a new Mustang, but it failed to arouse interest and the rotary programme was sold to John Deere in 1984.

HP

CURTISS (US) 1920–1921
Curtiss Motor Car Co., Hammondsport, New York.
The Curtiss was one of several aero-engined cars to be made in the United States just after World War I, others including the PRADO and the WHARTON. They all used the 90hp Curtiss OX-5 V8 engine, which in the Curtiss' case was made by the man who commissioned the cars, Glenn Hammond Curtiss. The engine was modifed for road use by Charlie Kirkham, chief engineer of the Curtiss Aeroplane & Motor Co., and the chassis was provided by Miles Harold Carpenter who made the PHIANNA. The number of Curtiss cars which were made is a mystery; possibly no more than one, a 2-seater roadster with dickey, although drawings exist of a dual-cowl tourer. The Curtiss Motor Car Co. was casually organised, and whatever cars were made were supplied to Curtiss' friends rather than seriously marketed.

NG

CUSTER (US) 1920–c.1960
Custer Specialty Co., Dayton, Ohio.
L. Luzern Custer made a series of miniature electric vehicles which could be driven by children, or adults for promotional and circus use. The Cootie was a child's car which sold for $95 in the early 1920s. One was used on the stage by the British comedian Lupino Lane, and was also licensed for road use. Other Custer products included the Cabbie, a miniature railway locomotive, the Chair, a 3-wheeled invalid car, the Carrier, a factory truck, and the Coupé, an attractive-looking coupé with electric lighting which could have been used on the road if the driver was prepared to put up with a maximum speed of 8mph (13km/h). After the war Custer made invalid cars and also a buckboard which could be powered by petrol or electricity.

NG

CUSTOCA (A) 1970–1986
1970–1974 Custoca Kunstoffkarosserien, Leoben.
1974–1986 Custoca Fiberglass Austria, Kraubath.
This Austrian glassfibre specialist was formed by Gerhard Holler and was ideally placed to manufacture beach buggies (under the name Amigo). Its other main product was the Strato, a car that was nominally inspired by the Lamborghini Marzal concept car – in shape only, it must be said, for underneath the glassfibre body lay a VW Beetle chassis and rear-mounted engine. This model was licence-produced in Switzerland as the ALBAR Jet, and an updated version was marketed as the Taifun. Also produced was the Hurrycane, a Ford GT40-inspired coupé designed to fit on to a Volkswagen Beetle floorpan. W or VW-Porsche engines could be fitted.

CR

CUSTOM CLASSICS (US) c.1981
Custom Classics, Bellflower, California.
The Karma I was a modified version of the KELMARK kit car. The doors were improved and a removable bonnet was incorporated at the front. This kit was later passed on to MAGNUM.

HP

CUSTOM CLOUD (US) c.1976
Custom Cloud Motors, Miami, Florida.
The 1973–76 Chevrolet Monte Carlo received a facelift from this kit car company in the form of pseudo-Rolls-Royce grill and trim, complete with 'Spirit of Ecstasy' bonnet ornament.

HP

CUSTOM COACHCRAFT (US) 1996 to date
Custom Coachcraft, Aledo, Texas.
This small kit car company made a replica of the Ferrari 308 that fitted on a Pontiac Fiero chassis.

HP

CUSTOM DESIGN ASSOCIATES (US) c.1984–c.1990
Custom Design Associates, Tacoma, Washington.
Ford Pintos were the donor car of preference for this kit car company. By sectioning the Pinto unit body, rewelding it back together and attaching fibreglass body panels, they created a vague replica of a Ferrari 308 GTB. The 508 GTF model used a Ford V8, while the 286 GTF relied on 2800cc Ford V6 power. They were available in kit or assembled form. Custom Design Associates also installed Pinto engines into Lotus Europas.

HP

CUSTOM LIMITED EDITIONS (US) c.1984
Custom Limited Editions Inc., Fort Worth, Texas.
This 427 Cobra replica was only available in fully assembled form. It was based on the STALLION kit and used a sturdy rectangular steel frame with the buyer's choice of big Ford V8 engines. Prices started at $55,000 in 1984.

HP

CUSTOM TRIKES BY STIRES (US) c.1985
Custom Trikes by Stires, Garden Grove, California.
Custom motorcycles were converted into open fibreglass-bodied 3-wheelers by this California company. The conversions retained the motorcycle front suspension but featured a wide 2-wheeled arrangement at the rear with Volkswagen Beetle engines and transaxles. Models included the Scorpion, Stallion, Stinger and Streak.

HP

CUSTOMOTIVE see CHIMO

CUTTING (US) 1909–1913
1909–1913 Clarke-Carter Automobile Co., Jackson, Michigan.
1913 Cutting Motor Car Co., Jackson, Michigan.
The Cutting was designed by Charles Cutting who had previously been responsible for the C.V.I., and was made in the same factory. It was a product of the Clarke-Carter Co., which is sometimes listed erroneously as a make in its own right.

Cuttings were well-built conventional cars powered by 32, 35, 40 or 60hp 4-cylinder engines by Milwaukee, Model or Wisconsin. Clarke-Carter was under-capitalised from the start, and was reorganised as the Cutting Motor Car Co. in 1913, but it was too late to save the firm. Only one model was listed for that year, a 40hp, and the company was sold up in October 1913.

NG

CV SHAPECRAFT *see* BIRCHFIELD and SHAPECRAFT

CVC *see* BEDOUIN

C.V.I. (US) 1908

C.V.I. Motor Car Co., Jackson, Michigan.

Designed by Charles Cutting, this car's name was sometimes rendered C.VI for Cutting Six, as it used a 40hp 6-cylinder engine. It was a conventional car made as a 5- or 7-seater tourer or 3/4-seater runabout, all priced at $4000. Output for 1908 was planned to be 50 cars, but it is not known if this figure was reached. Certainly the company did not last into 1909 when Cutting was involved with the 4-cylinder car that bore his own name and was made in the C.V.I. factory.

NG

C.V.R. (F) 1906–1907

Automobiles C.V.R., Boulogne-sur-Seine.

This company was formerly based at Neuilly and called Couverchel. As C.V.R. they made a wide variety of cars from a 12/16hp four to a 40/50hp six. All had shaft drive and 4-speed gearboxes, and Mutel, Peugeot or Tony Huber engines were generally used.

NG

C.W.S. (i) (GB) 1922

Co-operative Wholesale Society, Tyseley, Birmingham.

This 3-wheeler was a short-lived product of the Co-op whose other motor interests included Federal and Federation motorcycles made in the same factory from 1931 to 1937, and BELL (i) cars and commercial vehicles made in Manchester. The C.W.S. was powered by an 8hp J.A.P. V-twin engine, with Juckes 3-speed gearbox and chain drive to the single rear wheel. It was expensive at £150 (plus £3.15s (£3.75) for a hood), and production lasted only one season.

NG

C.W.S. (ii) (PL) 1925–1930

1925–1927 Centralny Zaklady Inzynierii, Warsaw.
1927–1930 Panstwowe Central Engineering, Warsaw.

The CZInz (Central Engineering Works) was set up by the Polish Army in 1918 as a manufacturing and service establishment. Part of it was called the CWS (Central Auto Works) intended for the major overhaul of military vehicles. In 1920 16 armoured Ford Model Ts were made there. In 1922 the CWS' director Captain Kazimierz Meyer decided to begin car production, and engaged Tadeusz Tanski as chief engineer. His design incorporated a 45bhp 2985cc ohv 4-cylinder engine, which was tested in 1923, and a complete car was ready by 1925. This had 4-wheel brakes and semi-elliptic springs all round. It was possible to disassemble (and assemble) the car using one spanner and a screwdriver. Production did not start until 1927, when it was called the T1. Open and closed bodies were made but most T1 chassis received van bodies for the Post Office or ambulances for the Red Cross. About 800 had been built when production ended in 1930.

In the same year the T8 was built with 2964cc side-valve straight-8 engine developing 80bhp. Only three prototypes were made, with 4-seater tourer, 2-seater roadster and faux-cabriolet bodies. They were followed by the T2, a 1500cc 4-cylinder derivative of the T8, but the world economic crisis put an end to production plans and to the whole CWS project.

RP

CYBERTECH (GB) 1992–1993

Cybertech Ltd, Birmingham.

The Predator was standard Lamborghini Countach replica fodder, offered in 200 (standard) and 250 (Anniversary) bodystyles.

CR

CYCLAUTO (F) 1919–1923

Sté Française du Cyclauto, Suresnes, Seine.

This 3-wheeler with single front wheel first appeared with a 496cc 2-cylinder 2-stroke engine with 2-speed epicyclic transmission and belt drive to the rear axle. It was made as a single seater on a 72in (1850mm) wheelbase, or as a 2-seater on a 77in (1950mm) wheelbase. For 1922 the 2-cylinder engine gave way to a 950cc single-ohc 4-cylinder C.I.M.E. engine, the wheelbase was lengthened to 92.5in (2350mm), and there was a conventional 3-speed gearbox and shaft drive. The engine was water-cooled and the front wheel was mounted ahead of the radiator. Apart from the 3-wheeled layout, it was more of a light car than a cyclecar but it could not compete against genuine light cars such as the Citroën 5CV.

NG

CYCLECARETTE *see* MONET-GOYON

CYCLEPLANE (US) 1914

The Cycleplane Co., Westerly, Rhode Island.

The Cycleplane was a product of the brief cyclecar fad in the United States, which lasted only for a year. The car's 'manufacturer' was Arthur W. Ball, MD, of Westerly, Rhode Island, whose wife registered the name as a trademark on 3 March 1914. The car was announced in *Cyclecar Age* that August. It was a tandem 2-seater, powered by a Spacke V-twin air-cooled engine. A planetary gearbox transmitted power to the rear wheels via the customary cyclecar belt drive. Suspension was by an inventive 'truss bridge frame', which used semi-elliptic springs as the upper and lower members. High, flat 'aeroplane mudguards' were said to act as shock absorbers! A single, small door was provided on the right side. The car's slogan, 'It rides over the dust', says much about the roads of the time.

A 4-cylinder water-cooled shaft-drive model, with selective gearbox, was advertised at $450; the V-twin Deluxe model was to sell at $400, and an entry-level $350 roadster was announced. Apparently, only one Deluxe model was ever built.

Dr Ball left the auto business at the end of August 1914, selling the rights to the car to a Mr Chrystie McConnell. That also appears to be the end of the Cycleplane.

KF

Further Reading
'The Cycleplane: A Short Flight of Fancy', Kit Foster,
Upper Hudson Valley Automobilist, July 1987.

CYCLOMOBILE (US) 1920

Cyclomobile Manufacturing Co., Toledo, Ohio.

Originally planned as a single seater, the Cyclomobile was widened to accommodate two passengers when it went into production. It was powered by a 13hp V-twin air-cooled Spacke engine, driving through friction transmission and chain drive. This was typical cyclecar specification, in fact, although the cyclecar boom had evaporated five years earlier. Nevertheless 206 cars were sold in 1920, followed by 181 in 1921. Production that year included a longer wheelbase version known as the Manexall. This name was a contraction of Manufacturers' & Exporters' Alliance Inc., a New York City firm set up to handle worldwide sales of the Cyclomobile. Probably some of the shorter Cyclomobiles were also sold under the Manexall name. The company merged with SUN (iv) in February 1922.

NG

CYCLOPE *see* AUGE

CYGNET (GB) 1982–1985

1982–1984 Cygnet Cars Ltd, Kislingbury, Northamptonshire.
1984–1985 Cygnet Cars Ltd, Wootton, Northamptonshire.

Quite why anyone bought a Cygnet Monaco kit is a mystery but quite a few were sold. This Ford Cortina-based 4-seater coupé was hideously styled (it had an upward-sloping front end and a concave roof) and completely disregarded any sense of quality. The Aston Martin-style grill alluded to the instigator's background at Newport Pagnell. A traditional-style roadster was also shown in 1983, but was stillborn.

CR

1905 Cyklon Cyklonette 3-wheeler.
NATIONAL MOTOR MUSEUM

1929 Cyklon 9/40PS saloon.
NATIONAL MOTOR MUSEUM

CYKLON (D) 1902–1929

1902–1922 Cyklon Maschinenfabrik GmbH, Berlin.
1922–1929 Cyklon Automobilwerke AG, Berlin-Charlottenburg; Mylau.
Cyklon began by making an unconventional motorcycle with the engine mounted over the front wheel, and followed this with a 3-wheeler called the Cyklonette using the same principle. The 450cc 3.5PS single-cylinder engine drove the wheel by chain, and the car was tiller-steered. A 2-cylinder engine of 1290cc and 10PS

soon followed, and the extra power allowed for 4-seater bodies and delivery vans. A landaulet was as popular as a taxi. They were of similar appearance to their rival, the PHÄNOMOBIL, and were made with little change up to 1922, although passenger cars made up a shrinking proportion of the output.

In 1919 Cyklon became part of Jacob Schapiro's combine, and in 1922 they turned to 4-wheeled cars called Cyklon rather than Cyklonette. The first was the 4-cylinder 1.3-litre 5/20PS with 2-seater coachwork, which was built for, and marketed by, Schapiro's associated company, Schebera. It was followed in 1926 by the 2350cc 6-cylinder 9/40PS, which was identical to the 9/40PS made by DIXI, which was also a member of the Schapiro group. They were made in saloon and tourer versions, and lasted until 1929 when Dixi went over to licence production of the Austin Seven, which in turn became the first BMW. The last cars to carry the Cyklon name were a small series of the 1.8-litre Typ D, built under licence from DONNET-ZEDEL.
HON

C.Y. PRODUCTIONS (US) c.1997 to date

Clint Young Productions, Costa Mesa, California.
This company dealt in movie and television series memorabilia. They built a replica of the Batmobile used in the 1960s *Batman* television series, and sold copies of it in assembled or kit form.
HP

CYRANO (F) 1899–1900

The original Cyrano voiturette was powered by a single-cylinder horizontal engine. This gave way in 1900 to a 2-cylinder unit, with belt-and-pulley transmission and final drive by spur gears to the rear axle. Bodies were a 2-seater or a 4-seater *vis-à-vis*.
NG

D.A. (GB) 1993

David Arthur, Warrington, Cheshire.

The D.A. Mongoose was only ever shown in prototype chassis form as a 3-wheeler designed for various engines from small diesels up to Honda CBR motorbike units. There were two seats in tandem and a single rear wheel. Intended kits never materialised.

CR

D.A.C. (US) 1922–1923

Detroit Air-Cooled Car Co., Detroit, Michigan.

The D.A.C. was debuted with the display of a touring car at the Detroit Automobile Show early in 1922 and elaborate plans were made for a sizeable annual production. The first D.A.C. cars were produced in Detroit, but a new factory was secured at Wayne, Michigan with production of more than 100 additional units before the company failed. The attractive air-cooled 6-cylinder cars were produced in both open and closed models.

KM

DACIA (RO) 1968 to date

Automobiles Dacia, Pitesti.

COMECON allowed Rumania to become a car-making country in the 1960s. As was often the case, foreign input was needed because designing locally would have taken too much time. The search for the licence for a middle-range family car started, and RENAULT, PEUGEOT, FIAT, ALFA ROMEO, and AUSTIN offered their models. In the end the Renault 12 was chosen. It was an innovative step, because the car was just a prototype back then, so Rumania was able to market a contemporary and modern design. As the contract was signed in 1966 and the 12 was slated for production in France three years later, another Renault, the 8, was chosen for the intervening years. The assembly plant was completed in Pitesti in the summer of 1968 and duly started production of the Dacia 1100 as it was called. Dacia was the name of the region when it belonged to the Roman Empire. The first one was offered to President Ceausescu himself. Every component of the 1100 arrived from France, and production lasted for three years.

Meanwhile, in 1969, the new Renault 12-based Dacia, called the 1300, entered the Rumanian market. Step by step the proportion of locally-made components increased. An estate version was added in 1973 and later a pick-up. For the elite a small number of Renault 20 models, known as the Dacia 2000 were also assembled.

The first update of the 1300 occurred in 1979 with new headlight treatment, modified interior and a new name, the 1310. Four years later two new engine variants joined the range: a 1.2-litre and a 1.4-litre. During the 1980s there was a short run of Dacia Sport models with coupé coachwork.

In the middle of the 1980s Russian designers created a light city car to be produced by Lada and Kamaz in a joint venture. Dacia also showed interest and started to produce the car under the name 500 Lastun in its Timisoara plant. It had a short life.

It seemed that the Renault 12-based Dacias would never be replaced, but times changed in Rumania as well. In 1996 a self-designed, boxy family car, the Nova, was introduced. It was powered by a 1.6-litre, 72bhp engine, and was, and continues to be, the sole product of the Pitesti Motor Works. In 1998 Dacia made an agreement with the Korean Hyundai, to assemble the Accent as part of a joint venture.

There were many stories about Dacia cars – they were built by prisoners, there was no quality control at all, etc. – but the facts were that it took years for someone to finally be permitted to get a Dacia and their quality was shameful. They looked like half-assembled kit-cars, gearboxes jammed in any gear at any time, doors refused to open, windows rolled down by themselves, and so on. Although owners were able to take their new cars to a repair service right away to sort them out, not everything could be foreseen, and that is one of the reasons Dacia will not be the most popular car in Eastern Europe for many years to come.

The Avo utility was sold in some Western markets as the Dacia Duster.

PN

DAEWOO (ROK) 1967 to date

Daewoo Motor Co., Seoul and Taegu.

The second most important Korean car maker (after HYUNDAI), Daewoo was founded by Woo-Choong Kim, who was still the company's chairman in 1998.

1989 Dacia Duster GL 4×4 utility.
DACIA CONCESSIONAIRES

1990 Dacia Demen 5-door estate.
DACIA CONCESSIONAIRES

1994 Daewoo Nexia saloon.
NATIONAL MOTOR MUSEUM

1997 Daewoo Lanos SX 5-door hatchback.
DAEWOO

1998 Daewoo Matiz hatchback.
DAEWOO

1999 Daewoo Korando 4×4.
DAEWOO

2000 Daewoo Nubira CDX estate.
DAEWOO

A clothing and textile company, Daewoo entered car manufacture by making various General Motors cars under licence and using their own names. These included the Maepsy-Na (Isuzu Gemini), Le Mans (Opel Kadett), which was sold in the US as the Pontiac Le Mans, Royale (Opel Rekord), and Royale Super Saloon (Opel Senator). In 1992 Daewoo severed its connection with GM, establishing instead a co-operation agreement with Honda. The range was extended to include the 800cc Tico, based on the Suzuki Alto, and the Arcadia (Honda Legend) while the Senator-based car was renamed Brougham Super Saloon.

Daewoo entered the European market in 1994 with the Nexia (named Cielo on the home market), and Espero, the former still Opel-derived, although restyled by IAD, the latter a Vectra-based Bertone-styled 4-door saloon with 1498cc 16-valve twin-cam or 1998cc single-ohc 8-valve 4-cylinder engines. Two new models which were the first to be conceived entirely by Daewoo, the Lanos and the Nubira were introduced in 1997. The former was made in 3- and 5-door hatchback form as well as a 4-door saloon, and used the single-cam 1498cc engine shared with the Nexia. The Nubira was slightly larger and made

in 4- and 5-door saloon form and as an estate car. Both had bold front ends which distinguished them from earlier Daewoos, and from other rivals.

For 1998 Daewoo extended the range at both ends. The new small car was the Matiz, a city car in the Fiat Seicento/Hyundai Atoz class, styled by Giugiaro and powered by a 796cc 3-cylinder engine. With a 5-door body, it offered many features associated with larger cars, such as power steering, electric windows and central locking. At the other end of the range was the Leganza, a 5-seater saloon using a 133bhp twin-cam 1998cc engine which was also available in the Nubira in 1998. An even larger saloon, between a BMW 5 and 7 Series in length, and with Daewoo's first 6-cylinder engine, was promised for 2000.

In January 1998 Daewoo took over another Korean car maker, SSANG YONG, which provided them with two new models not in the existing Daewoo line-up. These were the Musso range of 4x4 vehicles, and the Mercedes-Benz-based Chairman saloon, which would be a stop-gap luxury car until the arrival of the new six in 2000. Because of the downturn in the Korean economy, Daewoo renewed its links with General Motors in 1998, the American giant taking 50 per cent of Daewoo's capital. Daewoo had several manufacturing links with foreign countries. These included India, where Daewoo Motor India made the Matiz and Cielo, Romania, Egypt, Iran, Uzbekistan, Ukraine, and Poland where five models were made in the FSO factory, bought by Daewoo in 1997. These were the Tico, Lanos, Nubira, Espero and Leganza. The Romanian operation began in 1994 with manufacture of the Nexia, followed by the Tico and Espero. In 1999 these were replaced by the Matiz, Lanos and Nubira. These are sold under the name RODAE (ROmanian DAEwoo). Worldwide production of Daewoo cars in 1998 was 904,556 although cars represent a fairly small proportion of the conglomerate's activities. These include electronics, armaments, railways, ship building, clothing, hotels, property and financial services. In 1997 the Daewoo Group became the 18th largest company in the world. In the spring of 2000 Daewoo joined the ranks of the small MPVs with the Tacuma (Rezzo on the home market). A rival to the Renault Scenic, it offered a choice of 1.6- or 2-litre twin-ohc petrol or 1.9-litre diesel engines. Only 171in (4350mm) long, it seated five passengers with ample luggage space.
NG

D.A.F. (NL) 1958–1976
1958–1971 Van Doorne's Automobielfabriek N.V., Eindhoven.
1972–1976 DAF Car B.V., Born.
After the demise in 1925 of the first Dutch car manufacturer, the Spyker, the DAF car was on display at the Amsterdam exhibition, RAI for the first time in 1958. The firm made commercial trailers from 1928 and military 4×4 in 1940. After World War II they started to make commercial vehicles (1950). The DAF car went into production in 1959. It was produced with a step-free Variomatic-transmission, a fully automatic system using a centrifugal clutch and V-belt drive with a limited-slip differential. Power came from a front-mounted 600cc ohv air-cooled 22bhp flat-twin. All wheels had independent suspension.

With only a forward-and-reverse lever, the DAF was one of the easiest cars to drive of its time. After the introduction of the 750 and the Daffodil with the 30bhp engine in 1962 it looked bigger and, together with a higher top speed of 64mph (103km/h), it became more attractive for younger people. 20,000 a year were made at Eindhoven. They even used the automatic transmission in a light military 4×4 and a Formula 3 racing car. DAF won, along with the team prize in the 1966 Marathon de la Route, a number of other rally successes. In 1967 the basic model was still in production, but was joined by the bigger type 44, styled by Michelotti. It was a more powerful model with a 40bhp 844cc engine with a top speed of 75mph (120km/h). A year later the Type 55 with the 4-cylinder Renault engine went into production, followed by a charming sports coupé version. The fastest DAF listed in 1972 was the 63bhp Marathon 55 coupé with a 1440cc twin dual-choke carburettor engine giving 115mph (185km/h).

A De Dion back axle was fixed to the type 66, which replaced the 55 in 1972, but still with the Renault engine and a new centrifugal clutch incorporated in the Variomatic.

The same year VOLVO (i) took 33 per cent of the shares and the name of the firm became DAF Car B.V. The DAF dealers also got the facilities to sell Volvo cars. After taking 75 per cent of the shares in 1974 only the DAF 66 stayed in production; shortly thereafter the name was changed to the Volvo 66. The DAF-prototype 77 never came on the market. Volvo took the construction plans, improved them, and took it into production as the Volvo 343.
FBV

DAGMAR (US) 1922–1927

1922–1924 Crawford Automobile Co., Hagerstown, Maryland.

1924–1927 M.P. Möller Car Co., Hagerstown, Maryland.

One of the most distinguished sporting cars in the United States in its time, the Dagmar first appeared in 1922 as a 4-seater victoria speedster. The car featured straight-line or 'military' wings and all-brass trim instead of the then-conventional nickel. The cars were in fact standard Crawfords in modern dress, enhanced by wheel covers placed over the Crawford wooden-spoked ones. Named for the daughter of M. P. Möller, a Hagerstown pipe organ manufacturer, who had purchased the Crawford Automobile Company in 1905, the Dagmar was an instant hit with the affluent sporting crowd of its time and with such demand that the Crawford was discontinued, the factory gearing up for exclusive production. Powered by a 6-cylinder Continental 6T engine, additional closed and open body styles were added for 1923 and a year later conventional wings and nickel trim became available as options. Dagmar cars of the sporting type could be ordered in exotic colours, including, among others, orchid, lavender, pink, sky-blue, and eggshell white. By 1925 a smaller Dagmar was placed on the market, powered by a less powerful Continental engine. The smaller model 6-60 was devoid of the flash which sold the larger 6-70 (and later 6-80) Dagmars. The final year of Dagmar production was 1926, but the factory continued selling the cars with 1927 as the cut-off date. In that year an enormous 7-seater sedan was built for Mr Möller and his family for a trip to his native Denmark. Some 500 of the large Dagmars were built during their six years of existence, compared to relatively few of the smaller line. A number of the large sporting Dagmars remained unsold by 1927 and were available to the public as new cars through 1934 at increasingly lower prices annually. Möller also manufactured several brands of taxicab, the Elysee truck and prototypes for the Standish car of 1925, as well as custom body building and conversions.

KM

DAGONET (F) 1952–1958

Ateliers Jean Dagonet, Faverolles.

Dagonet's speciality was the production of modified Citroën 2CVs, all with drastically lowered bodywork. Year by year the bodywork would be changed, notably gaining an oval grill in a single-piece front end. Dagonets were also campaigned in motorsport. In 1956 a plastic-bodied coupé was presented under the name DF, again based on the 2CV, featuring a panoramic windscreen, but production did not begin. Jean Dagonet transferred his business to U.M.A.P.

CR

DAGSA (E) 1954–1955

Defensa Anti-Gas SA, La Granja.

This was a very simple light car, equivalent to the Citroën 2CV, with simple seats for four passengers, a folding fabric roof and four doors, with a 500cc 4-cylinder engine of German licence at the front. It was announced in 1955 for a price little more than a motorcycle. Defensa Anti-Gas was a specialist in military equipment such as anti-gas masks.

VCM

DAIHATSU (J) 1954 to date

1954–1974 Daihatsu Kogyo Kabushika Kaisha, Osaka; Ikeda.

1974 to date Daihatsu Motor Co. Ltd, Osaka; Ikeda.

The Daihatsu company was founded in 1907 to manufacture internal-combustion engines, under the name Osaka Hatsudoki Seizo Kabushiki Kaisha (Osaka Motor Manufacturing Co. Ltd). Its first vehicles appeared in 1930, and small 3-wheeled delivery trucks sold under the names Daihatsu or Tsubasa. In 1951 the company name was changed to Daihatsu Kogyo Kabushiki Kaisha, and during the 1950s and 1960s it produced a wide range of 3-wheeled commercial vehicles which enjoyed valuable tax concessions.

The first Daihatsu passenger car appeared in 1954. Called the Bee, it was a 3-wheeler with single front wheel, derived from a Daihatsu commercial chassis and powered by a 250cc 13.5hp V-twin engine. Despite having only a 2-door saloon body, the Bee became popular as a taxicab, for Japanese regulations authorised a charge of 60 yen per mile for a 3-wheeler compared with 100 yen per mile for a 4-wheeled cab. The Bee was made for a few years, after which Daihatsu concentrated on commercial vehicles until 1962, when it launched its first 4-wheeled car. Called the 700, it had a 678cc 4-cylinder engine which developed 30bhp and gave the

1966 DAF Daffodil Deluxe saloon.
NATIONAL MOTOR MUSEUM

1971 DAF 55 Marathon coupé.
NATIONAL MOTOR MUSEUM

1922 Dagmar sport victoria.
KEITH MARVIN

1926 Dagmar 6-60 roadster.
KEITH MARVIN

1964 Daihatsu Compagno Berlina saloon.
NATIONAL MOTOR MUSEUM

1973 Daihatsu Fellow Max GHL coupé.
NATIONAL MOTOR MUSEUM

1982 Daihatsu Domino saloon.
DAIHATSU

had been made. Three years earlier Daihatsu had entered the under 360cc K-class minicar field. This was an important sector of the Japanese market, accounting for 23.4 per cent of all domestic passenger car sales. Other companies which catered to this class included Honda, Mitsubishi and Subaru, so Toyota was obviously glad to get a foothold as well. The little Daihatsu was called the Fellow; it was a 4-seater saloon with all-independent suspension and a 356cc 2-cylinder 2-stroke engine. This developed 33bhp, but by 1972 there was a tuned version giving 40bhp. It was now called the Fellow Max, and was available as a saloon, hard-top coupé, and estate car. There was also a forward-control estate car and van which was the ancestor of the Daihatsu van so popular today.

The one millionth Daihatsu vehicle was delivered in 1971, a year after the company had opened a new factory at Tada. In 1973–74 two more factories, at Kyoto and Shiga, came into use. During the 1970s some larger models were made and these were based on Toyota models, the 1166cc Consorte (1973–75), a thinly-disguised Toyota Corolla, and 1407cc Charmant (1974–1986). A more individual vehicle was Daihatsu's first 4-wheel drive vehicle, the Jeep-like Taft of 1975, which had a 958cc 4-cylinder engine. This became an important part of the Daihatsu range, which is continued today in the Fourtrak.

Up to the mid–1970s the name Daihatsu meant little outside Japan, but in 1977 came a car which quickly made an impact on world markets. The Charade hatchback was powered by a 993cc 3-cylinder transverse engine driving the front-wheels. In its original form the 5-door hatchback had a speed of 82mph (133km/h), but the turbocharged version introduced in 1984 could exceed 100mph (160km/h). The Charade was voted Japanese Car of the Year in 1978, and in 1982 won a survey to find the most popular vehicle among Australian motorists. The Charade was the basis for several electric cars, including one built to order for the Australian distributor. This used the standard 5-door body shell and was powered by an 18.8bhp compound motor fed by eight 12-volt batteries housed at the rear. A Charade engine was used in the 1982 Charmant Hybrid, an experimental car in which the petrol engine generated electricity to be stored in batteries for town use. In 1982 the Charade engine became available in the De Tomaso-built INNOCENTI Mini, and a year later was standardised in these cars. In exchange De Tomaso provided know-how and equipment for the Charade De Tomaso Turbo of 1984, a hot 3-door hatchback with front air dam, side skirts, Campagnolo alloy wheels and a Momo steering wheel.

Meanwhile the Fellow Max had grown to 547cc by 1977 and a year later was replaced by the Cuore with restyled body and front-wheel drive. Sold on export markets as the Domino, it was soon available as a 3-door hatchback or 4-door saloon, and in Japan could be had with 4-wheel drive and a turbocharger. The latter gave 41bhp from 547cc, and was the smallest turbocharged car in the world. In 1986 the Cuore became a 5-door hatchback and the engine was enlarged to 846cc and 3 cylinders, although the 547cc unit was still available for the home market. It was joined for 1987 by the Leeza, a 2+2 coupé on a shorter wheelbase, whose 547cc engine gave 64bhp when turbocharged. This was the maximum power allowed by the Japanese government for sub-550cc minicars. In 1983 the Charade gained a wider variety of engines, including a diesel, and a 99bhp 12-valve turbo. Bodies were restyled in 1987, and in 1988 the Charade range was expanded to a 1295cc 4-cylinder car with saloon body and 4 × 4 option. The Charmant was dropped in 1986, by which time it had 1407 and 1587cc Toyota-built engines, and three years later came another mid-sized Daihatsu saloon, the 1587cc Applause. Unlike its predecessor it had front-wheel drive, and was still made in 1999.

The 4 × 4 off-roaders, which began with the tiny Taft in 1975, grew in size and variety. A 2530cc diesel engine came in 1978 to supplement the 1587cc petrol unit, and was enlarged to 2739cc in 1982. In 1984 came the Fourtrak with restyled body, 5-speed gearbox and a choice of 1988cc petrol or 2765cc diesel engines. Known in some markets as Rocky or Rugger, the Fourtrak was also sold under the name Toyota Blizzard. From 1998, it was available with the diesel engine only. A junior version of the Fourtrak was the Feroza, with 1598cc petrol engine, made from 1988 until 1997 when it was replaced by the Terios, a 5-door 4 × 4 with 1296cc engine.

The Charade was continued through 1999 with a restyling in 1993, but still the same 1295cc 4-cylinder engines, supplemented by 1499cc and 16-valve 1590cc units, and a choice of 3- or 5-door hatchback and 4-door saloon bodies. In contrast, the minicar line saw many changes and variants. The Cuore/Domino, which was also sold as the Mira, had a high-performance model in the Avanzato, which combined 0-62mph (100km/h) acceleration in under 9 seconds

2-door saloon a top speed of 68mph (110km/h). The following year the range was extended with the appearance of the 797cc Compagno, made as a saloon, estate or sports car. By 1966 the most powerful Compagno had a fuel-injection 65bhp 958cc engine and front disc brakes. In that year the Compagno became the first Japanese car to be sold on the British market, although this venture did not last beyond 1970, and regular imports of the make were not resumed until 1979.

In 1966 Toyota acquired a 34.5 per cent holding in Daihatsu, and this led to a change of models. As the Compagno was similar to the smaller 4-cylinder Toyotas there was no room for it, and production ended in 1970 after about 120,000

and a top speed of 120mph (190km/h) with luxury features such as electric windows, air-conditioning, power steering, and automatic windscreen wipers. The engine was a 659cc 3-cylinder unit, as the limit had been raised, but power was still governed to 64bhp. The performance figures quoted were for the ungoverned engine, which was permitted outside Japan. Other variants included the more rounded Opti 3-door and Classic 5-door hatchbacks and the Atrai luxury minibus based on the Hi–Jet. These were officially sold only in Japan, but they could be obtained in Europe as personal imports. A variant which was part of the regular export range was the Move, a high-roof short-bonneted 5-door hatchback which was virtually a new class of car. A rival was Suzuki's Wagon R. The Move had a 42bhp 847cc 3-cylinder engine, though the 64bhp turbo-charged 659cc was available in Japan. Also restricted to the Japanese market was an electric version of the Move. A larger and more conventional-looking estate car was the 1499 or 1590cc Grand Move.

A new model in 1998, slotting in between the Cuore and the Charade, was the Sirion, a 4-door saloon powered by an all-new 989cc 12-valve 3-cylinder engine giving 54bhp. Transmission was by a 5-speed manual or 4-speed automatic gearbox. For 1999 the Sirion's engine was used in a slightly enlarged Cuore and in a restyled Move.

In September 1998 Toyota increased their holding in Daihatsu from 34.5 per cent to over 50 per cent, effectively taking over the smaller firm. A possible result was that the Sirion might carry a Toyota badge. Daihatsu was small only by Japanese standards; with their 1998 production of 550,088 they beat Audi, Rover and Volvo. They also have production facilities, joint venture arrangements or technical agreements in Vietnam, China, Malaysia, Indonesia, Philippines, Thailand, and Italy. Some of these agreements, such as that in Italy, concern commercial vehicles only. Licence production of the Terios was due to start in Taiwan early in 1999.

Two new models were announced at the 1999 Frankfurt Show, an ultra frugal Sirion with a 3-cylinder direct-injection diesel engine consuming only 3 litres of fuel per 100km, and the NCX-2, an all-new Mini-MPV powered by a 1.3-litre 16-valve petrol engine. A further two models were also announced at the Tokyo Show the same year. The Kopen was a miniature sports car powered by a 660cc twin-cam 16-valve turbocharged 4-cylinder engine, mounted transversely at the front, and driving the front wheels via a 4-speed automatic gearbox. It was unusual in having a central driving position. The other model was the Naked, a high-roof 4-door saloon powered by a 660cc 12-valve 3-cylinder engine in two forms: normally aspirated, giving 56bhp, and turbocharged, giving 61bhp.

NG

DAIMLER (i) (D) 1886–1901

1886–1890 Gottlieb Daimler, Bad Cannstatt.
1890–1901 Daimler Motoren Gesellschaft, Bad Cannstatt.
Gottlieb Daimler (1834–1900) had worked for various engineering companies, including W.G. Whitworth (later Armstrong-Whitworth) before he joined the Deutz Gas Engine Works as technical director in 1872. He had already met Wilhelm Maybach (1846–1929) who became the chief engineer at Deutz. After disagreements with Gustav Otto of Deutz, he and Maybach moved to Cannstatt, where they developed a series of single-cylinder petrol engines. These were used to power a motorcycle (the world's first), a motor boat and, in 1886, a motorcar. Unlike the purpose-built chassis of Carl Benz, Daimler used a horse-drawn carriage with strengthened frame. The vertical engine had a capacity of 462cc and developed 1.1bhp at 600rpm. Ignition was by hot tube and transmission by pulley from the engine to a countershaft on which there were pinions which meshed with sprockets on the rear wheels. The carriage had four seats, but the rear seat passengers would have had their leg room severely restricted by the engine, which projected through the floorboards.

Daimler had his first trials with the car in the late summer of 1886, but did not follow it up with another for three years, as he was more interested in applying his engine to different modes of transport. However Maybach persuaded him to build a vehicle designed from the start as a motorcar. The 1889 car had a V-twin engine of 565cc developing 1.5hp and a tubular-steel frame with steel wheels, both supplied by NSU. It was known as the Stahlradwagen (steel wheel car), and was shown at the 1889 Paris World's Fair. The basic design of the engine was manufactured in France by Panhard et Levassor and used in the first Panhard and Peugeot cars. It is possible that two Stahlradwagens were made, but certainly no more.

1986 Daihatsu Domino hatchback.
NATIONAL MOTOR MUSEUM

1989 Daihatsu Charade Turbo hatchback.
DAIHATSU

1996 Daihatsu Cuore TR-XX Avanzato R4 hatchback.
DAIHATSU

1998 Daihatsu Terios 4x4 estate car.
DAIHATSU

1893 Daimler(i) Schroedterwagen 1.8PS 2-seater.
NATIONAL MOTOR MUSEUM

NICK BALDWIN

DAIMLER, GOTTLIEB (1834–1900)

Gottlieb Daimler lived and worked about 60 miles from Karl Benz, yet so far as is known they did not know each other and were not aware of each other's plans. Daimler was born in Schorndorf, a small town in Württemberg, where his father Johannes was a baker, a trade which the family had followed for four generations. The family name was originally Teimbler or Teumler, later Daumler, then Daimler. Johannes planned a career in the civil service for his son, but the revolutions which took place in several European countries in 1848 persuaded him that arms were going to be in great

demand. He therefore apprenticed him to a gunsmith. On completing his apprenticeship in 1852, Gottlieb attended the regional technical school, followed by two years in Stuttgart after which he went to work at a firm making railway carriages and, later, locomotives, at Grafenstaden in French Alsace. In 1856, at the age of 22, he was offered the position of foreman, but, believing that he lacked the necessary theoretical training, he put in two years' study at the Stuttgart Polytechnic before returning to Grafenstaden. Even as early as 1860 Daimler was unimpressed with the steam engine and when his request to work on alternative systems was turned down, he left Grafenstaden. He visited Paris to look at Lenoir's gas-fuelled internal-combustion engine, then spent the years 1862–63 in England, where he worked for, among others, W.G. Whitworth in Coventry, later part of Armstrong-Whitworth. Returning to Germany in 1863, he took a job managing the machine works at the Bruderhaus at Reutlingen, a Lutheran school for orphans and abandoned youngsters. One of the Bruderhaus pupils was Wilhelm Maybach, who was to become Daimler's right-hand man later on.

Daimler stayed at the Bruderhaus for six and a half years, longer than he had been with any other organisation, then moved to the Maschinenbau Gesellschaft Karlsruhe, at Karlsruhe, where Karl Benz had worked three years earlier. He took Maybach with him and, in 1872, both left Karlsruhe to join the Gasmotorenfabrik Deutz, run by Nikolaus August Otto and Eugen Langen. He became technical director, and held this post until July 1882. Otto perfected the 4-stroke engine in 1876, but it was Daimler and Maybach who prepared it for production, which began towards the end of that year. Daimler wanted it called the Deutz engine, as he said it was a joint effort, but Otto insisted on his own name when the design was patented in August 1877.

The 4-stroke was a great improvement on the 2-stroke engine, but it was still a large unit, and depended on a supply of town gas to power it. Daimler dreamed of a small, self-contained engine which could be powered by a

The Daimler Motoren Gesellschaft was founded in 1890 with finance from the Württembergischen Bank with two directors, Max Duttenhofer and Wilhelm Lorenz. Both were munitions makers and favoured a cautious policy of making low-speed stationary engines which sold well. Daimler and Maybach, however, were interested in the challenge of a high-speed engine which could be used in cars. In the autumn of 1892 they moved into the conservatory of the empty Hotel Hermann in Cannstatt where they continued their experiments. The most important work there was Maybach's invention of the atomising, or spray, carburettor. Probably no complete cars emerged from the Hotel Hermann, although one source claims that 12 cars were made there during 1893–95. Certainly a few cars were made by the 'official' Daimler company. Designed by Max Schroedter, they had vertical-twin engines, at first of 760cc but later of 1060cc, chain final drive and tubular frames, again by NSU. No more than 12 were made (some sources quote 19) up to 1895 when Daimler and Maybach were reconciled with the company and production began of a new design called the Riemenwagen (belt car) from the belt drive. Five sizes of engine were offered, all vertical twins, from 760 to 2190cc. Several bodies were available, a *vis-à-vis* and a victoria in which the driver sat over the rear axle, and a landau and cabriolet with the driver over the front axle. About 150 Riemenwagen were made during 1895–97, when they gave way to the Phoenix. This was the first to have a front-mounted engine, with 4-speed gearbox and chain final drive. The standard engines were a 1060cc 4hp 2-cylinder and 1845cc 6hp 4-cylinder, but more powerful models were made for competitions, including a 5.5-litre 24hp 4-cylinder driven by Emil Jellinek, Barons Arthur and Henri de Rothschild and Wilhelm Bauer. The latter was killed at the wheel of one in the Nice hill climb in March 1900, making it clear to Jellinek that this short-wheelbase, high car was not suitable for high-speed competition driving, and paving the way to the new car which was called the MERCEDES.

Jellinek, who was a director of Daimler, promised to take 36 cars designed to his specification if he could have the sole agency for France, Belgium, Austria-Hungary and the USA, and if they would bear a new name, that of his 11-year old daughter Mercedes. This name was unofficial at first, though mandatory in France where Panhard still had the right to the Daimler name. However, within

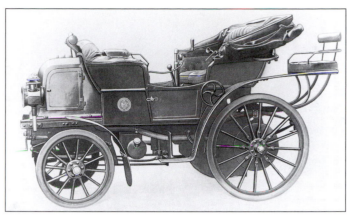

1897 Daimler(i) 6PS 'Phoenix' *vis-à-vis*.
NATIONAL MOTOR MUSEUM

1897 Daimler(i) 6PS 'Diligence'.
NATIONAL MOTOR MUSEUM

portable source. He chose petrol, then barely thought of as a fuel, although its heavier versions such as heavy oil and paraffin were used in small quantities for paint manufacture, as a lubricant, for home lighting where town gas was not available, and, earlier, as a patent medicine. His ideas found no favour with Otto, partly because they came from Daimler, with whom he had a bitter rivalry. In September 1881 Daimler was sent to Russia to explore the market for Otto engines and on reporting favourably he was invited to move to St Petersburg to manage a new factory which would be set up. He saw this as an ignominious exile, and promptly resigned. He moved to Bad Cannstatt because both he and his wife suffered from heart conditions, and they had found a magnificent house close to the medicinal springs. Here, he and Maybach set up a workshop in the greenhouse where they worked on a compact, high-speed engine fuelled by petrol. By the summer of 1885 this was sufficiently developed to power a vehicle; for simplicity they chose a 2-wheeler with small outrigger wheels which they named the Reitwagen (riding wagon). It was, in effect, the world's first motorcycle, although Daimler did not conceive it as such; it was merely the simplest way of testing the new engine. His son, 16-year old son Paul, made a number of trips along the 3km stretch between Bad Cannstatt and Unterturckheim.

In August 1886 Daimler took delivery of a 4-wheeled carriage from the coach builders Wimpf & Sohn, which he had taken to the engine works at Esslingen where a 462cc engine, nearly twice the size of that in the Reitwagen, was installed. The carriage made some successful journeys, but Daimler was refused a permit by the local police, and as he saw motor vehicles as only one of the applications for his engine, he did not carry on for a while. Even before the carriage ran he had used an engine in a boat, on the River Neckar which had taken eleven people at a time. Daimler engines were also used in a railcar in 1887, followed by trams for Stuttgart and Bremen, and a narrow-gauge locomotive in 1890. In 1888 the engine was tried in a tethered balloon, the Wolferrrt airship. Daimler and Maybach soon needed

larger premises, and as Deutz refused to co-operate, and the Esslingen Machine Works were too small, they set up their own engine factory at Cannstatt. Daimler was always more interested in making engines, which soon became widespread in motor boats, while Maybach was determined to make a proper car, rather than a motorised horse carriage. Though they remained in partnership their paths diverged; had it not been for Maybach, the Daimler car would probably never have come to production.

After the period 'in exile' at the Hotel Herrmann (see Daimler car entry), Gottlieb Daimler was made managing director of the reorganised company. However, he played a decreasing part in the business, and his heart problems confined him to bed for long periods from 1896 onwards. In the autumn of 1899 Kaiser Wilhelm asked to inspect all the models of Daimler vehicles. Daimler's second son Adolf took several months to organise this, but in February 1900 he gathered a group of 12 cars, trucks and buses, and paraded them before the family home before setting off for Potsdam to see the Emperor. Daimler was propped up in a chair by the bedroom window to see the parade of his life's work. Two weeks later, on 6 March, he died.

Daimler was married twice, first, in 1867, to Emma Kurz, by whom he had five children, Paul (1869–1945), Adolf (1871–1912), Ema, Martha and Wilhelm. She died, also from heart trouble, in 1888, and in 1893 he married Lina Hartmann, by whom he had two children, Gottlieb (1894–1916, killed during Ypres) and Émilie, born in 1897. Both Paul and Adolf joined the Daimler Motoren Gesellschaft, Adolf died young, and Paul left in 1923 to join Horch.

NG

Further Reading
Mercedes-Benz Personenwagen 1886–1986, Werner Oswald, Motorbuch Verlag, 1986.
The Star and the Laurel, Beverly Rae Kimes, Mercedes-Benz of North America, 1986.

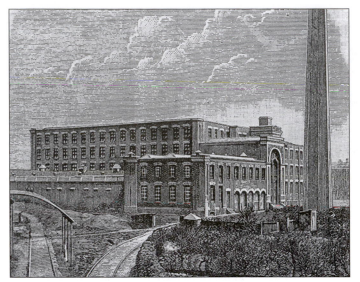

1896 Daimler (ii) Coventry factory, The Motor Mills.
NATIONAL MOTOR MUSEUM

1898 Daimler(ii) 6hp 4-seater dos-à-dos.
NATIONAL MOTOR MUSEUM

a year of the car's appearance at the Nice Speed Week in March 1901, the name was in general use, although the Daimler title was retained for commercial vehicles up to the merger with Benz in 1926.

NG

Further Reading
The Star and the Laurel, Beverly Rae Kimes,
Mercedes-Benz of North America,1986.
Mercedes-Benz Personenwagen 1886–1986, Werner Oswald,
Motorbuch Verlag, 1986.

DAIMLER (ii) **(GB)** 1896 to date
1896–1904 Daimler Motor Co. Ltd, Coventry.
1904–1910 Daimler Motor Co. (1904) Ltd, Coventry.
1910–1972 Daimler Co. Ltd, Coventry.
1972–1975 Jaguar, British Leyland UK Ltd, Coventry.
1975–1978 Leyland Cars, British Leyland UK Ltd, Coventry.
1978–1980 Jaguar-Rover-Triumph Ltd, Coventry.
1980 to date Jaguar Cars Ltd, Coventry.
Britain's oldest car company owed its origins to a meeting in 1888 between a young English businessman, Frederick Richard Simms (1863–1944) and a German manufacturer of gas engines, Gottlieb Daimler (1834–1900). Simms was impressed

with Daimler's petrol engines, which were used in small railcars and motor boats, and in February 1891 he acquired the licence to sell Daimler engines in Britain. Two years later he changed his company's name from F.R. Simms & Co. to the Daimler Motor Syndicate Ltd. Daimler engines were used in a variety of river and sea craft, from launches on the Thames to a Pembrokeshire lifeboat, and some were still operating after more than 20 years.

In October 1895 the company promoter Harry Lawson offered £35,000 for the Daimler Motor Syndicate. This was accepted by Simms and his fellow directors, one of whom was Gottlieb Daimler, and a month later Lawson refloated the company under the name British Motor Syndicate for £150,000. The aim of the new syndicate was to buy patents and to 'manufacture, sell, let on hire or otherwise deal in motors, cycles, carts, wagons, ships, boats, flying machines and carriages of all kinds'. Buying patents which he could sell on at a profit was Lawson's main aim, rather than making motorcars. To exploit the patents held by the British Motor Syndicate he formed the Daimler Motor Company in January 1896. He had already found a factory in the shape of a large, disused cotton mill at Foleshill, Coventry, but he did not exercise his option to buy until April 1896. He named the premises the Motor Mills, and several Lawson enterprises functioned there, including licence manufacture of the LÉON BOLLÉE tricar and E.J. PENNINGTON's experiments, as well as manufacture of M.M.C.and Daimler cars.

Although the Daimler Motor Company was established in January 1896, it was about 12 months before any Daimler cars left the Motor Mills. The name apart, they had no connection with the German Daimlers, being front-engined cars of Panhard type, with vertical-twin 4hp engines of 1526cc, with automatic inlet valves, tube ignition, 4-speed gearboxes, chain drive and tiller steering. It would not be correct to say that the engine was a copy of the Panhard, as there were significant differences such as the valves being on opposite sides. The first chassis left the Motor Mills in January 1897, bound for Hamilton in Scotland where carriage builder John Stirling fitted his own body and sold the result as a Stirling-Daimler. This car did, in fact, have a Panhard engine as no Coventry-built unit was ready, but Stirling subsequently purchased 100 genuine Daimlers.

The first all-Coventry Daimler made its maiden run in March 1897, and the first sale to a private buyer took place in April. Early production figures are uncertain, but the company claimed that 20 cars had been completed and sold by July, and in November output was said to be running at four cars per week. By the end of February 1898, 89 chassis had been sold, plus 24 engines for 'carriage, launch or other purposes'. Only chassis were made at the Motor Mills; they were transported by rail to Northampton where they received bodies by Mulliner. At first each had a different name according to the type of body fitted; Burleigh, Grafton, Rougemont, Universal, Wyley and the Jaunting Car.

The first 4-cylinder engine was completed in the autumn of 1897, to the order of Professor Boverton Redwood. It consisted of two 4hp motors in tandem, and by December four more of these 'coupled engines' had been made. A purpose-built 4-cylinder engine, rated at 12hp and of 3050cc, was made in 1899. It was designed by Sidney Straker, who later made Straker-Squire cars. One of the first customers was the Hon. John Scott-Montagu, who drove his car in the Tourist section of the 1899 Paris-Ostend Race, and in the Thousand Miles Trial of 1900, in which he was the only Member of Parliament to take part. Other improvements were the option of wheel steering in 1898 (several cars were retrospectively converted from tiller to wheel steering), and of electric ignition in 1900.

A new model in January 1899 was the Critchley voiturette, designed by J.S. Critchley to use up an unwanted stock of 50 4hp engines which were insufficiently powerful for the regular Daimlers. It was light and less expensive, selling for £200 when a 6hp twin cost £350–418 depending on body style, and a 12hp four £787–915. Unlike any other Daimler, it had belt final drive from the flywheel, and tensioning could only be varied by sliding the engine itself backwards and forwards. The years 1899–1901 saw several new models, but the company lacked direction, both in management and engineering. Indeed, in January 1899 there was a move to wind up the company, because of the falling value of its shares. Design was in the hands of Critchley until his resignation in May 1900, and Straker who was responsible for the 20hp 4-cylinder car of 1901. The cars were still on Panhard lines, but a new range appeared in 1902 designed by American-born Percy Martin (1871–1958) who joined Daimler in October 1901 and was to stay with the company until 1934. His range consisted of an 8hp twin, and fours of 12, 16 and 22hp. The Prince of Wales had taken delivery of his first Daimler in 1900, and three years later, as King Edward VII, ordered two of Martin's

1898/9 Daimler(ii).

NICK BALDWIN

SIMMS, FREDERICK RICHARD (1863–1944)

A versatile inventor, engineer, and businessman, he played a crucial role in bringing the automotive engine to Britain and was instrumental in starting its car production. He was born on 12 August 1863, in Hamburg, where his grandfather had set up Henry Simms & Co. as suppliers to the German high-seas fishing fleet. His childhood and school years were divided between Britain and the Continent.

He was building an aerial cable-lift with Mr Stansfield of Blackpool at the international exhibition in Bremen in 1888, when he saw a tiny tram powered by a Daimler internal-combustion engine. He was able to track down and meet Gottlieb Daimler, and the two formed a firm friendship. In 1890 he had a motor-launch with a 2hp Daimler engine built for him at Cannstatt. He took it to London and gave demonstration rides on the Thames, making plans for starting a motorboat industry at Putney. As a first step, he founded Simms & Co., consulting engineers, in partnership with A. Hendriks, a solicitor.

In 1892, they delivered a 38ft pinnace with a 10hp Daimler engine to the London County Council, and, for some years, Simms & Co. were England's biggest sellers of motor launches.

From 1890 to 1892 Simms had a seat on the Daimler Motoren Gesellschaft board of directors, and was privy to its role in starting a motor industry in France and Germany. He wanted to do the same in Britain, secured manufacturing rights to the Daimler patents, and established the Daimler Motor Syndicate Ltd in May 1893 in partnership with his cousin, Robert Gray, a wine merchant, and Theo Vasmer. They hired J. Van Toll from Berlin to serve as chief engineer, but never opened a factory, and sold out to H. J. Lawson in 1895.

As a private consultant to H.J. Lawson, he negotiated with Count Albert de Dion for manufacturing rights to the De Dion-Bouton tricycle and cars, which he obtained for the sum of £20,000 in 1896. The drawings from De Dion-Bouton were given to the New Beeston Cycle Co. which redesigned the vehicles for the British market. He also remained personally close to Gottlieb Daimler and helped him reorganise car production at Cannstatt in 1897, along the lines of the Daimler factory in Coventry. He may also have been influential in steering Daimler and Maybach towards shaft-drive to the rear axle.

Early in 1899, Simms demonstrated an invention he called the motor wheel (a single wheel carrying a 1½hp Daimler engine, easily attached to any kind of carriage) but this did not correspond to what the market wanted. During the automobile exhibition at Richmond in 1899, Simms demonstrated his Motor Scout, a motor quadricycle with armour plate on the front, armed with a Maxim repeater gun, and driven by an air-cooled 1½hp Simms engine. That led to a contract with Vickers, Sons & Maxim for a series of military vehicle designs from 1899 to 1901. In 1900 Simms also invented the armoured railway-car, fitted with Maxim machine guns, and intended for reconnaissance and communications duty in the Boer war.

In 1900, he organised a motor-vehicle department for George F. Milnes & Co. Ltd which developed into Milnes-Daimler Ltd, and set up a new Simms Manufacturing Co. Ltd plant in Kimberley Road, Kilburn, to produce the Simms-Welbeck car. In 1907, he reorganised the company as Simms Magneto Co. Ltd to make ignition equipment under Bosch licence. He founded the American Simms Magneto Co. at East Orange, New Jersey, in 1911.

Simms Magneto Co. Ltd became Simms Motor Units Ltd in 1920 and began making diesel injection equipment in 1935. He retired in 1935 and died at his home in Stoke Park on 22 April 1944.

JPN

1903 Daimler(ii) 22hp tonneau, The Hon. John Scott-Monagu at the wheel.
NATIONAL MOTOR MUSEUM

1906 Daimler(ii) 45hp tourer at Pately Bridge hill climb.
NATIONAL MOTOR MUSEUM

1912 Daimler(ii) 15hp tourer.
NATIONAL MOTOR MUSEUM

new 22hp cars. These had 5733cc engines with pair-cast cylinders and chain drive. The twins became less important as Daimler decided to go for the upper end of the market. Only 12 9hp twins were sanctioned for 1903 when the range was made up of 12, 14 and 22hp cars. Curiously, although magneto ignition was standard, tube ignition was retained as a standby, in case the magneto failed.

The 1904 season saw the largest Daimler yet, the 5.7-litre 28/36hp, as well as a new 3.3-litre 16/20hp. Surprisingly, a few cars with the ancient vertical twin engine were made. The 28/36 was the first Daimler to employ the finned top to the radiator tank, which has identified Daimlers ever since, although for a long time it has been purely decorative. Over the next few years wheelbases became longer and engine capacity grew, to 8462cc on the 35 and 10,431cc on the 45. The latter was the largest-engined Daimler passenger car ever built, and was said to require the strength of Sandow at the starting handle. Two batches of 10 were made in 1905 and a number were completed subsequently. King Edward VII and Queen Alexandra took delivery of one each in 1908. Some of the larger Daimlers of this period were made by DE LUCA in Italy. Unusually for a luxury car maker at that time, Daimler had their own coachbuilding department, but some chassis were supplied to outside coachbuilders.

Sleeve Valves and Shaft Drive

In 1908 Daimler made a complete change in design policy. Out went the old side-valve engines from 17 to 45hp, and in came a range of sleeve-valve units made under licence from the American, Charles Yale Knight. For the 1909 season these were offered in three models, a 3764cc 22hp, 6280cc 38hp and 9236cc 48hp. At the same time underslung worm drive replaced chains, although shaft drive had been tried experimentally in 1905, and in 1907 a small batch of 25 of the 17/21 had been sold with this system. Sales grew encouragingly, reaching about 2000 in 1910, but the heavy price paid for the Knight licence and for development work drained Daimler's finances, and by the end of 1909 they were on the brink of bankruptcy. They were saved by an amalgamation with the Birmingham Small Arms Co., familiarly known as BSA. This firm was already making cars and motorcycles, as well as small arms, and was a much richer company than Daimler. Their share capital was more than double Daimler's and they had no outstanding loans, whereas Daimler owed £51,000. *The Financial Times* described the merger as '. . .one of the most important ever effected in the motor industry'. This was certainly true in that it enabled Daimler to survive to become one of Britain's best-known makes. The merger brought several BSA directors on to the Daimler board, including F. Dudley Docker, whose son Sir Bernard Docker was to be BSA chairman from 1940 to 1956, and to have a considerable influence on Daimler in the 1950s.

In 1912 Daimler opened a new Coventry factory, known as the Radford Works. The Motor Mills continued in use until 1937, and were destroyed during a German air-raid in 1941. Radford built bus chassis between the wars, and survives today for the assembly of Jaguar engines, and front axle milling and machining.

The 1911 Daimler range consisted of six models; four fours and two sixes, from a 2612cc 15hp four to a 6246cc 38hp six. Also listed but not sanctioned for production was a 9420cc 57hp six. Presumably the engines had been completed the previous year and put into stock. King George V took delivery of eight of these monsters; the first in 1909 when he was still Prince of Wales, the last in 1924, although it is likely that the engines were all built before World War I. By 1914, apart from the British Royal Family, Daimlers were owned by the monarchs of Russia, Germany, Spain, Sweden, Greece, and Japan. Lord Montagu observed in *The Daimler Century*, 'its list of owners among the British aristocracy read like a digest of Debrett'. Daimlers were thought to be more respectable than Rolls-Royces; as an old chauffeur remarked, 'The "real people" had Daimlers; Rolls-Royces were for people who had made their money in jam and pickles and things like that!'

Daimler produced a wide variety of war materials during World War I, including 1000 ambulances, about 4000 lorries, shells, aero engines (RAF 1A V8s, RAF 4 V12s and Bentley-designed BR2 rotaries) and complete aircraft (BE2, DH10).

After the war 4-cylinder engines were dropped, apart from a short-lived 3306cc 20 in 1922 which used two thirds of the 6-cylinder 30 engine. This did not mean that Daimler made only large cars, for among their sixes was a tiny unit of 1541cc, the 12hp of 1923, although this grew the following year to 1870cc and 16hp. These engines were also used by BSA. Daimler's range became increasingly complex during the 1920s; in 1927 23 models were offered, using five engines and twelve wheelbase lengths. Front-wheel brakes were used on the 1924 35hp, and were standardised late in 1925 when light-alloy sleeves were adopted to improve specific output. For 1927 there was a striking V12 model, known as the Double Six. The Double Six had a 7126cc V12 engine with separate carburettor, cooling system and dual ignition, being essentially two 25/85 6-cylinder blocks set at an angle of 60 degrees on a common crankcase. Output was 150bhp and even with a heavy body on the longest of the two wheelbases (163ins (4140mm)) a top speed of 80mph (130km/h) could be reached. The downside of this was a fuel consumption no better than 10mpg. In August 1927 Daimler brought out a smaller V12, the Double Six 30, which used two banks of cylinders from the 16/50 to give a capacity of 3744cc. Both models of Double Six could be distinguished from lesser Daimlers by the vertical strip down the centre of the radiator. Exact production figures for the Double Six are not known, but it is unlikely that more than 800 were made in all. Manufacture of the original series ended in 1930, followed by improved Double Sixes with twin-coil ignition and no magnetos, and the fluid flywheel introduced on all Daimlers from 1931. These later Double Sixes, which were made in smaller numbers than the 50 and 30, had capacities of 5296 and 6511cc, and were made up to 1935. A further nine with a poppet-valve version of the bigger engine were made up to 1938; two of them went to the Royal Family.

Fluid Flywheels and Poppet Valves
The fluid flywheel had been developed in Germany in 1905 for use in steamships. Essentially it involved two halves of an enclosed casing, both with cups around their rings. There was no physical connection between the two, but the casing was filled with oil, and as the speed of the driving half increased, the oil was impelled into the cups of the driven member with such force as to create a solid coupling. When used in conjunction with an epicyclic gearbox, it resulted in virtually an automatic transmission. It was first used on the Double Six 30/40 introduced in September 1930, and was soon adopted in all Daimlers.

In December 1930 Daimler took over the old-established LANCHESTER company. It was stated that 'both cars will retain their individuality – in no way will there be any fusion of the Lanchester and Daimler cars'. This assurance proved

c.1914 Daimler(ii) 30hp Coupé.
NICK BALDWIN

to be absolutely hollow within a few years. The 1935–36 Lanchester Light Six was a close relative of the Daimler-built BSA Light Six, while the 1936–39 Lanchester Eighteen was essentially a Daimler Light 20 with a Lanchester grill. Whatever Lanchester enthusiasts may have thought about it, the merger was very good for Daimler, who now had an entry into the quality small car field, with prices starting at £310 in 1935, compared with £450 for the cheapest

NATIONAL MOTOR MUSEUM

LAWSON, HARRY JOHN (1852–1925)
A natural promoter, he also became an industrialist on a vast scale and has some claim to the title of 'founder of Britain's motor industry'. He was born within the walls of the city of London on 23 February 1852, as the son of a brass-turner. After elementary schooling, he was apprenticed to an engineering shop in 1868. At the age of 17 he built a safety bicycle, using parts from his own perambulator. He was granted a patent for the safety bicycle (No. 2649) on 27 June 1876.

He founded the Rudge Cycle Co. Ltd in 1887 to make safety bicycles, and was a co-founder of the Humber Bicycle Co. Ltd. He set up the Humber Extension Co. Ltd to handle peripheral activities and financial affairs (later to be integrated with the patent company). He also founded the London Scottish Investment Co., and Prestons of Liverpool, and organised the Licences

Insurance Co. to implement his scheme of compensating publicans whose licences were revoked or refused by the authorities. He also served as a director of the Beeston Tyre Co., suppliers to Humber and other makers of bicycles.

Always on the lookout for new business opportunities, he was one of the first in Britain to grasp the future role of the automobile. In 1895, he purchased the Daimler Motor Syndicate from F. R. Simms, securing British manufacturing rights to Daimler's patents, including engines and motor cars. He reorganised it as the British Motor Syndicate Ltd, and this was absorbed into the Daimler Motor Co. Ltd which he founded on 17 January 1896, with a capital of £100,000 in ten-pound shares. Among the directors were Gottlieb Daimler, F.R. Simms, the Hon. Evelyn Ellis, and Henry Sturmey. He exercised his option to purchase the old Coventry Cotton Mills, where he installed the Daimler Motor Co. Ltd with J.S. Critchley as works manager.

While he made the Daimler Motor Co. Ltd a going concern, he privately bought all varieties of motor-connected patents, covering steam cars, electric cars, as well as petrol-driven cars. He also got involved with Edward Joel Pennington and his automobile patents, which were the subject of several legal actions and earned a reputation as frauds.

On 14 May 1896, he consolidated these holdings into the Great Horseless Carriage Co. Ltd with a capital stock of £750,000, of which only half was actually paid up. The directors were H.J. Lawson, T. Robinson, J.C. Mace, T.H. Lambert, and E.J. Pennington. In October 1896 this syndicate purchased the Clément bicycle name and some of the Clément operations, including the Gladiator works at Pré-Saint-Gervais in Paris, forming Clément, Gladiator & Humber (France) Ltd, with Harvey du Cros, Ernest T. Hooley, and M.D. Rucker as directors. Before the end of the year, he also took over the New Beeston Cycle Works, and started car production there.

The Great Horseless Carriage Co. Ltd acquired a somewhat shady reputation in the press and the City, and in 1898 some of the shareholders sued for the return of their investment. Lawson seized this opportunity to reorganise and change the name, and the business resurfaced as the Motor Manufacturing Co. Ltd, which went on to seven years of mismanagement before paying its first dividend, and then withdrew to oblivion.

In 1904, Lawson went on trial in a fraud case (not connected with Daimler) and was sentenced to 12 months' hard labour.

In his later life, he stayed away from automobiles and out of the headlines, although he did write the occasional letter to The Autocar. He died in 1925, leaving no fortune, and forgotten by most.
JPN

1928 Daimler(ii) 35/120hp short tourer.
NATIONAL MOTOR MUSEUM

NATIONAL MOTOR MUSEUM

SCOTT-MONTAGU, The Hon. JOHN (1866–1929)

John Edward Douglas-Scott-Montagu was a tireless promoter of the motorcar and of motorists' interests in Britain, particularly through his position as a Member of Parliament, but also by his general enthusiasm. He was born on 10 June 1866 to Lord Henry Montagu-Douglas-Scott, second son of the sixth Duke of Buccleuch, who was created first Baron Montagu of Beaulieu in 1885, and his wife, the former Lady Cecily Stuart-Wortley. He was educated at Eton and New College, Oxford, but was not an enthusiastic scholar, and on coming down in 1889 he took the unheard of step for a young aristocrat of joining the workshops of the London & South Western Railway as a mechanic. He called himself 'Mr Douglas', and took lodgings in Vauxhall Bridge Road, close to his work at the Nine Elms depot of the railway. He received tuition in driving main line locomotives, which he continued to do occasionally until a few years before his death.

John's railway career came to an end in 1890 when he was selected as Conservative parliamentary candidate for the New Forest. In 1892 he was elected, and soon showed an interest in the problems of South Africa, where the unrest which would result in the Boer War was already brewing. He spent four turbulent months there in 1896, and five months after his return the Locomotives On Highways Act was passed by Parliamant, permitting cars to

travel at 14mph (22km/h) (later reduced to 12mph (19km/h)). John had his first ride on a motorcar in the autumn of 1897, on a Panhard from London to Windsor. He was immediately hooked on the new form of travel, and in the summer of 1898 he bought his first car, a 6hp Daimler. This began a connection between the Coventry firm and the Montagu family which has lasted to the present day.

He soon became active in the motoring world, joining the Automobile Club of Great Britain and Ireland (later the RAC) in January 1899. Four months later he took part in his first motoring competition, the Automobile Club's Easter Tour from London to Bournemouth. A stop was made at Palace House, Beaulieu, starting the tradition of Beaulieu's association with the motorcar which has continued to the present.

A very important year for John Montagu was 1899. In July he became the first MP to drive a petrol car into Palace Yard, Westminster. Electrics had been admitted for a few years, but internal-combustion cars were excluded on the grounds that they might set the buildings on fire. John claimed that this ban was contrary to his rights as an MP for 'free ingress and egress' to the Commons. The Speaker accepted his argument, and he was freely admitted. As a result of this victory he was made Chairman of the Parliamentary Automobile Committee, a position of great influence. In August he joined Charles Rolls in entering the Paris-Ostend race. This was the first time that Englishmen had competed in one of the great town-to-town races. John drove his new 12hp 4-cylinder Daimler to third place in the Tourist Class, and averaged the same travelling speed as the winner, although he was delayed by a broken cooling pipe, but still finished third. In 1900 he was one of the organisers of the famous Thousand Miles Trial, and was also a trustee of the Motor Vehicle Users' Defence Organisation, which was pledged to fight legal oppression. His 12hp Daimler was one 12 cars of that make in the Trial, and he was frequently called on to make speeches at the various stops during the Trial's progress around the country. As his biographer, Paul Tritton wrote, 'he, Rolls and others had assumed the role of motoring missionaries'. At the end of the Trial, Rolls was awarded a Gold Medal, John Montagu a Bronze.

In August 1900 (not 1899 as has long been believed) John was invited to lunch at Highcliffe Castle, where the Prince of Wales was staying. After the meal he took the Prince for a drive of about 20 miles, after which the heir to the throne was so delighted that he asked for advice about the choice of a car. John naturally recommended a Daimler, starting a link between that make and the Royal Family which lasted for more than 50 years.

The first issue of a new and up-market motoring magazine, *The Car Illustrated, a Journal of Travel by Land, Sea and Air* appeared on 28 May 1902. John's

376

Daimler. This was the 1805cc Fifteen, which used a 6-cylinder ohv version of the 1203cc Lanchester Ten. Introduced in 1933 it was the first Daimler since 1909 not to have sleeve valves, and the first since before World War I to sell for under £500. About 6100 were made of this and a slightly enlarged 2003cc version up to 1936. Increased production meant that Daimler could no longer build bodies for all their cars – closed Fifteens were mostly by Mulliner and the open version by Martin Walter. The theme was continued with the 2166 DB17 of 1937 and the DB18 of 1938–40. These cars were larger all round, with engines of 2166 and then 2522cc, underslung frames and ifs on the DB18.

There was also a complex range of larger 6-cylinder Daimlers and, from 1934, four sizes of straight-8. The sixes included the 2565cc Light 20 (1936–39) with sports saloon or 4-door cabriolet bodies and the EL24 (1937–40), a compact limousine with 3317cc engine, as the late Michael Sedgwick put it '. . .aimed at Mayors of modest means'. Production was approximately 860 Light 20s and 710 EL24s. The first straight-8 was the 3764cc V26 of 1934–35, made mostly in limousine form as the only available wheelbase was 142ins (3607mm). With a larger engine of 4624cc it became the 4.5-litre. About 475 were made, of which King George VI took ten, two of them with armour plating. Four of them were ordered with Lanchester radiators and bonnets because the King was a great Lanchester fan. At least three more straight-8s were 'Lanchesterised' for Indian maharajahs. More attractive owner/driver cars were the 3421cc Light Straight-8 and its development, the 3960cc 4-litre. These had very pleasing sports saloon and cabriolet bodies by such well-known firms as Charlesworth, Freestone & Webb, Vanden Plas and Tickford. Combined production was about 300.

1939 Daimler(ii) 2½-litre DB18 'Dolphin' special sport.
NATIONAL MOTOR MUSEUM

War and Peace

During World War II Daimler's activities were diversified through several 'shadow factories' to reduce the disruption caused by the expected air raids on Coventry. This was a wise decision as the Motor Mills and 70 per cent of the Radford works were destroyed in 1941. One of the 'shadow factories' was at Brown's

venture into publishing was aimed at a readership at the top end of the social scale (it cost 6d a copy, compared with 3d for *The Autocar* and 1d for *The Motor Car Journal*), was printed on high-quality paper and had a well-chosen staff of writers. The leading artist was Charles Sykes, who had been introduced to John Montagu by Claude Johnson of Rolls-Royce. Also introduced by Johnson was Eleanor Thornton, who had been Johnson's secretary, and who was to become not merely secretary but personal assistant and a vital part of John's staff on the magazine. It is generally accepted that she was the model for the Spirit of Ecstasy figure that Sykes sculpted for Rolls-Royce, and which was first seen on the cars in 1911.

From the Thousand Mile Trial onwards, John Montagu was at the forefront of most important motoring developments in Britain. In 1902 he sponsored the Motor Vehicles Registration Bill in which the unpopular idea of numbering cars was balanced by the suggestion of abandoning the speed limit. This optimistic *quid pro quo* did not meet with favour in the Commons or among motorists who thought the carrying of registration numbers was degrading, putting them on a level with common hackney carriages. Montagu's bill was heavily modified, and emerged as the Motor Car Act of 1903, in which the speed limit was raised to 20mph (32km/h), but the registration of cars went ahead, as from 1 January 1904. At least he managed to obtain some 'cherished numbers' including AA 19 and AA 20, which are still carried on Montagu-owned cars today.

In November 1905, on the death of his father, John became the second Baron Montagu of Beaulieu and owner of the 10,000-acre estate. Although Palace House, Beaulieu, became his home, he still travelled regularly to London to see to the running of *The Car Illustrated*, and to attend to his political life. Through his friendship with Charles Rolls he became increasingly involved with the Rolls-Royce company, and owned one of the five special versions of the 40/50 with ohvs giving 70bhp. He performed the opening ceremony at the new Rolls-Royce factory at Derby in July 1908 (two years earlier he had done the same for Argyll's 'Marble Halls') and through Rolls he became interested in flying. In 1908 he accompanied Rolls to see Wilbur Wright demonstrate his aeroplane at Le Mans, and this alerted him to the threat that aeroplanes presented to England's security. In 1909 he initiated the first air debate in Parliament, although, like so many prophets, he was not taken seriously. He was also active at the new Brooklands Motor Course, being a vice-president of the Brooklands Automobile Racing Club and presented the Montagu Cup at the first meeting. Indeed, Brooklands' founder, H.F. Locke-King, said that without John Montagu's encouragement, he would never have persevered with building the track.

At the outbreak of World War I John became Director of Organisation, Special Constabulary, taking charge of 'a kind of Dad's Army of 200 motorists and 1000 motorcycles' (Paul Tritton), but seven weeks later he took command of the Seventh Hampshire Reserve Battalion, with which he sailed to India in December 1914. He had a busy time in India, being Inspector of Motor Vehicles with particular interest in the North West Frontier. He made many recommendations for road and bridge building in the area, and also secured a reasonable allocation of trucks and armoured cars, though not as many as were needed. He returned to England in July 1915 to plead India's case at the War Office for motor transport, and also for aeroplanes, and sailed back to India in December on the P&O liner Persia. He only just escaped with his life after three days in an open boat when the ship was torpedoed in the Mediterranean on 30 December, but Eleanor Thornton was one of 335 who lost their lives.

He was back in India from November 1916 to March 1917, when he was concerned with providing adequate driving instruction for the Indian Army, and also inspected the road works he had recommended on the North West Frontier. On his return he was vociferous in arguing for a proper defence of London against air attacks, and also became a member of the Civil Aerial Transport Committee. For a number of years he was motoring correspondent of *The Times*, and reported regularly in road conditions on the Continent. He was always far-sighted in his predictions, foreseeing widespread air travel, motorways such as came to pass when the M1 opened in 1959, and overhead urban motorways such as the A40(M) Westway in West London. Despite his occasional journeys on the locomotive footplate, which included several stints as a driver during the General Strike, he did not see rail travel as playing an important part in the future. He died on 30 March 1929.

John Montagu was married twice, first to Lady Cecil Kerr, daughter of the ninth Marquess of Lothian, by whom he had two daughters, Helen and Elizabeth, and who died in 1919. In 1920 he married Pearl Barrington-Crake, by whom he had three daughters, Anne, Caroline and Mary Clare, and a son, Edward, who is the present Lord Montagu of Beaulieu, and who founded the Montagu Motor Museum (now National Motor Museum) in his memory.

NG

Further Reading
John, Lord Montagu of Beaulieu, a memoir, Laura, Lady Trowbridge and Archibald Marshall, Macmillan, 1930.
John Montagu of Beaulieu, Motoring Pioneer and Prophets, Paul Tritton, Golden Eagle/George Hart 1985.

1947 Daimler(ii) 2½-litre DB18 saloon.
NATIONAL MOTOR MUSEUM

1954 Daimler(ii) Conquest saloon, in 1954 Monte Carlo Rally.
NATIONAL MOTOR MUSEUM

1959 Daimler(ii) SP250 roadster.
NATIONAL MOTOR MUSEUM

Lane, Allesley, near Coventry; after the war it was used for production of cars and buses, and became the home of Jaguar in 1952. Daimler's wartime production included more than 50,000 Bristol aero engines, components for Bren and Browning guns, and the 4 × 4 Scout car which was powered by a modified version of the 2522cc engine used in the DB18. Between 1939 and 1945 Daimler made 6665 Scouts and 2764 armoured versions with larger engines.

The first postwar Daimlers were the DB18s, essentially a continuation of the 1939 models, though with restyled bodies which gave more luggage space, and two large cars, the DE27 with 4095cc six developed from the armoured car engine, and the DE36 with 5460cc straight-8 developing 150bhp. At 223in overall length and a wheelbase of 147in (3734mm), the DE36 was the world's largest production car, as well as being the last British-built straight-8. It and its slightly smaller DE27 sister, provided an ideal base for Britain's dwindling band of coachbuilders. Hooper built the most, including 25 limousines and state landaulettes for the Royal Family and the series of flamboyant cars that Sir Bernard Docker ordered at the instigation of his wife Norah, and which enlivened Earls Court Shows in 1951–53 (there were other 'Docker Daimlers', but they were on 6-cylinder chassis). There were also one or two convertibles by Hooper and a sports saloon by Freestone & Webb. Foreign monarchs who bought DE36s included the Emperor of Ethiopia, the Queen of the Netherlands, Prince Rainier of Monaco, and the Kings of Afghanistan and Thailand. A total of 205 DE36s were made. The DE27 was more popular for hire work, and 50 were supplied to Daimler Hire, in addition to the 205 sold to private buyers. It was also the basis of the DC27 ambulance, bodied initially by Barker and then by Hooper.

The DB18 was made until 1950, mostly as a saloon although there were some dropheads by Tickford, and also the Barker Special Sports Coupé, with more dramatic lines and two-tone colour scheme; 608 of these were made, and 3365 DB18s. They were replaced in 1950 by the Consort, with restyled body, the hydro-mechanical brakes from the Sports Special and a hypoid bevel rear axle replacing the traditional underslung worm. In 1953 it gave way to a more modern and less expensive saloon, the Conquest whose price (before Purchase Tax) was appropriately fixed at £1066. It had a short-stroke engine of 2433cc, an all-steel body which it shared with the Lanchester Fourteen, and torsion-bar ifs. Made from 1953 to 1956, it was joined and then supplanted by the Conquest Century (1954–58) with 100bhp thanks to larger valves and twin carburettors. A total of 9386 of both types was made, as well as about 234 drop-heads, 65 2-seater sports roadsters, and 54 drop-heads based on the roadster rather than the saloon.

The Conquest was the last Daimler-built popular saloon, for the next car in anywhere near the same class was the Jaguar-based 2.5-litre introduced in 1962. Meanwhile several versions of large Daimler were made, successors to the DE27 and DE36 though without their majestic appearance and enormous weight. The DK400 was a limousine with 4617cc 6-cylinder engine with Carbodies body which carried many echoes of Hooper styling. There was also a Sportsman saloon with the same engine and 4-light wrap-around rear window. These were very low-production cars, only 132 DK400s and 69 Sportsmen being made. More popular were the One-0-Four, Majestic and Majestic Major large saloons with 6-cylinder engines of 3468, 3794 and, in the Majestic Major, a 4561cc V8. The Majestic featured disc brakes all round and automatic transmission, while on the Majestic Major, power steering was optional to 1964, then standard to 1968. The three models were made from 1955 to 1968, a total of 3231 being built, together with 864 DR450 long wheelbase limousine versions of the Majestic Major.

In the Spring of 1959 there appeared a completely new car, Daimler's first entry into the sports car field. Originally called the Dart, until Dodge objected, the SP250 had a 2547cc V8 engine designed by Edward Turner who came from a motorcycle background, notably Ariel and Triumph. The camshaft was set high between the cylinder blocks, and operated inclined valves in hemispherical combustion chambers through short duralumin pushrods and valve gear similar to that on the Triumph Speed Twin. Unlike the motorcycle unit, the SP250 engine was markedly oversquare at 76.2 × 69.85mm. The distinctively styled 2-seater body was in fibreglass, and many journalists, while full of praise for the engine, felt that it deserved a better chassis and body. The standard gearbox was a 4-speed manual, but an automatic was an option for the US market. Automatic transmission was also preferred by the several British police forces, which bought the SP250; 2645 were made, and the engine went into a Jaguar Mk II body shell to make the 2.5-litre/V8-250 from 1962 to 1969. This was an excellent car, selling over 17,000 units. The veteran journalist Sammy Davis, who had been a Daimler

The Daimler "Twenty-five"

The model illustrated below is the Special Saloon at £1125.
Other coachwork styles are illustrated within

1976 Daimler(ii) DS420 limousine.
NATIONAL MOTOR MUSEUM

1989 Daimler(ii) Double Six V12 saloon.
JAGUAR CARS

1998 Daimler(ii) Super V8 saloon.
JAGUAR CARS

apprentice before World War I, said of it, 'This is not a Jaguar with a Daimler radiator grill and name plate. It can stand on its own'.

The sale of Daimler to Jaguar in June 1960 inevitably meant a loss of individuality. The last Daimler to have a distinctive appearance was the DS420 limousine which replaced the Majestic Major in 1968, and even this had a 4285cc Jaguar engine and floorpan, although considerably lengthened (by 21in (530mm)) to accommodate the 7-seater body. This was made by Motor Panels and finished and trimmed by Vanden Plas. Bare chassis were also supplied to other firms for hearse bodies to be fitted. Nearly all the DS420s bodied by Vanden Plas were limousines, but there were a few landaulettes. Production ended in September 1992, but the last hearse, made by Startin of Birmingham, was delivered in February 1994. The model's demise marked the end of the line for the famous twin-cam Jaguar engine, first seen in the XK120 sports car in 1948.

The limousine apart, all Daimlers of the past 30 years have been variants on successive models of Jaguar. The Sovereign in three series, made from 1969 to 1987, was a Jaguar XJ6, while for the Daimler version of Jaguar's V12, the name Double Six was revived. This was made from 1973 to 1992, mostly in saloon form though a 2-door coupé was offered during 1975–77. Although the new XJ40 was introduced in October 1986, the bonnet could not accommodate the V12 engine, so the older body shell was continued for the 12-cylinder cars, both those with Daimler and Jaguar badging. The very last, delivered in December 1992, was a Daimler Double Six which went into the company's museum. A new Double Six appeared shortly afterwards, in February 1993; this had the 5993cc 318bhp V12 also used in the Jaguar XJ12, and like all Daimler variants, was more luxuriously fitted out, with opening roof, heated seats, individual rear seats and lambswool carpets. The smallest 6-cylinder Daimler was the 4.0 with 3980cc 250bhp engine, the 3.2-litre Jaguar not being available in Daimler form. In 1997 the in-line six and V12 engines were replaced by a 3996cc four-cam V8. The Daimler versions were the V8 and Super V8, the latter with the modifications of the Jaguar XJR which included a supercharger boosting output from 294 to 375bhp. Both had new 5-speed automatic transmissions.

NG

Further Reading
Daimler Century, Lord Montagu of Beaulieu and David Burgess-Wise,
Patrick Stephens, 1995.
The Daimler Tradition, Brian Smith, Transport Bookman, 1972.
Britain's Motor Industry – the First Hundred Years, Nick Georgano (ed.),
G.T. Foulis & Co., Sparkford, 1995.
The Daimler Double Six, William Boddy, Profile Publications, 1966.

DAINO (I) 1923–1924
Fabbrica Automobili Daino, Cremona.
This company produced a very short-lived light car powered by a 1460cc ohv
4-cylinder engine which developed 16bhp.
NG

DAINOTTI (I) 1922–1923
Fabbrica Automobili Dainotti, Pavia.
The Dainotti was unusual in being a small car which was only made with
straight-8 engines. One used a 1492cc 2-stroke, while the larger model had a
2-litre 4-stroke engine, and was credited with 75mph (120km/h).
NG

DAISY (US) 1914
Daisy Cyclecar Co., Los Angeles, California.
The Daisy cyclecar was powered by a 10hp 4-cylinder air-cooled engine made
by the Pacific Mechanical Co., with friction transmission and double-chain drive.
A price of around $400 was planned, but production never started.
NG

DAKAR (GB) 1991 to date
Dakar Cars, Wilmington, Kent.
Dennis Adams' ROTRAX found favour as a utility/fun vehicle, but it called out
for a 4x4 drivetrain. Dakar Cars duly stepped in and bought the rights to make
the long wheelbase version exclusively for Range Rover mechanicals. It was a simple
body swap for the Range Rover, and boasted a very tough roll-over cage. American
V8 engines were optional. A Dakar appeared in the *Challenge Anneka* TV series,
securing widespread publicity.
CR

DAKOTA *see* DE TAMBLE

DALAT (VN) 1969–1975
Citroën Xe-Hoi Cong Ty, Saigon.
This was an open jeep-type vehicle based on the Citroën 602cc Mehari and using
Citroën mechanical elements.
NG

DALE (US) 1974–1975
Twentieth Century Motorcar, Los Angeles, California; Dallas, Texas.
The Dale was a 3-wheeled fibreglass coupé which its promoter Elizabeth Carmichael
claimed would outsell Detroit's Big Three. Annual sales of 3 million cars were
predicted, and among the Dale's slogans were 'Dollar for Dollar, the Best Car
Ever Built', 'The First Space Age Automobile', and 'Designed and built like it's
ready to be driven to the Moon'. Extolling the 3-wheeled layout, the catalogue
claimed 'The tri-wheel Dale is about to revolutionise the automobile industry.
It's the way more automobiles will be designed, from this day forward'. In fact,
only one prototype was ever built, powered by an 850cc 2-cylinder Onan engine
normally used to drive electric generators. Barely able to run, it surfaced again in
Dallas as the Revette. Carmichael was later revealed to be a man, Jerry Dean Michael,
and after years on the run, was jailed for fraud in 1989.
KB

DALEY (US) 1895–1898
M.H. Daley, Charles City, Iowa.
Daley was a maker of disc and lever harrows for farm work and he also hoped to
get into car manufacture. In 1895 he built a very light 2-seater weighing only 195
pounds (88kg) and powered at first by a rotary engine, then a more conventional
2-cylinder unit. The front wheels were held in bicycle-type forks, and could rise

1906 Dalhousie 2-seater.
NICK BALDWIN

1908 Dalhousie tourer.
NATIONAL MOTOR MUSEUM

up to 12in (305mm) on uneven ground. He announced production in December
1895, the cars to sell at $500 each, but he built no more than six. In 1898 he
informed *The Horseless Age* that he was 'still at it' and may have made one or two
more cars, but his main business was farm equipment.
NG

DALGLEISH-GULLANE (GB) 1907–1908
Haddington Motor Engineering Co., Haddington, East Lothian.
This company made a light 2-seater powered by an 8hp single-cylinder De Dion-
Bouton engine, with shaft drive. No more than ten were made, but one survives
today.
NG

DALHOUSIE (GB) 1906–1910
The Anderson-Grice Co. Ltd, Carnoustie, Angus.
Founded in 1860 to make foundry equipment and branching out into cranes in
1885, this company began limited manufacture of cars in 1906. The engines,
which were made in the factory, had four separately-cast cylinders. Two-seaters
were made at first, followed by quite large 4-seater tourers of distinctive appearance.
The radiator, bonnet louvres and dash all sloped backwards, at a time when
these items on nearly all cars were strictly vertical. The cars were named after the
Marquess of Dalhousie, a former Viceroy of India, and were designed by John
Williams and A.G. Grice, who was later concerned with GRICE and G.W.K.
cars. In 1910 the company decided to close its car department, remaining cars
and spares being bought by James Law of Arbroath, who may have assembled a
few more.
NG

DALILA (F) 1922–1923
Bouquet et Compagnie, Paris.
Powered by 6.9 or 7.5hp Ruby engines, the Dalila was a typical French light car
apart from its suspension. This consisted of inverted semi-elliptic springs which

c.1919 Daniels 8 sedan-limousine.
NATIONAL MOTOR MUSEUM

1921 Daniels 8 roadster.
JOHN A.CONDE

ran the whole length of the car, and were linked to the front and rear axles by metal arms. Whether this gave a more comfortable ride than conventional springing is not known, but it did not help to sell the Dalila, which lasted for only two seasons.
NG

DALLAS (F) 1981 to date
1981–1984 Automobiles Dallas, Neuilly-sur-Seine.
1984 to date Automobiles Grandin SA, Marne La Vallée.
The Americanesque name hinted that this was a leisure vehicle with styling (by Jean-Claude Hrubon) inspired by the Willys Jeep. To begin with, it was based on a Renault 4 platform and could be had either with front-wheel drive or Sinpar 4 × 4. In 1986, two years after being taken over by French singer Franck Alamo, came an all-new Dallas II model, which switched to Peugeot 205 mechanicals, including its engine (both petrol and diesel), in a box-section steel chassis. The open bodywork was in fibreglass with an optional hardtop, and there was space for up to four passengers.
CR

DALLISON (GB) 1913
Dallison Gearing & Motor Co. Ltd, Birmingham.
The Dallison cyclecar had a Precision V-twin engine which could be air-or water-cooled, and the makers helpfully said that any other make of engine could be supplied, if desired. It differed from most cyclecars in having a 5-speed gearbox and worm final drive. The body was quite streamlined, with a pointed radiator, and starting was by lever from the driver's seat. In March 1913, the makers announced that 30 cyclecars would be made each week, but after that little more was heard of the Dallison.
NG

DALTON (US) 1911–1912
Dalton Motorcar Co., Flint, Michigan.
Hubert K. Dalton was the manager of the WHITING Motorcar Co. when he decided to make a car under his own name. Very close to the Whiting in conception,

it had a 20hp 4-cylinder engine and was offered only as a 2-seater runabout at $900. He completed only three cars before moving to New York where he set up the Dalton Manufacturing Co. This was successful in making marine equipment during World War I.
NG

DAMA (CHI) 1991
Jiangyang Shipping Group Corporation Mini Auto Works, Yangzhou City, Jiangsu.
In 1991 about 1500 Dama (Large Horse) Suzuki-based minicars, pickups, vans and minibuses were built. Among them were 250 units of a 136in (3450mm)-long ugly-looking motor car named Dama HWC 1010, which was powered by a 4-cylinder 797cc engine made by the Dong'an Engine Works.
EVIS

DAMIRO (F) 1994–1995
The Damiro Alzane was a 1930s-style roadster powered, unusually, by an Alfa Romeo 4-cylinder engine. Sold either fully-built or in kit form, it was very short-lived.
CR

DANA (DK) c.1908–1914
Hakon Olsen, Maskinfabriek Dana, Copenhagen.
Olsen made several belt-driven cyclecars powered by 6hp Peugeot air-cooled engines, with 2-speed gearboxes. They were popular in country districts because their weight of about 570 pounds (260kg) was well within the 450kg limit above which cars were not permitted on some country roads. The abolition of this law forced the Dana out of the market.
NG

DANDY (GB) 1922–1925
James Sumner & Sons, Southport, Lancashire.
The Dandy was an unusual 2-seater 3-wheeler which could be folded to pass through a 32in (812mm) doorway. It was powered by a 998cc V-twin J.A.P. engine, driving through a 3-speed gearbox and chain drive to the rear axle. The side by side 2-seater body somewhat resembled a sidecar.
NG

DANGEL (F) 1968–1971
Automobiles Dangel, Sentheim.
Henri Dangel entered the motor industry expecting to find success in motor racing and sports car production. However, his business actually thrived in a very different area of the car market. Dangel's first vehicle was the 2-seat Barchetta of 1968, a fibreglass sports car aimed at Series Club racing, as well as being made available to regular road users. Power came from a rear-mounted Renault 8 Gordini engine. After just three years Dangel stopped production of its road racers, only to re-emerge in 1978 with a 4-wheel drive version of the Peugeot 504, and continues to make all-wheel drive conversion of various Peugeot and Citroën vehicles.
CR

DANIELS (US) 1916–1924
1916–1924 Daniels Motor Car Co., Reading, Pennsylvania.
1924 Levene Motor Co., Philadelphia, Pennsylvania.
The Daniels was a low production, highly esteemed luxury car built under the direction of its company's president, George E. Daniels, erstwhile president of Oakland and a vice-president of General Motors. It was at once a quality automobile and a heavy one, with weight on its closed models approaching 3 tons. It was powerful as well, all Daniels cars being equipped with side-valve V8 engines by Herschell-Spillman into 1919 and its own motor from then to the end of production in 1924. It featured a bore and stroke of $3\frac{1}{2} \times 5\frac{1}{4}$ins with a potential of 90bhp at 2000rpm. The Daniels was advertised as 'The Distinguished Car with just a little bit more power than you'll ever need' and identified by its high 'cathedral type' radiator, similar to the Fiat, and devoid of a radiator badge, identified only by the letter 'D' on its hubcaps. The Daniels was tailored by coachwork of the highest and best executed quality, first by the Keystone Vehicle Works of Reading and after 1920 by Fleetwood, also of that community and

prominent for custom coachwork for other contemporary expensive automobiles. The Daniels was a high-priced car with prices starting at $5350 for open models and rising after 1920. In 1921, top year for Daniels production, closed cars were priced from $6750 for the town brougham to $7800 for the 'California' limousine.

In 1924 the Daniels was taken over by the Levene Motor Co. of Philadelphia which specialised in supplying parts for orphan makes and servicing them. The Levene concern announced that it planned to continue production of the car, although it appears that this was just its way of completing cars from existing parts. Only a few of these last Daniels were completed, but at greatly raised prices, the suburban limousine from $7025 to $10,000. These cars proved to be faulty in their construction, a sad ending to a once proud automobile.

KM

DANILO (DK) 1958
This was a very short-lived microcar fitted with a 175cc engine.
CR

DANKAR (BR) 1979–c.1984
Dankar Ind. Com. de Veiculos Lda, Rio de Janeiro.
This firm built the Squalo, a mid-engined coupé using the running gear of the 1.6-litre Volkswagen Passat mounted in a central backbone chassis, with all-round disk brakes and torsion-bar suspension.
NG

DAN PATCH (US) 1910–1911
M.W. Savage Factories Co., Minneapolis, Minnesota.
This company was a prominent manufacturer of cattle feed and also marketed items such as stopwatches, cream separators, sewing machines and stoves, all of which were sold under the name Dan Patch, after a famous racehorse which they owned. In 1910 they added cars to their range, buying vehicles in from an Indiana manufacturer, probably McINTYRE. They were conventional-looking tourers and roadsters with 35 or 40hp engines. Savage said that they would sell 1500 cars in 1911, but far fewer than that actually reached customers. A few may have been sold into 1912 under the name Savage.
NG

DANSK (DK) 1901–1908
1901–1903 Dansk Automobil & Cyclefabrik, Copenhagen.
1903–1908 Dansk Automobilfabrik, Copenhagen.
These companies originated from a cycle shop started in 1896 by H.C. Christiansen. In 1899 he began to make tricycles powered by Cudell engines, and also built a prototype 4-wheeler which still exists. In 1901, with backing from the wealthy Fonnesbech-Wulff he formed the Dansk Automobil & Cyclefabrik, and offered a range of cars from 2 to 6hp, of which nine were exhibited at Copenhagen's Tivoli Gardens in 1902. They had two forward speeds but no reverse, with metal clutch and a separate chain drive for each gear. There was no differential. Christiansen provided Copenhagen's first motor taxi, but it proved too noisy in its original form, and the engine was replaced by an Oldsmobile. In 1903 a change of name indicated that bicycles were no longer made, and in 1904 Christiansen built Denmark's first motor bus, also using a 2-cylinder engine. However 1904 also saw his first 4-cylinder engine, a 12/16hp unit which drove through a leather cone clutch, 3-speed gearbox (presumably now with reverse), and shaft drive. After 1908 Christiansen turned to importing vehicles.
NG

D'AOUST (B) 1912–1927
Automobiles J. d'Aoust, Anderlecht; Berchem Ste Agathe.
Jules d'Aoust started in car manufacture in a Brussels suburb with small cars powered by French-built engines from Aster, Chapuis-Dornier or Decolonge. In 1914 he began making his own engine, an 1857cc 10/14CV 4-cylinder side-valve unit which powered a light car made in small numbers. D'Aoust had a number of sporting successes with one of these cars.

In 1919 he returned to production in a different factory a few miles away, first with the 12/14, to which he added a 3052cc 16hp with single-ohc. This model was called Circuit de Corse as it was intended to use it in this competition. It seems that few were made of this or an obscure 2296cc four, and that most production in the early 1920s rested on the 12/14. In 1922 there was a slightly

1899 Dansk prototype 2-seater.
HANS-OTTO NEUBAUER

1998 Dare DZ convertible.
DARE (UK)

larger (1991cc) short-chassis sport model with front-wheel brakes. These were also seen on two new small cars of 1923; the 6/8CV whose 1093cc engine was probably provided by Chapuis-Dornier or S.C.A.P., and the 1098cc 8CV whose engine was almost certainly a S.C.A.P. Both of these were available in sports form. In 1924 Arthur Duray drove a d'Aoust powered by a 9.4-litre Hispano-Suiza V8 aero engine, but this was purely a 'special'. The 10/14CV was continued up to the end of car production in 1927, as were the two smaller cars. In an attempt to diversify, Jules d'Aoust offered two commercial vehicles in his last few years of production, a 750kg van and a 2-tonne truck.
NG

DARBY (US) 1909–1910
Darby Motorcar Co., St Louis, Missouri.
Advertised as 'The Simplest Automobile on Earth', the Darby Model 20 had a 16hp 2-cylinder 2-stroke engine with friction transmission and chain drive. It was made in 3-seater roadster and 4-seater surrey form, on a 100in (2538mm) wheelbase, but few were sold.
NG

DARDO (BR) 1981
Corona SA, Diadema, Sao Paulo.
This rear-engined sports coupé used a 1.3-litre Fiat engine enlarged to 1500cc.
ACT

DARE (GB) 1991 to date
Dare (UK) Ltd, Colchester, Essex.
Dare was established by Ivor and Trevers Walklett, two of the founders of Ginetta. Rights to the Ginetta G4 and G12 had been bought by a Japanese company and Dare held the manufacturing rights. In essence, Dare was a sub-contractor to the Japanese importer.

DARE

1917 Darling (ii) Six tourer.
KEITH MARVIN

1937 Darmont V-twin sports car.
NICK GEORGANO/NATIONAL MOTOR MUSEUM

1902 Darracq 9½hp tonneau.
NATIONAL MOTOR MUSEUM

However, in 1998, came a completely new car, designed by Ivor Walklett. The Dare DZ aimed to provide a practical 2-seater with both generous luggage space and the broad style of an F1 car. The composite body was moulded to a space frame, there were front and rear wings, inboard front suspension, and a transverse Ford Zetec engine was mounted amidships, with a 210bhp supercharged option. Front wheels were exposed and had cycle wings while the rear wheels were enclosed in bodywork which housed twin side-radiators. It was available in open or gull-wing coupé form and the pop-up headlights were mounted on either side of a deep, sloping, windscreen.

MJL

DARLING (i) (US) 1901–1902
Beardsley & Hubbs Manufacturing Co., Mansfield, Ohio; Shelby, Ohio.
Volney Bearsdley and Charles Hubbs offered a wide variety of cars designed by Rollo R. Darling. They all had 10/12hp rear-mounted 2-cylinder engines, and were offered in seven body styles, from a 2-seater stanhope at $850 to a combination brake at $1200. In 1902 they moved their operations to Shelby, Ohio, but Darling had left them to try, unsuccessfully, to make a car in Cleveland. They made six Darlings a week for a while in 1902, then reorganised as the Shelby Motor Co. to launch the SHELBY car. Volney Beardsley later made an electric car under his own name in Los Angeles.
NG

DARLING (ii) (US) 1917
Darling Motors Co., Dayton, Ohio.
The Darling Six was a conventional car made only in 5-seater tourer form, powered by a 4964cc Continental 7N 6-cylinder engine. It had modern lines, with a form of dual-cowl body and wire wheels, but failed to sell, and production was discontinued within the year of its announcement. It was made in the former Wright-Martin aircraft factory.
NG

DARMONT (F) 1924–1939
R. Darmont, Courbevoie, Seine.
Together with the SANDFORD, the Darmont was France's best-known 3-wheeler, and like its rival, was derived from the MORGAN. For most of the Darmont's life it was more closely related to the British product than was the Sandford, being almost indistinguishable in appearance. Two models with side-valve engines were made, air-cooled and water-cooled, the former being called Étoile de France. The most powerful was the ohv Darmont Speciale which could exceed 100mph (160km/h) in supercharged form. All Darmonts used licence-built Blackburne V-twin engines.
The 3-wheelers were made up to 1939, and were joined in 1936 by a 4-wheeler, the Darmont Junior. This also had a Blackburne-type V-twin engine.
NG

DARNVAL (F) 1972–1973
Sté Darnval, Le Havre.
Francis Lechère and Vincent Mausset were behind the Darnval LM1 sports car. It was conceived as an inexpensive 2-seater coupé and used Renault mechanical components in its chassis; the handsome body was in fibreglass. A racing model was also produced with a multi-tubular chassis built by LENHAM in Britain.
CR

DARRACQ (F) 1896–1920
1896–1905 Sté A. Darracq, Suresnes, Seine.
1905–1920 A. Darracq et Compagnie (1905) Ltd, Suresnes, Seine.
Alexandre Darracq was one of the great entrepreneurs of the European bicycle industry which grew phenomenally between 1885 and 1900, making fortunes for several people, including Darracq. He was a businessman rather than an engineer, and must be the only man who gave his name to a famous make of car, yet never learnt to drive one. Indeed he was said to be unhappy even travelling as a passenger.
Born in Bordeaux in 1855, Darracq worked in an arsenal and then for sewing machine makers Hurtu & Hautin, who later branched into bicycles and then cars sold under the name HURTU. In 1891 he began to make bicycles himself, selling them under the name Gladiator, and undercutting the prices of the British cycles which were widely sold in France. Five years later he was bought out by a British group headed by Harvey du Cros, controller of Dunlop, on the condition that he did not engage in bicycle manufacture. Never one to worry about the spirit of an agreement, Darracq used his pay-off to build a large factory where he made bicycle components, adding motor tricycles and quadricycles.
In 1896 he made a few electric cars, then took out a licence to make the 4-wheeled cars designed by Léon Bollée (Bollée's 3-wheelers were made by Darracq's erstwhile employers, Hurtu). The 4-wheeled Bollées were not as successful as Darracq had hoped, and he quickly looked for another designer. He chose Paul Ribeyrolles who joined Darracq in 1900 and produced a design for an up-to-date light car with 6.5hp single-cylinder engine, 3-speed gearbox and shaft drive. Like his rival, Louis Renault, Darracq never made a chain-

384

driven car. Sixty of these cars were sold before the end of the year, and in 1901 sales were over 1000, which was a high figure for that time. After De Dion-Bouton, Darracq was the biggest car maker in France, and he also had a flourishing cycle component business.

Darracq's long involvement with racing began in 1901. Although the cars sold to the public were still small, Darracq's competition cars grew rapidly, to a 3770cc four in 1901, while by 1904 his Gordon Bennett cars had capacities of 11,259cc. An even larger car was the 200hp V8 of 1905, which used two blocks of the 1904 engine, with ohvs, to give a capacity of 22,518cc. It was too big for racing, but was used for record breaking. In December 1905 Victor Hemery set a new Land Speed Record of 109.65mph (176.45km/h). With smaller cars, Hemery won the 1905 Vanderbilt Cup and Louis Wagner the same event in 1906, but Darracq's efforts in the 1906 and 1907 Grands Prix were not crowned with glory, and after a second place in the 1908 Four Inch Race in the Isle of Man, Darracq did not race again until after World War I.

The touring cars also increased in size, although less dramatically. In 1903 2- and 4-cylinder engines were added to the range, and in 1904 the steel frames were pressed from a single sheet of metal. These were made by Arbel, and Darracq ordered 1000 in one batch. One of a three-model range was a 12hp 2-cylinder 2-seater that was later christened *Genevieve* and starred in the film of that name. Made in England in 1953, this light-hearted story of rivalry on the London-Brighton veteran car run gave an enormous boost to the old car movement worldwide, introducing many people to the pleasures of discovering and restoring veteran cars. By 1905 the largest Darracq had a 28hp 4-cylinder engine of 5.9 litres.

Commercially Darracq went from strength to strength. Profits rose from £75,000 in 1901 to £112,000 in 1904. British capital bought the company in 1903 and Darracq remained as managing director. Two years later a new company was formed under the name Alexandre Darracq & Co. (1905) Ltd, with 80 per cent of the share capital held in Britain. Even closer links with Britain were made in 1906, when a factory for assembling chassis and building bodies was opened at Kennington, South-East London. In 1907, when 2200 cars were sold, profits were £194,470.

Another foreign venture was set up in 1907, when Darracq formed an Italian company with headquarters and factory in Milan. It was called Società Italiana Automobili Darracq, later A.L.F.A. (Anonima Lombardo Fabbrica Automobili), and made small 2-cylinder Darracqs. This proved to be a mistake as the cars were insufficiently powerful for Italy's poor roads. They sold badly, and in 1910 the directors replaced them with new 4-cylinder cars designed by Giuseppe Merosi. These were called Alfas, and after 1915, ALFA ROMEOs.

Meanwhile, the French factory turned out a wide range of cars from an 1100cc single-cylinder voiturette to a 50hp 8140cc six with square cylinder dimensions (120 × 120mm). The singles disappeared in 1909, and the twins a year later. In 1912 Darracq had a costly encounter with the Henriod rotary-valve engine. Instead of trying this new design on one or two models, he tooled up for production of the rotary-valve unit for nearly all his cars. The engines developed less power than poppet-valve units of equivalent size, and Darracq sales slumped badly. In 1911 profits were £112,969, but a year later they amounted to just over £732. In June 1912 Darracq paid for his folly by resignation, which was presumably strongly recommended by the English directors. He played no further part in the motor industry, and died in 1928.

A new designer was hastily found in the person of Yorkshire-born Owen Clegg, who had designed a sound and up-to-date 12hp monobloc 4-cylinder engine for Rover, and now proceeded to produce a similar, slightly larger (2950cc) engine for Darracq. In 1914 electric lighting and starting were available on this car, which soon retrieved Darracq's reputation. In the summer of 1914 the company had 12,000 workers turning out 14 chassis per day. Darracq was now the third largest car maker in France, after Renault and Peugeot, and the fifth largest in Europe. The war saw the factory busy making aeroplanes of Breguet and Sopwith design and as with most engineering companies, Darracq ended the war in a very strong financial position.

Encouraged by wartime profits, Darracq's British directors decided to extend their coverage of the market by acquiring other companies. In 1919 they bought the Clement Talbot company of North Kensington, and the following year they added to their empire the Sunbeam Motor Co. Ltd of Wolverhampton, and the London-based commercial vehicle makers, W. & G. du Cros. A large issue of shares was made to finance these purchases, bringing capital to more than £1.5 million for the new combine which was called S.T.D. Motors Ltd.

1905 Darracq tourer in Coupe des Pyrénées.
NATIONAL MOTOR MUSEUM

1910 Darracq 25/30hp tourer.
NATIONAL MOTOR MUSEUM

1914 Darracq 16hp limousine.
NATIONAL MOTOR MUSEUM

The final Darracq models were the old Clegg-designed 16 and a new 4.5-litre V8 with coil ignition, spiral-bevel final drive and front-wheel brakes. They were initially called Talbot-Darracqs, but in 1920 the French company became Automobiles Talbot, and the Darracq name was gradually dropped (see TALBOT (ii)). In England, however, they remained Darracqs to avoid confusion with the London-built Talbots.

NG

Further Reading
Motoring Entente, Ian Nichols and Kent Karslake, Cassell, 1956.

1929/30 Datson [Datsun] prototype 2-seater.
NATIONAL MOTOR MUSEUM

DARRIAN (GB) 1986 to date
Team Duffee Engineering, Lampeter, Dyfed.
After a spell in modified form with CORRY, the original DAVRIAN was revived in Wales under the new name of Darrian. It was much modified, however, the bodywork being shortened at the rear and also widened. The construction method was either a fibreglass/Kevlar monocoque or a space frame chassis/roll cage. Mid-mounted Ford power was nearly always specified, though other options included Rover V8, Cosworth and Vauxhall 16V. This was a successful rally and road car. A further model was the Monte Carlo, a rear-engined replica of the Renault-Alpine A110.
CR

DARRIN (US) 1952–1958
Howard A. Darrin Automotive Design, Los Angeles, California.
Howard A. 'Dutch' Darrin was a legend in American classic car circles for his many original designs for American and European chassis during the pre-World War II period. He also did work for Kaiser, including the 1946 K-F sedan, but wanted to do a more sporting project. In 1946 he designed a fibreglass-bodied convertible, but production was shelved because of the poor quality of fibreglass of that time. He designed the Kaiser-Darrin sportscar in 1952 using his own money and without the knowledge of K-F executives. They accepted the design for production, although it did not join the line until 1954. Based on the Henry J chassis, it sported a Willys 2638cc ohv six with 90hp. Performance was leisurely, although an optional supercharger helped. The styling was attractive with a long nose and doors that slid into the mudguards, and the fibreglass body was built by GLASSPAR. After 335 Kaiser-Darrins were built, Kaiser closed down US operations, leaving Darrin with 100 unsold cars, which he powered with 304hp Cadillac V8s. In 1954 Darrin was rumoured to be the designer of a sleek fibreglass body for the Dyna-Panhard that was to have been sold by Robert Perreau of Los Angeles, but production failed to materialise. In 1957 Darrin was back in the sportscar business with the Flintridge-Darrin, also called the Darrin Mk II DKW. This was a rebodied DKW 3-cylinder sedan sold through Flintridge Motors in La Canada, California. The sporty convertible bodies were made of fibreglass by WOODILL Motors and a removable hard-top was available. Seating was on two bench seats that held up to six thin passengers.
HP

DARROW (US) 1903
Darrow Motor Vehicle Co., Owego, New York.
The Darrow was a light chain-driven runabout powered by a 3.5hp single-cylinder Thomas engine. Although Stuart Darrow formed a company and quoted a price of $550, only one car was made.
NG

DART (i) (US) 1914
Automatic Registering Machine Corp., Jamestown, New York.
This was a cyclecar built briefly by a company which claimed to be the largest maker of voting machines in the world. It had a 15hp 2-cylinder air-cooled engine, conventional gearbox and chain drive to one rear wheel only. The wheels were discs with spoke patterns pressed into them. Customers who disdained this rather ugly design could have wire wheels at $15 extra. The makers decided to concentrate on their main business before the year was out, so few Darts can have been made.
NG

DART (ii) see SCRIPPS-BOOTH

DART (iii) see MARTIN (iv)

DART (iv) (GB) 1991–1992
This was a very ugly and boxy roadster kit based on Morris Marina parts. After a disappointing debut in 1991, no more was heard from the company, although the project came up for sale in 1995.
CR

DARYL HOLLIDAY (US) 1984 to date
Daryl Holliday's Cobra Enterprise, Commerce City, Colorado.
MGB front suspension combined with a Jaguar IRS was featured on this very ARNTZ-like Cobra replica.
HP

DASH (GB) 1986–1993
1986–1989 Listair Ltd, Wrexham, Clwyd.
1989–1993 Dash Sportscars, Eardisley, Hereford.
The origins of the Dash can be traced back to Australia in 1978, when Peter Pellandine created the PELLAND. After making it in Britain for a while, in 1986 the design came to rest with a company called Listair, which modified it to a large degree and renamed it the Dash. The same confection of mid-mounted VW power in a monocoque fibreglass shell remained, along with the purpose-designed suspension system. In 1989 the Dash went to Dash Sportscars of Hereford, where the option of Alfasud power was added. Dash also made the M.C.A.
CR

DASSE (B) 1894–1930
Automobiles Gérard Dasse, Verviers.
Gérard Dasse (1842–1920) began his working life as a plumber, later manufacturing plumbing and electrical equipment, and in 1894, aided by his two sons Armand and Iwan, he built an experimental 3-wheeled car. It had a single front wheel and 2.5hp horizontal single-cylinder engine, with belt drive and a tubular frame. Ignition was by hot tube, and there was no suspension. In 1897 Dasse built another 3-wheeler, this time with two wheels at the front. This was inspired by a Léon Bollée voiturette which a local lawyer had bought and entrusted to the Dasse family for maintenance. A third car on similar lines was the first Dasse to be sold, and by 1900 they were making 4-wheelers with 2-cylinder engines, electric ignition, and chain drive. Several versions were made over the next few years, with front and rear engines.

At the 1904 Brussels Show, Dasse exhibited two cars with 16hp 2-cylinder and 24hp 4-cylinder engines, armoured wood frames, shaft drive and front suspension by a single transverse spring. A 2232cc 3-cylinder 15hp was introduced in 1905 and was made under licence by DÜRKOPP in Germany as the Dürkopp-Dasse. It was particularly popular as a taxi. From 1906 Dasse cars were characterised by round radiators. Commercial vehicles were also made, including a long-lived fire engine which was used by the Verviers fire brigade from 1906 to 1938.

By 1911 Dasse had 100 employees turning out more than 100 vehicles per year; these were made in five models, of 12, 16, 24, 30, and 50hp. In 1913 a 3560cc model with Henriod rotary-valve engine was offered. Gérard Dasse died in 1920 but the business was carried on by his sons. Two car chassis were made, a 12hp 2120cc with side-valves and a 20hp 3560cc with single-ohc. This layout was offered on the smaller car a year or two later. Front-wheel brakes arrived on the 1924 models. These cars were made in smaller numbers than before the war, about 20 of the 12hp and a handful of the 20hp per year. The last Dasse passenger car was a Six made in dwindling numbers from 1925 to 1930. It is possible that a few were made after that to special order only. Dasse concentrated on commercial chassis from the mid-1920s, including some with straight-8 Lycoming engines. These were made up to the late 1930s, when Dasse were also making Imbert producer gas engines under licence. After the war they

1948 Datsun DA Standard sedan.
NATIONAL MOTOR MUSEUM

concentrated on maintenance until the business closed in 1956, the year that Armand Dasse died. Iwan lived on until 1964.

NG

DAT; DATSON; DATSUN (J) 1914–1983

1914–1918 Kwaishinsha Motorcar Works, Tokyo.
1918–1925 Kwaishinsha Motorcar Co., Tokyo.
1925–1926 DAT Motorcar Co., Tokyo.
1926–1932 DAT Automobile Manufacturing Co. Ltd, Osaka.
1933–1934 Jidosha Seizo Co. Ltd, Yokohama.
1934–1944 Nissan Motor Co. Ltd, Yokohama.
1947–1949 Nissan Heavy Industries Corp., Yokohama.
1949–1983 Nissan Motor Co. Ltd, Yokohama.

For 50 years from 1933 to 1983, most of the passenger cars built by the Nissan Motor Co. were called Datsuns, but on 1 January 1984 the car name was changed to Nissan as part of a worldwide corporate identity programme.

The origin of the Datsun name dates back to 1914 when an American-trained engineer, Masujiro Hashimoto, built a prototype 4-cylinder car which bore the name DAT, after three men who financed the company, K. Den, R. Aoyama and A. Takeuchi. Dat is also the Japanese word for 'hare'. Hashimoto had built an earlier car, in 1912, on which the 1914 DAT may have been based, but its name is not known. In 1915 came the DAT Model 31, with 2-litre 4-cylinder engine, enlarged to 2.3 litres on the 1916 Model 41. This 20bhp car was made in small numbers until 1926; it was a conventional machine with side-valve engine, 3-speed gearbox and shaft drive. Top speed was no more than 25mph (40km/h).

Japanese car production was very limited in the early 1920s, and DAT's only rivals were the GORHAM 3-wheeler and the LILA. These were both made by the Jitsuyo Jidosha Seizo Company of Osaka, which merged with the DAT

1936 Datsun Phaeton 15 tourer.
NATIONAL MOTOR MUSEUM

Motor Co. in 1926. DAT moved their factory from Tokyo to Osaka and continued to make 10hp 4-cylinder Lilas in small numbers. No DAT cars were made between 1926 and 1931, although 2-ton trucks were made, mainly for the Japanese Army.

In 1932 DAT was bought by a large industrial group, Tobata Imono. Their president Moshisuke Ayukawa (1880–1967), had an ambition to make an inexpensive car which could compete with mass-produced American imports. Because Japanese roads were narrow, he envisaged a small car which was built in

1955 Datsun Type K110 convertible.
NATIONAL MOTOR MUSEUM

1959 Datsun Sport convertible.
NATIONAL MOTOR MUSEUM

1973 Datsun 120A Cherry coupé.
NATIONAL MOTOR MUSEUM

prototype form before the end of 1931. Christened the Datson (son of Dat), it had a 495cc 4-cylinder engine developing 10bhp and giving the little car a top speed of 35mph (56km/h). This was one of the smallest 4-cylinder engines ever made. In 1932 the name was changed to Datsun, as the word 'son' in Japanese means 'loss', hardly a suitable name for a car.

Production that first year was 150 cars, which were made with 2-seater roadster, 4-seater tourer or 4-seater saloon bodies. A general similarity in appearance to the Austin Seven has led to suggestions that the Datsun was a copy of the British car, but apart from the smaller engine, 495cc compared with 747cc, the Datsun had semi-elliptic rear suspension and worm drive, whereas the Austin favoured cantilever springs and bevel drive. It would be surprising if the Datsun's designer had been unaware of the Austin Seven, but there was no question of a direct

copy. Herbert Austin did order a Datsun to be sent to his Birmingham factory in 1935, but more out of curiosity than to investigate patent infringements.

The Osaka factory was sold to Ishikawajima in 1933 and operations moved to Yokohama, where a new factory was completed two years later. On 26 December 1933 the company name was changed to Nissan Motor Co. Ltd, which it has remained ever since. By mid–1934 1000 Datsun cars had been made, light trucks had joined the range, and the first cars had been exported (44 cars, sold mostly to Spain and Australia). In 1935 production reached 3800, rising to 6163 the following year. The engine was increased to 722cc and 16bhp in 1935, but otherwise changes were limited to styling until after World War II.

A larger car called the Nissan 70 was made from 1937 to 1940, but only in small numbers. It was an American design; Nissan had bought the engine tooling and body presses from GRAHAM-PAIGE of Detroit. The 3.7-litre 6-cylinder engine was also used in Nissan's range of trucks and buses. The last prewar design was the Nissan 50, a 4-door saloon resembling the Opel Olympia, powered by a 35bhp 1468cc 4-cylinder engine. Only a few were made, during 1940–42, and indeed passenger cars had taken second place to trucks for several years, as Japanese war preparations were stepped up.

Postwar Growth

Large numbers of aero engines and military vehicles were made during the war, and new factories were built. It was in an aero engine plant a Yoshiwara that the first postwar Datsun cars were made, as the Yokohama factory was reserved for truck production. The Standard DA 2-door saloon of 1947 was a utilitarian little car, still with the 722cc engine and with a narrow, high body less attractive than that of the prewar car. Only 4421 vehicles were made in 1947, mostly trucks. The 1948 figure was 8467, of which two were exported.

Improvements came on the 1951 DB2 models, which had 860cc 20bhp engines, hydraulic brakes and all-enveloping bodies resembling those of the American Crosley sedan. The Thrift of 1951–52 was the first 4-door saloon from Datsun, while there was also an attractive sports roadster with styling reminiscent of a prewar Singer or M.G., complete with humped scuttle and fold-flat windscreen. The roadster's engine was tuned to give 29bhp. Saloon bodywork was updated in 1955, but the 860cc engine soldiered on until 1958 when it gave way to an Austin-based 1189cc ohv unit on the first of the Bluebirds, a name still used by Nissan.

Austin's involvement with Nissan began in 1952, when the Japanese company signed an agreement to build the Austin A40 Somerset saloon under licence. This was replaced in 1955 by the A40 (later A50) Cambridge which was made until 1959. These cars were sold in Japan under the Austin name and, with their 1189cc engines, provided a useful larger car to sell alongside the little Datsuns. In 1956 the Cambridge was being built at the rate of 200 per month, probably more than the Datsun 110. Commercial vehicles still accounted for the bulk of Nissan's production right through the 1950s.

In 1958 Datsun exhibited at their first foreign motor show, the Imported Car Show in Los Angeles and this led to the establishment two years later of the American Nissan Motor Co. Also in 1960, the first Datsun car was sold in Europe. A Bluebird saloon, it was bought by a Norwegian customer and was still in use 16 years later, by which time it had covered more than 124,000 miles (200,000km).

The Bluebird marked the beginning of a modernisation programme which was to make Nissan one of the world's leading car manufacturers within ten years. It was a conventional design, like so many successful cars, with a 1189cc ohv engine derived from the Austin but made entirely in Japan, coil ifs and a 4-door saloon body. It was the smallest Datsun now, as the Austin Cambridge was replaced in 1961 by the Nissan Cedric with 1488 and 1883cc 4-cylinder engines, and, in 1966, a 1973cc six. These, together with the Silvia 1595cc sports coupé and President 3988cc V8 saloon and limousine were sold under the Nissan name until 1966, when the whole range was integrated under the name Datsun. The range also now included the Prince Skyline and Gloria saloons, made by PRINCE Motors of Tokyo which had been bought by Nissan.

These new models gave Datsun an increasingly complex range by the late 1960s, from the 988cc Sunny 2-door saloon to the 3988cc V8 President. One or two of these were made in long-wheelbase form for the Japanese Emperor. Production expanded dramatically, with the one millionth Datsun delivered in 1963, the three millionth in 1967 and the five millionth in 1969. By 1970 there were seven factories in Japan devoted wholly or partly to manufacture and assembly of passenger cars, as well as overseas plants in Mexico (since 1966), Peru (1967) and Australia (1968).

1975 Datsun 260Z 2+2 coupé.
NATIONAL MOTOR MUSEUM

The Datsun 240Z

Datsun was the first Japanese car maker to be involved in motor sport, taking part in the Australian Mobilgas Run from 1958, and starting a run of successes in the East African Safari in 1966. They had also made some sports cars such as the Fairlady 2000 of 1967, but the first sports car to come to international attention was the 240Z, which was made in its original form from 1969 to 1973. It was a conventional design, with a 2393cc single-ohc 6-cylinder engine developing 150bhp, although this was increased in later models. The gearbox was a 5-speed all-synchromesh unit and suspension was independent all round, with McPherson struts and anti-roll bars at the front, McPherson struts and lower wishbones at the rear. The integral construction 2-seater coupé body was styled by Albrecht Goertz.

The 240Z was a good example of the right car at the right time. The Austin Healey 3000 had recently ceased production, being forced out of the vital US market because of safety legislation, and there was a strong demand for a sturdy, uncomplicated sports car at a reasonable price. Nissan's engineers saw to it that there would be no complaints from safety-conscious officials in Washington, and they also wisely chose to go for a closed coupé rather than an open car, as the Austin Healey and the 240Z's predecessor, the Fairlady, had been. Within a year of its introduction, the 240Z had completely changed Datsun's image, and the series went on to become the best-selling sports car of all time. Sales of the 240Z and 260Z up to 1978 totalled 622,649, while the later 280ZX sold a further 414,358 up to the end of 1983. As with many cars, the earlier models were the lightest and fastest, with a top speed of 125mph (200km/h). The 260Z (1973–78) was heavier, particularly when Nissan responded to calls for four seats with the 2+2, and even with capacity increased to 2565cc (162bhp), top speed was not much above 120mph (192km/h). The bigger and heavier 280ZX had less performance still, thanks to emission controls dictated by the US market, but still found many buyers who wanted a stylish road car. In 1979 the US market took 70,000 of the 280ZX which was available with a turbocharger, and from 1981 there was an open version with Targa top.

Front-wheel Drive

Nissan joined the transverse-engine front-drive club in 1970 with the Cherry, which had an 1171cc ohv 4-cylinder engine developing 52bhp. Suspension was all independent, and there were disc brakes at the front. Body styles were 2- or 4-door saloons, estate car and, from 1973, a distinctively styled coupé. The Cherry was

1977 Datsun Laurel 2.4-litre Six saloon.
NATIONAL MOTOR MUSEUM

the first Datsun to sell in large quantities in Europe – Nissan UK was set up in 1970, selling just 1900 cars that year. Four years later the figure was 60,000, and in 1984 112,000 Britons bought Nissan cars. German imports began in 1972, with Nissan Motor Deutschland GmbH being set up in 1973 to co-ordinate all the distributors. In 1984 Germans took 67,000 Nissans.

The Cherry remained in production until 1986, having been regularly improved and updated. Front-wheel drive was adopted on larger Datsuns including the 1270 or 1488cc Sunny 4-door saloons and estates, the 1598cc or 1890cc Stanza 4-door saloon and 5-door hatchback, and the new 1809 or 1973cc Bluebird which went over to front-wheel drive in October 1983, only three months before the name change to Nissan. Two other models which became much better known as Nissans were the Micra, a 988cc 3-door hatchback introduced in 1982, and the Prairie, a high-roof 8-passenger estate car which was the first of the new breed of MPV (multi-purpose vehicle) or 'people carrier' adopted since by so many manufacturers in Japan and elsewhere. It used the 1488cc Sunny engine combined with the Stanza's floorpan. These and all other Datsuns became Nissans on 1 January 1984.

NG

1920 David cyclecar, winner of the cyclecar class of the Vuelta a Cataluña.
NICK BALDWIN

1922 David taxi-cyclecar.
V. CHRISTIAN MANZ

DAULON (F) 1950

This cigar-shaped single-seater 3-wheeler was created by M. Daulon in collaboration with the coachbuilder Gordia. It was powered by a Villiers 250cc single-cylinder 2-stroke engine, later changed to a JAP 350cc engine. It remained a prototype.
CR

D'AUX (F) 1924

Made by a firm of industrial belt manufacturers in Reims, the d'Aux was a cyclecar powered by a tiny 350cc single-cylinder Causan engine, with final drive by variable belts. Top speed was no more than 36mph (58km/h).
NG

DAVID (E) 1913–1923, 1951–1957

David SA, Barcelona.
The David cyclecar had a very strange origin, as it was based on wheeled bobsleighs. José Maria Armangué decided with some friends to organise downhill racing with very simple wheeled bobsleighs, first without engines and brakes. But as it took some time to get back to the top, he mounted a small JAP motorcycle engine, which was disconnected for the downhill run. Later, the David cyclecars were the best known of their kind in Spain, using 4-cylinder water-cooled engines, and front-wheel brakes. Armangué developed a special transmission for these cars, using variable pulleys and belt, that permitted 16 gears. He received several orders for this simple car, which was later fitted with engines from MAG, Ballot and also Elizalde. The 1922 catalogue listed different water-cooled engines with a single-cylinder 6/8hp, a 4-cylinder 6/8hp with thermosyphon circulation and a big 4-cylinder of 10/12hp. The Elizalde and a 1.8-litre Hispano-Suiza engine were specially used for racing cars. All Davids normally had a simple sporting two-seater body, but the manufacturer also took special orders for 3-seaters with one seat on the rear, a sports closed torpedo 2-seater body and a closed 3-seater with two comfortable rear seats and one front seat for the driver. These cars used ifs on two transverse springs.

David cyclecars won several important races. In the 1920s, the English Henderson Lane Co. wanted to buy the whole David production for export, but these plans failed. In 1919 David started production of taxi bodies on its cars. This was good business, and after finishing production of David cyclecars, the company successfully continued offering a Citroën taxi. The company was named distributor for Citroën and converted some of these cars into electric versions during the Spanish Civil War owing to the shortage of petrol.

In 1951 David offered a 3-wheeler minicar with single front wheel, using a single-cylinder 2-stroke 345cc air-cooled motorcycle engine of 10bhp. It had a 3-gearbox with final drive, just behind the front wheel. The car used a telescopic fork ifs. About 75 of the minicars were finally made, some of which have survived.
VCM

DA VINCI (US) 1925

James Scripps Booth, Indianapolis, Indiana.
The Da Vinci was an experimental car built by James Scripps Booth. It featured, among other things, an underslung worm drive, sleeve-valve engine and bonnet catches that operated from the car's interior, the latter a harbinger of today's electronically controlled principle. The car was a 5-seater sedan with a Sterling 8-cylinder engine with ohc. It was equipped with disc wheels and had a wheelbase of 105ins (2665mm).
KM

DAVIS (i) (AUS) 1901

Davis Cycle & Motor Works, Adelaide, South Australia.
In the days of penny-farthing cycles, Dick Davis was a prominent competitor who had his own cycle business, predating his venture into motors. His vehicle was a 4-seater *dos-à-dos* powered by a 3hp air-cooled petrol engine, driving via a countershaft and two belts which were brought into use by lever-controlled clutches. It was claimed that it could travel at 15mph (24km/h) on good roads. Unusually, its body was suspended on the chassis rather than the chassis being sprung on the axles. His car was an early Adelaide production but his cycle works closed in 1902 and he joined the Dunlop Co. in Brisbane.
MG

DAVIS (ii) (US) 1908–1929

George W. Davis Motor Car Co., Richmond, Indiana.
The Davis was one of the more successful small-production assembled cars on the American car market during the 1920s, featuring standard components throughout wedded to a considerable number of body styles and contrasting colour combinations. The outgrowth of a wagon company, the first Davis cars were high-wheelers in the style of the International Harvester and Schacht automobiles.

By 1911 Davis' offerings followed conventional lines, the cars powered by Continental 4-cylinder engines with a 6-cylinder series introduced for 1914, also powered by Continental, whose engines the company used exclusively throughout its existence, the four being dropped after 1915. Although the Davis production would remain relatively small with largest sales of nearly 1800 cars recorded in 1920, Davis also maintained an active export market after World War I. A sidelight to this market included two abortive attempts in Canada, first with the Winnipeg Six in 1923 and four years later with the Derby in Saskatoon, both basically rebadged Davises.

In 1928 the Davis was purchased by Villor P. Williams' Automotive Corp. of America, manufacturer of the Parkmobile, a mechanical addition which, when activated, lowered four small wheels, theoretically allowing a car to move sideways into tight parking places. Williams' plan was to include this device on subsequent Davis cars and in line with this, the Davis Six would be renamed the New York Six and the Davis Eight, introduced in 1927 to retain the Davis badge. It is doubtful that any of the 6-cylinder cars ever wore the New York Six badge although, to the contrary, an elaborate promotional flyer was distributed showing an illustration of the Parkmobile-equipped car bearing the badge plus some sketches showing the manner of the Parkmobile's operation. But by this time, Davis was running very tired and manufacturing ceased in 1928. Although the 1928 cars had been announced, only a handful were completed and marketed into 1929 as 1929 models. Perhaps as many as 15,000 cars were produced by Davis in its 21 years of existence.
KM

1947 Davis (v) 3-wheeler.
NATIONAL MOTOR MUSEUM

DAVIS (iii) (US) 1914
Davis Cyclecar Co., Detroit, Michigan.
Designed by William Norris Davis, this cyclecar was powered by a 10hp V-twin Spacke engine, with a conventional 3-speed gearbox and chain final drive. Although the transmission and final drive differed, the Davis bore a close resemblance to the Bedelia, having the driver in the rear seat.
NG

DAVIS (iv) see FLEETWOOD-KNIGHT

DAVIS (v) (US) 1947–1949
Davis Motorcar Co., Van Nuys, California.
Gary Davis was more of a publicist than a car designer and his frankly fatally flawed 3-wheeled design was presented as an advanced, aircraft-inspired, high-technology car. The Davis was a massive machine by 3-wheeled standards, at 15ft 5ins (4.7m) long. Davis claimed that his car would do sharp U-turns at 55mph (85km/h), but the reality was that the rear driving wheel would lift off the ground and spin freely, indicating a much higher speed on the speedometer! The first cars were powered by 2.2-litre 46bhp Hercules 4-cylinder engines, but later models came with 2.6-litre 57bhp Continental units. Davis claimed a top speed of 116mph (187km/h) and 30mpg, but again these claims later proved fanciful. The car was so wide that four people could be seated side-by-side on the single bench seat (again Davis extravagantly claimed five passengers), and a standard feature was a removable hard top. Some 17 running prototypes were built and the Davis was scheduled to sell at $1400 in 1949. However production never did begin despite assurances given to dealers to whom Davis had sold franchises netting around $1 million. This, combined with some financial irregularities, sent Mr Davis to jail and he was obliged to promise never to re-enter the car business.
CR

DAVRIAN (GB) 1967–1983
1967–1976 Davrian Developments, London.
1976–1980 Davrian Developments, Tregaron, Dyfed.
1980–1983 Davrian Developments, Lampeter, Dyfed.

1971/2 Davrian 875 coupé.
NATIONAL MOTOR MUSEUM

Adrian Evans built an open Hillman Imp-engined sports car called the Davrian as early as 1965, but kit-form sales did not begin until 1967, when a few open cars were made. The definitive Demon coupé arrived in 1968, boasting a tough fibreglass monocoque and fine handling, which made it a favourite of rally and circuit racers. Power options expanded to include Mini, VW Beetle and Ford, and detail improvements were made in successive Marks. The ultimate Mk8 version of 1980 was developed into a turn-key car (the Dragon) with Ford Fiesta power. That over-extended the company and it ended in bankruptcy in 1983. The Davrian metamorphosed to become the CORRY and the original designs were later re-engineered by DARRIAN at the same location.
CR

DAVY (GB) 1909–1911
Davy Engineering Ltd, Hulme, Manchester.
The Davy used a 15/20hp 4-cylinder Hewitt piston valve engine similar to that of the smaller CROWDY, and one Davy was shown on the Crowdy stand at the 1909 Olympia Show. The engine was made under licence from Hewitt Engines Ltd, and was designed by J.M. Hewitt. The 1909 Davy show car had a striking 'Canadian canoe' body, similar to the Labourdette skiff.
NG

1920 Dawson (iv) 11.9hp 2-seater.
NATIONAL MOTOR MUSEUM

1913 Day-Leeds 10hp 2-seater.
NATIONAL MOTOR MUSEUM

DAWSON (i) (US) 1899–1901

Dawson Manufacturing Co., Basic City, Virginia.
The Dawson Auto-Mobile was a light steam car with 2-cylinder engine, tiller steering and single-chain drive. George Dawson came from Cincinnati to make his car, but completed only one and could not obtain the necessary finance to build a second. He then returned to Cincinnati, having lost money but earned the distinction of having made the first car in Virginia.
NG

DAWSON (ii) (GB) 1900

H.T. Dawson & Son, Canterbury, Kent.
Henry Thomas Dawson built stationary gas engines in Clapham in partnership with Paris Singer. They planned to make a car, but before this was completed they quarrelled and Singer formed his own company to make the PARIS SINGER car. Dawson moved to Canterbury where he and his son made a few experimental cars. In 1903 the son, also called Henry, joined Henry Pavillet to make the CANTERBURY car.
NG

DAWSON (iii) (US) 1904

J.H. Dawson Machinery Co., Chicago, Illinois.
This short-lived car was powered by a 26hp 2-cylinder engine, with long, single-chain drive from the gearbox to the rear axle. The gearbox had two speeds: 'one slow and one fast', and two body styles were offered; 2-seater runabout and 4-seater tourer. A factory fire in March 1904 put an end to the Chicago Dawson.
NG

DAWSON (iv) (GB) 1919–1921

Dawson Car Co. Ltd, Coventry.
The Dawson was a well-designed and high quality car, the work of former Hillman works manager A.J. Dawson who had designed the 1913 Hillman Nine which did so much to save the fortunes of that company. In June 1918 he left

Hillman to set up his own business. Unlike many new postwar makes, the Dawson 11/22 was not an assembled product, but used a 1795cc single-ohc 4-cylinder engine of Dawson's own design and manufacture. The 3-speed gearbox and spiral-bevel drive were conventional enough but the Dawson had some unusual features such as an inspection lamp under the bonnet to aid repairs at night, and adjustable steering rake and pedals. Dawson did not make his own bodies, which were supplied mostly by Charlesworth, although there was at least one coupé by Cross & Ellis. They were expensive, with 1919 prices ranging from £600 for a 2-seater to £995 for a saloon. In 1920 they were even higher, and this must have been the main reason for Dawson's failure to sell many cars. The total made was 65 before the Dawson Car Co. was compulsorily wound up in February 1921. Later that year the factory was taken over by Triumph (iii).
NG
Further Reading
'The Dawson Story', M. Worthington-Williams, *The Automobile*, July 1995.

DAX *see* D.J.

DAYAN (US) c.1998 to date

Dayan Fat Factory, Orange, California.
This company made a fat-fendered custom pick-up truck body that sat on a 1966–96 Ford or Chevrolet truck chassis. The front featured dual rectangular headlights and dual grills, although other variations were available. They were sold in kit and finished form.
HP

DAY-LEEDS (GB) 1912–1924

Job Day & Sons Ltd, Leeds, Yorkshire.
This company was founded in 1901 although William Henry Day had been in business as a manufacturing chemist since 1886. The name Job Day came from William Henry's father, who did not play any part in the business. They soon became famous as makers of tea packaging machinery, and in 1912 added a bacon slicing machine, motorcycles and a cyclecar to their output. They had three factories in Leeds and the cyclecar was made in one of them. It was quite typical of the breed, although the 998cc inlet-over-exhaust V-twin was not a proprietary unit but was made in the factory, as were the motorcycle engines. Drive was by a 3-speed gearbox and belts to the rear wheels. A top speed of 50mph (80km/h) was claimed. Few of the cyclecars were made and at the 1913 Olympia Show, Day exhibited a shaft-driven light car powered by a 1130cc Turner 4-cylinder engine. Before the end of 1914 this had been replaced by a 1286cc T-head unit of Day's own manufacture. It was designed by W.L. Adams, who was also involved in the design of the MENDIP engine. Castings for both were initially made in Antwerp.
The same model was revived after the war, though the quoted cylinder dimensions of 63.5 x 100mm gave a capacity of 1266cc. Apart from electric lighting (but not starting), the 1920 Day-Leeds differed little from its prewar predecessor, apart from the price which had risen from £150 to £400. The 2-seater and coupé were bodied by Lockwood & Clarkson of Leeds. Demand for an expensive light car dwindled in the face of competition from mass producers such as Morris, and in 1926 the Day-Leeds car was discontinued. Production figures are not known but a good estimate would be 100 up to 1915, and 300 postwar. Day continued to make packaging machinery until it was absorbed by Baker-Perkins which also took over another packaging company, Rose-Forgrove. As Rose Brothers, they had made the Rose National or NATIONAL (ii) from 1905 to 1912.
NG
Further Reading
'The Day-Leeds Story', M. Worthington-Williams,
The Automobile, March 1995.

DAYTON (i) (US) 1909

W.O. Dayton Automobile Co., Chicago, Illinois.
This was a typical high-wheeler with horizontal twin engine and chain drive, formerly known as the RELIABLE DAYTON. William Dayton later made the Dayton (iii) cyclecar.
NG

DAYTON (ii) (US) 1911–1914

Dayton Electric Car Co., Dayton, Ohio.

This was one of many companies to offer electric cars in this period, and the Daytons did not differ from their rivals. Closed coupés and an open victoria were offered, with the option of chain or shaft drive. The latter were $100 more expensive. The drive systems were not mentioned on the 1913–14 models, which may indicate that chain drive was then no longer used.

NG

DAYTON (iii) (US) 1914

Dayton Cyclecar Co., Joliet, Illinois.

This cyclecar was made by William O. Dayton, who had built the RELIABLE DAYTON high-wheeler. Latching on to a new craze, he offered a cyclecar powered by a 9/13hp 2-cylinder Spacke engine, with hickory wood frame, friction transmission and belt final drive. Seating was either side by side or in tandem. Later in 1914 Dayton took a step away from the cyclecar by using an 18hp 4-cylinder engine. But by November 1914 he decided on a complete break with the past and introduced the 4-cylinder CRUSADER light car.

NG

DAYTON (iv) (GB) 1921–1922

Charles Day Manufacturing Co. Ltd, Shoreditch, London;
North Kensington, London.

Also known as the Day, this was a very light single-seater 3-wheeled cyclecar powered by a 4hp single-cylinder Blackburne engine, with chain drive to a 3-speed gearbox and final drive to the single rear wheel by belt. The price was a modest £115. It was exhibited at the Olympia Show in 1921, from the Shoreditch address, and some time afterwards Day moved to Stebbing Street, off Latimer Road in North Kensington. His company did not survive the following year.

NG

DAYTONA (US) 1956

Randall Products, Hampton, New Hampshire.

A rear-mounted 2hp Briggs & Stratton engine powered this lightweight minicar. It had no doors or weather protection.

HP

DAYTONA CLASSICS (GB) 1986–1987

Daytona Classics, Clacton, Essex.

This firm revived the SPIRIT SS as the Gatsby and also made the ex-A.D. 400 (now called the Magnum), plus a Cobra 427 replica and the 204GT, a Ferrari Dino lookalike that later became the DEON.

CR

DAY UTILITY (US) 1911–1913

Day Automobile Co., Detroit, Michigan.

As its name suggests, the Day Utility was designed to be a combination car. It had a 5-seater tourer body and a good load area under the two rows of seats. It was conventional in appearance, although higher than many tourers because of the load area; the 1911 model had a 21hp 4-cylinder engine and 100in (2538mm) wheelbase, and for 1912 this was quoted as a 26hp on a longer wheelbase. For 1913 power and wheelbase were increased again, to 33hp and 115in (2919mm), but Thomas Day could not find adequate finance to continue manufacture.

NG

D.B. (F) 1938–1961

Automobiles D.B., Champigny-sur-Marne, Seine.

D.B. was an unofficial partnership between Charles Deutsch and René Bonnet. It had to be unofficial because Deutsch was a civil servant – who eventually oversaw all French roads – and could not undertake a formal business arrangement. Deutsch inherited a workshop from his father and sold it to Bonnet in 1932. Bonnet was an entrepreneur and a fine mechanical engineer while Deutsch studied civil engineering and had an instinct for aerodynamics. The friends were interested in motor sport and, in 1936, booked a place in the French (sports car) Grand Prix. When the car they had hired did not arrive, they took their future into their own hands.

D.B.1 was based on Citroën 11CV *traction avant* mechanicals with a body inspired by George Eyston's Thunderbolt. It was completed in 1938 and Bonnet

1958 D.B. 850 Rallye coupé.
NATIONAL MOTOR MUSEUM

was able to run it in a handful of events before World War II broke out. By then D.B.2 had been built.

In 1945, the cars ran in the first postwar race meeting, in Paris, while a more advanced car was nearing completion. It had been started in Occupied France, at some risk to the two enthusiasts and it set the formula for all later D.B.s: low weight, low drag, and a tuned production engine.

Deutsch and Bonnet made a number of Citroën-based single-seaters and sports cars on a distinctive forked backbone chassis, but Citroën was not prepared to supply new components although Panhard was. Automobiles D.B., formed in 1949 used Panhard components almost exclusively. Among the competition cars the company essayed was a 500cc Formula Three car in 1950 and that became the basis for a Formula Two car, a twin-engined car, a 750cc supercharged Formula One car, an 850cc school car and, finally, a Formula Junior car up to 1960. And it was hopeless in every category. On the other hand, the sports and GT cars were subtle: many Panhard components were used and the aerodynamics were outstanding.

D.B.s appeared at Le Mans from 1949 on, but they were not successful until the mid-1950s when they began to dominate the 750cc in international events. There were numerous class wins at Le Mans, Sebring, in the Mille Miglia and, even, an outright win in the 1954 Tourist Trophy, which was run on handicap.

At the 1952 Paris Saloon, D.B. exhibited a road going coupé based on a box-section chassis and using Panhard Dyna suspension front and rear. The engines ranged from a 30bhp 610cc unit to a supercharged 850cc engine which gave 55bhp (from 1954). At first they had aluminium bodies, but fibreglass shells were used from 1955. By 1955 front disc brakes were an option and engines of 1000cc and even 1300cc were offered. Customers had a wide choice in the specification of their cars and D.B. developed the Panhard gearbox into an all-synchromesh unit before Panhard did so.

Over the years the bodywork changed, and became slimmer, but production of the road cars remained tiny, and no reliable road test figures are available for them. Besides, since the customer chose from a menu, hardly any two D.B.s were alike.

In 1961 the partners split: Bonnet wanted to use Renault running gear while Deutsch wished to stick with Panhard. A 750cc CD-Panhard (CD = Charles Deutsch) won its class and came 16th at Le Mans in 1962 and in 17th spot, and also a class winner, was a 1-litre Bonnet-Renault. It was the last year that there was a 750cc class at Le Mans.

René Bonnet continued to make cars under his own name and then was taken over by MATRA, while Deutsch became an independent engineering consultant whose work included the Bugatti circuit at Le Mans.

MJL

Further Reading
'D.B. stands for Deutsch-Bonnet', Griffith Borgeson,
Automobile Quarterly, Vol.XVIII, No.3.

D & B ENTERPRISES (US) 1995 to date

D & B Enterprises, Cheshire, Oregon.

The 1954 Maserati A6GCS was not the most common car for a kit car company to replicate, but that did not stop D & B. Their kit featured fibreglass bodywork

1910 Deasy 12hp tourer.
NATIONAL MOTOR MUSEUM

made in moulds pulled off an original car and a steel tube frame with fabricated suspension. Although originally intended for Alfa Romeo power, a Rover V8 with 5-speed transmission was more popular. They were sold in kit and completed form.

HP

DCA (E) 1995 to date

1992–1994 Drover Construcciones de Automóviles SL, Madrid.
1995 to date Fabricación Europea de Automóviles SL, Madrid.
Based on the English LOMAX 3-wheeler, the Spanish DCA was a 4-wheeler based on the Citroen 2CV. The fibreglass roadster body changed an old 2CV into an attractive 2-seater with classic styling, with details such as a one-part windshield, leather straps on the hood, a spoke steering-wheel, wooden dashboard and a lot of nice details made from fibreglass. With the 2CV engine these cars managed about 80mph (128 km/h). About fifty cars were built every year.

VCM

D.C. DESIGN (IND) 1993 to date

D.C. Design, Bombay.
Ex-GM designer Dilip Chabria was an incredibly prolific car designer and manufacturer, creating a vast range of new bodywork on Indian-made cars. Most were supplied as conversions. Chabria's first ever creation was the Hurricane, based on a Suzuki Gypsy with a shortened wheelbase, only two seats, contoured headlamps, a rear spoiler and wide wheels and tyres. An alternative model on the same chassis was the Ra, a Suzuki X90 lookalike. From a design point of view the most successful design was the Arya, based on the Tata Sierra but with Suzuki Swift upper bodywork and Fiat Coupé headlights. The Targa Sports Car was based on the Maruti 1000 (Suzuki Swift); the B.T.S. (which bizarrely stood for 'Better Than Sex') transformed the Maruti 800, changing to a mid-engined layout and completely revising the styling; the Vampire was a Plymouth Prowler-inspired creation on the Daewoo Nexia. Four-wheel-drive models included the Devak (on a Tempo Trax chassis) and the Quadro (on a Mahindra chassis), while D.C. also converted Hindustans and Opels into limousines.

CR

D & D (US) 1994–1998

D&D Corvette, Akron, Ohio.
The D & D Corvette Grand Sport was a replica of the Chevrolet racing car of the same name, of which only five had been built. D & D built a lot more replicas than that in both coupé and roadster forms. Body kits could be adapted to 1968–82 Corvettes, or D & D offered a round tube frame similar to the original but with new Corvette suspension and brakes. These kits proved to be very popular, but in 1998 D & D sold the project to ERA.

HP

D.D. (VN) 1949–1950

Marcel Degant had a plan to replace Vietnamese rickshaws, whose passengers were carried ahead of the driver, with a safer vehicle. He designed the car in France but set up finance to produce the car in Saigon. He hired Louis Descloitre to design a small open 3-wheeler powered by a 125cc Jonghi engine, with a single driver up front using handlebars and space for two passengers behind. Only six cars had been built before Degant decamped for Marrakech in Morocco, where a further 36 cars were made. Financial problems caused in part by Degant's alcoholism ended the project prematurely.

CR

DEAL (US) 1908–1911

Deal Motor Vehicle Co., Jonesville, Michigan.
The Deal Buggy Co. was set up in 1865, being renamed J.J. Deal & Son in 1891. George Deal motorised a buggy in 1905 and may have made a few more such conversions, but it was not until 1908 that the Deal Motor Vehicle Co. was formed and a production car turned out. This was the Deal 30, a 4-seater runabout whose solid tyres hinted at its buggy origins, although the wheels were of normal size. Its lack of doors at either front or rear was a rather primitive feature. In 1911 a more conventional 5-seater tourer was built, but this was the last year for Deal cars. Buggies continued to be made up to 1915.

NG

DEASY (GB) 1906–1911

Deasy Motorcar Manufacturing Co. Ltd, Coventry.
Deasy cars were built by a company headed by Captain Henry H.P. Deasy (1866–1947), whose father was the Lord Justice of Appeal in Dublin. He imported the Swiss MARTINI into England, and achieved fame by driving a 14hp Martini up the route of the Rochers de Naye rack railway in October 1903. Three years later he persuaded a group of wealthy friends to back him in a new car company. For a factory he acquired the premises at Parkside, Coventry, formerly occupied by the IDEN Motor Co., and his designer was E.W. Lewis, who came from ROVER. The first Deasy car had a 4.5-litre side-valve engine with cylinders cast en-bloc, which was a very early example of this practice. It also had a camshaft brake which Lewis had used on Rovers, full-pressure lubrication, transverse rear suspension, and an armoured wood frame. Both sets of brakes worked on the rear wheels, but by 1908 a transmission brake had been adopted. Larger Deasys included the 8.6-litre 35 and 12-litre 45. Relations between Deasy and Lewis were not good, and by the end of 1908 both men had lost their positions, although they continued with the firm; Deasy as a director and Lewis as a consulting engineer.

A smaller 2.9-litre 15 appeared in 1909, the year when J.D. Siddeley joined the company. The older Deasys were continued into 1910, but Siddeley introduced a new line of cars with thermosyphon-cooled engines ahead of dashboard radiators, and pressed-steel frames. Made in 2918cc 14/20hp and 4082cc 18/28hp models, they were called Deasy-J.D.S. to distinguish them from the older models which were called Deasy Standards. For 1911 there was a smaller Deasy-J.D.S., the 1944cc 12hp, but for 1912 the names of car and company were changed to SIDDELEY-DEASY. Captain Deasy had left at about the time that Siddeley joined the company. He returned to Ireland and, following in his father's footsteps, eventually became Lord Justice Baron Deasy of the Irish Court of Appeal.

NG

DeATLEY (US) c.1985

DeAtley Motor Sports, Portland, Oregon.
The DeAtley DMS 4.7 was a modified Mercedes 450SL with a 297hp engine, improved suspension and minor bodywork. The body was mildly restyled and dechromed, and a 5-speed transmission was installed. They were available built up from a new Mercedes, or the customer could bring their car in for conversion.

HP

DE BAZALAIRE (F) 1908–1928

F. de Bazalaire SA, Paris.
The De Bazalaire car appeared in public in 1907 when a team of three 1100cc 2-cylinder light cars competed in the Coupe des Voiturettes, although production did not start until the following year. Three models were listed in 1908; an 1100cc 8/9hp, 1.7-litre 12/14hp, both twins, and a 2-litre 4-cylinder model. They had L-head side-valve engines and rear-axle gearboxes. There was also a small six sold by Busson as the Busson-Bazalaire. Overhead inlet valves were adopted in 1910 when the largest model was a 2.5-litre six. In 1913 De Bazalaire

tried the Fischer side-valve engine but did not put it into production. Instead they made a range of five 4-cylinder cars using Ballot engines in the smaller models, and Janvier in the larger. Among these was the Type MM-Sport, with very long stroke (80 × 180mm) 3.6-litre T-head engine. The rear-axle gearboxes were retained up to the war.

The postwar De Bazalaires were conventional cars using mostly single-ohc S.C.A.P. engines of 1690cc, although the 3.6-litre Janvier was listed up to 1924.
NG

DE BEERS (GB) 1986
This company offered turn-key reproductions of the MG TD (on a Nissan Sunny basis) and the AC Cobra (on a Nissan 300 Cedric). The bodywork was in fibreglass and as much success as might be imagined awaited them.
CR

DE BOISSE (F) 1900–1904
J. de Boisse, Paris.
The De Boisse began life as a 3-wheeler with a single-cylinder engine mounted over the front-wheel, which it drove by chain. It was steered by a very long tiller, and had a 2-seater body. In 1902 came a more conventional car powered by a 6hp single-cylinder De Dion-Bouton engine, with shaft drive and a De Dion rear axle. In 1904 De Boisse offered a larger car with 12hp 2-cylinder De Dion engine.
NG

DEBONNAIRE (US) c.1955
Replac Corp., Euclid, Ohio.
This angular kit sportscar was based on 1941 to 1951 Ford running gear. The kit consisted of a fibreglass body with trim and an optional hard-top. Although it was also sold in kit form, a fully assembled Debonnaire cost $1800. Replac also sold a roadster kit called the Venture. It was styled by Phil Egan and the kit was only $650. It also fitted 1941 to 1951 Ford chassis.
HP

DE BRUYNE (GB) 1968
De Bruyne Motor Car Co. Ltd, Newmarket, Suffolk.
When the Gordon Keeble GT project failed, rights to the car were bought by John de Bruyne, an American. In 1968 de Bruyne took a stand at the New York Motor Show and displayed two rebadged Gordon Keebles and a new mid-engined coupé which had a 5.7-litre Chevrolet engine, a 5-speed transaxle, and a claimed top speed of 180mph (290km/h).
Nothing further was heard from de Bruyne.
MJL

DE CARLO (RA) 1959–1965
Metalmecanica Saic, Buenos Aires.
Metalmecanica was born in 1943. Production of the Paperino and Superpaperino scooters started in 1957. Tens of thousands of these were made. At the same time, automobile production was envisaged and this took form in the production of the De Carlo 600 and De Carlo 700 automobiles, which were in fact BMW 600 and 700 made under licence. Production started in 1959 and continued until 1965. 1,413 De Carlo 600s and 9,060 De Carlo 700s were made. Towards the end of 1965, Metalmecanica also made the Simca Ariane under licence. In early 1966 this model was also dropped, after 504 had been made.
ACT

DECATUR (i) (US) 1910–1911
Decatur Motorcar Co., Decatur, Indiana.
Mainly producers of commercial vehicles, this company offered the Decatur Utility Car, a 4-seater with rear seats which could be removed for carrying goods. The engine was a 12/14hp four, and at least 200 were made before the company returned to exclusive production of trucks.
NG

DECATUR (ii) (US) 1914–1915
Parcel Post Equipment Co., Grand Rapids, Michigan.
Most of these vehicles were built as mail delivery vans, in which the driver sat behind the load carrying area. However, a small number were turned out in

1910 De Bazalaire 10CV roadster.
NATIONAL MOTOR MUSEUM

1923 De Bazalaire 10CV tourer.
NATIONAL MOTOR MUSEUM

roadster form, with a seat replacing the box where the mail was carried. The engine was a 12/14hp four, and final drive was by chain.
NG

DECAUVILLE (F) 1898–1910
Sté des Voitures Automobiles Decauville, Petit Bourg, Seine-et-Oise.
The Société Decauville was founded in 1854 and engaged in a wide variety of engineering activities, but their speciality was narrow-gauge railway locomotives for branch lines and works use. At the end of 1897 a subsidiary company was formed to make a small car designed by Messrs Guedon and Cornilleau of Bordeaux, and this went into production in 1898. It was of very light construction, with tubular frame and powered by two 1.75hp De Dion-Bouton engines on the same crankcase, mounted under the seat and driving the rear axle through a 2-speed gearbox. Front suspension was independent, by a transverse spring and sliding pillars, and was the first known example of ifs on a petrol-engined car. There was no rear suspension at all. The car seated three, one seat facing the other two.

The little Decauville was a classic example of a voiturette, but as this name had been adopted by Léon Bollée, Decauville chose the name voiturelle for their little car. Production for 1898 was set at 600 cars, but only about 100 were delivered that year. Improved models were made in 1899, incorporating a water-cooled engine, rear suspension and a 3-speed gearbox. A larger engine of 5hp was available. The voiturelles proved very popular, took part in town-to-town races and were made under licence in Germany by WARTBURG and in Italy by MARCHAND.

In 1900 the engine was moved to the front, under a round bonnet with dashboard radiator. It was now an 8hp in-line twin of 1416cc, with 4-speed gearbox and shaft drive. It was followed by a 2090cc 10hp twin, with fully floating rear axle, one of which was bought by Henry Royce. He used several aspects of its design

1899 Decauville 3½hp single-cylinder voiturette.
NATIONAL MOTOR MUSEUM

1901 Decauville 10hp 2-cylinder tonneau.
NATIONAL MOTOR MUSEUM

1907 Decauville 16/20hp limousine.
NATIONAL MOTOR MUSEUM

in the first ROYCE car of 1904. The voiturelle was dropped at the end of 1902, and from then onwards Decauvilles were conventional cars, with dual ignition and chain drive on the larger models. A 12/14hp twin was listed until 1905, but thereafter all Decauvilles had four cylinders; 350 cars were delivered in 1904, which was probably Decauville's best year. Trucks and buses were also made at this time. Five models were catalogued in 1906, from 2.7 to 9.2 litres. Again there was licence production of some models in Germany and Italy, this time by EHRHARDT in Germany and by LUX in Italy. Production dwindled in the last few years as the cars failed to keep up with current developments. The last

cars were probably made in 1909 or 1910, and the automobile division of Decauville was closed in 1911.
NG

DE CEZAC (F) 1922–1927
Automobiles de Cezac, Perigueux, Dordogne.
The first De Cezac cars were made to special order, using Ballot engines, but from 1922 some attempt was made to market them commercially. Two sizes of 4-cylinder Ballot engine were used, 1590 and 1685cc. Tourers, saloons and coupés were offered, and the cars were of very conventional appearance and design. From 1925 a smaller C.I.M.E. engine of 1202cc was offered as well.
NG

DECHAMPS (B) 1899–1904
1899 Ateliers H.P. Dechamps, Brussels.
1900–1903 SA des Moteurs et Automobiles Dechamps, Brussels.
1903–1904 SA de Construction Mécanique et d'Automobiles, Brussels.
In March 1899 H.P. Dechamps exhibited a De Dion-Bouton-type tricycle and a voiturette powered by a front-mounted 3hp 2-cylinder engine, with 3-speed gearbox and chain drive. On 31 December 1899 the new company was formed, with larger premises which included a foundry and coachbuilding shop. The 1900 range consisted of three types, the tricycle, a 4.5hp 2-cylinder 2-seater voiturette and 8hp 4-seater car, while in 1901 the tricycle gave way to a 6hp single-cylinder voiturette, and the larger car was a 12hp. A variety of bodies was made, including a wagonette and light truck. Dechamps entered in town-to-town races such as Paris – Berlin for which they built a 20hp 4-cylinder car.
  In 1903 the company came under British control and the name was changed to SA de Construction Mécaniques et d'Automobiles, although the name Dechamps was still used for the cars. These were now larger, from a 2198cc 9/11hp twin to two fours, a 4396cc 14hp and a 5024cc 18hp, and they were all chain driven. In January 1904 the company brought out a new car under the name BAUDOUIN, and the Dechamps name was dropped.
NG

DECHAUX (F) 1947
Charles Dechaux displayed at the 1947 Paris Salon a chassis with a front-mounted transverse 4-cylinder air-cooled engine. Problems with the integrated automatic gearbox meant that the chassis was never bodied.
CR

DECKER (US) 1902–1903
Decker Automobile Co., Owego, New York.
Ward Decker was the president of the Decker Automatic Telephone Exchange Co. in Oswego, and designed a neat-looking shaft-driven small car powered by a 5.5hp single-cylinder engine mounted under a Renault-type bonnet. In early 1903 he formed a company to manufacture it, possibly with a factory in Binghamton, New York, but production never started.
NG

DECKERT (F) 1901–1906
H. Deckert et Compagnie, Paris.
Deckert cars were conventional machines made in four models, a 6hp single-cylinder, twins of 12 and 16hp and a 20hp four. The 6hp had a 2-seater body with a spider seat behind, and the larger cars had 5-seater tonneau bodies. Only one Deckert is known to survive, a 6hp owned by a Veteran Car Club member in Hampshire.
NG
Further Reading
'Deckert 8hp 1902', Debbie and Alan Coleman, *Veteran Car*, October 1996.

DE CLERQ (F) 1992 to date
Automobiles De Clercq, Provins, Seine-et-Marne.
This British-style 1930s roadster was exquisitely conceived by Benoît De Clercq, a co-director of the carrosserie Lecoq, and the car's body was realised in aluminium. In a tubular chassis, its choice of Ford engines ranged from a 130bhp 1.8, to a 220bhp Cosworth, to a 2.9-litre V6. There was Ford 5-speed transmission and 4-wheel disc brakes.
CR

DE CLEVES ET CHEVALIER (F) c.1907

Automobiles de Cleves et Chevalier, Neuilly, Seine.
This company made a chassis with 2120cc 10/14hp 4-cylinder pair-cast engine, on which two body styles were offered, a 5-seater tourer and 2-seater coupé. The chassis was conventional, with 3-speed gearbox and shaft drive.

KB

DECO (US) c.1985

Deco International Corp., Pacoima, California.
The Deco 427 Cobra replica used a shortened 1968 to 1982 Corvette chassis under a fibreglass body. Ford or Chevrolet engines were available and cars could be purchased in kit or completed form.

HP

DECOLON (F) 1957

Éts Decolon, Champigny-sur-Marne.
With dumpy 3-wheeled styling, the Decolon had a fibreglass open body using experience gained through the company's main business, making fairings for motorcycles. A 2-stroke Ydral air-cooled 5bhp 125cc or 10bhp 175cc engine was rear-mounted, driving the single rear wheel by chain, while a 250cc version was also mooted. Its relatively high price did it no favours in finding custom.

CR

DE COSMO (B) 1903–1908

De Cosmo et Compagnie, Liège.
Joseph de Cosmo had a varied career before he started to make cars under his own name. Born in Italy, he worked in Egypt in a railway locomotive repair shop, then for the Italian navy and several car firms including Gauthier-Wehrle and Delahaye in France, Singer in England, and F.N. in Belgium. In 1903 he left F.N. and started to make cars under his own name. They were large 4-cylinder machines of 24/30hp and 30/35hp, with 3-speed gearboxes and shaft drive. The 24/30 was to have been made under licence by WILKINSON in London, but the few Wilkinson-De Cosmos which appeared were probably Belgian-built. At the beginning of 1906 De Cosmo brought out a large 6-cylinder car with 4-speed gearbox and chain drive, whose capacity was 8270cc. This model was made by VIVINUS, but the smaller 4-cylinder models were continued, as De Cosmos. They also said that they were making trucks, buses and motor boats. The later cars had round radiators and bonnets of Delaunay-Belleville type.

NG

DECOSTER (B) 1898

J. & H. Decoster, Thielt.
The brothers J. and H. Decoster ran a wholesale and retail bicycle business, selling ordinary cycles, tandems and triplettes under the name Iris. In 1898 they made a few tricycles, quadricycles and voiturettes powered by De Dion-Bouton engines.

NG

DE COURVILLE see GATSBY

DE CROSS (US) 1913–1914

De Cross Cyclecar Co., Cincinnati, Ohio.
Called by its maker the Cy-Car, this was a typical cyclecar and was powered by a V-twin Spacke engine, with friction transmission and belt drive. Seating was in tandem, the driver being in the rear seat. To give him a better forward view, the passenger seat was lowered. The De Cross Cy-Car probably did not proceed beyond the prototype stage.

NG

D.E.C.S.A. (RSM) 1982–c.1987

D.E.C.S.A., San Marino.
The Lisa microcar was San Marino's first ever motor manufacturer, appearing in 1982, but that was just about the only exceptional thing about it. It had conventional-looking 2-seater fibreglass bodywork and a choice of 50cc and 123cc single-cylinder engines or a 250cc twin. Both 3- and 4-wheeled versions were built. Helped by French sales under Willam, it continued in production until about 1987.

CR

1902 Dechamps 8hp tonneau.
NATIONAL MOTOR MUSEUM

1902 Deckert 8hp 2-seater.
ALAN COLEMAN

DECUIR (US) c.1993

DeCuir Motor Co. Inc., Riverside, California.
DeCuir made a typical 427 Cobra replica with a mixture of fabricated and Ford Thunderbird suspension parts. They were sold in kit and turnkey form.

HP

DE DIETRICH (i) (F) 1897–1905

De Dietrich et Compagnie, Lunéville, Lorraine.
Still in business today, De Dietrich is one of the oldest industrial concerns in France. It was founded as an ironworks in 1684, and 100 years later it had three large factories in Alsace and Lorraine, as well as banking interests. The family suffered badly in the Revolution, but recovered to prosper in the nineteenth century, when they added railway rolling stock to their activities. The De Turckheim family came into the business in 1806 on the death of the then Baron de Dietrich and remained prominent well into the motor era. In 1871 Alsace became German territory after the Franco-Prussian war. While the Niederbronn factory became German, and later made the DE DIETRICH (ii), the family built a new factory on French soil at Lunéville in Lorraine, and it was here that they began making cars in 1897. They entered car manufacture by making the AMÉDÉE BOLLÉE design with horizontal 2-cylinder engines in 2.3- or 3-litre sizes. They were already quite old-fashioned, with tube ignition and a complex transmission system involving primary belt drive and final drive by two sets of bevels. The Lunéville factory turned out 72 of these cars in 1898 and 107 in 1900, but their poor performance in the 1901 Paris-Berlin Race demonstrated that a new design was needed. This was found in the shape of the TURCAT-MÉRY, a car being made in Marseilles on Panhard lines, with vertical front-mounted 2- and 4-cylinder engines, automatic inlet valves, tubular radiators, armoured wood frames and chain drive. In 1903 they were made with three sizes of 4-cylinder engines, 3, 4.1 and 5.4 litres. Mechanically-operated inlet valves arrived in 1904, and overhead inlet valves were used briefly in 1905.
During 1905 relations between Adrien de Turckheim and Eugene de Dietrich worsened. With financial backing from his father, his brother and Turcat-Méry

DE DIETRICH

1899 De Dietrich(i) streamlined racing car by Rothschild.
NATIONAL MOTOR MUSEUM

1902 De Dietrich(i) 16hp tonneau.
NATIONAL MOTOR MUSEUM

chairman Henri Estier, de Turckheim formed a new company for manufacture of the cars at Lunéville. It was called the Société Lorraine des Anciens Établissements de Dietrich et Compagnie. The cross of Lorraine featured on the badge and the cars were henceforth called LORRAINE-DIETRICH.

NG

DE DIETRICH (ii) (D) 1897–1904
De Dietrich et Compagnie, Niederbronn, Alsace.
Like its French counterpart, the German half of the De Dietrich empire made cars under Amédée Bollée licence for several years. To have a less expensive line of cars they acquired a licence to build the Belgian VIVINUS single-cylinder belt-drive voiturette. These were made in 1899 and 1900. Just as the French factory needed a new design and found it in the Turcat-Méry, Baron Eugene de Dietrich was highly impressed with the 4-cylinder car shown at the 1901 Milan Show by Ettore Bugatti. He persuaded the young Italian to come to Niederbronn where he designed a 4-cylinder chain-driven car called either De Dietrich, or De Dietrich-Bugatti. This was made in at least two engine sizes, a 5305cc called either a 20 or 24hp, and a 7430cc called a 24hp. In 1904 they were offered on the British market by the Burlington Carriage Co., and were called either De Dietrich-Bugatti or Burlington. Early in 1904 Bugatti parted company with De Dietrich and joined Emile Mathis for whom he designed the HERMES-SIMPLEX. No further cars were made at Niederbronn.

NG

DE DION-BOUTON (F) 1883–1932
1883–1894 De Dion, Bouton et Trépardoux, Paris.
1894–1897 De Dion, Bouton et Compagnie, Paris.
1897–1932 De Dion, Bouton et Compagnie, Puteaux, Seine.
As with Rolls and Royce, this famous French marque grew from the partnership of an aristocratic backer and a talented engineer. The backer was the Comte Jules Felix Philip Albert de Dion de Malfiance (1856–1946), who could trace his ancestry back to a thirteenth century crusader. The engineer was George Thadée Bouton (1847–1938), son of an artist and a music teacher. They met at the workshop which Bouton ran with his brother-in-law Charles Trépardoux (1853–1920), and which specialised in miniature steam engines and mechanical toys. De Dion had a mechanical bent, and offered the partners considerably more money than they were making, if they would work exclusively for him. A partnership, De Dion, Bouton and Trepardoux was formed, although some have wondered why De Dion did not simply employ the engineers, since his means and social position were so much higher than theirs. Perhaps they held valuable patents which earned them a partnership.

De Dion's ambitions reached much higher than mechanical toys, and before the year 1883 was out the new partnership had made a boiler capable of producing superheated steam for marine use, and a 4-wheeled steam carriage. This had a front-mounted boiler and 2-cylinder engine driving the front-wheels by leather belts. Steering was on the rear wheels. The belt drive caused many problems, which were ended when the machine caught fire and was destroyed.

In 1884 they built another 4-wheeler, of completely different conception. The boiler was smaller and coke fired, which reduced the risk of conflagration, the rear wheels were driven and the front steered, and it seated four people. An annular tube boiler generated steam at 170psi. This car still exists and has

NICK BALDWIN

DE DION, COUNT ALBERT (1856–1946)
The Count de Dion was probably the most patrician of all car makers, yet he was much prouder of his role in the infant motor industry than in his ancestry. He was born on 9 March 1856 at the family château of Maubreuil, at Carquefou, near Nantes, and was christened Jules Félix Philippe Albert de Dion de Malfiance. His father, the Marquis Albert Guilliaume Louis Joseph de Dion de Malfiance (1824–1901), traced his ancestry back to Jean de Dion of the Belgian village of Dion-le-Val, which he left in 1218 to join the Fifth Crusade. There followed a long line of knights to which the titles of Baron and Marquis were added. By the nineteenth century, engineering talent showed itself, when Henri de Dion (1828–78) pioneered the use of ornamental cast iron as a structural material.

Young Albert was sent to Munich to perfect his German (English was already a second language as he had an English grandmother), after which

398

been restored to running order, taking part in the 1996 London-Brighton Run in which it was the oldest competitor by seven years. In 1887 Comte de Dion drove in the 'race' organised by *Le Velocipede* magazine, in which he was the only competitor. He was said to have achieved a speed of 37mph (60km/h).

The partners built two more cars in 1885, both 4-seaters, one of which reverted to the original pattern of front-wheel drive and rear-wheel steering, the other with the conventional arrangement. They then turned to a much lighter design, a single-seater tricycle whose tiny 2-cylinder engine drove the rear wheel via a connecting rod, in locomotive style. Several of these were made and sold, and in 1892 Michelin pneumatic tyres were fitted for the first time. The first of a series of steam tractors was built in 1893. This incorporated what came to be known as the De Dion axle, but the design was probably the work of Trépardoux. It used a dead axle to carry the load, while drive was taken from the differential to the wheels by non-load-bearing half shafts with universal joints at each end. In the early vehicles the drive went not directly to the wheels, but to a countershaft from which the wheels were driven by chains. This tractor was coupled to the rear half of a horse-drawn victoria, and competed in the Paris-Rouen Trial of 1894 where it put up the best performance, but was disqualified from victory because it needed two men to operate it. Replicas of this tractor, which the makers called a 'boggie', were on sale in 1895, being advertised as suitable for drawing landaus, victorias, coupés, mail coaches or trucks. In 1897 one pulled a bus trailer carrying 35 passengers. The company also made rigid 4-wheeled steam vehicles for both goods and passenger work, up to 1904.

By the early 1890s, de Dion was having doubts about steam being the best motive power. He built two very advanced petrol engines, a 4-cylinder rotary and a 12-cylinder static radial, and by 1893 had convinced a somewhat sceptical

1895 De Dion-Bouton steam tractor with victoria trailer.
NICK GEORGANO

George Bouton of the advantages of internal combustion, certainly for passenger cars. Trépardoux would never be won over, and resigned from the partnership in January 1894. De Dion and Bouton then worked on a small petrol engine, initially of only 137cc, which could run at the astonishingly high speed of 3000rpm (the contemporary Benz engine turned at a maximum of 470rpm). The secret lay in the electric ignition in which a cam permitted not only the closing but also

he spent a number of years as a playboy in Paris society. He was accomplished in several sports, including duelling, and his activities seem to have been a gift to gossip writers of the day. Griffith Borgeson summed him up; 'He was clever, amusing, the life of any party and universally popular in high society in spite of his ignobly eccentric part-time obsession with nasty steam engines'.

It was this obsession that led him to the door of Charles Trépardoux, maker of a miniature steam engine that de Dion had seen in a gift shop. Trépardoux, his brother-in-law Georges Bouton and the young Count got on so well that they formed a partnership. De Dion was attracted to the idea of a small personal self-propelled vehicle in contrast to the large, bus-like machines being made by Amédée Bollée. It was the ability of Bouton and Trépardoux to miniaturise the steam engine which fascinated de Dion. Their first project was not, in fact, a car but a small boat for which a boiler capable of producing superheated steam was designed. This was patented in May 1883, the first of 394 patents granted to the firm or to de Dion himself. It is not certain how much of an innovator he was, but he was certainly full of ideas, despite a lack of engineering training. A plan to make boilers for the French Navy failed, bringing financial disaster to the partnership. De Dion's father was so incensed, whether because of the financial loss or the bad publicity it brought to the family name, that he declared that he was not responsible for Albert's debts, and obtained a court order preventing him from access to any of the family wealth. However, his personal allowance continued. The court order remained in force until 1892, when the success of the De Dion Bouton steam tricycle persuaded the Marquis that his son, now 36 years old, was not such an irresponsible spendthrift after all. As well as making a success with his tricycles he was now contributing papers to such prestigious journals as the *Bulletin de la Société des Ingenieurs Civils*. By the end of the 1880s, de Dion was becoming disenchanted with steam, and to avoid friction with his partners, especially Trépardoux who was the most conservative, he hired a small machine shop where he could work on petrol engines. He built a small 2-cylinder unit suitable for a tricycle, and also a 4-cylinder rotary radial and a 12-cylinder static radial. These very advanced engines, years ahead of their time, would have been suitable for aircraft, had there been any around, but as it was they had no future.

Apart from making cars Count de Dion was active in promoting the whole idea of automobilism. He was one of the Comité Organisateur des Courses,

which promoted the Paris-Bordeaux-Paris race of 1895, and following this was founded the Automobile Club de France. De Dion declined the presidency of this club, which was taken by the Baron de Zuylen, but he became vice-president. In 1895 he was on the organising committee of the first Salon de l'Automobile, so he was in at the formation of three of the leading organisations in France, and indeed in the world. The Comité Organisateur des Courses became the Commission Sportive Internationale (CSI), the governing body of today's motor sport, and the Automobile Club de France unified other clubs under the banner of the Fédération Internationale de l'Automobile (FIA). In 1900 he planned a series of road maps covering the whole of France, to be accompanied by a guide listing sites of interest, hotels, restaurants and garages. When it was complete he found that there was hostility from rival car makers who complained that he would earn too much publicity for his own cars. He therefore decided to hand it over to a neutral company, but one still with motoring connections. What better than a tyre manufacturer? Thus he gave the world another landmark, the Michelin Guide. He also founded the popular sports journal, *l'Auto*, which became *l'Équipe* after World War II.

Albert de Dion inherited the title of Marquis in 1901, on the death of his father and the following year he entered politics. From 1902 to 1923 he was a deputy and from then to 1941 a senator, being regarded as one of the most popular politicians in France. He was highly influential in the modernisation of France's roads, and his political career lasted long after car making ended. Much of his fortune was tied up in the business, and he was not a wealthy man when he died on 19 August 1946. His wife had died earlier, and Georges Bouton in 1938. Only his faithful Ethiopian chauffeur, Zélélé, who had joined the Count at the turn of the century, was still with him to the end. During the war, when petrol supplies were virtually non-existent, de Dion and Zélélé resurrected a steam tricycle of the 1880s and drove solemnly around Paris in it. The Marquis de Dion had no children, and on his death the title became extinct. He bequeathed the Château de Maubreuil to be a home for disabled soldiers.

NG

Further Reading
Images du Passé, Claude Baudin (ghosted autobiography), Paris, 1937.
'The Automotive World of Albert de Dion', Griffith Borgeson, *Automobile Quarterly*, Vol.15, No.3.

1901 De Dion-Bouton voiturette.
NATIONAL MOTOR MUSEUM

1905 De Dion-Bouton 15hp tourer.
NATIONAL MOTOR MUSEUM

1909 De Dion-Bouton 8hp roadster.
NATIONAL MOTOR MUSEUM

the rapid opening of the primary electrical circuit. For production the speed was reduced to 1800rpm. The single-cylinder engine was air-cooled, with an aluminium crankcase, with overhead inlet and side exhaust valves, and a flywheel on each side of the connecting rod to give ideal balance. It was installed in a tricycle which was pure bicycle back to the rear axle tube, and was therefore inexpensive to make. De Dion bought their bicycle frames from Decauville at this time. The original 137cc engine gave only 0.5bhp, which was insufficient, but the engine was easily scaled up, to 185cc in April 1896, 198cc in September 1896 and so on, up to 327cc in February 1900. The last tricycle, with 402cc water-cooled engine, was made in 1902.

An important year was 1898, because it saw the first De Dion-Bouton motorcycle and the first petrol-engined 4-wheeler. The latter was essentially a tricycle with two front-wheels and a seat between them. It paved the way for the introduction, in July 1900, of the famous *vis-à-vis* which had a water-cooled 402cc engine under the driver's seat, driving the rear wheels via a simple gearchange with a separate clutch for each of the two speeds, operated by a wheel on the steering column. An anticlockwise turn operated the low-speed clutch to move the car away from rest, while a turn in the opposite direction released the low-speed clutch and operated the high speed clutch. Final drive was by the De Dion axle. For 1903 the engine was moved to the front, under a coal scuttle bonnet, to make the Populaire, which became even more famous than the *vis-à-vis*. Two sizes of engine were offered; the 700cc 6hp Type N and the 942cc 8hp Type O. The former was for 2-seater bodies, had two forward speeds and no reverse, while the latter was suitable for 4-seater or light truck bodies and had three forward speeds and a reverse. By the end of 1903 there were two more Populaire variants, the Type Q with reverse gear, and the Type R with 942cc engine. The single-cylinder De Dion-Bouton was made until 1912, and production must have been in the region of 20,000 cars. Many have survived, and in 1999 there were 200 registered with the Veteran Car Club of Great Britain.

In contrast was the electric De Dion-Bouton, of which a very small number were made in 1901. They were 4-seaters, with batteries mounted below front and rear seats, and the 8hp motor centrally mounted under the floor. Two models were built; a cab with artillery wheels and an open 4-seater with wire wheels. They were not built in quantity because of limited range. Also, doubtless, the company was doing so well with petrol cars and steam trucks and buses, that they did not need a third string to their bow.

In 1900 De Dion claimed that more than 20,000 of their engines were in service, and in 1902 more than 30,000. These were by no means all in De Dion-Bouton cars, for they sold licences all over the world. It has been estimated that 140 makes worldwide used De Dion engines, some of the better known being Isotta Fraschini, Adler, Humber, Peerless, and Pierce-Arrow. During 1900–01 a factory in Brooklyn, New York, made a small number of American De Dion Motorettes in 2-seater, *vis-à-vis* or closed coupé forms, powered by American-made 3.5hp engines. In 1900 De Dion had 1300 employees, reaching 2500 in 1906, 4000 in 1912 and peaking at 6000 during World War I.

The first 2-cylinder De Dion-Bouton was the 1728cc Type S of 1903, and the first four, the 2545cc Type AD in 1904. The latter had a pressed-steel frame in place of the tubular frames used hitherto, these being used on the twins as well from 1905, and the singles from 1906. De Dion-Boutons were becoming steadily more conventional, with a foot-operated clutch and radiator in front of the bonnet replacing the coal scuttle type in 1906, though the single-cylinder Type AL retained the old expanding clutches. Mechanically-operated inlet valves were standard across the range by 1909. The largest fours that year ran to 4942cc (Type BU 30hp), but an important step forward was the V8, introduced at the 1910 Turin Show. The world's first series-produced V8 engine, the 6107cc Type CJ, had a single, centrally-mounted camshaft and twin-barrel carburettor. It was joined later in the year by a smaller model, the 3534cc Type CN. By 1918 the V8 had been made in twelve different sizes, from 2972 to 7773cc; an incredible variety, although some of the larger units went into commercial or military vehicles only. De Dion-Bouton's V8 was not especially successful, and probably made no profit for the company, but it inspired D. McCall White of Cadillac to develop a truly successful V8 a few years later. The De Dion axle was by no means universal on the cars made up to World War I, being supplemented by worm or bevel drive on several models. The 1914 range ran from the 821cc Type EJ2 twin, followed by the 1182cc EJ4 monobloc four, and six larger fours up to the 4398cc Type ET9, as well as the V8s.

Rotonde carriage body

Illustrated on model A L 2, 8 h.p. chassis

	Model :	AL 2, 8 h.p.			BN, 8 h.p.			BO, 9 h.p.			BQ, 10 h.p.		
		£	s.	d.	£	s.	d.	£	s.	d.	£	s.	d.
Chassis with tyres only		197	0	0	187	0	0	246	0	0	291	0	0
With Rotonde body ...		222	0	0	214	10	0	276	0	0	321	0	0
Extras :													
Waterproof hood as above		15	0	0	15	0	0	15	0	0	15	0	0
Cape-cart hood ...		12	0	0	12	0	0	12	0	0	12	0	0
Folding wind shield		8	10	0	8	10	0	8	10	0	8	10	0
Side doors		4	0	0	4	0	0	4	0	0	4	0	0
Box at back		5	0	0	5	0	0	6	0	0	6	0	0
Total, with body as illustrated		254	10	0	247	0	0	309	10	0	354	10	0

The above prices include with the carriage body, platform steps, as illustrated on next page, to all models except the 8 h.p. A L 2. On this the cost is £2 10s. extra.

For specifications of chassis, see pages 12, 14 and 16

Lamps not included; prices on application.

1913 De Dion-Bouton 26hp tourer.
NATIONAL MOTOR MUSEUM

1924 De Dion-Bouton 12/24 coupé.
NATIONAL MOTOR MUSEUM

1914 Deemster 10hp coupé.
NICK BALDWIN

De Dion-Bouton made a great variety of products during the war, including rifle components, bicycles, armoured vehicles, conventional trucks, aero engines, and magnetos. The latter were copies of the German Bosch, supplies of which had been cut off by the war. The company should have been well placed to compete in the postwar market, but in fact the 1920s saw a sad decline. This was in part due to the ages of the two partners – in 1919 de Dion was 63 and Bouton 72, neither had children in the business, and new designs were too few and too late. Several models of four and V8 were offered, one of the latter being as small as 2655cc. The fours had only two main bearing crankshafts, which limited revs to 1500rpm and made for a very sluggish performance, and the V8s were fragile due to poor quality metal. With the competition from Citroën, Renault and others in the low-price field, and modern luxury cars like

Hispano-Suiza, there was little reason for anyone to buy a De Dion-Bouton, and decreasingly few people did. The V8s were dropped after 1923, and there was a more modern four, the 1847cc Type IW with ohvs and front-wheel brakes. A new model for 1926 was the 1328cc JP, some of which were sold as the Model B1 BELLANGER, but the factory closed for most of 1927. When it reopened, two new models were offered. These were the 1982cc 4-cylinder Type LA and the 2496cc straight-8 Type LB, which was hastily enlarged to the 3072cc LP. Both had pushrod ohvs, and the 8 had Dewandre servo-assisted brakes. It was very expensive, at 102,000 francs for a coupé and 110,000 for a saloon. Very few were sold, and passenger car production ended in 1932. Commercial vehicles continued to be made in small numbers, especially low-floor coaches and refuse vehicles. The latter lasted until about 1950, and the 1947 Paris Salon saw an advanced prototype of a streamlined coach powered by a supercharged 6-cylinder opposed-piston engine. Part of the Puteaux factory became the Paris headquarters of Rover, and in the 1950s a few forward-control Land Rover fire engines carried De Dion-Bouton badges.

NG

Further Reading
'The Automobile World of Albert de Dion', Griffith Borgeson,
Automobile Quarterly, Vol. 15.
The Single-cylinder De Dion-Bouton, Anthony Bird, Profile Publications, 1966.
De Dion-Bouton, Anthony Bird, Ballantine Books, 1971.
'Charles Trépardoux, Automobile Pioneer', Francis Trépardoux,
The Automobile, April 1992.

DEEMSTER (GB) 1914–1924

Ogston Motor Co. Ltd, Acton, London.

The original Deemster light car was a development of the WILKINSON which used the same 844cc 4-cylinder engine that powered the company's Wilkinson-T.M.C. motorcycles. This had been introduced in 1912, but in January 1914 both motorcycle and car had been discontinued and the car design taken over by a new company, the Ogston Motor Co. headed by Scotsman J.N. Ogston. He originally planned to use his own name for the car, but by the time it appeared in April 1914 it had been rechristened Deemster, the name given to a judge in the Isle of Man. The engine, which was made in the works, had been enlarged to 1086cc, but otherwise the car was little changed until July 1914 when it was given a handsome vee-radiator and a starter which could be operated from the seat. The 2- and 4-seater open bodies were made by the Auto Sheet Metal Co. of nearby Shepherd's Bush. Very few had been completed before World War I brought car manufacture to an end. Ogston made field kitchens during the conflict, and in 1918 a new company, the Ogston Motor Co. (1918) Ltd, was formed. They bought land for a new factory, although still retaining the first, and announced four models – 2- and 4-seater tourers, a folding head coupé and a pointed tail sports car. However they were slow to get into production, and no cars at all were made in 1919 apart from five exhibited at the Olympia Show.

Production did get going in 1920, and in 1922 they turned to a 1496cc British Anzani engine, lengthening the wheelbase from 96 to 111in (2436 to 2817 mm) in September. Bodies were still made by the Auto Sheet Metal Co. Production ran at 15–20 per week for a while. In 1923 there were plans to make the Deemster in America, and the Deemster Corp. of Hazleton, Pennsylvania, was set up. Only one American Deemster was made, and it may well have come from Acton, though the track was 2in wider. Also in 1923, six Deemsters were sold to FRAZER NASH, who put their own badges on them. By 1924 the Deemster was becoming old-fashioned, with separate gearbox and rear-wheel brakes only, but the company could not afford to update the design, and did not survive into 1925.

NG

Further Reading
'Fragments on Forgotten Makes No. 29', Bill Boddy,
Motor Sport, November 1964.
'Deemster', M. Worthington-Williams, *The Automobile*, February 1990.

DEEP SANDERSON (GB) 1960–1969

Lawrencetune Engines Ltd, London.
Chris Lawrence Racing, London.

Deep Sanderson was named after a dance tune, 'Deep Henderson' by the Gilt-Edged Four, and the maiden name of the mother of racing driver and engineer, Chris Lawrence, the man behind the project.

During 1960–61 Lawrence built a handful of Formula Junior cars which raced without success. In late 1961, he launched the 301, a mid-engined coupé with Mini running gear, a backbone chassis and 'Lawrence Link' trailing link and coil spring suspension. It was perhaps the most competent Mini-based car of the 1960s.

After a false start with a bizarre body, the 301 was restyled. Lawrence subcontracted their construction to John Pearce, a former fabricator with Cooper. Pearce made about 20 cars, examples of which ran at Le Mans.

Lawrence's own company concentrated on prototypes including aerodynamic SLR bodies (one on a Triumph chassis, three on Morgan) and the chassis for the MONICA GT car.

MJL

DEERE-CLARK; DEERE (US) 1906–1907
Deere-Clark Motor Co., Moline, Illinois.

W.E. Clark had made the BLACKHAWK (i) in 1903 and two years later, with backing from the John Deere tractor company, he bought up the machinery of the defunct CLARKMOBILE company, and set up Deere-Clark in January 1906. It was a conventional car powered by a 25/30hp 4-cylinder engine, with shaft drive. Two body styles, a tourer and a limousine, were offered. For 1907 the car was known simply as the Deere, the wheelbase was lengthened by 6in and a Gentleman's Roadster added to the body range. Otherwise the design was unchanged. About 200 cars were made under both names, but by the end of 1907 the directors of John Deere decided not to remain in the car business. They continued with tractors and agricultural machinery, in which fields they are still active. The car side of the business was succeeded by the MIDLAND Car Co. early in 1908.

NG

DEERING MAGNETIC (US) 1918–1919
Magnetic Motors Corp., Chicago, Illinois.

The Deering Magnetic was a prestigious, if short-lived, luxury automobile equipped with an Entz transmission similar to that of the OWEN MAGNETIC. Powered by a Dorris 6-cylinder engine, the car was available with custom coachwork if so ordered. Designer of the Deering Magnetic was Karl H. Martin, formerly a custom coachbuilder in New York City who had previously designed the ROAMER, would design the KENWORTHY in 1920 and build his own WASP cars in Bennington, Vermont from 1919 to 1924. Wheelbase measured 132ins (3350mm) and prices were set at $4000 to $5000 for open models and from $4650 to $7000 for coupés, sedans, limousines and town cars. The failure of the Deering Magnetic was reportedly its difficulty in obtaining necessary parts when needed.

KM

DEETYPE (GB) 1974 to date
Deetype Replicas Ltd, East Hanningfield, Chelmsford, Essex.

Bryan Wingfield was one of the very first people to reproduce the Jaguar D-Type. In its initial guise, it was a fabulous and expensive machine with an aluminium monocoque realised by Williams & Pritchard. Any Jaguar XK engine could be fitted and Deetype even offered an expanded 4459cc 342bhp engine. Body styles included long-nose, short-nose and XK-SS, and there was also an abortive attempt to recreate the XJ13 racer. Bryan Wingfield branched out into engineering project work and also created a number of bespoke Ferrari replicas, including a Ferrari 400i-based modern re-interpretation of the GTO. He also made some 'genuine' Ford GT40s based on left-over chassis parts.

CR

DÉFI (F) 1973 to date
Défi Création et Construction Automobile, Lille.

Like so many other countries, France produced the British NOVA kit car under licence, here under the name Défi Sterling. It was sold complete or in kit form and could be powered by Volkswagen or Porsche engines, or later with Peugeot/Renault V6 power. A convertible model unique to France was also added. Another model – offered with less success – was the Irania, an open-topped jeep-style leisure vehicle using Volkswagen Transporter mechanicals.

CR

1962 Deep Sanderson 301 coupé.
NATIONAL MOTOR MUSEUM

1970 Deep Sanderson 2.6-litre V8 saloon, prototype for the Monica.
NATIONAL MOTOR MUSEUM

DEGUINGAND (F) 1927–1930
Sté des Nouveaux Ateliers A. Deguingand, Puteaux, Seine.

The old-established VINOT ET DEGUINGAND company closed its doors in 1926, but one of the partners, Albert Deguingand, was determined not to abandon car manufacture. The Vinot works were taken over by DONNET and Deguingand moved to smaller premises where he made a conventional light car powered by a 1170cc 4-cylinder S.C.A.P. engine made in side-valve (22bhp) or ohv (28bhp) form. A tourer and a saloon were offered, the latter having the unusual cost-cutting measure of two doors, both on the nearside of the car. A sports version with the ohv engine was announced but probably never built.

Deguingand quickly saw that these cars could offer no competition to mass producers such as Citroën, and so in 1928 he launched a smaller car, almost a revival of the cyclecar theme, with 735cc 4-cylinder 2-stroke engine designed by Marcel Violet. The cylinders were cast in pairs, each pair having a common combustion chamber and rising and falling together. The only moving parts were the four pistons, four bearings and the crankshaft. The 2-speed gearbox was in unit with the final drive, a separate lever being used to select reverse. Front suspension was by a single transverse spring. Three body styles were offered, 2- and 4-seater coupés and a doorless 2-seater sports car. The 2-stroke Deguingand had some success in rallies, but few were sold, and production ended in 1930. Three further attempts were made to market the design, however, by DONNET, GALBA and HUASCAR.

NG

DEHN (D) 1924
H.C. Dehn, Hamburg.

This was a 2-seater of simple design, powered by Dehn's own 2.5/8hp single-cylinder 2-stroke engine and with cycle-type wheels.

HON

DEHO (F) 1946–1948
Deho, Vanves.

The Deho was a 2-seater sports car based on Simca 8 mechanicals. This low-slung open sports car was designed by M. Turpin, and was built in collaboration with Auto-Avia. Deho also made performance parts for various Simca engines, and used the barquette to good effect to promote its tuning activities.

CR

1990 De La Chapelle roadster.
AUTOMOBILES DE LA CHAPELLE

1906 Delage 6hp 2-seater, sold in Great Britain as the Friswell Baby.
NATIONAL MOTOR MUSEUM

1914 Delage 15.9hp tourer.
NATIONAL MOTOR MUSEUM

DE JOUX (NZ) 1970

Ferris De Joux Design, Auckland, North Island.

A sports coupé which was produced by designing a fibreglass body to mate to the floorpan, bulkhead and sills of the Mini; the De Joux GT was significantly lower, wider and longer than the regular Mini but weighed 46kg less. The only mechanical revision was to locate the radiator at the front to achieve a lower bonnet line.

MG

DE LA CHAPELLE (F) 1985 to date

1985–1996 Automobiles De La Chapelle, Brignais.
1996–1997 D.L.C. Technologies, Brignais.
1997 to date Barré et Associés, Limonest.

This painstaking replica of the 1932 Bugatti Type 55 began life in 1978 as the STIMULA, changing in name in 1985 to De La Chapelle. It had the distinction of being the only replica sanctioned by the owners of the Bugatti name to carry the famous Bugatti plaque on its grill, a situation allowed to continue until 1988. There was a choice of 2- and 4-seater versions, all with fibreglass bodywork over a steel strengthening structure. The chassis was designed by Jacques Hubert of Matra and it was powered by a BMW 2-litre 6-cylinder engine or tuned Hartge 2.5-litre (258bhp) or Alpina 2.7-litre (210bhp) units. In 1989 De La Chapelle (under the auspices of Primwest-France) acquired a majority holding in the M.V.S. concern, manufacturers of the VENTURI. Filled with a spirit of optimism, in 1990 the company announced an ambitious new luxury MPV called the Parcours, to be built by Venturi. This had a 326bhp Mercedes-Benz 5-litre V8 engine and 4-wheel drive, but the immense (210in/5350mm) people carrier failed to reach production at its intended price of 1 million francs. At the 1992 Geneva Salon, another new model was shown, a car inspired by the Bugatti Type 57 Atalante. It could be bought as a 2-seater coupé or a 2+2 convertible. Finally a new Roadster model with modern Porsche Boxter-esque 2-seater bodywork was shown in 1996. Various engines were installed centrally: 135bhp and 167bhp 2.0-litre Peugeot 4-cylinder units and a 200bhp Renault V6. After financial instability, the Roadster's designer Bertrand Barré took over the company and finally productionised his car at the Mecasystème factory at Le Mans in 1998.

CR

DELACOUR (F) 1913–1920

Société des Automobiles Delacour, Paris.

The first Delacour was a light car powered by a 1778cc 4-cylinder engine, with friction transmission and shaft drive. Production was halted after the outbreak of war, but in 1920 the company announced two models, of 7 and 12hp, with what was described as 'patent progressive gear'.

NG

DELAGE (F) 1905–1953

1905–1912 Automobiles Delage, Levallois, Seine.
1912–1935 Automobiles Delage, Courbevoie, Seine.
1935–1953 Automobiles Delage, Paris.

'One drives an Alfa, one is driven in a Rolls – and one buys the girlfriend a Delage'. So car connoisseur David Scott-Moncreiff once said of this famous French marque. Like all generalisations it by no means tells the whole story, but there is no doubt that the Delages of the 1930s were eminently at home at the grander Concours d'Elegance, complete with Dior-clad lady and fashionably clipped poodle.

Louis Delage (1874–1947) founded Automobiles Delage in 1905 with a fellow ex-Peugeot employee, Augustin Legros (1880–1953). Their small workshop in the Paris suburb of Levallois carried out general engineering work for other companies until their own car was ready for production. It was a conventional little machine in the voiturette class. For his engines, Delage, like many others, went to De Dion-Bouton, while the chassis came from that well-known supplier of steel frames, Malicet et Blin.

Two cars were completed just in time for the Paris Salon held in December 1905. Their single-cylinder De Dion engines had capacities of 496 and 1059cc, and both had 3-speed gearboxes and shaft drive. The choice of engines was not ideal, for customers found the first too small, and the latter too large for a single, so in great haste Delage and Legros ordered another size from De Dion's large stock. This 697cc seemed just right, and by the time the Salon closed on 24 December the partners had a good number of orders, backed by cash deposits. They could not have asked for a better Christmas present, and this was soon followed by a loan of 150,000 francs from a wealthy admirer, with the sole condition that Delage gave his car-mad son a job.

Production began in 1906, although numbers were severely restricted by the size of the rickety barn in which the works were located. As his car did not differ from many others being made in and around Paris at that time, Delage decided to attract attention through racing. A second place in the Coupe des Voiturettes in November 1906 behind a Sizaire-Naudin of twice the engine capacity brought very welcome publicity just a month before the Salon, when Delage took so many orders that a larger factory became an urgent necessity.

In the Spring of 1907 Delage bought a new site of 0.75 acre (0.3 hectares) with a 0.5 acre (0.2 hectares) factory, also in Levallois, and moved production and offices there soon after Easter. Within a year he had outgrown this and erected a new brick building on the site, and this gave him nearly an acre (0.41 hectares) of factory floor space. He was helped by Henri Davene de Roberval, a director of Malicet et Blin, who not only provided a sizeable injection of cash, but also made available a regular supply of frames, gearboxes and axles. He was to remain on the board of Automobiles Delage until 1935.

Expansion enabled Delage to appoint dealers in the French provinces and abroad. His first foreign agent was the London firm of Charles Friswell & Co., who sold the 697cc car under the name Baby Friswell. In 1908 Delage turned to multi-cylinders, offering the 1206cc Type G twin and the 1767cc Type H four, both engines courtesy of De Dion-Bouton. During 1909 Delage contracted with Ernest Ballot to supply engines and with François Repusseau for bodies. In both cases he drove a very hard bargain; the engines were made both by Ballot and by Delage to the Delage design, but all bore the Delage name. The Levallois factory was now moving upmarket, with a quality 1460cc 8CV four which could carry 4-seater bodywork, followed by a 2566cc 16CV six in 1913, whose engine was designed by Arthur-Louis Michelat and made in the Delage factory. In 1909–10, before he had settled on Ballot engines, Delage bought some 4-cylinder units from Chapuis-Dornier. The last single-cylinder engines were listed in 1911. Delage moved to a new factory at Courbevoie on an 11 acre (4.475 hectare) site, which was to be the make's home for the rest of its independent existence.

Delage cars on the eve of World War I were the 12CV Type AI four and the 16CV Type AH six, both with Michelat-designed and Delage-built engines. During the conflict Delage and Legros planned their postwar programme, both deciding on a one-model range. Delage thought he could sell 3000 per year of a 3-litre six. When the car appeared, as the CO, it had grown to 4524cc, and they managed to sell only 1390 in the three years 1919–21. Michelat left during the early stages of the design, although he returned in 1934. He was replaced by an ex-Fiat engineer, Lovera, who stayed at Courbevoie for only two years, and who was succeeded in 1919 by Louis Delage's cousin Charles Planchon. He was responsible for some of Delage's finest designs, racing as well as touring cars.

1923 Delage GL 40/50hp tourer by Graham-White.
NATIONAL MOTOR MUSEUM

1926 Delage D1S 14hp 2-seater by Compton.
NATIONAL MOTOR MUSEUM

NATIONAL MOTOR MUSEUM

DELAGE, LOUIS (1874–1947)

Louis Delage was born in Cognac on 22 March 1874, the only son of Pierre Delage and Marie Longchamp. His father was an assistant station master, and was able to send his son to the École des Arts et Métiers at Angers, where he graduated in 1893. After military service he became a railway engineer at Bordeaux for a while, but was soon attracted by the motor car. He worked in Paris for Turgan-Foy and Peugeot, before starting his own company in a drawing office that doubled as a living room on the fifth floor of an apartment building in the rue Chaptal.

Automobiles Delage was founded in January 1905, and its success was undoubtedly helped by Louis' ability to drive a hard bargain. The contract he made with François Repusseau for the supply of bodies from 1909 to 1914 left the coachbuilder with practically no profit at all, and he obtained engines from Ballot on very advantageous terms. When René Thomas returned from America in 1914 with substantial prize money from his Indianapolis win and the sale of the car, Delage advised him to invest most of it in a company which owed Delage money. Fortified by Thomas' investment, the company was just able to settle its debts with Delage before it went bankrupt.

Delage was not a particularly rich man until World War I, when profits from army contracts made him very wealthy. In the 1920s he spent little time around the factory, and the man all the workers looked up to was Augustine Legros. In fact, Delage was not a popular man, and neither, apparently, was his son, Pierre. 'The Delage men were not people you would particularly want to know' said a former member of his staff. Women, on the other hand, found him attractive, or perhaps it was just his money, for he had what has been described as a 'public stable of actresses and dancers' as well as the magnificent Château de Pecq and an ocean-going luxury yacht, l'Oasis.

The failure of his company in 1935 left Delage and his family very badly off. He had poured his personal funds into an attempted company rescue, and lost everything. A sale to aero-engine makers Gnome et Rhône was frustrated by Madame Delage, it is said, through resentment of his affairs. His directorship under the Delahaye regime cannot have paid very much, and when a former employee encountered him in Paris just after World War II he was shabbily dressed, with a broken spectacle lens. He became very religious in his later life, making pilgrimages from Paris to Chartres on foot, and to Lourdes on a bicycle at the age of 73. He died on 14 December 1947. His son, Pierre, never made much money, dying in extreme poverty in 1964. His wife outlived them both, but was blind and helpless when she died in 1970.

NG

1938 Delage D6-75 Sport drophead coupé.
NATIONAL MOTOR MUSEUM

1927 Delage 17CV torpedo, with the dancer Mistinguett.
NICK BALDWIN

Delage urgently needed a replacement for the slow-selling CO, and in 1921 Planchon and Escure came up with the 2117cc 4-cylinder DE, a sound and sensible tourer with side-valve engine, 4-speed gearbox and 4-wheel brakes. With its more sporting variants, the 2121cc ohv DI, DIS and DISS with under slung frame, the D series remained in production until 1928, selling a total of 14,309 cars. The CO was improved by a pushrod ohv head, twin plugs and dual ignition, being marketed as the GS in 1921–23, and then the CO2; 300 of these were sold.

In 1923, with a sound basis provided by the DE, Delage decided to enter the luxury market with a car to rival the Hispano-Suiza. He brought in a new designer, Maurice Sainturat, who had worked for Delaunay-Belleville and Hotchkiss, giving him a free hand and an office of his own to design a world-beating luxury car. The result was the GL (Grand Luxe), with 5954cc 6-cylinder single-ohc engine developing 100bhp. The design included twin oil pumps, an X-braced frame, and hydraulic brakes. Three wheelbases were offered, of which the shortest was for a sporting model with a 130bhp engine. The GL was a very costly exercise, and it never recouped the money which had been spent on it. It was dropped after 1927, after just 100 had been made. Of these 20 were the short-chassis sports models.

The GL was followed by a series of smaller 6-cylinder cars, the 3181cc DM and 2170cc DR. Both were designed by Maurice Gaultier who had returned to Delage

after a 9-year absence, part of which was spent in prison where he had been sent, accused of making sub-standard munitions during the war. His greatest contribution to Delage was the D8 series, announced at the 1929 Paris Salon.

The D8 had a 4061cc straight-8 ohv engine with 5 main bearing crankshaft and Nelson-Bohnalite pistons which had aluminium crowns and lightweight cast-iron skirts. It developed 120bhp in standard form, while in the short-chassis D8SS a modified camshaft raised output to 145bhp. This gave a top speed of around 100mph (160km/h). The finest coachbuilders of the day went to work on the D8 chassis, especially Chapron, Fernandez et Darrin and Letourneur et Marchand. David Scott-Moncrieff observed, 'They built bodies of deathless elegance with funny little narrow windscreens like the slit of a pillarbox. They were lovely to look at, and the driving visibility was not nearly as bad as you might think'.

These custom-bodied D8s were very popular at the fashionable Concours d'Élégance held in Paris, Deauville and many other smart resorts. They were not expensive for such elegant cars, and nearly always carried off the prizes in their price class. In fact, they were underpriced, and Louis Delage made little, if any, profit on them. Despite this, customers were hard to find in the Depression years. Delage sold 3600 cars in 1928, but only 2000 in 1930. Even those 2000 did not sell quickly, and dealers blamed the company for not having less expensive cars to back them up. In fact, there were two 6-cylinder cars, the 2517cc DS and 3045cc D6, joined for 1933 by the 2001cc D6-II. In 1934 Gaultier widened the range with an eight using the same cylinder dimensions (75 × 75.5mm) as the D6-II, the 2668cc D8-15, and a four. This D4 had the smallest engine of any Delage since before World War I, at 1481cc. There were many interchangeable parts between the D4, D6-II and D8-15, but unfortunately the principle was extended too far – the rear axle that was just right for the D6-II was too heavy and expensive for the D4, and barely strong enough for the 8-cylinder car.

Confidence in Delage ebbed rapidly; sales dropped still further, key staff left for other companies and the prestigious Champs-Élysées headquarters were sold. Michelat was persuaded to return, and designed three new models, the 2678cc D6-75 and 3570cc D8-85 and D8-105 Sport. Together with Gaultier's cars they made up a complex range for 1935, but although they were well received, Automobiles Delage went into liquidation in April 1935. The company was bought for two million francs by Walter Watney, who owned AUTEX, the Paris agent for Delage. He soon found that the ailing company was more than he could cope with, and looked for an established car maker to take it over. After an agreement with Unic fell through, he signed an agreement with Delahaye, who would assemble the cars from their own components, but would still use the Delage name, badge and radiator. The Delage factory was sold to Ateliers GSP, a large manufacturer of machine tools After suffering bombing during the war, the remains were sold to truck maker Berliet.

Although he had lost all his fortune in his company's collapse, Louis Delage was allowed as a courtesy to remain on the board of the new company. The other survivor was the Michelat-designed D6-60 engine which powered the 6-cylinder Delages up to the end of production in 1953. Other components mostly came from Delahaye, and both marques carried Chapron-built bodies on their standard models. Several D6-60 chassis were delivered to Great Britain where they were bodied by local firms such as Coachcraft.

Delahaye at the wheel during the Paris-Marseille-Paris race in 1896.
NATIONAL MOTOR MUSEUM

DELAHAYE, ÉMILE (1843–1905)

The man who gave his name to the car was born in the city of Tours on 16 October 1843, the son of a tapestry worker. Having no inclination to follow his ancestry into the textile industry, he studied mechanical engineering at the École des Arts et Métiers in Angers, where he graduated in 1869. He found his first job in the drawing office of Ateliers J.F. Cail & Cie at Denain, near Douai, an important industrial enterprise that produced steam traction engines, locomotives, and railway equipment.

Called up for service as a military engineer in the war against Prussia in 1870, he found himself in Brussels when the fighting stopped, and promptly went to work for Halot & Cie, Cail's Belgian branch factory.

At the age of 30, he married Olympe Blanchet, a girl from his home town, and decided to return to his native Touraine. He found an opportunity in the small foundry of Louis Brethon, established in 1845, where the aging founder was ready to take on a younger partner. In 1879, Émile Delahaye and his wife purchased the foundry, and in about 1882 began making 4-stroke gas and petroleum engines of his own design, with 1-, 2-, or 4-cylinders, from 0.5 to 40hp.

In 1894 he began to design an automobile, for which he obtained a French patent in 1895. After a few one-off test cars, he was building cars on a production basis. He also drove his own cars in important races, and finished 10th overall in the 1896 Paris-Marseilles-Paris race. At such events, he also met many leaders of the industry and potential clients.

But he had no capital to expand his factory sufficiently to meet the demand. He was also ageing, not in the best of health, and his marriage was childless. He formed a close relationship with Georges Morane, who owned a Delahaye (and other cars), and the two came to terms on the sale of the Delahaye business. After the sale, Émile Delahaye gave freely of his experience, knowledge, and skills for three years, while car production was transferred from Tours to Paris.

He retired in 1901, sharing his time between his property at Vouvray and his vacation home in Saint-Raphael. He died at Vouvray in 1905.
JPN

c.1900 Delahaye 6CV 4-seater.
NICK BALDWIN

The last prewar Delage was the 4744cc D8 120; this had a straight-8 engine which was essentially the 6-cylinder Delahaye 135 with two extra cylinders. Chassis price was 105,800 francs compared with 65,500 for the Delahaye 135, and many of the leading coachbuilders produced elegant bodies for it. Other Delages made in 1939 were the 4-cylinder DI-50, based on the Delahaye 134, and the 6-cylinder D6-75. Production that year was about 400 cars.

The Delage name was revived in 1946 as the D6 3-litres, based on the 1939 D6-75 but with a slightly increased bore which raised capacity to 2984cc. There was also a prototype D-180 which used the 4553cc engine of the Delahaye 180 – hardly surprisingly there was no room for two such similar expensive cars and nothing more was heard of the D-180. As before, Delages were assembled in the Delahaye factory, but only about 120 cars were made postwar, compared with about 2000 Delahayes. Although the make lasted nominally until the end of Delahaye in 1954, the last Delage was delivered in October 1953.
NG

Further Reading
Delage, Notes et Souvenirs 1905–1935, Paul Yvelin, Published privately, 1971.
Automobiles Delage, Jacques Rousseau, Larivière, 1978.
'The Story of Delage', Griffith Borgeson, *Automobile Quarterly*, Vol.XIV, No.2.
The Delage D8, No. 14, Profile Publications, 1967.

DELAHAYE (F) 1895–1954
1895–1897 Emile Delahaye, Ingénieur-Constructeur, Tours.
1897–1901 Emile Delahaye & Cie, Paris.
1901–1906 Sté des Automobiles Delahaye, Léon Desmarais & Morane, successeurs, Paris.
1906–1916 Delahaye & Co. Limited, London and Paris.
1916–1954 Sté des Automobiles Delahaye, Paris.
1954 Sté Hotchkiss-Delahaye, Saint-Denis sur Seine.
Displayed in the automobile section of the 1895 Salon du Cycle in Paris, the first Delahaye car was neither typical of its age nor trend-setting. It may have owed something to Benz practice but also revealed a certain independence of Benz design. With a 74.8in (1898mm) wheelbase and 55.9in (1418mm) track, its dimensions were similar to a lot of horse-drawn carriages, and like them, had bigger wheels on the rear axle than on the front one – but the tyres were pneumatic (Michelin). The tubular steel frame was fabricated by bicycle-industry methods and was suitable for a great variety of coachwork.

The 2512cc paralle-twin had pushrod-operated overhead exhaust valves and automatic inlet valves (overhead), and delivered 7hp at 500 to 900rpm. It was mounted horizontally in the rear, with the transverse crankshaft at the back end, extending to a pair of belt-drive pulleys. The 3-speed gearbox, differential, and brake were mounted on a central jackshaft, both ends carrying sprockets for

1909 Delahaye 40/60hp tourer.
NATIONAL MOTOR MUSEUM

chain drive to the rear wheels. The rear wheel hubs also carried drums for contracting brake bands. The car had stub-axle steering without Jeantaud's geometry, operated by chain and sprockets from a vertical tiller shaft.

Delahaye produced 375 such chassis from 1895 to 1901 in a small factory that had grown from Louis Brethon's foundry. Emile Delahaye went into partnership with Brethon in 1879 and branched out into making 4-stroke gas and petroleum engines.

Type 2 had a bigger (3038cc) engine, geared for speeds up to 22mph (35km/h) in the same chassis, and Delahaye built 225 such cars from 1896 to 1901. During the same period, Delahaye also made 25 Type 3 cars with a 4046cc parallel-twin, geared for 28mph (45km/h).

On 30 December 1897, Emile Delahaye sold his enterprise to two Paris-based industrialists, Léon Desmarais and Georges Morane, for FrF802,959.02. Georges Morane (1874–1938) was the youngest son of Paul Morane, a self-taught engineer who took over a candle-making factory in Paris and branched out into building machinery for making candlesticks. In time, the product line expanded to include moulding machinery for iron foundries, and high-pressure hydraulic pumps. Georges Morane was a keen automobilist and one of the first in Paris to own a Delahaye. His brother-in-law, Léon Desmarais (1864–1916) was a graduate engineer from the École Centrale des Arts et Manufactures who took over his uncle's lubrication-oil and liquid-fuels business.

In 1898 they began a huge expansion of the Morane factory in the Gobelins district of Paris, erecting new buildings with a floor space of 6000m sq, and production of Delahaye cars was gradually transferred from Tours to Paris.

When this was accomplished in 1901, Emile Delahaye retired, but there was no question of changing the trade mark, which possessed considerable repute and goodwill. Emile Delahaye had also been instrumental in choosing the men who would take over his former responsibilities, Amédée Varlet and Charles Weiffenbach, who joined the company in 1898. Varlet was to direct the drawing office, and Weiffenbach would be in charge of production.

Emile Delahaye's last car design was Type 0, whose prototype was built in 1898. It was a much lighter car, powered by a 6hp 1099cc single-cylinder engine, though architecturally resembling its predecessors. About 250 units were built in 1901, before Varlet redesigned it, moving the engine to the front of the chassis, and increasing its size to 1330cc (with 8hp). Approximately 200 such cars, Type OA, were produced from 1901 to 1904, most of them with rear-entrance tonneau bodies by Védrine.

For the OA and the following models, Types 6, 7, and 8, Varlet maintained the horizontal engine installation. The 6, 7, and 8 were twins of 2194, 2200 and 3040cc, combined with the old-style drive line, belt drive from the flywheel to the gearbox/differential, and chain drive to the rear wheels.

In 1902 a vertical-twin appeared, as the first of a long-lasting generation of Delahaye cars. The 12hp 2194cc engine was first mounted in Type 10, introduced at the 1902 Salon in Paris. It also featured side exhaust valves, facing the automatic inlet ones, and a new drive line, with a short shaft from the flywheel to the gearbox (no longer transverse), with a separate differential with half-shafts carrying sprockets for the chain drive to the rear wheels. Type 11 was

a 4-cylinder version of Type 10, delivering 24 to 28hp at 950 to 1200rpm, with a 3-bearing crankshaft, geared for top speeds of 44 or 56mph (70 or 90km/h) according to coachwork type and weight. Delahaye made 250 Type 10 from 1902 to 1906, and 100 Type 11 from 1903 to 1904.

Several other models were made in smaller series. Type 13 of 1903–04 was basically a Type 11 chassis with a 5320cc 4-cylinder engine using a 2-main-bearing crankshaft. Type 15 of 1903–05 was based on Type 10, with an optional long-wheelbase chassis, and a choice of Type 10 or Type 11 engines. Types 16 and 17 had a 3396cc 4-cylinder 3-bearing engine derived from Type 11, with a peak output of 20hp at 1400rpm.

The first shaft-driven Delahaye was Type 20, an 8/10hp car with a 1460cc vertical-twin. The 3-speed gearbox was separately mounted, with a short, open propeller shaft having a flexible coupling at the front end and a universal-joint at the axle end. Introduced at the Salon in 1904, it was replaced a year later by Type 28, the 1460cc engine having been redesigned as an L-head with all valves mechanically operated, and output raised to 10–15hp at 1000 to 1500rpm. Type 28 also took the place of the aging Type 10 in the model line-up and was in production till the end of 1910, with total production estimated at 1650 cars.

By 1905 Georges Morane had disposed of all his non-automotive activities in order to expand production of cars, vans, trucks, buses, and marine engines. This would require important investments, of a scale that Léon Desmarais and Georges Morane could not handle by themselves. Their lawyers advised them of certain advantages offered by British laws on business and finance, and the possibility of raising capital on the London stock exchange. They registered a new company, based in London, as a holding for the Delahaye enterprise, on 25 June 1906, with several British directors, though Morane and Desmarais retained majority control. The British investors, however, were keen to take their profits as quickly as possible, and began selling their shares, some in London, some in Paris. By mid-1907, all but 5 per cent of the shares were back in French hands. But the London-based holding still offered financial and fiscal advantages, and was not dissolved until 22 August 1916, in the middle of World War I.

The London-based holding went hand-in-hand with increased car exports to the British market, which became an important outlet. Delahaye also appointed American agents in New York, where Delahaye taxicabs found a ready market. When the White Company of Cleveland, Ohio, wanted to begin building petrol-engine cars and phase out the steamers, Rollin H. White secured a licence from Delahaye.

Access to the German market was obtained indirectly, by granting a licence to Presto-Werke of Chemnitz, where local assembly of Delahaye Type 28, 21, and 27 began in 1906. But that lasted only a couple of years. Type 21 was a new departure in terms of engine design, for the 25–35hp 4933cc in-line four with its 3-bearing crankshaft was a T-head unit, made from 1904 to 1909. It had a 4-speed gearbox and chain final drive. Like Fiat, Benz, De Dietrich and Hotchkiss, Delahaye had some fear of using shaft drive with their highest-powered engines.

Type 27 was a colossal 7960cc T-head 4-cylinder unit with three main bearings and separately cast cylinders. It was Delahaye's flagship model from 1905 to 1915, updated in 1907 and again in 1912. The engine was rated at 60hp at 1500rpm, combined with a separate gearbox and chain final drive.

Final drive by chain was retained also for the Types 22, 24, 25, and 26. The 20–24hp 2915cc Type 22 appeared in 1904 with a fixed-head L-head engine and 4-speed gearbox. Its specifications had major revisions in 1905 and again in 1908. An elegant touring car on a 122 or 126.7in (3096 or 3215mm) wheelbase, engine size was increased to 3446cc in 1912.

Type 24 was intended as a replacement for Type 10, but was cancelled after a very short production run. Type 25 had an L-head 2915cc pair-cast engine delivering 20hp at 1400rpm, and Type 26 inherited the 4-cylinder T-head engine from Type 21 in a chassis with wheelbases of 124.6in (3162mm) or 133.86in (3397mm).

Type 32, first shown at the Paris Salon in 1907, was a big step forward, combining shaft drive with a 20hp (at 1600rpm) L-head 1944cc engine. The rigid frame had five cross-members and was available with three different wheelbases and rear suspension by 3/4-elliptic leaf springs (which soon spread across the model range as a means of shortening the frame and reducing chassis weight). The 2-bearing crankshaft helped convince Amédée Varlet that one bearing at each end of a 4-throw crankshaft would be enough even for engines of substantially higher displacement. Type 32 was produced until 1913 in substantial numbers (at least 2000) plus the 32 LC of 1912–14, with a 22hp 2292cc version of the same engine.

Due to ill health, Georges Morane had to cut back on his work effort in 1912. Through scholastic and business connections, Morane and Desmarais found their candidate for the succession in a recent engineering graduate from the École Centrale des Arts et Manufactures, Pierre Peigney, then in military service but free to join Delahaye in 1913. The company was then making some 1500 vehicles a year and ranked in the top ten of French car makers.

The 1907 to 1914 Type 37 was essentially a downscaled Type 32, with a 12hp 1208cc L-head engine, 3-speed gearbox and shaft drive to a 2-speed rear axle. Built on a 111.7in (2835mm) wheelbase, it was a very roomy car for its class, could reach 28mph (45km/h) and maintain it all day, for a very reasonable price, and it sold in important numbers.

Type 38, first shown at the 1907 salon, was a tentative upmarket version of the Type 32, with a 30hp L-head 3672cc engine having a one-piece cylinder block and two main bearings. Type 38 also featured a 4-speed gearbox, shaft drive, and 3/4-elliptic rear springs. It was produced up to 1912, when it was replaced by two bigger models launched in 1911, Types 43 and 44. Type 43 was a long-wheelbase touring car with 4-cylinder 2-main-bearing L-head engine, 4-speed gearbox and shaft drive. Type 44 had the same chassis with a 3174cc V6 engine delivering 28hp at 1400rpm. Both had a standard wheelbase of 120in (3046mm), with an optional 126in (3198mm).

The 1590cc 4-cylinder 10/12hp Type 47 was not so much a replacement for the 37 as a lower-priced alternative to the 32. The engine was not in the same

1923 Delahaye Type 87 tourer.
NATIONAL MOTOR MUSEUM

1927 Delahaye Type 92 12CV saloon.
NICK BALDWIN

1937 Delahaye Type 134 saloon.
NICK GEORGANO/NATIONAL MOTOR MUSEUM

1927 Delahaye Type 135 3½-litre drophead coupé.
AUTOMOBIELMUSEUM, DRIEBERGEN

VARLET, AMÉDÉE (1863–1938)

Born in Paris on 23 July 1863, the son of a shop foreman with Périn, Panhard & Cie, he was educated as an electrical engineer. From 1881 to 1892, he worked for Compagnie Edison in Paris. He set up the central power station in Avenue Trudaine and organised the distribution network. Next he joined the Établissements Oller and set up the electrical power supply for the Olympia. He also provided electric lighting for the Palais Garnier (opera), the Odéon theatre, the ex-Vaudeville, and the Gaité.

In 1896, he was invited by the Établissements Quillac at Anzin to get them started in the automobile industry; he designed a car for them, the Raouval, which had a number of innovations (channel-section steel frame, variable-ratio steering, and a raked steering column). It was produced at Anzin from 1897 to 1902.

Varlet returned to Paris in 1898 to design cars for Delahaye. He had married Hélène Weniger in 1889, and their son Jean was born in 1891. The family moved into a comfortable apartment at 15 boulevard du Palais. He designed all Delahaye models, including the racing cars, and drove part-way in the 1902 Paris-Vienna road race (his car broke down before arriving at Reims). He designed some very advanced marine engines, including a 4-cylinder unit with six valves per cylinder, in 1904, and created the first Delahaye fire-fighting vehicle in 1906.

The Tournesol motor plough of 1919 came from his drawing board, as did the next generation of Delahaye cars and trucks. He began working closely with the Pompiers de Paris and replaced their fleet of horse-drawn pumpers and ladders with motor trucks. Varlet designed the first French-built foam pumpers, and was the first in France to adopt the Magirus swivel-base extensible ladder.

He made Jean François chief engineer for cars in 1926 but kept a watchful eye on everything, even to the extent of accompanying the Delahaye racing team to Montlhéry and other tracks.

In 1936, Varlet invented a new type of articulated military vehicle, with power trains in both units, crawler tracks of trapezoidal periphery, and dual-model operation. A machine gun was mounted on a bridge pivoted between the front and rear units.

In about 1924, he had bought a house at Pomponne, on the Marne river about 25km east of Paris, which served as a weekend home and a place to entertain guests. His hobby was photography, and he had a big plate camera and his own dark-room at Pomponne. On the evening of 9 July 1938, he took his dog for a walk around Pomponne, but caught a virus thought to be just a cold. He went to bed that night and never woke up again. He and his wife are buried at Père Lachaise cemetery in Paris.

JPN

1938 Delahaye Type 135 roadster by Figoni et Falaschi.
NATIONAL MOTOR MUSEUM

tradition, for it had a roller-bearing crankshaft, and would run at 2100rpm. To assure adequate cooling, the radiator had a profiled cast-aluminium fan designed by the Établissements Chauvière of aviation fame.

Replacing the popular Type 28 was no easy task, and Delahaye did not attempt it until September 1910, by launching its Type 48 with a vertical-twin 1648cc L-head engine, 3-speed gearbox, and shaft drive. The rear axle was carried in a Hotchkiss-drive arrangement. Type 48 was in production until late in 1914.

For the 1912–1914 period, Type 58 substituted for the Type 38. At 3958cc it had the biggest one-piece cylinder block so far made by Delahaye, and true to form, it was an L-head fixed-head design with two main bearings. The chassis was derived from the 38s but changed from 3/4-elliptic rear springs to Hotchkiss drive.

Type 64, made from 1913 to 1914, was basically a taxicab, also available as a van and with other body styles. It had a lightweight but not flimsy chassis on a 123in (3096mm) wheelbase, and was powered by a 4-cylinder 2603cc L-head engine delivering 25hp at 1500rpm.

During the war Delahaye produced military trucks for 1½-ton payload, experimented with half-track vehicles, manufactured FN rifles under licence, and parts for Hispano-Suiza aircraft engines.

Léon Desmarais died in 1916, leaving his widow (née Marguerite Morane) and her brother, Georges Morane, in charge. Her son François was still in school but was named to the board of directors. Pierre Peigney was on active service at the front, and did not return to the company until 1919. Soon afterwards, he married Annic Morane, niece of Georges Morane.

There was a great deal of uncertainty about the automobile market after the war, but the directors of Delahaye were sure, in view of all the farmers and agricultural workers who had been killed at the front, that the demand for mechanized farm equipment would be great. Delahaye began production of the Tournesol motor plough in 1919, a huge machine 7m long and weighing 5tonne, mounted on four wheels in lozenge formation, with up to 16 ploughshares, half in front and half behind the driver, arranged in four rows.

Civilian versions of the military truck were also put on the market and car production resumed in 1919 with the prewar Type 64 (renamed 64 N). It had a 2612cc L-head (detachable) 4-cylinder engine delivering 27hp at 1600rpm. The crankshaft, typically, ran in two main bearings.

In 1921 François Desmarais graduated from the Ecole Centrale des Arts et Manufactures, and joined the Delahaye management. Amédée Varlet hired an assistant, Jean François, and both Varlet and Weiffenbach were seated on the board of directors in 1922.

Delahaye also introduced its Type 84 in 1919. It was basically an updated Type 43, now with aluminium pistons and a detachable L-head, and the same 2-bearing crankshaft. Power output from the 2940cc unit was raised to 40hp at 2000rpm. Amédée Varlet had also designed a 6-cylinder Type 82, and prototypes were on the road in 1919. It was an L-head design with two blocks of three cylinders, but a single head casting, and the crankshaft ran in four main bearings. From 1919 to 1922, Delahaye produced 1231 Type 84 cars and from 1920 to 1924, a total of 123 Type 82 chassis. The 4410cc engine put out 40hp at 1800rpm. For 1923 Type 82 lost the leather-cone clutch to receive a dry single-plate clutch, and 4-wheel brakes became optional. Type 84 became 84N late in 1922, when its crankshaft was put on ball bearings and output increased to 48hp at 2500rpm. A total of 309 cars were built to 84N specifications up to the end of 1924.

Delahaye did not intend to desert the 10CV medium-price market, but it took longer to get Type 87 ready for production. It was first displayed at the Paris Salon in 1921. Since moderate production cost was a major objective, it differed from the bigger cars in several ways. The gearbox was not mounted separately but bolted to the flywheel housing, and the L-head engine was cast en-bloc with an integral head. Adex-licence front wheel brakes became optional late in 1922, and other improvements were made in running order. It was a successful car and 3810 were built up to the end of 1926.

Type 97 was an alternative to the 87, with an estimated production of 500 cars from 1923 to 1926. The 1847cc 4-cylinder cast-en-bloc engine was Delahaye's first single-ohc car engine, with a vertical timing shaft and bevel gears. Output was 35hp at 2400rpm.

Type 84N was replaced by Type 92, arriving in October 1924, with a new 3-bearing 4-cylinder L-head 2513cc engine delivering 40hp at 2200rpm. It also had pushrod-operated overhead valves in a crossflow head. The chassis derived from Type 84N but had a longer wheelbase (130.8in (3320mm), up from 127.4in (3233mm)). Delahaye produced 339 Type 92 cars up to the end of 1928.

In 1926 Amédée Varlet placed Jean François in charge of all passenger-car engineering, leaving him freer to work on other projects, such as fire-fighting vehicles in particular, but he also developed new concepts in all-terrain vehicles.

Georges Morane held the title of president of Delahaye from 1922, but, despite being only 48 years old, he left the business affairs to the younger generation, Pierre Peigney and François Desmarais, while he spent his summers yachting on the Normandy coast and the winters on the French riviera.

Charles Weiffenbach, although his responsibilities were nominally restricted to production, was able to exert his influence at all levels including strategic planning. As early as 1922 he had tried to get his fellow directors and representatives of other car companies interested in forming an alliance to collaborate in purchasing, production, and marketing. At that time, it came to nothing. But in 1926, the heads of Unic and Chenard-Walcker began discussions, and when Weiffenbach got wind of it, he began planning a DUC union (Delahaye-Unic-Chenard) to which Pierre Peigney and François Desmarais seemed amenable.

1951 Delahaye 235 convertible by Saoutchik.
NATIONAL MOTOR MUSEUM

Formal negotiations began in May 1927, but by July, Unic was no longer involved. Delahaye and Chenard-Walcker acted speedily, and the model ranges of both makes expanded by shared production. The 1928 Delahaye 107M was also sold as a Chenard-Walcker 10CV, slightly disguised with its own radiator shell and other exterior details. In return, Delahaye obtained its own versions of the Chenard-Walcker 9CV and 16CV models. Delahaye built its Type 108 (14CV) for both organisations, while the Delahaye 109 (9CV) and 110 (12CV) were produced by Chenard-Walcker with two different badges. The first cracks in the union occurred in 1928 when Chenard-Walcker wanted to include Rosengart, and Chenard-Walcker dealers actually began selling the Rosengart 5CV. Charles Weiffenbach had an intense dislike for Lucien Rosengart, and would have vetoed it had he been asked. The cracks spread further when Weiffenbach learned that Chenard-Walcker had also begun buying shares in Ariès with a view to taking over that company. The union was dissolved with effect from 30 September 1931.

The joint acquisition of the coachbuilders Bargin & Beckerich in 1928, reorganised as SPCA (Société Parisienne de Construction Automobile) brought no lasting benefits for Delahaye, since it fell under Chenard-Walcker's control. On the other hand, Delahaye obtained lasting benefits of another kind: Varlet and François had become familiar with the short-stroke Chenard-Walcker engines and drew their conclusions from this experience.

Independently of the pact with Chenard-Walcker, Delahaye acquired part-ownership of Chaigneau-Brasier in 1929. While Varlet had no interest in the Chaigneau-Brasier's engine or front-wheel drive, it was Weiffenbach who wanted access to the company's plant at Ivry-Port, where he organised assembly of Delahaye trucks. In 1933, Delahaye obtained full ownership.

The Delahaye models that survived the union with Chenard-Walcker were obsolete by the end of 1931. Production of the 107M, which began in 1927, ended in 1929 after a run of 2605 cars. It was a 4-cylinder 38hp family car on a 122.4in (3107mm) wheelbase.

The 108 was essentially a 107M chassis with a 6-cylinder engine. While the 4-cylinder 107M engine had pushrod-operated overhead valves, the six was designed by Henri Toutée of Chenard-Walcker and had a Ricardo-type turbulent L-head. While most Delahaye engines of 1919–26 had 130mm stroke, the 108 engine had a stroke of only 107mm. Type 108 (renamed 108N late in 1931) was produced from October 1928 to mid-year 1933, with a total number of around 1200 units.

Type 112 was a Delahaye design from 1927, intended for production by Chenard-Walcker. It was powered by a 2872cc six with pushrod-operated ohvs, and differed from Delahaye practice in having a 110mm stroke and four main bearings. Chenard-Walcker made about 200 chassis called U8, then the tooling was transferred to Delahaye late in 1928, where another 187 units were completed in 1929.

True to his cartel-oriented reasoning, Weiffenbach clung to the idea of making a bigger profit by producing more. That meant also, selling at lower prices, which bore with it the risk of cutting costs while losing quality. Pierre Peigney and François Desmarais were not convinced. Delahaye's reputation and goodwill had not been won by building lots of cheap cars. Another difficulty was that Delahaye did not have the financial reserves needed for retooling the factory for rational and efficient high-volume production. In the end it was

Charles Weiffenbach (standing).
NATIONAL MOTOR MUSEUM

WEIFFENBACH, CHARLES (1870–1959)

For most of the world, he was 'Monsieur Delahaye', from the time of his early prominence after the end of World War I up to the end of car production at No. 10 rue du Banquier in Paris in 1954. An extrovert Alsatian who knew how to promote himself and his cause, he was born at Thann in the Vosges on 8 September 1870. There is a mystery as to how much schooling he had. No records exist of his being a student at the Arts et Métiers, of which some sources claim he was a graduate. In any case, Weiffenbach never denied it. He was energetic and had a natural affinity for getting things done. His ability to cope in 1909 with the production of ten separate touring car models plus a range of trucks, taxicabs, military vehicles, marine engines, and fire-fighting equipment, cannot be put in question.

His business-sense was one-directional, always oriented towards expansion, and he understood the ins and outs of the industry, from raw materials to parts and service. He was a pioneer of exploring 'economies of scale' and industrial collaboration with partners who were competitors in the marketplace. He knew everyone who mattered, and they all knew him. He would have lunch one day with Baron Petiet, the next day with Ettore Bugatti or Gabriel Voisin.

In 1944-45, he put the factories back on their feet and stayed with Delahaye until the merger with Hotchkiss. But he never fully retired from business, serving as president of Accumulateurs USL in France and chairman of the Fonderies Modernes de l'Automobile until his death towards the end of 1959.

JPN

Madame Léon Desmarais (1867–1938) who settled the matter. She was the biggest shareholder and she ruled that the honour of the Delahaye name must prevail. Its cars must show greatness, she felt, 'and if we sell fewer cars, we'll make fewer cars'. She was also receptive to the idea of racing as a means of publicity and promotion.

That was the signal Jean François needed. He was planning to simplify engine production down to one family of 4- and 6-cylinder units, with only two crankshafts, both of 107mm stroke. He also had an ifs system ready, with a low transverse leaf spring (based on a Sizaire design).

The 80mm bore 4-cylinder 2140cc version was originally designed for Type 114 which never went into production. The 3227cc (80 × 107mm) six was developed under code name 103 with a 4-main-bearing crankshaft and pushrod-operated ohvs. It was initially mounted in the Type 103 urban-delivery truck, which gave rise to the myth that Delahaye's later touring and sports/racing cars were powered by a truck engine.

The first into production was the 73.8mm bore 1831cc 4-cylinder version, installed in the 10CV Type 122 in 1932. It had the old 108N chassis with semi-elliptics all around, but timely styling and Michelin balloon tyres. The 80mm bore 2102cc engine went into the Type 124 delivering 40hp at 2600rpm.

The 6-cylinder 103 engine was mounted in the Type 126, shown at the Paris Salon in 1931, with a 75.5mm bore and 2860cc displacement. The chassis was dimensionally similar to the 108N's, but had an entirely new frame with deeper channel-section side members and five cross-members. Yet the suspension systems were the same as on the 108N. About 100 Type 126 chassis were built in 1932–33. The engine put out about 55hp at 3200rpm.

The first Delahaye with ifs was Type 134, shown at the 1933 Salon in Paris. It had the 2140cc (80 × 107mm) 4-cylinder engine with an output of 45hp at 3500rpm, 4-speed gearbox and Gleason spiral-bevel final drive. Standing on a 112.6in (2858mm) wheelbase, it was suitable for a number of body styles, including a series-produced coach by Manessius and a Sical faux-cabriolet.

The same front suspension was mounted on Type 132 which went into production in May 1934, replacing Type 123 and inheriting its 1831cc engine, revised for an output of 35hp at 3500rpm. Delahaye built some 100-odd 132s and approximately 900 134s up to mid–1936. The 134N was made from 1936 to 1938 in a series of 340 units, the 2140cc engine now delivering 50hp at 3800rpm. It was replaced by the 134G on which the engine was bored out to 84mm (2371cc) and rated at 59hp at 4200rpm, with a 6.92:1 compression ratio. Production continued at the same rate, but a military order for 99 units was received in the beginning of 1940, boosting the total to 376 chassis.

From the end of 1935, however, the memory of Delahaye is forever marked by the magic number 135. It came with the 3227cc 6-cylinder engine in its original sports version, and an 84mm bore 3557cc version in the 135 Compétition and 135 Spécial.

The frame was reinforced from the 134 design, but basically similar, with Bloctube side members and a sheet-steel platform welded to a number of cross-members. It had the same ifs and the same rear axle on semi-elliptic springs.

The single-carburettor 3227cc engine put out 95hp at 3600rpm, and the Triple-Solex version, 113hp at 3600rpm. A 4-speed gearbox with synchromesh on third and fourth was standard. Cotal semi-automatic was an extra-cost option.

The 135 Spécial was a short-wheelbase (106.3, not 116.1in (2698, not 2947mm)) model with a high-compression (8.4:1) Triple-Solex engine, delivering 152hp at 4300rpm. The 135 Compétition, on the other hand, put out a mere 120hp at 4200rpm. Since Delahaye never had its own coachwork shop, the 135 was a boon to France's coachbuilding industry. A special relationship was established with Henri Chapron, but Guilloré, Franay, de Villars, Figoni & Falaschi, and Antem also created elegant bodies on the 135.

In 1935 Delahaye acquired the Delage company, closed the Courbevoie factory, added Delage engine production at Rue du Banquier, and began assembly of Delage cars in the Delahaye plant. At the same time, the number of Delahaye models proliferated. Type 138, introduced in October 1933, combined a Type 126 chassis with the front suspension from Type 134, and a 90hp 3227cc six. About 300 cars of 138 specification were built in just over two years.

Counting all the model variations within the 135 family built in the prewar years, the total comes to approximately 1500 cars. Delahaye also produced 163 cars of Type 148 specification from mid–1936 to the end of 1939. It was a replacement for the Type 138, sharing the 90hp 3557cc six and the chassis with Type 135.

Jean François had designed a single-seat open-wheel racing car with a 60 degree V12 4496cc engine in 1936–37, and this engine was also mounted in six short-wheelbase chassis, derived from the 135, for road use. In this form, the engine put out 220hp (later 250hp) at 5400–5500rpm. Known as Type 145, two of the chassis were fitted with coupé bodies by Chapron, and one with a Franay cabriolet.

Delahaye did not neglect the 10CV to 12CV market segment, introducing Types 143 and 144 in May 1934, with 4-cylinder engines, 34hp from 1831cc in the 143 and 45hp from 2102cc in the Type 144. Both were grossly underpowered, since they had the old Type 126 chassis with engines from the 132 and 134, respectively. They did not sell well, production ending in October 1934 after a run of 24 Type 143s and 60 144s.

Two rogue models, Types 168 and 164, came into being in an odd deal with Renault. Renault's truck sales department had taken orders for a number of fire-fighting vehicles, a market whose light-duty end was dominated by Delahaye. Delahaye wanted those contracts, and Renault agreed on condition of Delahaye buying a quantity of Vivasport saloon bodies, stockpiled but not needed at Billancourt. They were put on modified Delahaye 134N chassis, with Delahaye radiator shells, bonnets and front wings, and sold in 1938–40.

1938 was marred by the deaths of three people prominent in Delahaye history. Amédée Varlet passed away in July, Madame Léon Desmarais in August, and Georges Morane in November. These events forced a realignment of executive positions, and François Desmarais became president of Delahaye, with Pierre Peigney as managing director. No one was appointed technical director, since Jean François, who had all the qualifications for the title, was suffering from a respiratory disease. He resigned from Delahaye in 1940 to seek health in the high alps, settling at Guillestre, where he died in April, 1944.

Under the German occupation, Delahaye produced its own prewar truck models for the Wehrmacht until 1942, when the order was given to produce machine guns and ammunition. Weiffenbach pointed out that his personnel had no experience in making arms, and the factory lacked the requisite tooling. The orders were changed to a variety of spare parts and Weiffenbach kept busy doing everything possible to disorganise production. At the end of 1942, Delahaye was told to begin production of a Hanomag field tractor at a rate of 100 units a month. When Paris was liberated in August 1944, not a single tractor had been completed.

Planning for the postwar era began early. In April 1941, Delahaye joined an association, the GFA (Générale Française de Construction Automobile), to co-ordinate purchasing and define product lines to avoid direct competition between the GFA members, which included SIMCA, Unic, Bernard, and Laffly. At the same time, Delahaye acquired Currus, thus providing itself with facilities for body production.

In August 1945, François Desmarais was killed in an accident, and Pierre Peigney took over the presidency and completed a full merger with Delage (which had been a subsidiary since 1935). In June 1946 an engineer named Morel was engaged as technical director. Weiffenbach went into semi-retirement, to act as adviser to the management and head of 'special missions'. On 1 October 1950, Pierre Peigney chose a representative of big shareholders in Delahaye, Bernard Guillin, as managing director.

The GFA grouping had been recognised by the government's Pons Plan for the automotive industry, but as Unic never resumed passenger-car production, and little ground existed for any sort of collaboration between fast-growing mass-market SIMCA and low-volume old-style luxury car maker Delahaye, its usefulness quickly evaporated.

Delahaye's postwar production got under way in 1945 with a 3½-ton truck, and the first postwar car was a Type 135M built in 1946. It was identical with the prewar 135, except for more powerful engines and wider track, front and rear. The 3557cc six was offered in versions of 95, 100, 115 and 125/130hp, the latter reserved for the 135 MS. They were taken out of production at the end of 1952 after a run of 1155 units.

A small series of 11 Type 148 cars with the 95hp 3557cc engine were also built for the government, followed by the 148L (légère = light) with the 105hp engine, of which 504 units were built up to the end of 1953.

The 4455cc 6-cylinder Type 175 engine was created by a full redesign including a 7-bearing crankshaft and a new block with 94mm bore. The 107mm stroke was retained. With a single carburettor, it put out 120/125hp; with two 140/148hp, and with the Triple Solex installation, 160/164hp. The 175 chassis was completely new, with Dubonnet front suspension and a De Dion tube at the back, with parallel semi-elliptics. This model was first shown at the 1947 Salon in Paris, and a total of 51 cars were made up to 1950.

The 120 and 140hp versions of the 4455cc six were also mounted in Types 178 and 180, which were extended wheelbase models of the 175, with a total of 54 cars made from 1947 to 1950. Type 182 was better known by the letters VLR (voiture légère de reconnaissance), a military project which found a ready civilian market. It had 4-wheel-drive, torsion-bar suspension all around, and a 63hp 1995cc aluminium-block engine. Production began in 1950 and ended in 1953 after a run of 9630 vehicles.

Delahaye's swan song was Type 235 – in reality just a modern dress on the old 135M. The prototype was built by Motto of Turin, in 1951, to designs by Philippe Charbonneaux, with a wide and low oval grill and full-width body sides. The same styling theme was followed, with variations, by Letourneur & Marchand, Figoni, Antem, Saoutchik, Faget & Varnet, Chapron and Beutler. Including the prototype, a total of 85 cars of 235 specification were produced.

Late in 1952, a smaller car was put on the drawing board. The 5-passenger saloon was proposed on a 112in (2842mm) wheelbase and a weight of 1150kg, powered by a 90hp 2500cc engine in either six or V8 configuration. Chausson was contacted to discuss body-shell production, but the talks foundered in May 1953.

Pierre Peigney reasoned that Delahaye would need a partner to survive as an auto maker, and he met with representatives of several other companies, including Salmson and Hotchkiss. By February 1954, all other partners were excluded and merger negotiations began with Paul Richard, president of Hotchkiss. The basic contract was signed on 19 March 1954, and Société Hotchkiss-Delahaye came into being on 9 June 1954. The makes Delage and Delahaye were suspended, and the only cars built after that date wore a Hotchkiss badge.

JPN

Further Reading
Delahaye, le Grand Livre, Jacques Dorizon, François Peigney, Jean-Pierre Dauliac, EPA, Paris, 1995.

DE LA MYRE-MORY (F) 1911–1914
Éts G. de la Myre-Mory, Neuilly, Seine.
This company made one model of 10hp 4-cylinder car, with 3-speed gearbox and shaft drive. They also made a 16hp 6-cylinder engine which they would supply to other manufacturers, although it is not known who their customers were.
NG

DE LANSALUT (F) 1899
The Paris-built De Lansalut was a voiturette powered by a 2.5hp single-cylinder air-cooled engine inclined at an angle of 45 degrees. Transmission was by belts.
NG

DELAUGÈRE (F) 1898–1926
SA des Éts Delaugère, Clayette Frères et Compagnie, Orleans, Loiret.
This regional car maker, little known even in its homeland let alone abroad, grew from a company which dated back to the middle of the nineteenth century. Jean-Pierre Delaugère (1810–1868) was a carriage and wagon maker whose son Emile and great-nephew Felix built a 3-wheeled car in 1898, followed by a 4-wheeler in 1900. The latter used a De Dion-Bouton engine, but a year later Delaugère were making 2-cylinder engines in their own factory, following these with a four in 1902. The cars were on Panhard lines, with automatic inlet valves and double-chain drive. The 20hp 4-cylinder car had a 4-speed gearbox. In 1904 Maurice Clayette joined the company, which became E. et F. Delaugère et M. Clayette, changing to its final title two years later.

By 1905 a wide range of cars was offered, from an 8/10hp twin to a massive 80/100hp four of 15 litres, as well as taxicabs and trucks. One model, the 16hp 4CCA, had shaft drive, and this gradually spread up the range which, by 1907 had shrunk to the twin and two fours, of 4.4 and 8 litres. They had 350 workers in 1909, production running at about two vehicles per day. The first monobloc engine came in 1911 in the shape of the 2.1-litre 10CV. Twins were still catalogued in 1912, along with the company's first six, the 5.2-litre Type 6N. A rear-axle gearbox was used on some models, as was the Fischer side-valve engine in the 2.7-litre Type SS. Although the marque never became well-known, even in France and their products were seldom written up in the press, some were exported as far

1921 Delaugère 2-door saloon.
NICK BALDWIN

1923 Delaugère 10CV tourer.
NATIONAL MOTOR MUSEUM

afield as Romania, the United States and Mexico.

During the war Delaugère made trucks and shells for the French Army, and resumed production in 1919 with three models; two fours of 2154 and 3176cc (Types 4 and 4Y), and a large six of 4764cc, the Type 6Z. They all had side-valve engines, 4-speed gearboxes and electric lighting and starting. They were continued through the 1922 season, when the Type 6Z 6-seater saloon had twin rear wheels. Front-wheel brakes were adopted on the 6Z in 1923 and across the whole range by 1925. For 1923 Delaugère turned to proprietary engines in place of their own, though the 6Z was continued up to 1925. The new engines came from Ballot, in three sizes, 1690, 2120 and 3327cc, all 4-cylinder side-valve units. Five body styles, made in-house, were listed for 1924, 3- and 4-seater tourers, 3- and 4-seater saloons and a *camionette Normande* or light truck. Larger commercial bodywork, including a hotel bus, was available with the 3327cc engine, and there was still a 3.5 ton truck. This was the LO3, with 4396cc engine, solid tyres and chain drive.

By 1925 Delaugère was struggling. The cheapest chassis cost 19,500 francs, whereas a Citroën B2 cost 14,200 francs for a complete car. Only one model, the 1690cc 10CV, was offered for 1926, and very few were made that year. The factory was bought by Panhard, who removed the machine tools to their plants at Paris and Rheims, and devoted the Delaugère factory to body manufacture. From it came famous Panhard bodies of the 1930s and 1940s, such as the Panoramique, Dynamic, and Dyna. Pierre Delaugère stayed on as a director, and a small staff of eight remained up to 1931 to ensure a supply of spare parts. The factory stood until 1973 when it was demolished to make way for a large block of flats.

NG

Further Reading
'Delaugère, Clayette et Cie', Alexis, *La Vie de l'Auto*, 29 August and 5 September 1985.

413

1909 Delaunay-Belleville Model 1A-6 park phaeton.
NATIONAL MOTOR MUSEUM

1913 Delaunay-Belleville 37.2hp Type FB6 tourer.
NATIONAL MOTOR MUSEUM

30 H.P. 6-Cyl. Delaunay Belleville Enclosed Landaulette. Type A.

1924 Delaunay-Belleville 30hp Type A enclosed landaulet.
NATIONAL MOTOR MUSEUM

DELAUNAY-BELLEVILLE (F) 1904–1948

SA des Automobiles Delaunay-Belleville, St Denis, Seine.

This company, maker of some of France's finest cars, was formed in the late 1860s by the partnership of naval engineer Louis Delaunay (1844–1912) and the Belleville firm, which made boilers for ships and locomotives. Louis married the owner's daughter and both he and the firm changed their name to Delaunay-Belleville. The firm prospered, selling its Dreadnought boilers to the British Admiralty as well as other customers. By 1900 they had 1000 employees.

A separate car division was formed in September 1903, and for design work they brought in Marius Barbarou, formerly with Benz and Clement. The Delaunay-Belleville cars appeared at the Paris Salon in December 1904. They were quality cars from the start, with 4-cylinder T-head engines, separately-cast cylinders, full-pressure lubrication, 4-speed gearboxes and chain drive. Three models, of 16, 24 and 30hp, were at first available. By 1907 the range extended to five 4-cylinder models from 10 to 40hp, and two sixes, of 15 and 40hp. These had L-head engines, a layout which was adopted on all Delaunays. They still had chain drive, although this had been superseded by shaft in 1910. The sixes had pair-cast cylinders.

From 1909 to 1914, a vast range of different chassis was listed, including a very small 10hp six of 2564 cc in 1909 and a 70hp six of 11,840cc from 1909 to 1911. This was called the SMT (Sa Majeste le Tsar) as the chassis was originally built to a special order from Czar Nicholas II of Russia, although a few were subsequently built for other customers. It was the last Delaunay to have chain drive.

From the beginning the Delaunay-Belleville was characterised by its round radiator and bonnet, said to have been inspired by the company's boiler-making tradition. Most carried fairly formal tourer, limousine or landaulette bodywork, and although a few roadsters were made, there was nothing suggesting a sports car, nor did the company engage in competitions until the 1920s, and even then, not with a works team. It was the chauffeur-driven car par excellence, and was as highly regarded as Panhard, Daimler or Rolls-Royce, although not as expensive. As well as the Czar, other notable owners included the kings of Greece and Spain, and President Poincaré of France. Rival car maker Fernand Charron said, 'No owner *ever* drives his Delaunay – it just isn't done'. Nevertheless the Editor-in-Chief's grandfather frequently drove the smaller of his two Delaunays, and his mother, aged 17, learnt to drive on it.

1928 Delaunay-Belleville S6 coupé de ville.
NICK BALDWIN

1933 Delaunay-Belleville DB4 saloon.
NATIONAL MOTOR MUSEUM

The best-known six was the Type H (1908) and its successor the HB (1910–14) which accounted for 2227 of the total of 7576 cars made from 1904 to 1914. Its 4426cc engine had only three main bearings, surprising perhaps in a car of its quality, but they seemed to suffice as the engine was slow revving and understressed. Up to 1914 production was divided about equally between fours and sixes. Barbarou left in 1912 to join Lorraine-Dietrich, and in the same year Louis Delaunay-Belleville died, to be succeeded by his sons Robert and Pierre.

It may be unfair to attribute the postwar decline of Delaunay to the absence of Louis Delaunay and Marius Barbarou, but they never regained their pre-eminent position among European car makers. Hispano-Suiza, Isotta-Fraschini and Rolls-Royce took over as the top luxury makes, and Delaunay-Belleville made little impact on the market. The round radiator was continued, now slightly pointed, and a variety of models was made. Some were quite small, such as the 2614cc P4B (1922–27) the 4-cylinder engine of which had ohc whereas most others had pushrods. The largest postwar model was a ponderous six of 7995cc, made from 1920 to 1922. In 1928 appeared the last genuine Delaunay-Belleville, the 3180cc S6, which became the U6 in 1930. Its 6-cylinder engine had pushrod-operated ohvs, the inlet valves being larger than the exhaust, a 7-bearing crankshaft and dual ignition. The brakes were of the Dewandre servo type, made by Delaunay-Belleville. The U6 Sport had a tuned engine giving a speed of 90mph (145km/h); among the make's rare sporting appearances was Poirier's entry of a U6 Sport in the 1930 Circuit des Routes Pavées.

The U6 was expensive to make and hard to sell in the Depression years, so for 1931 Delaunay installed a 4015cc straight-8 side-valve Continental engine in a slightly shortened U6 chassis. With a 6-light saloon body, this sold for 65,000 francs, compared with 88,000 francs for a similarly-bodied U6. They later offered a larger Continental engine of 5067cc in the standard 143in (3640mm) U6 chassis. This cost as much as a 'genuine' U6. Prices were lowered to 57,000 and 77,500 francs in 1935, but by then production was down to a trickle. In 1934 they turned to a smaller car, the 2308cc 4-cylinder RI-6 which used

Mercedes-Benz-type ifs by transverse semi-elliptic springs. The engine was also Mercedes 200-based, though with a longer stroke. The 4-door saloon and 2-door cabriolet bodies came from Chenard-Walcker. They also offered a Continental engine in this chassis, though it may not have been made. This resurfaced at the 1938 Salon in a new chassis with coil ifs and torsion bar rear suspension, but so far as is known it never received a body. The standard Delaunay of 1938–39 was the RI-6 with slightly modernised saloon and cabriolet bodies without running boards. This model was revived in 1946, now with an American-type waterfall grill and only offered in 4-door saloon form. It was made until 1948, but only 14 cars were completed, 13 saloons and one coupé bodied by Antem. The factory was later used for manufacture of the Rovin minicar.
NG

Further Reading
The 6-cylinder Delaunay-Bellevilles 1908–1914, Michael Sedgwick, Profile Publications, 1966.
'Delaunay-Belleville', Charles F. Kave, *Automobile Quarterly*, Vol. IV, No. 1.

DELAUNE *see* LE ROLL

DE LAVAUD (F) 1927–1930
Sté d'Expansion Technique E. Sensaud de Lavaud, Paris.
Sensaud de Lavaud exhibited his car at the Paris Salon each year from 1927 to 1930, yet it is unlikely that he sold any, though at least two were made. It was built to demonstrate his unconventional transmission, although other features of the car were quite unusual as well. The engine was a 2.3-litre six which was steam cooled, the radiator acting as a condenser. The cylinder head, like the frame and wheels, was made of Alpax, an alloy of aluminium and silicon. The Aluminium Française GRÉGOIRE built by Jean Grégoire during World War II used the same material. Suspension was independent all round, by rubber in vertical pillars. The transmission consisted of a swash plate at the end of the propeller shaft; the variable angle of the swash plate gave an infinite number of gear ratios and the makers claimed that the system combined economy, longevity of the components, high average speeds, comfort and safety. The system was tried by Gabriel Voisin in one of his cars, and he later took out a licence to produce it, though it never appeared on a production Voisin. A free wheel system on the rear axle replaced the usual differential.
NG

Further Reading
'Two of a Kind – Claveau and De Lavaud', M. Worthington-Williams, *The Automobile*, August 1997.

DE LA VERGNE (US) 1895–1896
De La Vergne Refrigerating Machine Co., New York City.
John Chester De La Vergne was a brewer turned maker of refrigerators whose company entered a Benz in the 1895 *Chicago Times Herald* race. He then commissioned several vehicles from the Hincks & Johnson Co. of Bridgeport, Connecticut, and Valentine, Linn & Son of Brooklyn. They were of Benz appearance, and probably owed a lot to the German design. At least four were made, called variously a motorcycle, motor drag or auto buggy, and the buyers included some of New York's richest and most prominent citizens, Astors, Rockefellers, and Goulds. John De La Vergne's death in May 1896 seems to have put an end to the make.
NG

DELCAR (US) 1947–1949
American Motors, Inc., Troy, New York.
Although the short-lived Delcar was initially built as a delivery van targeted to the crowded garment district of New York City, one, and possibly more, estate cars were produced. With a 60in (1523mm) wheelbase and a 4-cylinder engine located forward under the floor, it could seat six.
KM

DELECROIX (B) 1897–1899
The Delecroix voiturette was a very light 2-seater with engine mounted under the seat, and a tubular frame. The front-wheels were located in bicycle-type forks. Apart from this, the overall appearance was similar to that of the

Decauville voiturelle. Although he began experiments in 1897, it seems that Delecroix did not sell any cars until late 1898, and the following year he made a few with front-mounted vertical single-cylinder engine and chain drive.

NG

DE LEON (US) 1905–1906
Archer & Co., New York City.
Archer & Co. were the New York importers of HOTCHKISS cars, but they also assembled a few cars from imported parts of other French makes. The chassis were probably by Malicet et Blin. Sold under the name De Leon, the only model was a 35hp 4-cylinder tourer with double-chain drive.

NG

DELFIN (E) 1958
This Barcelona motorcycle company prepared some minicars using motorcycle engines. There was also an electric version with two small electric motors.

VCM

DELFOSSE (F) 1922–1926
Delfosse et Compagnie, Cambrai, Nord.
The Delfosse started out as a cyclecar and ended as a smart little sports car in the Amilcar idiom. It was built by Charles Delfosse (1895–1993), the first models using a 998cc in-line 2-cylinder Train engine and chassis supplied by Morain-Sylvestre, who wanted to proceed to 4-cylinder cars. They unloaded about 25 chassis on to Delfosse, who marketed them under his own name as the model DS II. Production began early in 1922, but by the end of the year he replaced the Train engine by a 960cc 4-cylinder Chapuis-Dornier, at the same time using wire wheels in place of the discs of the DS II. The new model was called the CD4; not more than six were made before Delfosse decided to make cars of his own design, though still using proprietary engines. The CD5 used a 1496cc Fivet engine and was intended for taxicab use in Poland. However the order was cancelled, and the dozen or so chassis were completed with bodies as tourers or (mostly) as light trucks. The CD6 and CD7 both used C.I.M.E. engines, the former a 1100cc pushrod ohv unit, and the latter a 1494cc with single-ohc which developed nearly 40bhp. With a light body the CD7 could reach 70mph (115km/h) in its first models, and 78mph (125km/h) later. Bodies were all of sporting appearance, with pointed tails and rather skimpy rear seats on the 3- or 4-seaters. One model could be transformed into a very claustrophobic-looking closed car by means of what later would be called a hard top. A feature of the CD6 and CD7 was the rear suspension, which was by a combination of semi-elliptics and reversed quarter elliptics.

For 1925 the CD6 and CD7 were continued but with a 1200cc pushrod engine replacing the 1100 on the CD6, and front brakes on both models. The former Rolls-Royce-shaped radiator gave way to an oval shape which was more in keeping with a sports car. A pointed-tail 2-door fabric saloon was available on both models. He also made a racing car with cowled radiator and no road equipment which had several successes. His last design, which was never built, was a little racer which very much resembled a Bugatti Type 35. The death in an accident of his leading driver, M. Lippens, ended Delfosse's racing programme, and at the end of 1926 he stopped production altogether. About 130 CD6s and 30 CD7s had been made. He then turned to selling motorcycles, followed by several important developments in railway signalling, and finally manufacturing agricultural machinery. Aided by his son, he was still active in this field in his 80s, when his company supplied 70 per cent of all the potato harvesting machines in France. He died at the age of 98.

NG

Further Reading
'Delfosse', Serge Pozzoli, *l'Album du Fanatique*, March and April 1975.

DELIN (B) 1899–1901
Usines Delin, Louvain.
Under the trade name Derby, J. Delin started making bicycles in 1890 and rapidly became one of the leading manufacturers in Belgium. By 1898, when he formed a limited company, he had 250 employees, and was already describing his activities as 'Fabrique d'Automobiles et de Cycles', although cars did not appear until the following year. At the Brussels Exposition in March 1899, Delin showed a 2-seater duc powered by a French Loyal flat-twin engine which he was

1901 Delin 3½hp voiturette.
NATIONAL MOTOR MUSEUM

making under licence. A year later he exhibited a very light voiturette on the lines of the PARISIENNE Victoria Combination, as well as a tricycle and a motorcycle. More individual cars appeared in 1901, a 2-seater voiturette with a 2.5hp engine, a 4-seater car and a delivery van with 4hp engines, and a 4-seater tonneau with an 8hp engine. The voiturette's steering column was vertical, but the others had inclined columns in the modern manner. They should have sold well but the competition was too great, and the company was liquidated in January 1902. Some of the machinery was sold to Eugene MATHIEU who made cars up to 1904.

NG

DELKIT (GB) 1984–1985
Delkit Fibreglass, Telford, Salop.
An ex-army officer called Derek Allen was behind the Delkit Camino, which was created by boat builder John Rock. It was an early example of a Ford Cortina Mk III/IV based coupé kit car, the mould quality was good, the interior looked professional, and the strong ladder chassis incorporated a sheet steel backbone. The problem was the styling, or lack of it: it was bulbous and unsubtle, and the project was therefore short-lived.

CR

DELLA FERRERA (I) 1924
Fratelli Della Ferrera, Turin.
Della Ferrera was a well-known name in the world of motorcycles, and made these from 1909 to 1948. Their venture into four-wheelers was brief, with a prototype cyclecar powered by a 707cc 2-stroke engine with four pair-cast cylinders set well back in the frame. The brake drums were integral with the wire wheels.

NG

DELLING (US) 1924–1927
Delling Steam Motor Co., West Collingwood, New Jersey.
Eric H. Delling was one of the more successful advocates of steam car design and production in the 1920s, a time during which a dozen or so attempts were made in the US toward a renaissance of steam-powered vehicles. Delling had made his mark in the automobile industry as the designer of the L-Head Mercer and after resigning his position at the Trenton, New Jersey company, he focused his attention on manufacturing a car of his own. Having designed a conventional petrol-powered prototype – the DELTA (iii) – with an idea of manufacture, he abandoned the idea, turning his attention to steam. For this he set up the Delling Steam Motor Co., in Philadelphia, Pennsylvania, moving the operation to West Collingwood, New Jersey in late 1923. Using a 3-cylinder double-action engine with poppet valves which he had designed himself, manufacturing began in early 1924. The Delling cars included a handsome sedan and a phaeton priced at $3250 and $2500 respectively. Delling cars were available with 126in (3148mm) or 132in (3350mm) wheelbases with disc wheels as standard equipment. The Delling clientele was limited and an estimated 100 cars were completed and sold by 1927 when the company ceased production of passenger cars. For a while the company existed on a limited basis, producing trucks on

417

1954 Dellow Mk II 10hp sports car.
NATIONAL MOTOR MUSEUM

1981 DeLorean DMC coupé.
NATIONAL MOTOR MUSEUM

special order. In addition to his own company, Eric Delling also served as the chief engineer for the Canadian Brooks Steam Motors of Stratford, Ontario which produced 180 fabric-covered sedans between 1923 and 1927.

KM

DELLOW (GB) 1949–1957

1949–1956 Dellow Motors Ltd, Alvechurch, Birmingham.
1956–1957 Dellow Engineering Ltd, Oldbury, Birmingham.

Ken Delingpole owned an engineering works and was a trials driver. Just after World War II, his general manager, Ron Lowe, built an outstanding trials car by mating a Ford Ten engine to an Austin Seven chassis and completing it with a simple body made on the *superleggera* principle.

Lowe was asked to make replicas whereupon Delingpole, who did not want to lose his works manager, suggested a partnership. Space was found at Delingpole's works in 1949 and the first Dellows were Ford/Austin specials sold as kits. Dellow then bought a stock of tubes which were originally the bodies of rockets designed to defend the south coast of England. These were used to make a high quality copy of the A7 chassis and Dellow cars were made complete and distributed through Ford agencies.

Coil springs and a Panhard rod replaced the Austin Seven-style quarter elliptics at the rear on the Mk II. The Mk III of 1952 was a long wheelbase 4-seater car – the prototype was built to accommodate Ron Lowe's growing family – and the Mk IV was a version with the Ford Consul engine. The Mk V of 1953 was a lightweight car with a slim body and the live front axle set on coil springs rather than the transverse leaf of the Austin Seven.

Dellows did well both in competition and in the market place (about 250 were made 1949–1952) but in 1952 restrictions on the UK car market were eased.

Not only did this change the market, it also changed motor sport which became specialised. All-rounders like Dellow (and Allard, HRG, etc.) suffered.

In 1955 the company was sold to Neville Nightingale who marketed the Mk IIC (an economy model built on traditional Dellow lines); the Mk IIE, which was a luxury version; and the Mk VI which had an enveloping aluminium body and ifs.

Nightingale made a handful of cars before closing in 1957.

MJL

DEL MAR (US) 1949

Del Mar Motors, San Diego, California.

The Del Mar was a postwar compact with a Continental 4-cylinder engine. It was available in convertible and sedan body styles and was to be sold for $1200. Although they intended to build the car in three factories across the US, only a few aluminium-bodied prototypes were made.

HP

DELMORE (US) 1921–1923

Delmore Sales & Service, New York, New York.

The Delmore was a curious vehicle for its time. This was a tri-car with its single wheel in the rear, a 68in (1726mm) wheelbase, and using a 2-cylinder Indian engine. It was theoretically available as a runabout, coupé, taxi or parcel delivery car although most, if not all, of its sparse advertising, mostly in newspapers, promoted the parcel principle emphasising its economy and minute size for negotiating the smallest back street operation. The seating arrangement was designed in true hansom-cab fashion with a single seat located at the rear of the seating area, provision for passengers being in front. Despite its probable advantages, it appears that the Delmore attracted few and the concern failed a little more than a year after its introduction.

KM

DELOREAN (GB) 1981–1982

DeLorean Motor Company, New York, New York;
factory at Dunmurry, Co. Antrim.

When former General Motors vice-president John DeLorean started his own company in 1974, he stated that he intended to build an 'ethical' rear-engined sports car. This was probably the last time that word was used regarding this company. After setting up production facilities in Northern Ireland, they developed a prototype mid-engined sports coupé with stainless-steel body panels and a hybrid plastic-fibreglass frame designed by former Pontiac engineer William T. Collins. This proved to be impractical to produce and the car was re-engineered with a steel backbone frame designed by Lotus. It was sturdy, if heavy, at 2840lbs with a 94.8in (2406mm) wheelbase. The first DMC-12 models were delivered in 1981 and immediately garnered negative press for indifferent quality control and lack of performance from the 130bhp Peugeot-Renault-Volvo V6 engine. The attractive Giorgio Guigiaro-designed body was well received and the gull-wing doors attracted a lot of attention but the stainless-steel panels tarnished easily and handling was not up to par. The 1982 models were improved but sales remained sluggish. Although the list price rose to over $30,000 by 1982, dealers began discounting them heavily. In 1982 the British government reacted to rumours of financial mismanagement by taking the plant into receivership. They had loaned DeLorean $138 million plus tax breaks in order to provide jobs for low-income Irish workers. DeLorean figures show that 4243 cars were built before the firm declared bankruptcy in December 1982. John DeLorean was subsequently arrested on drug racketeering charges relating to a supposed scheme to finance a cocaine smuggling operation that would have returned enough money to save his car company. He was later acquitted, but the shadow of failure was never lifted from the DeLorean company. The cars later received considerable publicity when they were featured in the *Back To The Future* movie series.

HP

Further Reading
'Dreaming the impossible dream: The DeLorean and its predecessors', Walt Woren, *Automobile Quarterly*, Vol. XXI, No. 2.

DELPEUCH (F) 1922–1925

Automobiles Delpeuch, Neuilly, Seine.

The Delpeuch was a conventional medium-sized tourer powered by a 2815cc 4-cylinder ohv engine with pair-cast cylinders. The 4-speed gearbox was separate from the engine, and brakes were on the rear wheels only. In 1924 the bore was increased by 2mm, giving a capacity of 2956cc, and the wheelbase lengthened. Production was very limited; indeed the great French historian Serge Pozzoli thought that possibly only one Delpeuch was made.

NG

DELSAUX (F) 1980–1983
Éts. N. Delsaux, Guesnain.

The Delsaux Modulo was a cheap, plastic-bodied 2-seater microcar with a 47cc rear-mounted Sachs engine, independent suspension all round and a weight of only 324lb. An improved version was sold from 1982 under the name Modulo Minimax.

CR

DELTA (i) (F) 1905–1915
M De Colange, Puteaux, Seine.

Delta cars were first advertised in 1905 when there was a wide range listed, 6, 8, 12, 14, 20 and 24hp. It is not certain how many of these were actually built, and the Delta name was not seen again until 1913 when it was carried on a 10/12hp 4-cylinder light car, usually made as a 2-seater. It was said to be manufactured throughout at the works. In the 1920s there was a De Colange proprietary engine, possibly made by the same company.

NG

DELTA (ii) (DK) 1918
Mammen & Drescher, Jyderup.

This company bought 20 chassis from the American firm Reed & Glaser in 1917, and stored them in New York until the end of the war. They were then imported into Denmark and fitted with 8.6hp 4-cylinder engines.

NG

DELTA (iii) (US) c.1923
The Delta was a one-off touring car, the prototype for a car which failed to go beyond the prototype stage. It was designed and built by Eric H. Delling who had designed the Mercer L-head car and carried a radiator similar to the Trenton, New Jersey car. The Delta was a touring car with a wheelbase of 133in (3375mm), powered by a 6-cylinder Continental 8A L-head engine. Further development of the Delta project was terminated when Delling decided to enter the steam car market as a manufacturer. The lone Delta survives.

KM

NICK BALDWIN

DE LOREAN, JOHN ZACHARY (born1926)
John Zachary De Lorean was born into a Detroit family of Lebanese extraction on 6 January 1926, and grew up in Detroit and Southern California. He graduated from Lawrence Institute of Technology in 1948 with a bachelor's degree in industrial engineering, went to work for Chrysler at Highland Park, and won a master's degree in automotive engineering from the Chrysler Institute in 1952. The following year, he left Chrysler to join Packard as head of technical research. At this point in his career, he was widely respected for his quick mind, progressive attitude, and cultivated a reputation as an inventor.

In 1956, he joined Pontiac Motor Division as director of advanced engineering. During his years with Packard, he had attended the Detroit College of Law, graduated as a master of business administration from the University of Michigan, and married Elizabeth Elaine Higgins. Pete Estes promoted him to assistant chief engineer of Pontiac in 1959, and he succeeded Estes as chief engineer in 1961. GM senior executives began to regard him as a potential candidate for the presidency of the corporation.

Tall, slim, athletic, and a sharp dresser, he became general manager of Pontiac in 1965, and a vice president of GM. Pontiac grew and prospered under his leadership, and in February 1969 he was named general manager of Chevrolet. He got the credit for selling more than 3 million Chevrolet vehicles in one year (1971). In October 1972, he climbed the corporate ladder to become group executive in charge of the car and truck group and a member of five GM policy committees (marketing, engineering, research, industrial relations, and personnel).

It looked as if nothing could derail his career. But something in his psyche changed. He let his hair grow and picked up a hippie style of dress, with oversize belt buckles and beads. He left his wife and later married the much younger Kelly Harmon, daughter of the golf pro, Tom Harmon. He resigned from GM and became a figurehead for the National Association of Businessmen, but he soon felt trapped in that office and moved to California. His marriage broke up again, though he remarried in 1974. He had plastic surgery to extend his chin, and repeated facelifts.

In 1976 he wanted to build the ideal sports car, and contacted Ital Design for styling suggestions. At first he wanted the car to be a 2-passenger coupé with an inboard-rear engine, but then decided it had to have a back seat, which pushed the engine out into the rear overhang. Renault had agreed to supply its 2975cc V6. He was able to raise a capital of approximately $10 million from investors, sponsors (including Allstate Insurance), and dealers.

For a time, De Lorean was negotiating with a bank in Puerto Rico about building the car there, and the government promised buildings on a former air-force base, tax concessions, and low-wage labour. But too many snags killed that project.

In 1977, De Lorean and his latest wife (Christina) flew to Ireland to look at the chances of building the car there. Irish contacts pointed out the possibility of getting subsidies from the UK government if he would locate the plant in Northern Ireland. It worked, and a greenfield factory was put up at Dunmurry, near Belfast. From 1978 to 1982, successive British governments poured £85 million into the operation. A total of 8583 cars were built before, in October 1982, the official receivers were called in.

The week before, John Z. De Lorean had been arrested in a Los Angeles motel room by federal drug agents and charged with participating in a $24 million scheme to distribute cocaine. It was not until August 1984 that he was acquitted on grounds of 'entrapment'. Christina then divorced him.

A Michigan grand jury was appointed to investigate the disappearance of $17,650,000 from the sports car project (assumed to be placed in a Swiss bank account for under-the-table payments to Colin Chapman and others associated with it). De Lorean was put before a Michigan court on charges of fraud and racketeering, but he was acquitted for lack of solid proof.

For the rest of his life, he faced certain arrest if he set foot on British soil. Because he never paid his lawyers their $150,000 fee for representing him during the bankruptcy proceedings of the De Lorean Motor Co., he would also be put under arrest if caught in Michigan. Finally, in April 1994, a circuit judge in Oakland, California, slapped a contempt-of-court ruling against him, making it risky to visit that state. He retired to a large estate at Bedminster, New Jersey, from which he was evicted by creditors in March 2000.

JPN

1908 Demeester 4-cylinder voiturette.
NATIONAL MOTOR MUSEUM

DELTA (iv) *see* YETI

DELTAYN (GB) 1985–1987
1985–1987 Deltayn Ltd, Finching Field, Essex.
1987 Deltayn Ltd, Appleby, South Humberside.
John Parradine ran a company importing dumper trucks, and decided to become a car maker by modifying the A.D. 400 to become the Deltayn Proteus. It was hardly recognisable when it was finished: noteworthy new features included six headlamps, a Lagonda-style grill, spoiler and skirts, and a T-bar targa top with a removable rear hard-top. The chassis was a massive ladder frame with cross-bracing and a backbone. Mechanically it was mainly Rover SD1 with Jaguar XJ suspension. In 1987, John Parradine ceased making the Proteus and formed a new company, PARRADINE, to make and market a new car, the Pegasus.
CR

DEL TECH *see* FOERS

DE LUCA (I) 1906–1910
SA Fabbrica Automobili de Luca, Naples.
Carmine de Luca SA was one of the leading engineering companies in Naples, founded in the mid-nineteenth century, and by 1905 having a work-force of 800. Its speciality was the manufacture of torpedoes and launching tubes under licence from Schneider. In April 1906 the four sons of the founder set up an automobile division, and took out a licence to build English DAIMLERs. Four models were listed, the 3308cc 16/24hp, 6786cc 28/40hp, 7964cc 32/55hp and 10,604cc 42/65hp. Probably only the smallest was actually made at Naples; Daimler refused consent to the 30hp being made by De Luca while they were still making them at Coventry. At least three 45hp Coventry-made cars were sold to De Luca at a special price for resale under the De Luca name.
   The 16/24hp made by de Luca differed from its Coventry equivalent in having shaft drive and a channel steel frame in place of armoured wood. The hubcaps bore the name De Luca with no mention of Daimler. In the Spring of 1908 Daimler began importing Naples-built chassis and fitting them with their own bodies. Three De Luca-Daimlers were shown on the Daimler stand at the 1908 Olympia Show, one of them having a sleeve-valve engine. De Luca had taken out a separate licence for this engine, which indicated that they hoped for serious production. However Daimler cancelled their order for De Luca-Daimlers, leaving the Naples company to rely only on the home market. This was insufficient, and manufacture at Naples ceased in 1910.
NG

DE LUXE *see* CAR DE LUXE

DE MARCAY (F) 1920–1921
De Marcay et Compagnie, Paris.
The De Marcay was a typical cycle car powered by a 987cc Anzani air-cooled V-twin engine, with 2- or 3-speed gearbox, shaft drive and no differential. Some had sliding pillar ifs on Sizaire-Naudin lines, while others had quarter-elliptic springs all round.
NG

DE MARS (US) 1905–1906
De Mars Electric Vehicle Co., Cleveland, Ohio.
William De Mars made a light 2-seater electric victoria with chain drive, which he sold under his own name for one season only. In February 1906 his company was bought by C.J. Blakeslee, and the name of car and company was changed to BLAKESLEE. About 20 were sold under this name, then new owners appeared and the car was renamed WILLIAMS. This lasted no more than a year, when the brothers John and William Byrider bought the company and named it after themselves. Their venture was marginally more successful that any previous one, lasting until 1910. During the four changes of name and ownership, design of the car changed little, although the Williams and Byrider had painted wheel flanges instead of polished brass.
NG

DEMATI (B) 1937–1939
Automobiles Demati, Brussels.
This unusual small car gained its name from those of the three men who promoted it, Defay, Matthys and Timberman. Matthys was a coachbuilder whose firm had been taken over by Imperia in 1928, and he applied his expertise to the integral construction tubular frame used in the Demati 2-door saloon. It was powered by a 600 or 980cc V-twin J.A.P. engine driving the front-wheels, and in order to avoid problems with driving and steering on the same axle, the partners gave the Demati rear-wheel steering. For the 1938 Brussels Salon they replaced the V-twin with a 950cc 4-cylinder Ruby engine, and in 1939 they abandoned the rear-wheel steering. By then it was too late to put the car into production, and the death of Eugene Matthys ended the project.
NG

DEMEESTER (F) 1906–1914
Automobiles Demeester, Courbevoie, Seine.
Léon Demeester began his motoring career on two wheels, coming to public attention when he won the motorcycle class in the 1901 Nice-Salon-Nice race on a Gladiator. In June 1905 it was announced that he would be making a small car at a reasonable price. He entered a 2-cylinder car in the Coupe des Voiturettes in November that year, but the first production Demeester of 1906 had a 6.5hp single-cylinder engine. He was soon convinced of the advantages of multi-cylinder engines, not least because they were a way round the bore restrictions imposed by Coupe des Voiturettes regulations (the bore was limited to 100mm, but the number of cylinders was not restricted). In 1907 he made an 8hp 4-cylinder engine, said to be the smallest of its kind in the world. Mechanically-operated inlet valves came in 1907, and in 1909 he bought ohv engines from Sultan. The 1912 Demeester range consisted of three fours, of 10, 12 and 16hp. For 1913–14 the smallest Demeester was the same as the 8hp SINPAR. This arrangement enabled Demeester to offer a smaller car than he was making himself at that time.
NG

DÉMISSINE (B) 1901–1902
O. de Ruyter, Brussels.
De Ruyter was a coachbuilder who offered a few electric cars under the name Démissine. They were exhibited at the 1902 Brussels Salon.
NG

DEMOCRATA (BR) 1967
Industria Brasileira do Automovel, Sao Paulo.
IBAP (Industria Brasileira do Automovel) was founded by Nelson Fernandes in 1964, in order to build the Democrata coupé, designed by Fernando Beraldin, then a Willys stylist. The body was made in fibreglass. Although the prototype was powered by a Chevrolet Corvair engine, Fernandes said the production engine would be a V-6 displacing 2498cc, with 120bhp output. A daily production of five cars was estimated, but apparently, only a few Democratas were made, while Fernandes saw himself tangled in legal and financial trouble.
ACT

DEMOT (US) 1910–1911
Demot Car Co., Detroit, Michigan.

This car's name was a contraction of Detroit Motorcar, alternatives being DeMotCar and Demotcar. It was an attractive-looking 2-seater, made as a tourer with windscreen and hood or as a racy roadster with neither of these features but a bolster tank behind the seat in the manner of the Mercer Raceabout. Power came from an 8/10hp 2-cylinder engine which drove through a 2-speed epicyclic transmission. The brake linings were made of asbestos and camel's hair. The backer, C.H. Ritter, later made the RITTER in Madison, Wisconsin.

NG

DE MOTTE (US) 1904

De Motte Motorcar Co., Valley Forge, Pennsylvania.

This company announced an ambitious programme of cars in various sizes, trucks and buses, and claimed that the same chassis was suitable for nearly all models. However, they did offer three sizes of engine; a 10hp for a runabout, 20hp four for a tonneau, and a larger unit for the commercials. All used chain drive. As the make lasted for less than a year, one may doubt that all these models were made.

NG

DEN HELD (NL) 1913–1914

Den Held used a 4-cylinder Ballot engine, Malicet et Blin chassis, and a body by the Rotterdam coachbuilder, Dolk. At least three were completed before World War I.

NG

DENISE COACHWORKS (US) c.1998

Denise Coachworks, Los Angeles, California.

The El Caprice body kit was a pick-up truck conversion for the big Chevrolet Caprice sedan. The top was cut off behind the front seats and the pick-up tail was grafted on. This greatly improved the looks of the whale-like Caprice and gave it a new functionality.

HP

DENNIS (i) (GB) 1899–1915

Dennis Bros Ltd, Guildford, Surrey.

John and Raymond Dennis were bicycle makers who also ran the Universal Athletic Stores in Guildford where they sold their cycles and other sporting goods. In 1899 they built a De Dion-Bouton-engined tricycle and exhibited this and a light car, also De Dion-powered, at the National Cycle Show in November that year. It was not built for sale, and the next Dennis cars, which were marketed, came in 1901. These had 8 or 10hp De Dion engines mounted in front under a De Dion-type bonnet, 3-speed gearboxes with direct drive on top, and shaft drive. The Dennises of 1903 had higher bonnets fronted by gilled-tube radiators. The small De Dion-engined cars were supplemented by larger models with 12/14hp 2-cylinder and 16/20hp 4-cylinder engines, both by Aster. The catalogue also contained a 'Gordon Bennett type racer' powered by a 40hp 4-cylinder Simms engine. In 1904 the famous overhead worm-drive was adopted and continued until the end of car production. On commercial chassis, worm drive survived up to the early 1930s. In 1906 a Dennis performed so well in a 4000 mile reliability trial that they were awarded the Dewar Trophy in the following year.

Like most makes Dennis cars grew larger over the years, the top model in 1906 having a 30/35hp 4-cylinder engine by White & Poppe. Dennis soon standardised on this Coventry engine maker, some being specially made to Dennis' specifications. In 1919 Dennis bought White & Poppe and later transferred production of their engines to Guildford. From 1909 to 1915 a wide range of reliable touring cars was built, from 15.9 to 60hp, the latter being a short-lived six made only during 1909–11. Gradually commercial vehicles assumed such importance for Dennis that passenger car production had to take second place. The last models were fours of 15.9 and 24hp. Even if World War I had not intervened, they would probably not have been made for much longer. Dennis has made commercial vehicles up to the present day. They are currently Britain's largest builders of bus chassis, and are also prominent in the fields of municipal vehicles and fire service vehicles.

NG

1910 Demot 8/10hp runabout.
SAH JOURNAL

1909 Dennis (i) 18hp tourer.
NATIONAL MOTOR MUSEUM

DENNIS (ii) (GB) 1911

John Dennis & Co., Harrow, Middlesex.

No connection with the well-known Dennis of Guildford, this firm made an early example of a cyclecar, powered by a 1.5-litre air-cooled V-twin engine, with a conventional 2-speed gearbox and worm final drive.

NG

DENNISON (NZ) 1900–1905

F.R. Dennison, Christchurch and Oamaru, South Island.

A strong contender for the laurel as the first internal combustion-engined vehicle made in New Zealand, Dennison's 1900 machine was a local production apart from the wheels, tyres and drive chains. The engine was a water-cooled unit with hot-tube ignition which ran on vaporised kerosene fuel. A cone clutch, a single gear, a countershaft and side chains comprised the drive line. It had a reputed speed of 15mph (24km/h) and a journey from Christchurch to Dennison's home town, Oamaru, a distance of some 174 miles over the tortuous route of that time, was made with much tribulation. On the return stage the machine caught fire during the descent to the Waitaki River and was completely burned out. By 1901, Dennison was again in Oamaru where he constructed a 3-wheeled vehicle powered by a 2.5hp De Dion-Bouton engine, which was capable of 22mph (35km/h) and attracted a buyer. In 1905 he built a 12-seater bus to the order of a client. This was wholly his own construction, apart from its tyres and bodywork.

MG

DE NOVO (GB) 1986–1992

1986–1990 De Novo Kits, Ponterwyd, Dyfed.
1990–1992 De Novo Kits, Halesowen, West Midlands.

Doug Pinchin displayed his K.N.W. one-off at various kit car shows in 1985, and the Lotus-like coupé received enough favourable comment for him to consider a production run. De Novo Kits (sometimes referred to as D.N.K.) productionised

1959 Denzel 1300 hard-top sports car.
NATIONAL MOTOR MUSEUM

1994 Deon Scoperta coupé.
NICK BALDWIN

the car as the Hornet II. The Ford Cortina provided the mechanical basis, the fibreglass body bonded on to a box section chassis, and there was a lift-out targa panel. Only a tiny handful were ever made.

CR

DENZEL (A) 1948–1960
Wolfgang Denzel, Vienna.
Garage owner, racer and engineer Wolfgang Denzel could so easily have enjoyed the same success as Porsche. He too produced open-topped sports cars in Austria using the mechanical platform of the Volkswagen Beetle. In fact, Denzels were often fitted with expanded 1281cc and 1290cc VW engines with up to 64bhp and, from 1954, with 1.5-litre Porsche engines. The first car was a 4-seater with wooden bodywork and VW wartime cross-country mechanicals. From 1951 Denzels switched from VW to purpose-designed tubular steel chassis, which were lighter, and the bodywork was now of aluminium. Wolfgang Denzel campaigned his car with success in the 1949 and 1954 Alpine Rallies. A coupé model was listed alongside roadster and convertible models from 1956 but the marque disappeared in 1960, before a new 1300 coupé prototype could be produced in series. Around 350 cars had been supplied in all, and Denzel went on to run a chain of successful car dealerships. The Denzel marque is also often referred to as W.D.

CR

DEON (GB) 1987–1993/1995–1998
1987–1988 J.H. Classics, Clacton, Essex.
1988–1991 J.H. Classics, Sutton Veny, Warminster, Dorset.
1991–1993 Deon Ltd, Ilminster, Somerset.
1995–1998 Deon Cars, Ilminster, Somerset.
The Ferrari Dino inspired this range of kit-form sports cars, initially sold under the name D.G.T., which emerged from the ashes of the DAYTONA CLASSICS operation. A multi-tube chassis with central backbone supported a steel-and-wood reinforced fibreglass shell. Lancia Beta front suspension was used at the rear and Fiat 124 at the front, a Lancia Beta engine was standard, although the Ford Cologne 2.9 V6 was an option (combined with an Escort RS Turbo gearbox). There was a coupé, the GTS-style targa coupé called the Scoperto, and a third Le Mans model - an original speedster style with no roof and a cut-down wind deflector. In 1992 the company took over the NOBLE P4 project and a more ambitious Mirabeau model was just about to be launched when Deon went bust in early 1993, after spectacular expenditure. You had to look twice to realise that the Mirabeau was not just a full convertible version of the Dino replica, but it was in fact heavily revised, with a smoothed-out front end, lip spoiler, wider wheel arches and new rear end treatment featuring a kick in the tail. The marque reappeared with the Mirabeau and Dino-style models in 1995.

CR

DE P (GB) 1914–1916
1914–1915 The Depford Co., Deptford, London.
1915–1916 The Depford Co., New Cross, London.
This light car took its name for the manufacturer, L.F. de Peyrecave, who had worked for DUO Cyclecars Ltd, and who took over Duo's works in September 1913. The name of his new company, Depford, was not inspired by the place of manufacture, but came from the names of de Peyrecave and his partner H.G. Burford who later made commercial vehicles under his own name. The De P car used an 8hp V-twin or a 10hp 4-cylinder Dorman engine and shaft drive.

NG

DE PALMA (US) 1905; 1916

1905 Ralph de Palma, New York City.
1916 De Palma Manufacturing Co., Detroit, Michigan.
The famous racing driver Ralph de Palma (1893–1956) made several attempts to enter car manufacture, but very few vehicles resulted. In 1905 he built two cars in New York to customers' specification, and in 1911 announced that he would build touring cars and roadsters, again to special order only. No details of these survive, but in 1916 he actually formed a company to produce aero engines and motorcars. These were racing cars, though it was announced that the company would build special speedsters for those who wanted cars of that type. Again, precise details are lacking, and probably production never reached double figures.

NG

DE PONTAC (F) 1955–1960

Éts S.E.P.A., Bordeaux.
Several attempts were made to produce a sports car based on the Citroën 2CV chassis in the 1950s, but none was stranger than the Marquis Jean-Marie de Pontac's. First presented in 1955, it featured a very low open 3-piece body whose front and rear plastic sections were symmetrical and interchangeable; the central aluminium section formed part of the chassis; and the headlamps swivelled into position. Unusually the suspension employed pneumatic damping (i.e. a tyre was the damper!), while the engine could be a standard 425cc 2CV twin or an enlarged 500cc version with 26bhp. At the 1957 Paris Salon, an example was shown with an inlaid flower pattern on the bodywork, a curious Plexiglass hardtop and a Panhard 850cc engine.

CR

DERAIN (US) 1908–1911

1908–1910 Simplex Manufacturing Co., Cleveland, Ohio.
1910–1911 Derain Motor Co., Cleveland, Ohio.
The Simplex company was founded by 20-year old Earl H. Sherbondy who planned initially to make 2-stroke engines rather than complete cars. At the 1908 Cleveland Auto Show, he exhibited a touring car simply to demonstrate his engine, but in August 1909 he announced that he would build a run of 25 30hp tourers to sell at $4000 each. That seems to have been the extent of Derain car production.

NG

DERBY (i) (F) 1921–1936

Éts B. Montet, Courbevoie, Seine; St Denis, Seine.
The Montet company was set up in 1912 by Bertrand Montet (1878–1928) and Georges Goett, and was engaged in general engineering. During World War I they specialised in tow hooks and couplings, and after the war dealt in ex-military Harley-Davidson motorcycles. When they decided to enter the cyclecar market, it was logical to use Harley engines. These were 998cc air-cooled V-twins (also used by RALLY in their first cars) driving through a 3-speed gearbox and shaft drive. Front suspension was by a transverse semi-elliptic spring, with semi-cantilevers at the rear. The body was a simple 2-seater, fronted by a handsome vee-radiator not unlike a miniature Bentley. The name Derby was chosen for its associations with the turf.

Alongside the V-twin at the 1921 Paris Salon was a racing model with 930cc 4-cylinder Chapuis-Dornier engine, and this pointed the way to future touring models. The Harley engine was carried on for one more season, joined for 1923 by several models using 4-cylinder Chapuis-Dornier engines, a 2-seater, a 3-seater and a *camionette voyageur* for commercial travellers. For 1924 the range was extended further, starting with a short-lived 2-seater powered by a 497cc single-cylinder 2-stroke engine and including a pointed-tail sports car, a 3-seater saloon and a delivery van. Engines were 961cc side-valve and 1097cc ohv fours. All were by Chapuis-Dornier, including the 2-stroke. Apart from the 2-stroke, these were continued without major change for 1925, although the sports model of the Chapuis-Dornier engine had three valves per cylinder, and a Cozette supercharger was available. Production was estimated at 50 per year in 1922–23, and 80 per year in 1924–25.

The Derby grew up in 1926; the tourers and saloon became larger, and on the sporting side there was a low 2-seater with cycle-type wings, similar in appearance to the Amilcar CGSS. As well as the Chapuis-Dorniers, engine options included

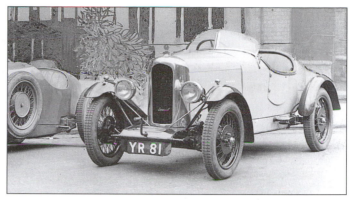
1927 Derby (i) 9hp sports models.
NATIONAL MOTOR MUSEUM

1931 Derby (i) FWD 1100cc saloon.
NATIONAL MOTOR MUSEUM

1933 Derby (i) 2-litre V8 saloon.
MICHAEL WORTHINGTON-WILLIAMS

a 1096cc S.C.A.P. and a 1097cc Ruby; both ohv units. With supercharger the S.C.A.P. gave 40bhp. Six-cylinder C.I.M.E. engines of 1200 and 1300cc were available in 1928. These were side-valve units, but had false ohv covers. Capacity of the C.I.M.E. six was increased to 1655cc for 1929 and to 1847cc for 1931. Some very handsome 4-seater torpedo, cabriolet and closed-coupé bodies were offered at this time, as well as low-slung sports and racing models. Derby production peaked at about 200 cars in 1925, but was down to around 100 a year from 1928 to 1931. Foreign involvement included licence assembly in Italy under the name Fadini during 1924–26, while both 4- and 6-cylinder models were sold in England under the name Vernon-Derby from 1927 to 1930. Although entirely French in manufacture, they carried the Vernon-Derby name on their radiators.

In 1930, following the death of Bertrand Montet two years earlier, Derby came under the control of English capital, with the racing drivers Douglas Hawkes and Gwenda Stewart in prominent positions. Design was headed by

1980 Desande roadster.
NICK BALDWIN

Étienne Lepicard (1891–1972) who came from Donnet, and who had built, on his own account, a prototype front-wheel drive V8 in 1929. Hawkes was attracted by this design, and in 1931 launched a front-drive Derby, though not, at first, with the V8 engine. Instead it was powered by a 1097cc 4-cylinder Ruby engine which, together with the drive unit, could be detached from the rest of the chassis. Three body styles were listed, and shown at the 1931 Salon, a saloon, a coupé and a roadster, all three being made by Macquet et Galvier of Courbevoie. A Chapron-bodied cabriolet was shown at the 1932 Salon. About 200 of these Derbys, called the L2 model, were made in 1931 and 1932 and about 50 in 1933 and 1934. Some were made with 1496cc Meadows 4ED engines, but these were not catalogued in France, and were probably assembled by Douglas Hawkes at his Brooklands workshops. Few were made, possibly no more than six, plus a forward-control delivery van.

At the 1933 Salon appeared the last Derby, which fulfilled Lepicard's ambition as it was a front-wheel drive V8. The engine was greatly altered from his 1929 prototype, with bigger bore and shorter stroke, giving a capacity of 1992cc. It had side inlet and overhead exhaust valves and developed 75bhp when announced, and this was raised to 85bhp after May 1934. Some very handsome long and low bodies featured in the catalogue, a 4-door saloon, 2-door cabriolet and roadster, all built by Duval as Macquet et Galvier had gone out of business. A handful of one-off coachwork was made such as a coupé by Labourdette and a 4-door saloon by Abbott of Farnham, Surrey. Probably the last V8 was bodied as a drophead coupé by Antem in 1936. A production run of 100 V8s was planned, but fewer were actually made. Serge Pozzoli thinks no more than 20. After the end of car production, George Goett concentrated on the towing hitch side of the business, which survived at least into the 1980s.

NG

DERBY (ii) (CDN) 1924–1927
Derby Motorcars Ltd, Winnipeg, Manitoba and Saskatoon, Saskatchewan.
When the WINNIPEG company failed in 1923, its vice-president, Louis Arsenault tried to market another car in the prairie city, but this time he chose to sell rather than manufacture. The last Winnipeg had been based on the DAVIS (i), and Arsenault continued the connection by importing the Davis, changing the nameplate to Derby, and adding Derby-labelled tyre covers. Sedan, tourer and roadster models were offered, all with the Davis' Continental 6-cylinder engine. Records indicate that no more than 31 Derbys were sold. Arsenault's office was originally in Winnipeg, then in Saskatoon, while conversion of the cars took place in the former Marshall tractor plant in Saskatoon.
NG

DER DESSAUER (D) 1912–1913
Anhaltische Automobil-und Motorenfabrik AG, Dessau.
This firm was a continuation of the MWD (Motor-Werke Dessau). The 2.1-litre 8/22hp model was continued, with power increased to 24hp. The quality was

quite acceptable, but financial problems forced the company to close down after less than two years.
HON

DEREK (GB) 1925–1926
Derek Motors Ltd, West Norwood, London.
The Derek was an undistinguished light car made in 9/20 and 10/25hp models, the former using a 1018cc side-valve Chapuis Dornier engine and the latter a 1247cc ohv Meadows. Both had 3-speed gearboxes, spiral bevel rear axles and quarter-elliptic suspension all round. Production was very limited.
NG

DE RIANCEY (F) 1899–c.1901
Sté des Automobiles de Riancey, Levallois-Perret, Seine.
This was a very light car on the lines of the PARISIENNE or Victoria Combination, with air-cooled 2-cylinder engine mounted on a centre-pivot front axle which it also drove. The complete engine and transmission turned when the car was steered.
NG

DE SALVERT (F) 1904–1906
Perrier et Compagnie, Paris.
This was a large car of conventional design, powered by a 24/30hp 4-cylinder engine.
NG

DESANDE (GB/B) 1979–c.1984
Desande Automobielen, Hulst.
The neo-classic Desande Roadster was a joint Belgian-British venture. It was based on a Ford Thunderbird chassis, incorporating that car's 116in (2944mm) wheelbase, box section frame, all-coil suspension, Ford 5-litre or 5.8-litre V8 power, Cruise-O-Matic transmission. Later examples were based on Chevrolet Impala station wagon chassis and had GM 5.0-litre V8 engines. The handcrafted aluminium body was built by London-based Grand Prix Metalcraft (which also made DEETYPE bodies) and there was an optional hardtop. The luxury interior featured leather trim, electric reclining seats, air conditioning and a wooden dash.
CR

DESBERON (US) 1901–1904
Desberon Motor Car Co., New York City; New Rochelle, New York.
The first Desberon was a neat-looking runabout powered by a 7hp 2-cylinder engine under a De Dion-Bouton-type bonnet, with shaft drive. It had two side by side seats and a precarious-looking 'spider' seat behind. By 1904 the Desberon was a much larger car, with 30/36hp 4-cylinder engine and tonneau body. Steam and internal-combustion-engined trucks were also made.
NG

DESCHAMPS (F) 1913
Deschamps et Compagnie, Paris.
This was a light cyclecar powered by a 638cc single-cylinder engine, transmission being by a 3-speed gearbox and shaft drive. A 2-seater was the only style listed.
NG

DE SCHAUM (US) 1908–1909
De Schaum Motor Syndicate Co., Buffalo, New York.
The man behind this car was born William Andrew Schaum, but somewhere during the move from his native Baltimore to Buffalo he became the more aristocratic De Schaum. The car he promoted was a high-wheeler with horizontal 2-cylinder engine, friction transmission and chain drive. A variety of engine sizes were quoted, from 10 to 20hp, as were six different wheelbases. For 1909 the cars were marketed under the name Seven Little Buffalos, but this did not help sales, which did not exceed 36. In 1910 De Schaum moved to Detroit to make the SUBURBAN car, but this was even less successful than the De Schaum.
NG

DESGOUTTES see COTTIN-DESGOUTTES

DESHAIS (F) 1950–1952
Automobiles Deshais, Paris.

With an all-up weight of only 180kg, the Deshais could be described as a sporty microcar, despite the fact that its air-cooled flat-twin engines of 125, 250, or 350cc were hardly powerful (starting at 6bhp and going up to 15bhp). The Deshais was also unusual in that it featured integral monocoque construction, with open 2-seater bodywork. From 1951 a larger 420cc transverse twin engine was fitted (as before, having front-wheel drive) but the car was too expensive to have much market impact.

CR

DE SHAW (US) 1907–1909
1907–1908 Charles De Shaw, Brooklyn, New York.
1908–1909 De Shaw Motor Co., Evergreen, New York.
Charles De Shaw was an enthusiast for the 2-stroke engine, and in 1907 he built a 12/14hp 3-cylinder engine which he installed in a light runabout. At first he had no company, and built cars to the order of friends, but in 1908 he became more ambitious and set up a company in which he was the mechanical engineer and superintendent. He also added a 5-seater tourer with a 28hp 4-cylinder engine, and a 14hp 4-cylinder runabout.

NG

DESIGN CLASSICS (US) c. 1981
Design Classics, Minnetonka, Minnesota.
The eMGe was an MG-TD replica that fitted on a Volkswagon Beetle chassis. Design Classics also built a 1957 Thunderbird replica called the Teebird that bolted onto a VW chassis. The rear-mounted engine left plenty of storage room up front where the V-8 should have been.

HP

DES MOINES (US) 1902
Des Moines Automobile Co., Des Moines, Iowa.
The Des Moines Motorette was a light tiller-steered 2-seater with single-cylinder engine under the seats and final drive by single chain. Larger models called Stanhope and Tonneau were also listed, and electric cars were announced but never built.

NG

DESMOULINS (F) 1920–1923
E. Desmoulins, Paris.
Two models of Desmoulins were made, a 7CV 4-cylinder tourer whose only unusual feature was a 5-speed gearbox, and a twin-engined car which used different sizes of engine mounted side by side and driving via twin propeller shafts to a double-drive underslung worm rear axle. There was no gearbox; the car normally ran on the larger engine, and for hill climbing the smaller was brought into play as well. The engines, both by Ballot, were of 1131 and 1590cc.

NG

DESOTO (i) (US) 1928–1960
Chrysler Motors Corp., Detroit, Michigan.
The year 1928 was very important for Walter Chrysler; within two months he bought the Dodge Brothers Co. for $170 million, and launched two new makes of car, Plymouth and DeSoto. The Plymouth was aimed at the low-price market dominated by Chevrolet and Ford, while the DeSoto was a step upmarket, although at first similar in appearance to the Plymouth and sharing many components. Both makes were built in the same factory.

Named after the sixteenth-century explorer Hernando de Soto, who discovered the Mississippi in 1541, the new car had a small side-valve 6-cylinder engine only a little larger than the Plymouth's four – 2866cc compared with 2790cc. It developed 55bhp and gave the car a lively performance, effectively curbed by Lockheed hydraulic brakes. Seven body styles were offered and these carried Spanish names such as Sedan de Lugo, Sedan Coche, and Cupe Business. Prices ran from $845 for a roadster to $955 for a de luxe sedan, and the car was a runaway best seller in its first year. Introduced on 4 August 1928 as a 1929 model, it had sold 34,518 by the end of the year; total production for the model year August 1928 to July 1929 was 81,065 cars. This beat other famous first-year sellers such as Chrysler, Graham-Paige, and Pontiac.

In January 1930 the six was joined by a 3404cc 70bhp straight-8 which was advertised as the world's lowest-priced straight-8, at prices from $985 to $1075. The engine and chassis shared many parts with the Dodge Model DC straight-8,

1929 DeSoto(i) K Series roadster.
NATIONAL MOTOR MUSEUM

1935 DeSoto(i) SG Airflow sedan.
NATIONAL MOTOR MUSEUM

1939 De Soto(i) S6 sedan.
NATIONAL MOTOR MUSEUM

1955 DeSoto(i) Fireflite convertible.
NATIONAL MOTOR MUSEUM

425

although DeSoto prices were $10 to $20 lower. This position was reversed in 1933 when DeSoto moved above Dodge and closer to Chrysler in price. It was probably because of its new position in the range that DeSoto was chosen to share with Chrysler the controversial Airflow styling introduced for the 1934 season. This was not only a styling exercise, because the Airflows had welded unitary construction and all seats within the wheelbase. To achieve this the passengers were moved forward 20ins (508mm) relative to the rear wheels, and the engine was relocated between the front wheels rather than behind them.

The Airflow was an efficient and logical design, and in the positioning of the engine and passengers it was a forerunner of all of today's cars. Unfortunately, the public found it was too radical a step away from what they thought a car should look like. In particular, the short bonnet and long passenger compartment were the antithesis of traditional elegance, as typified by the long-bonnetted Duesenbergs and Packards. The DeSoto Airflows sold slightly better than that of Chrysler, 15,000 to 11,000, but Chrysler also had a more conventional car for 1934, which took their total sales to just under 37,000. Unlike Chrysler, which offered three sizes of straight-8 in their Airflows, DeSoto's Airflow was made with a single six, of 3957cc.

For 1935 DeSoto had a more conservatively-styled car, the Airstream, as a companion to the Airflow, and sales for the model year jumped to 27,481. Both cars had the 3957cc engine, which developed 93bhp in the Airstream and 100bhp in the Airflow. The latter were priced at up to $300 higher, and customers were hard to find. Total Airflow sales in 1935 and 1936 were only 11,797, compared with 59,494 Airstreams.

The DeSoto Airflow was dropped after 1936, but Chrysler struggled on for another season. The 1937 DeSotos with 3738cc 6-cylinder engines, were conventional in design but attractively styled by Ray Dietrich, who headed Chrysler's styling department from 1936 to 1940. Sales for the 1937 model year were 82,000, helped by a long-wheelbase sedan which became popular as a taxicab. This model was introduced in 1936, when 3000 were made, including 2200 'Sunshine' cabs for New York City. Later renamed DeSoto Skyview, they featured European-style sliding roofs, which were offered on the regular sedans for 1939. DeSoto listed a long-wheelbase 7-seater car up to 1954, and was a major supplier to taxi operators right across the United States.

The next major changes came on the 1939 models, which had more streamlined bodies without projecting luggage boots, headlamps recessed into the wings, 2-piece windscreens and steering column gearchange. All 1939 DeSotos were closed models, but a convertible reappeared for 1940, now with a power-operated hood. The 3738cc engine was largely unchanged up to 1942, developing 93bhp in standard form and 100bhp with aluminium head. This was available on all models, and generally adopted on the long-wheelbase cars. Styling followed other Chrysler Corp. cars from 1939 to 1942, although a unique feature on the 1942 DeSotos was the retractable headlamps which disappeared behind a metal panel when not in use. DeSoto was the only American car to offer these, apart from the Cord 810/812, which was no longer in production. They were not revived after the war as they were not worth the cost and complexity. In 1941 both DeSoto and Dodge featured fluid drive, a semi-automatic transmission. As well as the headlamps, the 1942 DeSotos offered several unusual luxury features, including an automatic map light and an optional 8-programme push-button radio, the dial of which changed from red to green to violet according to the tuning. The speedometer changed colours too. Air-conditioning was an option, although it is not known if any were ordered. Only 24,771 of the 1942 models were made, before the effects of the war closed production lines on 9 February 1942.

Like most American cars, early postwar DeSotos were similar to the 1942 models and the only novelty for 1946 was an even longer wheelbase for the 9-seater Suburban with three rows of seats. This was intended for hotels as well as taxi operators and large families, and had a wheelbase of 140in (3543mm) and an overall length of 225in (5710mm). Styling was updated on the 1949 models, and again for 1955 with the 'Forward Look' employed on all Chrysler cars. The result was an 85 per cent increase in sales, to 129,767. The old side-valve 6-cylinder engine had been joined for 1952 by a hemispherical-head V8 which developed 160bhp from 4524cc; this was the first 8-cylinder DeSoto since 1931. The sixes did not feature on the 1955 cars, whose V8 engines were now of 4768cc, developing 185bhp from the standard Firedome engine and 200 from the Fireplate with 4-barrel carburettor. All DeSotos now had fully automatic transmissions, which were introduced on the 1954 models.

The mid-1950s saw the Chrysler Corp. putting much stress on power and performance. Each Division had its own high performance model, and DeSoto's was the Adventurer, introduced in 1956. This was available only as a 2-door hard-top coupé, and was powered by a 5594cc V8 developing 320bhp, thanks to twin 4-barrel carburettors, high-lift camshaft, stiffer valve springs and many other modifications. Top speed was 144mph (232km/h) and 0-60 mph (0-97km/h) took 10.5 seconds. The Adventurer retained its performance image until 1960, when the name was given to the top DeSotos, although these did not have any performance advantages. A DeSoto convertible was chosen as the Pace Car for the 1956 Indianapolis 500 Mile Race.

With 126,514 DeSotos finding customers, 1957 was a good year for sales, but the following year they dropped disastrously, to only 49,445; 1958 was a recession year for the industry generally, but Chrysler and its DeSoto Division were hit particularly badly. At the end of the year DeSoto suffered the indignity of being moved out of its own factory on Wyoming Avenue, which had been its home since 1935, and moving into one of the Chrysler factories. The situation was slightly better in 1959, but the 1960 models, which had unitary construction, sold only 26,081. By this time Chrysler had seven lines of car, the compact Valiant, low-priced Plymouth and Dodge Dart, the medium-priced Dodge and DeSoto, and the upmarket Chrysler and Imperial. DeSoto was squeezed at both ends, losing sales to Dodge and Chrysler, and there was really no room for it in the marketplace. In September 1960, DeSoto announced restyled 1961 models, but they were abruptly withdrawn two months later, after only 3034 had been made.

DeSoto Abroad

Several models of DeSoto were sold in the United Kingdom under the Chrysler name in the 1930s. The 1932 and 1933 sixes were the Chrysler Mortlake and Wimbledon, the 1934 Airflow, the Chrysler Croydon and the 1937 six, the Chrysler Richmond. The 1946–48 DeSotos were sold on some export markets under the Diplomat name, and for the Mexican market the DeSoto Diplomat had a Plymouth body with a modified DeSoto grill. The compression ratio was lower than for the home market, and the speedometer was calibrated in kilometres.

NG

Further Reading
The Plymouth and DeSoto Story, Don Butler, Crestline Publishing, 1978.
'DeSoto: Walter Chrysler's Stepchild', Jeffrey I. Godshall,
Automobile Quarterley, Vol. XX, No. 1.

DESOTO (ii) (AUS) 1947–1957

Chrysler Australia Ltd, Keswick, South Australia.

As Chrysler's postwar Australian assembly increased, its local content, a version of the PLYMOUTH P15, was offered as a DeSoto using the Canadian long-block, short-stroke engine. When the PLYMOUTH P24 was selected for manufacture in Australia, a rebadged version with a vertical grill was made as the SP24 Diplomat. The separate identities were discontinued when the CHRYSLER Royal became the sole name plate.

MG

DE SOTO (US) 1913–1914

De Soto Motorcar Co., Auburn, Indiana.

This company was a subsidiary of the ZIMMERMAN Manufacturing Co. which launched a big 6-cylinder tourer which was slightly larger and more expensive than the Zimmerman Model 6-46. Made only in touring form, the De Soto Six featured a compressed-air starter and electric lighting. For 1914 it was joined by a tandem-seated cyclecar with the usual V-twin engine and belt drive. For 1915 there were plans to rename the cyclecar the Motorette and move production to Fort Wayne, but John Zimmerman decided to discontinue the marque altogether. Even the Zimmerman lasted only one more season.

NG

DESSAVIA (D) 1907

Anhaltische Fahrzeugfabrik Robert Krause, Dessau.

This company made a friction-drive light 2-seater. Production was limited and did not last for more than a few months.

HON

Airflow DE SOTO

She: "HAVE you driven the new Airflow De Soto? Everyone is talking about it."

He: "Yes! It is the motor car with the new ride sensation . . . the latest Chrysler Motors engineering triumph."

OA-21

CHRYSLER EXPORT CORPORATION
DETROIT, MICHIGAN, U.S.A.

No. OA-21
Newspapers—February, 1935.
636 Lines—4 Cols. x 11⅜ Inches

1965 De Tomaso Vallelunga coupé.
NATIONAL MOTOR MUSEUM

1966 De Tomaso Vallelunga coupé.
NICK BALDWIN

1968 De Tomaso Mangusta coupé.
NICK GEORGANO

1975 De Tomaso Pantera GP4 coupé.
NATIONAL MOTOR MUSEUM

DESTA *see* INTHELCO

DE TAMBLE (US) 1908–1913
1908–1909 Speed Changing Pulley Co., Indianapolis, Indiana.
1909–1913 De Tamble Motor Co., Anderson, Indiana.
The first De Tamble, made in very small numbers, was a 2-seater runabout powered by a 16hp 2-cylinder engine. The engines were made by F.D. Carrico of Cincinnati, who had worked for the Speed Changing Pulley Co. and built an experimental car with them in 1896. When the company changed its name and relocated in Anderson, the 2-cylinder runabout was continued by at least three other companies, as the Breeze at Carthage, Ohio, the Dakota at Wimbledon, North Dakota, and the James at Lawrenceburg, Indiana. The Anderson-built De Tamble was a larger car, powered by 4-cylinder engines of 30, 36 and 40hp. Only open models were made. These were either runabouts or tourers. In its last year, a smaller De Tamble was made, with a 17hp 4-cylinder engine. The company suffered several closures and receiverships, the last in the summer of 1913. A restart of production was promised for 1 January 1914, but this never came about.
NG

D.ET.B. (F) 1896–1902
Cie des Automobiles David et Bourgeois, Paris.
D. et B. cars were large, heavy looking vehicles with Daimler-type bonnets and artillery wheels. The first model was powered by a 4-cylinder Pierre Gautier engine mounted in front, with a 4-speed gearbox and double-chain drive. In 1900 a lighter 6hp 2-cylinder model was introduced as well as the 16hp 4-cylinder model.
NG

DE TOMASO (I) 1965 to date
De Tomaso Automobili SpA, Modena.
Born in Argentina in 1928, Alejandro de Tomaso came to Italy in 1955, founded his company in 1959 and built six Formula One cars in 1961. Four years later came his first road car, the Vallelunga coupé, with mid-mounted Ford Cortina engine. About 50 of these were made, together with an open version the Pampero, and in 1967 De Tomaso bought up coachbuilders, Ghia, with finance from Rowan Industries of New Jersey, with which he had family connections through his American wife. A prototype Rowan electric city car was shown at the 1957 Turin Show, but did not go into production.

In 1969 De Tomaso launched a more powerful derivative of the Vallelunga which he called the Mangusta (mongoose) as these animals eat cobras! It was powered by a 4727cc Ford V8 engine, with a ZF 5-speed transaxle, backbone chassis, limited slip differential and servo-assisted Girling disc brakes. It was capable of 155mph (250km/h), and the American market cars featured air-conditioning. It led to a closer association with Ford, which was strengthened with the arrival of its successor, the Pantera, in 1971. Unlike the Mangusta this had integral construction, and used a larger and more powerful Ford V8 engine of 5763cc and up to 350bhp. In GTS form (from 1973) its speed was 175mph (282km/h). It was distributed in America through Lincoln-Mercury dealers. De Tomaso also made front-engined cars, the 2.9-litre Ford V6-powered Mustela coupé of 1969, of which little was heard, and the Deauville, a luxury 4-door saloon powered by a choice of 4727 or 5763cc (mostly the latter) Ford V8 engine with automatic transmission. Made from 1970 to 1988, its styling, by Ghia, was very close to that of the Jaguar XJ6. The Longchamp was a 2-door coupé version on a shorter wheelbase.

In 1976 De Tomaso bought control of Maserati from Citroën, and other acquisitions included the Benelli and Moto Guzzi motorcycle firms and Innocenti, Italian makers of the Mini. The Maserati link led to a hybrid, the Kyalami, which was effectively a Longchamp with a choice of Maserati V8 engines. De Tomaso sold Maserati to Fiat in 1990.

After the severance of the Ford link in 1974, the Pantera was made in dwindling numbers, but remained nominally available until 1996, by which date about 10,500 had been made. It was the only product until the mid-1990s, when two new models were announced, the mid-engined Guara coupé powered by a 3982cc BMW V8 engine with 6-speed gearbox, and the front-engined Bigua convertible powered by a 4601cc Ford V8 engine with 5-speed gearbox. For the American market the name Mangusta was revived for the Bigua. It featured a novel hardtop which could be set in three different positions to make a coupé, targa, or cabriolet. In 2000 De Tomaso was the only important Italian car maker

1999 De Tomaso Mangusta GP4 coupé .
DE TOMASO

independent of Fiat, though they had a strategic partnership with the American parts company, Visteon Automotive Systems. From 2000 the Mangusta was made by a seperate company, and was sold as the QVALE Mangusta.

NG

Further reading
De Tomaso Pantera, Jan Norbye, Osprey, 1980.
De Tomaso Automobili, Wallace Wyss, Osprey, 1981.

DETRICK (US) 1957

Forrest R. Detrick, Worthington, Ohio.
The Detrick S-101 was a prototype steam car designed by Lee Gaeke and built by William Mehrling. The Detrick engine had two cylinders with a 4in bore and 5in stroke. It used a 4-valve poppet arrangement with steam entering on one side of the cylinder and passing out through the other. The S-101 was built on a 1953 Ford F-100 pickup chassis stretched to 127in (3223mm). Although first shown with a crude classic-style body, a more stylish fibreglass body was planned. Detrick planned to sell the engine units for installation into other chassis.

HP

DETROIT (i) **(US)** 1899–1902

Detroit Automobile Co., Detroit, Michigan.
Although this company made very few cars, 20 at the most, it is important to historians as its chief engineer was Henry Ford, and it was the predecessor of the Cadillac Automobile Co. It was formed in July 1899 by wealthy Detroit businessman William H. Murphy, who had enough faith in Henry Ford to back him. A full line of vehicles was promised from the company, but all Henry had come up with by the end of the year was a single delivery wagon. He said that he had 'one and a half cars started' and a few more were completed during 1900. They had 2-cylinder engines mounted under the seat, epicyclic transmission and single-chain drive. In January 1901 the firm was officially dissolved, although Ford found other backers for his projects, which included the enormous Arrow and 999 racing cars. In August 1902, Murphy approached Henry M. Leland to value his company for sale; instead Leland suggested that it be continued, using his engines, and it was renamed the Cadillac Automobile Co.

NG

1983 De Tomaso Pantera GTS coupé.
NATIONAL MOTOR MUSEUM

1999 De Tomaso Guara coupé.
DE TOMASO

1912 Detroit Electric 2-seater.
NICK BALDWIN

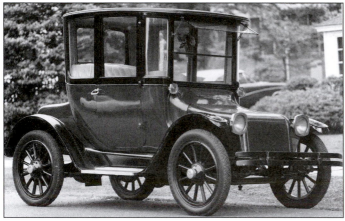

1917 Detroit Electric coupé.
NATIONAL MOTOR MUSEUM

DETROIT (ii) (US) 1904

Wheeler Manufacturing Co., Detroit, Michigan.

The Wheeler company manufactured auxiliary seats for cars, and this interest was manifest in the bodywork of their 15hp 2-cylinder car. This had three alternative styles, the basic version being a 2-seater runabout, behind which could be fitted either a tonneau for two additional passengers, or a delivery wagon. The engine was under the seat, with chain final drive, while the bonnet concealed fuel and water tanks. The car lasted less than a year, but the company continued with seat manufacture.

NG

DETROIT (iii) see CROWN (ii)

DETROIT (iv) (US) 1913–1914

Detroit Cyclecar Co., Detroit, Michigan.

Also known as the Little Detroit and Detroit Speedster, this was more of a light car than a cyclecar, having a 1.5-litre water-cooled 4-cylinder engine. At 860lbs (390kg) it was heavier than the average cyclecar. In the summer of 1914 the same design was made in a different factory as the Saginaw Speedster.

NG

DETROIT-DEARBORN (US) 1909–1910

Detroit-Dearborn Motorcar Co., Dearborn, Michigan.

This car was made in one model, a conventional 35hp 4-cylinder, whose most distinctive features were the names from classical mythology for its body styles, the Minerva tourer and Nike roadster. The first models were on the road in

November 1909, and the company was bankrupt by September 1910, after 110 cars had been made.

NG

DETROIT ELECTRIC (US) 1907–c.1939

1907–1910 Anderson Carriage Co., Detroit, Michigan.
1911–1918 Anderson Electric Car Co., Detroit, Michigan.
1919–c.1939 Detroit Electric Car Co., Detroit, Michigan.

The Detroit Electric was the most successful of the many electric cars of this type and led the field in longevity, hanging on to a rapidly dwindling market long after its fashion had passed into oblivion.

The Detroit Electric clientele consisted primarily of the woman owner-operator for shopping or social engagements. However, on a lesser scale, the cars, an underslung roadster and false front resembling a radiator, found a steady market also. The Detroit kept up with automotive styling and the factory reached its zenith in 1914 with a production of 4669 cars leaving the factory, priced between $2075 to $2275. Improvements continued on an annual basis, particularly with the increase in the possible mileage on a single charge – which could be made by a charging station or more commonly by a rectifier in the owner's garage.

The vogue in electric car popularity began to wane after 1916 and more Detroit Electric Cars featured false fronts to mask their motive power and otherwise avoid a freakish and obsolescent appearance in the contemporary traffic pattern, the dummy radiator shaped similarly to the contemporary Daniels, Fiat, and Kissel.

By 1921 Detroit prices peaked at $4000. Although prices dropped considerably after 1925, production did not increase. According to production figures by historian Beverly Rae Kimes, a scant 136 cars left the factory, further production listed as 1929, 26; 1930, 178; 1931, 131 and 1932, 59, later figures being unavailable.

The company maintained its archaic 'china closet' design to the end of production which came between 1939 and 1941. In 1930, however, an option was offered to buyers by masquerading the cars with bodies from Willys-Overland or Dodge, a notable exception being the Model 99 of 1932 which featured a smart-looking and specially designed 4-passenger coupé with a conventional steering wheel in place of the previous lever. It had a wheelbase of 112in (2842mm) and was priced at $4250.

An estimated 35,000 to 37,000 Detroits were built during their approximately 35 years in business.

KM

Further Reading
'Detroit Electric', Tom LaMarre, *Automobile Quarterly*, Vol. 27, No. 2.

DETROITER (i) (US) 1912–1917

1912–1916 Briggs-Detroiter Motorcar Co., Detroit, Michigan.
1916–1917 United Detroiter Corp., Detroit, Michigan.

Sometimes known as the Briggs-Detroiter, this car was promoted by Claude S. Briggs, former sales manager of the BRUSH Runabout Co., and was planned as a low-priced car which would be an improvement on the very basic Brush Runabout. The first Detroiter, made in one model only, was a 5-seater tourer powered by a 25hp 4-cylinder Continental engine, selling for a reasonable $850. It was a typical assembled car, with practically all components bought from outside sources. In 1913 rhd models were sold in England under the name Royal-Detroiter. By 1914 the range comprised seven models, three tourers, three roadsters and the Kangaroo Speedster, a rakish doorless car with the appearance of a junior Mercer 35. Only 150 of these were made, from a total 1600 cars made by the company in 1914. Only one size of Continental engine was offered, now increased from 2785 to 3153cc, and the variety of models was due to there being two lines, the more expensive having a better appearance and also featuring electric lighting and starting.

In 1915 Briggs answered complaints of sluggish performance by offering a 3502cc V8 engine by Massnick-Phipps in the same chassis and body styles as the four. This model F-8 was inevitably more expensive, and sold poorly – just 280 in the first half of 1915, compared with 450 of the fours. In June 1915 Detroiter was bankrupt, but the company was bought up by A.O. Dunk and relaunched with a 6-cylinder car called the Model 6-45. It was powered by a Continental 7W engine and offered with five body styles. However only 778 were sold before receivership loomed again in October 1917, and this time there was no second Dunk to save the Detroiter. A total of just over 6500 cars had been made, and of these about a dozen survive.

NG

Further Reading
'Detroiter – Assembled Car from the Motor City', Alan P. Smithee and Jennifer Bunker, *Automobile Quarterly*, Vol.37, No.4.

DETROITER (ii) (US) 1953
Detroit Accessories, St Clair Shores, Michigan.
This fibreglass-bodied convertible was normally based on a 1952–53 Ford V8 engine and chassis, but the prototype was built on a shortened Cadillac. Styled by industrial designer Ray Russell, the Detroiter used as many Ford parts as possible, including the glass, windshield frame, dash panel and floor mats. It resembled a customised Ford rather than a traditional sports car.
HP

DETROIT-OXFORD see OXFORD

DETROIT STEAM CAR (US) 1922–1923
Detroit Steam Motors Corp., Detroit, Michigan.
Initially appearing as the Truste-Detroit, very few of these touring cars were actually built. All had a 2-cylinder engine of their own design. A few prototypes carrying the Windsor name were built for projected sales in Canada.
KM

DEUTSCHLAND (D) 1904–1905
Motorenfabrik Deutschland, Berlin.
This company was one of the very few to offer steam cars in Germany. They used a Peter Stolz design with a 4-cylinder engine developing about 40bhp. Some were made in commercial vehicle form, and fewer as passenger cars.
HON

DEUTZ (D) 1907–1911
Gasmotorenfabrik Deutz AG, Cologne-Deutz.
This company was founded in January 1872 by Nikolaus August Otto and Eugen Langen, who had made the first satisfactory internal-combustion engine a few years earlier. Gottlieb Daimler was their technical director from 1872 to 1881. Only in 1907 did they start production of complete cars, designed for them by Ettore Bugatti. They had 4-cylinder ohv monobloc engines driven by curved tappets from an ohc, a layout similar to that which Bugatti used in his later Type 13 and Brescia models. They were offered in three sizes; the 4960cc 19/35hp with shaft drive, the 6400cc 24/45hp with the option of chain or shaft drive, and the 9900cc 38/65hp which was available only with chain drive. In 1909 there was also a smaller car with 3200cc engine and the same bevel-driven ohc. While he was working for Deutz Bugatti built a small car in the cellar of his house which became the Bugatti Type 10, prototype of the production Type 13. He left Deutz in 1910, and the following year they gave up car production. They continued to make engines, and in 1938 merged with truck and bus makers Magirus to form Magirus-Deutz. This firm was famous for air-cooled diesel engines from 1943, and continued to make Magirus-Deutz vehicles until 1975. They then merged with the heavy vehicle division of Fiat to form the Industrial Vehicles Corp., and their products were sold under the Iveco name, as they are still today.
HON

DEVAUX (US) 1931–1932
DeVaux-Hall Motor Car Corp., Grand Rapids, Michigan and Oakland, California.
Norman DeVaux had been president of the Chevrolet Motor Co. of California during Durant's presidency of General Motors and later in a similar capacity in the Durant Motors' West Coast operation. In 1930 with Col. Elbert J. Hall of Hall-Scott Motors, Oakland, California, the DeVaux-Hall Motor Car Corp. was formed and the first of the new DeVaux cars were completed for debut at both the New York and Chicago Automobile Shows in January 1931.
The DeVaux was built with an eye to the economy car marketplace, with a 6-cylinder L-head engine and with a wheelbase of 113ins (2868mm). The car's price bracket ran from $545 for the phaeton to $795 for the Custom Coupé and the Custom Sedan. The car met with considerable favour but was a victim of the Depression and a meagre 4808 found buyers for the 1931 calendar year. For 1932 the DeVaux's horsepower was increased from 70bhp to 80bhp, and,

1931 DeVaux 6-75 sedan.
NICK BALDWIN

unfortunately, so were the prices which were increased to a range of $725 to $895. In the winter of 1931–1932 the company was sold to Continental Motors which continued the DeVaux but, with the economic conditions worsening, were only able to sell 1358 of the 'DeVaux-Continental' cars.
DeVaux production ended. Continental redesigned the basic lines cosmetically to bring it up to date and introduced two sixes – the Ace and the Flyer, plus a bare-bones four – the Beacon – for 1933 under the Continental badge, continuing the Beacon into mid–1934 before closing down production altogether and returning exclusively to the manufacturing of engines.
Norman DeVaux attempted to resurrect the DeVaux by marketing an updated Continental Beacon designed as the DeVaux Four Forty-Four but was unsuccessful. In 1936 he launched his De-Vo for export. This existed as a lone prototype which was sent to South Africa where it survives.
KM

DE VECCHI (I) 1905–1917
1905–1908 De Vecchi, Stradea & Compagnia, Milan.
1908–1917 De Vecchi & Compagnia, Milan.
The first De Vecchi was a light car with a 10/12hp 4-cylinder engine with pair-cast cylinders and chain drive. This was unusual, as most contemporary Italian cars were considerably larger. The partners, de Vecchi and Stradea, were aided on the technical side by former racing cyclist F. Momo. Stradea left the company in 1908 and a reorganised firm offered a shaft-driven 16/20hp and a chain-driven 20/30hp. All cars had shaft drive from 1911. By 1914 there were three 4-cylinder cars, of 15/20, 20/25 and 25/30hp. The smallest had monobloc casting of cylinders, while the other two were pair cast. From 1914 most De Vecchi chassis were fitted with truck or ambulance bodywork, and after 1917 only aero engines were made. At the end of World War I, the company was in financial difficulties and was absorbed by the C.M.N. group.
NG

DEVILIN (GB) 1992
Devilin Cars, Darwen, Lancashire.
The Devilin Futura was an exotic kit-form coupé with a space frame chassis and a mid-mounted Renault V6 engine. It was seen at the 1992 Sandown kit car show but not thereafter.
CR

DEVIN (US) 1954 to date
Devin Enterprises, El Monte, California and Yucaipa, California.
Bill Devin pioneered many developments in American sports cars. In 1955 he built the first automobile engine with belt-driven ohcs, but did not patent the application. He then started one of the most successful kit car companies of all time, selling thousands of sleek fibreglass bodies that fitted everything from tiny Crosleys to muscular Corvettes. He followed that up with a line of sports cars of his design. The Devin SS was a ferocious Chevrolet V8-powered sports

1927 DEW (i) electric saloon.
HANS OTTO NEUBAUER

1913 Dewcar 4hp monocar.
NATIONAL MOTOR MUSEUM

car with a De Dion rear suspension, disc brakes and lightweight tubular chassis. The fibreglass body followed 1950s sports-racing car practice with a long bonnet and smooth, flowing lines. The Devin D followed, based on a sturdy steel chassis mounting Volkswagen front suspension and Porsche 356 or VW engines. The body retained many of the SS styling cues, but was shorter and had no grill opening. The Devin C was a modified D with a Corvair engine at the back. The D and C were sold in kit or assembled form. In 1965 Devin announced the Devin GT, a Devin C with a fastback hard-top. It was shown at the New York auto show and attracted much favourable attention, but Devin was unable to capitalise to go into production. Although Devin diversified into other ventures in 1965, he continued to sell cars on a limited basis.

HP

DE-VO (US) 1936

De-Vo Motor Car Corp., Hagerstown, Maryland.
The De-Vo was an attempt by Norman DeVaux, erstwhile manufacturer of the DEVAUX car of 1931 and 1932, to re-enter the automobile field, this time using a phonetic spelling of his name and targeting his sales exclusively to the export market. DeVaux's plan called for a small, 5-seater sedan featuring a right-hand steering position which would be reasonably priced in keeping with the export practice. DeVaux formed a corporation in Maryland during the latter part of 1936 and exhibited his prototype at the Waldorf-Astoria Hotel in New York City late that year or early in 1937. The De-Vo was built on a wheelbase of 102ins (2588mm) and powered by a 4-cylinder Continental engine, fabrication being at the M.P. Möller Co. of Hagerstown, erstwhile manufacturer of the Crawford and Dagmar cars and a wide variety of taxicabs. DeVaux's ambition ended with the completion of the lone De-Vo prototype, given serial number 1001 and shipped to South Africa where it exists today, fully restored, in a private collection.

KM

DEVON (i) see CLUB CAR

DEVON (ii) (AUS) 1938

Devon Motors Pty Ltd, Melbourne, Victoria.
The Fiat 500 Topolino was sold by the Victorian agent as the Devon 'Nippy Seven' fitted with 4-seater tourer and utility (pick-up) bodies.

MG

DEW (i) (D) 1927

Zschopauer Motorenwerke J.S. Rasmussen AG, Filiale Berlin, Berlin.
Danish-born Jürgen Skafte Rasmussen (1878–1964) was one of the great promoters of motor vehicles in Germany, starting with motorcycles and continuing with the SB cyclecar and, more famously, the DKW. The DEW was an integral construction electric car with wooden panels. It was commendably light but too flimsy to withstand daily use, especially for taxicab work for which many DEWs were destined.

HON

DEW (ii) see WILLIS (ii)

DEWALD (F) 1902–1926

Charles Dewald, Boulogne-sur-Seine.
Charles Dewald's business was in existence at least as far back as 1896, and in 1902 he was listed in a trade directory as engaged in *travaux pour amateurs,* which suggests that he built prototypes to order rather than production cars. From 1904 to 1912 six models with 4-cylinder engines were listed, the largest with a capacity of 7.4 litres. A new factory was opened in 1908, and production on a commercial scale started, although this was in very limited numbers. Trucks were made from 1912, and from then on these proved to be a major part of Dewald's business. A luxury car was listed from 1922 to 1926; the CD had a 4807cc straight-8 engine with single-ohc and 4-speed gearbox. It could have been a rival to the Delage CO or even the Hispano-Suiza, yet very little was heard of it outside the *Catalogue des Catalogues,* and production must have been very limited. Trucks were made until 1931, using chain drive to the end.

NG

DE WANDRE (B) 1924–1925

Éts Fr. de Wandre, Brussels.
The De Wandre was a Model T Ford considerably modified to give a more attractive appearance. Changes included a vee-radiator, disc or wire wheels and a chassis lowered by 5.5in (140mm) and lengthened by 18in (457mm). Four body styles were offered; tourer, saloon, town-landaulet and 3-seater roadster. Other Belgian firms who did similar work on the Ford included Emmel, Mineur, SACA and Speedsport.

NG

DEWCAR (GB) 1913–1914

D.E.W. Engineering Co. Ltd, Eynsford, Kent.
This car was the work of Harold E. Dew, who had built 13 prototypes of cyclecar, starting in 1910, before he essayed production. The first was a tubular-framed single-seater, but later models had a boat-type frame consisting of two ash planks joined at the front by a pointed metal prow. It could be described as a monocoque construction, because there was no body above the substantial planks. On one car, the driver sat astride the planks, but on the production car the frame was wide enough for him to keep his legs inside. Production started in April 1913, with a 4.5hp single-cylinder Precision engine powering the monocar and this was joined by a 2-seater with 8hp 2-cylinder Precision. Dew announced that the first 50 cars would all be single seaters, although it is not known if he fulfilled this pledge. In October 1913 the monocar's engine was uprated to 5/6hp and a more enveloping body was provided, although the basic 4.5hp model was still available at £75. The 8hp cost £95 with air-cooling and £115 with water-cooling.

Dew left the company in February 1914, later to make the D.ULTRA car. The Dewcar was renamed VICTOR, and production moved to Ealing, West London, for 1915.

NG

DEWITT (US) 1909–1910

Virgil DeWitt, North Manchester, Indiana.

Swiss-born Virgil DeWitt had worked for the KIBLINGER company, and his car bore signs of Kiblinger influence, being a high-wheeler powered by a 13.6hp 2-cylinder engine under the seat, with a piano box 2-seater body. About 200 were made before the factory was destroyed by fire in May 1910.

NG

DEXTER (F) 1906–1909
Constructions d'Automobiles Dexter, Lyons.
Headed by former racing cyclist A. Fauré, this company made a small number of very large cars, mainly for competitions. In these, 4- and 6-cylinder engines were used; of 50/60, 72 and 100hp, all cars having chain drive.

NG

DEY (US) 1917
Dey Electric Corp., York, Pennsylvania.
Having tried to make the DEY-GRISWOLD electric car before the turn of the century, Harry E. Dey made another attempt at manufacture in 1917. His 2-seater roadster looked like any petrol car, but had an electric motor integral with the rear axle, and the rotating armature drove one wheel and the rotating field the other. The planned price was $1000, but the car never went into production. An attempted revival in Jersey City, New Jersey, did not materialise.

NG

DEY-GRISWOLD (US) 1895–1898
Dey-Griswold & Co., New York, New York.
This was a most unusual electric car in which the motor forced oil through turbines attached to the rear wheels. This was a partial forerunner of the fluid drive employed by General Motors from the late 1930s. However, there was too much slippage for the system to be practical, and after a few cars had been made by the Pawtucket Motorcarriage Co., the idea was dropped. Dey later worked with the electrical engineer Charles Steinmetz, and made another attempt at car building with the Dey electric in 1917.

NG

DEZINA (GB) 1994–1998
Dezina Cars, Whitwick, Leicestershire.
Most people thought that, by the 1990s, the days of the VW Beetle-based exotic were dead and gone, but the Dezina DVS 5000 tried to prove them wrong. This was a kit-form Countach replica based on a stretched Beetle floorpan with engine options encompassing Fiat, Lancia, Ford, Alfasud, Golf and Rover V8. It was actually initially developed by BERKELEY (ii).

CR

D.F.P. (F) 1906–1926
Doriot, Flandrin et Parant, Courbevoie, Seine.
Auguste Doriot and Ludovic Flandrin met while working for Peugeot in the 1890s, and they then worked for a few years with Clément-Bayard before setting up their own company in 1906. They made a single-cylinder voiturette with shaft drive and transverse rear suspension. These were sold as Doriot-Flandrins until 1908, when Alexandre and Jules-René Parant joined them. A new company was formed and this bought out the former partners and their factory. Larger cars with 4-cylinder Chapuis-Dornier engines of 2.4 and 2.8 litres were introduced, and the singles were continued at least until 1910.

A smaller four, the 1592cc 10/12hp, was introduced in 1910. It had a side-valve monobloc engine, also by Chapuis-Dornier, thermo-syphon cooling and a 3-speed gearbox. There was also a less successful 3617cc 25/30hp 6-cylinder car in 1911. In 1912, D.F.P. started to make their own engines, the best-known being the 2-litre 12/15 with pressure lubrication, 3-bearing crankshaft and 4-speed gearbox. It was an ideal engine for tuning, and the best-known firm to do this was the London partnership of the brothers H.M. and W.O. Bentley. 'W.O.' fitted pistons made of an alloy of 88 per cent aluminium and 12 per cent copper, and took several records at Brooklands. He persuaded the makers to fit aluminium pistons on a production car, which appeared in 1914 as the 12/40hp, and was distinguished from the 12/15 by a vee radiator. It also had electric lighting and starting. Few of these were sold because of the outbreak of World War I.

D.F.P. never regained its prewar success in the 1920s. It has been suggested that when W.O. Bentley became a car maker in his own right, D.F.P. lost their

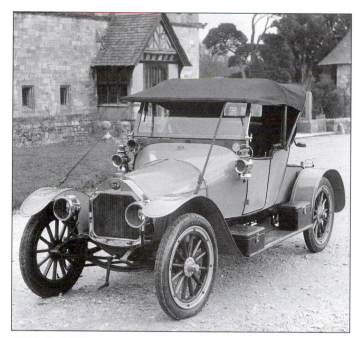

1913 D.F.P. 12/15hp 2-seater.
NATIONAL MOTOR MUSEUM

1920 D.F.P. 12/40hp 2-seater.
NATIONAL MOTOR MUSEUM

best export market, although they were represented in Britain by another company, B.S. Marshall Ltd. It is more likely that the cars were uncompetitive in the postwar market, which was not helped by the adoption of proprietary engines by Altos and Sergant. These were side-valve units of 1994 and 1843cc, and the cars were strictly touring style, with rather heavy saloon or tourer bodies. In 1922 the Sergant-engined 10/12 adopted American-style central gearchange and coil ignition, although they reverted to a magneto for 1923. Front-wheel brakes arrived in 1922, and in 1923 D.F.P. started making their own engines again, on the 1994cc ohv 13/50. This had the same dimensions as the Altos engine, and was possibly a conversion by D.F.P. of the side-valve Altos. Also in 1923 the company entered the light car field with the D.F. Petite, an Amilcar-sized car powered by a 1098cc C.I.M.E. engine, with 3-speed gearbox and differential-less back axle. This acquired front-wheel brakes in 1925, but a year later all production ended. The factory was bought by the makers of the LAFITTE light car.

NG

D.F.R. (F) 1924
Désert et de Font-Reault, Neuilly, Seine.
This company was better-known for motorcycles, which it made from 1921 to 1930, but in 1924 the company was reported in *l'Annual de l'Auto* as making cyclecars.

NG

1924 Diabolo 3-wheeler.
HANS OTTO NEUBAUER

D.G. (GB) 1982 to date

D.G. Motor Services, Wellingborough, Northamptonshire.

There was essentially only one British company that satisfied domestic demands for a chopper-style trike. D.G. adopted the American fashion for putting a VW Beetle engine in a basic box section chassis, adding extended motorbike front forks and a basic 2-seater fibreglass body. That gave you a trike called the Phoenix that could be driven on a motorcycle licence, and over 400 had been made by 1998. D.G. also made a US-style off-road 'sand rail' vehicle.

CR

D.G.T. *see* DEON

D. H. AIRCRAFT (US) c.1991

D. H. Aircraft Inc., Hicksville, Ohio.

This company sold plans for building a full size replica of the 1914 Stutz Bearcat sportscar. It used metal and wood construction and supposedly could be built for $2500.

HP

DHUMBERT (F) c.1920–1930

Automobiles Dhumbert, Voiron, Isère.

Little is known about Automobiles Dhumbert, which was listed in *l'Annuaire Général de l'Automobile* in 1923 as making 2- and 4-seater torpedos with 10CV engines, and again in 1930, when the cars were described as having 10 and 11CV 6-cylinder and straight eight engines in a chassis de grande luxe with independent suspension.

NG

DIABLE (F) 1921–c.1924

The Paris-built Diable was a 3-wheeler powered by a 1096cc 2-cylinder engine driving the single rear wheel by chain. It was possibly the same car as the German-built DIABOLO.

NG

DIABOLO (D) 1922–1927

Diabolo Kleinauto GmbH, Stuttgart.

This Morgan-like 3-wheeler, powered by a 1.1-litre V-twin Motosachoche engine was technically more refined than many of its contemporaries, and this was reflected in its relatively long life. However, it eventually succumbed to competition from 4-wheeled cars. A Diabolo was the first car of German film star Heinz Rühmann.

HON

DIAL (GB) 1970–1971

There were a number of racing orientated mid-engined kit cars around the beginning of the 1970s, of which the Dial Buccaneer was one of the better known. Its origins lay in an autocross special and it was very crude – indeed the kit was virtually unbuildable. It used a wide variety of parts in a space frame chassis: Triumph-based independent suspension all round, VW gearbox, and Ford in-line engines. The doors were gull-wing. Around 20 were made in total.

CR

DIAMANT (F) 1901–1906

Hammond, Mouter et Compagnie, Paris.
Sté la Française, Paris.

The Diamant was a conventional car of which the 1902 models had 5 or 7hp single-cylinder engines, a 9hp twin and a 12hp four. From 1904 a 24hp four was used. The cars were also known as La Française, a name born by the firm's motorcycles in later years, when they were controlled by ALCYON.

NG

DIAMANTE (US) 1978–c.1988.

1978–c.1980 Matthews Motor Coach Corp., Camarillo, California.
c.1980–c.1988 Mattco Corp., Ventura, California.

This was a neo-classic with Cord L29 and Mercedes-Benz overtones. Wheelbase was 136in (3533mm) and power was provided by a 7-litre Cadillac engine. Equipment included a picnic set complete with Minton china, and options were a 'tour car' hard top and carpets in vicuna or beaver.

NG

DIAMOND (i) *see* RICKETTS

DIAMOND (ii) **(US)** 1914–1915

The Cyclecar Co. of Wilmington, Wilmington, Delaware.

The Diamond was large for a cyclecar, with a 16/20hp 4-cylinder engine, and electric lighting and starting. For 1915 the makers called it a light car, although the company name remained the same.

NG

DIAMOND T (US) 1907–1911

Diamond T Motorcar Co., Chicago, Illinois.

C.A. Tilt was the son of a shoe manufacturer who had adopted the trademark of a T inside a diamond. It is not known if the shoes carried the name Diamond T, but when Tilt began car manufacture it seemed an eye-catching name. He built experimental cars from 1905, but did not enter the market until two years later when he offered a large and expensive 40hp car, made in runabout, tourer, and limousine models priced from $3250 to $4250. The 1908 and 1909 models were designated 50hp, but probably used the same size engine. For 1910 a smaller engine of 30hp was listed, and the limousine was no longer offered. Fifty cars were made in 1907, and total production probably numbered several hundred. In 1911 one of Tilt's customers asked for a truck, which Tilt built, using a car engine but chain drive in place of shaft. Trucks proved so popular that the cars were dropped. Diamond T became one of the best-known names in the American truck industry, surviving until 1966 when the firm merged with another former car maker, REO, to make the Diamond-Reo.

NG

DIANA (i) **(D)** 1922–1923

Diana Automobilwerk GmbH, Munich.

This was a 3-wheeler with tubular chassis, powered by a 4-cylinder engine.

HON

DIANA (ii) **(US)** 1925–1928

Diana Motors Co., St Louis, Missouri.

The Diana, introduced in mid-1925, was a more expensive companion car of the Moon. The Diana was heavily promoted prior to its debut and found considerable favour, both for its fetching design and excellent performance. In design, the Diana stood in a field of its own among other American cars, largely due to its impressive radiator, identical to that of the prestigious Belgian Minerva, both being named for Roman goddesses (Diana, Goddess of the Moon and Hunting; Minerva, Goddess of Wisdom), and set off by a striking radiator mascot – a standing Diana with a drawn bow. The Diana featured narrow windscreen posts that increased visibility and which the company used widely in its advertising. The Diana was equipped with a Continental 12Z straight-8 engine developing 72bhp at 2950rpm and was available in a variety of open and closed models in the $2000 range. For the fanciful buyer, a 'Palm Beach Roadster' was added to the line, featuring a bronze-plated radiator and wire wheels. In addition, a town car was available on special order priced at $5000.

The Diana was phased out of production in 1928 and would appear in modern dress a year later as the WINDSOR 'White Prince'.

KM

DIASETTI (US) c.1986

Diasetti Motors, Salt Lake City, Utah.
The Diasetti Z-Vette was a fibreglass body kit that added a Corvette-like nose, tail and wheel flares to a Datsun 240, 260 or 280 Z body.

They were sold in kit or assembled form.

HP

DIATTO (I) 1905–1927

1905–1909 Diatto-A. Clement Vetture Marca Torino, Turin.
1909–1918 Società Officine Fonderie Frejus Vetture Diatto, Turin.
1918–1919 Fonderie Officine Frejus Automobili Diatto, Turin.
1919–1923 Automobili Diatto, Turin.
1924–1927 Autocostruzione Diatto, Turin.

The Diatto company was established as a coachbuilder before 1835, in which year they built 15 2- and 4-wheeled carriages. Later they diversified into railway engineering and iron founding, but in 1905 decided to turn over the whole of their factory to car manufacture. This was a bold step, at a time when many engineering companies would have set up a car division and continued with their established business for a while. Their cars were made under licence from CLÉMENT-BAYARD and consisted of an 1884cc 2-cylinder 10/12hp and fours of 2724cc (12/16hp) and 3770cc (20/24hp). In 1908 a 4-litre 24hp pair-cast 6-cylinder car was built, and after one year this was superseded by the 2920cc monobloc 4-cylinder 16/20. There was also a 2049cc 12/15hp and a 4846cc 35hp, both of which had 4-cylinder engines, the 35 with the option of chain or shaft drive. All had T-head engines. The cars were originally to have been called Torino, but were generally known as Diatto-Cléments.

In 1909 Adolphe Clément ended the agreement and ceased to be a director, although cars of Clément design continued to be made for a few years. A new design was the L-head monobloc 2212cc 12/15 which was first made in 1910 and became the staple Diatto up to World War I. Called Tipo Unico, it superseded the Clément designs, and was enlarged to 2413cc in 1912 and to 2724cc by 1916.

During the war, Diatto opened a coachbuilding department in a separate factory, and also took over a factory from the French aero engine makers Gnome et Rhone. Here they built 8-cylinder Bugatti aero engines under licence, and also airframes. They also absorbed two other Turin car makers, NEWTON and SCACCHI, moving their machinery to their own factories. After the war they restarted car production with the 2724cc 25hp, which was probably a development of the Tipo Unico. This was the 4DA, and there was also a 2951cc version, the 4DC. In 1920 they also launched a light car with 1018cc 4-cylinder engine which was made in the former Gnome et Rhone factory. This was made until 1922, but the relatively small Diatto company was no match for Fiat in the popular car field. They wisely turned to a quality sporting car, and their most famous model, the Tipo 20. Designed by Giuseppe Coda (1883–1977), it had a 1996cc 4-cylinder engine with single-ohc driven by shaft and skew gears, a 2-bladed wooden fan mounted directly on the front of the camshaft, and a gasketless cylinder head joint. Long studs, screwed into the top of the crankcase, passed through the cast-iron block and head. The engine developed 40bhp, but after considerable tuning by Alfieri Maserati it produced 70bhp and was the basis for several Diatto racing cars. In 1923 came the Tipo 20S with a shorter wheelbase, four wheel brakes, and semi-elliptic rear springs in place of the cantilevers of the Tipo 20.

In 1923 Diatto was badly hit by the failure of the Banca Italiana di Sconto and went into liquidation in November. It was reformed as Autocostruzione Diatto in May 1924 with a new board of directors. Coda could not get on with the new board and left to join Citroën's Italian factory in 1925, but the Tipo 20A (touring) and 20S (sports) were continued until the 1926 season when the 20S was replaced by the 30. There was also a larger 2952cc Tipo 25 (touring) and Tipo 35 (sports). The 20A, 30 and a new 2632cc Tipo 35 were listed for 1927, but car production virtually ceased that year, although a few cars were assembled from parts in stock until 1928. Meanwhile the Maserati brothers had taken over the straight-8 racing car design and set up their own company to manufacture it as the Maserati Tipo 26. Diatto was reconstructed in 1931 to make industrial equipment and spare parts. In 1945 plans for a return to car production with a prototype designed for the Galileo Co., came to nothing.

NG

1926 Diana (ii) Eight roadster.
ELLIOTT KAHN

1927 Diana (ii) Eight roadster.
JOHN A. CONDE

1913 Diatto tourer.
NATIONAL MOTOR MUSEUM

Further Reading
'Diatto', Frank Lugg, *The Automobile*, October and November 1999.
Diatto, Sergio Massaro, Publicar, 2000.

1925 Diatto Tipo 30 tourer.
FRANK LUGG

1924 Diatto 2-litre tourer.
NATIONAL MOTOR MUSEUM

1917 Diaz y Grillo roadster.
NATIONAL MOTOR MUSEUM

DIAZ Y GRILLO (E) 1915–1922

Fábrica Española de Automóviles Diaz y Grilló, Barcelona.

The Diaz y Grillo or DyG was a sporting light car in the same category as the DAVID and the AMERICA, using 2- and 4-cylinder MAG engines. Some prototypes were equipped with English Blumfield engines; others used a transmission of variable pulleys and belt, like the David. The DyG series-built had torsion bar suspension and different bodies, including closed ones. Although not specially built for racing, DyG had success in several Spanish races. For some years the company represented Motosacoche, and after finishing car production they represented SENECHAL.

VCM

DICKINSON MORETTE (GB) 1903–1905

B.E. Dickinson & Co., Birmingham.

The Dickinson Morette was a very light 3-wheeler powered by a 1.5hp single-cylinder 2-stroke Ixion engine mounted just behind the front wheel. The flywheel carried a rubber wheel which acted directly on the tyre, in the manner of the Velosolex bicycle attachment of the 1950s. The starting system was most unusual; a lever below the steering tiller was pulled backwards, and was connected through clutches to the rear wheels. Each pull of the lever jerked the car forward, and as the front wheel was in direct contact with the flywheel, this, theoretically, started the engine. Raising the tiller freed the flywheel from the tyre, providing the action of a clutch. The first Morette was a single seater weighing only 90lbs (40.8kg), but it was said that 'when desired the vehicle can be enlarged and strengthened to carry two persons, a higher powered motor being in this case, of course, attached'. A later model had a 4hp 2-cylinder engine and drive to the front wheel by chain.

NG

DIEBEL (US) 1901

Diebel-Cox Manufacturing Co., Philadelphia, Pennsylvania.

William Diebel made a light runabout powered by a 7hp 2-cylinder air-cooled engine. The cooling was unusual, featuring rings with radiating arms shrunk on to the cylinder casting. The price was a reasonable $650, but the Diebel did not survive the year of its introduction.

NG

DIEBLER & RUSSELL (US) 1908

Diebler & Russell Co., Berlin, Wisconsin.

This was a large car powered by a 40hp Rutenber engine. Only three examples were made.

NG

DIECASTERS (AUS) 1946

Die Casters Ltd, Collingwood, Victoria.

As suppliers of components to the industry, this firm studied the possibilities of Australian motor manufacture prior to World War II. Several 10hp front-wheel drive ADLER Trumpf chassis were obtained, local bodies fitted and endurance tests were conducted during those years. Postwar, a group of subcontractors was assembled to supply components. When it became clear that G.M.H. had become the favoured manufacturer, this company directed its efforts elsewhere.

MG

DIEDERICHS (F) 1912–1914

Sté des Automobiles Diederichs, Charpennes, Rhône.

The brothers Charles and Frederic Diederichs had been involved in road vehicles for many years before they actually put a car on the market. Their family background was in textile machinery at Bourgouin, Isère, and Charles built a steam carriage there in 1878. The brothers made one or two prototype cars at the turn of the century, and then in 1912 they went into production with a conventional tourer powered by a 2154cc 10/12CV 4-cylinder Luc Court engine made in Lyons, and also used in LUC COURT cars for many years. The Diederichs, of which not more than 60 were made, had a Delaunay-Belleville-like round radiator and bonnet.

NG

DIEHLMOBILE (US) 1961

H. L. Diehl Co., South Willington, Connecticut.

This lightweight single-cylinder runabout looked like a 3-wheeled golf cart, but was designed to be disassembled quickly and stowed in a car trunk for easy transport. The single front wheel had a tiller-style steering mechanism and the two small rear wheels had trailer-style mudguards. There was a wide bench seat that could be removed for use outside the vehicle. The 3hp motor was mounted at the rear and used a chain drive to the rear axle.

HP

1912 Diederichs 10/12CV tourer.
NATIONAL MOTOR MUSEUM

DIE VALKYRIE (US) c.1952
Die Valkyrie, Cleveland, Ohio.
This special-bodied Cadillac was styled by well-known American designer Brooks Stevens. The bodies were made in West Germany by Spohn.

HP

DILE (US) 1914–1917
Dile Motorcar Co., Reading, Pennsylvania.
The Dile was an attractive small car powered by an 11hp 4-cylinder engine, with shaft drive, and offered only as a 2-seater roadster at $485. The name was derived from the first two letters of the partners who made it, Fred K. Dick and Irvin D. Lengel. A famous Dile customer was film star Pearl White who had hers specially painted in black and white stripes. In 1918 all uncompleted Diles, as well as patterns and blueprints, were taken over by Belmont Motors Corp. of Lewistown, Pennsylvania, but they did not continue production of the Dile. Instead they made trucks up to 1924.

NG

D.I.M. (GR) 1977–1983
D.I.M. Motor, George E. Dimitriadis & Co., Athens.
First displayed at the 1977 Geneva Motor Show, this small saloon car was based on the mechanicals of the Fiat 126, including its rear-mounted 594cc engine. The upright body was in fibreglass and could seat four people. It appeared at numerous motor shows in the ensuing years.

CR

DI NAPOLI (US) 1978–1980
Pacific Coachworks, Soleta, California.
With a Buick chassis and drive train and the centre section of a Buick hard-top body welded to a separate bonnet and boot, these cars, of which only five were built, were powered by a 3.8-litre turbocharged V6 engine.

NG

437

1978 Di Napoli coupé.
PACIFIC COACHWORKS

DINARG (RA) 1961–1962

Dinamica Industrial Argentina SA, Cordoba.

The Dinarg D-200 was announced in 1960. Production started in 1961. This was a minicar with a rear mounted 200cc, 2-cylinder, 2-stroke Sachs LDR200 engine, a closed 2-seater body and all around independent suspension. A maximum speed of 54mph (85km/h) was claimed. 300 units were made, although thousands had been promised.

ACT

DINGBAT (GB) 1971–1972

Cars & Car Conversions magazine sponsored this uniquely British buggy, which was unusually based on a Triumph Herald chassis. The glassfibre bodywork was angular in shape and featured a large roll-over centre section.

CR

DINGFELDER (US) 1903

Dingfelder Motor Co., Detroit, Michigan.

The Dingfelder was a light motor buggy powered by a 3.5hp single-cylinder engine, made by a company which also built stationary engines. Although the car was said by the press to have been very well received by the local trade, it survived less than a year.

NG

DINGWALL (GB) 1912–c.1949

G.H. Dingwall & Son (Engineers) Ltd, Dalston, London.

This company built hand-propelled tricycles from 1892, and in 1912 made their first powered carriage when they attached a 1¼hp Wall Autowheel to the rear of a hand-propelled tricycle. Pulling the wheel off the ground by a cable had the effect of a clutch, as in the Smith Flyer and Briggs & Stratton, which also used the Autowheel principle. The first conventional motor tricycle appeared in 1922 with a Villiers engine and 2-speed gearbox. It was steadily improved over the next 16 years, the peak being reached in 1938 with the first totally enclosed motor tricycle. Equipped with a streamlined body, windscreen, and hood, it was powered by a 198cc Villiers engine. Development ended at the outbreak of World War II.

In 1949 a new 3-wheeler was announced, with a flat-twin Coventry-Climax engine and chain drive to the single rear wheel. The body was a side-by-side 2-seater, and it took the concept beyond the usual invalid car. The prototype was shown to the Minister of Health at the 1949 Invalid Tricycle Association Rally in Richmond Park, but he ruled it out as being too expensive to supply to the NHS, and that brought Dingwall's business to an end.

NG

DININ (F) 1904–1906

Alfred Dinin et Compagnie, Puteaux, Seine.

The Dinin was a light electric car with a frontal bonnet under which some of the batteries were placed, the others being under the seat. The bonnet gave it the appearance of a petrol car. A correspondent remarked 'Dinin cars supersede the somewhat wanting look of the average electric car.'

NG

DINOS (D) 1921–1926

Dinos Automobilwerke AG, Berlin.

This company was a reorganisation of Loeb & Compagnie, which had made the LUC car. Two medium-sized cars were made under the Dinos name, the 2.1-litre 4-cylinder 8/35PS and 4-litre 6-cylinder 16/72PS, the latter in very small numbers. Both had single-ohc engines designed by Joseph Vollmer. In 1922 Dinos became part of the Stinnes concern, which also made AGA cars. Four years later the Dinos factory was turned over to additional production of Agas.

HON

DIO (US) c.1994 to date

Classic Antique Replicar Specialist, Oklahoma City, Oklahoma.

This sports car kit was a continuation of the Ambro kit bodies that had been made for racing cars in the 1950s. The original Ambros were not intended for street use and were thin fibreglass for light weight. The design was based on Maserati Birdcage and Lister-Jaguar lines and most had headrest fairings. Bill Bonadio rescued the design in 1994, when it had been long out of production. Like the Ambro, the Dio would fit on a Triumph chassis. CARS also sold a steel tube space frame that used Ford Mustang II suspension and Ford, Chevrolet or Triumph engines. The thick fibreglass body was intended for street use.

HP

DION (US) c.1992

Dion Sportscars, Long Beach, California.

The Porsche 911/912 was the basis of the attractive Dion kit car body. Unlike the popular slope-nosed kits from European firms like Ruf, the Dion was a complete body kit designed by James Kazaar. It had a rounded shape resembling a modernised Porsche Speedster. Although any 911 could be used, the Targa was the easiest to modify. Dion also offered an aluminium-bodied Cobra replica built on a chassis from CONTEMPORARY CLASSIC.

HP

DIRECT (B) 1904–1905

Sté de Constructions Mécaniques et d'Automobiles, Brussels.

The Direct was a large car powered by a 40/50hp 4-cylinder engine, which was said to be so flexible that no gearbox was needed. The drive was taken directly from the engine to a countershaft from which the rear wheels were driven by chains, hence the car's name. Any necessary reduction in gear ratio could be obtained by varying the pressure on the clutch. Made in very limited numbers in the factory which had previously seen production of BAUDOUIN and DÉCHAMPS cars, the Direct was designed by Robert Goldschmidt, who had previously worked for MIESSE where the prototype Direct had been built.

NG

DIRECT DRIVE *see* CHAMPION (iii)

DISAI (CHI) 1988 to date

Liuzhou Machinery Works, Liuzhou City, Guangxi Region.

The bodies of the Disai mini cars were made of glassfibre reinforced plastic. The design was based on a Daihatsu Charade, the engine a licence-built 2-cylinder Daihatsu type. The first models were all estate cars, named Disai LJ 720, later renamed Disai LJ 5010XA. A saloon car appeared later.

EVIS

DISBROW (US) 1916–1917

Disbrow Motors Corp., Cleveland, Ohio.

This car was promoted by the renowned racing driver Louis Disbrow, who was particularly famous for his exploits at the wheel of the 200hp Fiat-engined Jay-Eye-See (J.I.C.) car sponsored by CASE. His own car was an assembled product, but much larger and sportier than most of its kind. The 4-cylinder T-head Wisconsin engines were of 7.9 or 9.9 litres, the more powerful giving a claimed top speed of 90mph (145km/h). Other components came from well-known suppliers; steering, transmission and clutch from Warner, frame from Parrish & Bingham, radiator from Perfex, and wheels from Houk. The racy aluminium body was made by Disbrow, or at any rate in his factory. Also made in the factory was a special engine with aluminium block and 16 ohvs. Several Disbrow roadsters were sold but shortage of materials brought about by World War I ended the project during the summer of 1917.

NG

DISK (CS) 1924

Ceskoslovenska Zbrojovka, a.s., Brno.

When, in the 1920s, the demand for guns fell, the Czechoslovak Arms Factory, founded in 1919 in Brno, began to produce passenger cars. The first type, called Disk (or Diskos), a predecessor of the Enka and later of the well-known Z cars, was designed by Bretislav Novotny (famous for his Aero cars). The construction was remarkable for a self-supporting steel body and the friction gearing, which replaced the clutch and gearbox. Unusual also was the 2-stroke 4-cylinder in-line, 599cc 14bhp engine with side-valve gear. Only about 75 cars were sold, due to frequent failure of the friction gears. Another curiosity was that this car, priced 26,000 Kc, could be bought by the factory employees for only 15,000 Kc.

MSH

DISPATCH (US) 1910

Dispatch Motor Co., Minneapolis, Minnesota.

The first Dispatch was described in detail in the press in December 1910. It was a small roadster powered by a 2-cylinder 2-stroke engine, and was said to have been followed in 1912 by a larger car with a 23hp 4-cylinder Wisconsin engine. Roadster, tourer and coupé models were listed, at prices from $935 to $1210. Chain drive was said to be in use as late as 1918. In January 1919, *Motor Age* announced the end of manufacture, but there is no evidence that manufacture had ever started. The first car may have been built for the Dispatch Motor Co. by the M.B. Buggy Co. also located in Minneapolis. The continued publication of specifications with no cars to back them up is reminiscent of the British OWEN (i).

NG

DI TELLA (RA) 1959–1965

SIAM (Sociedad Industrial Americana de Maquinas) Di Tella Automotores, Monte Chingolo, Buenos Aires.

When in 1959 the old Siam Di Tella metallurgical firm decided to add automobiles to their line of products, an agreement was reached with B.M.C. to produce motor vehicles based on the British firm's 55bhp 1.5-litre Farina-styled saloons and station wagons, adding to these a pick-up truck. At first only the Morris-based Di Tella 1500 was produced, but by 1962 its offspring, the Argenta pick up truck and Traveller station wagon were also in production. To these, an MG-inspired Di Tella Magnette developing 75bhp was added. Di Tella production ceased in 1965, when all motor-manufacturing operations were acquired by Compania Industrial de Automotores SA, after 62,049 Di Tella vehicles had been made.

ACT

DIVA (GB) 1962–1968

1962–1965 Tunex Conversions Ltd, London.
1966–1967 Diva Cars Ltd, London.
1967–1968 Skodek Engineering, London.

Don Sim, one of the partners in Yimkin, was running a company called Tunex Conversions in 1962, when he designed the Diva GT. It was a compact car with a fibreglass body on a spaceframe, independent suspension all round, disc brakes on the front wheels, and an option of a variety of 4-cylinder Ford engines. It was offered in competition or road versions, the latter having upholstered seats, rubber engine mountings, etc. All 65 buyers chose the competition version, though some were used on the road.

Divas were phenomenally successful in the popular small-engine GT racing class. To serve a changing market, in 1965 Diva then made the Valkyr, a mid-engined coupé, which was primarily intended for racing. It was available with a range of engines from a Hillman Imp unit up to a 2.7-litre Coventry Climax FPF engine, but it was not as successful, or as popular, as the Diva. In 1967, the rights to both cars were sold, but the new owner had withdrawn by 1968.

MJL

DIXI (D) 1904–1928

1904–1920 Fahrzeugfabrik Eisenach, Eisenach.
1920–1928 Dixi-Werke AG, Eisenach.

From 1898 to 1904 cars made by the Fahrzeugfabrik Eisenach were sold under the name WARTBURG. They were then renamed Dixi (Latin for 'I have spoken', i.e., the last word). A completely new range of cars was designed by Willi Seck

1966 Diva GT coupé.
NATIONAL MOTOR MUSEUM

1966 Diva Valkyr coupé.
NATIONAL MOTOR MUSEUM

(1868–1955), who had come from SCHEIBLER. They were the 3456cc 16/20PS Typ S12 with shaft drive, and the chain-driven 4939cc Typ T. They were followed by several models with smaller engines, such as the single-cylinder 1240cc 7/9PS Typ T7 (1904–1907), 2-cylinder 1408cc S6 (1904–1905), and 4-cylinder 10/16PS Typ T14 (1905–1908). There was also a larger car with 6800cc 26/40PS engine made from 1907 to 1914. All these models had shaft drive. They had a good reputation both in Germany and abroad. In England they were sold under the name Leander and in France as Regina. The most popular model was the 1905cc Typ R8, of which 650 were made between 1908 and 1914.

Trucks were added to the range in 1908 and in 1910 aero engines, which were supplied to Dornier and to airship makers Flick & Heinig. In 1914 a low 3-seater, the Type B1 with 5/14PS 1320cc engine was announced. Only a few were made but it was revived after the war, being made up to 1921 along with other prewar designs, the 8/24, 13/39 and 20/55PS.

In June 1921 the Dixi works were bought by the Gothaer Waggonfabrik, makers of railway carriages, which was owned by the Russian-born financier Jacob Schapiro. The mainstay of postwar production was the Typ G1 6/18PS (6/24PS G2 from 1923) with 1568cc 4-cylinder side-valve engine, of which about 2300 were made up to 1928. Four-wheel brakes were adopted in 1925, and the model was made in tourer and limousine forms, the latter being often seen as a taxicab, and there were also sporting models (G5) which finished first, second and fourth in the 1922 AVUS races.

Schapiro also owned the CYKLON Automobilwerke, and in 1927 he put into production the 2350cc 6-cylinder Cyklon 9/40PS which was also badged as the Dixi 9/40PS. They had all-steel saloon and tourer bodies by Ambi-Budd, and Karmann made a few cabriolets. Though it was the cheapest six on the German market, fewer than 1000 were made. Two larger Dixi sixes were the 3.5-litre 13/60PS of which only four were made in 1926, and the 5.8-litre 23/70PS which was announced in 1924 but never saw production. In 1927 Dixi took out a licence to make the AUSTIN Seven, which they sold under the name Typ DA1 3/15PS. The first 100 came to Eisenach complete from Longbridge; the only

1904 Dixi 16/20PS tourer.
HANS-OTTO NEUBAUER

1914 Dixi Typ R12 10/26PS tourer.
NICK BALDWIN

1927 Dixi 9/40PS saloon.
NATIONAL MOTOR MUSEUM

1923 Dixie Flyer tourer.
JOHN A. CONDE

'manufacture' was the fitting of Dixi badges before they were delivered to customers. In October 1928 Dixi-Werke was bought by BMW for about one million marks, and from 1 January 1929 the cars were sold as BMW 3/15s. Apparently a few of the 9/40PS models were sold by Dixi as 1929 models.

NG

Further Reading
The Complete BMW Story, Werner Oswald and Jeremy Walton, Haynes, 1982.

DIXIE (i) (US) 1908–1910

Southern Motorcar Co., Houston, Texas.
The first car to carry the Dixie name was made in two models – a high-wheeler called the Junior and a conventional car called the Flier. The Junior was typical of its breed, with an air-cooled 10/12hp 2-cylinder engine under the seat, friction transmission and double-chain drive. The Flier had a 24hp 4-cylinder engine, conventional 2-speed gearbox and shaft drive. A 5-seater tourer was also available on this chassis, at an identical price of $2000. For 1909 the Junior was dropped and the 4-cylinder cars renamed Tourist, selling for $1500. However the failure of the company's bank prevented further development, and the Southern Motor Co. closed early in 1910. Total production is believed to have been no more than 17 cars.

NG

DIXIE (ii) (US) 1916

Dixie Manufacturing Co., Vincennes, Indiana.
This was a light car powered by a 13hp 4-cylinder engine. The only unusual features of its design were the use of coil springs and the availability of one model with a 36in (914mm) track, the other two having a standard 56in (1422mm) track. The wheelbase was identical on all three; a roadster with the alternative tracks and a 4-seater tourer on the standard track.

NG

DIXIE FLYER (US) 1916–1923

Kentucky Wagon Manufacturing Co., Louisville, Kentucky.
The Dixie Flyer was one of the more successful regional cars built in the Southern United States and was targeted for sales primarily in its area of manufacture. As it turned out, the Dixie Flyer was promoted on a national basis and sold with some success to a larger market outside Kentucky and Indiana, across the Ohio River from Louisville. This was a 4-cylinder assembled car which used a Herschell-Spillman engine between 1916 and 1919 and a more powerful model of that engine starting in 1920. A complete line of open and closed models comprised the Dixie Flyer catalogue, and sales peaked during the 1921 calendar year. Associated Motors & Corp. acquired the Dixie Flyer as well as both the Jackson of Jackson, Michigan and the National of Indianapolis, Indiana and what had been the Dixie Flyer became the National Model 'H' in 1924 until the National itself failed later that year. Dixie Flyer production reached about 7500 cars before it was discontinued.

KM

D.J. (GB) 1979 to date

D.J. Sportscars, Harlow, Essex.
D.J. Sportscars was the first British company to tackle a kit-form replica of the AC 427 Cobra under the name Dax, making its first fibreglass shell in 1979. It pioneered the engineering of chassis for Ford or Jaguar axles and offered a huge variety of engines, up to American V8s. The AC Ace chassis designer, John Tojeiro, became a director of D.J. in 1985 and the car was renamed Tojeiro in his honour. Options eventually expanded to encompass ladder, square tube or racing 'Supertube' space-frame chassis and Jaguar V12 power. Also available was a marginal Jaguar XJ6-based AC 289 replica. D.J. diversified into other kit car products, such as taking on the COVIN Speedster (also developing its own Californian model, a wide-arch Speedster) and substantially redesigning the K.V.A. GT40 replica in 1989. It also collaborated with MOHR of Germany to produce a British version of the Rush (a Lotus Seven lookalike) that was large enough to be fitted with V8 engines, or even a Cosworth engine and 4 × 4 transmission. Its most ambitious project of all was the Kamala, a novel supercar with a mid-mounted Ford Cosworth engine, a removable roof and potential 160mph (257km/h) top speed. However nothing matched the market pre-eminence of its Tojeiro 427, which was widely regarded as an industry leader.

CR

D.K. (DK) 1950

Bohnstedt-Petersen AS, Copenhagen.

This was an attempt to make a postwar car based on the prewar 2-cylinder D.K.W. The makers planned to use second-hand D.K.W. engines in a new conventional box-section frame, with hydraulic brakes and an all-enveloping body that slightly resembled the contemporary Borgward 1500. The plan was defeated by a shortage of suitable second-hand engines, and by the availability of new D.K.W.s which were being made in both West and East Germany.

NG

DKM (US) c.1978

DKM, Phoenix, Arizona.

Dennis Meecham was a Pontiac dealer who built the DKM Macho, a modified Trans-Am with more horsepower and lowered suspension. They were sold in carburetted and turbocharged form. The turbo version had 300hp.

HP

D.K.R. (DK) 1953–1954

Autofabriken D.K.R. AS, Roskilde.

Sixty-year old engineer S.A. Mathiesen (previously involved with the D.K.) joined forces with two others, Gabrielsen and Ahlmann-Ohlsen, to manufacture a plastic-bodied car in Denmark, which received support from the Danish government. The enveloping 4-door saloon body was mounted on an aluminium frame and was intended to offer American standards of roominess with European-style light weight. Initial plans called for a 3-cylinder engine but the eventual car was powered by an 1100cc Heinkel flat-4 45bhp engine mated to a ZF 4-speed gearbox and driving the front wheels. As many as 400 cars per month were planned to be built at a cost of 15,000 kronor each, but the Danish government withdrew its offer of assistance, scuppering the project.

CR

DKW (D) 1928–1966

1928–1939 Zschopauer Motorenwerke J.S. Rasmussen, Zschopau; Berlin-Spandau; Zwickau.

1950–1966 Auto Union GmbH, Dusseldorf; Ingolstadt.

The DKW name originated in 1916 when Jürgen Skafte Rasmussen (1878–1964) and a fellow Dane named Mathiessen experimented with a steam car design which they called simply the *Dampf Kraft Wagen* (steam car). Rasmussen began to make motorcycles in 1919, which he also called DKW, the initials now standing for *Das Kleiner Wunder* (the Little Wonder). By the late 1920s DKW was the largest maker of motorcycles in the world, and remained so until World War II.

The first car was shown at the Leipzig Fair in 1928. It followed the chassisless wooden construction used in the SB cyclecar and the DEW electric car, both of which were due to Professor Rudolph Slaby. It was made in the former D-WAGEN factory in Berlin. The engine was a 584cc 2-cylinder 2-stroke driving the rear wheels, and body styles were a 2-seater roadster and 2- or 4-seater cabriolets. A doorless 2-seater sports with pointed tail was offered in 1930 and 1931 only. More important was the F1 of 1931 which introduced front-wheel drive to the DKW range, and was made in far larger numbers than the rear-drive cars. It was powered initially by a 490cc 2-cylinder 2-stroke engine, which was soon replaced by a 584cc unit in the F2. It was made as the Reichsklasse from 1933 to 1940, while the later models on the same lines were the 692cc Meisterklasse (1935–1942), and the Front Luxus Cabriolet (1936–1940). The engines were mounted transversely in Mini fashion, and bodies were of fabric. Parallel to these front-wheel drive cars was a line of rear-drive models with larger engines; the V4 Schweberklasse and Sonderklasse, with capacities of 990cc to 1935 and 1054cc from 1936 to 1940. These were made in the Berlin factory, while the 2-cylinder cars came from the Audi factory at Zwickau. The twins were made in Switzerland from 1934 to 1940 as the Holka-DKW, while they were also the base for the TORNAX sports car. DKW joined the Auto Union group in 1932, and in 1934 held 15 per cent of the German car market, taking second place to Opel. Production of the 2-cylinder cars amounted to about 218,000, and of the fours about 26,000.

After World War II the old-style 692cc twins were made in the now-nationalised Audi factory under the name IFA F8, retaining their fabric bodies and prewar styling up to 1955. In West Germany DKW production was revived in a factory

1931 DKW Type FA.600 cabriolet.
NATIONAL MOTOR MUSEUM

1938 DKW Type F7 cabriolet.
NATIONAL MOTOR MUSEUM

1954 DKW Sonderklasse saloon.
NATIONAL MOTOR MUSEUM

at Dusseldorf. The 692cc twin and Meisterklasse name were revived for 1950, but the rounded styling was new, although based on a prewar design which never went into production. It was made as a 2-door saloon, Universal estate car and, in limited numbers, a 4-seater cabriolet by Karmann and a 2-seater coupé by Hebmuller. The same body shape was used for the Sonderklasse, which had an in-line 3-cylinder engine of 896cc, which had also been developed for a 1940 model. A similar shape and 3-cylinder engine were also made by IFA as the F9. The Meisterklasse was dropped after 1954, when 59,475 had been made, but the Sonderklasse was restyled several times up to 1963, being renamed 3/6 in 1955, when the first 4-door models were offered, and the Auto Union 1000 in 1958, when engine capacity went up to 980cc. This engine also went into the 1000SP coupé, which had completely different styling and was marketed as an Auto Union. From 1956 to 1958 the 3/6 engine, tuned to give 55bhp, powered the fibreglass-bodied Monza coupé which was made only in small numbers.

1962 DKW Junior saloon.
NATIONAL MOTOR MUSEUM

1915 D.L. 11.9hp 2-seater.
NATIONAL MOTOR MUSEUM

The 1957 Frankfurt Show saw a new model, the Junior 2-door saloon with 741cc 3-cylinder engine. This went into production in 1959 in a new factory at Ingolstadt. Capacity was increased to 796cc in the Junior De Luxe (1961–63) and to 889cc in the F12 (1963–65). The final development of this line was the F102 (1964–66) which had a 1175cc engine and completely restyled 2- and 4-door saloon bodies. Like all postwar DKWs it had a 2-stroke engine, but this was no longer acceptable to a wide market by the mid–1960s. A new 1696cc 4-cylinder 4-stroke engine was installed in the F102 body shell and the name AUDI was revived for this and subsequent models.

HON

DKW-VEMAG (BR) 1956–1967
Veiculos e Maquinas Agricolas, São Paulo.
The DKW-Vemag is considered the first genuinely Brazilian-made passenger vehicle. It was basically a German DKW Sonderklasse built in Brazil. There were some differences, however. For example, no heater was provided, for obvious reasons, and no coupés were made. The first vehicle to come out of the production line, in November 1956, was a station wagon. Then came the 4-door saloon. Later on, the Brazilian version of the Munga, called Candango, was made in 4 × 2 and 4 × 4 versions. DKW-Vemag's swan song was the Vemag-Fissore, a 2-door saloon designed in Italy and made in Brazil with standard DKW mechanical components. In 1967, Vemag, which had been founded in 1945, was absorbed by Volkswagen, and 2-stroke vehicle production stopped. 2,489 Fissores had been made.

ACT

D.L. (GB) 1913–1920
Dalziel Motor Manufacturing Co., Motherwell.
D.L. Motor Manufacturing Co., Motherwell.
Announced in December 1913, the D.L. was an attractive small car with vee-radiator initially offered in 8 and 10/12hp models, although mostly made only with the larger engine. This had a capacity of 1306cc and was rated at 11.9hp. Three body styles were listed; 2-seater, 4-seater and delivery van. There is some

evidence that a few were made after the war, although from 1919 the D.L.'s maker, William Guthrie, was busy with the Glasgow 3-wheeled agricultural tractor.

NG

D.L.G. (US) 1906–1907
D.L.G. Motorcar Co., St Louis, Missouri.
The initials of this company came from the names of the three men behind it – A.L. Dyke, B.L. Liebert and V.R. Givens. Dyke was a well-known supplier of components to the motor industry and who made the DYKE car earlier in the century, while the other men were both engineers. The car they came up with was an impressive-looking machine with Mercedes-type radiator, long bonnet and flared wings. It had a large 6-cylinder ohv engine. Prices were $4000 for a runabout and $4500 for a tourer, but very few of either were made.

NG

D.M.C. (GB) 1913–1914
Dukeries Motor Co. Ltd, Worksop, Nottinghamshire.
The D.M.C. was a very small 3-wheeler powered by a 4.5hp single-cylinder engine of the company's own manufacture. Final drive was by belt or chain to the single rear wheel, and the price was a modest £85. The maker's name came from the district called 'the Dukeries', because of several large ducal seats in the area.

NG

D.M.G. (PI) 1974–c.1982
1974–1979 D.M.G. Inc., Manila.
1979–c.1982 D.M.G. Inc., Quezon City.
The Volkswagen importer and assembly operation in the Philippines also made two special models locally. The first was the Toro, a good-looking coupé using Beetle mechanicals. Prototypes of a 2/3-seater metal-bodied estate were made in 1978 but it is thought that production never went ahead. A utility/jeep vehicle called the Sakbayan was also made, again based on a VW Beetle chassis. This vehicle originated in Australia and had steel bodywork with soft or hard tops.

CR

DMJ (US) c.1984
DMJ, Austin, Texas.
Kirsten Dodge and Joe Maxwell combined their initials with a 'J' for Jaguar to provide a name for their car company. They bought used Jaguar XJ-6 and XJ-12 sedans and completely reconditioned and modified them from the shell out. A number of engines were offered, from high-performance Jaguars to Chevrolet V8s. The body was customised with an air dam, side skirts and a rear wing. Prices ranged from $30,000 to 60,000 for a DMJ XJ-6.

HP

D.M.S. (GB) 1989–1993
Dorset Motor Services, Fordingbridge, Hampshire.
D.M.S. claimed that its Bullit was inspired by the Aston Martin Vantage but it did not look *anything* like it, more like a poorly converted Ford Capri Mk2/3, which was what it was. It was sold as a coupé or, more commonly, as a convertible. The conversion consisted of a set of fibreglass body panels for the bonnet, front wings, valance and boot, the rest gluing over the Capri body. Another project was the Predator, a Ferrari 250 GTO replica on a Datsun 240Z/260Z basis, but far more significant was the Venom, a budget 427 Cobra replica based on Ford Cortina/Granada parts. Another replica was the Abingdon, a copy of the MGA, but it seems unlikely that this reached production. CLASSIC REPLICAS assumed control of D.M.S in 1993.

CR

D.N.K. *see* DE NOVO

DOBI (E) 1919–1920
Autociclos Dobi, Madrid.
Assembled in a garage in Madrid, the Dobi was a short-lived cyclecar using a Douglas engine and belt drive. Some of the cars had a single headlamp on the front.

VCM

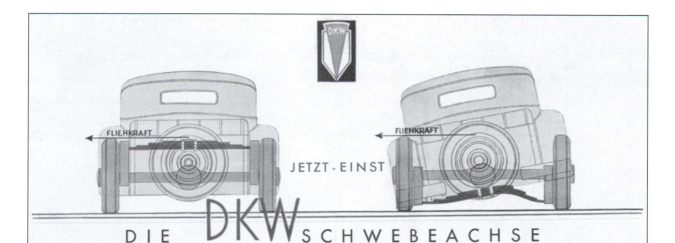

JETZT · EINST

DIE **DKW** SCHWEBEACHSE

Das Fahren im DKW-„Sonderklasse" gleicht wirklich einem „Schweben" über der Fahrbahn. Die hintere Querfederung ist so angeordnet, daß sie hinter den Fondsitzen und zwar in Rückenhöhe der Insassen am selbsttragenden Wagenkörper befestigt ist. Dadurch sitzt die Karosserie nicht mehr wie bisher **auf** den Federn, sondern sie hängt **in** der Feder. Daraus ergibt sich nicht nur ein großer Fortschritt für den Fahrkomfort der Insassen, sondern auch eine überragende Verbesserung von Straßenlage und Fahrsicherheit.

Seitlich wirkende Kräfte — wie sie in der Kurve auftreten und Schleudertendenzen hervorrufen können — greifen nicht mehr an einem großen Hebelarm an, sondern unmittelbar im Aufhängepunkt der Karosserie, so daß der Aufbau auch bei der schärfsten Fahrweise seine stabile Schwergewichtslage behält. Die DKW-Schwebeachse ist — wie kritische Fachleute betonen — eine ganz umwälzende Neuerung im modernen Automobilbau, deren Einführung durch die freitragende Karosseriebauweise von DKW ermöglicht wurde.

Schwebeachse!      Großer Radstand!
Freilauf!   Breite Spur!
Schnellgang-Getriebe   Ein repräsentativer Wagen!

AUTO · UNION · A-G

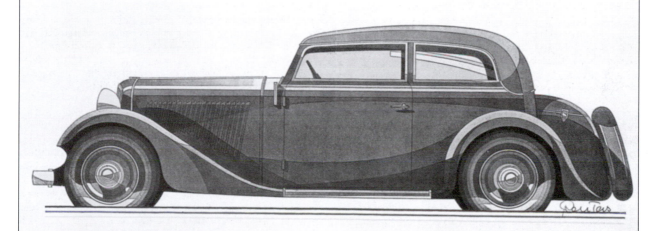

DIE VIERSITZIGE CABRIOLET-LIMOUSINE
Modell „1002"

ein ungemein geräumiger großer Wagen in wohltuend harmonischer Linienführung, dezent in den Farben, gediegen in Ausführung und Ausstattung. Selbsttragende, bewährt stabile Sperrholzkarosserie mit der unerreicht praktischen Kunstlederbespannung — elegante Stoffpolsterung — verstellbare Vordersitze (Stahlrohr) — sehr bequem zurückschlagbares, absolut wetterfestes Dach — großer, fest angebauter Kofferraum — breite Türen mit Spezialtürgriffen als Diebstahlsicherung — ganz reichhaltige Ausstattung: indirekt beleuchtetes

OFFEN

Armaturenbrett mit Bosch-Sicherheitszündschloß, elektrischer Ölstandskontrolle, Kraftstoffuhr, Tachometer, Amperemeter, Licht- und Winkerschalter, Freilaufschaltung, Starthelfgriff, Anlasser, elektrischer Zigarrenanzünder, Aschenbecher, Handschuhbehälter — Windschutzscheibe mit Einhandausstellvorrichtung — elektrische Beleuchtung des Innenraums — Scheinwerferabblendung durch Fußschalter — verchromte Schutzstange vorn — große Scheinwerfer — elektrischer Winker — elektrischer Doppelscheibenwischer — Radzierkappen

Modell SONDERKLASSE „1001" in gleicher Ausführung, jedoch mit Windschutzscheibe aus Sicherheitsglas, voll verchromten Scheinwerfern und Vigot-Wagenheber

1924 Doble E.24 coupé. Abner Doble's own car.
NATIONAL MOTOR MUSEUM

DOBLE (US) 1914–1931

1914–1915 Abner Doble Motor Vehicle Co., Waltham, Massachusetts.
1916–1917 General Engineering Co., Detroit, Michigan.
1917–1918 Doble-Detroit Steam Motors Co., Detroit, Michigan.
1923–1931 Doble Steam Motors Corp., Emeryville, California.

The Doble was the finest American steam car and although produced in tiny numbers, the later models set an example of what steam power could achieve if no expense were spared. Abner Doble (1895–1961) built his first steam car while at high school in San Francisco., and later, when at the Massachusetts Institute of Technology, visited the STANLEY brothers with whose rather basic cars he was unimpressed. He set about building the car he called the Model A. It had a 2-cylinder double-acting single-expansion engine mounted horizontally on the rear axle with watertube boiler and a radiator which condensed all the steam. The Model A was a handsome 2-seater roadster with wire wheels. Doble built five of these, sold four at $4000 each, and retained the fifth for further experiments.

The Abner Doble company was formed at the end of 1914 to produce a development of the Model A, which he called, logically, Model B. Despite capital of $500,000, largely provided by his wealthy father, Doble, who was still only 19 years old, could not make a commercial success of his company, and only one Model B was built. He then took his ideas to Detroit, where he attracted the attention of C.L. Lewis, former head of the Consolidated Car Co., which had built the ABBOTT-DETROIT. He backed Doble in the formation of a new company, the General Engineering Co., which was to make a new car derived from the Model B, called the Model C or G.E.C.-Doble. This was so successful at the 1916 Automobile Show that 11,000 orders were received. All seemed set for commercial success when World War I intervened, denying Doble a supply of essential components. He reorganised as the Doble-Detroit Steam Motors Co. and some cars were built for a year or so. Estimates of Doble-Detroit production range from three cars to 200; the former figure is probably closer to the truth. Certainly by 1919 Doble was disillusioned with Detroit; he sold manufacturing rights to the Amalgamated Machinery Co. of Chicago, which never built a single car, and moved to California.

In 1920 he formed Doble Steam Motors of California at San Francisco, and built a few experimental cars there. The Model D was an improved Doble-Detroit with monotube boiler, and the Doble-Simplex was a prototype assembled on a Jordan Big Six chassis. By 1923 a big factory at Emeryville had been completed,

and there Doble began production of his finest car yet, the Series E. He intended that this should rival the best internal-combustion cars, that it should be more flexible than a Packard Twin Six, quieter than a Rolls-Royce, and more powerful than a Hispano-Suiza. It had a 125bhp compound engine mounted on the rear axle, and gave a top speed of 95mph (153km/h). The electric firing and flash boiler meant that starting was very rapid compared with other steamers. In one test, a Doble Series E was left overnight in the street where the temperature was just on freezing. Operating pressure was reached in 23 seconds after switching on, and the car was ready to move off 41 seconds later, with four passengers. The Series E's 142in (3607mm) wheelbase was suitable for the finest custom coachwork. Eight body styles were offered, all by Murphy, although one chassis was sent to Hooper in London to be fitted with a shooting brake body for the Maharajah of Bharatpur. Among other customers for the Series E were film star Norma Talmadge and oil tycoon Howard Hughes, who had two. Unfortunately the prices of $8000 to $11,200 were among the highest in America, equal to the Locomobile Model 48 and only slightly lower than the Springfield-built Rolls-Royce. Wealthy buyers tended to be conservative and to shy away from the perceived eccentricities of steam, so Doble could find no more than 12 buyers for the Series E and even fewer of the improved Model F. Doble Steam Motors went into liquidation in April 1931, and the factory was taken over by the Besler brothers, George and William, sons of the chairman of the New Jersey Central Railroad. Their several experiments included a steam-powered aeroplane and at least one Buick sedan converted to steam. Abner Doble went to Europe where he worked with truck makers Sentinel in England and Henschel in Germany, developing advanced steam trucks and railcars.

NG

Further Reading
'The Steam Odyssey of Abner Doble', Maurice D. Henry, *Automobile Quarterly*, Vol. VIII, No. 1.

DOCTORESSE (F) 1899–1902

Sté Française d'Automobiles (système Gaillardet), Paris.
The Doctoresse was made in two models; 6 and 12hp, both with front-mounted 2-cylinder engines and chain drive. They were designed by Frederic Gaillardet, who had built a 5hp 3-wheeler in 1899, and after leaving Doctoresse became a consultant to MILDE.

NG

DODDSMOBILE (CDN) 1947

The Doddsmobile was presented as an economy 3-wheeler, with a small air-cooled engine driving the single rear wheel, open plywood bodywork and automatic transmission. Only one prototype was constructed.

CR

DODGE BROTHERS; DODGE (i) (US) 1914 to date

1914–1928 Dodge Brothers, Detroit, Michigan.
1928 to date Dodge Division, Chrysler Corp., Detroit, Michigan.
The Dodge name was familiar in Detroit for more than a decade before the first Dodge car appeared. The brothers John and Horace Dodge had in 1901 established a machine shop in which they made bicycle components and, later, engines and transmissions for the Curved Dash Oldsmobile. In 1903 they began to make engines, gearboxes and axles for Henry Ford, and soon almost all their output was for Ford. They supplied the engines for Ford's Models A, B and K. John Dodge became a Ford director in about 1904. In 1910 they opened a large factory in Hamtranck, a district of Detroit with a large Polish population. This would later be used for car manufacture.

By 1913 they had made a fortune as suppliers to Ford, but they realised that Henry was moving towards self-sufficiency, making more and more of his components. Also they resented, as John Dodge put it, 'being carried about in Henry Ford's vest pocket'. In the summer of 1914 the brothers ended their Ford contract, although they retained their valuable stock holding. Before they took this step they had been planning a car of their own, and the prototype appeared in November 1914. So high was their reputation in Detroit that 22,000 dealers had asked for a franchise even before a single car was built.

The Dodge Brothers car was a simple design intended for the mass market. The brothers were thoroughly familiar with the Model T Ford, but they thought that its weaknesses were the epicyclic transmission and low power of only 20bhp. Therefore their car had a conventional 3-speed gearbox with direct drive on top gear, and a 3480cc 35bhp 4-cylinder engine, which was nearly twice as powerful as the Ford. The only model was a 5-seater tourer, and, like Ford, the only colour was black. The body was an all-steel welded structure made for Dodge by the Edward G. Budd Co. of Philadelphia. This was the world's first mass-produced all-steel body. The price was inevitably higher than the Model T, at $785 compared with $450, but Dodge Brothers regarded their product as much more of a proper car. Asked why they had decided to make their own, John Dodge had replied, 'Just think of all those Ford owners who will some day want an automobile'.

Only 249 cars were made between 14 November and the end of the year, but 1915 saw production of 45,000 cars, followed by 71,400 in 1916. That year the Dodge was the fourth best-selling make in America, after Ford, Willys-Overland, and Buick.

Few changes were made to the Dodge in the early years (strictly speaking it was called Dodge Brothers up to 1930, but the cars were generally known as Dodge). A 2-seater roadster was added in 1915, a centre-door all-enclosed sedan in 1916, and a light truck in 1917. The tourer was widely used by the US Army, first in the 1916 Mexican border campaign against Pancho Villa, and from 1917 in Europe after America had entered World War I. General John Pershing used one as his staff car; his driver was Sgt Eddie Rickenbacker, who later became a flying ace and a car maker under his own name. In 1919, when production reached 105,398, an all-steel sedan joined the range, selling for $1900 compared with $1095 for a roadster. It was a very important design, and could be described as a forerunner of all the steel-bodied closed cars which are universal today, although many American manufacturers stayed with composite bodies until the early 1930s, and even Dodge offered a wood-framed coach body by Fisher in 1925. Up to 1924 mechanical changes were few, apart from increases in wheelbase in 1917 and 1924, larger brake drums in 1917 and slightly raked windscreens in 1920.

Both brothers died in 1920 and control of their company passed to their widows and a board of directors. Long-time employee Frederick Haynes became president and general manager and he occupied these posts until 1925, when the widows sold Dodge Brothers to the New York bank Dillon, Reed & Co. for $146 million, which was then the largest sum in the history of industrial finance. The one millionth car came off the line in the late autumn of 1923, but Dodge had dropped to sixth place in the US sales league. Worse was to come, and by 1928 they were in 13th place. The car became longer and lower in 1924, when three-

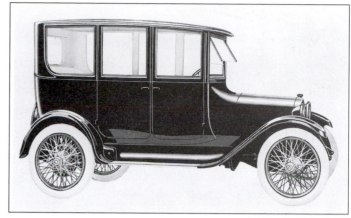
1919 Dodge(i) 4 sedan.
NATIONAL MOTOR MUSEUM

1932 Dodge(i) roadster.
NICK BALDWIN

1932 Dodge(i) DK victoria coupé.
NICK GEORGANO/NATIONAL MOTOR MUSEUM

quarter elliptic springs were replaced by semi-elliptics, but the old 3480cc 35bhp engine was continued until 1927, when output was upped to 44bhp. For 1928 Dodge joined the fashion for 6-cylinders, with 3408 and 3670cc engines developing 58 and 68bhp respectively, in Standard Six, Senior Six and Victory Six models. They were longer and lower than any previous Dodge, and for the first time the Dodge could be considered among the best-looking cars in America. They had, however, taken the company a long way from their original philosophy of making superior Fords at slightly higher prices. The new sixes cost from $945 to $1770, with the surviving four at $855 to $955, but Model A Ford prices in 1928 started at $480.

Faced with falling sales and being not especially interested in staying in the automobile business, Clarence Dillon looked for a way out. He found the answer in Walter P. Chrysler, who was anxious to extend his company into a lower price field. In a stock transaction rather than a cash deal, Chrysler bought Dodge from Dillon, Read for $170 million. The Chrysler company was only five years

1946 Dodge(i) De Luxe sedan.
NATIONAL MOTOR MUSEUM

were dropped. Sales were encouragingly up to seventh place with 121,457 Dodges finding customers during the 1928–29 model year. For 1930 two new models appeared; smaller, lighter, faster and yet less expensive than their predecessors. These were the 3110cc DD6 and the 3616cc DC8, the latter being Dodge's first and only straight-8. It was $450 less expensive than the old Senior Six, and as its weight was 550lbs (250kg) less, its performance was sparkling. Had it not been for the Depression, the Dodge Eight might have had a long and successful career, but it was dropped in the mid–1933 season, after 44,953 had been made.

During 1930 the name Dodge Brothers disappeared from company advertising, although the familiar badge with its six-pointed star was continued for a few more years. Dodge's niche was in the middle of the Chrysler group, initially more expensive than the companion DeSoto but later less so. From 1933 to 1937 Dodge held fourth place in US sales. Since the three makes ahead of it were the low-priced Chevrolet, Ford and Plymouth, this meant that Dodge was the best-selling car in the low-medium price range; Walter Chrysler must have been well pleased with his purchase.

Dodge cars were made in Canada from 1925, and in 1933 there was a Plymouth-like low-price small Canadian Dodge, the DQ, which had no US equivalent. This model was continued under various designations up to 1942, at prices around CDN$250 less than the 'regular' Dodge models. Another important overseas operation was in England, at Kew, Surrey, where an assembly plant turned out several models aimed at the UK market. As well as the 3570cc Victory six, Kew built a 2794cc six, while in 1938 the 4880cc Chrysler New York Special straight-8 carried Dodge badging for the UK market. During the 1930s Dodge at Kew also developed a range of trucks of British design. In

old and their acquisition of Dodge was likened to a sardine trying to swallow a whale. The Dodge factories were five times the size of Chrysler's, and the purchase gave Walter P. valuable foundry and forge shops. Without the acquisition of Dodge, he could never have launched the low-priced Plymouth, while the vast Dodge dealer network was also invaluable to him.

Chrysler's purchase was finalised on 31 July 1928, and as the 1929 models were about to be announced, there was little change for that year, although the fours

NICK GEORGANO

DODGE, JOHN (1864–1920) and HORACE (1868–1920)

When they died they were among the wealthiest men in America, but the brothers John and Horace Dodge were born in deep poverty, the sons of blacksmith Daniel Dodge, of Niles, Michigan. Although born four years apart, they were inseparable all their lives, their attachment being akin to that of identical twins. Growing up in their father's workshop, they began to tinker with machinery at an early age, and together took jobs at the Murphy Engine Co. in Detroit, when they were 22 and 18.

After four years they moved on to the Canadian Typograph Co. at Windsor, Ontario, and it was there that they leased part of the workshops to manufacture their first wheeled vehicle, the Evans and Dodge bicycle, although they had made one or two cycles for their own use while still at home in Niles. They stayed in the bicycle business from 1897 to 1901, when they returned to Detroit and set up their machine shop which was to build engines for Olds, and engines, transmissions and axles for Ford. While both were mechanically gifted, it was Horace who was primarily the engineer, while John looked after the business side.

It was the Ford connection which turned them into wealthy men, not so much from their fees as from the tremendous increase in the value of their

Ford stock. They were allocated 50 shares each in 1903, and a further 1000 each in 1908; when Henry Ford bought out the brothers in 1917, so that he could have complete control of the company, he paid them $25 million. They set up their car making company in 1914 because, as John said, they were tired of being carried round in Henry Ford's vest pocket.

Although the Dodges became millionaires, they were shunned by many people in the Detroit Social Register as 'gasoline aristocrats'. Their behaviour did not help them to gain acceptance, for both brothers drank heavily and conspicuously. John wrecked a bar during a brawl on at least one occasion. Refused membership of the Detroit Country Club, they bought a plot of land adjoining the club's grounds, planning to build an enormous house which would overshadow the club. Apparently this was never completed, and they continued to live at Grosse Pointe. However Horace gained some favour through his support of the Detroit Symphony Orchestra. He was one of its original patrons, and was the major contributor to the building of the Orchestra Hall. Victor Herbert composed The Dodge Brothers March for them, and Horace's daughter Delphine became a fine pianist.

Tragedy struck the Dodge family in 1920. While visiting New York for the Auto Show in January, Horace contracted influenza which turned to pneumonia. Although doctors despaired of his life, he recovered, but John, who was at his bedside day and night, caught flu himself and died on 11 January. Completely shattered by his brother's death, Horace never recovered his former vitality. On 10 December he died at his winter home in Palm Beach, Florida. The cause of death was given as cirrhosis of the liver; however that hackneyed phrase, 'a broken heart' was never more appropriate than in the case of Horace Dodge. Each brother left estates valued at more than $20 million. Five years later their widows sold out to Dillon Read for $146 million.

John Dodge married first, Ivy Hawkins in 1892 (d.1901), and second Matilda Rausch (1884–1967). Their son, John Duval Dodge operated a speedboat factory and tried to launch the rotary-valve Dodgeson car in 1926.

Horace Dodge married Scottish-born Anna Thompson (1866–1969) in 1896. They had two children, and Anna outlived them both. Delphine was thrice married at the time of her death in 1943, and Horace Jr was married to his fifth wife when he died in 1963.

NG

Further Reading
'The Brothers Dodge', Stan Grayson, *Automobile Quarterly*, Vol.17, No.1.

Norway the bus manufacturers Strommen Værkstad assembled Dodge cars from 1933 to 1940, including some 7-seater long-wheelbase saloons which were badged as Strommen. About 800 to 1000 were made each year.

Dodge engineering and styling in the 1930s followed the general development of the Chrysler Corp. Hydraulic brakes had arrived in 1928, free wheels in 1932 and synchromesh in 1933. The Dodge Division was spared the Airflow models made by Chrysler and DeSoto, which no doubt accounts for the way in which sales held up in the mid-1930s. However, Dodge did build a limited number of Airflow-styled trucks between 1934 and 1940, mostly for oil companies. Trucks became an increasingly important part of Dodge production in the 1930s.

After the demise of the straight-8, only one size of engine was offered. This was a 3570cc side-valve six developing 87bhp (1934–40) and 91bhp on the 1941 models. A larger engine of 3772cc and 105bhp was used in the short-lived 1942 range. An overdrive was an option for 1934, hypoid rear axles were introduced for 1937 and coil ifs for 1939. Along with other Chrysler Corp. makes, Dodge acquired a split grill and fully-faired headlamps on the 1939 models. Styling was close to that of DeSoto up to 1942, although Dodge never featured the controversial retracting headlamps of their sister make.

Passenger car production was halted by the war on 21 February 1942, and was not resumed until December 1945. Apart from minor styling changes, the 1946 to 1948 Dodges were similar to the 1942 models. For 1949 a new line was announced, with completely restyled bodies whose wings were faired into the front doors in the modern style. A fluid drive automatic transmission, which had been introduced in 1942, was an optional alternative to the 3-speed synchromesh gearbox. The engine was still the 3772cc side-valve six, and indeed this survived on the less expensive Dodges until 1959, although by then power was up from 105 to 135bhp.

A front-wheel drive prototype was tested in 1949–50, but was thought to be too radical, and Dodges continued to drive through the rear wheels until the arrival of the European-designed Omni in 1978. Sales held up well during the 1950s, but Dodge did not regain their excellent fourth place which they had enjoyed before the war; they were usually sixth to eighth in the league. Dodges were generally seen as rather staid cars, with no performance image, but this was to change with the introduction of the Red Ram V8 engine for 1953.

The 3954cc Red Ram was essentially a scaled-down version of Chrysler's 5426cc hemi-head V8 introduced in 1951. The hemispherical combustion chambers allowed larger valves set further apart, smoother manifolding and porting, all making for better thermal efficiency. In its 1953 form, the Red Ram developed 140bhp but its potential was much higher and within a few years a 5130cc version was giving 260bhp. By 1970, the ultimate development of this engine would be giving 425bhp from 6980cc.

The 1953 Dodges were the first Chrysler Corp. cars to be styled by Virgil Exner. They included the sporty-looking Coronet, which was available only with the V8 engine and featured wheel covers and a continental-style externally mounted spare wheel. Dodge's performance image began to be established during the V8's first year, with the breaking of 196 AAA stock car records at Bonneville Salt Flats. Perhaps in recognition of this new image, a Dodge was chosen for the first time as the Pace Car for the Indianapolis 500 in 1954. High-performance Dodges gained in power during the late 1950s, and by the end of the decade the 6276cc V8 optional in all Custom and Royal models was giving 345bhp.

In 1959 the old 3772cc side-valve six was discontinued, and this was replaced by a 3687cc ohv slant six used in the Dart. This was a new low-priced car aimed at the Ford-Chevrolet-Plymouth market, which nevertheless used the same styling as the more expensive Matador and Polara models. Even less expensive was the Lancer, introduced for 1961. This was Dodge's contribution to the new compact car market, and was closely related to the Plymouth Valiant. However this upmarket compact did not sell well, and was revised for 1963 as a new Dart, with an extra 4.5in (114mm) and fresh styling.

The full-sized Dodges gained even more power in the 1960s. In 1962 the Ramcharger 426, named for its capacity of 426 cu in (6980cc), developed 415bhp with single 4-barrel carburettor, and 425bhp with twin 4-barrels. Dodge won that year's NHRA (National Hot Rod Association) Championship, and became a strong contender in stock car racing organised by NASCAR (National Association for Stock Car Auto Racing). In 1964 Dodge finished 1-2-3 in the Daytona 500 stock car race, and together with Plymouth enabled Chrysler to take the Grand National title that year. This brought protests from Ford and General Motors that the 426 engine with hemi-head was not available in showroom cars,

1956 Dodge(i) Custom Royal Lancer convertible.
NATIONAL MOTOR MUSEUM

1970 Dodge(i) Challenger R/T coupé.
NATIONAL MOTOR MUSEUM

1980 Dodge(i) Omni 024 DeTomaso coupé.
NATIONAL MOTOR MUSEUM

1985 Dodge(i) Aries coupé.
DODGE

1986 Dodge(i) Diplomat sedan.
DODGE

1986 Dodge(i) 600 convertible.
DODGE

and after a lot of wrangling Chrysler withdrew from the 1965 season races. The following year they were back with Dodges and Plymouths powered by the 426 hemi which was offered in the hottest model of the Dodge Charger, a fastback coupé version of the Coronet sedan.

For 1968 Dodge announced a new Charger with semi-fastback styling and five engine options; 5211cc, 6276cc 2-barrel carburettor, 6276cc 4-barrel, 6980cc Hemi and 7210cc Magnum. The latter two were only available in a limited production model, the Charger R/T (Road and Track). The 426 was the most powerful of the options, at 425bhp compared with 375bhp for the larger but less highly-tuned 440 Magnum engine. Along with other sporty Dodges such as the Super Bee, Dart GTS and Coronet R/T, it wore bumble bee stripes around the rear deck and down the quarter panels. These cars were collectively known as Dodge's Scat Pack. The Charger was the most performance-orientated, with stiffer springs and shock absorbers, and larger disc brakes at the front. When *Road & Track* tested an automatic version, it recorded a top speed of 156mph (251km/h), and 0–60mph (0–97km/h) in 4.8 seconds. Even this performance was not enough to defeat the Fords in 1968 and 1969, and it was not until 1970 that the Chrysler Corp. again won the Grand National title, with the droop-snoot and aerofoil-equipped Dodge Daytona and Plymouth Superbird, both of which used the Hemi engine.

The Charger R/T of 1968–71 was one of the most famous performance cars in America. Frequently seen in films and on television, the best known Charger was probably the 'General Lee', the 4-wheeled star of the *Dukes of Hazzard* television series. This was very appropriate, as the whole stock car racing scene grew up in the country districts of the South-Eastern United States, typified by Hazzard County. The most wayout version of the Charger was the 1970 Daytona, which used the droopsnoot streamlined nose and aerofoils of the NASCAR cars. Only 505 of these were made, just enough to qualify the model as a production car for NASCAR racing. Its price was about $8900, compared with $3711 for the standard Charger R/T.

For 1971 Chrysler reduced its NASCAR entries to one car each from Dodge and Plymouth. This was the last year for the famous Hemi engine; insurance premiums on muscle cars such as the Charger R/T had become prohibitive,

and from 1 January 1972 all commercially available cars had to be able to run on regular fuels, which the Hemi could not. The R/T title was dropped for 1972, and although the Charger remained in Dodge catalogues until 1978, it was no longer a performance car, just another 'personal car'. During the 1960s Dodge generally held between sixth and eighth places in the league. Their best year was 1968 when their seventh place represented sales of 621,136 cars. As well as the exciting Chargers, the range included the compact Dart, intermediate Coronet, and full-size Polara and Monaco models, all available with a wide variety of body styles. Convertibles disappeared after 1971, the year in which Dodge began to import subcompact cars from Mitsubishi, which were sold under the name Dodge Colt.

Like all American cars, Dodges were downsized during the 1970s. The high-performance Charger had gone by 1972, and the larger touring models were reduced in both overall size and engine capacity. In 1972 the Monaco station wagon was 223in (5664mm) long, weighed 4568lbs (2072kg) and could be had with a 7210cc engine developing 330bhp. Ten years later the largest Dodge was the Diplomat sedan, 205in (5220mm), weighing 3507lbs (1591kg) and powered by a 5211cc engine developing 165bhp.

To make up for the decline of the large V8s, Dodge brought out several intermediate and smaller models. The Challenger coupé was an answer to Ford's Mustang and Chevrolet's Camaro; launched for the 1970 season, it was initially available with several engines up to the Hemi 426, and was made in convertible form until 1971. However, it appeared on the scene a bit too late to make a big impact on the market and was dropped in June 1974. From Europe came the Omni of 1978. This was a front-drive sedan with transverse 1716cc 4-cylinder engine, made in Britain and France as the Chrysler or Simca Horizon. It gained a 2212cc engine in 1982, and was offered as a sporty hatchback coupé called the 024 Charger. This had no European equivalent.

A larger front-drive car was the Aries made in sedan and station wagon forms and powered by transverse 4-cylinder engines of 2212cc Chrysler or 2556cc Mitsubishi manufacture. These were part of Chrysler's K range; others were the Chrysler LeBaron and Plymouth Reliant. There were also coupé and convertible models called the 400. These marked the return of the convertible after a 10-year absence. By 1986 only one Dodge was still rear-driven; the 5211cc V8 Diplomat sedan. Other models included the Colt hatchbacks, Conquest GT coupé and Vista 7-seater station wagon in 4×2 and 4×4 versions, all of which were imported from Mitsubishi, the Omni hatchbacks and Charger coupé, of which one model was prepared by Carroll Shelby, the Aries, Lancer and 600 4-door sedan and 2-door convertible. The Daytona coupé was derived from the Aries with the same engine options, and lines similar to those of the Charger.

The Diplomat was continued with little change until the end of the 1989 season, when it was dropped along with the other Chrysler rear-drive cars. Also dropped for 1990 were the Omni and Aries, leaving as the smallest Dodge the Shadow made in sedan or hatchback forms with the same engine options as the Aries; this was also badged as the Plymouth Sundance. Next in size was the Lancer H-car, sister to the Chrysler LeBaron GTS; launched in 1984 these were 5-door hatchbacks, although notchback sedan in shape, and used transverse 2212cc engines developing 93bhp in standard form up to 177bhp in the turbocharged Lancer Shelby. Almost identical in size, but made as a 4-door sedan only, was the Spirit, while the top of the 1990 range was the Dynasty sedan, cousin to the Chrysler New Yorker. For 1991 the Spirit could be had with Chrysler's Lotus-designed 16-valve head on the familiar 2212cc block, which gave 224bhp. This R/T version cost $17,871, which was $4000 more than the next costliest Spirit, and only 1400 were made in the 1991 and 1992 seasons.

The Shadow, Spirit, and Dynasty faded away in the mid-1990s, with little development money being spent on them. In their place came the Neon compact sedan and coupé, which were Plymouth Neons with Dodge badging, and the Intrepid, one of the LH family of 'cab forward' sedans similar to Chrysler's Concorde and Eagle's Vision. This had a choice of 3300cc pushrod or 3518cc ohc V6 engines. Early in 1995 the Spirit gave way to the Stratus, a lower-priced version of the Chrysler Cirrus sedan, powered by a choice of new Chrysler-built 2428cc four or Mitsubishi-built 2496cc ohc V6 engines. Another new model for 1995 was the Daytona-replacing Avenger coupé, based on the Mitsubishi Galant sedan. These, like the Galant and other Mitsubishi-designed models such as the Dodge Stealth coupé, were made at the Diamond Star factory at Normal, Illinois, set up jointly by Chrysler and Mitsubishi in 1988. Neon, Avenger, Stratus and Intrepid made up the mainstream 1998 range, together

1993 Dodge(i) Viper V10 sports car.
NATIONAL MOTOR MUSEUM

with the Caravan MPV, which had been made since 1984, and was now available in 4 × 4 form. Another Dodge 4 × 4 was the Durango sports utility station wagon derived from the Dakota pick-up, and powered by a choice of 3.8-litre V6 or 5.2-litre V8 engines. A 4 × 2 version was announced in mid-1998.

In 1992 there appeared a Dodge completely separate from the rest of the range. First seen as a concept car at the 1989 Detroit Show, the Viper was a traditional front-engined sports car in the Cobra mould. Indeed its development was entrusted to the 'father' of the Cobra, Carroll Shelby. Power came from a 7990cc V10 engine adapted from a truck unit, and this was the first use of a 10-cylinder engine in a passenger car. The simple 2-seater body was of all-steel construction, and the chassis was a conventional ladder frame design. Production Vipers had fibreglass bodies. A decision was taken in the summer of 1989 to put the Viper into production, although none went on sale until May 1992. At its launch, Chrysler chairman Bob Lutz said 'Sports cars have gotten too East Coast, effete, effeminate, with lots of whizzy little parts, too much electronics, too much sophistication'. His words were a clear dig at cars in the Ferrari/Lamborghini mould, although ironically it was Lamborghini, which Chrysler owned at the time, which did the development work of refining a truck engine into one for a sports car. In its production form it developed nearly 400bhp, and gave the Viper a top speed of 167mph (270km/h). At $50,000 it was not expensive compared with European supercars. By the end of 1997, Dodge had sold 8729 Vipers. The next stage in the Viper's development was the GTS coupé, seen as a concept at the 1993 Detroit Show and put into production in 1996. The coupé was much more than just a roadster with a top, being 90 per cent new, with a fresh body and interior, and a lightened engine now giving 450bhp.

Dodge built 372,832 passenger cars in 1997, together with 285,736 Caravans and 20,263 Durangos. They had six manufacturing plants in the United States, two in Canada and two in Mexico.

NG

Further Reading
The Dodge Story, Thomas A. McPherson, Crestline Publishing, 1976.

DODGE (ii) (US) 1914

Dodge Motorcar Co., Detroit, Michigan.
Although operating in the same city and in the same year as the famous Dodge Brothers company, there was no connection between the two. The Dodge

2000 Dodge(i) Neon coupé.
NICK GEORGANO

Motorcar Co. was formed by Alvan M. Dodge, who had previously been with the WAHL Co. He planned to build a light car with 25hp 4-cylinder engine, friction transmission and chain drive, in roadster or touring form. His car was announced several months before that of the Dodge Brothers, and Alvan M. sued them for use of his name. The matter was settled in 1916, in favour of the brothers who were by then successful car makers. Alvan M.'s car did not last beyond 1914, with very few completed.

NG

DODGE (iii) (AUS) 1947–1957

Chrysler Australia Ltd, Keswick, South Australia.
The establishment of Chrysler in Australian motor manufacturing led to the emergence of models not seen on the home market. A Dodge-badged version of the postwar PLYMOUTH appeared and when the 1953 Cranbrook was put into production with a 92 per cent local content, the Dodge Kingsway was a clone. This programme ran, with updates, until the CHRYSLER Royal put an end to badge engineering.

MG

1947 Dolo JB-4 coupé.
NICK BALDWIN

DODGE (iv) **(RA)** 1968–1982
1968–1980 Chrysler Fevre Argentina SA, Buenos Aires.
1980–1982 Volkswagen Argentina SA, Buenos Aires.
Local Valiant/Lancer variations started to be built in Argentina in 1968. These cars were joined by Dodge-badged cars. These were the Dodge Polara, Dodge GT, and Dodge Coronado models, all of them powered by a 3687cc 6-cylinder engine. A 5220cc V8 engine was offered from 1970 in the Dodge GTX Coupé. The Dodge 1500 (Hillman Avenger) was produced from 1973. In 1977 the Valiants were dropped and so were all the other big cars except the Coronado with 3687cc, 147bhp 6-cylinder engine, which continued in production until 1980. With the sale of Chrysler's overseas operations, Volkswagen stepped in and only the Avenger was produced, until 1982.
ACT

DODGE (v) **(BR)** 1969–1982
1969–1980 Chrysler do Brasil SA Ind e Com, São Bernardo do Campo.
1980–1982 Chrysler Motors do Brasil Ltda, São Bernardo do Campo.
Like Chrysler-Argentina, this firm built Hillman Avengers (badged as Dodge Polaras), first with 1500cc engines and later with 1800cc engines. Bigger American designs were also produced, these being the Dart and the Charger, the latter available from 1976 with a 215bhp 5220cc V8 engine and automatic transmission. Chrysler's financial troubles led to a Volkswagen take-over and production of Dodges continued only until 1982.
ACT

DODGESON (US) 1926
Dodgeson Motors Detroit, Michigan.
The Dodgeson was designed and engineered by John Duval Dodge, the son of John F. Dodge, a founder and president of the Dodge Brothers Motor Car Co. Its design incorporated a rotary engine designed by C.E. Wyrick. The straight-8 rotary valve engine had a bore and stroke of 63 × 127mm (3.2 litres) producing 72bhp at 3000rpm and was placed in a 4-point suspension position, supported between a channel section of side rails by rubber shock absorbers set in brackets. Aside from its engine the Dodgeson was assembled from standard components. A few chassis were presumably completed but the Dodgeson never proceeded beyond the prototype stage and it is doubtful if any coachwork was forthcoming.
KM

DODO (US) 1912
Auto Parts Manufacturing Co., Detroit, Michigan.
This was one of the first American cyclecars, powered by a 10/12hp 2-cylinder air-cooled engine which drove the front wheels. Although its standard track of 56in made it wide enough for side by side seating, the seats were in tandem. It was built by Auto Parts to the design of an employee, Karl Probst. Production never started, and Probst move to Toledo where he worked for the MILBURN company on their electric cars. Later he joined AMERICAN AUSTIN and while with their successors, American Bantam, he was one of the principal engineers responsible for the Jeep.
NG

DODSON (GB) 1910–1914
Dodson Motors Ltd (David Brown & Sons Ltd), Huddersfield, Yorkshire.
Built by the famous gear making firm of David Brown, the Dodson was almost identical to the Renault apart from a Zenith carburettor and modifications to the ignition and lubrication systems. Two 4-cylinder models, a 12/16hp and a 20/30hp were made.
NG

DOFRAL (US) c.1985–1989
Dofral Distributing Inc., Minneapolis, Minnesota.
The Classic T was a kit replica of the 1957 Ford Thunderbird. It was shortened 7ins (178mm) so that it would fit a custom frame that mounted Ford Pinto or Mustang II suspension and front-mounted engines.
HP

DOLLY (GB) 1920
The Dolly light car was powered by a 4-cylinder water-cooled engine, with separate gearbox and shaft drive. This was conventional enough, but the design was unusual in that the engine and propeller shaft slanted towards the rear, so that there was no need for a universal joint on the shaft, and an underslung worm gear could be used on the rear axle. It probably never passed the prototype stage.
NG

DOLO (F) 1947–1948

Éts Brun, Dolo, Galtier & Cie, Pierrefitte, Seine.

Few cars are more curiously styled than the Dolo, which looked like a melted steam train and was topped with the novelty of a Plexiglas dome. In prototype JB10 form as displayed at the 1947 Paris Salon, it was a 2-seater with a 3CV horizontally-opposed 571cc 4-cylinder engine developing 23bhp, driving the front wheels; 4-wheel independent suspension was also standard. In addition Dolo envisaged a 4/5-seater JB20 with a 6CV 8-cylinder engine of 1142cc capacity and 43bhp output (two 4-cylinder engines coupled together), but this project was scuppered as the company became embroiled in a financial scandal that ended in the courts.

CR

DOLORES (F) 1906

Dolores et Compagnie, Paris.

Little is known about Dolores et Compagnie except for an entry in *l'Annuaire Général de l'Automobile*, listing them as makers of 10, 16, 24 and 50hp cars. A reference to them as The Dolores Co. hints at an English or American connection.

NG

DOLPHIN (i) (GB) 1906–1909

The Two-Stroke Engine Co. Ltd, Shoreham, Sussex.

This company was formed by Ralph Ricardo to build marine engines, mainly for the local fishing fleet, but also for racing boats, yachts and barges. The engines were designed by his cousin Harry Ricardo (1885–1974), who favoured 2-strokes. At first he proposed a 15hp 2-cylinder unit, but this would have been seriously underpowered for the heavy tourer coachwork which a friend had ordered. Although he used a 2-cylinder car as a works hack, Ricardo designed a 25.8hp 4-cylinder engine for the cars which were given the name Dolphin, as it was widely used in the Shoreham area. The engines and gearboxes were built by LLOYD & PLAISTER of Wood Green, North London, and the chassis supplied by THORNYCROFT, with which company the Sassoons, backers of the Ricardos, had a family connection. Dolphins were exhibited at the 1908 and 1909 Olympia Shows, but very few were made. The best estimate is 12 of the 4-cylinder cars, plus the 15hp 2-cylinder prototype. Difficulties with suppliers and lack of family financial support brought about the end of the company in October 1909. Rights to the 2-cylinder engine, in smaller form, were bought by Lloyd & Plaister and used in their VOX cyclecar, of which about 50 were made.

NG

Further Reading

Dolphin Motors of Shoreham, M. Worthington-Williams, Sussex Industrial History, 1971.

DOLPHIN (ii) (US) c.1985

Dolphin Vehicles, Mountain View, California.

This high-performance 3-wheel coupé used a monocoque chassis with a motorcycle or electric engine. Plan sets for building the car were sold by designer Dann Parks.

HP

DOLPHIN (iii) (US) 1990–c.1993

Dolphin Vehicles, California.

Following the lead of several American companies, the Dolphin Vortex was designed to be built from a set of plans, meaning that you had to fabricate the metal subframes, create a triangulated plywood chassis and cover it all with a spruce-and-fibreglass body. Under the front end sat Triumph Spitfire double wishbones with coil/spring dampers, disc brakes and an anti-roll bar. Power could come from any one of a number of motorbikes, the prototype having a 4-cylinder Kawasaki 750cc unit. Drive to the single rear wheel was by Harley-Davidson toothed belt. Alternatively, you could install an array of eight 12 volt batteries and a 10hp electric motor. In this form, the compact motor drove the rear belt by direct belt drive. A range of 40–80 miles was quoted on a single charge, while a top speed of 60mph could be reached.

CR

1908 Dolphin (i) 40hp tourer.
NATIONAL MOTOR MUSEUM

DOLSON (US) 1904–1907

1904–1906 J.L. Dolson & Sons, Charlotte, Michigan.

1906–1907 Dolson Automobile Co., Charlotte, Michigan.

The first Dolson, the Model A, had a 15hp flat-twin engine, chain drive and a 5-seater tonneau body. With longer wheelbase and more powerful engine of 22/24hp, it was continued into 1906, but meanwhile more substantial 4-cylinder cars had appeared in the shape of the 28/32hp Model E (1905-06) and the 45/50hp Model F (1906-07). The F was made as a tourer and roadster, the latter called the Cannonball Roadster and capable of 75mph (120km/h). Described as of 55/60hp in 1907, they were large and substantial cars priced at $3250. Dolson advertising compared them with '. . . the parson's one-hoss shay, That ran a hundred years to a day'.

Certainly half of the approximately 700 Dolsons made were still on the road three years after production ceased, which was a creditable figure for the time.

NG

DOME (J) 1975 to date

Dome Co. Ltd, Higashioka.

This Japanese racing team started as early as 1965 racing a modified Honda S600, and it produced numerous racing cars and was connected with Tom's (a Toyota racing enterprise). Its first road car project was the dramatic Dome-0 of 1978, designed by four young Japanese: Minoru and Shoichi Hayashi, Akihiro Irimagi and Kenji Minura. It featured a steel monocoque chassis constructed by Hayashi Racing of Suzuka, all-independent suspension by coils and wishbones, a rear-mounted 2.8-litre Datsun 6-cylinder engine with a 5-speed ZF transaxle (later turbocharged, and Ford 3.0-litre V6 power was also tried). The 2-door coupé measured only 38½in high and the interior boasted computerised instruments. The car appeared at numerous motor shows, the intention being to launch a production run. However the company went on to concentrate on racing projects but in 1989 Dome engineered the JIOTTO prototype and in 1993 it showed the Pivot, a monobox passenger car prototype. 'Dome' is Japanese for 'children's dream'.

CR

DOMINION (CDN) 1910

Dominion Motors Ltd, Walkerville, Ontario.

This company planned to build a car on the lines of the American REGAL, to be called the Royal Windsor. When it appeared in the summer of 1910, its name had been changed to Dominion. It was a very conventional machine with 35hp 4-cylinder engine and tourer body, selling for CDN$1850. Few were made, and the promised 1911 models never appeared.

NG

DOMINO (i) (GB) 1986 to date

Domino Car Co., Southampton, Hampshire.

Richard Oakes designed the Domino Pimlico, which was made by a fibreglass boat and car body specialist. This was a fibreglass monocoque reinterpretation of the Mini, with ribbed contrasting lower bodywork, fatter wheel arches, no bumpers or doors and a targa roof. Other body styles followed: the Premier (with solid half-doors and sidescreens), the fully enclosed HT (or Hard Top), and the Pup pickup. At various times Domino also made and marketed the VINCENT Hurricane and WIZARD kit cars.

CR

1990 Donkervoort D10 sports car.
JOOP DONKERVOORT

1999 Donkervoort D8 sports car.
DON VAN DER VAART

DOMINO (ii) (ZA) 1993–1996
Datum Components, Cape Town.
The Domino 7 kit was developed as a Lotus 7 look-alike by Peter Colebank, whose main business was trailers and kit car components. Only three kits were sold.
CR

DOMINO (iii) (US) c.1995 to date
Domino Cars USA, Milford, Connecticut.
This company primarily imported kits from other countries, including a full range of fibreglass mini Cooper bodies in convertible and pick-up form. They also sold the Ninja-Mini-Cooper, which was a chopped Mini body on a custom space frame with motorcycle or Escort GT engines. They also briefly imported the Finale kit, which was later sold by PISA. Their most unusual kit was the Eurosport TR40, which transformed a Triumph TR-7 or TR-8 convertible into a pseudo-Ferrari F40-type car. The Eurosport X1/9 was a fat mudguard and scoops kit for the Fiat X1/9.
HP

DOMMARTIN (F) 1947–1950
Compagnie de Moteurs Dommartin, Dommartin, Somme.
Racing driver Giraud-Cabantous presented a redesigned version of the prewar S.E.F.A.C. 3.6-litre racer at Montlhéry in 1947 but a lack of finance prevented it ever racing. Instead, Dommartin turned to a new design of S.E.F.A.C. designer Emile Petit's – a curious open all-terrain vehicle. Under its open 4-seater forward-control bodywork lay an 800cc flat-twin air-cooled engine in the tail and a 5-speed gearbox.
CR

DOMUS (US) c.1980
Tharp Industries, Kansas City, Missouri.
This company made kits to convert Volkswagens into mini-trucks. The Flatback transformed the Beetle into a small flatbed truck. The Flatback II did the same thing to a VW Rabbit. The limited-edition Flatback III added a long pick-up-style tail and a relocated rear axle to a Rabbit for hauling motorcycles and other relatively lightweight objects.
HP

DONGFANGHONG (i) (CHI) 1960–1969
1960–1966 Beijing Auto Works, Beijing Municipality.
1966–1969 Beijing Dongfanghong Auto Works, Beijing Municipality.
After the appearance of the JINGGANGSHAN rear-engine car in 1958, the Dongfanghong BJ 760 was Beijing Auto Works' next try to mass produce a motorcar in China. Dongfanghong means 'The East is Red', a very popular theme in China at that time. The basic 4-door model was a clear Volga M21 twin, with only minor design differences such as flat sides missing the Volga mudguard imitations in the rear door. Even the engine was a Volga clone, with the same description as its Russian example – 2445cc 4-cylinder. Later these engines were used in China's work horse, the Beijing BJ 212 4 × 4 cross country car. Only 238 units were made. During the Great Cultural Revolution, a squared-off sedan type with a large Mao badge on the grill under the name Dongfanghong was developed. Probably only one was made. In the same year an estate car prototype of the same design was shown.
EVIS

DONGFANGHONG (ii) (CHI) 1991–1994
First Tractor Works Auto Sub-Works, Luoyang City, Henan Province.
In the early 1950s China's main tractor factory was built with strong Russian help. Caterpillar tractors of the Dongfanghong ('The East is Red') brand have been made since then. In 1965 a small heavy truck sub-factory started production, making Berliet-based military trucks.
In 1991 two motors cars were introduced: a 797cc 5-seat saloon and estate car, the Donghanghong LT 6390 was built on the Haerbin WJ 1010 chassis. The estate car was known as the Dongfanghong LT 5010JF. The other car, a bigger medium-sized saloon, was called the YITUO.
EVIS

DONGFENG (i) (CHI) 1958
First Auto Works, Changchun City, Jilin Province.
The Dongfeng ('East Wind', from the contemporary Chinese saying 'The East Wind prevails over the West Wind') CA 71 saloon is generally regarded as China's first self-made motor car. The First Auto Works was built during 1953–56 in a former Japanese military factory in Changchun, Manchuria. The main product, the Jiefang ('Liberation') truck, a ZIS copy, was built for 30 years from 1956. During the Great Leap Forward, the Dongfeng was developed. There is one photo existing of an earlier prototype with the grill having full-width horizontal strakes from 1957. The definitive version of the CA 71 was shown to Chairman Mao on 21 May 1958. There must have been a small batch of five cars, all equipped with a 1930cc square 4-cylinder 70bhp engine; wheelbase was 106in (2690mm). On the bonnet there was a very impressive Chinese dragon. The car preceded the HONGQI range. One of the Dongfeng cars remained and is still in the possession of the First Auto Works.
EVIS

DONGFENG (ii) (CHI) 1996 to date
Dongfeng Motors Corp., Shiyan City, Hubei Province.
In the second half of the 1990s, the Second Auto Works, renamed the Dongfeng Motors Corp., experimented with a small motor car called the Dongfeng EQ 7100. It was nicknamed Xiao Wangze (Little Prince). The car was a 4-door 5-seat hatchback, using the XIALI 1-litre 3-cylinder engine. For test reasons a pre-series of 77 units was used as taxicabs in Shiyan. At the same time, the Dongfeng name and logo was also used by a subsidiary of Dongfeng Motors, the Shenlong Auto Refit Works in Wuhan. The FUKANG cab and chassis (Citroën ZX) was the base of a pick-up, closed van, and an estate car called the Dongfeng EQ 714OU, which was quite similar to the contemporary Citroën C15.
EVIS

DONKERVOORT (NL) 1978 to date

1978–1985 Joop Donkervoort, Tienhoven, Utrecht.

1985 to date Donkervoort Automobielen BV, Nieuw Loosdrecht.

Joop Donkervoort was originally Caterham's Dutch agent but in 1978 he began producing his own Lotus Seven inspired car. Early cars had Ford 1600cc crossflow or RS2000 engines and live rear axles. There was a name change from Super Seven to Super 8 (or S8) from 1985 when the styling was retouched and a Ford 2-litre engine was adopted; later examples, called the S8A, switched to independent rear suspension. The S8AT gained turbocharging and a power output of 170bhp. The chassis in all cases was an asymmetrical steel space frame. A limited edition stripped-out D10 model from 1988 had cycle wings, a tiny wind deflector and half doors, and was powered by a 190bhp bored-out 2.2-litre turbocharged Ford engine allowing 0–60mph (0-97km/h) in 4.5 seconds. Next came the D8, an update of the S8 with Ford Zetec 1.8-litre power. A Cosworth-powered model was also listed from 1993, with 220bhp on tap. A dramatic successor to the D8 Cosworth in 1998 was the D20. Central to this car was a 2.8-litre 30V Audi V6 engine modified to produce 200bhp, allied to a new transaxle linked via an aluminium torque tube. Its body was much longer and wider, and sat on a longer wheelbase. A new factory was built in Lelystad to accommodate anticipated extra demand.

CR

DONNET-ZEDEL; DONNET (F) 1924–1936

1924–1928 SA des Automobiles Donnet-Zedel, Pontarlier, Doubs; Gennevillers, Seine; Nanterre, Seine.

1928–1934 SA des Automobiles Donnet, Gennevillers, Seine; Nanterre, Seine.

1935–1936, Donnet-Contin, Nanterre, Seine.

Donnet-Zedel was formed when wealthy industrialist Jerome Donnet, who had made a fortune in aircraft production during World War I, bought Automobiles ZEDEL of Pontarlier. The big 3168cc Zedel was dropped, but the smaller 2120cc CI-6 was continued under the Donnet-Zedel name, although it was an old design, dating back to 1912. Front-wheel brakes were optional. Jerome Donnet reduced the large number of body styles available on the CI-6, although it was still available with three open styles, two saloons and a landaulet taxi. For 1925 there was an additional sports model, a 4-seater torpedo with vee-windscreen, engine reduced to 1947cc and inlet-over-exhaust valve head designed by Ernest Henry of Peugeot and Ballot fame. He also designed a modified head for the 2120cc engine. The CI-6 was dropped at the end of 1928, but the engines continued to be used in commercial vehicles. Total production was about 15,000 cars, including those made under the Zedel name in 1922 and 1923.

The first new design under the Donnet-Zedel name was also Henry's work. Launched in 1925, the Type G (later G1) was a light car with a 1098cc side-valve engine and 4-speed gearbox. Unlike the CI-6 it had lhd and carried rather utilitarian bodies, 2-door saloons and cabriolets or 4-door tourers. Though completely lacking in glamour it was a worthy competitor for the smaller Citroëns, Renaults, and Peugeots, and helped Donnet to become France's fourth largest car maker in 1927–28. Exact production figures are not known, but Donnet certainly beat Mathis' output of 70 cars a day. In 1926 Jerome Donnet gained useful publicity by sending a stock Type G torpedo on a 10,000km trip from Paris to Constantinople and back, with no spare parts back-up or accompanying vehicle. There were also several sports versions of the Type G with 16-valve head designed by Étienne Lepicard, a Donnet-Zedel concessionaire from Arras who later became chief engineer for Derby.

The Type G was made in a former Donnet aircraft factory at Gennevilliers and this grew to be more important than the former Zedel plant at Pontarlier. This was sold in 1928, and with it disappeared the name Donnet-Zedel. Donnet also bought the Vinot et Déguingand factory at Nanterre. This factory was not large but it was surrounded by land which could be used for expansion later on.

Donnet's first six appeared for 1927; a 2540cc designed by Sainturat, and there were also smaller sixes of 1.3 and 1.8 litres. These were made into the 1930s, along with a 1304cc 7CV which was an enlarged version of Henry's Type G. More unorthodox designs were tried in the early 1930s, including an 11CV with front-wheel drive and ifs. This remained a prototype, but the little 4CV 2-stroke which had begun life as a Déguingand was made in small numbers, perhaps as many as 100, from 1931 to 1932. In Donnet guise, it was known as the

1927 Donnet G2 saloon.
NATIONAL MOTOR MUSEUM

1931 Donnet 11CV front-drive cabriolet.
NICK BALDWIN

Type 149 or Donnette. The conventional Donnets, which were made in dwindling numbers after 1930, received names in 1932. The 7CV became the Donnarex and a larger version (1474cc) of 1933–34 the Donnastar, the 1978cc four the Donnaquatre, while the 1996cc six was the Donnasix, and the 2538cc six the Donnamagna. The Donnastar was the only model listed for the 1934–35 season, but production ended in December 1934. The factory was sold to Henri-Théodore Pigozzi, who began production in 1935 of licence-built Fiats under the name SIMCA. Twelve Donnastars remained unsold; together with components and tools. They were bought by the electrical firm Contin-Souza who sold them off during 1935. They also made a handful of an improved model which they called the D35. These had fresh styling not unlike a contemporary Renault, pump-cooling in place of thermosyphon and improved ifs. They were listed into 1936.

NG

Further Reading

'Les Donnets de Nanterre', Eric Lepicard, *l'Album du Fanatique*, October 1976 – February 1977.

'Les Dernieres Donnets', Eric Lepicard, *La Vie de l'Auto*, 15 May 1983.

DONOSTI (E) 1928

Garage Internacional, San Sebastian.

Agent for the American MOON and with a repair workshop specialising in engines, the owner of Garage Internacional designed a special to participate in the 1923 Lasarte circuit race. However, the only car finished was the 1928 Donosti sportscar, which used a 3-litre 6-cylinder dohc-engine with four valves per cylinder. The body, with two banquets was made from aluminium, and the car participated as pace car in the Grand Prix of San Sebastian in 1928, and is still in existence.

VCM

1923 Dorris Model 6-80 tourer.
NATIONAL MOTOR MUSEUM

DORA (I) 1905–1906
Stà Industriale Dora, Genoa; Turin.
This company planned a range of electric passenger and commercial vehicles, but only a few prototypes were made, after which they turned to general electric engineering.
NG

DORAN (US) c.1994 to date
Doran Motor Company, Sparks, Nevada.
The Doran was a 3-wheeled electric vehicle that was built from a set of plans sold by Rick Doran. It was an attractive shape using a motorcycle-type power package with a single wheel at the back. The body was formed from fibreglass-over-foamcore construction and it was powered by a Prestolite 28hp motor with 9 batteries.
HP

DORAY (US) 1950
Doray Inc., Miami Springs, Florida.
This sports car was based on Willys Jeepster running gear. The body was steel and Jeepster windshield and doors were retained. A fibreglass bonnet gave the front a Cord-like appearance. A 6-cylinder Willys engine was used.
HP

DORCHESTER (US) 1906
Hub Motorcar Exchange, Dorchester, Massachusetts.
This company took over the factory of the Crest Manufacturing Co., which had recently discontinued the CRESTMOBILE, and began to make a very similar design under the Dorchester name. Instead of continuing where Crest had left off, they reverted to the earlier Crestmobile design, with the single-cylinder engine fully exposed at the front of the car, ahead of the front axle. Even at $400, the Dorchester was not an attractive proposition, and few were sold. The following year the company announced a slightly more sophisticated car called the HUB.
NG

DORÉ (F) c.1900
Sté G. Doré, Levallois-Perret, Seine.
This car used an electric *avant-train* unit, most of the bodies being taxicabs. Doré also made a petrol engine.
NG

DOREY (F) 1898–1913
W.H. Dorey, Paris.
Dorey was a French-Canadian car dealer and accessory merchant who advertised cars intermittently over quite a long period. At the Salon du Cycle in December 1898 he advertised a 2-seater voiturette with 653cc single-cylinder engine, patent carburettor and new gear change system in which 'a simple movement of the lever changed speeds without any shock or grinding of gears'. He called this a used car, in which case it may have been made by someone else, although he did advertise a catalogue of 2- and 4-seater cars. He also offered a catalogue of engines and components to 'Messieurs les constructeurs', which seems to have been his main business.

In 1906 Dorey was advertising voiturettes powered by single-cylinder De Dion-Bouton engines, as well as larger cars with 4-cylinder V.R. and Mutel engines. These lasted only into 1907, and the next Dorey car was a cyclecar with 2-cylinder air-cooled engine, advertised during 1912–13.
NG

DORIOT-FLANDRIN see D.F.P.

DORMANDY (US) 1903–1905
United Shirt & Collar Co., Troy, New York.
The Dormandy was probably the only automobile built in a shirt factory. The first of its four cars, a closed limousine type featuring a design well ahead of its time, was built for James Knox Polk Pine, president of the United Shirt & Collar Co., of Troy, New York, by Gary Dormandy, an employee who had an interest in automobiles and capability for such an undertaking. So delighted was Mr Pine with his car that he ordered two open touring models to be constructed for his two sons. Work on the open cars was accomplished in the nearby Troy Carriage Works and these proved so successful that Dormandy built one for himself, using certain Frayer-Miller components in the last one. When the first HARVARD cars were under construction in Troy ten years afterward, Dormandy was invited to affiliate with the builder, the Pioneer Motor Car Co., but declined.
KM

DORNER (D) 1927
Dorner Ölmotoren AG, Hanover.
Although not produced in series Dorner cars were noteworthy for their pioneering use of heavy oil engines. Designed by Hermann Dorner, they had 3/10PS V-twin engines. Unable to find financial support for his designs, Dorner took them to America where they were taken up by IHC (International Harvester Co.), their first diesel trucks being made in 1933.
HON

DORNIER DELTA see ZÜNDAPP

DORRIS (US) 1905–1925
1905–1906 St Louis Motor Carriage Co., St Louis, Missouri.
1906–1925 Dorris Motor Car Co., St Louis, Missouri.
George P. Dorris had already built two horseless carriages in his native city of Nashville, Tennessee in 1895 and 1897 respectively when, in 1905, he joined John L. French in founding the St Louis Motor Carriage Co., and commenced the production of a 4-cylinder car. A year later, his partner decided to move operations to Peoria, Illinois and Dorris reorganised the St Louis operation under his own name, the first cars using an in-house 30hp 4-cylinder ohv engine, launched at the 1906 New York City Automobile Show. From the outset of the company's existence, Dorris cars were built to meticulous standards, emphasising mechanical excellence, outstanding performance, conservative coachwork, and advanced design. The four was replaced with a 6-cylinder engine – which, with consistent updating, would power Dorris cars throughout their existence, eventually settling specifications of a 132in (3350mm) wheelbase and an engine affording 80bhp at 2600rpm. Maintaining a conservative image, the company slogan, 'Built up to a standard; not down to a price', exemplified the car perfectly in the marketplace of the time. Like the Dorris itself, the annual production was conservative as well with production seldom exceeding 250 units prior to 1920, these augmented by a line of Dorris commercial vehicles which had been produced since 1911 in sizes from 3/4 to 3 1/2 ton. Prices for Dorris cars were raised in 1920 from $4350 for the 7-seater touring car to $5800 for the limousine, production peaking that year with nearly 400 cars completed. Production, however, dropped by 65 per cent in 1921 due to the existing recession and thereafter would never exceed 116 units. A Dorris plan to manufacture the recently introduced Astra light car by Arrow Motors in St Louis in 1920 was abandoned before it got underway. By 1921, in addition to both its automobile and truck lines, Dorris built some large sedans and limousines on special order using its 3/4-ton truck chassis, notably a limousine with an $8000 custom-built body by the Walter M. Murphy Co. of Pasadena, California for oil magnate Henry R. Dabney which was completed in early 1923.

Dorris ended automobile production in 1924, its last cars being marketed as 1925 models.

KM

Further Reading
'When Dorris had his day: The Life and Cars of George P. Dorris', Curt McConnell, *Automobile Quarterly*, Vol. 37, No. 1.

DORT (US) 1915–1924
Dort Motorcar Co., Flint, Michigan.
Joshua Dallas Dort (1861–1925) was a personal friend and sometime partner of William Crapo Durant. They had formed the Flint Road Cart Co. in 1886, which later became the Durant-Dort Carriage Co., one of the largest makers of horse-drawn vehicles in the United States. Durant became involved with cars much earlier than Dort, starting with BUICK in 1904 and going on to found General Motors, while Dort stayed with carriages and buggies until 1915 when he launched the Dort Four. His chief engineer was Étienne Planche, designer of the ROEBLING-PLANCHE (ancestor of the MERCER), and later an associate of Louis Chevrolet. The Dort Four was a conventional well-built car powered by a 2.7-litre 4-cylinder Lycoming engine and 3-speed gearbox. The clutch and footbrake were combined in the same pedal, with the second pedal being an emergency brake, a curiosity which lasted until 1920. In 1915 and 1916 the only body style was a 3-door 5-seater tourer, which sold for $650; less expensive than the Dodge, which was a similar-sized car. For 1917 the tourer gained a fourth door, and there were also centre-door sedan and clover-leaf roadster models. The 3146cc Lycoming Model K engine was adopted on 1918 Dorts, and in 1920 conventional pedals and a hand-brake lever were adopted. That was Dort's most successful year, with 30,018 cars sold.

A Rolls-Royce-type radiator and longer wheelbases were introduced in 1921. Prices rose to $1215 for a tourer and as high as $1995 for a sedan and although they were dropped somewhat the following year, Dort was losing its way, being above the Chevrolet/Dodge price bracket, yet not perceived as having the quality of a Buick. For 1923, a 3205cc Falls 6-cylinder engine was added to the range, and this was the only engine for 1924. By now sales had fallen from the heady heights of 1920, to 5592 in 1923 and 2493 in 1924. J. Dallas Dort decided to cut his losses at the end of the year, and there were no 1925 models. The Canadian version, the GRAY-DORT, lasted one year longer. Total US production, over 10 years, had been just over 120,000.

NG

DOUGILL (GB) 1896–1899
A.W. Dougill & Co. Ltd, Leeds, Yorkshire.
This company made several experimental cars from 1896 to 1898. These featured rear-mounted horizontal engines with belt drive to a countershaft and chain final drive. In 1899 several Lawson Motor Wheels were assembled at Dougill's factory. Designed by Harry Lawson, these were self-contained power units, with wheel, petrol tank and brake, which could be used to motorise any horse-drawn vehicle. In fact, they were insufficiently powerful to drive more than a light 2-seater, and some complete 3-wheeled cars were made by Dougill. From 1904 to 1907 Dougill made several friction-driven FRICK cars and commercial vehicles.

NG

DOUGLAS (i) (GB) 1913–1922
Douglas Bros Ltd, Kingswood, Bristol.
Founded as general engineers in 1882, the Douglas firm first became involved in the motor business through supplying engine castings to Joseph Barter for his 'Fee' (later 'Fairy') motorcycles. When his own firm failed he moved to Douglas and was responsible for their subsequent range of flat-twin engines, which were used not only in Douglas motorcycles but in a variety of other uses at different times. Backed by greater resources than most cyclecar manufacturers, the 1913 design was quite luxurious and well-equipped, featuring shaft drive and an air-cooled engine of 'square' bore and stroke dimensions (88 × 88mm), priced at £200. Government contracts during World War I consolidated the company's prosperity and the postwar offering was increased in size, weight and price, the engine capacity being 1223 (92 × 92mm) and the price rising from £400 in 1920 to £500 in 1921 and 1922. At this price it was no longer viable and production ceased thereafter, the firm continuing with their increasingly successful motorcycles

1921 Dort Four coupé.
JOHN A. CONDE

c.1904 Dougill-built Frick 2-cylinder tonneau.
NATIONAL MOTOR MUSEUM

1914 Douglas (i) 10hp 2-seater.
NICK BALDWIN

1921 Douglas (i) 10.5hp 2-seater.
NATIONAL MOTOR MUSEUM

as their staple product. There are no original survivors but a replica assembled from parts in the 1940s continues to represent the breed.

DF

DOUGLAS (ii) (US) 1919–1920

Douglas Motors Corp., Omaha, Nebraska.

The Douglas was the continuation of the former Drummond which had previously produced cars under the banner of the Drummond Motor Co. before its acquisition by Douglas. With minor changes in specifications and price, the car retained its Herschell-Spillman V8 engine and limited its offerings to open body types. Later in 1919 the decision was made by Douglas to limit its production to trucks and it continued to build a line of half ton to 3½ton commercial vehicles until 1935. Although some listings carry the Douglas name into 1920, such cars would have been leftover 1919 models, presumably sold as 1920 cars.

KM

DOUGLAS (iii) (CY/GB) 1990 to date

Douglas Car Co., Barking, Essex.

The origins of this MG TF replica lay in Cyprus, but it was also made in Britain. Two kit-form versions were available: one based on the Triumph Herald/Vitesse/Spitfire, and another using a specially-designed chassis based on Ford Escort Mk I/II parts, though the front suspension was Cortina and a special multi-link rear end was supplied. Any Ford cross-flow engine was suitable. The 20-piece fibreglass body joined to a plywood floor.

CR

DOVAL (US) c.1979

Doval Coach Ltd, East Haven, Connecticut.

The Doval Shadow was a neoclassic car featuring a boat-tailed roadster body combined with an upright grill and abbreviated front mudguards. It was based on a Ford chassis with 5700cc Ford V8 engines. The body was aluminium and it was sold in fully assembled form.

HP

DOVE see BARCHETTA

DOW (US) 1905–c.1906

A.M. Dow, Braintree, Massachusetts.

Dow was a manufacturer of electrical components who built a car for his personal use. It had a 4-cylinder Trebert engine, A.O. Smith frame and body by Henry Emerson. Several friends asked him for replicas, and at least eight Dow cars were registered in Massachusetts in 1907. Whether any more were sold outside the state is not known.

NG

DOWAGIAC see LINDSLEY

DOW ELECTRIC (US) 1960

Dow Testing Laboratory, Detroit, Michigan.

As its name suggested, this was an electric microcar, only 74in (1878mm) long. The 2-seater car was powered by two 0.3hp motors, fed by three 12V and four 24V batteries. That gave a top speed of 20mph (32km/h) and a range of 30 miles (48km). No financial backing was secured, however.

CR

DOWEN (F) c.1906

Barret Frères, Lyons.

The only evidence of this car is an advertisement showing a conventional front-engined side-entrance tourer. The Établissements Dowen were said to be makers of cars, motorcycles and bicycles; Barret Frères may have been agents rather than manufacturers.

NG

DOWNING; DOWNING-DETROIT (US) 1913–1915

Downing Cyclecar Co., Detroit, Michigan.
Downing Motorcar Co., Cleveland, Ohio.

The Downing was made in both tandem and side by side seating versions, and also as a 4-seater and was more of a light car than a cyclecar, having an 18hp 4-cylinder engine, conventional selective gearbox and shaft drive. A 10hp 2-cylinder engine was also offered. In the summer of 1913, the firm announced that they would be manufacturing in Cleveland as well. This operation was called the Downing Motorcar Co., and the Detroit-built cars were renamed Downing-Detroit. The Cleveland-built cars were offered with similar engines but were on a shorter wheelbase and sold at a lower price.

NG

DOWNSHIRE see CHAMBERS

D.P.L. (GB) 1907–1910

Dawfield, Philips Ltd, West Ealing, Middlesex.

The D.P.L. had a 12/15hp flat-twin engine located under the floorboards halfway between front and rear axles, with 2-speed epicyclic transmission and final drive by chain. It was made mostly as a taxicab, although it was a convenient-sized small car for town use, and doubtless some were sold to private customers. Some taxicabs were exported to Australia. In 1908 the company announced the Baby Dawfield, a conventional light car with 9hp 2-cylinder engine and shaft drive.

NG

D&R (US) c.1992 to date

D&R Replicars, Kintnersville, Pennsylvania.

Well-built Lamborghini replicas were the stock and trade of this kit car company. They made replicas of the Countach and Diablo models scaled to fit standard length or stretched Pontiac Fiero running gear.

HP

D-RAD-RIKSCHA (A) 1951

This very short-lived Austrian 3-wheeled microcar was essentially a motorbike fitted with two rear wheels and basic open bodywork. It had a 12bhp 496cc engine and could seat three people.

CR

DRAGON (i) (US) 1906–1908

1906–1907 Dragon Automobile Co., Detroit, Michigan;
Philadelphia, Pennsylvania.
1907–1908 Dragon Motor Co., Philadelphia, Pennsylvania.

The Dragon was a conventional car powered by a 24/26hp 4-cylinder Herschell-Spillman engine, with 3-speed gearbox and shaft drive. Touring and runabout styles were offered, and for 1908 there was a rakish roadster with a larger engine of 35hp. However Dragon was practically out of business by this time. They moved from Detroit to Philadelphia, where they used part of the factory of J.G. Brill, famous makers of tramcars. Reorganisation as the Dragon Motor Co., which planned to build taxicabs did not help, as the new company inherited the large debts of the old. When they, too, went into receivership in March 1908, 70 incomplete Dragon chassis remained.

NG

DRAGON (ii) (F) 1913

P. Milhuet, Sancerre, Cher.

Coming from a town better known for wine than for cars, the Dragon was made in two models of light car, with a 6hp single-cylinder engine and a 10hp 4-cylinder engine.

NG

DRAGON (iii) (US) 1920–1921

Dragon Motors Corp., Chicago, Illinois.

The Dragon is a good example of high-geared stock-swindling which actually managed to produce some cars until the law put an end to the corporation. The Dragon was theoretically formed to build a line of sporting cars as well as a line of taxicabs. The taxicabs never materialised, although some 13 cars were completed and sold to, presumably, happy buyers. The Dragon, almost identical to the contemporary REVERE in appearance, was powered by a 4-cylinder engine developing 58bhp at 2400rpm. The car had a 120in (3045mm) wheelbase and sported wire wheels. A 4-seater touring car was priced at $3200, other styles including a roadster called a Pup, and a victoria. The enterprise was short-lived, functioning for a year before it was closed down.

KM

DRAGONFLY (i) (GB) 1981–1986

1981–1984 Dragonfly Cars, Hook, Hampshire.
1984–1986 Dragonfly Cars, Ash Vale, Hampshire.
The Dragonfly was a surprisingly satisfying way of turning an MG Midget into a 1930s-style roadster. The central body was left untouched, but the rear end was removed and replaced with a rounded fibreglass moulding, the front part of the chassis was lengthened by over ten inches, and a new tapering bonnet, flowing wings, vestigial running boards and a new radiator shell were fitted (all in fibreglass).

CR

DRAGONFLY (ii) (GB) 1994–1995

Dragonfly Cars, Toton, Nottinghamshire.
This Morgan-style trike was built as a one-off but was scheduled to be made as a kit car. It was unique among 3-wheelers in recreating almost exactly the form of the F-Type Morgan. A Z-section steel ladder frame chassis supported sliding pillar front suspension – an exact copy of the original Morgan system – and further enhanced the 1930s feel by borrowing its wheels from the Morris 8. A Hillman Imp steering rack was employed and, at the back end, the rear wheel was suspended on a Honda CX500 swinging arm. The motive power came from a Reliant Robin 848cc engine and gearbox, connected via the Honda CX shaft drive to power the rear wheel. The very basic bodywork was constructed by skinning a 1/2in plywood frame with steel.

CR

DRAKE (US) 1921–1922

Drake Motor & Tire Manufacturing Co., Knoxville, Tennessee.
The Drake Motor & Tire Manufacturing Co. was formed in 1921 to manufacture a line of automobiles, trucks, tractors and tyres. W.F. Drake, its president, initially planned to equip the cars and trucks with Drake tyres which, unfortunately, did not happen, as the planned construction of the tyre facility never got off the ground, due to the lack of finance. The cars, however, did, with attractive lines, a distinctive radiator and powered by a Herschell-Spillman Model 11000 6-cylinder engine. A tight budget restricted the Drake's promotion to factory literature which featured its slogan, 'Built like the rock of Gibraltar'. At least one truck and a single tractor appeared as prototypes but ended there. The Drake Six was available as a 5-seater touring car with a choice of artillery wood or disc wheels, and probably ten to fifteen cars were completed before the company failed, due largely to the recession of that time. One especially built 7-seater touring car was built for a silent-screen actress, her picture being included in factory literature. Ironically, the Drake Six and the lone truck were all equipped with Firestone tyres, a far cry from those which Drake had intended to produce alongside the cars.

KM

D.R.B. (AUS) 1981 to date

D.R.B. Enterprises, Southport, Queensland.
Denis Bedford built one-off cars before his Sabre coupé was offered as a fibreglass body kit for the Volkswagen platform in 1973. It was sold as a complete car from 1981 and was joined by a convertible in 1983. The Magnum and Sabre Mk 2 followed but those programmes were sold. The 1986 Taipan, a mid-engined coupé with a Nissan 1500cc power pack, was offered as a complete car in 1986. Cobra and GT40 replicas are current.

MG

DREAM MACHINE (US) c.1996

Dream Machine Productions, Gainesville, Florida.
This kit car company built a replica of the Dodge Viper that fitted on a Corvette chassis. Coupé and convertible versions were offered in kit and assembled form.

HP

DREXEL (US) 1916–1917

Drexel Motorcar Corp., Chicago, Illinois.
The Drexel succeeded the FARMACK, when Albert J. Farmer needed extra cash to bring out a new version of his Farmack car. This was powered by a 4-cylinder

1981 Dragonfly (i) sports car.
NICK GEORGANO

single-ohc Farmer engine also used in the first Drexel, the Model 5-40. Offered only as a 5-seater tourer at $985, this was something of a bargain for such an advanced design. Even more advanced was Farmer's engine offered in the Model 7-60, a twin-ohc four with 16-valves which developed 63bhp at 3600rpm, a specification which would not have been out of place in the 1980s. The makers were not exaggerating when they billed it as the most important engineering achievement of the year. How reliable it was is not known since, unfortunately, Farmer was not such a good businessman as he was an engineer. The company was bankrupt by the summer of 1917, and a projected car using a Ferro V8 engine was never built.

NG

DRIGGS (US) 1921–1923

Driggs Ordnance & Manufacturing Co., New Haven, Connecticut.
With its offices in New York City, the Driggs was an apt example of a carefully engineered smaller car to be sold at an attractive price but which just did not catch on in its appeal to an anticipated clientele. Widely advertised in the contemporary automotive press as being 'Built With the Precision of Ordnance', the Driggs, with a 4-cylinder L-head engine of its own design and a wheelbase of 104ins (2640mm), was available in both open and closed models with its touring car priced at $1275. Demand for the Driggs fell short of its predicted appeal and, overall, production probably did not exceed 150 completed units – most of them touring cars – when it was decided to withdraw the Driggs from the pleasure car field and restrict further operations toward the taxicab market. This Driggs did and remained in business into 1925.

KM

DRIGGS-SEABURY (US) 1915–1916

Driggs-Seabury Ordnance Corp., Sharon, Pennsylvania.
Driggs-Seabury was an armaments maker which built several cars for other firms to sell, and it also made a short-lived cyclecar under its own name. The Driggs-Seabury had a 4-cylinder engine and underslung frame, and was made as a tandem 2-seater with friction transmission and chain drive, and also as a side by side roadster with conventional 2-speed gearbox. Both sold for $395. Late in 1915 they renamed the car the Sharon after its place of manufacture. After the war they made the DRIGGS in another of their factories at New Haven, Connecticut, and also made the RITZ, TWOMBLY (iii) and VULCAN (ii) cars.

NG

DRI-SLEEVE (GB) 1971–1972

Dri-Sleeve Car Company, Warminster, Wiltshire.
Three partners took over the old OPUS premises in 1970 to build a Bugatti Type 35 replica. It was called the Dri-Sleeve Moonraker because a sleeve was supplied to protect the driver's right arm from the elements. The ladder chassis used a Ford rear axle, modified VW Beetle front end and Ford Cortina 1600GT engine (optionally supercharged to deliver 113bhp). The main body and bonnet were in aluminium, while the rear panel and cycle wings were in fibreglass. At £1954 in kit form and far more than that fully built, it was far too expensive and only six were made.

CR

1971 Dri-Sleeve Moonraker sports car.
NATIONAL MOTOR MUSEUM

1907 Drummond(i) 14/16hp 2-seater
NATIONAL MOTOR MUSEUM

1913 D.S.P.L. 15hp sporting tourer.
NATIONAL MOTOR MUSEUM

D.R.K. (GB) 1987–1998

D.R.K. Kits, Ellesmere Port, Cheshire.

Although officially a kit car, D.R.K. trikes were hand-crafted affairs with prices reflecting their quality. The body was built up on a hardwood frame using layers of plywood encased in aluminium. The chassis was designed to accept Renault 4/6 components, but a Renault 5 based version was soon added and became by far the more popular. About half a dozen each year were made.

CR

DRM (US) c.1994

Doug Rippie Motorsports, Plymouth, Minnesota.

Rippie had built a number of successful racing Corvettes and Camaros before he decided to build a street car. The DRM/400 1G was a modified Camaro introduced in 1994. V8 engines of 5700cc and 6300cc were offered, with up to 430hp. Top speed was around 185mph (298km/h). They were sold fully assembled from new Camaros or the components could be purchased individually. DRM also built a modified Corvette called the Black Widow.

HP

DRUMMOND (i) (GB) 1907–1909

North British Manufacturing Co., Dumfries.

D. McKay Drummond of the Dumfries Ironworks built a car for his own use in reliability trials, powered by a 20/24hp 4-cylinder engine. Encouraged by its success, he formed a company to make cars for sale; these were available with 14/16 and 20/24hp 4-cylinder engines, shaft drive and 2- or 4-seater bodies.

NG

DRUMMOND (ii) (US) 1915–1916

Drummond Motor Car Co., Omaha, Nebraska.

The Drummond was a short-lived Nebraska company which built both 4- and 6-cylinder cars before introducing a V8 for 1916, the latter using a Herschell-Spillman engine. Production remained small during Drummond's two-year existence and the company was succeeded by the Douglas Motor Corp. of Omaha which continued the car unchanged except by name – Douglas – into 1919. Production may have reached 300 units before it ended – at least under the Drummond badge.

KM

D.S. see STOEWER

D.S. MALTERRE (F) 1955–1956

Éts Malterre Frères, Paris.

Better known for its 125cc and 175cc motorcycles, D.S. Malterre essayed a 3-wheeled microcar in 1955. It was a fairly attractive 2-seater coupé, styled by M. Berlemont (designer of the Arista), with fibreglass bodywork and Plexiglas headlamp cowls. The tubular steel chassis featured 'Evidgum' suspension. The rear-mounted engine could be either a 6bhp 125cc or an 8bhp 175cc engine, from Ydral or Sotecma driven through a 3-speed gearbox. Like many microcars of the period, its high price forced it into competition with mass-produced small cars and few, if any, cars were sold.

CR

D.S.P.L. (F) c.1910–1914

Comte Pierre d'Hespel, Peranchies, Nord.

Comte d'Hespel was involved in sport before he became a car maker, having driven Corre (La Licorne) cars in the 1903 Paris-Madrid and Circuit des Ardennes races. He entered two cars under his own name in the 1910 Coupe des Voiturettes, but one overturned early in the race and the second withdrew '. . . after going furiously round the course ten times', reported *The Autocar*. D'Hespel does not seem to have formed a company, although he listed two models in 1912, a 12/16 of 2120cc and a 15hp of 2815cc. The latter, with vee-radiator and disc wheels, was shown at the 1913 Paris Salon in an unfinished state, without seats. The name was listed in *l'Annuaire Générale de l'Automobile* for 1921 and 1925, but without details.

NG

D.S.R. (F) 1908–1909

Sté d'Étude Dannadieu, Saussard et Robert, Paris.

The D.S.R. was a light car powered by a 4-cylinder valveless air-cooled engine. It had an unusual transmission in which an epicyclic gear was combined with the differential.

NG

D.U. (A) 1914

Dietrich & Urban, Graz.

This company made a car with 30PS 4-cylinder side-valve engine, one of which still exists.

NG

DUAL E TURCONI (I) 1899–1901

Dual e Turconi, Milan.

This was the name of a small workshop which assembled a few 3- and 4-wheeled voiturettes, mostly from imported components. Their Ideale had a front mounted

3.5hp single-cylinder engine, two speeds and belt drive. It was successfully driven from Milan to Paris and back.

NG

DUAL GHIA (US/I) 1955–1963

Dual Motors Corp., Detroit, Michigan.

Frank Sinatra, Peter Lawford and Eddie Fisher were a few of the celebrities who flocked to this Italian-American sports sedan. The prototype was called the Dodge Firebomb and was built in 1955. It used a modified Chrysler chassis with an attractive body by Ghia. The production Dual-Ghia, introduced in 1957, was made wider and longer to carry four people. Dual Motors was owned by Eugene Casaroll, and the engineering and production was overseen by Paul Farago. The frames were built in Detroit, shipped to Ghia in Italy for bodywork and returned again for final assembly. Dodge V8 engines produced up to 260hp. These big, opulent and expensive cars were popular with entertainers and other celebrities and about 200 of the first model were sold. All were convertibles except for two coupés. Several prototypes for a successor were made before the L6.4 model was approved. It used a unibody frame built entirely at Ghia using 1960 Chrysler suspension and running gear. The body was a striking fastback coupé with distinctive scooped taillights. However, after the prototype was built Casaroll dropped out of the project, leaving Farago and Ghia to build another 26 Ghia L6.4 models. Only the prototype carried the Dual-Ghia emblem.

HP

Further Reading
'Eugene Casaroll and the Dual-Ghia', John Matras and Paul Sable, *Automobile Quarterly*, Vol. 35, No. 3.

DUCATI (I) 1958

Ducati Meccanica SpA, Bologna.

It is remarkable how many motorcycle manufacturers have toyed with the idea of producing a car. In 1958 the Ducati brothers developed a 4-wheeled prototype called the Baptiste DU4, a 4-seater saloon conceived at a time when motorcycle sales were slumping. It was fitted with a 4-stroke V4 engine, in 16bhp 250cc and 18bhp 350cc forms, driving the front wheels. The search for an international partner to help produce the new car was not fruitful and the DU4 remained a prototype.

CR

DUCHESS (GB) 1984

M.F. Cawley, Arundel, Sussex.

Advertised in 1984, the Duchess Arunville was an MG Magna-inspired 2+2 roadster with an aluminium-over-marine ply body and Triumph Herald/Vitesse running gear and power. It is highly unlikely that production ever began.

CR

DUCK (US) 1913

Jackson Automobile Co., Jackson, Michigan.

Whether the Duck should be considered as a model of the Jackson or a short-lived independent make is a moot point. Nor was the advantage of its curious design ever explained. The Duck was actually a model of the Jackson Automobile which was operated from the rear seat. It is assumed that the company introduced the Duck in an effort to see if operating a car with passengers seated in front of the controls would appeal to buyers. We may assume that it did not since the car was discontinued in less than a year after its introduction. Jackson cars continued until 1923 with more conventional cars.

KM

DUCOMMUN (D) 1903–1904

Werkstätte für Maschinenbauvorm, Ducommun, Mulhouse, Alsace.

Apart from building buses and trucks, this company made a short-lived passenger car, in two models, a 12PS 2-cylinder and 24PS 4-cylinder. Commercial chassis lasted into 1905, and some Ducommun buses ran in London.

HON

DUCROISET (F) 1897–1900

Ducroiset et Fils, Grenoble.

1900 Ducroiset 8hp wagonette.
NATIONAL MOTOR MUSEUM

The Ducroiset was a heavy wagonette powered by a front-mounted 8hp horizontal 2-cylinder engine, with belt drive to a countershaft and chain final drive. It was sold in England under the name Hercules.

NG

DUDLY (US) 1913–1915

Dudly Tool Co., Menominee, Michigan.

The Dudly Bug was a cyclecar powered by a 10hp V-twin engine which drove through a 2-speed epicyclic transmission and final drive by long belts to the rear axle. The two seats were side by side but slightly staggered and the cycle-type front wings turned with the wheels. The 1913–14 Model A-1 cost $375, but the 1915 Model B-1 offered a 4-cylinder engine for only $10 more. However, it did not seem to help sales, because America was tired of cyclecars by then. H.F. Tideman, president of the Dudly Tool Co., then tried to make an electric car, the MENOMINEE, but this did not last out 1915.

NG

DUER (US) 1907–1910

Chicago Coach & Carriage Co., Chicago, Illinois.

The Duer started life as a typical high-wheeler, with 12hp 2-cylinder engine under the seat, and final drive by rope like its Chicago rival, the HOLSMAN. The 1908 models showed a move away from the buggy tradition as the engine was front-mounted under a bonnet. For 1909 bucket seats replaced the normal bench and a coupé was added to the open 2-seater. This was priced at $900, while the open car remained at $750 throughout the make's life.

NG

DUESENBERG (i) **(US)** 1919–1937

1919–1920 F.S. and A.S. Duesenberg, Newark, New Jersey.
1921–1925 Duesenberg Automobile & Motors Co., Indianapolis, Indiana.
1925–1926 Duesenberg Motors Co., Indianapolis, Indiana.
1926–1937 Duesenberg Inc., Indianapolis, Indiana.

The first production passenger car to carry the Duesenberg name did not appear until the end of 1920. Frederick (Fred) Duesenberg decided that the 4-cylinder walking beam engine had had its day, and sold the rights to the Rochester Motors Co. Inc., which supplied engines to several car makers, including ARGONNE, BIDDLE, KENWORTHY, REVERE, RICHELIEU and ROAMER. The big plant at Elizabeth, New Jersey, was sold to WILLYS, and the Duesenberg brothers worked on their own car at Newark. This was a single-ohc straight-8, although when the prototype was exhibited at New York's Hotel Commodore in November 1920 its straight-8 engine had the walking-beam valve system. All production cars had single-ohc driven by a vertical shaft. The 4260cc engine developed 100bhp. The Duesenberg Model A also had hydraulically-operated four-wheel brakes; these and the straight-8 engine were firsts for the American motor industry. Claims have been made for the Kenworthy Line-O-Eight which was announced at about the same time, but only a few prototypes were made.

1921 Duesenberg(i) Model A coupé by Bender.
NATIONAL MOTOR MUSEUM

1926 Duesenberg(i) Model A limousine.
NATIONAL MOTOR MUSEUM

Although the prototype Model A was built at Newark, all production cars came from a new factory in Indianapolis. It was some time before any cars reached the public as dealers did not get any to sell until 13 months after the New York launch. Just under 150 cars were made in 1922, of which 110 were complete, and the rest were bare chassis to be fitted with custom coachwork. Duesenberg did not have a body shop of their own, but they ordered various styles from Fleetwood, Rubay and particularly, Millspaugh & Irish. As they were made in small batches, these were obviously less expensive than a genuine custom body, but even so a Model A was not a cheap car; 1922 prices began at $6500, but were reduced to $5500 for a few months in 1923.

These prices put the Duesenberg among the ten most expensive cars in America, about the same as the Pierce-Arrow and more than $1000 above the Packard Twin Six. Although it was an advanced design and had handling and performance well above the average for an American car of the period, the Duesenberg had to struggle for sales against makes of proven renown. Nevertheless, more than 600 were sold between 1921 and 1926, which was a larger number than the more famous Model J sold in nine years. Little is known about Model A exports, though Duesenberg was represented in Germany in 1926, and one A was bodied as a roadster by the Berlin coachbuilders, Lehmann & Lindenheim.

Few changes were made to the Model A, so that by 1926 the rest of the industry had caught up with what had been such an innovative car. Straight-8 engines were almost commonplace, being offered on less expensive cars such as Packard, Locomobile and Stutz, while hydraulic brakes were no novelty either. Sales were down to two cars a week, and there was no money to develop a new model. Duesenberg would almost certainly have gone under had it not been for the intervention of Errett Lobban Cord, who had been general manager of Auburn since 1924, and became its president in 1926. He had worked wonders with

Auburn, but it was a middle-class car, and Cord set his sights on the top end of the luxury trade. Like Ettore Bugatti, he wanted to build a supercar to outshine all others. Duesenberg was exactly what he needed; a company with a high reputation but weak financially so that it could be bought cheaply.

In the autumn of 1926 the Auburn Automobile Co. bought Duesenberg for a claimed one million dollars, although the actual figure was probably less than half that, and set up a wholly owned subsidiary, Duesenberg Inc. Cord gave Fred a free hand to design a new car which would outclass and outperform the best that the United States or Europe could offer. While he was doing this, a small number of an improved Model A, known as the Model X, were made. Only 12 were completed, this being the number for which parts were on hand when Cord bought the Duesenberg company. Model X was never an official designation, but neither was Model A to start with. Initially the cars were advertised as the 'Eight In a Row' and later simply as the Duesenberg Straight Eight. The Model J has been so called because all drawings and parts numbers began with this letter, but it was not advertised as such, indeed, from about 1934 a car often did not feature at all in Duesenberg advertising. This showed an elegant yachtsman or lady with the caption 'He (or She) Drives a Duesenberg'.

The car which came to be called the Model J was launched in December 1928, and by any standards it was a remarkable machine. The engine was a twin-ohc straight-8 of 6882cc. Although twin ohcs had been used on Duesenberg racing engines, and also on several European sports cars such as Salmson and Sunbeam, they were virtually unknown on American touring cars and had never been tried on such a large engine. The marriage of advanced racing practice with great size was bound to result in enormous power, although exactly how much has been a source of controversy for years. Fred Duesenberg claimed 265bhp at 4250rpm, but most engines probably delivered less. The figure was for an engine which had been tuned for maximum output, a complex and time-consuming business

Frederick.
NATIONAL MOTOR MUSEUM

August.
NATIONAL MOTOR MUSEUM

DUESENBERG, FREDERICK (1876–1932) and AUGUST (1879–1955)

Frederick Samuel and August Samuel Duesenberg were born in Lippe, Germany, but in 1884 their widowed mother took them to the USA, where they settled on a farm at Rockford, Iowa. The brothers, who were always known as Fred and Augie, soon showed great mechanical aptitude, and from repairing farm machinery they progressed to making bicycles, and in about 1900 they made a small engine with rotary valves which they installed in one of their bicycles. Later Fred joined the Thomas B. Jeffery Co., maker of the Rambler car.

In 1905 Fred designed a 2-cylinder car, and the Mason Motor Car Co. of Des Moines, Iowa, was formed to produce it. He was joined by Augie, and they were both associated with Mason until 1913, although not continuously. It is known that Fred had another job in 1910-12, working for a car dealership in Des Moines, whether or not he was still with Mason. He was listed as an officer of Mason in late 1913 when a receiver was appointed, but by then the brothers had moved operations to St Paul,

1929 Duesenberg(i) Model J town car by Derham.
NATIONAL MOTOR MUSEUM

Minnesota. Fred developed the 4-cylinder engine with horizontal valves actuated by long vertical rocker arms, nicknamed the 'walking beam' engine. According to AAA rules they had to be raced under the Mason name in 1913, when they competed in the Indianapolis 500 and other races. Fred was able to use his own name from 1914 onwards and the engines were also sold to other makers of racing cars, and campaigned under other names including Braender Bulldog, Crawford and Sebring. Eddie Rickenbacker drove a Duesenberg into tenth place at Indy in 1914, and the marque scored its first victory on 4 July when Rickenbacker won a 2-mile dirt track race at Sioux City, Iowa.

The Duesenbergs' first venture outside the automotive field came in 1914, when they built two 50-litre 800hp in-line 12-cylinder engines for use in a racing hydroplane, Disturber IV. This became the first boat to exceed 60mph (97km/h). There followed 6- and 8-cylinder marine engines of Duesenberg design, which were made in considerable numbers by the Loew-Victor Manufacturing Co. of Chicago. As well as private buyers for fishing boats to luxury cruisers, customers included the Russian, Italian and US navies. In 1916 the brothers joined J.R. Harbeck, managing director of Loew-Victor, in a new company, Duesenberg Motors Corp. It is a tribute to the brothers' reputation that the new company was named after them, for they had no financial stake in it. A new factory was erected at Elizabeth, New Jersey, for the manufacture of aircraft engines, and was completed six months after the United States entered World War I. Here the 16-cylinder Bugatti-designed aero engines were made, but not more than 40 were completed before the end of the war, and the order for 2000 was immediately cancelled. The brothers were under contract to Duesenberg Motors until well into 1919. This was their primary employment, although it is thought that some racing activity originated on the premises. At some time in 1919 they set up a shop of their own in Newark, where the design and construction of racing cars (and the prototype passenger car chassis) was carried out. This lasted until April–May 1921 when everything was moved to Indianapolis. There they were contracted to a new company, Duesenberg Auto & Motors Inc., to which they sold the rights to build cars and engines under the Duesenberg name. This company built the production Model A, and at first sanctioned racing operations. After the success in 1921, when a Duesenberg won the French Grand Prix, the brothers operated their racing activities under the

name F.S. and A.S. Duesenberg in a separate location until the 1930s. This was a first-floor workshop across the street from the main plant, and as there was no lift the cars had to be moved in and out on a steep ramp.

During the 1920s the brothers divided their time between Duesenberg Automobile & Motors (Duesenberg Inc. from 1925), which made the road cars, Models A, X and J, and their racing cars, which were very successful at Indianapolis and elsewhere. Fred was involved in the massive Model J, which was made under the regime of Errett Lobban Cord, who hired him at $1000 a month. Augie was concerned with the racing cars. In July 1932 Fred was injured when his Model J left the road on the Lincoln Highway in Pennsylvania, and died from pneumonia shortly afterwards. Augie then became chief engineer and continued work on the supercharger which was used on the model SJ. He also contributed to the design of Auburn and Cord models up to the end of the A-C-D empire in 1937. He continued to occupy the small premises across the street, and worked with Ab Jenkins on the record-breaking Mormon Meteor cars. The first of these used an SJ chassis, but the most successful was the Meteor III, a completely new car powered by a Curtiss Conqueror engine. This took short and long-distance records in 1940, and in 1950, when Jenkins was 67 years old, he covered a mile at 190.68mph (306.8km/h).

There were plans to revive the Duesenberg name after the war, and Augie was again involved, but nothing came of them as it would have been too expensive to make a car worthy of the Duesenberg name. He died in 1955, and eleven years later his son Fritz announced a new Duesenberg, powered by a Chrysler V8 engine. Only one was made.

Fred Duesenberg married, in 1913, his secretary at Mason, Isle ('Mickey') Denny; they had one son, Denny, born in 1914.

Augie Duesenberg married Gertrude in about 1919; they had two children, Fritz and Dorothy.

NG

Further Reading
Duesenberg, the Pursuit of Perfection, Fred Roe, Dalton Watson, 1982.
'The Man Behind the Machines, Friedrich S. Duesenberg', Randy Ema, *Automobile Quarterly*, Vol.30, No.4.
'They Always Called Him Augie', George Moore, *Automobile Quarterly*, Vol.30, No.4.

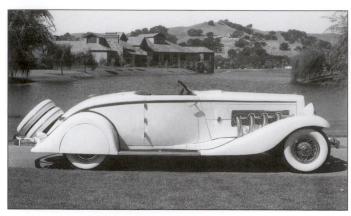

1935 Duesenberg (i) Model JN speedster by Rollston.
NATIONAL MOTOR MUSEUM

1966 Duesenberg (iv) sedan.
NATIONAL MOTOR MUSEUM

which was only done at extra cost. A more realistic figure for the average Model J would be 245 to 250bhp. Even this was remarkable when compared with the competition. The next most powerful American engine was the straight-8 Pierce-Arrow at 125bhp (the 175bhp V-16 Cadillac did not arrive until January 1930), while in Europe the 6.5-litre Speed Six Bentley developed 180bhp and the 8-litre Hispano-Suiza Boulogne 144bhp. Even the 9.4-litre Hispano-Suiza V12 that arrived in 1931 developed only 220bhp.

The Model J engine measured 48in (1220mm) from fan to flywheel, and the head contained 32 valves, four to each cylinder. It was made by Cord's Lycoming subsidiary to a Duesenberg design, and there was never any question of its being supplied to another car maker. The rest of the chassis was fairly conventional, although the frame was built on a massive scale, 8.5ins (216mm) deep at its maximum. The hydraulic brakes had drums 15ins (381mm) in diameter and 3ins (76.2mm) wide, with a vacuum booster available from mid-1929 onwards. Automatic lubrication was standard, with a red light to indicate when oil was running low. Another light reminded the driver to check the battery every 1400 miles.

The chassis price was $8500, and complete cars ranged from $11,000 to $14,000 in 1929, but prices rose and fell during the nine years that the Model J was made. Duesenberg still had no body department, and coachwork came from a variety of companies. Stylist Gordon Buehrig, who was later responsible for the Auburn 851 speedster and Cord 810, designed some bodies which were built to Duesenberg's specifications by Murphy, Derham and Brunn. Among the best known of these were the Beverly sport sedan by Murphy ($16,500 in 1932), the tourster by Derham and the torpedo phaeton by Brunn. Seven body styles were listed in the first catalogue. Many other coachbuilders made limited numbers or one-off bodies, including most of the American houses, Barker and Gurney Nutting in England, Franay and Saoutchik in France, Castagna in Italy and Graber in Switzerland. The largest and most expensive custom body was a 'Throne Car' by Bohman & Schwartz on a wheelbase extended to 178ins (4518mm).

Built for the evangelist Father Divine, it was said to have cost around $25,000.

The Model J quickly attracted a following in Hollywood, and although fewer were made than of the Model A it became much better known, and a higher proportion survives today. Among film stars who owned Js were Gary Cooper, Cary Grant, Marion Davies, and Mae West. Clark Gable used a Duesenberg, but there is no evidence that he actually owned one. Other notable owners included cosmetics maker Elizabeth Arden, oil tycoon J. Paul Getty, newspaper proprietor William Randolph Hearst, and mayors Jimmy Walker of New York City and Frank Hague of Jersey City. Duesenbergs were never common, though, and many Americans who lived away from the centres of wealth such as New York City, Florida and Hollywood, lived their whole lives without ever seeing a Duesenberg.

In Europe they were even rarer; about 60 crossed the Atlantic, of which a dozen had rhd. These went to Britain and Sweden, and some to India. Among British owners were financier Clarence Hatry and racing driver George Duller, while in Sweden the publisher Erik Akerlund had two Model Js. Several monarchs bought Js, including King Alfonso XIII of Spain, and Prince Nicholas of Romania. The prince had two, a cabriolet by Letourneur et Marchand and a chassis to which he fitted a light sporting body for racing at Le Mans. The last Model J chassis to be laid down was fitted in London with a Gurney Nutting body and sold to the Maharajah of Indore. However, it was not the last to be delivered – that honour belonged to a car ordered by the German artist Rudolph Bauer, which was to have carried a body of his own design and built by Erdmann & Rossi in Berlin. However, Bauer moved to the US before work began, so it was bodied by Rollson in New York and not completed until 1940.

In 1932 Fred Duesenberg decided that even more power was needed by some owners, and so created the SJ. This had a centrifugal supercharger turning at five times engine speed. Claimed output was 320bhp and top speed, with a reasonably light body, exceeded 130mph (210km/h). Only 36 supercharged cars were built, of which the last five had 'ram's horn' induction manifolds which boosted power to over 400bhp. There were probably fewer than 36 complete SJs built, as some Js were converted. A genuine SJ had tubular steel connecting rods in place of aluminium alloy, larger crankshaft bearings and stronger valve springs.

Cord's plan for the Model J was to build a first batch of 500 cars, followed by as many more batches as the market would take. He did not envisage a major redesign for at least ten years. In fact, there was never a second batch, and the company went out of business before even the first batch was completed. A total of about 480 were made, of which about 360 were sold in the first three years, 1929–31. After that the effects of the Depression reduced annual sales to a trickle, and Duesenberg did not have a less expensive car to back up the Model J. In 1934 there were plans for a smaller Duesenberg with striking streamlined body by Gordon Buehrig; a development of this later appeared as the Cord 810. Although the last Model J chassis (No. 2614) was laid down in 1935, the car was still listed up to 1937, and some were certainly sold through 1936. The Cord empire collapsed in 1937, ending production of Auburns and Cords, as well as Duesenbergs. The various companies were sold off and the factory became the home of Marmon-Herrington trucks. Fred had died in 1932 as a result of a road accident, but August (Augie) formed a new company, Duesenberg Marine Motor Co., which made engines for motor boats. In 1947 he was associated with a proposed new Duesenberg, but the plan was abandoned before even a prototype was built. He died in 1955, aged 76.

The Model J has a good survival rate – of the 480 or so made about 390 are known to exist today. In the mid-1970s they were still being discovered at the rate of about one per year, and as not more than 50 are known to have been broken up, there must still be a few 'out there' awaiting resurrection. They are among the most prized of collector cars, and according to *The Standard Catalog of American Cars* any J in good condition is worth in excess of $250,000.

Apart from replicas (see below), two cars have borne the Duesenberg name, both modern ideas of how a contemporary Duesenberg should look. The first was a Chrysler-powered sedan styled by Virgil Exner, dating from 1966, and the second a 1978 luxury limousine by Lehmann-Petersen on a stretched Cadillac frame. Only one car of each design was made.

NG

Further Reading
Duesenberg-the Pursuit of Perfection, Fred Roe, Dalton Watson, 1982.
'Duesenbergs in Europe', *Automotive History Review*, 1996.

DUESENBERG (ii) (US) 1947

Duesenberg, Indianapolis, Indiana.

Marshall Merkes bought what was left of the Duesenberg company and intended to reintroduce the line. August Duesenberg was hired to design an updated version of the original car, but none were built before the effort collapsed.

HP

DUESENBERG (iii) (US) 1959

Mike Kollins, Detroit, Michigan.

This attempt to reintroduce the Duesenberg name was based on a 1950 Packard chassis with a custom all-metal body. The body was a 2-seat sports car with a convertible top. A tall 'eggcrate' grill and raised bonnet line provided clearance for the Duesenberg engine. It was built by Mike Kollins, with chassis modifications by the A. O. Smith Co. A modified 1930 400hp Duesenberg straight-8 engine was used, but apparently only one car was built.

HP

DUESENBERG (iv) (US) 1966

Duesenberg Corp., Indianapolis, Indiana.

This relaunching was led by Fred F. Duesenberg, the son of August Duesenberg, as chairman. Styling was by legendary Chrysler stylist Virgil Exner and construction was by Ghia in Italy. The first model was to be the Model D sedan, a 4-door with low, sweeping lines and massive chrome grill surround. The chassis was based on Chrysler running gear and a 400hp Chrysler V8 was standard. With a 5700lb weight and a price of $19,500, it was not a success and only the prototype was built.

HP

DUESENBERG (v) (US) 1970–1979

Duesenberg Corp., Gardenia and Inglewood, California.

This company built a high-quality replica of an original SSJ Speedster. Dimensions were taken from an original car that had belonged to Gary Cooper. These replicas used an aluminium and steel body on a Dodge truck chassis powered by carburetted or supercharged Chrysler V8s. Although advertised at 500hp, they probably produced closer to 300hp. It was built on a 128in (3249mm) wheelbase and had 18in (475mm) diameter wheels with four-wheel drum brakes. Custom bodies resembling other Duesenbergs could be ordered. These assembled cars were very expensive.

HP

DUESENBERG II (US) c.1979 to date

Duesenberg Motors, Inc., Elroy, Wisconsin.
Elite Heritage Motors Corp., Elroy, Wisconsin.
Fall Motors Ltd, Genoa, Illinois.

This replica manufacturer made a full line-up of five Duesenberg models including the Model J Speedster, Royalton Phaeton, Torpedo Roadster, Torpedo Phaeton, and Murphy Roadster. These full-sized replicas were painstakingly created on Ford running gear. A 5700cc V8 with automatic transmission was combined with disc brakes, air conditioning and power steering. The bodies were fibreglass but, visually, the trim and wheels were very convincing. A price of $125,000 in 1984 to $195,000 in 1999 kept production totals low.

HP

DUESENBERG BROTHERS (US) 1978

Duesenberg Brothers, Mundelein, Illinois.

This boxy sedan was not a replica of the original classic, but a new design from a company formed by Harlan and Kenneth Duesenberg, nephews of original Duesenberg founders Fred and August. This somewhat lacklustre luxury car was based on Cadillac running gear with a 7000cc V8. At a projected price of $100,000, the venture did not succeed and only a single prototype was built.

HP

DUFAUX (CH) 1904–1906

1904–1906 Ch. & F. Dufaux Frères, Châtelaine, Geneva.

Charles (1879–1950) and Frédéric (1881–1962) Dufaux were two enthusiastic sportsmen living in Geneva. Several bicycle records had been made when they opened the Kursaal Garage in Geneva in 1903. They were agents for Werner, Griffon

1906 Dufaux 40hp tourer.
ERNEST SCHMID

1906 Dufaux 70/90hp 8-cylinder triple phaeton, by Geissberger.
ERNEST SCHMID

and Motosacoche motorcycles and soon produced their own model, which was designed especially for 'daring ladies'. Unfortunately there were not enough of them and their first business venture failed.

The brothers were not discouraged easily and ordered a special racing car from PICCARD & PICTET, who at the time produced water turbines and machinery. This car was designed by Charles Dufaux and incorporated many innovative ideas. The 8-cylinder in-line engine was cast in pairs and it was probably the first straight-8 designed as such – not simply by fitting together two 4-cylinder engines. Dimensions were 125 × 130mm, with a capacity of 12,756cc. Power output of the DUFAUX-PICTET was said to be 90bhp at 1200rpm. Frédéric was to drive this racer in the Gordon Bennett Cup event of 1904 but due to a broken steering arm the car did not start. However, he set a new Swiss record in the the Kilometre Lancé of Geneva with 71mph (115km/h). Late in 1904, Dufaux launched a 15hp and a 35/40hp passenger car, both with 4-cylinder engines. At the first Geneva Automobile Salon in spring 1905, Dufaux presented the 35hp model as a chassis and with a very luxurious limousine body. The main attraction however was the 80hp Gordon Bennett racing car and the still unfinished engine of a new 150bhp monster. For the Gordon Bennett race of 1905, Dufaux planned to run three cars but due to problems with the Swiss Automobile Club none was nominated. The 150hp racer was completed and Charles Stewart Rolls, always interested in the fastest cars available, had it shipped to England to start in the Brighton speed trials. It was not yet ready, failed miserably and was returned to Geneva. Late in 1905 the *mise-au-point* was completed and the Dufaux brothers transported it to Arles in southern France for an attempt to beat the land speed record. It had a huge 4-cylinder T-head engine of 225mm bore and 166mm stroke with a capacity of 26,400cc. With Frédéric at the wheel, the monster consisting of a light chassis, a huge engine and two bucket seats did indeed set a new record with 156.522 km/h (97.2mph) on 15 November 1905. It was officially timed by the ACF but for obscure reasons dropped from the official LSR lists before 1914. At the second Geneva Automobile Salon in 1906, Dufaux Frères displayed a new 8-cylinder 100/120hp racer and a very big and fast *berline de voyage* with a similar engine, a new 15hp 4-cylinder double phaeton and of course the 150hp record car. Towards the end of 1906, a new 16hp model with a 4-cylinder L-head engine of 4084cc and open tourer body was introduced.It had successfully completed a climb of the Simplon Pass. However, the economic situation and the stiff competition of the big companies forced Dufaux Frères to close down in 1907. The newly founded Italian company MARCHAND in Piacenza had secured some licence rights and built another straight-8 racing car for the GP of France. It was entered as the MARCHAND-DUFAUX and driven by Frédéric Dufaux but gave up with mechanical problems. One each of the 8-cylinder racing cars are in the Musée National de l'Automobile (formerly Collection Schlumpf), Mulhouse, and the Verkehrshaus der Schweiz in Lucerne.

FH

Further Reading
'Die Wagen von Charles und Frédéric Dufaux', Ferdinand Hediger,
Automobil Revue Berne, March 1966.

DUHANOT (F) 1907–1908
Sté des Automobiles Duhanot, Paris.
In 1907 Duhanot listed six different models, from 10 to 35hp, and one may doubt whether all of them were built. For 1908 the range was down to three, an 8/10hp 2-cylinder and two fours of 12/14 and 17hp. The 8/10hp was offered as a taxicab as well as for private use, and the company was well-known for taxis. At least one 1908 model had a radiator with revolving tubes 'constituted after the fashion of a windmill's sails'.

NG

DULOUX (US) 1994 to date
Duloux Motors Ltd, Castro Valley, California.
This kit car company built a pleasing replica of the 1937 Cord 812. They purchased the tooling from The CLASSIC FACTORY, who had been building them since 1981. Duloux based their kit on 1978 to 1983 General Motors chassis and V8 running gear. The body moulds had been pulled off an original car so the details and proportions were very accurate. They were sold in kit and assembled form.

HP

D. ULTRA (GB) 1914–1916
D.U. Manufacturing Co. Ltd, Clapham, London.
This was the second venture of Harold E. Dew, who had made the DEWCAR until he left that company in February 1914. Like the Dew, the D. Ultra (which presumably stood for Dew Ultra) was a cyclecar, but a more sophisticated design, with water-cooled Chater-Lea 8hp V-twin engine, a 4-speed friction transmission and chain drive. It was available as a 2-seater or a delivery van. Air- and water-cooled twins were offered for the 1915 season, together with a four powered by a 10hp water-cooled Lister engine.

NG

DUMAS (F) 1902–1903
M.A. Dumas fils, Champigny-sur-Marne, Seine.
The Dumas was an unusual-looking 3-wheeler powered by a 4.5hp single-cylinder Buchet engine mounted under a bonnet, ahead of which was the single front wheel which was driven by chain via a 2-speed transmission. Power was taken by belt to a short countershaft fitted to the steering head, so that, although the engine was fixed to the frame, the transmission mechanism turned with the wheel. This was facilitated by 'a novel arrangement', said *The Motor Car Journal*, without explaining it. The engine was automatically thrown out of gear when the brakes were applied.

NG

DUMONT (i) *see* SANTOS-DUMONT

DUMONT (ii) (F) 1912–1913
Automobiles Dumont, Asnières, Seine.
The Dumont was a light car powered by a large single-cylinder engine of 1334cc, and used a curious form of friction drive. The engine was transversely mounted and at each end of the crankshaft revolved a steel disc. Across the faces

of these, a friction disc was moved, giving 10 forward speeds, and from each disc power was transmitted by a long propeller shaft to bevel gears on the rear axle. The body was a 4-seater.

NG

DU MONTANT (F) 1974–1975
Jacques du Montant built a 1930s-style roadster of very lightweight construction (weighing only 580kg). Two versions were offered, with either Renault 4 or 6 platforms.

CR

DUMORE (US) 1918
American Motor Vehicle Co., Lafayette, Indiana.
Built for a short time only, this was a 2-seater cyclecar with an 1100cc 4-cylinder engine and chain or belt drive. The American Motor Vehicle Co. built the AMERICAN JUNIOR from 1916 to 1920.

KM

DUNALISTAIR (GB) 1925–1926
Dunalistair Cars Ltd, Nottingham.
The year 1925 was late for the introduction of a hand-assembled car with no outstanding features, so it is hardly surprising that the Dunalistair's life was short. It had a 2120cc 13.9hp 4-cylinder ohv Meadows engine, 4-speed Meadows gearbox and chassis frame from Mechins of Glasgow. The firm's solicitor's office was also in Glasgow, and the name hints at Scottish origins anyway. The 4-seater tourer bodies were made in Nottingham. Surprisingly for a car of this size and date, it had no front-wheel brakes. Only three or four were made.

NG

DUNAMIS (B) 1922–1923
Automobiles Dunamis, Antwerp.
Deriving its name from the Greek word for 'strength', the Dunamis was a luxury car powered by a 3386cc side-valve straight-8 engine, with 3-speed gearbox and 4-wheel brakes. A bare chassis and a saloon were shown at the 1922 Brussels Show, and made a second appearance a year later, after which no more was heard of the Dunamis. It was sponsored by tobacco merchant Theo Verellen and the prototypes were built for him in the MIESSE factory.

NG

DUNBAR (US) 1923
David Dunbar Buick Corp., Walden, New York.
The Dunbar dream was no more than a cleverly engineered stock swindle, largely made possible by the presence of David Dunbar Buick, founder and erstwhile president of the Buick Motor Car Co. After Buick had been edged out of his company by William C. Durant in 1908, he had proven that, despite his genius in plumbing 'furniture' and the valve-in-head engine, he was hardly a businessman, and his checkered career, including the manufacture of carburettors, was one of repeated failures. In 1921 Buick became president of Lorraine Motors Corp. of Detroit, Michigan, builder of a car of that name which had succeeded the earlier Hackett. This, too, was unsuccessful, and Buick faded from view until 1923. What apparently happened at that time was the formation of a corporation to manufacture a new car and as Buick was available, this was to be called the Dunbar, Buick's middle name. It is obvious that those in charge of the venture were more interested in financial gain than actually marketing a car and settled for a 'manufacturing site' in Walden, New York, on the west side of the Hudson River about 85 miles north of New York City. The *modus operandi* of the venture was obviously centred on the use of Buick's name and the promotion specified that the car was 'built by Buick', without actually saying it was Buick the man, and not the GM car, which was theoretically in back of the claim. One lone Dunbar roadster was built to promote the venture, a typically assembled car of the period with a 6-cylinder Continental engine. Although Buick probably was never aware of the chicanery involved, the sporting lines of the promotional car were successful, stock was sold, and those in charge of the David Dunbar Buick Corp. left the scene before buyers of the stock realised they had been 'taken'. (Buick himself then embarked on a series of careers – oilwells and Florida real estate – failing in all of them, and at the time of his death in 1929 held a desk job at the Detroit School of Trades. The David Dunbar Buick

1897/8 Dunkley gas-powered *dos-à-dos*.

Corp. attempted, unsuccessfully by mail, to continue its operation later in 1923 to no avail.)

KM

DUNHAM (US) c.1982

Dunham Coach Corp., Boonton, New Jersey.

This company made a boxy kit car that vaguely resembled a Rolls-Royce Silver Shadow. The proportions were a bit off and it only had two doors. Running gear came from a Corvette and power was courtesy of a 5700cc V8. It was based on a 98in (2487mm) wheelbase and was 185.3in (4703mm) long. Dunham also built another Corvette-based custom called the Caballista sporting a massive chrome grill, rectangular headlights and an angular top design.

HP

DUNKLEY (GB) 1896–c.1924

Dunkleys, Birmingham.

Dunkleys were pram manufacturers who made several unusual cars over a period of more than 20 years. Their first, announced in 1896, was a very unusual machine whose four wheels were arranged in diamond pattern. Unlike the Sunbeam-Mabley, which appeared a few years later, the Dunkley's wheels were of unequal size, those at the front and rear being considerably smaller than those at the side, through which the drive was taken. Seating was on the *dos-à-dos* pattern, and the car could be steered from either end, although the brake could only be operated by the rear-facing passenger. The engine was

1901 Dunkley gas-powered 4-seater.

powered by coal gas, and the body was of wicker construction. Dunkleys also made a 3-wheeler on the lines of an invalid carriage.

In 1901 Dunkleys brought out another 4-wheeler, also coal gas-powered, but a little more up to date in that the wheels were conventionally located and of the

1923 Dunkley Pramotor saloon.
NICK BALDWIN

1913 Duo cyclecar.
MICHAEL WARE

same size. The two seats were in tandem. They then abandoned the motorcar until 1913, when they brought out the ALVECHURCH cyclecar. Their next venture kept up their reputation for eccentricity. Introduced in 1922, the Pramotor consisted of a scooter minus the front wheel, which could be attached to any perambulator, preferably a Dunkley. Engines of 1 and 2.75hp were offered, and the Model 20 was a luxurious machine, with fully enclosed coupé body for the fortunate infant. Two factors worked against its success, though; a price of 135 guineas (£141.75) and the law which forbade the operation of powered vehicles on the pavement, consigning the power-crazed nanny to take her chances in the road with cars, buses and motorcycles.

NG

DUNN (US) 1916–1918
Dunn Motor Works, Ogdensburg, New York.
Walter Dunn was a builder of marine engines who decided to enter the cyclecar market just as most other Americans were leaving it. His car was unusual in having a 15hp V-4 engine of his own manufacture, and which was presumably also supplied for marine use. Other features of the car were a 2-speed gearbox, shaft drive and a very low price of $295.

NG

DUNSMORE (GB) 1987–c.1997
Dunsmore Motor Traction, Stretton-on-Dunsmore, Warwickshire.
The prototype of this attractive classic roadster kit used a Vauxhall Ventora engine and Austin Westminster rear axle but production versions used Jaguar mechanicals in an underslung steel ladder chassis, though any engine could in theory be fitted. Unusually there were fabric-covered plywood or steel body panels over a steel tube body frame. The character was distinctly antique: a beam front axle,

leaf spring suspension all round, friction dampers, non-servo drum brakes and a large diameter steering wheel.

CR

DUO (GB) 1912–1914
1912–1913 Duocars Ltd, Deptford, London.
1913–1914 Duo Cyclecars Ltd, Deptford, London.
The Duo was one of the more popular cyclecars, and was made with several engine options, including a 6/8hp single-cylinder Buckingham, 8hp air-cooled V-twin J.A.P., 10hp in-line twin Dorman, and 10hp 4-cylinder engines by Chapuis-Dornier or Mathis. The original model with J.A.P. engine had an armoured ash frame, two speeds and belt final drive. Shaft drive was used on the 4-cylinder cars which were announced for 1914. In September 1913, L.F. de Peyrecave took over the Duo works and the following year offered his DE P light car alongside the Duos. He left at the end of 1914 to make De Ps at New Cross.

NG

DUOPOWER (US) c.1993 to date
DuoPower, Inc., Santa Fe Springs, California.
DuoPower specialised in building concept cars. Company president Masao Watanabe had been a prolific designer in Japan before moving to the US in the 1980s. The Gila Monster was a 1994 design with a radical roadster body and a Cadillac V8 engine. The 1993 Koga 5.7 Afghan was a stunning front-engined coupé based on Chevrolet Camaro running gear with a 5700cc V8 engine. It was developed for a Japanese parts manufacturer that intended to have DuoPower build customer models in kit or assembled form with optional Corvette chassis and suspension parts. The Pandora was a restyled Mercedes 190 with a clean roadster body. It was featured at the 1992 Detroit Autoshow and attracted much interest, but only the prototypes of these three cars were built.

HP

DUPLEX (i) (GB) 1906–c.1909
Duplex Motor Engine Co., London.
This car was powered by a 4-cylinder 2-stroke engine rated at 30hp, and later at 35hp, and had chain drive, although later cars had shaft drive.

NG

DUPLEX (ii) (US) 1908–1909
Duplex Motorcar Co., Chicago, Illinois.
The Duplex was a high-wheeler powered by a 2-cylinder engine mounted transversely. There were two friction discs, one at each end of the crankshaft, and the driven discs had their own propeller shafts driving to a separate differential on the rear axle. The system was similar to that used on the DUMONT. Three models were listed for 1908; Stanhopes powered by 10 or 15hp engines, and a surrey. For 1909 the Duplex was a more conventional-looking car, with normal-sized wheels, a large bonnet and 4-seater body. The Duplex company was owned by the BENDIX company, which also made cars under its own name.

NG

DUPLEX (iii) (GB) 1919–1921
British Commercial Lorry & Engineering Co. Ltd, Manchester.
The 'Lorry' part of this company's name refers to commercial chassis sold under the name County, which had been made since 1915 by a predecessor company. In 1919 they announced a light car of conventional appearance but with a most unusual engine. It had eight cylinders, arranged in two rows of four parallel in the block. Each pair of cylinders was connected transversely at the top by a common combustion chamber, with a single sparking plug, and each piston was surrounded by its own sleeve valve. The sleeves were operated by two short connecting rods from two auxiliary crankshafts driven at half engine speed. The aluminium pistons were connected to the main crankshaft by different sized connecting rods, those on the nearside having substantial rods while those on the offside had 'slave rods' articulated from the 'master rods'. Capacity was 1479cc, but the eight cylinders gave it a rated 15.6hp, almost as much as the 3-litre Bentley's 15.9hp, with a correspondingly high annual tax.

The rest of the car was conventional enough, though quite up to date, with unit construction of engine and gearbox, and centre gear lever. Two- and 4-seater open bodies were listed, followed by all-weather and conventional saloons for

1921. It is not known how many Duplexes were sold with the 8-cylinder engine, but by the summer of 1920 an alternative 1498cc Coventry-Simplex engine was available, and doubtless the great majority of the 100 or so Duplexes made used this engine. The eight was not in evidence at the 1920 Olympia Show. The cars were unrealistically expensive, and the company was in receivership by August 1921.

NG

Further Reading
'Duplex light cars of Trafford Park', M. Worthington-Williams, *The Automobile*, December 1995.

DUPLEX (iv) (CDN) 1923

United Iron Works Co., Montreal, Quebec.
The Duplex used an unconventional 4-cylinder 2-stroke engine with two pistons per cylinder, which the makers claimed set a new record for fuel economy. It was mounted in a Hudson chassis and displayed at the 1923 Montreal Show, priced at CDN$1750. There was no production.

NG

DU PONT (i) *see* SPHINX (i)

DU PONT (ii) (US) 1920–1932

1920–1922; 1925–1930 Du Pont Motors Inc., Wilmington, Delaware.
1922–1925 Du Pont Motors Inc., Moore, Pennsylvania.
1930–1932 Du Pont Motors Inc., Springfield, Massachusetts.
Du Pont Motors was formed by E. Paul Du Pont, a member of the famous family which had widespread interests in munitions and textiles, and also bailed out General Motors after its collapse under William C. Durant. There was no business connection between Du Pont Motors and the family firm of E.I. Du Pont de Nemours & Co., even though both were located in Wilmington. The car making company grew out of Du Pont Marine Motors Co. which E. Paul had formed in 1917, and supplied engines to the US Navy. In 1919 he decided to build a high-quality car, and formed a team of experienced men. These included general manager Arthur Maris, formerly with BIDDLE, chief engineer John A. Pierson from the Wright-Martin Aircraft Co., and sales manager William A. Smith who came from MERCER.

Surprisingly for a car of its size and quality, the Du Pont Model A's engine had only four cylinders; it was a conventional side-valve unit of 4090cc and 55bhp, with a Brown-Lipe 3-speed gearbox and four body styles; tourer, roadster, sedan and suburban sedan. At prices from $4000 to $5600 it was far from cheap, yet its quality and doubtless the associations of the name, helped the company to sell 188 cars up to July 1923, when the Du Pont became a 6-cylinder car. The new unit, from Herschell-Spillman, was their 4730cc Model 90. The new Du Pont Model C was considerably lower in price, $2090–3085, but sold only 48 units in the 1924 season. For 1925 a 4323cc ohv Wisconsin six engine was chosen for the Model D, but the mid–1920s were lean years for Du Pont, and they sold only 27 Model Ds in two years, which was hardly more than one a month, and sales were largely to the East Coast. The assembly plant at Moore, Pennsylvania, to which they had moved in 1922, was closed and production concentrated at Wilmington, although bodies were made at Springfield.

The Model D's successor, the generally similar E, was made into 1928 and sold somewhat better, at 83 units. One Model E was fitted with a supercharger, but this was not a success. With wheelbase stretched from 125 to 136in (3175 to 3454mm), the E became the F, but only two of these were made. Much better known was the Model G, made from 1929 to 1932. This had a 5274cc straight-8 Continental engine, normally reckoned to give 114bhp, although Du Pont claimed 140bhp. The G was offered in twelve body styles, including designs from major coachbuilders such as Merrimac, Waterhouse and Derham. Prices were higher than before, from $4360 for a club sedan to $6125 for a 4-seater speedster. The Speedsters were made in very small numbers and had pointed radiator grills and skimpy wings. A 2-seater was bought by Mary Pickford as a gift for her husband Douglas Fairbanks, while two 4-seaters ran at Le Mans in 1929.

In May 1930, Paul Du Pont moved all his operations to Springfield, to be nearer body suppliers Merrimac. For a factory he bought that of the Indian Motorcycle Co. Total production of the Model G was 273 cars, brought to an end in January 1932 by the Depression. The last Du Pont was the Model H, which used the Continental

1920 Duplex (iii) 10hp 2-seater.
NATIONAL MOTOR MUSEUM

1929 Du Pont (ii) Model G speedster.
NATIONAL MOTOR MUSEUM

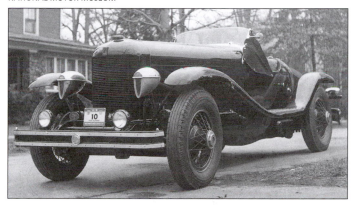
1929 Du Pont (ii) Model G roadster.
NATIONAL MOTOR MUSEUM

1931 Du Pont (ii) Model H phaeton by Locke.
NICK GEORGANO

1906 Duquesne (i) 16/21hp tourer.
NICK BALDWIN

1923 Durant Four tourer.
NATIONAL MOTOR MUSEUM

engine in a 146in (3708mm) Stearns-Knight frame. Only three of these magnificent cars were made, of which one, a Dual Cowl Sport Phaeton, survives. Production of all Du Pont models totalled only 537 cars.

NG

Further Reading
'Du Pont Motor Cars', S. Smith and A. Einstein Jr,
Automobile Quarterly, Vol.II, No.2; Vol.XIII, No.1.

DUPORT (F) 1977–1994

1977–1992 Éts Duport, St Ferréol, Faverges, Haute Savoie.
1992–1994 Sté Nouvelle Duport, St Ferréol, Faverges, Haute Savoie.
Teleski manufacturer Guy Duport was responsible for expanding the horizons of the 50cc-limited microcar class in France by persuading the authorities to sanction the fitment of larger-capacity diesel engines. His Caddy was the first diesel-powered microcar (using a 510cc Lombardini unit) and was claimed to be the world's smallest diesel car. It used Renault 4 steering and brakes. The 4-passenger Parco of 1980 also used many Renault trim parts. A departure into full-size vehicles with the 1983 720 was unsuccessful; this car was a leisure vehicle using a mid-mounted Renault 2-litre engine and a hardtop body. Another interesting model was the 1990 Onyx, a tiny fun car resembling a miniature Citroen Méhari. There was even a 654cc diesel-powered 'high performance' microcar called the GT. The company's swansong microcar, the Passion, cost as much as a Renault Clio.

CR

DUPRESSOIR (F) 1900–1914

Paul Dupressoir, Maubeuge, Nord.
Bicycle makers since 1892, Dupressoir was better known as a supplier of chassis under the name Rolling than as a maker of complete cars, although a few of these were made from time to time. Around 1900, some light voiturettes were made, powered by De Dion-Bouton or Aster engines mounted under the seat. They could be air- or water-cooled, of 2.5 or 3hp. In 1912 a range of complete cars, called Rolling, like the chassis, was announced. They had 4-cylinder monobloc Chapuis-Dornier engines of 7, 9, 10 and 12hp. The 9hp model was the basis for the English-built AVERIES light car of 1913–14.

NG

DUQUESNE (i) (US) 1904–1906

Duquesne Construction Co., Jamestown, New York.
The Duquesne Model C was a 5-seater tourer powered by a 16/21hp air-cooled 4-cylinder engine. Unusual features included a starter operated from the seat by a ratchet working on the flywheel, rear doors that opened when the front seats were tilted forward and headlights that turned with the steering. Despite these attractions, only five or six Duquesnes were sold. One of the partners, LeRoy Pelletier, later became Henry Ford's secretary and then a leading figure in the advertising business.

NG

DUQUESNE (ii) (US) 1912–1913

Duquesne Motorcar Co., Pittsburgh, Pennsylvania.
This Duquesne was a large assembled car powered by a 50hp 4-cylinder Wisconsin engine. Chief engineer was Frank Morse, who had been one of the founders of the Wisconsin Motor Manufacturing Co. For 1913 an even larger car with 6-cylinder Wisconsin engine of nearly 8 litres' capacity, on a 133in (3380mm) wheelbase, was announced, but very few were made of either model. Frank Morse later built the MORSE (iii) cyclecar.

NG

DURANT (US) 1921–1932

Durant Motors, Inc., New York, New York; Lansing, Michigan;
Muncie, Indiana; Elizabeth, New Jersey; Long Island City, New York;
Toronto and Leaside, Ontario, Canada and Syracuse, New York.
The Durant car was the keystone of William C. Durant's projected 'Second Empire' after he left as head of General Motors in 1920, previously heading a similar line-up during his first term as GM president. As he had left GM due to financial difficulties there, he was determined to produce a rival array of cars as competition, like GM producing various automobiles in all price ranges. These, over the years, included the 4-and 6-cylinder Durants, Star fours and sixes, Flint, Rugby (for export), and Locomobile, plus the Mason truck, the stillborn Eagle and Princeton, and an American version of the French Mathis which never got into production. The first Durant was fitted with a Continental 4-cylinder engine developing 35bhp at 2100rpm and with a 109in (2766mm) wheelbase and with the 5-seater touring car listed at $890. The first cars, built late in 1921, were used for promotion, attracting favourable public interest. Production began early in 1922 and with the addition of a larger six, this being built at Muncie, Indiana in the factory in which the Sheridan car had been produced, the Sheridan, formerly in the General Motors line-up, having been eliminated from it under the new GM management which sold the factory to Durant. The engine for the six was by Ansted, also of Muncie. The larger car's engine developed 70bhp at 3100rpm, and it had a wheelbase of 123½ins (3135mm). A touring car was priced at $1650. Production exceeded 22,000 units for the company's first year.

For 1923, specifications remained unchanged and with an increase in production of more than 8000 cars above the 1922 output, most of the sales being for the 4-cylinder line. In 1923 the six was dropped as sales had been disappointing, Durant reasoning that there was too much competition in the price range of the larger car. Production dropped severely during 1924 with an estimated 10,000 cars completed, this figure also including left-over Durant Sixes, the result of over-production. The four was continued unchanged for 1925, except for 4-wheel brakes and balloon tyres which were added as standard equipment. Sales dropped to less than 4500.

By 1926 Durant's 'Empire' was coming apart and the factory was closed down. Sales continued after a fashion but such cars as found buyers were presumably unsold 1925 models. Prices on them were also lowered.

The greater part of 1927 saw William C. Durant struggling with financial problems in a successful effort to resume production. The factories remained closed while a completely new series of Durants were planned. Production resumed and for 1928 four new models were introduced. These included a 4-cylinder line with prices starting at $695 and three sixes, the Series 55 with prices escalating upward with the Series 65 starting at $795, culminating with the Series 75 brougham at $1550. All 1928 models used a variety of Continental engines and production reached 22,000, considerably lower than a financial break-even figure. Historian Beverly Rae Kimes notes that these difficulties appeared almost insurmountable even before the stock market crash which was a 'staggering blow' and after which Durant attempted to solve his increasing problems with an infusion of $90 million of his own money. It was not enough to head off impending disaster for the company.

But Durant continued production. Production of 21,000 was recorded for 1930, a drop of 13,000 from the 1929 figures. Cosmetic changes resulted in an attractive

1930 Durant Six Sport roadster.
NATIONAL MOTOR MUSEUM

NICK BALDWIN

DURANT, WILLIAM CRAPO (1861–1946)

The founder of General Motors and Durant Motors was born in Boston, Massachusetts, on 8 December 1861. He was the grandson of Henry Howland Crapo (1804–1869), a former Atlantic whaler who moved to Flint, Michigan, in 1855, became a tycoon of the lumber trade, and was elected governor of Michigan in 1864.

His father, William Clark Durant, was a bank clerk whose wife divorced him in 1869. Billy Durant was 12 when his mother Rebecca, née Crapo, moved from Boston to Flint, where he attended local schools until he reached the age of 16 and went to work in one of his grandfather's stores. A year or so later he started an insurance agency, and, before he was 21, he had been asked to reorganise a gas company and sort out the tangled affairs of a local water works.

He entered the world of transport in September 1886, after being given a ride in a lightweight cart made by the Coldwater Road Cart Co. at Coldwater, Michigan. He went to Coldwater and bought the stock of finished and unfinished vehicles, parts, dies and patterns for $1500 (which he had borrowed from a bank in Flint), invited his friend Josiah Dallas Dort (1860–1925) to become a 50/50 partner for $1000, and organised the Flint Cart Co.

He had orders for 600 carts before building the first one. In fact, he had no production facilities, and contracted with William A. Paterson, owner of Flint's biggest wagon and carriage factory, for delivery of 1200 carts as soon as

possible. When Paterson tried to sell Flint carts direct to his customers, Durant and Dort broke off with him and leased factory space in an old cotton mill, where they began production. Their business was renamed Durant-Dort Carriage Co. in 1895; it continued to grow and spawned four subsidiaries.

He used his great wealth and leisure time to go to New York and study Wall Street and investment banking. Before the turn of the century he was ready for a new challenge, but it did not come until 1 November 1904, when James H. Whiting (1842–1919) hired him as general manger of the Buick Motor Co.

Salesman first, industrialist second, Durant got 1108 orders for the Model C Buick, when production capacity was only 5 to 8 cars a week. He arranged the recapitalisation of Buick and ordered the construction of a big factory in Flint. Buick became the No. 1 car-maker in the US.

He dealt with the Selden patent by taking over the Pope-Robinson licence and paid the ALAM a royalty of 1.25 per cent of Buick's wholesale price for every car. But Buick alone was not enough. In 1907, Durant proposed setting up a Buick-Ford-Reo-Maxwell-Briscoe cartel, but negotiations stalled, mainly due to Ford's intransigence.

His plans did not change-only the participants. He made Buick the backbone of a group of car companies that soon included Cadillac, Oldsmobile, Cartercar, Elmore, Ewing, Welch, Randolph, and Oakland. He called it the General Motors Co., formed on 16 September 1908 under the laws of New Jersey with a capital stock of $12,500,000 and headquarters in the Terminal Building, Park Avenue and 42nd street in New York City. In 1909, Durant tried again to buy Ford Motor Co., but failed.

He also bought supplier companies, such as the Weston-Mott Co., Champion Ignition Co., the Jackson-Church-Wilcox Co. (later Saginaw Steering Gear Division), Northway Motor & Manufacturing Co., Michigan Motor Castings Co., Heany Lamp Co., W.T. Stewart Body Corp., Dow Rim Co., and the Novelty Incandescent Lamp Co.

But Durant had no vision of how to stimulate co-operation and synergy within General Motors. Nor had he provided adequate sources of financing for the expansion he started. The bubble burst in November 1910, when the Wall Street bankers, Storrow, Lee, Higginson, J.W. Seligman, forced him to resign.

Within months of leaving GM, Durant was taking steps to establish a rival organisation. He bought the Flint Wagon Works from James H. Whiting, hired William H. Little away from Buick, and re-organised it as the Little Motor Car Co. Concurrently, he provided financial backing for Louis Chevrolet who started to build a car in Detroit. The Chevrolet Motor Co. was registered on 3 November 1911. Durant was also backing the Mason Motor Co. and the Sterling Motor Co. He set up Republic Motors Co. (under the laws of Delaware) as a holding for the manufacturing operations, and bought the Imperial Wheel Works in Flint, which was retooled to make Chevrolet cars.

William Crapo Durant; *continued*

In 1914, he began buying GM shares, and managed to bring the DuPont family along on this investment trail. When the GM board of directors met in the Belmont Hotel in Manhattan on 16 September 1915, Durant walked in and quietly announced 'Gentlemen, I control this company'.

General Motors Co. became the property of Chevrolet Motor Co. and it took some time to sort out the corporate structure. Durant did it by turning General Motors Co. into General Motors Corp. in May 1918, and made Chevrolet a division on a par with Buick and Cadillac.

Separately, Durant organised United Motors Co. as a holding for new supplier-industry businesses he had purchased, such as Hyatt and New Departure, Delco (Dayton Engineering Laboratories), Remy Electric, Perlman Rim, and Jaxon Steel Products. In December 1918, United Motors Co. was formerly made part of GM.

Durant also bought some car companies for GM, including Scripps-Booth and Sheridan, and, wanting to compete with Ford (Fordson tractor) in the farm-tractor market, bought the Janesville Machine Co. in Wisconsin and the Samson Sieve-Grip Tractor Co. of Stockton, California, for inclusion in GM.

But he had over extended GM's debt, and sacrificed a personal fortune of approximately $90 million to keep it afloat. He resigned on 30 November 1920. He was nearly 60 years old, but never hesitated to start his third motor-industry empire. Durant Motors Inc was registered in Albany, New York, on 12 January 1921, with a capital stock of $5 million.

He acquired a former Goodyear plant in Long Island City, New York, and displayed the Durant Four on 4 August 1921. He brought out the low-priced Star early in 1922. In 1921 he took over a vast factory (from Willys-Overland) at Elizabeth, New Jersey, and transferred Durant and Star assembly operations there. The 6-cylinder Flint was introduced in mid-year 1922, as a product of the Flint Motor Co. in Flint, Michigan. He bought the former Sheridan plant in Muncie, Indiana, from GM and used it for producing the Princeton car in 1923-24, sometimes badged as the Durant Six. In 1922, he purchased the Locomobile from the wreckage of Hare's Motors, and re-organised it. He then introduced the Mason truck, made in Flint, Michigan.

The Star was planned as a Ford rival, the Durant Four as an attack on the Chevrolet market, the Durant Six as an anti-Oldsmobile, the Flint as a Buick-beater, and the Locomobile to steal customers from Cadillac.

True to his style, he also picked New Process Gear out of the Willys basket, took over the Warner Transmission Corp., American Plate Glass Co., Adams Axle Co., and Associated Bodies Corp.

Privately (not included in Durant Motors Inc) he also held a block of shares in Hupmobile, Chandler, Peerless, and Paramount Cab when the stockmarket crashed late in 1929. Again, he sacrificed his personal savings to settle debts, but did not have enough. Durant Motors Inc was placed in receivership in 1931, and the company was liquidated in 1933.

In 1936, he was president of the Pomeroy-Day Land Co., with offices at 230 Park Avenue in New York City, but its assets were small real-estate properties in Flint, Michigan. He filed for personal bankruptcy on 8 February 1936, with debts approaching a million dollars. Later that year, he opened a diner-cum-mini superette in Asbury Park, New Jersey, which he intended as a pilot operation for starting a chain of such establishments. But he sold out in 1938, returned to Flint, and by 1940 was the owner of an 18-lane bowling alley.

He suffered a stroke during the night of 2 October 1942, and spent nine weeks recovering in Hurley Hospital. He and his wife then left for New York. He spent his last years in a wheelchair, struggling to write his memoirs. He died in his sleep in the early morning hours of 18 March 1946, in their apartment.

He was twice married, in 1884, to Clara Miller Pitt, by whom he had two children, Marjorie and Russell Clifford (Cliff). The marriage was dissolved in 1908, and a few hours after the divorce papers came through he married schoolgirl Catherine Lederer, who survived him.

JPN

1931 series and Durant announced that his company would introduce an American version of the Mathis car, having obtained a licence from the parent company in France. The Mathis prototypes were exhibited at the New York Automobile Show in January 1931 but production failed to get underway. A meagre 7000 Durants were produced that year.

The 1932 Durants were announced but in fact were only 1931 cars which had been updated by enough cosmetic changes to give them a more modern appearance, especially the attractive 6-22 series which featured a pointed grill. By 1 February production ceased permanently and Durant was out of business.

KM

DUREY-SOHY (F) 1899–1903

Automobiles Durey-Sohy, Paris.

The first products of this company were a voiturette powered by a vertical 2-cylinder engine and an electric hansom cab. The latter was still made in 1903, when they took over the range of petrol cars and motorcycles made by HANZER and marketed them under the Durey-Sohy name. These included 5hp and 6hp singles and a 9hp twin. They also sold a 12hp twin, presumably of their own design as it did not feature in the Hanzer range.

NG

DURIEZ (F) 1946–1951

Having made some electric vehicles during the war, Duriez turned itself to making forward-control vans and estate cars based on Citroën C4 chassis. It also made special bodies for the Renault 4CV from 1950 and worked on the LIVRY Atlas and a 4-speed gearbox that was used by both Citroën and D.B.

CR

DÜRKOPP (D) 1898–1927

1898–1913 Bielefelder Maschinenfabrik vorm. Dürkopp & Co. AG, Bielefeld.
1913–1927 Dürkopp-Werke AG, Bielefeld.

The origins of this company date back to 1867 when Nikolaus Dürkopp began to make sewing machines. He had branches in Graz, Austria and Bielefeld, and both branches soon added bicycles to their products. In 1898 they built their first cars, which were on Panhard lines, with front-mounted vertical 2-cylinder engines, double-chain drive and unequal-sized wheels. These were also made in France under the name Canello-Dürkopp. In 1899 there appeared a much smaller car with rear-mounted 6PS engine, wire wheels and tandem seating. The 1903 range consisted of 8 and 10PS twins, a 15PS 3-cylinder and 20 and 30PS 4-cylinder models, and an early example of a six was announced.

They had vertical T-head engines, with 3-speed gearboxes on the twins and 4-speeds for the fours, and chain drive. Some models were sold in England under the name Watsonia, after the importers, F. Watson.

Later models ranged from the 1560cc Typ KW 6/14PS (1909–14) to some enormous fours, the 8-litre Typ DG 30/70PS (1908–13) and 13-litre Typ DG 40/100PS (1912–14). Inevitably the big cars sold in very small numbers, but Dürkopp also offered a new range of smaller models under the name Knipperdolling. These had monobloc L-head engines of 1368cc and 1540cc.

After World War I they concentrated on the 2090cc Typ P8, made in 8/24 and 8/32PS forms. Normal output was 24 or 32bhp, but a supercharged engine developed 60bhp. This was in fact smaller, at 1991cc, to bring it within the 2-litre competition class. A few larger Dürkopps were also made, a six with the same dimensions as the P8, giving 3130cc, a 4164cc four (P16) and a 6246cc six (P24). Car production was given up in 1927, but commercial chassis lasted for three years longer, and included low-floor 4- and 6-wheel bus chassis. In 1948 Dürkopp returned to motorcycles with a range from 98 to 200cc, the best-known being the Diana scooter.

HON

DUROCAR (US) 1906–1911

Durocar Manufacturing Co., Los Angeles, California.

This car was designed by Watt Moreland, a former mechanic for WINTON, who had also been involved with the MAGNOLIA and TOURIST cars in California. In 1906 he joined forces with a Tourist dealer, William M. Varney to make the Durocar. This had a large 2-cylinder engine of 26hp, epicyclic transmission and shaft drive, and was available as a tourer, runabout or landaulette. Only seven cars had been made by September 1907, but thereafter output rose to five cars per day. Moreland resigned in 1908 because the directors would not agree to his suggestions for a 4-cylinder car, although they adopted a four in 1910, which was made in 35 and 45hp models. Sixty-seven Durocars were still running in California in 1917. Moreland moved to Burbank in 1911 and started the Moreland Motor Truck Co. which made trucks and buses up to 1941.

NG

DUROW (GB) 1985 to date
Durow Cars, Newthorpe, Nottinghamshire.
This was a rare British attempt at an American-style neo-classic, with gushingly expansive wings, a very long bonnet, obligatory whitewall tyres and an M.G. Midget centre body. The chassis was large but simple, and accepted Ford Granada mechanicals, with optional Rover V8 power. The choice of bodywork was very varied: fibreglass or stainless steel, 2-seater or 4-seater, and extra-long wheelbase limousine, fixed head or convertible styles. Model names included Deluge, Debonair, and Starr.

CR

DURSLEY-PEDERSEN (GB) 1912
Dursley-Pedersen Cycle Co., Dursley, Gloucestershire.
This famous bicycle maker announced a cyclecar powered by a 7.9hp 4-cylinder air-cooled engine, with 3-speed gearbox and shaft drive. The frame was of ash and total weight was only 450lb (203kg). The planned price was 100 guineas (£105), which would have been very good value had the car been produced, but there is no evidence that it was. Dursley-Pedersen bicycles were made from 1896 to 1914.

NG

DURYEA (i) (US) 1893–1914
1893–1898 Duryea brothers, Duryea Motor Wagon Co., Springfield, Massachusetts.
1898–c.1899 Duryea Manufacturing Co., Peoria, Illinois.
1899–1907 Duryea Power Co., Reading, Pennsylvania.
1908–1913 Duryea Motor Co., Reading, Pennsylvania.
1911–1914 Duryea Automobile Co.; Duryea Motor Co., Saginaw, Michigan.
There are several pretenders to the title of America's first petrol-engined car but, like Karl Benz in Germany, the Duryea brothers' claim rests on the fact that cars were made for sale within two years of the first prototype. Charles E. Duryea (1861–1938) and J. Frank Duryea (1869–1967) both had mechanical experience, with Charles selling and repairing bicycles, and Frank working as a toolmaker for the Ames Manufacturing Co. in Chicopee, Massachusetts. They were living in Springfield when they began work on their first car. In later years there was a lot of undignified argument between the brothers and their families about who was really responsible for its design. It seems that the idea was due to Charles, that the initial construction work was perhaps shared between the brothers, but that after Charles' departure to Peoria in September 1892, development work was solely down to Frank. Charles was perhaps disillusioned by the slow progress on the car, which would not run at all even after a year's work. Frank continued alone, with financial assistance from local businessman Erwin F. Markham.

The first Duryea car consisted of the body and frame of a horse-drawn buggy which had been bought second-hand for $70, and into which the brothers mounted a horizontal single-cylinder engine of 1302cc. This developed a theoretical 4hp. It had low-tension ignition, a spray carburettor and belt drive. It was driven for the first time on 21 September 1893; Charles said many years later 'It ran no faster than an old man could walk, but it did run'. In January 1894 it successfully completed a 6-mile run.

During 1894 Frank built a second car with 2-stroke (later converted to 4-stroke) engine, a purpose-built body and spur gear drive in place of the belt system. Individual clutches provided three forward speeds and a reverse. Pneumatic tyres were fitted. It was clearly a great advance on the first, and is sometimes called, for convenience, the Chicago car as it won the *Times-Herald* race held in the city in November 1895.

The third car was built in late 1895 and early 1896, and was sometimes called the Cosmopolitan car because it competed in that magazine's race from New York to Irvington, and was the only car to finish. The wheels were smaller and fitted with larger pneumatic tyres, the engine was smaller but higher powered, and belt

1901 Dürkopp 8PS tonneau.
NATIONAL MOTOR MUSEUM

1920 Dürkopp 8/24PS saloon.
NICK GEORGANO/NATIONAL MOTOR MUSEUM

1893 Duryea (i) 4hp buggy.
NATIONAL MOTOR MUSEUM

drive was again taken up. This was the basis of the production car.

The Duryea Motor Wagon Co. was founded in September 1895 and cars made from Spring 1896 to 1898. Several changes in design were made; the first 13 cars had belt drive, after which they went back to geared drive, wire wheels were adopted and dos-à-dos bodies to seat four passengers were provided. After the Motor Wagon Co. closed its doors, Frank Duryea made the HAMPDEN car, which later became the STEVENS-DURYEA. He had no further business links with his brother.

1906 Duryea (i) 15/18hp tonneau.
NATIONAL MOTOR MUSEUM

1981 Dutton Phaeton S2 sports car.
DUTTON CARS

1981 Dutton Sierra estate car.
NICK GEORGANO

Although Charles clearly kept an eye on what was happening at Springfield (and unfairly claimed more than his share of the credit), and was a partner in the Duryea Motor Wagon Co., he spent most of his time in Peoria on bicycle work, apart from a short spell in New Jersey. In February 1898 he incorporated the Duryea Manufacturing Co.. The cars had 3-cylinder engines made in the E.B. Hazen machine shop, epicyclic transmission, chain drive and a single front wheel controlled by a centre tiller. About 20 3-wheelers, known as the Duryea Trap, were made, as well as one machine gun-equipped armoured car and several motor boat engines. To increase seating capacity, a matching 2-wheeled trailer was offered. In 1900 Charles moved to Reading, Pennsylvania, where he continued the 3-cylinder 3-wheeler, adding a 4-wheeled version in 1902. These were his staple products until 1908; they had 3516cc 15hp engines (a 25/30hp was added for 1906 and 1907) with water-jacketed cylinder heads mounted transversely at the rear and driving via 2-speed gear in a power drum alongside the engine. Final drive was by chain. They had tiller steering, the tiller also acting as a gear selector and throttle. Charles championed the tiller on the grounds that it occupied only one hand, the other being free to hold a passenger's waist, a good five-cent cigar or, in inclement weather, an umbrella. Bodies were mostly open 2- or 4-seaters, although a fully enclosed Doctors' Phaeton was also offered. These Duryeas were made under licence in Coventry from 1902 to 1906 by Henry Sturmey, who was also editor of *The Autocar*, and in Liège, Belgium from 1900 to 1903. In Waterloo, Iowa, the Waterloo Gas Engine Co. made 21 Duryeas under licence from 1903 to 1905, selling them under the name Waterloo.

In the autumn of 1907 the Duryea Power Co. went into receivership after about 370 of the 3-cylinder cars had been built. Charles Duryea was not finished yet, though, and 1908 saw a new company, the Duryea Motor Co., and a new car the Buggyaut. This was a high-wheeled solid-tyred buggy, powered by a 15hp horizontally-opposed twin with drive by twin-grooved rollers on the crankshaft, which engaged with the rims of the rear wheels. Like the earlier cars it was tiller steered, the tiller being centrally mounted so that the car could be steered from either side. The Buggyaut was made until 1913, but from 1911 to 1914 Charles was also running the Duryea Automobile Co. at Saginaw, Michigan. Here, a modified version of the Buggyaut, called Electa, was made. This had a slightly more luxurious body with curved lines, but used the same running gear as the Buggyaut. A few Buggyauts were also made at Saginaw, or at any rate advertised. Production at both Reading and Saginaw had ended by January 1914.

It is worth recording that the youngest brother, Otho Cromwell Duryea (1880–1941) formed the Western Duryea Manufacturing Co. of Los Angeles in 1901 with plans to build cars and trucks of every description. No more than one prototype was made; Otho then returned East, to Butler, Pennsylvania, where he made a fortune in the mining and railcar industries.

NG

Further Reading
Charles E. Duryea, Automaker, George W. May, Edwards Brothers, 1973.

DURYEA (ii) **(US)** 1914–1915
Cresson-Morris Co., Philadelphia.
This car was designed by Charles Duryea but built for him by the Cresson-Morris Co. It was a cyclecar powered by a flat-twin engine and using the same drive system as the Buggyaut. It was priced at $400, but few were made. Cresson-Morris was also making a 4-cylinder light car for Henry Crowther, which he marketed from Rochester, New York, under the CROWTHER name. In 1916 he and Charles Duryea joined forces to make the CROWTHER-DURYEA.
NG

DURYEA GEM (US) 1916
Duryea Gem Manufacturing Co., Philadelphia, Pennsylvania.
Charles Duryea's last automotive venture was a 3-wheeled cyclecar with the same engine and drive as his 4-wheeler of 1914–15. The chassis was built by the Detroit Chassis Co. Despite being billed as 'The Biggest Idea in the History of the Motorcar and the Last Word in Automobile Construction', no more than six Gems were ever built. A 4-wheeler version was made only as a single prototype. Duryea wrote many technical books and articles until his death in September 1938. For 15 years he was technical editor of *Automobile Trade Journal*.
NG

DUTTON (GB) 1969 to date
1969–1971 Dutton Cars, Fontwell, West Sussex.
1971–1972 Dutton Sports Ltd, Fontwell, West Sussex.
1972–1979 Dutton Sports Ltd, Tangmere, West Sussex.
1979–1991 Dutton Cars Ltd, Worthing, West Sussex.
1991 to date Hacker Engineering Ltd, Worthing, West Sussex.
Dutton was perhaps the world's most prolific maker of kit cars. In all, it made about 8000 kits and, at one point, production reached 22 cars a week. Tim Dutton-Woolley's first special, the 'Mantis' was a gull-wing coupé based on a modified Lotus Eleven. When he assembled a Lotus Seven for someone else, he thought it was over-priced and it dawned on him that, in the late 1960s, there was no low-cost basic kit car on the market. He set about to build one along the lines of a Lotus Seven, although it emphatically was not a crib.

1982 Dutton Melos 4-seater sports car.
NICK GEORGANO

Dutton virtually re-invented the kit car market with the P1 of 1970. It was a simple spaceframe/body unit designed to take BMC running gear – a crashed Sprite was the ideal donor car – but they sold slowly. After two years just nine had been made, but revisions of the original theme, the B-series and the Malaga, which had Triumph Spitfire front suspension and a wide range of engine options, hit the right note. Dutton made its 500th kit in 1977 and doubled that in the next two years.

In 1979 came the Sierra, which had the appearance of an 'off-roader' and was perhaps the first kit ever not to be a sports car or fun vehicle. Ford had already registered the name and a minor legal skirmish ensued. The upshot was that Dutton renamed the vehicle the 'Dutton Sierra Kit' and, since the press perceived it as 'David and Goliath', Dutton received widespread publicity – cartoons appeared in the national press. The Dutton Sierra Kit is claimed to be the best-selling kit car ever offered. The Sierra Kit chassis was also offered in a Drophead version, with soft- and hard-tops, and was used for the Rico, a 2-door fastback saloon.

From 1979, all Duttons were sourced from Ford components. The Phaeton, a further development of the P1, arrived in 1980 and the following year saw the Melos, a 'traditional' 2+2 sports car with more creature comforts and a detachable hard-top. Its chassis was designed by Richard Oakes, perhaps the kit car industry's most accomplished freelance designer.

This chassis was then used for the Phaeton S2 and, in 1986, the Leggera, a 2-seat sports car, best described as a modern interpretation of the Austin-Healey 'Frogeye' Sprite. At the beginning of 1988 came the Beneto, an estate inspired by the Range Rover, and the Hacker, a Beneto with a shorter wheelbase which was available as a saloon, soft-top or pick-up.

Dutton had built a very rich range, with every model undergoing constant development to improve ease of build – early Duttons were poor in this department. They were popular and competitively priced, the most expensive kit, the Beneto, cost just £1395 + VAT. Then, at the height of the 1980s kit car boom, in 1989, Dutton sold every design to other companies.

Shortly afterwards, the kit car market went into recession and, one by one, the former Dutton projects folded.

1909 Dux D12 6/12PS tourer.
NATIONAL MOTOR MUSEUM

The company regrouped under the name Hacker Engineering and its first product was the Maroc, a convertible 2+2 built on a Ford Fiesta III with tubular bracing and fibreglass panels from the (raked) windscreen forwards. This sold in small numbers, as a kit or a turn-key car, was dropped in 1995 with the introduction of the Mariner, and was then revived again in a slightly modified version in 1999.

In the early 1990s, Tim Dutton acted as a consultant assisting a number of companies in Third World countries with local projects using fibreglass. This came to an end with the introduction of the Dutton Mariner in 1995. The Mariner was an amphibious 4-seat convertible, based on the Fiesta III, with a water jet propulsion system when being used on water.
MJL

DUX (D) 1908–1926
1908–1915 Polyphonwerke AG, Wahren, Leipzig.
1915–1926 Dux Automobilwerke AG, Wahren, Leipzig.
The Dux succeeded the POLYMOBIL in 1908. The first Dux was the Typ E12 with a 6/12PS 4-cylinder engine, 3-speed gearbox and shaft drive, and was followed

c.1901 Dyke 2-seater.
NATIONAL MOTOR MUSEUM

1925 D'Yrsan 8hp sporting 3-wheeler.
NATIONAL MOTOR MUSEUM

by the 1546cc 6/18PS which was made until after World War I, but only up to the end of 1919. Two models were made in the 1920s; the 4396cc 17/50PS 4-cylinder Typ S and the 4433cc 17/60PS Typ R. They both had 4-speed gearboxes, and the Typ R had optional 4-wheel brakes. They were similar in size, the R having a wheelbase only 21in (55mm) longer at 140in (3555mm), but there was a considerable difference in price, the S costing RM13,200 for a tourer, and the R, RM22,000.

HON

D & V (US) 1903

Devigne & Van Sickle, Paterson, New Jersey.
Jules Devigne and Levi Van Sickle made an assembled car of what they called 'simplified French type' with 12hp 3-cylinder engine and tonneau body. Few can have been built as the make did not last into 1904.

NG

D-WAGEN (D) 1924–1927

1924–1926 Deutsche Werke AG, Haselhorst, Spandau, Berlin.
1926–1927 Deutsche Kraftfahrzeugwerke AG, Berlin.
This state-owned former munitions factory took up motorcycles first (the famous D-Rad), followed by cars in 1924. The design was conventional, with a 1.3-litre 5/20PS 4-cylinder engine. The cars were renowned for their reliability, but competition in this sector was very fierce, and production was given up in 1927. American DURANT cars were made in the factory for a year, after which it became the site of DKW manufacture.

HON

DWORNIK see VINCENT

DYKE (US) 1901–1904

1901–1902 St Louis Automobile & Supply Co., St Louis, Missouri.
1903–1904 Dyke Auto Supply Co., St Louis, Missouri.

A. L. Dyke stands apart from *fin de siècle* automobile builders by offering buyers a choice of ready-made cars or those in kit form. As such, Dyke was very probably the first in America to offer cars in component form for home assembly by the purchaser. His first ready-made car was the Automotorette, a light petrol runabout with a tubular running gear, powered by a 5hp engine and weighing 750lb. The body of the Automotorette featured openings at the top and rear with corrugated water tanks which, let into the sides of the body, took the place of cooling tubes, the overall appearance resembling a steam car. Dyke's offerings in kit form included several designs with engines from a 5hp single to a 12hp twin, 2- or 5-seater open bodies and a choice of either solid or pneumatic tyres. The kits were priced between $700 and $1000. A. L. Dyke is remembered to this day as the author of *Dyke's Automobile and Gasoline Engine Encyclopaedia* of 1909.

KM

DYMAXION (US) 1933–1934

The Dymaxion was an experimental foray into an aerodynamic design for 'a car of the future'. It was designed by Buckminster Fuller, prominent in the field of futuristic designs for houses and boats, the first of the three Dymaxions being built in 1933 in the former Locomobile plant in Bridgeport, Connecticut. The car had three wheels, the single wheel at the rear, a 125in (3172mm) wheelbase and was powered by a Ford V8 engine. The Dymaxion was claimed to reach a speed of 120mph (193km/h) and economically designed to have 40mpg fuel potential. Largely constructed of balsa wood and duralumin, the car was involved in a fatal two-car collision near Chicago, Illinois, the publicity of which very probably killed any chances of marketability. Two more Dymaxions were completed in 1934, one of which was purchased by Leopold Stokowski, conductor of the Philadelphia Symphony Orchestra. One Dymaxion is known to survive.

KM

DYNAMOBIL (D) 1906

E.H. Geist Elektrizitätswerke AG, Cologne.
This company was a proponent of the 'mixte' or petrol-electric drive system. Their main work was with commercial vehicles, but they made a car chassis in 1906, powered by a 24hp petrol engine generating power for two 12hp electric motors.

HON

DYNA VERITAS see VERITAS

D'YRSAN (F) 1923–1930

Raymond Siran, Cyclecars d'Yrsan, Asnières, Seine.
The d'Yrsan was one of the three best-known French 3-wheelers, along with the Darmont and the Sandford, but was less directly derived from the Morgan than either of its rivals. Its maker, whose full name was Marquis Raymond Siran de Cavanac, had worked with Stewart Sandford, and left when he was apparently piqued that Mme Sandford said he could not build as good a car as her husband's. His Type A had a 904cc side-valve 4-cylinder Ruby engine and ifs by superimposed transverse leaves. The frame was tubular and final drive was by chain to the single rear wheel. The d'Yrsan could easily be recognised by the large 'Y' in the radiator. In 1926 this was joined by the Type BS with 25bhp 972cc ohv Ruby engine, while the most powerful was the 1097cc DS which gave 35bhp. The d'Yrsan was made in touring and sports forms, the latter with flared wings and pointed tail. There was a streamlined competition model called the Scarabee, of which a few were made in road-going form.

In 1927 Raymond Siran realised that the public was becoming disenchanted with 3-wheelers, and brought out a 4-wheeled light car which could be had with either the ifs of the 3-wheelers, or a beam front axle. Engines were either the 972 or 1097cc Ruby, although a 750cc Ruby was used in the 1929 Le Mans cars, to bring them within the smaller capacity class. They could be had in lowered frame as well as normal frame models, with 2-door coupé or sports bodies. Only 50 4-wheelers were made, compared with 530 3-wheelers, of which 490 were the BS model. Including seven special competition cars, total d'Yrsan production was 587. A proposed car with 1100cc 6-cylinder Aviation Michel engine was never built.

NG
Further Reading
'd'Yrsan ou l'Aventure Cyclecariste', Jacques Potherat, *l'Album du Fanatique*, May–July 1977.

E3D (F) 1982–c.1992

1982–1986 Études Design Développement et Diffusion des Produits sarl, Roissy-en-Brie.
1986–c.1992 International Motors Cars (Quatex Automobiles), Les Lilas.
Launched as the Jeepie in 1982, the E3D Chipie was a jeep-style leisure vehicle based on a shortened Renault 4 platform. The bodywork, in polyester, was designed by ex-Renault stylist Robert Sulpice and fitted over a riveted steel chassis with a tubular superstructure. The Chipie had also been built on the island of Martinique.

CR

EAC (US) c.1979

Electric Auto Corp., Troy, Michigan.
The EAC Silver Volt was a 4-seater station wagon with an electric motor and a continuously variable transmission. It used lead-cobalt batteries and had a range of 63 miles with a top speed of 70mph (113km/h). It also carried an on-board petrol generator that powered the air-conditioning, power steering and power brakes and provided extended driving range. It was to go on sale in 1979.

HP

EAGLE (i) see BADSEY

EAGLE (ii) (GB) 1901–1908

1901–1907 Eagle Engineering & Motor Co. Ltd, Altrincham, Cheshire.
1907–1908 St George's Motor Car Co., Leeds, Yorkshire.
The early history of the Eagle is closely tied up with that of the CENTURY (i). When Sydney Begbie took control of Century, the designer of the Century Tandem tricar, Ralph Jackson, set up a new business to make a thinly disguised version which he called the Eagle Tandem. In 1903 Jackson introduced the first Eagle 4-wheelers, a 9hp 2-cylinder and 18hp 4-cylinder, the latter with a 3-speed epicyclic transmission which he had patented in 1901. Tricars were still made, including a £100 single-seater runabout and the fearsome New Eagle Racer, a single-seater said to be capable of 80mph (130km/h).

Eagle went into voluntary liquidation in February 1905, but was not wound up until nearly two years later. Jackson then formed another company and made a limited number of 4-cylinder cars, of 10/12, 24/30 and 35/45hp which he called New Eagle. They were assembled at Broadheath Generating Station, Altrincham, and sold through St George's Motor Car Co. of Leeds. He made one further car, the JACKSON cyclecar, in 1913.

NG

Further Reading
'The Eagle Engineering & Motor Co. Ltd', R.J. Wyatt,
Old Motor, October 1963.

EAGLE (iii) (US) 1905

Eagle Auto Co., Buffalo, New York.
This short-lived company made two models, both with 4-cylinder air-cooled engines and chain drive. The Model A had a 12hp 2-cylinder engine and rear-entrance tonneau body, while the Model B had a 24hp 4-cylinder engine and a 5-seater side-entrance tourer body.

NG

EAGLE (iv) (US) 1905–1907

Eagle Automobile Co., Rahway, New Jersey.
Two 4-cylinder models of the Rahway Eagle were listed; a 20/24hp for 1906 and a 30hp for 1907. Possibly this was the same engine but the later version was slightly uprated. Final drive was by chain and the only body listed was a 5-seater tourer. Two of the partners in this company, Frank and Edwin Vandewater, later made the CORREJA car.

NG

EAGLE (v) (US) 1908

Eagle Motor Carriage Co., Elmira, New York.
This was a typical high-wheeler powered by a flat-twin engine, possibly by Brennan, with epicyclic transmission and final drive by rope or steel cable. Suspension was by long cantilever springs which ran from front to rear axles on each side. The price of the Eagle was a very low $350, but few cars were sold.

NG

1900 Eagle (ii) tandem 3-wheeler.
R. J. WYATT

1907 New Eagle (ii) 24/30hp tourer.
R. J. WYATT

EAGLE (vi) (US) 1909

Eagle Automobile Co., St Louis, Missouri.
Yet another Eagle which failed to live out the year of its introduction, this was a roadster with two seats plus a dickey, powered by a 14hp 2-cylinder air-cooled engine, driving through a friction transmission and shaft final drive. It looked quite rakish, but cannot have been much fun at any speed as it had solid tyres.

NG

EAGLE (vii) (US) 1911

Eagle Motor Car Co., Detroit, Michigan.
Only one example of the Detroit Eagle was made, to demonstrate inventor Martin Brazinski's patent aluminium tyres. These were built on to the wheels, with spring-loaded canvas and rubber sections surrounding the perimeter of the aluminium sidewalls. Apparently they gave a very bumpy ride, and Brazinski did not proceed with the idea. The car, still in existence, is a large tourer powered by a 60hp 6-cylinder Wisconsin engine.

NG

EAGLE (viii) (GB) 1912–1914

1912–1913 Eagle Motor Manufacturing Co., Shepherd's Bush, London.
1913–1914 Eagle Motor Manufacturing Co. Ltd, Barnes, London.
The Eagle cyclecar was made in two models, both with an 8/10hp air-cooled V-twin engine of Eagle's own manufacture, with shaft drive to a worm gear rear axle. The only difference in the two models was that one had a tubular frame, and the other was of pressed steel. Late in 1913 the company moved to the Beverley Works at Barnes; this factory was occupied in the 1920s by the makers of the BEVERLEY-BARNES. For 1914 Eagle offered a light car powered by a 1130cc 4-cylinder engine. The company was wound up at the beginning of 1914, and a new company, the Nova Motor Co. Ltd was founded in June. This was an inauspicious time to be starting a new car company, and so far as is known no cars were made under the Nova name.

NG

1913 Eagle (viii) 8/10hp cyclecar.
NICK BALDWIN

EAGLE (ix) (US) 1915–1916

Eagle Electric Automobile Co., Detroit, Michigan.

This company listed two models of electric car, a coupé and a limousine, offering them with or without batteries, the prices of the latter being $150 lower. They were announced from temporary premises, and may never have moved into their permanent factory. Only one Eagle Electric was registered in Michigan in 1916 and this suggests that only a prototype was made.

NG

EAGLE (x) (US) 1923–1924

Durant Motors Inc., New York, New York.

The Eagle turned out to be one of William C. Durant's stillborn automobiles (the other being the PRINCETON) which surfaced during the period Durant was forming his 'Second Empire', the purpose of which was to offer serious competition to General Motors with a line-up of cars in every price range. In advance promotion, the Eagle was announced as a contender in both 4- and 6-cylinder types, although the four never materialised. The six was unashamedly advertised as a competitor to Chevrolet and was launched in January 1924 at the New York Automobile Show, a touring car on a 115in (2918mm) wheelbase, priced at US$820. The car was equipped with 4-wheel brakes which, at the time, was exceptional for so cheap a car, but it never reached production, ending up as the FLINT 40, the main difference being in the substitution of a Continental 7U engine instead of the same company's 6Y in the Eagle prototypes.

KM

EAGLE (xi) (GB) 1981–1997

1981–1986 Eagle Cars, Lancing, Sussex
1986–1993 Eagle Cars, Storrington, Sussex
1993–1997 Eagle Cars, Arundel, Sussex

Under the banner 'The Eagle has landed' Eagle Cars launched the kit-form Eagle SS in 1981, a licence-built version of the American CIMBRIA SS. A VW floorpan was used, but in 1983 a new tubular steel ladder chassis for Ford Cortina components was launched for front-mounted engines up to V6. The same year came the +2, a 4 seater convertible derivative that was exclusively front-engined. Eagle also took over the RHINO jeep-style vehicle in 1983, renaming it the RV and, within months, developing a purpose-built ladder chassis for Cortina mechanicals. 4x4 versions based on Range Rover or Daihatsu Fourtrak chassis followed, with a Sierra-based option arriving in 1994. Another Eagle project was the P21 (and P25), which were re-engineered, restyled and rebadged versions of the Dutton Phaeton, acquired from DUTTON in 1989. Eagle also collaborated with European firms, first developing the Milan (also known as the M2) with a German company. This was to be a more up-market fully-built model, a four-seater convertible with modern styling and Ford Sierra components, but a production run did not ensue. Finally in 1994 came a Pontiac Fiero based Ferrari F40 replica called the Stendetto that was developed for a French company.

CR

EAGLE (xii) (US) 1987–1998

Jeep-Eagle Division, Chrysler Corp., Detroit, Michigan.

Chrysler's acquisition of American Motors resulted in the AMC Premier sedan, based on the Renault 25, receiving a new marque name, Eagle. This name had a long history with American Motors, dating back to the Willys Aero Eagle of 1952, and used on AMC's 4x4 cars in the 1980s. The Premier was joined by the Renault 21-based Medallion sedan, which was made in France for the US market, while the Premier was Canadian-built. Neither sold very well, and the Medallion was dropped after 1989; the Premier lasted until 1992. In 1990 there was a sister car to the Premier badged as the Dodge Monaco.

Although the Medallion was imported, Chrysler had intended the Eagle line to be one of import-beaters. However, in 1989 they decided to use imports, the sub-compact Summit sedan being the Mitsubishi Mirage (also badged as the Dodge Colt), and the Summit Wagon, the Mitsubishi Expo LRV. An imported design, but made at the Diamond Star factory at Normal, Illinois that was set up jointly by Chrysler and Mitsubishi, was the Talon, which also sold as a Plymouth Laser and Mitsubishi Eclipse. Described by *Autoweek* as 'fast, fun and affordable', the 1997cc twin-ohc 4-cylinder Talon could be had with 4-wheel drive and turbocharging; with both options it cost only $16,437 in 1990. For 1993 and 1994 only the Talon could be had with a single-ohc four of 1755cc.

For 1993 Eagle launched the Vision, a companion car to the 'cab forward' Chrysler LH series, with 3300 or 3518cc V6 engines. Vision sales were disappointing compared with those of the Chrysler Concorde and Dodge Intrepid, because it was perceived to be overpriced, and also because the Eagle name was still little known to American buyers. Sales tailed off, and it was dropped for 1998, leaving the Talon alone to carry the Eagle name. This it did until 5 February 1998, when the last one rolled off the line at the Diamond Star factory. A total of 216,743 Talons had been made.

NG

EAGLE AMERICAN (US) c.1980

Eagle American, Lincoln, California.

The Stallion was a Cobra replica, although it was longer than the original and had more ground clearance. Eagle American was started by Jim Kellison, who had built the KELLISON kit cars, and Mike Grant. The Stallion had a space frame with extra bracing. The rear end was a live axle and suspension was based on Ford parts. Although designed around the 7-litre Ford V8, other engines could be fitted as well.

HP

EAGLE COACH WORKS (US) 1973 to date

Eagle Coach Works, Lancaster, New York and Buffalo, New York.

Classic sportscars were replicated by this kit car manufacturer. They started with Bugatti, Alfa Romeo and Frazer-Nash kits based on the VW chassis. These were replaced in the 1980s by SS100 and XK-120 Jaguar replicas. Their line-up appears to have been identical to the cars sold by ANTIQUE AND CLASSICS.

HP

EAGLE-MACOMBER (US) 1916–1918

Eagle-Macomber Motor Co., Sandusky, Ohio.

The Eagle-Macomber was actually an extension of the earlier Eagle which had been produced by Walter C. Macomber, first in Los Angeles, subsequently in Chicago, Illinois and more recently in a larger place at Sandusky, Ohio. Like the earlier Eagle, it featured a rotary, 5-cylinder air-cooled engine which had a bore and stroke of 3¾ × 5in, a wheelbase of 118ins (2995mm) and a modern design emphasised by a pointed bonnet with a herringbone pattern. The ¾ angle view of the car as sketched appeared in the first of four promotional brochures. For any reader of the contemporary automotive journals, this design would readily have been recognised as identical with promotional material of the Bour-Davis car which otherwise had no connection with the Eagle-Macomber. The brochure sketch showed the car without the radiator cap of the Bour-Davis promotion but, in the side view illustration in the second flyer, the cap's removal had not been brushed out. Actually, of the handful of known prototypes carrying the Eagle-Macomber badge, none featured this sketched bonnet design. In July 1917 Macomber hosted a two-day 'open house' for those who had bought stock in the company. Originating in Albany, the special train carried some 200 persons for the event at the Sandusky factory where efforts for additional stock sales were the main programme of the event. Walter Macomber drove several thousand miles throughout the Eastern Seaboard to the Midwest of the country setting up agencies for the car but, unfortunately, production failed to get underway and the prototypes of the touring car constituted the entire output of the Eagle-Macomber. Stock was still being sold as late as July 1918, operations ceasing shortly afterward.

KM

EAGLE MANUFACTURING (US) c.1982
Eagle Manufacturing, Campbell, California.
Ferraris were the target of choice for this kit car manufacturer. The Eagle GT was a replica of the Dino 246 that fitted on a Porsche 914 chassis. The GTO kit was a replica of the 1962 Series I Ferrari 250 GTO that was based on Datsun 240-280Z running gear. The GTO kit project was sold to ALPHA Design Engineering in 1983.

HP

EAGLE PERFORMANCE (US) c.1991
Eagle Performance, Morristown, New Jersey.
This high-performance street car was a replica of the 1985 Lola-Chevrolet Corvette GTP racing car. Built by Jay Drake and Dennis Kazmerowski, it used a square tube frame and Corvette suspension with a DL transaxle. Engine choices included 5700cc Chevrolet V8s and the Eagle 10,184cc racing V8 with close to 900hp. They were sold in kit form for under $50,000, with fully assembled cars priced at $130,000. Air-conditioning was optional.

HP

EAGLET (i) (US) 1914–1915
Eagle Automobile Co., Los Angeles, California.
This was a cyclecar powered by a 2-cylinder engine, with epicyclic transmission and shaft drive. A 2-seater and a delivery van were offered, both priced at $425.

NG

EAGLET (ii) (GB) 1948
Silent Transport Ltd, Woking, Surrey.
Austerity-era electric cars made much more of an impact on the continent than in Britain but the Eaglet was a rare example of a car designed to sell at a time when there was no basic petrol ration. It was produced by a company engaged in converting road cars to electric power, and was a lightweight 3-wheeled coupé with a range of up to 30 miles per charge and a top speed of 30mph. At an expensive £412, it scored little success, and it is thought that only six or seven were made.

CR

EARL (i) (F) c.1903
This was a French car sold in England under the name Earl. It was a 4-seater rear-entrance tonneau powered by a 9½ hp 2-cylinder engine, with chain final drive. The announcement mentioned an 'occasional seat in the tonneau to take an extra passenger' but it must have been very cramped, given the limited area around the tonneau. The car's overall length was only 120in (3046mm), the same as that of the Mini.

NG

EARL (ii) (US) c.1907–1908
Earl Motor Car Co., Kenosha, Wisconsin.
Although prototypes may have been made in Milwaukee, production Earls came from Kenosha. It was made initially as a 2-seater roadster powered by a 15hp 2-cylinder engine, with friction transmission and chain drive. For 1908 the roadster was named the Tiger Roadster and power upped to 18hp, although it was probably the same sized engine. There was also a 4-seater tourer with 22hp 4-cylinder engine. Earl was out of business by the middle of 1908, and the factory was subsequently taken over by the makers of the PETREL.

NG

EARL (iii) (US) 1922–1923
1922–1923 Earl Motors Inc., Jackson, Michigan.
1923 Earl Motor Manufacturing Co., Jackson, Michigan.
The Earl was a revamped BRISCOE, and this was made by Briscoe's then recently appointed president Clarence Earl following Briscoe's departure from the company. The Earl Model 40 was a better-looking car than the Briscoe, on

1948 Eaglet (ii) electric 3-wheeler.
NATIONAL MOTOR MUSEUM

a 3in (76mm) longer wheelbase with four body styles (plus two delivery vans). The roadster had cycle-type wings, step plates and wire wheels which put it, if not exactly in the Kissel class, far removed from the utilitarian Briscoe. The engine was enlarged to 3182cc. Towards the end of 1922 Clarence Earl had a disagreement with his backers who wanted to restrict production, while he wanted to expand. He left, later becoming president of NATIONAL (i), while the company was reorganised as the Earl Motor Manufacturing Co. early in 1923. Production ended during the year, after about 2000 Earls had been made.

NG

EASOM (GB) 1988
Seen at the Newark kit car show in 1988 but never again, the Easom Macho was a Ginetta G11 replica based on Jaguar XJ6 parts.

CR

EASTBOURNE (GB) 1905–1906
Eastbourne Motor Works, Eastbourne, Sussex.
A South Coast holiday resort was an unlikely location for a car maker, and the Eastbourne was probably assembled by a local garage. It had a 12hp 2-cylinder Aster engine, 4-speed gearbox and shaft drive. With 4-seater tonneau body, it was priced at £300.

NG

EASTERN (US) 1910–1911
Eastern Motor Co., Brockton, Massachusetts.
Organised by Alonso R. Marsh, who had previously made the MARSH (i), this company offered a 24hp 4-cylinder tourer, but few were made. Marsh was later involved with the VULCAN (ii) and then with the second car to bear his name, the MARSH (ii) of Cleveland.

NG

EASTMAN (US) 1898–1900
Eastman Automobile Co., Cleveland, Ohio.
In 1898 bicycle maker Henry F. Eastman built a single example of an electric car which he called the Electro Cycle. It was a single-seater 3-wheeler steered by very long tiller to the front wheel. It had a tubular frame, bicycle wheels and an all-steel body said to be the first of its kind in America. In 1900 he established the Eastman Automobile Co. whose products were steamers rather than electrics. They were typical of their kind and date, with a single-cylinder engine driving the rear axle by single chain, tiller steering and full-elliptic suspension all round; the front spring was transverse. The body was all steel, like that of the Electro Cycle. Attractive though it was, the Eastman steamer did not survive the year 1900, and Henry Eastman organised a new company, the Eastman Metallic Body Co. After a while he moved to Detroit to continue bodybuilding.

NG

EASTMEAD-BIGGS (GB) 1901–1904
Eastmead & Biggs, Frome, Somerset.
Mr Eastmead was a manufacturer of lifts at Blackfriars, London, who was to sell the cars made by T.J. Biggs in Somerset. In fact, only three cars were made, the first with a 3.5hp Simms engine, which was destroyed by fire. The second had an

8hp Simms engine, French-made gearbox and Biggs' own worm-drive rear axle. The third had an 8hp 2-cylinder Aster engine and the gearbox, rear axle and body were all French made. This car was said to have given good service for several years. In 1905 Biggs designed a car for RALEIGH (i) with 4-cylinder Fafnir engine and chain drive.

NG

EASTON (US) c.1998 to date
Easton Armstrong Engineering, Houston, Texas.
The Easton EAE/GT was a Lamborghini Countach replica kit car based on Pontiac Fiero running gear. A semi-monocoque chassis was optional with fabricated suspension. They were sold in kit or assembled form.

HP

EAST WIND *see* DONG FENG

EATON (US) 1898–1900
1898–1899 Eaton Electric Motor Carriage Co., Boston, Massachusetts.
1899–1900 Eaton Motor Carriage Co., Boston, Massachusetts.
This company exhibited a light 2-seater electric car at the Mechanics' Fair in Boston in 1898. Few were made, but a small batch was said to have been exported to London. The change of company name in 1899 might indicate that they were not to concentrate exclusively on electrics, but there is no evidence of any other cars from this company.

NG

E.B.M. (i) (D) 1912
This little known car was listed as having a 3.8-litre 4-cylinder engine, but further details have not been found.

NG

E.B.M. (ii) (ZA) 1990s
E.B.M., Salt River, Cape Town.
The product of an engineering works, the E.B.M. Manx was described as a latter-day Lotus 7. A low-slung sports 2-seater with a T-bar roof, it used a space frame chassis, mid-mounted VW Golf engine and gearbox and double wishbone front and MacPherson strut/multi-link rear suspension. Fully-built cars and kits were available.

CR

E.B.M. (iii) (ZA) 1994 to date
E.B.M., Cape Town.
Established by Eric Booth, E.B.M. began building racing cars in 1994 before turning its attention to road car development. Its first road-legal vehicle was a mid-engined supercar, developed and constructed in South Africa. After three prototypes, the Tazio was launched in 1999, weighing less than 2200lb (1000kg), and offered with a variety of V8 engine options, including Chevrolet or BMW power. E.B.M. boasted that the Tazio's chassis could cope with engine power in excess of 800bhp, and a top speed of up to 206mph (331km/h) was claimed. The Tazio had a stainless steel chassis with fibreglass bodywork, available in a variety of closed coupé or roadster styles.

CR

EBS (D) 1924
Ernest Bauermeister & Sohn, Berlin-Baumschulenweg.
This very simple 3-wheeler combined the front end of a motorcycle, including the engine and driver's saddle, with a 2-seater cabin at the rear. Drive to the rear wheels was by chain to the gearbox and thence by shaft. Single-cylinder engines of 200, 250 or 350cc from various sources were used.

HON

ECCO (US) c.1982
Edwards Car Co., Arlington, Virginia.
This awkwardly proportioned coupé was a kit car designed to fit a Volkswagen Beetle chassis. The body was fibreglass and much of the assembly work was completed at the factory.

HP

ECHARRI (E) 1996 to date
Echarri Motor International SL, Lardero-La Rioja.
Echarri, specialist of roundabout and parish fair implements, presented a vintage-style open car with fibreglass tonneau body at the Barcelona Motor Fair in 1996. The car used a Fiat Cinquecento 30bhp engine and some mechanical parts, but had a purpose-built tubular chassis. Details such as special headlamps, a vertical windscreen, spoked wheels and an outside hand brake lever, as well as the chain-drive on the rear wheels and crank-starter (both mock-ups), gave the car an authentic appearance. In 1999 José Luis Echarri prepared a Jaguar 100 replica based on a Beetle chassis and engine, but using sheet metal for the body.

VCM

ECHO (US) c.1994 to date
Echo Enterprises, Chino, California.
The popularity of the 1989 *Batman* movie sparked a revival of interest in the 1960s television series of the same name. This company made a replica of the 'Batmobile' from the television series.

HP

ÉCLAIR (i) (AUS) 1904
Carbine & Collier 2-Speed Cycle Co., Pty Ltd, Melbourne, Victoria.
A type of French origin having a 'special design for Australia', powered by a 6hp water-cooled De Dion-Bouton engine which drove through a 3-speed gearbox, the Éclair was claimed to have 'Panhard-type' gearing and a 'Mercedes-like' bonnet. In deference to Australian conditions, the tyres fitted were Michelin's heaviest duty type. Whether or not there was any connection with the later Paris-built ÉCLAIR (ii) is unknown.

MG

ÉCLAIR (ii) (F) 1907–1908
SA des Constructions d'Automobiles l'Éclair, Paris.
This company made a conventional car with a 20hp 4-cylinder engine and shaft drive. Open and closed bodies were available. They were also listed as makers of electric vehicles.

NG

ÉCLAIR (iii) (F) 1920–1923
Lebeau-Cordier, Courbevoie, Seine.
This was a cyclecar powered by a 7/9hp v-twin Anzani engine, with shaft drive.

NG

ECLIPSE (i) (US) 1900–1903
Eclipse Automobile Co., Easton, Massachusetts.
The Eclipse was fairly typical of early steam cars, with a short wheelbase, wire wheels and tiller steering. It differed from the norm in having a 3-cylinder engine, while most steamers managed with two, and shaft drive in place of the usual single-chain. One was tried by the local post office, but this did not result in an order for a fleet of delivery vans. The Eclipse was the first design from Everett S. Cameron, who later made the TAUNTON (i) and then the better-known CAMERON.

NG

ECLIPSE (ii) (GB) 1901–c.1906
Eclipse Engineering & Motor Co., Wandsworth, London.
This company began by making engines, and their 1901 model was a vertical-twin with mechanically-operated inlet valves. An announcement in *The Motor Car Journal* describing this also made promise of 'a new light car...to which we hope to refer later on', but they did not do so. However, a few cars were assembled over the next few years, with 12hp 2-cylinder or 20/24hp 4-cylinder engines. One of the latter, second-hand but described as perfectly new by the makers, was offered for sale in 1906.

NG

ECLIPSE (iii) (US) 1904
Eclipse Manufacturing Co., Elmira, New York.
This company was a bicycle manufacturer who changed their name from Bicycle Co. to Manufacturing Co. when they put on the market a touring car

powered by a 20hp 4-cylinder air-cooled engine. They soon realised that two wheelers were a better bet, and for 1905 they became again the Eclipse Bicycle Co.

NG

ECLIPSE (iv) (US) 1905–1906
Krueger Manufacturing Co., Milwaukee, Wisconsin.
The Eclipse Model A had a single-cylinder engine made as a single casting, which the Krueger brothers claimed never overheated whatever the conditions. It was installed in a light 4-seater tourer with epicyclic transmission and shaft drive. They also offered a Model B with 22hp 2-cylinder engine; this became the Krueger Model C for 1906, when the single-cylinder car was no longer listed. The Eclipse/Krueger was one of the first lhd cars to be made in America.

NG

ECLIPSE (v) (US) 1916
Eclipse Motor Car Co., Detroit, Michigan.
This company advertised an ambitious range of four models, all with different sized engines. There were three fours, a 28hp roadster, 34 and 40hp tourers, and a 45hp V8 tourer. They also advertised truck, motorcycle and motor boat manufacture, but how much actually took place in the year that the company was in business is not known. They were on the look out for agents, but a condition of taking up the Eclipse agency was to take an Eclipse course with the Detroit Correspondence Institute of Motoring. This was possibly the same organisation as the Eclipse Motor Car Co.

NG

ECLIPSE (vi) (B) 1922–1923
This was a short-lived car assembled at Keumiée from mainly French components, including chassis frames from S.U.P. of Cons-La Granville in the Ardennes. The S.U.P. used a Sergant engine, and it is possible that the Eclipse's 8/10CV four also came from this source. The only body style available was a tourer.

NG

ECO (AUS) 1924–1926
Eco Motors Co. Ltd, Melbourne, Victoria.
George Hamilton-Grapes was from New Zealand, where he had been involved with the motor trade. At Melbourne in 1915 he took an interest in fuel efficiency and had, by 1919, patented his 'Gasifier'. Aiming to produce his own car, he visited the United States in 1921, where a prototype was constructed. Apart from the gasifier, the Eco also used much aluminium for weight saving, concealed spare wheel stowage, front suspension compliance, heat-dissipating aluminium wheels, a prominent aluminium collar around the radiator to 'force-draught' air through the core and hub caps which would be used as winding drums for de-bogging. At an Oakleigh facility, production had begun by 1924, assembled with US components, such as a 3180cc 40bhp Lycoming 4-cylinder engine, Borg & Beck clutch, Gemmer steering, and Stewart-Warner instruments. Wheelbase was 111ins (2820mm) and the tourer weighed 1145kg. The Eco name was abbreviated from guaranteed economy and because it could operate on kerosene.

MG

ECO 2 (GB) 1989–1992
Ringsped Ltd, Thorne, Doncaster, South Yorkshire.
Richard Oakes of Anglo Design styled this very small two-seater city car. Its most remarkable feature was that the 2½-inch chassis tubes were visible externally, the polypropylene body panels being simply bolted on between them. The doors were made of glass. Ford Fiesta mechanical parts were used, including a 1.0-litre engine, 5-speed gearbox, and 4-wheel disc brakes. It was intended to sell cars in kit form as well as fully-built, but the necessary finance for a production run never materialised, although at least five prototypes were built. A longer 4-seater model had also been under development.

CR

ECONOMIC (GB) 1921–1922
Economic Motors, London.
This was probably the lightest, simplest and cheapest car to be offered to postwar British motorists. A 3-wheeler with single front wheel and virtually

1991 Eco 2 coupé.
GUERNSEY PRESS

no body, certainly no weather protection, it had an ash frame whose flexibility rendered any kind of springing unnecessary, or so the makers claimed. The engine was an air-cooled 2-stroke flat-twin of 165cc, driving the offside rear wheel by chain via a 2-speed friction transmission. The magneto was located in the flywheel. Unladen, the Economic weighed 150lbs (68kg), top speed was 30mph (48km/h), and the price was £60.

The company also made a motorcycle with the same engine, and this sold for only £28.10s (£28.50). In 1923 the motorcycles' address was given as the Eynsford Engineering Co., of Eynsford, Kent, but it is not known if cars were made there as well.

NG

ECONOMY (i) (US) 1908–1911
Economy Motor Buggy Co., Fort Wayne, Indiana;
Kankakee, Illinois and Joliet, Illinois.
There were more changes of factory than of the design of this typical high-wheel buggy, which had a 2-cylinder air-cooled engine and double-chain drive. The company moved from Fort Wayne as it was sued for patent infringement by the makers of the SUCCESS buggy. Why they should have thought that a move to Illinois would render them safe from the charge is not known, but Kankakee proved to be unfruitful, because the right labour force could not be found, and they moved to Joliet where the Success people caught up with them again. Economy then turned to commercial vehicles which they made into 1912.

NG

ECONOMY (ii) (US) 1917–1921
Economy Motor Co., Tiffin, Ohio; Bellefontaine, Ohio.
The Economy was a conventional assembled car powered by a 22.5hp 4-cylinder engine offered in three body styles, tourer, sedan and Three-Dor tourer which was what in England would have been called a close-coupled body. The rear seat passengers had their own door on one side only, hence the name, and advertising said 'all five passengers are in the party and no one is slighted', which sounds as if seating was more cramped than in the conventional tourer. Both the Three-Dor and conventional tourer were identically priced at $1695, while the sedan was considerably more expensive at $2295.

Prices were reduced for 1918, when a 5-seater Chummy Roadster was listed at $1040; presumably this was the Three-Dor renamed. A Ferro V8 engine was an alternative to the four. Cars were made at both Bellefontaine and Tiffin up to the end of 1919, when the Bellefontaine branch was bankrupt and the Tiffin operation was reorganised as the Vogue Motor Car Co. The models which appeared in 1920 had 6-cylinder Continental engines and were called Economy-Vogue, and for 1921–22 the VOGUE name was used on its own for a car with a slightly longer wheelbase. This was considerably more expensive, with prices running from $2285 for a tourer to $3250 for a sedan.

NG

ECONOMYCAR (US) 1914
Economycar Co., Providence, Rhode Island.
This was a tandem seating cyclecar powered by a 9hp air-cooled V-twin engine, with epicyclic transmission and belt drive. In this specification it was quite

1989 Ecosse Signature coupé.
NICK BALWIN

1937 Edford V8 sports car.
NATIONAL MOTOR MUSEUM

1919 Edis 10hp sports car.
NATIONAL MOTOR MUSEUM

c.1994 Edran Spyder MK I coupé.
NICK GEORGANO

typical of its kind, but an unusual and old-fashioned feature was centre-pivot steering. It was sold by the International Cyclecar Co. of New York City which said that 6000 would be made in 1914. It is likely that far fewer were actually made.
NG

ECONOMY VEHICLES (US) c.1983
Economy Vehicles, Fort Meyers, Florida.
The Persona GT was a kit car rebody for the Volkswagen Beetle floorpan. It could be modified to take VW, V6, V8 or turbo diesel engines.
HP

ECONOOM (NL) 1912–1914
Hautekeet & Van Asselt, Amsterdam.
The Econoom was more or less a light car rather than a cyclecar. Two former employees of the SPYKER car manufacturer, Messrs Hautekeet and Van Asselt, founded a car firm for themselves in 1912 to meet the demand for small vehicles. They bought a French 4-cylinder 14bhp 1130cc Ballot engine as a base, together with the gearbox and rear axle of Malicet et Blin (MAB) to assemble a small car. The car, with a weight of only 400kg was very comfortable and easy to drive because of the half-elliptic springs at the front and three-quarter elliptic units at the rear.
Although successful and reliable, World War I stopped production at about 85 units, of which a number were exported to the Dutch East Indies.
After the hostilities the partners did not start car production again.
FBV

ECOSSE (GB) 1988–1990
Ecosse Car Company, Knebworth, Hertfordshire.
After Ford bought A.C., the separate enterprise which owned the rights to make the ME3000 was forced to change its name to Ecosse. A heavily revised version of the ME3000, called the Signature, was developed by John Parsons and ex-B.R.M. technical director Aubrey Woods. The more rounded fibreglass body now incorporated carbon fibre strengthening. The monocoque chassis featured double wishbone suspension all round and the engine choice switched from Ford to 165bhp Fiat Croma Turbo.
CR

EDFORD (P) 1930–1938
Ferreirinha et Irmao, Oporto.
The only known prewar Portuguese make of car, the Edford was a sports car using Ford components. The first models used lowered Model A chassis with roadster bodies and cycle-type wings, followed in 1936 by an attractive 2-seater powered by the 3622cc V8 engine. This had coil ifs in place of the Ford's transverse leaf suspension, a light aluminium body weighing only 330lbs (150kg), and a top speed of 110mph (177km/h).
NG

EDIS (E) 1918–1922
Carlos Jaummandreu Martorell, Barcelona.
Two different cars were offered under this name. A light car with a 2-cylinder 1108cc engine and a body with a very large bonnet, participated at the III Bajo Peñadés Race. The second car, called A-2, had a 4-cylinder engine.
VCM

EDISMITH (GB) 1905
Edwin Smith, Blackburn, Lancashire.
Edwin Smith ran the Circus Garage in Blackburn, and exhibited a light car powered by a 9hp single-cylinder De Dion-Bouton engine at the 1905 Manchester Show. He never formed a company, and the Edismith probably remained a one-off.
NG

EDISON (US) 1903–1904; 1914; 1927
Despite championing the electric car, the great electrical engineer Thomas Alva Edison never made a car for sale. In 1903–04 he built three large electric cars at West Orange, New Jersey, for his own use, and two more experimental cars used the Edison name, one built in 1914 in conjunction with Henry Ford, and a roadster

1958 Edsel Citation 2-door hard top.

in New York City in 1927. Several commercial vehicles were sold in England from 1914 to 1927 as Edisons, but these were built by General Motors, with GM chassis and Edison batteries.

NG

EDIT (I) 1924
Armino Mezzo, Turin.
Mezzo designed and built the unusual MOTOCOR 3-wheeler and the Edit was a more conventional car from his pen. It had a 1-litre air-cooled V-twin engine, 3-speed gearbox and shaft drive.

NG

EDITH (AUS) 1955–1958
Gray & Harper Pty Ltd, Oakleigh, Victoria.
The numbers of miniature cars appearing in postwar Europe prompted the manufacture of the Edith, which was a rear-engined 3-wheeler powered by a 197cc Villiers 2-stroke engine. A 4-speed gearbox took the drive to the single rear wheel, steering was by rack and pinion and suspension was independent all round. Weight was 305kg, tyres were 400 × 8 and 40mph (65km/h) was claimed. In 1956 the headlamps were enclosed and a 4-wheeled development appeared shortly before the programme was terminated in 1958. About twelve were produced and four rolling chassis were supplied for TILLI. The Edith name was that of Frank Gray's mother and daughter.

MG

EDM (US) c.1988–1990
Exotic Dream Machines, Rancho Cordova, California.
Rebody kits for the Porsche 911/912 are not common, but they were the main products of this kit car company. The Dream Speedster was an attractive kit that converted the 911 into an open roadster with an original design nose and tail. The California R59 updated a 911 into a facsimile of the Porsche 959 exotic car. There was also a 959-inspired convertible called the Intrigue Speedster and a 'customised' version called the R59S. EDM also sold a Lamborghini Countach replica but all these projects were put up for sale in 1990 to finance an original-design car that never materialised.

HP

EDMOND (GB) 1920–1921
Shand Motor & Engineering Co. Ltd, Lee Green, London.
This was a cyclecar powered by a 5/7hp Coventry-Victor air-cooled flat-twin engine, with 3-speed gearbox and shaft drive. It was made in the same factory as the NORTH STAR, which was owned by Sir J.F. Payne-Gallwey, Brown & Co. Ltd, whose other car interests included the CARROW and SWALLOW.

NG

EDMUND (GB) 1920
C. Edmund & Co. (1920) Ltd, Chester.
Charles Edmund was better known for his motorcycles, which were built from 1907 to 1923, than for his cars. These were cyclecars with 2-cylinder engines and shaft drive.

NG

EDRAN (B) 1993 to date
Edran, Limburg.
Designer and Porsche RSK replica importer André Hanjoul was inspired by the Porsche RS 60 Spider sports racer when creating the Edran Spider. It was an attractive mid-engined 2-seater coupé with fibreglass-and-Kevlar bodywork. Cars were either powered by a 2-litre Volkswagen or a Ford 1.8-litre engine, in either case mounted in the rear.

CR

EDSEL (US) 1957–1959
1957–1958 Ford Motor Co. (Edsel Division), Detroit, Michigan.
1958–1959 Ford Motor Co. (Mercury-Edsel-Lincoln Division), Detroit, Michigan.
The butt of countless jokes and the origin of a new word for failure, the Edsel was planned to give Ford an additional marque in the middle-class bracket. In the early 1950s Ford had something of an inferiority complex towards General Motors, sales lagging behind their rival by more than a million cars in 1954. They had only three marques, Ford, Mercury and Lincoln, compared with GM's five, and the Edsel was intended to bracket Mercury at either end, with a wide spread of models and engines.

At first the new car was to be all new, with its own engines and body shells, but Ford engineers soon found that this would be too expensive, so existing body shells were used; Ford in the lower-priced Ranger and Pacer models, Mercury for the more expensive Corsair and Citation. Two engines were offered from the new family of ohv V8s, a 303bhp 5915cc and a 345bhp 6718cc, which were not used by either Ford or Mercury, although they were of similar design. As the bodies and engines were familiar, a note of distinction had to be sounded somewhere, and this took the form of a vertical radiator grill, generally likened to a horse collar. Stylist Roy Brown had worked on the 1938 La Salle at GM's Art & Colour Studio and took his inspiration from that. 'Why don't we do something so old that it's brand new?' Another feature not found on any other Ford product was a push-button gear selector in the centre of the steering wheel.

When it was announced in September 1957 there were 13 models of Edsel in four series on three wheelbases, 116in (2946mm) (station wagons), 118 and 124in (2997 and 3150mm). As well as the wagons there were 2- and 4-door sedans, hard-tops and convertibles. Prices ran from $2519 for a 2-door Ranger sedan, a little above the Ford Fairlane on the same wheelbase but with a smaller engine, to $3810 for a Citation convertible, $317 less than a Mercury Park Lane convertible. Compared with rivals from other companies, these prices were lower than DeSoto or Oldsmobile, about on a par with Pontiac and slightly higher than Dodge.

Named after Edsel Ford, son of Henry I and father of Henry II, the new car was launched with a spectacular television show starring Bing Crosby, Frank Sinatra and Louis Armstrong, but sales were disappointing from the start. To break even Ford needed to sell 650 Edsels each day, but the best they managed was 409, and that only for the first ten days, after which it fell to around 300. There were many reasons for this. The market for medium sized cars, around 40 per cent when the Edsel was first planned, had dropped to 25 per cent by 1957 because of the inroads made by imports and smaller American cars such as the Rambler. The dealer network was unsatisfactory, for only 118 had exclusive franchises for Edsel, the rest were also selling Mercurys or even DeSotos, which were not Ford products at all. With sales hard to find, they were naturally likely to push the well-known brand rather than a newcomer. Quality control was poor, as Edsel production was squeezed into the end of each hour of Ford output, with the inevitable problems associated with rushed work. Dealers and buyers soon began to see Edsels as being of inferior quality to Fords and Mercurys. Above all, the Edsel failed to live up to the hype about its being a brand new car ('There's never been a car like the '58 Edsel') when all it was in effect was a Ford with a funny front.

Disappointing early sales ended the separate Edsel Division, and from January 1958 it was part of the M-E-L Division which also handled the small imports from British and German Ford factories. The range was slimmed down for 1959, to three lines, Ranger, Corsair and the station wagons, only one wheelbase (120in/3048mm) and four engines, a 3654cc economy six and V8s of 4785, 5440 and 5915cc. Sales slipped further; the horse-collar grill, which kept comedians busy, was blamed and was dropped for the 1960 Edsels. These looked somewhat like last year's Pontiac and public response was so poor that the plug was pulled on 19 November 1959, after only 2846 of the 1960 models had been made. Customers who had placed orders for Edsels were given a $300 credit towards the purchase of any other Ford product. It is said that the Edsel venture lost Ford $250 million; some say that it was the right car at the wrong time, others that it was the wrong car for any time. A more charitable summing up was that its aim was right but the target moved.

NG

Further Reading
'Of horse collars and lost Dollars: The unfortunately short history of the Edsel', John A. Heilig, *Automobile Quarterly*, Vol.31, No.1.

EDWARDS (i) (GB) 1913
J. Leslie Edwards, King's Norton, Worcestershire.
The Edwards cyclecar was marketed in two models, the Touring and the Brooklands, the latter having a doorless body and deeper scuttle. They were powered by an 8/10hp Precision engine, with friction transmission and chain drive to one rear wheel.

NG

EDWARDS (ii) (US) 1949–1955
E. H. Edwards Co., San Francisco, California.

Sterling Edwards was a wealthy Californian who wanted to build an American sports car to compete with European models on the track and in the showroom. The aluminium-bodied prototype was a combination street and race car designed by Norman Timbs and built by Indy car fabricators Emil Diedt, Lujie Lesovsky and Phil Remington. It used a ladder frame with independent suspension all round, disc brakes and a Ford V8 60 engine with Ardun cylinder heads. It was a successful racer and was followed by a Henry J-based version with a Chrysler V8. Edwards then dropped these racing versions to concentrate on street cars. A prototype street car with Henry J chassis and Oldsmobile engine followed, and the final production version of 1954 used a stylish Ghia-like fibreglass body designed by Edwards. It was available in hard-top and convertible versions with shortened Ford chassis and 205hp Lincoln V8s. Even with an expensive price tag, Edwards lost money on each car and only a reputed six were sold.

HP

EDWARDS-KNIGHT (US) 1912–1913
Edwards Motor Car Co., Long Island City, New York.
This car was the work of H.J. Edwards who had been with STODDARD-DAYTON and had designed the Stoddard-Knight for them. In February 1912 he and C.G. Stoddard left the company which had become part of Benjamin Briscoe's ill-fated United States Motor Co., and set up on their own as the Edwards Motor Co. Understandably Edwards used a Knight sleeve-valve engine, a 40/50hp 4.5-litre four. A 4-speed gearbox had direct drive in third, with fourth being an overdrive. It had a double-dropped frame giving a low appearance, and was made in five body styles, tourer, roadster, speedster, limousine and landaulette. Production began in December 1912 but not many were made as in October 1913 the design, licence and factory equipment were bought by John North Willys. The machinery was moved to Elyria, Ohio where the car went into production as the WILLYS-KNIGHT. This was made in greater numbers than any other American sleeve-valve car.

NG

E.E.C. (GB) 1952–1954
Electrical Engineering Construction Co. Ltd, Totnes, Devon.
Also known as the E.E.C.C. or the 'Workers' Playtime' (a then-popular radio programme), James Elliott's attempt to ride the bubble-car bubble created few ripples on the motoring scene. It was clothed in square-edged steel body with a front-opening door and was a foot higher than it was wide. An overheating Excelsior Talisman 250cc twin-cylinder engine could be found by the rear wheel. Despite a weight of only 588lbs and a price tag of £280 plus purchase tax, no sales records have been traced.

DF

EELCO (US) c.1975
EELCO Manufacturing and Supply Co., Inglewood, California.
Although this company sold a full line of drag racing parts, they also built a kit hot rod called the T Streetster. It was a conventional Model T rod with a simple ladder frame and was set up for V8 engines. They also made a heavy-duty frame for dune buggies that mounted any Manx-style body.

HP

EESTI (US) c.1985
Eesti Engineering, Poway, California.
The Eesti was not a kit car *per se*, but a set of plans for building a sports coupé from raw materials. Running gear was from General Motors front-wheel drive sedans with L4 and V6 engines placed amidships. The frame was a fabricated steel unibody with a fibreglass and polyurethane foam body made from the plan set. Although labour-intensive to build, the Eesti was a distinctive 2-seat coupé with angular wedge-like lines.

HP

EFP (US) c.1966–1980
Electric Fuel Propulsion Corp., Detroit, Michigan.
The 1966 Mars II was an electric car built out of a Renault R10 sedan. It used lead-cobalt batteries that could be recharged up to 200 times. This was accomplished by four 30-volt battery packs. During deceleration and coasting

the batteries were recharged by dynamic braking. In the early 1970s, EFP made electric powered versions of the AMC Hornet. The 1978 Transformer 1 was a $30,000 luxury electric car based on a General Motors mid-sized sedan body and chassis. It used a lead-cobalt battery system with a 32-volt DC motor. Top speed was supposedly 70mph (113km/h) and air conditioning and leather seats were standard. For longer trips, a mobile generator mounted on a small trailer could be towed behind to recharge the batteries during 2-hour fuel breaks. A proposed Transformer II was to be based on a Cadillac Seville chassis and body.

HP

1977 EFP Transformer I electric coupé.
NATIONAL MOTOR MUSEUM

E.G. (GB) 1987–c.1994

E.G. Autokraft Restorations (Arrow Spyder Ltd), Ponthenri, Llanelli, Dyfed.
This Welsh company was mainly involved in maintaining genuine Ferraris and converting real Daytona Coupés to Spyders, but it also made Daytona Spyder and Coupé replicas. This replica – initially called the P.K.A. V12 but later dubbed the Arrow Spyder – used a backbone chassis with Jaguar XJ12 or XJS mechanicals: the V12 engine was right and the suspension offered the right blend of sporting handling and superlative ride. The company entertained the idea of alternative power trains. The basis was a complex tubular chassis on to which was bonded an exacting body in a choice of fibreglass, fibreglass/Kevlar, steel or aluminium.

CR

EGAN (AUS) 1935–1936

Egan Motor Body Works, Geelong, Victoria.
The Egan works had been wholly involved with motor bodybuilding since 1916 and had been contracted to build the commercial bodies for Ford when it set up its car factory at Geelong. Will Egan's own car, which had US components fitted into a frame of his own fabrication, was exhibited at the 1935 Melbourne Motor Show. The 6-cylinder Lycoming engine produced 80bhp, the axles were Columbia, the steering was by Ross cam and lever and Bendix hydraulic brakes were fitted, while local products included springs, dampers and radiator. Although an aluminium high compression cylinder head ensured a satisfying performance, its riding qualities were unable to match those of cars then featuring independent suspension.

MG

1935 Egan Six sedan.
NATIONAL MOTOR MUSEUM

EGG & EGLI (CH) 1896–1919

1896–1900 Motorwagenfabrik Egg & Egli, Zürich.
1919 Rudolf Egg, Zürich.
Rudolf Egg (1866–1939), an engineer, built his first motorcar in 1893 for his personal use and fun. Three years later he met his partner Egli who was persuaded to finance and found a new company in Zurich. The Bollée-like 3-wheeler was of simple and solid design with side by side seating and belt drive and its proven De Dion single-cylinder engine of 3hp was water cooled and was mounted in the rear. With two on board, the little vehicle would climb 20 per cent gradients and had a top speed reputed to be 25mph. The price of SFr2000 covered the basic version. A folding hood and 2-seater trailer could be supplied at extra cost. In 1898 a licence was sold to BÄCHTOLD & Co, Steckborn who made six cars only, and to WEBER of Uster, who made about 50. In 1899 the design and all manufacturing rights were sold to Zürcher Patent-Motorwagenfabrik RAPID, which was managed by Jacques Syz and produced more than 100 cars which were sold under the name RAPID.

Rudolf Egg continued to develop light cars of his own. The 4-wheel voiturette, built on the lines of the Benz Velo, received a horizontal single-cylinder engine mounted in the rear and chain drive. Only a few were built. In 1900 Egg drove a RAPID 3-wheeler from Zürich to Paris to show it at the World Fair. In 1904 he helped to found the new EXCELSIOR automobile factory. Rudolf Egg, like many pioneer automobile engineers, became interested in aeroplanes, and based on his drawings, patents and a sample, the Maschinenfabrik Oerlikon built the first Swiss aeroplane engine of 50/60hp. He then returned to the development of passenger cars and built prototypes of light tourers.

During World War I, Rudolf Egg designed and developed a new car using a Zürcher proprietory 4-cylinder side-valve engine. It was shaft driven and the gearbox was in unit with the rear axle. One example, with a neat 2-seater body, has survived in a private collection. Small series of a similar car were produced by

1896 Egg & Egli 3-wheeler.
ERNEST SCHMID

MOSER, St Aubin. Rudolf Egg worked with Maschinenfabrik in Seebach after the war and designed a basically similar car but with an electric starter and equipment; this was produced in small numbers only and sold under the name SEMAG. Egg then took up the agency for Renault in Zürich until 1934. He died of a heart attack in 1939.

FH

Further Reading
'Schweizer Autopionier Rudolf Egg', Ferdinand Hediger,
Automobil Revue, February 1965.

1922 Ego 4/14PS phaeton.
NICK BALDWIN

1923 E.H.P. sports car.
NATIONAL MOTOR MUSEUM

1925 E.H.P. 6/8 CV Saloon.
NICK BALDWIN

EGO (D) 1921–1926

1921–1925 Mercur Flugzeugbau GmbH, Berlin.
1925–1926 Hiller Automobilfabrik AG, Berlin.
Like many aircraft makers, Mercur looked for a new activity after World War I, and began to make a light car with a 1016cc 4/14PS 4-cylinder engine of its own construction, also available in a twin-carburettor tuned version giving 24bhp. The Ego was more reliable than many rival small cars, and also became well known in sporting events. The great racing driver Rudolf Caracciola competed in an Ego in 1922, before joining Mercedes. In 1924 they turned to a larger car with 1.3-litre 5/25PS engine and a 4-seater body. This was not a success, and production ended soon afterwards.

HON

E.H.P. (F) 1921–1929

Établissements Henri Precloux, La Garennes-Colombes, Seine.
Named after its maker's company, the E.H.P. began life as one of the more attractive French cyclecars, with a low build, shaft drive, cantilever rear springs and a radiator resembling a 'miniature' Rolls-Royce. It was powered by a 1093cc

ohv Ruby OS engine, a little-known unit from the famous Courbevoie firm, though it was also used by Robert Sénéchal. An E.H.P. won its first hill climb victory on its first outing, at Argenteuil in April 1921. Production models of 1921–22 included a 2-seater tourer, 2-seater sports which had a windscreen of the Vutotal type seen on Chenard-Walckers in the late 1930s, and very light delivery vans. Bodies were made by Carrosserie Générale de l'Automobile of Courbevoie; this company took over E.H.P. in September 1922 and henceforth Precloux supplied chassis to C.G.A. who bodied them and arranged sales. Among the bodies were a 2-seater coupé, a drophead coupé, a mahogany-bodied skiff sports, a delivery van, and a miniature fire engine. Also in 1922, Precloux sold a licence to LORYC in Palma, Majorca, who built about 100 cars over the next four years, sold either as Loryc or Loryc-E.H.P.

From 1922 side-valve S.C.A.P. engines of 893 or 960cc were used, and for 1924 a new and larger E.H.P. was announced. The D4 (later DM) had a longer wheelbase suitable for 4-door coachwork, both open and closed. It was powered by a 1200cc ohv C.I.M.E. engine in a chassis made by BIGNAN which was among the firms to which C.G.A. supplied bodies. The long chassis version was called the DS. In 1925 there was the DT Speciale, a sports car powered by a 1495cc single-ohc C.I.M.E. engine. Only four or five were made; two tourers ran at Le Mans in 1925 and one example carried a very handsome 2-seater mahogany body; low built and with cycle-type wings and a pointed tail it resembled an Amilcar.

The DM and DS made up the range to 1928, joined at the 1927 Salon by the DV. This had a DS chassis lengthened by 1in (25.4mm) to 98in (2500mm), and was powered by side-valve 6-cylinder C.I.M.E. engines of 1215 or 1491cc. A sports car with supercharged 4-cylinder S.C.A.P. engine was also seen at the 1927 Salon, but was not put into production. E.H.P. had no stand at the 1928 Salon, although the DS and DV were listed into 1929. The C.G.A. was involved in Bignan's financial problems, and some of the last E.H.P.s were fitted with Bignan radiators. Henri Precloux made no further cars; in the mid-1960s he was working as a welder in a Paris suburb.

NG

Further Reading
'Les E.H.P', Serge Pozzoli, *l'Album du Fanatique*, March–June 1983.

EHRHARDT; EHRHARDT-SZAWE (D) 1904–1924

1904–1922 Heinrich Ehrhardt, Düsseldorf; Zella St Blasii.
1922–1924 Ehrhardt-Szawe Automobilwerk AG, Berlin; Zella St Blasii.
Heinrich Ehrhardt (1840–1928) was the founder of the Fahrzeugfabrik EISENACH AG, leaving in 1904 to set up a new factory at Düsseldorf which was run by his son Gustav. As with Eisenach, his cars were based on DECAUVILLE designs to begin with, and were sometimes sold as Ehrhardt-Decauvilles. In 1905 Ehrhardt launched a light car with 1272cc 2-cylinder engine of its own design, which was sold under the name Fidelio.

The Decauville designs were gradually given up and Ehrhardt made large cars of his own design. Among these was the 8-litre 31/50PS of 1913 which was the first German car to feature front-wheel brakes. After the war Ehrhardt built a few cars before combining with the coachbuilders Szawe, to make the Ehrhardt-Szawe. This had a 2.6-litre 10/50PS 6-cylinder engine with Soden automatic gearbox and, naturally, Szawe coachwork. It was a high-quality car but found few buyers in the austerity of 1920s Germany. Later the PLUTO light car was made in the factory at Zella-St Blasii.

HON

E.H.V. *see* COMPOUND

EIA (I) 1928

Società Lombarda Anonime Industriale Automobili.
This was a conventional 1-litre 4-cylinder car with 3-speed gearbox which never passed the prototype stage.

NG

EIBACH (D) 1924

Eichner & Bachmann GmbH, Berlin.
This was a 3-wheeler with single rear wheel powered by a 200cc DKW engine. The rear was like a motorcycle and two passengers sat in a forecar ahead of the rider.

HON

E.I.M. (US) 1915

Eastern Indiana Motor Car Co., Richmond, Indiana.
This was a light car with 4-seater body powered by an 18hp 4-cylinder engine, and with an underslung chassis. The engine was mounted on the frame rather than between the side members, which the company claimed prevented 'bedding' on rough ground. Only three cars were built, though the company's directors tried again with the LAUREL, which was made from 1916 to 1920.

NG

EINAUDI (F) 1927

Cyclecars Einaudi, Bois-Colombes, Seine.
This was a late example of the very small cyclecar which belonged more to the beginning of the decade. It had a 3.5hp single-cylinder engine, a 4-speed gearbox and a wheelbase of only 58½ins (1486mm). Its track was a mere 32½ins (825mm).

NG

EISENACH (D) 1898–1903

Fahrzeugfabrik Eisenach AG, Eisenach.
This company was best known for the light cars of DECAUVILLE design which were sold under the name WARTBURG. However, electric cars were also made and these were sold under the Eisenach name.

HON

EISENHUTH see COMPOUND

EKAMOBIL (D) 1913–1914

Ing. Erhard Brandis, Berlin.
This was a 3-wheeler with single front wheel, powered by a 6hp engine, with transmission by chain and shaft to the rear axle.

HON

ÉLAN (F) 1898–1900

Sté des Automobiles Élan, Paris.
This was a voiturette powered by a single-cylinder De Dion-Bouton engine driving the rear axle by chain. Some were made under licence in Belgium by GERMAIN. In 1900 Élan made a car powered by two single-cylinder De Dion engines, each driving a rear wheel separately.

NG

ELAND MERES see RHINO

ELBERT (US) 1914–1915

1914–1915 Elbert Motor Car Co., Seattle, Washington.
1915 Elbert Motor Car Co., Sunnyvale, California.
The Elbert was a tandem-seated cyclecar powered by an 18hp 4-cylinder engine with shaft drive to what was called a 'gearless differential'. It was offered with a standard or underslung frame, and cost a modest $295 for the passenger version, or $305 as a delivery van. The move to Sunnyvale was announced in March 1915, but apparently no production took place there as the premises consisted of a wayside blacksmith's shop.

NG

ELBURN-RUBY see RUBY

ELCAR (i) (US) 1916–1931

1916–1921 Elkhart Carriage & Motor Car Co., Elkhart, Indiana.
1921–1931 Elcar Motor Co., Elkhart, Indiana.
A well known small production make of car, the Elcar, was launched in 1916 by William B. and George B. Pratt, brothers who had manufactured the Pratt-Elkhart and the Pratt cars from 1909 at their family-owned carriage and buggy factory which had built horse-drawn vehicles since before the turn of the century. The first Elcars for 1916 and 1917 were typical assembled cars with Lycoming 4-cylinder engines. The 4-cylinder car was augmented by a larger 6-cylinder line in 1918 powered by a Continental 7R and both cars would be continued through 1924 with styling changed in keeping with the times, the 4-cylinder series using Lycoming engines and the sixes Continentals – the 7R through 1922, the 8R in 1923 and the 7U in 1924. During this period Elcar

1906 Ehrhardt 15/24PS tourer.
NATIONAL MOTOR MUSEUM

1927 Elcar (i) model 8-90 saloon by Theo Sprengers.
NICK BALDWIN

1930 Elcar (i)140 convertible sedan.
KEITH MARVIN

built cars on order for several other makes of cars which had no factories of their own and, in addition, produced a complete line of both 4- and 6-cylinder taxicabs to which both the Elcar and other badges were affixed. The taxis would be built until Elcar closed its doors in 1931.

In 1925 an 8-cylinder Lycoming-engined series was introduced augmenting its fours and sixes and in 1926 a Lycoming engine replaced the Continental 7U. Elcar dropped its four in 1927.

By 1928 Elcar offered four series – a six and three eights – at prices ranging from $1295 to $2595. These four lines of Elcars would be continued through 1929, the cheapest series being the Series 75 roadster for $995; the most expensive, the Model 120 eight 7-seater sedan with a 134in (3400mm) wheelbase, priced at $2645.

For 1930 Elcar debuted its Series 130 8-cylinder line on a wheelbase of 130ins (3300mm) and a horsepower potential of 140, making it the third most powerful car in the United States, only the Duesenberg 'J' and the Cadillac V16

1903 Eldredge 8hp runabout.
NATIONAL MOTOR MUSEUM

being more powerful. One series of eights was dropped for 1931, Elcar's final year. A six and two eights comprised the company's offerings, including the big Series 140, available only as a sedan, and a convertible sedan priced at $2120 and $1995, respectively.

Also projected but unsuccessful commercially was the Elcar-Lever, a car introduced at the New York Auto Show and featuring a design by Rev. Alvah Powell with a 6 × 8in bore and stroke. Elcar, over the years, had built a few cars on special order, the last of which were the two prototypes for the Mercer, an unsuccessful attempt to re-introduce the Mercer which had failed in 1926, the prototypes of which were basically Series 140 Elcars with a Mercer badge and minor cosmetic changes.

The Elcar failed during 1931 with a production of only 138 cars, its most successful year having been 1924 when 1836 cars had found buyers. Altogether, approximately 20,000 Elcars were completed in the company's 16 years of activity.

KM

ELCAR (ii) (US) 1975–1977
Elcar Corp., Elkhart, Indiana.
Elcar sold the Italian Zele electric cars, as well as the Cinderella, and electric vehicle resembling a 1903 Dargea. It had a 2hp motor and hydraulic brakes on the rear wheels only. It had a top speed of 20mph (32km/h).

NG

ELCO (US) 1915–1917
1915–1916 Bimel Buggy Co., Sidney, Ohio.
1916–1917 Bimel Automobile Co., Sidney, Ohio.
The Elco was initially planned to have been produced by the Elwood Iron Works of Elwood, Indiana, which also intended to introduce a V8 under the BAILEY-KLAPP name. Bankruptcy ended its plans before they began and the organisation was acquired by the Bimel Buggy Works which had been in business since 1844. They turned to car components in 1904 under the name Bimel Spoke & Auto Wheel Works, though they seem to have reverted to the original name when car production began. The Elco Four was a less interesting car than the Bailey-Klapp, thoroughly conventional, in fact, with a 30hp 4-cylinder Caille engine and made in two models, a 2-seater roadster and a 5-seater tourer, both priced at $585. A projected 6-cylinder car was never built. The Caille Engine Co. of Detroit was one of the country's leading manufacturers of slot machines and other more sophisticated gambling equipment, and also of outboard motors for boats. Because of the possible illegality and seizure of slot machines at the time, the makers always had another basic product to fall back on. In some cases it might be scales, safes and jukeboxes; Caille chose engines. Some of the last Elcos may have been sold under the Bimel name. The company was out of business by May 1917 and its assets, including leftover cars, were purchased by the American Motor Parts Co. of Indianapolis.

KM

ELDIN ET LAGIER (F) 1899–1901
Eldin et Lagier, Lyons.
This partnership sold De Dion-Boutons and assembled a small number of cars themselves from time to time, though there was no continuing series production. In 1899 they made a small car designed by Captain Barisien, with two front-mounted 1.75hp De Dion engines, while in 1901 they made a larger car with 20hp 4-cylinder engine for King Leopold II of Belgium. There is no evidence of car manufacture after 1901. In 1906 Alphonse Eldin was sales director of ROCHET-SCHNEIDER.

NG

ELDON see RACECORP

ELDREDGE (US) 1903–1906
National Sewing Machine Co., Belvidere, Illinois.
Thinking that it was a logical step from sewing machines to bicycles and then to cars, this company began making the former in 1894, and the latter in 1903. They were contracted to produce cars for sale by Oscar FRIEDMAN of Chicago under his own name, but apparently failed to deliver any. Nevertheless photographs of the Friedman and the first Eldredge show very similar cars, apart from the Friedman's lack of lights, which could well have been added later. The Friedman was described as a 6hp, the Eldredge as an 8hp, but both had 2-cylinder engines under the seat, tiller steering, chain drive, and a similar curved radiator. Later Eldredges had left-hand wheel steering.

NG

ELECTRA (i) (D) 1899–1900
H. Kruger, Berlin.
This was a very simple 2-seater 3-wheeler with electric motor.

HON

ELECTRA (ii) (US) 1913
Storage Battery Power Co., Chicago, Illinois.
This company's main business was the manufacture and supply of batteries and other components to the electric car industry, but for one year they advertised a complete car. It was a 2-seater roadster which sold for $750.

NG

ELECTRA (iii) (US) 1914–1915
Electra Manufacturing Co., Los Angeles, California.
This company offered one style of electric car, a 2-seater roadster with bonnet giving the appearance of a petrol car. The Model C on a 90in (2284mm) wheelbase sold for $750, while the Model D on a 96in (2436mm) wheelbase cost $1250. The difference lay not so much in the length as in the extra batteries of the Model D, which gave a 75 mile range, compared with 40 miles for the cheaper car.

NG

ELECTRA (iv) (US) c.1974
Die Mesh Corp., Pelham, New York.
Fiat 850 Spyders were converted to electric power by this company, using three 3.2hp motors. They had a range of 40 miles.

HP

ELECTRACTION (GB) 1976–1980
Electraction Ltd, Maldon, Essex.
Alongside ENFIELD, Electraction was the only serious British electric car project of the 1970s. The first model to see the light of day was the EVR-1 (also known as the Town Coupé and the Tropicana), which had Vauxhall Chevette headlamps and Vauxhall running gear. The glassfibre bodywork was styled by ex-Ford designer Roy Haynes. As well as the first coupé design, Electraction displayed a forward-control doorless buggy style called the Rickshaw (also known as the Bermuda), which had a 'Surrey' soft-top. There was also a van derivative of this model. A 7.5bhp Lansing-Bagnall electric motor powered all Electraction models. There were a number of appearances at international motor shows and the famous sports car maker A.C. was lined up to make up to 2400 cars a year, but nothing came of the plan.

CR

ELECTRA KING *see* B&Z

ELECTRAPH (F) 1942–c.1944
Raphael Bethenod, Cannes.
The Electraph 225 was an electric coupé with aerodynamic body by Brandome. It was designed by racing driver Raphael Bethenod, whose pseudonym was Raph, and had a range of 130 miles (205km) at an average speed of 25mph (40km/h). About 40 were made.
NG

ELECTRICA (US) 1981–c.1990
Jet Industries, Austin, Texas.
This was an electric conversion of the Dodge Omni, with a 22kW motor driving through the standard 4-speed manual gearbox.
NG

ELECTRICAR (i) (F) 1919–1924
Couillet, St Ouen, Seine.
Known as the Auto Bijou, this was a simple 3-wheeled electric car with single front wheel and wheel steering, the column of which could be moved to effect gear changing and braking. The motor was rated at no more than 0.5hp, and top speed was a leisurely 8mph (12km/h). Range was 30 miles (50km). Rear suspension was by semi-elliptic springs, but the front wheel was unsprung. The body was a single-seater without weather protection, but about 44lbs (20kg) of luggage could be carried as well, so long as the driver was not too heavy.
NG

ELECTRICAR (ii) (US) 1950–1966
Boulevard Machine Works, North Hollywood, California.
This relatively long-lived electric runabout was sold in three distinct versions. The Boulevard was a 2-seater with four 1/6hp electric motors, one for each wheel. The Cutie was a single-seater with one motor in front and one in the back. Finally the Cutie Junior had a single rear motor.
CR

ELECTRIC SHOPPER (US) 1952–1962
Electric Shopper, Long Beach, California.
This 3-wheeler was intended for short shopping errands and used a 1.5hp electric motor giving a range of 35 miles. It was available with a steel or fibreglass body with a rudimentary top and no side protection. A single front wheel was used.
HP

ELECTROBILE (US) 1951
Details of a 3-wheeled runabout with a DC electric motor appeared in 1951. If the reports were correct, this may have been one of the very first cars with a fibreglass body, but it is uncertain if any cars were actually built.
CR

ELECTROCICLO (E) 1946–c.1953
Electrociclos SA, Eibar, Guipúzcoa.
Announced in 1942, the small Electrociclo cars were built from 1946. There were three versions – 2-seater, delivery van, and 3-wheeled motorcycle. They used electric motors built by Spanish General Electric Co., and Tudor batteries.
VCM

ELECTROCYCLETTE (F) 1923–1925
Applications Eléctro-Mécaniques, Neuilly, Seine.
This company made a light electric cyclecar with the appearance of a petrol car, powered by a 0.75hp motor, with a range of 62 miles (100km) at an average speed of 12mph (20km/h). There were two models, the single-seater Type M at 4000 francs, and the 2-seater Type B at 5000 francs. Although the makers described the Electrocyclette as 'a dream car, without petrol or oil, without noise or fumes', they hedged their bets by adding the Type E which had a 5hp single- or 2-cylinder air-cooled petrol engine in the same chassis as the electric car. It was lighter than the electric, and had a top speed of 30mph (50km/h). They also listed the 4-cylinder Type O, with a speed of 44mph (70km/h).
In 1927 A.E.M. brought out a front-drive electric light car and delivery van under the name A.E.M.
NG

1976 Electraction EVR-1 coupé.
NATIONAL MOTOR MUSEUM

ELECTROGENIA *see* CHAMPROBERT

ELECTROLETTE (F) 1941–1943
P.A. André, Nice.
This was a very light electric car with 1.5hp motor which gave a speed of 12mph (20km/h). The cars had independent suspension all round, and could be had in open or coupé forms. During 1942 they were being made at the rate of two per day, but eventually wartime shortage of materials forced M. André to give up production.
NG

ELECTRO MASTER (US) 1962–1970
Nepa Manufacturing Co., Pasadena, California.
Produced during a spate of American electric car sales, this was a shopping car with a fibreglass body powered by a 2hp electric motor and fed by six 6V batteries. The top speed was 20mph (32km/h), the total range 40 miles (64km/h).
CR

ELECTROMOBILE (i) *see* CHAPMAN

ELECTROMOBILE (ii) (GB) 1902–1920
British Electromobile Co. Ltd, London.
The electric car was never as widespread in Britain as in the United States, but the Electromobile was the best-known of the British products and was familiar in the passenger car and commercial vehicle fields. The British & Foreign Electric Vehicle Co. Ltd of Lambeth in South London was founded in 1900, their business being the selling of French-built electrics, particularly the KRIEGER, under the names B.E.C. and Powerful. In November 1900 the name was changed to British Electromobile Co. Ltd and in 1902 they decided to sell cars under this name. They ordered 50 chassis from Greenwood & Batley of Leeds in October 1902, which were delivered in batches over the next six months. They had motors on the rear axle and had solid tyres. Bodies were made by a variety of firms in London, and also in Gloucester by the Gloucester Railway Carriage & Waggon Co. Ltd which had bodied some of the Bersey electric cabs in 1897–98.
From 1903 the Electromobile had motors combined with the rear axle made under French Contal patents, with double-reduction drive and pneumatic tyres. Bodies were mostly town broughams with the driver sitting above the front axle, although some open victorias were also made, one with the body suspended on C-springs on the chassis. In 1908 a fleet of 20 taxicabs went into service in London, some still being on the streets in the 1920s. It is difficult to establish the end of Electromobile production; they exhibited at Olympia up to 1907, but their stand in 1908 had an OPPERMAN electric landaulette and several OPEL petrol cars, for which they were the agents. In 1908 there were only Opels on the stand, although Electromobiles remained in buyers' guides until 1911. The total number of chassis supplied by Greenwood & Batley was 303, probably most of them before 1907. In 1904 they moved premises to

1907 Electromobile (ii) landaulet.
NATIONAL MOTOR MUSEUM

Hertford Street, off Curzon Street in the heart of Mayfair where many of their customers would have been found. Their garage there could accommodate 300 cars. They operated a hire service and for an annual payment of £325 a brougham could be hired with all maintenance and battery charging included. A driver could also be hired, but his wages were charged extra. The Electromobile company also sold and hired out Napier petrol-engined broughams.

In March 1914 the British Electromobile Co. Ltd went into voluntary liquidation, selling its business to its hire department, the Hertford Street Hiring Co. Ltd. They made one further attempt at manufacture after the war. At the 1919 Olympia Show they exhibited the Elmo, an electric car with short bonnet and limousine/landaulette body by Gill of Paddington. It was priced at £1050, plus £250 for batteries and £42 for tyres. Probably only one was built, and it made no further appearances at the show or anywhere else.

NG

ELECTROMOTION *see* COLUMBIA

ELECTRO MOTION (US) 1975–1976
Electro Motion Transportation Systems, Bedford, Massachusetts.
This was really a commercial vehicle but it was sold as a 4-passenger vehicle as well. It featured a tubular steel chassis with independent suspension and boxy aluminium bodywork with fibreglass opening panels. The electric motor was 20–35bhp with a central battery pack of 146v batteries, giving 40mph (64km/h) and a range of 30 miles (50km).

CR

ELECTRONIC (US) 1955
Electronic Motor Car Co., Salt Lake City, Utah.
The Electronic was an electric-powered sports car with a difference. Although the looks were conventional with a LA SAETTA fibreglass body, the running gear was not. Power was provided by an electric motor attached to the rear axle housing, and a small petrol or diesel motor powered a generator to recharge the 80-cell battery system. Future plans were for a system of radio transmitters installed coast-to-coast that would relay electronic signals to a receiver in the car. This signal would be changed into electricity that would recharge the batteries without need of the petrol motor. Although miniature versions of this system were successfully tested, this application was abandoned.

HP

ELECTRONOMIC *see* HOOD

ELECTRO-RENARD (F) c.1943–1946
This was a very small 2-seater electric car made at Lyons. A range of 45 miles (72km) per charge was claimed.

NG

ELEGANT MOTORS (US) c.1985 to date
Elegant Motors Inc., Indianapolis, Indiana.
This kit car company made a broad range of models. In addition to the usual Cobra replica, they also cloned copies of the Bill Thomas Cheetah, Auburn, Mercedes 500K, Lamborghini Countach, and Cord. They also made three models of a neoclassic design similar to a Duesenberg called the LaGrande Sportster. All were available in kit or assembled form. In addition to their regular Cobra replica, Elegant also built the Attack Cobra, a lengthened and widened version that would fit a Corvette chassis. It was distinguished by massive scoops, spoilers, and air dams.

HP

ELEKTRIC *see* AAA

ELFE (F) 1919–1921
Automobiles Defrance Frères, Vierzon, Cher.
The Elfe was one of several cars built by Eugene Mauve, who was called the father of the Bol d'Or, the 24-hour race for motorcycles and cyclecars held in the Foret de St Germain from 1922. The first production Elfe was a monocar or tandem 2-seater with front-mounted V-twin engine and V-belt drive to the rear wheels. Mauve also made a few competition Elfes powered by rear-mounted 1095cc Anzani V-twin engines, with driver and passenger seated on saddles, and single-chain drive. He competed in practically all the cyclecar events in 1920 and 1921, but without much success. In the 1921 Coupe des Voiturettes the Elfe was the slowest car on the course. Mauve was a lively fellow, though, and a journalist remarked that his repartee was faster that his car. In 1923 he began to make more conventional cars under the name MAUVE.

NG

ELFIN (AUS) 1959–1998
Elfin Sports Cars, Edwardstown, South Australia.
Elfin Sports Cars, Highett, Victoria.
Garrie Cooper, like many other specialist builders, began with his own specials before building for others. In 1959 a batch of sports racing cars carrying a name he remembered from a model aero engine, were produced; 24 were made. A clubman was introduced in 1961 and this remained available over a long period in road and track forms. Subsequently, cars were produced conforming with the regulations of every competition category. Cooper's own driving career was ended as a result of a heart condition in 1971, but his success as a builder was indicated by the 1976 claim that, with more than 300 built, he was the world's second largest competition car constructor. His untimely death in 1982 deprived Elfin of its driving force but it continued in other hands, in Victoria from 1994.

MG

ELGÉ (i) (B) 1912–1914
Lambin et Gendebien, Houffalize.
This car gained its name from the French for the initials (LG) of the two men behind it, René Lambin and Robert Gendebien. Their car was powered by a 12/14hp Fondu 4-cylinder monobloc engine of 2120cc. The crankcase and gearbox were protected by an aluminium casing which gave the impression of unit construction of the two components. The 12/14 was made with tourer or cabriolet bodies, and at the 1914 Brussels Show it was joined by a smaller car powered by a 1244cc Chapuis-Dornier engine.

Not more than 25 Elgés were made before the war put an end to the company. Lambin continued as a Studebaker agent into the 1930s. One Elgé was used by a Houffalize butcher up to 1938.

NG

ELGÉ (ii) (F) 1924
Roger-Louis Maleyre, Bordeaux.
Maleyre was mainly a bodybuilder, but in 1924 he made a series of 30 low-built sports cars powered by C.I.M.E. engines. They had aerodynamic coupé bodies. Maleyre also built an experimental airscrew-driven vehicle.

NG

1921 Elfe cyclecar.
NATIONAL MOTOR MUSEUM

ELGIN (i) (US) 1899

Elgin Sewing Machine & Bicycle Co., Elgin, Illinois.
Like the makers of the ELDREDGE, this was another sewing machine company which turned to the automobile. Their product was a light electric car capable of travelling 75 miles (120km) on one charge, but only at a speed of 8mph (12km/h). Only five were built before the company went out of business. By the end of 1899, the factory was taken over by a group of Chicago businessmen to make the WINNER (i).

NG

ELGIN (ii) (US) 1916–1924

1916–1923 Elgin Motor Car Corp., Argo, Illinois.
1923–1924 Elgin Motors Inc., Indianapolis, Indiana.
When several members of the famous Elgin watch and clock company decided to enter the car business, they took over the defunct NEW ERA (ii) Engineering Co., and moved the machinery to Argo. The first Elgin was a conventional car on the same lines as the New Era, although slightly larger and with a 6-cylinder ohv Falls engine. Open 2- and 4-seaters were made until 1918, when they were joined by a sedan. From mid-1917 to November 1918 the Elgin factory made trucks for the US Army and they launched their 1919 models with the assurance that they were 'a year and a half ahead of the times'. The most interesting Elgin was the 1922 six which had a Cutler-Hammer pre-selector transmission, double transverse rear springs and a luggage boot built into the rear of the bodywork.

Elgin production rose encouragingly, from 671 in 1916 to a peak of 4613 in 1920, but the postwar depression hit them hard. Sales dropped to 3173 in 1921 and 1161 in 1922. A new company was formed in 1923 and production moved to Indianapolis, but only 323 cars were made in 1924. Elgin Motors Inc. went into receivership in June of that year. Total Elgin production was 16,784 cars.

NG

ELIESON (GB) 1897–1898

Elieson Lamina Accumulator Syndicate Ltd, Camden Town, London.
This company made a light 4-seater electric car with chain drive and very narrow track front wheels. Taxicab and delivery van versions were offered, but it is not certain if they were made. Although the batteries were provided by Elieson, the cars were actually made by John Warrick & Co. Ltd of Reading, Berkshire, which later made the 3-wheeled Warrick parcel car.

NG

1897 Elieson electric car.
NATIONAL MOTOR MUSEUM

ELITE (i) (US) 1901–1902

D.B. Smith & Co., Utica, New York.
This was a typical light steam car with 2-cylinder engine and chain drive. It differed only in having very ornate bodywork, with compound curves and plenty of brass on lamps, dash, hubs and steering tiller. The company also made a 12hp petrol car called the Saratoga Tourist.

NG

ELITE (ii); ELITE-DIAMANT (D) 1919–1929

1919–1922 Elite Motorenwerke AG, Brand-Erbisdorf.
1922–1927 Elite-Werke AG, Brand-Erbisdorf.
1927–1929 Elite-Diamant-Werke AG, Brand-Erbisdorf.
Although founded in 1914 just before the outbreak of war, car production was not started until 1919. The first cars were based on the GEHA electric 3-wheeler, although a few 4-wheelers were made. These were supplemented from 1920 by petrol cars, in particular the 3130cc Typ E of 12/40PS. This was followed by the 4708cc 6-cylinder 18/70PS. Sports versions of this developed 90bhp. Several other models were made, including the 6020cc 4-cylinder E24

491

1925 Elite (ii) 18/70PS tourer.
NATIONAL MOTOR MUSEUM

1922 Elizalde Tipo 51 tourer.
GILI DE HEREDIA

1922 Elizalde Tipo 26 saloon.
GILI DE HEREDIA

c.1924 Elizalde 20/30hp tourer.
NATIONAL MOTOR MUSEUM

(1919–21), and the 6-cylinder 3128cc S12, 3650 and 3690cc S14. The later Elites were handsome cars, somewhat like the Mercedes-Benz Nurburg in appearance. The factory was sizeable, with 3500 workers in 1925, though this figure had dropped to 450 by 1929, in which year the works were acquired by Opel. About 3500 cars were made in all, and 1000 commercial vehicles.

HON

ELITE (iii) (US) 1971–1986
Elite Enterprises, Cocato, Minnesota.
Founded by racing driver Gerry Knapp, Elite built a line of high quality kit cars. Their first kit was an oddly proportioned coupé on a shortened VW platform called the Laser GT. Their best known model was the Laser 917, a loose recreation of the Porsche 917K that fitted on a VW Beetle floorpan. Porsche, Corvair, Mazda and General Motors V6 engines could be specified. Elite added a replica of the Allard J2X with a custom frame that used front-engined V8 or rear-engined VW engines. The Mini–18 was a VW-based kit that resembled a miniature semi-tractor truck. The Laser '49er was a fibreglass minivan body that also attached to VW running gear. In addition to these street cars, Elite also built a line of successful Formula Vee racing cars. Knapp passed away in 1986 and the company was bought by QUINT Industries. The Allard replica became a sales success for HARDY.

HP

ELITE JUNIOR (US) 1907
Hughson & Burchett Motor Co., Newark, New Jersey.
Although the Elite Junior had the appearance of a full-sized car, with bonnet, lamps, wings and an upholstered seat, it was a miniature vehicle designed for children of four to eight years of age, weighing not more than 60lbs (27kg) and for use on level and smooth surfaces only. It was powered by a coil spring, one windup giving power for one eighth of a mile.

NG

ELITEWAGEN (D) 1921–1923
Elitewagen AG, Ronneburg.
This company took over production of the REX SIMPLEX 13/40PS under the name Elitewagen, but production was limited, and instead the company concentrated on electric commercial vehicles, especially for municipal work.

HON

ELIZALDE (E) 1913–1928
1913–1915 Biada, Elizalde y Cia, Barcelona.
1915–1928 Fábrica Española de Automóviles Elizalde, Barcelona.
Arturo Elizalde produced precision components from 1908, and was also the representative of DELAHAYE in Spain, holding some shares of this company. His wife, Carmen Biada was involved with the first railways at Catalonia. In 1913, Biada, Elizalde y Cia – Biada was the name of Elizalde's brothers-in-law – presented its first car, Tipo 11, as a prototype. One year later production started with Tipo 20, equipped with a 4-cylinder 15/20hp engine with interchanging valves actuated by one crankshaft. The two Biada brothers left the company in 1915. In 1919 the Super 20, with four forward speeds and cantilever springing front and rear was introduced as a competition car. Thereafter all Elizaldes had a cylinder-head in bronze. First of a new generation of cars was the 'Queen Victoria Eugenia' (RVE), with 16/20hp, and the colossal Model 48, the largest car at the Paris Salon of 1921, with an 8-cylinder, 8143cc 160bhp engine. This big engine had four valves and two spark plugs per cylinder, and only six were built. This was followed by smaller cars such as the series 51: the 518 with 8-cylinder 125bhp, the 513 with 4-cylinder 28bhp, the 51 with 4-cylinder 33bhp, and the 517 with 4-cylinder 50bhp, which were built for many years, with different bodies. These cars were also sold as taxis. In 1927 Elizalde planned to build a new car, called the APTA, together with Ricart and España, but difficulties obliged the company to finish car production in 1928. About 650 Elizalde were made. After 1928 only aero-engines were built with good success until 1951, when the company was taken over by state-owned INI and incorporated into ENMASA, the former Mercedes-España.

VCM

ELKHART *see* CROWN-ELKHART and PRATT-ELKHART

ELLEMOBIL (DK) 1909–1913

J.C. Ellehammer, Copenhagen.

Ellehammer was an inventor who made a pioneer motor scooter in 1904. He made an aeroplane in 1906 and this was claimed to be the first European-built heavier-than-air flying machine. A typical inventor who lost interest in a project once it was successful, he made very few cars for sale. These included a 2-seater with air-cooled 2-cylinder engine, friction transmission and belt drive, which he offered in 1909 and 1910. In 1913 he built a car with 11hp horizontal 3-cylinder engine and hydraulic clutch, but this remained a prototype.

NG

ELLIS *see* TRIUMPH (i)

ELLSWORTH (US) 1907

J.M. Ellsworth, New York City.

John Mager Ellsworth made a few examples of a large and expensive car, with 40hp 4-cylinder T-head engine and the choice of shaft or chain drive. It had a patent clutch designed by Thomas Fay, formerly with SMITH & MABLEY, and the price was $5000. The partners soon decided to concentrate on the manufacture of chrome nickel-steel parts.

NG

ELMER SIX (US) 1911–1912

Elmer Auto Corp., Elkhart, Indiana.

This company bought the factory of the Elkhart Motor Car Co., which had made the STERLING (i) and KOMET for production of their conventional 6-cylinder car. Only prototypes were made before manufacture was transferred to Cleveland, where it became the GRANT. Some of the Elmer prototypes were called Lohr, and one of these exists today.

NG

ELMO *see* ELECTROMOBILE (ii)

ELMORE (US) 1900–1912

Elmore Manufacturing Co., Clyde, Ohio.

Brothers James and Burton Becker were bicycle makers who entered car production in 1900 with two light cars powered by single-cylinder engines, of 3.5hp in the runabout and 6hp in the trap. Both were on a 62in (1573mm) wheelbase, and had chain drive and tiller steering. Like all succeeding Elmores the engines were 2-strokes. The brothers championed this system with the slogan 'The Car That Has No Valves'. They only made 10 cars before they incorporated their company in 1902, but then output grew rapidly, to reach 400 in 1907. For 1903 2-cylinder models of 6 and 10hp joined the 5hp single for 1904 4-seater tonneau bodies were available, and the 2-cylinder models had dummy bonnets, though the engine remained under the seat.

A completely new range of shaft-driven cars was announced for 1906, with 24hp 3-cylinder and 35hp 4-cylinder engines under the bonnet, both with 5-seater tourer bodies. Prices were inevitably higher too; the 35hp tourer cost $2500, nearly twice as much as the 1905 2-cylinder canopy top tonneau. Closed bodies were introduced in 1909, the 24hp landaulette being popular as a taxicab. In 1907 the Beckers sold out to E.A. Goss who already controlled the E.R. Thomas Co., makers of the THOMAS Flyer. He, in turn, sold the company to Billy Durant two years later, as Durant thought that a 2-stroke would add variety to the range offered by his newly-formed General Motors Corp. Elmores grew in size from 1910 to 1912, when only 4-cylinder engines were used. These included a 46hp in 1910 and a 70hp on a 127.5in (3238mm) wheelbase in 1911. The collapse of Durant's empire in 1912 saw the end of Elmore production, as GM's directors closed all plants except for those in Detroit.

NG

EL MOROCCO (US) 1956–1957

R. Allender and Company, Detroit, Michigan.

Rubin Allender had made his fortune in the auto parts industry and wanted to build a car to market through his dealerships. El Moroccos started life as new 1956/57 Chevrolet hard-tops and convertibles, but fibreglass fins, massive bumpers and flashy side trim were added to make them look like contemporary Cadillac Eldorados. The design and production work was carried out at Creative Industries,

1921 Elizalde Tipo 48 chassis.
NICK BALDWIN

1904 Elmore 8hp tonneau.
NICK GEORGANO

which normally built show cars for Detroit manufacturers. They sold for about the same price as a stock Chevrolet sedan.

HP

ELSWICK (i) (GB) 1903–c.1907

Elswick Motor Co., Newcastle-upon-Tyne.

Described as 'new to the trade' in January 1903, the Elswick company assembled cars with several sizes of engines from various manufacturers. The 1904 range included a light car with 6hp single-cylinder De Dion-Bouton engine, and cars with 4-cylinder 20hp Brouhot and 24hp Mutel engines. The latter had a 3-speed gearbox and shaft drive. In 1906 they were offering the 6hp single- and two 4-cylinder cars, the 15/20 and 24/30. These sometimes carried the name S.P.Q.R., recalling for classical scholars the Latin Senatus Populusque Romanum (people and senate of Rome). Advertisements of 1906 stressed that Elswick cars were London-built, but the exact location is uncertain.

NG

ELSWICK (ii) (GB) 1981–c.1984

Elswick, Kings Coughton, Alcester, Warwickshire.

The Elswick Envoy was a William Towns-designed small car designed for wheelchair users. It used Mini mechanicals in a chassis engineered by G.K.N. Sankey. The angular glassfibre bodywork was built by RELIANT at its Tamworth plant. It featured a single rear door and a ramp for a wheelchair to mount the car and then be bolted in place (the driver then operated the car from the wheelchair).

CR

ELVA (i) (F) 1907

Voitures Elva, Paris.

Two models were listed by this company, a 6/8hp 2-cylinder 2-seater at 4350 francs, and a 12/14hp 4-cylinder double phaeton at 6500 francs.

NG

1964 Elva (ii) Courier Mk IV coupé.
NATIONAL MOTOR MUSEUM

1965 Elva (ii) GT160 coupé.
NICK BALDWIN

ELVA (ii) (GB) 1958–1968

1958–1961 Elva Engineering Co. Ltd, Bexhill, Sussex.
1962–1965 Trojan Ltd, Croydon, Surrey.
1965–1968 Ken Sheppard Customised Sports Cars Ltd, Shenley,
Hertfordshire.
In the early 1950s, Frank Nichols built up a garage business and commissioned
Mike Chapman to build him a competition car. The C.S.M. was a 1172cc Ford-
powered, cycle-winged sports car built on similar lines to the Lotus Mk VI.
It performed sufficiently well to encourage Nichols. With his mechanic, 'Mac'
Witts, Nichols made an improved version, which was christened 'Elva' (from
the French *elle va*, she goes). Witts also designed an overhead inlet valve
conversion for the Ford 1172cc side-valve engine.

The Elva Mk 1 spaceframe followed the broad layout of the C.S.M. (and the
Lotus Mk VI – Colin Chapman threatened legal action on the point) but Standard
Ten front suspension replaced the previous swing axles and it had a semi-enveloping
aluminium body.

The Elva Mk 1 achieved some success in British club racing and perhaps two
dozen were made. Further sports-racers followed and they were particularly
successful in America because they were designed to be forgiving. Further
expansion came with the introduction of the Courier road car in 1958. This was
built on a ladderframe with MGA running gear and a fibreglass body. It was a
cheap alternative to mainstream cars and was successful in racing. About 700
were sold, between 1958 and 1961, but the Courier was not available in Britain
until 1960, when it was sold as a kit.

In the early days of Formula Junior Elva was very successful, but was soon
overtaken by the likes of Lotus and Cooper. That hiccough apart, Elva seemed
destined for long-term success in America when the importer was gaoled for
financial irregularities. Elva was wiped out.

The Courier project was sold to Trojan and Nichols regrouped. Trojan made
about 100 examples of the Courier Mk III/IV. The Mk III reacted to the common
criticism that the cockpit was cramped by moving the engine forward, which
ruined the handling. The Mk IV redressed the balance but, by the time it arrived
in 1963, with independent rear suspension and a Ford engine option, the damage
was done.

Elva's designer, Keith Marsden, produced some excellent mid-engined sports
cars in the early 1960s – Elva introduced BMW to postwar motor racing and
also became the first company to be provided with Porsche engines.

In 1964 an Elva-BMW Mk VII became the basis for the 160 GT car with a
body designed by Trevor Fiore (born Trevor Frost, fiore is frost in Italian), but
Fissore, the coachbuilder, under-estimated the price, the British government
imposed swingeing import duties which further increased cost, and the body
itself was too heavy. Just three were made, one with a Rover V8 engine.

Ken Sheppard Sports Cars bought Elva from Trojan in 1965 and made 26 more
Couriers, all with 1800cc MG engines. Sheppard fitted a Rover V8 to a GT160,
but it handled badly while a 3-litre Ford-powered Mk IV coupé remained a
prototype. Elva ceased production in 1968.
MJL

Further Reading
'Elva…she goes!', Mike Taylor, *Automobile Quarterly,* Vol.35, No.4.

ELYSEE (GB) 1993 to date

1993–1998 Gemini Cars, Hucknall, Nottinghamshire.
1998 to date J.B. Sports Cars, Shepperton, Middlesex.
Basing a Lotus Elan replica on Vauxhall Chevette mechanicals was an odd
choice, and the chassis of the Elysee Sprint was not a backbone but a twin rail
ladder affair. Alternative engines included Ford crossflow and Fiat twin cam.
The fibreglass bodywork differed from the original Elan by having frogeye
headlamps, Mini-hinged doors and Chevette rear lamps. In 1998 a new Ford-based
chassis was under development.
CR

ELYSÉE (F) 1921–1925

Automobiles Elysée, Paris.
This was a light car made in two models, one with 780cc engine and belt drive,
and the other with 950cc engine and shaft drive. Both were 4-cylinder units.
NG

EMANCIPATOR (US) 1909

Emancipator Automobile Co., Aurora, Illinois.
Formerly known as the Aurora Motor Works which made the AURORA
runabout from 1907 to 1909, this company was renamed to celebrate the
introduction in January 1909 of a 20hp 4-cylinder car which they called
Emancipator because it was 'free from trouble'. It had a 2-speed epicyclic
transmission and shaft drive. Whether it was freer from trouble than any other
car of the time is not known, but the company was not free from financial
problems, and closed before the end of 1909.
NG

EMBEESEA (GB) 1975–1987

1975–1983 Embeesea Kit Cars, High Wycombe, Buckinghamshire.
1983–1984 M.B.C. Kit Cars, High Wycombe, Buckinghamshire.
1984–1986 D.J. Sportscars, Harlow, Essex.
1986–1987 M.D.B. Sportscars, Tredegar.
1987 Viking Sportscars.
Mike Carlton left Neville Trickett's SIVA to produce the Chepeko, a reworked
version of the Siva Saluki. The basic profile was just about recognisable, as were
the lift-up glass panels that were the doors, but the overall shape was heavier. As
before, a full-length Beetle floorpan was used. In 1977 the styling was beefed
up again and the model name changed to Charger. This had a deep front spoiler
and enlarged gull-wing doors, which included removable sunroof panels. The
Charger 2 joined this model in 1982, featuring a more rounded profile, double
skinning, 2+2 interior, a snout-like nose, deeper gull-wing doors, and different
glass treatment. Richard Oakes designed another model, the Eurocco notchback
coupé, in 1978 but this later emerged under different owners as the SN1.
Embeesea reworked the car into a fastback in 1981. It was based on a VW floorpan
with Alfasud/Lancia engine options. S&R Sports Cars subsequently produced
new versions of the Eurocco under the names SR1 and SR2. After passing to
D.J. Sportcars, the Chargers were resurrected as the Saratoga and Saturn by
M.D.B., then as the Dragonfire and Dragonfly by Viking. Several hundred had
been sold by that stage.
CR

EMBO (I) 1978–1982

Embo snc, Caramagna, Piemonte, Cuneo.

Using the Fiat Campagnola as a basis, Embo made a very short wheelbase 4x4 estate type vehicle. It shared its mechanical components with the Fiat, including 4-wheel drive and 2-litre petrol engines of 80bhp or 110bhp, or a 2.5-litre 72bhp diesel. Overall length was only 122in (3100mm). The model was restyled in 1980 and renamed the Mega but by 1982 it had abandoned 4×4 vehicles in favour of enhancing cars such as the Innocenti and Maserati Biturbo.

CR

EMBREE (US) 1909–1910

Embree-McLean Carriage Co., St Louis, Missouri.

Founded in 1889, this carriage company decided to enter the car business on a wide scale, with three engines, 30, 35 and 40hp, and three wheelbases, 105, 116, and 120in (2665, 2944, and 3046mm). They intended to make 500 cars in 1910 but were bankrupt by July with probably not one tenth of that figure completed.

NG

EMELBA (E) 1979–1987

Emelba SA, Barcelona.

This company prepared a lot of different special bodies using SEAT components. They first transformed Seat 127s into pick-ups and small delivery vans called the Samba 127, and later on created convertibles of the 127 and the Fura. The famous models of the Emelba range were the Pandita, a convertible using Panda components, the Poker, a small delivery van on Ritmo/Ronda chassis, and the Chato, a 6-seater car like the Fiat Multipla, using the Panda chassis of only 133in (3380mm) in length. This car had sliding doors. Based on the Ronda, Emelba developed a family car of modern design using composite plastic body, with seven transformable seats, like the Renault Espace, called the Siete (7). Only six were finally built, as Emelba had serious financial problems. The company intended to sell the Siete design to other companies, but failed.

VCM

EMERALD (GB) 1903–1904

Douglas S. Cox & Co., West Norwood, London.

The Emerald was a very light 2-seater voiturette powered by a 4hp single-cylinder engine. Drive was by a long belt from the 2-speed gearbox to the rear axle. Douglas Cox later acquired the works of the WELLER company, also at West Norwood, where he made the OSTERFIELD from 1906 to about 1909.

NG

EMERAUDE (F) 1913–1914

Constructions Industrielles Dijonnaises, Dijon.

This was the same design as the C.I.D. Baby, using the same 8hp single-cylinder Buchet engine and 4-speed friction transmission. However it had conventional semi-elliptic front springs in place of the Baby's single transverse spring, and unusual headlamps which were built into the top of the radiator shell.

NG

EMERSON (i) (US) 1907

Victor L. Emerson, Cincinnati, Ohio.

Victor Emerson claimed to be a pioneer car maker, with a 3-wheeler powered by 'gas from vaporising coal oil' on the road as early as 1885. He built another car with a Duryea-King engine in 1896, called the Emerson-Fischer, and in 1907 announced a very powerful machine that he called the Military. This had a 10.6-litre 60/70hp 6-cylinder rotary-valve engine, with only two forward speeds. He quoted a price of $8000 for a 3-seater roadster, but the numbers sold are not known; this was possibly none, because although Emerson was working for the American Auto Car Co. at the time, the Military was a private venture.

NG

EMERSON (ii) (US) 1917

Emerson Motor Co., Kingston, New York.

Backed by Robert C. Hupp, former maker of the HUPMOBILE, and the brothers Theodore and George Campbell, the Emerson was a very conventional car with 22hp 4-cylinder engine aimed clearly at the Ford Model T market. It had

1912 E.M.F. 30 tourer.
NATIONAL MOTOR MUSEUM

a 3-speed sliding gearbox instead of the Ford's epicyclic system, the wheelbase was 10in longer at 110in (2792mm). The price of $395 for a 5-seater tourer was not far above the Ford's $360, and way below the $835 asked for a Dodge. It seemed to be a successful proposition, but the company became embroiled in financial shenanigans including indictment of their brokers for using the mails to defraud. Robert Hupp resigned in March 1917, followed in September by the Campbells, who reorganised the company to make the generally similar CAMPBELL(ii). Emerson production probably totalled several hundred cars, all tourers.

NG

EMERY (GB) 1964

Paul Emery Cars Ltd, Fulham, London.

Paul Emery was an ingenious special builder who was the only constructor, apart from Ferrari, to make cars (called Emerysons) for the first four World Championship formulae. He was also involved in two production car efforts, both in 1964.

One was the Dart, an aluminium coupé built on a Minivan floorpan which had a longer wheelbase than a Mini. The idea was productionized as both the Mini-Marcos (see MARCOS) and the Mini-Jem.

The other was the Emery GT which was a mid-engined GT coupé with a spaceframe, all-independent suspension and Hillman Imp running gear. The prototype had an aluminium body (and was very successful in racing) while the three production cars had fibreglass bodies bonded to the spaceframe. Production ceased due to the death of Emery's backer.

MJL

E.M.F. (US) 1908–1912

Everitt-Metzger-Flanders Co., Detroit, Michigan.

The three men behind the E.M.F. had plenty of motor industry experience. Barney Everitt had grown rich in carriage and coachbuilding, and had made the WAYNE from 1904 to 1908, William E. Metzger was a brilliant salesman who had done wonders for CADILLAC in its early years, and Walter Flanders had been Henry Ford's production manager. They used two former car makers' factories – Northern and Wayne – and built a 30hp 4-cylinder car conventional in most respects apart from its combined gearbox and rear axle. This gave a lot of trouble and perhaps justified the unkind epithets which rivals used for the make's initials, 'Every Morning Fixit' or 'Every Mechanical Failure'.

Nevertheless, the E.M.F. attracted the attention of STUDEBAKER who were looking for a reasonably priced car that would sell in larger numbers than the expensive GARFORD which they were selling at the time. Studebaker agreed to take half of E.M.F.'s production for 1909; planned for 12,000 the actual figure was 8132, including 172 cars made in 1908. In 1910 output rose to 15,300, putting them in 4th place in the US production league. They were 2nd in 1911 with 26,827 and 3rd in 1912 with 28,032.

Everitt and Metzger, who had never been happy with the Studebaker agreement, left in May 1909 to make a car of their own called the EVERITT, while Flanders stayed on for a while. In July 1909, with Studebaker aid, he bought the factory of the defunct DE LUXE car, and made there a smaller 4-cylinder car named after himself (see FLANDERS).

1931 Émile Pilain 6CV saloon.
NATIONAL MOTOR MUSEUM

The E.M.F. was largely unchanged during its four year lifespan, though the troublesome thermosyphon cooling system was quickly replaced by a water pump; indeed early cars were recalled and fitted with pumps. The 2.7-litre 4-cylinder side-valve engine was continued to 1912, and a coupé was added to the range of open cars in 1911. Studebaker took over E.M.F. completely in 1912, and all subsequent cars were marketed as Studebakers. The three partners were reunited in the 1920s in the manufacture of the RICKENBACKER.

NG

Further Reading
'E & M & F…&LeRoy', Beverley Rae Kimes,
Automobile Quarterly, Vol.XII, No.1.

ÉMILE PILAIN (F) 1930–1931

SA des Établissements Émile Pilain, Levallois-Perret, Seine.
Émile Pilain left ROLLAND-PILAIN in 1927 and set up his own company three years later to make a small car powered by a 935cc 5CV side-valve engine with 3-speed gearbox and Perrot brakes. It was made as a 2-door saloon and faux-cabriolet; in addition, at the 1930 Paris Salon, Pilain exhibited an elegant little coupé de ville, described as the 'poor man's Hispano-Suiza', but this was probably a one-off. The cabriolet cost 24,000 francs, which was expensive compared with other 5CVs at the Salon, such as the Peugeot 190S at 15,750 and the Rosengart at 17,960 francs. For 1931 a 1226cc 7CV was added, which could carry a 4-door saloon body. The company was dissolved in December 1931. Production figures are not known, but they were probably less than 100, of which five are known to survive.

Even while he was making cars, Pilain advertised that he could supply new or second-hand cars of other makes, especially Citroën, Delage, Hotchkiss and Talbot.

NG

Further Reading
Rolland-Pilain, la Grande Aventure Automobile, Gilles Blanchet and Claude Rouxel, Edijac, 1985.

EMMEL (B) 1925–1926

Carrosserie Emmel, Brussels.
Like SPEEDSPORT, DE WANDRE and others, the Emmel was a Belgian conversion of the Model T Ford. Headed by coachbuilder M. van de Waele, the company lowered the Ford chassis and fitted a Ricardo head to the engine. Closed and open models were made, the latter capable of over 60mph (97km/h).

NG

EMMS (GB) 1922–1923

Emms Motor Co., Coventry.
The Emms was a conventional light car powered by a 4-cylinder Coventry Simplex engine of 1247 or 1368cc, with 3-speed gearbox, worm drive and quarter-elliptic suspension all round. It had disc wheels and three body styles were available; a 2-seater, a pointed-tail sports car and a closed coupé. An unusual feature was the mounting of the headlamps on the wings. *The Light Car & Cyclecar*

had their doubts about this: 'The advisability of mounting the headlights on the wings is open to question, for even in a minor mishap the wings usually suffer, and even if the lamps themselves are not damaged, the direction of the beam thrown from them is altered'.

NG

E.M.P. (GB) 1897–1900

Electric Motive Power Co., Balham, London.
This company began by converting horse-drawn vehicles to electric power, their first venture being a double-decker bus which was tried in Liverpool in 1894. Later vehicles included a 4-seater victoria with 2hp motor in 1897, a 5hp dog-cart and a 2hp 3-wheeler. Although the company exhibited at shows, the work was largely experimental, and few vehicles were sold to the public.

NG

EMPI (US) c.1960–1985

Engineered Motor Products Inc., Riverside, California.
This company sold an extensive line of Volkswagen repair, custom and performance parts. In the mid–1960s, owner Joe Vittone began selling Empi-modified VW sedans through Economotors, a VW dealership he also owned. These were called Empi GTVs. There were four models, all modified with speed and trim parts. The Mk IV model had an optional 1700cc engine and vastly improved handling. Empi also built a metal-bodied dune buggy called the Imp that had a decidedly utilitarian slant. There were four variations, including one for Corvair 6-cylinder engines. They later switched to a conventional fibreglass Meyers Manx-style body.

HP

EMPIRE (i) (US) 1899–1902

1899–1901 Empire Manufacturing Co., Sterling, Illinois.
1901–1902 Sterling Automobile & Engine Co., Sterling, Illinois.
The Empire was a typical light steam buggy with a V-twin engine geared directly to the rear axle. The rectangular boiler with horizontal tubes was placed transversely across the frame, under the seat. It had a tubular frame and bicycle-type wire wheels, and was priced at $750. In 1901 the Empire company was superseded by new owners, the Sterling Automobile & Engine Co., and the 1901–02 cars were generally known as Sterlings.

NG

EMPIRE (ii) (US) 1904

William T. Terwilliger & Co., Amsterdam, New York.
The Terwilliger brothers experimented with steam cars as early as 1897, but did not go into business until 1904 when they announced a car with 15hp 2-cylinder engine hung pivotally from the rear axle. The boiler was mounted amidships below the front seat of the 5-seater rear-entrance tonneau. Longer than most early steamers, it rode on an 87in (2210mm) wheelbase, and cost $2000.

NG

EMPIRE (iii) (US) 1909–1919

1909–1912 Empire Motor Car Co., Indianapolis, Indiana.
1912–1914 Greenville Metal Products, Greenville, Pennsylvania.
1914–1915 Connersville Wheel Co., Connersville, Indiana.
1915–1919 Empire Automobile Co., Indianapolis, Indiana.
The Empire began life as a neat-looking 20hp 4-cylinder car made only in 2-seater form, as a roadster or speedster, and dubbed The Little Aristocrat. The men behind the company included Arthur Newby, president of NATIONAL (i) and Carl Fisher, founder of Prest-O-Lite starters. They were also the leading lights behind the Indianapolis Motor Speedway, and the first Empire off the line was also the first car to be driven on the new brick circuit. Unfortunately the directors were so busy promoting the circuit and trying to make it pay, that the Empire was neglected. It received a new lease of life when new owners transferred production to Greenville, Pennsylvania, in the factory of Greenville Metal Products. Its president was Frank Fay, and in his honour the Empire 20 was named the Fay. There was a larger car with 25hp Teetor engine and 5-seater tourer body which still bore the Empire name.

In 1914 Empire was on the move again, to Connersville, Indiana, and finally, in 1915, back to Indianapolis, though to a different factory from their first one, which was now devoted to making Prest-O-Lite starters. The 1916 range included a six for the first time, a 25hp Continental, which carried 7-seater tourer bodywork and a 7-seater sedan in 1917. The last year for the Empire was 1919, when 191 cars were made. Total production was 4834 cars.

NG

EMPIRE STATE (US) 1900–1901
Empire State Automobile Co., Rochester, New York.
This was a typical light runabout powered by a 4.5hp single-cylinder engine under the seat, with single-chain drive, tiller steering and bicycle-type wire wheels without mudguards.

NG

EMPIRE STEAM CAR (US) c.1927
Cruban Machine & Steel Corp., New York, New York.
The Empire Steam Car was probably built for experimental purposes and the one car known to have been built and which survives was never completed. It was powered by a 3-cylinder compound steam engine of Cruban's own design. The car was designed by Carl Ubelmesser.

KM

EMPRESS (i) (F) 1899–1901
United Motor Industries, Paris.
This was one of a number of makes built in France for the UK market. The first model had a 2¼hp De Dion-Bouton engine mounted under the seat, and geared directly to the rear axle via a Didier 2-speed gear. It had a very light 2-seater body, suspended on C-springs at the rear, though an extra seat for one or two children could be fitted. By 1901 the Empress had a front-mounted engine, still a De Dion but now of 4½ hp, shaft drive and a 4-seater tonneau body. The drive to the wheels was by internally-toothed gear, as on the Milnes-Daimler commercial chassis.

NG

EMPRESS (ii) (GB) 1907–1910
Empress Motor Co. Ltd, Manchester.
This small company launched an ambitious range of cars in 1907, two fours of 16/20 and 20/24hp and two sixes of 24/30 and 30/36hp. All had pressure lubrication and detachable cylinder heads, and were shaft driven. In 1910 only the 4-cylinder models were listed, and in that year Frank Smith, who had designed the cars, turned his interests to aviation. There is no record of the Empress after 1910.

NG

EMSCOTE (GB) 1920–1921
Emscote Motor Co. Ltd, Warwick.
The Emscote was an unusual light car with frameless construction, unit engine and gearbox and front suspension by a single transverse semi-elliptic leaf spring which, with the axle, pivoted at the centre. Two engines were offered, an 8/10hp V-twin J.A.P. or an 11.9hp 4-cylinder Alpha. The company ordered 500 gearboxes from D.M.K. Marendaz, who built 260 before he realised that Emscote sales would not even justify that number, so he had to cut his losses. The number of Emscotes made is not known, possibly only 10 or 20. One of the partners was Seelhaft, who later went into business with Marendaz to make the MARSEAL.

NG

EMW (D) 1945–1956
Eisenach Motoren-Werke, Eisenach.
Eisenach had been the main BMW car plant before World War II, and in 1945 it was nationalised. The prewar Typ 321 2-door saloon and 327 cabriolet were made and at first sold with BMW badges. Pressure from BMW in Munich forced a change to EMW in 1952. Even in 1945, 68 321s were delivered, and a total of 9000 were made up to 1950. It was replaced by the 340, a 4-door saloon derived from the prewar BMW 326 but with an updated radiator grill. This was also made as an estate car, ambulance and delivery van, about 9500 being produced up to 1955. The best-looking of the EMWs were the 327 coupés and cabriolets, almost exact replicas of the prewar BMW apart from having front-

1912 Empire (iii) Model 25 2-seater.
NICK BALDWIN

1901 Empress (i) tonneau.
NATIONAL MOTOR MUSEUM

1952 EMW Type 327 cabriolet.
NICK GEORGANO/NATIONAL MOTOR MUSEUM

1952 EMW Type 340 saloon.
NICK GEORGANO/NATIONAL MOTOR MUSEUM

1907 Enfield (i) 15hp tourer.
NATIONAL MOTOR MUSEUM

1909 Enfield (i) 16/20hp tourer.
NATIONAL MOTOR MUSEUM

1914 Enfield (i) Autolette 2-seater.
NATIONAL MOTOR MUSEUM

hinged doors. The last of 505 cars was made in 1956, after which the factory was turned over to the manufacture of the WARTBURG (ii).

HON

ENCORE (i) (GB) 1992–c.1997

Encore Cars, Norwich, Norfolk.

This was a very convincing looking kit-form replica of the 1957 Lotus Elite, with very detailed duplication of the exterior and interior trim. However under the skin it was more pragmatic, with a separate steel backbone chassis in place of the original fibreglass monocoque. Typical of its cosmetic accuracy but practical engineering were dummy rear strut towers (the suspension was in fact by double wishbones all round). There was a choice of engines, though the prototype used Ford CVH power and a Sierra gearbox.

CR

ENCORE (ii) (US) 1999 to date

Encore Motors, Inc., Monroe, Mississippi.

The Primo was a replica of the 1953 Corvette that used a Chevrolet engine and running gear.

HP

ENDURANCE (i) (GB) 1899–1901

Endurance Motor Co. Ltd, Coventry.

Endurance cars were closely based on Benz designs, with 4.5 or 6hp horizontal single-cylinder engines and 2-speed belt transmission. One was entered in the Thousand Miles Trial of 1900, but it retired.

NG

ENDURANCE (ii) (US) 1924–1925

1924–1925 Endurance Steam Car Co., Los Angeles, California.
1925 Dayton, Ohio.

The Endurance was typical of a product capitalising on the 1920s steam car renaissance in the United States – a typical design with steam as its novelty and its selling point. The drawback appears to have been that, presumably because of its poorly organised planning, there were no cars to sell, good as they might have been. An outgrowth of the moribund Coats Steam Car of Sandusky, Ohio, the Endurance existed only as two or three prototypes, featuring a 124in (3147mm) wheelbase and with a projected touring car price of $1985. Moving its centre of operations to Dayton, Ohio early in 1925, a new design featuring an 8-cylinder poppet-valve engine was projected and, although promotion included a sketch of a hoped-for sedan, operations failed to get off the ground and the Endurance failed before any production.

KM

ENFIELD (i) (GB) 1906–1915

Enfield Autocar Co. Ltd, Redditch, Worcestershire.

The Enfield Autocar Co. grew out of the Enfield Cycle Co. which had made bicycles, motor tricycles, quadricycles and, from 1903, light cars under the name ROYAL ENFIELD. The cycle company continued, but more substantial cars were made by the new company. These had 4-cylinder side-valve engines of 4082cc (16/20hp) and 5878cc (24/30hp), followed by a smaller 3258cc 15hp in 1907. All had shaft drive. The directors were Albert Eadie who had been involved with Enfield bicycle manufacture since the 1890s, and E.H. Lancaster, a leading figure in the promotion of the CLEMENT car in England. The joint skills of these men were not enough to save Enfield from the problems of the motor industry slump of 1907–08, and they were forced to hand over to a new board of directors who put Enfield Autocar up for auction. It was bought by Alldays & Onions for a reputed £10,000. This would seem to have been a bargain because the sale included not only the Enfield works and machinery but also three finished cars and 10 partly completed chassis.

Alldays continued the Enfield designs for a year or two, but gradually the Enfield name was used for the more upmarket versions of Alldays designs. Thus the 1914 Enfield Nimble Nine light car was a badge-engineered Alldays Midget, though, curiously, these were similarly priced at £138. The 3018cc 18.4hp Enfield was equivalent to the 16/20 Alldays and was £25 more expensive at £425, and the 4082cc 24.9hp Enfield was equivalent to the 25/30 Alldays but cost £50 more at £480. The single-cylinder Enfield Autorette 3-wheeler of 1912–13

498

had no Alldays equivalent, and was dropped for 1914 in favour of the 8hp 2-cylinder 4-wheeled Autolette and the 4-cylinder Nimble Nine. Just after the Armistice in November 1918 the motor activities of the two companies were merged to form Enfield-Alldays Motors Ltd, all production taking place at Alldays, Birmingham factory.

NG

ENFIELD (ii) (GB/GR) 1969–1976
1969–1973 Enfield Automotive Ltd, London.
1973–1976 Enfield Automotive Ltd, Cowes, Isle of Wight.
No British electric car has ever been as successful as the Enfield. Greek shipping magnate J.K. Goulandris was the head of the parent company, which was based on the island of Syros in Greece; indeed some Enfields were built there, although final assembly was on the Isle of Wight in Britain. The Enfield 8000 had a steel tube frame chassis, coil spring suspension with ifs, rack and pinion steering and Dunlop Denovo tyres. The 8bhp DC motor was powered by eight 12v batteries and allowed a top speed of over 40mph and a range of up to 40 miles. Only 106 examples were made, most of which were bought by the Electricity Council, for the price was extortionate for most private car buyers. Enfield's Moke-style electric model, the Runabout, was stillborn. At almost the opposite end of the scale, Enfield also built two 4-wheel drive models. The first was the 1972 Safari, a large saloon based on a Jeep chassis. Its cumbersome lines never gave it a chance to compete with the Range Rover. In 1974 Enfield also built two prototypes of the Chicago, a 4×4 off-road 4-door saloon using Range Rover mechanicals.

CR

ENFIELD-ALLDAY (GB) 1919–1924
Enfield-Alldays Motors Ltd, Sparkbrook, Birmingham.
The prewar Enfield and Alldays cars had been conventional designs, but for the postwar market the directors of the newly-merged company decided on something quite revolutionary. Known as the Enfield-Allday Bullet, it had a 5-cylinder sleeve-valve radial engine of 1247cc in a tubular lattice frame with a 3-seater cloverleaf body mounted on tubular outriggers. The propeller shaft sloped downwards to the centrally-mounted 3-speed gearbox, and thence even more steeply to the helical bevel rear axle. It was announced in early 1919 at a price of £250, but by the Olympia Show in November the price had risen to £350. A chassis and three complete cars were exhibited, but these were probably the only Bullets ever made. A.C. Bertelli, who had been with the Grahame-White Aviation Co., was invited to give an opinion on the Bullet, and pronouced that it would need a great deal of development and would be uneconomic to produce. The designer, A.W. Reeves, then decided to make the car on his own under the name Reeves Radial, but never succeeded. Another sleeve-valve Enfield Allday, with 6 cylinders in line, had been announced in January 1919, but was dropped in favour of the Bullet and did not appear at the Show. However, one or two must have been made as William Storey used the oval radiator on the prototype of his 1920 STOREY car.

Two years in business with no cars sold was not a recipe for success, and Bertelli was invited to join Enfield-Allday as general manager to sort things out. He designed a conventional light car powered by a 1488cc 10/20hp side-valve 4-cylinder engine and this went on the market in 1921. The bodies were made by Bertelli's brother, Harry, who also built bodies for Aston Martin, and were handsome enough, but the 10/20 was overpriced at £575. Although prices were dropped for 1922 and even more for 1923 when there was also a 1750cc 12/30, Enfield-Allday struggled to sell around 100 cars in all. The company went into liquidation in April 1923, and was reorganised and relocated in a smaller factory at Small Heath, Birmingham. From there the 10/20 was offered with a bewildering variety of coachwork, in seven styles from the Warwick 2-seater at £575 to the Stratford 2-door saloon at £795. Interestingly, these names, as well as that of the Kenilworth drophead coupé, were used by Standard for their body styles a few years later. It is doubtful if these could have been an economic proposition, but anyway 1924 saw the collapse of the parent Alldays & Onions company, and Enfield-Allday was brought down with them. The company was reformed as Allday Motor Repair Ltd, but built no more cars, although the name survived on some lists up to 1926. Bertelli later made three racing cars sponsored by Woolf Barnato, and designed a 1.5-litre single-ohc engine which went into a prototype using an Enfield-Allday chassis. This was called the R & B (Renwick & Bertelli), and it became the basis for the 1927 ASTON MARTIN.

NG

1975 Enfield (ii) Bikini utility.
NATIONAL MOTOR MUSEUM

1922 Enfield-Allday 10/20hp all-weather tourer.
NICK BALDWIN

1924 Enfield-Allday 10/20hp Warwick 2-seater.
NICK BALDWIN

Further Reading
'The Enfield-Allday story', M. Worthington-Williams,
The Automobile, October 1989.

ENGELHARDT (D) 1900–1902
Hermann Engelhardt Motoren- und Automobilfabrik, Berlin.
This small enterprise developed from a repair shop to car production. Only one model was offered, with a 6.5hp engine. An interchangeable body, either passenger car or delivery van, was used.

HON

ENGER

1900 English Mechanic 3hp 2-seater.
NICK GEORGANO/NATIONAL MOTOR MUSEUM

1928 Enka 500cc saloon
NATIONAL MOTOR MUSEUM

ENGER (US) 1909–1917

Enger Motor Car Co., Cincinnati, Ohio.

The Enger company was unusual in that it progressed from two to 12 cylinders in seven years, making fours and sixes along the way. The first of Frank J. Enger's cars was a high-wheeler powered by a 14hp 2-cylinder engine, but he soon abandoned this for a conventional 35/40hp 4-cylinder car. Although advanced in having ohvs, it was made only as a $2000 tourer in 1910. For 1911 the car was called a 40hp, the wheelbase was 3in (76mm) longer at 119in (3020mm) and there were six body styles. The 40 was continued through 1914 with little change, being replaced for 1915 by the 6-50, made only as a tourer or roadster and both priced at $1495. Enger's masterpiece, the 55hp Twin Six, one of the first V12s made in America (or anywhere else), appeared in 1916. It could be converted to run on six cylinders by a lever which cut off the flow of fuel and opened the valves of one bank of cylinders. The Twin Six was made as a tourer or roadster, and sold for the very low price of $1095 (contemporary Packard Twin Six prices started at $3050 and rose to $5150). Enger's best year was 1916, with 1113 cars sold, and so it was ironic that Frank Enger should have killed himself in his office on 4 January 1917, having been diagnosed with cancer. He gave instructions for the company to continue, but his widow petitioned for receivership. Only 317 cars were made in 1917 when the range consisted of the Twin Six and a new, smaller four selling for $695.

NG

ENGLER (US) 1913–1914

W.B. Engler, Detroit, Michigan.

William B. Engler built in Pontiac, Michigan, a cyclecar with 10hp De Luxe air-cooled V-twin engine, friction transmission and belt drive. He moved to Detroit and made a small number of a modified version with shorter wheelbase and wider track for sale at $385, but he never formed a company for their manufacture.

NG

ENGLISH CARS OF DISTINCTION (GB) 1980s

A wide variety of classic Jaguars were reproduced by this enterprise, including the XK range (120, 140, and 150) and the E-Type.

CR

ENGLISH MECHANIC (GB) 1900–1913

The English Mechanic was not a make of car in the normal sense of the word, as there was no company or factory. The name came from the magazine, *The English Mechanic and World of Science & Art*, which published a series of articles and drawings by the engineer T. Hyler-White (1871–1920), on the design and construction of cars which could be built at home. The series started in May 1899 with a tricycle having a 1.75hp De Dion-Bouton engine. This was followed in January 1900 with the first of 56 parts on 'A small car and how to build it'. This design was based on the Benz Velo, and the author advised the use of a second-hand Benz engine. To keep down the costs of his amateur engineers, Hyler-White always suggested the use of second-hand components wherever possible, though castings, rough or machined to any degree of finish, could be obtained from his friend David J. Smith who had a workshop off Goswell Road in the East End of London. Over the next five years Hyler-White published numerous series of articles on building different designs, including a heavy 4-wheeled steam car (1901), a light steam 3-wheeler that somewhat resembled a Léon Bollée (1902), a petrol car with 8hp vertical-twin engine and shaft drive (1904) and a 5hp runabout on American lines with single-cylinder engine under the seat and single-chain drive. One of the steam cars was built in India, where it was subsequently converted to internal combustion; another was built not by the owner but completed for him by the engineers Lowke & Co. of Northampton.

It should be pointed out that while today we refer for convenience to these cars as English Mechanics, it is highly unlikely that their owners called them this when they were built. They are more likely to have gone by the owners' names, or the pen names which were so popular in the Edwardian era. One steam car builder signed himself 'Lacitcarp' ('practical' reversed) in correspondence with the magazine. Dr Alan Sutton, author of a definitive article on the English Mechanic, says that 'among their own circle of acquaintants, most builders carefully neglected to give any credit at all to either the magazine or Hyler-White'.

After July 1905 Mr Hyler-White turned his attention to other machines for his readers, including practical silversmithing, a self-playing piano and a reed organ. In 1909 he returned to cars with a series of articles on the E.M. runabout with a single-cylinder engine and belt drive, and finally, in 1913 he joined the cyclecar brigade with a proposal for a friction transmission, belt-driven machine. The number of cars made to Hyler-White's designs is not known, but at least four survive today, a Benz-type 2-seater of 1900, a steam dog-cart of 1903, a 1904 8hp tonneau, and a 1907 2-cylinder car.

NG

Further Reading

'Thomas Hyler-White and the Working Man's Motor Car', Alan Sutton, *Veteran Car*, February and April 1997.

ENGSTROM (S) 1900

C.A. Engströms Vagnfabrik, Eskiltuna.

The third petrol-engined car to be made in Sweden, Isak Engström's machine used a horizontal single-cylinder engine, adapted from an American-built stationary unit with two flywheels, which developed 3.5hp and gave a top speed of 22mph (35km/h). Final drive was by single chain and only one forward speed was provided. Although Engström quoted a price of 4000 kroner, only one prototype of his car was made.

NG

ENKA (CS) 1926–1930

Frantisek Kolanda a spol., tovarna na automobily, Praha-Liben.

After his arrival in Prague in 1925, designer Bretislav Novotny was busy with the production of small popular cars, and he constructed an automobile called Enka (or ENKA, from the first letters of the names of both designer Novotny and producer Kolanda, phonetically pronounced). Enka cars were very popular with a top speed of 47mph (75km/h), fuel consumption of 7 l/100km, and a price of 23,000 Kc for a 3-seater closed car. Enka was powered by a single-cylinder 499cc 10bhp 2-stroke water-cooled engine, with detachable aluminium cylinder head and aluminium pistons, later used in the AERO (ii) 10hp cars. Mechanical

ESSEX
THE CHALLENGER

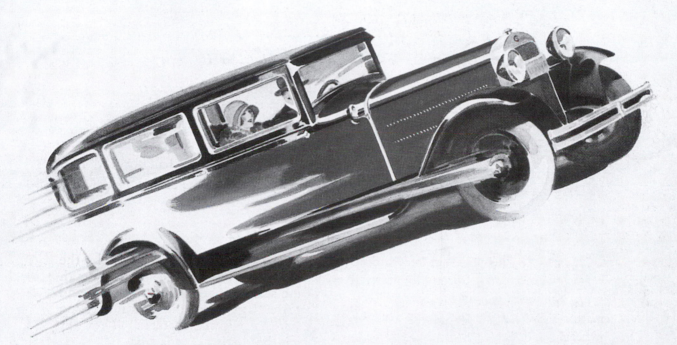

A SUPER-SIX

Challenging all Motordom on Acceleration, Performance, Endurance, Reliability, Economy, Beauty, Comfort, PRICE and VALUE.

c.1960 Enzmann 506 sports car.
NATIONAL MOTOR MUSEUM

c.1985 Entreposto Sado 550 saloon.
JEAN HAMMOND

brakes were only on the rear wheels and quarter-eliptic leaf springs in both ends served for better comfort. About 60 passenger cars and a few light vans were sold during 4 years of production.

MSH

ENNEZETA *see* ISO

ENSIGN (GB) 1913–1915
Ensign Motors Ltd, London.
This company was founded on 16 January 1913 under the name Florio Motors Ltd, and there is a strong suspicion that the cars sold as Ensigns were in fact FLORIOs. These were perhaps imported at first, although the 1914 Ensign brochure stated that the cars were manufactured in London. This is most unlikely to have been at the address in Brompton Road, South Kensington, but by 1914 the company had a factory at Willesden, North-West London, where commercial vehicle chassis were built. The 18hp Ensign had a 2949cc 4-cylinder monobloc engine, which according to *The Autocar*, 'followed Italian

lines'. Other sizes of engine were listed, including 2612 and 4250cc, and in these the cylinders were said to have been pair-cast, but it is not certain if any were built. After the war the Willesden factory was used for manufacture of the big BRITISH ENSIGN EP6, as well as smaller 4-cylinder cars which bore no resemblance to the prewar Ensign.

NG

ENTERPRISE (GB) 1983–1984
Chameleon Car Co., South Kensington, London.
Coming from a company whose main trade was customising Range Rover and Mercedes-Benz models, the Enterprise F16 was an extremely bold attempt to revolutionise luxury saloon car motoring. Over a tubular space frame chassis, its aerodynamic 4-door bodywork was in Kevlar – the first 'production' car to use this material exclusively – and featured photo-electric cells in the roof to absorb sunlight to charge the battery. A sophisticated specification included Ferguson 4-wheel drive, ABS and a turbocharged V8 engine. After a showing at the 1983 Geneva Motor Show, a price of £42,000 was announced but production never began.

CR

ENTERRA (US/CAN) c.1987–1996
Enterra Unlimited, Santa Ana, California; Barnaly, British Columbia.
The Enterra was introduced as a finished sport coupé with European styling and was sold through Pontiac dealers that also carried the Fiero it was based on. It was to be a higher-priced offering with an original body design. When Fiero production ended, the Enterra was made into a kit and sold through the Fiero Owners Club of America.
The Enterra was also manufactured at Barnaly in British Columbia in 1987.

HP

ENTREPOSTO (P) 1982–1986
Entreposto, Lisbon.
Virtually every European country has had a microcar maker and Portugal is no exception, in this case undertaken by the Nissan importer. The Entreposto Sado 550 featured a 2-seater fibreglass body on a steel tube chassis equipped with a Daihatsu 547cc 4-stroke 2-cylinder engine. This certainly made it faster than comparable microcars, listed as being capable of 69mph (110km/h). Other features included a 4-speed gearbox, rigid axles with leaf springs front and rear and hydraulic drum brakes.

CR

ENTROP (NL) 1909
De 's-Gravenhaagsche Rijwielen- en Motorrijwielenfabriek, 's-Gravenmoer.
After building bicycles for more than three years, Marinus Entrop started to manufacture a tiller-steered 3-wheeler powered by either a 417cc single- or 813cc 2-cylinder air-cooled engine mounted behind the front wheel. The Entrop had a weight of 400kg. The engine drove the gearbox by two Brampton chains, and both flywheels turned in the open air, but that was not a problem for the passengers, as they had a real body around them. The driver could use a steering wheel instead of a tiller when driving the luxurious 4-wheeler.

Only four Entrops were built in 1909; two of them were delivered in Holland and the others to the Dutch East Indies and Brazil.
FBV

E.N.V. (F) 1908
E.N.V. Motors Ltd, Courbevoie, Seine.
This was an English company with works in a Paris suburb, which was mainly known for its aero engines. The name came from the French 'en-v' meaning a vee layout engine. Its only car was shown at the 1908 Paris Salon. This had a 40hp V8 engine, 2-speed gearbox and 2-speed rear axle, giving four forward speeds. This would certainly have been simpler using an ordinary 4-speed gearbox. Production was very limited, if it happened at all.
NG

ENVEMO (BR) 1978–c.1994
Engenharia de Vehiculos e Motores, São Paulo.
Makers of tuning equipment for Chevrolets, the first Envemo was a convertible based on the Opala, with 2½-litre 4-cylinder engine and either manual or automatic transmission. From 1980 they produced Porsche 356 replicas using locally-built 1600cc Volkswagen Beetle engines.
NG

ENZMANN (CH) 1957–1967
Enzmann Automobile, Schüpfheim.
Emil Enzmann senior was the owner of the VW dealership, a hotel and a cinema in the rural village of Schüpfheim. His son, bearing the same forename, was a doctor of medicine. Together they produced in the early 1950s the prototype of a sporting roadster based on the platform chassis of the VW beetle. It had an aluminium body shaped over a wooden framework and served as the master for the fibreglass body of the production model. In order to keep the open-top body shell as stiff as possible, the Enzmann had no doors but did have a step-plate about halfway up the sidewalls. The attractive roadster with its very clean lines was shown for the first time at the "Comptoire Suisse" exhibition at Lausanne in September 1957 and shortly afterwards at the International Automobile Exhibition in Frankfurt. Enzmann was allocated booth number 506, hence the model designation Type 506 for all VW-based cars which followed. The standard version with the regular VW flat-four engine of 1192cc and 30bhp was on sale at SFr9300. Many of the buyers however preferred the 506 Super, with the modified 1295cc engine and MAG or Okrasa superchargers delivering 42 or 45bhp and a top speed of about 100mph (161km/h). For the most discriminating customers, Porsche 356 engines of 1582cc and up to 75bhp with Porsche brakes and wheels was available. In the 1960s the improved VW 1300 chassis was used, but as VW would no longer supply the chassis only, Enzmann had to buy complete cars, and this made the venture more expensive and less competitive.

There were various attempts to fit a soft- or hard-top and at least one true coupé with doors was built, but enthusiasts preferred the basic open-top version. In 1960 there was also one Enzmann coupé built on the DKW 1000 chassis. Production amounted to about 100 cars including some kits comprising the body shell and modifications. In the early 1990s a collector rebuilding an Enzmann decided to have the complete body remade with improvements and to offer new Enzmann roadsters or kits to the public but nothing more was heard of the project.
FH

ÉOLE (F) 1899–1901
J.B. Clement et Compagnie, Paris.
The original Éole voiturette used a 2.75hp Aster engine mounted at the front,

shaft drive to a 3-speed gearbox and final drive by chain. Instead of using a larger engine on their next model, the makers simply added a second one. The resulting 4.5hp car had a top speed of 35mph (56km/h). In 1901 a single 6hp Buchet engine, and a similar transmission to the original car, was used. In that year, the maker was given as Van Berendonck.
NG

EOLIA see TRACTION ARIENNE

EOS (i) (A) 1919–1920
Eos GmbH, Vienna.
This was a short-lived cyclecar of which no technical details are known.
HON

EOS (ii) (D) 1922–1923
Rossinech & Co., Berlin.
Formerly known as the Erco, this was a light car powered by a 5/20PS 3-cylinder 2-stroke engine.
HON

ÉPALLE (F) 1910–1914
Épalle et Compagnie, St Etienne, Loire.
A range of four cars was listed by this firm; an 8/10hp 2-cylinder, and three fours of 10/12, 12/16 and 14/20hp. They were all of conventional design with shaft drive.
NG

E. P. C. (US) c.1979
Electric Passenger Cars, San Diego, California.
EPC built a number of prototypes for electric car production. The Hummingbird I was based on a Volkswagen Type 181 'Thing', while the Hummingbird II used the more practical VW Rabbit as its base. It was powered by a 15hp motor and 12 6v batteries. The Hummingbird Hybrid Mk 1 used a combination of batteries and an onboard petrol generator to extend the range and performance. The Hummingbird Hybrid KSV was the same car with a damage-resistant safety body.
HP

E.P.C. (GB) 1970–1972
Essex Proto Conversions, Chelmsford, Essex.
Essex Proto Conversions, Dagenham, Essex.
E.P.C.'s main product was the Hustler beach buggy but it also produced the Pinza GS, an unusual sports/fun car cross-over for a VW Beetle chassis. This was sold in basic shell form or fully-built, and could be ordered with an optional gull-wing hardtop.
CR

EPOCAR (RSM) 1991–c.1993
Epocar SA, Galazzano, San Marino.
The Epocar Symbol joined a highly select group of cars produced in the tiny principality of San Marino. The style was a typical 'retro' 1930s-style convertible confection with a tubular chassis, Ford 2.0-litre power and fibreglass bodywork. The company claimed to be building three cars per month in 1992.
CR

ERA (US) 1980 to date
Era Replica Automobiles, New Britain, Connecticut.
Although Cobra replicas were as common as Volkswagens in the American kit car industry, ERA set itself apart with high-quality kits that were more authentic and better detailed than the industry at large. They sold well to better-heeled buyers who wanted a more realistic replica. They made replicas of the 427 S/C and 289 FIA Cobras, and followed with similar quality copies of the Ford GT-40 Mk I and II. These had stainless-steel monocoque chassis with fabricated suspension. The Mk I used 5000cc Ford engines, while the Mk II was designed for 7000cc engines. In 1998, ERA bought the rights to build Corvette Grand Sport replicas from D & D Manufacturing.
HP

1981 ERA Cobra replica.
NATIONAL MOTOR MUSEUM

c.1988 Erad Junior microcar.
NICK GEORGANO

1920 Eric-Campbell 10hp 2-seater.
NATIONAL MOTOR MUSEUM

E.R.A. (GB) 1980s
Under this name one of many Bugatti Type 35 replicas was marketed during the mid–1980s.

CR

ERAD (F) 1975–1997
Études et Réalisations du Douaisis sarl (Automobiles Erad), Aniche.
Erad was one of France's longest-lived producers of microcars, with a range of conventional and more adventurous vehicles, and sales exceeding 30,000 units, including 800 electric cars. Its first model was the Capucine, a plastic-bodied single-seater with 47cc Sachs engine and MacPherson strut front suspension. A 290cc Farymann diesel engine was offered from 1981, as well as a 123cc BCB petrol unit. A highly unusual model was the Midget of 1982, a charming replica

of the 1936 MG Midget only 9 feet (270cm) long and powered by a 125cc petrol or 600cc diesel engine. The Capucine was restyled for 1984 and offered in Plein Air convertible and 4-seater forms as well. A new budget model called the Junior was launched in 1988: at 35,000F it was the cheapest new car in France and featured a flop-forward canopy for entry. The 1990 Spacia 'monobox' looked like a miniature Renault Espace, predating the Twingo, and was powered by diesel engines up to 505cc or an electric motor. This was the first electric microcar to pass full EC crash tests. Another interesting model was the 1993 Agora, an ultra-basic canvas-roof 2-seater that Erad described as a '2CV for the year 2000'. Erad sank in 1997 but the products were revived by SAVEL.

CR

ERCO *see* EOS (ii)

ERDMANN (D) 1904–1908
Friedrich Erdmann, Gera.
This car was characterised by its friction transmission which was unusual in that it was used only for starting and steep gradients. For normal driving conditions, power was transmitted straight through by shaft from the engine to the rear axle. Various engines were used, including 2-cylinder Korting and 4-cylinder units by Fafnir and Horch. The cars were also sold under the name F.E.G., and the Erdmann friction-drive system was used by BERGMANN under licence.

HON

ERIC (GB) 1911–1914
P. & C. Syndicate Ltd, Northampton.
The Eric was one of the earliest cyclecars, making its appearance at the 1911 London Motor Cycle Show. It had a 6hp water-cooled flat-twin engine, 3-speed gearbox and chain drive to the single rear wheel. At the Olympia Show in November 1912 an air-cooled single-cylinder model at £105 was shown in addition to the water-cooled model, which was now shaft-driven and cost £135. The frame was a large diameter central tube with the body mounted on outriggers. This was said to eliminate swaying which led to the rear wheel skidding on corners. For 1914 the Eric became more car-like, with an 8hp 4-cylinder Salmons engine and the option of a closed coupé, though it remained a 3-wheeler.

NG

ERIC-CAMPBELL (GB) 1919–1926
1919–1921 Eric, Campbell & Co. Ltd, Cricklewood, London.
1922–1926 Vulcan Iron & Metal Works Ltd, Southall, Middlesex.
Unlike Eric Longden, there never was a Mr Eric Campbell; the name came from two men who founded the company, Hugh Eric Orr-Ewing and Noel Campbell Macklin. The latter was later responsible for the SILVER HAWK and INVICTA (iv) cars. Their product was an assembled light car, using a 1505cc Coventry-Simplex 4-cylinder engine with high-lift camshafts and drilled piston skirts, 3-speed gearbox and shaft drive. The prototype used a prewar Swift chassis. The body was a polished aluminium 2-seater which, with the tuned engine, clearly aimed the car at the sportsman rather than the family motorist. Two cars were entered in one of the first postwar races, the Targa Florio of November 1919. British cars were rare enough anyway in this gruelling Sicilian event, so it was even more remarkable that a hitherto unknown small make should take part. They had no success, but a decision was taken to lower capacity to 1498cc to bring the engine within the 1500cc competitions limit.
    Initially, Eric-Campbells were made in part of the Handley-Page aircraft factory at Cricklewood. Macklin left in May 1920 to make the Silver Hawk at Cobham, Surrey, and Eric-Campbell was soon in financial difficulties. This was not helped by their sporting programme which included a single-ohc racing car. In 1921 cars were being remaindered at bargain prices by Wood & Lambert of Stamford Hill, North London, but in 1922 production was taken over by the Vulcan Iron Works. They continued to make the Coventry-Simplex engined car, sold at considerably lower prices than in 1920, and in a wider range of body styles including, in 1924, a 2-door saloon. In its last years the Eric-Campbell was offered with two engines in addition to the Coventry-Simplex, a 1074cc and a 1496cc Anzani, both side-valve fours. A receiver was appointed in January 1926. Production has been estimated as high as 500; this is probably on the optimistic side.

NG

ERIC LONGDEN (GB) 1920–1927

1920–1922 Eric Longden, London.

1922–1927 Air Navigation & Engineering Co. Ltd, Addlestone, Surrey.

Eric Longden was an Australian-born steeplechase jockey who came to London to start a theatrical agency. In 1919–20 he started to assemble light cars in premises in Charing Cross Road (conveniently close to theatreland), next door to what is now Foyles Bookshop. The cars probably had Coventry-Simplex engines and Moss gearboxes, but little is known about them. They were not listed in insurance guides until 1922, when they were being made by the Air Navigation & Engineering Co at Addlestone, who were also making the BLERIOT WHIPPET. Surrey-built Eric Longdens had J.A.P. V-twin engines of 964 or 1088cc in 1922, and thereafter 1074 Alpha or, from 1924, 1320cc 4-cylinder Coventry-Simplex engines. Bodies were mostly open 2-seater sports models in polished aluminium, although a striking 2-door saloon with vee-windscreen and pointed tail was shown at Olympia in 1923. The 1923–24 Motor Trade Directory listed a new company, Eric Longden Cars Ltd, but it was probably a sales agency for the cars made by ANEC.

NG

ERIDANO (I) 1911–1914

Ditta Solavo, Turin.

This was a conventional light car powered by a 1693cc 4-cylinder engine, with 4-speed gearbox, selling for 5500 lire complete with 4-seater bodywork.

NG

ERIE (US) 1916–1919

Erie Motor Car Co., Painesville, Ohio.

The Erie company was formed to buy the VULCAN (ii) Manufacturing Co., also of Painesville, and as well as building Erie cars they serviced Vulcans. Their own car was a conventional machine with 33hp 4-cylinder engine made as a tourer or roadster, both priced at $795 in 1916–17 and $850 in 1918–19. A larger and more expensive tourer at $1975 was announced for 1920 but apparently never built. The company made the E.M.C. truck in 1917–18, but were not connected with another truck maker. Erie Motor Truck Co. of Erie, Pennsylvania, which was in business from 1914 to 1922.

NG

E.R.L. (S) c.1948–1951

Eskil Roland Lindström, Molndal.

Lindström built a small number of sports cars with prewar styling features such as cycle-type wings and cut-away doors, powered first by a motorcycle engine and later by a 600cc D.K.W. car unit. With the latter, top speed was about 60mph (100km/h).

NG

ERMINI (I) 1948–1962

Pasquale Ermini made a small number of sports cars throughout the 1950s, mainly for competition work and mainly in the 1100cc class. The Fiat 1100 engine block was used with special cylinder heads, sometimes with twin camshafts, plus a 5-speed gearbox and self-designed tubular chassis. Piero Scotti won his class in the Targa Florio, among others, in an Ermini. In 1953, Ermini offered a very pretty 1300 coupé with Frua coachwork and Fiat based engines. It also specialised in the transformation of Fiat engines with twin ohcs. In the 1950s Ermini ceased offering fully-built sports cars and concentrated on special bodies.

CR

ERNST (CH) 1905–1908

Ateliers Gustave Ernst, Geneva.

Gustave Ernst had been one of the first workers to be employed at the Daimler factory in Germany. In 1904 he returned to Switzerland and operated a workshop in Geneva, where he repaired automobiles. One year later he introduced his own make, a 12hp tourer. He made use of a chassis bought from Malicet & Blin, France and an ASTER 4-cylinder T-head engine of 2438cc with double magneto/coil ignition. Soon, larger 14hp and 16hp engines of 3402cc were fitted. Ernst cars, which had 3-speed gearboxes and chain drive, were quite successful in regional hill climbs and trials. In 1908 the limited production ceased.

FH

1923 Eric Longden 10hp saloon.
NICK BALDWIN

1905 Ernst 12.5CV tonneau.
ERNEST SCHMID

ERSKINE (US) 1927–1930

The Studebaker Corp, Detroit, Michigan.

The Erskine was the first of Studebaker's companion small car makes, the second being the ROCKNE. Named after Studebaker's president Albert Russel Erskine (1871–1933), it was billed as "The Little Aristocrat" and was intended to be a European-type quality small car. Unlike other Studebakers, it used a propietary engine, a 2392cc 6-cylinder Continental Model 8F, and many other components were bought in, though the bodies were made in Studebaker's Detroit factory where the Erskine was put together. They were styled by Ray Dietrich, while the engineering was the work of Leon A. Chaminade. The prototypes had two unusual features, fixed wire wheels with detachable rims, and fuel feed by electric pump, though these were discarded when the Erskine reached production, in favour of wood wheels and vacuum feed.

Four body styles were offered initially, tourer, sedan, business coupé, and custom coupé. Prices were high, at $975 for a sedan, when an Essex Six sold for $735 and a Super Six for $795. Nevertheless Erskine sold 24,893 units in its first season, and sales remained at about that level for the four years it was on the market. For 1929 the Erskine's engine capacity went up to 2528cc (Continental 9F), and for 1930 a 3364cc Studebaker Six engine was used and the wheelbase was increased from 109 to 114in (2766 to 2893mm). It now had little to distinguish it from the smaller Studebakers, and in May 1930 it was logically renamed the Studebaker Six. Total production was just over 95,000 cars.

NG

E.S.A. (A) 1920–1926

Egon Seilnacht, Atzgersdorf, Vienna.

Although Seilnacht only had a small workshop he made nearly every part of the car on his premises. Two models of the E.S.A. were made, a four and a six, both with side-valve engines. They were of conventional chassis design and, like most Austrian and German cars of the period, began with sharply-pointed vee radiators,

1926 Erskine sedan (prototype).
NATIONAL MOTOR MUSEUM

1917 Espana Tipo II tourer.
NATIONAL MOTOR MUSEUM

c.1908 Esperia 20hp tourer.
NICK BALDWIN

changing to a flat radiator in about 1922. Approximately 200 fours were made, and 30 to 40 sixes.

NG

E.S.A.P. (I) 1968
E.S.A.P. SpA, Venice.
The Minimach GT was a plain copy of the UNIPOWER GT, but with rectangular headlamps in place of round ones. Swift legal action by the British manufacturer of the Unipower forced the destruction of all E.S.A.P. tooling. Another Unipower copy was made in South Africa under the name Banshee, this time with no roof and a cut-down screen.

CR

ESCOL (B) 1926–1929
Éts Escol, Chatelet, Charleroi.
This company was founded before World War I by Jules Escol, a professor of mining engineering at Louvain University, to make mine winding machinery. In 1922 his two eldest sons, Felix and Maurice, built a prototype motorcycle, but it was not commercialised because of its high price. Four years later they decided to assemble cars, using 1.5-litre Fivet engines and chassis from S.U.P. They made their own coachwork. A small number were built, but in 1927 they turned to the more modern Chapuis-Dornier engine and fitted their chassis with four-wheel brakes. These were also made in small numbers, including an attractive pointed-tail 4-seater sports car, before the brothers abandoned car production in 1929. In 1933 they returned to motorcycles, which they made up to 1938.

NG

ESCULAPE (F) 1899
Automobile Union, Paris.
Named after the Greek god of medicine, Aesculapius, this was a very light voiturette with 2.25hp De Dion-Bouton engine which had an air-cooled cylinder head and water-cooled block, 2-speed gearbox and bicycle wheels. The engine was mounted at the rear of the tubular frame, behind the rear axle. The drive was taken forward by bevel gears to a 2-speed constant-mesh gearbox, and thence forward again to a countershaft in the centre of the frame and by side chains to the rear wheels.

NG

ESCULAPIUS see KNIGHT OF THE ROAD (i)

ESHELMAN (US) 1953–1960
Chester L. Eshelman Co., Baltimore, Maryland.
Tiny cars for children or a solitary adult were the speciality of this small-volume manufacturer. Their first model, the Sportabout, had a tall top and a Briggs & Stratton engine. Their best seller, introduced in 1955, was the Sport Car, a single-person roadster intended for short trips around the neighbourhood. It was only 54in (1370mm) long, had a 3hp B&S engine and could be adapted into a riding lawn mower.

HP

ESPAÑA (E) 1917–1928
Automóviles España, Fábrica Nacional F. Batlló SC, Barcelona.
Founded by Felipe Batlló y Godó, a member of one of the most important Catalonian families, the company built only one model in large numbers, and some peculiar prototypes. The Tipo I used a MAG 4-cylinder engine, but only the Tipo II, with French Altos engines, were built in series. It was a 24bhp 4-cylinder engine with 4-speed transmission. About 850 Tipo II were built. In 1922 the company presented the Tipo III, a prestigious car with a Rolls-Royce-like bonnet, with a 4-cylinder, 3690cc 58bhp engine. Three were built; one for King Alfonso XIII. They also built a prototype of Tipo IV, with a 4500cc 4-cylinder engine and with four valves-per-cylinder. Also several competition cars were built. España intended to create the Apta car together with RICART and ELIZALDE, but finally formed RICART-ESPAÑA to built a large luxury car.

VCM

ESPERIA (I) 1905–c.1910
Stà Automobili Lombarda, Bergamo.
This company exhibited two cars at the 1906 Paris Salon, both with 4-cylinder engines. The 20hp was a monobloc unit, while the 40hp had its cylinders cast in pairs. The latter offered the option of chain or shaft drive, but the smaller car was only shaft driven. The make, which was sometimes sold as Lombarda or S.A.L., was still listed in *l'Annuaire Générale de l'Automobile* in 1910, but it is not certain if it was then made.

NG

ESPRIT (US) c.1982
Esprit Coachworks, Corona, California and Hawaiian Gardens, California.
This kit car company was the distributor for several low-volume manufacturers.

They sold a DeTomaso Pantera replica that was based on a Volkswagen Beetle chassis and the attractive FIERRO 600 sports car kit. They also produced a unique Cobra replica that was built on a VW Beetle chassis. For those without the stomach for such blasphemy, a tube-frame version with a Ford V8 up front was also available.

HP

ESS EFF (US) 1912

Ess Eff Silent Motor Co., Buffalo, New York.

This primitive car used a 17hp 2-cylinder 2-stroke engine which was most unlikely to have lived up to the promise of silence in the company's name. Transmission was by friction discs and final drive by chains, which was very antiquated for 1912. The car's only redeeming feature was its low price of $350, but this did not attract many customers. The unusual name presumably referred to the makers, whose names began with 'S' and 'F', but their details have not survived.

NG

ESSEX (i) (US) 1901–1902

Essex Automobile & Supply Co., Haverhill, Massachusetts;
Lynn, Massachusetts.

This was a light runabout selling for $700 and powered, unusually for such a car, by a 4-cylinder engine. It had what was described as Upton direct transmission and single-chain drive. The 2-seater had tiller steering and was devoid of mudguards. In 1902 the company moved to Lynn to continue manufacture of the same car.

NG

ESSEX (ii) (US) 1906

Essex Motor Car Co., Boston, Massachusetts.

This was a late entrant into the field of New England steamers, introduced when most makers had gone over to internal-combustion engines or left the scene altogether. It had a 15/20hp 4-cylinder single-acting engine. Only one body style was offered, a 5-seater tonneau at $3000, which resembled the Serpollet. There were plans for the car to be made by the Bailey Carriage Co. of Amesbury, Massachusetts, but instead an electric car was introduced, undoubtedly a wise decision.

NG

ESSEX (iii) (US) 1918–1933

1918–1924 Essex Motors, Detroit, Michigan.
1924–1933 Hudson Motor Car Co., Detroit, Michigan.

In 1916 Hudson was a successful manufacturer, making 25,772 cars which put them in ninth place in the production league. However, secretary/treasurer Roscoe B. Jackson was worried about the threat from low-priced cars from mass producers such as Ford, Chevrolet and Dodge, and decided to build a competitor. A separate company, Essex Motors, was set up, and a former Studebaker factory in Detroit was leased for the new car. However, this was never used during the war, and when Essex production began it was in Hudson's own plant.

The Essex name was said to have been chosen after a study of a map of English counties, also, perhaps, because it implied six cylinders, although no Essex had more than four until 1924. The engine was an F-head (overhead inlet valves, side exhaust) of 2950cc developing 55bhp, which gave it a top speed of 60mph (100km/h) with a tourer body. Only three body styles were offered in the first season; a tourer, a roadster and a sedan. At $2250 the latter was considerably more expensive than the $1395 open cars. Production was planned to start in February 1918, but because of the demands of the war effort, only 92 cars left the factory that year. These were all tourers. It was a different story in 1919, with 21,879 delivered. This was more than the 18,175 made by the Hudson parent company.

The Essex Four had a good power-to-weight ratio, and the company soon entered cars in various record-breaking attempts. These included a long-distance endurance record of 3037 miles in 50 hours at the Cincinnati Speedway, and a 1061 mile journey through snowy Iowa roads in 24 hours, both in 1919. Other body styles such as a 2-door cabriolet were added in 1920 and 1921, but far more significant was the 2-door coach sedan introduced for 1922. This cost $1495, reduced to $1345 at the beginning of 1922 and to $1245 a few months later. This was only $200 more than the open tourer, and it was the first time that a closed car had been priced so close to an open car. The coach sedan was no beauty, being likened to 'a crackerbox on a raft'. However, its importance

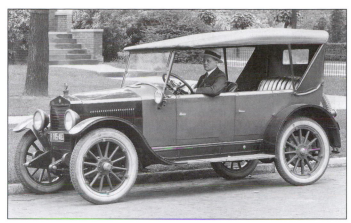
1922 Essex (iii) Four tourer.
NATIONAL MOTOR MUSEUM

1928 Essex (iii) Super Six sedan.
NATIONAL MOTOR MUSEUM

1932 Essex (iii) Pacemaker sedan.
NICK GEORGANO/NATIONAL MOTOR MUSEUM

was not lost on the industry; GM president Alfred P. Sloan wrote later that the introduction of the Essex coach was 'an event which was to profoundly influence the fortunes of Pontiac, Chevrolet and the Model T'.

By the end of the 1924 season, closed models were accounting for 90 per cent of Hudson-Essex production. A year later, when the coach had been redesigned with better proportions, its price of $765 was the same as the open tourer, and for 1926 was $100 less than the open car. A new 4-door sedan was the same price as the tourer. These sedans put Essex in the forefront of the trend which led to nearly 90 per cent of cars sold in America in 1929 having closed bodies. Ten years earlier, little more than 10 per cent had been closed.

For 1924 Essex became a six at last; the Four gave way to a conventional side valve six of 2130cc (increased to 2370cc in June 1924). It was no longer the performance leader that the Four had been, but was immensely popular, and helped Essex to sales of over 227,653 in 1929, when they reached third in the production league. Four-wheel brakes were optional in 1927 and standardised in 1928. The 1927 Super Six had a larger engine (2510cc), and came closer to Hudson in appearance when the original Rolls-Royce-type radiator gave way to a curved top. A particularly attractive model in the 1927 range was the speedabout; with its pointed tail it was, in fact, the cheapest model at $700. Today it is prized above all other 1927 Essexes. Engine capacity went up to 2645cc in 1929, which gave the same 55bhp as in the original Four of 1918. For 1930 the wheelbase was increased by 2.5in. Essexes became still closer to Hudson in appearance, having all-new styling with vee-radiators in 1932, when engine capacity went up to 3164cc. In July 1932 came a new model, the Essex Terraplane. These were substantially less expensive than the standard Essex, the twelve-model range running from $425 to $610, compared with $660-845. They were better-looking, and better-performing. For 1933 the Essex name was dropped and Hudson's junior range became simply TERRAPLANE.

NG

Further Reading
The History of Hudson, Don Butler, Crestline Publishing, 1982.

ESTANCIERA (RA) 1960–1970
IKA Renault SA, Cordoba.
Industrias Kaiser Argentina (IKA) started Jeep production in 1956. The Estanciera station wagon, based on the Jeep, with 3707cc, 6-cylinder engine, was introduced in 1960. At first it sold very well in car-starved Argentina: 44,147 Estancieras were sold in the 1960–1965 period. But as other, more sophisticated, vehicles became available, sales dropped, and in the last year of production only 415 Estancieras were made.

ACT

ESTEEM (GB) 1994–1996
Esteem Motor Co., Glencarnock, Ayrshire.
'The Finest Lamborghini Countach replica anywhere' was the bold claim of this Scottish company. Kit prices started extremely low but there was still a substantial steel chassis for V8 power, and an accurate late-model Countach fibreglass replica body.

CR

ETNYRE (US) 1910–1911
Etnyre Motor Car Co., Oregon, Illinois.
Designed by E.D. Etnyre, the Etnyre Four was a large car offered in tourer, roadster and coupé models, and powered by a 7.7-litre 50hp engine of Etnyre's own manufacture. The company was under-financed, and closed at the end of the 1911 season after only 10 cars had been made.

NG

EUCLID (i) (US) 1903–1904
Berg Automobile Co., Cleveland, Ohio.
The Euclid was a companion car to the BERG, both being made by Hart O. Berg. It was a more original car than its stable mate, which was closely based on the Panhard, although in fact it differed little from the many other American cars of its era. It had an 18hp 4-cylinder engine, shaft drive and a 5-seater tourer body. When Berg sold his business to the Worthington Automobile Co. in 1904, his car was continued, but the Euclid was not.

NG

EUCLID (ii) (US) 1907–1908
Euclid Motor Car Co., Cleveland, Ohio.
The second car to bear the Euclid name was no more successful than the first, but it was a more original design, having an air-cooled 3-cylinder 2-stroke engine, epicyclic transmission and double-chain drive. The roadster and tourer models were very conventional in appearance.

NG

EUCLID (iii) (US) 1914
Euclid Motor Car Co., West Haven, Connecticut.

The makers of this car called it a 'cycle-light car', a fair description as it was of cyclecar size with 40in track, but boasted such car-like features as a 1.6-litre 15hp 4-cylinder engine and shaft drive. Priced at $445, it was to have been called the Baby Grand, but Chevrolet claimed that name and threatened legal action, so Euclid renamed it the Grand Baby, which does not sound nearly so appealing. There were plans to build it in the CAMERON factory, but these never materialised.

NG

EUCORT (E) 1945–1953
Automoviles Eusebio Cortés SA, Barcelona.
Eusebio Cortés had the ambitious plan to start an important national manufacturer of 4-door sedans in 1945. The car used 2-cylinder 2-stroke 764cc engines with 23.5bhp, with front-wheel drive, and was delivered in several versions – sedan, station wagon and light van. The station wagon had a wooden body. At the end of 1948, the company introduced a new 3-cylinder 2-stroke engine of 32bhp, and this was offered together with the 2-cylinder engine. This 3-cylinder engined version also appeared as an attractive 2-door coupé, but only the prototype was produced. In 1949, the Victoria appeared. This was a redesigned version with integrated front lights. There also existed some racing bodies on the Eucort, a Capilla-designed convertible and a special one-box taxi prototype. The last Eucort had a Studebaker-looking design, with a radiator looking like a shell, and which was named Victoria Avión. Over 1500 Eucorts were made, but owing to the lack of finance and the impossibility of importing machine tools, the manufacturer closed in 1953.

VCM

EUDELIN (F) 1905–c.1908
M.A. Eudelin, Paris.
Eudelin advertised in *l'Annuaire Générale de l'Automobile* of 1906 that he could supply 'cars of all powers', using Barriquand et Marre engines, but it is not certain how many were actually made. In 1907 he made a 'cab de ville' with hansom cab-type body, although steered from the inside rather than from behind. It had a 14/16hp 4-cylinder engine, shaft drive and a round radiator. In 1908 Eudelin was said to be experimenting with a 'constant power' engine with opposed pistons.

NG

EUREKA (i) (US) 1899–1900
Eureka Automobile & Transportation Co., San Francisco, California.
The first car to carry the Eureka name was a 4-seater surrey powered by a rear-mounted 10hp 3-cylinder horizontal engine, with four forward speeds and single-chain final drive, vertical steering column and solid tyres. Top speed was 30mph (48km/h), although the makers admitted that this was too fast for ordinary Californian roads. The car was designed and built by J.M. Ough and George Waltenbaugh for Ough's employer Charles L. Fair, who was one of the partners in the company. This planned to make a variety of cars, delivery wagons and trucks in a large factory, but it never got started. Probably Fair's death in a racing accident in Europe did not help.

NG

EUREKA (ii) see PARISIENNE

EUREKA (iii) (F) 1906–1908
Automobiles Mainetty, La Garenne-Colombes, Seine.
This Eureka was powered by a 6hp single-cylinder De Dion-Bouton engine, with friction transmission and belt final drive. Unusually for such a light car, it had a 4-seater body.

NG

EUREKA (iv) (US) 1906–1907
Eureka Motor Car Co., Seattle, Washington.
This company admitted that they were going to be assemblers rather than manufacturers, 'buying the parts from the parts makers and assembling them here'. These parts included a 20/24hp 4-cylinder Duo engine, and a 2-seater runabout body. The Eureka was very expensive at $1900, and production was minimal.

NG

1946 Eucort 764cc saloon.
NICK GEORGANO/NATIONAL MOTOR MUSEUM

EUREKA (v) **(US)** 1907–1909

1907–1909 Eureka Motor Buggy Co., St Louis, Missouri.
1909 Eureka Motor Car Manufacturing Co., St Louis, Missouri.
This was a high-wheel buggy with a difference – several differences in fact. Its 10/12hp 2-cylinder engine was in unit with the conventional sliding gearbox, and final drive was by shaft, in place of the more usual friction transmission and belt, chain or rope drive. Although only one body style was listed in 1907–08, a 2-seater runabout, there were four alternative wheelbases. For 1909, in a new factory and with a different company name, maker Charles Zimmerman offered only one wheelbase but five bodies, including a delivery van. He had no connection with the Zimmerman family of Auburn, Indiana, which also made high-wheelers.
NG

EUREKA (vi) **(US)** 1907–1909

Eureka Motor Buggy Co., Beavertown, Pennsylvania.
This was a more typical high-wheeler than the St Louis product, for it had a friction transmission and chain drive. It was more car-like than some, with a bonnet in front. The 2-stroke Speedwell engines were a 12/14hp twin or 15/18hp 3-cylinder. In 1908 local businessman Maxwell Kearns invested heavily in the company, and in 1909 the cars were renamed KEARNS, though some were still marketed as Eurekas up to the end of the year.
NG

EUREKA (vii) **(US)** 1908–1909

Eureka Manufacturing Co., Rock Falls, Illinois.
Better known as makers of furniture and coffins, this company made a brief sortie into the car field, and made, like their contemporaries in St Louis and Beavertown, a high-wheel buggy. It was powered by a 15hp 2-cylinder engine, with epicyclic transmission and chain drive. Few complete cars were made, but Eureka became famous for hearse bodies on other people's chassis, and continued this business up to the early 1960s.
NG

EUREKA (viii) **(AUS)** 1974–1998

Eureka Sports Cars, Dandenong, Victoria.
Taking its name from the location of Australia's only armed uprising, the Eureka was a fibreglass kit design, known as Sterling in the United States and originated as the Nova in the UK, produced as a complete car by Allan Purvis. A roomier PL-30 with a powered entry hatch and Ford Cortina power, appeared in 1978. His own 1982 design did not reach production as the Purvis firm, which had also offered the Grant street buggy, failed. The Eureka continued with the F4 and a T-roof; 700 were sold by 1989 when a roadster appeared. The 1994 Boxer was a major re-engineering to replace the VW base.
MG

EURICAR (GB) 1930

J.V. and E.G. Eurich, Manchester.
This was a 3-wheeler with a rear-mounted 980cc V-twin J.A.P. engine, Sturmey-Archer gearbox and chain drive to the single rear wheel. The 2-seater body had a retractable metal hood, and the brakes were said to be 'hydraulic without friction' but this system was not explained to the press. The Euricar probably never went further than a single prototype.
NG

EUROCCO see EMBEESEA

EUROPA (GB) 1992 to date

Europa Engineering (Banks Service Station), Southport, Lancashire.
With much experience of the Lotus Europa, this operation was in a good position to produce a replica of the Lotus 47, which it called the 47R. Another model dubbed the 62 was more racing-orientated, with square headlamps and wider wheel arches. The concept was updated for the 1990s: the mid-mounted engine now came from Vauxhall or Alfa Romeo (or Renault, like the original), while the suspension was purpose-designed around Ford and Triumph hubs and components. Another route was to convert a genuine Lotus Europa.
CR

509

1922 Euston 2¾hp 3-wheeler.
NATIONAL MOTOR MUSEUM

EUROPÉENE (F) 1899–1903

Sté Européene d'Automobiles Paris.

This company built two types of steam car, made under the patents of Messrs Tatin and Tanière. These were a 3-wheeler with tiller steering to the single front wheel, and 2-seater body, and a 4-wheeler 4-seater *dos-à-dos*. Both had petrol-fired coiled-tube flash boilers and horizontal double-acting engines. They had 2-speed gearboxes, unusual on a steam car, and chain final drive. Top speed was a modest 16mph (25km/h). At the Paris Salon in July 1900 the 3-wheeler was not to be seen, and the 4-wheeler was now credited with 28mph (45km/h). They also made internal-combustion-engined cars, a 12hp 4-seater in 1900 and a 4-seater tonneau powered by a 6hp De Dion-Bouton engine in 1903.

NG

EUROSPORT (GB) 1990 to date

1990–1992 Eurosport, Rayleigh, Essex.
1992–1996 Eurosport, Sawston, Cambridgeshire.
1996 to date Rimmer Bros Ltd, Lincoln, Lincolnshire.

Eurosport was a Fiat X1/9 specialist offering fibreglass bodykits among other items. In 1990 it launched the most radical conversion of the Triumph TR7. The suggestion was that the TR40 resembled a Ferrari F40, but it all looked very odd on the front-engined Triumph. The fibreglass body panels attached over the standard TR7 (in either closed coupé or convertible forms).

CR

EURO WORKS (US) 1989 to date

Euro-Works Ltd, Dayton, Ohio.

The Lamborghini Countach was replicated in two forms by this kit car company. The Mirage S fitted onto a standard-length Pontiac Fiero chassis, while the Mirage K required that the Fiero chassis be lengthened by 5in (126mm). Turnkey models with V6 or V8 engines were sold as well as kits.

HP

EUSKALDUNA see CEYC

EUSTON (GB) 1922–1924

Fowler & Bigden, London.

This was a very light 3-wheeled monocar powered by a 2¾hp single-cylinder 2-stroke Villiers engine driving the front wheel. The body resembled a motorcycle sidecar, and was described as 'an attractive proposition for invalids'. Priced at £95, it was only 88in (1676mm) long and 36in (914mm) wide.

NG

E. V. A (US) c.1979

Electric Vehicle Associates, Inc., Cleveland, Ohio.

The EVA Metro was a 4-seater electric car based on the Renault 12 TL body powered by 19 6v batteries. It had a cruising speed of 55mph (88km/h) with a range of 30 to 55 miles. Luxury features included an automatic transmission, power steering and power brakes. The company also made electric-powered versions of the AMC Pacer and Pacer Wagon called the 'Change of Pace' models. Both used 15kW traction motors.

HP

EVANS (i) see SCORPION

EVANS (ii) (US) c.1993 to date

Evans Automobiles, Scottdale, Georgia.

John Evans built several street car designs based on mid-engined race car standards. The Evans Series I was based on a metal and composite semi-monocoque chassis with Corvette brakes. A 5700cc Chevrolet V8 was used with a ZF 5-speed transaxle. Gull-wing doors added visual appeal to what appeared to be a prototype racing car. It was sold, fully assembled, for $80,000. In 1996 the Evans Series II LM was introduced, designed to compete with the Jaguar XJ220 and McLaren F1 at Le Mans and in the super street car marketplace. The chassis was now a fully composite monocoque with pushrod suspension and computer-controlled shock absorbers. Engine choices included 7052cc Chevrolet or Donovan V8s and a ZF transaxle was offered. Price was up to $250,000 in 1996. A racing version was sold as well.

HP

EVANS HUNTER see MAELSTROM

EVANSVILLE see SIMPLICITY

EVANTE (GB) 1983–1994

1983–1991 Evante Cars Ltd (incorporating Vegantune), Spalding, Lincolnshire.
1992–1994 Evante Cars Ltd (Fleur de Lys Automobile Manufacturing), Newark, Nottinghamshire.

In form there was no doubt what car had inspired the Evante – the Lotus Elan. But despite the visual similarities, in construction it was a very different car, having a space frame chassis. Its Vegantune-manufactured VTA 1.6-litre (later 1.7-litre) twin cam engine developed either 140–150bhp or, in fuel-injected form, 160bhp. This drove through a Ford Sierra differential and 5-speed transmission, and there was all-independent suspension with double wishbones at the rear and 4-wheel disc braking. The fibreglass body was very like the Elan's, except for its spoilers and pop-up headlamps. Production of complete cars and kits got underway at the rate of one car per week. The car received styling, chassis and weather equipment improvements in 1991 but by the end of the year the company was in receivership. In 1992 the design was purchased by retro van manufacturer Fleur de Lys. It developed the car for 130bhp Ford Zeta 1.8-litre power, renaming it the Evante Gran and Gran Premio, but only nine such cars were built before the company closed its doors.

CR

EVASÃO (P) 1997 to date

Evasão, Vagos.

The microcar was very much the province of French manufacturers in the 1990s, and indeed the Evasão microcar was built in Portugal with French help. It was a conventional closed 2-seater with front-mounted engines. The range spanned the TXA315 and TXA325 (the number indicating engine capacity), as well as 4-seater and 500cc models.

CR

EVELYN (GB) 1913–1914

This was a light car sold by the Carette Company of Great Portland Street, London, the place of manufacture being uncertain. It had a 10hp 2-cylinder Dorman engine, Wrigley 3-speed gearbox and shaft drive. A 4-cylinder model was announced in the summer of 1914, but the outbreak of war prevented many from being made.

NG

EVERETT (i) (US) 1898–1899

Everett Motor Carriage Co., Everett, Massachusetts.

Messrs Milne & Killam made stationary steam engines of Whitney type, and in 1898 fitted one to a buggy. This worked sufficiently well for them to form a company, and this made a small number of replicas, but they did not proceed with this business beyond 1899, preferring to concentrate on engines and boilers. Frank Milne made one further steam car for his own use in 1901.

NG

1992 Evante roadster.
NICK BALDWIN

EVERETT (ii) (US) c.1956

Jay Everett, Los Angeles, California.

The Everett Astra, a one-off coupé with radical styling, was meant to be the prototype for a series of special built-to-order cars for wealthy patrons. It had a custom tubular frame with an Oldsmobile V8 engine driving through a Lincoln overdrive transmission. Suspension was by Ford transverse springs. The body was aluminium and had a fastback top with vertical tail lights and deeply scooped headlights.

HP

EVERETT-MORRISON (US) 1983 to date

Everett-Morrison Motorcars, Tampa, Florida.

Cobra replicas were the only product of this kit car company. They made a conventional tube frame kit that was adaptable to a wide variety of suspension donors, including Ford, Jaguar and Corvette. They also sold a turnkey model called the King Cobra that used Ford Thunderbird suspension and a 5700cc Ford V8.

HP

EVERGREEN (GB) 1993 to date

Evergreen Motor Co., Penzance, Cornwall.

Probably the most ridiculous name ever seen on a car – Evergreen Rudolph Sportwagen – was bestowed on this replica of the VW Karmann-Ghia Type 14, which had its origins in the German RUDOLPH replica. For once, the Beetle floorpan basis was quite in keeping. Evergreen added a steel support frame to enhance the rigidity of the fibreglass body, which was available in coupé and convertible guises. The project had connections with LEGEND.

CR

EVERITT (US) 1909–1912

Metzger Motor Car Co., Detroit, Michigan.

This company was formed by Barney Everitt and William Metzger, who had been in partnership with Walter Flanders in making the E.M.F. The first Everitt Four-30 was very similar to the E.M.F. 30, which was not surprising as they had taken E.M.F. designer William Kelly with them. In 1911 they added a larger four of 36hp, and in 1912 a six, the Six-48 on a 127in (3226mm) wheelbase. This was fitted with a compressed-air self starter, and sold for $1850–1900, compared with $1250–1500 for the 4-cylinder cars. Bodies were tourers and roadsters but Everitt offered no closed models. Late in 1912, Walter Flanders rejoined his former partners, and the Everitt company was reorganised as the FLANDERS Motor Co. The Everitt Six-48 became the Flanders Six, with the addition of electric lighting and starting, but this lasted only one year before Walter Flanders left to reorganise the United States Motor Co. During 1910–12 the Everitt 30 was made under licence in Canada by the TUDHOPE Motor Co. Ltd, at first as the Everitt or Everitt-Tudhope, and for 1912 simply as the Tudhope. Thomas J. Storey of the Brockville, Ontario firm Carriage Factories also bought components from Tudhope and assembled about 80 cars under the name BROCKVILLE 30.

NG

EVERYBODY'S (US) 1907–1909

Everybody's Motor Car Manufacturing Co., St Louis, Missouri.

This was a light 2-seater runabout powered by a 10hp 2-cylinder engine, with friction transmission and chain drive. Early examples were made in the factory of the SUCCESS Auto Buggy Co., but early in 1909 Everybody's moved into its own factory. The company failed shortly afterwards.

NG

EVERY DAY (CDN) 1910–1912

Woodstock Automobile Manufacturing Co. Ltd, Woodstock, Ontario.

The Every Day was a Canadian example of that familiar American type, the high-wheeler buggy, though it was more sophisticated than some in having a front-mounted 2-cylinder engine and shaft drive. Indeed the makers said in their advertisements, 'This is a shaft-driven car, not an automobile buggy'. Very few were made, and even the companion Oxford light truck sold only 33 units. The factory was later used for the manufacture of Bickle fire engines.

NG

1966 Excalibur (i) SS roadster.
NATIONAL MOTOR MUSEUM

1977 Excalibur (i) phaeton, with Brooks Stevens.
NATIONAL MOTOR MUSEUM

E.V.M. (F) 1907–1908

Voitures E.V.M., Paris.
The E.V.M. was made in three models, with 942cc 8hp single-cylinder and 10 or 12/14hp 4-cylinder engines of 1230 and 1814cc. All had 3-speed gearboxes and shaft drive. The 12/14hp chassis could carry double-phaeton or landaulette bodies. E.V.M. also supplied replacement parts for well-known makes such as Unic, Darracq, De Dion-Bouton, Renault and Mercedes cars. It is likely that E.V.M. stood for Emile Vauzelle-Morel, who had made cars under his own name a few years earlier.
NG

EVOLUTION (GB) 1993 to date

1993–1995 Mike Ryan, Cheltenham, Gloucestershire.
1995 to date Evolution Sports Cars, Avonmouth, Bristol.
As one of the myriad Lotus Seven style cars, the Evolution 1 tried to distinguish itself by offering Rover V8 power as well as the usual Ford engines (a wide variety of other power units could be fitted). Designed for budget builders, it featured aluminium main body panels, fibreglass wings and nose (with a prominent aerofoil) and a chassis with in-board pushrod suspension. You could either buy components from the manufacturer or create your own car from plans.
CR

E.W. (GB) 1990s

Chesterfield Motor Spares, Chesterfield, Derbyshire.
Ex-racing driver Eike Welhausen made a replica of the Lister Knobbly, with a space frame chassis, bespoke suspension, fibreglass bodywork and Jaguar engines. Its main market was replica racing.
CR

E.W.M. (GB) 1984–1985; 1988–1989

1984–1985 E.W.M. Kit Car Manufacturers, Salisbury, Wiltshire.
1988–1989 B&S Sports Cars, Birmingham.
Edward Waddington decided to launch a pair of Dutton competitors in the budget kit roadster market. The boxy Buccaneer was traditional in style, while the Brigand was more sporty with its droop-snoot and rear spoiler. Both used Ford Cortina mechanicals but were short lived. An attempted revival under the names B.S. Roadster and Sprint was equally unsuccessful.
CR

EXAU (F) 1922–1924

Cyclecars Exau, Paris.
The Exau was a neat-looking small car rather than a cyclecar, having an 893cc 4-cylinder S.C.A.P. engine and shaft drive.
NG

EXCALIBUR (i) (US) 1952–1953; 1965 to date

1952–1953 Beassie Engineering Co., Milwaukee, Wisconsin.
1965–1986 SS Automobiles, Milwaukee, Wisconsin.
1976 to date Excalibur Automobile Corp., Milwaukee, Wisconsin.
Excalibur designer Brooks Stevens was one of the most prolific designers in American specialist car history. The 1952–53 Excaliburs were heavily modified Kaiser Henry J chassis with cycle-mudguarded sports car bodywork. They were built to persuade Kaiser-Frazer to produce the design, but they went with the Kaiser-Darrin instead. Three cars were built and successfully raced with Willys and Jaguar engines. In 1963 Stevens built an experimental coupé called

MICHAEL LAMM

STEVENS, BROOKS (1911–1995)

Time magazine called him 'The seer that made Milwaukee famous.' During his 61 years as an industrial designer, Brooks Stevens served over 550 customers and styled thousands of products.

He was born in Milwaukee, Wisconsin in 1911 and, at age seven, contracted polio. For the next two years he lay in bed. To help pass the time, his father, an auto engineer and inventor, gave him pencil and paper. That's when Stevens began to draw cars. He slowly recovered but always used a cane.

In 1929, Stevens enrolled at Cornell to study architecture. His teachers soon pointed out that he spent much more time sketching the tiny cars in his architectural drawings than he did on his buildings. That immediately told him something: Maybe he ought to study car design instead of architecture.

Stevens left Cornell in 1932 and returned to Milwaukee with no particular plan in mind. In 1934, he entered a contest to redesign the Cutler-Hammer logo. One of the judges was Count Alexis de Sakhnoffsky. Stevens won the contest. This encouraged him to open his own industrial design firm in early 1935. Raymond Loewy, Walter Dorwin Teague, George W. Walker and others were proving to manufacturers that innovative designs and packaging could help sell products.

In time, Brooks Stevens' client list grew to include national and international accounts, among them Parker pens, Squibb, Budd, 3M, the Excalibur Hawk R2 in an effort to get Studebaker to put it into production. It was an attractive fastback design with a supercharged Avanti V8, but it remained a one-off. The first successful Excalibur was a cycle-mudguarded sports car on a Studebaker chassis with a Mercedes SSK-inspired body. Although conceived as a Studebaker show car, it was put into production with a 5362cc Chevrolet V8 engine in 1965. The first models were doorless roadsters, but in 1966 doors and a 4-seat phaeton were added to the line. Sales were brisk and in 1970 the old Studebaker-derived chassis was replaced with a special unit mounting Corvette suspension. This model was called the Excalibur II. In 1972 a 7445cc Chevrolet engine was made standard. In 1976 the Series III cars were introduced with more opulent bodywork, and this specification continued until 1981 when the Series IV replaced it. This was only available in phaeton form and engine size shrank to 5000cc, although it was bigger and longer than previous versions. Styling was altered to resemble the Mercedes 500/540K more than the SSK, although once again it was not an exact replica. In 1982 the roadster was reintroduced alongside the phaeton. In 1984 a special Signature 20th Anniversary model was

1914 Excelsior (i) 16hp landaulette.
NATIONAL MOTOR MUSEUM

Willys-Overland, Alfa-Romeo and Volkswagen. He styled outboard motors for Evinrude in 1935, designed the 'streamlined' Allis-Chalmers farm tractor for 1936, the round-window Hamilton clothes dryer in 1938, plus postwar Harley-Davidson motorcycles and Cushman scooters. He conceived glass-domed railcars, wide-mouth peanut butter jars, streamlined steam irons, luggage, bicycles, toys, playground equipment, metal garden furniture, high chairs, lawnmowers, snowmobiles and motorhomes.

His everlasting passion, though, was automobiles and especially automobile design. His first efforts were custom bodies for trucks and vans used by Wisconsin businesses: Johnson's Wax, Western Publishing Co., the Milwaukee breweries and coal companies.

During WW-II, he landed a contract with Willys-Overland and subsequently styled the 1946 Jeep all-metal station wagon and 1950 Jeepster. He also contributed to Kaiser-Frazer for 1948–51, did the 1800 Sprint for Alfa Romeo in 1951, designed a mid/transverse-engined 4wd pickup for Gutbrod; engineered, built and raced his own cycle-fendered Excalibur roadsters from 1950 to 1958, launched the Jeep Wagoneer in the 1960s, styled the 1955–74 Brazilian Aero Willys and Willys Rural wagon, and consulted for Studebaker from 1962 to the bitter end of that marque. He designed the 1962 Studebaker Hawk and created three prototypes for stillborn 1967 Studebakers. Stevens then worked with Volkswagen beginning in 1968 (on the 411) and American Motors/ Chrysler starting in 1969.

He styled the steam-powered, rear-engined 1950–52 Paxton Phoenix at the behest of California chainsaw/supercharger magnate Robert McCulloch, the 1956 Cadillac Valkyrie Paris salon car for a Cleveland business syndicate, Jim Gaylord's weird retractable hardtop of 1955, Olin Aluminum's three Scimitars for the 1958 Geneva show and built some 3600 of his own Excalibur SS neo-classics from 1964 through 1988.

Stevens was mild-mannered, ever-cheerful and highly charismatic. He exercised a thoughtful sense of history, both past and future, and revered antique, classic, one-off and race cars, collecting some of the choicest in his small museum in Mequon, Wisconsin. It was here that he kept the 1933 Marmon V12 prototype designed by Walter Dorwin Teague, Sakhnoffsky's prize-winning 1930 L-29 Cord coupé, Roscoe Hoffman's 1935 rear-X-engined experimental sedan built for the Fisher brothers, the Carraciola 1928 Mercedes, the King Alfonso 1925 Rolls-Royce phaeton, Tony Gulotta's 1933 Indy race car, a 1934 Miller Indy car, the Von Neumann 1939 SS-100 plus an assortment of additional pedigreed wonders.

The Stevens design organization grew from a 1935 one-man office to a firm that eventually employed 45 associates, with offices in Milwaukee and Chicago. Brooks Stevens Associates is still very much in business under the direction of his youngest son, Kipp.

During his semi-retirement, the elder Stevens taught at the Milwaukee Institute of Art & Design and gave spirited, articulate television interviews almost to the day he died. He passed away on 4 January 1995.

ML

c.1925 Excelsior (i) Adex C tourer.
BRYAN K. GOODMAN

1928 Excelsior (i) Albert I saloon, by Manessius.
NICK BALDWIN

announced, but in 1986 the company passed into bankruptcy. It was purchased from the Stevens family and reopened in 1987 with sedan and limousine models in addition to the convertibles. By the 1990s they had added Limited Edition models with higher price tags and styling similar to the original roadsters. In 1994 Excalibur added a fully assembled AC Cobra replica with a Ford V8 engine.

HP

EXCALIBUR (ii) **(GB)** 1985–1996
1985–1996 Excalibur Cars, West Looe, Cornwall.
The Excalibur began life as a close clone of the BONITO, also on a VW Beetle floorpan, but the company (a Cornish boatbuilder) quickly developed a special chassis for Ford Cortina components. The 2+2 seater fibreglass body had a steel frame bonded in for roll protection. 1992 saw the launch of Rover V8-powered and open-topped versions, the latter having a folding/detachable roof.

CR

1912 Excelsior (i) 14/20hp tourer.
NICK BALDWIN

1928 Excelsior (i) Albert I limousine, by Vanden Plas.
NICK BALDWIN

EXCEL (US) 1914
Excel Distributing Co., Detroit, Michigan.
The Excel was more substantial-looking than some cyclecars, and had a 1499cc 4-cylinder engine, although more typical of the breed were its friction transmission and belt drive. The 2-seater roadster cost $450. The company name implies that it marketed rather than manufactured the car.

NG

EXCELLENCE (CDN) 1985–c.1988
Excellence Motor Cars, Bromptonville, Québec.
This was a very typical large-scale neo-classic offering, first seen at the 1985 Montreal Motor Show. Like so many of its contemporaries, it used a Ford 5-litre V8 engine.

CR

EXCELSIOR (i) (B) 1903–1932
1903–1907 Compagnie Nationale Excelsior, Brussels.
1907–1909 A. de Coninck et Compagnie, Brussels; Liège.
1909–1929 SA des Automobiles Excelsior, Saventhem.
1929–1932 SA des Automobiles Imperia-Excelsior, Saventhem; Nessonvaux-les-Liège.
At the end of 1903 a young engineer, Arthur de Coninck, set up a small business with a grand name, the Compagnie Nationale Excelsior. He became an agent for French-built Aster engines, and made a few cars powered by these engines in single- or 2-cylinder form, with armoured wood frames. From 1905 he used larger Aster engines, 4-cylinder units of 16, 22 and 30CV, with Arbel steel frames and Malicet et Blin gearboxes. In 1907 he obtained more capital and larger premises, which enabled him to make his own engines and transmissions. He also represented the Cornilleau St Beuve car in Belgium. His first complete car was the 2950cc 14/20CV, with monobloc side-valve 4-cylinder engine, which was made up to 1914. In standard form it was the Type D, but there was also a more powerful Type DC Rapide and a town car, the Type B Fiacre (cab).

In 1909 de Coninck bought the factory of the defunct BELGICA company at Saventhem, near Brussels, and this allowed for further expansion. His first 6-cylinder car, the 4424cc D6 came in 1910, and was joined by the 5341cc Type F Roi des Belges in 1912. He also made a much larger six of 9100cc for racing, which was the first 6-cylinder car seen in Grands Prix. One finished sixth in the 1912 French Grand Prix and also sixth in the 1914 Indianapolis 500. By 1914 the Excelsior was established as a high-quality car, popular in export markets such as France and Great Britain as well as at home. The Belgian Royal Family were long-time customers of Excelsior. In 1913, the last full year of peace, 250 cars were made.

During the war the factory was occupied by the Germans, who confiscated all the machinery, but de Coninck had a new car, the Adex, ready in 1919. This name stood for Arthur de Coninck Excelsior and was also used for his patent designs, particularly the diagonally-compensated 4-wheel brakes used on the new car. The engine was similar to that of the prewar D6 but with a longer stroke giving a capacity of 4764cc. In October 1922 the engine dimensions were enlarged to those of the prewar Type F, and the valves were operated by an overhead camshaft. This beautiful engine gave 110bhp and was the only Excelsior model from 1925. It was inevitably very expensive, and not more than 100 were made each year. A 145bhp 3-carburettor sporting model was offered, and examples ran in the major long-distance events such as Le Mans, the Belgian 24 Hour Race, the Circuit de Routes Pavées and the Georges Boillot Cup. They won the 1926 Routes Pavées and 1927 Belgian 24 Hours.

At the end of 1926 Excelsior introduced the Albert I, named after Belgium's king. This was an improved version of the Adex, offered in 110bhp Tourist or 145bhp Sport forms. Two wheelbases were available, and the Adex braking system could be augmented by a Dewandre servo. The Albert I was a quality car in the same class at the Hispano-Suiza or Rolls-Royce, yet with chassis prices of £1150–1300 it was appreciably less expensive than either. However, sales declined in the late

1920s, and in 1927 Excelsior fell into the hands of Matthieu Van Roggen's empire, which also included Imperia, Métallurgique and Nagant. In 1929 components for the Albert I were sent to the Derihon factory at Liège, which already belonged to Imperia. Here a small number of chassis were assembled up to 1930 or 1931. The last appearance of Excelsior at a Brussels Salon was in December 1930. The factory at Saventhem was used for manufacture of Imperia bodies up to 1933, then sold.

NG

EXCELSIOR (ii) (CH) 1904–1907
Motorwagenfabrik Excelsior, Wollishofen-Zürich.
After manufacturing EGG & EGLI and RAPID 3-wheelers and selling licence rights to BÄCHTOLD and WEBER, Rudolf Egg was actively engaged in the foundation of the new Excelsior company in 1904. One year later, the first model was presented at the first National Automobile Show in Geneva. It was a new design, strongly resembling the Oldsmobile curved dash model 6C. It also had a single-chain drive of the rear wheels but instead of the tiller it was fitted with a proper steering wheel. The single-cylinder engine in the rear developed 6bhp. It was well received by the public but a fire in the factory in 1906 ruined the workshop, machinery and all plans for serial production. The application to display the car at the Berlin Automobile Show, which demonstrated the importance the firm placed in gaining export orders, also had to be cancelled. However, in 1906 a competely new model was launched. This was much more advanced, having its 4-cylinder in-line engine of 6PS supplied by Aachener Motorwerke of Germany under a bonnet and behind a brass honeycomb radiator with a pleasing, nearly round shell. The chassis with straight steel side members had around it semi-elliptic spring. Final drive was by shaft. The attractive 2-seater body was made by Chiattone of Lugano, from where the finished car was driven across the St Gotthard Pass to Zürich. Production was limited and in 1907 the marque disappeared.

FH

Further Reading
'Schweizer Autopionier Rudolf Egg', Ferdinand Hediger,
Automobil Revue, February 1965.

EXCELSIOR-MASCOT (D) 1910–1922
Excelsior-Werk für Feinmechanik GmbH, Cologne-Nippes.
This was an assembled car in the low-medium price category, offered with 3/8PS 2-cylinder engine, and fours of 6/14 and 8/18PS. Although it was made for some time, sales were largely confined to the local area.

HON

EXECUTIVE AUTO (US) c.1994
Executive Auto Brokers, Palm Springs, Florida.
The Ferrosa was a Fiero-based kit car with a Ferrari Testarossa-style body. It was sold in kit and assembled form.

HP

EXECUTIVE ENTERPRISES (US) c.1985
Executive Enterprises, San Bernardino, California.
In addition to assembling kits from other manufacturers, Executive Enterprises built a replica of the Porsche Speedsters.

HP

EXOR (D) 1923
Excelsior Machinen-GmbH, Berlin.
This was a light car powered by a 5/16PS 4-cylinder Atos engine.

HON

EXOTICA CUSTOM CARS (US) c.1987–1991
Exotica Custom Cars, Sumas, Washington.
The Freeman R/A was a handsome mid-engined sports car kit based on the Pontiac Fiero chassis. Designed by owners Glenn Freeman and Roy Anderson, it was inspired by several Italian exotic cars but was not a replica of any one of them. They were sold in coupé or convertible form and as kits or fully assembled cars.

HP

EXOTIC AUTOMOTIVE DESIGNS (US) c.1993
Exotic Automotive Designs, Ontario, California.
This kit car manufacturer sold replicas of the Ferrari Testarossa and the Lamborghini Countach in kit and turnkey form.

HP

EXOTIC COACHCRAFT (US) c.1984–1990
Exotic Coachcraft Inc., Diego, California.
Design Seigo, San Diego, California.
This Ferrari Daytona spyder replica was based on a Corvette chassis and running gear. The company was purchased by Seigo Takei who redesigned the kit for improved quality. Most were sold in fully assembled form, and many were exported to his native Japan.

HP

EXOTIC ENTERPRISES (US) c.1994 to date
Exotic Enterprises, Patterson, New Jersey.
Replicas of well-known exotic cars were the stock and trade of this kit car company. The Z Beamer-3 was a replica of the BMW M3 roadster based on Mazda Miata running gear. The Machiavelli 305 was a Ferrari 308 replica based on the Chevrolet Camaro or Pontiac Firebird, while the Firerossa was a Ferrari Testarossa replica on the same platform. They also sold replicas of the Lamborghini Countach, Diablo and Ferrari Testarossa on Pontiac Fiero chassis. The Mercedes 500SL was cloned onto Chrysler LeBaron or Ford Mustang chassis. They also had a number of moulds for older kits, including Ferrari and Tucker replicas and some original designs that they would build on special order.

HP

EXOTIC ILLUSIONS (US) c.1994 to date
Exotic Illusions, Dickson City, Pennsylvania.
Although their product line consisted of typical Lamborghini Countach replica kits, Exotic Illusions did lay claim to one of the most interesting names: their Countach replica was called the Eurosex 1000. It was based on the Pontiac Fiero chassis. At one time they were developing a Diablo replica, but, as of 1998, it had not been produced.

HP

EXOTIC REFLECTIONS (US) c.1990
Exotic Reflections, div. of RoboDesign, Costa Mesa, California.
This company made a replica of the Ferrari F40 for a Pontiac Fiero chassis. It was sold in kit form. They also built a Cobra replica.

HP

EXPERI-METAL (US) c.1983–1990
Experi-Metal Inc., Sterling Heights, Michigan.
The 1932 Chevrolet roadster was an unusual candidate for kit car replication, but EMI did just that. The all-steel body was formed on a 850-ton hydraulic press. All components were steel or cast metal and would interchange with the originals. Parts could be bought for restoration, or a complete car with L6, V6 or V8 engine could be ordered.

HP

EXPRESS (D) 1901–1910
Express-Werke AG, Neumarkt.
This company was mainly known for its bicycles and, from 1932, motorcycles, but in 1901 made an electric car, followed by a 2-cylinder light car. A 4-cylinder model remained a prototype.

HON

EXXACTA (US) c.1985
Exxacta Car Corp., Clearwater, Florida.
The 1953 Corvette was a likely candidate for production as a kit car, and this replica used a steel frame and running gear from General Motors mid-sized sedans. GM V6 and V8 engines were offered.

HP

1912 Eysink 6/8hp 2-seater.
NATIONAL MOTOR MUSEUM

E.Y.M.E. (GB) 1913

This was a cyclecar powered by a 964cc V-twin J.A.P. engine, with variable belt transmission and belt drive.

NG

EYSINK (NL) 1899–1920

M & A Eysink, Amersfoort.

The base of the Eysink car factory which later would grow to a very big motorcycle-manufacturer was laid on 6 May 1886 by D.H. Eysink at Amersfoort.

Eysink started building bicycles and assembling light units, but his sons Menno and August brought new modern ideas to the business. They saw the potential of introducing motorcycles and cars to fulfil the demand for motoring in general. First they started to assemble bicycles with small engines, but later on they constructed the first motorcar with a single-cylinder Benz petrol engine which made its first journey in 1897. This was the first Dutch car to go into production. The first Eysink had its engine at the front, wirewheels and a real steering wheel instead of a tiller. It had tubular frames, belt primary drive and chain final drive. After 1901 new 10 and 12hp 2-cylinder shaft-driven cars appeared. Until the outbreak of World War I a range of 4-cylinder cars was made with 10/12, 16/20, and 20/30 4-cylinder engines, as well as a 30/40hp 6-cylinder with two Zenith carburettors, an exception in those days. Alongside the earlier cars, in 1912 Eysink introduced a light car with a 6/8hp 4-cylinder engine and a 2-seater body; the steering gear and axles were bought from the French firm of Malicet et Blin. This light car had a troublesome form of pressure-lubrication operated by the exhaust gases. After 1919 it was re-introduced for a brief period with an old-fashioned brake system and a vee-radiator. It was not successful and too expensive compared to imported American cars. Around 1920, after about 400 units, Eysink stopped production of cars. Only one example exists in Holland, a 2-seater from 1912. From the production a small number were exported to the Dutch East Indies, Denmark, and Great Britain, where a number were used as taxicabs in London. The manufacturing of motorcycles was more successful. Eysink built a great number of them until 1956.

FBV

F.A.B. (B) 1912–1914

Fabrique Automobile Belge, Brussels.

This company took over the works of VIVINUS in the Brussels suburb of Schaerbeek, and announced two models, the 2120cc 12/16CV Type C, and the 3560cc 20/28CV Type B. Both had 4-cylinder monobloc side-valve engines, and 4-speed gearboxes. They were among the first makes to offer detachable wire wheels as standard on all their chassis. Bodies were mostly open 2- or 4-seaters, and the marque had several sporting successes, in Belgium and also in France and Sweden. The outbreak of World War I put an immediate end to car production.

NG

FACCIOLI (I) 1905–1906

Società Ing. Aristide Faccioli, Turin.

Faccioli had been F.I.A.T.'s first designer, but parted company with Giovanni Agnelli when the latter wanted to incorporate foreign ideas into the cars. Faccioli left in April 1901, and was involved in various projects for members of the Ceirano family, for whom he was working when his services were acquired by F.I.A.T. In 1905 he built two prototype cars, a single-cylinder 9hp and a 4-cylinder 12hp, but a reorganisation of the company put an end to the project. Faccioli later designed unsuccessful aero engines for S.P.A.

NG

FACEL VEGA (F) 1954–1964

Facel SA, Pont-à-Mousson.

The Facel name is a contraction of Forges et Ateliers de Construction d'Eure et de Loire, a company founded in 1938 by Jean Daninos, brother of the writer Pierre Daninos, who was famous for his Major Thompson books. Its original work was the manufacture of machine tools for the aircraft industry. During World War II they made gas generators for road vehicles, and resumed aircraft work when peace returned. They soon diversified into stainless steel kitchen furniture and car bodies, notably for Panhard, Simca and Ford (iv). The Ford Comète coupé had a Facel-designed and built body and they also built at least one striking coupé on the Bentley Mk VI.

In 1954 Daninos built a car initially called simply the Vega. It had a 4528cc DeSoto Firedome V8 engine with hemispherical combustion chambers which developed 180bhp. Also from the US came the 2-speed Torqueflite automatic transmission, although a 4-speed Pont-à-Mousson manual box was an option. The body was a handsome 4-seater 2-door coupé inspired by the Bentley design. The cars were inevitably very expensive, costing, in 1957, 3,250,000 francs compared with 2,750,000 for the Talbot-Lago coupé and only 1,900,000 for the Citroën DS. However, with the demise of Delage and Delahaye, followed by Talbot in 1959, the Facel was the only French luxury car, and sold quite well, both at home and abroad. About 70 per cent of production was exported, of which 75 per cent went to the United States, the best other markets being Great Britain and Germany. Prominent owners included the Shah of Iran and King Hassan II of Morocco.

Improvements included a wrap-around windscreen (the first on a French car) on the FVS of 1956, and regular increases in the size of the Chrysler-built engines. These reached a peak with the 360bhp 6276cc unit offered from 1958 onwards on the HK500. Disc brakes were standardised from 1960. A convertible was built in 1955, but it lacked rigidity and only six were made. More successful, but also criticised for lack of rigidity, was the Excellence 4-door pillarless saloon, of which 152 were made from 1956 to 1964. This was considerably costlier than the coupés, priced at 3,950,000 francs in 1957. The coupé was restyled in 1961, becoming the Facel II. This reverted to a conventional curved windscreen as the fashion for wrap-arounds was fading everywhere, and had a lower, more angular roof line and servo disc brakes. Power was up to 390bhp from 6767cc. Only 180 Facel IIs were made, compared with over 800 of the FV, FVS and HK500.

In 1959 Daninos made the unwise decision to move into a smaller-car market. Launched at the 1959 Salon, the Facellia had a family resemblance to the larger cars and a 1646cc twin-ohc 4-cylinder engine made by Facel's associated company, Pont-à-Mousson and designed by former Talbot engineer Carlo Marchetti. It was unreliable, with burnt-out pistons and serious oil leaks among its faults. Although rectified to some extent on later engines, the reputation badly damaged Facel. A 1780cc Volvo P1800 engine was substituted in the Facel

1912 F.A.B. 12/16hp limousine.
NATIONAL MOTOR MUSEUM

1956 Facel Vega Excellence saloon.
NATIONAL MOTOR MUSEUM

1961 Facel Facellia coupé.
NATIONAL MOTOR MUSEUM

III of 1963 which, like the Facellia, was available in convertible as well as coupé form. The final variation was the Facel 6 which used an Austin-Healey 3000 engine linered down to bring it within the 15CV tax bracket. Only 32 of these were made, compared with 1827 of the Facellia and Facel III. The company operated under receivership from the end of 1962 to mid–1964 when production ended. It was declared bankrupt in 1965.

NG

Further Reading

'Facel Vega: The Star-Crossed Career of a Grand Routière', Michael Sedgwick, *Automobile Quarterly*, Vol.XIV, No.3.

1911 Fafnir tourer.
NATIONAL MOTOR MUSEUM

FACTORY FIVE (US) 1994 to date
Factory Five Racing, South Dartmouth, Maine.
This kit car manufacturer made a Cobra replica that used a Ford Mustang 5.0 as its 'donor' car. Since most of the parts for this kit came off one car, it was inexpensive to build and many kits were sold.
HP

FADAG (D) 1921–1925
Fahrzeugfabrik Düsseldorf AG, Düsseldorf.
Although not many cars were made, the Fadag was better than most from small firms using good-quality engines. The 2020cc 8/35PS unit by Basse & Selve had a 3-bearing crankshaft and detachable head, while the 2450cc 10/50PS six by Siemens & Halske had a single-ohc driven by spiral bevel gear.
HON

FADINI see DERBY (i)

FAESING (US) c.1994
Faesing Motors, Wilmington, North Carolina.
The Faesing Husky was a unique high-performance roadster with a mid-engined Oldsmobile Quad-4 engine. The low-built body had no doors and separate windscreens for driver and passenger. It used a monocoque chassis with fabricated suspension. With a dry weight of 1400lbs, it was very quick. A turnkey Husky sold for $28,000 in 1994. Faesing also advertised a sports car kit called the Sebrace GT.
HP

FAFAG (D) 1921–1923
Fahrzeugfabrik AG, Darmstadt.
This was a small car powered by a 4/25Ps 4-cylinder engine with, unusually for cars of that class, a single-ohc.
HON

FAFNIR (D) 1908–1926
Aachener Stahlwarenfabrik Fafnir-AG, Aachen.
Originally a producer of motorcycle engines, this firm developed the Omnimobil kit containing an engine and a set of necessary components which enabled a number of bicycle manufacturers to become car makers. These included CITO and FELDMANN. In 1908 they began to make complete cars, with 1520 and 2012cc 4-cylinder engines with overhead inlet and side exhaust valves, the smaller with separately cast cylinders, the larger having them pair-cast. Several different sizes of engine were made, none of them large. The 1924cc 8/22PS Typ 472 (1912–14) had automatic lubrication.
After the war the 472 and another prewar design, the 2496cc 10/25PS Typ 384, were reintroduced, and were joined by the Typ 471 with a 1950cc engine developing

50bhp. It was made in sporting form, with some striking bodies, and with a supercharger gave 80bhp.
HON

FAGEOL (US) 1916–1917; 1921
Fageol Motors Co., Oakland, California.
Fageol was a major builder of 2- to 6-ton trucks from 1916 to 1939 and buses at another factory in Kent, Ohio. Shortly after the company was formed, a passenger car was designed which was to be one of the largest and most expensive cars ever built in the United States. With a wheelbase measuring as much as 145in (3680mm), the massive machine was powered by a 6-cylinder 13$\frac{1}{2}$-litre Hall Scott engine of 127 × 178mm bore and stroke capable of delivering 125bhp at 1300rpm. According to promotional material of the time, the Fageol would carry a chassis price of $9500 and complete cars from $17,000 and up – an enormous figure at the time – plus a complete line of open and closed coachwork. Two cars are known to have been completed. A victoria phaeton was featured prominently for exhibition, demonstration for potential buyers, and in promotion.
Whether this victoria was sold or not is speculative and in 1921 this car – or another similar to it – was advertised in London as available at the Oakland factory priced at $12,000.
KM

FAIRBANKS MORSE (US) 1908
Fairbanks, Morse & Co., Chicago, Illinois.
This company built a rail inspection car in 1905, and later became well-known for trucks and agricultural tractors, which they made up to the early 1920s. They built only one car, a tourer with 4-cylinder engine whose cylinders were separately cast, and double-chain drive. Called Model 1 Number 1, it was priced at $3850, but probably only the single example was built.
NG

FAIRFAX (GB) 1906
J.S. Fairfax & Co. Ltd, Chiswick, London.
The Fairfax was powered by a 7/9hp 2-cylinder White & Poppe engine mounted under the footboard. It had a sloping radiator and virtually no bonnet, to give maximum space for the tourer body on the short wheelbase of 81in (2055mm). It had a 3-speed gearbox, shaft drive and solid rubber tyres, the latter seriously out of date for 1906. Probably only a prototype was made.
NG

FAIRLEY (GB) 1950
Jas. Fairley & Sons Ltd, Sheffield, Yorkshire.
Amateur car constructor Mr R. Phillips made an Austin Seven-based special with Ballamy suspension, which was later converted to trials use with a Jowett Javelin engine. This inspired him to plan sales of a tubular-framed sports car designed for Jowett Javelin components, in 5-seater convertible and 2-seater competition styles. Series manufacture did not start but a number of subsequent one-offs were constructed.
CR

FAIRLITE see GINETTA

FAIRTHORPE (GB) 1954–1973
1954–1961 Fairthorpe Ltd, Chalfont St Peter, Buckinghamshire.
1961–1964 Fairthorpe Ltd, Gerrards Cross, Buckinghamshire.
1964–1973 Fairthorpe Ltd, Denham, Buckinghamshire.
Fairthorpe was founded in 1954 by the RAF war hero, Air Vice-Marshal Don 'Pathfinder' Bennett. Its first product was the rear-engined Atom which, curiously, was described as a sporty bubble-car. It was available with a number of BSA engines, 250 to 650cc, but found few buyers. It was replaced by the front-engined Atomota, some of which had Standard Ten engines, but it also failed to make much of an impact on the market.
In 1956 came the Electron, which was a kit car based on the Atomota chassis, with a Microplas Mistral body and 1100cc Coventry Climax FWA engine. About 30 were made and some of the later cars had a Fairthorpe body. That was followed by the Electron Minor, which was a 2-seater sports car using Standard

1917 Fageol 13½-litre tourer.
NATIONAL MOTOR MUSEUM

Ten components, which was a precursor of the Austin-Healey Sprite, although it lacked the Sprite's personality.

The Electron was largely the work of Fairthorpe's foreman, John Green, who later designed the Davrian. Another employee was Ken Lowe, who went on to make the Kenlowe electric cooling fan.

Fairthorpe used Standard-Triumph components because they were the best available – Ford's small cars were obsolete and since BMC was preparing the Sprite, it would not supply rivals. Fairthorpe continued to use S-T components after they became dated because S-T's chairman was Air Marshal Lord Tedder, Bennett's war-time chief.

The Electron Minor sold well at first, up to five a week, but the Sprite cost £631 to the £713 of an assembled Fairthorpe. The Electron Minor was available as a component car until 1973 and about 500 were sold. During 1961 to 1963 a 2+2 coupé version, the Electrina, was offered and about 20 were made.

In 1960 came the Zeta which had a tuned Ford Zephyr engine in an Electron chassis and it was one of the quickest cars, 0–100mph (0–160km/h), of its time. Despite a keen price, no more than 20 were made because, like all Fairthorpes, it was poorly made and ugly and, with the Zephyr engine, the handling was marginal.

It was succeeded by the Rockette which had a 70bhp Triumph Vitesse engine and a third, centrally-mounted, headlight. About 25 Rockettes were made during its production life, 1963 to 1967.

Don Bennett's son, Torix, was responsible for the TX range which began in 1967. It was notable for cross-over radius arms on the swing axle rear suspension to control the tendency of wheels to tuck in during hard cornering. Most of the underpinnings were Triumph GT6 and up to two dozen were built, the early cars on a Fairthorpe chassis, the later on a GT6 frame.

After 1970 the TX range was established as a separate marque, although it was still officially a badged Fairthorpe. Fairthorpe has been moribund for many years – there was an attempt to revive it in the late 1980s – but it still exists as a legal entity.

MJL

1955 Fairthorpe Atom coupé.
NICK GEORGANO

1958 Fairthorpe Atomota coupé.
NICK BALDWIN

1959 Fairthorpe Electron Minor sports car.
NATIONAL MOTOR MUSEUM

1969 Fairthorpe TX-S coupé.
NICK GEORGANO/NATIONAL MOTOR MUSEUM

1963 Falcon (vi) 515 coupé.
NICK GEORGANO/NATIONAL MOTOR MUSEUM

F.A.L. (US) 1909–1914

1909–1913 F.A.L. Motor Co., Chicago, Illinois.
1913–1914 F.A.L. Automobile Co., Chicago, Illinois.
This car gained its name from the three men behind the project, T.S. Fauntleroy, H.R. Averill and E.H. Lowe. Their car was a conventional machine powered by 4-cylinder Buda engine initially quoted as a 30hp, and from 1910 onwards as a 35/40hp, although doubtless it was the same unit. Various body styles were listed over the years, including toy tonneau, tourer, roadster, speed car and town car, at prices from $1750 to $3000. All were typical of their time, except for the last, the Grayhound introduced for 1914. This had a cyclops headlamp in the top of the radiator and a 2-seater roadster body, which could be converted into a bed; the seat cushion was pushed forward to act as a pillow and the sleepers' feet stretched towards the back of the body.
NG

FALCON (i) (US) 1907–1909

1907–1908 John M. Larsen, Chicago, Illinois.
1909 Falcon Engineering Co., Chicago, Illinois.
Before forming his company, Danish-born John Larsen built a roadster with a claimed 120bhp and a price tag of $7500. They were built to order and the number of orders received is not known, but they cannot have been many. Although he formed the Falcon Engineering Co., his next car was also built to order only. It was an enormous 9-seater tourer powered by a 10.5-litre 90hp 6-cylinder engine and priced at the very high figure of $12,500. As the finest 6-cylinder Peerless or Pierce-Arrow tourer cost less than half this, it is hardly surprising that Larsen received few orders, possibly none at all, but a photograph survives to show that at least one of his cars was built. He later returned to his native Denmark where he made a fortune in the ice cream business.
NG

FALCON (ii) (US) 1913–1914

Falcon Cyclecar Co., Staunton, Virginia.
This company originated from Cleveland, but all production of this cyclecar took place in Virginia. It had an air-cooled V-twin engine, friction transmission and belt final drive, but there were some features which set it apart from its many competitors. The control for the transmission was not by lever but by a wheel inset on the steering wheel, so the driver did not have to lean forward to change gear. A primitive feature outmoded by 1913 was centre-pivot steering in which the whole front axle turned with the wheels. The rounded bonnet was set far back behind the axle, and the body had no doors.
NG

FALCON (iii) (D) 1921–1926

1921–1922 Falcon Automobilwerke GmbH, Sontheim.
1922–1926 Falcon-Werke AG, Ober-Ramstadt.
This was a conventional car with the typical pointed radiator common to all German cars in the first half of the 1920s. It was available with 1250cc 6/20PS and 1496cc 6/36PS, the latter having some sporting potential. After production ended, the factory at Ober-Ramstadt was taken over by ROHR Auto AG.
HON

FALCON (iv) (US) 1921–1923

Moller Motor Car Co., Lewistown, Pennsylvania.
The Moller-built Falcon, frequently confused with the Falcon (v) of Newark, Ohio, with which it had no connection, was a small car built exclusively for the export market. Initially exhibited at the New York Automobile Salon at the Hotel Commodore in November 1921, three cars comprised the display, featuring a sedan with coachwork by New York City's Healey & Com. and two open models. Wire wheels were standard on all models. In addition to the frequent confusion with listings pertaining to the Newark, Ohio Falcon, the issue has been further complicated because of the Moller name. The Falcon was the product of the Lewistown factory headed by H. P. Moller, some of its cars being bodied by the M. P. Möller Co. of Hagerstown, Maryland, which was building Crawford and Dagmar automobiles at the time. However, there was no blood relationship between the two Mollers.
KM

FALCON (v) (US) 1921–1922

Halladay Motor Car Co., Newark, Ohio.
The Falcon, ostensibly a lower-priced companion car to the HALLADAY, albeit a sporting one, was announced in December 1921 and introduced at New York City's Grand Central Palace a month later. The car, priced at $1295, featured a trim, tastefully designed, streamlined body mounted on a 115in (2918mm) wheelbase and sporting wire wheels and individual aluminium step plates. Its 4-cylinder engine was advertised as being of its 'own' manufacture. Whether 'production' ever progressed beyond the exhibition car is doubtful as its parent company went into receivership shortly after the Falcon was shown to the public. The car is frequently confused with another contemporary car of the same name built in Lewistown, Pennsylvania. It is more than likely that neither Falcon enterprise was aware of the other's existence.
KM

FALCON (vi) (GB) 1958–1964

1958–1959 Falcon Shells Ltd. Watham Abbey, Essex.
1959–1961 Falcon Shells Ltd. Epping, Essex.
1961–1962 Falcon Cars Ltd. Epping, Essex.
1962–1964 Falcon Cars Ltd. Hatfield, Herts.

Falcon initially offered a twin-tube chassis 2-seater for 100E Ford mechanical components. Space frame chassis based on Len Terry's 1172 Formula Terrier special were also used, and later frames were built by the Progress Chassis Co. with coil suspension all round, independent at the front. Basic bodies, available over several years, included the Competition open 2-seater and the Caribbean GT coupé. Some 4-seaters were sold, including the Bermuda saloon. By 1962 kits to suit five engines were advertised – the 100E and 105E Fords, Coventry-Climax 1098cc and 1216cc, and the M.G.A. In 1963 the '515' was exhibited, with a GT body styled by T. Rohonyl, a Brazilian. This was bonded to the tubular frame, which was designed to accept Ford Cortina major mechanical parts.

DF

FALCON (vii) (GB) 1984 to date

1984–1987 Falcon Design, Birmingham.
1987–1990 Falcon Design, Rugby, Warwickshire.
1990–1993 Falcon Design, Stratford-upon-Avon, Warwickshire.
1993 to date The 2CV Centre, Frome, Somerset.

The specialist car world already knew Peter Bird before he set up Falcon, since he had co-created the STEVENS Cipher and helped develop the LOMAX. His first offerings were the Quarry and Chase, wedged-shaped utility-style vehicles intended for Citroën 2CV or VW engines, but these did not proceed beyond the prototype stage. More successful was the Falcon Sports, a Lotus 7 style kit designed – most unusually – for the Citroën 2CV/Dyane floorpan. The simple body was a plywood-and-aluminium sandwich (which could also be built from a set of plans) with fibreglass front and rear wings. A boat-tailed 3-wheeled version called the LX3 arrived in 1986.

CR

FALCON-KNIGHT (US) 1927–1928

Falcon Motor Corp., Detroit, Michigan; Elyria, Ohio.

The Falcon-Knight was marketed by John North WILLYS as a companion to the smaller Whippet and the Willys-Knight 70. It had a 109¹⁄₂in (2779mm) wheelbase and was powered by Knight 6-cylinder sleeve-valve engine. A complete line of closed and open models was offered, all with artillery wheels, except for the Gray Ghost roadster, which had wire wheels.

NG

FALKE (D) 1899–1908

1899–1907 Fahrrad- und Automobilwerke Albert Falke & Co., Mönchen-Gladbach.
1907–1908 Falke Motorfahrzeuge Albert Falke & Co., Mönchen-Gladbach.

Falke was one of a number of bicycle makers who turned to car production at the end of the nineteenth century. The first model had a strong resemblance to the DECAUVILLE Voiturelle, and it was followed in 1900 by a front-engined car with Falke's own 4PS 2-cylinder engine and shaft drive. Later, proprietary engines were used, by Fafnir and Breuer, twins of 700, 800 and 1250cc, and fours of 1500 and 1600cc. Falke cars were of sound design but were not sold very widely.

HON

F.A.M. (I) 1952

Fabbrica Auto Motoveicoli, Pesaro.

Having failed to productionise a microcar under the name B.B.C., Giuseppe Benelli tried again at the 1952 Turin Show. The F.A.M. was a boxy open 4-seater microcar with a separate chassis. Two unusual features were that the whole front bodywork lifted up to reveal the engine and the method of body construction (patented by Benelli) was by artificial leather over rubber, mounted on a steel latticework frame. The car was powered by a 21bhp 4-stroke V-twin engine of 500cc capacity.

CR

1928 Falcon-Knight Gray Ghost roadster.
NATIONAL MOTOR MUSEUM

FAMA (D) 1924

This was a light car made in Kiel, with 4/24PS engine and 2-seater body. The press said that the prototype had made a 7000km trial and that production would soon be starting, with the car selling at a modest price, but nothing more was heard.

HON

FAMOUS (US) 1908–1909

Famous Manufacturing Co., East Chicago, Indiana.

This was a typical high-wheeler with air-cooled 2-cylinder engine, epicyclic or optional friction transmission and chain drive. Unusual for so late a date were rear wheels which were slightly larger than those at the front. In 1909 the makers changed the car's name to Champion so that they could call it the 'Famous Champion', but this did not help sales.

NG

FANNING (US) 1901–1903

The F.J. Fanning Manufacturing Co., Chicago, Illinois.

The brothers John and Frank Fanning made both petrol and electric cars. The former had a 9hp air-cooled 2-cylinder engine with chain drive, and 2-seater runabout or 4-seater tonneau bodies. They had wheel steering whereas the 2hp electric runabout was tiller steered. The Fanning seemed to be a successful product, with several outlets on the East Coast, but a factory fire in May 1903 put an end to the business.

NG

FANTERA (US) c.1996

Fantera Ltd, Vista, California.

This Pontiac Fiero-based kit car was a replica of the DeTomaso Pantera. However, it was shorter and taller so the proportions were not accurate. It was inexpensive and could be completed for less than $5000 in 1996. They also made a replica of the Group 5 racing Pantera with flared mudguards, spoiler and a wing.

HP

FARMACK (US) 1915–1916

Farmack Motor Car Co., Chicago, Illinois.

Albert J. Farmer had plenty of automotive experience before he began to make his Farmack car. He was superintendent for the SMITH & MABLEY and RAINIER companies, followed by a spell with engine makers Northway. In 1914 he designed an advanced 4-cylinder engine with single ohc, which he put into a car the following year, backed by some Chicago investors. Among these was M.M. McIntyre who was the 'mack' in the name Farmack. Apart from the engine, the specification was conventional enough, the car being made in tourer, roadster and cabriolet models at quite reasonable prices of $855–1155. After a little over one year, fresh capital led to a change of name, and for 1916 the Farmack became the DREXEL.

NG

FARMAN (F) 1919–1931

Automobiles Farman, Billancourt, Seine.

The three Farman brothers, Dick (1872–1940), Henry (1874–1960) and Maurice (1877–1963), were born in France of English extraction, their father

1925 Farman A6B boat-tail tourer.
NATIONAL MOTOR MUSEUM

1927 Farman NF cabriolet, by Million-Guiet.
NICK BALDWIN

1928 Farman NF2 saloon.
NICK BALDWIN

being Paris correspondent of *The Standard*. They were successful racing cyclists in the 1890s, and took up motor racing at the turn of the century. Henry drove a Darracq in 1900, while he and Maurice both drove Panhards in the big town-to-town races, such as Paris-Vienna in 1902 and Paris-Madrid in 1903. They were also agents for several makes, and it has been claimed that they made a Farman car in 1902, but there is little evidence of manufacture. They then turned their interest to aviation, flying Voisin planes and then making their own, of which a large number were produced during World War I.

With the coming of peace they joined others who had been engaged in aircraft production or flying, VOISIN, FONCK, GNOME ET RHÔNE and the best-known, HISPANO-SUIZA, with a brand new luxury car at the 1919 Paris Salon. It is interesting that none of these people with aircraft experience considered making a popular car. Designed by Charles Waseige, the Farman A6 had a 6594cc single-ohc 6-cylinder engine with six welded steel cylinders surrounded by a welded-up sheet steel water jacket. The ohc was driven by vertical shaft. The 4-speed gearbox was separate from the engine on the prototypes, but when production began at the end of 1921 it was in unit with the engine and the cone clutch had been replaced by the multi-plate variety. Suspension was by semi-elliptic springs at the front and by cantilever at the rear. The production Farman had dual ignition and came in two models, the single carburettor standard and the twin-carb Sport. The latter soon received some striking bodies, including pointed tail 2- or 4-seater roadsters and a streamlined coupé with vee-windscreen and horizontal wings running from front to rear. Despite their sporty appearance, it seems that neither the roadster nor coupé were raced. In fact, the only Farman to take part in sport was an entry in the 1922 Circuit des Routes Pavées, and that was a standard tourer. A Type Sport was tested in 1922 by the famous journalist Charles Faroux, and reached a speed of 90mph (145km/h). Bodywork was by Gaborit or Grange, although from about 1922 Farman had their own coachwork department. The early cars had artillery wheels which gave them a rather heavy appearance, but by 1924 wire wheels were more usual, with disc covers on the sporting models. The 1924 catalogue mentioned a *type colonial surelevé* with greater ground clearance, but it is not known if any of these was made.

In order to reduce weight, the cylinder block was made of Alpax alloy with steel liners on the 1923 Type Sport, and this was extended to all Farmans from 1926. By then they had a complex suspension system involving transverse leaf springs at front and rear, with small cantilever helper springs. An even more complex compound steering system was employed, with separate steering mechanisms on each stub axle. It was supposed to avoid shocks being transmitted to the steering wheel, but was very heavy to operate. These features were continued on the 1929 Model NF (Nouvelle Farman) which also had an engine enlarged to 7065cc and wheelbase extended to 148in (3760mm). The pointed radiator was replaced by a rather bland flat shape which robbed the Farman of its former distinction. They had never been easy to sell, being among the most expensive French cars yet lacking the cachet of the Hispano-Suiza. Despite the support of some well-known customers such as the Shah of Iran and film star Pearl White as well as some maharajahs, Farman sold no more than 120 cars, perhaps fewer, in 10 years. The marque's last Salon appearance was in 1930, when an NF2 chassis cost 155,000 francs, and production ended during the course of 1931. There were plans to revive Farman in 1938, with a V8 engine (possibly a Ford) and body styled by artist Georges Ham, but this never even reached the prototype stage. Just four Farmans survive today.

NG

Further Reading
'Les Automobiles de Haut Luxe Farman', Serge Pozzoli,
l'Album du Fanatique, October 1972.
'The Brothers Farman', Frederick A. Usher,
Automobile Quarterly, Vol. 23, No. 4.

FARMAN-MICOT (F) 1898
Farman, Micot et Compagnie, St Maurice, Seine.
This was a light 3-seater car powered by an Augé Cyclope 2-cylinder engine. It is quite likely that one or more of the Farman brothers was involved, given their importance in the industry at the time, but this is not certain.
NG

FARNER (US) 1922–1923
Farner Motor Car Co., Streator, Illinois.
It is a moot point whether the Farner car existed beyond a handful of prototypes, the car being listed as an assembled one with a wheelbase of 115in (2919mm) and a Falls X9000 6-cylinder engine. The Farner appeared on numerous contemporary automobile rosters as well as automotive reference books of the period listing four body styles in both open and closed models with serial numbers 'A-1000 and up'. If any Farners were completed for exhibition purposes, it appears certain that the cars never reached the marketplace.
KM

F.A.R.T. (I) 1965
Fabbrica Autoveicoli Rimorchi Torino, Turin.
Under the exceedingly unfortunate name of F.A.R.T. Breack, this was a tiny cross-country vehicle powered by a rear-mounted Fiat 500 Giardiniera engine. The extremely simple forward control bodywork was entirely open and could seat four. Versions were offered with two sets of wheels per axle and there was an extra gear reduction, enabling it to mount a 40 per cent gradient and achieve a top speed of 40mph (64km/h).
CR

F.A.S. *see* STANDARD (iii)

FASCINATION (US) 1971–1977
Highway Aircraft Corp., Denver, Colorado and Sydney, Nebraska.
Designed by Paul Lewis, who made the prewar LEWIS AIROMOBILE, the Fascination was a truly weird car resembling an egg being chased by an aircraft wing. In its initial form, it claimed to have a flat air-cooled engine, but production was cut short by legal problems. After moving to Nebraska, designer Paul Lewis built a new version with a teardrop body, wing-like tail and four

1925 F.A.S.T. town car.
NATIONAL MOTOR MUSEUM

wheels with the front pair set close together. Engines considered for production included a steam powerplant, an electromagnetic motor run on static electricity and a 2-cycle engine with sealed cylinders operated by self-contained gas. The only three cars built, however, used Renault engines.
HP

F.A.S.T. (I) 1919–1925
1919–1923 Fabbrica Automobili Sport Torino, Turin.
1923–1925 Fabbrica Automobili Sport Torino di ing. Orasi, Turin.
This company was founded by Arturo Concaris out of the F.I.M.A. (Fabbrica Italiana Motori Aviazione) because of the falling demand for aero engines after World War I. His car had a large, long-stroke (84 × 135mm) ohv 4-cylinder engine of 2891cc, with a 3-speed gearbox and conventional chassis and brakes on the rear wheels only. The original Tipo Uno had a sporty body with pointed radiator, bulbous tail and an external exhaust pipe running the length of the car from engine to tail. Some examples took part in hill climbs, but did not make a notable mark on the sporting scene. In 1923 the firm was in difficulties, and was taken over by Alberto Orasi, who introduced the Tipo 2T. This used the same engine behind a flat radiator typical of Italian style at the time, and similar to that of an Itala, Diatto or O.M. It had a 4-speed gearbox and front-wheel brakes. There was also a short-wheelbase model called the 2S. Three F.A.S.T.s ran in the 1924 Targa Florio, but the best finished no higher than 19th. The marque's last show appearance was at Turin in 1925.
NG

FAST FORWARD (US) c.1993
Fast Forward, Little Rock, Arkansas.
The Fast Forward Icon was a Ferrari Testarossa replica based on Pontiac Firebird running gear.
HP

FASTO (F) 1925–1928
Fabriques d'Automobiles de St Ouen, Sainte-Éloy, Puy-de-Dome;
St Ouen, Seine.
This was a conventional touring car, intended to be economical and very strong, like the people of the Puy-de-Dome region where the prototypes were made. These were built in the works of the machine tool makers Établissements Audouard et Compagnie, Ateliers Mécaniques de Sainte-Éloy. The A2 had a 1597cc 4-cylinder side-valve engine which developed 25bhp, and a 3-speed gearbox. The prototype (A1) and the first 15 production A2s were made at Sainte-Éloy, but from late 1926 only the engines, gearboxes and rear axles came from there, the rest of the car being made in the Paris suburb of St Ouen. Fasto bodies were mostly tourers and heavy-looking saloons, but some were of fabric construction and presumably were not so heavy as they looked.

The 1926 Paris Salon saw two examples of the A2 and a 6-cylinder chassis, the C1, which used the same cylinder dimensions as the four to give a capacity of 2396cc. Like the smaller engine it had side-valves, but a false cover gave the appearance of an ohv unit. It is thought that only one was made. However, the 1927 4-cylinder A3 was a genuine ohv engine, with a capacity of 1617cc and output of 35bhp. A batch of 100 of these was ordered. The last model was the

1927 Fasto saloon.
NATIONAL MOTOR MUSEUM

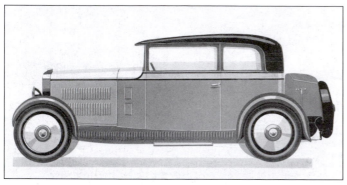

1928 Fasto 10CV saloon.
NICK BALDWIN

1907 Fawcett-Fowler 12hp tourer.
NATIONAL MOTOR MUSEUM

A4, with more economical side-valve engine of the same capacity as the A3, but with three bearings instead of two. The works at Sainte-Éloy closed in 1928, and reopened two years later as general engineers under the name Dupra et Tarbes.

NG

Further Reading
'Les Automobiles Fasto', Serge Pozzoli, *Le Fanauto,* July-September 1984.

FAUBER (US) 1914

Cyclecar Engineering Co., Indianapolis, Indiana.
The first car launched by William H. Fauber was a 2-wheeler which he called a bi-car. It had an 8hp 2-cylinder engine, motorcycle-type frame and tandem 2-seater body. Like other such cars, it had stabiliser wheels to hold it up when it was stationary. The price was only $295, and Fauber said that any man could save $100 by making it himself. Later in 1914 he offered a 4-wheeled cyclecar using the same engine in an 80in (2030mm) wheelbase, with 2-seater or light delivery van bodies. Surprisingly, this cost less than the bi-car, $285. Fauber said that he had built 100 cars in 1902, but these were made by Walter MARR for whom Fauber had worked.

NG

FAUGÈRE (F) 1898–c.1901

Faugère, Ochin et Dangleterre, Corbeil, Somme.
Sté des Automobiles Legères, Paris.
The first makers of this car were associated with coachbuilders Kellner in 1896, and in 1898 announced a light car powered by a 3hp horizontal engine with two flywheels. Transmission was by belt to a countershaft, and final drive by chain. The engine could be started by a lever from the driver's seat. The make has been erroneously listed as Faugue et Dangleterre.

NG

FAULKNER-BLANCHARD (US) 1910

Faulkner-Blanchard Motor Car Co., Detroit, Michigan.
This company was formed to make a tourer called the Gunboat Six, powered by a 33hp 6-cylinder engine. The rear of the body was rounded giving it a more sporting appearance than the average tourer. In September 1910 the company was said to be looking for a factory, so probably only a prototype or two were made.

NG

FAULTLESS *see* SAGINAW

FAUN (D) 1921–1928

Faun-Werke AG, Nuremberg.
This company was much better known for its commercial vehicles, which have been made from 1918 to the present day. A predecessor firm, the Fahrzeugfabrik Ansbach, had made a light car in 1910, and at the 1921 Berlin Show Faun brought out the Typ K1 with 1405cc 6/22PS single-ohc 4-cylinder engine. It did not go into production until 1924, when it was renamed the Typ K2 6/24PS. A number of sporting successes were achieved. In 1926 an enlargement of the bore raised capacity to 1550cc, and this model was known as the K3 6/30PS. By the time production ended in 1928 about 1500 Faun cars had been made. Faun later made a wide variety of commercial vehicles including heavy road tractors and buses. In recent years they have concentrated on ultra-large off-road dump trucks.

HON

FAURÉ *see* PIERRE FAURÉ

FAVEL (F) 1941–1944

Éts Favel, Marseilles.
This car's name was an acronym for Fabrication de Véhicules Automobiles Électriques Legères, which summed up its activities quite well. Like its contemporaries, it was built in response to an acute shortage of petrol in wartime France. It was a 2-door coupé with accommodation for five passengers, which was more than most of the wartime electrics. Sales were confined almost entirely to the Marseilles area.

NG

FAVIER (F) c.1925–1930

Automobiles Favier, Tullins, Isère.
This was a light car powered by a 4-cylinder Chapuis-Dornier engine. The company existed as a garage for some time before the start of car manufacture, which was on a very limited scale.

NG

FAVORIT (D) 1908–1909

Favorit Motorwagen-Fabrik Carl Hübscher, Berlin.
A 3-wheeled 2-seater built on motorcycle lines, but with wheel steering. The two rear wheels were driven by a cardan shaft.

HON

FAWCETT-FOWLER (GB) 1907–1909

Fowler, Preston & Co. Ltd, Liverpool.
The Fawcett-Fowler was one of several steam cars which suddenly appeared in England around 1907, others including the BOLSOVER, PEARSON-COX and RUTHERFORD. It had a 20/25hp 4-cylinder opposed engine under the bonnet, and a flash boiler over the rear axle, a reversal of the usual layout, which

kept the engine close to the axle to avoid the need for a long propeller shaft. In the Fawcett-Fowler there was a long shaft to a countershaft from which final drive was by chains. The designer was said to have followed as closely as possible petrol car practice, but in so doing lost the advantage of compactness available to the steam car. The body was a 5-seater tourer and the round condenser at the front gave the car the appearance of a Delaunay-Belleville. A later model had a Daimler-like 'radiator'. *The Steam & Electric Car Review* said that '...the new Fawcett-Fowler steam car should score a success second to none', but the make lasted less than three years.

NG

FAWICK (US) 1910–1912
Fawick Motor Car Co., Sioux Falls, South Dakota.
Thomas L. Fawick built at least two cars under the name Silent Sioux in 1908–09, a twin and a four. The latter had a 40hp Waukesha engine, which he continued to use when he renamed the car and company Fawick in 1910. The aluminium tourer body was built to Fawick's specificatioins by the Charles Abresch Co. of Milwaukee which also made trucks under the name Abresch-Cramer at the same time (it survived as body builders to 1965). Although Fawick fixed a price of $3000 for his car, he sold only five before turning to other interests, including the manufacture of clutches. The Fawick achieved its 15 minutes of fame when former President Theodore Roosevelt rode in one during a visit to Sioux Falls in 1910.

NG

FCA (US) c.1994
Frank's Classic Autos, Inc., Winter Haven, Florida.
The FCA 427SC was a Cobra replica based on a ladder-type chassis with Ford or Chevrolet engines and suspension.

HP

F.D. (i) (GB) 1911
Vining Tractor & Motor Manufacturing Co. Ltd, Shepherd's Bush, London.
The F.D., whose initials stood simply for Front Drive, was made in very small numbers, possibly just a prototype or two, but was a pioneering design in that its 4-cylinder engine was mounted transversely, driving the front wheels, preceding the Issigonis Mini design by 48 years. The gearbox was mounted ahead of the engine and driven by chain, while final drive was by spur gears to the front wheels. The Vining company had previously made front-drive taxicabs and small buses under the name V.H. or Vining-Hallett.

NG

F.D. (ii) (B) 1923–1925
Automobiles F.D., Roulers.
Made by Florent Depuydt (or De Puydt), this was a light car powered initially by a 1098cc C.I.M.E. ohv 4-cylinder engine, and available with five body styles; open 2-seater, 4-seater tourer, saloon, 2-seater sports (from 1924) and delivery van. Several other engines were available; a 1495cc single-ohc C.I.M.E., a 1994cc ohv Altos and a 1202cc ohv unit of uncertain origin. The larger-engined cars had front wheel brakes from the start, but the 1098cc did not get these until 1924. F.D.s took part in several rallies, such as the Tour de France, and one with a 4-seater pointed tail sports body ran in the 1924 Coupe Boillot at Boulogne, finishing seventh against strong opposition. Depuydt is reputed to have made cars in France, either at Colombes, near Paris, or at La Madeleine, Nord, but nothing is known about these activities.

NG

FEDELIA (US) 1913–1914
J.H. Sizelan Co., East Cleveland, Ohio.
A cyclecar with a track of only 38in (964mm) and a boat-tailed body, the Fedelia was powered by a 1.1-litre De Luxe engine.

NG

FEDERAL (i) (US) 1901–1902
Federal Motor Vehicle Co., Brooklyn, New York.
This was a typical light steam car with boiler and 10hp 2-cylinder engine behind the seat, and single-chain drive. Springs were full-elliptics, that at the front being a

1911 F.D. (i) 10/12hp tourer [left]; on the right is a 1909 Mors 12hp limousine.
NICK BALDWIN

1923 Federal (iii) Six tourer.
NICK GEORGANO

single transverse spring, and the frame was of angle iron. The body was of all-metal construction, and there were no wings or hood.

NG

FEDERAL (ii) (US) 1907–1909
1907 Federal Motor Car Co., Chicago, Illinois.
1907–1908 Federal Automobile Co., Chicago, Illinois.
1908–1909 Rockford Automobile & Engine Co., Rockford, Illinois.
Despite several changes of company, the Federal motor buggy design remained largely unaltered during its lifetime. It had a 14hp air-cooled opposed-twin engine with friction transmission, in which the flywheel acted as the driving disc, and belt final drive. The price increased steadily, from $475 to $600 and then $800, with pneumatic tyres at $100 extra. In May 1909 the Rockford company was bought by the Industrial Automobile Co. of Elkhart, Indiana, which may have assembled a few more Federals.

NG

FEDERAL (iii) (AUS) 1923–1924
Bradley Bros Ltd, Sydney, New South Wales.
A rebadged, but unidentified, US type, the Federal could have been so named because of the then activity which established Canberra as the Federal capital of Australia. Of conventional design, it used a 23hp 6-cylinder Falls engine, had a wheelbase of 117in (2972mm) and was fitted with wire wheels. In 1924 the more expensive Special 6 was listed, having a 25hp Continental engine in a chassis of 118in (2997mm). Other components included Liberty Bosch ignition, a Zenith carburettor, a Fuller clutch and Columbia axles. It was, however, missing from the lists before the year was out.

MG

FEE-AMERICAN (US) 1907–1908
Fee-Bock Automobile Co., Detroit, Michigan.
Fee-Bock was an agent for the 2-stroke ELMORE, and decided to enter the market with its own 2-stroke car, an 18/20hp 2-cylinder tourer. Few were made, and they soon returned to exclusive sales of Elmores.

NG

1954 Felber (i) 3-wheeler.
NICK GEORGANO/NATIONAL MOTOR MUSEUM

FEG *see* ERDMANN

FEIYUE (CHI) 1958–1960

Shanghai Mini-Auto Works, Shanghai Municipality.

Feiyue ('Flying Leap', another name for the 'Great Leap Forward', the mass-political movement 1958–59) mini-taxis were made in a small batch of about 25 units. It was an open, doorless, 4-passenger mini-car, weighing only 400kgs, producing a maximum speed of only 31mph (50 km/h). The fuel consumption was 5l/100km.

EVIS

FEJER (CDN) 1980s–1990s

Fejer Motor Car Co., Parry Sound, Ontario.

Fejer's main product, the Super Seven, was a self-explanatory version of the Caterham 7, fitted with a 1.6-litre Toyota Corolla engine. Two other models were offered: the Sidewinder, a VW-based plastic-bodied sand rail, and the Spyder, a modernised version of the Porsche RSK racer, powered by a VW 1.6-litre engine or, as an option, a 2.4-litre engine. By 1992 the company had turned to making Ferrari replicas on the Pontiac Fiero, with the name Mirage.

CR

FEJES (H) 1922–1932

1922 Magyar Lemezmotorgyár, Budapest.
1923–1932 Fejes Lemezmotor és Gépgyár Rt, Budapest.

Jen Fejes (1877–1951) was one of the greatest automotive engineers in Hungary. He contributed to the creation of MARTA, headed the automotive department of MAG and later became independent. In 1921 he patented his own engine made out of pressed-steel and welded sheet-iron, and a year later a chassis made out of the same materials. It was not surprising that he established a company to make cars following the pattern laid in his designs. The first model was a wooden-bodied tourer with one central headlight. It had a 4-cylinder, 24bhp engine and claimed to be 35 per cent lighter and 30 per cent more efficient than the usual touring cars available on Hungarian market. This car was hand-made, but Fejes wanted a bigger-scale operation, so he sought sponsors and established a limited company bearing his name. Various patents on car parts from sheet-iron followed, as well as work on cars and airplane engines.

Only a few had been made by 1925. Some of them were used by the Hungarian Post Office and not many found their way to private buyers. The Fejes range consisted of three 4-cylinder models, 15, 18 and 24bhp and a 6-cylinder variant as well. One of the interesting features of the car was the position of the headlights, above the radiator. Behind the scenes continuous financial problems prevented serious production. A Government loan was requested but turned down. Finally, a Fejes car made its appearance in London. Newspaper reports claimed that the car was cheap to make, but it was crude and suffered teething

problems. However, potential investors showed up and this gave Fejes new hope. Hungary didn't want his car, even the taxi companies said no. The newly founded Fejes Patents Syndicate Ltd in London was his final resort. Soon the ASCOT Motor Manufacturing Co. was registered to make Fejes cars under licence, but it went down within a year. The Fejes company ended its life in 1932 after 45 Fejes chassis had been made. It was again a case of much promise, but little realisation.

PN

FELBER (i) (A) 1952–1954

A.Felber & Co., Vienna.

This company began making motorcycle sidecars in 1923 and was well placed to make microcars in austere postwar years. Ernst Marold's first prototype was running in 1950 but production of the Felber Autoroller did not begin until 1952. A Rotax air-cooled 2-stroke twin 398cc 15bhp engine was mounted in the tail, driving the single rear wheel. The 2-seater had curious weather protection in the form of a rear-hingeing canopy. Around 400 cars were made in total.

CR

FELBER (ii) (CH) 1974–1985

W.H. Felber Automobiles, Morges, Vaud.

Willy H. Felber, a successful businessman, was a great enthusiast for extraordinary automobiles. As an agent for Ferrari and Rolls-Royce, he was in touch with a wealthy clientele. In 1971 he is said to have designed the first model which should bear his name. It took another three years until the FERRARI FF, a 2-seater roadster based on the Ferrari 330GTC, was shown at the Geneva Show of 1974. The body was reminiscent of the early Ferrari barchettas with a narrow aluminium body and separate wings. It was produced by PANTHER West Winds in Weybridge, England, and was certainly one of the most powerful and fastest replicas. Being shorter and lighter than the original 330GTC, it would reach 62mph (100km/h) in just 4.5 seconds with a top speed of 143mph (230km/h). The 330GTC was fading out of production in 1969 but apparently there were some frames and engines left at the Ferrari works of which Felber made good use. In the following three or four years ten similar, if not quite identical, cars were completed and sold. Its price was SFr 90,000.

For the man who wanted more luggage space in his Ferrari, Felber in 1977 offered the FF365 Croisette, a handsome estate car based on the Ferrari 365GTC designed by Willy Felber and built by Giovanni Michelotti. It was ordered by a high-ranking person in the Arabian Gulf region. Another Ferrari 365GTC was modified into the ultimate beach fun-car for the ruler of Qatar. This car is reported to have since returned to a Swiss collector. Simultaneously various LANCIAs were produced by Felber. The first was launched at the Geneva Show in 1975. It was the LANCIA FF roadster, which had a style recalling the fabulous D24 sports racer of the early 1950s, but instead of the two dohc V8, it had the more humble V4 engine of the Fulvia of 1300cc and 100bhp. The first car was also built by PANTHER but apparently there were capacity or other problems and the next three vehicles, the total production, were completed by Michelotti. These, however, were fitted with the FIAT-designed Beta engines and chassis. The LANCIA FF V was a modified Beta 2000 saloon with a new grill and a large rear window, and allowing access to the luggage space. The interior was much more luxurious and the price of SFr 36,000 was SFr 17,000 higher than the list price of the standard saloon. Nevertheless, about 20 were built by Michelotti. In 1977 the Felber Excellence was introduced. It was based on the PONTIAC Firebird but had a modified front and rear. The Felber grill, rather similar to the old LANCIA grills, and extensive modifications of the interior and dashboard made it a highly individual coupé or convertible. Total production amounted to 12 cars. With the petro-dollars flowing freely, Felber in 1978 launched his Oasis, a deluxe 4×4 model based on the INTERNATIONAL Scout. It could be ordered either with the original American V8 of 5653cc and 150bhp or with the ROLLS-ROYCE V8 engine of 7206cc and 'ample' bhp. Obviously Willy Felber had identified his customers' taste and the Oasis was the most successful Felber model, with about 70 cars sold in five years.

In 1979 Felber presented a luxurious small car, the Rubis, based on the LANCIA-AUTOBIANCHI A112, which remained in the programme for only a short time. One year later, the Felber Pacha, a modified BUICK Skylark, with new grill and improved interior but with the original V6 engine of 2838cc and

117bhp, was introduced. It cost SFr 37,600 and about 20 cars were produced. In 1981 a modified LANCIA Delta, named Felber Roberta, and a VW Golf appearing as the Felber Spécial Golf were exhibited at the Geneva Show. Both had beautiful interiors and the characteristic Felber grill. In 1985 a MASERATI quattroporte with Felber modifications was offered, but one year later production ceased.

Willy Felber had always designed and built cars to his personal liking and some were quite spectacular. For the enthusiast who wanted something out of the ordinary, Felber was a good address. The Haute Performance Co., owned by Willy Felber and his son, is still in business selling and repairing various makes.

FH

FELDAY (GB) 1966–1967
Felday Engineering Ltd, Dorking, Surrey.
Hillclimb champion Peter Westbury offered replicas of his tubular chassis Felday 6 from 1966. Unlike his other 4 × 4 specials, this had 2-wheel drive and a rear-mounted Ford 4.7-litre V8 engine driving through a Hewland gearbox and was intended for hillclimbing and Formula Libre. The bodywork was fibreglass and there was a road car project, but Westbury reverted to racing and engine preparation.

CR

FELDMANN (D) 1905–1912
Westfälische Automobilgesellschaft B. Feldmann & Co., Soest.
Feldmann was one of a number of firms which were helped into car production by using the Omnimobil components made by FAFNIR. A 2-seater with 6PS 2-cylinder engine was the first model, followed by more ambitious designs such as the 10/25PS 4-cylinder tourer and sports model with ohv engine which gave 40bhp. Production was on a small scale, and sales were limited mainly to the province of Westphalia.

HON

FELLPOINT see GINETTA

FEND (D) 1948–1953
Fend Kraftfahrzeug GmbH, Rosenheim.
Fritz Fend's 3-wheeler started as an invalid car which could be propelled manually. Later versions were motorised by a 38cc Victoria or 98cc Sachs engine. Bicycle wheels were used on the first models, but then there was a change to smaller wheels which made the vehicle more car-like. In addition a 100cc Ridel engine was available. All of these had been single-seaters, but a tandem 2-seater was launched in 1953, powered by a 174cc Sachs engine. This design was taken up by MESSERSCHMITT and made in much larger numbers than Fend had achieved, from 1953 onwards.

HON

FENGHUANG (CHI) 1958–1964
Shanghai Auto Works, Shanghai Municipality.
The first saloons made by the Shanghai Auto Works were called Fenghuang (Phoenix). The first prototype appeared in November 1958, and it was clearly a Plymouth-influenced vehicle. The engine was a 4-cylinder, 78hp unit. In January 1959 an American-styled version with dual headlights, heavy bumpers and a full-width grill, registered 3*00691, was introduced. There is only one photo of this car existing, this photo often printed with different backgrounds. The final version came in 1960, when a batch of 13 saloons was produced, using the Mercedes Benz 220 as a basis. It was renamed in 1964 and became famous as the SHANGHAI SH 760, remaining in production unchanged under this name until 1974.

EVIS

FENIX (E) 1903–1904
D. Támaro, Barcelona.
The partner of Emilio de la Cuadra abandoned the company to create his own, and offered cars from 0.75hp up to 30hp, with double chain transmission and the gearbox and differential in a single unit. In 1904 Domingo Támaro left Spain to work with TURCAT MERY.

VCM

FENTON (US) 1913–1914
Fenton Cyclecar Co., Fenton, Michigan.
The Fenton was a typical cyclecar with De Luxe 10hp air-cooled V-twin engine, friction transmission and belt drive. It had a striking vee-radiator reminiscent of an F.R.P. or a 90hp Mercedes. When announced, it was to be called the Signet, but Fenton was the name used for all the production cars, although there were probably not many of them. In 1914 the company was acquired by H.J. Koppin who renamed the car after himself. Apart from a $10 price increase to $385, there were no changes to the car, and as the Koppin it did not last beyond the end of 1914.

NG

FEORA (i) (US) 1981–1982
Chuck Ophorst, Los Angeles, California.
Half vintage fighter 'plane, half Star Wars out-take, the Feora was a highly unusual 3-wheeler. Its claimed drag coefficient 0.15 was achieved because of a very low frontal area, teardrop shape and extreme narrowness. The all-fibreglass bodywork sat atop a complex space frame chassis and the whole car weighed just 505lbs. There was seating for two in tandem, accessed by a folding canopy. With a 22bhp 175cc Honda 2-cylinder engine installed in the tail, a top speed of 92mph and a fuel consumption in excess of 90mpg was quoted. A production run of Feoras was planned but rejected because the projected price would have been prohibitive.

CR

FEORA (ii) (US) c.1984
Feora, Paramount, California.
The Feora was a radical trike design with an aircraft-like enclosed cockpit. It had a single headlight and the two front wheels had long fairings as on fixed-gear aircraft. It used 175cc or 400cc Honda motorcycle engines and running gear. Two occupants could ride in tandem after entering through a single gull-wing door. Front suspension and brakes were custom fabricated and the body could be quickly removed for maintenance. Feoras could be built to order, or plans could be purchased for home fabrication. No kits were sold.

HP

FERA (BR) 1981–1985
Industria de Artefatos Metalicos Bola SA, São Paulo.
The Fera XK4.1HE was a glassfibre replica of the Jaguar XK120, slightly wider, and with an XK150-type grill. Mechanical equipment came from the 4.1-litre 6-cylinder Chevrolet Impala.

NG

FERAL (F) c.1910–c.1921
A. Feral, Albi, Tarn.
This is one of those shadowy makes of which there is little evidence outside the pages of annuals. It first appeared in l'Annuaire Générale de l'Automobile in 1910, listed as a maker of 2-seater voiturettes, while in 1913 their entry referred to voiturettes and voitures extra-légères système Feral. They were back in the Annuaire in 1921, this time with voiturettes only.

NG

FERBEDO (D) 1923–1925
Ferdinand Benthauser, Nuremberg-Doos.
This maker of children's scooters and similar vehicles decided to go upmarket and made a 4-wheeled hybrid between a motorcycle and a car. Three passengers could sit in tandem as on a motorcycle, but steering was by a normal wheel. The engine was a 1.9PS Breuer. In 1925 the car was known as the Tom.

HON

FERGUS (i) (GB/US) 1915–1922
1915–1916 J.B. Ferguson Ltd, Belfast.
1921–1922 Fergus Motors of America, Newark, New Jersey.
1921 O.D. Cars Ltd, Belfast.
Machine tool makers J.B. Ferguson entered the motor trade in the early 1900s, becoming bodybuilders and agents for many leading British and Continental quality cars, and by 1914 they had the largest car repair works in Ireland. In 1915

1921 Fergus (i) sedan.
NICK BALDWIN

the company introduced a very advanced car powered by a 2.6-litre single-ohc 4-cylinder engine, designed, like the rest of the car, by J.A. McKee, helped by Roland Chilton and F. Eves. This was rubber mounted in a rigid box-section frame with cantilever springs all round. The chassis was pressure lubricated, and only needed oil at 11 lubrication points, and that only every six months. The tyres could be inflated by an engine-driven pump.

Such advanced designs often struggle in the market place, but the Fergus had less of a chance than most, appearing in the middle of World War I. A chassis was shown at the New York Automobile Show in January 1916, and was so well received that plans were laid to make it in the US, with a factory at Newark. Later in the year it was said that production could start in six months, that is early 1917, but by then the war caught up with the Fergus again, with the entry of the United States in April 1917. The Fergus did not reappear until 1920, by which time it had acquired front-wheel brakes and a 6-cylinder Northway engine. It also had an unrealistic price tag of $7500, raised to $8500 in 1922. Nobody bought it, although one of the two remaining chassis in Ireland was imported by an East Coast doctor and fitted with a Holbrook sedan body.

Back in Ireland there was a further attempt to market the design, which was renamed the O.D. (owner driver). Only one tourer was built, so total production was only three cars, the original chassis, the doctor's sedan and the O.D., whose makers became a garage and general engineering firm. After World War II its successors became the leading suppliers of electric hares for greyhound racing. The Ferguson name later became widely known for the tractors built by J.B. Ferguson's brother, Harry.

NG

FERGUS (ii) (US) 1949

Fergus Motors, New York, New York.
This company built the Fergus car from 1915 to 1922, but switched to importing British cars after World War II. The 1949 Fergus was a sports car based on the Austin A40 sedan. Only one is believed to have been built.

HP

FERGUS (iii) (GB) 1986–1987; 1991 to date

1986–1987 Fergus Engineering, Kingsbridge, Devon.
1991–1992 A.I.M.S., Kingsbridge, Devon.
1992 to date Projects of Distinction, Redditch, Worcestershire.
The Fergus Mosquito kit car was inspired by the great Aston Martin Ulster, and it looked very convincing. The donor mechanicals, from the humble Morris Marina, were chosen for their vintage feel and the job was quite well executed, with proper 18in wire wheels and dummy front leaf springs (Marina torsion bars were used in fact). Cars were supplied mainly in kit form, with a steel tube chassis and bodywork in fibreglass and aluminium.

CR

FERMI (I) 1947–1949

Fermi SA, Treviso.
Displayed at the 1948 Padua and 1949 Milan Shows, the Lucertola was a very small car that tried to look big by aping the style of the contemporary Chrysler convertible. In fact it only had a 358cc 14bhp 4-cylinder engine and could only

reach a top speed of 50mph (80km/h). Other features included ifs and a 4-speed gearbox, while a more powerful 650cc engine was planned. Like the car itself, nothing ever came of it.

CR

FERNA see H.H.

FERNANDEZ see LA SIRENE

FEROLDI (I) 1912

Enrico Feroldi, Turin.
Feroldi was a carburettor maker who offered one model of complete car. The Tipo Unico had a 3306cc side-valve 4-cylinder engine, the cylinders cast in pairs, developing 30bhp. In appearance it resembled a contemporary Fiat. Few were made, but Feroldi later made trucks using the same engine as the cars, in a new factory at Saluzzo.

NG

FERON ET VIBERT (F) c.1905–c.1907

Feron et Vibert, Soissons, Aisne.
This company made a small number of conventional touring cars with 4-cylinder engines and shaft drive.

NG

NICK BALDWIN

FERRARI, ENZO (1898–1988)

Son of Alfredo Ferrari, an artisan who made metal structures for railway stations (sheds, gangways, barriers), and his wife Adalgisa, Enzo Ferrari had two birth certificates, one stating his date of birth as 18 February 1898, the other, two days later. His family lived in Reggio Emilia, where a metalworking industry supplemented the agricultural and dairy economy of the land south of Parma.

He was drawn to motor racing from the day his father took him to see the Circuito di Bologna race in 1908. He broke off his studies at the Istituto Tecnico in Modena after the death of his father in 1915 and went to work as an instructor for the recruits of the Modena fire brigade.

Enzo was called up for military service in 1917, and in view of his metalworking experience, was given the job of shoeing mules for the mountain artillery in Val Seriana. In 1918 he was discharged as incurably stricken with Spanish 'flu, following two operations. The captain of the Modena fire brigade gave him a letter of introduction to someone at Fiat,

FEROX (GB) 1914

Ferox Light Car Co., Paisley, Renfrewshire.
The Ferox was a light car powered by a 1.3-litre 4-cylinder side-valve Ballot engine, with shaft drive. The standard body was a 2-seater.

NG

FERRARI (I) 1940 to date

1940–1945 Auto Avio Construzione, Modena.
1946–1960 Auto Construzione Ferrari, Modena.
1960 to date Società Esercizio Fabbriche Automobili e Corse
Ferrari Maranello, Modena.

The first car made by Enzo Ferrari, though it did not carry his name, was designed by Alberto Massimino using many Fiat parts, and was developed by Enrico Nardi, who later made cars under his own name. The engine was a 1500cc straight-8, based on two 4-cylinder Fiat engines, which gave around 75bhp. Two cars were completed in time for the 1940 *Gran Premio di Brescia della Mille Miglia*.

Ferrari's severance agreement with Alfa Romeo meant he could not use his own name for seven years, so the cars were called Auto Avia 815s. They showed promise, but neither finished. One of the drivers was a young motorcyclist, Alberto Ascari, who would win World Championships for Ferrari, 1952–1953.

Soon afterwards, Italy joined the war. Ferrari began the hostilities with a small workshop in Modena and ended it with a factory in nearby Maranello which

1950 Ferrari 195 berlinetta.
NATIONAL MOTOR MUSEUM

employed 150 people making machine tools and ball bearings. Ferrari then turned to Gioachino Colombo to design a new car, which now he could call a Ferrari. Colombo had worked with Ricart on a stillborn 1.5-litre supercharged flat-12 for Alfa Romeo and he decided on a single-ohc V12 of 1498cc with hairpin valve springs. It was designated Tipo 125 – 125cc was the capacity of each cylinder and that became Ferrari's method of labelling for some years.

and he went with high hopes to Turin, but had no success. He worked for a short period as a tester in a factory that made chassis frames in Via Ormea, Turin, before returning home.

He was not long unemployed, for he went to Bologna and was hired by the Giovannoni garage, which pioneered the business of stripping down second-hand light trucks and sending them to Milan to be fitted with lightweight torpedo or roadster bodies.

One of Ferrari's duties was to deliver the chassis to Milan, which brought him into contact with the racing driver Ugo Sivocci. Ferrari left Giovannoni and Bologna as soon as Sivocci found him a job in Milan, installing Isotta Fraschini engines into other chassis. In 1919-20 both Sivocci and Ferrari went to work for the SA Costruzioni Meccaniche Nazionali in Via Fatebenefratelli in Milan, makers of the CMN automobile. Here, Ferrari got his first experience as a racing driver.

It was in 1920 that he joined Alfa Romeo, followed shortly by Sivocci. For three years, Ferrari pursued two careers, one as a driver, another as a mechanic. In 1923 he married Laura Garello who persuaded him not to enter races, while at the same time he discovered that he was more interested in making engines than in racing them. For several years, his role was that of a test engineer attached to the Alfa Romeo racing team, with occasional racing engagements up to 1931. When his son Alfredo (known as Dino) was born on 19 January 1932, he gave up racing for good. From 1927 onwards, he was also the official Alfa Romeo agent for the Emilia-Romagna region.

He left Alfa Romeo at the end of 1928, and in February 1929, set up the Scuderia Ferrari at 11 Viale Trento e Trieste in Modena to race a team of Alfa Romeo cars.

The cars were distinguished from those of the official Alfa Romeo team by a yellow shield with a black prancing horse, painted on the sides of the body. This was copied from the emblem of the Baracca family, which had been painted on the fuselage of the planes flown by Francesco Baracca, Italy's premier fighter pilot in World War I who was shot down and killed near Treviso in 1918. Francesco Baracca's father, Count Enrico Baracca, first met Enzo Ferrari in 1923 in the pits of a race track, and they often saw each other at race meetings. Later, he also came to know Countess Paolina Baracca, the pilot's mother, who told him: 'Put my son's horse on your cars – it's sure to bring you luck'. From 1930 to 1940, the racing programme of Scuderia Ferrari achieved 124 victories, 82 second places, and 68 third places out of 343 starts.

In 1939, Enzo Ferrari founded Auto Avio Costruzioni which moved into a small factory at Maranello in 1943, working mainly as a sub-contractor for aircraft parts and machine tool supplier to the Compagnia Nazionale

Aeronautica di Roma, Piaggio SA of Pontedera, and RIV (Fiat's ball bearing subsidiary). Two Auto Avio cars were also built in 1940, and were entered in the short-circuit Mille Miglia.

The Maranello factory suffered severe bomb damage in 1944, and was rebuilt in 1946. In 1944-45 Ferrari began preparing for a fresh start in racing, building complete cars at Maranello. The prancing horse shield, framed in a rectangle, became the Ferrari badge.

The name Ferrari became famous, not only for winning races, but also for producing some of the world's fastest and most desirable sports cars. Italy's coachbuilders, led by Carrozzeria Touring, Pininfarina, Vignale, and Ghia, outdid themselves to make beautiful bodies for Ferrari chassis.

In contrast with prewar days, when Enzo Ferrari was directing the team from the pits, he no longer attended the races, but stayed home, waiting for a phone call to give him the results. In the 1960s, on the other hand, Laura Ferrari was practically a fixture on the pit counter.

He ruled Maranello as an autocrat, and no detail was too small to be worth his attention. He hired and fired racing drivers, engineers, salesmen, and mechanics, sometimes on a whim, sometimes calmly, sometimes with an outburst of temper.

It was a severe blow for him when Dino, his son and heir to Maranello, died on 30 June 1956, from muscular dystrophy. For many years he kept secret his illegitimate son, born in 1945 from a liaison with Lina Lardi, but the story leaked out when Piero Lardi was given a job in the racing department and his fellow workers noticed his striking physical resemblance to the 'Commendatore' (a title conferred upon Enzo in 1927). After the death of Laura Ferrari in 1978, he was given the name Piero Lardi-Ferrari and a seat on the board of directors.

Enzo Ferrari also held the title of Cavaliere del Lavoro from 1952, and in 1960 the University of Bologna conferred upon him an honorary degree in industrial engineering.

He resigned as chairman of the SEFAC-Ferrari board on 19 March 1977, but kept his office at Maranello and maintained a tight rein on the racing team. In 1978 he gave up the presidency of FOCA (Formula One Constructors' Association) because of his opposition to Bernie Ecclestone, head of Formula One (race organisers) and owner of TV rights to Formula One races.

He remained a power in the racing world until the age of 84, when ill health sapped his strength, though his mind remained perfectly lucid. He died peacefully on the morning of Sunday 14 August 1988.

JPN

1961 Ferrari 250GT berlinetta, by Pininfarina.
NATIONAL MOTOR MUSEUM

1961 Ferrari 400SA Super-America coupé.
NATIONAL MOTOR MUSEUM

1963 Ferrari 250 GTO coupé.
NATIONAL MOTOR MUSEUM

The first Ferrari engine was virtually the Alfa Romeo unit with a crease in it. In competition trim, with three downdraught twin-choke Webers, it gave up to 118bhp, delivered through a 5-speed gearbox, unusual at the time.

The prototype engine was run in September 1946 and, early in 1947, the first complete Tipo 125 was ready for testing. Its chassis was a cross-braced ladderframe with two oval main tubes, with double wishbone and transverse leaf front suspension, and a live rear axle and transverse leaf spring at the rear. Enzo Ferrari was 49 years old when the first car to bear his name was completed. Ferrari's reputation attracted the cream of drivers and, before long, his cars were winning races. By degrees, the engine was enlarged, though the chassis layout remained the same apart from variations in wheelbase. Versions were made ostensibly for road use, but these were merely de-tuned competition cars, sold to finance Ferrari's racing programme. The 2-litre Tipo 166 became Ferrari's first 'production' car and was made in small numbers, from 1948 to 1953.

In supercharged 1498cc form, the engine powered Ferrari's first grand prix car in 1948. Ferrari should have dominated in 1949, when Alfa Romeo withdrew for a year, but was twice beaten by ponderous 4½-litre Lago-Talbots which, being

normally aspirated, had superior fuel economy so lost less time refuelling.

Ferrari then turned to Aurelio Lampredi to design a 'big block' V12 which started at 3.3-litres and was gradually enlarged to the full 4.5-litres. Leaving aside Talbot and Delahaye, whose GP cars were derivations of their sports cars, Ferrari was the first manufacturer to make successful unblown grand prix cars for many years. Driving a Ferrari Tipo 375, Froilan Gonzalez won the 1951 British Grand Prix, inflicting the first defeat on Alfa Romeo since 1946.

A myth has arisen that Ferrari is inextricably linked to V12 engines, yet of more than 100 World Championship grand prix victories, Ferrari has won just 17 with V12s. It was V12 sports and GT cars which built Ferrari's reputation, taking seven World Sports Car Championships, from 1953 to 1961. Ferrari dominated the (Formula Two) World Championship, 1952–53, but thereafter enjoyed only spasmodic success in grand prix racing and, apart from the mid–1970s, it was usually when Ferrari employed British engineers.

Ferrari's fortunes were at such a low ebb in 1955 that, when Lancia was about to fold, Fiat brokered a deal whereby Ferrari took over the Lancia D50 F1 car with its designer, Vittorio Jano, and received a subsidy from Fiat. Juan-Manuel Fangio, driving a Ferrari-entered Lancia, won the 1956 World Championship.

Ferrari's first serious foray into the production car market was the 250 GT, made from 1954 to 1962. Unlike earlier efforts, the 250 GT was developed as a road car. It also became the basis for an unofficial competition among Italian coachbuilders which was won by Pininfarina. Since the late 1950s, Pininfarina has styled virtually all production Ferraris and the studio's flair has made an incalculable contribution to the marque's success.

A one-litre engine, intended for a 'popular' Ferrari was taken over by ASA. The 250 GT had a 3-litre version of Colombo's 'small block' V12 in a chassis similar to the original design and 905 examples were made. Disc brakes were fitted from late 1959 and the 4-speed gearbox had overdrive from 1960. A short wheelbase 250 GT (232 made) was almost always fitted with a Pininfarina body and became the first Ferrari standard production model. Lightweight versions were very successful in GT racing. From 1960, Ferrari became a significant producer of road cars with a 2+2 250 GT, the 330 GT America and the 330 GT 2+2 – all variations of the 250 GT. During 1960 to 1965, Ferrari production reached better than a car a day. A few 'big block' models, the America and Superamerica, were also made.

In 1961 Ferrari dominated F1 with its 1.5-litre V6 'sharknose' mainly because the British were slow in developing new engines. At the end of the year there was a mass walk-out by key personnel and the reason is typical of Ferrari's history. Enzo's son and heir, Alfredino ('Dino'), died in 1956 and Ferrari wished to recognise an illegitimate son, Piero Lardi. Ferrari's wife objected and began to meddle in the company, which led to eight senior men defecting to ATS.

Some Ferrari competition cars of the time were also practical road cars. Among them was the 250 GTO, a lightweight front-engined car developed by Giotto Bizzarrini, and the 250 LM, Ferrari's first mid-engined car. In 1962 came the 250 Lusso, a refined 250 GT SWB, and 350 were made. Ferrari had unequalled charisma – by 1965 he had won Le Mans nine times – but Maserati usually sold more road cars. Also in 1962, Ford entered discussion with Ferrari with a view to buying his company. Ferrari agreed, then changed his mind and Ford contracted Lola for a year to design a car (the GT 40) to beat Ferrari at its own game. Ford won Le Mans, 1966 to 1969, and apart from a dominant season in 1972, Ferrari was fading as a force in sports car racing.

In 1969 Fiat bought 50 per cent of Ferrari (increased to 90 per cent on Ferrari's death, the remaining stock going to Piero Lardi). Ferrari retained control of the racing division which Fiat funded.

The 275 GTB (Berlinetta) and GTS (Spider) of 1964 to 1967 used a chassis which could be traced back to 1947, but the suspension was all-independent. For competition work there was the lightweight 275 GTB/C. Twin ohcs appeared for the first time on a production Ferrari in 1966, boosting power to 300bhp, and these were designated GTB/4. There was no official Spider version, but Scaglietti built ten convertibles for the American importer. It was joined, from 1966 to 1968, by the 330 GTC and GTS with 4-litre 'quad cam' engines, and air conditioning was an option. As before, Ferrari made small numbers of very expensive cars (the Superfast 500) using the 'big block' engine. A few 4-litre 365 Californias were also made, from 1966 to 1967.

Most Ferraris made during the 1960s, could trace their origins to the original design and the 365 GT 2+2, made from 1967 to 1971, was no exception. It kept pace with modern developments, however, with power brakes, windows and

1971 Ferrari Dino 246 GT coupé.

steering. Air conditioning was standard, the rear seats could accommodate two adults, there was a large boot and attention had been paid to ergonomics. The single-ohc 4.4-litre V12 gave 320bhp. Cromodora alloy wheels were fitted until 1968, when they were replaced by Daytona-style five spoke alloys. Borrani wires were an option, but the day of the wire wheel was fast disappearing. It was soon joined by the 365 GTC and GTS (Spider) which were 2-seater variations on the same theme.

Enzo Ferrari had been devastated by the death of Alfredino, and competition V6 engines had been named 'Dino' in his memory. In 1967, Ferrari launched a new marque, Dino, and the Dino 206 GT had a 180bhp 2-litre V6 engine, built by Fiat, mounted amidships and drove through a 5-speed transaxle, while suspension was independent all round. Pininfarina's styling pointed the way for all mid-engined Ferraris, but the cockpit was noisy, luggage space was minimal and few more than 100 were built. Dino engines were also used by Fiat, in a model called 'Dino' and, in the future, Ferrari would supply engines for some Lancia models.

The replacement for the 275 GTB/4 was the 365 GTB/4, nicknamed the 'Daytona', after winning the Daytona 24-Hours, and one of the most desirable of all Ferraris. It used the 275 chassis but 352bhp from a 4.4-litre dry-sumped 'quad cam' meant 167+mph (270+km/h) (0–62mph (0–100km/h) in 5.9 seconds).

While the first Dino had disappointed, its replacement, the 246 GT and GTS ('Targa' top) was a different proposition. The engine was enlarged to 2.4-litres and, though it still did not have a Ferrari badge, about 4000 were made. In 1971 came the 365 GTC/4, a short-lived, but much admired model, which replaced both the 365GT 2+2 and the 365 GTC. The chassis was similar to the Daytona but a conventional 5-speed gearbox replaced the Daytona's transaxle.

Ferrari's replacement for the 365 GTC/4, the 365GT4, used that car's chassis, with a longer wheelbase and, with Fiat in charge, quality improved. A handsome 4-seat saloon, in 1976 the model received a fuel-injected 340bhp 4.8-litre engine, automatic transmission was an option, and it was renamed the 400i. Overall, sales were not high as Ferrari stopped selling its V12 cars in America rather than compromise the engines to meet emission laws. 1985 saw Bosch ABS and 4.9 litres; power remained at 340bhp, but torque was improved. Renamed the 412i, it stayed in production until 1988.

1985 Ferrari Testarossa coupé.

1987 Ferrari Mondial 3.2 cabriolet.

1988 Ferrari F40 coupé.
NATIONAL MOTOR MUSEUM

1999 Ferrari 360 Modena coupé.
FERRARI

In 1973, came the Dino 308 GT4 with a new 255bhp double-ohc 3-litre V8 engine (the 177bhp 208 was a 'tax break' car for Italy). The 308 was quicker than previous Dinos (149+mph (240+km/h), 0–62mph (0–100km/h) in 6.4 seconds). It had a 2+2 body by Bertone – the one production Ferrari not styled by Pininfarina – and, unlike the 246, it was badged as a Ferrari. The name 'Dino' was dropped from 1977. It was joined by the 365 GT4, a mid-engined coupé with an in-line 380bhp double-ohc 4.4-litre flat-12 engine and all-independent suspension. In 1976 the model was given a 5-litre engine and renamed '512 BB' – Berlinetta Boxer.

Ferrari had used the flat-12 configuration for some racing engines, but the 365 GT4 was the first road Ferrari not to have a vee-engine. Fuel injection came in 1981 and a few Targa-tops were made. The factory claimed a top speed of 186mph (300km/h), but this was widely doubted. The Berlinetta Boxer remained in production until 1985.

The Ferrari 308 GTB (and 308 GTS and the 'tax break' 208 GTB and GTS) was the true successor to the Dino 246 (the GT4 developed into the Mondial). Pininfarina was responsible for the styling, the chassis was broadly the same as its predecessors, and the 2921cc engine was dry-sumped. Models from 1977 had fibreglass body panels, which was novel for a production Ferrari.

In 1980 the GT4 was made over as the Mondial 8, with styling by Pininfarina and a longer wheelbase. It was Ferrari's first attempt at a 'world car' and, to meet emission controls, the 3-litre V8 had fuel injection. Meeting emission controls lost power and torque, but they were restored by the 240bhp *Quattrovalve* (4-valve) engine which was an option from 1982. 1983 saw the introduction of a cabriolet, the first soft top Ferrari had made since the Daytona Spider.

Meanwhile Ferrari made the Dino-derived 308i and 328 GTB and GTS, with 'tax break' 2-litre variants. The 3.2-litre engine of 1985 – also fitted to the Mondial – increased output to 260bhp, with improved torque. By the time the 308-series was replaced in 1988, it had become the most popular model in Ferrari's history.

In 1984, Ferrari built a new GTO. It resembled a 308 GTB, and used that car's engine, mounted north/south rather than east/west and, with twin IHI turbochargers and Weber-Marelli electronic fuel injection, it gave 400bhp. Ferrari claimed a top speed of 186+mph (300+km/h) (0–62mph (0–100km/h)

in 5 seconds). Road versions could have air conditioning and power windows. Just 200 examples were made, to homologate the model into Group B.

Also in 1984, came another new model with a famous name, the Testarossa. Pininfarina was responsible for the body which was of aluminium save for the roof and doors. The shape was evolved in a wind tunnel with special attention paid to downforce while the 'egg slicer' side grilles improved cooling. Larger overall than the 512 BB (it was 78in (1980mm) wide), it followed Berlinetta Boxer's broad chassis layout but was a little lighter. The 5-litre '4-valve' V12 had Bosch fuel injection and delivered its 380bhp to a 5-speed transaxle.

To celebrate Ferrari's fortieth anniversary, in 1988, the company introduced the F40, intended to be the world's fastest production car. In essence it was a GTO with different body panels. The engine was a short-stroke 471bhp variation of the 3-litre *Quattrovalve* V8 with twin IHI turbochargers. It was claimed to top 199mph (320km/h) and reach 62mph (100km/h) in under 4 seconds. A factory kit with larger turbochargers and different camshafts could add a further 200bhp.

It was also in 1988 that Enzo Ferrari died. He might have achieved even more success had he not run his factory as a Mediaeval city-state. He set his lieutenants against each other – Ferrari described himself as an 'agitator' of men. He was essentially an impresario, and a great one. He was responsible for arranging the creation of some of the most desirable cars in history and so perfectly did he promote his own legend that at least one obituary called him a designer.

He was, however, deeply conservative, which meant that Ferrari always lagged behind in terms of technology. He was conspicuously late to adopt disc brakes, for example, a mid-engined layout or, even, scientific aerodynamics. Many a Formula One designer looked at Ferrari's resources and could not believe why the Scuderia did not win every race it entered.

In the late 1980s there was a boom in classic cars and Ferraris changed hands for fabulous sums. In response, Fiat limited Ferrari production to 4000 cars a year to maintain *cachet*. After the market collapsed in 1990, Ferrari struggled to meet that target and short-time working was introduced for the first time.

Before that happened, Ferrari updated the 328 – the 348 had an enlarged engine (to 3405cc) which was located longitudinally and was five inches lower in the frame bringing a significant reduction in the centre of gravity. The new chassis was stiffer than previously and the 348 was also wider because the front radiator was replaced by a pair of side-mounted units.

A new Mondial, also introduced in 1989, shared the 348's layout and engine, but had a new 5-speed transmission, electronically controlled variable suspension, and a 3-position manual suspension selector.

At the end of 1991 came the 512 TR, a revised Testarossa with 422bhp and a claimed top speed of 193mph (310km/h).

Towards the end of 1992, Ferrari introduced the 456GT, the first new front-engined car it had made for more than 20 years. It was a 2+2 coupé with 442bhp from its 5.5-litre V12 engine with automatic transmission as an option.

A 348 Spider came in 1993 and both it, and the 348tb coupé, had 320bhp. They were replaced the following year by the 355 with a 3.5-litre V8 engine, 380bhp and a top speed of 171mph (275km/h). By general consent, it was the best all-round road car that Ferrari had ever built. It was soon available as a Spider and with a clutchless transmission, operated by paddles under the steering wheel, a system first developed by John Barnard for Formula One.

Later in 1994 came the F512M, a further make-over of the Testarossa, with a small increase in power and some shedding of weight. Finally, in 1994, the first photographs of the F50 were released. The F50 was a mid-engined sports car whose production was limited to 349 examples – the number was more memorable than 350. The 4.7-litre engine, derived from Ferrari's V12 F1 unit, drove through a 6-speed gearbox, was fitted to a carbonfibre monocoque/body, and delivered 520bhp, giving a top speed of 201mph (323km/h).

The 550 Maranello of 1997 was a front-engined 4-seat GT with a 478bhp 5474cc engine and a top speed of 197mph (318km/h). 1998 saw the 456 updated and offered as the 456M GT and the GTA, a more luxurious version with automatic transmission. In the spring of 1999 the F355 Berlinetta was replaced by the 360 Modena, a completely restyled coupé; with slightly larger engine of 3586cc and 405bhp. The same 40-valve layout was used, and also inherited from the F355 was the choice of standard gear-change or the paddle-operated, clutchless transmission. Ferrari expected about 80 per cent of customers to opt for the latter. Though longer and wider, the Modena was 77lb

1999 Ferrari 456 coupé.
FERRARI

(35kg) lighter than its predecessor, thanks to the extensive use of aluminium in its construction.

Ferrari has created mechanical artefacts which nonetheless fit easily in Italy's great tradition of art, sculpture, music, and style. Other makers have been more competent, but none can match Ferrari for sheer charisma.

MJL

Further Reading
Ferrari, Hans Tanner and Doug Nye, Haynes, 1974.
Ferrari, The Road Cars, Antoine Prunet, Haynes, 1987.
Ferrari, 1947–1997, Antonio Ghini, Rizzoli, 1997.
Ferrari Dino, Anthony Curtis, Crowood Auto Classics, 1990.

FERRARO MOTORS (US) c.1990

Ferraro Motors, Cheswick, Pennsylvania.
The Ferraro neoclassic kit car was based on Ford Escort or EXP bodies mounted on full-size Ford chassis. They were sold in coupé and convertible form and had the typical long mudguards and side-mounted spare tyres of the genre.

HP

FERRER (US) 1965–1966

Ferrer GT, Hialeah, Florida.
Designed and built by Frank Ferrer and his son Gary, the Ferrer GT was a kit sports car to fit on the Volkswagen Beetle chassis. It resembled a FIBERFAB Aztec kit car, which in turn drew inspiration from the Ford GT-40 and Porsche 904. However, it had better headlight treatment and doors than the Aztec and was a nicely finished out kit.

HP

FERRET (US) 1992 to date

Ferret Corp., c/o Pro Body, Holland, Michigan.
The Ferret was a very attractive mid-engined coupé with a steel frame. It was designed to accept Ford front suspension with General Motors transverse-mounted V6 engines mounted amidship. These fibreglass-bodied coupés were sold in kit form.

HP

FERRIS (US) 1920–1922

Ohio Motor Vehicle Co., Cleveland, Ohio.

1920 Ferris 6-cylinder tourer.
KEITH MARVIN

The Ferris was a highly regarded car of its time and although it was assembled from standard components throughout, its design and excellent coachwork set it apart from many of its peers. A Continental 9N 6-cylinder engine afforded power to the Ferris which rode on a wheelbase of 130in (3300mm). Disc wheels with matching side-mounted spares were standard. Three models were offered for 1920 and 1921 with a price range of $3350 to $4375, this being increased to a six-model offering in 1922 priced from $2595 for the 6-seater touring car to $3895 for the 4-seater sport sedan. The final Ferris cars comprising the Model '70' series, introduced in mid–1922, carried the newer Continental 6T engine with increased prices of $2795 for the 6-seater touring car to $4100 for the sport sedan. Production figures do not exist but a rule-of-thumb speculated guess would put the figure between 500 and 750 units.

KM

Further Reading
'Ferris, Car of Character', Stuart W. Wells,
Automobile Quarterly, Vol. 39, No. 1.

1969 Ferves Ranger.
NICK GEORGANO/NATIONAL MOTOR MUSEUM

FERRO (i) **(I)** 1935

Autorimessa Ferro, Genoa.

This was an aerodynamic 3-wheeler powered by a 650cc 4-cylinder engine, with 3-speed gearbox. Top speed was claimed to be 55mph (88km/h). It did not progress beyond the prototype stage.

NG

FERRO (ii) **(US)** c.1952

Ferro Corp., Santa Ana, California.

Ferro sold GLASSPAR G-1 fibreglass bodies for kit cars. Weight was 185lb (84kg) and it cost $700 in 1952.

HP

FERT (I) 1905–1906

Antonietti e Ugolino, Turin.

The Fert was powered by a 3.8-litre 4-cylinder German-built Fafnir engine and the chassis components were also imported. The company also acted as agent for the French PIVOT car, but both manufacture and agency had ceased by the end of 1906.

NG

FERVES (I) 1966–1971

Ferves srl, Turin.

Presented at the 1966 Turin Show, the Ferves Ranger was an attractive looking and extremely compact all-terrain vehicle. The rear-mounted engine was an 18bhp Fiat 500 unit, the all-independent suspension came from the Fiat 600D and all four wheels were driven. The open bodywork featured a folding windscreen and doors that could be fixed in the open position, and could seat four passengers. A Cargo pick-up version was also marketed. Later examples had 5-speedgearboxes (with an extra-low ratio), the option of 4 × 2 drive and a locking differential.

CR

FES *see* KESTREL

FESTIVAL (H) c.1956

Kálmán Szabadi, Vác.

The 1956 Revolution in Hungary put an official end to the Hungarian microcar efforts ALBA REGIA, BALATON, and UTTORO. But it didn't matter to Kálmán Szabadi, who built his Isetta 300 powered car between 1956 and 1960. As resin wasn't available, the smart decorator mixed pig fat and chicken feather with nitro shellac, added a layer of paint. The result was a material which was easy to form but smelled like a farm. The mix of gull-wing and conventional doors was a must as Szabadi was a tall man. Suspension came from Pannonia telescopic shock absorbers but as they were famous for their poor quality, every

wheel was held by a pair of them. The car looked big, but was only 3.1 metres long, and weighed 380kg. When the editor of Hungary's sole car magazine, *Autó-Motor*, saw the finished car he tried to convince the officials to make at least a small series, but the COMECON regulation which prohibited passenger car production in Hungary, was a stronger force, so the Festival remained a one-off.

PN

FEWMAL (US) 1914

Fewmal Motors Co., New York, New York.

Although called a cyclecar by its makers, the Fewmal was quite a substantial small car with sliding gearbox and shaft drive. The 18hp 4-cylinder engine had a single-ohc, very advanced for a $500 light car in 1914. Nevertheless, the makers did not last out the year and it is possible than only three Fewmals were made.

NG

F.H. (E) 1956–1960

Fábrica Hispano, Barcelona.

After the sale of HISPANO-SUIZA plants to PEGASO (ENASA), the company still continued its activity at a plant in Hostafranchs. They built two prototypes of new Hispano Suiza automobiles, one of them fitted with a Hugas body and Simca 1200cc engine. The technicians also developed a flat-4 engine in 1955, but then started the production of microcars, presented in 1956. Four types were offered, the F4 R with estate car body, the F pick-up, the J garden version, without doors, and the F2, a pick-up with or without a closed box. About 400 cars were made. The engine was a Hispano-Villiers single-cylinder of 9bhp. All these cars had independent front suspension, rack and pinion steering and hydraulic brakes. F.H. also sold the F5, with a twin-cylinder engine of 15bhp.

VCM

F.I.A.L. (I) 1906–1908

Fabbrica Italiana Automobili Legnano, Milan.

The F.I.A.L. was a light car powered by an 8hp vertical-twin or 10/12hp 4-cylinder engine. It was also known as the Legnano. Although production was small, two survive, one in the Museo dell'Automobile in Turin and another in Australia.

NG

F.I.A.M. (i) **(I)** 1924–1927

Fabbrica Italiana Automobili Motori, Turin.

This was a light car powered by a 750cc 2-cylinder 2-stroke engine.

NG

F.I.A.M. (ii) **(I)** 1978–c.1982

F.I.A.M., Coriano di Rimini.

The Johnny Panther was a 2-seater microcar powered by a 10bhp 124cc air-cooled Morini engine. It boasted all-independent springing, rear-wheel drive and automatic or 5-speed manual transmission, and could be bought with three or four wheels.

CR

FIAT (i) **(I)** 1899 to date

1899–1906 S.A. Fabbrica Italiana di Automobili, Turin.

1906–1943 S.A. Fabbrica Italiana Automobili Torino, Turin.

1943–1978 FIAT (Fiat) Società per Azioni, Turin.

1979 to date Fiat Auto S.p.A., Turin.

Not engineers and racing enthusiasts, but cold-blooded investors were the founders. Among them was 33-year-old Giovanni Agnelli, bearing a family name that has become identified with Fiat throughout his own and subsequent generations.

He was the one who had the management skills, the spark, however, came from Emanuele Cacherano di Bricherasio (1866–1904), an aristocrat and cavalry officer, but also a socialist. He had a vision of the automobile, not as the plaything of the idle rich, but as the answer to all the world's social problems: jobs for the masses, personal mobility for all, and a source of wealth to be tapped for welfare.

He was active in Turin's fledgling retail auto business, and on 1 July 1899, met in his home with a group of investors to draw up the papers of incorporation for Fiat. They were notarised on 11 July 1899, which stands as the official founding date.

Fiat began its activity by taking over two smaller businesses, a bicycle company owned by Giovanni Battista Ceirano which also had a prototype Welleyes car and held the automotive patents of Aristide Faccioli, and Società Italiana per la Costruzione ed il Comercio delle Automobili Torino, established by Bricherasio in 1898.

Along with the patents, Fiat also acquired the services of Aristide Faccioli, who was named technical director. Spacious premises were acquired in Corso Dante, Turin, where car production began on 19 March 1900.

The first Fiat 3½hp car was derived from the Welleyes, with a horizontal parallel-twin mounted under the driver's seat of the *vis-à-vis* body. About a dozen cars were made in makeshift premises in 1899, at first with 679cc units offering 4.2hp at 800rpm, later with 837cc units putting out 5 to 6hp at 1000rpm.

Aristide Faccioli was replaced in 1901 by Giovanni Enrico. Cesare Momo and Lauro Bernardi were also on Fiat's engineering staff in 1902.

In 1901 Fiat produced 80 8hp cars with front-mounted 1082cc vertical-twin engines, and the first 4-cylinder model appeared later that year, a 12/16hp 3768cc unit, supplemented by a 4181cc 16/20hp model in 1903. These cars seemed to follow along Panhard lines, but from 1904 onwards the Mercedes, influence was evident in all Fiat products.

Fiat produced 135 cars in 1903, but the investors had to wait for their returns. Fiat lost 18,000 Lire in 1900 and 10,000 Lire in 1901. The company broke even in 1902 and 1903, and paid its first dividends in 1904. Fiat's capital stock had been raised from 800,000 to 9 million Lire in 1900, but it was never fully paid up, which resulted in a lawsuit in 1906 against several Fiat directors for stock fraud, and it took over two years before they were cleared. New statutes were written on 18 March 1906, and the name Fiat was registered as a trade mark.

No dividends were paid in 1907 or 1908, but the entire capital stock was paid

1899 Fiat (i) 3½hp vis-á-vis.
NATIONAL MOTOR MUSEUM

up in 1908. By the end of the year, Fiat had 2700 workers and capacity for 5000 cars a year.

Guido Fornaca replaced Giovanni Enrico as technical director in 1906, and in the following years, T-head engines gave way to L-head designs, while shaft drive production began in 1908, followed by marine-diesel engines, railway locomotives and rolling stock, complete aeroplanes, and Fiat even set up its own steel foundries. He had a vision of the whole world as a market for Fiat cars, and promoted local production under licence. He sold manufacturing rights for the Fiat 15 Ter to Mitsubishi Heavy Industries in 1915, organised production of Fiat trucks by A.M.O. in Russia, opened a Spanish assembly plant at Guadalajara in 1919, put Austro-Fiat into gear in 1926, and got Polski-Fiat production going in 1931.

He purchased the NSU car factory at Heilbronn in 1929 to make Deutsche Fiat and put up financial backing for H.T. Pigozzi to establish Simca in 1932 and produce Fiat-origin cars in France. A Vickers subsidiary started Fiat assembly at Crayford in 1936 with 1,000 workers.

Leaving the day-to-day management of Fiat SpA to his trusted executives, he was elected Senator in 1923 to pursue a political career (and protest Fiat's interests at the highest level). He was able to block Ford's attempted takeover of Isotta-Fraschini in 1929 and prevail on the government to cancel Ford's building permit for an assembly plant at Leghorn, but lost his bid for control of Alfa Romeo in 1933. Agnelli wanted to merge Alfa Romeo with OM, but Mussolini wanted Alfa Romeo, one of Italy's major aero-engine makers, to operate under state governance.

Agnelli established IFI (Istituto Finanziario Industriale) on 27 July 1927 as a family holding mainly in order to stabilise the Fiat share price across all market fluctuations.

When Agnelli visited the US in May 1935, he was received in Dearborn as the honoured guest of Henry Ford.

In Rome, he was pragmatic on economic social policy but ardent in seeking military contracts for Fiat. He remained in Turin throughout the allied bombing in 1942 and the labour strikes of 1943, but developed relations with the anti-fascist movement as early as 1942, and secured O.S.S. support to prevent German looting and sabotage of the Fiat plants in 1945.

Worn out, he died in his Turin residence on 16 December 1945.

He married Clara Boselli of Florence in 1889, sister of a high-ranking official in the Navy. They had two children, Tina (1890–1928) and Edoardo (1892–1935).

JPN

AGNELLI, GIOVANNI (1866–1945)

He was born in the small Italian town of Villar Perosa on 13 August 1866, into a wealthy family whose fortune stemmed from the lumber trade. An only son, he attended a district school in Pinerolo until 1877 and later studied – with the monks – at San Giuseppe College in Turin.

In 1884 he entered the Military Academy of Modena and was commissioned into the Cavalry two years later. After a six-year military career, he resigned to look after the family estates and investments.

In 1899 he was a co-founder of Fiat, as well as a prominent shareholder and the company's secretary. He gained majority control of Fiat in 1906 and was named Cavaliere del Lavoro in 1907.

To Agnelli, Fiat was not just a motor vehicle manufacturer, but an organisation engaged in all forms of transport (and even beyond). Aero-engine

1902 Fiat (i) 12hp tonneau.
NATIONAL MOTOR MUSEUM

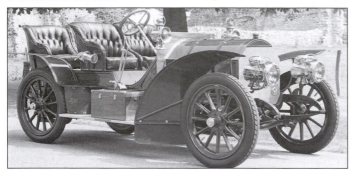

1904 Fiat (i) 75hp tourer.
NATIONAL MOTOR MUSEUM

1911 Fiat (i) 20/30hp landaulet.
NATIONAL MOTOR MUSEUM

replaced chain drive to the rear axle (though some high-powered models could be ordered with optional chain drive as late as 1910).

The first 6-cylinder Fiat was the 11,039cc 60hp model from 1907, a very high-priced car with a standard wheelbase of 127in (3240mm). There were no small Fiat cars in this period. The lowest-priced 1908 model was 'l Taxi' with a 2200cc 4-cylinder engine, designed specifically as a city taxi, and sold internationally, being popular in Paris, London, and New York. Over 2100 units were made over a 3-year period. The touring car range included the 4939cc 4-cylinder 20/30hp, the 7363cc 4-cylinder 28/40hp, the 7408cc 6-cylinder 35/45hp and the 7430cc 4-cylinder 50hp.

However, Agnelli was definitely steering Fiat towards the low-priced market. First came the 12/15hp Type I in 1910, with a 1846cc 4-cylinder engine – about

FIAT

AGNELLI, GIOVANNI 'GIANNI' (born 1921)

Grandson of Senator Giovanni Agnelli, co-founder of Fiat, and son of Edoardo Agnelli (1892–1935), he was born in Turin on 12 March 1921, and was destined to head the enterprise as well as the family in the second half of the twentieth century.

He was educated privately, graduated from the cavalry school at Pinerolo, and studied law at the University of Turin, which earned him the nickname 'l'Avvocato' to distinguish him from his brother Umberto and other Agnellis.

Drafted into the Italian Army in 1940, he was sent to fight on the Russian front in 1941, but was transferred to the desert army in Libya. When Mussolini was deposed in 1943, he returned to Turin but took to the hills, joining the Partisans who fought the German troops occupying northern Italy before he was attached to the Allied 4th Army under General Mark Clark.

After his grandfather's death in 1945, he was named Vice-Chairman of Fiat, but was mainly noted for his high-flying social life in an international élite of celebrities, heads of state, royalty and nobility, millionaires and politicians. One night in 1952 he ran his Ferrari into a truck on the Cannes–Nice highway, suffering permanent injuries to his right leg and foot.

He began to devote more of his time and attention to Fiat matters, and was appointed Managing Director in 1964. On 30 April 1966 he was elected Chairman of the board. The management culture that he inherited was centralised and hierarchical. He delegated greater responsibilities to middle management and rejuvenated the staff by instituting retirement at 65, except for members of the board.

When he saw that Fiat S.p.A. was getting 86 per cent of its 1968 income from cars and trucks, he felt the figure was 'too high' and began to invest in expansion of Fiat's non-automotive branches. He arranged Fiat's purchase of Lancia in 1969, at the same time securing majority control of Ferrari and placing Fiat executives in charge of Ferrari's production-car side. Fiat bought the earth-moving vehicle branch of Allis-Chalmers and moved it to southern Italy, merged with Fiat's construction equipment subsidiary. In 1974 he took over the Brazilian Alfa Romeo factory, and converted it to car production.

The Gilardini auto parts group came under Fiat's ownership in October 1974, and the former owner, Carlo De Benedetti (who had gone to college with Umberto Agnelli) joined Fiat as Director of Finance, Planning and Control. But he overstepped his authority by making decisions at a level that was Agnelli's prerogative, and was ousted in August 1976. The Gilardini group was merged into Magneti Marelli in October 1994. Agnelli then picked Clemente Signoroni to be his Director of Strategic Planning.

In December 1976, l'Avvocato raised $410 million by selling a 9.1 per cent stake in Fiat SpA to the Libyan Arab Foreign Investment Bank, which was also given two seats of the Fiat board of directors. Ten years later, the Libyan bank sold its Fiat shares in return for bonds issued by two of the Agnelli family's investment trusts (and cash payments from Agnelli's Italian and German bankers).

Fiat's truck and bus interests, including Unic in France and a stake in Magirus-Deutz, were merged into Iveco SpA. which grew by taking over Spain's ENASA (Pegaso) in 1990 and Ford's British truck branch in 1988.

In other deals, Fiat sold Grandi Motori Trieste (marine diesels) to IRI in a swap for plants making railway equipment and aero-engine parts. Agnelli was out-manoeuvered by Spain's INI (state industrial holding) over continued investment in SEAT, which ended in Fiat dumping its stake in SEAT in 1980.

Since becoming Chairman of Fiat, Agnelli often said he expected only four or five European car makers to survive. He was determined that Fiat should be one of them, even if it were in a partnership. In 1983–85 he held talks with Ford about merging their European passenger-car operations, but they were broken off because both sides wanted to be boss. In 1986 Fiat and Ford had a bitter duel for ownership of Alfa Romeo, which Ford lost. In 1987, Agnelli merged his latest acquisition into a new subsidiary of Fiat Auto, under the name Alfa-Lancia Industriale, SpA. Production of engines and other components for Alfa Romeo cars was co-ordinated with Fiat and Lancia, and all three began to share assembly facilities.

Agnelli was still interested in talking partnership with other captains of industry, and in 1989 he and Lee Iacocca discussed a worldwide merger of Fiat's and Chrysler's passenger-car activities. Those talks were fruitless, and were broken off in November 1990.

Negotiations with representatives of the Wallenberg family over the sale of Saab Automobiles to Fiat Auto began in 1988, but ended in November 1989 when Wallenberg sold 50 per cent of Saab Automobiles to General Motors. In October 1989 Fiat Auto S.p.A. paid GEPI $105 million for a 49 per cent stake in Maserati. Agnelli secured the balance in 1994, and in 1998 Maserati was placed under Ferrari control.

Originally opposed to any deals with Japanese partners, Agnelli relented and in 1988 set up Fiat-Hitachi to make hydraulic excavators at San Mauro Torinese. In 1999 he approved a joint venture with Mitsubishi to produce a 4x4 sport-utility vehicle to be sold with both badges. Assembly was contracted out to Pininfarina Industrie SpA.

Fiat's farm-tractor division was merged with Fiat-Allis in 1985, and named Geotech. In 1992, when Fiat bought control of New Holland from Ford, it was merged with Fiat's agricultural and construction equipment division to form New Holland Geotech.

When he was 65, l'Avvocato told Fiat shareholders that he would retire at 70. In 1991, he said he would stay on, but that some day, his brother Umberto, 15 years younger, would take over. But in December 1993, Umberto resigned from Fiat to run the family's IFI and IFIL holding companies. When l'Avvocato retired on his 75th birthday, it was Cesare Romiti who was named Chairman of Fiat S.p.A. Romiti stepped down in June 1998, and Paolo Cantarella was named Chief Executive Officer of Fiat SpA.

Yet l'Avvocato never gave up his supreme authority. On the occasion of Fiat's 100-year celebrations, 11 July 1999, it was Gianni Agnelli who gave the keynote speech.

In 1953 he married Marella Caracciolo di Castagneto, daughter of Prince Filippo, Duke of Melito, and his wife, the former Margaret Clarke of Peoria, Illinois. They had one son, Edoardo and one daughter, Margherita.

JPN

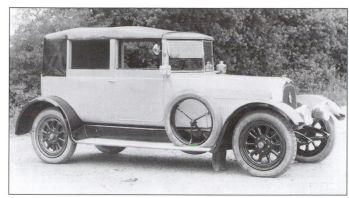

1921 Fiat (i) 510 20/30hp all-weather tourer, by Lanchester.
NATIONAL MOTOR MUSEUM

1922 Fiat (i) 501S tourer.
NATIONAL MOTOR MUSEUM

1927 Fiat (i) 509A 2-door saloon.
NATIONAL MOTOR MUSEUM

1000 were built in less than three years. This evolved into the IA; over 1300 being produced from 1912 to 1915. With the same engine in a smaller, lighter chassis, Fiat also produced 2041 Type Zero cars from 1912 to 1915.

From 1912 to 1920, total production of the 15/20hp Types 2A and 2B with a 2816cc 4-cylinder was 10,020 units. The big 3A with its 4396cc 4-cylinder engine was produced from 1912 to 1921, with a total production of 2150 units. Its third version, 3 Ter, was preferred by the military, and Fiat supplied 600 units in the 1912 to 1915 period.

There were 457 buyers for the 50/60hp Tipo 5, with a 9025cc 4-cylinder engine putting out 75bhp at 1000rpm. The same engine also went into the Tipo 6 – of which 86 were made.

1932 Fiat (i) Balilla coupé, by Pinin Farina.
NATIONAL MOTOR MUSEUM

1937 Fiat (i) 500 coupé.
NATIONAL MOTOR MUSEUM

1950 Fiat (i) 1400 saloon.
NATIONAL MOTOR MUSEUM

Production methods advanced, but did not keep pace with the rising demand. Production was increased mainly by taking on more workers. The payroll doubled, to 14,000 men from 1912 to 1920, while production tripled, to 12,000 cars. But change was coming. In April 1916 Fiat bought a 400,000m sq tract of open land in Turin, between Via Nizza and the railway tracks. Construction work began in March 1917, and car production at the Lingotto plant started in October 1923, with 6900 workers. By 1927 the 5-storey plant had capacity for 1200 cars a week, with 18,000 workers.

Production was organised by Ugo Gobbato. The stamping plant was on the ground floor, with some of the machine shops. The assembly lines occupied several floors, the complete cars coming off the belt on the top floor, going directly to the test track on the roof.

The first car made at Lingotto was the 501, designed by Carlo Cavalli and introduced in 1919. It was low-powered with its 1460cc 23bhp L-head engine, but it was a roomy car that found a ready clientele. Over a 7-year span, Fiat built 69,478 units. Fiat also made 42,421 Tipo 503 with the same 501 engine from 1926 to 1927.

Nearly 18,000 Fiat 505 with a 2296cc 4-cylinder engine were produced in Corso Dante from 1919 to 1925. It was replaced by the 507, built at the slow rate of 3701 units over a 2-year period. Over 13,500 Fiat 510, with a 3446cc 46bhp 6-cylinder engine, poured out of Corso Dante from 1919 to 1925, together with some 400 53bhp Type 510S. The 510 was replaced by the short-lived 512, taken out of production in 1928 after a run of 2583 cars.

1922 brought Agnelli an expensive lesson: it was not a good time for Fiat to enter the prestige-car market. No more than five Superfiats, Type 520, with a 6805cc ohv V12 engine, were built. Yet a slightly more modest 519, with a 4766cc ohv six, putting out 75–80bhp at 2600rpm, was kept in production from 1922 to 1927. This was also available as a high-performance 519S with lightweight frame and body, and a colonial 519C with heavy-duty suspension and higher ground clearance. Over 200 were produced.

The replacement for the 501 was the 509, first unveiled at the Paris Salon in October 1924, a compact economy car with a 990cc ohc engine rated at 22hp at an impressive 3400rpm. Cavalli directed the overall design of the 509, but the engine was the work of Bartolomeo Nebbia. Production began in the spring of 1925, and specifications were changed to 509A in 1926. In addition to the 509S and 509SM sports models, Fiat built 509 taxicab and commercial versions. When 509 production ended in 1929, over 90,000 units had been built. In 1928, about 55,000 cars were sold in Italy. That included 47,000 Fiat, 3000 Lancia, and 2000 Citroën. Though the 507 and the 512 had been disappointing for Agnelli, he could not give up his view of Fiat as a full-line car manufacturer. But Agnelli and his chief executive, Vittorio Valletta, lacked the self-confidence to pioneer Fiat concepts, opting instead for American inspiration. The 520, 521 and 525 had the architecture and styling of American cars. Shrewdly, Carlo Cavalli gave them smooth-running 6-cylinder engines, 2244cc in the 520, 2516cc in the 521, and 3739cc in the 525.

The Lingotto plant turned out over 20,000 each of the 520 (1927–29) and the 521 (1928–31), but the 525 had a slow start. Only 511 cars were made to the original specifications in 1928–29, but the 525 was redeemed by its modified issues. Over 2100 525S were produced from 1929 to 1931, in the same time span 1784 525N were built, plus a diminutive number of 525SS grand touring cars.

The 521 became the 522 in 1931, with the same 'old' looks, and the same 2516cc six was used in the 524. In spite of the depressed market, Fiat built over 6000 522 in the 1931–33 period. The 522S production run stopped at 732 cars. The 524, despite a styling remake in 1933, resulted in a 4-year total of only 2,275 units.

It became obvious that Fiat's growth could only be assured at the low-priced end of the market. The 514–styled like a miniature Oakland–replaced the 509 in 1929, powered by a 1438cc L-head engine, but only 36,970 units had been built by the end of 1932. There was also a 515, combining the 514 engine with the 522 body, but only 3405 units were made.

A major rethink was needed. Carlo Cavalli had been replaced by Tranquillo Zerbi in 1928, but Zerbi encountered inertia associated with mass production, and it took him some time to overcome it. In 1932 the 514 gave way to the 508 Balilla, with a new 995cc L-head engine in a traditional chassis designed by Emilio Martinotti (1892–1970). But the body looked as old as the 514. A restyling was ordered, and the 508B appeared in 1934, full of cues from Hudson, Studebaker, and Ford. Fiat built 41,395 units of the initial 508 and 72,769 of the restyled version from 1934 to 1937.

From a sales viewpoint, the Ardita series (4-cylinder 518 and 6-cylinder 527) were failures, but they were pleasant family cars that had the misfortune of being launched in a depressed market. Fiat made about 7500 518s and perhaps 1000 527 and 527S from 1933 to 1938, probably losing money on every one.

Dawn came with the 1500 which went into production in August 1935. Martinotti drew up a new chassis with cruciform frame and Dubonnet ifs. The styling concept came from Mario Revelli de Beaumont. The engine was a new ohv six of only 1493cc. Zerbi realised that streamlining would reduce the power requirement and fuel consumption, so that this model could serve as a replacement for the entire Ardita family. It was restyled more fashionably but less aerodynamically in 1939, and 42,500 cars were made from 1935 to 1948, more than 2800 1500E in 1948–49.

The 1500 set Fiat on a modern course, leading instead of following. The tiny 500, launched in the spring of 1936, confirmed the trend. The concept came from Antonio Fessia, who put Dante Giacosa in charge of the project. It made a lasting change in the small-car market, with its 570cc 4-cylinder engine mounted in the front overhang, ifs, and a pretty, eggshell-style 2-seater body. Fiat produced 122,000 of the initial version up to 1948, then 21,000 500B in 1948–49 and finally 376,370 restyled 500C from 1949 to 1955.

Fiat's leadership was again driven home by the 508C, arriving in 1937, styled like a shortened 1500, powered by an ohv 1089cc engine, with a frame based on that of the 500. It was a Giacosa creation, under Zerbi's responsibility, and a tremendous success. Fiat made over 250,000 of them in the opening 3-year period. Renamed 1100 (Millecento) in 1939, another 74,000 units were produced up to 1948. Its career ended with the 1100E, reaching an output of more than 58,000 from 1949 to 1953.

Fiat's biggest car since the 525N was taken out of production in 1931 was the 1938 Fiat 2800, styled like an overgrown 1500, with an 85hp 2852cc 6-cylinder engine. But due to the war, only 621 were made. As early as 1934 it was clear that Lingotto did not have enough capacity to meet future demand. Fiat began negotiating for the Mirafiori site, where construction work began in 1937. The entire production scheme was organised by Rambaldo Bruschi (1885–1966). But it did not become the main production centre for Fiat cars until after World War II.

From about 1950 Giacosa's attention was focussed on a replacement for the Fiat 500. Every possible engine and chassis configuration was designed, built and tested. Project 100, as it was known, went into production in 1955 as the

1955 Fiat (i) 600 saloon.
NATIONAL MOTOR MUSEUM

1957 Fiat (i) Nuova 500 roll-top saloon.
FIAT SPA

1971 Fiat (i) 127 hatchback.
NATIONAL MOTOR MUSEUM

Fiat 600, a 4-seater with a rear-mounted 4-cylinder water-cooled 633cc engine, a layout chosen purely on the basis of low manufacturing cost, not in the belief that it would make a better car. The van-style Multipla version appeared in 1956, and both were eminently successful in the market. Fiat 600 production lasted from 1955 to 1969, with a total output of 1,840,000 units.

The principles that guided Giacosa to the 600 were of paramount importance for an even smaller car, resulting in Project 110 appearing as the Fiat 'new' 500 in 1957, with a rear-mounted air-cooled horizontal parallel-twin. This was not

1983 Fiat (i) X1/9 sports car.
NATIONAL MOTOR MUSEUM

1991 Fiat (i) Tipo hatchback.
FIAT SPA

the initial success that Fiat expected, even with the addition of a 500 Sport in 1958 and a 500 Giardiniera (station wagon) in 1960. The 500 became the 500F in 1965, and 500R in 1972, while the 500 wagon was given to Autobianchi in 1968. Counting all types, 500 production exceeded 4 million units by the end of 1975.

From 1950 to 1959, Fiat restricted its model range to compact cars. The new family cars were called 1800 and 2100, powered by new sixes designed by Aurelio Lampredi. They were face-lifted in 1961, the 2100 being renamed 2300. There was also a Ghia-bodied 2300S coupé, built from 1961 to 1968. Total production of these cars came to approximately 186,000 units.

To fill the gap between the 1100 and the 1800, Fiat introduced the 1300 and 1500 saloons in 1961, sharing everything but the powertrains. Their 4-cylinder engines were basically the 1800/2100 sixes with two cylinders chopped off. Fiat produced about 600,000 of them over a 6-year time span.

The 1300 was replaced first, with the wide-track 124 in May 1966, a new car from the ground up. Its design and development were started by Vittorio Montanari and finished by Oscar Montabone. The 1500 was replaced in April 1967, by the 125 which sported a 1608cc twin-cam engine as standard. But it inherited the 1500 platform, updated by Angelo Mosso, and shared the doors and major body pressings with the 124.

The Fiat 124 saloon began life with a 1197cc engine. A Pininfarina-bodied 124 Spider appeared late in 1966, with a 1438cc version of the 125's twin-cam engine. That engine also powered the 124 coupé, launched in March 1967, and became optional in the 124 saloon in 1970.

The 124 Spider replaced the 1200 Cabriolet of 1959–63 and the 1500 and 1600S built from 1960 to 1963. Progressively bigger engines were offered, 1608cc, 1778cc and eventually 1997cc. Fiat made about 322,500 Spiders before giving it over to Pininfarina in 1982, who continued production with a PF badge. The 124 coupé reached a figure of nearly 280,000 units, its production run ending in 1975.

Over 4 million 124 saloons were produced in Italy and Fiat plants in other countries. The 125 was replaced by the 132 at the end of 1972, and the 121 succeeded the 124 in October 1974.

To fill the gap between the 600 and the 1100, Fiat introduced the 850 in 1964. Code-named 100G, it was closely related to the 600, with a more modern body and an 843cc engine, later increased to 903cc. Coupé and spider versions of the 850 were shown in Geneva in March 1965. The 850 spider was designed and produced by Bertone. The 850 station wagon was a boxy forward-control van,

produced from 1965 to 1975. Production of the 850 coach and coupé ended in 1971, the Spider being kept on for another year.

Fiat's growth could not be sustained without adding new plants, especially since Lingotto was scheduled for closing. The first of the new factories was Rivalta, which opened in 1968, immediately relieving Lingotto of assembling the 124 sports models and the Fiat Dino. Beginning in 1969, the Rivalta plant turned out vast numbers of the 128 and on a slow line, the 130. By 1971 the Rivalta plant had 16,000 workers and produced 2200cars daily.

The Dino was a sports model in the tradition of the 8V, a 1996cc V8 built from 1952 to 1954. Montanari had designed the 8V engine, and Fabio Rapi the body. One big difference was that the Dino V6 engine had a Ferrari pedigree. Fiat redesigned it and produced its own versions, first in 1987cc version, beginning in 1966, and from 1969 to 1972, a 2418cc version. Ettore Cordiano and Sergio Camuffo designed the Dino and 130 chassis. The Dino Spider was made by Pininfarina and the Dino coupé by Bertone.

The Fiat 130 was an attempt at the luxury car market, hitting the showrooms in 1969, on the heels of the look-alike Peugeot 604. Both sold in low figures, due to high prices and excessive fuel consumption. The Fiat 130 saloon was discontinued in 1971, but Pininfarina made a few hundred 130 coupé from 1971 to 1977.

Grandson of the founder, Giovanni (Gianni) Agnelli took over the chairman's seat from Valletta in 1968. He embraced Giacosa's plan to convert the entire Fiat line-up to front-wheel drive, and fell in with the government's plans to develop industry in the South of Italy. Fiat began construction work at Cassino (final assembly) and Termoli (engine plant) in 1970.

In 1972, Fiat had 14 basic models, a needless and wasteful spread, and started a $5 billion 5-year plan to rationalise the range. By 1982, there were only 5 basic models.

NICK BALDWIN

GIACOSA, DANTE (1905–1996)
Son of Piemontese parents, from Alba, he was born in Rome on 5 January 1905. He studied mechanical engineering and graduated from the Turin Polytechnic in 1927.

Almost immediately he found a position on the SPA engineering staff. Assigned to the military vehicle sector, he worked on the Pavesi P4 tractor, the CV-31 armoured vehicle, the Fiat 611 truck chassis, and the OM gun carrier.

After a brief spell in the enqine design office for passenger cars, he was transferred to the aircraft-engine office in June, 1932, where he was promoted to section head in November, 1932. His section worked on the Fiat A33 RC engine.

1998 Fiat (i) 20v Turbo coupé.
FIAT SPA

Early in 1935, Fessia involved Giacosa in his plans for a very small economy car. The initial version had front wheel drive, with a 500cc 4-cylinder water-cooled engine in the front overhang, and an ultra-simple rear suspension with quarter-elliptic springs. These features were retained for the production version, which had a live rear axle.

Once his chassis drawings were approved. he was named office manager of the automobile design department. He led the development of the 508C and became assistant director (under Fessia) of the Fiat automobile division from 1 January 1940.

He spent the war years mainly on aircraft-engine projects and preliminary studies for postwar cars and trucks. Beginning in 1944, he spent his spare time in drawing a small racing car chassis for Piero Ducamio (Cisitalia).

In 1945 Giacosa was named director of Fiat's technical projects division. In 1946 he instigated the 1100/103 protect and, with a view to replacing the 500, patented a powertrain layout with a transverse, horizontal 4-cylinder in-line engine mounted in the front overhang. driving the front wheels.

It was shelved while Giacosa turned instead to a rear-engine concept (600), but revived in 1961 when two events made Giacosa decide to adopt front-wheel-drive for most of Fiat's model range; first, the availability of low-cost constant-velocity universal joints, and second, the commercial success of the Austin/Morris Mini.

He also knew that the top management would not be ready to agree. He could not at that time get approval for a front-drive Fiat, but perhaps management would not forbid a front-drive Autobianchi. Working directly under Giacosa's eye. Ettore Cordiano designed the front-drive Autobianchi Primula, with a transversely mounted version of the Fiat 124 engine.

So intent was Giacosa on making a success of the Primula that he paid scant attention to the 124, its stablemate the 125, and their derivatives. He threw all his energy into developing smaller versions of the Primula, such as the Fiat 128, Fiat 127, and Autobianchi A-112, as well as the Primula's successor, the A-111. Enlarged versions were to follow when Lancia came into the Fiat fold, starting with the Lancia Beta in 1972.

Giacosa retired at the end of 1970, remaining as a consultant to the president's office and general management for another decade or more. Even in retirement. he stayed in his Turin apartment at No. 30 Viale Settimo Severo, where he died on 31 March 1996.

JPN

1998 Fiat (i) Barchetta LTD sports car.
FIAT SPA

1999 Fiat (i) Seicento Citymatic hatchback.
FIAT SPA

The first front-wheel drive Fiat was the 128, laid out by Giacosa and executed by Ettore Cordiano, launched in the spring of 1969 with a 1116cc single-ohc engine rated at 55bhp. This was the car Giacosa saw as the true replacement for the old 1100 (not the 124). In its first ten years, Fiat made more than 2.5 million 128s.

2000 Fiat (i) Multipla MPV.
FIAT SPA

2000 Fiat (i) Punto hatchback.
FIAT SPA

A smaller companion model, the 127, was launched in 1971, replacing the 850 and inheriting its 903cc engine. Produced in Italy, Spain, and Brazil, it hit the 5 million milestone by the end of 1981.

Cost considerations kept Fiat from making an immediate front-wheel drive successor to the 500. The 1972-model 126 continued the rear-mounted air-cooled twin, now 594cc capacity, in a neat looking body. Production was transferred to Poland in 1985.

Fiat also explored the centrally mounted engine in 2-seaters. Giuseppe Puleo created the X1/9 from 128 components, Bertone designed the body, and production began in 1972.

Giovanni Canavese was project manager for the Fiat 131, made as 2- and 4-door saloons and Estate wagons from October 1974, with 1297 and 1585cc single-ohc engines. Assembly was split between Mirafiori and Cassino.

In February 1978 twin-cam engines of 125 origin, with unchanged bore and stroke, replaced the earlier engines. Diesel engines became available in October 1978. From 1981 to 1984 a small series of Roots-blown 131 Abarth 2000 cars were made. The 132 was renamed Argenta in the spring of 1981, after turning out some 600,000 in a 9-year production run.

From 1975, Fiat's top priority became the development of a replacement for the 128, and Luigi Filtri was named project manager for the 138 and 136, which came on the market as the 1978 Ritmo and the 1983 Regata.

G. Puleo designed the chassis and the body came from Gianpaolo Boano at Fiat's styling centre. A Ritmo Diesel (designed by A. Lampredi) became optional in 1980. The 1116cc Ritmo Super 75 and 1498cc Ritmo Super 85 arrived in January 1981. The Ritmo was facelifted in September 1982 and again in May 1985. The 2 million production mark was passed at the end of March 1986. Ritmo assembly was split between Rivalta and Cassino, the Regata only at Cassino. The Lingotto plant was closed in 1986, its last car off the line being a Lancia Delta.

The Regata, though basically a notchback saloon version of the Ritmo, had the task of succeeding the 131. It was not a generational change; it was a conceptual change, like selling 128s to the traditional 1100 buyer. Still, 0.5 million units were built in the first three years.

Reducing the Ritmo definition to its very essence, Fiat came out with the low-cost Panda in 1980, a simple 2-box car with a choice of 652cc twin or 903cc 4-cylinder engines, offering vast versatility in a tiny package. Assembly was shared between Termini Imerese and the Desio plant (Autobianchi). In its first six years, Fiat produced 1,430,000 Pandas.

Vittorio Ghidella was the first chief executive of Fiat Auto S.p.A. which was founded on 1 January 1979. A mechanical engineer with a diploma from the Turin Polytechnic, he joined Fiat in 1955 and was production manager at Lingotto until 1963, when he was put in charge of RIV (ball bearings), returning

FIAT **THE 1100**L **TAXI**

1966 Fiat (ii) 1500 coupé.
ALVARO CASAL TATLOCK

to Fiat as director of passenger car production in 1978. He picked Paolo Scolari, a top engineer from Fiat-Allis (earth-moving equipment) to be his technical director, and gave him the task of replacing the old range of eight basically different car lines with a new range of just four platforms. The Uno replaced the 127 early in 1983; the Ritmo replaced the Argenta in 1985, the Tipo replaced the Ritmo in 1987; and the Tempra replaced the Regata in 1990. Made solely in Poland, the Cinquecento replaced the 126 in 1991.

The layout and packaging for all these cars were drawn up by an architect, Mario Maioli, who had joined Lancia in 1977 and was transferred to Fiat in 1980 to act as liaison officer between Fiat's styling centre and outside consultants. Ital Design provided the final designs for the Uno (146) and Croma (154) while the Tipo (160) and Tempra (159) were developed with I.DE.A. Institute.

An aggressive leader, Ghidella worked wonders for Fiat, but from 1985 on, there was increasing friction between him and the Fiat S.p.A. top management. Ghidella resigned on 25 November 1988, and his place was filled by Giorgio Garuzzo, who had led Iveco since 1984. At the end of 1990, Garuzzo was promoted general manager of Fiat S.p.A., and Paolo Cantarella became chief executive of Fiat Auto S.p.A. in February 1990, having joined Fiat in 1977 and worked in intersector industrial co-ordination, production systems, machine tools and robotics. At the end of 1995, he was called to a higher corporate office at Fiat S.p.A., opening the way for Roberto Testore, fresh from ten years at Comau (machine tools and robotics) who became chief executive of Fiat Auto S.p.A. on 1 January 1996. Born in Turin in 1952, he has a degree in mechanical engineering from Turin Polytechnic and joined Fiat's car sector in 1976.

The Uno was the best-selling car in Europe for years, but production was transferred to Poland late in 1993. The Panda is still in production but the big Croma was phased out in 1996.

The mass-market supermini class Fiat was the Punto, launched in 1993. It was made in 3- and 5-door models and, from 1994, as a cabriolet, with a range of five engines, from 1108cc (54bhp) to 1372cc (131bhp). A 5-speed gearbox was standard, with an optional 6-speed on the 1.1-litre model, and a 7-speed sequential box on the new Punto for 2000.

The Tipo was replaced by the Bravo/Brava (182) in August 1995. They were prepared in a record low-lead time of 36 months, under the direction of Mauro Bene, who had been with Alfa Romeo until 1986 (and was transferred to Ferrari in 1997). The chassis was developed by Renzo Porro, who had joined Fiat in 1962 as a test engineer.

The Bravo and the Brava share the 100in (2538mm) wheelbase, but the 2-door Bravo is only 158in (4025mm) in overall length, compared with 165in (4190mm) for the 4-door Brava. Their common engine line-up includes a 1370cc single-ohc engine with three valves per cylinder, 4-cylinder twin-ohc units of 1581 and 1747cc, a 5-cylinder 1998cc unit with twin-ohc, plus a 1929cc 4-cylinder diesel engine. They are assembled at the Cassino and Rivalta plants.

Nevio di Giusto became head of Fiat's styling centre in 1991, having joined Fiat in 1978, served as head of wind tunnel testing at Orbassano from 1979 to 1982, planned the architecture of future models from 1982 to 1985, and then directed body design and engineering for Lancia for six years.

Giuseppe Perlo, vice president of product since 1990, brought niche-market cars back to the Fiat range, beginning with the Fiat Coupé in 1993, Barchetta in 1995 and the Multipla in 1998. He had gone to work for Fiat at the age of

16, but his quick mind was soon spotted, and Fiat sent him to the Massachusetts Institute of Technology to study economics and business administration. He became marketing manager for Fiat Auto, and platform manager for the Lancia Thema and Fiat Croma in 1982–87.

The Coupé and Barchetta catered for the sporting market; the former was based on the Tipo and used a 16-valve 1747cc engine in normally-aspirated or turbocharged form, and from 1996 a 1998cc 3-cylinder unit. The Barchetta was an open 2-seater in the Mazda MX5/MGF class, based on the Punto and with a 1747cc engine.

The Multipla was an individually-styled 6-seater MPV with a short bonnet and a 1581cc petrol or 1910cc common-rail diesel engine.

The Fiat Marea (185), saloon and Weekend wagon, were launched in July 1996, replacing the Tempra and the Croma. The project manager was Renzo Porro, and Alessandro Piccone directed the engine design and line-up. It is assembled at Mirafiori which has a daily capacity for 650 Marea.

JPN

Further Reading
1899 Fiat 1999, Riccardo P. Felicioli, Automobilia, Milano, 1999.
Giovanni Agnelli, Valerio Castronovo, Unione Tipografico-Editrice Torinese, Torino, 1971.
50 years of Design with Fiat, Dante Giacosa, Automobilia, Milano, 1979.
Catalogo Bolaffi delle Fiat, Giulio Bolaffi Editore, Torino, 1970.
Fiat, Michael Sedgwick, Batsford, 1974.
Fiat and Lancia Twin Cams. A Collectors Guide, Phil Ward,
Motor Racing Publications, 1992.
Fiat XI/9, A Collectors Guide, Phil Ward, Motor Racing Publications, 1994.
Baby Fiats, Dave Randle, Sutton Publishing 2000.

FIAT (ii) (RA) 1960 to date

Fiat-Concord SAIC, Buenos Aires.

In 1919 Fiat started selling their automobiles in Buenos Aires, and in 1923 Fiat Argentina SA was established. However, local vehicle production had to wait until 1960, when the Argentine government laid out the rules for motor-vehicle production. They started producing the Fiat 600, Fiat 1100 and Fiat 2100 models. The 2100 was dropped after only 192 had been made, but the 1100 lasted until 1963, by which time 23,125 had been produced. The 600 continued to be Fiat's best-seller in Argentina for many years. By 1971 166,803 had been made and production continued until 1982, well after the Italian version of the 600 had given its last bow. The final series, known as 600S was powered by an 843cc engine.

In 1963 the Fiat 1500 was introduced, and in 1971, the Type 128. The 1500 was superseded by the 125 in 1973. There were 4-door sedan, station wagon, and sports versions. The 125 was produced until 1985. The 128 was discontinued in 1984.

The Spazio came in 1985, and was discontinued in 1996. The Duna was introduced in 1988 with a 1.3-litre petrol engine, which was superseded by the 1.7-litre engine in 1994. While station wagons and most other versions of the Duna were discontinued in 1996, the Duna SDL/CSD with 1.7-litre petrol engine was in production until 1997 and the Duna CS with 1697cc diesel engine was still being made in 1999, mainly for taxicab use. The Tempra 2-litre, lasted only from 1992 to 1996, but the Uno is particulary notable for its longevity. The 2-door sedan was introduced in 1985 and this model was still being made in 1999, also in a 4-door version. The Siena 4-door sedan was built from 1998 with 1580cc petrol engine or 1697cc diesel engine.

ACT

FIAT (iii) (NZ) 1973

Torino Motors Ltd, Auckland, North Island.

A special version of the 125 series assembled in New Zealand, the 125 T was the finale for its type, being aimed at production car racing. Fitted with a revised cylinder head, Scorpion camshafts obtained from South Africa and two Dellorto carburettors, it was the highest performing 4-cylinder car then to have come off local assembly lines. It was lowered 50mm, had a larger fuel tank and reduced luggage space, the wheels were locally made of alloy with wide rims, and it was distinguished visually by a matt-black grill and tail panels which carried a 125 T badge.

MG

FIAT (iv) (BR) 1976 to date

Fiat Automoveis SA, Betim.

Fiat's Brazilian factories have produced a variety of the well-known Italian models, including the 127, Uno, Tempra, and Punto, and also a number of models peculiar to the country. These included the 147, a 127 with 1049cc single-ohc engine, and a booted saloon and estate car versions of the Uno (Premio and Elba, respectively). Practically all the engines for these cars came from Fiat's factory in Argentina. In 1996 came the Palio, envisaged as a 'world car'. First made in Brazil, it was made in Argentina and Poland from 1997, while later planned production sites included Venezuela, South Africa, Egypt, Turkey, Russia, and Viet Nam. It was made in 3- and 5-door hatchback models, and as a 4-door saloon (the Siena) and estate car (the Weekend). Engines included 994, 1241, 1372, 1497, and 1581cc, the latter with twin-ohc and 16 valves. There was also a 1698cc turbo diesel. In 1998 the parent firm made a major investment in the Brazilian enterprise for production of the Marea at the rate of 4000 to 5000 per month.

NG

FIAT (v) (GR) 1970s–1980s

Auto Industrie Hellenica, Thiva.

The Greek arm of Fiat made two models especially for the local market during the late 1970s and early 1980s. The Poker was a Fissore-styled open utility/ leisure car based on a Fiat 126, while the Amico was a licence-built version of the FISSORE Scout.

CR

FIAT-BREVETTI (I) 1905–1912

1905–1912 Officine Meccaniche Ansaldi, Via Cuneo, Turin.

One of Piedmont's leading industrialists, Cavaliere Michele Ansaldi, had no part in Italy's auto industry until he decided, in 1904, to build cars. The company was established on 7 March 1905, with a capital stock of 850,000 Lire, 55 per cent held by Cav. Michele Ansaldi, and 45 per cent held by FIAT which provided technical assistance. The first Fiat-Ansaldi was a 10/12hp model with a 4-cylinder T-head engine, 3-speed gearbox and chain drive.

FIAT held a patent by Cesare Momo for a shaft-driven rear axle with torque tube, and wanted to field-test it before fitting it on Fiat cars. From 1906 onwards, all Fiat-Brevetti cars were shaft-driven, starting with the 15/25hp 3053cc 4-cylinder Tipo 2.

At the time, Fiat produced chassis only, but Fiat-Brevetti made complete cars at a rate of 500 units a year. They were designed by Alfredo Rostain, technical director of Societa Brevetti Fiat (and not by Momo who left Fiat in 1906 to work for Cantieri Aeronautici Ansaldo, makers of the SVA biplane, as an engine designer).

In 1908 Ansaldi began investing substantially in S.P.A. of Turin and sold his Fiat-Brevetti shares to Fiat, who continued car production at a slower rate in the Via Cuneo plant until the end of 1912. Approximately 1600 Fiat-Brevetti cars were built. During those years, shaft drive and torque tube were adopted for most new Fiat models. Having served its purpose, the Fiat-Brevetti car was discontinued and that factory handed over to Fiat Grandi Motori for production of marine diesel engines.

JPN

FIAT HISPANIA see HISPANO-GUADALAJARA

FIBERFAB (i) (US) c.1964–1996

Fiberfab, Sunnyvale, California; Fiberfab Division of Velocidad, Santa Clara, California; FiberFab, Boca Raton, Florida.

This company was one of the longest surviving kit car companies. It started out selling a range of kit car bodies, one of which resembled the Ford Cougar II show car. Their first big success was the Aztec, which came out in 1964. It was a low, angular coupé with hints of Lola GT, Ford GT-40 and Porsche 904 in the styling. It bolted to a Volkswagen Beetle floorpan and the roof and door area hinged up from the front to allow entrance to the cockpit. In 1965 Fiberfab added a special frame to take Corvair or Porsche running gear. A convertible version, the Azteca, appeared in 1965. The same basic body was cleaned up and fitted with a longer nose in late 1965 to become the Aztec II. It was replaced in 1967 by the Avenger, which was a more rounded interpretation of the Ford GT-40. It was a huge success, leading to special frames that accommodated Corvair running gear. The Valkyrie was an Avenger body with a steel tube frame

1999 Fiat (iv) Palio Weekend estate car.
FIAT SPA

1964 Fiberfab (i) Aztec 7 coupé.
HAROLD PACE

c.1968 Fiberfab (i) Valkyrie with Chevrolet V8 engine.
HAROLD PACE

mounting a Chevrolet V8 and modified Corvair transaxle. It was sold in kit and turnkey form. Another early kit was the Caribee, which was a front-engined coupé with gull-wing doors to fit on English sports car chassis like MG and Triumph. In 1968 it was replaced by the Jamaican, a very attractive coupé that fitted the same chassis as well as the VW. A V8 powered version was sold with a simple ladder frame. One of their most attractive kits was the Centurion, a replica of the Bill Mitchell-designed Corvette Sting Ray prototype. It fitted on early Corvette chassis. They also made a dune buggy kit called the Vagabond, a 3-wheeler and a 1930s Aston-Martin tourer replica called the Liberty SLR. One of their last designs was the Aztec 7, a VW-based kit that was inspired by the Bertone designed Alfa Carabo show car. Fiberfab was taken over by CLASSIC MOTOR CARRIAGES in the 1980s, relocated to Florida and dropped their old line of cars. Afterwards they produced variations on CMC designs like the Porsche Speedster, Cobra, MG-TD, 1933 Ford and 1934 Ford replicas and the Gazelle, a pseudo-Mercedes neoclassic design. Along with CMC, they were closed down by legal authorities in 1996.

HP

FIBERFAB (ii) (D) 1966–c.1982
1966–1973 Fiberfab-Karosserie, Ditzingen bei Stuttgart.
1974–c.1982 Fiberfab-Karosserie, Auenstein bei Heilbronn.
Like FIBERFAB (i), with whom they were originally associated, Fiberfab started by producing Volkswagen-based coupés. In 1975 they introduced the Sherpa, an open Jeep-type vehicle using Citroën 2CV engine and running gear.
NG

FIBERGLASS FABRICATORS (US) c.1986
Fiberglass Fabricators, Tucson, Arizona.
The Mark-1-41 was a fibreglass-bodied kit car that resembled a downsized 1941 Lincoln Continental convertible. It fitted on a full-length Volkswagen chassis. A hardtop was an optional extra. They were sold in kit or completed form.
HP

FIBERGLASS SPECIALTIES (US) c.1986
Fiberglass Specialties, Montgomery, Texas.
The James/Stone Speedster was an unusual kit that attempted to convert a Volkswagen Karmann Ghia into a Cobra replica. The nose clip bonded to the Ghia front end and two rear mudguard flares completed the trick, but not too convincingly.
HP

FIBER-JET (US) c.1994 to date
Fiber-Jet Industries, Roseville, California.
This company made a wide range of dune buggy bodies for the Volkswagen Beetle floorpan, as well as some other kit cars. In addition to conventional buggy bodies, their Super T kit resembled a Model T Ford and a stripped-down off-road buggy called the Sand Hopper. Other buggies were called the Enos 500, Cobra Buggy, Rough Terrain and Beach Comber. The Premier and Brauossa were rebody kits that gave Porsche 914s a quasi-Ferrari Testarossa look. The Fiber Jet 59 was a Porsche 959 replica that fitted on a Porsche 911 or 912 chassis. The Chop Top was a fibreglass VW Beetle body with a chopped, or lowered, top that bolted to a VW Beetle chassis.
HP

FIBERJET *see* TOTEM

FIBERSPORT (US) 1953–1955
John C. Mays, Towanda, Illinois.
Originally just a glassfibre body to mount on a Crosley chassis, later models used Mays' own tubular frame.
NG

FIBRE TECH (ZA) c.1988–1993
This company produced two kit designs. The first was the Badger, a VW Beetle-based Jeep CJ2 replica. Around 30 kits per year were supplied. The second model was the Rhino, an accurate replica of the Word War II Willy's CJ2 Army Jeep based on the Toyota Hilux pick-up in either 4×2 or 4×4 forms.
CR

FIBREGLASS DESIGNS (ZA) 1990s
Fibreglass Designs, Edenvale, Johannesburg.
The mainstay of this company was the Kango range of beach buggies and fun cars (indeed the company started trading as Kango Cars), but it also produced a variety of other vehicles. These included the Veep (a Jeep lookalike), Model T Ford bodies and the Beetle-based Van Wagon and Jirah estate. The Silhouette was an originally styled leisure vehicle using its own chassis designed for VW Golf power.
CR

FIBROMIRELI *see* MIRELI

FIDELIA (i) (F) 1905–1906
Voitures Fidelia, Angers, Maine-et-Loire.
The Fidelia was one of a crop of short-lived steam cars which appeared in France and England when the steamer was rapidly losing popularity everywhere. Like its contemporaries, the AUTO VAPEUR and WEYHER & RICHEMOND, it had a bonnet and condenser which gave it the appearance of a petrol car. It resembled one even more closely than its rivals, for under the bonnet was a vertical 4-cylinder engine, it had a leather cone clutch to allow the engine to run free when required, and shaft drive to the rear axle. The rear-mounted boiler was of Serpollet type.
NG

FIDELIA (ii) (US) 1914
J.H. Sizelan Co., Findlay, Ohio.
This was a typical light cyclecar with 10hp 2-cylinder De Luxe engine, friction transmission and final drive by a long belt. The hammock-like seats were in tandem, and the car had a single cyclops headlamp.
NG

FIDELIO *see* EHRHARDT

FIDES (I) 1905–1911
1905–1908 Fides Fabbrica Automobili Marca Brasier, Turin.
1908–1911 Fides Fabbrica Automobili Brevetti Enrico, Turin.
The Fides began as a licence-built BRASIER, but in 1908 former Fiat chief engineer Giovanni Enrico joined the company, added his name and designed two 4-cylinder side-valve engined cars which were made in small numbers. He also continued experiments with the oil-pressure-operated gear change which he had tried while at Fiat. The company was liquidated in 1911 and the factory was acquired by Lancia.
NG

FIEDLER (D) 1899–1900
Berliner Elektromobil und Acculatoren-GmbH, Berlin.
This company made electric vans, but also produced a few private cars for town use.
HON

FIELD (US) 1910–1911
Field Automobile Manufacturing Co., Lincoln, Nebraska.
This was a conventional 5-seater tourer powered by a 30/35hp 4-cylinder Continental engine. A price of $1500 was set, but very few were made.
NG

FIELDBAY *see* MAGNUM

FIELDMOUSE (GB) 1971–1972
This was an obscure Jeep-style vehicle with a steel body, designed for a Ford Popular chassis.
CR

FIERO FACTORY (GB) 1993 to date
The Fiero Factory Ltd, Birmingham, West Midlands.
From 1991, this company began importing and servicing Pontiac Fieros to Britain and went on to offer replacement body kits for the plastic-bodied Fiero from 1993. The Fierossa was the first: a fairly mild bodykit which was vaguely reminiscent of a Ferrari Testarossa. Other styles were the 308 Monza (a Ferrari 308GTB replica), Fiero F40 (another Ferrari lookalike) and the F282 (resembling the Ferrari F355). In all cases, the Fiero's plastic panels were removed, leaving the monocoque chassis entirely intact. Another product offered from 1995 was the Venom, an American-made Dodge Viper lookalike kit for Ford Granada or Chevrolet Corvette parts, while a new departure in 1998 was the Euro 427 Cobra replica using the Venom chassis with Ford Sierra donor components.
CR

FIERRO (US) 1982 to date
Joe Fierro, Diamond Bar, California.
No relation to the Pontiac product with a similar name (which it preceded), the Fierro was a kit car built by Joe Fierro. It was an attractive sports coupé based on the VW Beetle floorpan and running gear. Some were equipped with Mazda rotary engines and all were sold in kit form.
HP

F.I.F. (B) 1909–1914

Automobiles F.I.F., Etterbeek, Brussels.

This company was founded by a Luxembourg businessman, Felix Heck. He made mostly light cars in a variety of engine sizes, all with four cylinders, starting with a 10/12CV of 1592cc in 1909. The 1910 range included two larger models, the 2120cc 12/14CV and 2649cc 15/18CV. He entered several competitions without great success; for the 1911 Coupe des Voitures Legères he used an ohv engine of 2950cc. This was the largest to be employed in an F.I.F. and powered the 1912 18CV touring model. By then the smallest model was the 1460cc 8/10CV, which was probably a Fondu-built engine. All the engines had monobloc construction and Bosch magneto ignition.

The 1913 range included the smallest engine used in any F.I.F., the 1130cc 7/12CV; there was also a 1846cc 8/16CV. Both of these cars had attractive vee-radiators, and were made up to the war. Felix Heck (or Hecq in French spelling, which he used after the war) did not continue with complete cars after the armistice, but in the 1920s he made special-bodied Model T Fords under the name Lux Sport.

NG

FIGARI (I) 1925–1926

Gian Vittorio Figari and Prof. Francesco Bonavoglia of the Milan Polytechnic built an advanced small car with 840cc supercharged 4-cylinder 2-stroke engine which was said to develop 30bhp. There were plans to make the car at Monza, but the partners could not raise the necessary finance, and probably only the one prototype was made.

NG

FIGINI (I) 1900–c.1907

Ditta Luigi Figini & Compagnia, Milan.

Figini & Latta were among the earliest producers of motorcycles in Italy, making their first in 1898. They also made a few cars from time to time, starting with a single-cylinder voiturette and progressing to twins and fours. They were only a sideline to the 2-wheelers, which were made until 1910.

NG

FILIPINETTI (CH) 1967–1973

Georges Filipinetti, Grandson.

After completing his engineering studies in Germany, Georges Filipinetti (1907–1973) worked for Chrysler and Bugatti before entering his father's business. They were importers of Ferrari, and owned the Chateau de Grandson, including the motor museum. In 1962 he founded the Scuderia Filipinetti, for which Jo Siffert, Nino Vacarella, Mike Parkes and others raced. Franco SBARRO began working for him in 1963 and it was he who designed the Filipinetti 2+2 sports coupé with a fibreglass body. It had a tuned VW flat-four engine of 1584cc delivering 70bhp. Servo-assisted brakes had discs in front and drums in the rear. Top speed was about 110mph (177km/h). Two prototypes were completed in 1967 but regular production did not start. In 1972 a development of the FIAT 128 was exhibited at the Geneva Show and sports-racing versions with speeds of up to 135mph (217km/h) were announced. One year later a tuned version of the FIAT X1/9 with 190bhp was presented but, when Georges Filipinetti died, the plans to build 100 cars did not materialise.

FH

FILOQUE (F) 1902

FiloquePère, Bourgtheroulde, Eure.

This company advertised a 6/8hp voiturette, as well as 4-cylinder cars of 10, 15, and 20hp. It is not known how many were actually made.

NG

FILTZ (F) c.1899–c.1903

Sté des Moteurs et Voitures Automobiles Filtz, Neuilly, Seine.

The Filtz name was best-known for proprietary engines which were supplied to several car makers, notably TURGAN-FOY. However a Filtz car was shown at the 1899 Paris Salon. In 1902 there was a Filtz racing car with a 30hp 4-cylinder engine.

NG

F.I.M. (I) 1974–c.1980

Fabbrica Italiana Macchine srl, Angri, Salerno.

The Chihahua was a very small fibreglass-bodied 3-wheeler saloon or convertible with styling that was as comical as its name. Three engines were offered: a 50cc Morini, a 125cc BCB 4-stroke and a 250cc 2-stroke; in the latter case a top speed of 50mph was quoted.

CR

F.I.M.E.R. (I) 1947–1948

Fabbrica Italiana Motoveicoli e Rimorchi, Milan.

F.I.M.E.R. joined the ranks of immediate postwar microcar makers with the Superveturetta roadster. In prototype form it was doorless but the production version was redesigned with 'suicide' doors. A 7bhp 250cc 2-stroke twin was mounted in the tail driving through a 3-speed gearbox, the rear wheels being more narrow-set than the front pair. A lack of finance prevented a serious production run, although it is believed that some cars were built.

CR

FINAL CONCEPT (US) 1996 to date

Final Concept Inc., Port Charlotte, Florida.

Final Concept downsized the Lamborghini Countach shape to fit the Fiero chassis to make their Final Vision 2000 kit car. The Fiero chassis was reinforced and power train options included Chevrolet V8 engines on Pontiac, Oldsmobile or Cadillac transaxles. It was sold in kit or completed form.

HP

FINA-SPORT (US) c.1953

Perry B. Fina, New York, New York.

This sports-touring car was built for New York import car dealer Perry B. Fina. The body was styled by Vignale and it was built on a custom Ford-based chassis with a 210hp Cadillac V8. The appearance was similar to some Vignale-bodied Ferraris of the period. With a 115in (2919mm) wheelbase it was a large car and carried three passengers in the front seat and two in the back. Price in 1952 was a healthy $9800 and there was a 5-month delivery wait. Specifications were up to the customer and each car was expected to be different. Several were built, including one that had a Chrysler V8.

HP

FINCH LIMITED *see* PUNGS-FINCH

FINDLAY (US) 1910

Findlay Carriage Co., Findlay, Ohio.

This horse-drawn vehicle builder planned to enter car production with a 40hp 4-cylinder tourer, to sell for $2500. This was not a particularly high price for a large car, but few, if any, buyers came forward. The company continued to make carriages, and a handful of motor hearses, up to 1916 when the factory was destroyed by fire.

NG

FINE CAR STORE (US) c.1994 to date

Fine Car Store, San Diego, California.

This company sold high-quality, authentic reproductions of 1950s sports-racing cars. Their D-Type Jaguar and Aston-Martin DBR2 replicas were made in New Zealand by Tempero Coach. They used correct-specification engines and aluminium bodies. The Aston-Martin replica cost just under $200,000 in 1994, and they also sold expensive replicas of Ferrari racing cars.

HP

FINLAYSON (AUS) 1900–1904

Finlayson Bros & Co. Pty Ltd, Devonport, Tasmania.

This firm was a major foundry and engineering works which made a steam car for its own use. Under the seats it had a kerosene burning boiler which supplied a 2-cylinder, 6hp engine. As there was no condenser, the water consumption was high. Chain final drive, green-hide band brakes, 4-seater cedar bodywork and a claimed performance of 20mph (32km/h) were other features. Following a period of use, the engine was put to work in the factory and the remainder of the vehicle was stored in a loft, from which it was retrieved in 1960 and restored.

1902 Firefly 6hp tonneau.
NATIONAL MOTOR MUSEUM

1909 Firestone-Columbus high-wheel buggy.
NATIONAL MOTOR MUSEUM

A 2-cylinder 9hp petrol car was made later but automotive activity was concentrated, until about 1908, on the construction of several Gnome-engined buses for local operators. In 1964 the steam car led the procession at the opening ceremony of Hobart's Tasman bridge.

MG

FINOLA (GB) 1904

L.J. O'Higgins, Dublin.
Little is known of this car apart from an advertisement in the *Irish Motor News* in June 1904 for a 6hp light car with genuine De Dion engine, offered as a 2-seater at £147 and a 4-seater at £165. O'Higgins' business was described as the Central Automotor Agency and Garage, so the cars may have been made elsewhere. Possibly they were yet another product of Lacoste et Battmann.

NG

FIORE (I) 1974–1975

Fiore SpA, Naples.
This Fiat conversion company – which had nothing to do with the stylist Trevor Fiore – also presented at the 1974 Turin Show the Gipsy, an open 4-seater leisure vehicle based on the Fiat 127.

CR

FIORETTI (I) 1978–1981

Autofioretti srl, Rome.
The Fioretti F50 (also known as the Hallo) was a short-lived 3-wheeled microcar with a utilitarian fibreglass body. Its mechanical specification featured hydromechanical brakes, a 4-speed gearbox, and a 50cc Vespa engine driving the single front wheel.

CR

FIRE AERO (US) c.1985

Industrial Design Research, Laguna Beach, California.
This aerodynamic 3-wheeled coupé was based on a 750cc motorcycle engine and running gear. Volkswagen front suspension was used with Chevrolet steering, and a complete motorcycle engine and suspension was bolted on at the rear. The Fire Aero was designed by David Stollery of INDUSTRIAL DESIGN RESEARCH, who also designed the TRIHAWK.

HP

FIREFLY (GB) 1902–1904

Firefly Motor & Engineering Co. Ltd, Croydon, Surrey.
The Firefly company began by making shaft-driven light cars powered by 6hp Aster or De Dion-Bouton engines. They sold only in small numbers, and Firefly decided that commercial vehicles were a better proposition. However, a few more cars were made up to 1904, including larger models with chain drive and 9 or 12hp 2-cylinder Herald engines. The biggest were 16 and 24hp cars with 4-cylinder engines. Firefly also made the ingenious Firefly Portable Auto-Elevator, which lifted heavy loads from the ground to the floor level of the vehicle, using either manual or engine power. One of the directors of Firefly was William Glass, later famous for the motor trade bible, *Glasses Guide*.

NG

FIRESTONE-COLUMBUS (US) 1909–1915

1909–1914 Columbus Buggy Co., Columbus, Ohio.
1914–1915 New Columbus Buggy Co., Columbus, Ohio.
This company had built electric cars and high-wheelers under the Columbus name from 1903 and 1907 respectively, and when a proper car with conventional sized wheels was introduced for 1909 it took the name of the company president, Clinton DeWitt Firestone. For 1909 the Firestone-Columbus was made in only one body style, a 'Baby Tonneau' or small tourer, on a 110in (2791mm) wheelbase, with a 35hp 4-cylinder engine. Thereafter the range was extended to include runabouts, limousines and a 'family car', on wheelbases up to 130in (3299mm) and with a variety of 4-cylinder engines from 20/25 to 45hp. The company shunned annual model changes, saying that the directors met at nine o'clock every morning, and any changes thought necessary were put in hand immediately. These included a 60hp 6-cylinder car for 1913. The company went bankrupt that year and was reorganised under a new name and under the control of Charles A. Finnegan of the E.R. THOMAS Co. There were rumours that the Thomas Flyer might be built in Ohio, but this did not happen and in May 1915 the factory was sold, ending production of the Columbus Electric and Firestone-Columbus cars.

NG

FISCHER (i) (D) 1902–1905

Fischer & Co., Pfälzische Motoren- und Automobilfabrik, Hassloch/Pfalz.
This company made a few light cars using many bicycle components and a Fafnir engine.

HON

FISCHER (ii) (CH) 1908–1914

1908–1910 Fischer Wagen AG, Zürich.
1910–1914 Automobilfabrik Brunau, Zürich.
Martin Fischer (1866–1947), having worked for four years with Paul Vorbrodt to produce TURICUM cars, left to start his own company in 1908. With the help of some workers that followed Fischer, the first new car, a 14/16hp with a 4-cylinder engine and conserving the friction-disk transmission and chain final drive was completed. It was in fact a close copy of the Turicum. Production was taken up by Weidmann & Co., Zürich. The 4-cylinder side-valve engine of 2009cc capacity, later increased to 2544cc and 2609cc, was mounted into a conventional chassis with friction transmission which allowed a gradual change of speed without a clutch. The complete car with torpedo body cost SFr 6500 and in 1909–10 some 70 cars were completed and sold. Finances were provided by a wealthy silk dealer and this enabled Fischer to develop new models and to rent part of the Weidmann factory. In 1911 Fischer launched his new sleeve-valve 4-cylinder engine, which had two shafts with elliptic curves in the sump actuating crescent-shaped sleeves on either side of the cylinders. Another novelty was the special 4-speed gearbox with internal gearing, which was said to contain

at least 50 per cent less parts than any standard gearbox. Both inventions were patented. The engine of 2722cc delivered 35bhp. The sale price was SFr9500 and at the Berlin Auto Show of 1911, the car was well received.

Production in 1911–13 was nearly 200 cars, most of which were sold to Germany, Great Britain and Brazil. DELAUGERE, CLAYETTE Frères & Co. had taken the licence for the Fischer cars for France and exhibited at the Paris Show of 1913 a 24PS chassis and as well as a new type of touring body by Gangloff, Geneva with a hard-top, which had been built by Bazelaire. One year later Fischer made two 6-cylinder cars, their sleeve-valve engine having the same dimensions as the four for a capacity of 4084cc and supplying 40bhp at 2000rpm. Various US manufacturers were interested in the new engine and offered Fischer a position in their plants. However, he decided to sign a licence agreement with MONDEX-MAGIC of New York, through which 40 and 60hp versions built by PALMER-SINGER, of Long Island City, New York, were offered at $4500 and $6500 respectively in 1914–15. The outbreak of World War I forced the closing of the factory in Switzerland.

By 1919, Swiss statistics show 89 Fischer cars on the roads. Martin Fischer, who had continued his studies and designs of cars, proposed a cycle car with tandem seats to SIG Schweizerische Industrie Gesellschaft, Neuhausen. This had a MAG V2 motorcycle engine and friction drive, but after some prototypes were built the project was cancelled. A German company is said to have bought the licence rights of a new sleeve-valve engine but no production resulted. Martin Fischer died in 1947, aged 81. A Fischer chassis and tourer of 1912–13 are conserved by the Swiss Transport Museum in Lucerne.

FH

FISCHER (iii) (D) 1912–1913

Westautohaus Alex Fischer & Co., Berlin.

This dealer made light electric vans and also offered a passenger car version, but very few were made. Fischer was later associated with AAA and ALFI.

HON

FISCHER-DETROIT (US) 1914

The C.J. Fischer Co., Detroit, Michigan.

This was a light car powered by a 1.6-litre 4-cylinder Perkins engine, with 3-speed gearbox and shaft drive. It was offered in three models of 2-seater – speedster, tourist, and cabriolet – and also as a 4-seater sedan, the latter at the quite reasonable price of $845. In November 1914 there were plans to move to York, Pennsylvania, but production never started there.

NG

FISHER (i) (CDN) 1914–1915

Fisher Motor Car Co. Ltd, Walkerville, Ontario.

This company was formed to take over production of the TUDHOPE, which failed in the summer of 1913. By early 1914 the Fisher company, headed by ex-Canadian Studebaker manager Frank E. Fisher, was assembling cars of Tudhope design and selling them under the Fisher name. These were the 4-36 and 6-48, and were made in the Tudhope factory at Orillia, Ontario, although there were plans to build a large new factory at Walkerville. This never came about, and once the stock of Tudhope components had been used up, the 'manufacture' of Fishers came to an end. The factory was used for war work until 1918, and survived as a small scale supplier of automotive accessories up to 1928.

NG

FISHER (ii) see SYLVA

FISSON (F) c.1896–1898

L. Fisson, Paris.

Louis Fisson was among the first generation of car manufacturers in Paris, operating from a workshop at 14 rue Maublanc in the 14th Arrondissement, to the south of the city. He built at least two distinct types, one fairly closely based on the Benz, with rear-mounted engine, and the other with a vertical 2-cylinder engine of 2920cc at the front, driving through a 4-speed gearbox (with reverse available for all four speeds), and double-chain drive. Although a more up-to-date car on Panhard lines, it still retained three Benz features, lhd drive, a pot-type surface carburettor, and two levers for selecting the gears. The frame was of armoured wood, and the body on a surviving car dated 1898 is a rear-

1913 Fischer (ii) SS 10/33CV landaulet.
ERNST SCHMID

1913 Fischer (ii) SS 10/33CV tourer.
ERNST SCHMID

entrance waggonette, described as a Ralli cart. A single car was exhibited at the Paris Salon in December 1898, but few cars were made, and Louis Fisson disappeared from the motoring scene soon afterwards.

NG

FISSORE (I) 1971–1982

Fissore, Savigliano, Cuneo.

This famous coachbuilder, founded in 1936, also produced one vehicle that was listed as a regular production model. This was the Scout (initially launched as the Gipsy), a simple leisure vehicle first seen in 1971 and based on Fiat 127 mechanicals. It was designed by Franco Maina and production output reached as high as 180 units per month. Licensed Scout production was carried out in Spain by Emelba as the Samba and in Greece as the Amico. The Scout was still being made as late as 1982.

CR

FITCH (i) (US) 1949

Sport and Utility Motors, White Plains, New York.

Champion racing driver John Fitch built two prototypes for a line of sports cars early in his career. The Fitch Model A was built in his engineering shop, and the lessons learned were applied to the Type B. In order to keep prices low, production parts were used throughout. The chassis was a modified Fiat 1000 with a restyled Crosley Hot Shot body. Power was from a Ford V8-60 engine with 105hp. It proved to be a very quick, if unreliable, race car. Fitch intended to sell them for $2850 in street trim, but production was stopped as Fitch's racing career blossomed.

HP

FITCH (ii) (US) c.1964–1970

John Fitch, Falls Village, Connecticut.

John Fitch rejoined the ranks of vehicle manufacturers when the Chevrolet Corvair caught his attention. He offered a package of modifications that turned it into the Fitch Corvair Sprint. These included minor engine upgrades, improved

1966 Fitch (ii) Phoenix sports car.

suspension, better brakes and faster steering. The most notable change was an extended top with 'flying buttresses'. The Fitch Toronado Phantom was a first-series Oldsmobile Toronado with improvements to the suspension, brakes, transmission and trim. All were painted two-tone grey and white, and could only be ordered fully assembled from Oldsmobile dealers. Fitch also made modified Pontiac Firebirds with improved suspension, brakes and trim. The 1966 Fitch Phoenix was a Corvair-powered sports car with a steel body and chassis built in Italy by Intermeccanica. It had a wild, angular shape designed by artist Coby Whitmore. Initially it had been designed for use as a mudguarded street car, or with mudguards removed, as a formula racing car. Much of the design input was from Gerald Mong, designer of the Bobsy line of racing cars. However, the racing option was dropped by the time the prototype was unveiled in 1966. Although Fitch had orders for many cars, Chevrolet dropped the Corvair and only the prototype Phoenix was completed.

HP

F.L. (F) 1909–1914
Sté Générale des Voitures Automobiles Otto, Paris.
The Otto company made their first cars in 1901 and listed them until about 1904, after which there was an apparent gap until they launched the CULMEN in 1907, followed by the F.L. in 1909. It was a conventional car with 2009cc 12/16hp 4-cylinder monobloc engine in which the engine, flywheel assembly and gearbox were all connected as a single unit, and was joined by a six with the same cylinder dimensions, giving a capacity of 3014cc. The name probably came from that of the Eiffel tower, pronounced eff ell. An alternative explanation is that the cars sold in England by R.M. Wright of Lincoln (who made the GODIVA earlier in the century) carried the letters FL on the badge, standing for Floreat Lindum or (long) flourish Lincoln. However these letters would be meaningless to a Frenchman, so presumably R.M. Wright simply adapted them for their own badge, which featured Lincoln Cathedral.

NG

FLAC (DK) 1915
Mammen & Drescher, Jyderup.
This short-lived Danish make was powered by a 10hp 4-cylinder American engine of uncertain origin, possibly a Perkins judging from its size, and had friction transmission and final drive by chain running in an oil bath. Only 25 were made.

NG

F.L.A.G. (I) 1905–1908
Fabbrica Ligure Automobili Genoa, Genoa.
This was a solidly-built touring car made in three sizes, a 12/16hp and 16/24hp with shaft drive, and a chain-driven 40hp. All were 4-cylinder engines with pair-cast cylinders. The company was the Italian agent for THORNYCROFT cars, and it has been suggested that the F.L.A.G. was based on the English car, or even a licence-built Thornycroft, but the makers hotly denied this.

NG

FLAGLER (US) 1914–1915
Flagler Cyclecar Co., Chicago, Illinois; Cheboygan, Michigan.
The first Flagler was a neat-looking little cyclecar with a 10/12hp 2-cylinder engine, friction transmission and belt drive. After the company moved to a former pea-canning factory at Cheboygan, the Flagler grew up, having an 18hp 4-cylinder Farmer engine and shaft drive. About 100 Flaglers were made.

NG

FLAID (B) 1920
Ateliers Depireux, Liège.
Although built in Belgium, the Flaid was apparently destined for the British Market. A stand was taken at the 1920 White City Show (the overflow hall from Olympia), to be shared with TH. SCHNEIDER, but the Flaid never put in an appearance. However at least one was sold by a dealer in Great Portland Street. It was a conventional small car powered by a 1095cc 4-cylinder engine.

NG

FLANDERS (i) (US) 1909–1912
Everitt-Metzger Flanders Co., Detroit, Michigan.
The Flanders was a light car designed by Walter Flanders, formerly a partner in E.M.F., and was intended as a direct competitor for the Model T Ford. In the summer of 1909 the Flanders' $750 price tag was lower than the Model T's by $75, but by 1911 the position was reversed because Henry lowered prices every year. The Flanders was made by Studebaker in the former De Luxe car factory, and had a 20hp 4-cylinder engine. A 2-speed gearbox was employed in 1909 only, replaced by 3-speed for 1910. Open models were made in 1909–10, but a coupé was added for 1911. Total production of the Flanders 20 was 31,514. Despite the success of his car. Walter Flanders irritated his employers, Studebaker, by devoting too much time to other projects such as his electric car and a 4-cylinder motorcycle, and they parted company with him before the end of 1912. After

1912 the Flanders name was dropped, and the car became the Studebaker SA25.

A quite different car was the Flanders Six, which was the Everitt Six renamed for the 1913 season.

NG

FLANDERS (ii) (US) 1912–1915

1912–1913 Flanders Manufacturing Co., Pontiac, Michigan.
1913–1914 Tiffany Electric Co., Flint, Michigan.
1914–1915 Flanders Electric Co., Pontiac, Michigan.

Designed by LeRoy Pelletier, advertising manager for E.M.F., and sponsored by Walter Flanders, this was an attractive-looking electric car, which was about 12in (305mm) lower than most of its rivals and featured worm drive. Two body styles were made; the closed Colonial coupé and open Victoria coupé, both priced at $1775. Fewer than 100 were made before the Flanders Manufacturing Co. was in difficulties. In 1913 Pelletier bought the company, renamed it Tiffany and set up a separate factory at Flint. The Tiffany name was used from October 1913 to March 1914, after which Pelletier moved back to Pontiac and resumed the Flanders name. Production of the Tiffany and second generation Flanders Electric probably amounted to fewer than the first.

NG

FLANDRIA see CLAEYS-FLANDRIA

FLEETBRIDGE (GB) 1904–1905

J.T. Bentley & Co., Blackfriars, London.

The Fleetbridge was one of the smallest and cheapest cars of its day. It was powered by a 3.5hp single-cylinder engine with single-chain drive, a tubular frame and 2-seater body. The price was £70, and for 1905 there was a more powerful model with 5hp Fafnir engine at 80 guineas (£84.00). The Fleetbridge was also known as the Royal Fleetbridge or Ludgate.

NG

FLEETWOOD-KNIGHT (CDN) 1923

Davis Dry Dock Co., Kingston, Ontario.

John Davis' Dry Dock Co. had a fine reputation for high quality yachts, launches and lifeboats, and he hoped that his car would maintain his high standards. It had a 6-cylinder Knight sleeve-valve engine and was originally planned to be a tourer. Davis' son Lloyd completed it as a sedan, but it was soon badly damaged by fire and rebuilt as a roadster. The projected price of CDN$5000–6000 was too high, and no further cars were made. The prototype was kept by the family for many years, and was reported to be still in service in Renfrew, Ontario, in 1967, with more than 300,000 miles on the clock.

NG

FLETCHER (GB) 1967

Norman Fletcher Ltd, Walsall, Staffordshire.

Design company OGLE made the Mini-based SX1000 coupé between 1961 and 1963, and left behind a couple of interesting prototypes, one with a modified front and another with a modified rear. Boatbuilders Norman Fletcher acquired the Ogle moulds used both new designs to make one, updated model called the Fletcher GT. The nose featured a new inset headlamp arrangement behind perspex cowls, while the tail had a new sharp bustle and different light clusters. Fletcher returned to boat-making but interestingly became the parent company of RELIANT two decades later.

CR

FLEUR DE LYS (GB) 1983–1994

Fleur de Lys Automobile Manufacturing, Newark, Nottinghamshire.

This company picked up on the success of the defunct ALBANY by launching a range of vintage-style commercial vehicles with the name Newark. After many years producing these vans, it offered a passenger Landaulet version in 1991 and subsequently other vintage models under the names Lincoln and Belgravia. It also acquired the EVANTE concern in 1992 but became financially overstretched.

CR

FLINT (i) (US) 1902–1904

Flint Automobile Co., Flint, Michigan.

1912 Flanders (i) 20hp 2-seater.
NATIONAL MOTOR MUSEUM

1912 Flanders (ii) electric coupé.
NATIONAL MOTOR MUSEUM

This company was formed by A.B.C. Hardy, who had been a partner in the Durant-Dort Carriage Co., and who realised the potential of the automobile before Billy Durant or Joshua Dallas Dort did. He left their firm in 1901 and began to make a light 2-seater, which he called the Flint Roadster, although sometimes it went under his own name, Hardy. It had an 8hp single-cylinder engine, chain drive and left- or right-hand tiller steering, and was priced at $850. Hardy made 52 of these runabouts before ending production because he was unwilling to pay royalties to the Association of Licenced Automobile Manufacturers in respect of the Selden patent. He then rejoined Durant who had just become a car maker with his acquisition of BUICK. Hardy's later career involved management of GM's MARQUETTE (i) division and then vice-president and general manager of CHEVROLET.

NG

FLINT (ii) (US) 1923–1927

1923 Flint Division, Durant Motors Corp., Long Island City, New York.
1924–1926 Flint Motor Co., Flint, Michigan.
1926–1927 Flint Motor Co., Flint, Michigan.

The Flint was a product of Durant Motors by default. Its prototype was to have been the Chrysler Six, its development underway at the former Willys Corp. plant in Elizabeth, New Jersey, which had been temporarily rented by Walter P. Chrysler, by the Zeder-Breer-Skelton engineering team when that plant was acquired by William C. Durant. Under a prior arrangement, the car's prototype also became a Durant holding. With minor modifications, work on the new car was continued, its result being Durant's new Flint which was introduced at Hotel Commodore in New York City during January 1923. The Flint was fitted with a 7-bearing crankshaft and a steel tube for added reinforcement. A well-

1926 Flint (ii) sedan.
NATIONAL MOTOR MUSEUM

1979 Flipper 50cc microcar.
NATIONAL MOTOR MUSEUM

1906 Florentia tourer in the Coppa d'Oro, Bologna.
NATIONAL MOTOR MUSEUM

designed, and equally well-engineered car, the Flint would occupy a prominent niche in William C. Durant's automotive empire, various models during its existence of more than four years, priced from $960 to $2750 with a complete line of both open and closed body styles. All Flint cars were powered by Continental 6-cylinder L-head engines 6E, 7U, 9L, and 14U, with wheelbases of 115in (2919mm) and 120/130in (3046/3300mm). Disc wheels were standard on all Flint cars except for the Models 40 and Z–18, the smaller Flints which were fitted with the wood artillery type.

The Flint occupied the sales position between the Durant Six and the Locomobile in the contemporary Durant line. Another proposed car, the Princeton, planned to fit in between the Flint and Locomobile, was abandoned at the pilot stage when it became the senior Flint line.

Flint sales peaked in 1924 when 14,778 cars found buyers; total Flint production from 1923 to 1927 was nearly 37,000 cars.

KM

FLINTLO (US) 1905
Flint & Lomax Co., Denver, Colorado.
When this company exhibited their car at the Denver Automobile Show in April 1905, it was unfinished and had no name, and in the earliest reports it was called the Flint-Lomax. Soon afterwards it was given the abbreviated name Flintlo. It was a 5-seater tourer with a 14hp 4-cylinder engine and had ohvs, which was an advanced feature for its day. Transmission was conventional through a 3-speed gearbox and shaft drive. It did not survive into 1906.

NG

FLINTRIDGE see DARRIN

FLINTRIDGE-DARRIN see DARRIN

FLIPPER (F) 1978–1984
Flipper sarl, Villejuif.
The Flipper was one of the most idiosyncratic of all French microcars. Its curious plastic bodywork was moulded in two halves and then joined to make a monocoque. Most notably it surmounted a pair of narrow-set front wheels. The 47cc engine was attached to these wheels and was able to turn with them through 360 degrees. It had a 47cc Sachs or 50cc Motobécane engine, independent suspension and drive to front wheels via 2-speed automatic transmission. Pedal-power was provided for emergency propulsion. More conventional front-wheel drive arrived for 1980 and an open version, the Flipper Donky, was offered from 1981. The final Flipper model was a much more conventional microcar and featured a 50cc Polymécanique engine.

CR

FLIRT (I) 1913–1914
Ditta Ing. P. Pestalozza, Turin.
There was nothing flirtatious about this car, the name of which came from the Latin words *Fortis Levis Jucunda Rapida Transeat* (strong, light, cheerful, speedy, it goes). It was a conventional car with 20/30hp 4-cylinder T-head engine and a pear-shaped radiator, like that of the contemporary Fiat, Isotta-Fraschini or Züst.

NG

FLORENTIA (I) 1903–1912
Fabbrica di Automobili Florentia, Florence.
The first Florentias were conventional 2-cylinder cars designed by Giustino Cattaneo and Antonio Chiribiri, both of whom went on to greater things; Cattaneo as the long-time designer at ISOTTA-FRASCHINI and Chiribiri making cars under his own name. In 1905 Florentia took out a licence to make ROCHET-SCHNEIDER cars, initially the 16 and 24hp models which had 4-cylinder T-head engines, 4-speed gearboxes, honeycomb radiators and chain drive. In 1906 came a shaft-driven 18/22hp of 4.4 litres, and in 1907–08 there were some larger chain-driven models including the 9.9-litre 4-cylinder 40/50 and a 6.6-litre 6-cylinder car. Florentia bought the Venice-based S.V.A.N. shipbuilding company in 1906, and this took an increasing amount of their attention. They were still listed as car makers in 1912, but production may not have lasted as long as that.

NG

F.N.

FLORIO (I) 1912–1916
Florio Automobili de G. Beccaria & Compagnia, Turin.
Beccaria was a well-known metal forging firm which supplied chassis to several Italian car makers, including Fiat and Storero. In 1912, they began to manufacture 4-cylinder cars of 3- and 5-litre capacity, to the order of Cav. Vincenzo Florio of Targa Florio fame. They were represented in England by Florio Motors Ltd, which became Ensign Motors in November 1913, and there is a strong suspicion that the first Ensigns, at any rate, were Florios.
NG

FLYER (US) 1913–1914
1913–1914 Flyer Motor Car Co., Elizabeth, New Jersey.
1914 Flyer Motor Car Co., Mount Clemens, Michigan.
The Flyer was an example of a large car in miniature, for although only a 2-seater on a 100in (2538mm) wheelbase, it had a 20hp 4-cylinder water-cooled engine, shaft drive, and full electric lighting and starting. The price was a very reasonable $495, though raised in 1914 to $600. The company was lured to Mount Clemens by the promise of exemption from taxes and free water for five years, but did not live to enjoy these benefits.
NG

FLYING FEATHER *see* SUMINOE

FLYING SCOTSMAN *see* SCOTSMAN (i)

FLYING STAR (F) 1906
Voitures Flying Star, Lyons.
This was a 10/12hp 4-cylinder car made in very small numbers.
NG

F.M.R. *see* MESSERSCHMITT

F.N. (B) 1899–1935
Fabrique Nationale d'Armes de Guerre, Liège.
The F.N. was the longest-lived Belgian make of car, and was built in quite large numbers, though it never achieved the international fame of Métallurgique or Minerva. As the name implies the company's background was in armaments and it dated back to 1886, when several arms makers formed a union which, three years later, became the Société de Fabricants d'Armes de Guerre. The Belgian government placed a very large order for 150,000 Mauser rifles for the army and civil guard, which enabled the group to flourish for several years. Then in 1896 the arms side of the business was largely taken over by the German Lowe group, makers of the Mauser. F.N. looked for other business and chose bicycles, followed by motorcars.
The first F.N. car was designed by Italian-born J. de Cosmo. It had a front-mounted 3.5hp 2-cylinder engine, air-cooled on the prototype but later water-cooled, 2-speed belt transmission and chain final drive. The prototype was shown at the Brussels Show in March 1899, and production began in the spring of 1900. One hundred cars were made during the year. For 1901 a 4.5hp engine was used, and 280 cars were built. A wide variety of body styles was available, many with names derived from horse carriages, such as Duc, Jardinière, Tonneau, Victoria and Wagonette. Although it was not a production car, it is worth mentioning the enormous petrol-electric tonneau which F.N. built for Count Pierre de Caters in 1901. Designed with the help of racing driver and land speed record holder Camille Jenatzy, it had a 60hp 4-cylinder engine which charged batteries to drive the rear wheels. The petrol engine could be connected directly to the rear axle at the same time as the batteries, giving a total of 100hp.
In December 1901, F.N. began to make motorcycles and these were so successful that cars took a back seat for several years. In fact, from 1902 to 1906 they made no cars of their own, as they were the Belgian representatives for DE DION-BOUTON. These were imported as chassis and fitted with F.N. bodies. In 1906 F.N. returned to car manufacture with another French design, but one very different from the little De Dion. This was the ROCHET-SCHNEIDER, a large and expensive car closely based on the Mercedes. Up to 1908 they carried the names La Locomotrice or RSB (Rochet-Schneider Belge) and looked almost identical to the French product, but later cars had F.N. radiators. They had 6.9-litre 4-cylinder engines, the cylinders cast in pairs, and double-chain drive. A total of

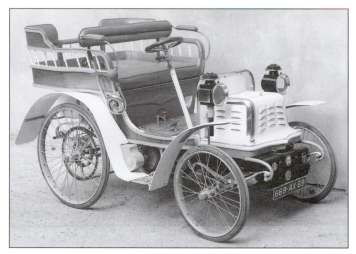
1901 F.N. 2-cylinder tonneau.
NATIONAL MOTOR MUSEUM

1914 F.N. 10hp 2-seater.
NATIONAL MOTOR MUSEUM

1921 F.N. 16/20hp tourer.
NATIONAL MOTOR MUSEUM

125 of these large cars was made up to 1913, and customers included the German Crown Prince, King Peter of Serbia and the Shah of Persia.
Shortly after the introduction of the RSB, F.N. brought out a smaller car to reach a wider market. The 1994cc Type 2000 had four pair-cast cylinders with L-head valves, and was joined in 1908 by the still smaller 1385cc Type 1400. These were followed by several models of small to medium-sized car in the years up to 1914, including the 1250, 1950, 2400 and 2700, the numbers referring to the approximate capacity in cubic centimetres. The 2400 of 1912 was the first monobloc four, while the 1950 of 1913 was unusual in having the outmoded

555

F.N.

1932 F.N. Type 832 saloon.

layout of side-valves in a T-head. By 1914 more than 3600 F.N. cars had been made, many of them exported to France, Germany, Holland and Great Britain, as well as to the Belgian Congo and several countries of the British Empire. All coachwork was made in F.N. factories, which also turned out large quantities of motorcycles, bicycles, rifles, pistols and cartridges.

During World War I the F.N. factories were requisitioned by the German Army and used for the repair of military vehicles. The first postwar cars, which appeared in the summer of 1920, were developments of the 1250, 1950 and 2700, joined for 1921 by a larger car, the 3800. This was a luxury car, seen as a successor to the old Rochet-Schneider-based models, and unlike most F.N.s it was supplied as a chassis to be bodied by the best Belgian coachbuilders. It was made up to 1925, and the engine was also used in commercial vehicles.

For the rest of the 1920s, F.N. concentrated on light to medium-sized 4-cylinder cars. The 1250 was the inspiration for the German AGA light car which, in turn, was made in Sweden by the aircraft builders THULINverke of Landskrona. Left-hand drive and a central gear lever appeared on the 2200 of 1922, and the first F.N. to have ohvs was the 1300 which replaced the 1250 in 1923. This was one of the most successful designs ever made by the firm; between 1923 and 1927 a total of 2781 were built, of which 200 were the Type Sport. These were fitted with 2- or 4-seater bodies, some of the latter being very handsome dual-cowl phaetons with pointed tails.

In 1925 F.N. made 1500 cars, putting them in second place among Belgian manufacturers, just behind Minerva. The 1300 was replaced in 1927 by the generally similar 1400, now with a 4-speed gearbox. Two of these made the first land journey from Belgium to the Congo in 1928, continuing to Cape Town. After about 200 had been made, the 1400 was replaced in the summer of 1929 by the 11CV Type Tolée. This was similar mechanically, but used steel bodies in place of fabric. Among its features were sliding front seats and a ceiling light which illuminated when the doors were opened, conveniences taken for granted today but unusual in a modestly priced car in 1929. The engine was enlarged to 1625cc in October 1931 and to 2 litres in 1933. This was the Prince Baudouin model, which reverted to side-valves. It was joined in December 1934 by the 2260cc Prince Albert, of which 499 were made before all passenger car production was halted in September 1935. This decision was taken because earlier in the year the Belgian government ordered a massive reduction of import duties on American components which brought down the cost of Ford and General Motors cars assembled in Belgium. Companies such as F.N., which made rather ordinary cars in small numbers, could not compete with Ford V8s and Chevrolet Sixes which cost less than a 4-cylinder Prince Albert.

The most interesting F.N. of the 1930s was the 832, which had a 3257cc straight-8 side-valve engine giving 75bhp. This was designed on American lines, though with a 4-speed gearbox and choice of lhd or rhd. The bodies were very American in styling, and the 832 could easily be mistaken for a Dodge or Hupmobile. A team of three roadsters won the Coupe du Roi in the 1932 Spa 24-Hour Race, and another won the Liège-Rome-Liège Rally. Despite the purchase of five 832s by the Belgian Royal Family, the model did not sell well, and only 571 found customers between 1930 and 1935. Apart from a prototype

cross-country car in 1934, the only passenger car activity was the assembly of the Peugeot 202, 302 and 402 from 1937 to 1940.

After the war production of motorcycles and commercial vehicles was resumed. The 2-wheelers lasted until 1962 and the trucks, latterly mostly for the Army, to 1965. F.N. made Rolls-Royce and General Electric jet engines, and had a licence to produced the Hawk missile. They were also involved in the development of Belgium's nuclear power station programme.

NG

FNM (BR) 1960–1963
Fabrica Nacional de Motores (FNM), Rio de Janeiro.

FNM had been making lorries since 1957. In 1960, they introduced the FNM-200. This was the Model JK. These initials honoured President Juscelino Kubitschek, who gave a great impulse to the Brazilian automobile industry. The manufacturer acknowledged that the FNM-200 was an ALFA ROMEO 4-door saloon under a different name. It was powered by a 122bhp engine and a 100mph (160 km/h) top speed was claimed. It took FNM over a year to have a regular production line and even after that few vehicles were made and most of them were delivered to the government. It is common knowledge that there were always quality-control problems with these cars.

ACT

F.N.M. (I) 1985
Fratelli Negri Macchine.

A diesel engine specialist showed a 4-wheel drive estate vehicle at the 1985 Turin Motor Show. Called the Pepper, it was a conventional-looking but compact off-roader powered by a 1.3-litre 4-cylinder engine developing 60bhp.

CR

F.O.D. (I) 1925–1927; 1948–1949
Fonderie Officine De Benedetti, Turin.

Francesco De Benedetti ran a large foundry which supplied the aircraft industry during World War I, and later the motor industry. He had personally acquired more than 300 patents, and decided to apply some of these to the design of a light car. It had a very small 4-cylinder engine of only 565cc, but with ohc and widespread use of aluminium alloys, which were also found in the clutch, gearbox components and steering gear. The frame was a platform type, and several body styles were offered including open 2-seater, 2-seater cabriolet, saloon, sports and light van. No parts were bought-in except for electrical equipment and tyres, though the Turin factory was more of an assembly plant. Chassis and bodies were supplied by S.A.M. of Legnano, which made cars of their own.

De Benedetti planned an initial run of 500 cars, but this number had not been achieved when production ended in 1927, due to his failure to compete with Fiat. De Benedetti became an industrial designer, though his three daughters fared less well, becoming factory workers for rival firms. In 1948 he returned to the light car idea, with a small 4-seater coupé powered by a 300cc 2-cylinder engine which he called the Debe. A 250cc 2-seater coupé followed in 1949, but he was not able to raise the necessary finance to put the Debe into production.

NG

FOERS (GB) 1977 to date
1977 to date J.A. Foers Engineering, Rotherham, Yorkshire.
1990–c.1995 Del Tech Ltd, Rotherham, Yorkshire.

From workshops in Rotherham, John Foers made a popular Mini-based utility called the Nomad. Unusually for a kit car, it had an all-aluminium body, mounted on a steel chassis. Body styles included a basic pick-up, a convertible and a van/estate. Almost 200 were made. In 1985 came the more sophisticated Triton using Metro subframes and mechanicals. The styling was a little sleeker, though still with flat glass all round, and there was only one body style: a 3-door estate. The third and final Foers model was the Ibex, a boxy Land Rover-based utility vehicle with a Foers-designed chassis. On the launch of this model, the smaller cars were passed on to Del Tech Ltd.

CR

FOIDART ET ROSENTHAL (B) 1900

Éts Foidart et Rosenthal, Brussels.

This company exhibited two cars at the 1900 Brussels Show, of 3 and 7hp with single-cylinder horizontal engines and 3-speed gearboxes. There seems to have been no development of these, but in 1914 Foidart announced a steam wagon whose production was frustrated by the war.

NG

FOLGORE (I) 1900–1902

Sebastiano Castagneri, Alessandri.

This was a light car powered by a 1.75hp engine of which no further details are known.

NG

FONCK *see* RENÉ FONCK

FONDU (B) 1906–1912

Automobiles Charles Fondu, Vilvorde, Brussels.

The Usines Fondu was set up in 1860 by Jean-Baptiste Fondu to supply material to the Belgian National Railway Co. His son Charles took over the business in 1896 and turned his attention to cars at the beginning of the twentieth century. In 1906 he launched the first Fondu on the market; the Type 1 CHF was a substantial car with 3768cc 20/24CV 4-cylinder engine, 3-speed gearbox and shaft drive. It was designed by a young Swiss engineer, Julien Potterat, who later became director of the car division of Usines Fondu. In 1907 the 20/24 was enlarged to become the 4082cc 24/30CV, and there was also a 50CV six of 6123cc. In 1908 Charles Fondu sold a licence to the Russko Baltiskij Vagonnij Zavod of Riga, also a railway wagon builder, to make the 24/30 under the name RUSSO-BALTIC. It was the first series produced car in Russia. (Riga, now capital of Latvia, was then part of the Russian Empire.) Although the engines were the same, the Russo-Baltic and the Fondu were not identical; small differences included the shape of the front axle.

Potterat left Fondu to supervise the Russo-Baltic project, and later Fondus were smaller cars of 1131, 1690 and 2120cc. The last year in which they made complete cars was 1912, but their engines were widely supplied, not only at home to firms such as ELGE, F.I.F, LINON and S.A.V.A, but also to C.L.E.M. in France, MATHIS in Germany and TURNER in England. Fondu engines were still sold in the 1920s, and from 1924 to 1933 the factory housed Établissements, Blavier S.A., makers of La Mondiale motorcycles.

NG

FONLUPT (F) 1920–1921

Éts Fonlupt, Levallois-Perret, Seine.

This short-lived car was advertised in two models, a four and an eight, with the same cylinder dimensions (70 × 140mm), giving capacities of 2154 and 4308cc respectively. A cyclecar was introduced in 1921, with 950cc S.C.A.P. engine. Établissements Fonlupt also made Triplex tipping bodies for trucks, Veritas speedometers, Simplex petrol pumps and Rapid electric starters.

NG

FONTAUTO (I) 1971–1972

Fontauto SNC, S. Dalmazzo, Cuneo.

Created by the Italian Volkswagen importer, the Fontauto Hobbycar (presented at the 1971 Turin Show) was a VW Beetle-based fun car of a style that was distinctly different from the usual beach buggy fare. It also benefited from brand new Beetle mechanicals. Fontauto is still in business today as a carrozzeria.

CR

FORCE 4 (GB) 1991–1992

Force 4 Engineering, King's Lynn, Norfolk.

Offered by a restoration company, the Force 4 Bretsa was a replica of the ISO Grifo coupé. It used Jaguar XJ mechanicals and had a glassfibre replica body with carbon fibre strengthening. The prototype used a Jaguar V12 engine.

CR

1906 Fondu limousine, by Decunsel.
NATIONAL MOTOR MUSEUM

FORD (i) (US) 1903 to date

Ford Motor Co., Detroit, Michigan.

Henry Ford built his first experimental car in a workshop behind his home on Bagley Avenue, Detroit, in 1896. The first production car, produced by the Ford Motor Co. which was founded on 16 June 1903 was, logically, called the Model A. It was quite typical of American practice at the time, with a 1645cc horizontally-opposed 2-cylinder engine mounted under the seat, driving through a 2-speed epicyclic transmission and single-chain drive. The body was a 2-seater with a detachable rear-entrance tonneau which made it into a 4-seater. The price was $850, $100 more than the contemporary Cadillac which, the engine apart, was a very similar design as the Cadillac's layout had been planned by Henry Ford the previous year.

The first sale of a Model A was to a Chicago dentist, Dr E. Pfennig, on 15 July 1903; other orders followed and before the end of the year the Ford Motor Co. was in a healthy financial state. The factory was still mainly an assembly plant, for engines and running gear was supplied by the Dodge brothers, bodies by the C.R. Wilson Carriage Co., tyres by the Hartford Rubber Co. and wheels came from the Prudden Co. The Model A was discontinued in October 1904 after 670 had been made. This is the official Ford figure, although other sources quote 1708. It was replaced by three models; the AC was similar to the A but with a larger engine (1975cc), the C had this larger engine and a bonnet and vertical radiator, although the engine remained under the seat. The Model B was a completely new car with a front-mounted vertical 4-cylinder engine of 4646cc developing 24bhp. Unlike the smaller Fords it had shaft drive and a side-entrance tourer body. At $2000 it was more than double the price of the smaller models, and Henry was not happy with it or with his partner Alexander Malcolmson, whose idea it was. Henry was determined that cars should cater for as wide a section of the populace as possible, and so they had to be inexpensive and made in large numbers. He managed to ease out Malcolmson in 1906. Production figures for the Model B are not known, but they must have been quite small.

Towards the end of 1904, a new factory on Piquette Avenue came into use and by April 1905 Ford had 300 employees making an average of 25 cars a day. In the summer of 1906 daily production was up to 100 cars. These were mainly the 2-cylinder Model F, derived from the C, and a new 4-cylinder Model N with 2442cc 18bhp engine mounted at the front. Priced at $500 it was less than half the price of the F, although it had only two seats. At the other end of the scale was the 6636cc 6-cylinder Model K, which was a Malcolmson project and sold for $2500. Henry hated it, dealers found it hard to sell, but were nevertheless told to take one Model K for every ten of the popular Model N they were allocated, Henry made this stipulation for the 1907 season, by which time the K's price had risen to $2800. Only 584 were made in the two seasons, and Henry did not make another 6-cylinder car until 1941.

Smaller Fords in 1907 and 1908 were the Models R and S. The R had running boards instead of step plates and the S had a single rear seat. They were the direct ancestors of the Model T which, when it was introduced in October 1908, replaced all other models.

1903 Ford (i) Model A tonneau.
NATIONAL MOTOR MUSEUM

1907 Ford (i) Model K tourer.
NATIONAL MOTOR MUSEUM

1909 Ford (i) Model T tourer. AM 1371 said to be the first Model T sold in England.
NATIONAL MOTOR MUSEUM

Enter the Model T

The Model T's engine was slightly larger than that of the S, at 2896cc and 20bhp, and incorporated two very significant improvements; monobloc casting and a detachable cylinder head. Transmission was the same 2-speed epicyclic system used on all previous Fords, but an innovation was left-hand steering. Five body styles were offered initially, a 2-seater runabout at $825, 5-seater tourer at

NICK BALDWIN

FORD, HENRY (1863–1947)

When Henry Ford died, a Detroit newspaper carried the banner headline 'The Father of the Automobile Dies'. This was not strictly accurate, but he had become so much identified with the motorisation of America that no one bothered to argue about it.

Henry's father, William Ford (1826–1905), had crossed the Atlantic as a steerage passenger in 1847, a refugee from the Irish potato famine, and in 1861 married Mary Litogot (1839–76). Other Fords were already living in Michigan and gave William support in lending him money to buy a farm and purchasing his produce. A myth has grown up that Henry Ford was a poor boy who pulled himself up from nothing, but in fact, by the time of his birth on 30 July 1863, his parents were among the more important families in the Irish farming community around Dearborn, owning several hundred acres. Henry was the eldest of six surviving children, and as such his father hoped that he would stay on the farm and eventually take it over. However, according to his autobiography, his 'road to Damascus conversion' came when he encountered his first self-propelled road vehicle, a steam traction engine which completely captivated him. He was no scholar, and the niceties of spelling and grammar eluded him all his life, but his father described him as 'a lad with wheels in his head'. While still at school he earned some pocket money mending friends' watches, and at 16 he took a job at the James Flowers & Brothers Machine Shop in Detroit. This was followed by a stint at the Detroit Dry Dock Co., after which he returned to the farm. He soon acquired a property of his own; 80 acres of forest land which he worked, felling trees with a Westinghouse steam engine.

After about nine years, Henry, now married and as yet childless, moved back to Detroit and took a job with the Edison Illuminating Co. Here he met the famous electrical engineer Thomas Alva Edison, who was to be a close friend until his death in 1931. It was during his time at Edison, where he was Chief Engineer, that Henry Ford built his first car. Like all other car makers of his day, he had no ready-made components with which to work. The cylinders for his engine came from a length of scrap pipe from a steam engine cut in half and bored out to the right diameter; the flywheel came from an old lathe; the wheels and seat came from bicycles, and the horn was a domestic doorbell screwed to the front. Several of the components had been located for Ford by his friend Charles Brady King, who had a car running a few weeks earlier, and who later made the King 4- and 8-cylinder cars in Detroit. Ford completed his car in June 1896, but in his enthusiasm to get it finished he had failed to consider how he was to get it out of his tiny workshop. Finding the door too narrow he demolished the frame with a pickaxe, and after removing some bricks he was able to manhandle his little car on to Bagley Avenue. It ran at 20mph (32km/h), much faster than King's heavier car, and after running around Detroit for several trials, Ford felt confident to submit it to the biggest test for cars of those days, country roads. His particular problem was that the roads were deeply rutted, and that as the track of his car was smaller than that of ordinary wagons, he was forced to drive with one side of the car in the ruts and the other several inches higher, with the car sharply tilted. This was hardly helpful to the primitive mechanism, let alone the comfort of his wife and 3-year old son Edsel.

Like all inventors, Ford was impatient to move on, and by the end of 1896 he had sold his quadricycle, as he called the first car, for $200. He used the money to build a second car, which was running by the Spring of 1898. This was a much more sophisticated vehicle than the Quadricycle. The chain drive was now to the centre of the rear axle rather than to the side and there was proper buggy-type seating (though the modified Quadricycle shared this improvement). There were stylish mudguards over front and rear wheels, and two headlights. It sufficiently impressed some wealthy Detroiters, including Mayor William Maybury, to back Henry in forming his own company, the Detroit Automobile Co.

Only one vehicle was completed and shown to the press by this concern, although other experimental cars were made. The demonstrator was a $^1\!/_2$-ton delivery van which proved so fragile and difficult to repair that it could not be sold. The Detroit Automobile Co. was wound up in January 1901, and Henry devoted his attention to making racing cars. One of these was the enormous 999 with an 18.9-litre 4-cylinder engine which took a number of records, including a mile at 91.37mph (147.01km/h) on the frozen Lake St Clair, with Henry himself driving. However, his backers were businessmen rather than sportsmen, and seeing no profit in racing cars, they had parted company with Ford before this. His chief backer, William Murphy, brought in Henry Leland as a production consultant. In March 1902 Ford resigned in disgust, with only $900 compensation and a promise from Murphy that he would not use the Ford name in connection with any car. Murphy was true to his word, and the Henry Ford Co. was reorganised as the Cadillac Automobile Co.

Ford had quarrelled with two partners in a little over two years and still had made no money from making or selling cars. An impartial observer might have forecast that he would fizzle out like countless contemporary tinkerers, warranting no more than a few lines in a specialist encyclopedia. However, in 1902 he found a new supporter. In his days with the Edison Illuminating Co., one of his jobs had been to buy coal, and the best merchant to go to was Alexander Young Malcomson who marketed his coal as 'Hotter Than Sunshine'. The men remained friends, and in August 1902 he agreed to provide funds for the manufacture of a new Ford car. Knowing Ford's doubtful reputation he kept his involvement quiet at first, but in November he agreed to the formation of a company called Ford & Malcomson. On 16 June 1903 it was reorganised as the Ford Motor Co., the title it still bears today. This time Henry was successful, and the new company sold 670 cars in its first 16 months. The company went from strength after that, although there a problem over Malcomson's support for a more expensive product, which led to his leaving the company in 1906. In that year Ford made more cars than any other manufacturer, a position he was to hold for the next 20 years.

Ford achieved a notable victory in January 1911, when an appeal court ruled that he did not have to pay royalties to the Association of Licenced Automobile Manufacturers in respect of the Selden Patent. The A.L.A.M. had been founded in 1903 by a group of most of the leading car makers, and Ford's approaches had been rejected on the grounds that, as Olds treasurer Fred L. Smith said, 'the Ford outfit is nothing but an assemblage plant'. Ford's attitude was 'If you can't join them, beat them', and he fought the claims through numerous court battles. When he won, the A.L.A.M. was disbanded, and the American industry was rid of a heavy burden that no one else had had the courage to challenge.

His earlier cars had made him a wealthy man, but with the Model T he became a multi-millionaire. In 1919 he bought out the other stockholders for $105,820,894, and this represented only 41.5 per cent of the stock. A few years later he received an offer of $1000 million for the entire stockholding from the investment firm of Hornblower & Weeks, but he turned it down.

Ford used his great wealth in a variety of ways. The most foolish was the Peace Ship, in which he and 55 delegates sailed to Europe in December 1915, hoping to persuade the warring powers to give up their struggle. The ship, named *Oscar II* after the peace-loving Swedish king of that name, got no further than Oslo when Ford was taken ill and returned to America on another ship. He was mocked in some sections of the American press, but many people agreed with Rabbi Joseph Krauskopf who said 'It is a thousand times better to be branded a fool in the service of humanity, than to be hailed a hero for having shed rivers of blood'.

If the Peace Ship made Ford look like a foolish saint, his campaign against the Jews, pursued through his own newspaper *The Dearborn Independent*, was more sinister, especially in the light of the inspiration he gave to Adolf Hitler. Ford was the only American to be mentioned in *Mein Kampf*. However, he was motivated no so much by racism as by the Mid-Western farmer's natural suspicion of big city financiers. He always boasted that he made things, not money. Many of the postwar developments, such as short skirts and jazz music, which others of his generation also found distasteful, he attributed to Jewish influence. He felt that they were destroying the traditional country, homespun, square dancing way of life in which he had been brought up. Certainly he had no admiration for the practical policies of Nazi anti-Semitism, and when he was shown film of the concentration camps in 1945, he suffered a serious stroke. However there is little doubt that his prejudices harmed the company. His erstwhile friend Rabbi Leo Franklin returned the Model T that Henry had given him, and Jewish customers lost to other makes were not easily won back.

Ford showed his love of his roots in the establishment of Greenfield Village, an extensive museum to the American way of life, particularly as it was lived on the farms and in rural communities. Begun in 1929, the building and stocking of Greenfield Village became a major interest for Henry in his later years. He spent much time and money tracking down artefacts from his past, including the original Westinghouse steam engine which he had used on his first property in 1882. Not that he ever gave up his interest in the company. Although Edsel became the nominal president in 1918, Henry continued to make the important decisions almost up to his death in April 1947. Indeed he had to take over the presidency again when Edsel died in May 1943, though he was not up to it, and two years later handed over to his grandson Henry II.

On the day that he died there was been a power cut at his home, Fair Lane, so, in the words of his biographer Robert Lacey, 'Henry Ford left the world as he had entered it, lit by candles and warmed by coal fires'.

Henry Ford's position in history, pre-eminent in his lifetime, is likely to remain unchallenged for many years to come. In countless polls from the 1920s onwards he was voted among the greatest living men, greatest living Americans, 'the person I would most like to meet' and so on. Not everyone has been so uncritical; historian Bernard Weisberger rated him the single most overrated figure in American history. He based this on the facts that Ford did not invent the automobile, nor the assembly line, nor mass ownership of cars. However he contributed mass ownership to a greater extent than any other car maker, and will always be though of as the man who put the world on wheels.

Henry Ford married, in 1888, Clara Jane Bryant (1866–1950). They had one child, Edsel (1893–1943).

NG

Further Reading
My Life and Work, Henry Ford with Samuel Crowther, Heinemann, London, 1922; Doubleday, New York, 1923.
Ford, the Times, the Man, the Company, Allan Nevins and Frank Ernest Hill, Charles Scribner's Sons, New York, 1954.
Ford; Expansion and Challenge, Allan Nevins and Frank Ernest Hill, Charles Scribner's Sons, New York, 1957.
Ford; Decline and Rebirth, Allan Nevins and Frank Ernest Hill, Charles Scribner's Sons, New York, 1963.
The Public Image of Henry Ford; an American Folk Hero and his Company, David L. Lewis, Wayne State University Press, 1976.
Ford, the Men and the Machine, Robert Lacey, Heinemann, London, 1986.

1926 Ford (i) Model T Fordor sedan.
NATIONAL MOTOR MUSEUM

1929 Ford (i) Model A roadster.
NATIONAL MOTOR MUSEUM

1932 Ford (i) V8 Model 18; two Tudor sedans and a 4-door phaeton.
NATIONAL MOTOR MUSEUM

1938 Ford (i) Model 81A sedan.
NATIONAL MOTOR MUSEUM

$850, 2-seater coupé at $950, 7-seater landaulette at $950 and 7-seater town car at $1000. A total of 10,660 Model Ts was made in its first fiscal year, 1 October 1908 to 30 September 1909. The majority were tourers and runabouts, and the more expensive closed models were made in very small numbers, 236 town cars and 47 coupés. Most components were now made by Ford, apart from tyres which he bought from his friend Harvey Firestone, and bodies which came from several suppliers, notably Kelsey and O.J. Beaudette. The inspiration behind the T was due to Henry Ford, but several others played vital roles in its development, particularly Childe Harold Wills, the metallurgist who had been with Ford since 1902, and was later to make his own car, the WILLS SAINTE CLAIRE, the Hungarian-born draughtsman Joseph Galamb, and foreman pattern maker Charles Sorensen who came from Denmark.

The first Model Ts were made in the Piquette Avenue factory in Detroit, but Henry had already purchased a large plot of land outside the city at Highland Park. The new factory was ready for production by April 1910, and it was there that the production lines were set up which enabled Ford to outstrip all his competitors, although they already headed the US production league, and had done so since 1906. The moving production lines went into action in August 1913, increasing output that year from 170,211 to 202,667. In 1914, the first full year of mass production, Highland Park turned out 308,162 cars. Two years later the figure was 734,811, more than five times as many as Ford's nearest rival, Willys Overland. In April 1911 Ford opened the industry's first branch assembly plant, at Kansas City, Missouri.

As production grew, the unit price came down and by 1915 the tourer cost only $440. This was little more than half the 1908 figure, and for a much better equipped car. The original Model T was a pretty basic vehicle; standard equipment consisted of three oil lamps, two at the side and one at the rear. Headlamps, windscreen, hood, horn, bumpers and speedometer were all extras. By 1915 these were all included in the price, except for the bumpers, which were seldom seen on Model Ts. A debit from 1914 onwards was that the only available colour was black. This was because japan black enamel was the only paint which would dry quickly enough to keep up with the assembly line. Earlier Model Ts had been offered in a variety of colours, although dark blue predominated after 1910. The all-black tradition came to an end in 1926 when quick-drying Duco lacquer came into use. However Model Ts assembled in Copenhagen for the Danish market were painted in light grey, with black wings, from 1923.

Relatively few changes were made to the Model T during its 19-year lifespan; a fully-enclosed 3-door sedan was introduced for 1915, and the brass radiator gave way to a painted one of different shape for 1917, but engine size and power, transmission and wheelbase remained constant. This was surprising in view of the changes taking place in the rest of the industry, but as the car sold so well there seemed no need to make alterations. Ford may not have kept up with their rivals in technology, but they were way ahead in the sales charts. Lack of annual changes and expensive research and development kept the price down too. The lowest-priced Ford was the 1924 2-seater roadster which sold for $260, compared with $490 for the equivalent Chevrolet. The Model T virtually sold itself, and from 1917 to 1923 all advertising was suspended, apart from that by local dealers. This was another important factor in keeping prices low.

The peak production year for the Model T was 1923, when 1,817,891 were made. That year they outsold Chevrolet by six to one, but three years later the proportion was only two to one, and anxiety spread through the company, affecting everyone but Henry himself. Now aged 63, he stubbornly refused to admit that his beloved T was desperately old-fashioned, and that a prosperous America was prepared to pay more for a car with conventional transmission, six cylinders and front-wheel brakes, to mention only three items which the T lacked. Admittedly, the 1926 Fords had several improvements such as wire wheels and bumpers, but these were extras. Because the car was quite basic, an enormous trade grew up in accessories. The Sears Roebuck catalogue offered as many as 5000 items for the Model T, fancy lamps, horns, disc wheels and almost anything that could be bolted or screwed on to a car. Some firms offered complete body kits to transform the T's homely appearance, others provided ohv conversions to boost its performance. Some transformations can be regarded as new makes. Examples of these include MAYFAIR (ii) in the US, MAIFLOWER in England, MONTIER in France, EMMEL and SPEEDSPORT in Belgium.

On 25 May 1927 the Ford Motor Co. announced that it would be bringing out a new car, and Model T production officially ended at Highland Park the following day. However, serial numbers indicate that some cars were built into early June, and trucks were continued for some time longer. The Model T engine was made in considerable numbers for marine and industrial use up to 1931, and a few at a time up to 1941. A total of 15,007,033 Model Ts had been made in the US and Canada, with many more coming from foreign assembly plants in England, Ireland, France, Belgium, Denmark, Germany, Italy, Spain, Brazil, Argentina, and Japan. The T was widely mourned, and several enthusiasts bought six or seven cars, so that they would last them the rest of their lives, and avoid the need to master a conventional gearbox.

'Henry's Made a Lady Out of Lizzie'
Rumours about the T's successor abounded – an X-8 engine was tried but found to be too complex for mass production, an in-line six was predicted by some in the industry, but Henry was still wary of sixes after the Model K. Anyway, Ford's main rivals, Chevrolet and the new Chrysler-built Plymouth, had four cylinders, so the new Ford, christened the Model A, would have the same. It was a 3286cc side-valve unit which developed 40bhp, double the output of the Model T, giving a top speed of 60mph (100km/h). As was expected, the gearbox was conventional 3-speed sliding, and there were brakes on all four wheels. The bodies were gracefully styled by Edsel Ford and Joe Galamb, giving rise to the song 'Henry's Made a Lady Out of Lizzie'. Or, as Ford's biographer Robert Lacey put it, 'the Ford image changed overnight from country cousin to country club'.

The change took a little more than overnight in fact. Today, old models are seldom discontinued until their successors are well into production, but this was not Henry's way. The A was not launched until December 1927, after an interval of seven months in which 60,000 men were thrown out of work in Detroit alone, across the nation 23 assembly plants were shut down and dealers had to survive

1950 Ford (i) Custom convertible.
NATIONAL MOTOR MUSEUM

by selling spare parts. When production restarted Henry had a new factory, the enormous River Rouge plant outside Dearborn, on land which he had bought in 1915. This took over from Highland Park, and is still the centre of Ford production.

Curiosity about the new car was greater than for any other before or since. In New York people began gathering outside the Broadway showroom at three in the morning, and in Cleveland mounted police had to be called out to control the crowds. By Christmas nearly half a million firm orders had been taken, though there were virtually no cars available for a test drive. The new cars were so scarce that they were driven around the country, stopping for no more than a few hours in each city before speeding on to the next.

NICK BALDWIN

FORD, HENRY II (1917–1987)
Blessed by destiny, as his early career seemed, he came to look more like its victim in later life. As the chief executive and part owner of the Ford Motor Co. from 1945 to 1980, his personality and business methods changed over the years. The respectful and modest young man who showed a talent for knowing the difference between good advice and bad, and never guessed wrong in picking men for positions of leadership, ended up as a despot with a vacillating mind. Alternatively charming and stubborn, shrewd and foolish, his once-ordered private life turned into a scandal-filled, self-indulgent one.

Eldest son of Edsel Ford, he was born in Detroit on 4 September 1917. He attended Detroit University School and the Hotchkiss School near Lakeville, Connecticut. He was admitted to Yale University in 1936, but left before graduating, in 1940. He was drafted for military service in 1941 and went to the Great Lakes Naval Training School as an Ensign. He was discharged from the US Navy upon his father's death in May 1943 to assume his responsibilities at the Ford Motor Co. (where he had held the title of Director since December 1938). In April 1944 he was named executive Vice-President; in September 1945 he presented his grandfather with a letter of resignation for the increasingly senile Henry Ford to sign, and took the title of President. The company was then losing money at the rate of $10 million a month.

He ended the confusion of executives giving conflicting orders, set up a policy committee in October 1945, and began drawing up an organisation chart. He needed new management, and responded favourably to a letter from Charles B. Tex Thornton (1913–1981) proposing the wholesale hiring of a team of former US Air Force officers who had taken courses from the Harvard Business School. They became trainees, and those who stayed with Ford achieved high office. One (Arjay Miller) served as president of the Ford Motor Co. from 1963 too 1968.

To fill Ford's most urgent needs, he lured Ernest R. Breech away from Bendix to serve as chairman of the Finance Committee (effective from 1 July 1947), who brought in former GM men, Harold T. Youngren (1892–1969) as vice-president of engineering and Del S. Harder as vice-president of production.

Henry Ford II stopped the financial haemorrhaging, sold off the rubber plantation in Brazil, and severed the joint tractor-production agreement with Harry Ferguson. He set up Ford Division in 1949 as a separate unit from Lincoln-Mercury, and in 1955 Ford sold more cars in the US than Chevrolet.

In 1961 he made himself Chairman of the Board after Breech's departure. He resigned from the company in September 1979.

He married, first Anne McDonnell in 1940 (marriage dissolved in 1964), secondly Maria Christina Vettore Austin, in 1965 (marriage dissolved in 1980), thirdly, Kathleen Roberta DuRoss, in 1980. By his first wife he had a son, Edsel Ford II, who became president of the Ford Motor Credit Co. in 1990, and two daughters, Charlotte and Anne. He died on 3 October 1987 from complications following a bout of pneumonia.

JPN

Further Reading
Ford, Robert Lacey, William Heinemann Ltd, 1986.

1955 Ford (i) Thunderbird convertible.
NATIONAL MOTOR MUSEUM

1964 Ford (i) Fairlane 500 hard-top sports coupé.
NATIONAL MOTOR MUSEUM

In styling the A bore some resemblance to the Lincoln, although its wheelbase was too short for real elegance. Body options were similar to those on the T, with the addition of a taxicab and a delivery van. For 1929 the range was extended from 9 to 18 models, including bodies by Briggs and Murphy as well as Ford, and two new styles, a station wagon at $650 and a town car at $1400. The latter was something of a folly and only 1065 were made, but the station wagon was another matter. Although sales were slow at first, with only 4954 delivered out of a total for the Model A of 1,310,147, they picked up later to become an integral part of the Ford range, while the style was copied by most US manufacturers.

Ford's sales were seriously hit by the Depression, falling to 627,104 in 1931. In July of that year Henry announced layoffs of 70,000 workers and the temporary closure of 25 of the 36 assembly plants across the country. Sales of the Model A were being challenged by Chevrolet's new low-price six, but Henry would still have nothing to do with a 6-cylinder engine. 'We're going from a four to an eight', he said, 'because Chevrolet is going to a six'. This time he chose the well-tried V8 layout and in March 1932 he launched the world's first low-priced, mass-produced V8 car.

The V8
The new engine had a capacity of 3622cc and developed 65bhp. The body styles were similar to those of the Model A, and with 65 per cent more power and very little extra weight, performance was remarkable, with more than 80mph (128km/h). At 106in (2690mm), the wheelbase was only 2.5in (63mm) longer than the Model A's, and this combined with transverse leaf suspension inherited from the

Model T and A, made handling exciting and sometimes dangerous. However, the glamour of a V8 engine, which Chevrolet did not have until 1955, helped sales through the 1930s. The Model A was dropped almost immediately, but its engine was available in the V8 chassis as the short-lived Model B. This was made only from March to September 1932, although the 4-cylinder engine was available as an option on passenger cars and light commercials until 1934, and was continued by the British Ford factory later still.

The bodies of the first series V8, known as the Model 18, were not unlike those of the A, but the wings were fully crowned (more deeply curved), and the slight vee of the radiator made the new cars instantly recognisable. Fourteen body styles, in Standard and De Luxe versions, were available, at prices from $460 to $650. From 1933 a longer wheelbase and double dropped frame gave the V8 a more modern appearance. Edsel Ford was increasingly involved in styling. The V8's performance soon attracted the attention of dirt track racers who found that a V8 stripped of wings, running boards and roof could beat almost anything on the track. The engine was highly suitable for tuning, and thus began the hot-rod craze which reached a peak after World War II, leading to the formation of the NHRA (National Hot Rod Association), with its highly specialised machines of today. Although highly modified Model Ts with ohv conversions had been raced in the 1920, even appearing at Indianapolis, Ford was not prominent in sport until the advent of the V8. In the 1933 Elgin (Illinois) Road Race, Fords took the first seven places, and many other successes followed. In Europe the V8 made its mark in the Monte Carlo Rally with a win in 1936 by the Romanians P.G. Cristea and Ion Zamfirescu in a stripped roadster, and in 1938 by the Dutchmen Bud Bakker Schut and Klaas Barendricht in a stock sedan. In the 1938 Rally 26 Fords were entered, and 19 won trophies.

Changes in the 1930s were mostly in styling, although the long-awaited hydraulic brakes arrived on the 1939 models and steering column gear change for 1940. The transverse leaf springs were not replaced until 1948. Ford lost their lead to Chevrolet in 1936, and apart from the war years did not regain it until 1959. There were two attempts at making a less expensive car, the 2228cc V8-60 of 1937, and the 3700cc six of 1941. The small V8 engine was used in British and French Fords, but was under-powered for the US market, and sold poorly. The six lasted only for the 1941 and 1942 seasons, the latter cut short by America's entry into World War II. It was revived after the war and made until 1951.

The Ford factories were busy during the war making aircraft engines (57,000), Jeeps (278,000), tanks and reconnaissance cars. An enormous new factory at Willow Run, Michigan, turned out 8600 Liberator bombers, but was sold after the war to Henry J. Kaiser for the manufacture of KAISER and FRAZER cars.

In May 1943 Edsel Ford died of cancer, in his 50th year. His father, then aged nearly 80, resumed the title of company president which he had given up 25 years before, but his grandson, 26-year old Henry II, was recalled from the Navy to take over the running of the business. He became president in September 1945.

The postwar Ford cars, launched on 3 July 1945, were 1942 models with mild restyling and V8 engine size increased to 3917cc. The only significant new model for the next three years was the Sportsman, which was a convertible with station wagon-type wood panelling, in the style of the Chrysler Town & Country. In June 1948 came a completely new Ford, with all-enveloping body and coil ifs replacing the transverse leaves. The new cars were 3in lower than their predecessors, and were among the sleekest looking of any of the new generation of American cars. Styling was by George Walker and Richard Caleal. Only the engines were unchanged, being the familiar 3700cc six and 3917cc V8.

Gradual changes were made during the 1950s, the most important being the option of automatic transmission for 1950, a 3528cc ohv six with almost square cylinder dimensions (89.67 × 91.44mm) for 1952 and a brand new 3923cc ohv V8 for 1954. For the 1955 season Ford brought out the Thunderbird, a 2-seater personal car with sporting overtones which was their answer to Chevrolet's

Corvette. Thunderbird styling was lower and quite different from the regular Fords, and it had a 198bhp 4785cc V8 engine which was also used in police versions of the sedans. With greater power than the Corvette and the option of a manual gearbox, as well as comfort features such as wind-up windows and a power-operated hood, the Thunderbird outsold its rival by more than four and a half to one in its first three years. Ford decided that a 4-seater version would sell even better, and this was introduced for 1958. It did sell better, but it had a bulky appearance, and enthusiasts regretted the disappearance of the crisply styled 2-seater T-bird. This soon became a collector's car, and numerous replicas have been offered in kit form or complete. The best were the SHAY T-Bird and REGAL ROADSTERS versions. It was retrospectively nicknamed the Little Bird, while the 4-seater became the Big Bird or Square Bird. In 1967 the Thunderbird lost what little sporting image it had with the introduction of a 4-door sedan, although in the 1980s it was again a performance car, with a turbocharger from 1984 to 1988, and then a supercharger. Ford dropped the Thunderbird name in 1998.

From 1955 Ford joined other US manufacturers in the horsepower race, and by 1960 the largest engine displaced 5768cc and developed 360bhp. A novelty of 1957 was the Skyliner with power-operated retractable hard-top. This very

NICK BALDWIN

IACOCCA, LEE (b.1924)

One of the most important figures in postwar Ford history, Lido Anthony Iacocca was born in Allentown, Pennsylvania, to Italian parents who had arrived in America three years earlier. His father Nicola, owned the Orpheum Wiener House, making hotdogs, and later diversified into car rentals, running an all-Ford fleet, first Model Ts and then Model As and V8s. Lee was a very studious boy, spending more time with his books than playing with friends, studied industrial engineering at Lehigh University where he completed the four-year course in three, then did a master's degree at Princeton. He was recruited to Ford by a talent scout who arrived in a Lincoln Continental, 'that car really turned my head', Iacocca recalled, 'One glimpse of it and one whiff of the leather interior were enough to make me want to work at Ford for the rest of my life'.

While at Princeton he announced his intention of becoming a Ford vice-president by the age 35; few youthful ambitions are so nearly realised, for it was a month after his 36th birthday that Henry Ford II gave him command of the Ford Division, the premier division of the company. He got there through the route of successful sales, putting the Philadelphia district at Number One in the Ford National Sales League, and in 1956 he went to Dearborn where he was put in charge of Ford truck marketing.

In November 1965 he was appointed vice-president, Car & Truck Group, controlling Ford, Lincoln, Mercury and truck divisions, but by then he had already launched his greatest contribution to Ford – the Mustang. This was

originally to have been a mid-engined 2-seater, but, car buff though he was, Iacocca's enthusiasm was tempered with common sense. 'When I looked at the guys praising it, the off-beat crowd, the real buffs, I said "that's sure not the car we want to build because it can't be a volume car. It's too far out"'. He ordered a new model, with front engine and four seats, and this was the car which was launched in April 1964 to become one of Ford's greatest successes. Among the accolades that the Mustang brought to Iacocca were cover stories in both Time and Newsweek. He was also responsible for dropping a V8 engine in the hitherto unexciting Falcon, and for Ford's re-entry into NASCAR racing.

On 10 December 1970 Iacocca moved up to the presidency of Ford, only one step away from the top job, the chairmanship, which was held by Henry II. He was to remain in the presidency for 7½ years, and at one point Henry said, rather reluctantly, that the Italian would succeed him, but it never came to that. Relations between the two men deteriorated and in August 1978 Iacocca was fired. He was given three months until he reached his 54th birthday, occupying an inferior office and with little executive power. He gave as his reason for the dismissal, 'Henry just doesn't like strong guys around', and indeed Henry had given much the same treatment to Bunky Knudsen nine years before. Also, Henry felt that Lee gave himself airs, ordering the best linen, china and silverware on the company planes, while Henry was happy with his sandwich and the fruit basket.

Lee Iacocca did not have to wait long for fresh employment; by November 1978 he was at the helm of Chrysler, where he was horrified at the lack of accounting, 'the lousy cars, bad morale and deteriorating factories'. He was, however, helped by a number of key men who he had brought with him from Ford, including 'father of the minivan' Harold Sperlich, and financial wizard Gerald Greenwald. By 1983 he had turned the situation around completely, thanks to new models such as the K-cars, and federal loan guarantees which he managed to extract from a reluctant Congress. The loans were for ten years, but amazingly, he managed to repay them in full within three. However, he lost his touch in the late 1980s with an unwise purchase of Gulfstream Aviation, while the purchase of American Motors in 1987, in order to obtain the valuable Jeep business, while ultimately of great benefit to Chrysler, cost a great deal at the time. Early in 1993 he handed over the chairmanship to Robert Eaton, who had been in charge of GM Europe.

Lee Iacocca married first Mary McCleary, with whom he had two daugthers, Kathryn Lisa and Lia Antionette. Mary died in 1983, and three years later he married Peggy Johnson (marriage dissolved in 1987). In 1991 he married Darrien Earle, who owned and managed a retuarant in Los Angeles

NG

Further Reading
Iacocca, an Autobiography, Lee Iacocca with William Novak, Bantam Books, 1984.
Iacocca, America's Most Dynamic Businessman, David Abodaher, Zebra, 1985.

complex design involved three drive motors and four lock motors, ten power relays and 610ft of wiring; the roof disappeared completely into the luggage boot in less than one minute. In 1957 it cost only $337 more than the soft-top Sunliner convertible, but the price margin increased over the next two seasons, and it was withdrawn after the 1959 season, having sold a respectable 49,394 units.

In 1959 Ford built their 50 millionth car, and overtook Chevrolet to sell 1,528,592 cars. Since World War II they had opened 22 new assembly plants in the US, and 21 new parts depots. For 1960 they brought out a compact car to rival Chevrolet's Corvair and Plymouth's Valiant. Named the Falcon, it was more conventional than its rivals, with a front-mounted 2365cc 6-cylinder engine, and easily outsold them. Body styles were 2- and 4-door sedans, joined later by a station wagon and Ranchero pick-up truck. The Falcon series was continued up to 1970, gaining a V8 engine in addition to the sixes in 1963. For two seasons, 1963 and 1964, Ford made a major onslaught on European rallies with the Falcon, winning the Tulip and Geneva Rallies in 1963 and the Geneva in 1964.

NATIONAL MOTOR MUSEUM

McPHERSON, EARLE STEELE (1891–1960).
The inventor of the suspension system that bears his name had a long and creative career, leaving big footprints in the annals of several companies. He was born in Highland Park, Illinois, in 1891, educated at local schools, and graduated from the University of Illinois in 1915.

He found his first job with the Chalmers Motor Co., but he spent most of World War I in Europe, working on aircraft engines for the US Army. From 1919 to 1922 he was an engineer with the Liberty Motor Car Co. in Detroit, and then joined Hupmobile as a design engineer, working on engines, transmissions, axles, steering and suspension. He was the chief engineer for the 1929 Model E, and was promoted to assistant chief engineer of Hupmobile in 1931.

In 1934 he moved to a position in General Motors's central engineering office and was assigned to Chevrolet where he became a design engineer in 1935. He had a hand in the redesign of the 6-cylinder engine for 1937, and led several chassis projects.

In 1945 he was named chief engineer of the Light Car Project (Cadet), which featured his patented spring-leg suspension system front and rear. When GM decided not to put it into production, he left Chevrolet and joined Ford in September, 1947. at Harold T. Youngren's invitation,

He designed radically new cars for Ford of Britain (1950 Consul and Zephyr) and was vice president of engineering on his return to Dearborn in 1952. He led the design of a modern 6-cylinder car engine and laid down the basic concept for the Ford Falcon concept car. He retired in the spring of 1957 and died in 1960.

JPN

Mustang

Big V8s continued to be made in the 1960s, reaching a peak with the 375bhp 7030cc of 1969, although the slightly smaller 6997cc '427' was more powerful at 425bhp. However, the most important Ford of the decade, and one of the most significant postwar American cars, was the Mustang. The brainchild of Lee A. Iacocca, who had worked his way from a salesman in Chester, Pennsylvania, to company vice-president in five years, the Mustang was planned as a personal car, rather as the original Thunderbird had been. Using many Falcon components, Iacocca and his team produced a crisply-styled 4-seater in coupé or convertible form, initially with a choice of five engines, from a 101bhp 2781cc six to a 271bhp 4727cc V8. Aiming at as wide a market as possible, Iacocca gave the Mustang six transmissions, three suspension packages, three brake systems, three wheel sizes and many other performance and comfort options. This wide market coverage was later used in the Anglo-German Ford Capri, although with not so many options. Within five months of its launch in April 1964, the Mustang became the third most popular car in the United States; half a million cars were sold in 18 months and by June 1967 the 1$^{1}/_{2}$ millionth Mustang was delivered.

The 6-cylinder Mustang appealed to young professional men and women who sought a sporting image without being too demanding about their car's performance. The V8 was a fine performer, but lacked the handling to match until Carroll Shelby got his hands on it (see SHELBY). The regular Mustangs received their first major revision for the 1967 season; bodies were longer and wider, and styling more aggressive, a trend continued on the 1969 models, in which engine options ran from a 115bhp six to a 360bhp V8. The latter was fitted to the Mach 1, which was available only with a fast-back coupé body. Sharing the same body were the Boss 302, 351 and 429, the numbers representing engine capacity in cubic inches. The most powerful was the 375bhp Boss 429, of which only 852 were made. In 1974 the Mustang underwent a dramatic change, with a much smaller body and 2294cc 4-cylinder engine. A V8 was back in the range from 1975 but these later models, called Mustang II from 1974 to 1978, and then plain Mustang, lacked the glamour of the pre-fuel crisis cars.

The 1970s Onwards

Ford entered the 1970s with a wide range of cars, in contrast to the one-model days of the Model T, A, and V8. Smallest was the sub-compact Pinto launched in October 1970, a 2-door sedan (a 3-door hatchback was added in mid-1971), powered by a choice of 4-cylinder engines, a 1616cc pushrod ohv British Ford or a 1999cc single-ohc from Ford of Germany. The latter was more powerful (100bhp) and much more popular among American buyers. One size up from the Pinto was the compact Maverick, a Falcon replacement powered by a 2785cc six and available originally (1970) in 2-door form only, although later made as a 4-door sedan. Next came the intermediate Torino and full-sized Galaxie XL and XLD in addition to the Mustang and Thunderbird. The latter was now a full-sized 2- or 4-door hard-top coupé (2-door only after 1972).

The last year for convertibles was 1973, but they would reappear ten years later. Although big V8s up to 7.5 litres were made up to 1978, the average size of American Fords dropped from mid-decade onwards. The Granada of 1975 was pitched between the Maverick and Torino in size and price; inspired by the European Granada it was made in 2- and 4-door versions and sold very well for a new model. The Maverick disappeared in 1978, replaced by the 3277cc 6-cylinder Fairmont, and for 1981 the Pinto gave way to the transverse-engine front-drive Escort. This was the US-market version of Ford's 'world car' also made in Britain and Germany. Engines were built in the US and Germany, manual transmissions and running gear by Mazda in Japan, and automatic transmissions in the US. Body styles were a 3-door hatchback and 5-door station wagon. Although engines of 1298cc or 1599cc were planned, only the larger was offered on the US Market. The Escort was an immediate best seller, with more than 320,000 finding customers in its first season, when it was America's second most popular car, after Chevrolet's similar sized Chevette. In 1982 the Escort captured the number one spot. The Mustang was fourth and the Fairmont fifth, but the bigger Fords trailed behind their equivalents from Buick, Chevrolet and Oldsmobile.

On 15 November 1977, Ford built its 100 millionth car in the United States, and worldwide production reached 150 million during the following year, which also saw Ford's 75th birthday as a car manufacturer. However the next few years were difficult, with a deepening recession and problems among top executives. The workforce was cut from 190,000 to 115,000 during 1979–81, and

1984 Ford (i) Mustang Turbo GT convertible, with a 1964 Mustang convertible in the background.
NATIONAL MOTOR MUSEUM

in 1979 a clash between Henry Ford II and Lee Iacocca led to the latter's resignation and move to head the Chrysler Corp.

New models of 1982 included the ExP, an Escort-based 2-seater coupé built only for the US Market, with no European versions, and a return to high performance for the Mustang. The top model now had a 157bhp 4950cc V8 giving 0–60mph (100km/h) acceleration in under 8 seconds. A Mustang convertible was available from 1983, and the 1984 season saw an important new model, the front-drive Tempo. This was a 2- or 4-door sedan with styling similar to the European Sierra, but with more luggage space. Engines were a 53bhp 1983cc diesel or a 85bhp 2294cc petrol unit. A rival to the GM X-cars or Chrysler's K-cars, the Tempo replaced the rear-drive Fairmont, and was available with a 100bhp fuel-injection engine from 1985. In the following year it was joined by the larger Taurus, which had been under development since 1979 and was known as the DN5 project (D for the size, N for North America). Also badged as the Mercury Sable, the Taurus had styling links with the European Scorpio and was the most aerodynamic American sedan ever made, with a drag coefficient of 0.33 for the Taurus and 0.32 for the slightly longer and sleeker Sable. Even the station wagon achieved 0.35. Engine options were an 88bhp 2507cc four or a 140bhp 2982cc V6, both new engines specially developed for the new cars.

With an investment of more than $3 billion, the DN5 was crucial for Ford, which had lost $2 billion for two years in a row. Fortunately the new models were runaway successes. Despite a shortened season (they were launched on 26 December 1985), sales of the 1986 Taurus reached 236,362, while the 1987 Taurus was the best-selling Ford, beating the Escort by just seven cars to reach 374,772. In 1987 the Taurus was the best-selling American-designed car, though just beaten to first place by the Honda Accord. The 1989 season included the Taurus SHO (Super High Output) with a Yamaha-engineered 24-valve V6 engine with single camshaft to each bank of cylinders. This developed 220bhp and propelled the six-seater sedan to 60mph(96km/h) in 7 seconds. Despite its performance, the SHO was a slow seller because of its relatively high price and absence of automatic transmission until 1993. The whole Taurus range was mildly restyled for 1992 and sales soared to 368,000 for the 1992 model year and to 459,000 for 1993. The SHO was dropped, but the regular Taurus continued to be Ford's best selling car. In 1997 they sold 357,162 compared with the Escort's 283,898. Significantly the truck-derived Explorer 4×4 station wagon beat them to both with sales of 383,852.

The smaller Fords of the 1990s were more closely linked to the Far East. The budget-priced Festiva was a Mazda 121 (Kia Pride when the Korean company took over the design from Mazda), which gave way to the Aspire, which was also Kia-built but with more modern lines. The Aspire was made from 1994 to 1997. Escorts of 1990 were based on the Mazda 323, using a 1786cc twin-ohc Mazda or 1868cc single-ohc Ford engine. Escorts were made in Mexico as well as Michigan, and the range was redesigned again for 1996 along the lines of the contemporary Mazda 323. Another Japanese-inspired model was the Probe, made from 1989 to 1997 in the factory at Flat Rock, Michigan, owned jointly by Ford and Mazda. Based on the Mazda MX-6, it was an American-styled sporty coupé powered by a 2184cc Mazda 4-cylinder engine, joined in 1990 by a 2982cc Ford V6 as used in the Taurus. The Probe was redesigned for 1993 on a new-generation MX-6 platform, although with more dramatic styling than the Japanese car. Power was now exclusively Mazda; a 2310cc four for the base model and a 2507cc V6 for the sporty GT. When it was launched, the Probe was to have been called a Mustang, but there were massive protests from enthusiasts who thought it sacrilege that the sacred name should go on a car of foreign design and with front-wheel drive. The Mustang name was reprieved to be carried by a new 'native' design in 1993, with 218bhp 4604cc V8 engine, joined later by the 32-valve Cobra version giving 238bhp. It was still made in 1998. Another familiar name was Thunderbird, restyled in

1987 Ford (i) Taurus sedan.
FORD MOTOR COMPANY

1983 and again in 1988. The standard engine was a 3802cc V6 developing 140bhp (210bhp with turbocharger), but a 4950cc V8 was an option. It was continued through the 1990s with little change, but the turbocharger was dropped. The more sporting SC model with ABS and optional 5-speed manual transmission accounted for only 6 per cent of sales, an indication that the typical Thunderbird buyer was not performance-orientated. Ford finally discontinued the Thunderbird in the summer of 1998.

The traditional full-sized Crown Victoria sedan was continued throughout the 1990s. It was completely restyled for 1992 (the announcement was actually made in December 1990 and cars reached the showrooms in March 1991) with styling following that of the Taurus, and an all-new modular V8 engine also used in the Mustang. Previous Crown Victorias, dating from 1979, had been nicknamed 'cars for the shuffleboard set', but the new models were more agile and responsive, and even came with a handling and performance package. After the demise of the big rear-driven General Motors cars, they were the sole representatives of the traditional American car. As such they were popular with taxicab operators and police forces, for whom special versions were made. They were still made in 2000, coming from Ford's Canadian factory at St Thomas, Ontario.

Other models in the 2000 line-up included the Contour sedan with 1983cc four or 2540cc twin-cam V6 engines, based on the European Mondeo, and several models of 4×4 station wagon. This line dated back to the Bronco of 1965, and its junior version, the Bronco 2, introduced in 1982. This was renamed Explorer in 1990, while the Bronco became the Expedition in 1995. They were massive vehicles, the Expedition being 212in (5380mm) long and 79in (2005mm) wide, with engines up to a 232bhp 5.4-litre V8. They were nevertheless highly popular, the Explorer outselling any of the passenger cars in 1997, with sales of 383,852. Even this figure was put in the shade by the F-105 pick-up truck, which registered 712,267 sales in 1997. The bulk of these went to private buyers, indicating a massive change in American lifestyles. A new, smaller 4×4 to challenge the Honda CR-V and Toyota RAV4 appeared in 2000. Called the Escape, it had a 2-litre Zetec 4-cylinder or Duratec V6 engine, with a turbodiesel option for the European market. Ford's contribution to the 'one-box' MPV family was the Aerostar launched in 1986 with 3-litre V6 engine and made to the end of the 1997 season. A larger version was the Windstar which was based on a Taurus platform.

Frank Hershey (centre) working on a 1935 Pontiac model.
MICHAEL LAMM

HERSHEY, FRANK (1907–1997)

Franklin Quick Hershey was born 23 July 1907 in Detroit. His family moved to California in 1910. Frank's mother knew Henry Leland and always drove Cadillacs. Frank confessed later that his mother's interest in Cadillacs sparked his fascination with automobiles.

In 1927, while Frank was attending Occidental College, he showed some styling drawings to a friend. The friend suggested that Frank apply for a job with Walter M. Murphy, the Pasadena coachbuilder. Murphy didn't care for Frank's sketches, but his general manager, Frank Spring, hired Hershey anyway.

Frank left Murphy in 1928 to work in Harley Earl's fledgling Art & Colour section. He returned to Murphy after the stock-market crash of 1929 and designed dozens of custom bodies. Murphy produced many of these on Duesenberg, Packard, Cord L-29 and other chassis. Frank also designed the 16-cylinder Peerless prototype at Murphy.

When Frank Spring moved to Hudson in 1931, he asked Hershey to join him. Hershey wasn't happy at Hudson, however, and when Harley Earl called him in the spring of 1932 to design an alternate for the stymied 1933 Pontiac, Hershey accepted. General Motors was on the verge of discontinuing Pontiac, and the 1933 body design would be critical. Earl gave Hershey two weeks to come up with an alternate body. Frank based the new car's lines on his favorite Bentley, and Earl accepted it. The resulting 1933 Pontiac sold well and saved Pontiac.

Hershey was soon made head of the Pontiac design group. In that capacity, he styled the 1935 Pontiac, including the hallmark Silver Streak. Frank told two stories about the Silver Streak: 1) that it was inspired by the British beach racers' hood-mounted oil coolers and, 2) that it came about when he took a grooved ribbon of warm clay out of the extruder and draped it along the hood of a full-sized model before leaving for the day. When Earl saw the ribbon than night, he liked it so much that Hershey turned it into the Silver Streak.

Frank subsequently served as head of the Buick studio and, from 1936 to 1941 was chief designer for Holden in Australia, Opel in Germany and Vauxhall in England. Frank joined the Navy in 1942 but received a military discharge in 1944 and came back to GM as temporary head of the Cadillac studio.

It was here and in an experimental styling area that Hershey and Ned Nickles designed the 1948 Cadillac, taking inspiration for the trendsetting tailfins from the Lockheed P-38 Lightning twin-boom fighter airplane.

In 1948, against GM policy, Frank and two friends started an outside business. When Harley Earl found out, he fired him. Frank then went freelance and did some designs for Reo Motors Inc., the truckmaker. In 1952, he took a job with Packard but moved to Ford in early 1953 as director of styling.

As he arrived at Ford, a colleague from GM told Frank about the forthcoming Corvette, and Frank independently began to lay out the car that became the 1955 2 seater Thunderbird. When Henry Ford II asked George Walker at the Paris auto show why Ford couldn't build racy two-seaters like the Europeans, Walker remembered Hershey's project and told HF-II about it. Ford Division rushed the Thunderbird into production. Hershey remained with Ford until 1956.

Frank returned to California that year to oversee the industrial-design department of Kaiser Aluminum. Eight years later, he moved to Rite Autotronics, where he did packaging and product design. He retired in 1978 and lived out the rest of his life in the California desert. Frank Hershey passed away at age 90 on 20 October 1997.

ML

1989 Ford (i) Thunderbird coupé.
FORD MOTOR COMPANY

NICK BALDWIN

TELNACK, JACK (born 1937)

In 1987, Fortune magazine named John J. Telnack one of the year's 50 most fascinating people in American business. Jack was born in Henry Ford Hospital on 1 April 1937. He grew up in Dearborn, Michigan and, as a youngster, liked to bike over to Ford's test track across from Greenfield Village. There, sitting atop the serpentine brick fence, he and his friends would watch the pre-release Fords go by.

A few years later, his pride and joy became a lowered, channeled 1941 Mercury convertible. That's when he made up his mind to become a Ford designer. Jack drove out to Pasadena and enrolled in Art Center College of Design. He graduated in 1958 and went to work, naturally enough, at Ford. He led a fairly undistinguished early career, one high point of which was designing the wheelcovers for the 1965 Mustang.

Telnack's first break came in 1966 when Ford vice president Gene Bordinat sent him to Australia. 'Go down there and do something,' ordered Bordinat, 'just don't make my phone ring.' In other words, Jack was on his own.

Previous Australian Fords had been designed in Dearborn. Telnack succeeded in making Ford products more attractive to Australians. Bordinat brought Telnack back to Dearborn in 1969 but shipped him off again in 1973, this time to Ford of Europe. Jack became an overseas vice president. He returned to the U.S. in 1976 as Ford's director of international special vehicles and advanced concepts design office. As such, he campaigned to make American Fords more genuinely aerodynamic, starting with the slant-front 1979 Mustang.

In those days of the box-like 1978 Fairmont and 1980 Thunderbird, Ford chairman Donald E. Petersen asked Telnack if he really liked Ford's styling direction. Telnack said no, and Petersen encouraged Jack to try something new. From that direction came the 1983 Thunderbird, the next generation of aero design following the success of the 1979 Mustang.

Don Kopka had authored the highly aerodynamic Ford/Ghia Probe concept vehicles. From those, indirectly, came the more European 1984 Tempo/Topaz and Continental Mark VII. These transitional models were intended to familiarize Americans with Ford's aero direction, all of which ultimately led to the 1986 Ford Taurus, Telnack's great contribution to American auto design. The Taurus was done by a team of designers who'd worked in Ford's German design studios: Ray Evert, Fritz Mayhew and Bob Zokas. Credit went – and rightly so – to their boss, Jack Telnack.

Ford's hot-selling trucks and sport utilities were another of Telnack's design responsibilities. Among his homeruns in this area were the F-Series, Ranger, Explorer, Expedition, Mountaineer and Navigator.

Telnack became Ford's vice president of design in 1987 and global design chief in 1993. He pioneered the 'electronic studio' that linked Ford's seven major worldwide design operations, including Jaguar, Ghia and the California Concept Center. Jack introduced 'new edge' design with the Lincoln Sentinel, Mercury MC4, the European Ford Ka, Puma, and the 1999 Cougar. New edge combines soft, sculpted forms intersected with sharp lines and creases. Jack retired on 31 December 1997 and is currently designing yachts in Florida.

ML

567

MICHAEL LAMM

WALKER, GEORGE (1897–1993)

When Time magazine did a cover article on Ford design vice president George W. Walker in November 1957, they called him the 'Cellini of Chrome.' Walker loved the sound and sparkle of that title. It compared him with the great 16th-century Italian sculptor and silversmith. But according to Gene Bordinat, his successor at Ford, the Time editors also had in mind Cellini the sexual acrobat, another area in which Walker excelled.

If Bordinat and others can be believed, Walker boasted of bedding his high-school English teacher, and his trysts on the $30,000, inch-deep, black lambswool carpet of his private office at Ford were legendary, especially after the installers had to keep coming back to cut out soiled spots and replace them with plugs of fresh carpet.

George William Walker was born on 22 May 1897 in Chicago. His mother was an Oklahoman and part Cherokee, a fact in which Walker took great pride. His father, a conductor for the Erie Railroad, kept moving the family as his routes changed. As a result, George's schooling suffered. But he grew up big and husky and, at 15, became a semi-pro football player. He later played professionally with Jim Thorpe for the Cleveland Panthers. His main source of income to age 27 was football.

After many broken fingers and a flattened nose (later fixed), Walker decided to take advantage of an artistic bent. He attended the Cleveland School of Art and also attended the Otis Art Institute. After graduating, Walker opened an illustration studio in Cleveland and began doing artwork for bodymaker Baker-Raulang as well as for ad agencies, a paint company and Dura Corp., manufacturers of automotive door hardware.

Walker's business success, both at this early stage of his career and later, rested on his extremely upbeat and jovial personality. He was outgoing and vital and had great powers of persuasion. People just plainly liked him. He also carefully crafted a long list of social and business connections by becoming a member of dozens of clubs and fraternal organizations. He prided himself on being a 32nd-degree Mason and belonging to country clubs all over America. As president of Detroit's elite Recess Club (1939–49) high atop of the Fisher Building, Walker controlled who could join and who couldn't, and when a friend of someone like Harley Earl applied, it gave Walker another of his many bargaining chips.

Walker lucked out in the timing of his career, because American business was just growing style conscious in the late 1920s and early 1930. He came in on the coattails of industrial design's founding fathers, people like Raymond Loewy, Walter Dorwin Teague, Norman Bel Geddes and Henry Dreyfuss. After opening an office near GM headquarters in Detroit's New Center Building, Walker decided he needed to put his name before the Detroit business community, so he hired a publicist. His publicist did such a good job that Walker found himself getting assignments from as far away as Europe.

Not that he wasn't a skillful and motivated designer, but his real strengths lay in the politics and salesmanship of design. He soon built a sizable clientele, including Burroughs office machines, Admiral radios, International Harvester, Packard, and Nash-Kelvinator.

He also had a knack for hiring the right people. To service his automotive accounts, he took on former Chrysler designer Don Mortrude, who did the 1939 Nash. Through Mortrude, Walker claimed to have had a hand in designing the 1941 Packard Clipper, but if so, his role was minimal.

One automotive account Walker kept trying to get was Ford. He'd sold the senior Henry Ford some Dura door handles in the early 1930s by showing his samples on black velvet while his rivals laid theirs on the bare table. In 1935, Walker put together an elaborate, expensive portfolio of futuristic car designs to show to Henry Ford, not realizing that Edsel made most of the styling decisions. When Henry opened the huge portfolio, the binding broke and all the pages dropped out. Without a word, Henry got up and left. Walker didn't try to woo Mr Ford again after that.

Walker finally did land a Ford assignment in 1946 after his friend, Ernest Breech, asked him to submit designs in competition with E.T. (Bob) Gregorie for the 1949 Ford. Walker lucked into a beautiful clay model created by a Studebaker design group and presented it as his own. Breech and Henry Ford II liked it, and Walker's model became the 1949 Ford.

After Bob Gregorie left, Breech offered Walker a contract to become a styling consultant to Ford. Walker's group dominated Ford design activities and, in 1955, Ford hired Walker and his key people permanently and made Walker a Ford vice president.

George Walker would find himself in various moral and legal scrapes throughout his career, but somehow he always squeaked through. Once, when a grand jury investigated him for non-payment of taxes, his attorney literally pleaded him 'dumb', saying a designer of Walker's stature couldn't be bothered with attending to anything so mundane as taxes. Walker, sitting tanned and impressively dressed, told of smiling at the women on the jury. Needless to say, he got off.

Walker's group designed the 1952 Ford and used that format for all Ford Motor Company passenger cars through 1959, including Mercury and Lincoln. Even the classic 1955 Thunderbird and the misbegotten 1958 Edsel shared the general lines and attributes laid down by the 1952 Ford.

For many years, Walker owned a third interest in a Detroit company called Trim Trends. Trim Trends supplied stamped brightwork to nearly all U.S. automakers. After Walker got the 1949 Ford contract, he made sure that Trim Trends supplied all of Ford's stamped brightwork. And for many years afterward, Trim Trends kept getting Ford Motor Company orders. Walker, of course, encouraged his designers to specify stampings rather than cast trim.

The Walker styling touch extended not only to his clients' products but also to himself. He proudly maintained a huge and elegant wardrobe and racks of expensive shoes. His office, his cars and his dogs were all dramatically colour coordinated in black and white. According to Time, he once had Saks Fifth Avenue make him four 'cocktail suits': the male equivalent of cocktail dresses. These featured white fabric trimmed in different colours of braiding. He decided at the last minute not to wear his cocktail suits in public, lest he be considered 'eccentric'. Time also mentioned that Walker wore so much Faberge cologne '...that it lingers on long after he leaves the room'.

As politically savvy as Walker was, he didn't get along at all well with William Clay (Bill) Ford, the one Ford family member who cared as much about styling as his father, Edsel, had. Walker referred to Bill Ford as 'the fuckin' kid' behind his back and, of course, that returned to haunt him.

George Walker left Ford in 1961. He retired to Gulfstream, Florida and, at age 80, was elected town mayor. He later became Gulfstream's police commissioner and also served as a director of the Palm Beach County Hospital District and two Florida banks. Around 1980, still spry and sprightly, Walker built himself an elaborate home on a golf course in Tucson, Arizona, where he passed away on 19 January 1993. He was 96 years old.

ML

NICK BALDWIN

ENGEL, ELWOOD (1917–1986)

Elwood P. Engel was born in Newark, New Jersey. His father died when Elwood was seven, and his mother remarried and moved to Malvern, New York, on Long Island. Elwood showed such a strong aptitude for drawing that his art teacher enrolled him at Pratt even before he graduated high school.

At Pratt, Elwood earned side money by designing women's wear and working on designs for the 1939 New York Worlds Fair. After graduating in industrial design, he enrolled in Harley Earl's school for designers in Detroit. Here he met Joe Oros, a fellow student. Both completed the school and went to work for GM Styling, where they stayed until World War II. During the war, Engel became a cartographer for the Army in Europe and the Pacific.

Oros had taken a job with George Walker's industrial design firm and arranged for Engel to join him after the war. Together, they helped design the 1949 Ford under Walker's short-term contract with Ford Motor Company. When Walker received a permanent contract, Oros and Engel became his principal executive designers, with Oros in charge of Ford cars and trucks and Engel overseeing Lincoln and Mercury. Elwood is best remembered for spearheading the design of the 1961 Lincoln Continental.

In 1961, when George Walker retired from Ford, he wanted Engel to follow him as Ford's design vice president. Ford, however, appointed Gene Bordinat. Walker then convinced Chrysler to hire Engel to replace Virgil Exner, who had had a heart attack and was being edged out of his vice presidency.

At Chrysler, Engel is remembered for a relaxed, casual management style. He would sometimes pitch pennies with the clay modelers and behaved more like 'one of the boys' than an executive. While at Chrysler, he won the Pratt alumni prize, divorced his first wife and married his secretary. Engel had a flair for the dramatic, and when a design wasn't going well, he might pound his fist into a clay model or lash out verbally.

One of his first projects at Chrysler was to style the 1963 gas-turbine cars. These took their cue from his 1961 Continental, a theme he repeated again in the 1965 Imperial. Among his most memorable designs at Chrysler were the 1968 Dodge Charger, the 1970 Challenger/Barracuda and the entire line of full-sized 1970 models.

Engel retired in 1973 but stayed on as a Chrysler consultant until June 1974. He'd built a vacation home on 40 acres near Northport, Michigan, where he delighted in gardening, planting trees and simply going into the little town of Northport to socialize at the coffeeshop. He died on 24 June 1986 after a 10-year battle with cancer.

ML

After a rocky decade in the 1980s, Ford flourished in the 1990s, with record profits in 1997. Apart from 1991, when Chevrolet outsold them by 40,000 units, Ford has been the bestselling American car, thanks to the leadership of Harold A. Poling as chairman and Philip Benton Jr as president (1990–93), followed by British-born Alex Trotman who combined both posts from late 1993 to December 1998 when he gave way to William Clay Ford Jr, Henry's great-grandson, who was the first Ford to have his name on the door of the chairman's office for nearly 20 years. Australian-born Jac Nasser remained as chief executive.

NG

Further Reading
The Ford Road, Lorin Sorensen, Silverado Publishing Co., 1978.
'Ford, 1903–1984', The Auto Editors of *Consumer Guide,*1984.
Ford, the Men and the Machine, Robert Lacey, Heinemann, London, 1986.
The Ultimate Mustang Book, Nicky Wright, Multimedia,1986.
The Cars that Henry Ford built, Beverly Rae Kimes,
Automobile Quarterly Publications.
Mustang! The Complete History of America's Pioneer Ponycar,
Gary L. Witzenburg, Automobile Quarterly Publications.

FORD (ii) (CDN) 1904 to date

1904–1953 Ford Motor Co. of Canada Ltd, Walkerville, Ontario.
1953 to date Oakville, Ontario.

Ford's Canadian operation was opened on 17 August 1904, little more than a year after production began in Detroit. It was formed by Gordon McGregor of the Walkerville Wagon Co., with Detroit banker John Gray as president and Henry Ford as vice-president. In 1906 Henry stepped up to the presidency, which he retained until 1927 when he was succeeded by Edsel.

The first car to emerge from the Walkerville Wagon Works in October 1904 was a Model C. Only 117 cars were made in 1904, of which seven were the 4-cylinder Model B, and the balance, Model Cs. Until the arrival of the Model T, production was slow to grow, with only 667 cars being made up to the middle of 1908. These were assembled from US-built components rather than manufactured, although bodies were made by William Gray & Sons of Chatham, Ontario, who later made the GRAY-DORT car. The arrival of the Model T boosted output; 1280 cars were made in 1909–10, 11,600 in 1912–13 and 15,675 in 1913–14. By 1927 a total of 757,888 Model Ts had been made at Walkerville. Generally they followed the American design, although they had a one-man hood and swing-out 2-piece windscreen in 1920, three years before Detroit. An interesting sideline was the Ford boat, made from 1922 in co-operation with the Gidley Boat Co. of Penetang, Ontario. This not only used a Model T engine, but had the car's windscreen, sidescreens and hood.

The original agreement gave Ford of Canada sales rights in all countries of the British Empire, but in 1907 Henry took away the concession for the British Isles, setting up a factory at Manchester in 1911. However, assembly plants in South Africa and Australia were set up by Ford of Canada, as well as distribution branches in Singapore, Malaya and India.

Walkerville started Model A production in December 1927, and it built its millionth car in 1931. Like the parent company, they launched the V8 in 1932 and the Mercury in 1938, but Walkerville never built the Lincoln or Lincoln Zephyr. Postwar Canadian Fords carried their own brand names, and some differed in trim from their US counterparts. The Meteor was a 1949 Ford with a Mercury grill, and there was also the Monarch (1946–51), a slightly restyled Mercury, and the Frontenac of 1960 which was based on the Ford Falcon. From 1962 to 1979 the name Meteor Montcalm was used for a Canadian-styled Mercury, and other variations included the Meteor Niagara (1954–59 Ford Custom), Meteor Rideau (1954–-59 Ford Fairlane) and Rideau Victoria (1955–56 Ford Victoria). Apart from these locally named cars, several familiar Fords were built in Canada under their own names, such as the Mustang, Maverick and Pinto. The Crown Victoria was built only in Canada, for export to the United States; this enabled Ford to keep their CAFE (Corporate Average Fuel Economy) lower than if it had included the high-consumption V8 engine. CAFE is based only on US-built cars.

In 1953 a new plant at Oakville was opened and took over from Walkerville. Another plant dedicated to compacts was opened at St Thomas in 1968, although later production there was extended to include the Crown Victoria. As well as the Crown Victoria, the Windstar was built in Canada at the Oakville plant.

NG

2000 Ford (i) Taurus sedan.
FORD MOTOR COMPANY

FORD (iii) **(GB)** 1911 to date

1911–1931 Ford Motor Co. Ltd, Trafford Park, Manchester.
1921–1984 Ford Motor Co. Ltd, Cork, Irish Republic.
1931 to date Ford Motor Co. Ltd, Dagenham, Essex.
1964–1966 Ford Advanced Vehicles Ltd, Slough, Buckinghamshire.

Ford's first European assembly plant was set up at Trafford Park industrial estate, in a former tramcar factory. Here Model Ts came in crates direct from Detroit and up the Manchester Ship Canal. In 1914 Trafford Park turned out 7310 cars; this was 29 per cent of total British production and the largest number from a single factory in the whole of Europe. In 1917 Ford opened a plant at Cork, initially for tractor manufacture, although cars were added in 1921, and a wide variety of British Fords were made there until the plant was closed in 1984. The first specifically European Ford was the Model AF, similar to the Model A but with a smaller engine of 2043cc. This was fitted to most of the 14,516 Model As made at Trafford Park and Cork during 1929–31.

A new Ford factory was opened at Dagenham, Essex, in October 1931. Its first product was a Model AA 1.5ton truck, but in February 1932 came a small British Ford designed for the European market. The Model Y had a 933cc 4-cylinder side-valve engine, a 3-speed gearbox with synchromesh on the upper two ratios, and the same transverse leaf suspension as the Models T, A, and pre–1948 V8s. The 2- and 4-door saloon bodies were designed by Bob Gregorie when he was working in the Lincoln styling department, and anticipated the styling of the 1933 American Fords. They were later called the Tudor and Fordor models, although these names were not used in 1932. The former was priced at £120, reduced to £100 in 1935. This was the first British saloon to be sold for this magic figure, but it lasted only two years. When the Y was replaced in late 1937, the new 8hp Tudor saloon cost £117.

The Model Y was a great success in Britain, and gave Ford a 41 per cent share of the market for cars of 8hp and under in 1936, compared with 22 per cent the previous year. Production at Dagenham and Cork was 157,668, and the Model Y was also made in France, Germany, Spain and New Zealand. Its successor, the Model 7Y (April 1937 to 1939), had the same engine and suspension with a new body, Girling brakes and pressed steel wheels instead of wire. Just over 65,000 were made up to 1939 when it was replaced by the Anglia. This was generally similar, apart from a new bonnet and grill, but only about 6000 were made before the war halted production in 1941. The Anglia was revived in 1945 to become one of the most important postwar British Fords.

2000 Ford (i) Crown Victoria LX sedan.
FORD MOTOR COMPANY

1966 Ford (ii) Meteor Montcalm convertible.
NATIONAL MOTOR MUSEUM

1936 Ford (iii) Ten CX Fordor saloon.
NICK GEORGANO

1936 Ford (iii) V8-22 saloon.
NATIONAL MOTOR MUSEUM

1939 Ford (iii) Prefect drophead coupé.
NATIONAL MOTOR MUSEUM

1948 Ford (iii) Anglia 10hp export saloon.
NATIONAL MOTOR MUSEUM

In 1935 Ford of Britain extended their range with the 1172cc Model C Ten, made in Tudor, Fordor and open tourer versions. This classic engine, a 3-bearing side-valve four generally similar to the smaller 8hp, remained in the Ford range until 1962, and was used to power countless trials specials as well as the DELLOW, NORDEC and other small-production sports cars. In 1937 the Model C was replaced by the 7W Ten De Luxe with styling similar to that of the 7Y, and this in turn gave way for 1939 to the generally similar Prefect. When wartime demands ended Prefect production in 1940, a total of 179,704 of the Model C, 7W and Prefect had been made.

The Eights had made up the bulk of prewar Dagenham production, being ideally suited to the British market. Larger cars were also made, the Model B during 1932–34, and the V8 from 1932 to 1939. Like the A, the B came with two engine sizes, 2043 and 3285cc, the smaller being known as the BF. The 3622cc V8 was not made in large numbers at Dagenham, only 13,508 in eight seasons, but there was also a smaller V8 using the 2227cc engine that had not been a success in the US. This engine was used in American-styled bodies similar to those of the big V8s for the 1936 season, but in 1937–39 there was a smaller, more compact 4-light saloon, the V8-62, of which 12,226 were made.

The Dagenham factory was quick to get back into production after the war – the first Anglia came off the lines in May 1945 and the first Prefect a month later. They were identical to the prewar models, although the Prefect tourer and cabriolet were not revived, but in 1949 they were mildly restyled. The V8 also made a brief comeback in the shape of the Pilot. This had a 4-light saloon body similar to that of the prewar V8-62, but with the larger 3622cc engine. The Pilot gave Ford of Britain some of their first rallying successes when Ken Wharton won the 1950 Tulip and Lisbon rallies. A total of 22,155 Pilots were made between 1947 and 1950. Nearly all were saloons, but a few estate cars were made by outside coachbuilders, and there were also some pick-ups and a handful of 6-light 7-seater limousines.

A New Generation
At the 1950 London Motor Show Ford showed their first all-new postwar cars, the 1508cc Consul and 2262cc Zephyr. These had ohv engines with the same oversquare dimensions (79.37 × 76.2mm) for the 4-cylinder Consul and 6-cylinder Zephyr. They shared the same all-enveloping 4-light saloon body which was of semi-monocoque construction, with substantial chassis members welded to the floorpan. The Zephyr had an extra 4in of wheelbase to accommodate its longer engine. They were, in effect, American-type cars for the European Market and shared with the 1949 US Fords the body designer George Walker and suspension expert Earl McPherson, whose coil springs in independent struts have been used in European Fords ever since. They were the first British Fords to have hydraulic brakes. The new cars were among the most modern popularly priced British saloons, and the 68bhp Zephyr was a good performer. Racing driver Raymond Mays reported that it cornered like a racing car, better than some racing cars in fact, and that one could make maximum and cruising speed synonymous. From 1952 there were convertibles in both models, and from 1953 there was a DeLuxe version of the Zephyr called the Zodiac. The first series was made up to 1956, by which time a total of nearly 400,000 had been made; 227,732 Consuls, 148,629 Zephyrs and 22,634 Zodiacs. They were followed by the restyled Mk II (1956–62; 682,400) and Mk III (1962–68; 291,900) versions with larger engines of 1703 and 2553cc. There was no Consul in the Mk III series, the 4-cylinder car being called the Zephyr 4. The Mk IV Zephyr, which was made from 1968 to 1972, had fresh styling, and vee engines – a 1996cc V4 and 2995cc V6. The Zodiac Executive had a 2994cc V6, and power steering from October 1967.

The small 4-cylinder Anglia and Prefect gained Consul-style full-width bodies and McPherson suspension in 1954, although they kept the old side-valve engines for a further five years. Meanwhile the old Anglia with prewar styling was continued under the name Popular. In 1959 came an all-new Anglia with 997cc ohv engine, so the 1954-styled Anglia took the name Popular and had another three years of life. The new Anglia, known as the 105E, had a very oversquare engine (80.96 x 48.4mm) which gave a low piston speed and longer life. Capacity went up to 1198cc in 1962, although the smaller engine was continued. This was the first of the Kent engines which were used for more than 20 years. The 105E had distinctive styling, with a reverse angle rear window, which was seen on the larger Consul Classic. The 105E was made up to 1968, and production was 1,083,960.

1952 Ford (iii) Prefect saloon.
NICK GEORGANO

Meanwhile, Dagenham launched for 1963 one of their best-selling cars ever, the Cortina. This was a conventionally styled and engined saloon powered by 1198 or 1498cc Kent engines, with 4-speed all-synchromesh gearboxes, automatic available from 1964 and front disc brakes from 1965. The Cortina was not as distinctive-looking as the 105E Anglia, but it quickly became one of Britain's favourite family cars, was widely used by fleet operators and was the basis for some very successful competition cars. The Cortina Mk I GT (1963–66), had front disc brakes from the start and an 83bhp engine, but the real flyer was the Lotus Cortina which used a 105bhp 1588cc twin-cam Lotus

Elan engine (based on a Ford block) in a lowered Cortina body shell. It had coil rear suspension and disc brakes at the front, and top speed of 108mph (173km/h). The Lotus Cortina was very successful in rallying and saloon car racing, and was also popular as a sporting road car. Only 3301were made of the Mk I, compared with 76,947 GTs and 933,143 of the Cortina 1200 and 1500.

In 1967 came the restyled Cortina Mk II, which also had its GT and Lotus variants, although the latter were not so exciting as the Mk Is, and were known as Cortina Lotus rather than the other way round. They were built at Dagenham, whereas the original Lotus Cortina was assembled at Lotus' factory at Cheshunt. With the Mk III (1970–76), the Cortina gained a larger body, so that it was nearly as big as the Zephyr/Zodiac range. These were officially replaced in 1972 by the Granada, which had basically similar styling to the Cortina Mk III, but employed all-independent suspension and a choice of 1996cc V4 or 2994cc V6 engines. For 1975 the V4 was replaced by a 1993cc ohc in-line four developed for the American Ford Pinto. The Cortina continued in Mk IV (1976–79) and Mk V (1979–82) versions, with a greater variety of engines from a 1297cc in-line four to a 2293cc V6. Styling was shared with the German Ford Taunus. Both Cortina and Taunus were replaced by the Sierra in 1982.

The GT40

During the 1960s, the American Ford company became heavily involved in motor sport, campaigning on four fronts, drag racing, stock car racing, track racing and international sports/prototype racing. The biggest challenge in the latter field was the 24-Hour Race at Le Mans, and it was to win this event that Ford started the GT40 project. It was an international undertaking, for the initiative came from Detroit, although the cars were built at Ford's Advanced Vehicles factory at Slough. The later Mk IIs were finished by Kar Kraft, a Detroit-based Ford subsidiary.

NICK BALDWIN

PERRY, PERCIVAL LEE DEWHURST (1879–1957)

A child of the Black Country, Percival Lee Dewhurst Perry; was raised in Birmingham, Britain's engineering heartland. He won a scholarship to King Edward's School, but was prevented from continuing his education by the poverty of his family.

He responded to a newspaper advertisement for an office job in London, which turned out to have been placed by H.J. Lawson, and suddenly he was on the inside of the motor business, and his interest in automobiles swelled. He learned to drive a De Dion-Bouton tricycle and Daimler horseless carriages.

Parting with Lawson, he joined a firm of printers in Kingston-upon-Hull, where he had an aunt and an uncle (and was to meet his future wife). But after a few years of moderate prosperity, he decided that he really belonged in the motor trade, and again began looking for openings in London.

This coincided with the return of one of his personal friends from America, who had brought three Ford cars back with him, and was selling rights for Ford cars in Britain for a five-year term. They agreed to go into partnership, and founded the American Motor Car Co. with offices at 117 Long Acre, London, in 1904. The pace of their business was restrained only by Ford's terms of f.o.b. settlement of all invoices. As the sales curve rose, they fell deeper in debt.

That was when Perry had the idea of going to America and getting Ford to finance its British sales organisation. He went in 1906, and met with Ford's export manager, R.M. Lockwood in New York, before travelling to Detroit where he met Ford's banker, John S. Gray, who introduced him to C.H. Wills and Henry Ford. He also met James Cousins and Norval Hawkins, but failed in his main purpose. He did, however, establish friendships and a position of trust with the Ford family and several Ford Motor Co. officials, which smoothed things and speeded up the business.

The American Motor Car Co. changed its name to Central Motor Co. in 1905, remaining in Long Acre where the fully assembled cars arrived from Detroit in big wooden boxes.

In 1908 Perry went back to Detroit, and this time the discussions achieved his aims. He went on the payroll of a new branch of the Ford Motor Co., established at 55 Shaftesbury Avenue, in London, as general manager. From that base, he built a nationwide sales organisation.

He founded the Ford Motor Co. (England) in 1909, and two years later moved headquarters to Trafford Park, Manchester, setting up a local assembly plant. The cars were no longer shipped complete, but crated as knocked-down kits. The company was reorganised as Henry Ford & Son, Ltd.

Perry was awarded a CBE in 1917 and a KBE in1918 for his voluntary service in many government departments. In 1927 he secured a huge tract of Thames-side land near Dagenham, Essex, and Ford's architects and industrial engineers prepared plans for a true manufacturing plant. The Dagenham plant came on stream in 1931. Its first passenger car product was the Model A, followed two years later by the Model Y, a scaled-down chassis with more modern styling. On the opening of the Dagenham plant, the company became Ford Motor Co. Ltd, under Perry as managing director (the Americans called him president) and chairman.

In 1938 he became Lord Perry of Stock Harvard. He retired in 1948, and Sir Rowland Smith took over as chairman. He died on 17 June 1957.

JPN

1959 Ford (iii) Zodiac saloon.
NATIONAL MOTOR MUSEUM

The GT40, so called because its roof was 40in (1016mm) from the ground, was developed from Eric Broadley's Lola GT, a Ford-powered sports/racing coupé of 1963. The original GT40 had a mid-mounted 4.2-litre V8 engine driving through a Colotti transaxle, and a sheet steel monocoque body with fibreglass panels and doors. They showed great potential in racing, but failed to finish a single event in 1964 due to cracking of the light alloy blocks, so for 1965 the 4767cc engine was used. They still had only one major win (the Daytona 1000km), but in 1966, with a 6997cc engine, they swept the board, finishing 1-2-3 at Daytona and Le Mans, and 1-2 at Sebring. A total of 107 GT40s were made at Slough, of which about 31 were road-going versions with detuned engines and more comfortable interiors. It is difficult to be dogmatic about figures as some road cars were converted for racing and vice versa. The Mk III of 1967–69 was intended to be the definitive road car with better silencing and interiors and even some space for luggage. A batch of 20 was planned but only seven were completed, of which four had lhd. From the 1980s onwards, several companies on both sides of the Atlantic have offered GT40 replicas in kit or complete forms. The best were ERA and SAFIR.

Towards the European Ford

Despite building cars for much the same markets, the British and German Ford companies made no common models or even interchangeable parts until the mid–1960s. The Transit van, introduced in 1965, was the first design to be made in both countries. However, in 1967 a new controlling company named Ford of Europe was formed, under the direction of Ford of Germany's head, John Andrews. The first passenger car to be born from this new organisation was the Escort. For this and later Fords see FORD (ix).

One purely English car which carried the Ford name, although not made by them, was the RS200 mid-engined 4-wheel drive coupé specially designed for Group B rallying and announced in 1984. Built for Ford by RELIANT, it had a 250bhp 1.8-litre fuel-injected 4wd which gave a top speed of 140mph (225km/h). The 200 necessary for homologation were not ready until early 1986, but their rallying career was short-lived. In the Portuguese Rally, an RS200 was involved in a fatal accident in which three spectators died; this and the deaths of Henry Toivonen and Sergio Cresto in the Corsican Rally led to the banning of the ultra-fast Group B cars at the end of 1986. Ford set about marketing the

1961 Ford (iii) Popular Saloon.
NICK GEORGANO

1963 Ford (iii) Anglia Super saloon.
NATIONAL MOTOR MUSEUM

1966 Ford (iii) Cortina MKI 4-door saloon.
SIDNEY GEORGE WARREN

1938 Matford (Ford (iv)) F92A saloon.
NICK GEORGANO/NATIONAL MOTOR MUSEUM

RS200 as a road car. With interior trim by Tickford the cars cost £50,000, the highest price ever charged for a Ford.

NG

Further Reading
The Big Idea, the Story of Ford in Europe, Dennis Hackett, Ford Motor Co. Ltd, Dagenham, 1978.

FORD (iv) (F) 1916–1954

1916–1925 Automobiles Ford, Bordeaux; Asnières, Seine (1925–1939).
1934–1940 SA Française Matford, Strasbourg.
1939–1954 Ford S.A.F., Poissy, Seine.

The first French Ford factory was an assembly plant set up at Bordeaux by Percival Perry, the head of the English Ford Motor Co. Model Ts were assembled there until 1925, when a new factory was acquired at Asnières, near Paris. This built Model Ts up to 1927, Model As from 1927 to 1931 and Model Ys from 1932 to 1934. These little cars did not sell so well in France as in Britain or Germany, nor did the V8 which was imported from America and incurred heavy import duties which priced it out of the market. In order to find proper manufacturing facilities instead of a mere assembly plant, Maurice Dollfuss, head of Automobiles Ford, proposed a merger with the old-established MATHIS company of Strasbourg. They had a large factory and a few years earlier had been the fourth largest car maker in France, but by 1934 their sales had slumped badly.

A new company called SA Française Matford was formed in September 1934. They rented the Strasbourg factory from Emile Mathis, and retained the Asnières factory as well. The plan was that Ford-based Matfords should be made alongside the existing Mathis models, but apart from a few hybrid cars called Quadruflex, which had Ford V8 engines in Mathis all-independently sprung chassis, the factory was soon making only Matfords.

The 1935 Matfords were identical in appearance to the American Ford V8-48, and were available only with the 3622cc engine. A more individual French design emerged in 1936. This was the V8 Alsace, which had a swept-tail 4-light saloon body, unlike anything made in Detroit. Two engine sizes were now offered; 2227 and 3622cc V8s, and from 1937 additional body styles included a cabriolet and a hatchback *commerciale* for travelling salesmen. The hatchback, so widespread today, was pioneered in France, where Berliet, Chenard-Walcker, Citroën and Renault also offered this style in the 1930s. In 1938 Matford added a wood-bodied station wagon to their range.

The Matford sold well in France, where buyers appreciated the power of a V8 engine concealed discreetly under a bonnet no longer than that of many 4-cylinder cars. Apart from the Chenard-Walcker Aigle 8, which also had a Ford engine, the Matford was the only V8 made in France. Sales rose from 1049 in 1935 to 8898 in 1938, but dropped to less than half this figure in 1939, as the Matford factories increased their output of trucks for the French Army.

As war threatened, Maurice Dollfuss decided that a safer factory location than Strasbourg must be found. He bought a 60-acre (24 hectare) site at Poissy, on the Seine about 25 miles from Paris, and built a completely new factory, which opened in 1939. He also ended his links with Emile Mathis, forming a new company, Ford S.A.F. (Société Anonyme Française) in August 1939.

In June 1940 the Poissy factory came under the control of the invading German forces, and built trucks for the Wehrmacht for the next four years. After the war the factory quickly returned to car production with the F-472, which was very similar to the prewar small V8. Because of the prevailing austerity and shortage of petrol, the larger V8 was not reintroduced for several years. The only factory body style was the 4-light saloon, but a few attractive cabriolets were built on the F-472 chassis by Antem and Guilloré.

In the autumn of 1948 the F-472 was replaced by the Vedette. This used a slightly smaller edition of the V8 engine (2158cc) but otherwise it was all new, with coil ifs, a cruciform-braced frame and an all-enveloping saloon body which bore a family resemblance to that of the 1949 Mercury. The Vedette had, in fact, been planned as a small Ford to be built in America, only to be dropped as dealers reported practically no public interest in a small car. Dollfuss had seen prototypes during a visit to Detroit in June 1945, and expressed interest, so when the parent company decided against the small car project, it fell conveniently into the hands of the French organisation.

The Vedette was made initially only as a 4-door saloon, but for 1950 a 2-door coupé and cabriolet were offered, and in Spring 1952 came the Abeille, which had a hatchback in the prewar style, and could carry a cargo of 500kg. Two other derivatives of the Vedette were the Vendome with 3917cc engine in the same body, and the Comète sports coupé. This had a sleek 4-seater body designed by Jacques Brasseur of Facel Métallon who made the bodies for Ford. Later, they launched their own car, the FACEL VEGA.

Handsome though the Comète was, it did not sell well, being underpowered and too expensive. With the 66bhp 2158cc engine, it could only do 80mph (130km/h), yet it cost 1,368,000 francs in 1951, compared with 851,000 francs for a Vedette saloon and only 628,000 for the Citroën 15CV six. In order to improve performance Ford gave the Comète the 3917cc V8 engine in 1954, which boosted top speed to just over 92mph (150km/h). This model, with wire wheels and a mesh grill instead of the Comète's single bar, was known as the Monte Carlo. Unfortunately the bigger engine took it over the 15CV tax bracket, which meant that a Monte Carlo owner paid 77,420 francs a year, compared with 22,540 for a Comète.

This tax burden also hit sales of the Vendôme, so when Ford brought out a new car for 1955, only the smaller engine was available. This new Vedette came into line with the production of Dagenham and Cologne, having a unitary construction saloon body and McPherson strut ifs. The 4-light saloon body was more up to date than Dagenham's, with a wrap-around rear window. Engine capacity was increased to 2351cc and power to 80bhp. Top speed was 87mph (140km/h) and the cars came in three models; basic Trianon, mid-range Versailles and luxury Régence, the latter with wire wheels and 2-tone paintwork.

Relatively few of these cars were made under the Ford name, for in November 1954 Ford headquarters in America sold the French operation to SIMCA Industries. They retained 15.2 per cent of the equity, but even this was sold four years later. The reason for the sale was that the Vedette was too large to reach the mass market, and to develop a new smaller car would have been too costly. Twenty years later they would doubtless have put a British or German design into production, but in 1954 the concept of a European Ford was still a long way off. However, the Vedette survived and was made under the Simca name until 1962.

NG

Further Reading
The Big Idea, The Story of Ford in Europe, Dennis Hackett, Ford Motor Co. Ltd, Dagenham, 1978.
Vedette, Le Grand Livre, D. Paignieux, La Boutique du Collectionneur, 1999.

FORD (v) **(D)** 1925 to date
1925–1931 Ford Motor Co. AG, Berlin.
1931–1939 Ford Motor Co. AG, Cologne.
1939 to date Ford-Werke AG, Cologne.
The first Ford operation in Germany was a parts depot set up in Hamburg in 1912. The Ford Motor Co. AG was not established until 1925, when an assembly plant was built at Plotzensee, Berlin. Here Model T trucks were assembled from April 1925, and cars from June 1926. A total of 3771 Model T cars were turned out before the Model A took over. As in Britain, two versions of

1953 Ford (iv) Vedette 13CV saloon in 1954 Monte Carlo Rally.
NATIONAL MOTOR MUSEUM

1953 Ford (iv) Comète coupé.
NICK GEORGANO

1935 Ford (v) Model Y Köln cabriolet.
NATIONAL MOTOR MUSEUM

the A were made, with 2043 or 3285cc 4-cylinder engines, and these were followed in 1932 by the B and BF using the same engines in the V8 chassis. The 3622cc V8 was not German-built until 1935, by which time the company had moved to a new factory at Cologne. The site for this factory was offered to Ford by Konrad Adenauer, the Mayor of Cologne and after the war the celebrated Chancellor of the Federal German Republic. Unlike Berlin, Cologne was a proper manufacturing plant, with a growing number of German-made components in the cars. By 1937 the Ford Eifel was 100 per cent German-made. The Berlin plant was closed in April 1931 after 44,209 cars and trucks had been assembled there.

Production at Cologne started in May 1931, and the factory built the Model A well into 1932, several months longer than Detroit or Dagenham. They also made the models B and BF, and continued to use the 3285cc 4-cylinder engine in the V8 chassis and body up to 1936. This peculiarly German model was known

1948 Ford (v) Taunus saloon.
NATIONAL MOTOR MUSEUM

1953 Ford (v) Taunus 12M saloon in the 1954 Monte Carlo Rally.
NATIONAL MOTOR MUSEUM

1964 Ford (v) Taunus 17M saloon.
NATIONAL MOTOR MUSEUM

1966 Osi-Ford (Ford (v)) 20 M/TS coupé.
NICK GEORGANO

as the Rheinland. In 1933 Cologne began production of the 933cc 4-cylinder Model Y, called in Germany the Köln (Cologne). This was almost identical to the British-made car, although the 4-door saloon was never made in Germany, and there were some cabriolets which were never offered by Dagenham. These were bodied by Deutsch, who made open models of German Ford up to 1971. The Köln was dropped in 1936, after 11,121 had been made. It did not sell very well, being less powerful and more expensive than the contemporary small Opel. More successful was the 1172cc Eifel, which sold 61,495 units between 1936 and 1940. This began as a German copy of the British 10hp Model C, but in 1937 acquired more individual styling, resembling a scaled down V8. The Deutsch-bodied cabriolets were particularly attractive. About 200 roadster bodies for the Eifel were made for Ford by another car maker, STOEWER of Stettin. In 1939 the Eifel was joined by the Taunus, named after the mountains near Cologne, the name being carried on successive models of German Ford up to 1982. The Taunus used the same 1172cc engine in a slightly longer chassis with hydraulic brakes, which were not seen on British Fords until the 1951 season and even then only on the Consul and Zephyr. It had a streamlined body with faired headlamps in the style of the 1939 American Ford V8. Military and essential civilian orders kept the Taunus in production until 1942, by which time 7100 had been made.

In addition to the 4-cylinder cars, Cologne built 15,336 V8s, mostly with the 3622cc engine, but 442 had the small-block 2227cc unit. Styling was similar to American models in 1935–36, but the later German models differed slightly, never having the faired headlamps of the American cars. Like the Eifel, the V8 was available with a handsome cabriolet body by Deutsch.

The Cologne factory was less badly damaged during the war than most German car plants, and they were able to restart production of trucks in May 1945. Although damage was relatively small, Ford-Werke received from the US approximately $1.1 million as compensation for the bombing of the Cologne plant. Passenger cars were not built until November 1948, when the Taunus began to come off the lines again. At first it was very similar to the prewar model, but a new radiator grill came in 1950, and from 1951 the split windscreen gave way to a single one. A total of 74,128 were made, including estate cars, taxicabs and delivery vans, before the new Taunus 12M appeared in 1952. Henry Ford II visited Cologne in 1948, and discussed plans to buy up Volkswagen, but these came to nothing because of the uncertain ownership of VW.

The 12M was an all-new car apart from the faithful old 1172cc engine. The body was completely restyled and of integral construction, the new Taunus falling into line with American and British Fords in having McPherson strut ifs. The success of the 12M helped Ford to exceed their best prewar year (1938) by a handsome margin in 1952, with 40,344 sales. The head of Ford-Werke at this time was Ehrhart Vitger who had been put in charge by the Allied Military Government in 1946. Ford had lost 236 dealers to the Eastern zone, but within five years Vitger, had come close to replacing these, in many cases taking over dealerships from Adler, who no longer made cars. Between 1950 and 1960 Ford-Werke increased output by nearly 800 per cent, overtaking Ford of Canada in 1958, and making twice as many cars as Canada in 1962. On the domestic front, Ford kept a steady third place, behind Volkswagen and Opel.

In 1955 a 1.5-litre ohv engine was introduced for the 12M bodyshell, the new car being called the 15M. It was a short-stroke design, similar to the British Consul, but with different dimensions. Slightly smaller at 1498cc, compared with the Consul's 1508cc, it was nevertheless more powerful; 55bhp against 47bhp, and had the advantage of a 4-speed gearbox. On the debit side, no Taunus had four doors until the 1698cc 17M of 1957. The old 1172cc side-valve engine was continued in the 12M until 1962, when a completely new German Ford appeared. Still called the Taunus 12M, it had a V4 engine driving the front wheels, and had been planned as a sub-compact for the American market, called the Cardinal and to have been built at the Louisville, Kentucky, factory. Two engine sizes were offered, a 1183cc 40bhp and a 1498cc giving 50 or 55bhp according to tune. Originally the only body styles were a 2-door coupé and station wagon, and the usual limited production cabriolet by Deutsch.

The 4-wheel drive 12M was very successful, with 1,063,931 being made between 1962 and 1970. The vee engine became universal on German Fords for nearly a decade; other models were the V4 17M (1498 and 1699cc), the V6 20M (1998 and 2293cc) and the V6 26M (2550cc). Several high-performance models were made, although there was no German equivalent of the Lotus Cortina. The 15M/RS gave 75bhp from its 1699cc, with a top speed of 98mph

(158km/h), while the most powerful of the V6s was the 108bhp 20M/TS (106mph/ 170km/h). A limited production sports coupé of 1966–68 was the OSI-Ford 20M/TS with fastback 2-seater body by OSI of Turin, and a choice of 1998 or 2293cc V6 engines. These cost around DM15,000, compared with DM10,340 for the regular 4-seater 20M/RS coupé; 870 were sold with the 2-litre engine and 409 with the 2.3-litre.

In January 1968 the Escort went into production at Cologne, marking the beginning of European Fords common to both British and German operations. For this and later models, see FORD (ix).

NG

Further Reading
The Big Idea, The Story of Ford in Europe, Dennis Hackett,
Ford Motor Co. Ltd, Dagenham, 1978.

FORD (vi) (AUS) 1926 to date
Ford Motor Co. of Australia Pty Ltd, Geelong, Victoria.
Ford Motor Co. of Australia Pty Ltd, Campbellfield, Victoria.
Established by the Ford Motor Co. of Canada, a plant on the lines of the Toronto facility was constructed, quickly becoming a major builder of standardised bodies. While generally following overseas programmes, local requirements led to the development of the 'Ute', which has become part of Aussie folklore. While a light commercial pick-up body on a car chassis was common, the Ford initiative was to build a coupé, with all the car appointments, having an integrated tray area instead of a luggage/dickey seat space. It was a regular production model and marketed as a car body type rather than as a commercial. Farmers, for example, could justify purchase on the grounds of work use but suffered no loss of car amenities.

It continued on the popular models and its acceptance ensured that other producers followed. Beginning on the 1934 Ford V8, it was also fitted to the English 8/10hp models, the Consul and Zephyr and has been ongoing through the Falcon's currency. The saloon body for the postwar Anglia and Prefect had a prominent luggage trunk and an Anglia tourer, by Martin & King, was Australia's lowest priced car for some years.

Wholly Australian manufacture followed the erection of a new factory, which had 7 hectares under one roof and the selection of the Falcon, a US compact with a 6-cylinder 2365cc engine, for production in 1960. Initially unchanged, its acceptance was marred by mechanical weakness but its option of automatic transmission was a sales advantage. As following revisions gradually drifted away from equivalent home models, larger engines of 2783 and 3277cc became available. A wholly new XR series of 1966 had US styling but much local design input. It was larger, with a 111in (2819mm) wheelbase and the option of a 4740cc V8 engine. The upmarket Fairlane was so based with 116in (2946mm) wheelbase and it filled a market gap in an economic fashion, to be rewarded in the showrooms. A high-performance GT model also appeared.

Exports of rhd cars were made from this time and revisions included disc brakes and a 4953cc V8. In 1970 with the XY series, the 6-cylinder engines were 3277 and 4100cc. In 1972 the Cortina TC was fitted with the locally made 6 – the Ford contribution to the 'shoe-horned six' fad. This ran through the TE revision until replaced in production by the MAZDA 626-based Telstar. The president of Ford Asia Pacific, Bill Bourke, then announced that the basic Fiera, developed in Australia, was an entrant into motor manufacturing programmes of countries such as Indonesia, Korea, Malaysia, the Philippines, and Thailand. An Australian XA Falcon of 1972 formed the basis of a family of models, including the Fairlane ZF and a 121in (3073mm) wheelbase LTD luxury version with a 5752cc V8 engine. Its 2-door companion was the Landau and the coupé body also became available on the Falcon.

In 1976 emissions regulations were met by fitting cross-flow cylinder heads. The 1979 XD had a crisply styled body with large window areas and the Falcon, which had suffered during the energy crisis from the success of the smaller Holden Commodore, gradually achieved supremacy. The 6-cylinder engine gained an alloy cylinder head, handling was sharpened and the Fairlane was visually distinguished by having a third window. The V8 option was deleted in 1982 and the fuel injection fitted to the sixes gave improved power and economy. Coil rear suspension was fitted in 1983 while unleaded fuel engines, 5-speed manual gearbox and 4-wheel disc brakes arrived in 1986. A wholly new body shell was used for the 1988 EA model, which had 3.2- and 3.9-litre ohc

1939 Ford (vi) Tudor sedan.
EDDIE FORD

1971 Ford (vi) Fairlane 500 sedan.
NATIONAL MOTOR MUSEUM

1999 Ford (vi) Falcon AU Forte sedan.
FORD AUSTRALIA

engines and rack and pinion steering. Companion models were the Fairlane NA and the DA series LTD.

An alliance with NISSAN resulted in a clone of the front-drive Pintara being marketed as the Corsair. The 1990s revisions to the Falcon included the reintroduction of the Windsor 'small block' V8, the automatic transmission became 4-speed and a range of safety features were incorporated. A wholly Australian designed Falcon AU series was released in 1998, and this incorporated constructional advances to give a lighter and more economically manufactured structure, good air penetration and the option of irs. Coincidentally announced was that the new president and chief executive of Ford's corporate empire was Australian Jac Nasser. In 1999 came a Tickford-tuned version of the Falcon, with a 270bhp V8 engine and 4-speed automatic transmission with steering wheel mounted control.

MG

Further Reading
The History of Ford Australia, Norm Darwin, Eddie Ford Publications, 1986.

1981 Ford (viii) Corcel II saloon.
ALVARO CASAL TATLOCK

FORD (vii) (RA) 1962 to date

Ford Motors Argentina SA, Buenos Aires.

Ford Motor Company's first branch in South America, was inaugurated in Buenos Aires, in 1913. The first automobiles sold were model Ts. By 1916 a total of 3,549 vehicles had been sold and an assembly plant was built in 1917. The first model A to come out of that plant, was the 100,000th vehicle Ford assembled in Argentina. After Henry Ford II visited Argentina in 1959, it was decided to start local manufacture in a new plant built in General Pacheco, Buenos Aires. In 1960 production started. Only Ford F100 and Ford F600 commercial vehicles were made there, until in 1962, Falcon production commenced too. Falcon production, as in Australia, was destined to continue long after manufacture of this model ceased in the USA.

The early Argentine Falcons were designated 170, because of their engine capacity in cubic inches. They had a 2786cc, 6-cylinder engines, and only 4-door sedans were produced. From 1962 to 1965, 38,419 were made. In 1964 the Falcon Futura 188 with 3064cc engine was introduced. The engine was to be enlarged again in 1967, to 3620cc. In that same year the Falcon station wagon was introduced. The Ford Fairlane came in 1969, with two engine options: V8 4785cc or 6-cylinder 3620cc. A version of the German 2.3-litre Taunus was added in 1975. The Taunus came in saloon and coupé versions. The 1980s brought along the Escort. Although exports of Falcons to neighbouring countries petered out around 1984, the model continued to be offered locally until 1990, when production stopped for good. Later on came the Sierra, which survived until 1994. 1999 production was limited to the Escort in 4-door, 2-door and station wagon configurations, with either 1796cc, 54bhp or 1753, 60bhp engines.
ACT

FORD (viii) (BR) 1965 to date

1965–1967 Ford Brasileira, Rua, São Paulo.
1967 to date Ford-Willys do Brasil SA, São Paulo.

On 24 April 1919, it was decided by Ford Motor Company to create Ford Brasileira. Initial investment would be $25,000, a sum then raised to $30,000 at Mr. Henry Ford's suggestion. In 1921, an assembly line was inaugurated at the Solon street address in São Paulo. The Model T would rapidly become Brazil's most popular automobile, but actual manufacture of *Brazilian* vehicles would have to wait until 1957 when $24 million were invested in order to start lorry production. Brazilian Ford automobiles started to be produced when a local version of the Galaxy was announced in 1965. This was powered by a 4.5 litre V-8 engine.

In 1967 Ford merged with Willys. The resulting range was an extraordinary international mix-up, with Renault Dauphines being built alongside the 2.7-litre Aero-Willys 6-cylinder ioe engine sedan and its deluxe variant, the Itamaraty, the Jeep-based Rural Willys station wagons, and the Galaxy. The 1969 Ford V8s came with 4752cc units, power assisted steering and air-conditioning as standard. There was also a new small 4-cylinder, 4-door sedan, called the Corcel I, available

from 1968 in 1289cc 68bhp standard and 1400cc, 80bhp GT forms. The Corcel name was publicist Mauro Salles' idea, in order to stay in tune with other horse-related Ford models. Styling was by Ford's Roberto Araujo, with design along Renault lines, with fwd, coil-and-wishbone ifs, and a rigid axle and coils at the rear. The Corcel became very popular. In 1969 the 2-door coupé version was introduced, and by 1971 127,000 Corcel cars had been made. In 1972 a local version of the Ford Maverick was introduced, in 4-door, 2-door coupé and station wagon versions (of these last only 100 were made). The Maverick was originally fitted with Willys or Ford V8 engines, though a 2.3-litre ohc four was standard from 1976. The Maverick was not listed after 1979. A restyled Corcel II came in 1977, with a 1.8-litre option available a year later. These Corcels were made in coupé and station wagon guises. The 4-door luxury sedan, introduced in 1981, was called Del Rey. In 1979 the first alcohol-powered engines were fitted to Brazilian Ford Corcels. Escort production started in 1983. The Corcel II was discontinued in 1987. In 1993 a new Escort, and also the Verona, Fiesta, Versailles and Hobby were presented.

1999 production included the Fiesta 2- and 4-door sedans with 1299cc 60bhp engine and the new Ka 2-door sedan with 4-cylinder, 1299cc 60bhp engine.
ACT

FORD (ix) (EU) 1967 to date

The new controlling company, Ford of Europe, was set up in June 1967, and although the Ford Motor Co. in Britain and Ford-Werke in Germany continued separate corporate existences, and models distinct to each country were made for a while, it is convenient to group them together from this date. The first fruit of collaboration was the Escort, announced in January 1968, although it had been under development since 1964. A replacement for the 105E Anglia, it was a conventional saloon offered in 2- or 4-door models with, initially, 1098 or 1298cc ohv 4-cylinder engines. It was not made in existing Ford factories but in three new plants, in Britain at Halewood near Liverpool and on the Continent at Genk in Belgium, which came under the control of Ford of Germany, and (from January 1970) at Saarlouis in south-west Germany. More powerful Escorts were also offered; the 1298cc giving 75bhp in place of the regular 1300's 53bhp, and the Twin Cam, which had the 105bhp 1558cc Lotus Elan engine and running gear in a strengthened Escort bodyshell. This was good for 115mph (185km/h) and was seen as a direct replacement for the Lotus Cortina. The first 25 were assembled at Henry Taylor's Ford competition workshop at Boreham, Essex, but production Twin Cams were made at Halewood from May 1968 onwards. They were replaced in 1970 by the RS1600 which used a 16-valve Cosworth BDA twin-cam engine of 1599cc and 120bhp. These were made at Ford's Advanced Vehicles Operation at South Ockenden, Essex, and most were used for racing or rallying. Engines of up to 2 litres and 245bhp were fitted on occasions. The RS1600's success in the 1970 London-Mexico World Cup Rally provided the name for the next high-performance Escort, the Mexico. Made from 1970 to 1974, it was a less powerful but more usable version of the RS1600, with 86bhp Cortina GT engine. The Escort became a household name in rallying for more than ten years. The Twin Cam won the Rally Constructors' Championship in 1968 and 1969, and Escorts won the RAC Rally in eight consecutive years, 1972 to 1979. In the latter year they took the World Rally Championship for makes with five wins and three second places.

The Escort Mk II arrived in 1974. This had been under development for two years, with the code-name Brenda, from a secretary at Ford of Britain's product development division. Changes were mainly in the restyled and somewhat anonymous bodies, for the engines were the existing 1098, 1298 and 1599cc, the latter appearing in a mainstream Escort for the first time. Several high-performance versions were made, including the RS1800, RS Mexico and RS2000. The latter, with 1993cc Pinto engine, was the most tractable of the RS models. Apart from a few early RS1800s which were assembled at Halewood, all the Mk II RS models were made in Germany. Nearly all RS models had two doors, although a few 4-door Mexicos were made to special order, and some wedge-nosed RS2000 with four doors were made in Australia. The Escort replaced Germany's front-drive Taunus models in 1970, although the Escort itself was to adopt front drive in 1980.

Before continuing the Escort story, we must return to 1969 and the introduction of the car many called Europe's answer to the Mustang. The Capri was a 4-seater coupé with a variety of engine options, originally 1300 and 1600 in-line fours, 2000 V4 and 3000 V6 models, with power outputs from 61 to 140bhp. Later

1971 Ford (ix) Capri 2000GT coupé.
NATIONAL MOTOR MUSEUM

RS versions gave 150bhp in road-going form, and as much as 400bhp from a 3.4-litre 4-camshaft Cosworth V6 for racing. Front disc brakes were standard on all models. All British-built Capris were made at Halewood, but from 1977 they were made only in Germany. The Mk II with opening hatchback came in 1974, and the restyled 4-headlamp Mk III in 1978. The 1300 engine was dropped for 1982, and the 3000 was replaced by a 160bhp fuel-injected 2800, known as the 2.8i. The most luxurious Capri, made only in small numbers, was the Tickford version, introduced in 1983, with an IHI turbocharger and Garrett intercooler which raised output to 205bhp and top speed to 140mph (225km/h). The body was restyled by the use of skirts and airdams and the interior was very luxurious. Prices started at £17,200, compared with £10,599 for the standard 2.8i. The final run of 1038 2.8is, all painted Brooklands Green, was unofficially known as the Brooklands model. The last Capri left the line at Cologne on 19 December 1986, ending a production run of 1,866,647 cars.

Ford's larger saloons in the 1970s were the Cortinas in Mk III, IV and V forms already described under British Ford, and the Taunus which, from 1970, shared the Cortina body shell. There were, however, some 2-door coupés peculiar to the Taunus range, with no Cortina equivalents. Engines were 1300 and 1600 fours, and 2000 or 2300 V6s. The top of the Taunus range was the 2300 GXL made in saloon or coupé forms. The Granada was the largest Ford, a roomy 4-door saloon or estate car, with several engine options, a 1993cc single-ohc in-line four, 1996cc ohv V4, and V6s of 2495 or 2994cc. From 1974 to 1977 there was a Granada coupé with the 1993 or 2994cc engines. The Mk II Granada included a 2498cc diesel engine in the range, and was made from 1977 up to 1985. The smaller engined models in the Granada range were called Consuls in Germany up to the end of 1975, when the whole range carried the Granada name. In the spring of 1985 the Granada gave way to the Scorpio which had an aerodynamic body not unlike that of the Sierra, and came with

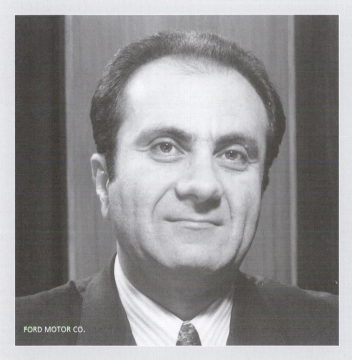

FORD MOTOR CO.

NASSER, JACQUES (born 1947)
Familiarly known as Jac, Nasser was born in the Lebanon, but moved with his family to Australia when he was four years old. His father worked briefly as a foreman for General Motors in Melbourne, and went on to build up a property business. Jac gained a degree in business studies at the Royal Melbourne Institute of Technology, and joined Ford Australia as a financial analyst in 1968. Like Lee Iacocca, he was a Ford enthusiast from the start. In 1973 he moved to Dearborn, then had postings to Asia and Latin America. He learnt about the problems of emerging countries first hand when armed workers seized a Ford plant in Argentina and took him hostage. He negotiated and resumed control himself, and the plant was eventually restored to Ford with some help from the Argentine Army.

In 1990 he moved from Autolatina, the joint Ford-VW enterprise in Argentina and Brazil, to Australia where Ford was making big losses. By cutting the workforce and revamping marketing he turned loss to profit within three years, and was rewarded by being made chairman of Ford Europe in 1993. Among his achievements there was the introduction of the Ka, which was later made in Brazil as well. In January 1999 he took over from Alex Trotman as chief executive of Ford worldwide, with headquarters at Dearborn. He is a firm believer in niche marketing, seeing a big future for a greater variety of lifestyle machines of all kinds. Ever conscious of Ford's image, he flew to the British plant at Dagenham in October 1999, to confer with union leaders about serious episodes of racist bullying at the plant, which has a 40 per cent black and Asian workforce.
NG

1983 Ford (ix) Fiesta Popular Plus hatchback.
FORD MOTOR COMPANY

1983 Ford (ix) Sierra Ghia hatchback.
FORD MOTOR COMPANY

1991 Ford (ix) Escort convertible.
FORD MOTOR COMPANY

1991 Ford (ix) Scorpio 4x4 saloon.
FORD MOTOR COMPANY

five engine options from 1796 to 2933cc. It was the first car in its price range to be equipped with ABS (Anti-lock Brake System) in all models. Later in 1985 came a 4 × 4 Scorpio, and from January 1986 a 2498cc Peugeot diesel engine was available. The Scorpio name was used everywhere except for the British market, where they continued to be called Granadas.

The last of 4,279,079 Cortinas was made on 22 July 1982. It was replaced by the Sierra, a conventionally-engineered rear-drive car with Cortina-type engines of 1294, 1594, 1998, 2294 and 2792cc, the three largest being V6s. The bodies were completely new aerodynamic shapes by Uwe Bahnsen, made in 3- and 5-door hatchback forms, and an estate car. In the spring of 1983, the Sierra gained a high-performance version in the shape of the XR4i. This had a 150bhp fuel-injected 2792cc engine, and a 3-door body with biplane rear spoiler. Top speed was 130mph (206km/h). In 1985 it was replaced by the XR 4x4 with the same engine and main gearbox, an FF 4-wheel drive system and a 5-door hatchback. It was less dramatic looking than the XR4i, but was more practical and with better handling. There was still a high-performance 3-door hatchback, the RS Cosworth with 1993cc 4-cylinder engine with Cosworth-built 16-valve aluminium cylinder head and Garrett T3 turbocharger. Top speed was more than 140mph (230km/h). A booted version of the Sierra called the Sapphire appeared in 1987 and and in 1988 this also received the Cosworth treatment. In 1989 Sierras gained new twin-ohc engines aimed at economy and low emission levels rather than performance. They were made until 1993 when they gave way to the front-drive Mondeo, leaving the Scorpio as the only rear-driven European Ford passenger car. The Scorpio was dropped in August 1998 due to poor sales.

Ford Goes Front Drive

When the Escort replaced the Anglia in 1968, Ford no longer had a really small car to face the challenge of the 'super mini' typified by the Renault 5 and Fiat 127. Their answer was the Fiesta, a front-wheel drive hatchback offered initially in 957 and 1117cc versions, later joined by 1297 and 1599cc models. The latter was the sporting model, known as the XR2. All had 4-speed gearboxes with no automatic option until the Daf-developed CVS (Continually Variable System) was offered on the larger-engined Fiestas. From 1989 Ford made this transmission at their new Bordeaux plant and sold them to Fiat for use in the Tipo and Uno. They were adopted in the Escort and Orion for 1990. The Fiesta was an international car, with bodies and engines being made in two new factories at Valencia, Spain, transmissions at Bordeaux, and cylinder blocks, radiators and carburettors at Dagenham. Final assembly was divided between Saarlouis and Valencia. The Fiesta was launched in September 1976 and became the fastest-selling European car. Half a million had been made by September 1977, and the millionth was delivered in 1979. By the end of 1984 production had reached 3,312,000. It was face-lifted in 1984 and revised in 1989 when a 5-door version was offered for the first time.

At the end of 1980 the Escort went over to front-wheel drive, with all-round independent suspension and servo disc brakes on all but the most basic version. Engines were a 1117cc pushrod ohv, or single-ohc 1297 and 1599cc units. As on the Fiesta, they were transversely-mounted, and drove through 4-speed gearboxes, with an automatic option. A 1608cc diesel engine was available, and the largest petrol engine powered the sporting XR3. This became the fuel-injected XR3i in 1983, with 5-speed gearbox, 105bhp and a top speed of 115mph (185km/h). Even more powerful were the 1982–83 RS1600i, and 1984 RS Turbo, with 130bhp and a speed of 130mph (206km/h). A convertible Escort was available from 1984, while 1983 saw a booted 4-door saloon version called the Orion. The front-drive Escort was very much a European car; engine, steering, brakes, suspension and interior were developed by Ford's British R&D centre at Dunton, Essex, while styling, engine structure and transmission were the responsibility of the German equivalent at Merkenich. United Kingdom market cars were built at Halewood, although engines were made by Ford's engine plant at Bridgend, South Wales, which had opened in 1978. Capable of producing 500,000 engines per year, Bridgend supplied Ford's engine needs over a wide range worldwide, apart from the big American V8s.

In 1993 the Sierra was replaced by the Mondeo, a car of roughly the same size but with transversely mounted 4-cylinder engines, twin-cam units of 1597, 1796 and 1988cc and a single-ohc diesel of 1953cc. Made in 4-door saloon and estate forms, the Mondeo was more of a world car than any Ford since the Model T, being made in the USA as well as in Europe, where production was concentrated at Genk. It had been planned as long ago as the mid–1980s, with

1998 Ford (ix) Mondeo Verona 4-door saloon.
NATIONAL MOTOR MUSEUM

original development taking place in the USA, before being transferred to Europe in 1987 and shared between Britain and Germany. A 170bhp 2544cc V6 engine joined the Mondeo range in 1994, and the 1999 range consisted of this and the 1988cc four, plus the diesel, now of 1753cc. The V6 was available in two models, with 170 or 200bhp known as the ST24 and ST200. A restyled and larger Mondeo with revised rear suspension and a new range of direct-injection petrol and diesel engines, was to be introduced in autumn 2000, most cars being made at the Belgian plant at Genk. It was no longer a world car, as the slow-selling American versions, Ford Contour/Mercury Mystique, were dropped. A coupé based on the ST24 floorpan and engine was the Cougar, announced at the 1998 Detroit Motor Show. It went on sale in America in April 1998, coming to Europe five months later. Seen by some as a true replacement for the Capri, it could be had on the European Market with a 1988cc 4-cylinder engine.

The Fiesta was continued into the 1999 Ford range, production having been transferred from Valencia to Dagenham. As well as 3- and 5-door hatchbacks, there was a Fiesta-derived coupé, the Puma, launched in July 1997 and available with 1388 or 1679cc 16-valve engines, while the largest Fiesta engine was an 8-valve 1388cc. The Puma was the first Ford whose styling was designed entirely on computer. A high performance model called the Racing Puma was anounced in January 2000, with a 153bhp Zetec engine and body modifications by Tickford. The Fiesta was given for a facelift in late 1999. The top performer was the Zetec S with 104bhp 1.6-litre engine. A completely new Fiesta was due in 2001, with the sharper New Edge styling as seen on the Ka and Focus.

The Fiesta's replacement on the Spanish production lines was the Ka, an idiosyncratically-styled 3-door hatchback available with a single engine, the 60bhp 1299cc. The Ka was made in two models, the basic Ka which lacked central locking, power steering and electric windows, all available on the more expensive Ka 2 and 3.

The autumn of 1998 saw the eventual replacement for the Escort, although there would be an overlap, with the older car continuing for a year or two. Its replacement, the Focus, shared New Edge styling with the Ka, and had a brand-new platform and body, initially only a 3- or 5-door hatchback, but saloon and estate versions appeared in January 1999. It was slightly longer and wider than the Escort, but the biggest difference lay in the height, 3in (80mm) more. The Focus had new independent rear suspension derived from that of the Mondeo estate. Four petrol engines were offered, of 1388, 1596, 1796 and 1988cc, the smallest came from the Fiesta and the two larger units from the Mondeo and Cougar. A 1753cc turbo diesel was added to the range in January 1999. A 200bhp Cosworth-powered 3-door model was promised for mid-2000.

In 1996 Ford entered the MPV field with the Galaxy, a 9-passenger front-drive vehicle made in a form very similar to the Volkswagen Sharan and Seat

1998 Ford (ix) Ka hatchback.
FORD MOTOR COMPANY

1999 Ford (ix) Focus Zetec hatchback.
FORD EUROPE

Alhambra. All were made in the same factory in Portugal, but the Galaxy had 4-cylinder or V6 Ford engines, while the others were both VW-powered. In 1997 Ford made 1,177,879 cars in Europe, putting them in fourth place, behind Volkswagen, Renault, and Fiat.

NG

1907 Forman 14/16hp tourer.
NATIONAL MOTOR MUSEUM

FORDHAM *see* DAYTONA

FORDS ONLY (US) c.1985
Fords Only, Ventura, California.
The Lust Cobra was a low-cost Cobra replica kit based on Mustang II running gear.
HP

FOREST (US) 1905–1906
Forest Motor Car Co., Boston, Massachusetts.
The makers of the Forest claimed years of experience with gas and petrol engines from 2 to 100hp. Their car had a 20hp flat-twin engine with a very long stroke (114.3 × 178mm), giving a capacity of 3646cc. It had a conventional 3-speed gearbox and 5-seater tourer body.
NG

FORGEOT-TRAYSSAC (F) 1924
Les Automobiles Forgeot-Trayssac, Levallois, Seine.
This was one of several transformations of the Model T Ford, and as far as the appearance went, more complete than many. It featured a Rolls-Royce-type radiator and a coachbuilt sedanca de ville body by Mom, with carriage side lamps. The Ford's transverse springs were replaced by conventional semi-elliptics, and wire wheels were fitted.
NG

FORMAN (GB) c.1904–c.1907
Forman Motor Manufacturing Co. Ltd, Coventry.
Forman was a well-known engine maker who supplied power units to several firms including Brown, Hallamshire, Horbick, and Velox. They also made a few cars powered by their own 12/14hp 2-cylinder or 14hp 4-cylinder engines, with shaft drive.
NG

FORMULA 27 (GB) 1992 to date
Sterling Autoparts (Formula 27 Cars), Brinscombe, Stroud, Gloucestershire.
This Lotus Seven clone was originally launched as a plans-built car, the only factory parts you needed to buy being the fibreglass nose and wings. The rest you made yourself, including the square tube steel space frame chassis and aluminium main body tub. There was a choice of Ford, Fiat, Vauxhall or Rover V8 engines. Factory-made chassis were optional and gradually full kits became available. A new model in 1998 was the Blade, a lightweight version powered by a 135bhp Honda Fireblade motorbike engine.
CR

FORMULA AERO (US) c.1987
Formula Aero, Mishawaka, Indiana.
This company made a body kit that converted a Pontiac Fiero into a semi-Dino 246 replica. However, the Dino's proportions did not make the transition intact. It was available in kit or completed form on a new Fiero chassis, or the company would install the kit for free on a customer's car.
HP

FORREST (GB) 1907–1916
J.A. Wade & Co. Ltd, Liverpool.
This was a light car powered by an 8hp V-twin engine, with friction transmission and shaft drive. Later models used a small 4-cylinder engine. A light van was offered from 1908, and later production concentrated on these rather than passenger cars. There was also a taxicab with front-opening hansom-cab body style. The Forrest was sold in London under the name Realm-Forrest.
NG

FORSTER (i) **(CDN)** 1920
Forster Motor Car & Manufacturing Co. Ltd, Montreal.
Designed by Captain M.L. Fitzgerald, this was a large car powered by a 6-cylinder Herschell-Spillman engine, with a Rolls-Royce-type radiator and two body styles, a tourer and a coupé called the Princess Pauline. It was intended for the British market rather than Canada and Fitzgerald had reportedly arranged with a London firm, Southgate Ltd of Regent Street, to supply them with 10,000 cars over the next ten years. He acquired a factory in Montreal, but the only illustrations of the car were artist's impressions, so possibly not even a prototype was built.
NG

FORSTER (ii) **(GB)** 1922
Forster Light Cars Ltd, Richmond, Surrey.
J.H. Forster had designed the GLOBE (ii), which had been made before the war as the SPHINX-GLOBE in France and as the Globe in London. In 1922 he tried again, using his own name for a light car powered by a 10hp 2-cylinder engine, and priced at £225. Probably only prototypes were made.
NG

FORT PITT *see* PITTSBURGH (ii)

FORWARD (DK) 1911–1912
Paul Christensen, 'Kronborg', Copenhagen.
Christensen was the Danish representative for Napier cars, and also sold Birmingham-built bicycles under the name Forward. His car was an unusual design, a 3-wheeler with rear-mounted water-cooled 8hp V-twin engine driving through a 2-speed epicyclic transmission and chain to the single rear wheel. Steering was by tiller. A 4-wheeled version appeared in 1912, one of which survives. It has been suggested that the Forward was based on the Coventry-built CROUCH, or even that it was a Crouch imported and renamed. The presence of a carburettor by the Brooklyn Valve Co. suggests an American origin. The 3-wheeler might have been a MOTORETTE, but there was never a 4-wheeled Motorette.
NG

FORZARI (GB) 1996–1998
Forzari Developments, Ceredigion, Wales.
This Group C-style kit-form coupé boasted an advanced structure of carbon fibre and aluminium honeycomb monocoque centre hull, stressed Renault V6 mid-mounted engine and gearbox, rose-jointed double wishbone suspension and 4-piston calliper vented disc brakes.
CR

FOSSUM (N) 1906–1907
Marcus Hansen Fossum of Oslo built two cars, the first of the high-wheeled buggy type with 2-cylinder air-cooled engine, the second with a single-cylinder water-cooled engine and the appearance of a Curved Dash Oldsmobile. He could not raise the finance to put either into production.
NG

FOSTER (i) **(US)** 1901–1904
1901–1903 Foster Automobile Manufacturing Co., Rochester, New York.
1904 Artzberger Automobile Co., Allegheny, Pennsylvania.
This company made steam and electric cars, three models of steamer, described as the Light Roadster, Touring Wagon and Surrey, and a single model of electric runabout. By the end of 1901 they had built 165 cars. They ran into patent problems with the steamers, as in 1902 they were sued by the WHITNEY Wagon Co. for patent infringement. This led to a switch to petrol cars for 1903,

with 9 and 12hp 2-cylinder engines. However, they were bankrupt by the end of the year. In 1904 the steamer was made by W.H. Artzberger who also offered steam cars under his own name.
NG

FOSTER (ii) *see* AUTOGEAR (i)

FOSTLER (US) 1905
Chicago Motocycle Co., Chicago, Illinois.
This was a runabout powered by a front-mounted single-cylinder engine, with 2-speed epicyclic transmission and single-chain drive. It was exhibited at the 1905 Chicago Show by the company that had also made the CALORIC and CHICAGO (i), alongside these three-year old designs. The Fostler name may have come from the customer who ordered the car, and it is possible that a few replicas were made, although the company's main business was in repair work.
NG

FOSTORIA (i) **(US)** 1906–1907
Fostoria Motor Car Co., Fostoria, Ohio.
The 16hp 2-cylinder Fostoria was a revival of the DETROIT-OXFORD, and lasted only a year before designer William Radford joined the newly-formed Hudson Motor Car Co., later being involved in the design of the Warren-Detroit, Pilgrim (ii) and Balboa cars.
NG

FOSTORIA (ii) **(US)** 1915–1916
Fostoria Light Car Co., Fostoria, Ohio.
As the company name implied the second car to be called Fostoria was a genuine light car powered by a 2.1-litre 4-cylinder ohv Sterling engine, and offered in four models; tourer, roadster, speedster and coupé. By September 1916, 293 had been made, but engine quality was suspect and Fostoria switched to Le Roi. Before any Le Roi-powered cars were made they changed the name of car and company to SENECA.
NG

FOTH (D) 1906–1907
Carl Foth Maschinenfabrik, Domitz.
This company made a limited number of voiturettes with 8PS single-cylinder engines and friction transmission.
HON

FOUCH (US) 1914–1915
James R. Fouch, Los Angeles, California.
The Fouch was an attractive-looking light car made in roadster form only, with a 4-cylinder engine in unit with a 3-speed gearbox and shaft drive. A price of $495 was quoted, but Fouch, who ran a small machine shop, never formed a company. He later designed a vehicle as far removed as possible from the little Fouch, the enormous Bulkely-Rider road tractor with 90hp engine and final drive ratio in bottom gear of 96:1.
NG

FOUCHER ET DELACHANAL (F) 1897–c.1900
Foucher et Delachanal, Paris.
These partners were listed as bicycle makers in 1892. Their car had a horizontal twin engine with belt drive to pulleys on a countershaft behind the rear axle, and final drive by double-chains. It had a 3-seater body and tiller steering.
NG

FOUILLARON (F) 1900–1914
G. Fouillaron, Levallois-Perret, Seine.
Gustav Fouillaron started in business with a bicycle shop at Angers in 1899, and in 1900 patented a transmission system which he used in all the cars that he made from then until the outbreak of World War I. This involved belts running over expandable pulleys, essentially the same system used by Daf more than fifty years later. The belts were made of chrome leather and cat gut, and control was by a small lever on the steering column. Apart from the transmission, the Fouillaron followed conventional design, always using proprietary engines.

1902 Fouillaron 10hp tonneau.
NATIONAL MOTOR MUSEUM

The 1902 range consisted of two light cars with single-cylinder De Dion-Bouton engines, a 6hp 2-seater and 8hp 4-seater tonneau, a 12hp 2-cylinder with Roi-des-Belges tourer body and three 4-cylinder cars, of 12, 16 and 24hp. The largest of these engines was by Buchet. Honeycomb radiators and Malicet et Blin steering gear arrived in 1904, and shortly afterwards shaft final drive was standardised on the larger models. During 1906–08 Fouillarons had round radiators, and some had diagonally mounted engines and transmissions with the propeller shaft driving to one rear wheel. Shaft drive was universal by 1910, and the last years of peace saw a variety of models, from an 8hp 1-litre single to a 16/20hp 3.7-litre four. In between these came the only 6-cylinder offered by Fouillaron, the 2.8-litre 15/18hp. Bodies for the larger cars were made by Vicart, a neighbour of Fouillaron.

In addition to cars, the Fouillaron company made variable speed systems, presumably on the same principles as in the cars, used in the manufacture of paper, chocolate, cement, earthenware and pottery.
NG

FOULKES (GB) 1981–1988
Foulkes Developments Ltd, Dartmouth, Devon.
The Impala utility kit car was the very first British kit ever to use the Fiat 500/126 as a basis. It had a simple one-piece fibreglass body on a ladder chassis with optional weather equipment. Early ones had squared wheel arches, post–1984 ones round arches. Foulkes' prototype Ford-based 2+2 coupé of 1987 was stillborn.
CR

FOUR WHEEL DRIVE (US) 1904–1906
Four Wheel Drive Wagon Co., Milwaukee, Wisconsin.
As its name implies, this company was mainly concerned with building 4 × 4 delivery wagons and trucks, but they did make a few touring cars powered by 40hp 4-cylinder Rutenber engines. A truck chassis was used, hence the wheelbase of 132in (3350mm), very long for the period. There was no connection with the better-known Four Wheel Drive Auto Co. of Clintonville, Wisconsin, makers of Badger cars and F.W.D. cars and trucks.
NG

FOURNIER (i) *see* MARCADIER

FOURNIER (ii) *see* SEARCHMONT

FOURNIER (iii) **(F)** 1913–1924
SA des Anciens Éts, Fournier, Levallois-Perret, Seine.
The 1913–14 examples of this maker had 6/8hp single-cylinder engines, and were also known as Baby Silvestre. Like all Fournier's cars they had friction transmission. Postwar models had 990cc V-twin Train engines, or small fours by Ruby (904cc) or Ballot (1131cc). In addition to the usual open models, the 1921 range included a neat closed coupé, which was unusual on so small a chassis.
NG

1933 Framo 200cc 3-wheeler.
NATIONAL MOTOR MUSEUM

FOX (i) **(F)** 1912–1923
1912–1914 M.L. van der Eyken, Neuilly, Seine.
1919–1923 M.L. van der Eyken, Puteaux, Seine.
Five models of Fox were made before the outbreak of war. Each of these were fitted with 4-cylinder monobloc engines, which were of 9hp, 10/12, 12/15, 14/16 and 18/20hp, the latter having a capacity of 3.6 litres. After the war it was made in only one model, with 1816cc 4-cylinder ohv Chapuis-Dornier engine, with cone clutch and 4-speed gearbox. It is not known why the Dutch-sounding builder should have chosen such an English name as Fox for his cars.
NG

FOX (ii) **(D)** 1920–c.1927
Fox Automobil-AG Paul Rollmann, Cologne.
The Fox, or Fox-Kleinauto, was an unusual example of a German car built by an Englishman. George Morrison (1896–1976) served in the Occupation Forces in Germany and after demobilisation in April 1919, decided to remain in the country. With a German friend, Paul Rollmann, he set up the Fox company to make a light sports car powered by a 4.98PS 4-cylinder engine, possibly a proprietary unit. The bodywork was made in Coblenz and came in three models, open and coupé 2-seaters and a pointed-tail sports model. The end of production is not certain; it certainly lasted to 1923, when the firm, like so many others, was badly hit by the drastic inflation which hit Germany. Morrison returned to England in February 1927, so the Fox did not last beyond then.
NG
Further Reading
'The Fox-Kleinauto', M. Worthington-Williams, *The Automobile*, May 1991.

FOX (iii) **(US)** 1921–1923
Fox Motor Car Co., Philadelphia, Pennsylvania.
Ainsley H. Fox had made the Fox shotgun before the war, and in 1914 formed the Fox Motor Co. to make air-cooled engines. In 1919 he decided to make complete cars, forming the Fox Motor Car Co. which absorbed his engine-building concern. It was two years before the car appeared, but when it did it was a handsome-looking large car on a 128in (3249mm) wheelbase, powered by a 4-litre air-cooled 6-cylinder engine with aluminium pistons and ohvs. The six separately-cast cylinders were cooled by a fan blower. Two bodies were offered initially, a tourer at $3900 and a sedan at $4900, with a 3-seater coupé at $4900 being added for 1923. The wheelbase was increased to 132in (3350mm) for 1922. The fact that it had an air-cooled engine provoked comparison with the Franklin, but the Fox was a larger car in a higher price bracket (1921 Franklin prices started at $2400), more comparable with Cadillac. There were no criticisms of the Fox's quality, but the small make struggled in a very competitive market. Production did not get under way until May 1922, and ended in December 1923. Estimates of production vary widely, between 25 and 3000. The true figure was probably a few hundred.
NG

FOY-STEELE (GB) 1913–1916
S.M.C. Syndicate Ltd, Willesden, London.
The Foy-Steele was a conventional light car powered by a 4-cylinder monobloc Coventry-Simplex engine of 2303cc, with 3-speed gearbox and shaft drive. Body styles were open 2- and 4-seaters, together with a 'speed model' and a Colonial tourer with higher ground clearance. The name was taken from Foy steel, an alloy used in the car's universal joints and other components. The makers, the S.M.C. Syndicate, had earlier made the S.M. or Shave-Morse steam car and truck, but it has been suggested that the Foy-Steele was made in the works of the WAVERLEY (ii).
NG

F.R. (F) 1927–1928
Fehr & Rougouchin, Paris.
This was a light 3-wheeler powered by a 500cc Hannissard 2-cylinder 2-stroke engine. It looked not unlike a Morgan, and used the same type of sliding pillar with vertical coil front suspension.
NG

F.R.A. (GB) 1998 to date
The Toy Shop, Sandyford, Newcastle-upon-Tyne.
This was a monocoque fibreglass replacement shell for the Mini, offered in saloon, Clubman, hatchback and cabriolet forms.
CR

F.R.A.M. *see* CANTONO

FRAM KING *see* FULDAMOBIL

FRAMO (D) 1932–1937
Framo-Werke GmbH, Frankenberg/Saxony; Hainichen/Saxony.
J.S. Rasmussen of DKW fame owned this firm but he did not incorporate it into the Auto Union combine. As Metallwerke Frankenberg it was formed in 1922 to make motorcycle components, and in 1926 the first Framo 3-wheeled delivery vans were made, using DKW engines. A combination car version for passengers and goods appeared in 1932 and in 1933 came the Piccolo, the first Framo aimed purely for passenger use. It had a 200cc DKW engine mounted over the single front wheel. A completely different layout was chosen for the Stromer coupé, which had two front wheels powered by DKW 2-stroke engines of 200, 400 or 600cc, and a neat 2-seater coupé body. The next step was a 4-wheeler which had a rear-mounted 300cc engine (later reduced to 200cc), again by DKW. Production of passenger cars was given up in 1937, but vans, both 3- and 4-wheelers, were continued. In 1945 the firm was nationalised, and the 4-wheeled vans were continued under the name IFA Framo, and then as Barkas up to the reunification of Germany in 1990.
HON

FRANCE JET *see* AVOLETTE

FRANCKE (US) 1904–1905
George O. Francke Auto Co., Milwaukee, Wisconsin.
Francke offered a rear-entrance tonneau powered by a 12hp 2-cylinder engine bought from the H. Fast machine shop, also of Milwaukee. Chassis and body were of Francke's own construction, but very few were made and Francke soon returned to his previous business of selling cars.
NG

FRANCO (I) 1907–1912
Automobili Franco, Sesto San Giovanni, Milan.
This company made large cars on Fiat lines, with 4-cylinder engines of up to 7 litres' capacity, and chain drive. The make's greatest claim to fame was their victory in the 1910 Targa Florio with a 6.8-litre car.
NG

FRANÇON (F) 1922–1926
1922–1925 Truelle et Compagnie, Rueil-Malmaison, Seine-et-Oise.
1925–1926 Truelle et Compagnie, St Ouen, Seine.

The Françon was a light car powered by a 2-cylinder 2-stroke engine designed by Chedru on Trojan lines. The earliest cars had separate cylinders and a capacity of 458cc, but from 1923 the cylinders were cast in one block, and capacity was increased to 664cc. In this form it gave 14bhp and a top speed of 40mph (64km/h). The engine was water-cooled, with aluminium pistons. Transmission was by a 5-speed friction disc system, and final drive by a single chain running in an oil bath. The open body was a 3-seater, the space next to the rear passenger being reserved for luggage. The first cars had wooden chassis, soon replaced by steel. The makers also built industrial and marine engines.

NG

FRANKEL (F) 1898
Automobile Union, Paris.

The first Frankel was a tiller-steered single-seater tricycle powered by a single-cylinder horizontal 2hp engine, but 2-seaters and quadricycles were advertised, with engines up to 3.5hp. The price was the equivalent of £80, and H.O. Duncan, writing in *The Autocar*, said that M. Frankel had orders for more than 100 tricycles. Large-scale manufacture by well-known cycle makers in France and England was promised, but little more was heard of the Frankel.

NG

FRANKLIN (US) 1902–1934
1902–1917 H.H. Franklin Manufacturing Co., Syracuse, New York.
1917–1934 Franklin Automobile Co., Syracuse, New York.

The Franklin was the best-known American air-cooled car, and indeed, before the advent of the Volkswagen, probably the best-known in the world. It was also most unusual for using a wooden chassis as late as 1928, and full-elliptic springing up to 1932.

For much of its life the Franklin was the work of one man, John Wilkinson, who designed a car with transverse 4-cylinder engine in 1898, just after graduating from Cornell University. His first backers, the New York Automobile Co., failed to pay him for his two prototypes, but the design was taken up by Herbert H. Franklin (1866–1956), a manufacturer of die castings at Syracuse. Helped by finance from Alexander T. Brown, Franklin bought up the New York Automobile Co., took John Wilkinson on to his payroll, and put his design into production in the summer of 1902. This first Franklin had a 4-cylinder 1.7-litre engine, with ohv, an advanced feature for the period, and Franklin never made a side-valve engine. As on the prototypes it was mounted transversely, driving though a 2-speed epicyclic transmission and single-chain final drive. Long-time Franklin features such as wooden frame and full-elliptic springs were already present in the first cars.

The first sale was made in June 1902, and 12 more cars were sold that year. The figure for 1903 was 183 and for 1904, 400. A 4-seater rear-entrance tonneau was available that year, and for 1905, when sales reached 1500, a new model appeared with longitudinally-mounted engine under a rounded Delaunay-Belleville-like bonnet. This was made until 1911, when a Renault-type bonnet was adopted, followed by the sloping 'horse collar' shape in 1921 and a vertical false radiator from 1925. The small 12hp transverse engine was continued until the end of 1906, but larger cars were the order of the day, including a 30hp six. There was always a six in the range from then on, and the last four was made in 1913.

Franklin's full-elliptic suspension gave an excellent ride; tyre life was up to 20,000 miles, and for this reason the company did not fit detachable rims as standard until 1922. An automatic ignition advance and retard was fitted in 1907, and in 1908 a gear-driven fan. In 1910 the fan was incorporated in the flywheel to give a suction-cooling system, and this was continued until 1923 when a sirocco fan was geared to the front of the crankshaft.

Although air-cooling and wooden frames had been abandoned by all other car makers in the Franklin's class, the cars from Syracuse were by no means backward in design. Closed sedan bodies were available from 1913, and full electric equipment a year later. Aluminium pistons were adopted in 1915. Franklin were never very interested in competitions, and their proposed straight-8 racing car for the 1905 Vanderbilt Cup did not get beyond the eliminating trials. They did, however, take part in several demonstrations to prove that air-cooled cars did not overheat – these included a 1916 drive from Walla Walla, Washington, to San Francisco (802 miles/1290kms) entirely in bottom gear.

1924 Françon 664cc tourer.
NATIONAL MOTOR MUSEUM

1898 Frankel motor tricycle.
NATIONAL MOTOR MUSEUM

1902 Franklin 2-seater.
NATIONAL MOTOR MUSEUM

Production increased considerably in the 'teens, from 1214 in 1912 to just under 9000 in 1917. Only one model was offered, the 3630cc 6-30, which was reduced slightly in capacity (3263cc) and wheelbase from 1917 onwards. Franklins were in the upper-medium price bracket, running in 1917 from $1850 for a 5-seater tourer to $3000 for a 7-seater town car. There was little change in design in the early 1920s apart from the introduction of the 'horse collar' grill in 1921, which made for a less attractive car than with the previous Renault-type

1919 Franklin Series 9 sedan.
JOHN A. CONDE

1923 Franklin 25hp sedan.
NICK GEORGANO

bonnets. Franklin customers tended to be very loyal, but by the mid–1920s the message began to come back from the dealers that a new and less controversial car was needed. Led by Ralph Hamlin, who had sold Franklins in Southern California since 1905, the dealers threatened to give up their franchises unless the design was changed. 'New car or no car' was their slogan. Herbert Franklin was agreeable to a change but not John Wilkinson, who believed that his front-hinged bonnet was perfectly functional. Franklin and his board sought a new design from the Walter Murphy body company and Wilkinson resigned in protest. He subsequently built a prototype water-cooled car under his own name. In fact the design that was eventually adopted was not Murphy's, but came from Frank de Causse. Franklin had admired de Causse's work for Locomobile, and gave him a free hand to restyle his car from front to rear. A wide, rectangular 'radiator' gave the car the appearance of a water-cooled design; the body lines, though far from streamlined, were much cleaner and lighter than most contemporary designs. In particular, the framework surrounding the windscreen and doors was lightened in appearance by the use of slim but strong metal pillars in place of wooden ones. A custom body department was set up, headed by de Causse, and designs were commissioned from such famous names as Brunn, Derham, Holbrook, Locke, Merrimac, and Willoughby. Prices were inevitably higher, and a 1926 Series 11 cost $685 more than a 1925 Series 10. By

DE CAUSSE, FRANK (1880–1928)

J. Frank de Causse (rhymes with rose) had come to the US from Paris, a distinction that probably gave him a fashion edge in selling his ideas and services to American automakers. According to biographer Walt Gosden, de Causse studied art, architecture, design and art history in France.

As a teenager, de Causse became interested in cars and took a job as a drafting apprentice with Kellner, the Paris coachbuilder. Here he soon found himself involved not only with making body drafts but also with designing, and he soon discovered a knack for presenting his designs to Kellner's customers. It was by combining these three talents – designing, drafting and salesmanship – that de Causse became Kellner's assistant manager in 1904.

In 1914, the Locomobile Co. of Bridgeport, Connecticut decided to offer its own line of custom bodies. To start the project, Locomobile needed a custom body designer, someone with experience and a name, preferably French. To find such a person, Locomobile sent a representative to the Paris Salon to interview candidates. De Causse was hired and arrived at Locomobile's New York office in the autumn of 1914. Here he soon built up a small design staff, which included the superb watercolorist, Roland L. Stickney.

Locomobile's 'custom department' commissioned only about 40 or so cars a year, none actually built by Locomobile. De Causse created many of the designs, which Stickney rendered and Locomobile published in catalogue form. Agents sold specific designs to customers from these catalogues, and de Causse then farmed the work out to independent coachbuilders in and around Manhattan, notably Healey, Locke, Demarest and Holbrook. Owners of custom Locomobiles included the Vanderbilts, the Carnegies, the Wanamakers, Chicago chewing-gum magnate William Wrigley and even General 'Black Jack' Pershing.

The first de Causse Locomobile bodies appeared on the Healey stand at the 1916 New York Salon. Here de Causse introduced one of the earliest examples

(perhaps the earliest) of a dual-cowl, double-windshield phaeton. Later, de Causse also designed Locomobile's production bodies. But when the Locomobile Co. of America went into receivership in 1922, de Causse found himself without a steady income.

By this time, LeBaron Carrossiers was doing business in New York as an architectural autobody design firm. After Locomobile let him go, de Causse decided to capitalize on the same idea. He would design but not construct custom bodies for individual customers.

Like LeBaron, de Causse rented offices in midtown Manhattan, and like LeBaron, too, he sold many of his designs to factory sales agents. Taking one final page from LeBaron's book, de Causse arranged with local coachbuilders to put his designs on wheels. Among his first customers was the New York agent for Benz automobiles, for whom de Causse designed four distinctive body styles.

In 1923, de Causse received a frantic phone call from the Franklin Automobile Company. Franklin's sales manager was upset because several dealers had threatened to give up their franchises if Franklin's future aircooled cars didn't show a more conventional 'radiator' design. Franklin management, prodded by their influential Southern California distributor, asked for styling proposals from the Walter M. Murphy Company in California and from J. Frank de Causse in New York. Franklin ended up choosing the de Causse design, and de Causse ended up reshaping not just the grille, with its distinctive circle at the bottom, but the entire line of bodies for the 1925 Franklins.

Concurrently, W.C. Durant hired de Causse to style his new Flint automobile. Durant had by then taken over Locomobile and, when he heard about de Causse working for Franklin, told de Causse that he was still under exclusive contract to Locomobile. Not at all, said de Causse, and these two very strong wills argued loudly. De Causse finally won.

H.H. Franklin asked de Causse to create custom designs for his company as well as several for production. De Causse was given a small studio inside Franklin's Syracuse engineering offices. It wasn't long before Franklin was offering boattail speedsters and other much more sporting designs than the company ever had before.

Meanwhile, de Causse kept his Manhattan office and did additional designs for various private clients. He also arranged for special-bodied Franklins to have their coming-out at the salons in New York, Chicago and Los Angeles. He later traveled to the European motorshows on Franklin's behalf. And in 1926, de Causse began working for Locke & Company, doing their full-sized body drafts.

Things were going well, but late in 1926 or early 1927, Frank de Causse was diagnosed with throat cancer. He traveled to Paris for treatment, but nothing helped. He passed away at age 48 on 10 May 1928.

ML

1934 Franklin V12 Club brougham.
NICK GEORGANO

the late 1920s Franklin prices were in the range $2490 to $3800, with the custom models running as high as $7200. However, the new designs proved very popular with the public, and Franklin enjoyed their peak year in 1929, with more than 14,000 cars sold. Among Franklin enthusiasts was the aviator Charles Lindbergh, who had captured the headlines with his solo transatlantic flight in May 1927. The 1928 Franklins were called the Airman series after Lindbergh, and were the first to feature front-wheel brakes, internal-expanding Lockheed hydraulics, although the contracting typewas more generally favoured in the USA. Franklins also used a steel frame for the first time in 1928. This was not because H.H. distrusted wood from an engineering viewpoint, but the ash timber did not grow locally to Syracuse but had to be transported across the Continent from the Pacific Northwest, then left to season for five years. With increased production, the company could not wait that long.

A little-known result of the popularity of the de Causse cars was Herbert Franklin's decision to enter a more popularly priced market with a 4-cylinder car, to sell for no more than $1000. He put James Yarian, who had joined the company in 1918, in charge of the project which was started in 1924. It was plagued with problems, cracked cylinders, troubles with camshafts, valves, big-end bearings, and only one Franklin Model Z was built. To maintain Franklin's high standards, it would have needed to cost well over his target figure of $1000, and H.H. closed down the project, dismissing the seven men involved in it including James Yarian. He took the Model Z and tried to build it himself under his own name (see YARIAN).

Despite occasional flights of fancy such as de Causse's boat-tail speedster, Franklin's image was that of a staid sedan for the middle aged or elderly. In order to attract younger buyers, the company hired the well-known competition driver Erwin 'Cannonball' Baker who set a new coast-to-coast record of 69 hours 31 minutes, without once stopping the engine. He also broke the Pike's Peak hill climb record with a specially-built 4-wheel drive Franklin racing car. The new image was reflected in the 1930 Pirate models which had concealed running boards. The 4490cc 6-cylinder engine gave 87bhp, and this was raised to 100bhp for 1931. Unfortunately the Depression hit Franklin badly; from their 1929 peak of 14,432, sales dropped to 6036 in 1930, 2851 in 1931 and only 1905 in 1932. Despite the collapse of businesses and banks across the country, this was the era of the multi-cylinder car; Auburn, Cadillac, Lincoln, Packard and Pierce-Arrow all offered V12s, and Franklin joined them in April 1932 with a big 6810cc 150bhp car. It was the first Franklin to use semi-elliptic springs and the traditional Franklin-made tubular axles were replaced by conventional proprietary axles bought from Columbia. These were cost-cutting

1924 Franklin Model Z sedan.
KEITH MARVIN

1929 Franklin Airman Limited sedan.
NICK GEORGANO

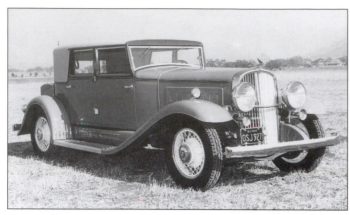

1931 Franklin series 15 convertible brougham.
NATIONAL MOTOR MUSEUM

1933 Franklin Olympic sedan.
NICK GEORGANO

measures, but the V12 was still expensive, at $3885 for a sedan and $4185 for a 7-seater limousine. For the 1934 season prices were drastically cut, by $1000 across the V12 range and up to $440 for the 6-cylinder Airman, but at these prices the company could not possibly have made a profit. By then it did not really matter as Franklin was insolvent anyway. In October 1932 they introduced a new model at the opposite end of the scale from the V12. The Olympic combined the 6-cylinder air-cooled engine with the chassis and bodies of the REO Flying Cloud, and sold for $1385–1500. Apart from the engine the Olympic had nothing to distinguish it from many other medium-priced cars. Franklin sold only 1011 cars in 1933, and 360 in 1934, which was the company's final last year.

The factory was taken over by Air Cooled Motors Corp., headed by former Franklin engineers Carl Doman and Edward Marks, who made engines for aeroplanes and helicopters; a converted flat-6 helicopter engine powered the 1948 TUCKER. In honour of the cars the company name was later changed to the Franklin Engine Co., and continued in business until the early 1970s, when the factory was demolished to make way for a high school.

NG

Further Reading
The Franklin Automobile Company, Sinclair Powell,
Society of Automobile Engineers, 1999.
'Franklin–the twelve at the end of the road', Stan Grayson,
Automobile Quarterly, Vol.XVII, No.3.
'A matter of principle: The Wilkinsen Era at Franklin', John F. Katz,
Automobile Quarterly, Vol.26, Nos.2 and 3.

FRANKLINITE (AUS) 1909
Keep Bros & Wood, Melbourne, Victoria.
As suppliers to the coachbuilding trade, this firm was aware that the opportunity to engage in the growing motor trade was being missed because it was being taken up by the cycle trade. It tried to tempt it by importing the motor components of the KIBLINGER, later MCINTYRE, motor buggy and building the vehicle with local material and skill. The air-cooled flat-twin was available with 14 or 18hp, driven via epicyclic transmission and chains to the solid-tyred high wheels. Advertising that it was 'supplied by the coach-building trade' failed to attract the horse lovers.

MG

FRANTZ (US) 1901–1902
Frantz Automobile Co., Cherryville, Ohio.
The Frantz was one of only three known examples of cars made by clergymen (the others were the AURORA and the LUCK UTILITY). The Revd Hiram Frantz combined his pastoral duties with inventing various useful devices such as a sewing machine motor and a tin opener. 'He combines theology and mechanics thoroughly', said Motor Age. By May 1901 he had built four light steam cars which used his patent burner, and were typical of their kind, with tiller steering, wire wheels and single-chain drive. He announced at the time that he was ready to build petrol cars also, and was to open a larger factory for the purpose, but it seems that the steamers were the only Frantz cars made. By the end of 1902 he had returned to the full-time ministry of the gospel.

NG

FRANZ see WETZIKON

FRASER (i) (GB) c.1911
Douglas S. Fraser & Sons Ltd, Arbroath, Angus.
This company built three steam cars with poppet-valve engines, coil tube boilers and vaporising paraffin burners. Two had 3-cylinder engines, and one a 4-cylinder. Although production for general sale was planned, the three cars all went to members of the Fraser family.

NG

FRASER (ii) (NZ) 1988 to date
Fraser Cars New Zealand, Auckland, North Island.
A clubman type sportscar made by Neil Fraser, the FC 7 was built on an elaborately constructed, comprehensively triangulated frame and incorporated a De Dion-type rear axle. The regular engine was a 2-litre Toyota twin-ohc unit fitted with two dual-throat carburettors, which gave 134bhp but for competition use, a lighter, higher powered Ford-Cosworth BDA engine could be specified. The make was marketed in both Australia and Japan; production having reached 174 by 1996.

MG

FRAYER-MILLER (US) 1904–1909
1904–1907 Oscar Lear Automobile Co., Columbus, Ohio.
1907–1909 Oscar Lear Automobile Co., Springfield, Ohio..
The design of this car was the work of three men, Lee A. Frayer and William J. Miller who had worked together since 1902, and Oscar S. Lear with whom they joined forces in 1904 to make an air-cooled car. Their pooled ideas resulted in a 24hp 4-cylinder car with air-cooled engine in which a rotary blower forced air through aluminium jackets which surrounded the cylinders. The side-valves were in a T-head, and the car featured a 3-speed gearbox and shaft drive. A tourer was the only model until 1907 when a runabout and limousine were added. A 36hp six was added in 1905, and the first example delivered to a customer, on 1 November, was said to be the first 6-cylinder car sold in America. The six was made up to 1907, in which year there was also a short-lived 50hp four, but the staple product was the 24hp four which was made through to the end of car production in 1909. The company then decided to concentrate on commercial vehicles. In 1910 the name of company and vehicles was changed to Kelly, and two years later to Kelly-Springfield.

NG

FRAZEN (US) c.1952
Ray Greene Co., Toledo, Ohio.
The Frazen sports car was intended to supplement the Ray Greene Co.'s steady boat sales. This fibreglass-bodied car was sold in fully assembled form on a Henry J chassis with a 6-cylinder engine. The interior was trimmed in leather

and it had a padded dash and a removable hard-top. The body was dumpy and rounded, resembling a cartoon caricature of a sports car. It could also be ordered in kit form.

HP

FRAZER *see* KAISER (iii)

FRAZER NASH (GB) 1924–1957

1924–1925 Frazer Nash Ltd, Kingston on Thames, Surrey.
1925–1926 William G. Thomas & Frazer Nash Ltd, Kingston on Thames, Surrey.
1926–1957 A.F.N. Ltd, Isleworth, Middlesex.

The Frazer Nash was a peculiarly British phenomenon – an unconventional and in some ways old-fashioned car made in tiny quantities which captured the imagination of sports car enthusiasts all over the world. In 33 years of production, just over 400 were made – a morning's output from a major manufacturer – yet the make has an almost fanatical following, and there is a section of the Vintage Sports Car Club devoted to the prewar Frazer Nash.

Frazer Nash Ltd was founded in 1922 by Captain Archibald Frazer-Nash (1889–1965) who had previously built the G.N. cyclecar with his friend Ron Godfrey. A few cars were made with shaft drive, two or three had Ruby engines and five or six were DEEMSTERs with Frazer Nash radiators. In 1924 Frazer-Nash adopted the form of transmission he had employed on the G.N. This was a chain-drive system in which a separate chain was used for each speed. The chain-driving sprockets were engaged by dog clutches, and transmitted power from a countershaft to the rear axle. Initially three forward speeds were provided, with a fourth optional in 1927 and standard from 1928 onwards. Reverse was obtained by an additional chain outrigged from the bevel box, which made use of the sprockets giving second forward speed.

The advantages of this system were that it was lighter and absorbed less power than a conventional gearbox, and in skilled hands could be operated very quickly. The sprockets could be changed rapidly to give different ratios to suit various courses, such as hill climbs or speed trials.

The rest of the Frazer Nash design included quarter-elliptic suspension all round, rack-and-pinion steering and cable-operated brakes. On the first car of 1924 these worked on the rear wheels only, but front-wheel brakes were optional from 1925, and soon standardised. Although bodywork became lower over the years, the main changes in the Frazer Nash between 1924 and 1939 were concerned with the engines. The first few cars had 1496cc ohv Plus Power engines, but these were soon replaced by side-valve Anzani units of the same size, which were used up to 1932. In 1928 the 50bhp ohv Meadows 4ED of 1496cc began to be offered, and the works tuned individual cars to over 80bhp, while other power units available in the 1930s were the 60bhp single-ohc Gough, designed by Albert Gough and made by Frazer Nash themselves, and the 1660cc 6-cylinder twin-ohc Blackburne which gave 75bhp. Two cars were powered by the 1911cc 6-cylinder BMW engine, after Frazer Nash became the British BMW concessionaires in 1934.

Frazer Nashes were offered with a confusing variety of names, mostly referring to sporting venues where the cars performed, not always with as much distinction as one might have expected. The best-known model was the TT Replica, of which 86 were made between 1932 and 1938, yet the marque never finished in the first three in the Ulster Tourist Trophy. Other model names evoking races, hill climbs or trials included the Boulogne (1926–32), Nurburg (1932–33), Shelsley (1934–36), Colmore (1932–39) and Exeter (1932). They usually referred to body styles rather than engines, so a TT Replica might have a Meadows, Gough or Blackburne engine, according to its date. The bodies were mostly open 2-seaters, although the earlier cars, called Interceptor or Sportop, could seat three or four at a pinch, as could the Colmore. Only two saloons were ever made, one by Weymann for the 1928 Tourist Trophy, the other by Wylder, although three sports cars were rebuilt into saloons.

Considering the variety of models, the number of Frazer Nashes made was very small. The best years were the earliest, with one car per week leaving the factory in 1925 and 1926. However, little if any profit was made on these cars. In October 1925 Archie Frazer-Nash merged with William G. Thomas, converters of ex-War Department trucks, who had larger premises across the road, and in 1928 he sold the company to Richard Plunket-Greene, from whom H.J. Aldington took control, moving production to Isleworth in 1930. He and his brothers Bill

1925 Frazer Nash 3-seater.
NATIONAL MOTOR MUSEUM

1934 Frazer Nash TT replica in 1939 MCC Lands End Trial.
NATIONAL MOTOR MUSEUM

1949 Frazer Nash Le Mans replica in 1954 Eastbourne Rally.
NATIONAL MOTOR MUSEUM

(W.H.) and Don (D.A.) ran the company until the end of car making in 1957.

Under the Aldington regime the cars became profitable but production was cut back. In 1930, when 12 models were listed, only 14 cars were made, and the best year thereafter was 1934 when 39 were delivered. After that the sale of BMWs became a much more important part of the business, and the 'chain gang' Frazer Nashes were made virtually to order. Fourteen were made in 1935, eleven in 1936, while the last three years of the decade saw only four made. The last, delivered in January 1939, was a Colmore 3-4 seater. In contrast, A.F.N. sold 707 BMWs between December 1934 and September 1939. They carried badges reading Frazer Nash BMW, and most were imported complete from Germany, although some were assembled at Isleworth, and a few were fitted with

1904 Fredonia 9hp tonneau.
KEITH MARVIN

British coachwork by a number of coachbuilders, including Abbott of Farnham. Some of the BMWs sold by A.F.N. carried different model numbers. Thus the German Typ 315 was the Type 34, the 315 and 319 were the Type 40, and the Typ 315 sports was the Type 55. The later models, Typs 326, 327 and 328 carried the same numbering in both countries.

During World War II, all three Aldington brothers served in the forces. 'D.A.' was transferred to the Ministry of Supply, which brought him into contact with the Bristol Aeroplane Co., and led to the adoption of the BMW engine in the new car which Bristol were to produce after the war. 'H.J.' became a director of Bristol, and was instrumental in bringing to England the drawings for the successful BMW 328 sports car, and also some engines and components. He also hired the BMW designer Fritz Fiedler, whose ingenious horizontal pushrod engine was used in Bristol and Frazer Nash cars.

The new car was originally to have been called the Frazer Nash Bristol, but the aeroplane company thought this unacceptable, and preferred the simple name Bristol. This went on the 2-door saloon made at Bristol, while the sports models would be built by Frazer Nash at Isleworth, and called Frazer Nash. Their Fiedler-designed 1971cc uprated BMW engines and gearboxes were made at Bristol.

Between 1948 and 1957, seven models were offered under the Frazer Nash name, although, as in prewar days, output was small. The best known was the Le Mans Replica which had a simple open 2-seater body and cycle-type wings; 34 were sold between 1948 and 1953, and among their sporting successes were the third place of Norman Culpan and H.J. Aldington at Le Mans in 1949 (hence the name; the model was originally called the High Speed), and Franco Cortese's victory in the 1951 Targa Florio, the first time a British car had won the gruelling Sicilian race. Other Bristol-powered models all had full-width bodies – they included the Mille Miglia, Targa Florio and Sebring open 2-seaters, and a fixed-head coupé of which only eight were made. One of the Targa Florios was fitted with a 2660cc Austin engine at the suggestion of Austin's Leonard Lord, and shown at the 1952 Earls Court Show. Also at the Show was Donald Healey's 100 powered by the same engine. It was this car that Lord chose for production as the Austin Healey 100. However, he was suitably apologetic to the Aldingtons, and refunded their expenses on the project.

In the 1950s the Frazer Nash began to go the way of the prewar chain-driven version, but the foreign cuckoo in the Isleworth nest was no longer BMW but Porsche. A.F.N. began to import these in 1953, and they soon became more lucrative than making Frazer Nashes. They also imported 3-cylinder D.K.W.s for a while; one of these was the basis for a one-off roadster with a part-fibreglass body styled after the Frazer Nash Mille Miglia. By the middle of the decade production was down to less than 10 cars per year. The last Frazer Nash was a coupé powered by the 3168cc BMW V8 engine. Called the Continental, it cost £3751 which was hardly competitive with the Aston-Martin DB2/4 at £3076, still less with the Jaguar XK140 coupé at only £1711. Only one Continental was made in 1957, although the make lingered on in some lists up to 1960. Total production of the postwar Frazer Nashes was 84, which added to the prewar figure of 323 gives a total of 407. A good proportion survives today, and the Frazer Nash section of the VSCC has over 200 members, with about 200 chain-driven cars.

A.F.N. Ltd continued as a retail distributor for Porsche, while Porsche Cars Great Britain Ltd was the importer and distribution centre. Archie Frazer-Nash had little to do with the cars after the Aldingtons took over, but he became famous for his gun turret which was used on many well-known aircraft during World War II. The company name survived on various products, including small electric vehicles such as golf buggies, and in 1998 was carried on a road vehicle again, when Frazer Nash bought up Robin Hood Vehicle Industries, makers of a midicoach, which they renamed the Eastleigh 100.

NG

Further Reading
The Chain Drive Frazer Nash, David Thirlby,
Macdonald & Co., 1965.
From Chain Drive to Turbocharger, Denis Jenkinson,
Patrick Stephens, London, 1984.

FRAZIER (US) 1955
Larry Frazier, Los Angeles, California.
The Frazier was one of the most radical experimental cars of its time. Built by automotive engineer Larry Frazier, it used a rear-mounted 5-cylinder radial engine with 5 camshafts to produce 75hp at 3800rpm. There was a single master rod that acted directly on the single-throw crank, with 4 parasite rods pinned to the master. Suspension was by hydraulic struts that operated through oil and air bladders in a cylinder, somewhat similar to the Hydrolastic suspension later used by BMC in England. It had no shock absorbers or springs. The body was an attractive coupé with fibreglass and magnesium panelling. Price was expected to be in the $8000 range, but it appears that only the prototype was made.
HP

FREDCAR (F) 1987
Fredcar, Vocance.
This was an ultra-simple plastic/fibreglass utility body designed for any Citroën 2CV, Dyane or Ami chassis. Doors with windows and a hard-top were optional.
CR

FREDERICKSON (US) 1914
Frederickson Patents Co., Chicago, Illinois.
This was a cyclecar powered by a new type of 2-cylinder 2-stroke engine, in which compression took place not in the crankcase but on the underside of the piston, 'the engine being built with a crosshead like a steam engine'. Otherwise it was typical of its kind, with friction transmission and belt drive. Tandem or staggered seating was offered, and 'even with the wind resistance caused by side by side seating', the company claimed a top speed of 55mph (88km/h), which was a good speed for a cyclecar. The designer, Clayton E. Frederickson, later made the LITTLEMAC.
NG

FREDERIKSEN see ANGLO-DANE

FREDONIA (US) 1902–1904
Fredonia Manufacturing Co., Youngstown, Ohio.
This company built a car in 1895, and one or two more the following year, one of which was said to be the Booth-Crouch (see CROUCH (i)). The engine of this car was built by W. Lee Crouch and the body designed by its customer, Dr Carlos Booth, but possibly it was put together by the Fredonia company. They did not offer a line of cars for sale until September 1902, when the 9hp single-cylinder runabout and 10hp tonneau were listed. They had tiller steering, single-chain drive and a front similar to the contemporary Cadillac and Ford. For 1904 the engine was quoted as a 10/12hp, wheel steering was provided, and there was a frontal bonnet on De Dion-Bouton lines, although the engine was still under the seat. The Fredonia engine was unusual in that the mixture was pre-compressed in an annular chamber before admission to the cylinder.
NG

FREE SPIRIT see HUDSON

FREIA (D) 1922–1927

1922–1923 Kleinautobau AG, Greiz.

1923–1927 Freia Automobil AG, Greiz.

This company made expensive small cars powered by a 1320cc 5/14PS 4-cylinder engine, followed by a 1472cc 6/30PS and 1807cc 7/35PS. These were made by Freia themselves and also by Steudel. The 1925–27 5/20PS was an attractive-looking car with an underslung frame and wire wheels. It was made as a tourer or coupé. The Freia's designer Arthur Schuh later joined J.K. Rasmussen and became technical director of Audi.

HON

FREJUS *see* DIATTO

FREMONT (US) 1920–1922

Fremont Motors Corp., Fremont, Ohio.

The Fremont was a typical assembled car powered by a 3205cc 6-cylinder Falls engine. Its appearance was more distinctive than many, with horizontal bonnet louvres, cycle-type wings and step plates instead of running boards. It was built in a plant that had been home to several trucks, Burford, Fremont-Mais and Lauth-Juergens, and a Fremont truck was also part of the programme. Initially, Fremont cars were for export only, but very few cars were built. The sales manager was Fred M. Guy who had designed the disc valve engine used in the ACE (iii).

NG

FRENAY (B) 1913–1914

Automobiles Frenay, Liège.

The Frenay was a light car powered by a 1460cc 10/12hp 4-cylinder Ballot engine, with dynamo lighting and starter. It had a handsome radiator similar to that of the Métallurgique. It was announced at the end of 1913, but production did not get going until May 1914, leaving little time for many to be made before the outbreak of war. At least one came to England, where it was advertised in 1920 at more than double the 1914 list price of £250.

NG

FRENETTE (GB) 1981–1982

Peter Frenette, St Neots, Cambridgeshire.

This Mini Moke Californian replica, made by a gunsmith, was unusual in only one respect: it had a stainless steel body. The mechanical side was entirely derived from the Mini.

CR

FRERA (I) 1905–1913

Corrado Frera & Compagnia, Tradate.

Frera was a well-known name in the motorcycle world, being in business from 1906 to the mid–1950s. Their cars were much rarer, being confined to a few light machines with air-cooled 2-cylinder engines sold under the name Piccolo. From about 1910 to 1913 they produced the ZEDEL under licence.

NG

FRICK (i) (GB) 1904–1906

A.W. Dougill & Co. Ltd, Leeds, Yorkshire.

Dougills had made experimental cars from 1896, and also built the Lawson Motor Wheel self-contained power unit. In 1904 they announced a light car with 7hp single-cylinder engine and friction transmission incorporating two driven discs. This was made under MAURER patents. Final drive was by chain. In 1906 a 2-cylinder engine was adopted, but soon afterwards Dougill concentrated on commercial vehicles which were made up to the end of 1907.

NG

FRICK (ii) (US) c.1955

Bill Frick Motors, Rockville Centre, Long Island.

Bill Frick was one of the pioneers in American road racing, working with Briggs Cunningham and being the first to install a Cadillac engine into the Allard J2, thereby creating a legend. Frick liked the 5400cc Cadillac V8 with its ohvs and 210hp. For street use he installed them into 1949–1950 Ford sedans, which went very quickly. He sold over 200 of these Fordillacs to everyone from Cunningham

1926 Freia 1300cc 2-seater.
NATIONAL MOTOR MUSEUM

1922 Fremont Six tourer.
KEITH MARVIN

1904 Frick (i) 7hp tonneau.
NATIONAL MOTOR MUSEUM

to Luigi Chinetti. He built about half that many Studillacs, which used the same engine shoehorned into the sleek 1953 Studebaker coupé. The Thunderlac that followed was a Cadillac-powered 1955 Ford Thunderbird. In 1955 he created an entire car of his own design, with a box-section chassis and the Cadillac engine in various stages from stock to supercharged. Transmission options included Cadillac automatics and a Z-F 4-speed manual. The aluminium body was designed by Michelotti and built by Vignale. The Frick Special was similar to the 340-series Ferraris, only larger. Price in 1955 was a hefty $9000, and only two coupés and a convertible were made.

HP

1959 Frisky 3-wheeler.
NICK GEORGANO/NATIONAL MOTOR MUSEUM

FRIEDMAN (US) 1900–1903

Friedman Automobile Co., Chicago, Illinois.

Chicago florist Oscar J. Friedman built a 3-wheeled car with 3hp 2-cylinder engine in 1900, before setting up his company which was to make 4-wheelers and airships. The latter remained a dream, but the cars were offered, although made for Friedman by the National Sewing Machine Co. of Belvedere, Illinois. They had 6hp 2-cylinder engines and tiller steering. Friedman ordered 525 cars, but far fewer were delivered, and in April 1903 he sued the National Sewing Machine Co. for breach of contract. They subsequently made a very similar design which they called the ELDREDGE.

NG

FRIEND (US) 1921

Friend Motors Corp., Pontiac, Michigan.

The Friend was little more than the Olympian car with badge engineering, the Olympian having been acquired in 1920 by Otis B. Friend. Fewer than 50 cars had been completed when the Friend failed. The Friend featured its 'own' 4-cylinder engine and, with a 112in (2842mm) wheelbase, was offered only as a '5-passenger touring' model, in reality a 5-seater 2-door roadster. Wooden artillery or wire wheels were options and, in an effort to remain in business, its price was reduced from $1585 to $1185, but to no avail.

KM

FRISBIE (US) 1901–1909

Frisbie Motor Co., Cromwell and Middletown, Connecticut.

Russell Abner Frisbie (1874–1968) was a sporadic builder of cars whose main business was the provision of engines to other companies, particularly for marine work. His first car of 1901 was a light 2-seater runabout powered by a 2-cylinder engine, which he said was for his own use. This still survives. He built another in 1902 and in 1905 made two 6-cylinder engines, one of which went into a large touring car, the other into a high-speed launch. By 1909 he had built several more cars, some of which may have been offered for sale. His factory later made aircraft components and although retired in the 1920s, he continued to service Frisbie marine engines which powered most of the local fishing boats. Another branch of the family formed the Frisbie Pie Co. at Bridgeport, Connecticut. This gave a new word to the language when it was found that the pie plates had aerodynamic qualities which provided an enjoyable pastime for young and old.

NG

FRISKY (GB) 1957–1964

1957–1958 Henry Meadows (Vehicles) Ltd, Wolverhampton, Staffordshire.
1958–1959 Frisky Cars Ltd, Wolverhampton, Staffordshire.
1959–1961 Frisky Cars (1959) Ltd, Wolverhampton, Staffordshire.
1961–1962 Frisky Cars (1959) Ltd, Sandwich, Kent.
1963–1964 Frisky Spares and Service Ltd, Queenborough, Kent.

The purple racing colours of Egypt were only ever painted on one car: the PHOENIX sports car, the brainchild of British businessman Captain Raymond Flower who was then based in Cairo. While still in Egypt, he also developed a microcar of very strange appearance (featuring a single up-and-over door) but that was never marketed and Flower returned to his native Britain in the middle of the Suez crisis. Developing his Phoenix microcar, he collaborated with engine maker Henry Meadows Ltd, who eventually built the production cars. As the Frisky first appeared in Britain in 1957, it sported attractive lines penned by Michelotti and now had gull-wing doors. The new car was claimed to offer seating for five. However, this was judged an impractical production proposition and the Frisky was restyled with open bodywork, conventional doors and sharper lines (including tail fins). The fibreglass body was made in the nearby Guy lorry works and was mounted atop a separate ladder chassis. The rear wheels were set so close together that no differential was required. The 249cc Villiers 2-stroke engine drove the rear wheels by chain through a motorbike gearbox; reverse was obtained by reversing the engine. The front suspension was Dubonnet-type independent. Very shortly after launch, a 324cc Villiers 16bhp engine was also offered as an option. The first cars were called the Friskysport, and the little car lived up to its name: it could manage 65mph (105km/h) while returning 56mpg. Both coupé and convertible versions were sold. Another project, the 1958 Friskysprint, did not enter production in Britain. It was a dramatic-looking open car designed by Gordon Bedson and was much more of a sports car, measuring only 37.5in (952mm) high. Its 492cc 3-cylinder 2-stroke Excelsior engine developed 30bhp and Meadows claimed it would do 85mph (137km/h). The project re-emerged in Australia as the Lightburn Zeta Sports. Meanwhile, Captain Flower decided to press ahead with a more basic Frisky, which he called the Family Three. This was a 3-wheeler with accommodation for four people, using 197cc, then 250cc 2-cylinder engines. Production concentrated on 3-wheelers after 1961. A larger version, the Prince, was offered from 1960 with a 324cc or 328cc engine. The only other Frisky was also called the Frisky Sport. Not much is known about this model, which was a larger and more conventional-looking car. Whether it went into production is not known. After its fourth successive change of premises, Meadows abandoned production of the Frisky in 1964.

CR

FRISWELL see DELAGE

FRITCHLE (US) 1905–1920

Fritchle Automobile & Electric Storage Battery Co., Denver, Colorado.

Oliver Parker Fritchle started in business by making batteries which, from the beginning, had an exceptional storage capacity. His first electric cars were made in very small numbers for a local clientele, one in 1905, two in 1906 and 17 in 1907. In 1908, when he made 33 cars, he attracted valuable publicity by challenging other makers of electrics to a long distance run. Nobody took up his challenge, so he made the journey himself, from Lincoln, Nebraska, to New York, a distance of 2140 miles (3444km). During this journey the Fritchle electric frequently covered 100 miles on one battery charge, a very high figure then or now. The resulting publicity helped sales into three figures, 187 in 1909, 214 in 1910 and a peak of 323 in 1911. The car was advertised as 'The 100 Mile Electric'.

The Fritchle was made in a variety of body styles; in addition to the usual closed coupés, there was an open 5-seater tourer on a 100in (2538mm) wheelbase. Up to 1912 chain or shaft drive were offered, the latter costing $100 more. The most expensive Fritchle was the 5-seater brougham of 1913–15 which cost $3600. For 1916 they offered a petrol-electric coupé with a 4-cylinder air-cooled engine, but it was not a success, and did not feature in the 1917 catalogue. By then the waning popularity of the electric car was felt in Denver as elsewhere; sales dropped to 23 cars in 1918, 17 in 1919, and just six in 1920.

NG

FROGEYE (GB) 1986–c. 1996

The Frogeye Car Co., Ryde, Isle of Wight.

During the development of this Austin-Healey Sprite Mk1 replica, both Geoffrey and Donald Healey were impressed enough with it to give it their endorsement – although the Healey name could not be used because the rights were owned by other parties. This high quality replica used a steel box section chassis and meticulous fibreglass bodywork. Cars were sold complete, but many customers opted to turn their old MG Midget into a Frogeye replica (the company initially called their offering a 'restoration kit'), or used Austin A30/A35 mechanicals as per the original Sprite.

CR

FRONT DRIVE (US) 1905

Auto Front Drive Manufacturing Co., St Louis, Missouri.

This company made a front-drive axle which could be fitted to any car, and to demonstrate the system they built a car powered by a 16hp 4-cylinder Streite engine. Drive was taken to the front axle by chain, and it seemed a crude design. They invited enquiries from firms willing to manufacture the car, or failing that, the axles, but there were no takers. Probably the single prototype with tourer body was the only Front Drive made.

NG

FRONTENAC (i) (US) 1906–1913

Abendroth & Root Manufacturing Co., Newburgh, New York.

This company was a well-established maker of boilers, tubes and other metal goods, whose history dated back to the 1870s. When they entered the motor business it was with a large and expensive design, with a 40/45hp 4-cylinder Continental engine and shaft drive. They made a tourer, runabout and limousine, all on the same 124in (3147mm) wheelbase, strange in that the limousine and tourer bodies were so much larger than the runabout. Prices were high, the limousine costing $5000. About a dozen cars were made in 1906 and 100 in 1907, after which sales dropped. Although the Frontenac was listed up to 1913, production was negligible for the last few years, the company preferring to concentrate on the business they knew best.

NG

FRONTENAC (ii) (US) 1921–1924

Frontenac Motor Corp., Indianapolis, Indiana.

The Frontenac's initial design was that of an advanced touring car designed by Louis Chevrolet – who had become prominent for the design of his racing cars – and Cornelius W. van Ranst. Backed by Stutz officials and sometimes called the Stutz-Frontenac, it featured a 3.2-litre single-ohc 4-cylinder unit with thermo-syphon cooling, unusual on an American high-performance car at this date. Unfortunately, the Frontenac Motor Co. failed and the car never reached the marketplace. Undaunted, with Chevrolet as president, the reorganised company started work on a new design with power by an 8-cylinder single-sleeve valve Burt-type engine; the American rights had been obtained by Louis Chevrolet from the owner of the Burt patent in Europe on a time-limit agreement. A phaeton was completed featuring a 140in (3553mm) wheelbase, 4-wheel hydraulic brakes and balloon tyres with wire wheels. The Burt engine developed 80bhp at 2600rpm. Initial plans were made to exhibit the cars at the 1925 auto shows. Production ended because the American rights to the Burt engine's time limit had run out and Frontenac had been unable to raise the necessary funds to continue further operation.

KM

FRONTENAC (iii) (CDN) 1931–1933

Dominion Motors Ltd, Leaside, Ontario.

This company was formed to take over DURANT's Canadian operation, and to try to make a success of car making just as Durant was failing in the US. Introduced in August 1931, and named after Count Frontenac, an eighteenth century governor of 'new France', the Frontenac 6-70 was a more powerful and luxurious version of the Durant Six, with 72bhp 3570cc 6-cylinder engine. It was distinguished by a slightly vee'd-radiator, and was made as a sedan, coupé and sport roadster. As well as the Frontenac, 4- and 6-cylinder Durants and Reo Flying Clouds were built at the Leaside factory. In May 1932 came the Frontenac 6-85, which was a DE VAUX made under licence. Powered by a 3517cc Continental Red Seal engine, it was made in sedan, coupé and convertible models, and was priced about CDN$200 more than the slightly smaller 6-70. Total Frontenac sales in 1932 were less than 1000, and for 1933 they tried a lower-priced car, based on the CONTINENTAL (vi). This had a 2345cc 4-cylinder engine in the C-400 which was the equivalent of the Continental Beacon, or 6-cylinder 3517cc in the C-600 (Continental Flyer). There was also the more luxurious Ace, but this was not made in Canada, being a Detroit-built Ace imported complete. None of them sold well and production at Leaside ended just before Christmas 1933.

NG

FRONTENAC (iv) see FORD (ii)

1915 F.R.P. Model 45 Series C tourer.
HENRY AUSTIN CLARK

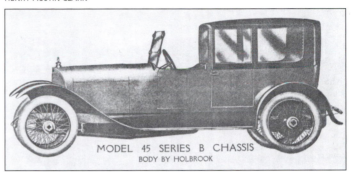

1916 F.R.P. Model 45 Series B town car, by Holbrook.
KEITH MARVIN

FRONTMOBILE (US) 1917–1918

Safety Motor Co., Greenloch, New Jersey.

The Frontmobile was the last and most unorthodox car designed by C.H. Blomstrom, who had also to his credit the QUEEN, BLOMSTROM, GYROSCOPE, and REX (ii). As its name implied, the Frontmobile was a front-wheel drive car with a 26hp 4-cylinder Le Roi engine, gears mounted on the differential housing and worm final drive. The gear lever passed through the dashboard to the right of the steering column. The frame was dropped immediately behind the engine to give a low centre of gravity, and suspension was by transverse springs. A roadster and a tourer were listed, at $1000 and $1200 respectively, but it is thought that not more than five Frontmobiles were made, of which one survives. This has a G.B. & S. engine. Blomstrom later formed Camden Motors Corp. in Camden, New Jersey, to make a similar car, but probably not a single one was made there.

NG

F.R.P. (US) 1914–1916

Finley-Robertson-Porter Co., Port Jefferson, Long Island, New York.

Finley Robertson Porter was the designer of the T-head 4-cylinder MERCER of 1910 and was affiliated with that company until the advent of the L-head Mercer whereupon he left that company and organised one of his own. His plans called for a powerful, quality automobile using his initials for the name of the new car. One might speculate at the brute power potential of the F.R.P. In its promotional brochure it carried a statement that 'The horsepower rating of the Model 45 motor according to the S.A.E. formula adopted by some states as a means of classifying licence rates is 34hp. The actual development at 1000 feet of piston speed was 52hp and at its maximum speed of 2500rpm 170hp.'

This put the car in a category of its own as by far the most powerful road car in the country. It could be ordered in three wheelbase sizes. These were: the Series A, used for the racing models at 110in (2792mm); Series B at 140in (3553mm); and Series C at 130in (3299mm), all chassis priced at $5000. Labelled in the brochure as 'America's Foremost Pleasure Car', claiming the car afforded 'No waste through a lack of knowledge either in design or manufacture'.

Photos included a racing car, a victoria and a town car, all featuring bodies by Holbrook, plus a 7-seater touring car with a body by M. Armstrong & Co.

1983 FSM Beskid.
ROBERT PRZYBYLSKI

c.1964 FSO Warszawa saloon.
ROBERT PRZYBYLSKI

c.1970 FSO Syrena saloon.
NICK GEORGANO

A full-page advertisement appeared in several magazines – both general and automotive – featuring the Holbrook-bodied town car which was exhibited at New York City's Hotel Astor during the week of 3–8 January 1916. The number of F.R.P.s completed is unknown. Three were bought by a Wisconsin industrialist, all of which were described as touring cars with Brewster bodies, who placed an order for six to ten more cars. Another was sold to a party in Massachusetts while Mr Porter built one for his personal use. Whether any of the subsequent cars ordered by the man in Wisconsin were completed and sold is not known.

The Porter factory was occupied by the government at the start of World War I, leaving Robertson with sufficient parts for 30 to 40 more cars. He went to Wright Field at Dayton, Ohio to head up the motor department there which was testing Liberty engines.

At the conclusion of hostilities, Robertson opted not to continue further F.R.P. manufacture and sold the remaining parts to the American & British Manufacturing Corp. of Bridgeport, Connecticut which started production of the PORTER luxury car of which 34 would be completed between 1919 and 1922. Finley Robertson Porter was named as a consultant in this venture and his son, Robert, became chief engineer. One F.R.P. survives.
KM

F.S. (US) 1911–1912
F.S. Motors Co., Milwaukee, Wisconsin.
These initials stand for Filer & Stowell, which was well-known for their Corliss steam engines, and which was the parent company of F.S. Motors. They entered car manufacture by buying up the PETREL Motor Car Co. and the Beaver Manufacturing Co. who made engines. The F.S. naturally used Beaver engines, of 22, 30 and 40hp, in a conventional shaft-driven chassis. Bodies included two sizes of runabout and a torpedo tourer, as well as a parcel car with 12hp engine.
NG

FSM (PL) 1972–1992
Fabryka Samochodow Malolitrazowych, Bielsko-Bialo.
When Edward Gierek replaced Wladyslaw Gomulka as secretary-general of the Polish communist party, it was decided that FSM would make a popular car. In 1972 production of the Syrena 105 was transferred to Bielsko from the FSO factory in Warsaw. In October 1971 Poland bought the licence for the manufacture of the Fiat 126 which went into production in new factories at Bielsko and Tychy. Two years later the first vehicles were assembled, and in the next year local manufacture, as opposed to assembly, began. The 126 received a 650cc engine in 1976, and three years later FSM became the sole supplier of the 126 on all markets.

During the late 1970's and early 1980's the factory's R & D department prepared many prototypes of small cars. With one exception, they were all based on the 126, including a front-drive model. The most interesting was the Beskid, with monocoque body and front-wheel drive. It was designed to accomodate engines from a longitudinally-mounted 700cc twin to a transverse 1100cc four. Seven prototypes were made in 1983, but the Beskid was shelved.

Parallel to 126 production the Syrena was continued, in saloon, pick-up, and delivery van versions. It was thought that the Fiat Panda would replace the Syrena, but this plan was disturbed by Martial Law, and the Syrena was continued up to 30 June 1983. Altogether 344,077 Syrenas were made in the FSM factory. In 1987 the 126B, with horizontally-mounted water-cooled engine, was put into production, but proved unpopular. The same year a licence for the Fiat Cinquecento was taken out, and four years later it went into production. In 1992 Fiat acquired the FSM factory. The millionth Cinquecento was made in 1997, and the following year the Seicento replaced it. However, the Fiat 126 (with catalytic converter) was still made. Up to early 1999 about 3,300,000 126s had been made.
RP

FSO (PL) 1951 to date
1951–1996 Fabryka Samochodow Osobowych, Warsaw.
1996 to date Daewoo-FSO, Warsaw.
Although the Polish state planned to continue the association with Fiat after World War II (see POLSKI-FIAT), an agreement was signed instead with the Soviet Union for licence manufacture of the GAZ M-20 Pobieda saloon. The first of the 2120cc side-valve 4-cylinder cars, called Warszawa, came off the line late in 1951, but it was five years before all major parts were actually manufactured in Poland. The factory had ambitious plans to modernise the design, and commissioned a body from Ghia. However, when the Polish Communist Party leader Wladyslaw Gomulka saw the prototypes he thought they were too bourgeois, so the round-back Pobeida style was continued. A 70bhp ohv engine was introduced in 1962, and in 1964 a notchback saloon body was introduced (Model 203 with ohv engine, 204 with side-valve), and the following year the Warszawa estate car (Model 203K) went on sale. After protests from Peugeot, these model numbers were changed to 223 and 224. During their 21 years of production, 245,471 Warszawa cars were made.

1995 FSO Polonez saloon.
ROBERT PRZYBYLSKI

In 1957, after four years development, a new smaller car was introduced. Called the Syrena, its engine was based on the prewar DKW, with 744cc 27bhp in-line 2-cylinder 2-stroke engine, front-wheel drive and a 2-door saloon body. Made on a shoe-string budget without proper tooling, the cars were rather unreliable, but were nevertheless the only transport available to ordinary Polish citizens. In 1961 a prototype Syrena Sport was announced, with flat-twin 4-stroke engine, and in 1966 the Syrena gained a 843cc 3-cylinder 2-stroke engine with power up to 40bhp, and a synchromesh gearbox. This model was designated the 104, and was made by FSO up to 1972, when production was transferred to the FSM plant. Total Syrena output in Warsaw was 177,234.

In the early 1960s it was apparent that new technology was needed if production at FSO was to be raised from about 25,000 per year to more than 100,000. New models of Syrena and Warszawa were planned, but in 1965 a licence was acquired for manufacture of the Fiat 125. Following huge investments in FSO and about 100 other factories, production began in 1968. Two engines were available, 1295cc/60bhp and 1481cc/75bhp. At first only the 4-door saloon body was made, but from 1973 an estate car was added. This included a high-roof version for ambulances, and an extra-long-wheelbase model. During the mid-1970s three prototypes of sports cars were made, and also of a 4 × 4 estate car. In 1976 production hit record levels with 122,790 made. Production of the Polski Fiat 125P ended in 1991 when car no. 1,455,699 was completed. Other models assembled between 1973 and 1983 included the Fiat 127, 128, 131, 132, and the Zastava 1100. The total for all these was 73,266.

Late in1977 production began of a restyled car called the Polonez. It had the same 1265cc or 1481cc Fiat engines in a new 5-door hatchback body. A family of new engines in the 1.6 to 2-litre range was planned but shelved, though the Fiat engine was increased to 1.6 litres. At the same time a Polonez truck with 1000kg payload was introduced, and in December 1985 the Nysa truck factory was taken over by FSO. Also assembled there, from 1995, were the Citroën C-15 and from 1998 Berlingo.

In 1985 a prototype of the Wars popular car modelled on the Opel Kadett with 1.3-litre engine and front-wheel drive was built, but did not go into production. Three years later the Fiat Uno was planned as a replacement for the Polonez, but the Ministry of Industry opposed the idea, and the Polonez was continued.

1978 FSO Polonez hatchback.
NATIONAL MOTOR MUSEUM

1981 FSO Polski-Fiat 125P saloon.
NATIONAL MOTOR MUSEUM

c.1953 Fuldamobil N-2 coupé.
NICK GEORGANO/NATIONAL MOTOR MUSEUM

Production reached an all-time low (44,801 units) in 1991 and the factory was in the red. The Citroën diesel engine was added the same year, and up-dating of the Polonez continued, including Rover 1.4 engines from 1993. The FSO factory was put up for sale in 1990 with Opel as a possible buyer, but in 1996 Daewoo acquired it. They continued the Polonez, adding an estate version in 1999, and added their own Lanos to the production lines. In 1999 Daewoo-FSO made 212,191 cars, the most popular being the Matiz (79,443) and the Lanos (61,945). Only 13,273 Polonez cars were made.

RP

FUCHS (A) 1922–1925
Inzersdorfer Industriewerke Hans Fuchs AG, Vienna.
This firm built specialist components for several car makers, and also offered a car of its own. This had a 1180cc 5/15PS 4-cylinder engine. The open body seated three passengers in a cloverleaf layout.

HON

FUGITIVE see U.V.A.

FUHR (US) c.1980
Fuhr Motors, Lake Grove, New York.
The Fuhr Osage was a 2-seat gull-winged sports car that fitted on a Volkswagen Beetle chassis. The body was fibreglass with a foam inner layer. It had a wedge-shaped body with awkward angular window treatment so flat-paned glass could be used.

HP

FUJI (J) 1957–1958
Fuji Toshuda Motors Corp., Tokyo.
The Fuji Cabin was one of a handful of Japanese 3-wheeled microcars. It had a 5.5bhp air-cooled single-cylinder 123cc 2-stroke engine giving a top speed of 37mph. It looked rather like a mobile kidney bean, with its ultra-rounded 2-seater coupé shape realised in fibreglass, and it featured a single front headlamp. Some 85 examples were built in all.

CR

FUJIOKA (US) 1922–1923
Fujioka Motor Car Co., Los Angeles, California.
Little is known of the small Fujioka car, which was built for export to Japan, other than that a few units were completed and shipped. The car was designed by Earl A. Spencer and the company was headed by Fred J. Fujioka who operated the F. & K. Garage and was manager of the Japanese Automobile Club of Southern California, both of which shared the same address, 231 N. San Pedro Street in Los Angeles. The venture was short-lived and Mr Fujioka returned to full-time management of the garage. Earl A. Spencer tried again to project a car for the Japanese market and built a pilot model of a viable small car – named for himself – for that purpose, but failed to progress beyond the construction of a single prototype.

KM

FUKANG (CHI) 1990 to date
Shenlong (Dongfeng-Citroën) Automobile Corp. Ltd,
Wuhan City, Hubei Province.
The Citroën ZX Volcane was rebaptised the Fukang in China ('Prosperity and Health'). The 1360cc hatchback (DC 7140) was produced by a joint venture agreed between the Dongfeng Motors Corp. and S.A. Citroën. Dongfeng owned 70 per cent, Citroën, Société Generale, and BNP 30 per cent. The contract was signed in 1990, and the joint venture started in 1992. The first assembly took place in 1990 in a factory in Xiangfan. Later a completely new factory was built in Hanyang District, Wuhan City. Potential capacity was 150,000 units per year, with a possibility to enlarge the factory to produce 300,000 units. In 1997 four versions of the Fukang were made: a 1360cc 4-speed RX and RS, a 5-speed RG and a 1587cc 5-speed AL, with Bosch fuel injection. In August 1998 a saloon version was introduced, which was especially designed for China by Citroën partner Heuliez. The car was named Fukang 988 DC 7160 when serial production started. A third product, a chassis with cab, was the basis of the DONGFENG (ii) EQ 7140 van and pick-up. Local assembly of the Citroën XM V6 Exclusive and Xantia under the Fengsheng brand also took place in a small workshop in Huizhou City, Guangdong Province.

EVIS

FULDAMOBIL (D) 1950–1960
Elektromaschinenbau Fulda GmbH, Fulda.
This was a 3-wheeled coupé with a single rear wheel driven by a single-cylinder 250cc Ilo or 360cc Sachs single-cylinder engine. The first examples had a wooden frame with alloy panels; the next step was an all-steel body and in 1957 a fibreglass body which gave the Fuldamobil a more handsome appearance than it had formerly. During 1954–55 it was built under licence by NWF (Nordwestdeutscher Fahzeugbau AG) of Wilhelmshaven with a 200cc Ilo engine. Some export models were made with twin rear wheels mounted close together. Some cabriolets were made and the Netherlands-built Bambino was offered in doorless roadster form.
The Fuldamobil design was made in a surprising number of other countries. It was offered in Britain as the Nobel 200 by York Noble Industries, being made by various firms including LEA-FRANCIS and shipbuilders Harland & Wolff, in Sweden as the Fram King Fulda, in the Netherlands as the Bambino, in Greece as the Attica and Alta, in India as the Hans Vahaar, and in Chile as the Bambi.

HON

FULGURA see BERGMANN

FULLER (i) (US) 1908–1911
Angus Automobile Co., Angus, Nebraska.
The three Fuller brothers were builders of buggies and wagons. They fitted an engine to one of their buggies, and sold it to a local doctor. The formation of the Angus Automobile Co. led to more ambitious machines, full-size cars offered with two sizes of 4-cylinder engine, 22/26hp and 35/40hp, and a 60hp six. For such a powerful car, the latter was not expensive, at $2500 for a roadster and $3500 for a tourer. The makers boasted that they were the only car makers in Nebraska, which was possibly true during the years that they were active, but there were several others before. Their car was sometimes known as the Angus.

NG

FULLER (ii) (US) 1909–1910
Fuller Buggy Co., Jackson, Michigan.
This Fuller was the idea of George A. Matthews, who owned the Fuller Buggy Co. and was a director of the JACKSON Automobile Co. Wanting to see the name of his Fuller company on a car, he made a high-wheeler with a 22hp 2-cylinder engine and chain drive, and also a conventional 4-cylinder car with a 23/30hp engine. By 1911 the high-wheeler had been dropped and the 25/30 absorbed into the Jackson range.

NG

FULMEN (E) 1921
Ernesto Rodriguez Franco, Barcelona.
Short lived, The Fulmen was a cyclecar whose designer was, amongst other things, the author of *Enciclopedia del Automóvil*.

NG

1909 Fuller (ii) motor buggy.
NATIONAL MOTOR MUSEUM

FULMINA (D) 1913–1926

1913–1921 Fulmina-Werke Paul Hoffmann GmbH,
Mannheim-Friedrichsfeld.
1921–1926 Fulmina Werk GmbH, Mannheim-Friedrichsfeld.
This company began production with three medium-sized cars, of 8/25, 10/30 and
16/45PS. Both open and closed bodies were offered. Postwar production concentrated
on the 8/22PS, a very conventional 4-cylinder car. Manufacture was continued
sporadically until 1926, but output was very small.

HON

FULTON (US) 1920

Fulton Motor Truck Co., Farmingdale, New York.
There was quite a vogue in America in the early 1920s for small cars built entirely
for export. Examples included the ALSACE, FREMONT and HERMES (iii).
The Fulton truck company built at least one prototype of such a car, powered
by a 4-cylinder engine and with rhd, but it never went into production. Fulton
were in business as truck makers from 1917 to 1925.

NG

FULTON AIRPHIBIAN see AIRPHIBIAN

FUQI (CHI) 1989–1993

Fuqi Auto Works, Fuzhou City, Jiangxi Province.
The Fuqi FQ 6400 was a plastic-bodied motor car made in 4-door saloon and
5-door hatchback version. The body was inspired by the Daihatsu Charade.
The factory also made cross country-vehicles and pick-ups.

EVIS

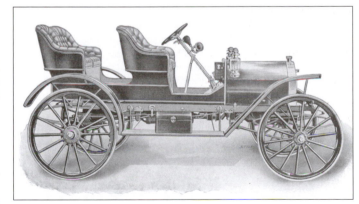

1908 Fuller (i) Model B 16/18hp tourer.
NICK BALDWIN

FUSI FERRO (I) 1948–1949

Stà Fusi Ferro, Turin.
The extraordinary Fusi Ferro Aurora 8 was shown at the 1948 Turin Motor Show.
Two unusual features of this 6-seater car were the central driving position and
the removable, transparent Plexiglas roof with an electric blind sited behind it.
The engine was also extraordinary: it was a 1086cc straight-8 cylinder unit composed
of two Fiat Topolino blocks joined together, with a unique ohv cylinder head and
twin carburettors. Its output was rated at 60bhp. The transmission had four speeds
and the suspension was all-independent. The long, low, full-width bodywork had
enclosed wheels and faired-in headlamps, all on an exceptionally long 116in (2950mm)
wheelbase, and was created by Costruzione Automobili e Motoscafi srl of Como.
A top speed of 78mph (125km/h) was claimed.

CR

1909 F.W.D. Battleship 45hp tourer.
JOHN A.CONDE

1967 F.W.M. GT coupé.
NATIONAL MOTOR MUSEUM

FUTURA (GB) 1971
Fellpoint Ltd, Penn, Buckinghamshire.
The Futura was built by Robin Statham, whose company Fellpoint Ltd also briefly made the MINIJEM. A humble VW Beetle floorpan lay underneath an incredible wedge-shaped body, whose windscreen hinged up sideways to allow the passengers to enter by climbing over the nose. That meant that the four headlamps were positioned behind the screen, but this fell foul of the law, so pop-up units were developed. The money required to develop it eventually sank

Fellpoint in 1971, and the prototype was cut up and exported to Brazil, although two Futura bodies were moulded at a later stage, one of which reached the road in 1979.
CR

FUXING (CHI) 1994–1998
Xinhua Industrial Corp., Shenzhen City, Guangdong Province;
Beifan Vehicle Research Institute, Beijing Municipality;
Qinchuan Machinery Works, Xi'an City, Shaanxi Province.
Several small prototypes were made by three plants under the Fuxing name ('Lucky Star'). The first prototype was a 2-door, 4-seater minicar named Fuxing C987, was powered by a 700cc engine. A concept car (2-door, 3-seater) designed by the Italian I. DE. A studios, called the Gritto, was exhibited by the Beifan Institute as a Chinese product. In 1995 the Beifan Xiao Fuxing QCJ 7085 was the most important of this range. This 5-door 4-seater motor car was designed by the Hong Kong designer Kak Lee. He used the Suzuki Alto (1988–93) platform, 800cc engine and gearbox. The design of the Fuxing was inspired by a fish, which is a symbol in Chinese culture for wealth.
EVIS

F.W.D. (US) 1909–1912
1909–1911 Badger Four Wheel Drive Automobile Co., Clintonville, Wisconsin.
1911–1912 Four Wheel Drive Automobile Co., Clintonville, Wisconsin.
Well known as truck makers until quite recently, the F.W.D. was originated by two machinists. They were Otto Zachow and his brother-in-law William A. Besserdich, who invented a double-Y universal joint encased in a ball-and-socket which allowed for the front wheels of a vehicle to be powered and steered at the same time. They tried their system out first in a steam car which did not work, then with a 45hp petrol engine in a car they called 'The Battleship'. In 1909, with backing from Dr W.H. Finney, they formed the Badger Four Wheel Drive Automobile Co. to make a large touring car on the lines of 'The Battleship', which was initially called the Badger or Badger-F.W.D. In 1911 Dr Finney dropped out (unwisely as it turned out) and the Badger name was dropped. Zachow and Besserdich offered three body styles on their F.W.D. for 1911 and 1912, a tourer, runabout and roadster. They also began to make trucks, and soon realised that these were a better bet, so cars were discontinued after only 12 had been made. Their trucks became some of the best-known vehicles of World War I; 15,000 were made, not only by F.W.D. but also by Kissel, Mitchell and Premier. Their Model SU-COE was equally famous in World War II, and they continued to make custom-built trucks into the 1990s.
NG

F.W.M. (GB) 1960s
F.W.M. Engineering Co., Southport, Lancashire.
Three different GT coupés were offered by F.W.M., each based on Ford mechanicals with 997cc, 1198cc and 1498cc engines. The chassis was a tubular space frame using all-independent suspension and front disc brakes, while the bodywork was in fibreglass with a Perspex rear screen.
CR

Glossary

A guide to some of the more frequently used technical and general terms which may not be familiar to the reader.

ALAM formula rating. *See* horsepower.

All-weather. In the immediate post-World War 1 period this name was applied to cars which could be opened to the elements, but which had comprehensive arrangements against wind and rain when they were closed. This would normally have included glass windows in metal frames, which either folded down into the doors or were stowed away in a special compartment. This was in contrast to a tourer, which had only a rudimentary hood and, possibly, canvas side-curtains which rolled down. The complexity and expense of these systems meant that all-weather bodies were confined to expensive chassis. In America such a design was known as a Springfield Top.

Automatic inlet valves (aiv). Inlet valves opened atmospherically, without any mechanical control. A primitive system, soon replaced by mechanical actuation (*see also* moiv).

Avant-train. A 2-wheeled power unit consisting of engine, gearbox, final drive, steering wheel, and other controls, which could be attached to a horse-drawn vehicle, or to enable various bodies to be used with the same engine. *Avant-train* units were the earliest examples of front-wheel drive, but were outmoded soon after 1900. Electric as well as petrol engines were used.

Belt drive. A system whereby the final drive is a conveyed from countershaft to rear axle by leather belts.

bhp. *See* horsepower.

Blower. *See* supercharger

Brake. *See* shooting brake.

Brougham. Based on its horse-drawn forerunner, the brougham was a highly formal design, distinguished by the separate nature of the passenger compartment, which often retained its own carriage lamps. Even when the chauffeur's area became enclosed the passenger saloon was made wider, usually by use of a 'D-front' - so called because of its shape as seen from above. Another distinguishing feature was the brougham's sharp-edged appearance in profile; this applied both to the roof-line and to the shape of the door, and the 'brougham door' - curved forward at the toe - continued to appear as a feature of otherwise conventional designs well into the thirties.

Cabriolet de Ville. This version of the cabriolet implies merely that the front portion of the folding head can be opened separately into the de ville position, usually by being rolled up; the later term for a similar, although less formal, design was a three-position drophead coupé. *See also* Salamanca.

Cabriolet. Of all coachbuilding terms, this is the one whose meaning has evolved the most over the years. Originally a cabriolet was a four-door, four- or six-light drophead body with a division, and without even having enclosed drive. Soon, however, the requirement for the division was dropped, and it came to mean the same as an all-weather; it began to replace that name during the mid-twenties. (A variation, the coupé cabriolet, had only two doors.) The increasing popularity of the style in the thirties, and some borrowing of features from Germany where it was even more popular, led to a further widening of its definition; it could now, for example, describe a body (sometimes known as a saloon cabriolet) where only the fabric roof itself opened, leaving windows and frames standing, and indeed some commentators tried to restrict its use to such bodies (leaving drophead coupé for the alternative type). Later, the requirement for four doors evaporated, and a cabriolet came to be synonymous with a drophead coupé.

Cardan (shaft). The driving shaft which conveys power from gearbox to rear axle. More usually known as the propeller shaft, the word was widely used in France (transmission à cardan) in the early days to distinguish shaft drive from chain drive. The principle is said to have been invented by the Italian philosopher Girolamo Cardano (1501 – 1576).

Catalytic Converter or **Catalyst.** A device in which a chemical reaction is induced in order to change the chemical composition of the gases flowing through it. The automotive catalyst consists of a 'washcoat' usually containing platinum and rhodium, on a ceramic or metallic core, fitted into the exhaust system in order to clean up exhaust gases after they leave the engine. Two types are commonly used. The two-way catalyst removes half to two-thirds of CO and HC and can be retrofitted relatively easily. It is commonly used on diesel engines. The three-way catalyst in addition removes NOx, but this requires it to be 'regulated' and integrated with the engine management system as this can only be achieved when the engine is run at a relatively rich stoichiometric mixture. It can then remove up to 95% of toxic emissions under ideal conditions. Both types are damaged by lead and require the use of unleaded fuel.

Chain drive. A system whereby the final drive is conveyed from countershaft to wheels by chains. Double-chain drive was widely used on powerful cars until about 1908, but could still be found on some old-fashioned machines as late as 1914. Indeed, Frazer-Nash used three chains, one for each forward speed, as late as 1939. A number of light cars used a centrally-mounted single-chain drive to a live axle.

Close-coupled. Originally, implied that all seats were within the wheelbase (often to make more luggage space), and that rear seating room was therefore limited. Later, when engines had been moved forward and seating within the wheelbase had become the norm, the term came to mean merely that the body was shorter than normal.

Clover-Leaf. An arrangement of three seats, usually in an open car or coupé, where the third seat is placed behind and between the two front ones so that its occupant's legs are between the front seats. In vogue during the twenties.

Common rail. A type of direct injection diesel engine developed by Fiat and Bosch in the 1990s. It achieves the very high injection pressures needed in two stages. The first stage pressurises a tube-like chamber – the common rail – from which the injectors build up the remainder of the required pressure before injection into individual cylinders. It is technically less demanding than the alternative unit injector approach whereby very high technology injection pumps - the unit injectors - build up the required pressure for each cylinder individually.

Continental Coupé. A popular style in the late-1920s and early 1930s. The intended image was of a fast, close-coupled car which would be ideal for Continental touring; it was reinforced by making the luggage container in the form of a separate trunk rather than an integral part of the body, since this was perceived to be a French style of the time.

Convertible. An all-embracing term which has come to mean any car with a folding head. *See also* all-weather.

Coupé de Ville. Similar to a cabriolet de ville, but the rear part of the head is fixed instead of folding. Where it was intended to make clear that the design had only two doors and no division, it was sometimes called a sedanca coupé.

Coupé. The French word coupé means 'cut'. As applied to coachbuilding, it originally referred to the centre part of a horse-drawn carriage, between the 'box' in front and the 'boot' at the rear. Thus for a car it also means foreshortened - ie close-coupled - but it is applied specifically to a 2-door, 2- or 4-light, close-coupled body with either a fixed or an opening head; in the latter case it must have normal glass windows - fixed, lifting or sliding - otherwise it becomes a sports body. A coupé can have two or four seats enclosed under the head.

Cowl. A scuttle, 'cowl' being the preferred term in America. A dual-cowl design (usually a phaeton) had a second cowl in front of the second row of seats.

CV. *See* horsepower.

Cycle Wing. A wing on the front wheel which closely follows the wheel's curvature, like the mudguard on a bicycle. Sometimes actually turned with the wheel. *See also* helmet wing.

Cyclecar. A simple light car whose design owed much to motorcycle practice, of which a large variety were made from 1912 until about 1922. The typical cyclecar had an engine of fewer than four cylinders, was often air-cooled, and final drive was by belts or chains. Cyclecars flourished in England, France, and the US, but disappeared with the coming of mass-produced 'genuine light cars', such as the Austin Seven and Citroën 5CV.

De Dion axle. A system of final drive in which the rear axle is 'dead', or separate from the driving shafts. The drive is transmitted by independent, universally-jointed half-shafts. The system was first used on the De Dion-Bouton steamers of the 1890s, but was abandoned by the firm after 1914. It is, however, used on a number of modern sports cars.

De Ville. Implies a body style where the front (ie driver's) compartment is either open to the skies or can be made to be. Originally all 'de ville' designs had four doors.

Dickey-Seat. Usually found on two-seater coupés of the twenties; a lid behind the hood lifted up to form an additional seat.

Dos-à-dos. A 4-seater car in which the passengers sat back to back. Seldom seen after about 1900, this lay-out was revived briefly in the Zundapp Janus of 1956.

Drophead Coupé. A coupé with an opening head.

Drophead. A design where the head can be folded flat to make the car open.

Epicyclic gearbox. A form of gear in wehich small pinions (planetary pinions) revolve around a central or sun gear, and mesh with an outer ring gear or annulus. Bset known for their use on the Ford Model T, epicyclic gearboxes were found in a wide variety of early US cars. In the US they are known as planetary transmissions.

Estate car. *See* shooting brake.

Fast and loose pulleys. A system of transmission in which the countershaft carried a loose pulley for neutral, and two fixed pulleys meshing with spur gears of different ratios on the axle. Moving a belt from loose to fixed pulley provided a clutch action. The system was used on early Benz, New Orleans, and other cars.

Faux-Cabriolet. The French word 'faux' means false; these bodies looked like dropheads because they had fabric-covered roofs, and often dummy hood-irons, but in fact their roofs were fixed.

F-head. Cylinder head design incorporating overhead inlet and side exhaust valves. Also known as inlet-over-exhaust (ioe). *See also* L-head; T-head.

Fixed-head Coupé. A coupé with a solid, immovable head (although it might possibly be fitted with a sunshine roof).

Flexible Fuel Characteristics. Ability of an engine type to run on more than one type of fuel. External combustion engines often have this advantage; it means an engine is less dependent on a possibly finite fuel source.

Friction transmission. A system of transmission using two disks in contact at right angles. Variation in gear ratio was obtained by sliding the edge of one disk across the face of the other. This theoretically provided an infinitely variable ratio, although in some systems there were a limited number of positions for the sliding disk.

GDI. Gasoline direct injection, the term used by Mitsubishi for its direct injection petrol engine, the first of a new generation of such engines, which promise greater fuel efficiency and lower emissions.

Helmet Wing. Similar to a cycle wing, but the bottom kicks backwards away from the wheel rather in the manner of a Roman helmet.

HEV or Hybrid-electric Vehicle. A vehicle which has a dual powertrain one of which is electric. In practice most examples have a heat engine – usually internal combustion – generating electricity, which is then used to power electric motors which drive the wheels. Two types exist, parallel hybrid in which either the heat engine or full electric drive from batteries can be used allowing the vehicle to operate in zero emissions mode in urban areas and as a normal internal combustion car elsewhere. More elegant is the series hybrid, which uses the advantages of internal combustion and electric vehicle in order to create a more efficient powertrain than in a conventional car.

High-wheeler. A simple car with the appearance of a motorised buggy, which enjoyed a brief period of popularity in the US and Canada between 1907 and 1912. Over 70 firms built high-wheelers, the best known being Holsman, International, and Sears.

Horsepower. (hp, bhp, CV, PS) The unit used for measuring the power output of the engine, defined mechanically as 33,000 foot-pounds per minute. Up to about 1910 the horsepower quoted by makers was meant to correspond to the actual output, although it was often used with more optimism than accuracy. Sometimes a double figure would be quoted, such as 10/12 or 24/30; here the first figure represented the power developed at 1000rpm, while the second was the power developed at the engine's maximum speed. In 1904 the Automobile Club of Great Britain & Ireland's rating of horsepower (the RAC rating from 1907 onwards) was introduced, calculated on the bore of the engine only, and as engine efficiency improved the discrepancy between rated and actual horsepower grew. Thus, by the mid-1920s a car might be described as a 12/50 or a 14/40, where the first figure was the rated hp, and the second the actual hp developed at maximum revs. RAC ratings were widely used until after World War II, but when taxation by horsepower was abandoned in January 1948, manufacturers soon stopped describing their cars as Eights or Tens.

The American ALAM (later NACC) horsepower rating followed the British system of calculation on the cylinder bore alone, but French (CV) and German (PS) ratings were based on different formulae, with the result that a 15hp British car might be called an 11CV in France or a 9PS in Germany. The French rating was introduced in 1912 and the German at about the same time. Prior to this the terms CV and PS were used to denote actual brake horsepower. Today horsepower rating has largely been abandoned; engine capacity is indicated in litres, and power in developed or brake horsepower.

Hot-tube ignition. An early system in which the mixture was ignited by a small platinum tube, open at its inner end, which was screwed into the cylinder head. The outer, closed end was heated to red heat by a small petrol-fed burner, and when the mixture passed into the tube, it ignited. The system was outdated by 1900, although some firms continued to fit tubes as an auxiliary to electric ignition.

Indirect Injection Diesel. This is the traditional diesel engine, where the actual combustion process is started in a pre-chamber connected to the combustion chamber itself. Combustion then spreads to the combustion chamber itself in a controlled manner. It offers reduced engine noise at the expense of higher fuel consumption, compared to the alternative direct injection diesel engine, where the combustion process is started in the conventional manner within the actual combustion chamber.

Inlet-over-exhaust valves (ioe). *See* F-head.

Landaulet. (*Also spelt* landaulette.) A very popular style amongst the moneyed classes before and after World War I. Based on a well-known style of horse-drawn carriage, its distinguishing feature was that only the rear portion of the roof opened - ie that part covering the back-seat passengers. Originally it was assumed not to have an enclosed driving compartment, so in later years the term enclosed landaulet (or sometimes limousine landaulet) made the distinction. It was further assumed to have a division; when this was omitted, it became a saloon landaulet. Finally, it might be a three-quarter, single or coupé landaulet (this last sometimes shortened to coupélette), according to whether it had six, four or two lights.

Lean-burn. A process whereby the amount of fuel burnt in the engine is minimized in favour of air, leading to hotter and more efficient combustion with a useful reduction in emissions of CO and HC, although NOx emissions increase, as the air is heated to higher temperatures. Diesel engines are naturally lean-burn.

L-head. Cylinder head design in which inlet and exhaust valves are mounted on one side of the engine. It was the most commonly-used design for all but high-performance engines from about 1910 until after World War II. Also known as side valves (sv), *See also* T-head.

Light. A light in coachbuilding terms is a side-window; hence it is convenient to classify a saloon, for example, as 4-light or 6-light.

Limousine de Ville. A limousine with a folding roof extension above the driver's seat.

Limousine. The essential qualities of a limousine are that it should be roomy (usually through having a long wheelbase), its roof should be fixed, and it should have a division. The driver's compartment may not have been enclosed in the early days, but the passenger compartment always was. The massive leg room in the rear usually permitted the addition of two further 'occasional', i.e., folding, seats. What was not normal was a luggage compartment, since a limousine was used for town work rather than touring; there was often, however, a folding luggage grid. Later, a demand grew for a dual-use body which could combine both formal and touring requirements, which became known as a sports limousine or later touring limousine; this retained the division, but sacrificed some rear leg-room, and usually the occasional seats, to permit the addition of a luggage-boot. The sports limousine often dispensed with a quarter-light.

Live axle. An axle which transmits power, as opposed to a dead axle, where the power is either carried by separate half-shafts (*see* De Dion axle) or by side chains.

Mechanically operated inlet valves (moiv). *See* automatic inlet valves.

Monocar. Single-seater car. The expression is never used for racing cars, most of which have been single-seaters since the late 1920s (these are sometimes known as *monopostos*), but for ultra-light single-seater cyclecars of the 1912 to 1915 period.

Motor buggy. *See* high-wheeler.

Overhead valve. Cylinder head design in which the valves are mounted above the combustion chamber, either horizontally or inclined at an angle. Generally abbreviated to ohv.

Over-square. An engine in which the cylinder bore is greater than the stroke (e.g., 110mm × 100mm). A 'square' engine is one in which the bore and the stroke are identical (100mm × 100mm).

Phaeton. An alternative term for a tourer. This was the preferred description in America, where the dual-cowl phaeton was particularly popular.

Pillarless. A fixed-head body where there is no obstruction above the waist-line between the windscreen pillar and the rear quarter. Can apply to both two- and four-door designs.

Planetary transmission. *See* epicyclic gearbox.

Power-train. Term commonly used for the subassemblies of the car that make it move; i.e. engine, clutch, gearbox and final drive.

PS. *See* horsepower.

Quarter-light. Originally a light, or window, alongside the rear seat which was fixed in the rear quarter of the car rather than being part of a door. Later, when it became common to arrange swivelling ventilation windows in the front section of front doors, these also became known as quarter-lights, and it became necessary to distinguish between front and rear ones.

RAC rating. *See* horsepower.

Roadster. The term originated in America, and meant an open body with one wide seat capable of taking two or three abreast, possibly also having a dickey-seat. It was the American equivalent of the British 2-seater. In recent years it has come to mean the same as a two-seater sports car.

Roi des Belges. A luxurious type of open touring car, named after King Leopold II of Belgium. The style is said to have been suggested to the King by his mistress, Cléo de Mérode. The style was sometimes also known as the Tulip Phaeton.

Rotary valves. Valves contained in the cylinder head whose rotary morion allows the passage of mixture and exhaust gases at the appropriate times.

Runabout. A genereal term for a light 2-seater car of the early 1900s, especially those made in the US.

Salamanca. Sometimes called a salamanca cabriolet, this design was conceived by Count de Salamanca who was the Rolls-Royce agent in Madrid. It was no more than a formal, four-light cabriolet de ville, but luxurious in execution; the term was used exclusively in connection with Rolls-Royce chassis.

Saloon Limousine. Similar to a Sports Limousine, in that it had a division but being built on a shorter chassis than a normal limousine had to sacrifice some rear leg-room. Unlike a sports limousine, however, it normally had a quarter-light - ie it was a six-light design - and would not have had a luggage-boot.

Saloon. Probably the term which has least changed in meaning over the years. It has always meant a vehicle which has a fixed roof (although possibly with a sunshine roof fitted), which is completely enclosed, and which does not have a division. It can have four lights or six, and either four doors or two, although during the thirties the last type became increasingly difficult to distinguish from a fixed-head coupé, and indeed was sometimes named saloon-coupé.

Scuttle. That part of the bodywork between the engine compartment and the windscreen, forming an apron over the legs of the front passengers.

Sedanca de Ville. The word sedanca is in theory synonymous with de ville, so to describe a body as a sedanca de ville is illogical in the extreme. In practice it implied a de ville design with a large, saloon-like rear compartment often having four side-windows.

Selective transmission. The conventional transmission in which any gear mey be selected at will, as distinct from the earlier progressive transmissions, where the gears had to be selected in sequence.

Shooting brake; brake; estate car; station bus; station wagon. The original brake or shooting brake was similar to the wagonette (*qv*), and was used on large estates to carry members of shooting parties. The station bus was used for conveying guests and servants, and was usually a closed vehicle, whereas early brakes were open. After World War I both types declined in use, but the names were reincarnated in the wood-panelled station wagon which US manufacturers began to offer as part of their ranges in the 1930s. By 1941 all the popular makers were listing station wagons, and the fashion spread to Europe, where the name estate car was more often used, after World War II.

Side valves. Cylinder head design in which the valves are mounted at the side of the combustion chamber. They may be side-by-side (L-head), or on opposite sides of the engine (T-head). The usual abbreviation, sv, applies to the L-head design; the rarer T-head design being specifically mentioned.

Sleeve valves. Metal sleeves placed between the piston and the cylinder wall. When moved up and down, holes in them coincide to provide passage for gases at the correct times.

Speedster. An American term for a sporting open car with sketchy bodywork, usually no doors, a raked steering column and bolster fuel tank behind the seats.

Spider. A French term for a very light sporting voiturette, often with a sketchy dickey seat, around the turn of the century. It was revived by Alfa Romeo for their sports cars in the 1950s, and by Porsche as the Spyder.

Sportsman's Coupé. A 2-door, 4-light fixed-head coupé with built-in luggage-locker. The provision of covered luggage accommodation was quite an innovation in Europe in 1927, when the intense but short-lived fad for this type of design started. It was achieved by 'close-coupling', ie moving the rear seats forward so that the rear passengers' feet were in floor wells under the front seats.

Sportsman's Saloon. This was a 4-door, 4-light close-coupled saloon; the craze for this type of body took over, around 1929-30, from that for the sportsman's coupé. The name was later shortened to sports saloon.

'Square' engine. *See* over-square.

Station bus; station wagon. *See* shooting brake.

Sunshine Saloon. During the latter half of the twenties, particularly in the UK, numerous styles were named 'sunshine saloons' by their builders. They ranged from saloons with what we would now call a sliding or sunshine roof, to semi-cabriolet designs where the whole roof folded back.

Supercharger. A compressor (colloquially a 'blower') fitted to an engine to force the mixture into the cylinders at a pressure greater than that of the atmosphere. First seen on the 1908 Chadwick, the supercharger was widely used on sports and racing cars in the 1920s and 1930s, and on Formula 1 racing cars until 1954. Differs from a turbocharger (*qv*) in that it runs at a constant speed.

Surrey. An open 4-seater car, often with a fringed top.

T-head. Cylinder head design in which inlet and exhaust valves were mounted on opposite side of the engine. Two camshafts were needed, and in order to make do with only one, the L-head (qv) design was developed. The T-head was outmoded after about 1910.

Three-quarter. An older coachbuilding term, little used after the twenties. A three-quarter body had a quarter-light; its opposite, a single body, did not; thus a 4-door, 6-light landaulet would be referred to as a 'three-quarter landaulet', whereas a 4-door, 4-light version would be a 'single landaulet'.

Tonneau Cover. A covering for an open tourer or sports car for use when no sidescreens have been erected. It comes from a very early motoring term describing the passenger-carrying part of a body (from the French word for a barrel).Because they were built on a short chassis, early tonneaus had a door at the back, between the two seats, these being known as rear-entrance tonneaus. These gave way to the side-entrance tonneau, which was in fact, synonymous with the tourer, though early examples would have had doors for the rear seats, but not for those at the front.

Torpedo. An early term for what was in effect a large 4- or 5-seat tourer. Although bearing little resemblance to a torpedo, its name came from its smooth contours, free from intricate mouldings, and from the continuos horizontal line formed by the bonnet and waist-line, often accentuated by a secondary scuttle or cowl between the two rows of seats.

Tourer. Always an open body with a collapsible hood, and usually having four or five seats. The feature which distinguishes it from a cabriolet or drophead coupé is that its side windows - if it has any at all - are in the form of light-weight detachable side-screens which can be removed and stowed in a locker.

Trembler coil ignition. Ignition by induction coil and electromagnetic vibrator, which broke the primary circuit and induced the high-tension current in the secondary windings. Used by Benz and many other pioneers, but superseded by the De Dion-Bouton patent contact breaker, invented by Georges Bouton in 1895.

Turbocharger. A compressor fitted to an engine to force mixture into the cylinders at a pressure greater than that of the atmosphere. Unlike a supercharger, a turbocharger is usually driven by exhaust gases from the engine, so that the faster the engine is running, the greater the boost provided by the turbocharger, and vice versa. First seen on a production car in the Chevrolet Corsair Monza Spyder in 1962, the system became well-known in the BMW 2002 Turbo (1973), and Porsche 911 Turbo (1975). It was introduced to ordinary production saloons by Saab on their 99 of 1977.

Vee-radiator. A honeycomb radiator coming to a more or less sharp point. The first production car to use the design was probably the Métallurgique in 1907, and by 1914 a large number of makes had vee-radiators. They were especially popular in Germany, and from 1919 to 1923 there was hardly a single German or Austrian car without a vee-radiator. They should not be confused with the vee-shaped grill found on many cars of the later 1930s, whose flamboyant design concealed an ordinary, flat radiator.

Victoria Hood. A type of hood which is cantilevered out from its point of attachment to the front of the seat it is intended to cover, with no support from the windscreen. Only feasible for 2-seaters (although at least one 4-seater design had two such hoods, one for each row of seats).

Vis-à-vis. A 4-seater car in which two passengers sat facing the driver.

Voiturette. A French term for a light car, initially used by Léon Bollée for his 3-wheeler of 1895, but soon applied by manufacturers and journalists to any small car.

Waggonette. A large car, usually for six or more passengers, in which the rear seats faced each other. Entrance was at the rear, and the vehicles were usually open. See also shooting brake.

Further reading.
The Complete Book of Automobile Body Design, Ian Beattie, Haynes Publishing. 1977.

Contributors

NICK GEORGANO
Editor in Chief

Nick Georgano was born in London in February 1932. He began his career as a motoring writer at the age of 7 when he prepared a truck catalogue which was typed out by his long-suffering mother. He was 16 when he first attempted to write an 'encyclopedia'.

On coming down from Oxford in 1956 he became a preparatory schoolmaster during which time he helped his friend Ralph Doyle to revise his *The World's Automobiles* – Nick completed this after Ralph's death in 1961, an invaluable apprenticeship for editing the *Complete Encyclopedia of Motorcars*, first published in 1968. On the strength of this he abandoned the schoolroom for the typewriter and has since edited or written 31 titles including *The Complete Encyclopedia of Commercial Vehicles* (editor), *The Encyclopedia of Motor Sport* (editor), *A History of Transport* (editor), *History of Sports Cars*, *History of the London Taxicab*, *Early Days on the Road* (with Lord Montagu of Beaulieu), *The American Automobile – a Centenary*, *The Art of the American Automobile*, *Britain's Motor Industry – The First 100 Years* (editor). For the latter and for *The Complete Encyclopedia of Motorcars* he was awarded the Montagu Trophy of the Guild of Motoring Writers. He was Head Librarian at the National Motor Museum from 1976 to 1981. He is a member of the National Motor Museum Advisory Council and Trustee of the Michael Sedgwick Memorial Trust and the Horseless Carriage Foundation, California.

KENNETH BALL

Born in August 1929, Kenneth Ball attended Accrington Grammar School and studied engineering at Blackburn Technical College. He has an HNC in Mechanical Engineering and in Automobile Engineering, and is a graduate of the Institute of Mechanical Engineers.

Since his youth, Kenneth Ball has collected and dealt in rare motoring publications. He also founded Autobook Publishers Ltd, which, during the 1960s and early 1970s, was the world's largest publisher of motor car workshop manuals. He sold his publishing interests in 1972 to concentrate on collecting and dealing in rare motoring publications.

DAVID FILSELL

Born in March 1934, David started collecting material for a motor encyclopaedia soon after. When he went to Bryanston he was delighted to find a like-minded pupil in Nick Georgano. David chose a career in hospital administration, but his pervasive interest in all things motoring manifested itself in a variety of ways – rallying, marshalling, cigarette cards, model collecting and so on, as well as motoring history. He was a major contributor to *The Complete Encyclopedia of Motorcars* and *The Encyclopedia of Motor Sport*. He has been an active Vintage Sports Car Club (V.S.C.C.) member since 1954. Having recently retired, he intends to spend more time with his Barrington motors, his collection of Clynos and on original research.

CHRISTOPHER 'KIT' FOSTER

Holding BSc and MSc degrees in Electrical Engineering, 'Kit' Foster served as engineer and project manager for the US Department of Defense for over 25 years. He is currently a freelance motoring journalist and contributing editor to *Special Interest Autos*. He has contributed regularly to *Automobile Quarterly*, *Collectible Automobile*, and *Classic Car Mart*. Previous credits also include *Classic and Sportscar*, *The Automobile*, *Old Cars Weekly* and *Car Collector*. From 1989 to 1995 he was editor of the *Society of Automotive Historians' Journal* and *Automotive History Review*.

AUSTIN MAXWELL 'MAX' GREGORY

Max Gregory was born in March 1935. After a long career as a dairy farmer in Australia, he was forced to retire in 1995 following a motor accident. Since then, he has concentrated on his hobby as a motoring writer and historian. He has been a contributor to *Restored Cars* magazine since 1974, and has also had articles published in New Zealand and the US.

PAUL FERDINAND
HEDIGER

Born in February 1934 in Switzerland, Ferdinand Hediger's interest in engines and motor vehicles started in his childhood. He became sales manager, and later general manager, of a target arms factory exporting pistols worldwide, from which he retired in 1995.

From 1965 his freelance articles, mainly on motoring history, were published by the Swiss weekly *Automobil Revue*, as well as various German, Austrian, British, US, and Spanish magazines. His first book *Klassische Wagen Vol. II* was published in 1972, followed by *Oldtimer* in 1978, and *Klassische Wagen 1919-1939* in 1988, for which he obtained the Award of Distinction by the SAH.

ERIK H. F. van INGEN
SCHENAU

Erik van Ingen Schenau was born in April 1947. Following an early career in social work, he has worked in the tourist industry since 1982 and is currently director of a travel agency in The Netherlands. In 1966 he began researching automotive developments in the People's Republic of China, travelling extensively in China and developing his specialism in Chinese automobiles. He founded the China Motor Vehicle Documentation Centre, a large library of Chinese automobile reference material, based in The Netherlands. His freelance writing has been published across the European motor press and he is a correspondent for the German *Auto Katalog*.

MARGUS HANS
KUUSE

Margus Hans Kuuse was born in December 1943 in Tartu, Estonia, and trained as an engineer at Tallinn Technical University. Since 1971 he has held the position of editor for numerous motoring magazines, including *Tehnika Ja Tootmine*, *Autorev__*, *Autoposter*, and *Autopluss*. He is currently news/contributing editor for *Eesti Ekspress*, *Autoleht*, and *Motor News* in Russia, Ukraine and Belorussia.

As a freelance writer, his work has appeared in leading motor magazines and newspapers internationally, including a period in the 1970s and 1980s as Soviet correspondent to the British *Autocar* magazine. Book credits include Estonia's main auto history book *Sada Autot*. He has also worked as a consultant for Estonian television.

MICHAEL LAMM

Born in February 1936, Michael Lamm has followed a career as a publisher, writer and editor in the US. From 1959, his early work as an editor included the *Foreign Car Guide*, *Motor Life*, and *Motor Trend*. He turned to freelance work in 1965, in 1970 became founder and editor of *Special-Interest Autos*, and since 1971 has been a contributing editor to *Popular Mechanics*. Michael is owner of the Lamm-Morada Publishing Co. Inc. which he founded in 1978. He has authored and published many articles and books, including *A Century of Automotive Style*.

MIKE LAWRENCE

Mike Lawrence was a teacher until 1982, when, at the age of 40, he became a motoring journalist. He has been editor of *Motor Sport*, motoring editor of the *Portsmouth News*, and has contributed to many journals internationally. He was the historical consultant to BBC2's history of motor racing, *The Power And The Glory*, and consultant to the Goodwood *Festival of Speed* videos. Mike has written, or co-written, more than 25 books, and is a consultant to Brooks the Auctioneers. Living near Goodwood, he masterminded the campaign to support the return of racing to the circuit.

Mike's poetry and plays have won awards and, in 1996, he gained a PhD for his research into Shakespeare's dramatic techniques. As Dr Lawrence, he teaches courses on Shakespeare for the Universities of Sussex and Gothenburg.

VOLKER CHRISTIAN
MANZ

Born in January 1956 in Hamburg, Germany, Christian has lived in Spain for the last twenty years. He published his first story at the age of 13, but entered professional journalism in 1982, after a career in hotel management. He is a correspondent for *Automobil-Revue* and other German language magazines, and contributes to several Spanish car magazines. His articles have been translated into 16 languages and published in 22 countries. Christian is co-editor of *Hispano-Suiza/Pegaso*, *A Century of Trucks and Buses*, and editor of electric car bulletins.

KEITH MARVIN

Keith was born in July 1924, and followed a career in the newspaper industry in the US between 1948 and 1974. He then turned to freelance writing and editing, his publications including several books on automotive history, with indepth studies of Dagmar, Wasp, and McFarlan cars, and two books on number plate history. His articles and book reviews have been published widely in the US, Canada, and the UK. He has also had several books of verse published.

Keith was a founding member of the Society of Automotive Historians, and has worked as a designer of number plates for various governments.

PÁL NÉGYESI

Pál was born in Hungary in November 1973, and is a graduate in librarian and communication studies. He has contributed to various Hungarian car magazines, including *Autô-Motor*, *Sport Auto*, and *4 × 4 Magazin*. He wrote for the short-lived *British Alternative Car World*, and several articles for *Classic Car Mart*. In 1997 he became editor of *AutoClassic*, Hungary's premier classic car magazine. His first book, which covers the history of the first Hungarian motorcycle factory, Méray, was published in 1998.

HANS-OTTO NEUBAUER

Hans-Otto was born in July 1929 in Altona, Germany. After working with BP in Germany, he became a freelance writer and editor, specialising in all German makes and aspects of the automobile in social history. He contributed to the first edition of the *Encyclopedia of Motorcars*, and was editor of *Die Chronik des Automobils* and *Die Geschichte des Automobils*. His articles have been published in numerous magazines and the press. Hans-Otto is a founder member of the Automobilhistoriche Gesellschaft, and is editor of the *Automobilhistorische Nachrichten*.

PAUL NIEUWENHUIS

Born in May 1954 in The Netherlands, Paul was educated in Australia, Belgium, Spain, and the UK. He graduated from the University of Edinburgh with an MA and PhD in General Linguistics. Paul joined the Motor Industry Research Unit in Norwich in 1986, followed by the Centre for Automotive Industry Research at Cardiff Business School in 1990. His publications include *Japanese Commercial Vehicles*, as well as co-authoring *The Green Car Guide* and *The Death of Motoring?*, and co-editing *Motor Vehicles in the Environment*. He has contributed to a number of magazines and journals, particularly on environmental and strategic issues affecting the motor industry.

JAN P. NORBYE

Jan Norbye was born in August 1931 in Oslo, Norway. He graduated from Oslo Commercial College in 1951, and held positions with Esso and Volvo up to 1961. He became technical editor of *Car and Driver* in 1961 until 1964, followed by automotive editor of *Popular Science* until 1974, and international editor of *Automotive News* until 1980. Jan then turned to freelance writing and has authored many books including *Autos Made in Japan*, *The Complete History of the German Car*, *The Wankel Engine*, *The Gas Turbine Engine*, *Modern Diesel Cars*, and *The 100 Greatest American Cars*.

HAROLD W. PACE

Harold Pace was born in July 1952 in the US. He has been a freelance commercial photographer in the advertising industry since 1980. He began writing for automotive publications in 1993, and has been a contributor to many motor magazines including *Automobile Quarterly*, *Excellence*, *Forza*, *Vintage Motorsports*, and *Sports Cars International*. His specialist interest is in limited-production kit, sports and racing cars. In 2000 he published a comprehensive survey of these machines, *The Big Guide to Kit and Specialty Cars*. Harold has also competed in drag, slalom, SCCA and historic racing.

ROBERT PRZYBYLSKI

Robert was born in August 1962 in Poland. In 1991 he became a freelance writer, working for car-enthusiast magazines. He moved to Motomagazyn in 1993 as a staff writer, and is currently editor-in-chief. He has also been a contributor to newspapers and yearbooks. Other publications include *A Big Three – A 100 Years of the American Automobile*.

CHRIS REES

Born in October 1963, Chris Rees is a full-time motoring journalist and author with a passion for specialist cars. He has been editor of *Alternative Cars* magazine, and has worked on the staff of numerous specialist, mainstream, internet and classic car titles. Books to his credit include *British Specialist Cars*, *Three-Wheelers*, *Microcar Mania*, *Classic Kit Cars*, *Caterham Sevens*, *Original Alfa Romeo Spider*, and the annual *Classic Car Buyers Guide*.

HALWART SCHRADER

Halwart Schrader was born in February 1935 in Germany, and is a graduate of Art History and Commercial Graphics. He started work in the advertising department of *Der Spiegel*, then moved to the editorial staff of Auto Union customers' magazine *Copilot*. He launched the *BMW Journal* in 1962, staying three years. In 1973 he started his own publishing business, becoming editor/publisher of Germany's first classic car magazine *Automobil Chronik*. He has written more than 50 books on motoring history and related subjects.

MARIAN
ŠUMAN-HREBLAY

Born in March 1950, Marian graduated from Charles University in Prague with an MA in Librarianship. He worked as a librarian before moving into motor bookselling in 1990, and is now owner of the Autoantikvariat bookselling and consulting firm. He has been a member of the Society of Automotive Historians since 1985.

ALVARO CASAL
TATLOCK

Born in January 1940, Alvaro has been a journalist in Uruguay since 1962. From 1971 he spent four years as the South American correspondent of the *Veteran and Vintage Magazine*. He has had numerous books published since 1982, on motoring and other subjects. His latest book, *The Automobile in South America*, was published in 1996. With support from the Uruguayan Automobile Club, he founded Uruguay's first motor museum in 1983.

FRANS B.
VRIJALDENHOVEN

Born in October 1928, Frans received technical training at Saurer, Jaguar Cars, and Daimler-Benz. In 1951 he became service manager for Holland for Mercedes-Benz cars and trucks. This was followed by similar positions with Skoda, IFA, Steyr, OM and Büssing trucks, and Adler motorcycles. In 1955 he became vice-managing director of a General Motors dealership in The Hague. Prior to retirement, he held the position of adviser at the National Association for the Dutch car trade.

Frans is currently an automotive historian and freelance publisher. His published work includes books on the cars of Prins Bernhard of The Netherlands, and Dutch royal motoring in general since 1904. He has written other specialist publications on Dutch coachbuilders, assembly plants in Holland, and the cars of the German Kaiser Wilhelm II.

NICK WALKER

Nick Walker was born in August 1936. Although trained as an engineer, he spent most of his career in marketing and general management. After retiring early, he took up writing on motoring matters, concentrating on coachbuilding and coachbuilders. He has written regularly for *Classic Car Mart* and also for *The Automobile*. Other published work includes the *A-Z of British Coachbuilders*. Nick is honorary librarian for the Vintage Sports Car Club (V.S.C.C.), and honorary archivist of IBCAM. An Alvis owner for many years, he is Midlands Chairman of the Alvis Owners Club.